INDEX to
RECORD AND
TAPE REVIEWS

A Classical Music Buying Guide

1980

ANTOINETTE O. MALEADY

CHULAINN PRESS

San Anselmo, California 1981

ISBN 0-917600-06-1
Library of Congress Catalog Card No. 72-3355
Manufactured in the United States of America
Copyright © 1981 by Antoinette O. Maleady
CHULAINN PRESS
Post Office Box 770
San Anselmo, California 94960

To Kathryn

CONTENTS

Introduction   vii

Abbreviations   ix

I.   Composers   1

II.   Music in Collections   583

III. Anonymous Works   703

IV.   Performer Index   709

v

INTRODUCTION

This Index brings together in one volume a listing of all classical music recordings reviewed in 1980 in the major reviewing media of the United States, England and Canada.

The Index has four sections. Section I is a straight listing by composer. Section II, "Music in Collections", lists records or tapes with several composers on one disc or tape. Section II main entries are arranged alphabetically by name of the manufacturer, and then serially by the manufacturer's number within each entry. The work of any composer in each of these collections appears in Section I under the name of that composer, with a reference to the Section II entry. Section III lists, alphabetically by title, anonymous works with a reference to their location in Section I or Section II. Section IV is a Performer Index to recordings listed in Sections I and II, with reference by citation number to its location within the section. Each cittation gives, if available, complete entries for each composition; performers; the disc label and number; variant labels and numbers; tape cassette, cartridge or reel numbers; quadraphonic disc or tape numbers; reissues; location of the reviews and the reviewers evaluation of the recording. The main entry for each recording is in upper case letters. Tapes or discs reviewed in 1980 that were also reviewed in 1979, 1978, 1977, 1976, 1975, 1974, 1973, 1972 and/or 1971 have all the reviews brought together in the 1980 Index.

A key is provided for understanding the entries of the four sections. The entries are fictitious entries to show the various possibilities of form.

Section I

MACONCHY, Elizabeth
1219 Ariadne, soprano and orchestra. WALTON: Songs: Daphne; Old Sir
[entry   Faulk; Through gilded trellises. Heather Harper, s [Heather
  no.]   Harper, soprano]; Paul Hamburger, pno [Paul Hamburger, piano];
         ECO [English Chamber Orchestra]; Raymond Leppard [conductor].
         Columbia M 30443 [disc number] (2) [number of discs in set]
         Tape (c) MT 30443 [cassette number] (ct) MA 30443 [cartridge
         number] (r) L 30443 [reel number] (Q) MQ 30443 [quadraphonic
         disc number] Tape (c) MAQ 30443 [quadraphonic tape cartridge
         number].   (also CBS 72941) [recording also available on CBS
         label].
                    ++Gr 9-75 p1025 [evaluation excellent; review in Gramo-
                            phone, September 1975, page 1025]
                    +-NR 2-78 p4 [evaluation mixed, review in New Records,
                            February 1978, page 4]
                    -St 7-79 p55 tape [evaluation poor, review in Stereo
                            Review, July 1979, page 55]
                    +NYT 7-23-80 pD38 [evaluation good, review in New York
                            Times, July 23, 1980, pagd D38]

Section II

LONDON

OS 36578 (also Decca SXL 3315) [label number. Also available on Decca
    label] (Reissue from OS 3716) [Reissue from London OS 3716]
2395 Baroque flute sonatas. BLAVET: Sonata, flute, no. 3, F major.
[entry GAULTIER: Suite, G minor. HANDEL: Sonata, flute, op. 1, no.
    no.] 5, G major. LOEILLET: Sonata, flute, F major. VINCI: Sonata,
    flute, D major. Jean-Pierre Rampal, flt [Jean-Pierre Rampal,
    flute]; Raymond Leppard, hpd [Raymond Leppard, harpsichord];
    Claude Viala, vlc [Claude Viala, violoncello]; AMF [Academy
    of St. Martin-in-the-Fields]; Raymond Leppard [conductor]
            +—MQ 4-79 p53 [evaluation mixed, review in Musical
                        Quarterly, April 1979, page 53]
            +STL 1-15-80 p30 [evaluation good, review in Sunday
                        Times, London, January 15, 1980, page 30]

Section III

Kyrie trope: Orbis factor. See no. 1315. [Anonymous works, appears
    in Section I, citation number 1315]

Section IV

Baker, Janet, mezzo-soprano (contralto) 231, 494, 939, 1367, 1786,
    2513 [performer, listed in reviews as mezzo-soprano or contralto.
    Citation numbers in Section I and II where artist has performed]

ABBREVIATIONS

Periodicals Indexed

AR	American Recorder
ARG	American Record Guide
ARSC	Association for Recorded Sound Collections Journal
Audio	Audio
CJ	Choral Journal
CL	Clavier
FF	Fanfare
FU	Fugue
Gr	Gramophone
GTR	Guitar Review
Ha	Harpers
HF	High Fidelity
HFN	Hi-Fi News & Record Review
HPD	Harpsichord
IN	The Instrumentalist
LAMR	Latin American Music Review
LJ	Library Journal/School Library Journal Previews
MJ	Music Journal
MM	Music & Musicians
MQ	Musical Quarterly
MR	Music Review
MT	Musical Times
MU	Music/American Guild of Organists
MUM	Music Magazine
NCM	Nineteenth Century Music
NR	New Records
NYT	New York Times
OC	Opera Canada
ON	Opera News
Op	Opera, London
OR	Opera Review
PNM	Perspectives of New Music
PRO	Pro Musica
RR	Records and Recording
SFC	San Francisco Examiner and Chronicle
SR	Saturday Review/World
St	Stereo Review
ST	Strad
STL	Sunday Times, London
Te	Tempo

Performers

Orchestral

AMF	Academy of St. Martin-in-the-Fields
BBO	Berlin Bach Orchestra
BeSO	Berlin Symphony Orchestra
BPhO	Berlin Philharmonic Orchestra
BPO	Boston "Pops" Orchestra
Brno PO	Brno State Philharmonic Orchestra
BRSO	Berlin Radio Symphony Orchestra
BSO	Boston Symphony Orchestra
CnSO	Cincinnati Symphony Orchestra
CO	Cleveland Orchestra
COA	Concertgebouw Orchestra, Amsterdam
CPhO	Czech Philharmonic Orchestra
CSO	Chicago Symphony Orchestra
DBS	Deutsche Bach Solisten
ECO	English Chamber Orchestra
FK	Frankfurt Kantorei
HCO	Hungarian Chamber Orchestra
HRT	Hungarian Radio and Television
HSO	Hungarian State Symphony Orchestra
LAPO	Los Angeles Philharmonic Orchestra
LOL	Little Orchestra, London
LPO	London Philharmonic Orchestra
LSO	London Symphony Orchestra
MB	Munich Bach Orchestra
MPAC	Munich Pro Arte Chamber Orchestra
MPO	Moscow Philharmonic Orchestra
MRSO	Moscow Radio Symphony Orchestra
NPhO	New Philharmonia Orchestra
NSL	New Symphony, London
NWE	Netherlands Wind Ensemble
NYP	New York Philharmonic Orchestra
ORTF	O.R.T.F. Philharmonic Orchestra
OSCCP	Orchestre de la Societe des Concerts du Conservatoire du Paris
OSR	L'Orchestre de la Suisse Romande
PCO	Prague Chamber Orchestra
PH	Philharmonia Hungarica
PhO	Philharmonia Orchestra, London
PO	Philadelphia Orchestra
PSO	Prague Symphony Orchestra
ROHO	Royal Opera House Orchestra, Covent Garden
RPO	Royal Philharmonic Orchestra
SBC	Stuttgart Bach Collegium
SCO	Stuttgart Chamber Orchestra
SDR	Stuttgart S.D.R. Symphony Orchestra
SSO	Sydney Symphony Orchestra
VCM	Vienna Concentus Musicus
VPM	Vienna Pro Musica
VPO	Vienna Philharmonic Orchestra
VSO	Vienna Symphony Orchestra
VSOO	Vienna State Opera Orchestra

Instrumental

acc	accordion	mand	mandolin
bal	balalaika	mar	marimba
bs	bass	ob	oboe
bsn	bassoon	ond	ondes martenot
c	celesta	org	organ
cimb	cimbalon	perc	percussion
cld	clavichord	pic	piccolo
clt	clarinet	pno	piano
cor	cornet	rec	recorder
dr	drums	sax	saxophone
Eh	English horn	sit	sitar
flt	flute	tpt	trumpet
Fr hn	French horn	trom	trombone
gtr	guitar	vib	vibraphone
harm	harmonica	v	viol
hn	horn	vla	viola
hp	harp	vlc	violoncello
hpd	harpsichord	vln	violin
lt	lute	z	zither

Vocal

bar	baritone	ms	mezzo-soprano
bs	bass	s	soprano
con	contralto	t	tenor
c-t	countertenor		

Qualitative Evaluation of Recordings

++	excellent or very good	/	fair
+	good	–	poor
+–	mixed	*	no evaluation

ABAELARD, Peter
    O quanta qualia. See no. 3960
ABBIATE, Louis
1   Sonata, piano, no. 3, op. 34, E flat major. Bernard Ringeissen,
        pno. Calliope CAL 1872
            +HFN 12-80 p131
ABREU
    Tico Tico. See no. 3568
ABSIL, Jean
    Pieces en quatuor. See no. 3718
2   Suite sur des themes populaires roumains. CLERISSE: Introduction
        et scherzo. PIERNE, G.: Introduction et variations sur une ronde
        populaire. PIERNE, P.: Trois conversations. Nova Saxophone
        Quartet. Crystal S 153
            +FF 9/10-80 p283   ++NR 12-78 p9
            +IN 11-79 p10
ABT, Franz
    Laughing. See no. 3791
ACHAVAL
    Milonga del andariego. See no. 3614
ACHRON, Joseph
    Hebrew dance, op. 35, no. 1. See no. 3964
    Hebrew lullaby, op. 35, no. 2. See no. 3964
    Hebrew melody, op. 33. See no. 3964
    Stimmung, op. 32, no. 1. See no. 3964
ADAM
    Songs: The blessed day; O holy night. See no. 3933
ADAM, Adolphe Charles
    Le chalet: Villons de l'Helvetie. See no. 3979
    Le chalet: Vive le vin l'amour et le tabac. See no. 3631
    Giselle: Peasant pas de deux. See no. 3666
    Le postillon de Longjumeau: Mes amis ecoutez l'histoire. See no.
        3558
    Si j'etais roi. See no. 63
    Le toreador: Ach Mama. See no. 3872
    Le toreador: Ah vous dirai-je Maman. See no. 3559
    Le toreador: Qui le vie. See no. 3631
ADAM DE LA HALLE
    Fines amouretes ai. See no. 3864
3   Le mans d'amor. RAIMBAULT DE VAQUERAS: Kalenda maia. RICHARD I,
        King: Ja nun ma pris. ANON.: 22 pieces. Gerald English, t;
        Jaye Consort. Everest 3447 (From Pye GSGC 14092)
            +ARG 7-79 p49   *NR 6-79 p12
            +-FF 7/8-80 p178

Rondeaux (4). See no. 3910
Tant con je vivrai. See no. 3864
ADAMS
　　Songs: The star of Bethlehem; Thora. See no. 3874
ADDINSELL, Richard
　　Dangerous moonlight: Warsaw concerto. See no. 3790
　　Warsaw concerto. See no. 3605
ADDISON, John
　　A bridge too far. See no. 3786
ADLER, Samuel
　　Canto VIII. See no. 3859
　　Sonata breve. See no. 3859
ADSON, John
　　Courtly masquing ayres (3). See no. 4000
AGUILLERA DE HEREDIA, Sebastian
　　Pange lingua a tres voces. See no. 3756
　　Salve de lleno. See no. 3756
　　Tiento de falsas de quatro tono. See no. 3756
　　Tiento lleno de primer tono. See no. 3756
AHO, Kalevi
4　Quintet, oboe and strings. CRUSELL: Divertimento, op. 9. MOZART:
　　　　Quartet, oboe, K 370, F major. Jauko Teikari, ob; Hannele
　　　　Segerstam, Olavi Palli, vln; Pentii Mikkonen, vla; Veli-Pekka
　　　　Bister, Risto Poutanen, vlc. Finlandia FA 320
　　　　　　　　+HFN 10-80 p111

AHRENS
　　Es kommt ein Schiff geladen. See no. 4036
AHROLD, Frank
5　Songs: Second coming; Song without words. LEWIS: Nuances II.
　　　　Philip Langridge, t; RPO, LSO: Robert Hall Lewis, Harold Farber-
　　　　man. CRI SD 389
　　　　　　　　+FF 7/8-78 p47　　　　　　　　++SFC 8-3-80 p33
　　　　　　　　+NR 8-78 p2
AICHINGER, Gregor
　　Jubilate Deo. See no. 3970
　　Laudate dominum. See no. 3814
AITKIN
　　Maire my girl. See no. 3875
AKSES, Necil Kazim
6　Scherzo. ERKIN: Kocekce. SAYGUN: Bes halk Turkusu. TUZUN: Esin-
　　　　tiler. Ayhan Baran, bs; Budapest Philharmonic Orchestra; Hikmet
　　　　Simsek. Hungaroton SLPX 12073
　　　　　　　　+FF 9/10-80 p294　　　　　　　+MQ 7-78 p418
　　　　　　　　+-HFN 12-80 p151　　　　　　　+-NR 11-80 p3
ALABIEFF (Alabiev), Alexander
　　Die Nachtigall. See no. 3559. See no. 3872
7　Quintet, winds, C minor. IPPOLITOV-IVANOV: Evening in Georgia, op.
　　　　69a. RIMSKY-KORSAKOV: Quintet, B flat major. Alexei Nasedkin,
　　　　pno; Valentin Zveroz, flt; Anatoly Lyubimov, ob; Vladimir Soko-
　　　　lov, clt; Sergei Krasavin, bsn; Anatoly Demin, hn; Emilia Mosk-
　　　　vitina, hp. United Artists UACL 10018
　　　　　　　　+-Gr 1-80 p1171　　　　　　　　/HFN 2-80 p103
　　Songs: Die Nachitgall; Solovei. See no. 3770
ALAIN, Jehan
　　Choral Dorien, op. 47. See no. 4023

Danses (2). See no. 3963
8   Litanies, op. 79. Variations sur un theme de Jannequin. BACH:
       Chorale prelude, S 633, Liebster Jesu wir sind hier; S 632, Wenn
       wir in hochsten Noten sein; S 641, Herr Jesu Christ dich zu uns
       wend. Toccata and fugue, S 565, D minor. BRUHNS: Prelude and
       fugue, E minor. FRANCK: Chorale, no. 3, A minor. Almut Rossler,
       org. Ursina Motette M 1025
                    +-ARG 9-80 p48   +-FF 7/8-80 p169
     Litanies, op. 79. See no. 3658. See no. 3733. See no. 4062
     March in the style of Handel. See no. 4067
9   Suite, no. 1, organ. POULENC: Concerto, organ, timpani and strings,
       G minor. Kjell Johnsen, org; Swedish Royal Orchestra Members;
       Kjell Ingebretsen. Propius 7785
                    +St 2-80 p129

ALBENIZ, Isaac
     Cantos de Espana, op. 232: Baja la palmera; Cordoba. See no. 3816
     Espana, op. 165: Capricho catalan. See no. 3975
     Espana, op. 165: Tango. See no. 3555. See no. 3935
10   Iberia, Bks I and II. Ricardo Requejo, pno. Claves D 8003/4 (2).
                    +Gr 8-80 p240   +HFN 10-80 p101
11   Iberia, Bks I and II. Claudio Arrau, pno. Odyssey Y 35229 (From
       Columbia ML 4194)
                    ++FF 5/6-80 p34   +SFC 9-30-79 p45
                    +HF 1-80 p63   +St 1-80 p112
                    +NYT 11-11-79 pD19
     Iberia: Carnival in Seville. See no. 3621. See no. 3665
12   Iberia: El corpus en Sevilla; Triana (orch. Fernandez Arbos).
       FALLA: El amor brujo: Pantomime; Ritual fire dance. The three-
       cornered hat: Final dance. La vida breve: Spanish dance, no. 1.
       GRANADOS: Goyescas: Intermezzo. TURINA: Danzas fantasticas, op.
       22: Orgia. LSO; Morton Gould. Chalfont SDG 302
                    +-ARG 11-79 p31   +HFN 1-80 p115
                    +-HF 11-79 p116   +St 10-79 p92
     Iberia: Triana. See no. 3825
     Navarra. See no. 3665
13   Piezas caracteristicas: Torre bermeja. BACH: Partita, violin, no.
       2, S 1004, D minor: Chaconne (trans. Newman). SAINZ DE LA MAZA:
       Campanas del alba. TURINA: Fandanguillo, op. 36. Michael New-
       man, gtr. Sheffield LAB 10
                    ++ARG 11-79 p31   +-HF 11-79 p116
                    +FF 11/12-79 p15   +SFC 12-23-79 p40
                    +FF 7/8-80 p174   ++St 11-79 p104
     Piezas caracteristicas: Torre bermeja. See no. 3665. See no. 3722
     Recuerdos de viaje, op. 71: Rumores de la caleta. See no. 3665.
       See no. 3676
14   Songs to Italian texts (6). BAUTISTA: Songs dedicated to Andalusian
       cities. MORENO: Aztec songs (4). RODRIGO: Sephardic songs (4).
       Victoria de los Angeles, s; Geoffrey Parsons, pno. Columbia M
       35139 (also CBS 76833 Tape (c) 40-76833)
                    ++FF 3/4-80 p181   ++NR 12-79 p11
                    +-Gr 2-80 p1288   +-NYT 10-28-79 pD24
                    +-HFN 2-80 p99   +-RR 2-80 p90
                    +-HFN 10-80 p117   +St 2-80 p138
15   Suite espanola, op. 47: Asturias (Leyenda); Sevillanas (arr. A.
       Romero). TORROBA: Piezas caracteristicas. Burgalesa. Fandan-

guillo. RODRIGO: Elogio de la guitarra. ROMERO, C.: Preludes
(2). Angel Romero, gtr. Angel S 37312 Tape (c) 8XS 37312 (ct)
8XS 37312
      +FF 1/2-80 p172   ++St 5-79 p117
      +-NR 4-79 p14
  Suite espanola, op. 47: Asturias. See no. 3975
  Suite espanola, op. 47: Cadiz. See no. 3603
  Suite espanola, op. 47: Granada, Asturias. See no. 3635
  Suite espanola, op. 47: Granada, Sevilla. See no. 3549. See no.
    3607. See no. 3775
  Suite espanola, op. 47: Granada, Sevilla, Castilla. See no. 3609
  Suite espanola, op. 47: Sevilla. See no. 3883. See no. 3964
ALBENIZ, Melchior
  Sonata, D major. See no. 3676
d'ALBERT, Eugene
16 Tiefland (The lowlands). Gre Brouwenstijn, Judith Hellwig, Ruth
    Mixa, Kerttu Metsala, Dodi Protero, s; Waldemar Kmentt, Hans
    Hopf, t; Paul Schoffler, Eberhard Wachter, bar; Oskar Czerwenka,
    bs; VSOO Chorus; VSO; Rudolf Moralt. Philips 6768 026 (2)
        +FF 5/6-80 p34
  Tiefland, excerpts. See no. 4071
  Tiefland: Pedro's dream. See no. 3770
  Tiefland: Sein bin ich. See no. 3774
ALBINONI, Tommaso
17 Adagio, G minor. BACH: Cantata, no. 147, Jesu joy of man's desiring.
    Cantata, no. 140, Sleepers awake. Suite, orchestra, S 1068, D
    major: Air on the G string. CIMAROSA: Concerto, guitar, D major.
    MARCELLO: Concerto, guitar, D minor. VIVALDI: Concerto, guitar,
    D major. Liona Goyd, gtr; ECO; Andrew Davis. Columbia M 35853
        +-MUM 3/4-80 p33   +-NR 8-80 p14
18 Adagio, G minor. PACHELBEL: Canon, D major. TELEMANN: Concerto,
    flute, violin and violoncello. Jean-Pierre Rampal, flt; Colleg-
    ium Musicum Paris; Roland Douatte. Everest SDBR 3462
        +NR 7-80 p16
19 Adagio, G minor. Concerto, op. 9, no. 8, G minor. Concerto, op. 9,
    no. 1, B flat major. Concerto, op. 10, no. 8, G minor. Maria
    Teresa Garatti, org; Leo Driehuys, Heinz Holliger, Maurice Bour-
    gue, ob; Felix Ayo, Roberto Michelucci, vln; I Musici. Philips
    6570 085 Tape (c) 7310 085 (From AXS 3005, 6580 001)
        +FF 9/10-78 p10   +RR 11-79 p65
        +-Gr 11-79 p801   ++SFC 7-9-78 p54
        +HFN 11-79 p157   +STL 12-9-79 p41
        +HFN 1-80 p123 tape
20 Adagio, G minor. BONPORTI: Concerto, violin, op. 11, no. 6: Reci-
    tativo. VIVALDI: Concerto, bassoon, RV 501. Concerto, oboe,
    op. 11, no. 6. Concerto, orchestra. Jean-Francois Paillard
    Chamber Orchestra; Jean-Francois Paillard. RCA GL 2-5239 Tape
    (c) GK 2-5239
        +Gr 1-80 p1162   +-HFN 1-80 p123 tape
        +-HFN 10-79 p167   +-RR 4-80 p127 tape
  Adagio, G minor. See no. 31. See no. 3602. See no. 3912. See
    no. 3942. See no. 3943. See no. 3999. See no. 4030
21 Concerti, op. 2 (12). I Solisti Veneti; Claudio Scimone. Erato
    STU 71234 (2)
        +-Gr 4-80 p1549   -MT 12-80 p783
        +-HFN 4-80 p100   +RR 4-80 p52

22   Concerti, op. 7, nos. 1-2, 4; op. 9, no. 3, F major; op. 1, B major.
       Ingo Goritzki, Jochen Muller-Brincken, ob; Jorg Ewald Dahler,
       hpd; Monteverdi Instrumental Academy; Hans Ludwig Hirsch.   Claves
       D 601
               +–Gr 7-80 p157   +–HFN 8-80 p93
23   Concerti, op. 7, nos. 2-3, 5-6, 8-9, 11-12. Heinz Holliger, Hans
       Elhorst, ob; Camerata Bern. DG 2533 409 Tape (c) 3310 409
               +FF 3/4-80 p34   ++NR 2-80 p5
               +Gr 11-79 p801   +NYT 12-2-79 pD22
               ++HF 4-80 p104 tape   +RR 11-79 p67
               +HFN 11-79 p133   ++SFC 4-20-80 p34
24   Concerto, op. 7, no. 3, B flat major. HERTEL: Concerto, trumpet
       and oboe a 6. HUMMEL: Concerto, trumpet, E flat major. Andre
       Bernard, tpt; Heinz Holliger, ob; ECO; George Malcom. CBS 35856
       Tape (c) MT 35856 (also CBS 76862)
               +–FF 9/10-80 p137   +–NYT 5-18-80 pD32
               +Gr 11-79 p854   ++RR 11-79 p66
               +HFN 11-79 p151   ++St 10-80 p108
25   Concerto, op. 7, no. 4, G major. LECLAIR: Concerto, violin, op. 7,
       no. 3, C major. MOZART: Andante, K 315, C major. PERGOLESI:
       Concerto, flute, no. 1, G major (attrib.). Alexandre Magnin,
       flt; Heidelberg Chamber Orchestra. Da Camera Magna SM 91037
               -FF 1/2-80 p173
     Concerto, op. 76, no. 6, D major. See no. 31
     Concerto, op. 9, no. 1, B flat major. See no. 19
26   Concerti, op. 9, nos. 2, 5, 8, 11. Heinz Holliger, ob; I Musici.
       Philips 9502 012 Tape (c) 7313 012
               +FF 3/4-80 p34   +NR 8-80 p7
               ++HF 4-80 p104 tape   +NYT 12-2-79 pD22
     Concerto, op. 9, no. 2, D minor. See no. 31
     Concerto, op. 9, no. 3, F major. See no. 22
27   Concerti, op. 9, nos. 3, 6, 9, 12. Maurice Andre, Guy Touvron, tpt;
       Wurttemberg Chamber Orchestra; Jorg Faerber. Angel SZ 37736
       Tape (c) 4ZS 37736
               +ARG 11-80 p14   +NYT 5-18-80 pD32
               +FF 7/8-80 p40   +SFC 4-20-80 p34
               +NR 7-80 p3
     Concerto, op. 9, no. 8, G minor. See no. 19
28   Concerti, op. 10. Piero Toso, Giuliano Carmignola, vln; Daniele
       Roi, hpd; I Solisti Veneti; Claudio Scimone. Erato STU 71311 (2)
               +Gr 11-80 p660   ++HFN 12-80 p131
     Concerto, op. 10, no. 1, B major. See no. 22
     Concerto, op. 10, no. 8, G minor. See no. 12
     Concerto, trumpet, C major. See no. 3563
     Concerto, trumpet, F major. See no. 3999
29   Concerto, trumpet, op. 6, no. 4, D minor. MARCELLO: Concerto, trum-
       pet, C minor. HAYDN: Concerto, trumpet, E flat major. TELEMANN:
       Concerto, trumpet, F minor. Maurice Andre, tpt; LPO; Jesus Lopez-
       Cobos. HMV ASD 3760 Tape (c) TC ASD 3760 (also Angel S 37513)
               +FF 11/12-79 p158   ++HFN 12-79 p185 tape
               ++Gr 9-79 p477   +–RR 9-79 p66
               ++HFN 9-79 p119   +–RR 4-80 p128 tape
     Sinfonia, B flat major. See no. 31
     Sonata, C minor. See no. 31
30   Sonata, trumpet, C major. BACH: Ave Maria (Gounod). Cantata, op.

63: Choruses. Easter oratorio, S 249: Sinfonia. MALOTTE: The
Lord's prayer. TELEMANN: Heidenmusik. David Hickman, tpt;
William Neil, org; Baroque Consort. Crystal S 702
　　　　　+FF 5/6-80 p195　　　　　　　　+NR 4-80 p6
Suite en sol. See no. 4001

31　Works, selections: Adagio, G minor (arr. Giazotto). Concerto, op.
9, no. 2, D minor. Concerto, op. 7, no. 6, D major. Sinfonia,
B flat major. Sonata, C minor. Maurice Andre, tpt; Jacques
Chambon, ob; Georg-Friedrich Hendel, vln; Saar Radio Chamber
Orchestra; Karl Ristenpart. Erato STU 70231 Tape (c) MCE 70231
　　　　　+Gr 4-76 p1587　　　　　　　　+HFN 9-80 p115 tape
　　　　　+FF 11/12-79 p20　　　　　　　+NR 3-74 p14
　　　　　+-HFN 5-76 p91　　　　　　　　+RR 4-76 p35

ALBRECHTSBERGER, Johann

32　Concerto, organ, B flat major. BACH, C.P.E.: Concerto, organ, E
flat major. HAYDN: Concerti, organ, C major, F major. HAYDN,
M.: Concerto, organ and viola, C major. Jane Parker-Smith, org;
Lubomir Maly, vla; PCO; Steuart Bedford. HMV SQ SLS 5164 (2)
Tape (c) TC SLS 5164
　　　　　+Gr 6-79 p31　　　　　　　　　+MT 3-80 p181
　　　　　+HFN 7-79 p117　　　　　　　　+RR 8-79 p82
　　　　　+HFN 9-79 p123 tape

33　Concerto, trombone, B flat amjor. ANGERER: Luctus Gaudium. LARS-
SON: Concertino, trombone and strings. MOZART, L.: Concerto,
trombone, D major. Branimir Slokar, trom; Southwest German Cham-
ber Orchestra; Paul Angerer. Claves D 707
　　　　　+HFN 5-80 p133
Concerto a cinque, E flat major. See no. 3563

ALCOCK

34　Out of the deep. BYRD: Exalt thyself O God, anthem. EAST: O Lord
of whom I do depend; When Israel came out of Egypt; When David
heard that Absalom was slain. Magnificat: Nunc dimittis. HAR-
RIS, W.: Almighty and most merciful father; I was glad when they
said unto me; Come down O lord divine; King of glory king of
peace. Lichfield Cathedral Choir; Peter King, org; Jonathan
Rees-Williams. Alpha APS 311
　　　　　+-Gr 11-80 p728

ALCOCK, John
　Voluntary, D major. See no. 3656. See no. 4041

ALEXIUS, Carl

35　Sonatina. GERSHWIN: Rhapsody in blue (arr. Dokschitzer). HINDE-
MITH: Sonata, trumpet and piano. MARTINU: Sonatina. Edward Tarr,
tpt; Elisabeth Westenholz, pno. BIS LP 152
　　　　　+HFN 10-80 p112

ALFANO
　Risurrezione: Katyusha's scene. See no. 3928

ALFONSO X, King

36　Las cantigas de Santa Maria. Clemencic Consort; Rene Clemencic.
Harmonia Mundi HM 977/9 (3)
　　　　　+-FF 11/12-80 p54　　　　　　　　++HFN 3-79 p129
　　　　　+Gr 3-78 p1605
Cantigas, nos. 159, 200, 277, 281. See no. 3760
Rosa das rosas. See no. 3647

ALFORD, Kenneth
　Old Panama. See no. 3617

ALFVEN, Hugo
    Swedish rhapsody, no. 1, op. 19. See no. 3915
37   Symphony, no. 4, op. 39, C minor. Elizabeth Soderstrom, s; Gosta
      Windbergh, t; Stockholm Philharmonic Orchestra; Stig Westerberg.
      Bluebell Bell 107
              +FF 3/4-80 p35

ALKAN, Charles
38   Concerto, piano, no. 2, C sharp minor. BERWALD: Concerto, piano,
      D major. CZERNY: Divertissement de concert, op. 204. LISZT:
      Malediction, G 121. Michael Ponti, pno; Southwest German Cham-
      ber Orchestra; Paul Angerer. Turnabout TV 34740
         +-ARG 3-80 p49   +-FU 4-80 p47
         +-FF 5/6-80 p99
39   Esquises, op. 63, no. 45: Les diablotins. LISZT: Malediction.
      WAGNER: Siegfried Idyll. John Bingham, pno; Ensemble 13 Baden
      Baden; Manfred Reichert. Harmonia Mundi 1C 065 99843
         +-FF 5/6-80 p99   +RR 2-80 p63

ALLEGRI, Gregorio
40   Miserere. MUNDY: Vox patris caelestis. PALESTRINA: Missa Papae
      Marcelli. Alison Stamp, treble; Tallis Scholars; Peter Philips.
      Classics for Pleasure CFP 40339 Tape (c) TC CFP 40339
         +Gr 10-80 p523   +HFN 10-80 p110
         +Gr 12-80 p889 tape   +HFN 12-80 p159 tape
    Miserere. See no. 3939

ALONSO (16th century Spain)
    La tricotea Samartin. See no. 3864. See no. 4002

ALTENBURG, Johann
    Concerto, trumpet, D major. See no. 3674

ALTER
    Akavyah. See no. 3922

ALVARADO, Diego de
    Tiento. See no. 3871

ALVAREZ
    La mantilla. See no. 3901
    Suspiros de Espana. See no. 3921

ALVARS
    La mandoline. See no. 3678

ALWYN, William
    Derby day. See no. 3829

d'AMBROSIO, Alfredo
    Serenade, no. 4. See no. 3964

AMIROV, Fikret
41   Sevil. Eleanora Andreyeva, Lyudmila Simonova, L. Imanov, I. Budrin,
      L. Isaeva; MRSO and Chorus. Melodiya 33D 019415-20
         +FF 7/8-80 p40

AMMERBACH, Elias
    Ich sag ade. See no. 3590

AMON, Johann
42   Quartet, horn, F major. MOZART, L.: Sinfonia da caccia, G major.
      Sinfonia da camera, D major. ROSETTI: Concerto, horn, F major.
      Hermann Baumann, Christoph Kohler, Mahir Cakar, Jean-Pierre
      Letetit, hn; Jaap Schroder, vln; Wiel Peeters, vla; Anner Bylsma,
      vlc; Concerto Amsterdam; Jaap Schroder. HNH 4033 (also Acanta
      DC 22752)
         +FF 9/10-79 p177   ++SFC 7-15-79 p47
         +NYT 12-2-79 pD22   ++St 9-79 p96
        ++RR 1-80 p83

AMRAM, David
    Fanfare. See no. 3740
    Portraits. See no. 3739
ANCHIETA, Juan de
    Songs: Con amores la mi madre. See no. 3698
ANDERSEN, S.
    Der flyvver saa mange Fugle. See no. 3774
ANDERSON
    Fiddle faddle. See no. 3962
    The syncopated clock. See no. 3962
ANDRIENSSEN, Hendrik
    Fantasie. See no. 3612
    Variations and fugue on a theme by Kuhnau. See no. 3818
ANERIO, Giovanni
    Christus factus est. See no. 3763
ANGERER, Paul
    Luctus Gaudium. See no. 33
ANGLADA
    Brindo a tu salud. See no. 3930
ANGLES, Rafael
    Adagio, D minor. See no. 3942
d'ANNIBALE
    O paese d'o sole. See no. 3667
ANTHEIL, George
43 Symphony, no. 5. MAXWELL DAVIES: St. Thomas Wake. Louisville Orch-
        estra; Richard Duffallo. Louisville LS 770
                +-FF 11/12-80 p134   +NR 11-80 p3
APPLETON, Jon
    In deserto. See no. 44
    Mussems sang. See no. 44
    The Sydsing camklang. See no. 44
    Syntrophia. See no. 44
44 Works, selections: In deserto. Musseums sang. The Sydsing camk-
        lang. Syntrophia. Zoetrope. Jon Appleton, synclavier and
        other digital systems. Folkways 33445
                +-ARG 2-79 p10   +NR 1-80 p15
    Zoetrope. See no. 44
ARAUJO, Juan de
    Los cofla desde la estleya. See no. 3849
    Villancico. See no. 3708
ARBEAU, Thoinot
45 L'Orchesographie: Branle de Poictou. Branle d'Escosse. Pavane
        "Belle qui tiens ma vie". Gaillardes: Si j'aime ou non; J'ay-
        meray mieulx dormir seulette; Anthoinette; La traditore. Branle
        de La Haye. Branle de l'Official. Bransles de Champagne: Le
        guerre; Cassandre; Pinagay; Aridan; Charlotte. Branle de Chan-
        elier. Branle des Hermites. Branle de Malte. Branle des
        Lavandieres. Branle de pois. Branle des Sabots. Branle de
        chevaux. Allemandes. Volte. Basse danse et retour Joyssance
        vous donneray. Tourdion. Branle double. Branle simple. Branle
        gay. Branle de Bourgoigne. Branle de la Montarde. Gavottes.
        Michel Block, Remy Dubois, Claude Flagel, Anne-Marie Hess, Sophie
        Jacques de Dixmude, Annick and Jacques Ledent, Jerome Lejeune,
        Catou Pecher, Bernard Vanderheijden, Marion Vergruggen; Georges
        Octors, early instruments; Claude Flagel. Le Chant de Mond LDZ
        74649

+—HFN 8-80 p93   +—RR 8-80 p64

ARCADELT, Jacques
    Ancidetimi pur.   See no. 3683
    Ave Maria. See no. 3934
    Che piu foc'al. See no. 3806
    Da si felice sorte. See no. 3683
    Donna quando pietosa. See no. 3683
ARCHER, Violet
46   Sonata, clarinet and piano. Sonata, horn and piano. Sonata, alto
        saxophone and piano. Paul Brodie, sax; George Brough, Armas
        Maiste, Gloria Saarinen, pno; Pierre Del Vescova, hn; James Camp-
        bell, clt. Radio Canada International 412
            +FF 3/4-80 p36
    Sonata, horn and piano. See no. 46
    Sonata, alto saxophone and piano. See no. 46
ARDITI, Luigi
    Parla waltz. See no. 3695
    Songs: Il bacio; L'Incantrice; Leggiero invisible. See no. 3770
ARENSKY, Anton
    Concerto, violin, A minor: Tempo di valse. See no. 3964
    Valse. See no. 3882
ARIOSTI, Attilio
47   Sonatas, viola d'amore, A major, D minor. CORRETTE: Sonata, viola
        d'amore, A major. MILANDRE: Andantino and menuetto, D major.
        STAMITZ: Sonata, viola d'amore, D major. Gunther Lemmen, vla
        d'amore; Alfred Lessing, vla da gamba; Fritz Neumeyer, hpd. Toc-
        cata FSM 53624
            +HFN 5-80 p134
ARIOSTI
    La profezio d'Eliseo nel'assedio di Amaria: Ma per destin peggiore
        ...Prole tenera. See no. 3729
ARMA, Paul
48   Sonata, solo violoncello. BACH: Suite, solo violoncello, no. 2,
        S 1008, D minor. Roy Christensen, vlc. Gasparo GS 106
            +—FF 9/10-80 p50   +NR 7-80 p13
ARNAUD, Leo
49   Fanfares: Olympic theme; La chasse; Olympiad. GRAINGER: Lincolshire
        posy. Shepherd's hey. VAUGHAN WILLIAMS: English folk song suite.
        Toccata marziale. Cleveland Symphony Winds; Frederick Fennell.
        Telarc DG 10050
            +Gr 8-80 p326   +HFN 9-80 p114
ARNDT, Felix
    Marionette. See no. 4045
ARNE, Thomas
50   Air and gigue. BRITTEN: Symphony symphony, op. 4. ELGAR: Serenade,
        op. 20, E minor. Toronto Chamber Orchestra; Boyd Need. Ultra-
        Fi ULDD 10
            +FU 6-80 p45
    As you like it: Under the greenwood tree. See no. 3795
    Concerto, harpsichord, G minor. See no. 3691
    Sonatas, harpsichord, F major, E minor. See no. 3745
    Songs: Where the bee sucks. See no. 3778. See no. 3840
ARNOLD
    Wenn der Herrgott net will. See no. 3711
ARNOLD, Malcolm
    Beckus the dandipratt. See no. 57. See no. 3829

51   Concerto, flute, no. 2, op. 111. Concerto, flute and strings, op.
       45. Serenade, small orchestra. Sinfonietta, no. 3, op. 81.
       Richard Adeney, flt; Bournemouth Sinfonietta; Ronald Thomas. HMV
       ASD 3868 Tape (c) TC ASD 3868
                   ++Gr 7-80 p135   +HFN 9-80 p115 tape
                   +Gr 8-80 p548 tape   +RR 8-80 p36
     Concerto, flute and strings, op. 45. See no. 51
52   Concerto, harmonica. BENJAMIN: Concerto, harmonica. VILLA-LOBOS:
       Concerto, harmonica. Tommy Reilly, harm; London Sinfonietta;
       David Atherton. Argo ZRG 905
                   ++Gr 1-80 p1137   ++RR 12-79 p82
                   +HFN 12-79 p175
53   Concerto, 2 violins, op. 77. MARTIN: Concerto, violoncello. Step-
       hen Kates, vlc; Paul Kling, Peter McHugh, vln; Louisville Orches-
       tra; Jorge Mester. Louisville LS 731
                   +FU 3-80 p46
     Cornish dances, op. 91. See no. 58
     Fantasy, op. 86. See no. 3588
     Peterloo overture, op. 97. See no. 58
54   Scottish dances, op. 59 (4). Symphony, no. 3, op. 63. LPO; Malcolm
       Arnold. Desto DS 6448 (Reissue)
                   +ARG 9-78 p18   +SFC 5-7-78 p46
                   +FF 7/8-80 p41
55   Serenade, guitar and strings. CASTELNUOVO-TEDESCO: Concerto, guitar,
       no. 1, op. 99, D major. DODGSON: Concerto, guitar, no. 2. John
       Williams, gtr; ECO; Charles Groves. CBS 76634 Tape (c) 40-76634
       (also Columbia M 35172)
                   ++FF 9/10-80 p95   ++NR 2-80 p4
                   +-Gr 12-77 p1067   +RR 1-78 p43; 1-78 p15
                   ++Gr 2-78 p1471 tape   +RR 2-78 p95 tape
                   +HFN 1-78 p117   ++St 3-80 p93
                   +HFN 3-78 p155 tape
     Serenade, small orchestra. See no. 51
     Sinfonietta, no. 3, op. 81. See no. 51
     Solitaire. See no. 57
56   Sonata, oboe and piano. JACOB: Sonata, oboe and piano. POULENC:
       Sonata, oboe and piano. SAINT-SAENS: Sonata, oboe and piano,
       op. 166, D major. Sonia Trubashnik, ob; Lara Trubashnik, pno.
       Pavane ADW 7007
                   +-Gr 5-80 p1689
57   Symphony, no. 1. Beckus the dandipratt. Solitaire. Bournemouth
       Symphony Orchestra; Malcolm Arnold. HMV ASD 3823 Tape (c) TC
       ASD 3823
                   +-Gr 6-80 p31   ++RR 6-80 p38
                   ++HFN 6-80 p102
     Symphony, no. 3, op. 63. See no. 54
58   Symphony, no. 5, op. 74. Cornish dances, op. 91 (4). Peterloo
       overture, op. 97. Birmingham Symphony Orchestra; Malcolm Arnold.
       HMV ASD 2878
                   +Audio 12-77 p48   ++HFN 5-73 p978
                   ++FF 3/4-80 p38   +RR 5-73 p39
                   +-Gr 5-73 p2041
59   Symphony, brass instruments, op. 123. PREMRU: Music for Harter
       Fell. SALZEDO: Capriccio, op. 90. Philip Jones Brass Ensemble;
       Howard Snell. Argo ZRG 906 Tape (c) KZRC 906

      ++Gr 11-79 p801   +HFN 12-79 p177
      +Gr 2-80 p1302   ++RR 11-79 p67

60   Three shanties. FARKAS: Ancient Hungarian dances. IBERT: Pieces
        breves (3). NIELSEN: Quintet, op. 43. Frosunda Wind Quintet.
        BIS LP 136
             +HFN 4-80 p115   +RR 3-80 p75
             ++NR 3-80 p8   +St 4-80 p136

ARZRUNI, Sahan
    Invocation. See no. 3851
    Mentations, no. 1. See no. 3851
    Heterophonic suite, excerpts. See no. 3851

ASHFIELD, Robert
    The fair chivalry. See no. 3524

ASHFORTH, Alden
61   Byzantia (Two journeys after Yeats). Dennis Heath, t; James Bros-
        sert, org; Alden Ashforth, synthesizers. Orion ORS 74164 Tape
        (c) OC 829
             ++HF 10-75 p70   ++NR 10-75 p11
             +HF 8-80 p87 tape   +NR 9-80 p1 tape

ASHRAFI, Mukhtar
62   Mukhabbat, ballet suite. Uzbek Navoi Bolshoi Theatre Orchestra;
        Mukhtar Ashrafi. Melodiya 33M30 35923/4
               -FF 7/8-80 p41

ATTAIGNANT, Pierre
    Branles (5). See no. 3683
    Galliard. See no. 3590
    La guerre. See no. 3612
    La Magdalena. See no. 3612
    Pavane et galliarde. See no. 3754
    Tordion. See no. 3754

ATTERBERG, Kurt
    Symphony, no. 6, op. 31, C major. See no. 4071

ATTWOOD, Thomas
    Come holy ghost. See no. 3815
    Psalm, no. 98. See no. 3567
    To all that breathe the air of heaven. See no. 3873

AUBER, Daniel
63   Fra Diavolo. Overtures: ADAM: Si j'etais roi. BOIELDIEU: La dame
        blanche. THOMAS: Mignon. Cecila Fusco, Margaret Simoncini, s;
        Giuseppe Campora, Romano Grigolo, t; Marco Stecchi, Palo Mazzotta,
        bar; Vito Susca, Alfredo Mariotti, bs; Teatro Giuseppe Verdi Or-
        chestra, Monte Carlo Opera Orchestra; Arturo Basile, Louis Fre-
        maux. DG 2726 072 (Reissue)
             +FF 7/8-80 p41   -NYT 12-16-79 pD21
             -NR 2-80 p11   +SFC 1-6-80 p43
    Fra Diavolo: Pour toujours disait-elle. See no. 3558
    Fra Diavolo: Romance; Welches Gluck ich arme. See no. 3770
    Manon Lescaut: L'eclat de rire. See no. 3770
    La muette de Portici: Air du sommeil. See no. 3770

AUFDERHEIDE, May
    Pelham waltzes. See no. 4045

AURIC, George
64   Les facheux. MILHAUD: Le train bleu. SATIE: Jack in the box (Mil-
        haud). Monte Carlo National Orchestra; Igor Markevitch. Varese
        VS 81097

                    +–ARG 3-80 p53   +FF 11/12-80 p156
    Les facheux. See no. 3908
    Interludes (3). See no. 3862
AVISON, Charles
65   Concerti grossi, nos. 1-12. Iona Brown, Malcolm Latchem, vln; Den-
        nis Vigay, vlc; Nicholas Kramer, hpd; AMF; Neville Marriner.
        Philips 6769 018 (3)
                    ++ARG 5-80 p10   +MT 1-80 p33
                    ++FF 3/4-80 p39   ++NR 5-80 p3
                    ++FU 4-80 p44   +NYT 5-25-80 pD21
                    +Gr 9-79 p453   ++RR 9-79 p66
                    ++HF 7-80 p52   +SR 3-1-80 p29
                    +HFN 9-79 p100   +STL 12-2-79 p37
66   Concerti grossi, op. 2, nos. 1, 3, 8-10, 12 (ed. Robertson/ Thomas).
        Bournemouth Sinfonietta; Ronald Thomas. HMV ASD 3842 Tape (c)
        TC ASD 3842
                    +Gr 4-80 p1549   +RR 4-80 p53
                    +HFN 4-80 p100   +STL 5-11-80 p38
                    +–MT 11-80 p709
AYALA, Hector
    Serie americaine. See no. 3706
AZALAIS DE PORCAIRAGUES
    Ar em al freg temps vengut; Vida. See no. 3749
AZZAIOLA, Filippo
    Chi passa per sta strada. See no. 4042
BABBITT, Milton
67   Arie da capo. MARTINO: Concerto, clarinet, bass clarinet and con-
        trabass clarinet. Anand Devendra, Dennis Smylie, Leslie Thimmig,
        clt; Group for Contemporary Music; Harvey Sollberger. Nonesuch
        H 71372
                    +–ARG 7/8-80 p28   +NR 5-80 p8
                    +FF 5/6-80 p100   ++St 6-80 p117
BABELL, William
    Sonata, oboe, no. 1, B major. See no. 3542
BABOU, Rene
68   Fantaisie des trompettes basses et hautes. CHAUMONT: Suite sur le
        2nd ton. SCRONX: Echo, F major, C major. Jozef Sluys, org.
        Zephyr ZO 6
                    +–Gr 7-80 p153   +HFN 9-80 p114
BACEWICZ, Grazyna
69   Concerto, orchestra. Musica sinfonica in tre movimenti. Overture.
        Pensieri notturni. Warsaw Philharmonic Orchestra; Witold Rowicki.
        Muza SX 0274
                    +FF 7/8-80 p121
    Divertimento. See no. 3857
    Kleine Triptychon. See no. 4024
70   Music, strings, trumpets and percussion. MALAWSKI: Symphonic etudes.
        PENDERECKI: Threnody for the victims of Hiroshima. Regina Smend-
        zianka, pno; Warsaw Philharmonic Orchestra; Witold Rowicki, Stan-
        islaw Wislocki. Muza SX 0171
                    +FF 7/8-80 p121
    Musica sinfonia in tre movimenti. See no. 69
    Overture. See no. 69
    Pensieri notturni. See no. 69

BACH, Carl Philipp Emanuel
71   Concerti, flute, A minor, B flat major, A major, G major. Aurele
       Nicolet, flt; Netherlands Chamber Orchestra; David Zinman. Phil-
       ips 6747 444 (2)
                  +-Gr 11-80 p660   +HFN 10-80 p101
72   Concerto, flute, D minor. STAMITZ: Concerto, flute, op. 29, G major.
       VIVALDI: Concerto, flute, RV 428, D major. Eugenia Zukerman, flt;
       ECO; Pinchas Zukerman. Columbia M 35879
                  +NR 12-80 p5
73   Concerti, flute, D minor, G major. Hans-Martin Linde, flt; Lucerne
       Festival Strings; Rudolf Baumgartner. DG 2547 021 Tape (c) 3347
       021 (From 198435)
                  +Gr 8-80 p258   +HFN 9-80 p115 tape
                  +Gr 9-80 p413 tape
74   Concerto, flute, D minor. HOFFMEISTER: Concerto, flute, no. 6, D
       major. Ingrid Dingfelder, flt; ECO; Charles Mackerras. Enigma
       K 53575 (also Nonesuch H 71388)
                  +Gr 4-79 p1696   +RR 3-79 p55
                  +Audio 12-80 p89
75   Concerto, flute, D minor. Concerto, violoncello, A major. Jean-
       Pierre Rampal, flt; Robert Bex, vlc; Huguette Dreyfus, hpd; Cham-
       ber Orchestra; Pierre Boulez. Harmonia Mundi HMU 545
                  +HFN 7-80 p117   -ST 11-80 p500
                  -RR 7-80 p48
76   Concerto, harpsichord, D minor. Concerto, oboe, E flat major. Gus-
       tav Leonhardt, hpd; Helmut Hucke, ob; Collegium Aureum; Franz-
       josef Maier. Harmonia Mundi 065 99828
                  +Gr 9-80 p326   +MT 12-80 p783
                  +-HFN 7-80 p117   +RR 7-80 p48
77   Concerto, 2 harpsichords. BACH. J.S.: Concerto, harpsichord, S 1052,
       D minor. Gustav Leonhardt, Alan Curtis, hpd; Collegium Aureum.
       Harmonia Mundi 065 99785
                  +HFN 11-80 p131
78   Concerto, 2 harpsichords, F major. BACH, J.C.: Concerto, piano, op.
       7, no. 6, G major. BACH, W.F.: Concerto, harpsichord, C minor.
       Robert Veyron-Lacroix, pno and hpd; Huguette Dreyfus, hpd; Saar
       Radio Chamber Orchestra; Karl Ristenpart. Musical Heritage Soci-
       ety MHS 4047
                  +FF 3/4-80 p49
79   Concerti, oboe, B flat major, E flat major. Peter Pongracz, ob;
       Ferenc Liszt Chamber Orchestra; Janos Sandor. Hungaroton SLPX
       12120
                  +HFN 12-80 p131
     Concerto, oboe, E flat major. See no. 76.
     Concerto, organ, E flat major.   See no. 32
80   Concerto, violoncello, A major. COUPERIN: Pieces en concert (arr.
       Bazelaire). VIVALDI: Concerti, violoncello, G minor, G major
       (arr. Malipiero). Lynn Harrell, vlc; ECO; Pinchas Zukerman. HMV
       ASD 3899 Tape (c) TC ASD 3899
                  +-Gr 11-80 p684   +HFN 12-80 p159 tape
                  +HFN 10-80 p111
     Concerto, violoncello, B flat major. See no. 75
81   Duets (4). BACH, J.C.: Sonata, 2 harpsichords, op. 15, no. 5, G
       major. BACH, J.S.: Canons (14). BACH, W.F.: Concerto, 2 harp-
       sichords, F major. Rolf Junghanns, Bradford Tracey, hpd. Toc-
       cato 53622 (also Nonesuch H 71357 Tape (c) N5 71357)

+FF 9/10-80 p50   +MT 11-79 p920
+-HFN 7-79 p116   +NR 5-79 p14
+-HFN 12-79 p110 tape   +NYT 4-22-79 pD25
++MQ 10-77 p563   +RR 7-79 p96

82   Fantasia, C major. Rondo, no. 1, C major. Sonata, harpsichord,
     no. 1, G major. HAYDN: Sonatas, piano, B major, D major. Fritz
     Neumeyer, cld. Harmonia Mundi 065 99798
                    +FF 7/8-80 p98   +-RR 2-80 p76
                    /HFN 1-80 p101

83   Fantasia, C minor. Fantasias, C minor (2). BACH, J.S.: Chromatic
     fantasia and fugue, S 903, D minor. BACH, W.F.: Fantasia, D
     minor. MOZART: Fantasia, K 397, D minor. Colin Tilney, cld.
     DG 2533 326
                    ++AR 2-80 p176   +MT 12-78 p1055
                    +ARG 3-77 p39   +-NR 7-77 p14
                    ++Gr 4-78 p1750   +-RR 4-78 p75
                    ++HF 5-77 p100   ++SFC 9-11-77 p42
                    ++HFN 4-78 p109   ++St 6-77 p91

     Fantasias, C minor (3). See no. 83

84   Fantasia and fugue, C minor. Sonata, organ, G minor. BACH, W.F.:
     Fugues (5). KREBS: Prelude, B flat major. SCHNEIDER: Fantasia
     and fugue, D minor. Volker Lutz, org. Audite FSM 53183
                    +-FF 5/6-80 p184

85   Fantasia and fugue, C minor. Sonata, organ, no. 2, B flat major.
     BACH, J.M.: Wenn wir in hochsten Noten sein. BACH, J.S.: Chor-
     ale preludes, S 659, Nun komm der Heiden Heiland; S 671, Kyrie
     Gott heiliger Geist. Prelude and fugue, S 552, E flat major.
     Gerald Gifford, org. Vista VPS 1088
                    ++NR 12-80 p10

     Fantasia and fugue, C minor. See no. 3618
     March. See no. 3569
     Rondo, no. 1, C major. See no. 82

86   Sinfonias, nos. 1-4. ECO; Raymond Leppard. Philips 9502 013
                    ++FF 7/8-80 p42   ++St 6-80 p83
                    ++NR 7-80 p3

87   Sinfonias, nos. 1-6. English Concert; Trevor Pinnock. DG 2533 449
                    +Gr 10-80 p487   +HFN 10-80 p101

88   Sinfonias, nos. 1-6; C major, D major. Academy of Ancient Music;
     Christopher Hogwood. L'Oiseau-Lyre DSLO 557/8 (2) Tape (c) KDSL
     2-7064
                    +Gr 11-79 p802   +RR 4-80 p128 tape
                    +HFN 11-79 p133   +STL 12-2-79 p37
                    ++RR 11-79 p68

89   Sonata, flute, A minor. STAMITZ, C.: Concerti, flute, D major, G
     major. James Galway, flt; New Irish Chamber Orchestra; Andre
     Prieur. RCA RL 2-5315 Tape (c) RK 2-5315
                    +Gr 11-80 p660

     Sonata, flute, A minor. See no. 4006

90   Sonata, flute and harpsichord, D major. BENDA: Sonata, flute and
     harpsichord, D major. FREDERICK II, King: Sonata, flute, no. 48,
     E minor. QUANTZ: Sonata, flute, op. 1, no. 1, A minor. Hans-
     Martin Linde, flt; Johannes Koch, vla da gamba; Hugo Ruf, hpd.
     Harmonia Mundi 065 99865
                    +-HFN 7-80 p117   +-RR 8-80 p73

91   Sonata, flute and violin, D minor. FREDERICK II, King: Symphony,

D major. GRAUN: Trio sonata, F major. QUANTZ: Concerto, flute,
G major. Hans-Ulrich Niggemann, flt; Emil Seiler Chamber Orches-
tra; Stuttgart Chamber Music Ensemble; Carl Gorvin. DG 2547 014
Tape (c) 3347 014 (From SAPM 198319)
>   +Gr 8-80 p258
Sonata, harp, F major. See no. 3819
Sonata, harp, G major. See no. 3564
92   Sonatas, harpsichord, F major, B minor. BACH, J.C.F.: Sonatina, A
minor. BACH, W.F.: Sonata, harpsichord, B flat minor. Rolf
Junghanns, cld. Telefunken 6-42073
>   +FF 5/6-80 p192
93   Sonatas, harpsichord, nos. 1-6. Bob van Asperen, hpd. Telefunken
EK 6-35378 (2)
>   ++Audio 2-80 p43   ++HFN 4-79 p117
>   +FF 3/4-80 p39   ++NYT 1-27-80 pD20
>   ++Gr 6-79 p74   +RR 4-79 p92
Sonata, harpsichord, no. 1, G major. See no. 82
94   Sonata, harpsichord, no. 1, E minor: Andante. Sonata, harpsichord,
no. 3, B minor: Cantabile. BACH, J.S.: Anna Magdalena notebook,
S 508: So off ich meine Tabakspfeife. Chorale prelude, S 691,
Wer nur den lieben Gott lasst walten. Marcia, S Anh 122, D major.
Menuets, S Anh 114-115, S 121. Musette, S Anh 126, D major. The
well-tempered clavier, Bk 1: Preludes, S 846, 853-854, 856, 858,
862, 867; Bk II: S 881, 889. Denis Vaughan, cld. Arabesque LP
8044 Tape (c) 9044
>   +ARG 6-80 p15   +HF 6-80 p96 tape
>   +FF 7/8-80 p51   +NYT 1-6-80 pD18
Sonata, harpsichord, no. 3, B minor: Cantabile. See no. 94
Sonata, oboe, G minor. See no. 3542. See no. 3753
95   Sonata, organ, no. 1, D major. COUPERIN: Messe pour les couvents:
Elevation, Offertoire sur les grands jeux. Cromorne en taille.
Messe pour les paroisses: Tierce en taille, Kyrie couplet V.
KERCKHOVEN: Fantasias (3). MUFFAT: Toccata, no. 1, D minor.
Gustav Leonhardt, org. Harmonia Mundi 065 99612
>   +RR 3-80 p83
Sonata, organ, no. 2, B flat major. See no. 85
96   Sonata, organ, no. 6, G minor. BACH, J.S.: Concerto, flute, violin
and harpsichord, S 1044, A minor. Toccata and fugue, S 916, G
major. PURCELL: Fantasia: Three parts on a ground, D major.
Marie Leonhardt, vln; Frans Bruggen, flt; Gustav Leonhardt, hpd,
org; Leonhardt Consort; Gustav Leonhardt. Telefunken 6-41356
>   ++FF 11/12-80 p213
Sonata, organ, no. 6, G minor. See no. 84
97   Trio, E major. BACH, J.S.: Sonata, 2 flutes and harpsichord, S
1039, G major. BACH, W.F.: Duo, 2 flutes, F major. Trio, A
minor. Stephen Preston, Nicholas McGegan, flt; Anthony Pleeth,
vlc; Christopher Hogwood, hpd; Jane Ryan, vla da gamba. L'Oiseau-Lyre DSLO 518
>   +-Audio 9-78 p110   +MT 12-78 p1051
>   +-FF 9/10-80 p64   ++RR 4-78 p76
>   +Gr 4-78 p1738   +SFC 5-14-78 p38
>   ++HFN 5-78 p126
98   Trio sonatas, C minor, B flat major, E major. Ars Rediviva. Supraphon 111 1675
>   ++FF 11/12-80 p55   +HFN 10-80 p102
>   +Gr 10-80 p511   +NR 10-80 p8

BACH, Jan
99   Laudes. LECLERC: Par monts et par vaux. PERSICHETTI: Parable II.
     New York Brass Quintet. Crystal S 210
                    ++ARG 9-80 p50   ++NR 5-80 p8
                    +FF 5/6-80 p129
BACH, Johann Bernhard
100 Du Friedensfurst, Herr Jesu Christ, partita.** Passacaglia (Cha-
     conne), B major.** BACH, Johann Christoph: Aus meines Herzens
     Grunde. Prelude and fugue, B flat major.** Wach auf mein Herz
     und singe.** Warum betrubst du dich mein Herz.** BACH, Johann
     Ernst: Fantasia and fugue, F major.** BACH, Johann Lorenz: Pre-
     lude and fugue, D major. BACH, Johann Michael: Chorale preludes:
     Allein Gott in der Hoh sei Ehr;** Wenn wir in hochsten Noten sein.
     BACH, J.S.: Capriccio, S 993, E major.** Fantasia, S 904, A
     minor.* Chorale prelude, S Anh 78, Wenn wir in hochsten Noten
     sein.** Prelude and fugue, S 542, G minor.* Prelude and fugue,
     S 547, C major.* Toccata and fugue, S 565, D minor.* Wilhelm
     Krumbach, org. Telefunken 6-35273 (2) Tape (c) 6-35273 (*from
     SAWT 9503; **from SAWT 9551)
                    +-Gr 2-76 p1359   +HF 1-80 p91 tape
     Passacaglia, B major. See no. 100
BACH, Johann Christian
101 Arias: Ach dass ich Wassers g'nug hatte. BUXTEHUDE: Aria: Muss der
     Tod denn nun doch trennen. Jubilate domino, cantata. TELEMANN:
     Ach Herr strafe mich nicht. Rene Jacobs, c-t; Kuijken Consort.
     Accent ACC 7912
                    ++HFN 6-80 p101   +RR 6-80 p13
     Aria with 15 variations, A minor. See no. 4022
102 Concerto, bassoon, B flat major. HUMMEL: Concerto, bassoon, F major.
     Gabor Janota, bsn; Liszt Ferenc Chamber Orchestra; Janos Rolla.
     Hungaroton SLPX 12014
                    ++ARG 12-80 p34   ++NR 7-80 p4
                    +FF 11/12-80 p126
     Concerto, piano, op. 7, no. 6, G major. See no. 78
     Quintet, D major. See no. 3543
103 Quintets, op. 11, nos. 1, 3-4, 6. Heidelberg Baroque Ensemble. Da
     Camera SM 92813
                    ++FF 9/10-80 p50
104 Sinfonias, op. 3, nos. 1-6. Simon Preston, hpd; AMF; Neville Mar-
     riner. Philips 9502 001 Tape (c) 7313 001 (From 6707 013)
                    ++FF 11/12-79 p21   +HFN 11-80 p129
                    +Gr 11-80 p660   ++SFC 6-10-79 p45
                    ++HF 9-79 p109   ++St 10-79 p146
     Sinfonias, op. 9, no. 2, E flat major. See no. 105
     Sinfonias, op. 18, no. 1, E flat major. See no. 107
105 Sinfonia concertante, C major. Sinfonia, op. 9, no. 2, E flat maj-
     or. SALIERI: Concerto, flute and oboe, C major. Sinfonia, D
     major. Richard Adeney, flt; Peter Graeme, ob; James Brown, ob;
     Emanuel Hurwitz, vln; Keith Harvey, vlc; ECO; Richard Bonynge.
     London STS 15510
                    +-FF 11/12-80 p116
106 Sinfonia concertanti, C major, F major, E flat major. Collegium
     Aureum; Franzjosef Maier. Harmonia Mundi 065 99790
                    +HFN 2-80 p85   ++RR 2-80 p45
107 Sinfonia concertante, violin and violoncello, A major. Sinfonia,

op. 18, no. 1, E flat major. Franzjosef Maier, vln; Angelica
   May, vlc; Collegium Aureum; Reinhard Peters. Harmonia Mundi 1C
   065 99827
                 +FF 3/4-80 p40   +RR 4-80 p55
                 +HFN 4-80 p117
108 Sonatas, harpsichord, C major, A major, F major. BACH, Johann
   Christoph: Sonata, harpsichord, A major. MOZART: Sonata, piano,
   C major. Luciano Sgrizzi, Michele Delfosse, hpd. Alpha DB 189
                 +FF 11/12-80 p208
   Sonata, 2 harpsichords, op. 15, no. 5, G major. See no. 81
   Sonata, 2 organs, C major. See no. 4027
BACH, Johann Christoph
   Aus meines Herzens Grunde. See no. 100
   Prelude and fugue, E flat major. See no. 100
   Sonata, harpsichord, A major. See no. 108
   Wach auf mein Herz und singe. See no. 100
   Warum betrubst du dich mein Herz. See no. 100
BACH, Johann Christoff Friedrich
109 Die Kindheit Jesu. Esther Himmler, s; Ingeborg Russ, alto; Urs
   Dettwyler, t; Bruce Abel, bs; Trossingen Martin Luther Church
   Choir; Gerd Witte. Musical Heritage Society MHS 4086 (also FSM
   53034)
                 -FF 7/8-80 p42
   Sonata, harpsichord, A major. See no. 3834
   Sonatina, A minor. See no. 92
BACH, Johann Ernest
   Fantasia and fugue, F major. See no. 100
BACH, Johann Lorenz
   Prelude and fugue, D major. See no. 100
BACH, Johann Michael
   Chorale preludes: Allein Gott in der Hoh sei Ehr; Wenn wir in hoch-
   sten Noten sein. See no. 100
   Wenn wir in hochsten Noten sein. See no. 85
BACH, Johann Sebastian
110 Allabreve, S 589, D major. Canzona, S 588, D minor. Toccata and
   fugue, S 566, E major. Toccata and fugue, S 538, D minor. Carl
   Weinrich, org. Westminster MCA 1407
                 ++FF 11/12-80 p63
   Allabreve, S 589, D major. See no. 245. See no. 247
111 Anna Magdalena notebook, S 508, excerpts (23). Robert Radaelli, pno.
   Pavane ADW 7012
                 +-HFN 3-80 p86   +RR 4-80 p91
   Anna Magdalena notebook, S 508: So offich meine Tabakspfeife. See
   no. 94
   Applicatio, S 994, C major. See no. 218
   Aria, S 587. See no. 246
112 Air and variations in the Italian style, S 989, A minor. Variations,
   harpsichord, S 988. Rosalyn Tureck, hpd. CBS 79220 Tape (c) 40-
   79220 (also Columbia M2 35900)
                 ++ARG 9-79 p8   +HFN 2-80 p86
                 +-CL 11-79 p6   +-MT 11-80 p709
                 ++FF 11/12-80 p62   +-NYT 1-27-80 pD20
                 +Gr 2-80 p1281   +RR 1-80 p96
                 -HF 12-79 p84
   Aria variata alla maniera Italiana, S 989, A minor. See no. 219

BACH (cont.)   18

Arias: Ach windet Euch nicht so geplagte Seelen, S 245c. See no.
144
Arias: Unschuld Kleinrod reiner Seelen. See no. 149
113 Ave Maria (Gounod, arr. Gamley). SCHUBERT: Ave Maria, G 839 (arr.
Gamley). Luciano Pavarotti, t; National Philharmonic Orchestra;
Kurt Herbert Adler. London L 15 20102
                    +NR 12-80 p1
Ave Maria. See no. 30. See no. 3624. See no. 3770. See no. 3961
114 Brandenburg concerti, nos. 1-6, S 1046-1051. Los Angeles Chamber
Orchestra; Gerard Schwarz. Angel DSB 3901 (2) Tape (c) 4Z2S
3901 (45 rpm) DSSC 4504
        +ARG 12-80 p14   ++NYT 6-8-80 pD20
        +-FF 9/10-80 p52   ++SFC 6-22-80 p36
        +-HF 10-80 p71   +St 9-80 p78
        +-NR 8-80 p6
115 Brandenburg concerti, nos. 1-6, S 1046-1051. Wendy Carlos, synthesizer. Columbia M2X 35895 (2) Tape (c) M2T 35895 (also CBS 79227
Tape (c) 40-79227. From 73163, 73395 (nos. 2-5)
        +FF 9/10-80 p54   +NYT 5-25-80 pD21
        +Gr 7-80 p167   +-RR 7-80 p49
        +-HF 6-80 p67   +SR 8-80 p83
        ++HFN 7-80 p105   +-St 10-80 p108
        ++HFN 9-80 p115 tape
116 Brandenburg concerti, nos. 1-6, S 1046-1051. Stuttgart Chamber
Orchestra; Karl Munchinger. Decca JB 61/2 Tape (c) KJBC 61 (From
5BB 130/1)
        +Gr 1-80 p1137   +RR 12-79 p45
        +HFN 12-79 p179
117 Brandenburg concerti, nos. 1-6, S 1046-1051. BPhO; Herbert von
Karajan. DG 2707 112 (2) Tape (c) 3370 030
        -FF 11/12-80 p56   ++NR 9-80 p2
        +-Gr 6-80 p31   +-RR 6-80 p39
        +Gr 8-80 p275 tape   +SFC 7-13-80 p33
        +-HF 10-80 p71   +-St 9-80 p78
        +-HFN 6-80 p102   +SR 8-80 p83
        +-HFN 8-80 p109 tape
118 Brandenburg concerti, nos. 1-6, S 1046-1051. Suites, orchestra,
S 1066-1069. Collegium Aureum. Harmonia Mundi 197 53000/3 (4)
        +-HFN 12-80 p153
119 Brandenburg concerti, nos. 1-6, S 1046-1051. Polish Chamber Orchestra; Jerzy Maksymiuk. HMV SLS 5155 (2) Tape (c) TC SLS 5155
(also Angel SZB 3873)
        -ARG 4-80 p14   +NR 2-80 p3
        +FU 3-80 p44   +-RR 9-79 p67
        +-Gr 9-79 p454   ++SFC 11-18-79 p47
        +-HFN 9-79 p101   +-St 9-80 p78
        +-HFN 1-80 p123 tape
120 Brandenburg concerti, nos. 1-6, S 1046-1051. Gerard Jarry, vln;
Jean-Pierre Rampal, flt; Pierre Pierlot, ob; Maurice Andre, tpt;
Anne-Marie Beckensteiner, hpd; Jean-Francois Paillard Orchestra;
Jean-Francois Paillard. Musical Heritage Society MHS 4019/20 (2)
        +FF 9/10-79 p33   +-St 9-80 p78
121 Brandenburg concerti, nos. 1-6, S 1046-1051. Collegium Aureum;
Franzjosef Maier. Quintessence 2PMC 2705 (2) (From RCA)
        +Audio 2-80 p42   ++FF 11/12-79 p21

122 Brandenburg concerti, nos. 1-6, S 1046-1051. Leonhardt Consort;
     Gustav Leonhardt. RCA RL 3-0400 (2) (Also ABC)
                 +-FF 9/10-80 p51
123 Brandenburg concerti, nos. 1-6, S 1046-1051. VSOO Members; Hermann
     Scherchen. Westminster MCA 2-9500 (2) (From WST 307)
                 -FF 11/12-80 p57
     Brandenburg concerti, nos. 1-6, S 1046-1051. See no. 320
     Brandenburg concerto, no. 2, S 1047, F major: 3rd movement. See no.
     3999
     Brandenburg concerto, no. 3, S 1048, G major: 1st movement. See no.
     3526. See no. 3883
124 Brandenburg concerto, no. 5, S 1050, D major. Suite, orchestra,
     S 1069, D major. Stephen Preston, flt; Simon Standage, vln;
     Trevor Pinnock, hpd; English Concert. DG 2533 440 Tape (c) 3310
     440
                 +-FF 9/10-80 p62   +NYT 6-8-80 pD20
                 +Gr 6-80 p31   +RR 6-80 p39
                 +-HF 11-80 p61   +St 9-80 p78
                 +-HFN 6-80 p102   ++STL 5-11-80 p38
                 +NR 8-80 p6
     Brandenburg concerto, no. 5, S 1050, D major. See no. 229
     Brandenburg concerto, no. 6, S 1051, B major: Allegro II. See no.
     4028
     Canons (14). See no. 81
     Canons, S 1087 (14). See np. 4035
125 Cantatas, nos. 1, 4, 6, 11 (Ascension oratorio), 12, 44, 61, 64-65,
     67, 104, 111, 121, 124, 158, 171, 182. Christmas oratorio, S
     248. Magnificat, S 243, D major. Edith Mathis, s; Anna Reynolds,
     ms; Peter Schreier, t; Dietrich Fischer-Dieskau, bar; Munich Bach
     Orchestras and Choirs; Karl Richter. DG 2722 018 (11) (From
     SAPM 198353/5, 198197, 2722005, 198465)
                 +Gr 1-76 p1222   +-MM 7-76 p31
                 +Gr 7-80 p154   +-MT 1-76 p39
                 +-HFN 12-75 p147   +-RR 1-76 p53
     Cantata, no. 4: Sinfonia. See no. 3943
126 Cantatas, nos. 11, 58, 78, 198. Christiane Baumann, Uta Spreckel-
     sen, s; Naoko Ihara, con; John Elwes, Vincent Girod, t; Philippe
     Huttenlocher, bs; Lausanne Chamber Vocal Ensemble and Orchestra;
     Michel Corboz. Erato STU 71099 (2)
                 +Gr 5-78 p1909   +HFN 4-80 p100
                 +HFN 5-78 p125   +-RR 2-78 p81
127 Cantata, no. 14, War Gott nicht mit uns diese Zeit; Unsre Starke
     heisst zu schwzch. Cantata, no. 24, Ein ungefarbt Gemute; Alles
     nun ihr wollet. BEETHOVEN: Quintet, 3 horns, oboe and bassoon,
     E flat major. MOZART: Concerto, horn, no. 1, K 412, D major.
     Quintet, horn, K 407, E flat major. Hermann Baumann, hn; Ad
     Mater, ob; Adrian van Woudenberg, Werner Meyendorf, hn; Brian
     Pollard, bsn; VCM, Esterhazy Quartet, Leonhardt Consort; Vienna
     Boys Choir, Chorus Viennensis; Nikolaus Harnoncourt, Gustav
     Leonhardt. Telefunken AP 6-42321 Tape (c) 4-42321 (From AS
     6-41272, 6-42173, EX 6-35030, AW 6-41251)
                 ++ARG 2-80 p50   *HF 2-80 p102 tape
                 -FF 1/2-80 p170   +-HFN 3-79 p139
                 +Gr 7-79 p223   +RR 3-79 p100
128 Cantatas, nos. 21, 34, 39, 51, 55-56, 60, 68, 76, 93, 106, 129, 175,

189, 201, 211-212. Edith Mathis, Adele Stolte, Elizabeth Speiser,
s; Anna Reynolds, Hertha Topper, Eva Fleischer, Ingeborg Springer,
ms; Peter Schreier, Ernst Hafliger, Hans-Joachim Rotzsch, t;
Dietrich Fischer-Dieskau, Kurt Moll, Theo Adam, Gunter Leib,
Siegfried Lorenz, bs; Munich Bach Orchestra and Choir, Leipzig
Gewandhaus Orchestra, Berlin Solistenvereinigung, Berlin Chamber
Orchestra; Kurt Thomas, Helmut Koch. DG 2722 019 (11)
>   +Gr 12-75 p1086   +-HFN 1-76 p102
>   +Gr 7-80 p154   +-RR 12-75 .p87
>   +MM 7-76 p31

Cantata, no. 24, Ein ungefarbt Gemute; Alles nun das ihr wollet.
See no. 127

Cantata, no. 29: Sinfonia. See no. 325. See no. 4062

129 Cantata, no. 45, Es ist dir gesagt. Cantata, no. 176, Es ist ein
Trotzig. Sheila Armstrong, s; Norma Proctor, alto; Kurt Equiluz,
t; Erich Wenk, bs; Gachinger Kantorei; Helmut Rilling. Stauda
SDG 610119
>   +-HFN 8-80 p93   -RR 7-80 p85

130 Cantata, no. 59, Wer mich liebet der wird main Wort halten. Cantata,
no. 134, Ein Herz das seinen Jesum lebend weiss. Arleen Auger,
s; Helen Watts, alto; Adalbert Kraus, t; Niklaus Tuller, bs; Bach
Ensemble, Gachinger Kantorei; Bach Collegium, Stuttgart; Helmuth
Rilling. Musical Heritage Society MHS 4119
>   +-FF 5/6-80 p35

131 Cantata, no. 68, Also hat Gott die Welt geliebt. Cantata, no. 172,
Erschallet ihr Lieder. Ursula Buckel, s; Irma Keller, alto; Theo
Altmeyer, t; Jakob Stampfli, bs; Kassel Vocal Ensemble; German
Bach Soloists; Klaus Martin Ziegler. Stauda SDG 610114
>   +-RR 8-80 p77

Cantata, no. 79, Gott der Herr ist Sonn und Schild. See no. 3569

132 Cantata, no. 80, Ein feste Burg ist unser Gott. Cantata, no. 140,
Wachet auf ruft uns die Stimme. St. Thomas Choir, Leipzig;
Leipzig Gewandhaus Orchestra; Erhard Mauersberger. DG 2547 024
Tape (c) 3347 024 (From 198407)
>   +Gr 8-80 p246   +-HFN 10-80 p117 tape
>   +Gr 9-80 p413 tape   +RR 6-80 p83
>   +-HFN 7-80 p117

133 Cantata, no. 80, Ein feste Burg ist unser Gott. Chorale prelude,
S 657, Nun danket alle Gott. Chorale prelude, S 720, Ein feste
Burg ist unser Gott. Frederick Grimes, Nancianne Parrella, org;
Diane Higginbotham, s; Jacqueline Pierce, ms; Gene Tucker, t;
Daniel Pratt, bar; Holy Trinity Lutheran Church Bach Orchestra
and Choir; Frederick Grimes. Holy Trinity Church HTL 1979
>   +MU 1-80 p14   +-St 4-80 p122

Cantata, no. 80, Ein feste Burg ist unser Gott. See no. 4054

134 Cantata, no. 82, Ich habe genug ich habe den Heiland. Concerto,
violin, oboe and strings, S 1060, D minor. Easter oratorio, S
249: Adagio. Okko Kamu, vln; Brynjar Hoff, ob; Knut Skram, bs;
Canticum Novum Kammerorkester; Alf Ardal. BIS LP 101
>   +FF 5/6-80 p40   +-RR 3-80 p45

135 Cantatas, nos. 84-90. Wilhelm Wiedl, Marcus Klein, treble; Paul
Esswood, c-t; Kurt Equiluz, t; Ruud van der Meer, Max van Egmond,
bs; Tolzer Boys Choir, Hanover Boys Choir, Collegium Vocale,
Ghent; Leonhardt Consort, VCM; Nikolaus Harnoncourt, Gustav
Leonhardt. Telefunken EX 6-35364 (2)
>   ++ARG 3-80 p14   ++HF 4-80 p75

```
      +FF 11/12-79 p22              +HFN 7-79 p101
      +FU 11-79 p44                 +-RR 7-79 p100
      +-Gr 7-79 p237
```

136 Cantatas, nos. 91-98. Detlef Bratschke, boy soprano; Paul Esswood,
     c-t; Kurt Equiluz, t; Ruud van der Meer, Max van Egmond, Philippe
     Huttenlocher, bs; Tolzer Boys Choir; VCM, Leonhardt Consort;
     Nikolaus Harnoncourt, Gustav Leonhardt. Telefunken 6-35441/2 (4)
```
         ++ARG 7/8-80 p14             +HF 4-80 p75
         +-ARG 9-80 p14              +HFN 2-80 p85
         +-FF 7/8-80 p43            +-NYT 1-20-80 pD22
         +-Gr 1-80 p1181            +-RR 1-80 p105
         +Gr 3-80 p1424             +-RR 2-80 p83
```

137 Cantata, no. 93, Wer nur den lieben Gott. Cantata, no. 117, Sei
     Lob und Ehr dem hochsten Gut. Ingeborg Reichelt, s; Lotte Wolf-
     Matthaus, alto; Johannes Feyerabend, t; Hans-Olaf Hudemann, bs;
     Gottinger Stadt-Kantorei, Frankfurt Cantata Orchestra; Ludwig
     Doormann. Stauda SDG 610102
```
         -RR 8-80 p77
```

138 Cantatas, nos. 99-102. Wilhelm Wiedl, Detlef Bratschke, treble;
     Paul Esswood, alto; Kurt Equiluz, t; Philippe Huttenlocher, bar;
     Max van Egmond, bs; Tolzer, Boys Choir, Hanover Boys Choir, Ghent
     Collegium Vocale, VCM, Leonhardt Consort; Nikolaus Harnoncourt,
     vlc and cond; Gustav Leonhardt. Telefunken EX 6-35443 (2)
```
         +Gr 12-80 p859              +-HFN 11-80 p115
```

139 Cantata, no. 106, Gottes Zeit ist die allerbeste Zeit. TELEMANN:
     Du aber Daniel gehe hin, funeral cantata. Elly Ameling, s;
     Maureen Lehane, con; Kurt Equiluz, t; Barry McDaniel, bar; Aachen
     Cathedral Choir; Collegium Aureum Members; Rudolf Pohl. Harmonia
     Mundi 1C 065 99751 (From HMS 30847, BASF 2021449-9)
```
         +FF 1/2-80 p34              +-HFN 11-78 p165
         +-Gr 10-78 p717            +RR 9-78 p87
```

140 Cantata, no. 106, Gottes Zeit ist die allerbeste Zeit. Cantata, no.
     140, Wachet auf ruft uns die Stimme. Margareta Hallin, s; Margot
     Rodin, con; Ulf Bjorkegren, t; Hakan Hagegard, bar; Stockholm
     Bach Choir; Baroque Ensemble; Anders Ohrwall. Meridian E 77016
```
         +-Gr 9-79 p488              +MT 4-80 p248
         +HFN 9-79 p100             ++RR 9-79 p110
```
     Cantata, no. 106: Sonatina. See no. 3795
     Cantata, no. 110, Unser Mund sei voll Lachens. See no. 228
     Cantata, no. 117, Sei Lob und Ehr dem hochsten Gut. See no. 137
141 Cantata, no. 118 O Jesu Christ mein's Lebens Licht. PURCELL: Fun-
     eral music for Queen Mary. SCARLATTI, D.: Stabat mater. Amor
     Artis Chorale; Johannes Somary. Westminster MCA 1404 (From Decca
     DL 710114)
```
         +ARG 11-80 p39             +FF 7/8-80 p163
```

142 Cantata, no. 126, Erhalt uns Herr bei deinem Wort. Cantata, no. 149,
     Man singet mit Freuden vom Sieg. Elly Ameling, s; Janet Baker,
     ms; Theo Altmeyer, t; Hans Sotin, bs; South German Madrigal
     Choir; Consortium Musicum; Wolfgang Gonnenwein. Seraphim S 60339
```
         ++NR 9-80 p7
```
     Cantata, no. 134, Ein Herz das seinen Jesum lebend weiss. See no.
     130
143 Cantata, no. 140, Wachet auf. Cantata, no. 148, Bringet dem Herrn
     Ehre. Elly Ameling, Janet Baker, s; Theo Altmeyer, t; Hans Sotin,
     bs; South German Madrigal Choir; Consortium Musicum; Wolfgang
     Gonnenwein. Seraphim S 60328 (From SME 91658)

+Audio 2-80 p42   +SFC 12-9-79 p42
+FF 1/2-80 p34   -St 4-80 p122
+ON 12-15-79 p36

Cantata, no. 140, Sleepers awake. See no. 17. See no. 132. See
    no. 140. See no. 145. See no. 324. See no. 3602
Cantata, no. 140, Wachet auf ruft uns die Stimme: Chorale. See no.
    325
Cantata, no. 147, Jesu joy of man's desiring. See no. 17. See no.
    324. See no. 3531. See no. 3602. See no. 3624. See no. 3640.
    See no. 3663. See no. 3737. See no. 3777. See no. 3835. See
    no. 3912. See no. 3938. See no. 3999
Cantata, no. 147, Jesu joy of man's desiring: Chorale. See no. 325
Cantata, no. 148, Bringet dem Herrn Ehre. See no. 143
Cantata, no. 149, Man singet mit Freuden vom Sieg. See no. 142
Cantata, no. 156: Arioso. See no. 326
144 Cantata, no. 160, Ich weiss dass mein Erloser lebt. Cantata, no.
    189, Meine Seele ruhmt und preist. Aria: Ach windet Euch nicht
    so geplagte Seelen, S 245c. Peter Schreier, t; Lucerne Festival
    Strings; Peter Schreier. Vanguard VSD 71226
                ++ARG 9-79 p15   +NR 1-80 p11
                +Audio 2-80 p42   ++SFC 6-10-79 p45
                +FF 7/8-79 p16   ++St 10-79 p130
Cantata, no. 172, Erschallet ihr Lieder. See no. 131
Cantata, no. 176, Es ist ein trotzig. See no. 129
Cantata, no. 189, Meine Seele ruhmt und preist. See no. 144
145 Cantata, no. 201, Sheep may safely graze. Cantata, no. 140, Wachet
    auf. Fugue, S 578, G minor. Gigue. Passacaglia and fugue, S
    582, C minor. Toccata and fugue, S 565, D minor. FRESCOBALDI:
    Toccata. HANDEL: Water music: Minuet; Air; Hornpipe; Allegro
    maestoso. PACHELBEL: Canon, D major. Canadian Brass. RCA ARL
    1-3554 Tape (c) ARK 1-3554
                +ARG 11-80 p30   +NR 7-80 p6
                +-FF 7/8-80 p186   -SFC 4-20-80 p34
                +HF 10-80 p98 tape
Cantata, no. 201, O yes just so. See no. 3774
146 Cantatas, nos. 202, 209, 211, 212. Elly Ameling, s; Gerald English,
    t; Siegmund Nimsgern, bs; Collegium Aureum. Quintessence PMC
    2704 (2)
                +FF 3/4-80 p41   ++SFC 2-10-80 p41
147 Cantata, no. 202 (last movement missing). HANDEL: Giulio Cesare:
    V'adoro pupille; Hercules my father. MOZART: Cosi fan tutte,
    K 588: Amore e un ladroncello. Don Giovanni: Mi tradi. Die Ent-
    fuhrung aus dem Serail, K 384: Martern aller Arten, Welch ein
    Geschick. Le nozze di Figaro, K 492: Deh vieni non tardar.
    Elisabeth Schwarzkopf, s. Rococo 5374
                +NR 1-80 p8
148 Cantata, no. 208, Was mir behagt. Helen Donath, Elisabeth Speiser, s;
    Wilfried Jochims, t; Jakob Stampfli, bs; Figuralchor Stuttgart;
    Bach Collegium; Helmut Rilling. Stauda SDG 610206
                +-RR 8-80 p77
Cantata, no. 208, Sheep may safely graze. See no. 324. See no.
    3640. See no. 3795. See no. 3860. See no. 3936
149 Cantata, no. 210, O holder Tag erwunschte Zeit. Unschuld Kleinod
    reiner Seelen, aria. Ursula Buckel, s; German Bach Soloists;
    Helmut Winschermann. Stauda SDG 610201

+HFN 12-80 p132   +RR 7-80 p86

150 Cantata, no. 215, Preise dein Glucke. Erna Spoorenberg, s; Werner
     Krenn, t; Erich Wenk, bs; Figuralchor der Gedachtniskirche; Bach
     Collegium, Stuttgart; Helmuth Rilling. Musical Heritage Society
     MHS 4060 (From Barenreiter BM 30 LS 1355)
                +FF 1/2-80 p34

151 Cantata, S 249a, Entflieht entweichet ihr Sorgen. Edith Mathis, s;
     Hetty Plumacher, alto; Theo Altmeyer, t; Jakob Stampfli, bs;
     Gachinger Kantorei; Figuralchor der Gedachtniskirche; Bach Col-
     legium; Helmuth Rilling. Stauda SDG 610204
                +HFN 12-80 p132

Canzona, S 588, D minor. See no. 110. See no. 246. See no. 247

Capriccio, S 992, B flat major. See no. 217. See no. 219

Capriccio, S 992, B flat major: Postillion's aria and fugue in imi-
     tation of the postillion's horn. See no. 3569

Capriccio, S 993, E major. See no. 100

Chaconne. See no. 3976

Chorale prelude, In dulci jubilo: Fantasia. See no. 4066

Chorale preludes, Jesu meine Freude; O haupt voll blut und Wunden;
     Herzlieber Jesu was hast du Verbrochen. See no. 3912

Chorale prelude, Nun komm der Heiden Heiland. See no. 3973

Chorale prelude, O sacred head surrounded. See no. 3970

Chorale prelude, Prepare thyself Zion. See no. 3992

Chorale prelude, Von Himmel hoch. See no. 3972

Chorale prelude, S Anh 78, Wenn wir in hochsten Noten sein. See
     no. 100

Chorale preludes, S 572, 690-713, 727, 736. See no. 243

152 Chorale preludes, S 599-609, 751. Fugue on the magnificat, S 733.
     Pastorale, S 590, F major. Prelude and fugue, S 547, C major.
     Arwed Henking, org. Mitra OSM 16159
                +HFN 5-80 p134   +RR 6-80 p70

Chorale prelude, S 599, Nun komm der Heiden Heiland. See no. 3777

Chorale preludes, S 599, Nun komm der Heiden Heiland; S 600, Gottes
     Sohn is kommen; S 601, Herr Jesu Christ der ein'ge Gottes Sohn;
     S 603, Puer natus in Bethlehem; S 604, Gelobet seist du Jesu
     Christ; S 606, Vom Himmel hoch da komm ich her; S 607, Vom Him-
     mel kam der Engle Schar; S 608, In dulci jubilo. See no. 3591

Chorale preludes, S 603-615. See no. 251

153 Chorale preludes, S 605, Der Tag der ist so freudenreich; S 615, In
     dir ist Freude; S 641, Wenn wir in hochsten Noten sein. DISTLER:
     Nun komm der Heiden Heiland, partita. MENDELSSOHN: Prelude and
     fugue, D minor. Arno Schonstedt, org. Pape 202
                +FF 7/8-80 p169

Chorale prelude, S 605, Der Tag der ist so freudenreich. See no.
     4040

154 Chorale preludes, S 606, Vom Himmel hoch da komm ich her; S 645,
     Wachet auf; S 650, Kommst du nun Jesu vom Himmel herunter. Fan-
     tasia and fugue, S 542, G minor. Prelude and fugue, S 548, E
     minor. Karl Richter, org. London STS 15489
                +FF 3/4-80 p43

Chorale preludes, S 608/729/751, In dulci jubilo. See no. 3836

155 Chorale preludes, S 615, In dir ist Freude; S 617, Herr Gott nun
     schleuss den Himmel auf; S 639, Ich ruf zu dir Herr Jesu Christ;
     S 637/705, Durch Adams Fall ist ganz verderbt; S 645, Wachet auf
     ruft uns die Stimme; S 659, Nun komm er Heiden Heiland; S 665,

Jesus Christus unser Heiland; S 667, Komm Gott Schopfer heiliger
Geist; S 734, Nun freut euch lieben Christen g'mein. BRAHMS:
Chorale preludes, op. 122, nos. 4-5, 8-11. (all arr. Busoni).
Paul Jacobs. Nonesuch H 71375

    ++ARG 12-80 p24   ++HF 8-80 p64
    +-FF 9/10-80 p146   +-SFC 6-22-80 p36

Chorale prelude, S 615, In dir ist Freude. See no. 3663
Chorale prelude, S 622, O Mensch bewein dein Sunde gross. See no.
    249. See no. 3742
Chorale prelude, S 630, Heut triumphiere Gottes Sohn. See no. 3736
Chorale prelude, S 632, Herr Jesu Christ dich zu uns wend. See no.
    3742
Chorale prelude, S 632, Wenn wir in hochsten Noten sein. See no. 8
Chorale prelude, S 633, Liebster Jesu wir sind hier. See no. 8
Chorale preludes, S 635b, 727, 728, 736. See no. 242
Chorale prelude, S 639, Ich ruf zu dir Herr Jesu Christ. See no.
    3777

156 Chorale prelude, S 641, Wenn wir in hochsten Noten sein; S 767,
    O Gott du frommer Gott: Partita. Toccata and fugue, S 565, D
    minor. DUPRE: Versets pour les Vepres du commun des fetes de la
    Sainte Vierge, op. 18: Antiphon; Magnificat, nos. 1 and 6.
    FRANCK: Fantaisie, A major. KARG-ELERT: Lake Constance, op. 96,
    no. 1: Pastel. Rondo alla campanella, op. 156. Ralph Downes,
    org. Vista VPS 1089

    +Gr 5-80 p1694   +RR 4-80 p94
    +MT 11-80 p712

Chorale prelude, S 641, Wenn wir in hochsten Noten sein. See no. 8
157 Chorale preludes, S 643, Alle Menschen mussen sterben; S 737, Vater
    unser im Himmelreich. Fantasia and fugue, S 542, G minor. Pas-
    sacaglia and fugue, S 582, C minor. Toccata, S 540, F major.
    Michael Murray, org. Telarc DG 10049

    ++Gr 10-80 p517   ++NR 10-80 p12

158 Chorale preludes, S 645-648. Concerto arrangements from Telemann
    and Vivaldi. ORTIZ: Recercada, no. 2. Francis Hardy, tpt;
    Francois-Henri Houbart, org. Harmonia Mundi HM 1029

    -HFN 6-80 p115

Chorale preludes, S 645-650. See no. 248
Chorale preludes, S 645-650; S 726, Herr Jesus Christ dich zu uns
    wend; S 729, In dulci jubilo; S 728, Jesus meine Zuversicht; S
    730/731, Liebster Jesu wir sind hier; S 732, Lobt Gott ihr Chris-
    ten allzugleich; S 735, Valet will ich dir geben; S 737, Vater
    unser im Himmelreich; S 763, Sei gegrusset Jesu gutig: Partita;
    Vom Himmel hoch, S 769: Variations. See no. 245

159 Chorale preludes, S 645, Wachet auf ruft uns die Stimme; S 646, Wo
    soll ich fliehen hin; S 654, Schmucke dich O liebe Seele; S 734,
    Nun freut euch lieben Christen g'mein. Passacaglia and fugue, S
    582, C minor. Toccata, adagio and fugue, S 564, C major. Gabor
    Lehotka, org. Hungaroton SLPX 12025

    +-FF 5/6-80 p42

Chorale preludes, S 645, Wachet auf ruft uns die Stimme; S 646, Wo
    soll ich fliehen hin; S 654, Schmucke dich O liebe Seele; S 734,
    Nun freut euch lieben Christen g'mein. See no. 250
Chorale prelude, S 645, Wachet auf ruft uns die Stimme. See no.
    249. See no. 326. See no. 4038
Chorale prelude, S 646, Wo soll ich fliehen hin. See no. 159

Chorale prelude, S 649, Ach bleib bei uns. See no. 249
160 Chorale preludes, S 654, Schmucke dich; S 658, Von Gott will ich
    nicht lassen; S 659, Nun komm der Heiden Heiland; S 662, Allein
    Gott in der Hoh (2); S 665, Jesus Christus unser Heiland; S 667,
    Komm Gott Schopfer. Hermann Harassowitz, org. Ursina Motette
    M 1011
                  /MU 11-80 p18
161 Chorale prelude, S 654, Schmucke dich. Concerto, organ, no. 5,
    S 596, D minor. Passacaglia and fugue, S 582, C minor. LANGLAIS:
    Mors et resurrection, op. 5, no. 1. SCHUMANN: Canon, op. 56, no.
    6, B major. Edmund Wright, org. Wheaton College unnumbered.
                  +MU 10-80 p10
Chorale prelude, S 654, Schmucke dich o liebe Seele. See no. 159
162 Chorale prelude, S 657, Now thank we all our God. FLETCHER: Festi-
    val toccata. HOLZGRAF: Mormon hymns: Come come ye saints; Oh my
    father. Variations on "Londonderry air". Lloyd Holzgraf, org.
    M & K Real time RT 113
              +ARG 4-80 p51   +ARG 2-80 p48
Chorale prelude, S 657, Nun danket alle Gott. See no. 133
163 Chorale prelude, S 658, Von Gott will ich nicht lassen. Prelude and
    fugue, S 541, G major. Prelude and fugue, S 544, B minor. BOHM:
    Prelude and fugue, A minor. MURSCHHAUSER: Aria pastoralis vari-
    ata. SWEELINCK: Unter der Linden grune. Gabor Lahota, org.
    Hungaroton SLPX 11980
              +FF 1/2-80 p167   +NR 6-80 p13
164 Chorale prelude, S 659, Nun komm der Heiden Heiland. Prelude and
    fugue, S 544, B minor. BRUHNS: Prelude, E minor. BUXTEHUDE:
    Prelude, D major. PACHELBEL: Chaconne, F minor. Peter Seymour,
    org. Gaudeamus KRS 32
              +MT 11-80 p712   +RR 1-80 p98
Chorale prelude, S 659, Nun komm der Heiden Heiland. See no. 85
165 Chorale prelude, S 667, Komm Gott Schopfer: Veni creator. DANDRIEU:
    Livre de noels: Noels pour l'amour de Marie; Sortons de nos
    chaumiers. FANTINI: Ballet et caprice. SENNY: Plain chant pour
    une cathedrale. Abbey of Bec Hellouin Schola; Marie-Andree
    Morriset-Balier, org; Michel Morisset, tpt. Grand Orgue 45 T
    MBM 790512
              +FF 5/6-80 p190   +MU 3-80 p8
Chorale prelude, S 667, Komm Gott Schopfer. See no. 4038
Chorale prelude, S 668, Vor deinen Thron tret ich hiermit. See no.
    4038
Chorale prelude, S 668, Wenn wir in hochsten Noten sein. See no.
    224
Chorale preludes, S 669/672, Kyrie Gott Vater in Ewigkeit, S 670/
    673, Christe aller Welt trost; S 671/674, Kyrie Gott heiliger
    Geist; S 675/676/677/716, Allein Gott in der Hoh sei Ehr; S 678/
    679, Diess sind die heil'gen zehn Gebot; S 680/681, Wir glauben
    all an einen Gott; S 682/683, Vater unser im Himmelreich; S 684/
    685, Christ unser Herr zum Jordam kam; S 686/687, Aus tiefer Not
    schrei ich zu dir; S 688/689, Jesus Christus unser Heiland; S
    714, Ach Gott und Herr; S 719, Der Tag der ist so freudenreich;
    S 721, Erbarm dich mein O Herre Gott; S 723, Gelobet seist du
    Jesu Christ; S 724, Gottes Sohn ist kommen; S 733, Meine Seele
    erhebt den Herren. See no. 244
166 Chorale preludes, S 669-689. Prelude and fugue, S 552, E flat major.

Lionel Rogg, org. Harmonia Mundi HM 775/6 (2)
    +FF 7/8-80 p45
Chorale preludes, S 671, Kyrie Gott Heiliger Geist. See no. 85
Chorale preludes, S 678, Sei Gegrusset Jesus gutig; S 679, Vom
    Himmel hoch: Variations. See no. 248
Chorale prelude, S 680, Wir glauben all an einen Gott. See no. 4055
Chorale prelude, S 691, Wer nur den lieben Gott lasst walten. See
    no. 94
Chorale prelude, S 712, Ich dich hab ich gehoffet Herr. See no.
    3736
Chorale preludes, S 715, Allein Gott in der Hoh sei Ehr; S 720,
    Ein feste Burg ist unser Gott; S 722, Gelobet seist du Jesu
    Christ; S 738, Von Himmel hoch; S 766, Christ der du bist: Par-
    tita. See no. 241
Chorale prelude, S 720, Ein feste Burg ist unser Gott. See no. 133
Chorale prelude, S 720, En feste Burg. See no. 326
Chorale prelude, S 727, Herzlich tut mich verlangen. See no. 3939
Chorale prelude, S 729, In dulci jubilo. See no. 3784
Chorale prelude, S 729, In dulci jubilo: Fantasia. See no. 251
167 Chorale preludes, S 730/731, Liebster Jesu wir sind hier. HEILLER:
    Improvisation, no. 1, on a twelve-tone theme by Nikolas Fheodor-
    off. Improvisation, no. 2, on the hymn "Ach wie fluchtig, ach
    wie nichtig". PACHELBEL: Chaconne, F minor. Anton Heiller, org.
    Preiser SPR 9824
        ++RR 2-80 p78
Chorale preludes, S 731, Liebster Jesu wir sind hier. See no. 249
Chorale prelude, S 734, Nun freut euch lieben Christen g'mein.
    See no. 159. See no. 3783
Chorale prelude, S 751, In dulci jubilo. See no. 3682
168 Chorale preludes, S 766, Christ der du bist der helle Tag: Partita.
    Fantasia and fugue, S 542, G minor. Prelude and fugue, S 552, E
    flat major. Sonata, organ, no. 6, S 530, G major. Hans Pfluger,
    org. Impromptu SM 193280
        -FF 5/6-80 p39
169 Chorale prelude, S 768, Sei gegrusset Jesu gutig: Partita. Passa-
    caglia and fugue, S 582, C minor. Toccata and fugue, S 538, D
    minor. Karl Richter, org. DG 2533 441
        +-Gr 8-80 p240   +-RR 8-80 p67
        +-HFN 9-80 p99
Chorale prelude, S 768, Sei gegrusset: Partita. See no. 3732
Chorale preludes, S 770, Ach was soll ich Sunder machen; S 771,
    Allein Gott in der Hoh sei Ehr. See no. 246
Chorale preludes of diverse kinds (18). See no. 248
170 Christmas oratorio, S 248. Gundula Janowitz, s; Hertha Topper, con;
    Christa Ludwig, ms; Dietrich Fischer-Dieskau, bar; Keith Engen,
    bs; Munich Bach Orchestra and Chorus; Karl Richter. DG Tape
    (c) 3335 369
        +RR 4-80 p127 tape
171 Christmas oratorio, S 248. Heiner Hopfner, t; Nikolaus Hillebrand,
    bs; Regensburg Cathedral Choir, Collegium St. Emmeram; Hanns-
    Martin Schneidt. DG 2710 024 (3) Tape (c) 3376 012
        +ARG 3-80 p16   ++NR 1-80 p11
        ++Gr 10-79 p685   +-NYT 10-7-79 pD24
        +-HF 1-80 p68   +ON 12-15-79 p36
        +-FF 1/2-80 p30   +-RR 11-79 p116
        +-HF 5-80 p90 tape   ++SFC 12-9-79 p42

    +HFN 12-79 p133   +-St 12-79 p136
    +NR 12-79 p1

172 Christmas oratorio, S 248. Hans Buchhierl, treble; Andreas Stein,
     alto; Theo Altmeyer, t; Barry McDaniel, bar; Tolzer Boys Choir;
     Collegium Aureum; Gerhard Schmidt-Gaden. Harmonia Mundi 1C 153
     99640/2 (3)
         +FF 11/12-80 p58

173 Christmas oratorio, S 248. Elly Ameling, s; Brigitte Fassbaender,
     con; Horst Laubenthal, t; Hermann Prey, bs; Tolzer Boys Choir;
     Bavarian Radio Chorus; Bavarian Symphony Orchestra; Eugen Jochum.
     Philips 6703 037 (3) Tape (c) 7699 097
         +AR 2-74 p22   +MJ 1-74 p41
         +Gr 9-73 p517   ++NR 12-73 p11
         +HF 2-74 p89   ++RR 9-73 p102
         +HFN 3-80 p107 tape ++St 1-74 p106
         +LJ 11-74 p45

    Christmas oratorio, S 248. See no. 125
    Christmas oratorio, S 248: Pastorale. See no. 325

174 Chromatic fantasia and fugue, S 903, D minor. Concerto, harpsichord,
     S 971, F major. Duets, S 802-805. Rosalyn Tureck, pno. Colum-
     bia M 35822 (also CBS 76899)
         ++ARG 7/8-80 p15   +NR 3-80 p14
         +-FF 5/6-80 p38   +NYT 6-8-80 pD20
         +Gr 6-80 p53   +RR 6-80 p70
         ++HFN 5-80 p117   +St 7-80 p78
         +-MT 11-80 p709

175 Chromatic fantasia and fugue, S 903, D minor. Concerto, harpsichord,
     S 971, F major. French suite, no. 5, S 816, G major. Toccata, S
     912, D major. George Malcolm, hpd. London STS 15491
         +-FF 3/4-80 p43

176 Chromatic fantasia and fugue, S 903, D minor. Duets, S 802-805.
     Partita, harpsichord, no. 5, S 829, G major. Robert Smith, hpd.
     Towerhill T 1005
         +-FF 9/10-80 p55   +St 7-80 p78

    Chromatic fantasia and fugue, S 903, D minor. See no. 83. See no.
     217. See no. 219. See no. 220. See no. 3751
    Clavierubung, Pt 1. See no. 3659

177 Clavierubung, Pt 3. Ton Koopman, org. Telefunken DX 6-35375 (2)
         +-FF 3/4-80 p42   +-RR 12-78 p87
         +-HF 8-80 p64   ++St 3-80 p93
         +HFN 12-78 p148

    Clavierubung, Pt 3. See no. 248
    Concerto arrangements from Telemann and Vivaldi. See no. 158

178 Concerto, flute, violin and harpsichord, S 1044, A minor. Suites,
     orchestra, S 1066-1068. Stephen Preston, flt; Simon Standage,
     vln; English Concert; Trevor Pinnock, hpd and cond. DG 2533
     410/11 (2) Tape (c) 3310 410/11
         ++ARG 1-80 p16   +HFN 5-79 p118
         +-FF 1/2-80 p40   +NYT 6-8-80 pD20
         +Gr 5-79 p1880   +-RR 5-79 p48
         ++HF 11-79 p88   +St 10-79 p131

    Concerto, flute, violin and harpsichord, S 1044, A minor. See no.
     96. See no. 320

179 Concerto, harpsichord, S 971, F major. Duets, harpsichord, nos.
     1-4, S 802-805. Partita, harpsichord, no. 7, S 831, B minor.
     Mireille Lagace, hpd. Calliope CAL 1657

+FF 11/12-80 p62
180 Concerto, harpsichord, S 971, F major. Partita, harpsichord, S 831,
     B minor. French suite, no. 5, S 816, G major. Andras Schiff,
     pno. Decca SDD R 564
                    ++Gr 4-80 p1568   +-RR 5-80 p80
                    +-HFN 4-80 p101   +STL 4-13-80 p39
181 Concerto, harpsichord, S 971, F major. Concerto, harpsichord, S
     972, D major. Partita, harpsichord, no. 7, S 831, B minor.
     Trevor Pinnock, hpd. DG 2533 424
                    +FF 7/8-80 p44   +NYT 6-8-80 pD20
                    +Gr 12-79 p1002   +-St 7-80 p78
                    ++NR 5-80 p13   +STL 2-10-80 p40
182 Concerto, harpsichord, S 971, F major. CHOPIN: Andante spianato and
     grand polonaise, op. 22, E flat major. MOZART: Sonata, piano,
     no. 15, K 545, C major. SCHUBERT: Scherzo, no. 1, D 593, B flat
     major. Friedrich Gulda, pno. Everest SDBR 3455 (From Mace 9060)
                    +-ARG 7/8-80 p49   +-NR 6-80 p12
                    -FF 5/6-80 p188
183 Concerto, harpsichord, S 971, F major. Partita, harpsichord, no. 7,
     S 831, B minor. Prelude, fugue and allegro, S 998, E major.
     Gustav Leonhardt, hpd. Harmonia Mundi 065 99867
                    +-HFN 10-80 p113
184 Concerto, harpsichord, S 971, F major. Partita, harpsichord, no. 7,
     S 831, B minor. Rosalyn Tureck, pno. HMV SXLP 30416 Tape (c)
     TC SXLP 30416 (From ASD 372)
                    +Gr 1-80 p1171   +-HFN 4-80 p121 tape
                    +Gr 5-80 p1717 tape   +RR 1-80 p97
                    +HFN 1-80 p121
185 Concerto, harpsichord, S 971, F major. French suite, no. 5, S 816,
     G major. Partita, harpsichord, no. 1, S 825, B flat major. Toc-
     cata and fugue, S 565, D minor. Constance Keene, pno. Laurel
     Protone LP 16
                    -ARG 7-79 p14   +SFC 1-13-80 p40
                    +-FF 11/12-80 p64   +-St 6-79 p124
                    -NR 4-79 p13
186 Concerto, harpsichord, S 971, F major. Duets, S 802-805. Partita,
     harpsichord, no. 7, S 831, B minor. Blandine Verlet, hpd.
     Philips 9500 588
                    +FF 1/2-80 p36   ++SFC 2-10-80 p41
                    +HF 4-80 p75   +-St 7-80 p78
                    ++NR 3-80 p15
     Concerto, harpsichord, S 971, F major. See no. 174. See no. 175.
        See no. 217. See no. 219
     Concerto, harpsichord, S 971, F major: Allegro. See no. 4028
     Concerto, harpsichord, S 972, D major. See no. 181
187 Concerti, harpsichord, S 973, G major; S 976, C major; S 978, F
     major (trans. Zabaleta). HANDEL: Concerti, organ, op. 4, no. 5,
     F major; op. 7, no. 4, D minor (trans. Zabaleta). Nicanor Zaba-
     leta, hp; ECO; Garcia Navarro. DG 2531 114
                    +Gr 3-80 p1379   +NR 11-80 p4
                    +HFN 3-80 p89   +RR 3-80 p67
     Concerto, harpsichord, S 976, C major. See no. 187
     Concerto, harpsichord, S 978, F major. See no. 187
188 Concerti, harpsichord, nos. 1-2, 4, S 1052, 1053, 1055. ECO; Ray-
     mond Leppard. Philips 9502 002 Tape (c) 7313 002

+HFN 4-80 p119   +RR 4-80 p53
+HFN 8-80 p109 tape

189 Concerti, harpsichord, nos. 1, 4-5, S 1052, 1055, 1056. Concerto,
3 harpsichords, S 1064, C major. Concerto, violin, oboe and
strings, D minor (reconstructed). Peter-Lukas Graf, flt; Helmut
Hucke, ob; Rainer Kussmaul, Gunnar Crantz, Kathrin Rabus, vln;
Cologne Philharmonic Orchestra; Helmut Muller-Bruhl. Claves P
712/4
+-HFN 8-80 p93

190 Concerti, harpsichord, nos. 1, 4-5, S 1052, 1053-1056. Michele
Boegner, pno; Les Solistes de France; Jean-Claude Hartemann.
Calliope CAL 1615
+-HFN 8-80 p93   -RR 8-80 p37

191 Concerti, harpsichord, nos. 1, 4-5, S 1052, 1055-1056. Andras
Schiff, pno; ECO; George Malcolm. Denon OX 7182
+FF 11/12-80 p59

192 Concerti, harpsichord, nos. 1, 4-5, S 1052, 1055-1056. Ralph Kirk-
patrick, hpd; Lucerne Festival Strings; Bernard Baumgartner.
DG 2547 010 Tape (c) 3347 010 (From SAPM 198013, 198189)
+-Gr 4-80 p1595   +RR 4-80 p53
+-HFN 6-80 p117

Concerti, harpsichord, nos. 1-7, S 1052-1058. See no. 320

193 Concerto, harpsichord, no. 1, S 1052, D minor. Concerto, harpsi-
chord, no. 4, S 1055, A major. Concerto, harpsichord, no. 5,
S 1056, F minor. Maria-Joao Pires, pno; Gulbenkian Foundation
Chamber Orchestra; Michel Corboz. Erato STU 70891
+HFN 4-80 p100   +RR 10-79 p73

194 Concerto, harpsichord, no. 1, S 1052, D minor. MOZART: Concerto,
piano, no. 21, K 467, C major. Carl Post, pno; Grand Prix Festival Orchestra; Carl Post, Hans Peeters. Grand Prix GP 9001
-FF 5/6-80 p35

195 Concerto, harpsichord, no. 1, S 1052, D minor. Concerto, harpsi-
chord, no. 2, S 1053, E major. Concerto, harpsichord, no. 4, S
1055, A major. Raymond Leppard, hpd; ECO; Raymond Leppard.
Philips 9502 002 Tape (c) 7313 002 (From 6747 194)
+FF 11/12-79 p26   +SFC 6-10-79 p45
+Gr 7-80 p166 tape

Concerto, harpsichord, no. 1, S 1052, D minor. See no. 77
Concerto, harpsichord, no. 2, S 1053, E major. See no. 195
Concerto, harpsichord, no. 4, S 1055, A major. See no. 193. See
no. 195
Concerto, harpsichord, no. 5, S 1056, A major. See no. 193. See
no. 203

196 Concerto, harpsichord, no. 6, S 1057, F major. Concerto, 3 harpsichords, S 1063, D minor. Concerto, 3 harpsichords, S 1064, C
major. Concerto, 4 harpsichords, S 1065, A minor. Zoltan Kocsis, Andras Schiff, Sandor Falvai, Imre Rohmann, pno; Lorant
Kovacs, Istvan Matuz, flt; Franz Liszt Music Academy Orchestra;
Albert Simon. Hungaroton SLPX 11752
+-FF 5/6-80 p36

197 Concerto, harpsichord, no. 8, S 1059, D minor. Concerto, 2 harpsichords, S 1060, D minor. Concerto, 3 harpsichords, S 1064, C
major. Gerard Jarry, Catherine Gabard, Brigitte Angelis, vln;
Jacques Chambon, ob; Luciano Sgrizzi, hpd; Jean-Francois Paillard Chamber Orchestra; Jean-Francois Paillard. Musical Heritage
Society MHS 4071

+FF 1/2-80 p36
Concerti, 2 harpsichords, S 1060-1062. See no. 320
Concerto, 2 harpsichords, S 1060, C minor. See no. 197
Concerti, 3 harpsichords, S 1063-1064. See no. 320
Concerto, 3 harpsichords, S 1063, D minor. See no. 196. See no. 200
Concerto, 3 harpsichords, S 1064, C major. See no. 189. See no. 196. See no. 197
Concerto, 4 harpsichords, S 1065, A minor. See no. 196. See no. 320
Concerto, oboe, S 1055, A major. See no. 320
Concerto, organ, A minor. See no. 4039
198 Concerti, organ, nos. 1-5, S 592-596. Gerald Gifford, org. Vista VPS 1067

+-ARG 8-79 p11   +NR 8-80 p13
++Gr 3-79 p1589   +MT 8-79 p656
+HFN 8-79 p99

Concerti, organ, nos. 1 and 2, S 592, S 593. See no. 243
199 Concerto, organ, no. 2, S 593, A minor. Concerto, organ, no. 5, S 596, D minor. VIVALDI: Concerti, op. 3, no. 8, A minor; no. 11, D minor. Bruno Salvi, Romana Pezzani, vln; Angelicum String Orchestra; Alessandro Esposito, org; Alberto Zedda. Musical Heritage Society MHS 4100 (From STA 8961)

+FF 7/8-80 p151   -HF 7-80 p78

Concerto, organ, no. 3, S 504. C major. See no. 241
Concerto, organ, no. 5, S 596, D minor. See no. 161. See no. 199. See no. 241
Concerto, organ, no. 6, S 597, E flat major. See no. 245
200 Concerti, violin and strings, S 1041-1043. Concerto, 2 violins and strings, S 1043, D minor. Concerto, 3 harpsichords and strings, S 1063, D minor. Concerto, violin, oboe and strings, S 1060, D minor. Christian Altenberger, Ernst Mayer-Schierning, Jurgen Kussmaul, Wolfgang Kussmaul, vln; Ingo Goritzki, ob; German Bach Soloists; Helmut Winschermann. Arabesque 8075-2 Tape (c) 9075-2

+-HF 12-80 p66   ++NR 11-80 p4

201 Concerti, violin and strings, S 1041-1042. concerto, 2 violins and strings, S 1043, D minor. Thomas Magyar, vln; Netherlands Chamber Orchestra; Szymon Goldberg, vln and cond. Philips 6570 010 Tape (c) 7310 010

+-Gr 3-80 p1379   +-HFN 8-80 p109 tape
+-Gr 7-80 p166 tape   +RR 3-80 p45
+-HFN 3-80 p85

202 Concerti, violin and strings, S 1041-1042. Concerto, 2 violins and strings, S 1043, D minor. Arthur Grumiaux, Hermann Krebbers, vln; Solistes Romandes; Arpad Gerecz. Philips 9500 614 Tape (c) 7300 731

+FF 11/12-80 p60   +MUM 10-80 p32
+HF 12-80 p66   ++NR 9-80 p6

Concerti, violin and strings, S 1041-1043. See no. 320
203 Concerto, violin and strings, S 1041, A minor. Concerto, harpsichord, S 1056, F minor. TELEMANN: Concerti, flute, C major, D major. Jean-Pierre Rampal, flt; Saar Chamber Orchestra; Karl Ristenpart. Erato STU 70241

+-HFN 4-80 p101   +RR 10-79 p74

204 Concerto, violin and strings, S 1041, A minor. Concerto, violin and strings, S 1042, E major. Concerto, 2 violins and strings, S

1043, D minor. Stoika Milanova, Georgi Badev, vln; Sofia Chamber Orchestra; Vassil Kazandjiev. Harmonia Mundi HM 113
　　+-HFN 3-80 p85　　　　　　　　　-RR 4-80 p54
205　Concerto, violin and strings, S 1041, A minor. Concerto, violin and
strings, S 1042, E major. Concerto, 2 violins and strings, S
1043, D minor. Denes Kovacs, Maria Balint, vln; Budapest Phil-
harmonic Orchestra; Miklos Erdelyi. Hungaroton SLPX 12096
　　+-ARG 3-80 p15　　　　　　　　+-HFN 12-79 p157
　　+-FF 1/2-80 p35
Concerto, violin and strings, S 1042, E major. See no. 204. See
no. 205
Concerto, 2 violins: Largo. See no. 3943
Concerto, 2 violins and strings, S 1043, D minor. See no. 200.
See no. 201. See no. 202. See no. 204. See no. 205. See no.
3964. See no. 3968
Concerto, violin, oboe and strings, S 1060, D minor. See no. 134.
See no. 189. See no. 200. See no. 320
Duets, S 802-805. See no. 174. See no. 176. See no. 179. See no.
186
Easter oratorio, S 249: Adagio. See no. 134. See no. 325
Easter oratorio, S 249: Sinfonia. See no. 30
206　English suites, nos. 1-6, S 806-811. Zuzana Ruzickova, hpd. Erato
ERA 9040/2 (also Musical Heritage Society MHS 3950/2)
　　+FF 5/6-80 p36　　　　　　　　+RR 7-73 p66
207　English suites, nos. 1-6, S 806-811. French suites, nos. 1-6, S
812-817. Alan Curtis, hpd. Telefunken 6-35452 (4)
　　+-FF 11/12-80 p60
English suites, nos. 1-6, S 806-811. See no. 219
208　English suite, no. 2, S 807, A minor. Partita, harpsichord, no. 2,
S 826, C minor. Toccata, S 911, C minor. Martha Argerich, pno.
DG 2531 088 Tape (c) 3301 088
　　　　　　+CL 9-80 p14　　　　　　　　++NR 6-80 p12
　　　　　　+-FF 7/8-80 p50　　　　　　　++NYT 6-8-80 pD20
　　　　　　++Gr 4-80 p1571　　　　　　　+RR 4-80 p90
　　　　　　+Gr 5-80 p1717 tape　　　　+St 8-80 p92
　　　　　　-HF 11-80 p71　　　　　　　　+STL 4-13-80 p39
　　　　　　+HFN 3-80 p86
English suite, no. 2, S 807, A minor. See no. 220
English suite, no. 3, S 808, G minor: Sarabande, Gavotte, Musette.
See no. 3964
English suite, no. 6, S 811, D minor: Gavottes, nos. 1 and 2. See
no. 3964
Fantasia, C major. See no. 4001. See no. 4043
Fantasia, C minor. See no. 220
Fantasia, S 562, C minor. See no. 246. See no. 247. See no. 4063
Fantasia, S 563, B minor. See no. 244
Fantasia, S 570, C major. See no. 241
Fantasia, S 571, G major. See no. 246
209　Fantasia, S 572, G major. Prelude and fugue, S 552, E flat major.
REUBKE: Sonata on the 94th psalm. Jennifer Bate, org. Unicorn
RHS 368
　　　　　　+-Gr 3-80 p1411　　　　　　　+-MT 5-80 p323
　　　　　　/-HFN 4-80 p101　　　　　　　+RR 3-80 p86
Fantasia, S 572, G major. See no. 243. See no. 247. See no. 249
Fantasia, S 904, A minor. See no. 100

Fantasia, S 906, C minor. See no. 217. See no. 219

Fantasia, S 921, C minor. See no. 3825

210 Fantasia and fugue, S 537, C minor. Fantasia and fugue, S 542, G
     minor. Passacaglia and fugue, S 582, C minor. Toccata and
     fugue, S 565, D minor. Lionel Rogg, org; Harmonia Mundi HM 771
     Tape (c) HM 40 771 (also Desto 7188)
                   -FF 11/12-80 p63   +-HFN 1-80 p121
                   +HFN 3-79 p139 tape   +-RR 1-80 p98

Fantasia and fugue, S 537, C minor. See no. 241. See no. 247

211 Fantasia and fugue, S 642, G minor. Passacaglia and fugue, S 582,
     C minor. Toccata and fugue, S 538, D minor. Toccata and fugue,
     S 565, D minor. Helmut Walcha, org. DG 2547 011 Tape (c) 3347
     011 (From SAPM 198304, 198305, 198002)
                   +Gr 4-80 p1595   +RR 5-80 p80
                   +-HFN 6-80 p117

212 Fantasia and fugue, S 542, G minor. Fugue sopra il Magnificat, S
     733. FRANCK: Pastorale, op. 19, E major. PURCELL: Trumpet tune.
     VIERNE: Fantasiestucke, op. 54: Carillon de Westminster. Pierre
     Labric, org. Grande Orgue LCM 760110
                   -FF 1/2-80 p172   -HFN 5-80 p134

Fantasia and fugue, S 542, G minor. See no. 154. See no. 157. See
     no. 168. See no. 210. See no. 243. See no. 247. See no. 3732.
     See no. 3942

Fantasia and fugue, S 904, A minor. See no. 218. See no. 219

Flocks in pastures green abiding. See no. 3533

213 French suites, nos. 1-6, S 812-817. Kenneth Gilbert, hpd. Harmonia
     Mundi HMU 438 (2)
                   +FF 7/8-80 p46   ++RR 1-79 p69
                   +-Gr 8-76 p318   +STL 8-8-76 p29
                   +HFN 3-79 p119

French suites, nos. 1-6, S 812-817. See no. 207. See no. 219

French suite, no. 5, S 816, G major. See no. 175. See no. 180.
     See no. 185

Fugue, G minor. See no. 4043

Fugue, S 574, C minor. See no. 246. See no. 247

Fugue, S 576, G major. See no. 246

Fugue, S 577, G major. See no. 241. See no. 3615. See no. 3616

Fugue, S 578, G minor. See no. 145. See no. 246. See no. 247.
     See no. 324. See no. 326

Fugue, S 579, B minor. See no. 245. See no. 247

214 Fugue, S 1026, G minor. Sonatas, 2 violins, S 1021, S 1023-1024.
     Boston Museum Trio. Titanic TI 80
                   ++St 12-80 p116

Fugue, S 1080, D minor. See no. 248

215 Fugue, lute, S 1000, C minor. Sonata, solo violin, S 1001, G minor:
     Adagio. Suite, lute, S 997, C minor. WEISS: Suite, lute, D
     minor. Tombeau sur la mort de Mr. Cajetan, Baron d'Hartwig.
     Konrad Junghanel, lt. Accent ACC 7801
                   ++ARG 5-80 p52   +HFN 6-80 p101
                   -FF 9/10-80 p273   ++RR 6-80 p31

216 Fugue, lute, S 1000, G minor. Prelude, fugue and allegro, S 998,
     E flat major. SOR: Fantasia, op. 54. Sonata, guitar, op. 15,
     C major. Goran Sollscher, gtr. DG 2531 195
                   +HFN 10-80 p101

Fugue, lute, S 1001, G minor. See no. 225. See no. 319. See no.
     321. See no. 3577

Fuga sopra il Magnificat, S 733. See no. 152. See no. 212. See
   no. 4050
Gavottes, nos. 1 and 2. See no. 324
Gigue. See no. 145
217 Harpsichord works: Capriccio, S 992, B flat major. Chromatic fantasia and fugue, S 903, D minor. Concerto, harpsichord, S 971,
   F major. Fantasia, S 906, C minor. Toccata and fugue, S 916, G
   major. Ralph Kirkpatrick, hpd. DG 2547 031 Tape (c) 3347 031
   (From SAPM 198565, 198183, 198185)
        +—Gr 12-80 p847   +—HFN 12-80 p153
218 Harpsichord works: Applicatio, S 994, C major. Fantasia and fugue,
   S 904, A minor. Inventions, 2 part, S 772-786 (15). Inventions,
   3 part, S 787-801 (15). Preludes, S 924-390, 939-942, 999 (12);
   933-938 (6). Minuets, nos. 1-3, S 841-843. Suites, S 818a, S
   819, A minor, E flat major. Variations, harpsichord, S 988. Das
   wohltemperierte Klavier, S 846-893. Toccatas, S 912-916. Ralph
   Kirkpatrick, Helmut Walcha, Karl Richter, hpd. DG 2722 015 (11)
        +—Gr 6-75 p67   +—HFN 6-75 p84
        +—Gr 7-80 p154
219 Harpsichord works: Aria variata alla maniera Italiana, S 989, A
   minor. Capriccio, S 992, B flat major. Chromatic fantasia and
   fugue, S 903, D minor. English suites, nos. 1-6, S 806-811.
   Fantasia, S 906, C minor. French suites, nos. 1-6, S 812-817.
   Fantasia and fugue, S 904, A minor. Concerto, S 971, F major. Partitas, harpsichord, nos. 1-6, S 825-830. Partita, harpsichord,
   S 831, B minor. Huguette Dreyfus, Ralph Kirkpatrick, hpd. DG
   2722 020 (10) (From 2533 138/9, SAPM 198003/5, 198655, 198183,
   198185)
        ++Gr 1-76 p1216   +RR 11-75 p67
        +Gr 7-80 p154
220 Harpsichord works: Chromatic fantasia and fugue, S 903, D minor.
   Fantasia, C minor. English suite, no. 2, S 807, A minor. Partita, harpsichord, no. 1, S 825, B flat major. Preludes and
   fugues, C major, C minor, B flat major, G major. Harold Samuel,
   pno. Pearl GEMM 147
        +Gr 11-80 p697   +NR 3-80 p14
        +HFN 2-80 p103   +RR 2-80 p68
Inventions, 2 part, S 772-786. See no. 218. See no. 3883
Inventions, 3 part, S 787-801. See no. 218
Kleines harmonisches Labyrinth, S 591, C major. See no. 241
Komm heiliger Geist, fantasia, S 651. See no. 4057
221 Die Kunst der Fuge (The art of the fugue), S 1080. Marie-Claire
   Alain, org. Erato STU 70878/9 (also Musical Heritage Society
   MHS 4154/5)
        +—FF 9/10-80 p51   ++RR 10-79 p116
        +HFN 4-80 p100
222 Die Kunst der Ruge, S 1080. Jean-Francois Paillard Orchestra; Jean-
   Francois Paillard. Erato STU 71122/3 (2)
        +—Gr 5-80 p1651   +—RR 4-80 p89
        ++HFN 4-80 p100
223 Die Kunst der Fuge, S 1080. Gustav Leonhardt, hpd. Harmonia Mundi
   1C 99793/4 (2)
        ++FF 3/4-80 p40   +—MT 1-80 p33
        ++Gr 10-79 p671   ++RR 10-79 p116
        +HFN 10-79 p169   +STL 12-2-79 p37

224 Die Kunst der Fuge, S 1080. Chorale prelude, S 668a, Wenn wir in
       hochsten Noten sein. Wolfgang Rubsam, org. Philips 6768 038 (2)
              +—HFN 5-80 p117   +RR 7-80 p74
     Die Kunst der Fuge, S 1080. See no. 248
     Die Kunst der Fuge, S 1080: Contrapunctus, nos. 3 and 9. See no.
       3675
     Die Kunst der Fuge, S 1080: Contrapunctus, no. 9. See no. 4001
225 Lute works: Fugue, S 1000, G minor. Prelude, S 999, C minor. Pre-
       lude, fugue and allegro, S 998, E flat major. Suite, lute, S 996,
       E minor. Suite, lute, S 997, G minor. Suite, lute, S 995, G
       minor. Suite, lute, S 1006a, E major. John Williams, gtr.
       Columbia M2 33510 (2). (also CBS 79203 Tape (c) 40-79203)
              +AR 5-80 p34   +RR 11-75 p68
              ++Gr 1-75 p652   +RR 1-76 p65 tape
              ++HFN 12-75 p173 tape   +—SFC 10-27-75 p24
              ++HFN 11-75 p148   ++St 12-75 p116
              +NR 10-75 p13   ++STL 10-5-75 p36
226 Magnificat, S 243, D major. STRAVINSKY: Symphony of psalms (rev.
       version). Anna Tomova-Sintow, s; Agnes Baltsa, ms; Peter Schrei-
       er, t; Benjamin Luxon, bs; German Opera Chorus; BPhO; Herbert von
       Karajan. DG 2531 048 Tape (c) 3301 048
              -ARG 5-80 p15   +NR 3-80 p10
              +—FF 3/4-80 p44   +—NYT 1-20-80 pD22
              -Gr 11-79 p886   +—RR 12-79 p105
              -HF 3-80 p86   -SFC 3-9-80 p39
              +—HFN 12-79 p157   +—St 4-80 p123
227 Magnificat, S 243, D major. Mass, S 232, B minor. Rachel Yakar,
       Jennifer Smith, s; Birgit Finnila, con; Anthony Rolf Johnson, t;
       Philippe Huttenlocher, bar; Jose Van Dam, bs; Lausanne Vocal En-
       semble and Chamber Orchestra; Michel Corboz. Erato STU 71314 (3)
              +—Gr 11-80 p710   +HFN 12-80 p132
228 Magnificat, S 243, D major. Cantata, no. 110, Unser Mund sei voll
       Lachens. Walter Camert, Peter Hinterreiter, s; Andreas Stein,
       alto; Theo Altmeyer, t; Siegmund Nimsgern, bs; Tolzer Boys Choir;
       Collegium Aureum; Gerhard Schmidt-Gaden. Harmonia Mundi 065
       99750 (From BASF KMB 21584)
              +—FF 1/2-80 p34   +—RR 7-79 p102
              +—HFN 7-79 p118
229 Magnificat, S 243, D major. Brandenburg concerto, no. 5, S 1050,
       D major. Anna Bathy, Judit Sandor, Magda Tiszay, Labos Somogy-
       vari, Gyorgy Littasy; Budapest Chorus; Tibor Ney, vln; Janos
       Szebenyi, flt; Annie Fischer, pno; Budapest Orchestra; Otto Klem-
       perer. Hungaroton LPX 12160
              +—Gr 12-80 p881   +HFN 12-80 p149
230 Magnificat, S 243, D major. KUHNAU (Bach): Der Gerechte kommt um.
       Judith Nelson, Emma Kirkby, s; Carolyn Watkinson, con; Paul El-
       liott, t; David Thomas, bs; Christ Church Cathedral Choir; Acad-
       emy of Ancient Music; Simon Preston. L'Oiseau-Lyre DSLO 572
       Tape (c) KDSLC 572
              +—Gr 1-80 p1182   +RR 1-80 p106
              ++HFN 1-80 p101
     Magnificat, S 243, D major. See no. 125
     Magnificat, S 243, D major: The cathedral. See no. 3841
     Magnificat, S 243, D major: Esurientes. See no. 3795
     Marcia, S Anh 122, D major. See no. 94
     Masses, S 232-236. See no. 323

231 Mass, S 232, B minor. Elisabeth Schwarzkopf, s; Marga Hoffgen, ms;
     Nicolai Gedda, t; Heinz Rehfuss, bar; Vienna Gesellschaft Orch-
     estra and Chorus; PhO; Herbert von Karajan. HMV RLS 746 (3)
     (From Columbia 33CS 1121/3)
                    +–Gr 4–80 p1575   +–RR 4–80 p105
                    +–HFN 4–80 p119
232 Mass, S 232, B minor. Margaret Marshall, s; Janet Baker, ms; Robert
     Tear, t; Samuel Ramey, bs; AMF and Chorus; Neville Marriner.
     Philips 6769 002 (3) Tape (c) 2-7699 076
                    +–ARG 2–79 p11   +MJ 12–78 p45
                    +FF 3/4–79 p20   +–MT 10–80 p633
                    +–Gr 9–78 p517   +⊦NR 1–79 p9
                    +Gr 12–78 p1178 tape   +RR 9–78 p86
                    +–HF 2–79 p67   +RR 2–79 p101 tape
                    +HF 12–79 p110 tape   +⊦SFC 10-15–78 p43
                    +HFN 9–78 p137   +⊦St 12–78 p144
                    +HFN 11–78 p187 tape
233 Mass, S 232, B minor. Teresa Stich-Randall, s; Anna Reynolds, ms;
     Ernst Hafliger, t; John Shirley-Quirk, bar; RIAS Chorus; BRSO;
     Lorin Maazel. Philips 6770 024 (2)
                    +–NYT 6-8–80 pD20
     Mass, S 232, B minor. See no. 227
     Minuets, S Anh 114-115, S 121. See no. 94
     Minuets, nos. 1-2. See no. 324
     Minuets, nos. 1-3, S 841-843. See no. 218
234 Motets, S 225-230. Westminster Choir; Chamber Orchestra; Wilhelm
     Ehmann. Westminster Choir College WC 1/2 (also Peters PLE 124/5)
                    +–FF 1/2–80 p34   +MU 3–79 p14
                    +MJ 2–79 p43
235 Motets, S 225-231. Barmen Gemarke Kantorei; Collegium Aureum. Har-
     monia Mundi 151 99616/7
                    +–HFN 4–80 p119   +–RR 4–80 p106
236 Motets, S 225, Singet dem Herrn ein neues Lied; S 226, Der Geist
     hilft; S 227, Jesu meine Freude. St. Thomas Choir; Leipzig Ge-
     wandhaus Orchestra; Kurt Thomas.   DG 2547 009 Tape (c) 3347 009
     (From SAPM 198019)
                    -Gr 4–80 p1595   +–HFN 6–80 p119
237 Motets: S 227, Jesu priceless treasure. Songs (partsongs): God
     liveth still, S 461; Breath of God life giving, S 445; It is fin-
     ished, S 458; Jesus is this dark world's light, S 474; Lord pour
     not thy vengeance on me, S 463; Now is the mournful time, S 450;
     O Jesu so meek O Jesu so kind, S 49. King's College Chapel Choir;
     Bernard Richards, vlc; Francis Baines, bs; Simon Preston, org;
     David Willcocks. Argo ZK 67 Tape (c) KZKC 67
                    +Gr 10–80 p523   +–HFN 10–80 p115
238 Motets, S 227, Jesu meine Freude; S 225, Singet dem Herrn. Peter
     Lawson, pno; Leipzig Gewandhaus Orchestra; Kurt Thomas. DG
     2547 024
                    -RR 6–80 p82
     Motets: Furchte dich nicht, S 228; Der Geist hilft unser Schwach-
     heit auf, S 226; Ich lasse dich nicht, S Anh 159; Jesu meine
     Freude, S 227; Komm Jesu komm, S 229; Lobet den Herrn, S 230;
     Sei Lobe und Preis, S 231; Singet dem Herrn, S 225. See no. 323
     Musette, S Anh 126, D major. See no. 94
239 Ein musicalische Opfer (A musical offering), S 1079. Musica Anti-
     qua Cologne; Reinhard Goebel. DG 2533 422 Tape (c) 3310 422

                +FF 3/4-80 p46   +−MT 4-80 p248
            +−Gr 11-79 p854   +−NR 2-80 p7
            +HF 6-80 p71   +−NYT 6-8-80 pD20
            ++HFN 11-79 p133   +RR 11-79 p110
240 Ein musicalische Opfer, S 1079. AMF; Neville Marriner. Philips
         9500 585 Tape (c) 7300 708
                ++FF 5/6-80 p39   +−HFN 3-80 p85
            ++Gr 3-80 p1379   +NR 3-80 p5
            +−HF 6-80 p71   +−NYT 6-8-80 pD20
            +HFN 2-80 p107 tape   +−RR 3-80 p45
     Ein musicalische Opfer, S 1079. See no. 322
     Ein musicalische Opfer, S 1079: Fugue (orch. Webern). See no. 3493
     Ein musicalische Opfer, S 1079: Ricercare a 6. See no. 3916
241 Organ works: Chorale preludes, S 715, Allein Gott in der Hoh sei
         Ehr; S 720, Ein feste Burg ist unser Gott; S 722, Gelobet seist
         du Jesu Christ; S 738, Von Himmel; S 766, Christ der du bist:
         Partita. Concerti, organ, no. 3, S 594, C major, no. 5, S 596,
         D minor. Fantasia and fugue, S 537, C minor. Fantasia, S 570,
         C major. Fugue, S 577, G major. Kleines harmonisches Labyrinth,
         S 591, C major. Preludes and fugues, S 532, D major; S 534, F
         minor; S 553-560. Sonata, organ, no. 6, S 530, G major. Toccat-
         as and fugues, S 538, D minor; S 565, D minor. Trio, S 584, G
         minor. Peter Hurford, org. Argo D207D3 (3) Tape (c) K207K33
                ++Gr 11-80 p698   +HFN 11-80 p115
242 Organ works: Chorale preludes, S 635b, 727, 728, 736. Prelude, S
         943, C major. Prelude and fugue, S 536, A major. Trio sonata,
         S 525, E flat major. Trio sonata, S 526, C minor. Andre Isoir,
         org. Calliope CAL 1713 Tape (c) CAL 4713
                +−Gr 8-80 p240   +RR 8-80 p66
            +−HFN 8-80 p93
243 Organ works: Chorale preludes, S 572, 690-713, 727, 736. Fantasia
         and fugue, S 542, G minor. Preludes and fugues, S 533, S 536,
         S 541. Sonata, organ, no. 4, S 528, E minor. Sonata, organ,
         no. 5, S 529, C major. Concerti, organ, nos. 1-2. Fantasia, 572.
         Peter Hurford, organ.   Decca D120D3 (3) Tape (c) K120K32
                +Audio 4-79 p81   ++HFN 4-79 p133 tape
            +FF 3/4-80 p47   +MT 3-79 p224
            ++Gr 11-78 p921   +RR 12-78 p87
            +Gr 5-79 p1940 tape   +SFC 7-13-80 p33
            +HFN 11-78 p163
244 Organ works: Chorale preludes, S 669/672, Kyrie Gott Vater in Ewig-
         keit; S 670/673, Christe aller Welt trost; S 671/674, Kyrie Gott
         heiliger Geist; S 675/676/677/716, Allein Gott in der Hoh sei
         Ehr; S 678/679, Diess sind die heil'gen zehn Gebot; S 680/681,
         Wir glauben all an einen Gott; S 682/683, Vater unser in Himmel-
         reich; S 684/685, Christ unser Herr zum Jordam kam; S 686/687,
         Aus tiefer Not schrei ich zu dir; S 688/689, Jesus Christus unser
         Heiland; S 714, Ach Gott und Herr; S 719, Der Tag der ist so
         freudenreich; S 721, Erbarm dich mein, O Herre Gott; S 723, Ge-
         lobet seist du Jesu Christ; S 724, Gottes Sohn ist kommen; S 733,
         Meine Seele erhebt den Herren. Fantasia, S 563, B minor. Pre-
         lude and fugue, S 552, E flat major. Prelude and fugue, S 543,
         A minor. Toccata and fugue, S 566, E major. Peter Hurford, org.
         Decca D138D3 (3) Tape (c) K138K32
                ++Gr 5-79 p1913   +HFN 7-79 p119 tape

++Gr 9-79 p534 tape   ++SFC 7-13-80 p33
++HFN 5-79 p118

245 Organ works: Allabreve, S 589, D major. Chorale preludes, nos. 1-6,
    S 645-650; S 726, Herr Jesu Christ dich zu uns wend; S 729, In
    dulci jubilo; S 728, Jesus meine Zuversicht; S 730/731, Liebster
    Jesu wir sind hier; S 732, Lobt Gott ihr Christen allzugleich;
    S 735, Valet will ich dir geben; S 737, Vater unser im Himmel-
    reich; S 763, Sei gegrusset Jesu gutig: Partita; Vom Himmel hoch,
    S 769: Variations. Concerto, organ, no. 6, S 597, E flat major.
    Fugue, S 579, B minor. Preludes and fugues, S 544, B minor; S
    545, C major. Sonatas, organ, no. 1, S 525; no. 3, S 527. Trio,
    S 583, D minor. Peter Hurford, org. Decca D150D3 (3) Tape (c)
    K 150K32

            +Gr 7-79 p224   +MT 2-80 p105
            ++Gr 12-79 p1065 tape   ++RR 5-79 p79
            ++HFN 9-79 p100   ++RR 8-79 p100

246 Organ works: Aria, S 587. Canzona, S 588, D minor. Chorale pre-
    ludes, S 770, Ach was soll ich Sunder machen; S 771, Allein Gott
    in der Hoh sei Ehr. Fantasias, S 562, C minor; S 571, S 771,
    Allein Gott in der Hoh sei Ehr. Fantasias, S 562, C minor; S
    571, G major. Fugues, S 574, C minor; S 578, G minor; S 576, G
    major. Passacaglia and fugue, S 582, C minor. Pastorale, S 590,
    F major. Pedal-Exercitium, S 598. Preludes, S 567, C major; S
    569, A minor. Preludes and fugues, S 546, C minor; S 547, C
    major. Sonata, viola da gamba and harpsichord, no. 1, S 1027, G
    major. Peter Hurford, org. Decca D177D3 (3) Tape (c) K177K32

            +Gr 12-79 p1027   +MT 9-80 p565
            ++HFN 12-79 p157   +-RR 12-79 p91

247 Organ works: Allabreve, S 589, D major. Canzona, S 588, D minor.
    Fantasias, S 562, C minor; S 572, G major. Fantasias and fugues,
    S 537, C minor; S 542, G minor. Fugues, S 574, C minor; S 578, G
    minor; S 579, B minor; S 1080, D minor. Passacaglia and fugue,
    S 582, C minor. Pastorale, S 590, F major. Preludes and fugues,
    S 531-536, S 539, S 541, S 543-552. Trio sonatas, nos. 1-6, S
    525-530. Toccata, adagio and fugue, S 564, C major. Toccatas
    and fugues, S 538, D minor; S 540, F major; S 565, D minor. Hel-
    mut Walcha, org. DG 2722 014 (8) Tape (c) 3376 004 (From 2722
    002/1)

            *Gr 8-75 p347   +HF 6-76 p97 tape
            +-Gr 1-77 p1183 tape   +-HFN 7-75 p72
            +Gr 7-80 p154

248 Organ works: Chorale preludes, S 645-650. Chorale preludes of di-
    verse kinds (18). Chorale preludes, S 678, Sei gegrusset Jesus
    gutig; S 679, Vom Himmel hoch: Variations. Clavierubung, Pt 3.
    Die Kunst der Fuge, S 1080. Helmut Walcha, org. DG 2722 016 (8)
    (From 2722 003)

            ++Gr 4-76 p1631   ++RR 12-75 p77
            +Gr 7-80 p154

249 Organ works: Chorale preludes, S 622, O Mensch bewein; S 645, Wachet
    auf; S 649, Ach bleib bei uns; S 731, Liebster Jesu. Fantasia,
    S 572, G major. Prelude and fugue, S 552, E flat major. Pre-
    lude and fugue, S 545, C major. Toccata and fugue, S 565, D
    minor. Noel Rawsthorne, org. HMV ESD 7090 Tape (c) TC ESD 7090

            +Gr 8-80 p240   +-HFN 10-80 p117 tape
            +-HFN 9-80 p99   +RR 8-80 p67

250 Organ works: Chorale preludes, S 645, Wachet auf ruft uns die Stimme;
       S 646, Wo soll ich fliehen bin; S 654, Schmucke dich o liebe
       Seele; S 734, Nun freut euch liben Christen g'mein. Passacaglia
       and fugue, S 582, C minor. Toccata, adagio and fugue, S 564, C
       major. Gabor Lehotka, org. Hungaroton SLPX 12025
                      +NR 6-80 p13
251 Organ works: Chorale preludes, S 603-615. Chorale prelude, S 729,
       In dulci jubilo: Fantasia. Variations on "Vom Himmel hoch", S
       769. Pastorale, S 590, F major. Nicholas Jackson, org. Spec-
       trum SR 117
                      +FF 11/12-80 p59
252 Orgelbuchlein, S 599-644. Andre Isoir, org. Calliope CAL 1710/11
       (2) Tape (c) CAL 4710/11
                      ++Gr 5-80 p1690   +RR 6-80 p71
                      +HFN 5-80 p117
     Partita, flute, C minor. See no. 3845
253 Partita, flute, S 1013, A minor. Sonatas, flute and harpsichord,
       S 1030, 1032, 1034-1035. Sonata, 2 flutes and harpsichord, S
       1039, G major. Lucius Voorhorst, Masahiro Arita, flt; Anneke
       Uittenbosch, hpd; Veronica Hampe, vla da gamba. Seraphim SIB
       6110 (2)
                      +-ARG 9-79 p12   +-FF 5/6-80 p36
254 Partitas, harpsichord, nos. 1-6, S 825-830. Gustav Leonhardt, hpd.
       Harmonia Mundi 1C 149 99840/2 (3)
                      +FF 5/6-80 p39   +-MT 5-80 p321
                      +-Gr 3-80 p1412   +-RR 2-80 p14
                      +HFN 3-80 p105
     Partitas, harpsichord, nos. 1-6, S 825-830. See no. 219
     Partita, harpsichord, no. 1, S 825, B flat major. See no. 185. See
       no. 220. See no. 3777
     Partita, harpsichord, no. 1, S 825, B flat major: Minuets (2). See
       no. 3659
     Partita, harpsichord, no. 2, S 826, C minor. See no. 208
     Partita, harpsichord, no. 5, S 829, G major. See no. 176
     Partita, harpsichord, no. 7, S 831, B minor. See no. 179. See no.
       180. See no. 181. See no. 183. See no. 184. See no. 186.
       See no. 219
     Partitas, violin, nos. 1-3, S 1002, 1004, 1006. See no. 321
255 Partita, violin, no. 2, S 1004, D minor: Chaconne (arr. Busoni).
       FRANCK: Prelude, chorale and fugue. MOZART: Rondo, piano, K 511,
       A minor. Artur Rubinstein, pno. RCA RL 1-3342 Tape (c) RK 1-3342
                      +Gr 6-80 p53   +HFN 6-80 p115
                      +Gr 10-80 p548 tape   +RR 6-80 p78
     Partita, violin, no. 2, S 1004, D minor: Chaconne. See no. 13. See
       no. 325. See no. 326. See no. 327
256 Partita, violin, no. 3, S 1006, E major. SCARLATTI, D.: Sonatas,
       guitar (5). Eliot Fisk, gtr. Levinson MAL 6
                      +FF 5/6-79 p10   +NYT 6-1-80 pD19
     Partita, violin, no. 3, S 1006, E major: Gavotte. See no. 327. See
       No. 3549. See no. 3775
     Partita, violin, no. 3, S 1006, E major: Loure; Gavotte; Menuet;
       Gigue. See no. 319
     Partita, violin, no. 3, S 1006, E major: Minuets, nos. 1 and 2. See
       no. 3964
     Partita, violin, no. 3, S 1006, E major: Preludio. See no. 326

257 Passacaglia and fugue, S 582, C minor. Pastorale, S 590, F major.
       Prelude and fugue, S 535, G minor. Prelude and fugue, S 544, B
       minor. Ferdinand Klinda, org. United Artists UACL 10014
              +FU 5-80 p46   +–RR 12-79 p92
              +HFN 1-80 p101
258 Passacaglia and fugue, S 582, C minor. BUXTEHUDE: Prelude, fugue
       and chaconne. REGER: Choral fantasies, op. 67, nos. 3 and 41.
       Roger Fisher, org. Vista VPS 1044
              +Gr 8-77 p327   +–MU 8-77 p10
              +–HF 7-77 p95   +NR 1-80 p12
              +–HFN 6-77 p131   +RR 6-77 p82
              ++MU 1-78 p17
       Passacaglia and fugue, S 582, C minor. See no. 145. See no. 157.
         See no. 159. See no. 161. See no. 169. See no. 210. See no.
         211. See no. 246. See no. 247. See no. 250
       Pastorale, S 590, F major. See no. 152. See no. 246. See no. 247.
         See no. 251. See no. 257
       Pedal-Exercitium, S 598. See no. 246
       Prelude, D minor. See no. 3944
       Prelude, S 567, C major. See no. 246
       Prelude, S 569, A minor. See no. 246
       Preludes, S 924-930, 929-942, 999, 933-938. See no. 218
       Prelude, S 926, D minor. See no. 327. See no. 3775
       Prelude, S 929, G minor. See no. 327
       Preludes, S 933-938: Little preludes (2). See no. 3659
       Prelude, S 934, E minor. See no. 327
       Prelude, S 940, D minor. See no. 327
       Prelude, S 943, C major. See no. 242
       Prelude, S 999, C minor. See no. 225. See no. 319. See no. 321.
         See no. 327. See no. 3549
259 Preludes and fugues (48). Anthony Newman, org. Vox QSVBX 5479/80
       (2) Tape (c) CBX 5479
              +–HF 9-77 p98   -NR 9-77 p14
              -HF 4-80 p104 tape   +St 3-80 p107 tape
              ++MU 4-77 p15
       Prelude and fugue, D major. See no. 3944
       Prelude and fugue, E minor. See no. 3728
       Preludes and fugues, C major, C minor, B flat major, G major. See
         no. 220
       Preludes and fugues, S 531-536, S 539, S 541, S 543-552. See no.
         247
       Prelude and fugue, S 532, D major. See no. 241
       Preludes and fugues, S 533, S 536, S 541. See no. 243
       Prelude and fugue, S 534, F minor. See no. 241
       Prelude and fugue, S 535, G minor. See no. 257
       Prelude and fugue, S 536, A major. See no. 242
       Prelude and fugue, S 541, G major. See no. 163
       Prelude and fugue, S 542, G minor. See no. 100
       Prelude and fugue, S 543, A minor. See no. 244
       Prelude and fugue, S 544, B minor. See no. 163. See no. 164. See
         no. 245. See no. 257
       Prelude and fugue, S 545, C major. See no. 245. See no. 249. See
         no. 325
       Prelude and fugue, S 546, C minor. See no. 246
       Prelude and fugue, S 547, C major. See no. 100. See no. 152. See
         no. 246

260 Prelude and fugue, S 548, E minor. Trio sonata, no. 4, S 528, E
     minor. COUPERIN, F.: Messe pour les paroisses. SWEELINCK: Fan-
     tasia, D minor. Rudolf Heinemann, org. Ursina Motette 1004
                    -FF 5/6-78 p10   +MU 10-80 p12
     Prelude and fugue, S 548, E minor. See no. 154
261 Prelude and fugue, S 552, E flat major (orch. Schoenberg). BRAHMS:
     Quartet, piano, no. 1, op. 25, G minor (orch. Schoenberg). CSO;
     Robert Craft. CBS 61887 (From SBRG 72358/9, 72546/7)
                  +-Gr 8-80 p214   +-RR 7-80 p60
                  -HFN 4-80 p119
     Prelude and fugue, S 552, E flat major. See no. 85. See no. 166.
     See no. 168. See no. 209. See no. 244. See no. 249. See no.
     3781. See no. 3939
     Preludes and fugues, S 553-560. See no. 241
     Prelude and fugue, S 895, A minor. See no. 327
     Prelude, fugue and allegro, S 998, E flat major. See no. 183. See
     no. 216. See no. 225. See no. 321. See no. 3577
     Presto. See no. 3637
     Quia respexit. See no. 324
     St. John Passion, S 245. See no. 264
262 St. John Passion, S 245: Ruht wohl ihr heiligen Gebeine. St. Matt-
     hew Passion, S 244: Da nahmen die Kriegsknechte des Landpfleger
     Jesum; O Haupt voll Blut und Wunden. HANDEL: Israel in Egypt:
     He sent a thick darkness; He smote all the firstborn of Egypt.
     Judas Maccabaeus: See the conquering hero comes. Samson: Then
     round about the starry throne. Messiah: Hallelujah. Saul: Mourn
     Israel mourn. HAYDN: The creation: The heavens are telling the
     glory of God. The seasons: Come gentle spring. Soloists; Buda-
     pest Chorus and Children's Chorus; Hungarian State Orchestra;
     Tamas Zaszkaliczky, org; Miklos Erdelyi. Hungaroton SLPX 12116
                    +-FF 9/10-80 p249   +NR 9-80 p7
263 St. Matthew Passion, S 244 (sung in English). Felicity Lott, s;
     Alfreda Hodgson, ms; Robert Tear, Neil Jenkins, t; John Shirley-
     Quirk, Stephen Roberts, bar; Bach Choir, St. Paul's Cathedral
     Boys Choir; Thames Chamber Orchestra; David Willcocks. Decca
     D139D4 (4)
                    +Audio 12-79 p100   +-MT 10-80 p633
                    +Gr 3-79 p1594   +-RR 5-79 p93
                    +HFN 5-79 p118
264 St. Matthew Passion, S 244. St. John Passion, S 245. Irmgard See-
     fried, Antonia Fahberg, Evelyn Lear, s; Hertha Topper, con; Ernst
     Hafliger, t; Dietrich Fischer-Dieskau, bar; Keith Engen, Max
     Proebstl, Hermann Prey, bs; Munich Bach Orchestra and Choir;
     Munich Boys Choir; Karl Richter. DG 2722010 Tape (c) 3376 001/2
     (From SAPM 198009/12, 198329/30)
                    +Gr 11-74 p935   +HF 11-75 p149 tape
                    +-Gr 1-77 p1185 tape   +-RR 12-74 p19
                    +Gr 7-80 p154
265 St. Matthew Passion, S 244. Edith Mathis, s; Janet Baker, ms; Peter
     Schreier, t; Dietrich Fischer-Dieskau, bar; Matti Salminen, bs;
     Munich Bach Choir, Regensburg Cathedral Choir; Munich Bach Orch-
     estra; Karl Richter. DG 2723 067 (4) Tape (c) 3376 016 (also DG
     2712 005 Tape (c) 3376 016)
                    +FF 9/10-80 p56   ++NR 7-80 p8
                    +Gr 5-80 p1699   +-NYT 6-8-80 pD20

```
        ++Gr 7-80 p166 tape         +-RR 4-80 p106
        +-HF 9-80 p82               +St 10-80 p108
        +-HFN 7-80 p105             ++STL 6-8-80 p38
        +-HFN 8-80 p109 tape
```

266 St. Matthew Passion, S 244. Cathedral Church of St. Paul, Detroit.
     Magnetic Recording Service Tape cassettes unnumbered (3)
                    +MU 1-80 p14
267 St. Matthew Passion, S 244. Agnes Giebel, s; Marga Hoffgen, con;
     John Van Kesteren, Ernst Hafliger, t; Walter Berry, Franz Crass,
     Leo Ketelaars, bs; Netherlands Radio Chorus, St. Willibrod's
     Church Boys Choir; COA; Eugen Jochum. Philips 6770 018 (4) Tape
     (c) 7650 018 (Reissue)
                    ++FF 3/4-80 p47   ++NR 7-79 p12
                    +-HF 12-79 p110 tape   +NYT 10-7-79 pD24
     St. Matthew Passion, S 244: Be near me Lord. See no. 3939
     St. Matthew Passion, S 244: Da nahmen die Kriegsknechte des Land-
     pfleger Jesum; O Haupt voll Blut und Wunden. See no. 262
268 St. Matthew Passion, S 244: Kommt ihr Tochter; Da Jesus diese Rede
     vollen; Herzliebster Jesu; Da versammleten sich die Hohenpriester;
     Ja nicht auf das Fest; Da ging hin der Zwolfen einer; Da kam Jes-
     us mit ihnen; O Mensch bewein dein Sunde Gross; Erbarme dich; Auf
     das Fest aber hatte der Landpfleger; Da nahmen die Kriegsnechte;
     O Haupt voll Blut und Wunden; Und von der sechsten Stunde; Wenn
     ich einmal soll scheiden; Wir setzen uns. Agnes Giebel, s; Marga
     Hoffgen, con; Ernst Hafliger; Walter Berry, Leo Ketelaars, bs;
     Netherlands Radio Chorus, St. Willibrod Church Boys Chorus; COA;
     Eugen Jochum. Philips 6570 011 Tape (c) 7310 011 (From SAL 3562/
     5)
                    +Gr 3-80 p1424   +-HFN 4-80 p121 tape
                    +Gr 7-80 p166 tape   +-RR 2-80 p84
                    +-HFN 2-80 p105
     St. Matthew Passion, S 244: O sacred head surrounded. See no. 3938
     Siciliano. See no. 324. See no. 3555
     Sonata, flute, S 1013, A minor. See no. 322
269 Sonata, flute and harpsichord, S 1020, G minor. HANDEL: Sonata,
     oboe, op. 1, no. 6, G minor. VIVALDI: Sonata, oboe, RV 53, C
     minor. Heinz Holliger, ob; Edith Picht-Axenfeld, hpd; Marcal
     Cervera, vlc. Philips 9502 019
                    ++FF 5/6-80 p88   +NR 5-80 p7
     Sonata, flute and harpsichord, S 1020, G minor. See no. 322
270 Sonatas, flute and harpsichord, S 1030, 1032, 1034-1035. Marc Beau-
     coudray, flt; William Christie, hpd. Harmonia Mundi HM 10065
                    -FF 9/10-80 p60   ++HFN 6-80 p102
     Sonatas, flute and harpsichord, S 1030, 1032, 1034-1035. See no.
     253
     Sonatas, flute and harpsichord, S 1030-1035. See no. 322
     Sonatas, flute and harpsichord, S 1031, E flat major: Siciliano.
     See no. 3777
     Sonatas, flute and harpsichord, S 1035, E major. See no. 4020
     Sonatas, 2 flutes and harpsichord, S 1039, G major. See no. 97.
     See no. 253. See no. 322
271 Sonata, harpsichord, S 964, Dminor. FUX: Harpeggio and fuga, G
     major. Chaconne, D major. Suite, A minor. Robert Kohnen, hpd.
     Accent ACC 7805
                    +FF 3/4-80 p48   +RR 6-80 p27
                    +HFN 6-80 p101

Sonatas, organ, nos. 1 and 3, S 525 and S 527. See no. 245
Sonatas, organ, no. 4, S 528, E minor. See no. 243
Sonatas, organ, no. 5, S 529, C major. See no. 243
Sonatas, organ, no. 6, S 530, G major. See no. 168. See no. 241

272 Sonatas, viola da gamba and harpsichord, nos. 1-3, S 1027-1029.
     Catherina Meints, vla da gamba; Doris Ornstein, hpd. Gasparo
     GS 212
                +NR 10-80 p7

273 Sonatas, viola da gamba and harpsichord, nos. 1-3, S 1027-1029.
     Mary Cyr, vla da gamba; John Grew, hpd. McGill University Re-
     cords 78007
                ++MUM 3/4-80 p34   +ST 7-80 p195

274 Sonatas, viola da gamba and harpsichord, nos. 1-3, S 1027-1029.
     Marcal Cervera, vla da gamba; Rafael Puyana, hpd. Philips 9502
     003 (From 6500 005)
                ++FF 11/12-79 p27   +HFN 11-80 p129
                -Gr 11-80 p684   ++SFC 6-10-79 p45

275 Sonatas, viola and harpsichord, nos. 1-3, S 1027-S 1029. Janos
     Starker, vlc; Zuzana Ruzickova, hpd. Supraphon 111 2485
                +FF 11/12-80 p64   ++NR 10-80 p8
                +-HFN 10-80 p101
     Sonatas, viola da gamba and harpsichord, nos. 1-3, S 1027-1029.
     See no. 322
     Sonatas, viola da gamba and harpsichord, no. 1, S 1027, G major.
     See no. 246
     Sonatas, violin, nos. 1-3, S 1001, 1003, 1005. See no. 321
     Sonatas, violin, no. 1, S 1001, G minor. See no. 3964
     Sonatas, violin, no. 1, S 1001, G minor: Adagio. See no. 215
     Sonatas, violin, no. 1, S 1001, G minor: Fugue. See no. 3549. See
     no. 3775
     Sonatas, violin, no. 3, S 1005, C major. See no. 3964
     Sonatas, 2 violins, S 1021, S 1023-1024. See no. 214

276 Sonatas, violin and harpsichord, S 1014-1019. David Oistrakh, vln;
     Hans Pischner, hpd. DG 2726 002 (also DG 2539 055/6. From SLPM
     1961, 1966, 1968)
                +FF 5/6-80 p40   -HFN 4-73 p776
                +-Gr 4-73 p1922   +-RR 4-73 p71

277 Sonatas, violin and harpsichord, S 1014-1019. Sigiswald Kuijken,
     vln; Gustav Leonhardt, hpd. Harmonia Mundi 1C 151 99820/1 (2)
                +-FF 9/10-80 p60   +-RR 2-80 p68
                ++Gr 2-80 p1276   ++ST 3-80 p836
                ++HFN 2-80 p105

278 Sonatas, violin and harpsichord, S 1014-1019. Henryk Szeryng, vln;
     Helmut Walcha, hpd. Philips 6768 029 (2)
                +-ARG 11-79 p19   ++SFC 6-10-79 p45
                +-FF 7/8-80 p47   ++St 11-79 p83

279 Sonatas, violin and harpsichord, S 1014-1019. Arthur Grumiaux, vln;
     Christiane Jaccottet, hpd. Philips 6769 017 (2)
                +-FF 7/8-80 p47   +-NYT 6-8-80 pD20
                ++NR 5-80 p7

280 Sonatas, violin and harpsichord, S 1014-1019. Josef Suk, vln; Zuz-
     ana Ruzickova, hpd. Quintessence PMC 2703 (2)
                +-FF 3/4-80 p41

281 Sonatas, violin and harpsichord, S 1014-1019. Carol Lieberman, vln;
     Mark Kroll, hpd. Titanic TI 33/4 (2)

```
        +ARG 7/8-80 p16              +NYT 6-8-80 pD20
        +FF 5/6-80 p42              +St 6-80 p110
        +-HF 7-80 p59
```

Sonatas, violin and harpsichord, S 1014-1019. See no. 321

282 Sonatas, violin, harpsichord and viola da gamba. Taskin Harpsichord
       Trio. Wealden WS 174
                        ++RR 2-80 p64

283 Sonatas and partitas, solo violin, S 1001-1006. Oscar Shumsky, vln.
       Musical Heritage Society MHS 4032/4 (3)
                 +FF 1/2-80 p38   +-St 12-79 p136

284 Sonatas and partitas, solo violin, S 1001-1006. Felix Ayo, vln.
       Philips 6770 950 (2)
                ++Gr 3-80 p1412   +RR 2-80 p68
                +HFN 2-80 p86   ++ST 11-80 p500

285 Sonatas and partitas, solo violin, S 1001-1006. Christian Ferras,
       vln. Sine Qua Non SAS 2028 (3) Tape (c) C 2028
                +-ARG 5-79 p14   +-HF 12-79 p126 tape
                +-FF 1/2-80 p38   +SFC 4-8-79 p49

Songs: Ach das nicht, S 439; Die bittre Leidenzeit, S 450; Brich
    entzwei, S 444; Dir dir Jehova, S 452; Eins is not, S 453; Es
    kostet viel, S 459; Gib dich zufrieden, S 521; Gott lebet noch,
    S 461; Gott wie gross, S 462; Die guldne Sonne, S 451; Ich lass
    dich nicht, S 467; Ich steh an deiner Krippen, S 469; Ihr Gestirn,
    S 476; Komm susser Tod, S 478; Kommt Seelen, S 479; Kommt wieder,
    S 480; Der lieben Sonne Licht, S 446; Liebster Herr Jesu, S 484;
    Mein Jesu, S 487; O Jesulein, S 493; So gehst du nun, S 500; So
    gibst du nun, S 501; Steh ich bei meinem Gott, S 503; Vergiss
    mein nicht, S 505; Wie wohl ist mir, S 517; Wo ist mein Schaf-
    lein, S 507. See no. 323

Songs (partsongs): God liveth still, S 461; Breath of God life giv-
    ing, S 445; It is finished, S 458; Jesus is this dark world's
    light, S 474; Lord pour not thy vengeance on me, S 463; Now is
    the mournful time, S 450; O Jesu so meek O Jesu so kind, S 49.
    See no. 237

Songs: Nain Jeesusta vain; Puer natus in Bethlehem. See no. 3592

Suites, S 818a, S 819, A minor, E flat major. See no. 218

286 Suites, lute. BUXTEHUDE: Suites, klavier. PACHELBEL: Suites, lute.
       Walter Gerwig, lt. Nonesuch 71229 Tape (c) N5 1229
                   +HF 4-80 p104 tape

Suites, lute, S 995-997, 1006a, G minor, E minor, C minor, E major.
    See no. 321

Suites, lute, S 995, G minor. See no. 225. See no. 3577

287 Suites, lute, S 996-998. Martha Goldstein, lt. Pandora PAN 111
                   +-FF 3/4-80 p190

Suites, lute, S 996, E minor. See no. 225

Suites, lute, S 996, E minor: Allemande. See no. 3549

Suites, lute, S 996, E minor: Allemande; Bourree. See no. 319. See
    no. 3775

Suites, lute, S 997, C minor. See no. 215. See no. 225

Suites, lute, S 1006a, E major. See no, 225

Suites, orchestra, S 1066-1068. See no. 178

288 Suites, orchestra, S 1066-1069. Munich Bach Orchestra; Karl Rich-
       ter. DG 2547 008 Tape (c) 3347 008 (From SAPM 198272/3)
                +Gr 4-80 p1595   +-HFN 6-80 p117
                +-Gr 7-80 p166 tape   +-RR 6-80 p40
```
```

289 Suites, orchestra, S 1066-1069. English Concert; Trevor Pinnock.
    DG 2723 072 (2) Tape (c) 3310 175 (From 2533 410/11, 2533 440)
                +-Gr 12-80 p824   +-HFN 12-80 p132
290 Suites, orchestra, S 1066-1069. German Bach Soloists; Helmut Win-
    schermann. Musical Heritage Society MHS 4203/4 Tape (c) MHC
    6203/4
                +HF 12-80 p66
291 Suites, orchestra, S 1066-1069. Roger Bourdin, flt; BRSO; Lorin
    Maazel. Philips 6770 031 (2) Tape (c) 7650 031
                +-FF 9/10-80 p64
292 Suites, orchestra, S 1066-1069. Hans-Martin Linde, transverse flt;
    Collegium Aureum; Franzjosef Maier. Quintessence 2PMC 2702 (2)
    (also Harmonia Mundi 1C 151 99618/9)
                +Audio 2-80 p42   +-FF 9/10-79 p36
                +-ARG 8-79 p12   +-St 9-79 p92
293 Suites, orchestra, S 1066-1069. Busch Chamber Players; Marcel Moyse,
    flt; Fritz Busch. WRC SHB 68 (2)
                +HFN 12-80 p132
    Suites, orchestra, S 1066-1069. See no. 118. See no. 320
294 Suite, orchestra, S 1067, B minor. TELEMANN: Suite, flute, A minor.
    Ransom Wilson, flt; Los Angeles Chamber Orchestra; Gerard Schwarz.
    Angel DS 37330 Tape (c) 4ZS 37330 (also HMV ASD 3948)
                +ARG 12-80 p16   +RR 9-80 p100
                +FF 9/10-80 p61   +SFC 7-6-80 p27
                +-Gr 9-80 p326   ++St 12-80 p116
                +NR 9-80 p12
295 Suite, orchestra, S 1067, B minor (arr.). VIVALDI: Concerto, 2
    trumpets. Steven Seward, tuba; Vicki Berneking, pno; Eric Ander-
    son, euphonium. Golden Crest RE 7083
                +NYT 5-18-80 pD42
296 Suite, orchestra, S 1067, B minor. GLUCK: Orfeo ed Euridice: Dance
    of the blessed spirits. MOZART: Concerto, flute, no. 2, K 314,
    D major. Claude Monteux, flt; LSO; Pierre Monteux. London STS
    15493
                +-FF 3/4-80 p120
    Suite, orchestra, S 1067, B minor: Badinerie. See no. 3640
    Suite, orchestra, S 1067, B minor: Minuet; Badinerie. See no. 3951
    Suite, orchestra, S 1067, B minor: Rondo and Badinerie. See no.
    3999
297 Suite, orchestra, S 1068, D major. Suite, orchestra, S 1069, D
    major. New Chamber Soloists; George Malcolm. Merlin MRF 78901
                +-ARG 6-80 p16   +HFN 7-79 p101
                +Audio 6-80 p113   +-RR 8-79 p71
                ++FF 7/8-80 p48   ++St 4-80 p88
                +Gr 6-79 p31
298 Suite, orchestra, S 1068, D major: Air on the G string. HANDEL:
    Berenice: Minuet. Solomon: Arrival of the Queen of Sheba.
    Water music: Air and hornpipe. HAYDN: Concerto, trumpet, E flat
    major. MOZART: Divertimento, no. 17, K 334, D major: Minuet.
    Serenade, no. 13, K 525, G major. AMF; Neville Marriner. Argo
    ZRG 902 Tape (c) KZRC 902 (From ZRG 442, 697, 543, 679)
                +-Gr 8-80 p233   +RR 8-80 p49
                +HFN 8-80 p103
299 Suite, orchestra, S 1068, D major: Air on the G string. HANDEL:
    Water music: Suite. PACHELBEL: Canon, D major. PH; Zoltan Rozsn-
    yai. M & K Realtime RT 206, PS 1007

-HF 11-80 p86

Suite, orchestra, S 1068, D major: Air on the G string. See no. 17.
See no. 324. See no. 325. See no. 326. See no. 3589. See no.
3602. See no. 3663. See no. 3715. See no. 3912. See no. 3943.
See no. 4030

Suite, orchestra, S 1069, D major. See no. 124. See no. 297

300 Suites, solo violoncello, nos. 1-6, S 1007-1012. Andre Navarra,
vlc. Calliope CAL 1641/3 (3) Tape (c) 4641/3
      ++FF 11/12-80 p64   ++RR 6-80 p70
      +-Gr 9-80 p368   +ST 11-80 p500
      ++HFN 5-80 p117

301 Suites, solo violoncello, nos. 1-6, S 1007-1012. Maurice Gendron,
vlc. Philips 6770 005 (3) Tape (c) 7650 012
      +ARG 8-79 p10   +HFN 4-79 p117
      ++Audio 12-79 p100   ++RR 5-79 p80
      +FF 1/2-80 p39   ++SFC 5-6-79 p61
      +-Gr 5-79 p1913

302 Suites, solo violoncello, nos. 1-6, S 1007-1012. Pierre Fournier,
vlc. Sine Qua Non SAS 2026 (3) Tape (c) 2026
      +ARG 5-79 p14   +HF 10-79 p126 tape
      +FF 1/2-80 p38

303 Suites, solo violoncello, nos. 1-6, S 1007-1012. Milos Sadlo, vlc.
Supraphon 111 1701/3 (3)
      +-ARG 8-79 p10   +HFN 2-80 p86
      +FF 1/2-80 p39   +RR 1-80 p96

Suites, solo violoncello, nos. 1-6, S 1007-1012. See no. 322

Suites, solo violoncello, no. 1, S 1007, G major: Menuetto and
courante. See no. 3569

Suites, solo violoncello, no. 1, S 1007, G minor: Prelude. See no.
327. See no. 3549. See no. 3775

Suites, solo violoncello, no. 1, S 1007, A major: Prelude; Allemande; Courante; Sarabande. See no. 319

Suites, solo violoncello, no. 1, S 1007, A major: 3 movements. See
no. 3975

304 Suites, solo violoncello, no. 2, S 1008, D minor. CRUMB: Sonata,
solo violoncello. HINDEMITH: Sonata, violoncello, op. 25, no. 3.
Frans Helmerson, vlc. BIS LP 65
      +-ARG 9-79 p16   +NR 7-80 p13
      +HFN 7-79 p115   +RR 7-79 p82

Suites, solo violoncello, no. 2, S 1008, D minor. See no. 48

Suites, solo violoncello, no. 3, S 1009, C major: Courante. See
no. 3549. See no. 3775

Suites, solo violoncello, no. 3, S 1009, C major: Suite. See no.
3722

Toccata, S 540, F major. See no. 157. See no. 3524

305 Toccatas, S 910, F sharp minor; S 912, D major; S 913, D minor.
Glenn Gould, pno. Columbia M 35144 Tape (c) MT 35144 (also CBS
76881)
      +-ARG 7-79 p14   +-MT 6-80 p382
      -CL 11-79 p8   +-MUM 3/4-80 p35
      +-FF 7/8-79 p18   +NR 3-80 p14
      +-Gr 3-80 p1412   +RR 4-80 p91
      +HF 7-79 p127   +-St 7-79 p94
      +HFN 3-80 p85   +-STL 4-13-80 p39
      ++MJ 11/12-79 p49

306 Toccatas, S 911, C minor; S 914, E minor; S 915, G minor; S 916, G
     major. Glenn Gould, pno. Columbia M 35831 Tape (c) MT 35831
                +ARG 11-80 p15   +-NR 5-80 p11
                +FF 7/8-80 p49   +NYT 6-8-80 pD20
                +-HF 11-80 p61   +St 8-80 p92
     Toccata, S 911, C minor. See no. 208
     Toccatas, S 912-916. See no. 218
     Toccata, S 912, D major. See no. 175
     Toccata, S 914, E minor. See no. 306
     Toccata, S 915, G minor. See no. 306
     Toccata, S 916, C major. See no. 306
     Toccata, adagio and fugue, S 564, C major. See no. 159. See no.
        247. See no. 250. See no. 307. See no. 308. See no. 3658.
        See no. 3664
307 Toccata and fugue, S 538, D minor. Toccata and fugue, S 540, F
     major. Toccata and fugue, S 565, D minor. Toccata, adagio and
     fugue, S 564, C major. Andre Isoir, org. Calliope CAL 1701
     Tape (c) CAL 4701
                +Gr 8-80 p240   +RR 8-80 p66
                +-HFN 8-80 p93
308 Toccatas and fugues, S 538, D minor; S 540, F major; S 565, D minor.
     Toccata, adagio and fugue, S 564, C major. Joan Lippincott, org.
     Gothic 68005
                -NR 12-80 p10
     Toccata and fugue, S 538, D minor. See no. 110. See no. 169. See
        no. 211. See no. 241. See no. 247
     Toccata and fugue, S 540, F major. See no. 247. See no. 307. See
        no. 308
309 Toccata and fugue, S 565, D minor. RUSSELL: The bells of St. Anne
     de Beaupre. VIVALDI: Concerto, organ, D minor: Largo. WAGNER:
     Tannhauser: Grand march. Lloyd Holzgraf, org. M & K Real Time
     RT 114
                +ARG 4-80 p51   +ARG 2-80 p48
     Toccata and fugue, S 565, D minor. See no. 8. See no. 100. See
        no. 110. See no. 145. See no. 156. See no. 185. See no. 210.
        See no. 211. See no. 241. See no. 247. See no. 249. See no.
        307. See no. 308. See no. 3615. See no. 3616. See no. 3624.
        See no. 3625. See no. 3658. See no. 3660. See no. 3664. See
        no. 3743. See no. 3838. See no. 3938
     Toccata and fugue, S 566, E major. See no. 244
     Toccata and fugue, S 916, G major. See no. 96. See no. 217
     Trio, S 583, D minor. See no. 245
     Trio, S 584, G minor. See no. 241
310 Trio sonata, C major. FASCH: Trio sonata, G major. FESCH: Trio
     sonata, no. 4, G minor. STAMITZ: Trio sonata, G major. Los
     Angeles Baroque Players. Crystal S 703
                +ARG 7/8-80 p51   +NR 4-80 p6
                +-Audio 8-80 p73   ++SFC 3-9-80 p40
                +FF 3/4-80 p198
311 Trio sonatas, S 525-530. Jean-Pierre Rampal, flt; Robert Veyron-
     Lacroix, hpd. RCA ARL 1-3580 Tape (c) ARK 1-3580
                +FF 9/10-80 p64   +SFC 6-15-80 p36
                +NR 7-80 p7
     Trio sonatas, S 525-530. See no. 247
312 Trio sonatas, S 527-530. Andre Isoir, org. Calliope CAL 1714
                +-HFN 9-80 p99

Trio sonata, S 525, E flat major. See no. 242
Trio sonata, S 526, C minor. See no. 242
Trio sonata, S 528, E minor. See no. 260. See no. 4063
313 Variations, harpsichord, S 988. Rosalyn Tureck, hpd. CBS 79220
       (2) (also CBS M2 35900)
                +-FF 11/12-80 p62   -STL 2-10-80 p40
                -NYT 6-8-80 pD20
314 Variations, harpsichord, S 988. Trevor Pinnock, hpd. DG 2533 425
                +Gr 12-80 p847   +-HFN 12-80 p132
315 Variations, harpsichord, S 988. Blandine Verlet, hpd. Philips
       6768 074 (2)
                -FF 3/4-80 p43   +-NYT 1-27-80 pD20
                +HF 4-80 p75   ++SFC 2-10-80 p41
                -NR 2-80 p14
316 Variations, harpsichord, S 988. Gustav Leonhardt, hpd. Quintes-
       sence PMC 7151
                +FF 11/12-80 p61
317 Variations, harpsichord, S 988. John Gibbons, hpd. Titanic TI 30/1
       (2)
                +-FF 5/6-80 p36   ++NYT 1-27-80 pD20
     Variations, harpsichord, S 988. See no. 112. See no. 218
     Variations on "Vom Himmel hoch", S 769. See no. 251
318 Das wohltemperierte Klavier, S 846-893. Helmut Walcha, hpd. DG
       2714 004 (5)
                +-ARG 6-79 p10   ++NR 6-79 p14
                +-FF 11/12-80 p65   ++SFC 4-8-79 p49
                +-HF 9-79 p110
     Das wohltemperierte Klavier, S 846-893. See no. 218
     Das wohltemperierte Klavier, S 846, 853-854, 856, 858, 862, 867;
       Bk II: S 881, 889. See no. 94
     Das wohltemperierte Klavier, S 846: Prelude. See no. 3628
     Das wohltemperierte Klavier, S 846: Prelude and fugue, no. 6, D
       major. See no. 3737
     Das wohltemperierte Klavier, S 853: Prelude. See no. 327
319 Works, selections: Fugue, lute, S 1000, G minor. Partita, solo
       violin, S 1006, E major: Loure; Gavotte; Menuet; Gigue (arr.
       Gerwig). Prelude, S 999, C minor. Suite, lute, S 996, E minor:
       Allemande; Bourree. Suite, solo violoncello, no. 1, S 1007, A
       major: Prelude; Allemande; Courante; Sarabande (arr. Gerwig).
       Walter Gerwig, lt. Desto DC 7186 (also Nonesuch H 71137)
                +FF 11/12-80 p63   +St 11-80 p78
320 Works, selections: Brandenburg concerti, nos. 1-6, S 1046-1051. Con-
       certo, flute, violin and harpsichord, S 1044, A minor. Concerti,
       harpsichord, nos. 1-7, S 1052-1058. Concerti, 2 harpsichords, S
       1060-1062. Concerti, 3 harpsichords, S 1063-1064. Concerto, 4
       harpsichords, S 1065, A minor. Concerto, oboe, S 1055, A major.
       Concerti, violin and strings, S 1041-1043. Concerto, violin,
       oboe and strings, S 1060, D minor. Suites, orchestra, S 1066-
       1069. Karl Richter, Hedwig Bilgram, Iwona Futterer, Ulrike Schott,
       Ralph Kirkpatrick, hpd; Spiros Rantos, Rudolf Baumgartner, Otto
       Buchner, Eduard Melkus, vln; Aurele Nicolet, flt; Heinz Holliger,
       Edgar Shann, ob; Munich Bach Orchestra; Lucerne Festival Strings;
       Vienna Capella Academica; Eduard Melkus, Rudolf Baumgartner, Karl
       Richter. DG 2722 011 (11)
                +Gr 12-74 p1114   +-RR 12-74 p19
                +Gr 7-80 p154

321 Works, selections: Fugue, lute, S 1000, G minor. Partitas, violin,
     nos. 1-3, S 1002, 1004, 1006. Prelude, S 999, C minor. Prelude,
     fugue and allegro, S 998, E flat major. Sonatas, violin, nos.
     1-3, S 1001, 1003, 1005. Sonatas, violin and harpsichord, S 1014-
     1019. Suites, lute, S 995-997, 1006a, G minor, E minor, C minor,
     E major. Wolfgang Schneiderhan, Henryk Szeryng, vln; Karl Rich-
     ter, hpd; Narciso Yepes, 1t. DG 2722 012 (7) (From SAPM 198381/
     2, SLPM 139270/2, 2708030)
              ++Gr 12-74 p1158   +-RR 12-74 p19
              +Gr 7-80 p154
322 Works, selections: Das Musikalisches Opfer, S 1079, C minor. Son-
     ata, solo flute, S 1013, A minor. Sonatas, flute and harpsichord,
     S 1020, G minor. Sonatas, flute and harpsichord, S 1030-1035.
     Sonata, 2 flutes and harpsichord, S 1039, G major. Sonatas,
     viola da gamba, nos. 1-3, S 1027-1029. Suites, solo violoncello,
     nos. 1-6, S 1007-1012. Aurele Nicolet, Christiane Nicolet, flt;
     Karl Richter, Christiane Jaccottet, Eduard Muller, Hedwig Bilgram,
     hpd; Johannes Fink, August Wenzinger, vla da gamba; Pierre Four-
     nier, Fritz Kiskalt, vlc; Otto Buchner, Kurt Gunter, vln; Sieg-
     fried Meinecke, vla; Karl Richter, cond. DG 2722 013 (7)
              +Gr 5-75 p1980   +HFN 7-75 p71
              +Gr 7-80 p154
323 Works, selections: Masses, S 232-236. Motets: Furchte dich nicht,
     S 228; Der Geist hilft unser Schwachheit auf, S 226; Ich lasse
     dich nicht, S Anh 159; Jesu meine Freude, S 227; Komm Jesu komm,
     S 229; Lobet den Herrn, S 230; Sei Lobe und Preis, S 231; Singet
     dem Herrn, S 225. Songs: Ach das nciht, S 439; Die bittre Leid-
     enzeit, S 450; Brich entzwei, S 444; Dir Dir Jehova, S 452; Eins
     is not, S 453; Es kostet viel, S 459; Gib dich zufrieden, S 521;
     Gott lebet noch, S 461; Gott wie gross, S 462; Die guldne Sonne,
     S 451; Ich lass dich nicht, S 467; Ich steh an deiner Krippen, S
     469; Ihr Gestirn, S 476; Komm susser Tod, S 478; Kommt, Seelen,
     S 479; Kommt wieder, S 480; Der lieben Sonne Licht, S 446; Lieb-
     ster Herr Jesu, S 484; Mein Jesu, S 487; Jesulein S 493; So gehst
     du nun, S 500; So gibst du nun, S 501; Steh ich bei meinem Gott,
     S 503; Vergiss mein nicht, S 505; Wie wohl ist mir, S 517; Wo
     ist mein Schaflein, S 507. Maria Stader, Renate Krahmer, Elisa-
     beth Speiser, s; Hertha Topper, Annelies Burmeister, con; Ernst
     Hafliger, Peter Schreier, t; Dietrich Fischer-Dieskau, Keith
     Engen, Theo Adam, bs; Regensburg Cathedral Choir; Vienna Capella
     Academica; Dresden Kreuzchor; Munich Bach Orchestra and Choir;
     Dresden Philharmonic Orchestra; Hedwig Bilgram, positiv organ;
     Karl Richter, Martin Flamig, Hans-Martin Schneidt. DG 2722 017
     (S 232, reissue from 2710 001)
              +Gr 7-80 p154
              +Gr 9-75 p499   +RR 8-75 p60
              +HFN 9-75 p70
324 Works, selections: Fugue, G 578, G minor. Gavottes, nos. 1 and 2.
     Menuets, nos. 1 and 2. Suite, orchestra, S 1068, D major: Air
     on the G string. Siciliano. Cantata, no. 208: Sheep may safely
     graze. Cantata, no. 140: Sleepers awake. Cantata, no. 147: Jesu
     joy of man's desiring. Prelude, C major. Quia respexit. Laur-
     indo Almeida, gtr. Orion Tape (c) OC 824
              +NR 8-80 p1 tape
325 Works, selecdtions: Cantata, no. 29: Sinfonia. Cantata, no. 140,

Wachet auf: Chorale. Cantata, no. 147, Jesu joy of man's desiring: Chorale. Christmas oratorio, S 248: Pastorale. Easter
oratorio, S 249: Adagio. Partita, violin, no. 2, S 1004, D min-
or: Chaconne. Prelude and fugue, S 545, C major. Suite, orchestra, S 1068, D major: Air on the G string. Rainer Kussmaul,
vln; Wolfgang Hochstein, hpd; Helmut Winschermann, ob; German
Bach Soloists; Helmut Winschermann. Quintessence PMC 7160
                    +FF 11/12-80 p65
326 Works, selections: Cantata, no. 156: Arioso. Chorale preludes,
     S 645, Wachet auf ruft uns die Stimme; S 720, Ein feste Burg.
     Fugue, S 578, G minor. Partita, violin, no. 2, S 1004, D minor:
     Chaconne. Partita, violin, no. 3, S 1006, E major: Preludio.
     Suite, orchestra, S 1068, D major: Air on the G string. LSO;
     Leopold Stokowski. RCA GL 4-2921 (From ARL 1-0880)
          +-HFN 4-80 p117   +-RR 4-80 p55
327 Works, selections: Partita, violin, no. 2, S 1004, D minor: Chaconne.
     Partita, violin, no. 3, S 1006, E major: Gavotte. Preludes, S
     926, D minor; S 929, C minor; S 934, E minor; S 940, D minor;
     S 999, C minor. Prelude and fugue, S 895, A minor. Suite, solo
     violoncello, no. 1, S 1007, G minor: Prelude. Das wohltemperier-
     te Klavier, Bk I, S 853: Prelude. (all arr. Zelenka, Segovia)
     Milan Zelenka, gtr. Supraphon 111 2263
          +FF 11/12-80 p62   +St 11-80 p78
BACH, Wilhelm Friedemann
     Air. See no. 3772
     Concerto, harpsichord, C minor. See no. 78
     Concerto, 2 harpsichords, F major. See no. 81
     Duo, flute and oboe, F major. See no. 328. See no. 331
     Duo, flute and violin, E flat major. See no. 328. See no. 331
     Duos, 2 flutes, E flat major. See no. 331
     Duos, 2 flutes, F minor. See no. 331
328 Duos, 2 flutes, F minor, E flat major. Duot, flute and oboe, F
     major. Duo, flute and violin, E flat major. Trio sonatas, D
     major, F major, B flat major, C major. Freiburg Baroque Soloists.
     Audite FSM 53194/5
          +FF 9/10-80 p66
     Duo, 2 flutes, F major. See no. 97
     Fantasia, D minor. See no. 83
     Fugues (5). See no. 84
     Sonata, flute and oboe, D major. See no. 331
     Sonata, flute and violin, D major. See no. 331
329 Sonatas, harpsichord (6). Hans Kann, fortepiano. Musical Heritage
     Society MHS 4029
          -FF 9/10-80 p67
     Sonata, harpsichord, B flat minor. See no. 92
330 Sonata, 2 harpsichords, F major. BLANCO: Concerto, 2 harpsichords,
     G major. COUPERIN, F.: Livres de clavecin, Bk II, Ordre no. 9.
     SOLER: Concerto, 2 harpsichords, no. 3, G major. Ton Koopman,
     Anneke Uittenbosch, hpd. Telefunken AW 6-42227
          +-FF 3/4-80 p183   /RR 5-78 p47
          +Gr 5-78 p1890   +-SFC 2-10-80 p41
          +-HFN 5-78 p143
     Sonatas, oboe and violin, F major, C major. See no. 331
     Trio, A minor. See no. 97
     Trio sonatas, D major, F major, D flat major, C major. See no. 328

331 Works, selections: Duos, 2 flutes, E flat major. Duo, flute and
oboe, F major. Duo, 2 flutes, F minor. Duo, flute and violin,
E flat major. Sonata, flute and oboe, D major. Sonata, oboe
and violin, F major, C major. Sonata, flute and violin, D major.
Freiburg Baroque Soloists. Musical Heritage Society MHS 4052/3
(2)
+FF 3/4-80 p48
BACHELET, Alfred
Chere nuit. See no. 3985
BACK-Sven-Erik
332 Quartet, strings, no. 2. EKLUND: Quartet, strings, no. 4. ELIAS-
SON: Designo, string quartet. HEMBERG: Zona rosa. Crafoord
Quartet. Caprice CAP 1139
+FF 9/10-79 p179   ++RR 5-80 p76
+Gr 6-80 p53
BACKER-GRONDAHL, Agathe
Undomssang, op. 36, no. 6. See no. 4024
Visnet, op. 39, no. 9. See no. 4024
BACON, Ernst
Parting. See no. 3884
BADINGS, Henk
Stabat mater. See no. 3934
BAENA, Lope de
Arcangel San Miguel. See no. 4002
BAERMANN, Heinrich Josef
Adagio, clarinet and strings, D flat major. See no. 837
BAIRD, Tadeusz
333 Concerto lugubre, viola. Love sonnets (4). Goethe Briefe. Stefan
Kamasa, vla; Andrzej Hiolski, bar; Polish Radio Orchestra; Jacek
Kasprzyk, Jan Krenz. Muza SX 1576
++FF 9/10-80 p68
Goethe Briefe. See no. 333
Love sonnets (4). See no. 333
334 Novelettes (4). Songs: Chansons des trouveres; Epiphany music; Four
songs. Krystyna Szostek-Radkowa, ms; Warsaw Philharmonic Orches-
tra; Witold Rowicki. Muza SX 0462
+FF 7/8-80 p121
Songs (5). See no. 3857
Songs: Chansons des trouveres; Epiphany music; Four songs. See no.
334
BAIRSTOW, Edward
Let all mortal flesh keep silence. See no. 3527
Songs: Jesu the very thought of thee. See no. 4019
Though I speak with the tongues of men and of angels. See no. 3528
BAKER, Ernest
Cantilena. See no. 3644
BAKER, Larry
Before assemblages III. See no. 3655
BAKFARK, Balint
Fantasia. See no. 3966
335 Fantasia, no. 2. Madrigal and motet transcriptions: Faulte d'argent
(Josquin des Pres); Cantibus organicus, Fundite cantores, Venite
filii, Servitore domino (Gombert); Che piu foc'al (Arcadelt);
Veni in hortum meum (Lassus); Jesu nomen sit nomen (Clemens non
Papa). Daniel Benko, lt. Hungaroton SLPX 11987

+–ARG 4-80 p15   –FF 9/10-80 p272
Madrigal and motet transcriptions: Faulte d'argent (Josquin des
   Pres); Cantibus organicus, Fundite cantores, Venite filii, Servitore domino (Gombert); Che piu foc'al (Arcadelt); Veni in hortum
   meum (Lassus); Jesu nomen sit nomen (Clemens non Papa). See no.
   335
BALADA, Leonardo
336 Homage to Sarasate. BRANT: On the nature of things after Lucretius.
   CORDERO: Symphony, no. 2, in one movement. Louisville Orchestra;
   Jorge Mester. Louisville LS 765
                +–FF 9/10-80 p104
BALAKIREV, Mily
337 Islamey. Russia. Overture on 3 Russian themes. GLINKA: Russlan
   and Ludmila: Magic dances. Life for the Czar: Overture. SCRI-
   ABIN: Day dreams, op. 24. USSR Symphony Orchestra; Yevgeny
   Svetlanov. HMV ASD 3709 Tape (c) TC ASD 3709
                +–Gr 7-79 p322   +–MM 11-79 p29
                +–Gr 10-79 p727 tape   +RR 8-79 p73
                +HFN 9-79 p119   +RR 3-80 p105 tape
                +–HFN 11-79 p157 tape
   Islamey. See no. 3622. See no. 3678
   Overture on 3 Russian themes. See no. 337. See no. 2535
   Russia. See no. 337
338 Russian folk songs, piano, 4 hands (3). Victoria Postnikova,
   Gennady Rozhdestvensky, pno. Melodiya S 10 07565-6
                +FF 7/8-80 p51
339 Suite, piano, 4 hands. LISZT: Grand valse di bravura, op. 6.
   ONSLOW: Sonata, piano, op. 7, E minor. WAGNER: Polonaise, D
   major. Richard Boldrey, Elizabeth Buccheri, pno. Spectrum SR
   113 Tape (c) SC 213
                +FF 3/4-80 p189   +HF 6-80 p96
340 Symphony, no. 1, C major.* BORODIN: Prince Igor: Polovtsian dances
   (orch. Rimsky-Korsakov). RPO, Beecham Choral Society; Thomas
   Beecham. HMV SXLP 30171 Tape (c) TC EXE 193 (*From SXLP 30002)
                +FF 5/6-80 p42   +HFN 6-76 p105 tape
                +Gr 10-74 p676   +RR 10-74 p33
341 Symphony, no. 1, C major. PhO; Herbert von Karajan. HMV XLP 60001
   Tape (c) TC XLP 60001 (From Columbia LX 1323/8)
                +Gr 7-80 p135   +–HFN 9-80 p115 tape
                +Gr 10-80 p548 tape   +RR 7-80 p49
                +–HFN 7-80 p115
342 Symphony, no. 2, D minor. GLAZUNOV: Cortege solennel, op. 91, G
   major. MRSO; Gennady Rozhdestvensky. Columbia M 35155 (also
   Melodiya 33C 10 08851-52)
                +ARG 1-80 p17   +–HF 10-79 p93
                +FF 9/10-79 p39   +SFC 7-1-79 p44
                +FF 11/12-79 p29   +St 11-79 p83
BALASSA, Sandor
343 The man outside. Ilona Tokody, s; Sandor Palcso, Attila Fulop, t;
   Jozsef Gregor, bs; Hungarian Radio Chorus; Budapest Symphony
   Orchestra; Gyorgy Lehel. Hungaroton SLPX 12052/3 (2)
                +NR 8-80 p10   +SFC 11-23-80 p21
BALAZS
   Songs: Song; Spring landscape; Carillon. See no. 3803
BALBASTRE, Claude
   Votre bonte. See no. 3733

BALDELLI
A suon di baci. See no. 3981
BALFE, Michael
344   The Bohemian girl. Leigh Munro, Ellen Sussman, Roberta Peters, s;
        Alice Garrott, alto; Vinson Cole, William Martin, Anthony Marlow,
        t; Peter Strummer, Will Roy, Gary Jordan, Howell Glynne, bs; Cen-
        tral City Opera Festival Orchestra and Chorus, ROHO; Paul Poliv-
        nick, Thomas Beecham. VOCE 17 (3)
                    +-FF 11/12-80 p66
      Come into the garden Maud. See no. 3774. See no. 3874
      Killarney. See no. 3947. See no. 4070.
BALFOUR-GARDINER
      Evening hymn. See no. 3531
BALLARD, Robert
      Ballet de Monsieur le Dauphin. See no. 3612
      Branles de village. See no. 3612
BANCHIERI, Adriano
      Fantasia terza decima. See no. 3597
345   Festino nella sera del Giovedi grasso avanti cena. Elisabeth and
        Guy Roberts, lt; The Scholars. Arion ARN 38411 (also Musical
        Heritage Society MHS 4039)
                    +FF 3/4-80 p50   +RR 7-79 p22
                    +Gr 7-79 p237   ++St 2-80 p120
      Ricercare del 5 and 6 tuono. See no. 3813
      Sonata sopra l'aria musical del Gran Duca. See no. 3956
BAND
      General Burgoyne's march. See no. 3971
BANTOCK, Granville
346   Fifine at the fair. DELIUS: Songs of sunset. Maureen Forrester,
        con; John Cameron, bar; Beecham Choral Society; RPO; Thomas
        Beecham. HMV SXLP 30440 Tape (c) TC SXLP 30440 (From HMV DB
        21145/8, ALP 1983)
                    +Gr 10-80 p523   +-HFN 10-80 p115
347   The pierrot of the minute. BRIDGE: Suite, string orchestra. Sum-
        mer. There is a willow grows aslant a brook. BUTTERWORTH: The
        banks of green willow. Bournemouth Sinfonietta; Norman Del Mar.
        RCA RL 2-5184 Tape (c) RK 2-5184
                    +-Gr 12-79 p1002   +RR 1-80 p63
                    +-HFN 2-80 p103   +RR 3-80 p104 tape
                    +HFN 2-80 p107 tape   ++ST 7-80 p197
348   Sapphic poem. HOLBROOKE: Concerto, piano, no. 1. MACKENZIE: The
        little minister overture, op. 57. Gillian Thoday, vlc; Philip
        Challis, pno; Hull Youth Orchestra; Geoffrey Heald-Smith. Gough
        & Davy GD 2003
                    +FF 1/2-80 p95   +Gr 2-79 p1413
BARBE, Helmut
      Ein Jager langs dem Weiher ging. See no. 3662
BARBER, Samuel
      Adagio, strings. See no. 353. See no. 3623
      Commando march. See no. 4012
349   Concerto, violin, op. 14. BLOCH: Sonata, violin, no. 1. Louis
        Kaufmann, vln; Pina Pozzi, pno; Lucerne Festival Orchestra; Wal-
        ter Goehr. Orion ORS 79355 (From Concert Hall)
                    +-ARG 5-80 p16   +-NR 2-80 p4
                    +-FF 3/4-80 p63

350 Concerto, violoncello, op. 22. BRITTEN: Serenade, op. 31. Raya
       Garbousova, vlc; Charles Bressler, t; Ralph Froelich, hn; Musica
       Aeterna; Frederic Waldman. Varese VC 81057 (From Decca, 1966)
                 +–ARG 6-79 p16   ++St 5-79 p115
                 +–FF 5/6-80 p43
     Dover beach. See no. 353
     Essays, orchestra, no. 2, op. 17. See no. 353
     Medea's meditation and dance of vengeance, op. 23a. See no. 353
     Overture to School for scandal, op. 5. See no. 353
351 Quartet, strings, op. 11: Adagio. BARTOK: Roumanian folk dances.
       BRITTEN: Simple symphony, op. 4. RESPIGHI: Ancient airs and
       dances, Set 3: Suite. I Musici. Philips 6570 181 Tape (c) 7310
       181
                 ++FF 11/12-80 p223
     Quartet, strings, op. 11, B minor: Adagio. See no 3565
     Sonata, piano, op. 26, E minor. See no. 3622
352 Sonata, violoncello and piano, op. 6. DELLA JOIO: Duo concertato.
       KODALY: Sonata, violoncello and piano, op. 4. Jeffrey Solow, vlc;
       Albert Dominguez, pno. Pelican LP 2010
                 +FF 5/6-80 p43   ++St 9-80 p77
353 Works, selections: Adagio strings. Dover beach. Essay, orchestra,
       no. 2, op. 17. Medea's meditation and dance of vengeance, op.
       23a. Overture to School for scandal, op. 5. Dietrich Fischer-
       Dieskau, bar; NYP, Juilliard Quartet; Thomas Schippers. CBS
       61898 Tape (c) 61898
                 +Gr 12-80 p889 tape   +HFN 9-80 p115 tape
                 +HFN 8-80 p94   +RR 7-80 p31
BARBIREAU, Jacques
     Songs: En frolyk weson. See no. 3795
BARBLAN, Otto
     Canon, D minor. See no. 3734
     Chaconne on BACH. See no. 3734
BARDO, Lajos
     Fire-rainbow. See no. 3803
BARES, Peter
354 Magnificat. Peter Bares, org. Musikwissenschaftliche Verlags-
       Gesellschaft WA 102
                 +FF 9/10-80 p270
BARGINGANT
     L'Omme bany da sa plaisance. See no. 3880
BARNARD, Charlotte (Claribel, pseud.)
     Come back to Erin. See no. 4070
     Songs: Come back to Erin. See no. 3947
BARNBY, Joseph
     Home they brought her warrior dead. See no. 3791
BARNES, Milton
     Fantasy. See no. 3607
     Fantasy. See no. 3635
BARNHART
     When stars looked down. See no. 3737
BARON, Ernst
355 Concerto, guitar, no. 1, C major. GALILEI: Studies, guitar (6).
       GIULIANI: Sonata, violin and guitar, op. 25, E minor. SCHEID-
       LER: Sonata, flute and guitar, D major. Diego Blanco, gtr;
       Gunilla von Bahr, flt. BIS LP 90
                 +FF 7/8-80 p78   ++NR 5-80 p7

+-HFN 4-80 p115   ++RR 3-80 p30
BARRERA Y CALLEJA
    Adios Granada. See no. 3551
BARRETT, John
    Voluntary, C major. See no. 3866
BARRIOS MANGORE, Agustin
    Aconquija maxixa. See no. 4030
    Cancion de la hilandera. See no. 3607. See no. 3635
    La catedral. See no. 3614
    Danza de la gitana. See no. 3609
    Danza paraguaya. See no. 3614. See no. 3634
    Valse, op. 8, no. 4. See no. 3607. See no. 3635
BARSANTI, Francesco
356 Concerto, 2 horns, op. 3, no. 4, D major. HANDEL: Concerto, 2
        horns, F major. TELEMANN: Concerto, horn, D major. Concerto, 3
        horns, D major. Suite, 2 horns, F major. James Stagliano, Art-
        hur Berv, hn; Kapp Sinfonetta; Richard Dunn. Westminster MCA
        1422 Tape (c) 1422
                        +NR 12-80 p6
    Sonata, recorder, G minor. See no. 3990
BARTEVIAN, Ara
    For children. See no. 3851
BARTHELEMY
    Pesca d'amore. See no. 3774
    Songs: Adorables tourments; Triste ritorno. See no. 3945
    Songs: Sulla bocca amorosa; Triste ritorno; Serenamente. See no.
        3981
BARTLETT, John
    Sweet birdes deprive us never. See no. 3877
    Whither runneth my sweetheart. See no. 3879
BARTOK, Bela
357 Allegro barbaro. BRAHMS: Rhapsodies, op. 79. ENESCO: Sonata, piano,
        no. 3, op. 24, D major. TRENKNER: Arabesques, op. 28. Evalinde
        Trenkner, pno. Orion ORS 80379
                        +-FF 9/10-80 p118   +NR 8-80 p12
358 Bluebeard's castle, op. 11. Sylvia Sass, s; Kolos Kovats, bs; LPO;
        Georg Solti. Decca SET 630 Tape (c) KCET 630 (also London OSA
        1174)
                        +-Gr 8-80 p265   +-NR 12-80 p8
                        ++Gr 12-80 p889 tape   +-RR 8-80 p28
                        +-HFN 8-80 p94   +St 12-80 p116
                        +MT 12-80 p783
359 Bluebeard's castle, op. 11. Julia Varady, s; Dietrich Fischer-
        Dieskau, bar; Bavarian Symphony Orchestra; Wolfgang Sawallisch.
        DG 2531 172
                        +AR 11-80 p16   +NYT 3-30-80 pD23
                        +FF 9/10-80 p70   +Op 3-80 p270
                        +Gr 1-80 p1195   +RR 12-79 p38
                        +-HF 8-80 p59   +-St 10-80 p107
                        +-HFN 1-80 p101   +STL 12-2-79 p27
                        +NR 7-80 p9   +STL 2-10-80 p40
360 Bluebeard's castle, op. 11. Birgit Nilsson, s; Bernard Sonnersted,
        bar; Danish Radio Orchestra; Lavard Friisholm. Historical Re-
        corder Enterprises HRE 225
                        +FF 11/12-80 p67

361 Bluebeard's castle, op. 11. Mihaly Szekely, bs; Klara Palankay, ms;
    Budapest Philharmonic Orchestra; Janos Ferencsik. Hungaroton
    SLPX 11011
                +ARG 8-79 p13   ++NR 6-79 p11
                +FF 1/2-80 p42   +-RR 4-79 p48
                +Gr 5-79 p1929   ++SFC 7-8-79 p43
                +HFN 3-79 p119
362 Bluebeard's castle, op. 11. Dance suite. The miraculous mandarin,
    op. 19. The wooden prince, op. 13. Olga Szonyi, s; Mihaly Szek-
    ely, bs; LSO, BBC Orchestra and Chorus, PhO; Antal Dorati. Mer-
    cury SRI 3-77012 (3) (From SR 90183/311/416/426)
                +ARG 11-80 p16   +NYT 3-30-80 pD23
                +FF 7/8-80 p52   ++SFC 5-4-80 p42
                +-HF 8-80 p60
363 Concerto, orchestra. Orchestra; Ferenc Fricsay. DG 2535 701
                +ARSC Vol 12, nos. 1-2, 1980 p124
364 Concerto, orchestra. CPhO; Karel Ancerl. Quintessence PMC 7152
    Tape (c) 7152
                +FF 11/12-80 p67
365 Concerto, orchestra. PO; Eugene Ormandy. RCA ARC 1-3421
                ++Gr 7-80 p135   ++RR 7-80 p50
                -HF 12-79 p79   ++SFC 9-16-79 p61
                +-HFN 7-80 p105   +-St 11-79 p86
                +NYT 3-30-80 pD23
366 Concerti, piano, nos. 1-3. Sonata, 2 pianos and percussion. Martha
    Argerich, Stepehn Bishop-Kovacevich, pno; Willy Goudswaard,
    Michael de Roo, perc; LSO, BBC Symphony Orchestra; Colin Davis.
    Philips 6768 053 (2) (From 9500 043, SAL 3779, 9500 434)
                +-FF 9/10-80 p69   +-NR 7-80 p5
                +Gr 2-79 p1413   +RR 2-79 p54
                +HFN 2-79 p115   ++SFC 5-4-80 p42
367 Concerti, piano, nos. 1 and 2. Maurizio Pollini, pno; CSO; Claudio
    Abbado. DG 2530 901 Tape (c) 3301 901
                +-ARG 1-80 p18   ++HFN 8-79 p99
                +FF 3/4-80 p50   ++NYT 3-30-80 pD24
                ++FU 4-80 p44   ++RR 9-79 p68
                +Gr 7-79 p191   ++SFC 9-16-79 p61
                +Gr 9-79 p533 tape   ++St 1-80 p95
                +HF 2-80 p83
    Concerti, piano, nos. 1 and 2. See no. 3705
368 Concerto, piano, no. 3, E major. Concerto, viola. Geza Nemeth,
    vla; Dezso Ranki, pno; Budapest Philharmonic Orchestra, Hungarian
    State Symphony Orchestra; Andras Korody, Janos Ferencsik. Hun-
    garoton SLPX 11421 Tape (c) MK 1018
                +Gr 3-76 p1458   +NR 3-76 p3
                +-HF 8-76 p79   +RR 2-76 p24
                +HF 5-80 p90   ++SFC 2-8-76 p26
369 Concerto, piano, no. 3, E major. RAVEL: Concerto, piano, G major.
    Julius Katchen, pno; LSO; Istvan Kertesz. London STS 15494
                +FF 7/8-80 p53
370 Concerto, viola (completed Serly). HINDEMITH: Der Schwanendreher.
    Daniel Benyamini, vla; Orchestre de Paris; Daniel Barenboim. DG
    2531 249
                +-ARG 12-80 p18   +/HFN 10-80 p109
                +-FF 9/10-80 p69   +MT 12-80 p783
                +Gr 4-80 p1549   -NR 7-80 p2

```
              +HFN 5-80 p117                    +RR 5-80 p52
       Concerto, viola.  See no. 368
371    Concerto, violin, no. 2, B minor.  Pinchas Zukerman, vln; LAPO;
       Zubin Mehta.  Columbia M 35156 Tape (c) MT 35156 (also CBS 76831
       Tape (c) 40-76831)
              +-FF 7/8-80 p52                   +NR 5-80 p4
              /Gr 3-80 p1379                    +NYT 3-30-80 pD24
              +Gr 5-80 p1717 tape              ++RR 4-80 p56
              ++HF 7-80 p60                    ++St 7-80 p76
              +HFN 3-80 p86                     +-ST 9-80 p339
              +HFN 6-80 p119 tape
372    Concerto, violin, no. 2, B minor.  RAVEL: Introduction and allegro.
       Tibor Varga, vln; Nicanor Zabaleta, hp.  DG 2535 704
              +ARSC Vol 12, nos. 1-2, 1980 p124
       Contrasts.  See no. 377
       Dance suite.  See no. 362
373    Divertimento, strings.  Music for strings, percussion and celeste.
       AMF; Neville Marriner.  Argo ZRG 657 Tape (r) F 657
              +RR 5-80 p90 tape                 +SFC 10-18-70 p32
374    Divertimento, strings.  CORIGLIANO: Concerto.  Hilde Somer,
       pno; San Antonio Symphony Orchestra, BBC Symphony Orchestra;
       Victor Allessandro, Antal Dorati.  Mercury SRI 75118
              +-ARG 12-79 p40                   +NYT 8-5-79 pD20
              +FF 1/2-80 p43                   ++SFC 10-21-79 p57
375    Divertimento, strings.  MOZART: Divertimento, no. 11, K 251, D maj-
       or.  Adelaide Chamber Orchestra, Kammermusiker Zurich; Brenton
       Langbein.  SARFC ACR 1001
              +-RR 4-80 p68
376    Hungarian peasant suite (arr. Arma).  HUGHES: Sonitudes.  PETERSON:
       Capriccios (42).  VILLA-LOBOS: Assobio a joto (Jet whistle).
       Janet Millard, flt; Loren Brown, vlc; Wayne Peterson, pno.  1750
       Arch S 1760
              +-FF 11/12-80 p212                +SFC 1-20-80 p47
              +NR 9-80 p4
377    Mikrokosmos: Tale; In the style of a folk song; Wrestling; From the
       island of Bali; Bulgarian rhythm; Fifth chords; Peasant dance;
       Alternating thirds; Fourths; Syncopation; Bagpipe; Free variations;
       From the diary of a fly; Dances, nos. 1-6, in the Bulgarian rhy-
       thm.  Contrasts.  Bela Bartok, pno; Joseph Szigeti, vln; Benny
       Goodman, clt.  CBS 61882 (also CBS 235484)
              +Gr 2-80 p1276                   ++RR 2-80 p70
              +HFN 2-80 p86
378    The miraculous Mandarin, op. 19.  Music, strings, percussion and
       celesta.  PO; Eugene Ormandy.  HMV ASD 3655 Tape (c) TC ASD 3655
       (also Angel SZ 37608)
              -FF 1/2-80 p43                    +HFN 9-79 p101
              +FU 5-80 p46                      +HFN 9-79 p123 tape
              +Gr 7-79 p191                     +NYT 3-30-80 pD23
              +Gr 9-79 p533 tape              ++RR 7-79 p46
              +HF 12-79 p79                   ++SFC 9-16-79 p61
       The miraculous mandarin, op. 19.  See no. 362
379    Music, strings, percussion and celesta.  STRAVINSKY: Apollon musa-
       gette.  BPhO; Herbert von Karajan.  DG 2542 134 Tape (c) 3342
       134 (From 2530 065)
              +Gr 7-80 p135                     +HFN 10-80 p117
```

Music, strings, percussion and celesta. See no. 373. See no. 378
380 Quartets, strings, nos. 1-6. Hungarian Quartet. DG 2728 011 Tape
  (c) 3373 011
                +ARG 12-80 p17   +NYT 3-30-80 pD24
381 Quartet, strings, no. 3, C sharp major. RAVEL: Quartet, strings, F
  major. Sequoia String Quartet. Delos DMS 3004
                +HF 8-80 p80   ++NYT 3-30-80 pD24
                +HFN 4-80 p101   +RR 4-80 p88
                +NR 2-80 p6   ++St 6-80 p120
382 Quartet, strings, no. 4, C major. SHOSTAKOVICH: Quartet, strings,
  no. 7, op. 108, F sharp minor. STRAVINSKY: Pieces, string quartet (3). WEBERN: Bagatelles, op. 9 (6). Slovak Quartet. RCA
  PRL 1-9060
                +-FF 11/12-80 p220
Rhapsody, no. 1. See no. 3915
383 Rumanian folk dances. SCHUBERT: German dances (6). SCHUMANN: Symphony, no. 1, op. 38, B flat major. Orchestra; Sergiu Celibidache. Rococo 2132
                +-NR 5-80 p3
Rumanian folk dances. See no. 351. See no. 3785
384 Sonata, piano. BERG: Sonata, piano, op. 1. BUSONI: Sonatina, no.
  2. WEBERN: Variations, op. 27. Franzpeter Goebels, pno. Musicaphon BM 30 SL 1525
                +-HFN 10-80 p113
Sonata, 2 pianos and percussion. See no. 366
385 Sonata, solo violin. Sonatas, violin and piano (3). Jenny Abel,
  vln; Robert Szidon, pno. Harmonia Mundi HA 227 073 (2) (also
  157 99783/4)
                -FF 5/6-78 p12   +-ST 3-80 p837
386 Sonata, solo violin. Hanna Lachert, vln; NYP. Telarc 5033
                ++NYT 3-30-80 pD24
Sonatas, violin and piano (3). See no. 385
387 Sonatas, violin and piano, nos. 1 and 2. Gidon Kremer, vln; Yuri
  Smirnov, pno. Hungaroton SLPX 11655
                +Gr 1-75 p1361   +SFC 10-16-77 p47
                +-HF 1-80 p68   +-St 7-75 p94
                +NR 5-75 p9
388 Sonatas, violin and piano, nos. 1 and 2. Sandor Vegh, vln; Peter
  Pettinger, pno. Telefunken 6-42417
                +HF 1-80 p68   +St 2-80 p120
                ++NYT 3-30-80 pD24
389 Suite, no. 1, op. 3. Two pictures, op. 10. Detroit Symphony Orch-
  estra; Antal Dorati. Decca SXL 6897 (also London 7120)
                ++ARG 1-80 p19   +NYT 3-30-80 pD23
                +NR 3-80 p1   +RR 10-79 p76
390 Suite, op. 14. LEES: Sonata, piano, no. 4. PROKOFIEV: Sonata, piano,
  no. 2, op. 14, D minor. Gary Graffman, pno. Odyssey Y 35203
                +-FF 1/2-80 p126   +SFC 9-16-79 p61
Two pictures, op. 10. See no. 389
The wooden prince, op. 13. See no. 362
BARTOLINO DA PADOVA
  Per un verde boschetto. See no. 4032
BARTOLUCCI, Domenico
391 Christus natus es. MARENZIO: Innocentes por Christo infantes. PAL-
  ESTRINA: Cantabo domino; Dextera domini; Exaltabo te; Improperium

exspectavit; Paucitas dierum; Tota pulchra es; Vox dilecti mei;
Vulnerasti cor meum. ANON. (16th c.): Dio s'e fatto fanciullo;
Supra il fieno colcato. Sistine Chapel Choir, Vatican Boys Choir;
Domenico Bartolucci. Acanta DC 21841 Tape (c) DF 31841
+-Gr 1-80 p1194   +RR 10-79 p142
++HFN 9-79 p123

BARTSCH, Charles
    Bagatelles. See no. 3809
BASHFORD, Rodney
    Cavalry walk. See no. 4029
BASTON, John
    Concerto, D major. See no. 3795
BATCHELAR, Daniel
    Mounsiers almaine. See no. 3577
BATES
    Songs: Come life Shaker life; Mount Zion; Ode to contentment; Rights
        of conscience. See no. 3848
BATESON, Thomas
    Songs (madrigals): Those sweet delightful lilies. See no. 3893
BATH, Hubert
    Love story: Cornish rhapsody. See no. 3790
BATTISHILL, Jonathan
    Amidst the myrtles. See no. 3873
BAUER
    X-N-trick rag. See no. 3679
BAUMANN, Max
    Sonatina, organ, no. 2: Toccata II, allegro vivace. See no. 4034
    Suite, op. 67, no. 1: Toccata I, agitato brillante. See no. 4034
BAUMGARTNER
    0 du mein Heimatland. See no. 3626
BAUR, Jean-Pierre
392 Sonatas, harp and harpsichord, op. 6, no. 3-4; op. 7, nos. 1-2; op.
        8, nos. 3-4. Marielle Nordmann, hp; Brigitte Haudebourg, hpd.
        Arion ARN 38533
                ++HFN 8-80 p94   +RR 7-80 p75
BAUR, John
393 The moon and the yew tree. CHATMAN: Whisper baby. RHODES: Visions
        of remembrance. Carol Wilson, Christine Anderson, s; Lorraine
        Manz, ms; Elizabeth Baur, flt; Robert Weirich, pno; John Burton,
        vlc; Maura Chatman, pno; Carleton Contemporary Ensemble; Univ.
        of British Columbia Chamber Singers; William Wells, Cortland
        Hultberg. CRI SD 426
                +NR 10-80 p11
BAUTISTA, Julian
    Songs dedicated to Andalusian cities. See no. 14
BAX, Arnold
394 Coronation march (arr. O'Brien). BLISS: Processional (arr. O'Brien).
        ELGAR: Imperial march, op. 32. Pomp and circumstance march, op.
        39, no. 1, D major (arr. Farrell). WALTON: Orb and sceptre (arr.
        McKie). Crown imperial (arr. Murrill). Christopher Herrick,
        Timothy Farrell, org. Vista VPS 1055
                +-Gr 10-77 p712   +-RR 8-77 p44
                ++NR 4-80 p14   +RR 1-78 p70
    Far in a western brookland. See no. 3837
    Malta GC: Introduction and march. See no. 3786

Mediterranean. See no. 3964
395 Quartet, strings, no. 3, F major. Amici Quartet. Guadeamus KRS 31
                +Gr 11-79 p854   ++RR 11-79 p102
                +-MT 1-80 p33   +ST 1-80 p691
396 Tintagel. DELIUS: Irmelin. A song of summer. A village Romeo and
         Juliet: The walk to the paradise garden (arr. Beecham). IRELAND:
         A London overture. LSO; John Barbirolli. HMV ESD 7092 Tape (c)
         TC ESD 7092 (From ASD 2305)
                +Gr 11-80 p234   +HFN 9-80 p115
                +Gr 12-80 p889 tape

BAY PSALM BOOK
     Psalms, nos. 23, 100. See no. 3848
BAYLE, Francois
397 Espaces inhabitables. Reves d'oiseaux (3). Tremblement de terre
         tres doux. Harmonia Mundi INA Gramme 9101
                +FF 7/8-80 p16
398 Grande polyphonie. Harmonia Mundi INA GRM AM 72704
                +FF 7/8-80 p16
     Reves d'oiseaux (3). See no. 397
     Tremblement de terre tres doux. See no. 397
BAZZINI, Antonio
     La ronde des lutins, op. 25. See no. 3552. See no. 3788. See no.
         3964
BEACH, Amy
     Improvisation, op. 118. See no. 4024
399 Theme and variations, op. 80. FOOTE: A night piece. HOOVER: Diver-
         timento. Diane Gold, flt; Alard Quartet. Leonarda LPI 105
                +FF 11/12-80 p68   ++NR 9-80 p4
     Trio, op. 150. See no. 4065
BEALE, William
     The humble tenant. See no. 3873
BEAUCARNE
     Christopher Colomb. See no. 3760
BECKLER, Stanworth
400 Little suite, op. 59. FARKAS: Antiche danze Ungheresi. PAUER:
         Quintet, winds. SCHULLER: Suite. Pacific Arts Woodwind Quintet.
         Orion ORS 79345
                +FF 7/8-80 p182   +NR 6-80 p8
BECKWITH, John
401 Quartet, strings. SCHAFER: Quartet, strings, no. 2. Orford Quar-
         tet. Melbourne SMLP 4038
                +MUM 12-80 p32
BEDYNGHAM, John
     Songs: Mon seul plaisir ma doulce joye; Zentil madona. See no. 3880
BEESON, Jack
402 Dr. Heidegger's fountain of youth. Carol Wilcox, s; Judith Christ-
         in, ms; Grayson Hirst, t; Robert Shiesley, bar; Alfred Anderson,
         bs-bar; Chamber Orchestra; Thomas Martin. CRI SD 406
                +ARG 9-80 p18   +NR 2-80 p11
                +FF 3/4-80 p51   ++St 5-80 p82
BEETHOVEN, Ludwig van
403 Adagio, op. 150, E flat major. Sonatina, C major. Sonatina, op.
         150, C minor. Theme and variations, D major. HUMMEL: Sonata,
         mandolin, C major. Hugo D'Alton, mand; John Beckett, forte-
         piano. Saga 5350 Tape (c) CA 5350

+HFN 6-80 p117   +RR 4-74 p67
+RR 7-80 p75   ++RR 9-75 p77

Ah perfido, op. 65. See no. 582. See no. 3367

Allegro and minuet, 2 flutes, G major. See no. 621

Andante favori, F major. See no. 413. See no. 501

404 Bagatelles, WoO 59, A minor (2). Bagatelle, no. 25, A minor. Rondo, op. 51, no. 2, G major. HAYDN: Andante and variations, F minor. MOZART: Gigue, K 574, G major. Rondo, piano, K 511, A minor. Suite, K 399, C minor: Allemande. SCHUBERT: Klavierstucke, no. 2, D 946, E flat major: Allegretto. Kupelweiser Walzer, G major. Landler, no. 3, D 790. Jorg Demus, pno. Harmonia Mundi 065 997 96

++FF 7/8-80 p164   +MT 10-80 p638
+-HFN 3-80 p105   ++RR 4-80 p95

405 Bagatelle, no. 25, A minor. Sonata, piano, no. 17, op. 31, no. 2, D minor. Sonata, piano, no. 28, op. 101, A major. Oxana Yablon-skaya, pno. Orion Tape (c) In Sync C 4037

+NR 9-80 p10 tape

406 Bagatelle, no. 25, A minor. Bagatelles, op. 126 (6). Bagatelles, op. 119. Hans Boepple, pno. Orion ORS 80375

+CL 9-80 p14   -NR 5-80 p12
+-FF 7/8-80 p53

407 Bagatelle no. 25, A minor. Sonata, piano, no. 14, op. 27, no. 2, C sharp minor. Sonata, piano, no. 18, op. 31, no. 3, E flat major. Bella Davidovich, pno. Philips 9500 665 Tape (c) 7300 763

+ARG 2-80 p18   +-HF 1-80 p73
+-FF 7/8-80 p56   +NR 1-80 p14
+-FU 5-80 p47

Bagatelle, no. 25, A minor. See no. 404. See no. 413. See no. 3677

408 Bagatelles, op. 33, nos. 1-7. MOZART: Sonata, piano, no. 4, K 282, E flat major. Sonata, piano, no. 8, K 310, A minor. Alicia de Larrocha, pno. London CS 7179

+FF 11/12-80 p141   +St 10-80 p114
+SFC 10-19-80 p20

Bagatelles, op. 119. See no. 406

409 Bagatelles, op. 126 (6). Rondo, op. 51, no. 2, G major. Sonatas, piano, nos. 24, 30-31. Jorg Demus, pno. Harmonia Mundi 1C 151 99655/6 (2)

+Gr 4-80 p1571   +RR 4-80 p92
+-HFN 3-80 p105

Bagatelles, op. 126 (6). See no. 406

410 Concert movement, WoO 5, C major. Romance, no. 1, op. 40, G major. SCHUBERT: Konzertstuck, D 345, D major. Polonaise, D 580, B major. Rondo, D 438, A major. Gidon Kremer, vln; LSO; Emil Tchakarov. DG 2531 193 Tape (c) 3301 193

+-FF 7/8-80 p55   +NR 7-80 p13
+Gr 1-80 p1137   +RR 1-80 p65
+HFN 1-80 p102   ++St 9-80 p77

411 Concerti, piano, nos. 1-5. Fantasy, op. 80, C minor. John Lill, pno; Scottish National Orchestra; Alexander Gibson. Classics for Pleasure CFP 78253 (4)

+HFN 2-80 p105   +RR 2-80 p46

412 Concerti, piano, nos. 1-5. Fantasia, op. 80, C major. Daniel

Barenboim, pno; John Alldis Choir; NPhO; Otto Klemperer. HMV SLS
5180 (4) Tape (c) TC SLS 5180 (From SLS 941)
<table>
<tr><td>+Gr 9-79 p454</td><td>+HFN 2-80 p107 tape</td></tr>
<tr><td>+HFN 10-79 p169</td><td>+-RR 11-79 p69</td></tr>
<tr><td>+HFN 12-79 p185 tape</td><td>+RR 2-80 p97 tape</td></tr>
</table>

413 Concerti, piano, nos. 1-5. Bagatelle, op. 25, A minor. Andante
favori, F major. Polonaise, op. 89, C major. Variations and
fugue, op. 34, F major. Artur Schnabel, pno; LPO, LSO; Malcolm
Sargent. World Records SHB 63 (4) Tape (c) TC SHB 63
<table>
<tr><td>+Gr 10-80 p542</td><td>++HFN 12-80 p132</td></tr>
</table>

414 Concerto, piano, no. 1, op. 15, C major. Concerto, piano, no. 2,
op. 19, B flat major. Radu Lupu, pno; Israel Philharmonic Orchestra; Zubin Mehta. Decca SXDL 7502 Tape (c) KSXCD 7502 (also
London LDR 10006 Tape (c) LDRS 10006)
<table>
<tr><td>+-FF 11/12-80 p69</td><td>+-HF 12-80 p68</td></tr>
<tr><td>+Gr 4-80 p1550</td><td>+HFN 4-80 p101</td></tr>
<tr><td>+HF 10-80 p98 tape</td><td>++RR 4-80 p59</td></tr>
</table>

415 Concerto, piano, no. 1, op. 15, C major. Artur Benedetti Michelangeli, pno; VSO; Carlo Maria Giulini. DG 2531 302 Tape (c) 3301
302
<table>
<tr><td>+Gr 10-80 p487</td><td>+SFC 10-19-80 p20</td></tr>
<tr><td>+HFN 10-80 p102</td><td>+STL 9-14-80 p40</td></tr>
<tr><td>+HFN 11-80 p131 tape</td><td></td></tr>
</table>

416 Concerto, piano, no. 1, op. 15, C major. Christoph Eschenbach, pno;
BPhO; Herbert von Karajan. DG 2535 273 Tape (c) 3335 273 (From
SLPM 139023)
<table>
<tr><td>+FF 11/12-80 p81</td><td>+HFN 6-78 p135</td></tr>
<tr><td>+Gr 6-78 p38</td><td>+-RR 7-78 p43</td></tr>
<tr><td>+-Gr 9-78 p564 tape</td><td></td></tr>
</table>

417 Concerto, piano, no. 1, op. 15, C major. Sonata, piano, no. 5, op.
10, no. 1, C minor. Stephen Bishop-Kovacevich, pno; BBC Symphony
Orchestra; Colin Davis. Philips 6570 134 Tape (c) 7310 134
(From 7300 116)
<table>
<tr><td>+Gr 5-80 p1651</td><td>+HFN 9-80 p115 tape</td></tr>
<tr><td>+-HFN 5-80 p135</td><td>+RR 5-80 p54</td></tr>
</table>

418 Concerto, piano, no. 1, op. 15, C major. Sonata, piano, no. 26, op.
81a, E flat major. Claudio Arrau, pno; COA; Bernard Haitink.
Philips 6570 167 (From PHM 5570, 5-970, 6770 014)
<table>
<tr><td>+FF 1/2-80 p44</td></tr>
</table>

419 Concerto, piano, no. 1, op. 15, C major. Alfred Brendel, pno; LPO;
Bernard Haitink. Philips 9500 252 Tape (c) 7300 563 (From 6767
002)
<table>
<tr><td>++Gr 10-79 p631</td><td>++RR 10-79 p79</td></tr>
<tr><td>+HFN 12-79 p185 tape</td><td>+RR 2-80 p97 tape</td></tr>
</table>

420 Concerto, piano, no. 2, op. 19, B flat major. Concerto, piano, no.
4, op. 58, G major. Wilhelm Kempff, pno; BPhO; Ferdinand Leitner.
DG 2542 136
<table>
<tr><td>+-HFN 12-80 p153</td></tr>
</table>
Concerto, piano, no. 2, op. 19, B flat major. See no. 414

421 Concerti, piano, nos. 3-5. Concerto, violin, op. 61, D major. Egmont, op. 84: Overture. Leonore overture, no. 3, op. 72a. MOZ-
ART: Concerto, violin, no. 5, K 219, A major. Concerto, horn,
no. 3, K 447, E flat major. Serenade, no. 13, K 525, G major.
Dresden Staatskapelle; Karl Bohm. EMI 1C 137 53500/5 (5)
<table>
<tr><td>+FF 9/10-80 p291</td></tr>
</table>

422 Concerto, piano, no. 3, op. 37, C minor. Maurizio Pollini, pno;
     VPO; Karl Bohm. DG 2531 057 Tape (c) 3301 057
                    +ARG 7-79 p22   ++HF 9-79 p111
                    ++CL 2-80 p6   +HFN 5-79 p118
                    ++FF 11/12-79 p30   +HFN 8-79 p123 tape
                    ++FU 9-79 p50   +-NR 7-79 p7
                    +-Gr 4-79 p1696   ++RR 5-79 p50
                    +Gr 8-79 p382 tape   ++SFC 4-29-79 p53
423 Concerto, piano, no. 3, op. 37, C minor. Stephen Bishop-Kovacevich,
     pno; BBC Symphony Orchestra; Colin Davis. Philips 6570 135 Tape
     (c) 7310 135 (From 6500 315)
                    +Gr 4-80 p1549   +HFN 9-80 p115 tape
                    +Gr 7-80 p166 tape   +RR 4-80 p58
                    +HFN 4-80 p119   +RR 8-80 p93 tape
424 Concerto, piano, no. 3, op. 37, C minor. Artur Rubinstein, pno;
     LPO; Daniel Barenboim. RCA ARL 1-1418 Tape (c) ARK 1-1418 (ct)
     ARS 1-1418 (From CRL 5-1415)
                    +ARG 7-79 p22   +-NR 6-79 p7
                    +-HFN 9-80 p115   ++RR 8-80 p37
                    +-HFN 11-80 p131 tape
425 Concerto, piano, no. 4, op. 58, G major. MOZART: Concerto, piano,
     no. 23, K 488, A major. PFITZNER: Concerto, piano, op. 31.
     SCHUMANN: Concerto, piano, op. 54, A minor. Walter Gieseking,
     pno; Orchestras; Marc Andreae, Robert Heger, Joseph Keilberth.
     Bruno Walter Society IRI 363 (2)
                    +-NR 3-80 p5
426 Concerto, piano, no. 4, op. 58, G major. Sonata, piano, no. 19, op.
     49, no. 1, G major. Sonata, piano, no. 20, op. 49, no. 2, G
     major. Radu Lupu, pno; Israel Philharmonic Orchestra; Zubin
     Mehta. Decca SXL 6886 Tape (c) KSXC 6886 (also London CS 7108
     Tape (c) CS 5-7108)
                    +FF 9/10-79 p43   +HFN 11-78 p187 tape
                    +Gr 9-78 p462   ++MM 7-79 p40
                    +Gr 12-78 p1177 tape   +NR 1-80 p4
                    +-HF 8-79 p83   +-RR 7-78 p43
                    +HFN 9-78 p139   +SFC 9-9-79 p45
427 Concerto, piano, no. 4, op. 58, G major. Arturo Benedetti Michel-
     angeli, pno; Belgrade Philharmonic Orchestra. Rococo 2113
                    -NR 5-80 p4
428 Concerto, piano, no. 4, op. 58, G major. MENDELSSOHN: Concerto,
     violin, op. 64, E minor. Jascha Heifetz, vln; Artur Rubinstein,
     pno; RPO; Thomas Beecham. World Records SH 1005
                    +ARSC Vol 12, no. 3, 1980 p240
     Concerto, piano, no. 4, op. 58, G major. See no. 420
429 Concerto, piano, no. 5, op. 73, E flat major. Radu Lupu, pno;
     Israel Philharmonic Orchestra; Zubin Mehta. Decca SXDL 7503
     Tape (c) KSXDC 7503 (also London LDR 10005)
                    +ARG 4-80 p17   +-HFN 9-79 p101
                    +-FF 1/2-80 p44   +-NR 7-80 p5
                    +-FU 6-80 p43   +-RR 11-79 p70
                    +-Gr 9-79 p459   ++St 12-80 p117
                    +Gr 12-79 p1065 tape   ++SFC 9-9-79 p45
                    +-HF 12-80 p68   +RR 2-80 p97 tape
430 Concerto, piano, no. 5, op. 73, E flat major. Maurizio Pollini,
     pno; VPO; Karl Bohm. DG 2531 194 Tape (c) 3301 194

```
        +-CL 9-80 p64                  +HFN 1-80 p102
        +-FF 7/8-80 p54               -NR 4-80 p5
        +Gr 1-80 p1138               ++RR 1-80 p64
       ++Gr 3-80 p1446 tape          ++SFC 2-3-80 p45
```

431 Concerto, piano, no. 5, op. 73, E flat major. Alicia de Larrocha,
    pno; LAPO; Zubin Mehta. London CS 7121 Tape (c) CS 5-7121 (also
    Decca SXL 6899 Tape (c) KSXC 6899)

```
        +-FF 11/12-79 p31            +-HFN 8-79 p123 tape
        /FU 11-79 p43                +MM 7-79 p40
       ++Gr 5-79 p1880               +NR 1-80 p4
        +Gr 9-79 p534 tape          ++RR 5-79 p50
        +-HF 8-79 p83                +St 8-79 p108
        +HFN 5-79 p119
```

432 Concerto, piano, no. 5, op. 73, E flat major. Walter Gieseking, pno;
    Berlin Reichsender Orchestra; Artur Rother. Varese VC 81080
    (Reissue, 1936)

```
        +ARG 4-79 p17                +HFN 1-80 p119
       ++CL 11-79 p11                +NR 5-79 p6
        +FF 9/10-79 p44              +-RR 1-80 p65
        +Gr 1-80 p1138              ++St 6-79 p124
        +HF 5-79 p81
```

433 Concerto, violin, op. 61, D major. STRAUSS, R.: Sinfonia domestica,
    op. 53. Erich Rohn, vln; BPhO; Wilhelm Furtwangler. Bruno Wal-
    ter Society IGI 364 (2)

```
        +NR 8-80 p6
```

434 Concerto, violin, op. 61, D major. Kyung-Wha Chung, vln; VPO; Kiril
    Kondrashin. Decca SXDL 7508 Tape (c) KSXCG 7508 (also London LDR
    10010 Tape (c) 5-10010)

```
       ++FF 11/12-80 p70            +-HFN 7-80 p105
        +-Gr 8-80 p214              ++NR 10-80 p6
        *Gr 10-80 p548 tape         ++RR 7-80 p50
        +Gr 9-80 p413 tape           +St 11-80 p78
        +HF 12-80 p68
```

435 Concerto, violin, op. 61, D major. Anne-Sophie Mutter, vln; BPhO;
    Herbert von Karajan. DG 2531 250 Tape (c) 3301 250

```
        +Gr 9-80 p331                +HFN 10-80 p117 tape
       ++Gr 10-80 p548 tape         +-NR 12-80 p6
        +-HFN 9-80 p100
```

436 Concerto, violin, op. 61, D major. Wolfang Schneiderhan, vln; BPhO;
    Paul van Kempen. DG 2548 299 Tape (c) 3348 299 (From 18099)

```
       ++Gr 3-80 p1385              +-RR 3-80 p46
        +HFN 3-80 p86              ++ST 7-80 p196
```

437 Concerto, violin, op. 61, D major. David Oistrakh, vln; French
    National Radio Orchestra; Andre Cluytens. HMV SXLP 30168 Tape
    (c) TC SXLP 30168, TC EXE 197 (also Angel S 35783) (From Colum-
    bia SAX 2315)

```
        +Gr 11-74 p889               +HFN 3-76 p94 tape
        +-HFN 10-80 p117 tape        +RR 10-74 p36
```

438 Concerto, violin, op. 61, D major. Erich Gruenberg, vln; NPhO;
    Jascha Horenstein. Nonesuch H 71381

```
        +FF 11/12-80 p70            ++St 11-80 p78
```

439 Concerto, violin, op. 61, D major. Romance, no. 1, op. 40, G major.
    Romance, no. 2, op. 50, F major. Arthur Grumiaux, vln; NPhO,
    COA; Alceo Galliera, Bernard Haitink. Philips 6570 051 Tape (c)
    7310 051 (From 900222, 802719, Epic BC 1120)

+FF 9/10-78 p18   +HFN 1-79 p127 tape
+Gr 10-78 p696   +RR 10-78 p24
+Gr 5-79 p1940 tape   ++RR 6-79 p122 tape
+HF 12-80 p68   +SFC 5-28-78 p41
+HFN 10-78 p137

440 Concerto, violin, op. 61, D major. Hermann Krebbers, vln; COA;
     Bernard Haitink. Philips 6580 115
                +Gr 2-76 p1337   +HFN 10-80 p113
                +Gr 10-80 p487   +-RR 2-76 p25
                +-HFN 2-76 p92

441 Concerto, violin, op. 61, D major. Leon Spierer, vln; Frankfurt
     Radio Orchestra; Hermann Michael. Schwann VMS 2071
                +-ARG 11-79 p34   +NR 10-80 p5
     Concerto, violin, op. 61, D major. See no. 421. See no. 3964.
     See no. 3968

442 Concerto, violin, violoncello and piano, op. 56, C major. Anne-
     Sophie Mutter, vln; Yo Yo Ma, vlc; Mark Zeltser, pno; BPhO;
     Herbert von Karajan.   DG 2531 262 Tape (c) 3301 262
                +-ARG 12-80 p20   +NYT 9-21-80 pD22
                ++FF 9/10-80 p70   ++RR 5-80 p53
                +Gr 5-80 p1632   ++RR 8-80 p93 tape
                ++HF 9-80 p84   ++SFC 4-27-80 p35
                +HFN 5-80 p118   ++STL 5-11-80 p38
                +-NR 7-80 p5

443 Concerto, violin, violoncello and piano, op. 56, C major. Geza Anda,
     pno; Wolfgang Schneiderhan, vln; Pierre Fournier, vlc; Berlin
     Radio Symphony Orchestra; Ferenc Fricsay. DG 2535 153 (From 136
     236)
                +FF 1/2-80 p54   -RR 1-76 p31
                +-Gr 2-76 p1332

444 Concerto, violin, violoncello and piano, op. 56, C major. Henryk
     Szeryng, vln; Janos Starker, vlc; Claudio Arrau, pno; NPhO;
     Eliahu Inbal. Philips 6570 070 Tape (c) 7310 070 (From 6500 129)
                +-Gr 12-79 p1007   +HFN 2-80 p107 tape
                +HFN 12-79 p179   +-RR 1-80 p65

445 Concerto, violin, violoncello and piano, op. 56, C major. Angel
     Reyes, vln; Samuel Mayes, vlc; Theodore Lettvin, pno; Univ. of
     Michigan Symphony Orchestra; Gustav Meier. University of Michi-
     gan SM 0010
                +-ARG 12-80 p20   +IN 11-80 p60
                +-FF 7/8-80 p54

446 Contretanze, WoO 14. Deutsche Tanze (German dances), WoO 8. Min-
     uets, WoO 7 (12). AMF; Neville Marriner. Philips 9500 567 Tape
     (c) 7300 704
                +ARG 1-80 p21   +-HFN 10-79 p171 tape
                +FF 1/2-80 p45   ++NR 12-79 p4
                +Gr 8-79 p322   -RR 9-79 p69
                +-Gr 11-79 p924 tape   ++SFC 10-7-79 p49
                +HFN 8-79 p99

447 Coriolan overture, op. 62. Egmont, op. 84: Overture. Fidelio, op.
     72: Overture. Leonore overture, no. 3, op. 72b. LSO; Josef
     Krips. Everest 3461
                +FF 5/6-80 p46
     Coriolan overture, op. 62. See no. 462. See no. 554. See no. 555.
     See no. 557. See no. 575. See no. 594. See no. 3843. See no.
     3898

448 Deutsche Tanze (12). Minuets (12). Vienna Bella Musica Ensemble.
    Harmonia Mundi HM 1017
                +–FF 9/10–80 p73   +NR 6–80 p8
                +Gr 4–80 p1567   +RR 3–80 p46
                +HFN 3–80 p86   +St 8–80 p92
    Deutsche Tanze (6). See no. 3601
    Deutsche Tanze, no. 6. See no. 3964
    Deutsche Tanze, no. 12. See no. 3897
449 Egmont, op. 84: Overture. LISZT: Les preludes, G 97. MERCURE:
    Kaleidoscope. SAINT-SAENS: Danse macabre, op. 40. Winnipeg
    Symphony Orchestra; Piero Gamba. CBS SM 334
                ++MUM 3/4–80 p34
450 Egmont, op. 84: Overture. LISZT: Les preludes, G 97. MOZART: Sere-
    nade, no. 13, K 525, G major. SMETANA: Ma Vlast: The Moldau.
    BPhO, BRSO; Ferenc Fricsay. DG 2535 406 (From Decca and DG orig-
    inals)
                +FF 9/10–80 p290
    Egmont, op. 84: Overture. See no. 421. See no. 447. See no. 462.
    See no. 555. See no. 557. See no. 591. See no. 3860
    Fantasia, op. 80, C minor. See no. 411. See no. 412
    Fantasia, op. 80, C minor. See no. 623
451 Fidelio, op. 72. Leonie Rysanek, Irmgard Seefried, s; Ernst Haflig-
    er, Friedrich Lenz, t; Dietrich Fischer-Dieskau, bar; Keith Engen,
    Gottlob Frick, bs; Bavarian State Opera Orchestra and Chorus;
    Ferenc Fricsay. DG 2726 088 (From 138390/1)
                +FF 5/6–80 p44   +NYT 6–29–80 pD18
452 Fidelio, op. 72. Hildegard Behrens, Sona Ghazarian, s; Peter Hof-
    mann, David Kubler, Robert Johnson, t; Theo Adam, Gwynne Howell,
    Philip Kraus, bar; Hans Sotin, bs; CSO and Chorus; Georg Solti. Lon-
    don 3LDR 10017 (3) (also Decca D178D3 Tape (c) K178K32)
                +–FF 9/10–80 p71   ++Op 6–80 p575
                +–Gr 4–80 p1584   +RR 4–80 p38
                +Gr 9–80 p413 tape   +SFC 4–27–80 p35
                +–HF 8–80 p61   ++St 8–80 p98
                +–HFN 5–80 p117   +STL 4–13–80 p39
                +–NYT 6–29–80 pD18
453 Fidelio, op. 72. Sena Jurinac, Maria Stader, s; Jan Peerce, t; Gus-
    tav Neidlinger, bs; Bavarian State Opera Orchestra and Chorus;
    Hans Knappertsbusch. Westminster MCA 3-14300
                +FF 11/12–80 p70   ++SFC 6–15–80 p36
454 Fidelio, op. 72, excerpts. Maria Cebotari, s; Peter Anders, t;
    Walburga Wegner, s; Orchestra; Hans Schmidt-Isserstedt. Acanta
    BB 23311
                +–Gr 9–80 p408
455 Fidelio, op. 72, excerpts (arr. Sedlak). Southwest German Radio
    Orchestra Wind Octet. Artaria SM 92812
                +FF 5/6–80 p54
    Fidelio, op. 72: Abscheulicher. See no. 3931
    Fidelio, op. 72: Abscheulicher wo eilst du hin; Hat man nicht auch
    Gold beineben. See no. 3774
    Fidelio, op. 72: Gott welch Dunkel hier...In des Lebens Fruhlings-
    tagen. See no. 3558
    Fidelio, op. 72: Hat man nicht auch Gold beineben. See no. 3712
    Fidelio, op. 72: Jetz Schatzchen jetz sind wir allein. See no. 3538
    Fidelio, op. 72: Life is nothing without money. See no. 3905

Fidelio, op. 72: Overture. See no. 447. See no. 462. See no. 554.
See no. 555. See no. 600

Die Geschopfe des Prometheus (The creatures of Prometheus), op. 43:
Finale. See no. 623

Die Geschopfe des Prometheus, op. 43: Overture. See no. 564. See
no. 565. See no. 592. See no. 597

Grosse Fuge, op. 133, B flat major. See no. 477. See no. 479

Konig Stefan (King Stephen), op. 117: Overture. See no. 607. See
no. 608

456 Leonore. Edda Moser, Helen Donath, s; Richard Cassilly, Eberhard
Buchner, Rainer Goldberg, t; Karl Ridderbusch, Theo Adam, Hermann
Christian Polster, Siegfried Lorenz, bs; Leipzig Radio Chorus;
Dresden Staatskapelle Orchestra; Herbert Blomsted. Arabesque
8043-3 (3) Tape (c) 9043

      +FF 5/6-80 p46   +-ON 2-2-80 p28
      +HF 6-80 p96 tape   ++St 5-80 p90
      +NYT 1-6-80 pD18

Leonore overtures, nos. 2 and 3, op. 72. See no. 554

Leonore overture, no. 2, op. 72. See no. 563. See no. 579. See
no. 584

Leonore overture, no. 3, op. 72a. See no. 421. See no. 447. See
no. 462. See no. 555. See no. 559. See no. 580. See no. 583.
See no. 607. See no. 608

Masonic march. See no. 3844

457 Mass, op. 86, C major. Emilija Markova, s; Lilijana Parachikova,
con; Christo Kamenev, t; Ivan Petrov, bs; Rodina Choir; Sofia
Philharmonic Orchestra; Constantin Iliev. Harmonia Mundi HM 109

      +-HFN 1-80 p102   +RR 12-79 p106

458 Mass, op. 86, C major. Jennifer Vyvyan, s; Monica Sinclair, con;
Richard Lewis, t; Marian Mowakowski, bs; Beecham Choral Society;
RPO; Thomas Beecham. HMV SXLP 30284 Tape (c) TC SXLP 30284
(From ALP 1674)

      +ARSC Vol 12, no. 3,   +-HFN 6-79 p117 tape
         1980 p252   +MT 9-79 p747
      ++Gr 4-79 p1755   ++RR 5-79 p95
      ++Gr 7-79 p259 tape   ++RR 9-79 p135 tape
      +HFN 5-79 p133

459 Mass, op. 86, C major. Christiane Eda-Pierre, s; Patricia Payne,
con; Robert Tear, t; Kurt Moll, bs; LSO and Chorus; Colin Davis.
Philips 9500 636 Tape (c) 7300 741 (From 6769 001)

      ++ARG 4-80 p16   +NYT 10-7-79 pD24
      -FF 1/2-80 p46   +ON 2-2-80 p28
      +Gr 10-79 p686   ++RR 10-79 p134
      +HFN 11-79 p155   +SFC 11-4-79 p40
      +HFN 1-80 p123 tape   +St 3-80 p92
      +NR 12-79 p8

460 Mass, op. 123, D major. Edda Moser, s; Hanna Schwarz, con; Rene
Kollo, t; Kurt Moll, bs; Netherlands Broadcasting Foundation
Chorus; COA; Leonard Bernstein. DG 2707 110 (2) Tape (c) 3370
029

      ++ARG 1-80 p17   ++NR 12-79 p8
      +-FF 3/4-80 p56   ++NYT 10-7-79 pD24
      +-FU 2-80 p44   +-ON 2-2-80 p28
      +Gr 8-79 p358   +RR 9-79 p112
      +Gr 9-79 p534 tape   ++SFC 11-4-79 p40
      ++HF 1-80 p71   ++St 4-80 p123

```
        +-HF 5-80 p90 tape              +-HFN 10-79 p147
461  Mass, op. 123, D major.  Elisabeth Schwarzkopf, s; Christa Ludwig,
        ms; Nicolai Gedda, t; Nicolas Zaccaria, bs; Vienna Singverein,
        PhO; Herbert von Karajan.  HMV SLS 5198 (2) Tape (c) TC SLS 5198
        (From 33CS 1634/5, World Records ST 914/5)
              +Gr 7-80 p157               +-HFN 7-80 p117
     Mass, op. 123, D major: Gloria, excerpt.  See no. 623
     Minuets (12).  See no. 448
     Minuets, WoO 7 (12).  See no. 446
     Modlinger dances, nos. 1, 4, 6, 8.  See no. 3989
     Opferlied, op. 121b.  See no. 3844
462  Overtures: Egmont, op. 84.  Coriolan, op. 62.  Fidelio, op. 72b.
        Leonore, no. 3, op. 72a.  Ruins of Athens, op. 113.  BPhO; Herbert
        von Karajan.  DG 2542 141 Tape (c) 3342 141 (From SLPM 13900,
        64362B/30)
              +Gr 10-80 p487              +HFN 11-80 p129
463  Polonaise, op. 89, C major.  Sonata, piano, no. 28, op. 101, A major.
        Sonata, piano, no. 30, op. 109, E major.  Lee Luvisi, pno.  River-
        gate Recordings
              +-CL 4-80 p12
     Polonaise, op. 89, C major.  See no. 413
     Prelude, op. 39, no. 1.  See no. 3628
464  Quartets, piano, nos. 1-4.  Martinu Piano Quartet.  Supraphon 111
        2211/2
              +FF 1/2-80 p46             -MT 12-79 p1006
              +Gr 10-79 p662             +-NR 10-79 p5
              +-HFN 8-79 p101            +-RR 7-79 p72
465  Quartet, strings, nos. 1-6, op. 18.  Cleveland Quartet.  RCA ARL
        3-3486 (3) Tape (c) ARK 3-3486
              +-ARG 9-80 p18             ++NR 3-80 p9
              +-FF 9/10-80 p74           +NYT 2-10-80 pD24
              +-Gr 9-80 p354             +-SFC 2-17-80 p44
              +-HF 8-80 p65              ++St 6-80 p111
              +-HFN 10-80 p102
466  Quartet, strings, no. 2, op. 18, G major.  Quartet, strings, no. 3,
        op. 18, D major.  Quartet, strings, no. 10, op. 74, E flat major.
        MOZART: Quartet, strings, no. 17, K 458, B flat major.  Quartet,
        strings, no. 19, K 465, C major.  Quartet, strings, no. 23, K
        590, F major.  Budapest Quartet.  Odyssey Y3 35240 (3)
              ++FF 3/4-80 p57            ++NYT 2-10-80 pD24
              ++NR 3-80 p8
467  Quartet, strings, no. 3, op. 18, D major.  Quartet, strings, no. 4,
        op. 18, C minor.  Lindsay Quartet.  Enigma K 53587
              +Gr 1-80 p1167            +RR 11-79 p103
              +HFN 11-79 p135           +STL 12-2-79 p37
     Quartet, strings, no. 3, op. 18, D major.  See no. 466
     Quartet, strings, no. 4, op. 18, C minor.  See no. 467
468  Quartet, strings, nos. 7-11.  Alban Berg Quartet.  HMV SLS 5171 (3)
        Tape (c) TC SLS 5171
              +-Gr 12-79 p1024          +-MT 9-80 p565
              +HFN 2-80 p87             +-RR 12-79 p83
              +HFN 2-80 p107 tape
469  Quartets, strings, nos. 7-11.  Cleveland Quartet.  RCA ARL 4-3010
        (4)
              +ARG 12-79 p27            ++HFN 10-79 p147
              -FF 1/2-80 p47            +-RR 11-79 p104
```

```
                +-Gr 10-79 p662              +-SFC 7-15-79 p47
                +HF 11-79 p90               ++St 11-79 p75
```
470 Quartets, strings, nos. 7-11. New Hungarian Quartet. Vox SVBX
     5113 (3)
```
                +-FF 1/2-80 p47             +-HF 5/6-80 p65
```
471 Quartet, strings, no. 7, op. 59, no. 1, F major. HAYDN: Quartet,
     strings, op. 103, D major: Minuet. Busch Quartet. CBS 61888
```
                +Gr 4-80 p1567             +RR 5-80 p75
                +HFN 4-80 p101             +STL 4-13-80 p39
```
472 Quartet, strings, no. 8, op. 59, no. 2, E minor. Smetana Quartet.
     Denon OX 7178
```
                +FF 11/12-80 p72
```
     Quartet, strings, no. 8, op. 59, no. 2, E minor: Finale. See no.
     623
473 Quartet, strings, no. 9, op. 59, no. 3, C major. Quartet, strings,
     no. 10, op. 74, E flat major. Talich Quartet. Calliope CAL 1636
```
                -HFN 12-80 p132
```
474 Quartet, strings, no. 9, op. 59, F major. Quartet, strings, no. 11,
     op. 95, F minor. Quartet, strings, no. 15, op. 132, A minor.
     Busch Quartet. World Records SHB 27 Tape (c) TC SHB 27 (From HMV
     DB 2109/12, DB 1799-800, DB 3375-80)
```
                +Gr 9-80 p413 tape         +RR 1-75 p37
                +Gr 1-75 p1361            ++STL 2-9-75 p37
```
475 Quartet, strings, no. 10, op. 74, E flat major. Quartet, strings,
     no. 11, op. 95, F minor. Allegri Quartet. Argo ZK 81
```
               ++Gr 12-79 p1024            +RR 1-80 p94
                +HFN 12-79 p158            +ST 4-80 p927
```
476 Quartet, strings, no. 10, op. 74, E flat major. Quartet, strings,
     no. 11, op. 95, F minor. Gabrieli Quartet. Decca SDD 551 Tape
     (c) KSDC 551
```
                +Gr 3-80 p1403             +-RR 3-80 p68
                +-HFN 2-80 p87
```
     Quartet, strings, no. 10, op. 74, E flat major. See no. 466. See
     no. 473
     Quartet, strings, no. 11, op. 95, F minor. See no. 474. See no.
     475. See no. 476
477 Quartets, strings, nos. 12-16. Grosse Fuge, op. 133, B flat major.
     Aeolian Quartet. Argo D155D4 (4)
```
                +-FF 11/12-80 p72          +-RR 7-79 p73
                +-Gr 9-79 p478             +-ST 11-79 p529
                -HFN 9-79 p101
```
478 Quartet, strings, no. 12, op. 127, E flat major. Quartet, strings,
     no. 16, op. 135, F major. Talich Quartet. Calliope CAL 1640
     Tape (c) CAL 4640
```
                +Gr 6-80 p44               +-HFN 11-80 p115
                +Gr 12-80 p842             +RR 6-80 p65
                +-HFN 6-80 p102            +ST 9-80 p342
```
479 Quartet, strings, no. 13, op. 130, B flat major. Grosse Fuge, op.
     133, B flat major. Talich Quartet. Calliope CAL 1637 Tape (c)
     4637
```
                +-HFN 11-80 p115
```
480 Quartet, strings, no. 13, op. 130, B flat major. Orford Quartet.
     CBS SM 321
```
                +-MUM 3/4-80 p32
```
481 Quartet, strings, no. 14, op. 131, C sharp minor. Talich Quartet.

Calliope CAL 1638
+Gr 12-80 p842   +—HFN 11-80 p115
+HFN 8-80 p94   +RR 7-80 p69

482 Quartet, strings, no. 14, op. 131, C sharp minor. LaSalle Quartet.
DG 2530 921
−FF 7/8-80 p56   +—NR 8-78 p9

483 Quartet, strings, no. 14, op. 131, C sharp minor. VPO; Leonard
Bernstein. DG 2531 077
+FF 5/6-80 p47   +—NYT 11-18-79 pD24
++Gr 1-80 p1138   +—RR 4-80 p59
+HF 7-80 p61   +SFC 2-17-80 p44
+++HFN 3-80 p86   +SR 1-5-80 p39
+MT 10-80 p633   +St 3-80 p96
+NR 1-80 p5   ++ST 7-80 p196

484 Quartet, strings, no. 15, op. 132, A minor. Talich Quartet. Cal-
liope CAL 1639 Tape (c) CAL 4639
+Gr 6-80 p44   +—HFN 11-80 p115
+Gr 12-80 p842   +RR 6-80 p65
+—HFN 6-80 p102   +ST 9-80 p342

Quartet, strings, no. 15, op. 132, A minor. See no. 474
Quartet, strings, no. 16, op. 135, F major. See no. 478
Quintet, 3 horns, oboe and bassoon, E flat major. See no. 127

485 Quintet, piano, op. 16, E flat major. DUKAS: Villanelle. MARAIS:
Le Basque. MALIPIERO: Dialogue, no. 4. Ferrier interview Montreal 10 March, 1950. Kathleen Ferrier, con; Instrumental accompaniment. Arabesque 8070
+NR 11-80 p8

486 Quintet, piano, op. 16, E flat major. MOZART: Quintet, piano, K
452, E flat major. Nash Ensemble. CRD CRD 1067 Tape (c) CRDC
4067
+Gr 3-80 p1398   +HFN 4-80 p121 tape
++Gr 7-80 p166 tape   ++RR 3-80 p68
+HFN 3-80 p86

487 Quintet, piano, op. 16, E flat major. Serenade, op. 25, D major.
Abbey Simon, pno; Richard Woodhams, ob; George Silfies, clt;
George Barry, bsn; Roland Pandolfi, hn; Jacob Berg, flt; Max
Rabinovitsi, vln; Darrel Barnes, vla. Turnabout TVC 37004 Tape
(c) CT 7004
+—FF 1/2-80 p50   +HF 1-80 p91 tape

Quintet, piano, op. 16, E flat major: Finale. See no. 623

488 Quintet, strings, op. 29, C major. MENDELSSOHN: Quintet, strings,
no. 2, op. 87, B flat major. Guarneri Quartet; Pinchas Zuker-
man, vla. RCA ARL 1-3354 Tape (c) ARK 1-3354
+FF 11/12-79 p33   +MT 12-80 p784
+Gr 2-80 p1276   +RR 2-80 p64
+—HFN 4-80 p103   +—ST 9-80 p339

489 Romance, no. 1, op. 40, G major. Romance, no. 2, op. 50, F major.
MENDELSSOHN: Concerto, violin, op. 64, D minor. SCHUBERT: Kon-
zertstuck, D 345, D major. Ronald Thomas, vln; Bournemouth Sin-
fonietta. CRD 1069 Tape (c) CRDC 4069
+—Gr 8-80 p214   +HFN 12-80 p159 tape
+—HFN 8-80 p105   +—STL 8-10-80 p30

Romance, no. 1, op. 40, G major. See no. 410. See no. 439. See
no. 3964

490 Romance, no. 2, op. 50, F major.* BRAHMS: Concerto, violin and

violoncello, op. 102, A minor.* MOZART: Concerto, violin, no. 3,
   K 216, G major. SHOSTAKOVICH: Trio, piano, no. 2, op. 67, E
   minor. David Oistrakh, vln; Milos Sadlo, vlc; Dmitri Shostakovich, pno; CPhO, Prague Radio Orchestra; Karel Ancerl. Supraphon 010 2371/2 (2) (*From Supraphon LPV 244)
                +-ARSC Vol 11, no. 2-3   ++HFN 7-79 p116
                     1979 p194   ++NR 10-79 p3
                +FF 7/8-80 p173   +RR 7-79 p64
                +Gr 8-79 p327

Romance, no. 2, op. 50, F major. See no. 439. See no. 489. See
   no. 810. See no. 3964. See no. 4009
Rondo, op. 51, no. 1, C major. See no. 3820
Rondo, op. 51, no. 2, G major. See no. 404. See no. 409
Die Ruinen von Athen, op. 113: Chorus of dervishes Turkish march.
   See no. 3964
Die Ruinen von Athen, op. 113: Incidental music. See no. 592
Die Ruinen von Athen, op. 113: Overture. See no. 462. See no. 565
Die Ruinen von Athen, op. 113: Turkish march. See no. 3625
491 Septet, op. 20, E flat major (orch. Druzecky). Collegium Musicum
   Pragense. Musicaphon BM 30 SL 4113
                +-HFN 10-80 p113
Serenade, op. 25, D major. See no. 487
Serenade, op. 41, D major. See no. 621
Sonata, flute, B flat major. See no. 621
492 Sonata, horn and piano, op. 17, F major. Variations on Mozart's
   "Bei Mannern welche Liebe fuhlen". WOELFL: Grand duo, op. 31, D
   minor. Bonnie Hampton, vlc; Nathan Schwartz, pno. Orion ORS
   78325
                +FF 1/2-80 p50
493 Sonata, horn and piano, op. 17, F major. Trio, 2 oboes and cor
   anglais, op. 87, C major. Variations on Mozart's "La ci darem
   la mano", C major. Heinz Holliger, Hans Elhorst, ob; Maurice
   Bourgue, ob; Heinz Holliger, cor anglais; Jurg Wyttenbach, pno.
   Philips 9500 672 Tape (c) 7300 676
                ++FF 9/10-80 p78   ++NR 7-80 p7
                ++Gr 11-80 p684   ++St 10-80 p109
                +HFN 10-80 p102
Sonata, horn and piano, op. 17, F major. See no. 622
494 Sonatas, piano, nos. 1-3, 15. Glenn Gould, pno. Columbia M2 35911
                +SFC 12-80 p94
495 Sonatas, piano, nos. 1-7. Artur Schnabel, pno. HMV RLS 753 (3)
   Tape (c) TC RLS 753
                +Gr 10-80 p542   +HFN 12-80 p153
496 Sonatas, piano, nos. 1-7. Bernard Roberts, pno. Nimbus D/C 901 (4)
                +-Gr 9-79 p484   +-RR 7-79 p83
                +-HFN 10-79 p149   +St 4-80 p125
497 Sonatas, piano, nos. 1-7. Malcolm Binns, fortepiano. L'Oiseau-
   Lyre D182D3 (3)
                +Gr 10-80 p517   +HFN 9-80 p100
498 Sonatas, piano, nos. 1-32. Variations on a theme by Diabelli, op.
   120. Anton Kuerti, pno. Aquitaine Records 90361/74 (14)
                +MQ 1-78 p113   +MUM 3/4-80 p37
499 Sonatas, piano, nos. 1-32. Wilhelm Kempff, pno. DG 2740 228 (10)
   (From DGM 18105, 18079, 18071, 18106, 18019, EPL 30245, DGM
   18071, 18079, 12020, 18076, 18055, 18056, 18021, 18089, 18135,
   18145, 18146)

+Gr 11-80 p698

500 Sonatas, piano, nos. 1-32. Anton Kuerti, pno. Odyssey Y4 34646/9
     (13)
                +ARG 7-78 p19   +MUM 3/4-80 p37
                +-FF 7/8-78 p17   +-NYT 8-6-78 pD16
                +-HF 11-78 p105   -SFC 4-30-78 p46
                +MJ 7-78 p56

501 Sonatas, piano, nos. 1-32. Andante favori, F major. Alfred Brendel,
     pno. Philips 6768 004 (13)
                ++Audio 4-79 p81   +-MUM 3/4-80 p37
                +-CL 2-79 p9   +NR 1-79 p14
                ++Gr 11-78 p922   +-NYT 12-3-78 pD19
                +-HF 2-79 p64   +RR 10-78 p91
                ++HFN 10-78 p121

502 Sonata, piano, nos. 1-32. Artur Schnabel, pno. Seraphim 1C 6063/6
     (4) (From IC 6065, 6066)
                +ARG 5-71 p48   +SR 12-80 p94
                +MUM 3/4-80 p37   +ST 4-71 p85
                +SFC 12-20-70 p33

503 Sonata, piano, no. 1, op. 2, no. 1, F minor. Sonata, piano, no. 20,
     op. 49, no. 2, G major. Sonata, piano, no. 26, op. 81a, E flat
     major. Alfred Brendel, pno. Philips 9500 507 Tape (c) 7300 667
     (From 6768 004)
                +Gr 5-79 p1914   +-MUM 1/2-80 p34
                +HFN 6-79 p117 tape   +RR 5-79 p81

504 Sonata, piano, no. 3, op. 2, no. 3, C major. Sonata, piano, no. 11,
     op. 22, B flat major. Alfred Brendel, pno. Philips 9500 450
                +-MUM 1/2-80 p34
     Sonata, piano, no. 3, op. 2, no. 3, C major. See no. 3976

505 Sonata, piano, no. 4, op. 7, E flat major. Sonata, piano, no. 9,
     op. 14, no. 1, E major. Sonata, piano, no. 10, op. 14, no. 2, G
     major. Vladimir Ashkenazy, pno. Decca SXL 6961 Tape (c) KSXC
     6961 (also London 7191)
                +Gr 12-80 p847   +-HFN 12-80 p133
     Sonata, piano, no. 4, K 282, E flat major. See no. 408
     Sonata, piano, no. 5, op. 10, no. 1, C minor. See no. 417
     Sonata, piano, no. 7, op. 10, no. 3, D major: Largo e mesto. See
     no. 3832

506 Sonatas, piano, nos. 8-15. Bernard Roberts, pno. Nimbus D/C 902 (4)
                +-RR 2-80 p71

507 Sonatas, piano, nos. 8, 14, 21, 23-24, 26, 29. Wilhelm Kempff, pno.
     Quintessence PMC 2707 (2)
                +ARG 3-80 p17

508 Sonatas, piano, nos. 8, 14, 23. Rudolf Serkin, pno. CBS 61937 Tape
     (c) 40-61937 (From SBRG 72148)
                ++Gr 12-79 p1028   +-HFN 2-80 p107 tape
                +-HFN 12-79 p179   ++RR 12-79 p93

509 Sonatas, piano, nos. 8, 14, 23. Vladimir Horowitz, pno. Columbia
     M 34509 Tape (c) MT 34509 (Reissues) (also CBS 76892 Tape (c)
     40-76892. From 73173, SBRG 72180)
                +-Gr 3-80 p1412   +-MT 5-80 p321
                +HF 2-78 p104 tape   +NR 8-77 p14
                +-HFN 2-80 p87   +-RR 2-80 p72
                +-HFN 3-80 p107 tape

510 Sonatas, piano, nos. 8, 14, 24, 26. Wilhelm Kempff, pno. Quintes-

sence PMC 7081
>   +FF 3/4-79 p33   +MUM 3/4-80 p37

511 Sonata, piano, no. 8, op. 13, C minor. Sonata, piano, no. 14, op.
>   27, no. 2, C sharp minor. Sonata, piano, no. 28, op. 101, A
>   major. Misha Dichter, pno. Philips 9500 319 Tape (c) 7300 591
>   /FF 5/6-78 p15   +HFN 10-80 p117 tape
>   +-Gr 5-80 p1690   /MJ 7-78 p56
>   +Gr 8-80 p275 tape   +NR 6-78 p11
>   +HF 5-78 p95   +RR 5-80 p81
>   +HF 5-79 p103 tape   ++St 6-78 p138
>   +-HFN 5-80 p118

512 Sonata, piano, no. 8, op. 13, C minor. Sonata, piano, no. 14, op.
>   27, no. 2, C sharp minor. Sonata, piano, no. 23, op. 57, F min-
>   or. Solomon. Seraphim M 60286
>   +ARG 12-77 p20   ++NR 12-77 p13
>   ++FF 9-77 p4   +St 1-78 p96
>   +MUM 3/4-80 p37

>   Sonata, piano, no. 8, op. 13, C minor. See no. 3811
>   Sonata, piano, no. 9, op. 14, no. 1, E major. See no. 505
>   Sonata, piano, no. 10, op. 14, no. 2, G major. See no. 505
>   Sonata, piano, no. 11, op. 22, B flat major. See no. 504

513 Sonata, piano, no. 12, op. 26, A flat major. Sonata, piano, no. 23,
>   op. 57, F minor. Sviatoslav Richter, pno. RCA VICS 1427 Tape
>   (r) V8S 1006
>   *ARG 11-70 p156   +MUM 3/4-80 p37

514 Sonata, piano, no. 13, op. 27, no. 1, E flat major. Sonata, piano,
>   no. 14, op. 27, no. 2, C sharp minor. MOZART: Rondo, piano, K
>   485, D major. Rondo, piano, K 511, A minor. Malcolm Bilson,
>   fortepiano. Nonesuch H 71377 Tape .(c) Advent E 1056
>   +FF 9/10-80 p167   ++St 11-80 p79
>   +NYT 7-27-80 pD20

515 Sonatas, piano, nos. 13-14, 16. Vladimir Ashkenazy, pno. London CS
>   7111 (also Decca SXL 6889 Tape (c) KSXC 6889)
>   +-FF 11/12-79 p34   ++NR 1-80 p13
>   ++FU 10-79 p43   +-RR 10-79 p120
>   +-Gr 10-79 p672   +RR 8-80 p93 tape
>   ++HF 11-79 p90   ++SFC 4-29-79 p53
>   +HFN 10-79 p147

516 Sonatas, piano, nos. 14, 17, 26. Wilhelm Kempff, pno. DG 2535
>   316 Tape (c) 3335 316 (From SKL 904)
>   +Gr 3-80 p1417   +RR 2-80 p72
>   +-HFN 2-80 p105   +RR 2-80 p97 tape

517 Sonatas, piano, no. 14, 21, 26. Guiomar Novaes, pno. Vox 531 500
>   (also Turnabout THS 65171)
>   +FF 11/12-80 p74   +MUM 3/4-80 p37

518 Sonatas, piano, nos. 14, 26, 32. Guiomar Novaes, pno. Vanguard
>   10014
>   +MUM 3/4-80 p37

519 Sonata, piano, no. 14, op. 27, no. 2, C sharp minor. Sonata, piano,
>   no. 15, op. 28, D major: Andante. Sonata, piano, no. 23, op. 57,
>   F minor. Paul Badura-Skoda, pno. Harmonia Mundi 1C 065 99769
>   (Reissues)
>   +FF 1/2-80 p51   +NYT 7-27-80 pD20
>   +HFN 6-80 p117   +RR 5-80 p82

>   Sonata, piano, no. 14, op. 27, no. 2, C sharp minor. See no. 407.

See no. 511. See no. 512. See no. 514. See no. 3811. See no. 3856. See no. 3944

520 Sonata, piano, no. 14, op. 27, no. 2, C sharp minor: Adagio; Presto. CHOPIN: Nocturne, op. 37, no. 2, G major. Nocturne, op. 48, no. 1, C minor. MENDELSSOHN: Songs without words, op. 67, no. 4: Spinning song. SCHUBERT: Impromptus, op. 42, nos. 2-3, D 935. Ignace Jan Paderewski, pno. Everest SDBR 3453
        -FF 9/10-80 p261   +NR 3-80 p13

Sonata, piano, no. 14, op. 27, no. 2, C sharp minor: Adagio sostenuto. See no. 623

Sonata, piano, no. 14, op. 27, no. 2, C sharp minor: 1st movement. See no. 3907

Sonata, piano, no. 15, op. 28, D major: Andante. See no. 520

521 Sonatas, piano, nos. 16-25. Bernard Roberts, pno. Nimbus DC 903 (4)
    +-Gr 9-80 p375

522 Sonata, piano, no. 17, op. 31, no. 2, D minor. Sonata, piano, no. 18, op. 31, no. 3, E flat major. Vladimir Ashkenazy, pno. London CS 7088 Tape (c) CS 5-7088 (also Decca SXL 6871 Tape (c) SXC 6871)

+-Gr 3-79 p1589	++NR 1-80 p14
+-HF 4-79 p78	+NYT 12-3-78 pD19
++HFN 3-79 p121	+RR 3-79 p106
++HFN 4-79 p133 tape	++SFC 2-11-79 p47
+MM 7-79 p40	+STL 12-2-79 p37

Sonata, piano, no. 17, op. 31, no. 2, D minor. See no. 405

Sonata, piano, no. 18, op. 31, no. 3, E flat major. See no. 407. See no. 522

Sonata, piano, no. 19, op. 49, no. 1, G minor. See no. 426

Sonata, piano, no. 20, op. 49, no. 2, G major. See no. 426. See no. 503

523 Sonatas, piano, nos. 21, 23, 29. Wilhelm Kempff, pno. Quintessence PMC 7130
        +ARG 3-80 p17   +MUM 3/4-80 p37
        +FF 3/4-80 p59

524 Sonatas, piano, nos. 21, 28-32. Solomon, pno. Turnabout THS 65068/70
        +MUM 3/4-80 p37   +St 1-78 p96

525 Sonata, piano, no. 21, op. 53, C major. SCHUBERT: Fantasia, op. 15, D 760, C major. Ilana Vered, pno. Decca PFS 4433 (also London SPC 21183 Tape (c) SPC 5-21183)
        +FF 9/10-80 p76   +HFN 12-78 p148
        +-Gr 12-78 p1130   +-NR 1-80 p13
        ++ HF 3-80 p71   +RR 12-78 p88

526 Sonata, piano, no. 21, op. 53, C major. Sonata, piano, no. 31, op. 110, A flat major. Harris Goldsmith, pno. Musical Heritage Society MHS 4005
        +FF 11/12-80 p75   +St 7-80 p76
        +HF 3-80 p71

527 Sonata, piano, no. 21, op. 53, C major. Sonata, piano, no. 23, op. 57, F minor. Walter Gieseking, pno. Odyssey 3216 0314
        +MUM 3/4-80 p37

Sonata, piano, no. 21, op. 53, C major: 1st movement, excerpt. See no. 623

528 Sonata, piano, no. 22, op. 54, F major. LISZT: Annees de pelerinage, 2nd year, G 161: Il penseroso. Sonata, piano, G 178, B

minor. Viktor Friedman, pno. Orion ORS 79334
    -FF 3/4-80 p112   -NR 1-80 p13
Sonata, piano, no. 23, op. 57, F minor. See no. 512. See no. 513.
    See no. 520. See no. 527

529 Sonatas, piano, nos. 24, 30-31. Jorg Demus, pno. Harmonia Mundi
     151 99655/6 (2)
            +Gr 4-80 p1571   +RR 4-80 p92
            +-HFN 3-80 p105
     Sonatas, piano, nos. 24, 30-31. See no. 409
     Sonata, piano, no. 26, op. 81a, E flat major. See no. 418. See no.
     503

530 Sonatas, piano, nos. 28-30. Paul Badura-Skoda, pno. Astree AS
     47/8 (2)
            +Gr 5-80 p1690   +RR 5-80 p82

531 Sonata, piano, no. 28, op. 101, A major. Sonata, piano, no. 30,
     op. 109, E major. Stephen Bishop-Kovacevich, pno. Philips 9500
     569 Tape (c) 7300 702
            +-CL 9-80 p14   /NR 5-80 p12
            +FF 9/10-80 p76   ++SFC 3-16-90 p31
            +MUM 5/6-80 p32   ++St 6-80 p110
     Sonata, piano, no. 28, op. 101, A major. See no. 405. See no. 463.
     See no. 511
     Sonata, piano, no. 28, op. 101, A major: Allegretto ma non troppo.
     See no. 3811

532 Sonata, piano, no. 29, op. 106, B flat major. Daniel Barenboim,
     pno. Sine Qua Non 7750
            /NR 5-80 p12

533 Sonata, piano, no. 30, op. 109, E major. Sonata, piano, no. 31, op.
     110, A flat major. Ludwig Olshansky, pno. Monitor MCS 2161
     Tape (c) 55013
            +ARG 11-80 p18   +NR 8-80 p9
            +-FF 7/8-80 p57   +SFC 8-31-80 p31
     Sonata, piano, no. 30, op. 109, E major. See no. 463. See no. 531

534 Sonata, piano, no. 31, op. 110, A flat major. Sonata, piano, no.
     32, op. 111, C minor. Inger Sodergren, pno. Calliope CAL 1648
     Tape (c) CAL 4648
            +FF 9/10-80 p783   +HFN 8-80 p94
            +Gr 7-80 p153   ++RR 6-80 p72
     Sonata, piano, no. 31, op. 110, A flat major. See no. 526. See no.
     533

535 Sonata, piano, no. 32, op. 111, C minor. SCHUMANN: Faschingsswank
     aus Wien, op. 26. Sviatoslav Richter, pno. Bruno Walter Society
     IGI 309
            +NR 5-80 p12

536 Sonata, piano, no. 32, op. 111, C minor. SCHUMANN: Faschingsswank
     aus Wien, op. 26. Sviatoslav Richter, pno. I Grandi Interpreti
     IGI 309
            +FF 7/8-80 p57
     Sonata, piano, no. 32, op. 111, C minor. See no. 534

537 Sonata, 2 pianos, op. 6, D major. MOZART: Sonata, piano, 4 hands,
     K 497, F major. WEBER: Pieces, piano, op. 3 (6). Rolf Junghans,
     Bradford Tracy, fortepiano. Toccata FSM 53625
            +HFN 5-80 p133

538 Sonatas, violin and piano, nos. 1-10. David Oistrakh, vln; Lev
     Oborin, pno. Philips 6768 036 (4) (From SAL 3416/20)

```
       +Gr 12-79 p1027              ++RR 1-80 p98
       +HFN 12-79 p179             +ST 7-80 p196
```

539 Sonatas, violin and piano, no. 1-10. Henryk Szeryng, vln; Ingrid
    Haebler, pno. Philips 6769 011 (5)
```
       +Gr 10-80 p511              ++NR 11-80 p6
       ++HFN 10-80 p102
```

540 Sonata, violin and piano, no. 1, op. 12, no. 1, D major. Sonata,
    violin and piano, no. 5, op. 24, F major. Arthur Grumiaux, vln;
    Claudio Arrau, pno. Philips 9500 055 Tape (c) 7300 473
```
       +FF 5/6-80 p48              ++HFN 5-76 p95
       +-Gr 5-76 p1776             +NR 1-80 p5
       +Gr 10-76 p658 tape         +-RR 5-76 p64
       +-HF 4-80 p78
```
    Sonata, violin and piano, no. 1, op. 12, no. 1, D major. See no.
    817

541 Sonata, violin and piano, no. 2, op. 12, A major. Sonata, violin
    and piano, no. 4, op. 23, A minor. Arthur Grumiaux, vln; Claudio
    Arrau, pno. Philips 9500 263
```
       +FF 9/10-80 p77             ++NR 6-80 p8
       +Gr 8-77 p313              +-NYT 7-6-80 pD15
       ++HFN 7-77 p107            ++RR 9-77 p81
```
    Sonata, violin and piano, no. 4, op. 23, A minor. See no. 541
    Sonata, violin and piano, no. 5, op. 24, F major. See no. 540

542 Sonata, violin and piano, no. 7, op. 30, no. 2, C minor. Sonata,
    violin and piano, no. 8, op. 30, no. 3, G major. Arthur Grum-
    iaux, vln; Claudio Arrau, pno. Philips 9500 220 Tape (c) 7300
    784
```
       +FF 5/6-80 p48             +-HFN 3-77 p99
       +-Gr 3-77 p1416            +-NR 8-80 p9
       +-HF 4-80 p78              +RR 3-77 p75
```
    Sonata, violin and piano, no. 8, op. 30, no. 3, G major. See no.
    542
    Sonata, violin and piano, no. 9, op. 47, A major. See no. 3964
    Sonatas, violoncello, nos. 1-5. See no. 622
    Sonatina, C major. See no. 403. See no. 3730
    Sonatina, op. 105, C minor. See no. 403

543 Songs: Adelaide, op. 46; Ich liebe dich, G 235; Der Kuss, op. 128;
    Resignation, G 252. SCHUBERT: An die Dioskuren; An die Laute,
    D 905; Die Forelle, D 550; Im Abendrot, D 799; Der Musensohn, D
    764. SCHUMANN: Dichterliebe, op. 48. Fritz Wunderlich, t; Hub-
    ert Giesen, pno. DG 139125
```
       +RR 8-80 p14
```

544 Songs: Adelaide, op. 46; Ich liebe dich, G 235; Der Kuss, op. 128;
    Resignation, G 252. SCHUBERT: An die Dioskuren; An die Laute,
    D 905; An die Musik, D 547; An Sylvia, D 891; Der Einsame, D 800;
    Fruhlingsglaube, D 868; Heidenroslein, D 257; Die Forelle, D 550;
    Im Abendrot, D 799; Der Musensohn, D 764; Standchen, D 889.
    SCHUMANN: Dichterliebe, op. 48: Songs (6). Fritz Wunderlich, t;
    Hubert Giesen, pno. DG 2535 614
```
       +RR 8-80 p14
```

545 Songs: Abendlied unterm gestirnten Himmel, WoO 150; Adelaide, op.
    46; An die Ferne geliebte, op. 98; Das Baschlein in unserm Strass-
    chen, op. 108, no. 25; Das Hirtenmadchen, WoO 155/3; Den Goldwein
    kredenzt, WoO 154/6; Elegie auf den Tod eines Pudels, WoO 110;
    En schwur es mir beim Scheiden, WoO 154/12; Gesangesmacht, WoO

152/2; Die Gondel, WoO 157/12; Der Knabe vom See, WoO 155/24;
Der Kuss, op. 128; Liebe und Gluck fahrt hin, WoO 152/20; Lied
aus der Ferne, WoO 137; Marmotte, op. 52, no. 7; Mignon, op. 75,
no. 1; Mit einem gemalten Band, op. 83, no. 3; Morgen fur Grillen,
WoO 152/21; Neue Liebe neues Leben, op. 75, no. 2; Nur wer die
Sehnsucht kennt, WoO 134; O Zaub'rin leb wohl, op. 108, no. 18;
Prufung des Kussens, WoO 89; Der Scheidekuss, WoO 155/25; Son-
nenschein, WoO 153/13; Spar die Schwanke, WoO 156/5; Der Traum,
WoO 155/14; Die Trommel geruhret, op. 84, no. 1; Vergebens ist's,
WoO 153/15; Wonne der Wehmut, op. 83, no. 1. Maria Muller,
Marta Fuchs, s; Helena Rott, Emmi Leisner, con; Peter Anders,
Walther Ludwig, Lorenz Fehenberger, t; Arno Schellenberg, Karl
Schmitt-Walter, bar; Kurt Bohme, bs; Piano accompaniments.
Odyssey Y2 35242 (2)
                +─FF 3/4-80 p51   -NR 3-80 p12
546 Songs: An die ferne Geliebte, op. 98. HAYDN: Schottische und Walis-
     ische Lieder. STRAUSS: Orchesterlieder (5). Fritz Wunderlich,
     t; Walter Weller, vln; Ludwig Beinl, vlc; Heinrich Schmidt, pno;
     Bavarian Radio Orchestra; Jan Koetsier. Philips 6520 022
                +RR 8-80 p14
547 Songs: Irish songs: The British Light Dragoons; Come draw we round
     the cheerful ring; The kiss dear maid thy lip has left; O harp
     of Erin; On the massacre of Glencoe; The pulse of an Irishman;
     The return to Ulster; Tis sunshine at last. Scottish songs: Cease
     your funning; O Mary at thy window be; Sally in our alley.
     Welsh songs: Cupid's kindness; Good night; The vale of Clwyd;
     When mortals all to rest retire. Songs of various nationality:
     The soldier. Robert White, t; Samuel Sanders, pno; Ani Kavafian;
     vln; Yo Yo Ma, vlc. RCA ARL 1-3417
                +ARG 1-80 p20   +NYT 10-14-79 pD24
               ++FF 3/4-80 p52   +ON 2-2-80 p28
                +HF 12-79 p88   +RR 2-80 p49
                +Gr 2-80 p1282   +SFC 9-9-79 p45
                +NR 12-79 p11   +St 5-80 p86
548 Songs: An die ferne Geliebte, op. 98. BRAHMS: Ernste Gesange, op.
     121 (4). SCHUMANN: Belsazar, op. 57; Die beiden Grenadiere, op.
     49, no. 1; Dichterliebe, op. 48: Ich grolle nicht; Liederkreis,
     op. 24: Schone Wiege meine Leiden; Lotusblume, op. 25, no. 7;
     Widmung, op. 25, no. 1. Norman Bailey, bar; John Constable, pno.
     Saga 5450 Tape (c) 5450
                +Gr 3-80 p1449
549 Songs: Folksong arrangements from England, Scotland, Wales and Ire-
     land. Accademia Monteverdiana; Denis Stevens. Schwann VMS 2059
                -FF 11/12-80 p71
     Songs: Aus Goethes Faust, op. 75, no. 3; Ich liebe dich, WoO 123.
     See no. 3573
     Songs: In questa tomba oscura. See no. 3774. See no. 3903
550 Symphonies, nos. 1-9. OSCCP; Carl Schuricht. Angel (Japan) EAC
     30113/9
                ++ARSC Vol 12, nos. 1-2, 1980 p82
551 Symphonies, nos. 1-9. Gre Brouwenstijn, s; Kersten Meyer, con;
     Nicolai Gedda, t; Frederick Guthrie, bs; St. Hedwig's Choir;
     BPhO; Andre Cluytens. Classics for Pleasure CFP 78251 (8)
                -HFN 2-80 p105   +─RR 3-80 p45
552 Symphonies, nos. 1-9. Joan Sutherland, s; Marilyn Horne, con;

James King, t; Martti Talvela, bs; VSOO Chorus; VPO; Hans Schmidt-
Isserstedt. Decca JBA 500/5 (6) (From SXL 6437, 6232, 6274,
6396, 6329, 6447, 6233)
+Gr 4-80 p1550   +-HFN 3-80 p105
553 Symphonies, nos. 1-9. Gwyneth Jones, s; Hanna Schwarz, alto; Rene
Kollo, t; Kurt Moll, bs; VSOO Chorus; VPO; Leonard Bernstein.
DG 2740 216 (8) Tape (c) 3378 090
    ++ARG 9-80 p20   +NR 6-80 p1
    +-FF 5/6-80 p14   +-NYT 4-27-80 pD21
    +FF 11/12-80 p75   +RR 4-80 p56
    +Gr 3-80 p1380   +-RR 5-80 p105 tape
    +-Gr 5-80 p1717 tape   +-SFC 5-11-80 p35
    +HF 7-80 p61   +St 8-80 p94
    ++HFN 4-80 p101   +-STL 4-13-80 p39
554 Symphonies, nos. 1-9. Fidelio, op. 72: Overture. Coriolan overture, op. 62. Leonore overtures, nos. 2 and 3, op. 72. Elisabeth Schwarzkopf, Elisabeth Hongen, s; Hans Hopf, Otto Edelman,
bar; Bayreuth Festival Orchestra and Chorus, VPO, BPhO, Stockholm Philharmonic Orchestra; Wilhelm Furtwangler. Electrola
149 53432/9 (8)
    ++NYT 4-27-80 pD25
555 Symphonies, nos. 1-9. Coriolan overture, op. 62. Egmont, op. 84:
Overture. Fidelio, op. 72: Overture. Leonore overture, no. 3,
op. 72b. Kiri Te Kanawa, s; Julia Hamari, ms; Stuart Burrows, t;
Robert Holl, bs; LSO; Eugen Jochum. HMV SQ SLS 5178 (8) (From
ASD 3376, 3484, 3583, 3627) (also Angel SZH 3890. From S 37410,
37529, 37463, 37530, 35731, 37463)
    +-ARG 9-80 p20   +-NR 6-80 p3
    ++Gr 11-79 p802   +NYT 4-27-80 pD21
    +-HF 6-80 p68   +-RR 12-79 p46
    +-HFN 2-80 p86   +-SFC 3-16-80 p31
556 Symphonies, nos. 1-9. Joan Sutherland, s; Norma Procter, con;
Anton Dermota, t; Arnold van Mill, bs; Chorale du Brassus; OSR;
Ernest Ansermet. London STS 15464/9 (6) (From London discs 1954-
1957)
    +-FF 1/2-80 p51
557 Symphonies, nos. 1-9. Coriolan overture, op. 62. Egmont, op. 84:
Overture. Ingeborg Wenglor, s; Annelies Burmeister, alto;
Martin Ritzmann, t; Rolf Kuhne, bs; CPhO and Chorus; Paul Kletzki. Supraphon 110 2461/8 (8)
    +NR 8-80 p2   +SFC 8-31-80 p31
558 Symphony, no. 1, op. 21, C major. Symphony, no. 2, op. 36, D major.
CO; Lorin Maazel. CBS 76854 Tape (c) 40-76854 (From 79800)
    +Gr 8-80 p214
559 Symphony, no. 1, op. 21, C major. Leonore overture, no. 3, op. 72b.
RPO, LSO; Antal Dorati. Mercury SRI 75121
    +FF 7/8-80 p59   +NR 5-80 p4
560 Symphony, no. 1, op. 21, C major. Symphony, no. 8, op. 93, F major.
Leipzig Gewandhaus Orchestra; Kurt Masur. Philips 6570 131 Tape
(c) 7310 131 (From 6747 135)
    +Gr 2-80 p1263   +-HFN 4-80 p121 tape
    +Gr 7-80 p166 tape   -RR 2-80 p46
    +HFN 2-80 p105   +-RR 5-80 p105 tape
561 Symphony, no. 1, op. 21, C major. Symphony, no. 8, op. 93, F major.
Bavarian Radio Orchestra, BPhO; Eugen Jochum. Quintessence PMC
7128

                        +—FF 1/2-80 p52
562 Symphony, no. 2, op. 36, D major. HAYDN: Symphony, no. 93, D major.
     Symphony, no. 99, E flat major. Symphony, no. 104, D major.
     LPO; Thomas Beecham. HMV RLS 734 (2) (From Columbia LX 586/9,
     721/3, 505/7, 856/8)
                    +ARSC Vol 12, no. 3,   +HFN 6-79 p115
                       1980 p247   +RR 6-79 p80
                    +—Gr 6-79 p41
563 Symphony, no. 2, op. 36, D major. Leonore overture, no. 2, op. 72.
     COA; Eugen Jochum. Philips 6570 168 (From 6500 088)
                    +FF 1/2-80 p53
564 Symphony, no. 2, op. 36, D major. Creatures of Prometheus, op. 43:
     Overture. LPO; Bernard Haitink. Philips 9500 257 Tape (c) 7300
     545 (From 6747 307)
                    +—FF 5/6-78 p16   +HFN 6-80 p119 tape
                    +—Gr 12-79 p1002   +RR 11-79 p70
                    +HFN 11-79 p153   +—RR 5-80 p105 tape
565 Symphony, no. 2, op. 36, D major. Creatures of Prometheus, op. 43:
     Overture. Ruins of Athens, op. 113: Overture. BPhO; Bayreuth
     Radio Orchestra; Eugen Jochum. Quintessence PMC 7109
                    +FF 1/2-80 p53
     Symphony, no. 2, op. 36, D major. See no. 558
566 Symphony, no. 3, op. 55, E flat major. NYP; Zubin Mehta. CBS 35883
     Tape (c) HMT 35883
                    +—Gr 9-80 p326   +—HFN 12-80 p159 tape
                    +—HFN 10-80 p103   +STL 9-14-80 p40
567 Symphony, no. 3, op. 55, E flat major. BPhO; Andre Cluytens. Clas-
     sics for Pleasure CFP 40076 Tape (c) TC CFP 40076
                    +—HFN 8-80 p109 tape
568 Symphony, no. 3, op. 55, E flat major. BPhO; Herbert von Karajan.
     DG 2535 302
                    +—MUM 10-80 p37
569 Symphony, no. 3, op. 55, E flat major. BPhO; Rafael Kubelik. DG
     2535 412 Tape (c) 3335 412 (From 2740 155)
                    +—Gr 11-80 p660   +HFN 11-80 p131 tape
                    +—HFN 12-80 p153
570 Symphony, no. 3, op. 55, E flat major. VPO; Erich Kleiber. London
     23202
                    +MUM 9/10-80 p37   +NYT 1-16-77 pD13
                    +NR 5-77 p4   ++SR 5-28-77 p42
571 Symphony, no. 3, op. 55, E flat major. RPO; Antal Dorati. Mercury
     SRI 75123
                    +—FF 11/12-80 p76   +NR 7-80 p4
572 Symphony, no. 3, op. 55, E flat major. Columbia Symphony Orchestra;
     Bruno Walter. Odyssey Y 33925
                    +MJ 10-76 p25   +MUM 9/10-80 p37
573 Symphony, no. 3, op. 55, E flat major. CO; Georg Szell. Odyssey Y
     34622 Tape (c) YT 34622 (From Epic BC 1001, Columbia M7X 30281)
                    ++FF 5/6-78 p16   +MJ 9-78 p35
                    +HF 5-78 p96   +MUM 9/10-80 p37
574 Symphony, no. 3, op. 55, E flat major. COA; Eugen Jochum. Philips
     6570 088
                    +—MUM 9/10-80 p37
575 Symphony, no. 3, op. 55, E flat major. Coriolan overture, op. 62.
     Leipzig Gewandhaus Orchestra; Kurt Masur. Philips 6570 165 Tape

(c) 7310 165 (From 6747 135)
    +Gr 5-80 p1651   +-HFN 8-80 p109 tape
    -HFN 4-80 p117   +-RR 4-80 p58

576 Symphony, no. 3, op. 55, E flat major. CPhO; Lovro von Matacic.
Quintessence PMC 7089
    +FF 5/6-79 p27   ++SFC 3-25-79 p41
    ++MUM 9/10-80 p37

577 Symphony, no. 3, op. 55, E flat major. NBC Symphony Orchestra; Arturo Toscanini. RCA VICS 1655
    +MUM 9/10-80 p37

578 Symphony, no. 3, op. 55, E flat major. VPO; Wilhelm Furtwangler.
Turnabout THS 65020
    +MUM 9/10-80 p37

579 Symphony, no. 3, op. 55, E flat major. Leonore overture, no. 2, op.
72. VPO, LSO; Felix Weingartner. Turnabout THS 65174
    +-Audio 8-80 p72   ++NR 5-79 p4
    ++ARG 5-79 p15   +FF 5/6-79 p26

580 Symphony, no. 3, op. 55, E flat major. Leonore overture, no. 3, op.
72b. VPO; Wilhelm Furtwangler. World Records SH 375
    +Gr 12-80 p880   +HFN 8-80 p94

Symphony, no. 3, op. 55, E flat major: Allegro con brio, excerpt.
See no. 623

581 Symphony, no. 4, op. 60, B flat major. Symphony, no. 8, op. 93, F
major. CO; Lorin Maazel. CBS 76855 Tape (c) 40-76855 (From
79800)
    +-Gr 6-80 p31   +-RR 6-80 p40
    +-HFN 6-80 p115

582 Symphony, no. 4, op. 60, B flat major.* Ah perfido, op. 65. Birgit
Nilsson, s; LSO, ROHO; Pierre Monteux, Edward Downes. London STS
15394 (*From Victrola 1102)
    +FF 1/2-80 p54

583 Symphony, no. 4, op. 60, B flat major.* Leonore overture, no. 3,
op. 72b. LPO, Bernard Haitink. Philips 9500 258 Tape (c) 7300
661 (*From Philips 6747 307)
    +-Gr 12-79 p1002   ++HFN 1-80 p123 tape
    +HFN 11-79 p153   +RR 11-79 p70

584 Symphony, no. 4, op. 60, B flat major. Leonore overture, no. 2,
op. 72. BPhO; Eugen Jochum. Quintessence PMC 7139 (From DG
138694)
    ++FF 5/6-80 p48

585 Symphony, no. 5, op. 67, C minor. Symphony, no. 8, op. 93, F major.
BSO, CO Members; Rafael Kubelik. DG 2535 407 Tape (c) 3335 407
    ++FF 11/12-80 p77   +/HFN 12-80 p159 tape

586 Symphony, no. 6, op. 68, F major. ECO; Michael Tilson Thomas. Columbia M 35169 Tape (c) MT 35169 (also CBS 76825 Tape (c) 40-76825)
    +FF 5/6-80 p50   +NR 3-80 p2
    +FU 6-80 p43   +NYT 12-9-79 pD25
    +Gr 1-80 p1138   +-RR 1-80 p63
    +Gr 2-80 p1302 tape   -RR 5-80 p106 tape
    +HF 4-80 p78   ++SFC 12-9-79 p43
    /-HFN 1-80 p102   +St 3-80 p92
    +-HFN 2-80 p107 tape

587 Symphony, no. 6, op. 68, F major. LAPO; Carlo Maria Giulini. DG
2531 266 Tape (c) 3301 266

+–Gr 6-80 p32   +HFN 8-80 p109 tape
+HFN 6-80 p102   -RR 6-80 p40

588 Symphony, no. 6, op. 68, F major. BPhO; Lorin Maazel. DG 2535 274
     Tape (c) 3335 274 (From 138642)
                 +–FF 1/2-80 p55   +SFC 7-15-79 p47

589 Symphony, no. 6, op. 68, F major. Orchestre de Paris; Rafael Kube-
     lik. DG 2535 413 Tape (c) 3335 413 (From 2740 155)
                 +Gr 11-80 p665

590 Symphony, no. 6, op. 68, F major. PO; Riccardo Muti. HMV ASD 3854
     Tape (c) TC ASD 3854 (also Angel S 37639 Tape (c) 4ZS 37639)
                 +–FF 9/10-80 p77   ++NR 7-80 p3
                 +–Gr 5-80 p1652   +–NYT 5-11-80 pD24
                 +–HFN 5-80 p118   +–RR 5-80 p53
                 +HFN 8-80 p109 tape   +St 11-80 p79

591 Symphony, no. 6, op. 68, F major. Egmont, op. 84: Overture. NPhO;
     Carlo Maria Giulini. HMV SXLP 30313 Tape (c) TC SXLP 30313
     (From ASD 2535)
                 /-Gr 1-80 p1137   +HFN 4-80 p121 tape
                 +HFN 4-80 p117   +–RR 4-80 p105 tape

592 Symphony, no. 6, op. 68, F major. Creatures of Prometheus, op. 43:
     Overture. Ruins of Athens, op. 113: Incidental music. Leipzig
     Gewandhaus Orchestra; Kurt Masur. Philips 6570 133 Tape (c) 7310
     133 (From 6747 135)
                 +Gr 5-80 p1651   +HFN 9-80 p115 tape
                 +HFN 5-80 p135   +–RR 5-80 p53

593 Symphony, no. 6, op. 68, F major. COA; Eugen Jochum. Philips 6570
     159
                 +–FF 1/2-80 p55

     Symphony, no. 6, op. 68, F major. See no. 3585

594 Symphony, no. 7, op. 92, A major. Coriolan overture, op. 62. LSO;
     Eugen Jochum. Angel SZ 37531
                 +–FF 1/2-80 p52   +NYT 12-9-79 pD25
                 +–NR 12-79 p4   ++SFC 10-7-79 p49

595 Symphony, no. 7, op. 92, A major. RPO; Colin Davis. HMV SXLP 20038
     Tape (c) TC SXLP 20038, TC EXE 138 (also Angel S 37027)
                 +Gr 7-75 p254 tape   +–HFN 10-80 p117 tape
                 +RR 7-75 p69 tape   +–RR 5-78 p76 tape

596 Symphony, no. 7, op. 92, A major. RPO; Thomas Beecham. HMV SXLP
     30286 Tape (c) TC SXLP 30286 (From ASD 311)
                 -ARSC Vol 12, no. 3,   +HFN 7-79 p119 tape
                    1980 p252   +MT 9-79 p747
                 -Gr 5-79 p1885   +RR 5-79 p49
                 ++Gr 8-79 p382 tape   +–RR 9-79 p135 tape
                 +HFN 5-79 p131

597 Symphony, no. 7, op. 92, A major. Creatures of Prometheus, op. 43:
     Overture. VPO; Claudio Abbado. London STS 15495
                 +FF 3/4-80 p60

598 Symphony, no. 7, op. 92, A major. Columbia Symphony Orchestra;
     Bruno Walter. Odyssey Y 35219 (From Columbia MS 6082)
                 /FF 9/10-79 p48   +–MUM 3/4-80 p35
                 +FU 3-80 p44   +NYT 6-17-79 pD32

599 Symphony, no. 7, op. 92, A major. FRESCOBALDI: Gagliarda (Stokow-
     ski). PALESTRINA: Adoramus te (Stokowski). Symphony of the Air;
     Leopold Stokowski. Quintessence 7110 Tape (c) P4C 7110
                 +–ARG 9-80 p20   +HF 7-80 p82 tape
                 +–FF 7/8-80 p59

600 Symphony, no. 7, op. 92, A major. Fidelio, op. 72: Overture. Leip-
    zig Gewandhaus Orchestra; Kurt Masur. Philips 6570 048 Tape (c)
    7310 048 (From 6747 135)
                +Gr 4-80 p1550   +HFN 6-80 p119 tape
                +Gr 7-80 p166 tape   +RR 3-80 p46
                +HFN 3-80 p105   +-RR 5-80 p105 tape
601 Symphony, no. 7, op. 92, A major. BPhO. Saphir INT 120924
                +Gr 12-80 p880
602 Symphony, no. 8, op. 93, F major. Symphony, no. 9, op. 125, D minor.
    Gundula Janowitz, s; Hilde Rossl-Majdan, con; Waldemar Kmentt,
    t; Walter Berry, bar; Vienna Singverein; BPhO; Herbert von Kara-
    jan. DG 2725 101 (2) Tape (c) 3374 101 (From SLPM 138807/8)
                +Gr 12-79 p1007   +RR 10-79 p78
                +HFN 11-79 p153   +RR 5-80 p106 tape
603 Symphony, no. 8, op. 93, F major. Symphony, no. 9, op. 125, D
    minor. Carole Farley, s; Alfreda Hodgson, con; Stuart Burrows,
    t; Norman Bailey, bs; Brighton Festival Chorus; RPO; Antal Dor-
    ati. Mercury SRI 2-77013
                +FF 5/6-80 p51   +-NR 3-80 p4
    Symphony, no. 8, op. 93, F major. See no. 560. See no. 561. See
    no. 561. See no. 581. See no. 585
    Symphony, no. 8, op. 93, F major: Allegretto. See no. 3897
604 Symphony, no. 9, op. 125, D minor. Soloists; LSO; Bruno Walter.
    Bruno Walter Society BWS 742
                +FF 7/8-80 p60   +-NYT 6-17-79 pD32
605 Symphony, no. 9, op. 125, D minor. Lucine Amara, s; Lili Chooka-
    sian, con; John Alexander, t; John Macurdy, bs; Mormon Tabernacle
    Choir; PO; Eugene Ormandy. CBS 30111 Tape (c) 40-30111
                +-Gr 1-80 p1203   +-RR 12-79 p48
                +-HFN 1-80 p119
606 Symphony, no. 9, op. 125, D minor. Lucia Popp, s; Elena Obraztsova,
    ms; Jon Vickers, t; Martti Talvela, bs; CO and Chorus; Lorin
    Maazel. CBS 76999 Tape (c) 40-76999 (From 79800)
                +-Gr 1-80 p1138   +-RR 1-80 p64
                +HFN 1-80 p119   +-RR 5-80 p106 tape
                +-HFN 3-80 p107 tape
607 Symphony, no. 9, op. 125, D minor. Leonore overture, no. 3, op. 72.
    King Stephen, op. 117: Overture. Aase Nordmo Lovberg, s; Christa
    Ludwig, ms; Waldemar Kmentt, t; Hans Hotter, bar; PhO and Chorus;
    Otto Klemperer. HMV SXDW 3051 (2) Tape (c) TC2 SXDW 3051 (From
    Columbia 33 CX 1574/5, SAX 2276/7, 2542, 2373)
                +Gr 1-80 p1138   +-HFN 4-80 p117
                +Gr 5-80 p1717 tape   +-HFN 4-80 p121 tape
608 Symphony, no. 9, op. 125, D minor. Konig Stefan, op. 117: Overture.
    Leonore overture, no. 3, op. 72b. NPhO; Otto Klemperer. HMV
    Tape (c) TC SXLP 30313
                +RR 5-80 p106 tape
609 Symphony, no. 9, op. 125, D minor. Adele Addison, s; Jane Hobson,
    ms; Richard Lewis, t; Donald Bell, bar; CO and Chorus; Georg
    Szell. Odyssey Y 34625 Tape (c) YT 34625 (From Epic)
                +FF 9/10-79 p50   /MUM 5/6-80 p33
                +-MJ 9/10-79 p51
610 Symphony, no. 9, op. 125, D minor. Elisabeth Soderstrom, s; Regina
    Resnik, con; Jon Vickers, t; David Ward, bs; LSO; London Bach
    Choir; Pierre Monteux. Westminster WG 8364/2 (2)
                -ARG 3-80 p18   +FF 1/2-80 p54

Symphony, no. 9, op. 125, D minor. See no. 602. See no. 603. See no. 3710

Theme and variations, D major. See no. 403

Trio, bassoon, flute and piano. See no. 621

611 Trio, clarinet, op. 11, B flat major. Trio, piano, no. 4, op. 70, no. 1, D major. Franzjosef Maier, vln; Hans Deinzer, clt; Rudolf Mandalka, vlc; Jorg Demus, pno. Harmonia Mundi 1C 065 99839

+FF 5/6-80 p52   +RR 4-80 p84
+HFN 5-80 p118   +ST 9-80 p342

612 Trio, clarinet, op. 11, B flat major. BRAHMS: Trio, clarinet, violoncello and piano, op. 114, A minor. Bob Wilber, clt; Leo Winland, vlc; Janos Solyom, pno. Phontastic Artemis ARTE 7107

+FF 5/6-80 p52   +Gr 11-80 p691

Trio, 3 flute, G major. See no. 621

Trio, 2 oboes and cor anglais, op. 87, C major. See no. 493

613 Trio, piano, no. 4, op. 70, no. 1, D major. Trio, piano, no. 5, op. 70, no. 2, E flat major. Henryk Szeryng, vln; Pierre Fournier, vlc; Wilhelm Kempff, pno. DG 2530 207 Tape (c) 3342 118

+Gr 7-80 p166 tape   +RR 2-80 p97 tape

614 Trio, piano, no. 4, op. 70, no. 1, D major. Trio, piano, no. 5, op. 70, no. 2, E flat major. Henryk Szeryng, vln; Pierre Fournier, vlc; Wilhelm Kempff, pno. DG 2542 125 Tape (c) 3342 125 (From 2720 016)

+Gr 8-80 p234   -RR 8-80 p93 tape
+HFN 7-80 p117

Trio, piano, no. 4, op. 70, no. 1, D major. See no. 611

Trio, piano, no. 5, op. 70, no. 2, E flat major. See no. 613. See No. 614

615 Trio, piano, no. 6, op. 97, B flat major. HAYDN: Sonata, piano, no. 50, D major. Solomon, pno; Henry Holst, vln; Anthony Pini, vlc. Arabesque 8032 Tape (c) 9032 (From HMV originals)

+FF 7/8-80 p60   +NR 8-80 p9
+HF 6-80 p72   +NYT 1-6-80 pD18

616 Trio, piano, no. 6, op. 97, B flat major. Beaux Arts Trio. Philips 6833 033 (From SAL 3530)

+Gr 9-80 p354

Trio, piano, no. 6, op. 97, B flat major: Allegro moderato, excerpt. See no. 623

617 Trio, strings, op. 8, D major. DOHNANYI: Serenade, op. 10, C major. Itzhak Perlman, vln; Pinchas Zukerman, vla; Lynn Harrell, vlc. Columbia M 35152 Tape (c) MT 35152 (also CBS 76832)

++ARG 2-80 p19   +MT 6-80 p382
++FF 3/4-80 p59   +RR 3-80 p68
+Gr 2-80 p1281   +St 2-80 p124
++HFN 2-80 p87   +ST 7-80 p195

Variations, C minor (32). See no. 619. See no. 3944

Variations, op. 76, D major. See no. 619

Variations, opp. 105 and 107. See no. 621

Variations, op. 105, no. 1, G major. See no. 623

618 Variations and fugue, op. 34, F major (6). MENDELSSOHN: Variations serieuses, op. 54, D minor. MOZART: Variations on "Unser Dummer Pobel", K 455 (10). HAYDN: Variations, F minor. Lydia Artymiw, pno. Chandos ABR 1013 Tape (c) ABT 1013

+Gr 10-80 p548 tape   +HFN 9-80 p113
+Gr 9-80 p380   +HFN 10-80 p117 tape
+STL 9-14-80 p40

619 Variations and fugue, op. 34, F major (6). Variations, op. 76, D
     major (6). Variations, C minor (32). Variations and fugue, op.
     35, E flat major (15). Rudolf Buchbinder, pno. Telefunken 6-
     42070 Tape (c) 4-42070
                    +FF 5/6-80 p53   ++HF 9-80 p86
     Variations and fugue, op. 34, F major. See no. 413
     Variations and fugue, op. 35, E flat major. See no. 619
     Variations on a Swiss air, F major (6). See no. 3819
     Variations on a theme by Diabelli, op. 120. See no. 498
620 Variations on a theme from Mozart's "The magic flute". BRAHMS:
     Concerto, violin and violoncello, op. 102, A minor. Alfred Cor-
     tot, Nicholas Mednikoff, pno; Jacques Thibaud, vln; Pablo Casals,
     vlc; Casals Orchestra; Alfred Cortot. Pearl GEMM 175
                    +-HFN 6-80 p103
     Variations on a theme from Mozart's "Die Zauberflote" (7). See no.
     3906
     Variations on Handel's "See the conquering hero comes" (12). See
     no. 622
     Variations on Mozart's "Bei Mannern welche Liebe fuhlen". See no.
     492. See no. 622
     Variations on Mozart's "Ein Madchen oder Weibchen". See no. 622
     Variations on Mozart's "La ci darem la mano", C major. See no. 493
621 Works, selections: Allegro and minuet, 2 flutes, G major. Serenade,
     op. 41, D major. Sonata, flute, B flat major. Trio, 3 flutes,
     G major. Trio, bassoon, flute and piano. Variations, op. 105
     and op. 107. Jean-Pierre Rampal, flt; Robert Veyron-Lacroix,
     pno; Christian Larde, flt; Alain Marion, flt; Paul Hongne, bsn.
     Everest 3468/3
                    +-ARG 7/8-80 p16   +-NR 3-80 p9
622 Works, selections: Sonata, horn and piano, op. 17, F major. Sonatas,
     violoncello and piano, nos. 1-5. Variations on Mozart's "Ein Mad-
     chen oder Weibchen". Variations on "Mozart's "Bei Mannern welche
     Liebe fuhlen". Variations on Handel's "See the conquering hero
     comes". Miklos Perenyi, vlc; Dezso Ranki, pno. Hungaroton SLPX
     11928/30 (3)
                    +ARG 11-80 p20   +-FF 11/12-80 p74
623 Works, selections: Fantasia, op. 80, C minor: Finale. Die Geschopfe
     des Prometheus, op. 43: Finale. Mass, op. 123, D major: Gloria,
     excerpt. Quartet, strings, no. 8, op. 59, no. 2, E minor: Finale.
     Quintet, piano, op. 16, E flat major: Finale. Sonata, piano, no.
     14, op. 27, no. 2, C sharp minor: Adagio sostenuto. Sonata,
     piano, no. 21, op. 53, C major: 1st movement, excerpt. Symphony,
     no. 3, op. 55, E flat major: Allegro con brio, excerpt. Trio,
     piano, no. 6, op. 97, B flat major: Allegro moderato, excerpt.
     Variations, op. 105, no. 1, G major. Various soloists and orch-
     estras. Turnabout TV 34803
                    +NR 2-80 p4
     Zapfenstreichen, no. 2, C major. See no. 4029
BELCHER, Supply
     Carol. See no. 3849
BELL'HAVER, Vincenzo
     Toccata del 1 tuono. See no. 3813
BELLINI, Vicenzo
     I Capuleti ed i Montecchi: Se Romeo t'uccise. See no. 3770
624 Concerto, oboe, E flat major. HUMMEL: Introduction, theme and

variations, op. 102, F major/minor. MENDELSSOHN (arr. Angerer): Songs without words, op. 30, no. 1; op. 38, no. 2; op. 53, no. 4; op. 85, no. 3. SINIGAGLIA: Romanze, op. 3. Branimir Slokar, trom; Southwest German Chamber Orchestra; Paul Angerer. Claves D 906

> ++ARG 6-80 p53

625 Concerto, oboe, E flat major. CIMAROSA: Concerto, oboe, C major. DONIZETTI: Concertino, cor anglais, G major. SALIERI: Concerto, flute and oboe, C major. Heinz Holliger, ob, cor anglais; Aurele Nicolet, flt; Bamberg Symphony Orchestra; Peter Maag. DG 2535 417 Tape (c) 3335 417 (From SLPM 139152)

> ++Gr 12-80 p842   +-HFN 12-80 p159 tape
> ++HFN 12-80 p153

626 Norma. Renata Scotto, s; Tatiana Troyanos, Ann Murray, ms; Giuseppe Giacomini, Paul Crook, t; Paul Plishka, bs; Ambrosian Opera Chorus; National Philharmonic Orchestra; James Levine. Columbia M3 35902 (3) (also CBS 79327 Tape (c) 40-79327)

> +-ARG 10-80 p10   +OC Summer 1980 p47
> +-FF 7/8-80 p61   +ON 5-80 p44
> +-Gr 7-80 p161   +-Op 9-80 p910
> +-HF 7-80 p64   +RR 7-80 p42
> +-HFN 7-80 p106   +St 7-80 p76
> +NYT 3-23-80 pD25

627 Norma. Maria Callas, Edda Vincenzi, s; Christa Ludwig, ms; Franco Corelli, Piero de Palma, t; Nicola Zaccaria, bs; La Scala Orchestra and Chorus; Tullio Serafin. HMV SLS 5186 Tape (c) TC SLS 5186 (From Columbia SAX 2412/4)

> +-Gr 6-80 p60   +-Op 9-80 p910
> +HFN 6-80 p119   ++RR 6-80 p34

Norma: Al del tebro. See no. 3899
Norma: Casta diva; Ah bello a me ritorna. See no. 3770
Norma: Ite sul colle. See no. 3368. See no. 3930
Norma: Keusche Gottin. See no. 3774
Norma: Mira Norma. See no. 3792

628 Norma: Sediziose voci...Casta diva...Ah bello a me. PONCHIELLI: La gioconda: Suicidio. VERDI: Macbeth: Nel di della vittoria... Ambizioso spirto...Veni t'affretta...Or tutti sorgete; La luce langue. La traviata: E strano...Ah fors' e lui che l'anima... Sempre libera. Il trovatore: Vanne; Lasciami...D'amor sull'ali rosee. Sylvia Sass, s; Ambrosian Singers; National Philharmonic Orchestra; Lamberto Gardelli. Decca SXL 6921 Tape (c) KSXC 6921 (also London OS 26609)

> +-ARG 7/8-80 p47   +-ON 2-25-80 p45
> +-FF 5/6-80 p175   +-Op 6-79 p575
> +-Gr 4-79 p1768   +RR 4-79 p48
> +HFN 4-79 p129   +St 4-80 p142

Norma: Sediziose voci...Casta diva...Ah bello a me ritorna. See no. 3948

629 Il pirata: Oh s'io potessi; Col sorriso d'innocenza. DONIZETTI: Anna Bolena: Piangete voi; Al dolce guidami castel natio. THOMAS: Hamlet: A vox jeux; Partagez-vous mes fleurs; Et maintenant ecoutez ma chanson. Maria Callas, s; Monica Sinclair, con; John Lanigan, t; Joseph Rouleau, bs; Duncan Robertson, t; PhO; Nicola Rescigno. HMV ASD 3801 Tape (c) TC ASD 3801 (From Columbia SAX 2320)

+Gr 11-79 p912   +Op 3-80 p271
+HFN 11-79 p155   ++RR 11-79 p48
+-HFN 2-80 p107 tape

630 I puritani. Montserrat Caballe, s; Julia Hamari, ms; Alfredo Kraus,
     t; Matteo Manuguerra, bar; PhO; Riccardo Muti. Angel SZCX 3881
               +SFC 12-7-80 p33
     I puritani: A te o cara. See no. 3672
     I puritani: A te o cara; Ah viene al tempio; Qui la voce. See no.
     3770
     I puritani: Cinta di fiori. See no. 3899
     I puritani: Viene fra queste braccia. See no. 3774
     Sonata, organ. See no. 3762
     Songs: Almen se non poss'io; Malinconia ninfa gentile; Vaga luna
     che inargenti. See no. 3596
     Songs: Fenesta che lucive. See no. 3771
631 Songs: Il fervido desiderio; Vaga luna. MONTEVERDI: Ahi troppo
     duro; Quel sguardo sdegnosetto. PIZZETTI: Levommi il mio pen-
     sier; Donna Lombarda; La pesca dell'anello; La prigioniera; Quel
     rosignuol. ROSSINI: La gita in gondola; La promessa; Il rimpro-
     vero. Anna Gabrieli, s; Piotr Wolny, pno. Orion ORS 78307
               -NR 2-79 p11   +-ON 1-23-80 p45
     La sonnambula: A te diletta...Come per me sereno...Sovra il sen la
     man mi posa. See no. 3774
     La sonnambula: Ah non credea; Ah perche non posso odiarti; Vi
     ravviso. See no. 3770
     La sonnambula: Ah perche non posso odiarti; Prendi l'anel ti dono;
     Son geloso. See no. 3981
     La sonnambula: Prendi l'anel ti dono. See no. 3977
632 Les Troyens: Les Grecs ont disparu; Que la deesse nous protege; Non
     je ne verrai pas; Du roi des dieux; Royal hunt and storm; Pardon-
     ne lopas; Tout n'est que paix et charme autour de nous; Vallon
     sonore inutiles regrets; Ah ah je vais mourir; Adieu fiere cite.
     Berit Lindholm, s; Josephine Veasey, Anne Howells, Elizabeth
     Bainbridge, ms; Heather Begg, con; Jon Vickers, Ryland Davies,
     Ian Partridge, David Lennox, t; Peter Glossop, Roger Soyer,
     Anthony Raffell, Pierre Thau, Raimund Herincx, Dennis Wicks, bs;
     ROHO and Chorus; Colin Davis. Philips 6570 098 (From 6500 161)
               +Gr 6-80 p60
BELSAYAGA, Cristobal
     Magnificat. See no. 3707
BEMBERG, Herman
     Nymphes et Silvains. See no. 3774
     Songs: Les anges pleurent; Chant venitien; Chanson des baisers. See
     no. 3770
BENATZKY, Ralph
     Ich muss wieder einmal. See no. 3738
633 White Horse Inn. Ingeborg Hallstein, s; Erika Koth, s; Rudolf
     Schock, t; Gunther Philipp, pno; Bavarian Radio Chorus; Munich
     Radio Orchestra; Johannes Fehring. Eurodisc 80838 (2)
               +-ARG 10-80 p38   +NYT 8-31-80 pD14
634 White Horse Inn. Anneliese Rothenberger, Grit van Juten, Elke
     Schary, s; Peter Minich, Norbert Orth, Peter Kraus, t; Munich
     Children's Choir; Bavarian Radio Chorus; Munich Radio Orchestra;
     Gunther Salber, vln; Peter Dosch, zither; George Schwenk, acc;
     Willy Mattes. HMV SQ SLS 5184 (2) Tape (c) TC SLS 5184 (also
     Angel SZBX 3897, EMI 1C 157-45414/5)

+—ARG 10-80 p38   +HFN 6-80 p119 tape
+—FF 7/8-80 p63   +NR 5-80 p11
+Gr 11-79 p922   +NYT 7-13-80 pD20
+—HF 7-80 p64   +RR 11-79 p46
+HFN 1-80 p102   ++St 7-80 p77

BENDA, Frantisek
635 Concerto, flute, E minor. RICHTER: Concerto, flute, D major. Jean-
       Pierre Rampal, flt; Viktorie Svihlikova, hpd; PCO; Milan Munclin-
       ger. Quintessence PMC 7140
                +FF 5/6-80 p138   +SFC 2-17-80 p44
BENDA, Jiri (Georg)
     Sonatina, flute and harpsichord, D major. See no. 90
BENEDICT, Julius
     Il carnevale di Venezi. See no. 3559
BENJAMIN, Arthur
     Concerto, harmonica. See no. 52
     Fanfare for a festive occasion. See no. 3959
     Fanfares: For a state occasion; For a brilliant occasion; For a gala
       occasion. See no. 3959
     An ideal husband. See no. 3786
BENNET, John
     All creatures now are merry-minded. See no. 3995
     Eliza her name gives honor. See no. 3995
     Weep O mine eyes. See no. 3893
BENNETT, Richard Rodney
     Alba. See no. 4048
636 Aubade. Spells. Jane Manning, s; Bach Choir; PhO; David Willcocks,
       David Atherton. Argo ZRG 907
                +Gr 1-80 p1182   +MT 4-80 p248
                ++HFN 1-80 p102
637 Impromptus (5). MOREL: Me duele Espana. WALTON: Bagatelles (5).
       Michael Lauke, gtr. Radio Canada International RCI 457
                +MUM 10-80 p36
     Lady Caroline lamb, theme. See no. 3786
638 Madrigals. FAURE: Madrigal. HINDEMITH: La belle dame sans merci.
       Chansons (6). ROUSSEL: Poemes de Ronsard. Gregg Smith Singers;
       Gregg Smith. Grenadilla GS 1034
                +—FF 1/2-80 p164   -NR 10-79 p8
     Spells. See no. 636
     Yanks, theme. See no. 3786
BERBERIAN
     Prelude. See no. 3850
BERCHEM, Jachet de
     O vos omnes. See no. 3763
BERG, Alban
     Arias: Der Wein. See no. 645
639 Chamber concerto: Adagio. DEBUSSY: Prelude a l'apres-midi d'un
       faune. SCHOENBERG: Chamber symphony, no. 1, op. 9, E major.
       Boston Symphony Chamber Players. DG 2531 213 Tape (c) 3301 213
                +FF 9/10-80 p197   +NR 5-80 p4
                +—Gr 5-80 p1652   +NYT 10-19 pD24
                ++HF 10-80 p74   +RR 4-80 p78
                +—HFN 3-80 p103   ++St 10-80 p120
640 Concerto, violin. STRAVINSKY: Concerto, violin, D major. Itzhak
       Perlman, vln; BSO; Seiji Ozawa. DG 2531 110 Tape (c) 3301 110

++FF 9/10-80 p78   ++NR 5-80 p4
++Gr 3-80 p1385   ++NYT 7-6-80 pD15
++Gr 5-80 p1717 tape   ++RR 3-80 p47
++HF 7-80 p60   ++SFC 4-6-80 p31
+HFN 3-80 p87   ++St 7-80 p82
+HFN 8-80 p109 tape   ++ST 9-80 p340
+MT 10-80 p633   ++STL 3-9-80 p41
+MUM 10-80 p32

641 Concerto, violin. Pieces, orchestra, op. 6. Ulf Hoelscher, vln;
     Cologne Radio Orchestra; Hiroshi Wakasugi. Harmonia Mundi 1C
     065 99848
               +-Gr 10-80 p494   +-FF 9/10-80 p79

642 Concerto, violin. Pieces, orchestra, op. 6 (3). Arthur Grumiaux,
     vln; COA, LSO; Igor Markevitch, Antal Dorati. Philips 6539 061
     (From SAL 3650, 3539)
               +-Gr 10-80 p494

643 Lulu. Anja Silja, s; Trudeliese Schmidt, ms; Brigitte Fassbaender,
     con; Horst Laubenthal, Josef Hopferwieser, Werner Krenn, t; Hans
     Hotter, bar; Harald Proglhof, Walter Berry, Kurt Moll, Manfred
     Schenck, Alfred Sramek, bs; VPO; Christoph von Dohnanyi. Decca
     D48D3 (3) Tape (c) K48K32 (also London OSA 13120 Tape (c) OSA 5-
     13120)
               +-ARG 10-79 p6   +NR 4-80 p11
               +-FF 9/10-79 p51   +ON 12-1-79 p44
               +Gr 12-78 p1162   ++Op 3-79 p252
               +Gr 5-79 p1940 tape   +-RR 12-78 p42
               +HF 8-79 p84   +RR 11-79 p126 tape
               +HFN 12-78 p149   ++SFC 7-8-79 p43
               +MT 3-79 p224   +St 10-79 p131

644 Lulu. Teresa Stratas, s; Yvonne Minton, Hanna Schwarz, ms; Robert
     Tear, Kenneth Riegel, Helmut Pampuch, t; Toni Blankenheim, Franz
     Mazura, bar; Gerd Nienstedt, Jules Bastin, bs; Paris Opera Orch-
     estra; Pierre Boulez. DG 2740 213 Tape (c) 3378 086 (also DG
     2711 024 Tape (c) 3378 086)
               +FF 1/2-80 p56   +ON 3-8-80 p29
               +Gr 10-79 p694   +ON 2-80 p10
               +Gr 3-80 p1446 tape   +Op 2-80 p163
               ++HF 3-80 p69   ++RR 11-79 p36
               ++HFN 1-80 p102   +RR 6-80 p94 tape
               ++MT 7-80 p444   ++SFC 12-16-79 p60
               ++NYT 12-16-79 pD21   ++St 3-80 p104
               +OC Summer 1980 p46   +STL 12-2-79 p37

645 Lulu: Suite. Arias: Der Wein. Judith Blegen, Jessye Norman, s;
     NYP; Pierre Boulez. CBS 76575 (also CBS M 35849)
               +FF 11/12-80 p79   +RR 9-79 p69
               +Gr 8-79 p327   ++SFC 8-10-80 p29
               +HFN 8-79 p101

646 Lyric suite. SCHOENBERG: Verklarte Nacht, op. 4. Ramor Quartet;
     Edith Lorincz, vln; Zsolt Deakey, vlc. Turnabout TVC 37012 Tape
     (c) CT 70012
               +-FF 9/10-80 p80

647 Lyric suite: 3 movements. SCHOENBERG: Verklarte Nacht, op. 4. NYP;
     Pierre Boulez. CBS 76305 Tape (c) 40-76305 (also Columbia M
     35166 Tape (c) MT 35166
               -ARG 3-80 p36   +NR 12-79 p4

BERG (cont.)   88

+-FF 1/2-80 p142   +RR 8-77 p62
                         +-Gr 9-77 p423   +RR 11-77 p121
                         ++HFN 9-77 p137   ++SFC 12-16-79 p60
                         +HFN 10-77 p169 tape   -St 2-80 p132
    Pieces, orchestra, op. 6. See no. 641. See no. 642
    Sonata, piano, op. 1. See no. 384
648 Songs: Fruhe Lieder (7). SEGERSTAM: Songs of experience. Taru
    Valjakka, s; Austrian Radio Orchestra; Leif Segerstam. BIS LP
    83
                         +ARG 2-80 p20   +NR 10-79 p10
                        ++FF 5/6-80 p54   +RR 4-80 p107
                         +HFN 3-80 p86
649 Wozzeck. Isabel Strauss, s; Ingeborg Lasser, con; Albert Weiken-
    mèier, Fritz Uhl, Richard Van Vrooman, Gerard Dunan, t; Karl
    Donch, Raymond Steffner, bar; Walter Berry, Walter Poduschka, bs;
    Paris Opera Orchestra and Chorus; Pierre Boulez. CBS 79251 (2)
    (From 72509/11)
                         +Gr 9-80 p386   +Op 10-80 p1016
                        ++HFN 10-80 p115
BERG, Josef
650 Eufrides in front of the gates of Tymenas. GIDEON: Seasons of time.
    HUNDLEY: Ballad on Queen Anne's death; Some sheep are loving;
    Spring; Wild plum. RIETI: Poemes de Max Jacob (4). Paul Sperry,
    t; Gerard Schwarz, tpt; Thomas Muraco, pno; Mise en Scene and
    electronic effects by Michael Lobel. Serenus SRS 12078
                         +ARG 11-79 p56   +NYT 9-16-79 pD24
                        ++FF 9/10-80 p241
BERGER, Theodor
    Legend of Prince Eugen. See no. 3898
    Rondino giocoso, op. 4. See no. 3710
BERGMANN, Erik
651 Aubade, op. 48. SIBELIUS: Finlandia, op. 26. Legends, op. 22:
    Lemminkainen and the maidens of Saari. Helsinki Philharmonic
    Orchestra; Jorma Panula. Finlandia FA 314
                         -FF 11/12-80 p175
BERIO, Luciano
652 Allelujah II. Concerto, 2 pianos. Nones. Bruno Canino, Antonio
    Ballista, pno; LSO, BBC Symphony Orchestra; Pierre Boulez, Luci-
    ano Berio. RCA ARL 1-1674
                         +ARG 4-77 p14   ++MM 1-79 p30
                        ++FF 3/4-80 p61   +MT 12-77 p1014
                         +Gr 8-77 p292   ++NR 3-77 p7
                        ++Gr 3-78 p1539   +-RR 9-77 p57
                         +HF 6-78 p88   ++SFC 12-19-76 p50
                         +HFN 10-77 p152   +-St 4-80 p126
                         -MJ 10-77 p29   ++Te 12-77 p34
653 Chamber music, female voice, clarinet, violoncello and harp. Dif-
    ferences, 5 instruments and tape. Pieces, violin and piano (2).
    Sequenza III and VII. Cathy Berberian, voice; Heinz Holliger,
    ob; Juilliard Ensemble Members; Luciano Berio. Philips 6500 631
                         +Gr 7-80 p157   ++RR 7-80 p70
                         +HFN 7-80 p117
    Concerto, 2 pianos. See no. 652
654 Coro. Cologne Radio Orchestra and Choir; Luciano Berio. DG 2531
    270

              +Gr 9-80 p380   +STL 8-10-80 p30
              ++HFN 11-80 p116
      Differences, 5 instruments and magnetic tape. See no. 653
655   Laborintus II. Christiane Legrand, Janette Baucomont, s; Claudine
      Meunier, con; Eduardo Sanguinetti, speaker; Musique Vivante En-
      semble; Lucian Berio. RCA LSC 3267 (also Harmonia Mundi HM 764)
              +ARG 10-72 p698   -NR 7-72 p12
              +FF 3/4-80 p61   *NR 8-80 p2
              +FF 7/8-80 p63   ++RR 4-80 p107
              +-HF 8-72 p64   ++SFC 5-14-72 p42
              +HFN 3-80 p107   +-SR 5-20-72 p49
              -MQ 7-73 p488   +-St 10-72 p120
      Nones. See no. 652
      Pieces, violin and piano. See no. 653
      Sequenza I. See no. 4017
      Sequenza III. See no. 653
      Sequenza VII. See no. 653
656   Surabaya Johnny (Weill). BOULEZ: Eclat. CRUMB: Night music I.
      DLUGOSZEWSKI: Fire fragile flight. Orchestra of Our Time; Joel
      Thome. Candide CE 31113
              +ARG 1-80 p52   ++NYT 9-16-79 pD24
              +-FF 11/12-79 p58   ++SFC 12-21-79 p57
              +HF 10-79 p124
BERIOT, Charles de
      Prendi per me sei libero. See no. 3770
657   Scene de ballet, op. 100. RESPIGHI: Concerto gregoriano. Kurt
      Stiehler, Carl Taschke, vln; Leipzig Radio Orchestra, Leipzig
      Philharmonic Orchestra; Ernst Borsamsky, Herbert Kegel. Varese
      VC 81090 (From Urania URLP 7100, 7166)
              +-FF 11/12-79 p116   +SFC 5-25-80 p41
              +-HF 11-79 p108   +-St 2-80 p130
BERKELEY
      Poems of St. Teresa of Avila. See no. 3562
BERKELEY, Lennox
658   Antiphon. BERKELEY, M.: Meditations. IRELAND: Concertino pastor-
      ale. Westminster Cathedral String Orchestra; Colin Mawby. Uni-
      corn UNS 260
              +FF 9/10-80 p138   +-RR 4-80 p65
              +Gr 3-80 p1385   +St 11-80 p90
              +HFN 3-80 p104
659   Fantasia, op. 92. BOELLMAN: Suite gothique, op. 25: Toccata.
      FRANCK: Cantabile. Choral, no. 3, A minor. Piece heroique.
      KARG-ELERT: Harmonies du soir. Lynne Davis, Arnold Mahon, org.
      Michael Woodward MW 916
              ++Gr 12-80 p859   +MU 6-79 p10
              +HFN 9-79 p121
BERKELEY, Michael
      Meditations. See no. 658
BERLIN, Irving
      White Christmas. See no. 3933
BERLINSKY, Herman
      Psalm, no. 23. See no. 3892
      Sing joyfully, psalm, no. 81. See no. 3922
BERLIOZ, Hector
      Beatrice et Benedict: Overture. See no. 692. See no. 3556

660 Benevenuto Cellini, op. 23: A boire a boire...; Une heure encore; La
    gloire etait ma seule idole; Teresa Cellini; Un meurtre avec en-
    levement; Seul pour lutter; Sur les monts les plus sauvages;
    Teresa Teresa ici; Du metal du metal. Christiane Eda-Pierre,
    Jane Berbie, s; Nicolai Gedda, Derek Blackwell, t; Robert Massard,
    Roger Soyer, bar; Jules Bastin, Robert Lloyd, bs; ROHO Chorus;
    BBC Symphony Orchestra; Colin Davis. Philips 6570 094 Tape (c)
    7310 094 (From 6707 019)
                +Gr 6-80 p60   +HFN 9-80 p115 tape
                +HFN 7-80 p117   +RR 7-80 p42
661 Benvenuto Cellini, op. 23: Overture. Le Corsaire, op. 21. LISZT:
    Tasso, lamento e triunfo, G 96. WEBER: Turandot: Overture. MRSO:
    Gennady Rozhdestvensky. HMV ASD 3714
                +Gr 8-79 p327   +-MT 2-80 p106
                +HFN 8-79 p119   ++RR 8-79 p83
    Benvenuto Cellini, op. 23: Overture. See no. 3556
662 Le carnival romain, op. 9. TCHAIKOVSKY: Romeo and Juliet: Fantasy
    overture. VERDI: La forza del destino: Overture. Halle Orches-
    tra, NPhO; John Barbirolli. Barbirolli Society SJB 103
                +HFN 1-80 p115   +RR 2-80 p62
    Le carnival romain, op. 9. See no. 692. See no. 3556. See no.
    3581. See no. 3621. See no. 3666. See no. 4072
    Le Corsaire, op. 21. See no. 3556
    Le Corsaire, op. 21: Overture. See no. 661. See no. 692
663 La damnation de Faust, op. 24. Yvonne Minton, ms; Placido Domingo,
    t; Dietrich Fischer-Dieskau, bar; Jules Bastin, bs; Orchestre de
    Paris and Chorus; Daniel Barenboim. DG 2709 087 (3)
                +ARG 1-80 p21   +-ON 3-15-80 p45
                +-FF 1/2-80 p63   +-RR 9-79 p114
                +Gr 9-79 p488   +-SFC 9-23-79 p37
                +HFN 10-79 p149   ++St 2-80 p120
                +-MM 10-79 p38
    La damnation de Faust, op. 24: Autrefois un Roi de Thule; D'amour
    l'ardente flamme. See no. 3630
    La damnation de Faust, op. 24: D'amour l'ardente flamme. See no.
    3632
    La damnation de Faust, op. 24: Hungarian march, Dance of the sylphs,
    Minuet of the will-o-the-wisps. See no. 4069
    La damnation de Faust, op. 24: Maintenant chantons a cette belle...
    Devant la maison. See no. 3770
    La damnation de Faust, op. 24: Marche hongroise, Ballet de slyphes,
    Menuet de follets. See no. 3556
664 La damnation de Faust, op. 24: Minuet of the will-o-the-wisps;
    Dance of the sylphs; Rakoczy march. SCHUBERT: Rosamunde, op. 26,
    D 797: Overture. STRAUSS, R.: Don Juan, op. 20. WAGNER: Die
    Meistersinger von Nurnberg: Prelude. COA; Willem Mengelberg.
    Past Masters PM 27 (From Telefunken 78s)
                +FF 7/8-80 p192
665 La damnation de Faust, op. 24: Rakoczy march. BIZET: L'Arlesienne:
    Suite, no. 2. CHABRIER: Espana. GOUNOD: Faust: Ballet music.
    BPhO; Herbert von Karajan. HMV ASD 3761 Tape (c) TC ASD 3761
                ++Gr 9-80 p352   ++HFN 11-80 p127
666 La damnation de Faust, op. 24: Rakoczy march. BIZET: Carmen: Pre-
    lude. BRAHMS: Hungarian dance, no. 5, G minor. GINASTERA:
    Panambi suite. PH; Zoltan Rozsnyai. M & K RT 203

+–ARG 5-80 p45   +HF 5-80 p70
+–FF 9/10-80 p42
667 La damnation de Faust, op. 24: Rakoczy march. ROSSINI: Il barbiere
    di Siviglia: Overture. La gazza ladra: Overture. Guillaume Tell:
    Overture. PH; Zoltan Rozsnyai. M & K RT 204, DBS PS 1005
                    -HF 11-80 p86
    La damnation de Faust, op. 24: Rakoczy march. See no. 3709. See
    no. 3897. See no. 3962. See no. 3969
    La damnation de Faust, op. 24: Serenade. See no. 3979. See no.
    3982
    La damnation de Faust, op. 24: Song of the flea; La Valanga che
    volge. See no. 3771
    La damnation de Faust, op. 24: Su queste rose. See no. 3980
    L'Enfance du Christ, op. 25: O misere des rois. See no. 3631
    L'Enfance du Christ, op. 25: Trio des jeunes. See no. 3556
    Hamlet, op. 18: Funeral march. See no. 692
668 Harold in Italy, op. 16 (trans. Liszt). Aldo Bennici, vla; Daniel
    Rivera, pno. Dischi Ricordi RCL 27054
                    +–Gr 11-80 p691   +HFN 12-80 p133
669 Harold in Italy, op. 16. Yehudi Menuhin, vla; PhO; Colin Davis.
    HMV SXLP 30314 Tape (c) TC SXLP 30314 (From ASD 537)
                    ++Gr 1-80 p1141   +RR 1-80 p66
                    +HFN 1-80 p119   +RR 7-80 p97 tape
                    +HFN 4-80 p121 tape
    Herminie. See no. 671
    King Lear, op. 4. See no. 3585
670 La mort de Cleopatre. ELGAR: Sea pictures, op. 37. Yvonne Minton,
    s; BBC Symphony Orchestra, LPO; Pierre Boulez, Daniel Barenboim.
    CBS 61891 Tape (c) 40-61891 (From 76576, 76579)
                    ++Gr 8-80 p247   +–HFN 10-80 p117 tape
                    +–HFN 8-80 p107   +RR 8-80 p78
671 La mort de Cleopatre. Herminie. Janet Baker, ms; LSO; Colin Davis.
    Philips 9500 683 Tape (c) 7300 778
                    +FF 11/12-80 p78   ++NR 7-80 p11
                    ++Gr 8-80 p247   +NYT 6-15-80 pD29
                    +–HF 9-80 p86   +RR 8-80 p77
                    +HFN 7-80 p106   ++SFC 6-8-80 p36
                    +HFN 9-80 p115 tape   +–St 11-80 p80
                    +MUM 11/12-80 p32   +STL 6-8-80 p38
672 Requiem, op. 5. Kenneth Riegel, t; CO and Chorus; Lorin Maazel.
    Decca D137D2 (2) Tape (c) K137K22 (also London OSA 12115 Tape
    (c) OSA 5-12115)
                    -ARG 6-80 p16   +–HFN 11-79 p157 tape
                    -FF 3/4-80 p62   +–MT 5-80 p321
                    +–Gr 10-79 p686   +NR 4-80 p9
                    +Gr 12-79 p727 tape   +NYT 11-18-79 pD24
                    +–HF 1-80 p74   +RR 10-79 p134
                    +HFN 10-79 p149
    Reverie et caprice, op. 8. See no. 4009
673 Romeo et Juliette, op. 17. Yvonne Minton, ms; Francisco Araiza, t;
    Jules Bastin, bs; Orchestre de Paris and Chorus; Daniel Baren-
    boim. DG 2707 115 (2) Tape (c) 3370 036
                    +–Gr 11-80 p717   +NYT 12-14-80 pD38
                    +HFN 11-80 p116
674 Romeo and Juliet, op. 17, excerpts. PROKOFIEV: Romeo and Juliet,

op. 64, excerpts. TCHAIKOVSKY: Romeo and Juliet, excerpts. San
Francisco Symphony Orchestra; Seiji Ozawa. DG 2535 422
+-HFN 12-80 p153

675 Romeo and Juliet, op. 17: Love scene. PROKOFIEV: Romeo and Juliet:
Ballet suites, excerpts. TCHAIKOVSKY: Romeo and Juliet: Fantasy
overture. San Francisco Symphony Orchestra; Seiji Ozawa. DG
2530 308 Tape (c) 3300 284, 3335 422

+Gr 5-73 p2058	/HFN 6-73 p1189 tape
-HF 7-73 p98	++NR 5-73 p2
+-HFN 5-73 p995	+-RR 5-73 p68
+HFN 11-80 p131	+St 7-73 p112

Romeo et Juliet, op. 17: Premiers transports. See no. 3630
Romeo et Juliet, op. 17: Queen Mab scherzo. See no. 3556
Romeo et Juliet, op. 17: Romeo alone and celebration at the Capulets.
See no. 692

676 Symphonie fantastique, op. 14. NYP; Leonard Bernstein. CBS 61910
Tape (c) 40-61910 (also Columbia M 31843 Tape (c) MT 31843)

+-HFN 4-80 p103	+RR 5-80 p106 tape
+HFN 8-80 p109 tape	+RR 5-80 p54

677 Symphonie fantastique, op. 14 (trans. Liszt). Bruno Mezzena, pno.
CBS 76861

+Gr 10-80 p517	/-HFN 10-80 p102

678 Symphonie fantastique, op. 14. NYP; Zubin Mehta. Decca SXDL 7512
Tape (c) KSXDC 7512 (also London LDR 10013)

+Gr 6-80 p32	+RR 6-80 p42
+-Gr 12-80 p889 tape	+SFC 6-22-80 p36
++HF 8-80 p66	+-St 11-80 p80
++HFN 6-80 p103	

679 Symphonie fantastique, op. 14. Orchestre de Paris; Daniel Barenboim.
DG 2531 092 Tape (c) 3301 092

+ARG 1-80 p21	+HFN 7-79 p101
+-FF 1/2-80 p66	+-MM 11-79 p38
+-FU 4-80 p45	+-NYT 3-2-80 pD26
+-Gr 6-79 p41	+-RR 7-79 p49
+-HF 11-79 p85	

680 Symphonie fantastique, op. 14. BPhO; Herbert von Karajan. DG 2535
256 Tape (c) 3335 256 (From SLPM 138964)

+FF 11/12-80 p81	+HFN 6-78 p133
+Gr 5-78 p1852	+MUM 7/8-79 p34
-Gr 9-78 p564 tape	+-RR 6-78 p48

681 Symphonie fantastique, op. 14 (trans. Liszt). Francois Duchable,
pno. EMI 2C 069 73004
+HFN 12-80 p133

682 Symphonie fantastique, op. 14. PhO; Ling Tung. Enigma K 53593

-Gr 1-80 p1141	+-RR 1-80 p66
+-HFN 1-80 p103	

683 Symphonie fantastique, op. 14 (trans. Liszt). Idil Biret, pno.
Finnadar SR 9023

+ARG 7-79 p22	+-NR 7-79 p14
+-FF 11/12-80 p80	+-NYT 10-19-80 pD24
++Gr 8-79 p352	+-SFC 4-15-79 p41
+MJ 11/12-79 p49	+St 10-79 p134

684 Symphonie fantastique, op. 14. LSO; Andre Previn. HMV ASD 3496
Tape (c) TC ASD 3496 (also Angel S 37485)

+ARG 1-80 p21	+HFN 2-79 p101

```
              +FF 11/12-79 p44           +HFN 4-79 p133 tape
              +-Gr 2-79 p1414            +RR 3-79 p62
              +-HF 11-79 p85             +-RR 9-79 p135 tape
```

685 Symphonie fantastique, op. 14. French National Radio Orchestra;
    Thomas Beecham. HMV SXLP 30295 Tape (c) TC SXLP 30295 (From ASD
    399)

```
              +ARSC Vol 12, no. 3,       +HFN 11-79 p153
                 1980 p253               +HFN 1-80 p123 tape
              ++Gr 11-79 p809            ++RR 11-79 p71
```

686 Symphonie fantastique, op. 14. NYP; Zubin Mehta. London LDR 10013

```
              +-FF 9/10-80 p81           ++HFN 6-80 p103
              +Gr 6-80 p32               +RR 6-80 p42
              +-Gr 12-80 p889 tape       +SFC 6-22-80 p36
              ++HF 8-80 p66              +-St 11-80 p80
```

687 Symphonie fantastique, op. 14. COA; Colin Davis. Philips 6500 774
    Tape (c) 7300 313 (r) G 6500 774

```
              +-Gr 3-75 p1647            +RR 3-75 p23
              +-HF 5-75 p73              +-RR 3-75 p73 tape
              +HF 9-75 p116 tape         +SFC 12-29-74 p20
              +HF 11-80 p88 tape         +St 7-75 p94
              ++NR 2-75 p1
```

688 Symphonie fantastique, op. 14. LSO; Colin Davis. Philips 6570 031
    Tape (c) 7310 031 (From Philips 6580 127, SAL 3441)

```
              +HFN 6-80 p115            +RR 6-80 p42
              +HFN 9-80 p115 tape
```

Symphonie fantastique, op. 14. See no. 3557

689 Symphonie funebre et triomphale, op. 15. Musique des Gardiens de
    la Paix; Desire Dondeyne. Calliope CAL 1859 Tape (c) CAL 4859
    (also Nonesuch H 71368)

```
              +FF 1/2-80 p64            ++RR 2-77 p43
              +Gr 3-77 p1392            ++SFC 9-23-79 p37
              +-HFN 2-77 p113           ++St 12-79 p136
              ++NR 12-79 p15
```

690 Symphonie funebre et triomphale, op. 15. Musique des Gardiens de
    la Paix; Desire Dondeyne. Erato STU 70493 (Feom Westminster WST
    14066, Musical Heritage Society MHS 1276)

```
              +ARG 3-80 p18             +-HFN 12-80 p153
              -FF 11/12-79 p45
```

Les Troyens: Chasse royale et orage. See no. 3556
Les Troyens: Chers Tyriens. See no. 3770

691 Les Troyens: Les grecs ont disparu; Que la deesse nous protege; Non
    je ne verrai pas; Du roi des dieux; Royal hunt and storm; Par-
    donne Iopas; Tout n'est que paix et charme autour de nous; Val-
    lon sonore; Inutiles regrets; Je vais mourir; Adieu fiere cite.
    Berit Lindholm, s; Heather Begg, Josephine Veasey, ms; Jon
    Vickers, t; Peter Glossop, Roger Soyer, bar; ROHO and Chorus;
    Colin Davis. Philips 6570 098 Tape (c) 7310 098

```
              +HFN 7-80 p117            +RR 7-80 p42
              +HFN 11-80 p131
```

Les Troyens: Royal hunt and storm. See no. 692

692 Works, selections: Beatrice et Benedict: Overture. Le carnival ro-
    main, op. 9. Le Corsaire, op. 21: Overture. Hamlet, op. 18:
    Funeral march (arr. Harty). Romeo et Juliette, op. 17: Romeo
    alone and celebration at the Capulets. Les Troyens: Royal hunt
    and storm. Halle Orchestra, LPO; Hamilton Harty. World Records
    SH 148 (From various Columbia 78s)

+FF 11/12-80 p80

BERMUDEZ, Pedro
    Domine ad adjuvandum me festina. See no. 3708
BERNARD DE VENTADORN
    Can l'erba; vida. See no. 3749
    Quqnd vei la lauzeta mover. See no. 3748
BERNARDI, Steffano
    O quam tu pulchra es. See no. 3546
BERNSTEIN, Charles Harold
693 Apologyana. Glory of Samothrace. In appreciation. Poem tones,
        violoncello and bassoon. Trilogy, flute. The woman speaks.
        Toby Saks, vlc; Arthur Grossman, bsn; Felix Skowronek, flt;
        Gary Gray, clt; Milton Thomas, vla; Soni Ventorum. Laurel LR 113
            +NR 11-80 p6
     Glory of Samothrace. See no. 693
     In appreication. See no. 693
     Poem tones, violoncello and bassoon. See no. 693
     Rhapsodic outline and drawings. See no. 694
     Trilogy, flute. See no. 693
694 Les trois Jonas. Rhapsodic outline and drawings. Charles Brennand,
        vlc. Laurel LR 108
            ++FF 11/12-79 p45   +-St 2-80 p121
            +-NR 4-79 p14
     The woman speaks. See no. 693
BERNSTEIN, Leonard
     Candide: Overture. See no. 3638. See no. 3797
695 Fancy free. CHAVEZ: Daughter of Colchis.* Ballet Theatre Orches-
        tra; National Symphony Orchestra of Mexico; Leonard Bernstein,
        Carlos Chavez. Varese VC 81000 (From Decca DL 6023, 7512)
            +HF 6-80 p73   ++NR 4-79 p4
     Fancy free. See no. 696
696 Serenade, violin, strings and percussion. Fancy free. Gidon Kremer,
        vln; Israel Philharmonic Orchestra; Leonard Bernstein. DG 2531
        196
            +FF 5/6-80 p55   +NR 8-80 p3
            +Gr 2-80 p1263   ++RR 2-80 p49
            ++HF 6-80 p73   +SFC 5-4-80 p42
            +HFN 2-80 p87   ++St 7-80 p67
697 Sonata, clarinet and piano. DELLA JOIO: Concertante, clarinet and
        piano. POLIN: Margo'a. Synaulia II. RUSSO: Studies, clarinet
        and piano (2). John Russo, clt; Lydia Walton Ignacio, pno; Lor-
        en Lind, flt. Orion ORS 79330
            +-ARG 7/8-80 p50   +NR 3-80 p7
            +-FF 11/12-80 p213
     West side story: Prologue. See no. 3643
BERRY, Wallace
698 Sonata, piano. SWIFT: Great praises. Summer notes. Anna Carol
        Dudley, s; Dady Mehta, Marvin Tartak, Paul Hersh, pno. CRI SD
        412
            +-ARG 6-80 p17   /+NR 5-80 p12
            +-FF 11/12-80 p193   +SFC 1-13-80 p41
BERWALD, Franz
     Concerto, piano, D major. See no. 38. See no. 703
     Concerto, violin, op. 2, C sharp minor. See no. 703
699 Duo, violin and piano, D major. NIELSEN: Sonata, violin and piano,
        no. 2, op. 35. Josef Grunfarb, vln; Greta Erikson, pno. Caprice

CAP 1053
+-Gr 5-80 p1677   +RR 5-80 p83
Estrella di Soria. See no. 703
Festival of the Bayaderes. See no. 703
Memories of the Norwegian Alps. See no. 703
Play of the elves. See no. 703
700 Quartet, strings, G minor. WIKMANSON: Quartet, strings, op. 1, no.
     2, E minor. Chilingirian Quartet. CRD CRD 1061
               +Gr 5-80 p1678   +MT 5-80 p321
               +HFN 3-80 p87   +RR 3-80 p71
     Queen of Golconda: Overture. See no. 703
     Racing. See no. 703
701 Septet, B flat major. HUMMEL: Septet, op. 74, D minor. Nash En-
     semble. CRD CRD 1044 Tape (c) CRDC 4044 (also Vanguard VSD 71260)
               +FF 3/4-80 p105   ++RR 8-78 p80
               ++Gr 8-78 p348   ++RR 1-79 p91 tape
               +HFN 8-78 p101   ++St 3-80 p96
               +HFN 9-78 p159 tape   +STL 7-9-78 p38
               ++NR 1-80 p5
     Serious and joyful fancies. See no. 703
702 Sinfonie singuliere. LIDHOLM: Ritornello. ROMAN: Symphony, E min-
     or. Swedish Radio Orchestra; Herbert Blomstedt. SR Records SRLP
     1339
               +FF 7/8-80 p64
     Symphonies, C major, G minor, D major, E flat major. See no. 703
703 Works, selections: Concerto, piano, D major. Concerto, violin, op.
     2, C sharp minor. Estrella di Soria. Festival of the Bayaderes.
     Memories of the Norwegian Alps. Play of the elves. Queen of
     Golconda: Overture. Racing. Serious and joyful fancies. Sym-
     phonies, C major, G minor, D major, E flat major. Marian Migdal,
     pno; Arve Tellefsen, vln; RPO; Ulf Bjorlin. Seraphim SID 6113 (4)
               +ARG 2-80 p24   +MUM 2-80 p32
               +FF 11/12-79 p46   +NYT 9-2-79 pD20
               +-FU 4-80 p45   +St 12-79 p140
               +HF 12-79 p88
BESARD, Jean
     Air de cour. See no. 3966
     Branle. See no. 3966
     Guillemette. See no. 3966
     Volte. See no. 3966
BESTOR, Charles
704 Sonata, piano. BREHM: Variations, piano. PLESKOW: Pentimento.
     WATTS: Sonata, piano. Dwight Peltzer, pno. Serenus SRS 12069
               +-ARG 2-78 p38   +HF 5-78 p114
               +FF 3/4-80 p184   +NR 12-77 p12
BEVILACQUA, Matteo
     Canzonette veneziane (3). See no. 3600
BIBER, Carl Heinrich
705 Battalia, D major. Sonata a 4, D minor. Sonata, no. 8, B flat
     major. Sonata a 6, B flat major. MUFFAT: Concerto, D minor.
     Suite, E major. VCM; Nikolaus Harnoncourt. DG 2547 004 Tape
     (c) 3347 004 (From SAPM 198362)
               +Gr 4-80 p1595   +HFN 6-80 p117
     Harmonia artificiosa ariosa, no. 1, D minor. See no. 3767
706 Serenade, C major. BOCCHERINI: Quintet, strings, op. 30, no. 6, C

C major. MOZART: Serenade, no. 13, K 525, G major. VIVALDI:
Concerto, op. 10, no. 2, G minor. James Galway, flt; Karl Ridderbusch, bs; Lucerne Festival Strings; Rudolf Baumgartner. Vanguard VSD 71266 (also RCA GL 2-5309 Tape (c) GK 2-5309. From LRL
1-5085)
        +-Audio 11-80 p86   +SFC 8-31-80 p31
        +Gr 11-80 p139   +St 12-80 p137
        +NR 9-80 p6
Sonata a 4, D minor. See no. 705

707 Sonata a 6, B flat major. HAYDN: Concerto, trumpet, E flat major.
HUMMEL: Concerto, trumpet, E flat major. Timofei Dokshitser, tpt;
Moscow Chamber Orchestra. Quintessence PMC 7135 (From Angel SR
40123)
        ++ARG 6-80 p52   +HF 1-80 p100
        ++FF 5/6-80 p88
Sonata a 6, B flat major. See no. 705
Sonata a 7. See no. 3569
Sonata, no. 8, B flat major. See no. 705
Sonata, trumpet, C major. See no. 3674
Sonata, solo violin, no. 6. See no. 3729

BIELAWA
Sweet was the song. See no. 3993

BIGELOW, Frederick
Our director. See no. 3617

BILIK, Jerry
708 Symphony, band. They walked in darkness. Joe Falkerson, narrator;
Tennessee Technological University Band; Jerry Bilik, Wayne Pegram. USC Sound Enterprises KM 3857
        +-FF 5/6-80 p55
They walked in darkness. See no. 708

BILLI
E canta il grillo. See no. 3770

BILLINGS, William
Songs: Bethlehem; Boston; Judea. See no. 3849
Songs: The bird; Thanksgiving anthem, O praise the Lord of heaven
(Psalm, no. 148). See no. 3848
Thus saith the Lord, the lofty one. See no. 3971

BINCHOIS, Gilles de
Je ne veis onques la pareille. See no. 3880

BINGHAM
Green isle of Erin. See no. 4070

BIRTWISTLE Harrison
709 Punch and Judy. Jan DeGaetani, ms; Phyllis Bryn-Julson, s; Stephen
Roberts, bs-bar; Philip Langridge, t; London Sinfonietta; David
Atherton. Decca HEAD 24/5 (2)
          +Gr 9-80 p391   +STL 9-18-80 p40
          ++HFN 8-80 p94   +STL 12-14-80 p38

BISHOP
The pilgrim of love. See no. 3774

BITSCH, Marcel
710 Concertino. MATTHEWS: Summer is icumen in: Lhude sing. NOON: Motets and monodies. VILLA-LOBOS: Ciranda des sete notas. Joseph
Polisi, bsn; Thomas Schmidt, pno; Ronald Roseman, ob; John Snow,
English hn. Crystal S 341
        +ARG 1-80 p50   +FF 9/10-80 p282

BIZET, Georges
    Agnus Dei. See no. 3888
    Agnus Dei: Intermezzo. See no. 3961
711 L'Arlesienne: Suite. Carmen: Suite. Lss Musiciens de l'Opera;
     Georges Gabon. Everest SDBR 3477
           -NR 12-80 p5
712 L'Arlesienne: Suites, nos. 1 and 2. Jeux d'enfants, op. 22. CO;
     Lorin Maazel. Decca SXL 6903 Tape (c) KSXC 6903
         +Gr 12-80 p824   +-HFN 12-80 p133
713 L'Arlesienne: Suites, nos. 1 and 2. Carmen: Suites, no. 1. Carmen:
     Suite, no. 2: Pastorale; Minuet; Farandole. Lamoureux Concerts
     Orchestra; Igor Markevitch. Philips 6570 107 Tape (c) 7310 107
     (From SFL 14048)
         +Gr 5-80 p1659   +NR 12-78 p4
         +-HFN 5-80 p135   +-RR 5-80 p55
         +-HFN 10-80 p117 tape
714 L'Arlesienne: Suites, nos. 1 and 2. Carmen: Suites, nos. 1 and 2.
     LSO; Neville Marriner. Philips 9500 566 Tape (c) 7300 715
         +FF 3/4-80 p63   +/HFN 10-79 p171 tape
         +Gr 8-79 p327   +NR 3-80 p5
         +Gr 10-79 p727 tape   +RR 8-79 p75
         +-HFN 9-79 p104   +St 3-80 p92
    L'Arlesienne: Suites, nos. 1 and 2. See no. 3557. See no. 4069
    L'Arlesienne: Suite, no. 1. See no. 726. See no. 728
715 L'Arlesienne: Suite, no. 2. Carmen: Suites, nos. 1 and 2. PO;
     Eugene Ormandy. RCA ARL 1-3343 Tape (c) ARK 1-3343
         +ARG 9-80 p24   ++NR 5-80 p2
         +FF 5/6-80 p56
    L'Arlesienne: Suite, no. 2. See no. 665
    L'Arlesienne: Suite, no. 2: Minuet. See no. 3890
716 Carmen. Rosa Ponselle, Hilda Burke, Thelma Votipka, s; Helen Old-
     heim, ms; Rene Maison, Giordano Paltrinieri, t; Julius Huehn,
     George Cehanovsky, bar; Louis d'Angelo, bs-bar; Metropolitan
     Opera Orchestra; Gennaro Papi. Metropolitan MET 7 (3)
         -FF 7/8-80 p64   +ON 6-80 p45
         +-HF 3-80 p75   +SR 1-5-80 p39
         +OC Winter 1980 p51
717 Carmen. Martha Angelici, Germain Chellet, s; Solange Michel, Ray-
     monde Notti, ms; Raoul Jobin, Frederic Leprin, t; Michel Dens,
     Julien Thirache, Jean Vieuille, bar; Xavier Smati, bs; Paris
     Opera Orchestra and Chorus; Andre Cluytens. Trianon TRI 33308-10
     (3)
         +ARSC Vol 12, nos. 1-2, 1980 p102
718 Carmen, excerpts. Elizabeth Hongen, alto; Torsten Ralf, t; Dresden
     State Opera Orchestra and Chrus; Karl Bohm Acanta BB 21362
         -Gr 11-80 p736   +-HFN 9-80 p100
    Carmen: Dut-il m'en couter la vie; En vain pour eviter; Habanera.
     See no. 3770
    Carmen: Entr'acte, Act 3. See no. 3890
    Carmen: Et la garde descendante, La cloche a sonne...Dans l'air nous
     souvons. See no. 3553
    Carmen: Fantaisie. See no. 3665
    Carmen: Habanera; Seguidilla; Card scene. See no. 3928
    Carmen: Il fior che avevi a me; La tua madre...Mia madre vedo ancor.
     See no. 3981

Carmen: La fleur que tu m'avais jetee. See no. 3774
Carmen: La fleur que tu m'avais jetee; Il fior che avevi a me dato.
    See no. 3946
Carmen: Micaela's aria. See no. 3987
Carmen: Prelude. See no. 666. See no. 3638. See no. 3969
719 Carmen: Prelude; Habanera; Duet; Seguidilla; Toreador song; Quintett;
    Flower song and finale; Card trio; Micaela's aria. Elizabeth
    Robson, Rita Hunter, s; Ann Robson, ms; Patricia Johnson, con;
    Donald Smith, John Stoddart, t; Raimund Herincx, Julian Moyle,
    bar; Leon Greene, bs; Sadlers Wells Orchestra and Chorus; Colin
    Davis. HMV ESD 7081 Tape (c) TC ESD 7081 (From CSD 1398)
        +Gr 3-80 p1434   +HFN 6-80 p119 tape
        +Gr 7-80 p166 tape   +RR 3-80 p40
        +HFN 3-80 p107
Carmen: Prelude; L'amour est un oiseau rebelle. See no. 3666
720 Carmen: Preludes, Act 1-4; Avec la garde montagne; Danse boheme.
    The fair maid of Perth: Suite. FRANCK: Le chasseur maudit. Col-
    umbia Symphony Orchestra, RPO; Thomas Beecham. CBS 61877 (From
    Columbia 33CX 1037, LX 8790/1 8813/4)
        +ARSC Vol 12, no. 3   +HFN 1-80 p119
         1980 p251   +RR 12-79 p49
        +Gr 12-79 p1007
Carmen: Prelude, Act 4. See no. 3555
Carmen: Sontag war's. See no. 3646
Carmen: Suite. See no. 711
Carmen: Suites, nos. 1 and 2. See no. 714. See no. 715
721 Carmen: Suite, no. 1. Carmen: Suite, no. 2, excerpts. GRIEG: Peer
    Gynt, opp. 46/55, excerpts. St. Louis Symphony Orchestra; Leon-
    ard Slatkin. Telarc 10048
        +FF 5/6-80 p56   ++NR 10-80 p4
        +-Gr 5-80 p1659   +RR 5-80 p55
        +-HFN 5-80 p118   +SFC 12-9-80 p33
Carmen: Suite, no. 1. See no. 713. See no. 4069
Carmen: Suite, no. 2, excerpts. See no. 721
Carmen: Suite, no. 2: Pastorale; Minuet; Farandole. See no. 713
Carmen: Toreador song. See no. 3899
722 Jeux d'enfants, op. 22. RAVEL: Ma mere l'oye. SAINT-SAENS: Le
    carnaval des animaux. Peter Katin, Philip Fowke, pno; Scottish
    National Orchestra; Alexander Gibson. Classics for Pleasure
    CFP 40086 Tape (c) TC CFP 40086
        +-Gr 6-75 p35   +-RR 5-75 p38
        ++HFN 7-75 p77   +-RR 7-80 p97 tape
        +HFN 8-80 p109 tape
Jeux d'enfants, op. 22. See no. 712. See no. 725. See no. 727
La jolie fille de Perth. See no. 725
La jolie fille de Perth: Quand la flamme de l'amour. See no. 3770
La jolie fille de Perth: Suite. See no. 720. See no. 3557. See
    no. 4069
Patrie overture. See no. 3557
723 Les pecheurs de perles (The pearl fishers). Pierrette Alarie, s;
    Leopold Simoneau, t; Rene Bianco, bar; Xavier Depraz, bs; Elisa-
    beth Brasseur Chorus; Lamoureux Concerts Orchestra; Jean Fournet.
    Philips 6747 404 (From Epic)
        +FF 9/10-80 p81
Les pecheurs de perles, excerpts. see no. 3696

724 Les pecheurs de perles: A fond du temple saint. PUCCINI: La boheme:
     O Mimi tu piu non torni. Manon Lescaut: Ah Manon mi tradisce;
     Presto in fila...No pazzo son. VERDI: Aida: Tu amonasro. Don
     Carlo: Io l'ho perduta...Qual pallor. La forza del destino: Sol-
     enne in quest'ora. Otello: Si per ciel. Rigoletto: Questa o
     quella; Bella figlia dell'amore. Il trovatore: Deserto sulla
     terra; Di qual tetra luce...Ah si ben mio; Di quella pira. Zinka
     Milanov, Roberta Peters, Anna Maria Rota, Licia Albanese; Jussi
     Bjorling, t; Enrico Campi, Franco Calabrese; Robert Merrill, bar;
     Leonard Warren, Fedora Barbieri, ms; Boris Christoff, bs; RCA
     Victor Orchestra, Rome Opera Orchestra; Renato Cellini, Jonel
     Perlea. RCA RL 4-3243 Tape (c) RK 4-3243
               +-Gr 8-80 p269   +-RR 8-80 p33
               +Op 11-80 p1112
     Les pechuers de perles: Au fond du temple saint. See no. 3538
     Les pecheurs de perles: C'etait le soir...Au fond du temple saint.
       See no. 3792
     Les pecheurs de perles: Del tempio al limitar. See no. 3900. See
       no. 3945
     Les pecheurs de perles: Della mia vita; Mi par d'udir ancora; Non
       hai compreso. See no. 3981
     Les pecheurs de perles: Je crois entendre encore; De mon amie fleur
       endormie. See no. 3926
     Les pecheurs de perles: Me voila seule dans la nuit. See no. 3886
     Les pecheurs de perles: Me voila seule dans la nuit...Come autre-
       fois. See no. 3793
     Les pecheurs de perles: Mi par d'udir ancora. See no. 3988
725 Symphony, C major. Jeux d'enfants, op. 22. La jolie fille de Perth.
     ORTF; Jean Martinon. DG 2535 238 Tape (c) 3335 238 (From DG
     2530 186)
               +ARG 9-80 p25   +-HFN 10-77 p169 tape
726 Symphony, C major. L'Arlesienne: Suite, no. 1. Savaria Symphony
     Orchestra; Janos Petro. Hungaroton LSPX 11908
               +-FF 9/10-80 p84
727 Symphony, C major. Jeux d'enfants, op. 22. COA; Bernard Haitink.
     Philips 9500 443 Tape (c) 7300 649
               +FF 5/6-80 p58   ++NR 1-80 p2
               +-Gr 11-79 p809   +RR 11-79 p71
               ++HFN 11-79 p135   ++SFC 10-28-79 p53
               +HFN 1-80 p123 tape   ++St 2-80 p121
728 Symphony, C major. L'Arlesienne: Suite, no. 1. PO; Eugene Ormandy.
     RCA ARL 1-3640 Tape (c) ARK 1-3640
               ++NR 11-80 p2   ++SFC 11-23-80 p21
729 Symphony, C major. PSO; Jindrich Rohan. Supraphon 110 2428
               /ARG 12-80 p22   +NR 7-80 p2
               +FF 9/10-80 p82   +SFC 7-27-80 p34
     Symphony, C major. See no. 3557
730 Te deum. POULENC: Gloria, G major. Kari Lovaas, s; Siegfried
     Jerusalem, t; Philharmonic Vocal Ensemble; Stuttgart Philharmonic
     Orchestra; Hans Zanotelli. Candide QCE 31104 (also Turnabout TVS
     37134 Tape (c) KTVC 37134)
               +-ARG 6-79 p15   +-NYT 10-7-79 pD24
               +-FF 5/6-79 p34   +-ON 1-13-79 p33
               +-Gr 12-79 p1033   +-RR 12-79 p106
               -HFN 1-80 p103   -SFC 2-25-79 p41
               +NR 3-79 p10

BLAKE, Eubie
     The chevy chase. See no. 3679
BLANCHARD
     Prelude avec trompette du "Te deum". See no. 3736
BLANCO, Jose
     Concerto, 2 harpsichords, G major. See no. 330
     Concerto, organ, G major. See no. 4035
BLAND
     Carry me back to old Virginny. See no. 3831
BLANGINI, Giuseppe
     Per valli per boschi. See no. 3770
BLASCO, Manuel
     Piece, 2 flutes and harpsichord. See no. 3707
BLAVET, Michel
     Sonata, flute, op. 2, no. 2, F major. See no. 3544
BLECH, Leo
     Telefonische Bestellung. See no. 3738
BLISS, Arthur
     Christopher Columbus suite. See no. 3786
731 Discourse. Edinburgh overture. Meditations on a theme by John
        Blow. Birmingham Symphony Orchestra; Vernon Handley. HMV ASD
        3878
                    +-Gr 8-80 p214   +RR 8-80 p38
                    +-HFN 7-80 p106
     Edinburgh overture. See no. 731
     Fanfare for a coming of age. See no. 3959
     Fanfare for a dignified occasion. See no. 3959
     Fanfare for heroes. See no. 3959
     Fanfare for the bride. See no. 3959
     Fanfare for the Lord Mayor of London. See no. 3571. See no. 3959
     Fanfare, homage to Shakespeare. See no. 3959
     Interlude. See no. 3959
     Meditations on a theme by John Blow. See no. 731
     Music for an investiture. See no. 4029
     Music for strings. See no. 3585
     Processional. See no. 394
     Royal fanfare. See no. 3959
     Royal fanfare, no. 1: Sovereign's fanfare. See no. 3959
     Royal fanfares, nos. 5 and 6. See no. 3959
     Salute. See no. 3660
732 Sonata, viola and piano. VAUGHAN WILLIAMS: Suite, viola and piano.
        Emanuel Vardi, vla; Frank Weinstock, pno. Musical Heritage
        Society MHS 4043
                    ++FF 1/2-80 p66   ++St 2-80 p134
     Things to come: Epilogue. See no. 4046
BLOCH, Agustyn
     Meditations. See no. 3857
BLOCH, Ernest
733 Avodah. Baal Shem. Sonata, violin and piano, no. 2. Michael
        Davis, vln; Nelson Harper, pno. Orion ORS 79344
                    +ARG 3-80 p20   +St 3-80 p93
                    -NR 2-80 p7
     Baal Shem. See no. 733
734 Concerto grosso, no. 1. MARTIN: Petite symphonie concertante.
        Osian Ellis, hp; Simon Preston, hpd; Philip Ledger, Francis Grier,

pno; AMF; Neville Marriner. Angel S 37577 (also HMV ASD 3732)

  +-ARG 9-79 p32   +NYT 5-25-80 pD21
  ++FF 11/12-79 p98   ++RR 5-80 p64
  +-Gr 3-80 p1385   +SFC 7-1-79 p44
  +-HFN 4-80 p103   ++St 10-79 p142
  +MT 9-80 p565   +-ST 8-80 p268
  ++NR 10-79 p2   +STL 3-9-80 p41

735 Four episodes. CRESTON: Choric dances, op. 17a. MUCZYNSKI: Dance
  movements, op. 17. Serenade for summer, op. 38. Arizona Chamber
  Orchestra; Robert Hull. Laurel LR 110
    +FF 9/10-79 p72   +SFC 10-12-80 p21
    +-NR 7-79 p5

 Prelude. See no. 3734

736 Sacred service. Louis Berkman, bar; Zemel Choir, London Chorale,
  London Concord Singers; LSO; Geoffrey Simon. Chandos ABR 1001
  Tape (c) ABT 1001
    +-Gr 1-80 p1182   +MT 9-80 p565
    +-Gr 7-80 p166 tape +RR 3-80 p91
    +HFN 2-80 p87

737 Sinfonia breve. MCPHEE: Tabuh-Tabuhan. SCHULLER: Studies on themes
  of Paul Klee (7). Eastman Rochester Orchestra, Minneapolis Symphony Orchestra; Paul Hanson, Antal Dorati. Mercury SRI 75116
  (Reissues)
    +FF 11/12-80 p82   ++SFC 3-9-80 p39
    ++NR 5-80 p4

 Sonatas, violin, nos. 1 and 2. See no. 3964
 Sonata, violin, no. 1. See no. 349
 Sonata, violin and piano, no. 2. See no. 733

BLOMDAHL, Karl-Birger
 Little suite, bassoon and piano. See no. 3588

BLOW, John
738 Salvator mundi. HUMFREY: O Lord my god. LOCKE: How doth the city
  sit solitary. PURCELL: Motets and anthems. Monteverdi Choir;
  English Baroque Soloists; John Eliot Gardiner. Erato STU 71276
    +MUM 12-80 p35

 Salvator mundi. See no. 3530
 Suite, D minor. See no. 3745

BLUMENFELD, Harold
 Rilke. See no. 4026

BOCCHERINI, Luigi
739 Concerto, flute, op. 27, D major. MERCADANTE: Concerto, flute, E
  minor. TARTINI: Concerto, flute, a 5, G major. Severino Gazzelloni, flt; I Musici. Philips 6500 611 Tape (c) 7300 334
    +Gr 2-75 p1473   ++RR 1-75 p34
    +HF 4-75 p97   ++RR 7-75 p72 tape
    +HFN 7-80 p117   +RR 9-75 p79 tape
    +NR 3-75 p5   +-RR 8-80 p55
    +SFC 10-5-75 p38

740 Concerto, violoncello, G major. LEO: concerto, violoncello, F minor
  (ed. Welsh). TARTINI: Concerto, violoncello, D major (ed. Welsh).
  VIVALDI: Concerto, violoncello, RV 401, C minor. Moray Welsh,
  vlc; Scottish Baroque Ensemble; Leonard Friedman. Abbey ABY 812
    +Gr 10-80 p504   +HFN 9-80 p114

 Minuet. See no. 3605. See no. 3909

741 Quartets, strings, op. 1, no. 1, C minor; op. 39, A major; op. 44,

no. 4, G major. Molard Quartet. Musical Heritage Society MHS
4054
　　　　+FF 11/12-80 p83
742 Quartets, strings, op. 6, nos. 1 and 3. Quartet, strings, op. 58,
no. 2. Quartetto Italiano. Philips 9500 305
　　　++Gr 3-80 p1403　　　　　　+NR 6-78 p7
　　　++HFN 2-80 p87　　　　　　　+NYT 6-4-78 pD15
　　　+MJ 1-79 p46　　　　　　　　+RR 3-80 p72
　　　+-MT 6-80 p382　　　　　　　++St 6-78 p139
Quartet, strings, op. 39, A major. See no. 741
Quartet, strings, op. 44, no. 4, G major. See no. 741
Quartet, strings, op. 58, no. 2. See no. 742
743 Quintet, guitar. CASTELNUOVO-TEDESCO: Quintet, guitar. GIULIANI:
Quintet, guitar. Siegfried Behrend, gtr; Zagreb Quartet. Acanta
EA 22780
　　　　+-HFN 7-80 p114　　　　　　++RR 7-80 p71
744 Quintet, guitar, D major. DVORAK: Trio, piano, no. 4, op. 90, E
minor. David Starobin, gtr; Bruno Canino, pno; Daniel Phillips,
Pina Carmirelli, Joseph Genualdi, vln; Jerry Grossman, Marcy
Rosen, vlc; Philipp Naegele, vla. Marlboro Recording MRS 13
　　　　+ARG 5-80 p9
745 Quintet, guitar, no. 1, D major. SCHNABEL: Quintet, guitar, C maj-
or. Siegfreid Behrend, gtr; Zagreb Quartet. Da Camera Magna SM
93606
　　　　+FF 11/12-80 p83
746 Quintets, guitar, nos. 4-6. Pepe Romero, gtr; AMF Chamber Ensemble.
Philips 9500 621 Tape (c) 7300 737
　　　　+Gr 11-80 p691　　　　　　+NR 12-80 p7
　　　　+HFN 11-80 p116
747 Quintets, strings, op. 13, no. 3, F major; op. 40, no. 2, D major;
op. 30, no. 6, C major. Quintetto Boccherini. Musical Heritage
Society MHS 4131
　　　　+St 7-80 p77
Quintet, strings, op. 13, no. 5, E major: Minuet. See no. 3794
748 Quintet, strings, op. 25, no. 4, C major. HUMMEL: Septet, op. 74,
D minor. Marlboro Music Festival. Columbia M 35163
　　　　+FF 3/4-80 p104　　　　　　+NYT 10-14-79 pD24
　　　　++NR 10-79 p6　　　　　　　++St 3-80 p96
Quintet, strings, op. 30, no. 6, C major. See no. 706. See no. 747
749 Quintet, strings, op. 31, no. 4, C minor; op. 40, no. 2, D major;
op. 42, no. 4, G minor. Richte van der Meer, vlc; Quartetto
Esterhazy. Telefunken 6-42353 Tape (c) 4-42353
　　　　+FF 11/12-80 p83　　　　　　+HFN 1-80 p103
　　　　+Gr 2-80 p1281　　　　　　　+St 7-80 p80
Quintet, strings, op. 40, no. 2, D major. See no. 747. See no. 749
Quintet, strings, op. 42, no. 4, G minor. See no. 749
750 Stabat mater, op. 61. Tamara Hert, Kumiko Oshita, s; Jean-Claude
Orliac, t; La Follia Instrumental Ensemble; Miguel de la Fuente.
Arion ARN 38500
　　　　+Gr 1-80 p1182　　　　　　+RR 12-79 p107
BOECK, Auguste de
Menuet. See no. 3889
BOELLMAN, Leon
Menuet gothique. See no. 3963
751 Sonata, violoncello and piano, op. 40. FAURE: Elegie, op. 24, C

C minor. Papillon, op. 77. Serenade, op. 98. SAINT-SAENS: Al-
legro appassionato, op. 43. Le carnival des animaux: Le cygne.
Andre Navarra, vlc; Annie d'Arco, pno. Calliope CAL 1854
   +Gr 9-80 p356   +RR 8-80 p74
   +HFN 8-80 p105

752 Suite gothique, op. 25. GIGOUT: Minuetto. JONGEN: Sonata eroica,
  op. 94. MULET: Tu es petrus. David Sanger, org. Saga 5471
    +Gr 4-80 p1572   +MT 10-80 p633
    +HFN 5-80 p135   +RR 4-80 p92
 Suite gothique, op. 25. See no. 3958
 Suite gothique, op. 25: Priere a Notre Dame. See no. 3624
 Suite gothique, op. 25: Toccata. See no. 659. See no. 3582. See
  no. 3664. See no. 3838. See no. 4034

BOELY, Pierre Alexandre
 Reveillez-vous, pastoreux. See no. 4061

BOHM, Georg
 Christ lag in Todesbanden. See no. 3757
 Prelude and fugue, A minor. See no. 163

BOHRER, Anton and Max
753 Duo, violin and violoncello, no. 1, op. 41. REICHA: Duo, violin
  and violoncello, no. 2, op. 84, F major. Roseline Peveteau, vln;
  Jan Stegenga, vlc. Musical Heritage Society MHS 4016
    /FF 1/2-80 p67

BOIELDIEU, Francois
 The Calif of Bagdad: Overture. See no. 3847
754 Concerto, harp, C major. DITTERSDORF: Concerto, harp, op. 4, no. 6,
  B flat major. Marisa Robles, hpd; AMF; Iona Brown. Argo ZRG 930
    ++Gr 9-80 p331   +RR 8-80 p45
    +HFN 8-80 p105   ++STL 7-13-90 p38
 La dame blanche: Ce domaine. See no. 3770
 La dame blanche: Overture. See no. 63

BOISMORTIER, Joseph Bodin de
 Concerto, op. 37, no. 6, E minor. See no. 3547
 L'Hyver: Cantata, no. 4. See no. 3610
 Sonatas, bassoon, E minor. See no. 3804
 Sonata, flute, op. 91, no. 2, G minor. See no. 3544
755 Sonata, saxophone, no. 2, A minor (arr. Watters). LINN: Saxifrage
  blue. BONNEAU: Caprice in the form of a waltz. PELUSI: Concert
  piece, baritone, saxophone, brass quintet and percussion. Mark
  Watters, sax; Assisting artists. Crystal S 152
    +FF 9/10-80 p283   +NR 7-79 p9
756 Suites, nos. 1-4, op. 59. Mireille Lagace, hpd. Calliope CAL 1865
  Tape (c) CAL 4865
    +-Gr 8-80 p241   +RR 7-80 p76
    +HFN 8-80 p94

BOITO, Arrigo
 Mefistofele: Ave signor; Son io spirito che nega. See no. 3899
 Mefistofele: Ave signor; Son lo spirito che nega; Ecco il mondo.
  See no. 3927
 Mefistofele: Ave signore degli anteli e del santi...Ave Signor; Son
  io spirito che nega. See no. 3773
 Mefistofele: Dai campi dai prati; Giunto sul passo. See no. 3988
 Mefistofele: Dai campi dai prati; Ogni mortal mister gustai...Giunto
  sul passo estremo. See no. 3671
 Mefistofele: L'altra notte in fondo al mare. See no. 3789. See no.
  3869

Mefistofele: L'altra notte; Dai campi dai prati. See no. 3774
757 Mefistofele: Prologue. VERDI: Pezzi sacre: Te deum. John Cheek,
    bs; Morehouse Spelman Chorus; Young Singers of Callanwolde; At-
    lanta Symphony Orchestra and Chorus; Robert Shaw. Telarc DG
    10045

+FF 9/10-80 p84	+ON 7-80 p37
+-Gr 9-80 p380	+St 10-80 p109
+HF 11-80 p84	+SFC 9-7-80 p32
++HFN 11-80 p116	

Mefistofele: Spunta l'aurora pallida. See no. 3770
Nerone: Queste ad un lido; Ecco la Dea. See no. 3984
758 Sinfonia, A minor. MERCADANTE: Sinfonia on themes from Rossini's
    "Stabat mater". PUCCINI: Capriccio sinfonico. Edgar: Prelude.
    Preludio sinfonico, A major. VERDI: The battle of Legnano: Over-
    ture. Monte Carlo Opera Orchestra; Claudio Scimone. Erato STU
    71040 (also Erato ZL 30614, Musical Heritage Society MHS 3984)

++ARG 10-79 p56	+ON 1-19-80 p37
+FF 1/2-80 p182	+RR 6-78 p58
+Gr 6-78 p76	+St 11-78 p131

BOLLING, Claude
759 Concerto, guitar and piano. Angel Romero, gtr; George Shearing,
    pno; Shelly Manne, drum; Ray Brown, bs. HMV EMD 5535 Tape (c)
    TC EMD 5535 (also Angel DS 37327 Tape (c) 4ZS 37327)

++FF 9/10-80 p85	+HFN 6-80 p103
++Gr 6-80 p69	++NR 10-80 p5
+Gr 10-80 p548 tape	

760 Picnic suite. Jean-Pierre Rampal, flt; Alexandre Lagoya, gtr;
    Claude Bolling, pno; Guy Pedersen, bs; Daniel Humair, drums.
    CBS M 35864 Tape (c) MT 35864

+FF 11/12-80 p84	+-St 11-80 p86

BOND, Carrie Jacobs
    Songs: I love you truly. See no. 3831
BOND, Victoria
761 Monologue. Peter Quince at the clavier. GILBERT: Interrupted suite.
    Transmutations. Penny Orloff, s; Zita Carno, Delores Stevens,
    Richard Grayson, Susan Savage, pno; Ronald Leonard, vlc; Thomas
    Harmon, org; Scott Shepherd, Penny Orloff, perc; Gary Gray, clt.
    Protone PR 150

+-FF 11/12-80 p84	

Peter Quince at the clavier. See no. 761
BONNEAU
    Caprice in the form of a waltz. See no. 755
BONNET, Joseph
    Pieces, op. 7: Elves. See no. 3958
BONONCINI, Antonio
762 Stabat mater. CALDARA: Crucifixus. LOTTI: Crucifixus. Felicity
    Palmer, s; Philip Langridge, t; Paul Esswood, alto; Christopher
    Keyte, bs; St. John's College Chapel Choir; Philomusica; George
    Guest. Argo ZRG 850

++FF 7/8-79 p36	++NR 5-80 p9
+Gr 3-78 p1599	+RR 3-78 p64
+HFN 4-78 p111	++St 6-79 p126
+-MT 9-78 p769	

BONONCINI, Giovanni
763 Care luci del mio ben. Ecco Dorinda il giorno. Misero pastorello.

Siedi amarilli. Rene Jacobs, alto; Sigiswald Kuijken, Lucy van
Dael, vln; Wieland Kuijken, vlc; Robert Kohnen, hpd. DG 2533 450
        +Gr 10-80 p524   +STL 11-9-80 p40
        +HFN 11-80 p116
   Divertimento, F major. See no. 3990
   Ecco Dorinda il giorno. See no. 763
   Misero pastorello. See no. 763
   Siedi amarilli. See no. 763
BONPORTI, Francesco Antonio
764 Concerti, op. 11, nos. 4, 6, 8-9. I Musici. Philips 9502 004
        +ARG 6-80 p18   +NR 8-80 p7
        ++FF 5/6-80 p58   +NYT 5-25-80 pD21
   Concerto, op. 11, no. 6: Recitativo. See no. 20
BORDEAU, Eugene
765 Solo, bassoon and piano. HINDEMEITH: Sonata, oboe and piano. MES-
   SIAEN: Le merle noir. VIVALDI: Sonata, flute, oboe, bassoon and
   harpsichord, RV 103, D minor. Dawn Weiss, flt; David Weiss, ob;
   Abraham Weiss, bsn; Zita Carno, pno. Crystal S 354
        +FF 9/10-80 p282   ++IN 7-79 p8
        +HF 6-79 p94   +NR 4-79 p7
BORLET (14th century)
766 He tres doulz roussignol. JACOB DE SENLECHES: Fuions de ci. En ce
   gracieux. TREBOR: Quant joyne euer. Se Alixandre et Hector.
   ANON.: Ma tredol rosignol. Mass of Barcelona. Atrium Musicae
   Madrid; Gregorio Paniagua. Musical Heritage Society MHS 3980
        +FF 9/10-80 p99
BORODIN, Alexander
767 In the Steppes of Central Asia. Prince Igor: Polovtsian dances.
   MUSSORGSKY: A night on the bare mountain. TCHAIKOVSKY: Overture,
   the year 1812, op. 49. Orchestra; Ferenc Fricsay. DG 2535 727
        +-ARSC Vol 12, nos. 1-2, 1980 p124
768 In the Steppes of Central Asia. Prince Igor: Polovtsian march.
   Symphony, no. 2, B minor. USSR Symphony Orchestra; Yevgeny Svetlanov. Quintessence PCM 7165 Tape (c) 7165
        +-FF 11/12-80 p85
769 In the Steppes of Central Asia. MUSSORSKY: A night on the bare
   mountain. RIMSKY-KORSAKOV: Antar, op. 9. Brno PO; Jiri Belohlavek. Supraphon 110 2279
        +-NR 10-80 p3
   In the Steppes of Central Asia. See no. 3962
770 Prince Igor: Dance of the Polovtsian maidens; Polovtsian dances
   (orch. Rimsky-Korsakov/Glazunov). MUSSORGSKY: Khovanschina:
   Entr'acte, Act 4; Dance of the Persian slave (orch. Rimsky-
   Korsakov). Pictures at an exhibition (orch. Ravel). PhO; Herbert von Karajan. HMV SXLP 30445 Tape (c) TC SXLP 30445 (From
   SAX 2421, 2294, 2296, 33CS 1421)
        ++Gr 9-80 p331   +-HFN 10-80 p113
   Prince Igor: Lentement baissee le jour. See no. 3774
771 Prince Igor: Overture (arr. Glazunov); Polovtsian dances (orch.
   Rimsky-Korsakov). STRAVINSKY: The firebird (1919 version). At-
   lanta Symphony Orchestra and Chorus; Robert Shaw. Telarc DG
   10039
        ++ARG 4-79 p50   +-HFN 12-79 p158
        ++FF 1/2-79 p22   +RR 1-80 p87
        +-HF 3-79 p110   ++St 2-79 p136

772 Prince Igor: Polovtsian dances. RIMSKY-KORSAKOV: Russian Easter
      overture, op. 36. TCHAIKOVSKY: Overture, the year 1812, op. 49.
      COA; Igor Markevitch. Philips 6570 191 Tape (c) 7310 191
                    +NYT 9-7-80 pD29
     Prince Igor: Polovtsian dances. See no. 340. See no. 767. See
      no. 1232. See no. 3807. See no. 4072
     Prince Igor: Polovtsian march. See no. 768
     Prince Igor: Vladimir's aria. See no. 3926
773 Quintet, piano, C minor. MENDELSSOHN: Sextet, op. 110, D major.
      Vienna Octet Members. London STS 15502 (Reissue)
                    ++FF 9/10-80 p86
774 Symphony, no. 2, B minor. RIMSKY-KORSAKOV: The tale of the Tsar
      Sultan: Suite. Monte Carlo Opera Orchestra; Roberto Benzi.
      Philips 6570 105 Tape (c) 7310 105
                    ++Gr 7-80 p166 tape   /-HFN 8-80 p109 tape
                    +-Gr 10-80 p494   +RR 4-80 p60
                    +-HFN 4-80 p117
     Symphony, no. 2, B minor. See no. 768
BORTNIANSKY, Dimitri
775 Sing ye people. DEGHTYAROV: All nations have seen. VEDAL: Today
      the master of the creation is crucified. Holy Trinity-St.
      Sergius Monastery Choir, Holy Trinity Cathedral Mixed Choir;
      Archimandrite Matthew, Deacon Pavel Gerasimov. Ikon IKO 11
                    +-Gr 12-80 p871
776 Songs: I see thy bridal chamber. DVORESKY: O gentle light. TRAD.:
      The archers; Cherubic hymn: Old chant; Come let us bless Joseph;
      Give rest with the righteous; Greek chant: Let my prayer be set
      fort (arr. Glinka); Let God arise and Christ is risen; The
      resurrection O Christ our saviour; Simonov Monastery melody.
      Nicolai Gedda, t; Russian Cathedral Choir, London; Michael For-
      tounatto. Ikon IKOS 10
                    +Gr 5-80 p1711
BOSC
     Rose mousse: Entr'acte. See no. 3962
BOSSI
     Cantate domino. See no. 3933
BOSSI, Marco Enrico
777 Intermezzo goldoniani, op. 127. MERCANDANTE: Concerto, clarinet,
        op. 101, B major. PUCCINI: Minuet, no. 1, A major. Minuet,
        no. 2, A major. SINIGAGLIA: Adagio tragico, op. 21. Jorg Fadle,
        clt; RIAS Sinfonietta; Jiri Starek. Schwann Music Mundi VMS
        2046
                    +FF 3/4-80 p196
BOSSLER, Kurt
     Kaleidoskop. See no. 4035
BOTTEGARI, Cosimo
     Songs: Morte da me Tant aspettata; Zefiro torna. See no. 3600
BOTTESINI, Giovanni
     Ero e Leandro: Romanza d'Ero. See no. 3770
BOULANGER, Lili
     Cortege. See no. 3964. See no. 4065
     D'un matin de printemps. See no. 3822
778 Faust et Helene. Pour les funerailles d'un soldat. Lyne Dourain,
        ms; Andre Mallabrera, t; Michel Carey, bar; Monte Carlo Opera
        Orchestra and Chorus; Igor Markevitch. Festival Classique FC 441

(also Varese VC 81095)
        ++ARG 3-80 p20   /FF 9/10-80 p86
        +FF 11/12-78 p32   +NYT 4-13-79 pD26

Nocturne. See no. 3822. See no. 4065
Nocturne, F major. See no. 3964
Pour les funerailles d'un soldat. See no. 778

BOULEZ, Pierre
779 Domaines. Michel Portal, clt; Musique Vivante Ensemble; Diego Masson. Harmonia Mundi HM 930 (From RCA SB 6849)
        +FF 11/12-80 p86   /+HFN 8-79 p101
        +Gr 8-79 p347   +RR 8-79 p76

Eclat. See no. 656
780 Le marteau sans maitre. Jean Deroubaix, ms; Severino Gazzelloni, flt; Georges van Gucht, xylorimba; Claude Ricou, vibraphone; Jean Batigne, perc; Anton Stingl, gtr; Serge Collot, vla; Pierre Boulez. Harmonia Mundi 1C 065 99831
        +-FF 11/12-80 p86   ++HFN 5-80 p135
        +-Gr 5-80 p1700   +RR 5-80 p56

781 Sonata, piano, no. 1, CHAVEZ: Estudio a Rubinstein. Caprichos (5) SESSIONS: Sonata, piano, no. 2. Alan Mark, pno. CRI SD 385
        +-FF 3/4-80 p65   ++SFC 10-21-79 p57
        +NYT 2-25-79 pD21

782 Sonata, piano, no. 2. KRENEK: sonata, piano, no. 4. David Burge, pno. Musical Heritage Society MHS 3874
        +FF 3/4-80 p184   +-St 8-79 p108

Sonata, piano, no. 2. See no. 3705

BOURGEOIS
Psalm, no. 8. See no. 3848

BOURGEOIS, Derek
Wind symphony: Hock theme. See no. 3571

BOUSSET, Jean-Baptiste de
Air a boire. See no. 3764

BOUTRY, Roger
Interference, bassoon and piano. See no. 3588
Pieces a quatre (5). See no. 3653

BOYCE, William
Alleluia. See no. 3814
783 Concerti grossi, B flat major, B minor, E minor. Overture, F major. Cantilena; Adrian Shepherd. Chandos ABR 1005 Tape (c) ABT 1005
        +-Gr 12-79 p1007   +HFN 2-80 p91
        +Gr 8-80 p275 tape   /RR 1-80 p69
        -HF 12-80 p70

Overture, F major. See no. 783
784 Songs (choral): I have surely built thee an house; O be joyful; O give thanks; Save me O God; Turn thee unto me. Worcester Cathedral Academy and Choir; Donald Hunt. Abbey ABY 811
        +Gr 3-80 p1424   +HFN 12-80 p133
        +-HFN 2-80 p87   +RR 3-80 p92

785 Songs (choral): By the waters of Babylon; I have surely built thee an house; O where shall wisdom be found; Turn thee unto me O Lord. Voluntaries, organ, nos. 1-2, 4, 10. Arthur Wills, org; Ely Cathedral Choir; Arthur Wills. Saga 5440 Tape (c) CA 5440
        +Gr 3-77 p1437   +-HFN 4-79 p131
        +-HF 12-80 p70   +RR 3-77 p88
        +-HFN 3-77 p99   ++RR 11-77 p119 tape
        +HFN 11-77 p187 tape   +RR 4-79 p109

Songs: Tell me lovely shepherd. See no. 3778
786 Symphonies, nos. 1-8. AMF; Neville Marriner. Argo ZRG 874 Tape (c)
       KZRC 874 (r) B-C F 874
                        ++FF 3/4-79 p42   ++HFN 5-78 p146 tape
                        +-Gr 3-78 p1556   +-MT 8-78 p687
                         +Gr 4-78 p1771 tape   ++RR 3-78 p30
                        ++HF 1-79 p73   ++RR 4-78 p104 tape
                        ++HF 11-79 p124 tape   ++RR 4-80 p128
                        ++HFN 3-78 p133   ++SFC 5-6-79 p61
787 Symphonies, nos. 1-8. Menuhin Festival Orchestra; Yehudi Menuhin.
       Classics for Pleasure CFP 40326 (From HMV HQS 1302)
                        +-Gr 3-80 p1449   +-RR 2-80 p49
                        ++HFN 4-80 p119
788 Symphonies, nos. 1-8. Bournemouth Sinfonietta; Ronald Thomas. CRD
       CRD 1056 Tape (c) CRDC 4056
                        +Gr 6-79 p42   +MT 8-79 p656
                        +HFN 6-79 p105   +RR 6-79 p72
                        +HFN 10-79 p171 tape   +-RR 4-80 p128 tape
     Symphony, no. 1, B flat major. See no. 3691
     Symphony, no. 4, F major. See no. 3639. See no. 4030
     Voluntaries, organ, nos. 1-2, 4-10. See no. 785
BOYKAN, Martin
789 Quartet, strings, no. 2, GIDEON: Nocturnes. Songs of youth and
       madness. Judith Raskin, s; Ronald Roseman, ob; Gordon Gottlieb,
       vibraphone; Da Capo Chamber Players, American Composers Orches-
       tra, Pro Arte Quartet; John DeMain, James Dixon. CRI SD 401
                        +ARG 9-79 p28   +NR 1-80 p6
                        +-FF 5/6-80 p79
BOZZA, Eugene
     Agrestide. See no. 3714
     Nuages. See no. 3718
BRACKETT
     Simple life. See no. 3848
BRADE, William
     Festive dances (2). See no. 4000
BRAGA
     Engenho novo. See no. 3965
BRAHMS, Johannes
     Academic festival overture, op. 80. See no. 861. See no. 863.
       See no. 878. See no. 886
     Aus vier fruhe Kompositionen: O Traurigkeit O Herzelied. See no.
       4036
790 Ballades, op. 10. Variations on a theme by Paganini, op. 35, A
       minor. Earl Wild, pno. Vanguard Tape (r) D 10006
                        +HF 2-80 p102
     Ballades, op. 10, no. 1, D minor. See no. 3953. See no. 3954
     Canons (4). See no. 3741
791 Chorale preludes, op. 122 (11). Fugue, A flat minor. Bernard
       Lagaci, org. Titanic TI 38
                        +FF 7/8-80 p66   ++St 2-80 p121
     Chorale preludes, op. 122, nos. 3, 9-11. See no. 820
     Chorale preludes, op. 122, nos. 4-5, 8-11. See no. 155
     Chorale preludes, op. 122: Herzliebster Jesu was hast du verbrochen;
       O Welt ich muss dich lassen; Schmucke dich o liebe Seele; Herz-
       lich tut mich verlange. See no. 4036
792 Concerto, piano, no. 1, op. 15, D minor. Maurizio Pollini, pno;

VPO; Karl Bohm. DG 2531 294 Tape (c) 3301 294
                +—Gr 12-80 p824   +HFN 12-80 p159 tape
                +—HFN 11-80 p116
793 Concerto, piano, no. 1, op. 15, D minor. Emil Gilels, pno; PhO;
     Eugen Jochum. DG 2542 126 Tape (c) 3342 126 (From 2707 064)
                +Gr 7-80 p166 tape   +—HFN 8-80 p109 tape
                ++Gr 10-80 p494   +—RR 8-80 p39
                +—HFN 8-80 p107   +—RR 8-80 p95 tape
794 Concerto, piano, no. 1, op. 15, D minor. John Lill, pno; Halle
     Orchestra; James Loughran. Enigma K 53570 Tape (c) K 4-53570
                +Gr 1-79 p1278   +HFN 2-80 p91
                ++Gr 5-79 p1940 tape   +—RR 1-79 p55
795 Concerto, piano, no. 1, op. 15, D minor. Garrick Ohlsson, pno;
     LPO; Klaus Tennstedt. HMV ASD 3762 Tape (c) TC ASD 3762 (also
     Angel S 37568)
                +ARG 6-80 p19   ++NR 1-80 p4
                +—FF 3/4-80 p66   +NYT 6-22-80 pD20
                +Gr 9-79 p459   +—RR 9-79 p70
                +—HF 6-80 p76   +RR 2-80 p98 tape
                -HFN 10-79 p151   ++St 2-80 p122
                -HFN 12-79 p185 tape
796 Concerto, piano, no. 1, op. 15, D minor. Claudio Arrau, pno; COA;
     Bernard Haitink. Philips 6570 014 Tape (c) 7310 014 (From 6700
     018)
                +Gr 2-80 p1263   +—HFN 3-80 p105
                +—HFN 2-80 p107 tape   +RR 3-80 p48
797 Concerto, piano, no. 1, op. 15, D minor. Concerto, piano, no. 2,
     op. 83, B flat major. Misha Dichter, pno; Leipzig Gewandhaus
     Orchestra; Kurt Masur. Philips 6769 013 (2)
                +Gr 9-80 p331   +HFN 9-80 p100
798 Concerto, piano, no. 1, op. 15, D minor. Misha Dichter, pno; Leip-
     zig Gewandhaus Orchestra; Kurt Masur. Philips 9500 410 Tape (c)
     7300 618
                +—ARG 7/8-80 p17   +—NR 5-80 p5
                +—CL 7/8-80 p8   +—NYT 6-22-80 pD20
                +—FF 5/6-80 p58   +SFC 2-3-80 p45
                +—HF 6-80 p73   ++St 8-80 p92
799 Concerto, piano, no. 2, op. 83, B flat major. Geza Anda, pno; BPhO;
     Herbert von Karajan. DG 2535 263 (Reissue from 139034)
                +FF 11/12-80 p81   +—Gr 12-78 p1094
800 Concerto, piano, no. 2, op. 83, B flat major. Misha Dichter, pno;
     Leipzig Gewandhaus Orchestra; Kurt Masur. Philips 9500 414 Tape
     (c) 7300 619
                +—ARG 7/8-80 p17   +—NR 5-80 p5
                +—CL 7/8-80 p8   +—NYT 6-22-80 pD20
                +—FF 5/6-80 p58   +SFC 2-3-80 p45
                +—HF 6-80 p76   ++St 8-80 p92
801 Concerto, piano, no. 2, op. 83, B flat major. Stephen Bishop-
     Kovacevich, pno; LSO; Colin Davis. Philips 9500 682 Tape (c)
     7300 777
                ++NR 12-80 p6
     Concerto, piano, no. 83, B flat major. See no. 797. See no. 894.
     See no. 3709
802 Concerto, violin, op. 77, D major. Nathan Milstein, vln; VPO;
     Eugen Jochum. DG 2530 592 Tape (c) 3300 592

+Audio 11-76 p111   +─NR 4-76 p3
+─Gr 12-75 p1031   +RR 12-75 p22
+─HF 5-76 p80   +RR 4-76 p81 tape
+─HF 1-77 p151 tape   +SFC 2-29-76 p25
+HFN 3-76 p113 tape   +St 6-76 p101
+MJ 5-76 p29   +STL 1-11-76 p36
+MUM 5/6-80 p37

803 Concerto, violin, op. 77, D major. Pinchas Zukerman, vln; Orchestre
     de Paris; Daniel Barenboim. DG 2531 251 Tape (c) 3301 251
                    +Gr 4-80 p1553   /HFN 6-80 p103
                    +Gr 7-80 p166 tape   +NR 12-80 p5
                    -HF 12-80 p72   +RR 5-80 p56

804 Concerto, violin, op. 77, D major. MOZART: Concerto, violin, no.
     5, K 219, A major. TCHAIKOVSKY: Concerto, violin, op. 35, D
     major. David Oistrakh, vln; Staatskapelle; Franz Konwitschny.
     DG 2726 087 (2)
                    +FF 7/8-80 p172   +NR 4-80 p5

805 Concerto, violin, op. 77, D major. Georg Kulenkampff, vln; BPhO;
     Hans Schmidt-Isserstedt. Past Masters PM 24 (From Telefunken 78s)
                    +FF 5/6-80 p59

806 Concerto, violin, op. 77, D major. Hermann Krebbers, vln; COA; Ber-
     nard Haitink. Philips 6570 172 Tape (c) 7310 172
                    +FF 11/12-80 p87   +─HFN 3-80 p105
                    +Gr 7-80 p166 tape   +HFN 6-80 p119 tape
                    +HF 4-80 p80   +RR 3-80 p48

807 Concerto, violin, op. 77, D major. Salvatore Accardo, vln; Leip-
     zig Gewandhaus Orchestra; Kurt Masur. Philips 9500 624 Tape (c)
     7300 729
                    +─FF 5/6-80 p59   +NYT 7-6-80 pD15
                    +HF 6-80 p73   +SFC 2-3-80 p45
                    -NR 5-80 p5

808 Concerto, violin, op. 77, D major. Henryk Szeryng, vln; LSO; Pierre
     Monteux. RCA VICS 1028
                    +MUM 5/6-80 p37

809 Concerto, violin, op. 77, D minor. Lydia Mordkovich, vln; PhO; Kurt
     Sanderling. RCA RL 2-5231 Tape (c) RK 2-5231
                    +Gr 4-80 p1553   +RR 2-80 p50
                    +─HFN 1-80 p103

810 Concerto, violin, op. 77, D major. BEETHOVEN: Romance, no. 2, op.
     50, F major. Yehudi Menuhin, vln; Lucerne Festival Orchestra,
     PhO; Wilhelm Furtwangler. Seraphim 60232 (From HMV/Victor orig-
     inals, 1949, 1953)
                    +HF 2-75 p89   +St 2-75 p84
                    +MUM 5/6-80 p37

811 Concerto, violin, op. 77, D major. Nathan Milstein, vln; PhO; Ana-
     tole Fistoulari. Seraphim S 60265
                    +MUM 5/6-80 p37   +St 3-77 p126
                    +─NR 6-76 p6

812 Concerto, violin, op. 77, D major. Albert Spalding, vln; Vienna
     Tonkunstler Orchestra; Wilhelm Loibner. Varese VC 81059 (From
     Remington R 145)
                    +─HF 12-80 p72
     Concerto, violin, op. 77, D major. See no. 894. See no. 3709.
     See no. 3772. See no. 3968

813 Concerto, violin and violoncello, op. 102, A minor. Itzhak Perlman,

vln; Mstislav Rostropovich, vlc; COA; Bernard Haitink. Angel SZ
37680 Tape (c) 4ZS 37680 (also HMV ASD 3905 Tape (c) TC ASD 3905)
    ++FF 11/12-80 p87   +HFN 12-80 p157 tape
    +Gr 10-80 p494   ++NR 10-80 p6
    ++HF 12-80 p72   ++NYT 9-21-80 pD22
    +HFN 12-80 p133

814 Concerto, violin and violoncello, op. 102, A minor. WAGNER: Sieg-
    fried Idyll. Isaac Stern, vln; Leonard Rose, vlc; NYP; Bruno
    Walter. Odyssey Y 34721
        +FF 5/6-78 p22   ++NR 2-78 p7
        ++MUM 5/6-80 p37

815 Concerto, violin and violoncello, op. 102, A minor. Variations on
    a theme by Haydn, op. 56a.* Salvatore Accardo, vln; Heinrich
    Schiff, vlc; Leipzig Gewandhaus Orchestra; Kurt Masur. Philips
    9500 623 Tape (c) 7300 728 (*From 6769 009)
        +-FF 9/10-80 p87   +-NR 8-80 p7
        +Gr 12-80 p824   +NYT 7-6-80 pD15
        +HF 6-80 p73   +SFC 7-6-80 p27
        +-HFN 12-80 p133   +St 8-80 p93

816 Concerto, violin and violoncello, op. 102, A minor. SAINT-SAENS:
    Concerto, violoncello, no. 1, op. 33, A minor. Nathan Milstein,
    vln; Gregor Piatigorsky, vlc; Robin Hood Dell Orchestra, RCA
    Symphony Orchestra; Fritz Reiner. RCA AVM 1-2020
        +-ARG 5-77 p16   +MJ 10-77 p27
        +-ARSC Vol 10, no. 1,   +-MUM 5/6-80 p37
        1978 p86

817 Concerto, violin and violoncello, op. 102, A minor. BEETHOVEN:
    Sonata, violin and piano, no. 1, op. 12, no. 1, D major. Chris-
    tian Ferras, vln; Paul Tortelier, vl; Pierre Barbizet, pno; PhO;
    Paul Kletzki. Seraphim S 60049
        +MUM 5/6-80 p37
    Concerto, violin and violoncello, op. 102, A minor. See no. 490.
    See no. 620. See no. 894. See no. 3906. See no. 3964

818 Ein deutsches Requiem, op. 45. BRUCKNER: Te deum. Elisabeth Grum-
    mer, Agnes Giebel, s; Marga Hoffgen, con; Dietrich Fischer-
    Dieskau, bar; Josef Traxel, t; Gottlob Frick, bs; St. Hedwig's
    Cathedral Choir; BPhO; Rudolf Kempe, Karl Forster. Arabesque
    8007-2 (2) Tape (c) 9007-2 (From Electrola 90003/4, 80010, RCA
    LM 6050)
        +-ARG 4-80 p18   +NYT 1-6-80 pD18
        +HF 3-80 p77

819 Ein deutsches Requiem, op. 45. Variations on a theme by Haydn, op.
    56a. Kiri Te Kanawa, s; Bernd Weikl, bar; CSO and Chorus; Georg
    Solti. Decca 135D2 (2) Tape (c) K 135K22 (also London OSA 12114
    Tape (c) OSA 5-12114)
        +-ARG 1-80 p22   +NR 3-80 p9
        +FF 9/10-79 p56   +NYT 6-10-79 pD24
        ++FU 10-79 p42   +ON 3-8-80 p29
        +-Gr 9-79 p495   +-RR 9-79 p115
        ++Gr 2-80 p1302 tape   ++SFC 6-3-79 p48
        +-HF 9-79 p112   +-St 11-79 p84
        +-HFN 10-79 p149   +STL 12-2-79 p37
        +MT 4-80 p248

820 Ein deutsches Requiem, op. 45. Chorale preludes, op. 122, nos. 3,
    9-11. Fugue, A flat minor. Prelude and fugue on "O Traurig-

keit, O Herzleid". Helen Donath, s; Kurt Widmer, bs; South Ger-
man Madrigal Choir; Ludwigsburger Festival Orchestra; Werner
Jacob, org; Wolfgang Gonnenwein. Harmonia Mundi 1C 157 99703/4
    +–Gr 11–80 p717   +–HFN 12–80 p133
Ein deutsches Requiem, op. 45: How lovely are thy dwellings fair.
    See no. 3835
F-A-E sonata: Allegro. See no. 848
821 Fantasias, op. 116. Variations and fugue on a theme by Handel, op.
    24, B flat major. Daniel Graham, pno. Vivace VCR 1101
        +–Audio 11–80 p86   –NR 8–80 p12
        +CL 9–80 p16   +–St 12–80 p119
Fugue, A flat minor. See no. 791. See no. 820. See no. 3858
Hungarian dances. See no. 894
822 Hungarian dances, nos. 1–10. Variations and fugue on a theme by
    Handel, op. 24, B flat major. Andre Gorog, pno. Calliope CAL
    1626
        +–FF 11/12–80 p89
823 Hungarian dances, nos. 1, 3, 10. DVORAK: Slavonic dances, op. 46,
    nos. 1, 8. LISZT: Les preludes, G 97. SMETANA: Ma Vlast: Vltava.
    CSO; Daniel Barenboim. DG 2531 054 Tape (c) 3301 054
        +FF 1/2–80 p182   +NR 7–79 p2
        +Gr 10–78 p752   +RR 12–78 p74
        +HFN 12–78 p167   +–RR 5–79 p124 tape
        +HFN 3–79 p139 tape
Hungarian dances, nos. 1, G minor. See no. 3964
824 Hungarian dances, nos. 2, 6, 9, 16. PAGANINI: Cantabile, op. 17, D
    major. Le streghe, variations on a theme by Sussmayr, op. 8.
    SCHUBERT: Sonatina, violin and piano, no. 2, op. 137, D 385, A
    minor. Vladimir Spivakov, vln; Boris Bechterev, pno. HMV SQS
    1413 (also Angel SZ 37574)
        +–ARG 1–80 p51   +HFN 8–79 p119
        +–FF 11/12–79 p104   +RR 8–79 p112
        +Gr 8–79 p351   ++St 11–79 p104
        ++HF 11–79 p106   +ST 1–80 p692
Hungarian dances, no. 5, G minor. See no. 666. See no. 3601. See
    no. 3679. See no. 3969
Hungarian dances, nos. 5 and 6. See no. 3709
Hungarian dances, nos. 11–16. See no. 3950
825 Hungarian dances, nos. 17–20. LISZT: Hungarian fantasia, G 123.
    Hungarian rhpasody, no. 4, G 244, E flat major. Hungarian rhap-
    sody, no. 5, G 244, E minor. Shura Cherkassky, pno; BPhO; Her-
    bert von Karajan. DG 2535 175 Tape (c) 3335 175
        +FF 11/12–80 p81
Let nothing ever grieve thee, op. 30. See no. 3660. See no. 3970
826 Liebeslieder, op. 52. Neue Liebeslieder, op. 65. Duo Crommelynck.
    Pavane ADW 7010
        +Gr 1–80 p1167   +/RR 4–80 p93
        +HFN 3–80 p87
Motets, op. 110: Ich aber bin elend; Ach arme Welt; Wenn wir in
    hochsten Noten sein. See no. 853
Neue Liebeslieder, op. 65. See no. 826
827 Pieces, piano, op. 76 (3); op. 116; op. 118 (6); op. 119 (4).
    Rhapsodies, op. 79. Walter Gieseking, pno. Seraphim IB 6117
    (2) (From Angel 35027/8)
        +–ARG 11–80 p20   /NR 6–80 p13
        +–HF 8–80 p67   ++NYT 6–22–80 pD20

Pieces, piano, op. 76: Capriccio. See no. 3953. See no. 3954
Pieces, piano, op. 116. See no. 827
828 Pieces, piano, op. 117: Intermezzi. Pieces, piano, op. 118, nos.
     1-6. Rhapsodies, op. 79, nos. 1-2. Inger Sodergren, pno. Cal-
     liope CAL 1679 Tape (c) CAL 4679
                +–Gr 10-80 p518   +–HFN 10-80 p102
                +FF 11/12-80 p87
Pieces, piano, op. 117: Intermezzi. See no. 3550. See no. 3811
829 Pieces, piano, opp. 118 and 119. Rhapsody, op. 72, no. 2, G minor.
     Radu Lupu, pno. Decca SXL 6831 (also London CS 7051)
                ++ARG 3-80 p22   +MT 2-79 p134
                ++FF 3/4-80 p67   +–NR 6-80 p13
                +Gr 11-78 p927   +RR 11-78 p86
                ++HF 12-79 p92   ++St 1-80 p94
                +HFN 11-78 p167
Pieces, piano, op. 118. See no. 827. See no. 828
Pieces, piano, op. 118: Romance. See no. 3953. See no. 3954
830 Pieces, piano, op. 119. Variations and fugue on a theme by Handel,
     op. 24, B flat major. Rudolf Serkin, pno. Columbia M 35177
     Tape (c) MT 35177
                +FF 9/10-80 p91   +NYT 6-22-80 pD20
                ++HF 8-80 p67   ++St 9-80 p77
831 Pieces, piano, op. 119. DEBUSSY: Images: Reflets dans l'eau; Hom-
     mage a Rameau; Mouvement. Sylvia Traey, pno. Pavane ADW 7005
                –HFN 8-80 p95
Pieces, piano, op. 119 (4). See no. 827
832 Pieces, piano, op. 119, nos. 1-3. SCHUMANN: Kreisleriana, op. 16.
     Ludwig Olshansky, pno. Monitor MCS 2160
                –FF 9/10-79 p71   –HF 5-80 p81
Prelude and fugue on "O Traurigkeit, O Herzleid". See no. 820
833 Quartets, piano, nos. 1-3. Beaux Arts Trio; Walter Trampler, vla.
     Philips 6747 068 (3)
                +–Audio 12-75 p105   +NR 5-75 p8
                –HF 9-75 p83   ++SFC 8-24-75 p28
                +HFN 11-80 p116   ++St 10-75 p106
                ++MJ 10-75 p39
Quartets, piano, nos. 1-3. See no. 895
834 Quartet, piano, no. 1, op. 25, G minor (orch. Schoenberg). German
     Philharmonic Youth Orchestra; Hans Zender. DG 2531 198
                +–Gr 5-80 p1659   ++RR 6-80 p42
                +HFN 6-80 p103
835 Quartet, piano, no. 1, op. 25, G minor. Emil Gilels, pno; Amadeus
     Quartet. DG 2542 140 Tape (c) 3342 140 (From 2530 133)
                ++Gr 12-80 p842   +HFN 12-80 p153
Quartet, piano, no. 1, op. 25, G minor. See no. 261
Quartets, strings, nos. 1-3. See no. 895
836 Quartet, strings, no. 1, op. 51, C minor. Quartet, strings, no. 2,
     op. 51, A minor. LaSalle Quartet. DG 2531 255 Tape (c) 3301 255
                +–Gr 12-80 p846   ++STL 11-9-80 p40
                +HFN 12-80 p135
Quartet, strings, no. 2, op. 51, A minor. See no. 836
837 Quintet, clarinet, op. 115, B minor. BAERMANN: Adagio, clarinet and
     strings, D flat major. Jack Brymer, clt; Allegri Quartet. Argo
     ZK 62 Tape (c) KZKC 62
                +Gr 2-80 p1281   ++HFN 2-80 p86
                +Gr 7-80 p166 tape   ++RR 3-80 p73

838 Quintet, clarinet, op. 115, B minor. George Silfies, clt; St. Louis
       Symphony Members. Turnabout 37000 Tape (c) CT 7000
                +HF 1-80 p91 tape
       Quintet, clarinet, op. 115, B minor. See no. 895
839 Quintet, piano, op. 34, F minor. Maurizio Pollini, pno; Quartetto
       Italiano. DG 2531 197 Tape (c) 3301 197
                +Gr 10-80 p548 tape   +HFN 10-80 p117 tape
                +-Gr 9-80 p359   +RR 8-80 p59
                +HFN 8-80 p95
840 Quintet, piano, op. 34, F minor. Sviatoslav Richter, pno; Borodin
       Quartet. Saga 5448
                +-Gr 7-77 p192   +-HFN 4-80 p119
                +-HFN 6-77 p137   +-RR 11-77 p79
                ++RR 5-80 p76
       Quintet, piano, op. 34, F minor. See no. 895
       Quintet, strings, nos. 1 and 2. See no. 895
       Rhapsodies, op. 79. See no. 357. See no. 827. See no. 828
       Rhapsodies, op. 79, no. 2, G minor. See no. 829
       A rose has bloomed. See no. 3663
       Die schone Magelone, op. 33, no. 12: Muss es ein Trennung. See no.
         3774
841 Serenade, no. 1, op. 11, D major. Symphony of the Air; Leopold
       Stokowski. Varese VC 81050 (From Decca DL 710031)
                +FF 3/4-79 p44   +HFN 1-80 p103
                +Gr 2-80 p1263   ++St 11-78 p118
842 Serenade, no. 2, op. 16, A major. Variations on a theme by Haydn,
       op. 56a. LPO; Adrian Boult. Angel SZ 37648
                +-ARG 12-79 p30   +NR 12-79 p3
                +FF 11/12-79 p48   +NYT 6-22-80 pD20
                +-HF 11-79 p92   +-SFC 8-5-79 p53
                +MUM 5/6-80 p34
843 Serenade, no. 2, op. 16, A major. WAGNER: Siegfried Idyll. South
       German Philharmonic Orchestra; Karl Ristenpart. Nonesuch H 71383
                +-FF 9/10-80 p88   +St 11-80 p80
                +NYT 6-22-80 pD20
       Sextet, strings, nos. 1-2. See no. 895
       Sonatas, clarinet and piano, nos. 1-2. See no. 895
844 Sonata, clarinet and piano, no. 1, op. 120, F minor. Sonata, clari-
       net and piano, no. 2, op. 120, F sharp minor. Bruce Nolan, clt;
       Robert Spillman, pno. Golden Crest RE 7094
                +-ARG 10-80 p41   +-St 10-80 p110
       Sonata, piano, no. 2, op. 120, F sharp minor. See no. 844
845 Sonata, piano, no. 1, op. 1, C major. Sonata, piano, no. 2, op. 2,
       F sharp minor. Krystian Zimerman, pno. DG 2531 252
                +Gr 6-80 p53   ++RR 6-80 p73
                +HFN 6-80 p103   ++St 12-80 p82
                ++NR 11-80 p9   ++STL 5-11-80 p38
       Sonata, piano, no. 2, op. 2, F sharp minor. See no. 845
846 Sonata, 2 pianos, op. 34b, F minor. Variations on a theme by Haydn,
       op. 56a. Alfons and Aloys Kontarsky, pno. DG 2531 100 Tape (c)
       3301 100
                +-Gr 8-79 p347   +NR 1-80 p14
                ++FF 1/2-80 p67   +-NYT 6-22-80 pD20
                +HF 10-80 p98 tape   ++RR 8-79 p104
                +HFN 8-79 p103   +-RR 2-80 p98 tape
                +MT 2-80 p105

847 Sonatas, violin and piano, nos. 1-3. Trio, horn, op. 40, E flat
     major. Stoika Milanova, vln; Dora Milanova, pno; Vladimir Grig-
     orov, hn. Harmonia Mundi HM 115/6
            +-HFN 8-80 p95   ++RR 8-80 p68
848 Sonatas, violin and piano, nos. 1-3. F.A.E. sonata: Allegro. Jenny
     Abel, vln; Leonard Hokanson, pno. Harmonia Mundi 151 99705/6
            +-HFN 6-80 p117   +ST 9-80 p342
            /RR 5-80 p83
     Sonatas, violin and piano, nos. 1-3. See no. 895
849 Sonata, violin and piano, no. 1, op. 78, G major. FRANCK: Sonata,
     violin and piano, A major. Angelica May, vlc; Leonard Hokanson,
     pno. Musicaphon BM 30 SL 4007
            +-HFN 8-80 p95   +-RR 7-80 p79
     Sonata, violin and piano, no. 2, op. 100, A major. See no. 3964
850 Sonata, violin and piano, no. 3, op. 108, D minor. FRANCK: Sonata,
     violin and piano, A major. David Oistrakh, vln; Sviatoslav Rich-
     ter, pno. Quintessence PMC 7133 (From Musical Heritage Society
     MHS 3956, Angel S 40121)
            -FF 1/2-80 p68
     Sonata, violin and piano, no. 3, op. 108, D minor. See no. 3964
     Sonatas, violoncello and piano, nos. 1 and 2. See no. 895
851 Songs: Ach wende diesen Blick, op. 57, no. 4; Agnes, op. 59, no. 5;
     Alte Liebe, op. 72, no. 1; Auf dem Kirchhofe, op. 105, no. 4;
     Der Jager, op. 95, no. 4; Madchenlied, op. 107, no. 5; Maienkatz-
     chen, op. 107, no. 4; Nicht mehr zu dir zu gehen, op. 32, no. 2;
     Schon war das ich dier weihte, op. 95, no. 7; Sommerabend, op. 85,
     no. 1; Die Trauernde, op. 7, no. 5; Vergebliches Standchen, op.
     84, no. 4; Wie Melodien zieht es, op. 105, no. 1; Wie rafft ich
     mich auf, op. 32, no. 1; Zigeunerlieder, op. 103. Sena Jurinac,
     s; Georg Fischer, pno. Acanta EA 22670
            -HFN 2-80 p91   +-STL 2-10-80 p40
            +-RR 2-80 p84
852 Songs: Lieder, op. 59, no. 8. Lieder, op. 86, no. 5. Lieder, op.
     94, nos. 1, 5. LOEWE: Ballad, op. 123, no. 2; Lieder, op. 9,
     no. 5; Odins Meeresritt. SCHUBERT: Greisengesang, D 778; Die
     Liebe hat gelogen, D 751; Orest auf Tauris, D 548; Die Schafer
     und der Reiter, D 517; Schiffers Scheidelied, D 910; Totengrabers
     Heimweh, D 842. WOLF: Italinische Liederbuch, no. 5. Morike
     Lieder: Fuffreise. Hans Hotter, bar; Michael Raucheisen, pno.
     Acanta BB 23037
            +HFN 12-79 p173   +STL 4-13-80 p39
            +RR 11-79 p40
853 Songs (choral): Fest und Gedenkspruche, op. 109; Schaffe in mir
     Gott, op. 29, no. 2; Warum ist das Licht gegeben, op. 74, no. 1.
     Motets, op. 110: Ich aber bin elend; Ach arme Welt; Wenn wir in
     hochsten Noten sein. Barmen-Germarke Singers; Helmut Kahlhofer.
     Harmonia Mundi 1C 065 99830
            ++FF 5/6-80 p60   +-HFN 12-80 p133
            +-Gr 10-80 p524
854 Songs: Der bucklichte Fiedler, op. 93, no. 1; O susser Mai, op. 93,
     no. 3; Waldesnacht, op. 62, no. 3. MENDELSSOHN: Songs, op. 48
     (6). SCHUMANN: Der Konig von Thule, op. 67, no. 1; Im Walde, op.
     75, no. 2. REGER: Es waren zwei Konigskinder; Ich hab heut Nacht
     getraumet. Marburg Vocal Ensemble. Musicaphon BM 30 SL 1337
            +-HFN 10-80 p111

855 Songs: Agnes, op. 59, no. 5; Botschaft, op. 47, no. 1; Dein blaues
        Auge, op. 59, no. 8; Der Fruhling, op. 6, no. 2; Heimweh, op. 63,
        no. 8; Immer leiser wird mein Schlummer, op. 105, no. 2; In der
        Beeren, op. 84, no. 3; Der Jager, op. 95, no. 4; Komm bald, op.
        97, no. 5; Des Liebsten Schwur, op. 69, no. 4; Das Madchen
        spricht, op. 107, no. 3; Sandmannchen; Spanisches Lied, op. 6,
        no. 1; Die Trauernde, op. 7, no. 5; Vergebliches Standchen, op.
        84, no. 4; Von ewiger Liebe, op. 43, no. 1; Von waldbedkranzter
        Hohe, op. 57, no. 1; Wiegenlied, op. 49, no. 4. Elly Ameling,
        s; Dalton Baldwin, pno. Philips 9500 398
                 +ARG 3-79 p13   +NR 12-78 p13
               ++FF 5/6-79 p35   +NYT 3-4-79 pD23
                 +Gr 5-79 p1921   ++RR 5-79 p96
               ++HF 3-79 p91   ++SFC 12-31-78 p42
                 +HFN 4-79 p118   ++St 3-79 p86
                 +MM 8-79 p29   +STL 2-10-80 p40
                 +-MT 12-79 p1006

856 Songs: Botschaft, op. 47, no. 1; Geistliches Wiegenlied, op. 91,
        no. 2; Gestille Sehnsucht, op. 91, no. 1; Immer leise wird mein
        Schlummer, op. 105, no. 2; Die Mainacht, op. 43, no. 2; Meine
        Liebe ist grun, op. 63, no. 5; O komme holde Sommernacht, op. 58,
        no. 4; Standchen, op. 106, no. 1; Therese, op. 86, no. 1; Der Tod
        das ist die kuhle Nacht, op. 96, no. 1; Von ewiger Liebe, op. 43,
        no. 1; Wie Melodien zieht es mir, op. 105, no. 1. Jessye Norman,
        s; Geoffrey Parsons, pno; Ulrich von Wrochem, vln. Philips
        9500 785 Tape (c) 7300 859
                 +Gr 7-80 p158   ++NR 11-80 p8
               ++HFN 8-80 p95   +-RR 7-80 p87
               ++HFN 10-80 p117 tape

857 Songs: Motet, op. 74, no. 1; Marienlieder, op. 22; Songs (10).
        Gulbenkian Foundation Symphony Chorus; Michel Corboz. RCA ARL
        1-3350
               ++HF 11-79 p102   +ON 3-8-80 p29
               ++NYT 10-7-79 pD24   ++SFC 11-18-79 p47

858 Songs: Das Madchen spricht, op. 107, no. 3; Die Mainacht, op. 43,
        no. 2; Nachtigall, op. 97, no. 1; Von ewiger Liebe, op. 43, no.
        1. SCHUBERT: Songs: Die abgebluhte Linde, D 514; Heimliches
        Lieben, D 922; Minnelied, D 429; Der Musensohn, D 764. SCHUMANN:
        Frauenliebe und Leben, op. 42. Janet Baker, ms; Martin Isepp,
        pno. Saga 5277 Tape (c) CA 5277
                 +FF 11/12-80 p173   +HFN 10-76 p185 tape
                 +-Gr 2-77 p1322 tape   +HFN 9-79 p123
                 +HF 11-76 p124   ++RR 9-79 p127

859 Songs: Liebeslieder, op. 52. Zigeunerlieder, op. 103. MARX: Der
        bescheidene Schafer; Hat dich die Liebe beruhrt; Und gestern hat
        er mir Rosen gebracht; Valse de Chopin; Windrader. SCHUBERT: Im
        Walde, D 834. Ljuba Welitsch, s; Ernest Lush, Frederick Stone,
        Joseph Marx, pno; Irmgard Seefried, s; Elisabeth Hongen, con;
        Hugo Meyer-Welfing, t; Hans Hotter, bar; Friedrich Wuhrer, Her-
        mann von Nordberg, pno. World Records SH 373
                 +Gr 9-80 p408   +-RR 8-80 p78
                 +-ON 12-20-80 p52
     Songs: Am Wildbach die Weiden; Die Berge sind spitz; Nun stehn die
        Rosen in Blute; Und gehst du uber den Kirchhof. See no. 3952
     Songs: An die Nachtigall, op. 46, no. 4; An die Tauben, op. 63, no.
        4; Nachtigallen schwingen, op. 6, no. 6. See no. 3537

Songs: Auf dem See, op. 59, no. 1; Es Schauen die Blumen, op. 96,
no. 3; Der Jager, op. 95, no. 4; Ruhe Sussliebchen in Schatten.
See no. 3562
Songs: Auf den Kirchhofe, op. 105, no. 5; Die Mainacht, op. 43, no.
2. See no. 3573
Songs: Der eifersuchtige Knabe; All meine Herzgedanken. See no.
3662
Songs: Ernste Gesange, op. 121. See no. 548
Songs: Geheimnis, op. 71, no. 3; Das Madchen spricht, op. 107, no.
3. See no. 3541
Songs: Liebestreu, op. 3. no. 1; Vergebliches Standchen, op. 84, no.
4. See no. 3551
Songs: Vier ernste Gesange, op. 121; Sapphische Ode, op. 94, no. 4;
Komm bald, op. 97, no. 5. See no. 3863
Songs: Wiegenlied, op. 49, no. 4. See no. 3928
Songs of Mary, op. 22: A cry to Mary. See no. 3531

860   Symphonies, nos. 1-4. Halle Orchestra; James Loughran. Classics
for Pleasure CFP 78252 (4)

       +HFN 2-80 p105   +RR 3-80 p48

861   Symphonies, nos. 1-4. Academic festival overture, op. 80. Tragic
overture, op. 81. CSO; Georg Solti. Decca D151D4 (3) Tape (c)
K151K44 (Symphony, no. 4 from SXL 6890) (also London 2406 Tape
(c) 5-2406)

+ARG 5-80 p18	+—HF 2-80 p83
+—FF 3/4-80 p67	+HF 7-80 p82 tape
+Gr 9-79 p459	+NYT 12-9-79 pD25
+Gr 2-80 p1302 tape	+RR 9-79 p72

862   Symphonies, nos. 1-4. Tragic overture, op. 81. BPhO; Herbert von
Karajan. DG 2740 193 (4) (also DG 2711 022 Tape (c) 3371 041)

++ARG 5-79 p22	+—MJ 9/10-79 p51
+—FF 5/6-79 p36	++NR 2-79 p1
+—Gr 10-78 p678	++NYT 12-3-78 pD19
+Gr 1-79 p1331 tape	+—RR 12-78 p48
+HF 4-79 p80	+RR 1-79 p90
+HF 12-79 p110 tape	++SFC 12-24-78 p39
+HF 7-80 p82 tape	+St 4-79 p133
+HFN 10-78 p123	

863   Symphonies, nos. 1-4. Academic festival overture, op. 80. Tragic
overture, op. 81. Variations on a theme by Haydn, op. 56a.
Leipzig Gewandhaus Orchestra; Kurt Masur. Philips 6769 009 (4)
Tape (c) 7699 109

-ARG 5-80 p18	+HFN 11-79 p157 tape
/-FF 5/6-80 p60	+—NR 1-80 p3
+—Gr 9-79 p459	+—RR 9-79 p71
+—HF 2-80 p83	+SFC 11-4-79 p40
+HFN 10-79 p151	

Symphonies, nos. 1-4. See no. 894

864   Symphony, no. 1, op. 68, C minor. Orchestre de Paris; Charles Munch.
Arabesque 8056 Tape (c) 9056

       ++NR 5-80 p5   +—SFC 3-23-80 p35

865   Symphony, no. 1, op. 68, C minor. WAGNER: Rienzi: Overture. PO;
Leopold Stokowski. Cameo GOCLP 9009 (From Matrix A37483/92,
D1499-1503, A37004, A37700/1, DB 1226-7)

       +Gr 8-80 p215

866   Symphony, no. 1, op. 68, C minor. VPO; Zubin Mehta. Decca SXL
6796 Tape (c) KSXC 6796 (also London CS 7017 Tape (c) CS 5-7017)

++ARG 12-79 p28   +NR 3-80 p2
++FF 9/10-79 p58   +NYT 6-22-80 pD20
++Gr 3-79 p1562   ++RR 5-79 p51
+-HF 9-79 p113   ++St 9-79 p92
+-HFN 4-79 p118

867 Symphony, no. 1, op. 68, C minor. BPhO; Wilhelm Furtwangler. DG
     2530 744 (also DG 2535 162)
                    +ARG 11-76 p16   +-NR 10-76 p2
                    ++FF 3/4-80 p223   +RR 5-76 p23
                    +Gr 5-76 p1772   ++STL 1-9-77 p35
                    +-HF 11-76 p105

868 Symphony, no. 1, op. 68, C minor. VPO; Claudio Abbado. DG 2542 138
     Tape (c) 3342 138 (From 2530 424)
                    +Gr 12-80 p831   +-HFN 12-80 p153

869 Symphony, no. 1, op. 68, C minor. PhO; Carlo Maria Giulini. EMI
     (Japan) EAC 30292
                    +-ARSC Vol 12, nos. 1-2, 1980 p88

870 Symphony, no. 1, op. 68, C minor. BPhO; Wilhelm Furtwangler. Ev-
     erest SDBR 3437
                    -ARG 7-79 p23   +-NR 7-79 p4
                    -FF 1/2-80 p70   +-St 9-79 p92

871 Symphony, no. 1, op. 68, C minor. Symphony, no. 2, op. 73, D major.
     Slovak Philharmonic Orchestra; Ludovit Rajter. Musical Heritage
     Society MHS 4115/6 (2)
                    +-ARG 12-80 p22   +-FF 11/12-80 p88

872 Symphony, no. 1, op. 68, C minor. Dresden State Orchestra; Kurt
     Sanderling. RCA GL 2-5191 Tape (c) GK 2-5191 (From SB 6873)
                    +Gr 7-80 p136   +-HFN 9-80 p115 tape
                    +Gr 9-80 p413   +RR 8-80 p39
                    +HFN 8-80 p107

873 Symphony, no. 1, op. 68, C mionr. PhO; Guido Cantelli. World
     Records SH 314 Tape (c) TC SH 314 (From ALP 1152, RCA LHMV 1054)
                    +-FF 9/10-80 p89   +HFN 1-80 p103
                    ++Gr 10-79 p633   ++RR 3-80 p47

874 Symphony, no. 2, op. 73, D major. Tragic overture, op. 81. Nation-
     al Philharmonic Orchestra; Leopold Stokowski. CBS 76667 (also
     Columbia M 35129)
                    +ARG 12-80 p22   +-HFN 8-78 p102
                    ++FF 9/10-80 p90   +NYT 6-22-80 pD20
                    +Gr 8-78 p324   +RR 8-78 p52

875 Symphony, no. 2, op. 73, D major. NYP; Zubin Mehta. Columbia M
     35158 Tape (c) MT 35158 (also CBS 76830 Tape (c) 40-76830)
                    +ARG 12-79 p28   +-HFN 1-80 p123 tape
                    -FF 9/10-79 p59   ++NR 6-79 p6
                    +Gr 12-79 p1007   +-NYT 6-10-79 pD24
                    +-HF 9-79 p113   -RR 11-79 p72
                    +-HFN 11-79 p135   -SFC 7-29-79 p49

876 Symphony, no. 2, op. 73, D major. PhO; Carlo Maria Giuliani. EMI
     (Japan) EAC 30293
                    +-ARSC Vol 12, nos. 1-2, 1980 p88

877 Symphony, no. 2, op. 73, D major. Tragic overture, op. 81. FRANCK:
     Symphony, D minor. SCHUBERT: Symphony, no. 5, D 485, B flat
     major. Symphony, no. 8, D 759, B minor. TCHAIKOVSKY: Symphony,
     no. 5, op. 64, E minor. LPO; Thomas Beecham. HMV RLS 733 (4)
     (From Columbia LX 515/9, LS 638/9, LS 904/8, 785/8, 666/8, 869/73)

              +ARSC Vol 12, no. 3,   +HFN 8-79 p115
                 1980 p247   +MT 9-79 p747
              +FF 7/8-80 p191   +—RR 6-79 p74
              +—Gr 4-79 p1729
878 Symphony, no. 2, op. 73, D major. Academic festival overture, op.
     80. LSO; Pierre Monteux. Philips 6570 108 Tape (c) 7310 108
     (From SAL 3435)
              +Audio 2-80 p42   ++HFN 11-79 p157 tape
              +Gr 11-79 p810   +MUM 7/8-79 p37
              +HFN 10-79 p171 tape   +—RR 9-79 p80
              +HFN 9-79 p121
879 Symphony, no. 2, op. 73, D major. Tragic overture, op. 81.   Dresden
     State Orchestra; Kurt Sanderling. RCA GL 2-5266 Tape (c) GK 2-
     5266 (From SB 6875)
              +—Gr 4-80 p1550   +—HFN 8-80 p109 tape
              +Gr 9-80 p413 tape   +RR 4-80 p60
              +—HFN 4-80 p119
     Symphony, no. 2, op. 73, D major. See no. 871
880 Symphony, no. 3, op. 90, F major. Tragic overture, op. 81.   PhO;
     Carlo Maria Giulini. EMI (Japan) EAC 30294
              +—ARSC Vol 12, nos. 1-2, 1980 p88
881 Symphony, no. 3, op. 90, F major. Symphony, no. 4, op. 98, E minor.
     Slovak Philharmonic Orchestra; Ludovit Rajter. Musical Heritage
     Society MHS 4169/70 (2)
              +—ARG 12-80 p22
882 Symphony, no. 3, op. 90, F major. PhO; Guido Cantelli. Seraphim
     S 60325
              +ARSC Vol 12, nos. 1-2,   +MUM 7/8-79 p37
                 1980 p117   +MUM 5/6-80 p34
              +FF 9/10-79 p62   +NYT 7/8-79 pD24
              +—HF 10-79 p99
883 Symphony, no. 3, op. 90, F major. SCHUMANN: Symphony, no. 4, op.
     120, D minor. PhO; Guido Canteli. World Records SH 315 Tape
     (c) TC SH 315 (From BLP 1083, 1044, RCA LHMV 13)
              +—FF 9/10-80 p89   +HFN 1-80 p103
              +Gr 10-79 p633   ++RR 3-80 p47
     Symphony, no. 3, op. 90, F major: 3rd movement.   See no. 3605
884 Symphony, no. 4, op. 98, E minor. NYP; Zubin Mehta. CBS M 35837
     (also CBS 76949 Tape (c) 40-76949)
              +—FF 9/10-80 p91   +MUM 11/12-80 p32
              +FF 11/12-80 p88   +—NYT 6-22-80 pD20
              +—Gr 9-80 p332
885 Symphony, no. 4, op. 98, E minor. NYP; Zubin Mehta. CBS 76949
     (also Columbia M 35857 Tape (c) MT 35857)
              +HFN 9-80 p100
886 Symphony, no. 4, op. 98, E minor. Academic festival overture, op.
     80. LSO, BPhO; Claudio Abbado. DG 2542 120 Tape (c) 3342 120
     (From 2720 061, 135112)
              +Gr 7-80 p136   +—RR 5-80 p106 tape
              +HFN 5-80 p135   +—RR 6-80 p42
              +HFN 8-80 p109 tape
887 Symphony, no. 4, op. 98, E minor. CPhO; Dietrich Fischer-Dieskau.
     Quintessence PMC 7094 (From Supraphon 410 2077)
              +—FF 9/10-79 p55   +—NYT 6-10-79 pD24
              +HF 2-80 p84

Symphony, no. 4, op. 98, E minor. See no. 881. See no. 3585. See
  no. 3710
Tragic overture, op. 81. See no. 861. See no. 862. See no. 863.
  See no. 874. See no. 877. See no. 879. See no. 880
Trio, clarinet, op. 114, A minor. See no. 612. See no. 895
888 Trio, horn, op. 40, E flat major. Trios, piano, nos. 1-3. Suk
  Trio; Zdenek Tylsar, hn. Supraphon 111 2251/2
   +-FF 1/2-80 p70   ++NR 12-79 p7
   +-Gr 10-79 p667   +-RR 7-79 p73
   +-HFN 8-79 p101
Trio, horn, op. 40, E flat major. See no. 847. See no. 895
889 Trios, piano, nos. 1-3. Pro Arte Trio. BIS LP 98/9 (2)
   +-Gr 9-80 p359   ++NR 5-80 p7
   +-HFN 3-80 p87   +RR 3-80 p72
890 Trios, piano, nos. 1-3. Gyorgy Pauk, vln; Ralph Kirshbaum, vlc;
  Peter Frankl, pno. HMV SLS 5115 (2)
   +Gr 12-79 p1027   +RR 1-80 p94
   +HRN 1-80 p103   ++STL 2-10-80 p40
   ++MT 4-80 p248
Trios, piano, nos. 1-3. See no. 888. See no. 895
891 Trio, piano, no. 2, op. 87, C major. San Francisco Trio. Sound
  Storage SSR 2010
   -FF 11/12-80 p89   +SFC 12-9-80 p33
892 Variations and fugue on a theme by Handel, op. 24 (25). Waltzes,
  op. 39 (16). Leon Fleisher, pno. Odyssey Y 35920 (From Epic LC
  3331, Columbia 61670)
   +-FF 3/4-80 p70   +-NYT 6-22-80 pD20
   +-HF 8-80 p67   ++SFC 7-20-80 p34
   +-MUM 10-80 p36
Variations and fugue on a theme by Handel, op. 24, B flat major.
  See no. 821. See no. 822. See no. 830
893 Variations on a Hungarian song, op. 21, no. 2. CHOPIN: Variations,
  op. 12. MENDELSSOHN: Andante con variazioni, op. 82, E flat
  major. Fantasies, op. 16 (3). Prelude and fugue, op. 35, E
  minor. Rondo capriccioso, op. 14, E major. Phyllis Moss, pno.
  Orion ORS 80369
   +-CL 9-80 p16   +NR 5-80 p11
   +FF 5/6-80 p105
Variations on a theme by Haydn, op. 56a. See no. 815. See no. 819.
  See no. 842. See no. 846. See no. 863. See no. 894. See no.
  2908
Variations on a theme by Paganini, op. 35, A minor. See no. 790.
  See no. 3976
Waltzes, op. 39 (16). See no. 392. See no. 3882
894 Works, selections: Concerto, piano, no. 2, op. 83, B flat major.
  Concerto, violin, op. 77, D major. Concerto, violin and violon-
  cello, op. 102, A minor. Hungarian dances. Symphonies, nos. 1-
  4. Variations on a theme by Haydn, op. 56a. Yehudi Menuhin,
  vln; Willi Boskovsky; Emanuel Brabec; Edwin Fischer, pno; BPhO,
  VPO; Wilhelm Furtwangler. EMI/Electrola 159 53240/6 (7)
   +NYT 6-22-80 pD20
895 Works, selections: Quartets, piano, nos. 1-3. Quartets, strings,
  nos. 1-3. Quintet, clarinet, op. 115, B minor. Quintet, piano,
  op. 34, F minor. Quintets, strings, nos. 1, 2. Sextets, nos. 1
  and 2. Sonatas, clarinet and piano, nos. 1, 2. Sonatas, violin
  and piano, nos. 1-3. Sonatas, violoncello and piano, nos. 1, 2.

Trio, clarinet, op. 114, A minor. Trio, horn, op. 40, E flat
major. Trios, piano, nos. 1-3. Arthur Grumiaux, Daniel Gullet,
Alfred Malacek, Rudolf Hartmann, vln; Gyorgy Sebok, Hephzibah
Menuhin, Menahem Pressler, pno; Janos Starker, Bernard Green-
house, Peter Steiner, vlc; Kunio Tsuchiya, vla; Beaux Arts Trio,
BPhO Octet, Quartetto Italiano. Philips 6768 146 (15)
+—Gr 9-80 p356   +HFN 11-80 p116

BRANDMULLER, Theo
    Hommage a Perotin. See no. 4038
BRANDTS BUYS, Jan
    Serenade, op. 25, D minor. See no. 3818
BRANT, Henry
    On the nature of things after Lucretius. See no. 336
896 Orbits. SAMUEL: What of my music. Bay Bones Trombone Choir and
        Assisting Artists; Int. Soc. of Bassists and Percussion; Amy
        Snyder, voice; Nalga Lynn, s; Gerhard Samuel. CRI SD 422
                +—Audio 10-80 p134   ++SFC 6-1-80 p35
                +—FF 9/10-80 p289   +—St 11-80 p82
                +NR 7-80 p6
BREHM, Alvin
    Colloquy and chorale. See no. 3821
    Variations, piano. See no. 704
BRESGEN, Cesar
    Die Jagd. See no. 3662
BRETON, Tomas
    La Dolores: Estratto del duetto. See no. 3770
BREVELLE-SMITH
    The witch of Bowden. See no. 4007
BREVI, Giovanni
    O spiritus angelici. See no. 3546
BREWER
    The fairy pipers. See no. 3903
    Marche heroique. See no. 4064
BRIAN, Havergal
    The Cenci: Fanfare. See no. 3566
897 Doctor Merryheart. English suite, no. 1, F major. Fantastic vari-
        ations on an old rhyme. Hull Youth Orchestra; Geoffrey Heald-
        Smith. Cameo GOCLP 9010
                +—Gr 4-80 p1553
    English suite, no. 1, F major. See no. 897
    Fantastic variations on an old rhyme. See no. 897
    Festival fanfare. See no. 3959
898 Symphony, no. 10, C minor. Symphony, no. 21, E flat major. Leices-
        tershire Schools Symphony Orchestra; James Loughran, Eric Pink-
        ett. Unicorn RHS 265 (From RHS 313)
                +Gr 12-80 p831   +HFN 12-80 p153
    Symphony, no. 21, E flat major. See no. 898
BRIDGE, Frank
    Allegro moderato. See no. 901
899 Characteristic pieces (4). Poems (3). Sonata, piano. Three lyr-
        ics. Eric Parkin, pno. Unicorn RHS 359
                +Audio 2-80 p44   +MT 10-79 p836
                +Gr 11-79 p874   +RR 12-79 p93
                +HFN 11-79 p135
    First book of organ pieces. See no. 4053

900 Idylls, string quartet (3). Noveletten, string quartet (3). BRIT-
     TEN: Phantasy quartet, op. 2. Quartet, strings, D major. Janet
     Craxton, ob; Gabrieli Quartet. Decca SDD 497 (also London STS
     15439)

++FF 11-77 p13	+NR 6-80 p8
+-FF 3/4-80 p70	+RR 6-77 p73
+Gr 6-77 p69	++St 1-80 p90
+-HFN 6-77 p117	+ST 8-77 p343
++MM 10-77 p44	+-Te 12-79 p32
+MT 7-78 p601	

     Noveletten, string quartet (3). See no. 900
901 Oration, concerto elegiaco for cello. Poems (2). Allegro moderato.
     Julian Lloyd Webber, vlc; LPO; Nicholas Braithwaite. Lyrita SRCS
     104

+Gr 1-80 p1141	++RR 12-79 p49
+HFN 12-79 p158	

     Poems (2). See no. 901
     Poems (3). See no. 899
     Sally in our alley. See no. 3996
     Sonata, piano. See no. 899
     Suite, string orchestra. See no. 347
     Summer. See no. 347
     There is a willow grows aslant a brook. See no. 347
     Three lyrics. See no. 899
BRIDGE, Frederick
     God's goodness. See no. 3524
     The goslings. See no. 3791
BRINDLE, Reginald
     El polifemo de oro. See no. 3967
BRITTEN, Benjamin
     Antiphon. See no. 3525
902 Canticle, no. 2, Abraham and Isaac, op. 51. Canticle, no. 3, Still
     falls the rain, op. 55. A ceremony of carols, op. 28: Interlude.
     Folksongs: she's like the swallow; I married a wife; I will give
     my love an apple; Master Kilby. SCHUBERT: Andante, D 604, A
     major. Landler, D 366 (4). Quartet, strings, no. 8, D 112, B
     flat major: Minuet and trio. Quartet, strings, no. 12, D 703, C
     minor. Quintet, piano, op. 114, D 667, A major: Theme and vari-
     ations; Finale. Quintet, strings, op. 163, D 956, C major:
     Adagio and scherzo. Scherzo, D 593, D flat major. Sonata, pi-
     ano, no. 18, D 894, G major: Minuet and trio (arr. Bream). Songs:
     Amalia, D 195; Der Fluchtling, D 402; Der Jungling am Bache, D 30;
     Licht und Liebe, D 352; Nur wer die Sehnsucht kennt, D 887; Sehn-
     sucht, D 636; Der Ungluckliche, D 713. Die Winterreise, op. 89,
     D 911: Die Wetterfahne; Erstarrung; Die Krahe; Der Wegweiser;
     Die Post. Janet Baker, ms; Peter Pears, t; Hermann Prey, bar;
     Sviatosvla Richter, Leonard Hokanson, Dalton Baldwin, Graham
     Johnson, pno; Alan Civil, hn; Julian Bream, gtr; Anthony Pleeth,
     vlc; Rodney Slatford, double bs; Clifford Curzon, pno; Amadeus
     Quartet. CBS 79316 (3) (also Columbia M3 35197)

+-FF 1/2-80 p178	+NR 1-80 p15
+Gr 7-79 p223	+ON 4-19-80 p28
++HFN 7-79 p113	+RR 7-79 p79

     Canticle, no. 3, Still falls the rain, op. 55. See no. 902
903 A ceremony of carols, op. 28. The golden vanity, op. 78. Missa

brevis, op. 63, D major. Marisa Robles, hp; Robert Bottone, pno; Clement McWilliam, org; Winchester Cathedral Choir; Martin Neary. Pye TPLS 13065

+Gr 1-76 p1225   +MU 4-80 p11
+HFN 1-76 p104   +RR 1-76 p55

904 A ceremony of carols, op. 28. TRAD. (arr. Ellis): English carols: Deck the halls; Ding dong merrily on high; Away in a manger; I saw three ships; Coventry carol; Once in Royal David's city; We've been awhile a-wandering. Osian Ellis, hp; Vienna Boys Choir; Uwe Christian Harrer. RCA ARL 1-3437 Tape (c) ARK 1-3437 (also RL 3-0467)

+ARG 12-79 p15   +ON 12-15-79 p36
+-FF 11/12-79 p52   +-RR 1-80 p107
+-HFN 6-80 p103   +SFC 12-9-79 p43
++NR 12-79 p1   +St 12-79 p137

A ceremony of carols, op. 28: Interlude. See no. 902
Corpus Christi carol. See no. 3778. See no. 3992
The eagle has two heads. See no. 3571
Festival Te Deum, op. 32. See no. 3530
Gloriana, op. 53: soliloquy and prayer. See no. 3948
The golden vanity, op. 78. See no. 903
Hymn to the virgin. See no. 3528
Jubilate Deo, C major. See no. 3527

905 Les illuminations, op. 18. Serenade, op. 31. Robert Tear, t; Dale Clevenger, hn; CSO; PhO; Carlo Maria Giulini. DG 2531 199 Tape (c) 3301 199

+FF 7/8-80 p66   ++NR 8-80 p2
+Gr 1-80 p1182   ++NYT 6-15-80 pD29
+Gr 5-80 p1717 tape   +-RR 4-80 p108
+-HF 8-80 p70   ++SFC 4-6-80 p31
+HFN 4-80 p103   ++St 10-80 p110

Lachrymae, op. 43. See no. 3996

906 The little sweep. Sam Monck, Cato Fordham, David Glick, Colin Huehns, treble; Catherine Benson, Catherine Wearing, Mary Wells, Katherine Willis, s; Heather Begg, ms; Robert Tear, t; Robert Lloyd, bs; Finchley Children's Music Group, Kings College Choral Scholars; Medici String Quartet; Francis Grier, pno; Tristan Fry, perc; Philip Ledger. HMV ASD 3608 Tape (c) TC ASD 3608

+FF 5/6-80 p62   ++HFN 1-79 p116
+Gr 11-78 p955   +HFN 1-79 p127
+Gr 5-79 p1940 tape   ++RR 1-79 p48

907 Matinees musicales, op. 24. Soirees musicales, op. 9. Variations on a theme by Frank Bridge, op. 10. PhO, Bath Festival Orchestra; Robert Irving, Yehudi Menuhin. Classics for Pleasure CFP 40308 (From HMV CLP 1172, ASD 637)

+-FF 9/10-80 p92   +HFN 4-79 p131
++Gr 6-79 p42   +RR 4-79 p71

Missa brevis, op. 63, D major. See no. 903
Nocturnal, op. 70. See no. 3967
Phantasy quartet, op. 2. See no. 900
Quartet, strings, D major. See no. 900
The rape of Lucretia, op. 37: Duet, Act 2. See no. 3562
Russian funeral. See no. 3571
Scherzo. See no. 3795
Serenade, op. 31. See no. 350. See no. 905

908 Simple symphony, op. 4. ELGAR: Serenade, op. 20, E minor. WARLOCK:
       Capriol suite. WILLIAMSON: English lyrics (6). Yvonne Lea, ms;
       Scottish Baroque Ensemble; Leonard Friedman. Abbey ABY 810
              +Gr 8-80 p215   +-HFN 8-80 p105
     Simple symphony, op. 4. See no. 50. See no. 351
909 Sinfonietta, op. 1. LUTOSLAWSKI: Dance preludes. PROKOFIEV: Quin-
       tet, op. 39, G minor. West Jutland Chamber Ensemble. BIS LP 87
              +FF 7/8-78 p67   +RR 4-80 p88
              +HFN 6-80 p115
910 Sinfonietta, op. 1. COPLAND: Appalachian spring. VARESE: Octandre.
       Stratford Ensemble; Raffi Armenian. CBS SM 5000
              +-MUM 12-80 p33
     Soirees musicales, op. 9. See no. 907
911 Songs: (Folksong arrangements): The foggy foggy dew; The miller of
       Dee; The ploughboy. Winter words, op. 25. WOLF: An eine Aeol-
       sharfe; Bei einer Trauung; Im Fruhling; Jagerlied; Lied eines
       Verliebten; Denk es o Seele; Heimweh. Peter Pears, t; Benjamin
       Britten, pno. Aldeburgh Festival-Snape Maltings Foundation AF
       001
              +Gr 10-80 p533
     Songs: Come you not from Newcastle; The foggy foggy dew; The holy
       sonnets of John Donne, op. 35; The king is gone a-hunting; O
       waly waly; The ploughboy; Sonnets of Michelangelo, op. 22. See
       no. 3776
     Songs: She's like the swallow; I married a wife; I will give my love
       an apple; Master Kilby. See no. 902
912 Suite, harp, op. 83. SCHAFER: The crown of Ariadne. TAILLEFERRE:
       Sonata, harp. Judy Loman, hp. Aquitaine MS 90570
              +MUM 7/8-80 p31
913 Variations on a theme by Frank Bridge, op. 10. VAUGHAN WILLIAMS:
       Fantasia on a theme by Thomas Tallis. PhO; Herbert von Karajan.
       HMV SXLP 60002 Tape (c) TC SXLP 60002 (From Columbia 33CX 1159)
              +Gr 7-80 p136   +HFN 10-80 p117 tape
              +Gr 10-80 p548 tape   +RR 8-80 p39
     Variations on a theme by Frank Bridge, op. 10. See no. 907
     Young person's guide to the orchestra, op. 34. See no. 3955
BROADWOOD
     Songs: Birth of the flowers; The keys of heaven. See no. 3560
BROSCHI, Carlo
     Idapse: Ombra fedele anch'io. See no. 3636
BROUWER, Leo
     Airs populaires cubaine (3). See no. 3706
     Canticum. See no. 3599
     Danza caracteristica. See no. 3599. See no. 3614
     Elogio de la danza. See no. 3599
     Micro piezas. See no. 3816
     Tarantos. See no. 3686
BROWN, Christopher
     Laudate dominum. See no. 3532
BROWN, Earle
914 Small pieces for large chorus. FOSS: Three airs on O'Hara's angels.
       REYNOLDS: The emperor of ice cream. RICHARDS: Though under med-
       ium... Gregg Smith Singers; Oresta Cybriwsky, pno; David Staro-
       bin, mand; Joseph Passaro, Gordon Gottlieb, perc; Michael Willens,
       bs; Gregg Smith. Turnabout TV 34759
              +FF 9/10-80 p249

BRUBECK, Dave
915 La fiesta de la posada. Phyllis Bryn-Julson, s; Gene Tucker, t;
     Jake Gardner, bar; John Stephens, bs; Dave Brubeck, pno; Dale
     Warland Singers, St. Paul Chamber Orchestra, Edith Norberg's
     Carillon Choristers; Dennis Russell Davies. CBS 73903 Tape (c)
     40-73903
                  +Gr 8-80 p276   +-RR 5-80 p93
                  +HFN 4-80 p103
BRUCH, Max
916 Adagio appassionata, op. 57. Concerto, violin, no. 3, op. 58, D
     minor. Romance, op. 42. Salvatore Accardo, vln; Leipzig Ge-
     wandhaus Orchestra; Kurt Masur. Philips 9500 589 Tape (c) 7300
     711 (From 6768 065)
                  +ARG 1-80 p24   +HFN 5-80 p135
                  +Audio 2-80 p42   +HFN 9-80 p115
                  ++FF 3/4-80 p71   ++RR 5-80 p57
                  ++Gr 5-80 p1659   ++SFC 11-18-79 p47
                  ++HF 4-80 p80   ++St 2-80 p122
     Adagio appassionato, op. 57. See no. 923
     Concerti, violin, nos. 1-3. See no. 923
917 Concerto, violin, no. 1, op. 26, G minor. LALO: Symphonie espag-
     nole, op. 21, D minor. Pinchas Zukerman, vln; LAPO; Zubin Mehta.
     CBS 76726 Tape (c) 40-76726 (also Columbia M 35132 Tape (c) MT
     35132)
                  ++ARG 11-79 p19   +-HFN 4-79 p134 tape
                  ++FF 1/2-80 p71   ++RR 3-79 p76
                  ++Gr 2-79 p1415   ++RR 6-79 p123
                  +-HFN 2-79 p103
918 Concerto, violin, no. 1, op. 26, G minor. GLAZUNOV: concerto, vio-
     lin, op. 82, A minor. Pierre Amoyal, vln; RPO; Claudio Scimone.
     Erato STU 71164 (also Musical Heritage Society MHS 4109)
                  +ARG 5-80 p22   +-HFN 9-79 p104
                  -FF 7/8-80 p67   +RR 10-79 p84
                  +Gr 9-79 p460
     Concerto, violin, no. 1, op. 26, G minor. See no. 3964. See no.
     3968
     Concerto, violin, no. 1, op. 26, G minor: Adagio. See no. 3625
919 Concerto, violin, no. 3, op. 58, D minor. SPOHR: Overture to
     "Faust", op. 60. Albert Pratz, vln; CBS Festival Orchestra;
     Victor Feldbrill. Canadian Broadcasting Corporation SM 329
                  +ARG 1-80 p24
     Concerto, violin, no. 3, op. 58, D minor. See no. 916
920 In memoriam, op. 65. Serenade, op. 75. Salvatore Accardo, vln;
     Leipzig Gewandhaus Orchestra; Kurt Masur. Philips 9500 590
     Tape (c) 7300 712 (From 6768 065)
                  +ARG 7/8-80 p18   +HFN 6-80 p119 tape
                  +FF 5/6-80 p62   +NR 4-80 p15
                  +Gr 10-80 p496   +NYT 7-6-80 pD15
                  +HF 4-80 p80   ++RR 3-80 p48
                  ++HFN 3-80 p105   ++SFC 1-20-80 p47
     In memoriam, op. 65. See no. 923
921 Konzertstuck, op. 84. Scottish fantasia, op. 46. Salvatore Accar-
     do, vln; Leipzig Gewandhaus Orchestra; Kurt Masur. Philips 9500
     423 Tape (c) 7300 641
                  +-ARG 8-79 p16   +MJ 7/8-79 p57

                    +FF 11/12-79 p53   +NR 10-79 p12
                    +HF 8-79 p87   ++RR 3-80 p48
                  ++HFN 3-80 p105   +SFC 7-29-79 p49
                    +HFN 8-80 p109 tape   ++St 9-79 p93
      Konzertstuck, op. 84. See no. 923
      Odysseus: Ich wob dies Gewand. See no. 3774
922   Pieces, clarinet, viola and piano, op. 83. SCHUMANN: Marchenerzah-
        lungen, op. 132. John Weigand, clt; Emanuel Vardi, vla; Frank
        Weinstock, pno. Musical Heritage Society MHS 4130
                    /FF 9/10-80 p92
      Romance, op. 42. See no. 916. See no. 923
      Scottish fantasia, op. 46. See no. 921. See no. 923. See no.
        3964
      Serenade, op. 75. See no. 920. See no. 923
923   Works, selections: Adagio appassionato, op. 57. Concerti, violin,
        nos. 1-3. In memoriam, op. 65. Konzertstuck, op. 84. Romance,
        op. 42. Scottish fantasia, op. 46. Serenade, op. 75. Salvatore
        Accardo; Leipzig Gewandhaus Orchestra; Kurt Masur. Philips 6768
        065
                    +Gr 3-80 p1449   +ST 1-80 p691
BRUCK, Arnold von
      O du armer Judas. See no. 3765
BRUCKNER, Anton
      Christus factus est. See no. 3531
      Helgoland, op. 150. See no. 940
      Locus iste. See no. 3528
      Psalm, no. 150. See no. 940
924   Quintet, F major. WOLF: Italian serenade. Melos Quartet; Enrique
        Santiago, vla. Turnabout 37005 Tape (c) CB 7005
                    +HF 1-80 p91 tape
925   Requiem, D minor. Herrad Wehrung, s; Hildegard Laurich, ms; Fried-
        rich Melzer, t; Gunter Reich, bs; Laubacher Kantorei; Werner
        Keltsch Instrumental Ensemble; Hans Michael Beuerle. Nonesuch
        H 71327 (also Cantate 658231)
                    -ARG 11-76 p19   +NR 9-76 p8
                    +HF 11-76 p106   +SFC 12-5-76 p58
                    +HFN 12-80 p135
926   Symphony, no. 1, C minor. Dresden State Orchestra; Eugen Jochum.
        HMV ASD 3825 Tape (c) TC ASD 3825
                  ++Gr 2-80 p1264   +MT 9-80 p565
                    +HFN 3-80 p87   +RR 2-80 p50
                    +HFN 4-80 p121 tape   +RR 5-80 p106 tape
927   Symphonies, nos. 4,* 7-9. VPO, BPhO; Wilhelm Furtwangler. DG 2740
        201 (5) (From 2535 161, LMP 18854, Unicorn UNS 109/110, *new to
        UK)
                    +Gr 1-80 p1141   +-HFN 1-80 p103
928   Symphony, no. 4, E flat major. Munich Philharmonic Orchestra; Rud-
        olf Kempe. Acanta EB 22739 (2)
                    +Gr 3-80 p1386   +-RR 3-80 p49
                    +-HFN 3-80 p105
929   Symphony, no. 4, E flat major. BPhO; Eugen Jochum. DG 2535 111
        Tape (c) 3335 111 (From SLPM 139134/5)
                    +ARG 11-78 p21   +HFN 8-75 p87
                    /FF 11/12-78 p40   +HFN 10-75 p155 tape
                    +Gr 8-75 p321   +NYT 5-28-78 pD13
                    +HF 7-80 p32 tape   ++RR 6-75 p34

930 Symphony, no. 4, E flat major. PhO; Otto Klemperer. HMV SXLP 30167
        Tape (c) TC SXLP 30167, TC EXE 75 (ct) 8X EXE 75 (From Columbia
        SAX 2569) (also Angel 36245)
                    +Gr 7-74 p200   +-HFN 10-80 p117 tape
                    +Gr 9-74 p595 tape   ++RR 7-74 p35
931 Symphony, no. 4, E flat major. Leipzig Gewandhaus Orchestra; Kurt
        Masur. Vanguard VSD 71238 Tape (r) B C E 71238 (From Eurodisc)
                    +-ARG 3-79 p19   -NR 5-79 p4
                    +FF 3/4-79 p44   +SFC 12-24-78 p39
                    +HF 1-80 p91 tape   +-St 5-79 p98
                    ++MJ 7/8-79 p58
     Symphony, no. 4, E flat major. See no. 3710
932 Symphony, no. 5, B flat major. PO; Eugene Ormandy. CBS 61818 Tape
        (c) 40-61818 (From 77222)
                    +-Gr 5-80 p1659   +-RR 5-80 p106 tape
                    /-HFN 6-80 p115   +RR 6-80 p45
                    +HFN 8-80 p109 tape
933 Symphony, no. 5, B flat major. CSO; Daniel Barenboim. DG 2707 113
        (2)
                    +-ARG 5-80 p19   +NR 2-80 p2
                    +-FF 5/6-80 p63   +-NYT 12-9-79 pD25
                    +-Gr 11-79 p810   +RR 11-79 p73
                    +-HF 5-80 p67   +-SFC 5-11-80 p35
                    +HFN 12-79 p159
934 Symphony, no. 5, B flat major. Munich Philharmonic Orchestra;
        Rudolf Kempe. Odyssey Y2 35243 (2) (also Acanta HA 22526)
                    ++FF 5/6-80 p63   +HFN 12-80 p135
                    +HF 5-80 p67   ++SFC 5-11-80 p35
                    +-NR 2-80 p2
935 Symphony, no. 5, B flat major (orig. version). Leipzig Gewandhaus
        Orchestra; Kurt Masur. Vanguard VSD 71239/40 (2) Tape (r) L
        71239
                    +ARG 8-79 p18   +HF 1-80 p91 tape
                    +Audio 11-79 p130   +-MJ 7/8-79 p58
                    ++FF 7/8-79 p41   ++NR 6-79 p6
                    +FU 10-79 p43   +SFC 6-3-79 p48
                    +HF 1-79 p76
     Symphony, no. 5, B flat major. See no. 3710
936 Symphony, no. 6, A major. CSO; Georg Solti. Decca SXL 6946 Tape
        (c) KSXC 6946 (also London CS 7173)
                    +Gr 5-80 p1659   ++RR 6-80 p45
                    +-HF 12-80 p72   ++SFC 8-17-80 p36
                    +-HFN 5-80 p118   +St 12-80 p119
937 Symphony, no. 6, A major. BPhO; Herbert von Karajan. DG 2531 295
        Tape (c) 3301 295
                    +-Gr 11-80 p665   +HFN 12-80 p159 tape
                    +HFN 11-80 p116
938 Symphony, no. 6, A major. BRSO; Eugen Jochum. DG Tape (c) 3335 415
                    +HFN 11-80 p131 tape
939 Symphony, no. 7, E major. Dresden State Orchestra; Eugen Jochum.
        Angel SZB 3892 (2)
                    ++HF 12-80 p74   +-St 12-80 p119
                    +NR 10-80 p4
940 Symphony, no. 7, E major. Helgoland, op. 150. Psalm, no. 150.
        Ruth Welting, s; CSO and Chorus; Daniel Barenboim. DG 2707 116
        (2)

```
                +–Gr 9-80 p332                      +NYT 12-14-80 pD38
                +HFN 9-80 p100
```
941 Symphony, no. 7, E major. Te deum. NYP; Bruno Walter. Odyssey Y2
     35238 (2)
```
                +FF 1/2-80 p72                      ++MU 9-80 p10
                +–MJ 7/8-79 p58                     +NYT 6-17-79 pD32
```
942 Symphony, no. 7, E major. WAGNER: Siegfried Idyll. COA; Bernard
     Haitink. Philips 6769 028 (2) Tape (c) 7699 113
```
                +ARG 5-80 p19                       +HFN 3-80 p107 tape
                +FF 5/6-80 p65                      ++NR 2-80 p2
                +Gr 1-80 p1142                      +NYT 12-9-79 pD25
                +Gr 3-80 p1446 tape                 ++RR 1-80 p69
                +HF 5-80 p67                        ++RR 5-80 p106 tape
                +HF 7-80 p82 tape                   +SFC 5-11-80 p35
                +HFN 1-80 p105                      +–St 4-80 p126
```
943 Symphony, no. 7, E major. Danish Radio Orchestra; Kurt Sanderling.
     Unicorn RHS 356 Tape (c) UKC 356
```
                +–FF 7/8-80 p68                     +–HFN 11-80 p131 tape
                +Gr 7-79 p197                       +–RR 7-79 p50
                ++HF 12-80 p74                      ++SFC 5-25-80 p41
                –HFN 7-79 p103
```
944 Symphony, no. 7, E major. Leipzig Gewandhaus Orchestra; Kurt Masur.
     Vanguard VSD 72142
```
                +–ARG 11-79 p20                     +SFC 7-29-79 p49
                –FF 5/6-80 p65                      +–St 4-80 p126
```
945 Symphony, no. 7, E major. Cincinnati Symphony Orchestra; Max Rud-
     olf. Westminster MCA 1412 (From Decca DL 710139)
```
                –FF 11/12-80 p90                    –HF 12-80 p74
```
946 Symphony, no. 8, C minor. BPhO; Eugen Jochum. DG 2726 077 (2)
     Tape (c) 3372 077 (From SLPM 138918/9)
```
                +FF 7/8-79 p42                      +NYT 8-5-79 pD19
                +Gr 1-78 p1255                      +–RR 1-78 p42
                +HF 7-80 p82                        ++SFC 4-29-79 p53
                +–MJ 7/8-79 p58
```
947 Symphony, no. 8, C minor. Cologne Radio Orchestra; Gunter Wand.
     Harmonia Mundi 1C 153 99853/4 (2)
```
                +–FF 9/10-80 p93
```
948 Symphony, no. 9, D minor. BPhO; Eugen Jochum. DG 2535 173 Tape
     (c) 3335 173
```
                +ARG 11-79 p20                      +HF 7-80 p82
                +FF 11/12-79 p54                    +St 12-79 p137
```
949 Symphony, no. 9, D minor (orig. version). BPhO; Herbert von Kara-
     jan. DG 2542 129 Tape (c) 3342 129 (From SLPM 139011)
```
                +Gr 4-80 p1553                      +HFN 8-80 p109 tape
                +Gr 7-80 p166 tape                  +RR 5-80 p106 tape
                +HFN 7-80 p115                      +RR 8-80 p39
```
950 Symphony, no. 9, D minor. Cologne Radio Symphony Orchestra; Gunter
     Wand. Harmonia Mundi 065 99804
```
                +–FF 9/10-80 p93                    +–HFN 9-79 p104
```
951 Symphony, no. 9, D minor. Columbia Symphony Orchestra; Bruno Wal-
     ter. Odyssey Y 35220
```
                ++FF 1/2-80 p72                     +MJ 7/8-79 p58
                ++FU 3-80 p44                       +NYT 6-17-79 pD32
```
952 Symphony, no. 9, D minor. Leipzig Gewandhaus Orchestra; Kurt Masur.
     Vanguard VSD 71245

+–ARG 11-79 p20   +–HF 9-79 p114
-FF 5/6-80 p65   +St 12-79 p137
Te deum. See no. 818. See no. 941
BRUHNS, Nicolaus
953 Nun komm der Heiden Heiland. Toccatas, nos. 1-3, E minor, G minor.
     HANFF: Chorale preludes, Ach Gott von Himmel sich darein; Ein
     feste Burg ist unser Gott; Erbarm dich mein. Wolfram Syre, org.
     Ursina Motette M 1005
                 -ARG 1-80 p25   +MU 2-80 p10
              +FF 11/12-79 p160
     Nun komm der Heiden Heiland. See no. 954
     Prelude, E minor. See no. 164
954 Preludes, nos. 1-3. Nun komm der Heiden Heiland. SCHEIDT: Passa-
     mezzo. Gillian Weir, org. Argo ZK 65
               ++Gr 11-80 p698   +RR 6-80 p73
              +HFN 6-80 p103
     Prelude and fugue. See no. 3656
     Prelude and fugue, E minor. See no. 8. See no. 3742
     Toccatas, nos. 1-3, E minor, G minor. See no. 953
BRUINS, Theo
955 Studi (6). DE LEEUW: Men go their ways. SCHAT: Anathema, op. 19.
     VAN BAAREN: Sonatina, piano. Theo Bruins, pno. Composers Voice
     CV 7904
                 +FF 9/10-80 p247
BRUMEL, Anton
956 Mater patris et filia, motet. JOSQUIN DES PRES: Mater patris et
     filia missa. Motets: O Domine Jesu Christe. Schola Cantorum
     Sankt Foillan, Aachen; Wilhelm Eschweiler. Da Camera Magna SM
     94053
                 ++FF 1/2-80 p99
     Songs: Noe noe; Tandernac. See no. 3702
BRUNA, Pablo
     Tiento de falsas de segundo tono. See no. 3756
     Tiento sobre la letania de la virgen. See no. 3756
BUCHARDO
     Jujena. See no. 3965
BUCHT, Gunnar
     Klarinettstudie, op. 59. See no. 3650
BUDEL
     Lancan li jorn. See no. 3760
BULL, John
     Fancy. See no. 3719
     Fantasia. See no. 3855
     Galliarda. See no. 3755
     In nomine. See no. 3855
     The king's hunt. See no. 3648. See no. 4044
     Lord Lumley's pavan and galliard. See no. 3755. See no. 4014
     My grief. See no. 3648. See no. 4044
     My self. See no. 3648. See no. 4044
     Pavana. See no. 3755
     Piper's galliard. See no. 3745
     Prelude and fantasia. See no. 4014
     The prince's galliard. See no. 4014
BULLIVANT, Gerald
     Te deum, E flat major. See no. 3533. See no. 3936

BULLOCK, Ernest
    Give us the wings of faith. See no. 3528
BUNS, Benedictus
    Sonata finalis, op. 5, no. 15. See no. 3818
BUONAMENTE, Giovanni
    Sonata 3 violini. See no. 369
BURGK, Joachim
    Der Herr mit seinen Jungern. See no. 3765
BURKHARD, Willy
957 Serenade, op. 71, no. 3. FALLA: Homenaje, guitar. Spanish popular
        songs (5) (arr.). PAGANINI: Caprices, op. 1, nos. 9 and 11.
        Sonatas, violin and guitar, nos. 1 and 4. Hansheinz Schneeberg-
        er, vln; Rudolf Wangler, gtr. Da Camera SM 95059
                +FF 5/6-80 p188
    Suite, op. 98. See no. 3629
BURTON, Stephen
958 Symphony, no. 2. Diane Curry, ms; Stephen Dickson, bar; Syracuse
        Symphony Orchestra; Christopher Keene. Peters PLE 128
                +-ARG 4-80 p19   +FF 5/6-80 p66
BUSATTI, Cherubino
    Morte son io. See no. 3997
BUSCH, William
    Rest. See no. 3778
BUSH, Geoffrey
    Yorick. See no. 3829
BUSNOIS, Antoine
959 Fortuna desperata, chanson. JOSQUIN DES PRES: Fortuna desperata
        missa. Motets: In principio erat verbum. Boston Camerata; Joel
        Cohen. Titanic TI 22
                ++FF 1/2-80 p99
    In hydraulis. See no. 2441
    Songs: Est il mercy de quoy l'on puest finer; J'ay moins de bien.
        See no. 3880
BUSONI, Ferruccio
    Elegie, no. 5. See no. 3678
    Rondo Arlecchinesco. See no. 961
    Sonatina, no. 2. See no. 384
960 Sonatina, no. 6. SZYMANOWSKI: Variations on a Polish folk tune, op.
        10. TOCH: Burlesken, op. 31. WEBER: Aufforderung zum Tanz, op.
        65. Evelinde Trenkner, pno. Orion ORS 80382
                +NR 11-80 p10
961 Turandot: Suite. Rondo Arlecchinesco. Melitta Muszely,
        s; Melanie Geissler, ms; Fritz Uhl, t; Gottfried Fehr, Charles
        Gillig, bs; Bern City Orchestra, RPO; Otto Ackermann, Jascha
        Horenstein. Bruno Walter Society IGI 361 (2)
                +-NR 3-80 p11
    Turandot: Suite. See no. 961
BUTTERWORTH, George
    The banks of green willow. See no. 347
962 Love blows as the wind blows. ELGAR: Pleading, op. 48, no. 1.
        Song cycle, op. 59. Songs, op. 60. VAUGHAN WILLIAMS: On Wen-
        lock edge (orch. composer). Robert Tear, t; Birmingham Symphony
        Orchestra; Vernon Handley. HMV ASD 3896 Tape (c) TC ASD 3896
                +Gr 9-80 p380   +HFN 12-80 p159 tape
                +HFN 11-90 p123

A Shropshire lad: Loveliest of trees; When I was one and twenty;
    Look not in my eyes; Think no more lad; The lads in their hund-
    reds; Is my team ploughing. See no. 3837
A Shropshire lad: Songs. See no. 3991
BUTTERLY, Nigel
    The white throated warbler. See no. 3795
BUXTEHUDE, Dietrich
963 Cantatas: Herr ich lasse dich nicht; Ich suchte des Nachts; Mein
        Herz ist bereit; O Gottes Stadt. Helen Donath, s; Theo Altmeyer,
        t; Jakob Stampfli, bs; Stuttgart Bach Collegium; Helmuth Hilling.
        Cantate 658 214
                +-HFN 10-80 p102
     Canzone, no. 1: Passacaglia. See no. 965
964 Canzonettas, G major, E minor. Chorales: Gelobet seist du Jesu
        Christ; Gott der Vater wohn uns bei; Komm Heiliger Geist Herre
        Gott; Vater unser in Himmelreich. Preludes, C major, G minor, E
        minor. Prelude, fugue and chaconne, F major. Toccata, F major.
        Verset on the chorale "Vater unser im Himmelreich". Bernard
        Lagace, org. Calliope CAL 1731 Tape (c) CAL 4731
                +Gr 8-80 p241
     Canzonettas, G major, E minor. See no. 964
     Chorales: Gelobet seist du Jesu Christ; Gott der Vater wohn uns bei;
        Komm Heiliger Geist Herre Gott; Vater unser im Himmelreich. See
        no. 964
     Erschienen ist der herrlich Tag. See no. 4041
     In dulci jubilo. see no. 4068
     Jubilate Domino. See no. 101
     Muss der Tod denn nun doch trennen, aria. See no. 101
     Nun bitten wir den heiligen Geist. See no. 4036
965 Nun freut euch. Canzone, no. 1: Passacaglia. Prelude and fugue,
        no. 1, C major; no. 17, F major. Armin Schoof, org. Ursina
        Motette 1015
                -FF 9/10-80 p94   ++MU 11-80 p18
     Prelude, D major. See no. 164
     Preludes, C major, G minor, E minor. See no. 964
     Prelude and fugue, A minor. See no. 3971
     Prelude and fugue, D major. See no. 3742
     Prelude and fugue, G minor. See no. 4022
     Preludes and fugues, no. 1, C major; no. 17, F major. See no. 965
     Prelude, fugue and chaconne. See no. 258
     Prelude, fugue and chaconne, F major. See no. 964
     Sonata, 2 violins, op. 1, no. 5, C major. See no. 3767
     Suites, klavier. See no. 286
     Toccata, F major. See no. 964
     Toccata and fugue, F major. See no. 3664
     Verset on chorale "Vater unser im Himmelreich". See no. 964
BUZZI-PECCIA, Arturo
     Lolita. See no. 3945
     Mal d'amore. See no. 3774
BYRD, William
     Agnus Dei. See no. 4033
     Alleluia. See no. 4001
     Alleluia ascendit Deus. See no. 3783
     Almand. See no. 3755
     Ave verum corpus. See no. 3835

Exalt thyself O God, anthem. See no. 34
Calino casturame. See no. 3745. See no. 3755
Carmans whistle. See no. 3648. See no. 4044
Coranto. See no. 3855
Dances (2). See no. 3718
Earl of Salisbury pavan. See no. 3566
Fantasia, C major. See no. 3595
Galiarda. See no. 3719
Galiardas passamezzo. See no. 3755
Galliard. See no. 971. See no. 3855
In fields abroad. See no. 3719
John come kiss me now. See no. 3755
Laudibus in sanctis. See no. 3532
Lavolta Lady Morley. See no. 4044
The leaves be green. See no. 3795
Lord Willoughby's welcome home. See no. 971. See no. 3648
Malt's come down. See no. 3745

966 Mass, 4 voices. DAVIES: Psalm, no. 23. NOBLE: Magnificat and nunc
      dimittis. WESLEY, S.S.: Ascribe unto the Lord. Cathedral Sing-
      ers of Ottawa; Frances MacDonnel. Christ Church Cathedral un-
      numbered
                    +MU 6-80 p8
Miserere. See no. 3595. See no. 3755

967 Motets (6). TALLIS: Lamentations of Jeremiah. King's Singers.
      Moss Music Group MMG 1107
                    +NYT 8-17-80 pD18

968 My Lady Nevells booke. Christopher Hogwood, hpd. L'Oiseau-Lyre
      D29D4
                    ++ARG 6-78 p26   +NR 6-78 p13
                    +Gr 1-77 p1160   +RR 2-77 p77
                    +Gr 5-80 p1690   +SFC 1-28-79 p43
                    +HFN 1-77 p103   ++St 5-78 p89
                    +-MT 9-77 p735

969 My Lady Nevells booke: The fourth pavan and galliard; Qui passe; The
      battell; Sellinger's round; Monsieur's alman; Hugh Ashton's
      ground; A galliard's gigge; The second ground; The fifth pavan
      and galliard; The carman's whistle; A voluntary. Christopher
      Hogwood, virginals, hpd, org. L'Oiseau-Lyre DSLO 566
                    ++HFN 5-80 p118   +RR 5-80 p84
The noble famous queen. See no. 3997
Pavan. See no. 971. See no. 3855
Pavana bray. See no. 971
Prelude. See no. 3595
The queen's alman. See no. 3995
Rowland, or Lord Willoughby's welcome home. See no. 4044
Sing joyfully unto God. See no. 3530

970 Songs (choral): Cibavit eos; O quam suavis; Oculi omnium. MENDEL-
      SSOHN: Lauda Sion, op. 73. VICTORIA: Lauda Sion; O sacrum con-
      vivium; Tantum ergo. Mavis Beattie, s; Nancy Long, ms; John
      Dudley, t; Anthony Shelley, bar; Patrick Russill, org; London
      Oratory Choir; John Hoban. Abbey ABY 818
                    +-Gr 11-80 p731   +HFN 12-80 p149
Songs: Ah silly soul; All is as a sea; O dear life; When I was
      otherwise. See no. 4025
Songs: Ave verum corpus; Lullaby my sweet little baby. See no. 3941

Songs: From virgin's womb this day did spring; Laudibus in sanctis.
  See no. 3525
Songs (madrigals): Lullaby my sweet little baby; Though Amaryllis
  dance. See no. 3893
Songs: The day Christ was born; Haec dies. See no. 3894
This sweet and merry month of May. See no. 3995
La volta. See no. 3755
Watkin's ale. See no. 3648. See no. 4044
Will you walke the woods soe wylde. See no. 971
Wolsey's wilde. See no. 971
971 Works, selections: Galliard. My Lord Willoughbys welcome home.
  Pavana bray. Pavane. Will you walke the woods soe wylde. Wol-
  seys wilde. DOWLAND: A fancy. Forlorn hope fancy. The King of
  Denmarks galliard. My Lady Hunsdon's puffe. Mignarda. Pavana.
  The Earl of Essex galliard. Sir Henry Guilfordes almaine. Paul
  O'Dette, lt. Nonesuch H 71363 Tape (c) N 5-1363
              +ARG 9-79 p48   +HFN 11-79 p149
              +FF 9/10-80 p272   +NYT 4-22-79 pD25
              ++Gr 11-79 p885   +RR 12-79 p96
              +HF 4-80 p104 tape   ++St 12-79 p155

CABALLERO
  El cabo primero: Yo quiero un hombre. See no. 3774
CABANILLES, Juan
  Corrente italiana. See no. 3756
CABEZON, Antonio de
  Ave maris stella. See no. 3590
  Ay joly bois. See no. 972
  Ayme que vouldra. See no. 972
  Diferencias sobre el canto de La dama le demanda. See no. 972. See
    no. 3864
  Diferencias sobre el canto Llano del caballero. See no. 4021
  Diferencias sobre la Gallarda milanesa. See no. 972
  Fabordones. See no. 972
  Magnificat: Versos. See no. 972
  Pavana italiana. See no. 972
  Susanne en jour. See no. 972
  Tientos, nos. 2 and 3. See no. 972
  Ultimi miei sospiri. See no. 972
  Versos im 7 ton. See no. 972
972 Works, selections: Ay joly bois. Ayme que vouldra. Diferencias
  sobre el canto de La dama le demanda. Diferencias sobre la
  Gallarda milanesa. Fabordones. Pavana italiana. Susanne en
  jour. Tientos, nos. 2 and 3. Ultimi miei sospiri. Versos im
  7 ton. Magnificat: Versos. Gertrud Mersiovsky, org. Harmonia
  Mundi 065 99678
              +-RR 7-80 p77
CACCINI, Giulio
973 Euridice. Judith Mok, Anne Perret, Veronique Diestchy, ms; Carlos
  Manuel Soto Chavarria, t; Francisco Javier Valls Santos, bar;
  Instrumental Ensemble; Rodrigo de Zayas. Arion ARN 238 023 (2)
              +Gr 9-80 p391   +-HFN 12-80 p135
  Songs: Amarilli mia bella. See no. 3600
CAGE, John
  And earth shall bear again. See no. 977
974 A book of music, 2 prepared pianos. Sonatas and interludes, pre-

prepared piano. Joshua Pierce, Maro Ajemian, pno. Tomato 2-1001
(2)

++ARG 5-78 p22	++MQ 4-78 p261
++CL 11-78 p6	*NYT 3-12-78 pD19
+FF 5/6-78 p26	++SFC 7-23-78 p45
+HF 6-80 p74	+St 4-78 p123
+MJ 7-78 p57	

975 Etudes australes, nos. 1-16. Grete Sultan, pno. Tomato TOM 2-1101
(2)

-FF 11/12-80 p90	+St 4-80 p124
+HF 6-80 p74	

Haiku (7). See no. 977
Pastorales. See no. 977
Quartet, 12 tom-toms. See no. 977
A room. See no. 977

976 The seasons. WUORINEN: Two-part symphony. American Composers
Orchestra; Dennis Russell Davies. CRI SD 410

+ARG 7/8-80 p20	+NR 4-80 p3
+Audio 12-80 p87	+NYT 2-24-80 pD20
+FF 3/4-80 p14	+SFC 3-9-80 p39
+HF 4-80 p80	+St 4-80 p124

She is asleep. See no. 977
Sonatas and interludes, prepared piano. See no. 974
Totem ancestar. See no. 977
Wonderful widow of 18 springs. See no. 4026

977 Works, selections: And the earth shall bear again. Haiku (7). Pastorales. Quartet, 12 tom-toms. A room. She is asleep. Totem
ancestar. Jay Clayton, singer; Joshua Pierce, pno; Paul Price
Percussion Ensemble; Joshua Pierce. Tomato TOM 7016

+FF 11/12-79 p55	++MJ 5/6-79 p47
+FF 11/12-80 p90	+St 4-80 p124
+HF 6-80 p74	

CAILLIET
Variations on "Pop goes the weasel". See no. 3962

CAIX d'HERVELOIS, Louis de
978 Pieces de viole, 1st livre. Suite, no. 1, 3rd oeuvre. Jordi Savall,
Ariane Maurette, vla da gamba; Hopkinson Smith, baroque gtr and
theorbo; Ton Koopman, hpd. Telefunken AW 6-42126

+-FF 3/4-80 p78	+HFN 7-78 p96
+-Gr 7-78 p213	+RR 5-78 p47
+HF 3-80 p77	

Suite, no. 1, 3rd oeuvre. See no. 978

CALDARA, Antonio
La costanza in amor vince l'inganno: Selve amiche; Come raggio sol.
See no. 3687
Crucifixus. See no. 762

CALKIN
Breathe soft ye winds. See no. 3791

CALLCOTT
O snatch me swift. See no. 3873

CALVERT, Morley
Chanson melancolique. See no. 4043
Introduction, elegy and caprice. See no. 3620
The Monteregian hills: Suite. See no. 3740

CALVI, Carlo
La bertazzina. See no. 3956

CAMERON, Richard
     Variations. See no. 3650
CAMIDGE, Matthew
     Gavotte. See no. 3582. See no. 3618
CAMILLERI, Charles
979 African dreams. Etudes, Bks I and II. Sonatina, no. 1. Sonatina
          semplice. Angela Brownridge, pno. Bedivere BVR 302
                    +HFN 12-80 p135
     Etudes, Bks I and II. See no. 979
     Sonatina, no. 1. See no. 979
     Sonatina semplice. See no. 979
CAMPIAN, Thomas
     Fair if you expect admiring. See no. 3719
     Jack and Joan. See no. 3876
980 Songs: Author of light; The cypress curtain of the night; Fair if
          you expect admiring; I care not for these ladies; It fell in a
          summer's day; There is a garden in her face. DANYEL: Eyes look
          no more; Like as the lute delights; What delight can they en-
          joy. HOLBORNE: The night watch. Pavan and galliard. ROSSETER:
          Prelude, galliard and almain. Songs: No grave for woe; Shall
          I come if I swim; Sweet come again; What then is love but mourn-
          ing; Whether men do laugh or weep. James Bowman, c-t; Robert
          Spencer, lt. Saga 5470
                    +Gr 4-80 p1584   +RR 5-80 p95
                    +HFN 5-80 p129
     Songs: Come let us sound; When to her lute. See no. 3877
     Songs: If you longst so much to learn; Fain would I wed; Never love
          unless you can; Oft have I sighed. See no. 3778
     Suites, nos. 1-3. See no. 3963
     Sweet exclude me not. See no. 3600
981 Works selections (Songs, consort pieces and masque music): All
          looks be pale; Come ashore merry mates; The cypress curtain of
          the night; Fain would I wed; Fair if you expect admiring; Fire
          fire; Harden now thy tired heart; I care not for these ladies;
          It fell on a summer's day; Jack and Joan they think no ill; Move
          now with measured sound; Never love unless you can; Never weather-
          beaten sail; Now hath Flora rob'd her bowers; So sweet is thy
          discourse to me; Sweet exclude me not; What if a day; While danc-
          ing rests. London Camerata; Glenda Simpson, s; Barry Mason, lt.
          Meridian E 77009
                    +Gr 8-79 p363   +-MT 1-80 p33
                    +HFN 7-79 p103   +RR 6-79 p111
CAMPOS
     Danzas. See no. 3645
CAMPRA, Andre
982 Requiem mass. Judith Nelson, Dinah Harris, s; Jean-Claude Orliac,
          Wynford Evans, t; Stephen Roberts, bs; Monteverdi Choir; English
          Baroque Soloists; John Eliot Gardiner. Erato STU 71310
                    +Gr 10-80 p524   +-HFN 12-80 p135
     Tancrede: Suite. See no. 3610
CANFIELD, David
983 Cat dances. Cats. Dog trots. Improvisation on thoughts in the
          mind of a cat. Sonata, violin and piano. Karen Hagerman, s;
          David Brunell, pno; David DeBoor Canfield; Andres Cardenes, vln;
          Concentus Felices; Richard Allen Fiske. Enharmonic EN 79 001

+–FF 3/4-80 p72

Cats. See no. 983

Dog trots. See no. 983

Improvisation on thoughts in the mind of a cat. See no. 983

Sonata, violin and piano. See no. 983

CANNABICH, Christian

Sinfonia, B flat major. See no. 3703

Sinfonia concertante, C major. See no. 3703

CANNIO

O surdato 'nnammurato. See no. 3667

CAPLET, Andre

Ballades francaises (5). See no. 3861

Divertissements. See no. 3564

Ecoute. See no. 3892

CAPUA, Eduardo de

Mari Mari. See no. 3900. See no. 3988

O sole mio. See no. 3771. See no. 3981

Songs: Mari Mari; O sole mio. See no. 3667

CARA, Marchetto

Non e temp. See no. 3864

CARDILLO

Core 'ngrato. See no. 3949

CARISSIMI, Giacomo

984 Cantatas: Amor mio che cosa e questo; Apritevi inferni; Bel tempo
    per me se n'ando; Deh memoria; In un mar di pensieri; No no mio
    core; Suonera l'ultima tromba; V'intendo v'intendo occhi. Martyn
    Hill, t; Trevor Jones, vla da gamba; Robert Spencer, lt; Chris-
    topher Hogwood, hpd, org. L'Oiseau-Lyre DSLO 547
                    +Gr 9-79 p495   +MT 8-80 p504
                    +HFN 9-79 p105   +RR 9-79 p116

Songs: No non mi speri; Vittoria mio cuore. See no. 3687

Vittoria: Vittoria mio core. See no. 3901

CARLETON, Nicholas

Praeludium. See no. 3590

CARLSTEDT, Jan

985 Quartet, strings, no. 4. MENDELSSOHN: Quartet, strings, no. 6, op.
    80, F minor. Saulesco Quartet. Philips 6519 008
                    +–FF 7/8-80 p68

CARMICHAEL, Hoagy

Stardust. See no. 3882

CARMINA BURANA: Plaintes mariales du jeu de la passion. See no.
    3747

CARON

Cente mille escus. See no. 3880

CAROSO, Fabricio

Bassa savella. See no. 3612

CARR

Trumpets of victory. See no. 3971

CARR, Richard

986 Division upon an Italian ground. PARCHAM: Solo, G major. PEPUSCH:
    Sonata, recorder, no. 4, F major. VAN EYCK: Doen Daphne. Eng-
    els Nachtegaeltje. Pavane lachrymae. Frans Bruggen, rec; Niko-
    laus Harnoncourt, vla da gamba; Anner Bylsma, vlc; Gustav Leon-
    hardt, hpd. Telefunken 6-42050 Tape (c) 4-42050
                    -FF 1/2-80 p170

CARRENO, Teresa
    Intermezzo scherzo, op. 34. See no. 4024
    Quartet, strings, B minor. See no. 4065
    Reverie-Barcarolle "Venise", op. 33. See no. 4024
CARTER, Elliot
987 A mirror on which to dwell. Symphony of three orchestras. Specu-
        lum Musicae, NYP; Pierre Boulez. Columbia M 35171 Tape (c) MT
        35171
                +NYT 9-28-80 pD31
988 Pastoral. CASTELNUOVO-TEDESCO: Sonata, clarinet and piano, op. 128.
        FROHNE: Study, solo clarinet, op. 17. Elsa Ludewig-Verdehr, lt;
        David Liptak, Ralph Votapek, pno. Grenadilla GS 1018
                +-FF 3/4-80 p72   +-NR 10-79 p4
989 Sonata, piano. CASELLA: Ricercari sul nome B-A-C-H (2). HONEGGER:
        Prelude arioso fughette sur le nom de Bach. LISZT: Fantasia and
        fugue on the name B-A-C-H, G 529. Evelinde Trenkner, pno.
        Orion ORS 79342
                +-CL 4-80 p12   +-NR 5-80 p12
                +-FF 5/6-80 p67
    Symphony of three orchestras. See no. 987
    Tell me where is fancy bred. See no. 4026
CARULLI, Fernando
    Divertimento per il Decacordo. See no. 3686
CASALS, Pablo
    O vos omnes. See no. 3571. See no. 4059
CASCARINO, Romeo
    Songs (8). See no. 3891
CASELLA
    Ricercari sul nome B-A-C-H. See no. 989
CASSADO, Gaspar
990 Suite, solo violoncello. CHOPIN: Sonata, violoncello and piano, op.
        65, G minor. SCHUBERT: Sonatina, violin and piano, no. 1, op.
        137, D 384, D major. Janos Starker, vlc; Shigeo Neriki, pno.
        Denon OX 7171
                +FF 9/10-80 p94
CASTELNUOVO-TEDESCO, Mario
991 Alghe. Alt Wien. Piedigrotta. La sirenette e il pesce turchino.
        Michael McFrederick, pno. Orion ORS 80370
                +FF 9/10-80 p97   +NR 10-80 p14
    Alt Wien. See no. 991
    Concerto, guitar, no. 1, op. 99, D major. See no. 55. See no.
        3612. See no. 3798
    Etudes d'ondes: Sea murmurs. See no. 3964
    Fantasia. See no. 3642
    Piedigrotta. See no. 991
    Quintet, guitar. See no. 743
    La sirenette e il pesce turchino. See no. 991
    Sonata, clarinet and piano, op. 128. See no. 988
    Sonata, guitar: Vivo ed energico. See no. 3549. See no. 3775
    Tango. See no. 3552. See no. 3788
    Tarantella, A minor. See no. 3798
    Valse. See no. 3964
CASTEREDE, Jacques
    Sonatine. See no. 3653

CATALANI, Alfredo
Loreley: Ah dunque ei m'amera. See no. 3774
Loreley: Nel verde maggio. See no. 3988
La Wally: Ebben ne andro lontano. See no. 3770. See no. 3789
La Wally: T'amo ben mio. See no. 3982
CAVALLI, Pier Francesco
992 Ercole amante. Colette Alliot-Lugaz, Marilyn Hill-Smith, Yvonne
Minton, ms; Ulrik Cold, John Tomlinson, bs; English Bach Festi-
val Orchestra; Michel Corboz. Erato STU 71328 (3)
+/Gr 10-80 p533   +STL 12-14-80 p38
+STL 11-9-80 p40
Lamento di Cassandra: L'alma fiacca svani; Son ancor pargoletta.
See no. 3687
CAVENDISH, Michael
Come gentle swains. See no. 3893
CAZZATI
Sonata, trumpet and strings. See no. 3716
CELLI, Joseph
993 S for J. Sky. GOLDSTEIN: A summoning of focus. SCHWARZ: Extended
oboe. STOCKHAUSEN: Spiral. Joseph Celli, ob; Various electron-
ics. 0.0. Records 1
+-ARG 2-80 p52
Sky. See no. 993
CEREMUGA, Josef
994 Symphony, no. 3, KRCEK: Symphony, no. 1. CPhO, Plzen Radio Orch-
estra; Jiri Belohlavek, Mario Klemens. Supraphon 110 2290
-FF 11/12-80 p91   +-NR 11-80 p3
CEREROLS, Juan (Joan)
995 Missa pro defunctis. Pues para en la sepultura. Vivo yo. Mont-
serrat Escolania and Capella de Musica; Ireneu Segarra. Harmonia
Mundi 065 99715
+HFN 5-80 p118   ++RR 4-80 p108
Pues para en la sepultura. See no. 995
Vivo yo. See no. 995
CERNOHORSKY, Bohuslav
Fuga moderato. See no. 3752
CERTON, Pierre
J'ay le rebours. See no. 4042
Songs: Amour a tort; C'est grand pitye; Ce n'est a vous; De tout le
mai; En esperant; Entre vous gentilz hommes; Heilas ne fringue-
rons nous; Je l'ay ayme; Je ne veulx poinct; Martin s'en alla;
Plus ne suys; Que n'est elle aupres de moy; Si ta beaulte; Ung
jour que Madame dormait. See no. 996
996 Sus le pont d'Avignon, mass. Songs: Amour a tort; C'est grand pitye;
Ce n'est a vous; De tout le mai; En esperant; Entre vous gentilz
hommes; Heilas ne fringuerons nous; Je l'ay ayme; Je ne veulx
poinct; Martin s'en alla; Plus ne suys; Que n'est elle aupres de
moy; Si ta beaulte; Ung jour que Madame dormait. Boston Camerata;
Joel Cohen. Harmonia Mundi HM 1034
+FF 9/10-80 p97   +RR 8-80 p78
++Gr 5-80 p1700   +-St 11-80 p82
+HFN 6-80 p106
CESAR
Causerie, op. 40, no. 6. See no. 3887

CESTI, Pietro
997 Cantatas: Pria ch'adori; Amanti io vi disfido; Lacrime mie; Mia
       tiranna. Judith Nelson, s; Rene Jacobs, c-t; William Christie,
       hpd; Jaap Ter Linden, vlc; Konrad Junghanel, theorbo. Harmonia
       Mundi HM 1018
                 ++Gr 10-79 p686   +HFN 12-79 p159
                 +HF 8-80 p78   ++RR 9-79 p117
CHABRAN, Carlo
998 Sonata, violin, op. 1, no. 5, G major. NARDINI: Sonata, violin,
       no. 1, B flat major. TARTINI: Sonata, violin, G minor. Sergiu
       Luca, vln; Barbara Bogatin, vlc; James Richman, hpd. Nonesuch
       H 71361
                 +ARG 12-79 p58   +NYT 4-22-79 pD25
                 ++FF 1/2-80 p165   +RR 11-79 p115
                 +HFN 11-79 p149   ++St 8-79 p116
CHABRIER, Emmanuel
999 Bourree fantasque. Pieces pittoresques: Idylle; Scherzo valse.
       DEBUSSY: Preludes, Bk 1: Le vent dans la plaine; Les colines d'
       Anecapri; Bk 2: Les terrasses des audiences; Les tierces alter-
       nees. SATIE: Gymnopedies (3). SAINT-SAENS: Concerto, piano,
       op. 11. Etudes, op. 52. Toccata, op. 111. Cecile Ousset, pno.
       Aurora AUR 5068 (From Decca SDD R 435)
                 +-Gr 1-80 p1172   +RR 12-79 p98
                 +-HFN 12-79 p179
1000 Espana. CHAUSSON: Viviane, op. 5. DUKAS: Sorcerer's apprentice.
       ENESCO: Roumanian rhapsody, op. 11, no. 1, A major. Pro Musica
       Orchestra; Hans-Jurgen Walther. CMS/Summit 1064 Tape (c) X 41064
                 +HF 6-80 p96 tape
1001 Espana. FALLA: El sombrero de tres picos: Suites, nos. 1 and 2.
       RAVEL: Rapsodie espagnole. PO; Riccardo Muti. HMV ASD 3902
       Tape (c) TC ASD 3902 (also Angel DS 37742 Tape (c) 4ZS 37742)
                 ++Gr 12-80 p831
1002 Espana. DUKAS: The sorcerer's apprentice. DEBUSSY: Nocturnes:
       Fetes. Prelude to the afternoon of a faun. PH; Zoltan Rozsnyai.
       M & K RT 202
                 +ARG 5-80 p45   /FF 9/10-80 p38
     Espana. See no. 665
     Espana: Rhapsody. See no. 4069
     Marche joyeuse. See no. 3666. See no. 3799
     Pieces pittoresques: Idylle; Scherzo valse. See no. 999
     Pieces pittoresques: Scherzo valse. See no. 3953. See no. 3954
1003 Songs: Ballade des gros dindons; Les cigales; Chanson pour Jeanne;
       Credo d'amour; L'Invitation au voyage; L'ile heureuse; Lied; Pas-
       torale des cochons roses; Serenade de Ruy Blas; Sommation irres-
       pectueuse; Tes yeux bleus; Toutes les fleurs; Villanelle des
       petits canards. Bruno Laplante, bar; Janine Lachance, pno.
       Calliope CAL 1880
                 +RR 8-80 p18
     Songs: Ballade des gros dindons; Pastorale des cochons roses; Vil-
       lanelle des petits canards. See no. 3861
1004 Trois valse romantiques. SAINT-SAENS: The carnival of the animals.
       SEVERAC: Le soldat de plomb. Marylene Dosse, Annie Petit, pno;
       Wurttemberg Chamber Orchestra; Jorg Faerber. Turnabout TVS
       34586
                 +Gr 1-80 p1142   +RR 12-79 p74
                 +-HFN 12-79 p175   -St 6-76 p108
                 +NR 2-76 p14

CHAGRIN, Francis
    Helter skelter. See no. See no. 3829
CHAIX, Charles
    Chorales (2). See no. 3734
CHAMINADE, Cecile
    Air de ballet, no. 3, op. 37. See no. 4024
1005 Concertstuck, piano. DOHNANYI: Capriccio, op. 28, no. 6, F minor.
        Capriccio brillante, op. 2, no. 4. A dedication, op. 13, no. 1.
        Postludium, op. 13, no. 10. Rhapsody, op. 11, no. 2. James
        Johnson, pno; RPO; Paul Freeman. Orion ORS 78296 (also DBS GS
        2005)
                        +-ARG 8-79 p19   +FF 9/10-79 p69
                        +ARG 5-80 p45   +FF 9/10-80 p38
                        +CL 12-79 p11   +NR 12-79 p5
    L'Enjoleuse, op. 50. See no. 4024
    Songs: L'ete; Chanson slave. See no. 3770
    Trio, no. 1, op. 11, G minor. See no. 4065
    CHANTS A LA COUR DE CHARLES QUINT. See no. 3578
CHAPI Y LORENTE, Ruperto
    La bruja: Jota. See no. 3919
    El milagro de la virgen: Flores purisimas. See no. 3983
    Moreno. See no. 3919
CHAPMAN, Edward
    Christ is the flower within my heart. See no. 3531
CHARPENTIER, Gustave
    Louise: Depuis le jour. See no. 3554. See no. 3770. See no. 3886.
        See no. 3985
    Louise: Depuis le jour; Depuis longtempes j'habitais cettre chambre.
        See no. 3774
CHARPENTIER, Marc-Antoine
    Beatus vir. See no. 1007
    Carols (3). See no. 1011
1006 Easter eve mass. DELALANDE: Psallite domino. ANON.: Messe de Tou-
        louse. Messe de Tournai. Schola Cantorum New York; McNeil Rob-
        inson, org and cond. Musical Heritage Society MHS 4133 Tape (c)
        MHC 6133
                        +-FF 9/10-80 p99   +-HF 11-80 p88 tape
    L'Enfant prodigue. See no. 1015
    In nativitatem Domini canticum. See no. 4068
1007 Le Judgement dernier. Beatus vir. Evelyn Brunner, Helena Vieira,
        s; Naoko Ihara, con; Alain Zaepffel, c-t; Alejandro Ramirez, t;
        Philippe Huttenlocher, bs; Gulbenkian Foundation Orchestra and
        Chorus; Michel Corboz. Erato STU 71222
                        +Gr 8-80 p248   +RR 5-80 p93
                        /-HFN 5-80 p119   ++STL 7-13-80 p38
1008 Judith. Colette Alliot-Lugaz, Lynda Russel, s; John York-Skinner,
        alto; Anthony Roden, Michael Goldthorpe, t; Richard Jackson, John
        Tomlinson, bs; English Bach Festival Chorus; English Baroque Or-
        chestra. Erato STU 71282
                        +Gr 10-80 p524
1009 Lecons de tenebres. Judith Nelson, Anne Verkinderen, s; Rene Jacobs,
        c-t; Wieland Kuijken, bs viol; William Christie, org and hpd;
        Konrad Junghanel, theorbo. Harmonia Mundi HM 1005/7 (3) Tape
        (c) HM 40 1005/7
                        ++FF 5/6-80 p68   ++HFN 3-79 p139 tape
                        +Gr 7-78 p232   +NYT 8-10-80 pD17

+HFN 6-78 p119   +RR 5-78 p59

1010 Lecons de tenebres du Vendredy Sainct, nos. 1-3. Repons du Mercredy
     Sainct: 2nd and 3rd nocturnes. Judith Nelson, Anne Verkinderen,
     s; Rene Jacobs, c-t; Wieland Kuijken, treble viol and bs viol;
     William Christie, hpd and org; Konrad Junghanel, theorbo; Adel-
     heid Glatt, bs viol. Harmonia Mundi HM 1008/9 (2)
               ++FF 11/12-80 p91   +MT 11-79 p922
               ++Gr 8-79 p358   +NYT 8-10-80 p1917
               +HFN 8-79 p103   +RR 7-79 p103
1011 Magnificat. Te deum. Carols (3). Pro Cantione Antiqua Soloists;
     Collegiate Church of St. Mary Choir; La Grande Ecurie et la Cham-
     bre de Roy; Jean-Claude Malgoire. CBS 76891
               +HFN 6-80 p106   ++STL 5-11-80 p39
               +RR 6-80 p83
1012 Messe de minuit pour noel (Midnight mass on French Christmas carols).
     Sonata a six. Boston Camerata; Joel Cohen. Desmar DSM 1016G
               ++AR 8-80 p85   +NR 8-79 p8
               ++ARG 12-79 p15   ++SFC 12-9-79 p43
               +FF 7/8-79 p43   +St 4-79 p134
               +HF 8-79 p88
1013 Messe pour les trepasses. Miserere des Jesuites. Karine Rosat,
     Jennifer Smith, s; Hanna Schaer, con; John Elwes, Fernando Sera-
     fim, t; Philippe Huttenlocher, bar; Michel Brodard, bs; Gigino
     Maestri, Ortwin Noeth, Carlos Laredo, vln; Ricardo Ramalho, Car-
     los Franco, flt; Peter Healey, Paulo Teixeira, ob; Elias Ariz-
     curen, vlc; Antoine Sibertin-Blanc, org; Gulbenkian Foundation
     Orchestra and Chorus; Michel Corboz. Erato STU 70765/66 (2)
     (also Musical Heritage Society MHS 4098/9 (2))
               +FF 7/8-80 p69   ++RR 7-74 p74
     Miserere des Jesuites. See no. 1013
1014 Missa Assumpta est Maria. English Bach Festival Soloists; Orches-
     tra and Chorus. Erato STU 71281
               +HFN 12-80 p135
     Repons du Mercredy Sainct: 2nd and 3rd nocturnes. See no. 1010
1015 Sainte Caecila vierge et martyre. L'Enfant prodigue. Les Arts
     Florissants Vocal and Instrumental Ensembles; William Christie.
     Harmonia Mundi HM 10066
               +FF 9/10-80 p98   +HFN 6-80 p106
               +Gr 5-80 p1700   +HFN 6-80 p106
     Sonata a six. See no. 1012
     Te deum. See no. 1011
CHASE, Allen
     Fugue for brass sextet. See no. 3740
CHATMAN, Stephen
1016 Hesitation. On the contrary. HUDSON: Fantasy/refrain. MORGAN:
     Trio, flute, violoncello and harpsichord. Robert Onofrey, clt;
     John Loban, Linda Quan, vln; Maura Chatman, celeste; Carole Mor-
     gan, flt; Barbara Haffner, Andre Emelianoff, vlc; Lambert Orkis,
     hpd; John Graham, vla; Eastman Musica Nova; Sydney Hodkinson.
     CRI SD 414
               +-HF 10-80 p72   ++NR 10-80 p6
     On the contrary. See no. 1016
     Whisper baby. See no. 393
CHAUMANT, Lambert
     Suite sur le 2nd ton. See no. 68

CHAUN, Frantisek
1017 Ghiribizzo. Pictures (5). HAVELKA: Hommage a Hieronymus Bosch.
        Josef Hala, pno, CPhO; Vaclav Neumann, Zedenek Kosler. Panton
        110 597
                    ++FF 1/2-80 p90
     Pictures. See no. 1017
CHAUSSON, Ernst
1018 Concerto, violin and piano, op. 21, D major. Lorin Maazel, vln;
        Israela Margalit, pno; Cleveland Orchestra. Telarc 10046
                    +-FF 11/12-80 p92   ++NR 10-80 p5
                    +Gr 12-80 p831   +SFC 8-17-80 p36
                    +-HF 10-80 p72
     Concerto, violin and piano, op. 21, D major. See no. 3964
1019 Poeme, op. 25, E major. RAVEL: Tzigane. SAINT-SAENS: Introduction
        and rondo capriccioso, op. 28. Havanaise, op. 83. Kyung-Wha
        Chung, vln; RPO; Charles Dutoit. Decca SXL 6851 Tape (c) KSXC
        6851 (also London CS 7073)
                    +-FF 11/12-80 p211   +RR 9-79 p84
                    ++Gr 9-79 p474   ++RR 3-80 p104 tape
                    +HFN 9-79 p117   +ST 1-80 p692
                    +NYT 7-6-80 pD15
1020 Poeme, op. 25, E major (arr. Ysaye). RHEINBERGER: Suite, op. 166,
        C major. VITALI: Chaconne, G minor. Pierre d'Archambeau, vln;
        Michele Johns, pno; Marilyn Mason, org. Orion ORS 79336
                    +-FF 1/2-80 p132   +-NR 7-79 p10
1021 Poeme, op. 25, E major. RAVEL: Tzigane. SAINT-SAENS: Havanaise,
        op. 83. Introduction and rondo capriccioso, op. 28. Igor Oist-
        rakh, vln; MRSO; Gennady Rozhdestvensky. Quintessence PMC 7132
                    +FF 3/4-80 p73
     Poeme, op. 25, E major. See no. 3772
1022 Songs: Cantique a l'epouse, op. 36, no. 1; Le charme, op. 2, no. 2;
        Le colibri, op. 2, no. 7; Les heures, op. 27, no. 1; Les papil-
        lons, op. 2, no. 3; Poeme de l'amour et de la mer, op. 19; Sere-
        nade italienne, op. 2, no. 5; Serres chaudes, op. 24. Bruno La-
        plante, bar; Janine Lachance, pno. Calliope CAL 1860
                    +RR 8-80 p18
1023 Songs: Amour d'Antan; La caravane; Le charme; Le colibri; Les papil-
        lons; Temps des lilas. RACHMANINOFF: A passing breeze; The ans-
        wer; Christ is risen; How long since love; The harvest of sorrow;
        Lilacs; Oh do not grieve; To the children. Jan DeGaetani, ms;
        Gilbert Kalish, pno. Nonesuch H 71373
                    ++ARG 9-80 p38   ++NYT 6-15-80 pD31
                    +-FF 9/10-80 p101   ++St 6-80 p80
                    +NR 6-80 p11
1024 Trio, piano, op. 3, G minor. FAURE: Trio, piano, op. 120, D minor.
        Guarneri Trio. Broekmans Van Poppel BP 201
                    +Gr 7-80 p148
     Viviane, op. 5. See no. 1000
CHAVEZ, Carlos
     Caprichos (5). See no. 781
     Daughter of Colchis. See no. 695
     Estudio a Rubinstein. See no. 781
1025 Sinfonia india. GALINDO: Sones de Mariachi. HALFFTER: Don Lindo
        de Almeria. MONCAYO: Huapango. National Symphony Orchestra of
        Mexico; Kenneth Klein. Unicorn RHS 365

         +—FF 5/6-80 p69   ++SFC 5-11-80 p35
         ++Gr 1-80 p1162   +St 9-80 p87
         +—RR 11-79 p74

CHAYNES, Charles
     Impulsions. See no. 3653
CHEDEVILLE, Nicolas
1026 Le printems ou les saisons amusantes. STAMITZ: Concerto, viola d'
     amore, no. 1, D major. TELEMANN: Concerto, oboe d'amore, D major.
     Concert suite, sopranino recorder. Jean-Philippe Vasseur, vla
     d'amore; Michele Fromenteau, hurdy gurdy; Michel Sanvoisin, rec;
     Jacques Vandeville, ob d'amore; Grenoble Ensemble Instrumental;
     Stephane Cardon. Arion ARN 38525
                   +RR 5-80 p58
CHEMIN-PETIT, Hans
     Und in dem Schneegebirge. See no. 3662
CHERUBINI, Luigi
1027 Marches (8). PACHELBEL: Canon sur une basse obstinee (trans. Barbo-
     teu). Suites, B flat major, G major. ANON.: Die Bankelsanger-
     lieder: Sonata, excerpt. Ars Nova Brass Quintet. Erato STU
     71265
              ++Gr 5-80 p1689   +HFN 8-80 p105
              +HFN 5-80 p131   +—RR 5-80 p77
1028 Medea (ed. Lachner). Sylvia Sass, Magda Kramar, s; Klara Takacs,
     Veronika Kincses, Katalin Szokefalvy-Nagy, ms; Veriano Luchetti,
     t; Kolos Kovats, bs; Hungarian Radio and Television Chorus; Buda-
     pest Symphony Orchestra; Lamberto Gardelli. Hungaroton SLPX
     11904/6 (3)
              +—ARG 3-79 p20   +OC Vol XX, no. 2, p 51
              +—FF 3/4-79 p47   +—ON 2-23-80 p45
              +—HF 6-79 p32   +SFC 2-25-79 p41
              +—NR 3-79 p12   +St 9-79 p93
     Medea: O amore viene a me. See no. 3723
1029 Requiem, C minor. Morski Zvutsi Chorus; Bulgarian Radio & TV Orch-
     estra. Harmonia Mundi HM 143
                   -HFN 9-80 p100
1030 Requiem, C minor. ORTF and Chorus; Lamberto Gardelli. Philips 9500
     715 Tape (c) 7300 805
                   +NR 11-80 p6
1031 Requiem, D minor. Brassus Chorale, Lausanne Pro Arte Chorus; OSR
     and Chorus; Horst Stein. Decca SXDL 7518
              +Gr 11-80 p717   +HFN 11-80 p116
1032 Requiem, D minor. CPhO and Chorus; Igor Markevitch. DG 2535 404
     Tape (c) 3335 404
              +FF 9/10-80 p102   ++St 11-80 p84
     Sonata, horn. See no. 3839
     Sonata, 2 organs, G major. See no. 4027
CHICOREL
     Let your house. See no. 3922
CHIHARA, Paul
1033 Ave Maria Scarborough fair. Magnificat. Missa carminum brevis.
     CURTIS-SMITH: Masquerades. William Albright, org; New England
     Conservatory Chorus, University of California L. A. Men's Glee
     Club; Lorna Cooke de Varon, Don Weiss. CRI SD 409
              ++FF 3/4-80 p74   +NR 3-80 p10
     Magnificat. See no. 1033

Missa carminum brevis. See no. 1033
CHION, Marcel
1034 Requiem. Harmonia Mundi GRM AM 68905
        +FF 7/8-80 p16
CHOPIN, Frederic
1035 Allegro de concert, op. 46, A major. LISZT: Totentanz. MENDELSSOHN:
        Capriccio brilliant, op. 22, B minor. Michael Ponti, pno; BeSO;
        Volker Schmidt-Gertenbach. Turnabout 34735
                +CL 9-80 p16   -FF 11/12-80 p129
1036 Andante spianato and grande polonaise, op. 22, E flat major. Con-
        certo, piano, no. 2, op. 21, F minor. Krystian Zimerman, pno;
        LAPO; Carlo Maria Giulini. DG 2531 126 Tape (c) 3301 126
                +Gr 10-80 p496   +-HFN 10-80 p117 tape
                +HFN 10-80 p103
1037 Andante spianato and grande polonaise, op. 22, E flat major. Con-
        certo, piano, no. 2, op. 21, F minor. Nocturne, op. posth., C
        sharp minor. Tamas Vasary, pno; BPhO; Janos Kulka. DG 2535 221
        Tape (c) 3335 221 (From SLPEM 36452)
                ++Gr 8-79 p328   +-NYT 4-6-80 pD22
                +HFN 8-79 p121   +RR 7-79 p50
     Andante spianato and grande polonaise, op. 22, E flat major. See
        no. 182. See no. 1068. See no. 1069
1038 Ballades, nos. 1-4, opp. 23, 38, 47, 52. Impromptus, nos. 1-3, opp.
        29, 36, 51. Tamas Vasary, pno. DG 2535 284 Tape (c) 3335 284
        (From SLPEM 136455)
                +-FF 9/10-80 p102   +-HFN 5-79 p133
                +-Gr 5-79 p1914   +RR 5-79 p83
1039 Ballades, nos. 1-4, opp. 23, 38, 47, 52. Colin Horsley, pno. Meri-
        dian E 45001
                +Gr 12-80 p848   +-HFN 12-80 p135
1040 Ballades, nos. 1-4, opp. 23, 38, 47, 52. Fantaisie-Impromptu, op.
        66, C sharp minor. Impromptu, no. 1, op. 29, A flat major; no.
        2, op. 36, F sharp major; no. 3, op. 51, G flat major. Agustin
        Anievas, pno. Seraphim S 60336
                +-FF 7/8-80 p70   +NYT 4-6-80 pD22
                +-NR 5-80 p13
1041 Ballade, no. 1, op. 23, G minor. Ballade, no. 4, op. 52, F minor.
        STRAVINSKY: Petrouchka: 3 scenes. Etudes, op. 7 (4). Arthur
        Ozolins, pno. Aquitaine MS 90588
                +MUM 10-80 p33
1042 Ballade, no. 1, op. 23, G minor. Ballade, no. 2, op. 38, F major.
        Barcarolle, op. 60, F sharp minor. Fantasie, op. 49, F minor.
        Prelude, op. 28, no. 15, D flat major. Shura Cherkassky, pno.
        Tudor 73018 Tape (c) 73518
                +Gr 12-80 p848   +-HFN 9-80 p100
1043 Ballade, no. 2, op. 38, F major. Preludes, op. 28, nos. 1-24.
        Waltz, op. 34, no. 1, A flat major. Vladimir Ashkenazy, pno.
        London CS 7101 Tape (c) CS 5-7101 (also Decca SXL 6877 Tape (c)
        KSXC 6877)
                +FF 7/8-79 p44   ++NR 1-80 p14
                +Gr 7-79 p229   +RR 7-79 p88
                ++HF 4-79 p88   ++SFC 10-28-79 p53
                ++HFN 7-79 p104   ++St 5-79 p100
     Ballade, no. 2, op. 38, F major. See no. 1042
     Ballade, no. 3, op. 47, A flat major. See no. 1065. See no. 1066

Ballade, no. 4, op. 52, F minor. See no. 1041. See no. 3820

Barcarolle, op. 60, F sharp major. See no. 1042. See no. 1067.
See no. 3777

1044 Berceuse, op. 57, D flat major. SCHUBERT: Impromptu, op. 142, no. 3,
D 935, B flat major. SCHUMANN: Arabesque, op. 18, C major.
Blumenstuck, op. 19, D major. Faschingsschwank aus Wien, op. 26:
Intermezzo. Fantasiestucke, op. 12: Warum, Fabel, Traumeswirren,
In der Nacht, Des Abend. Nachtstucke, op. 23, no. 4. Jorg Demus,
hammerflugel. Harmonia Mundi 1C 065 99797
      ++FF 7/8-80 p164

Berceuse, op. 57, D flat major. See no. 1066. See no. 1067. See
no. 3825. See no. 3902. See no. 3953. See no. 3954

Chants polonaise, op. 74: My joys. See no. 3678. See no. 3902

1045 Concerto, piano, no. 1, op. 11, E minor. Emil Gilels, pno; PO;
Eugene Ormandy. CBS 61931 Tape (c) 40-61931 (From SBRG 72338)
      ++Gr 9-79 p467   +/RR 9-79 p85
      +HFN 10-79 p169   +RR 2-80 p98 tape
      +-HFN 11-79 p157 tape

1046 Concerto, piano, no. 1, op. 11, E minor. Krystian Zimerman, pno;
LAPO; Carlo Maria Giulini. DG 2531 125 Tape (c) 3301 125
      +ARG 11-79 p23   +-HFN 8-79 p123 tape
      +-CL 4-80 p14   +NYT 4-6-80 pD22
      +-FF 1/2-80 p74   +RR 5-79 p53
      +Gr 5-79 p1886   ++SFC 6-17-79 p41
      +HF 9-79 p116   ++St 9-79 p93
      +-HFN 6-79 p105

1047 Concerto, piano, no. 1, op. 11, E minor. Mazurkas, op. 7, no. 1,
B flat major; op. 67, no. 3, C major; op. 68, no. 2, A minor;
op. posth., D major. Tamas Vasary, pno; BPhO; Jerzy Semkov. DG
2535 206 Tape (c) 3335 206 (Reissues)
      +FF 1/2-80 p74   +HFN 1-77 p119
      +-Gr 1-77 p1141   ++RR 12-76 p53
      +Gr 3-77 p1458 tape

1048 Concerto, piano, no. 1, op. 11, E minor. Maurizio Pollini, pno;
PhO; Paul Kletzki. HMV SXLP 30160 Tape (c) TC SXLP 30160, TC
EXE 66 (ct) 8X EXE 66 (From ASD 370) (also Seraphim S 60066)
      ++Gr 6-74 p45   ++RR 5-74 p30
      +-HFN 10-80 p117 tape

1049 Concerto, piano, no. 1, op. 11, E minor. FAURE: Ballade, op. 19.
Earl Wild, pno; RPO, Metropolitan Symphony Orchestra; Malcolm
Sargent, Charles Gerhardt. Quintessence PMC 7141
      +-ARG 4-80 p19   +St 3-80 p94
      +-FF 5/6-80 p69

Concerto, piano, no. 1, op. 11, E minor. See no. 1069. See no.
3777

1050 Concerto, piano, no. 2, op. 21, F minor. SCHUMANN: Concerto, piano,
op. 54, A minor. Martha Argerich, pno; National Symphony Orchestra; Mstislav Rostropovich. DG 2531 042 Tape (c) 3301 042
      +ARG 11-78 p877   +-NR 7-79 p7
      +-ARG 10-79 p48   +NYT 4-6-80 pD22
      +-CL 9-79 p60   ++RR 12-78 p71
      +-HF 9-79 p116   +RR 4-79 p126 tape
      +-HFN 12-78 p153   +SFC 6-3-79 p48
      +-HFN 2-79 p117 tape   +St 8-79 p116
      +MUM 7/8-79 p34

Concerto, piano, no. 2, op. 21, F minor. See no. 1036. See no. 1037. See no. 1069

Contredanse, G flat major. See no. 1064. See no. 1068

1051 Etudes (3). Preludes, nos. 1-26. Nikita Magaloff, pno. Philips 6570 071

          +HFN 7-80 p117   +-RR 7-80 p78

1052 Etudes, opp. 10 and 25. Fou Ts'ong, pno. CBS 61886 Tape (c) 40-61886

          +-Gr 5-80 p1690   +-HFN 8-80 p109 tape
          +-Gr 8-80 p275 tape   +-RR 6-80 p75
          +-HFN 5-80 p119   -RR 8-80 p95 tape

1053 Etudes, opp. 10 and 25. Tamas Vasary, pno. DG 2535 266 Tape (c) 3335 266 (From SLPEM 136454)

          +Gr 7-78 p220   +-NYT 4-6-80 pD22
          +-HFN 6-78 p135   +RR 6-78 p77
          +HFN 9-78 p157 tape

1054 Etudes, opp. 10 and 25. Polonaise, opp. 26, 40, 53, 61. Preludes, op. 28, nos. 1-24. Maurizio Pollini, pno. DG 2740 230 (3) (From 2530 291, 2530 550, 2530 659)

          +Gr 8-80 p241   +STL 9-14-80 p40
          +HFN 10-80 p113

1055 Etudes, opp. 10 and 25. Nouvelles etudes (3). GODOWSKY: Studies on Chopin etudes, nos. 4, 13-15, 25, 26, 33, 36, 45, 47-48. Symphonic metamorphsis on themes from "Die Fledermaus". Symphonic metamorphosis on "Artist's life waltz". David Saperton, pno. IPA 118/9 (2)

          ++FF 3/4-80 p74   +NR 10-79 p11
          +-MT 4-80 p249

1056 Etudes, opp. 10 and 25. Alfred Cortot, pno. World Records Tape (c) TC SH 326

          +Gr 9-80 p413 tape

Etudes, opp. 10 and 25. See no. 1070

Etudes, op. 10, nos. 3, 5, 12. See no. 3907

Etudes, op. 10, no. 4, C sharp minor. See no. 3678

Etudes, op. 10, no. 5, G flat major. See no. 3902

1057 Etudes, op. 10, no. 10, A flat major. Polonaise-Fantaisie, op. 61, A flat major. LISZT: Sonata, piano, G 178, B minor. Diana Kacso, pno. DG 2535 008

          +-HFN 10-80 p103

Etudes, op. 25, nos. 1 and 2. See no. 3678

Etudes, op. 25, nos. 2 and 9. See no. 3902

Etudes, op. 25, no. 2, F minor. See no. 3944

Etudes, op. posth., A flat major. See no. 3944

1058 Fantasie, op. 49, F minor. Scherzo, no. 2, op. 31, B flat minor. SCHUMANN: Carnival, op. 9. SMETANA: Reves. Esquisses. Frantisek Rauch, pno. Supraphon 111 2741/2 (2)

          -FF 9/10-80 p201   +NR 8-80 p13

Fantasie, op. 49, F minor. See no. 1042. See no. 1065. See no. 3550

Fantaisie-Impromptu, op. 66, C sharp minor. See no. 1040. See no. 1066. See no. 3902. See no. 3953. See no. 3954

Fantasy on Polish airs, op. 13, A major. See no. 1069

Funeral march, op. 72, no. 2, C minor. See no. 1064

1059 Grand duo concertante. Introduction and polonaise, op. 3. Sonata, violoncello and piano, op. 65, G minor. Anner Bylsma, vlc; Gerard van Blerk, pno. Acanta EA 21577

+—HFN 3-80 p87   +RR 2-80 p74
+MT 6-80 p382   ++ST 7-80 p195
Impromptus, nos. 1-3, opp. 29, 36, 51. See no. 1038
Impromptus, no. 1, op. 29, A flat major. See no. 1040. See no.
   1066. See no. 3902
Impromptus, no. 2, op. 36, F sharp major. See no. 1040. See no.
   3811
Impromptus, no. 3, op. 51, G flat major. See no. 1040
Introduction and polonaise, op. 3. See no. 1059
Krakowiak, op. 14, F major. See no. 1069
Mazurkas, B flat major, G major. See no. 1064
Mazurkas, op. 6. See no. 1068
Mazurkas, op. 7, no. 1, B flat major. See no. 1047. See no. 1067
Mazurkas, op. 33, no. 2, D major. See no. 1067. See no. 3953. See
   no. 3954
Mazurkas, op. 41, no. 3, B major. See no. 1067
Mazurkas, op. 50 (3). See no. 1065
Mazurkas, op. 50, no. 3, C sharp minor. See no. 3777
Mazurkas, op. 56, no. 1, B major. See no. 3833
Mazurkas, op. 56, no. 2, C major. See no. 1067. See no. 3811
1060 Mazurkas, op. 59, nos. 1-3. Polonaise, op. 53, A flat major.
   Polonaise-Fantaisie, op. 61, A flat major. Sonata, piano, no.
   3, op. 58, B minor. Martha Argerich, pno. DG 2542 110 Tape (c)
   3342 110 (From SLPM 139317)
                 +Gr 10-80 p1171   +RR 2-80 p98 tape
Mazurkas, op. 67, no. 3, C major. See no. 1047
Mazurkas, op. 68, no. 2, A minor. See no. 1047. See no. 1064
Mazurkas, op. 68, no. 4, F minor. See no. 1067
Mazurkas, op. posth., A flat major. See no. 1067
Mazurkas, op. posth., D major. See no. 1047
Mazurkas, a Emile Gailliard, A minor. See no. 1065
Nocturne. See no. 4003
1061 Nocturnes, complete. Claudio Arrau, pno. Philips 6747 485 (2)
   Tape (c) 7699 088
                 ++ARG 3-80 p22   ++HFN 7-79 p103
                 +Audio 12-79 p100   ++HFN 10-79 p171 tape
                 ++FF 5/6-80 p70   ++NR 12-79 p13
                 +—FU 12-79 p43   +NYT 11-11-79 pD19
                 +Gr 6-79 p79   +RR 6-79 p103
                 +Gr 10-79 p727 tape   ++SFC 9-30-79 p45
                 +HF 1-80 p63   ++St 1-80 p112
1062 Nocturnes (19). Ivan Moravec, pno. Connoisseur CS 1065/1165 (2)
   Tape (c) IN SYNC C 4025/6
                 +NR 9-80 p2   +RR 2-75 p51
1063 Nocturnes, nos. 1-21. Garrick Ohlsson, pno. Angel SZB 3889 (2)
   Tape (c) 4Z2X 3889
                 -ARG 7/8-80 p20   +SFC 1-6-80 p43
                 +NR 3-80 p14   +St 6-80 p110
                 ++NYT 4-6-80 pD22
Nocturnes, op. 9, no. 2, E flat major. See no. 3677. See no. 3902.
   See no. 3906. See no. 3964
Nocturnes, op. 15, no. 1, F major. See no. 1067
Nocturnes, op. 15, no. 2, F sharp major. See no. 3625. See no.
   3856
Nocturnes, op. 27, no. 2, D flat major. See no. 3777. See no. 3964

Nocturnes, op. 32, no. 1, B major. See no. 3622
Nocturnes, op. 37, no. 2, G major. See no. 519
Nocturnes, op. 48 (2). See no. 1065
Nocturnes, op. 48, no. 1, C minor. See no. 519. See no. 1066
Nocturnes, op. 62, no. 1, B major. See no. 3811
Nocturnes, op. 62, no. 2, E major. See no. 1067
Nocturnes, op. 72, E minor. See no. 1064. See no. 3677
Nocturnes, op. posth., C sharp minor. See no. 1037. See no. 3772
Nouvelles etudes (3). See no. 1055. See no. 1079
Nouvelles etudes, A flat major. See no. 1067

1064 Piano works: Contredanse, G flat major. Funeral march, op. 72, no. 2, C minor. Mazurkas, op. 68, no. 2, A minor; B flat major; G major. Nocturne, op. 72, E minor. Polonaise, op. 71, no. 2, B flat major. Rondo, op. 73, C major. Sonata, piano, no. 1, op. 4, C minor. Waltzes, op. posth., A flat major, E flat major. Vladimir Ashkenazy, pno. Decca SXL 6911 Tape (c) KSXC 6911
+Gr 11-80 p703   +HFN 11-80 p117

1065 Piano works: Ballade, no. 3, op. 47, A flat major. Fantaisie, op. 49, F minor. Mazurkas, op. 50 (3). Mazurka, a Emile Gailliard, A minor. Nocturnes, op. 48 (2). Prelude, op. 45, C sharp minor. Tarantelle, op. 43, A flat major. Vladimir Ashkenazy, pno. Decca SXL 6922 Tape (c) KSXC 6922 (also London CS 7150
+FF 11/12-80 p93   ++HFN 5-80 p119
+Gr 5-80 p1693   ++RR 6-80 p74

1066 Piano works: Ballade, no. 3, op. 47, A flat major. Berceuse, op. 57, D flat major. Fantaisie-Impromptu, op. 66, C sharp minor. Impromptu, no. 1, op. 29, A flat major. Nocturne, op. 48, no. 1, C minor. Polonaise, op. 53, A flat major. Scherzo, no. 2, op. 31, B flat minor. Waltz, op. 64, no. 2, C sharp minor. Earl Wild, pno. Quintessence PMC 7131
+FF 1/2-80 p74   +St 3-80 p93

1067 Piano works: Barcarolle, op. 60, F sharp major. Berceuse, op. 57, D flat major. Mazurkas, op. 7, no. 1, B flat major; op. 33, no. 2, D major; op. 41, no. 3, B major; op. 56, no. 2, C major; op. 68, no. 4, F minor; op. posth., A flat major. Nouvelle etudes, A flat major. Nocturne, op. 15, no. 1, F major. Nocturne, op. 62, no. 2, E major. Prelude, op. posth., A flat major. Variations, op. 12. Waltz, op. 64, no. 3, A flat major. Peter Serkin, pno. RCA ARL 1-3344 Tape (c) ARK 1-3344
+ARG 12-79 p39   +-NR 10-79 p11
+CL 10-79 p38   +NYT 4-6-80 pD22
+-FF 7/8-80 p71   ++SFC 8-12-79 p49
+-HF 12-79 p92   -St 1-80 p94

1068 Piano works: Andante spianato and grande polonaise, op. 22, E flat major. Contredanse, G flat major. Mazurkas, op. 6. Polonaise, op. 53, A flat major. Tarantella, op. 43, A flat major. Variations, op. 12. Malcolm Frager, pno. Telarc DG 10040
+-ARG 6-79 p51   +-HFN 5-80 p119
++Audio 8-79 p86   +NR 11-80 p9
+-CL 10-79 p37   /RR 6-80 p74
+FF 7/8-79 p12   ++St 6-79 p140

1069 Piano works: Andante spianato and grande polonaise, op. 22, E flat major. Concerto, piano, no. 1, op. 11, E minor. Concerto, piano, no. 2, op. 21, F minor. Fantasy on Polish airs, op. 13, A major. Krakowiak, op. 14, F major. Variations on Mozart's "La ci darem la mano", op. 2, B flat major. Abbey Simon, pno; Hamburg Symp-

hony Orchestra; Heribert Beissel. Vox SVBX 5126 (3) (Q) QSVBX
     5126 Tape (c) CBX 5126
          +HF 9-74 p92   +NYT 8-11-74 pD22
          +HF 4-80 p104 tape   +St 11-74 p124
          ++NR 7-74 p5   +St 3-80 p109 tape
1070 Piano works: Etudes, opp. 10 and 25. Preludes, op. 28, nos. 1-24.
     Prelude, op. 45, C sharp minor. Songs, op. 74: Spring: The ring.
     Alfred Cortot, pno. World Records SH 326/7 (2). (From HMV DB
     2027/9, 2308/10, 2015/8, 2108, DA 1682)
          +Gr 3-80 p1417   +RR 6-80 p75/76
          +HFN 7-10 p106   +STL 7-13-80 p38
1071 Polonaise, opp. 26, 40, 44, 53, nos. 1-6. Lazar Berman, pno. DG
     2531 094 Tape (c) 3301 094
          +-CL 7/8-80 p8   +-NR 5-80 p13
          +FF 7/8-80 p71   +-NYT 4-6-80 pD22
          +-Gr 12-79 p1028   +-RR 1-80 p98
          +HFN 2-80 p91   +St 6-80 p111
          +-MT 9-80 p566
1072 Polonaise, opp. 26, 40, 44, 53, 61, nos. 1-7. Antonio Barbosa, pno.
     Orion Tape (c) In Sync C 4023
          +NR 9-80 p2 tape
1073 Polonaise, opp. 26, 40, 44, 53, 61, nos. 1-7. Nikita Magaloff, pno.
     Philips 6570 137 Tape (c) 7310 137 (From 6768 067)
          -Gr 3-80 p1417
     Polonaise, opp. 26, 40, 44, 53, 61, nos. 1-7. See no. 1054
1074 Polonaise, op. 40, no. 1, A major. Scherzo, no. 4, op. 54, E major.
     Sonata, piano, no. 3, op. 58, D minor. Waltz, op. 64, no. 2, C
     sharp minor. Daniel Epstein, pno. Sonar SD 170
          +FF 9/10-80 p103   +St 2-80 p122
          +/NYT 4-6-80 pD22
     Polonaise, op. 40, no. 1, A major. See no. 3902. See no. 3953.
     See no. 3954
1075 Polonaise, op. 40, nos. 3-4; op. 53, no. 6. Sonata, piano, no. 3,
     op. 58, B minor. Emil Gilels, pno. DG 2531 099
          ++CL 4-80 p8   +-NR 3-80 p14
          +-FF 7/8-80 p70   +NYT 4-6-80 pD22
          +Gr 1-80 p1171   ++RR 2-80 p73
          +-HF 9-80 p87   ++St 7-80 p81
          +HFN 3-80 p87   +STL 2-10-80 p40
     Polonaise, op. 53, A flat major. See no. 1060. See no. 1066. See
     no. 1068
     Polonaise, op. 71, no. 2, B flat major. See no. 1064
     Polonaise-Fantaisie, op. 61, A flat major. See no. 1057. See no.
     1060
     Preludes, nos. 1-26. See no. 1051
1076 Preludes, op. 28, nos. 1-24; op. 45, C sharp minor; op. posth., A
     flat major. Fou Ts'ong, pno. CBS 61944 Tape (c) 40-61944
          +Gr 11-80 p703   +HFN 12-80 p159 tape
1077 Preludes, op. 28, nos. 1-24. Grant Johannesen, pno. Golden Crest
     CRS 4182
          +-ARG 4-80 p20   +NYT 6-4-80 pD22
1078 Preludes, op. 28, nos. 1-24. Claudio Arrau, pno. Odyssey Y 35934
          +-FF 9/10-80 p102   +NYT 4-6-80 pD22
1079 Preludes, op. 28, nos. 1-24. Prelude, op. 45, C sharp minor. Pre-
     lude, op. posth., A flat major. Nouvelles etudes (3). Nikita
     Magaloff, pno. Philips 6580 118 Tape (c) 7310 071

-Gr 2-77 p1307 +-RR 11-76 p89
+-HFN 9-80 p115 tape
1080 Preludes, op. 28, nos. 1-24. Bella Davidovich, pno. Philips 9500
666 Tape (c) 7300 764
+CL 10-79 p37 +NR 1-80 p14
-FF 3/4-80 p76 +-NYT 4-6-80 pD22
+-HF 1-80 p73 -SFC 10-28-79 p53
1081 Preludes, op. 28, nos. 1-24. Prelude, op. 45, C sharp minor. Al-
fred Cortot, pno. World Records Tape (c) TC SH 327
+Gr 9-80 p413 tape
Preludes, op. 28, nos. 1-24. See no. 1043. See no. 1054. See no.
1070
Preludes, op. 28, no. 15, D flat major. See no. 1042. See no.
3906. See no. 3907
Preludes, op. 28, no. 17, A flat major. See no. 3907
Preludes, op. 28, no. 23, F major. See no. 3678
Preludes, op. 45, C sharp minor. See no. 1065. See no. 1070. See
no. 1076. See no. 1079. See no. 1081
Preludes, op. posth., A flat major. See no. 1067. See no. 1076.
See no. 1079
Rondo, op. 73, C major. See no. 1064
1082 Scherzi, nos. 1-4, opp. 20, 31, 39, 54. Nicolai Petrov, pno. Clas-
sics for Pleasure CFP 40333
+-Gr 12-80 p848 -HFN 11-80 p117
1083 Scherzi, nos. 1-4, opp. 20, 31, 39, 54. Sviatoslav Richter, pno.
United Artists UACL 10016
++Gr 12-79 p1028 ++RR 12-79 p94
+HFN 1-80 p105 ++STL 2-10-80 p40
Scherzo, no. 2, op. 31, B flat minor. See no. 1058. See no. 1066
Scherzo, no. 4, op. 54, E major. See no. 1074
Sonata, piano, no. 1, op. 4, C minor. See no. 1064
1084 Sonata, piano, no. 2, op. 35, B flat minor. Sonata, piano, no. 3,
op. 58, B minor. Martha Argerich, pno. DG 2531 289 Tape (c)
3301 289 (From 2530 530, 139317)
+Gr 10-80 p518 +HFN 10-80 p117 tape
+-HFN 10-80 p113
1085 Sonata, piano, no. 2, op. 35, B flat minor. Sonata, piano, no. 3,
op. 58, B minor. Tamas Vasary, pno. DG 2535 230 Tape (c) 3335
230 (From SLPEM 136450)
++Gr 8-79 p352 +RR 7-79 p87
+Gr 12-79 p1106 +-RR 11-79 p85
+HFN 3-80 p107
1086 Sonata, piano, no. 3, op. 58, B minor. Steven Gordon, pno. Refer-
ence Recordings RR 5
++St 2-80 p122
1087 Sonata, piano, no. 3, op. 58, B minor. PROKOFIEV: Sonata, piano,
no. 7, op. 83, B flat major. Anthony di Bonaventura, pno. Ultra
Fi ULDD 13
-FU 4-80 p45 ++HF 4-80 p82
Sonata, piano, no. 3, op. 58, B minor. See no. 1060. See no. 1074.
See no. 1075. See no. 1084. See no. 1085. See no. 3777
Sonata, piano, no. 3, op. 58, B minor: Scherzo molto vivace; Largo.
See no. 3832
1088 Sonata, violoncello and piano, op. 65, G minor. GRIEG: Sonata,
violoncello and piano, op. 36, A minor. Claude Starck, vlc;

Ricardo Requejo, pno. Claves D 703
        +–HFN 8-80 p95
1089 Sonata, violoncello and piano, op. 65, G minor. SZYMANOWSKI: Son-
     ata, violin and piano, op. 9, D minor. Jerzy Kosmala, vla; Barry
     Snyder, pno. Orion ORS 79349
              ++FF 1/2-80 p75
     Sonata, violoncello and piano, op. 65, G minor. See no. 990. See
     no. 1059
1090 Songs, op. 74: Bacchanal; Der Bote; Fruhling; Die Heimkehr; Madchens
     Wunsch; Mein Geliebter; Meine Freuden; Melodie; Melancholie;
     Litauisches Lied; Leichen (2); Mir aus den Augen; Der Reiters-
     mann vor der Schlacht; Das Ringlein; Trube Wellen; Was ein
     junges Madchen liebt. Kari Lovaas, s; Roland Hermann, bar; Geof-
     frey Parsons, pno. Claves D 502
              +Gr 7-80 p158   +–HFN 11-79 p135
     Songs, op. 74: Spring; The ring. See no. 1070
     Tarantelle, op. 43, A flat major. See no. 1065. See no. 1068.
     See no. 3678
1091 Trio, piano, op. 8, G minor. SMETANA: Trio, piano, op. 15, G minor.
     Beaux Arts Trio. Philips 6500 133
              /Gr 4-80 p1567   ++HFN 6-80 p117
     Variations, op. 12. See no. 893. See no. 1067. See no. 1068
1092 Variations on Mozart's "La ci darem la mano", op. 2, B flat major.
     POULENC: Aubade. Joela Jones, David Syme, pno; LSO, NPhO; Paul
     Freeman. Orion ORS 74139, ORS 76221 Tape (c) OC 822
              ++NR 9-80 p10 tape
     Variations on Mozart's "La ci darem la mano", op. 2, B flat major.
     See no. 1069
1093 Waltzes (14). Leonard Pennario, pno. Angel DS 37332
              +SFC 12-21-80 p22
1094 Waltzes (14). Krystian Zimerman, pno. DG 2530 965 Tape (c) 3300
     965
              ++ARG 7-79 p29   +HFN 2-79 p117 tape
              +–FF 1/2-80 p74   +–MJ 11/12-79 p49
              ++Gr 11-78 p927   ++MM 6-79 p34
              +Gr 5-79 p1940 tape   +RR 12-78 p89
              +–HF 6-79 p82   +–St 5-79 p100
              +HFN 12-78 p153
1095 Waltzes, nos. 1-14. Claudio Arrau, pno. Philips 9500 739 Tape (c)
     7300 824
              +Gr 9-80 p375   +–HFN 10-80 p103
1096 Waltzes, nos. 1-19. Nikita Magaloff, pno. Philips 6590 050 Tape
     (c) 7310 050 (From Philips 6580 173)
              +–Gr 3-80 p1417   +HFN 9-80 p121 tape
              +–HFN 2-80 p105   +RR 2-80 p72
              +–RR 8-80 p95 tape
     Waltzes, op. 18, E flat major. See no. 3856. See no. 3902. See
     no. 3907
     Waltzes, op. 34, no. 1, A flat major. See no. 1043. See no. 3605.
     See no. 3777
     Waltzes, op. 34, no. 3, F major. See no. 3678
     Waltzes, op. 42, A flat major. See no. 3902. See no. 3935
     Waltzes, op. 64, no. 1, D flat major. See no. 3951. See no. 3953.
     See no. 3954
     Waltzes, op. 64, no. 2, C sharp minor. See no. 1066. See no. 1074.
     See no. 3902

Waltzes, op. 64, no. 3, A flat major. See no. 1067
Waltzes, op. posth., E flat major, A flat major. See no. 1064
Waltzes, op. posth., E flat major. See no. 3976
CHOVI
    Pepite greus. See no. 3921
    CHRISTMAS SONGS. See no. 3572. See no. 3724. See no. 3787. See
        no. 3865
CHUKHAJIAN
    Impromptus. See no. 3850
CIBBINI-KOZELUH, Katharina
    Valses, op. 6 (6). See no. 4024
CILEA, Francesco
    Adriana Lecouvreur: Del sultana Amuratte...Io sono l'umile ancella.
        See no. 3774
    Adriana Lecouvreur: Ecco respiro appena...Io son l'umile ancella;
        Poveri fiori. See no. 3789
    Adriana Lecouvreur: Io son l'umile ancella. See no. 3869
    Adriana Lecouvreur: La dolcissima effigie; L'anima ho stanca. See
        no. 3671. See no. 3827
    Adriana Lecouvreur: L'anima ho stanca. See no. 3981
    L'Arlesiana: Come due tizzi accesi. See no. 3771
    L'Arlesiana: E la silita storia. See no. 4031
    L'Arlesiana: Esser madre. See no. 3928
    Songs: Lontananza. See no. 3981
CIMA, Andrea
    Canzona francese. See no. 3846
CIMAROSA, Domenico
    Concerto, guitar, D major. See no. 17. See no. 3602
    Concerto, oboe, C minor. See no. 625
1097 Il fanatico per gli antichi Romani: Sinfonia. Il maestro di cappel-
        la. Il matrimonio segreto: Sinfonia and aria di Geronimo. Phil-
        ippe Huttenlocher, bar; Lausanne Chamber Orchestra; Armin Jordan.
        Erato STU 71059 (also Musical Heritage Society MHS 4040)
                    ++FF 11/12-79 p57   +HFN 4-78 p113
                    +-Gr 2-78 p1456   +RR 8-78 p46
                    +HF 1-80 p74
    Il maestro di cappella. See no. 1097
1098 Il matrimonio segreto. Julia Varady, Arleen Auger, ms; Julia Ham-
        ari, ms; Ryland Davies, t; Dietrich Fischer-Dieskau, bar; Alberto
        Rinaldi, bs; Richard Amner, hpd; ECO; Daniel Barenboim. DG 2709
        069 (3) (Also DG 2740 171)
                    +-ARG 12-77 p26   +NR 12-77 p9
                    +Gr 9-77 p470   +ON 2-4-78 p33
                    +Gr 8-80 p265   +-RR 9-77 p36
                    +HF 11-77 p95   ++RR 8-80 p29
                    +HFN 9-77 p140   +-SFC 8-28-77 p46
                    +HFN 8-80 p107   ++St 1-78 p84
                    +-MM 9-78 p29   ++STL 8-10-80 p30
                    +MT 5-78 p426
1099 Il matrimonio segreto: Cara cara; Io ti lascio. MASSENET: Manon:
        Act 2. Werther, excerpts (3). MOZART: Don Giovanni, K 527: Duet,
        Act 1; Il mio tesoro. Bidu Sayao, s; Rosa Ponselle, ms; Aldo
        Noni, Tito Schipa, t; Orchestras and conductors. MDP Records 024
                    +FF 5/6-80 p176
    Il matrimonio segreto: Pria che spunti. See no. 3977

Il matrimonio segreto: Sinfonia and aria di Geronimo. See no. 1097
1100 Requiem. Elly Ameling, s; Birgit Finnila, ms; Richard van Vrooman,
     t; Kurt Widmer, bs; Montreux Festival Chorus; Lausanne Chamber
     Orchestra; Vittorio Negri. Philips 9502 005 Tape (c) 7313 005
     (From 839752, SAL 3796)
                  +ARG 10-79 p41   +HFN 3-80 p107
                  ++FF 11/12-79 p57   +HFN 4-80 p121 tape
                  +-Gr 2-80 p1287   ++MT 12-80 p784
                  ++Gr 9-80 p413   +RR 2-80 p84
                  +HF 9-79 p116   ++SFC 6-10-79 p45
     Songs: Quoniam tu solus sanctus; Gloria patri. See no. 3766
CLARKE
     Street music. See no. 3791
CLARKE, Herbert
     The bride of the waves. See no. 1101
     Caprice brilliante. See no. 1101
     Carnival of Venice. See no. 1101
     From the shores of the mighty Pacific. See no. 3654
     Rondo caprice. See no. 1101
     Showers of gold. See no. 1101
     The southern cross. See no. 1101
     Stars in a velvety sky. See no. 1101
     Valse brilliante. See no. 1101
     La veta caprice. See no. 1101
1101 Works, selections: Bride of the waves. Caprice brilliante. Carni-
     vale of Venice. Rondo caprice. Showers of gold. The southern
     cross. Stars in a velvety sky. Valse vrilliante. La veta cap-
     rice. HERBERT: Prince Arianias: Ah Cupid. LEVY: Russian fanta-
     sie. Sousa Band, Victor Orchestra. Crystal S 450
                  +NR 6-80 p14   +NYT 5-18-80 pD32
CLARKE, Jeremiah
     English suite, D major. See no. 3866
     Trumpet voluntary. See no. 3545. See no. 3640. See no. 3616.
     See no. 3663. See no. 3895. See no. 3916. See no. 4029. See
     no. 4030. See no. 4067
     Trumpet voluntary, D minor. See no. 3615
1102 Voluntary, D major (Prince of Denmark's march). HAYDN: Concerto,
     trumpet, E flat major. PURCELL: Sonata, trumpet, D major. Trum-
     pet tune and air, D major. Voluntary, 2 trumpets, C major. VIV-
     ALDI: Concerto, 2 trumpets, C major. Rogin Voisin, tpt; Orches-
     tra; Harry Dickson. Westminster MCA 1417 (From Unicorn)
                  +NR 11-80 p5
CLARKE, Rebecca
1103 Trio, violin, violoncello and piano. HOOVER: Trio, violin, violon-
     cello and piano. Suzanne Ornstein, vln; James Kreger, vlc;
     Virginia Eskin, pno; Rogeri Trio. Leonarda LPI 103
                  +FF 9/10-80 p104   +-NR 8-80 p10
CLEMENCIC, Rene
     Chronos, no. 2. See no. 1104
1104 Maraviglia, no. 3, Chronos, no. 2. Sesostris. Clemencic Consort.
     Scorpios SC 1094013
                  *RR 8-80 p39
1105 Moliere. Film Sound Track. Harmonia Mundi HM 1020
                  +-ARG 12-80 p52   +RR 5-80 p40
                  ++NR 8-80 p3

Sesostris. See no. 1104
CLEMENS NON PAPA
    Jesu nomen Sit nomen. See no. 3806
    O crux benedicta. See no. 3763
CLEMENTI, Muzio
    Andante convariazioni. See no. 3819
    Montferrin, op. 49. See no. 1107
1106 Sonatas, piano, op. 13, no. 6, F minor; op. 24, no. 2, B flat major;
        op. 25, no. 2, F sharp minor; op. 37, no. 2, G major. Jos van
        Immerseel, pno. Chandos Accent 7911
                +HFN 6-80 p101   +RR 6-80 p31
1107 Sonatas, piano, op. 14, no. 3, F minor; op. 26, no. 2, F sharp minor;
        op. 31, no. 1, A major. Montferrine, op. 49 (3). Luciano
        Sgrizzi, pno. Abbey Alpha DB 195
                +FF 11/12-80 p94   +HFN 12-80 p135
                +Gr 12-80 p848
    Sonatas piano, op. 24, no. 2, B flat major. See no. 1106
    Sonatas, piano, no. 25, no. 2, F sharp minor. See no. 1106
1108 Sonatas, piano, op. 26, no. 2, F sharp minor. Sonatas, piano, op.
        36, no. 2, G major. LISZT: Annees de pelerinage, 2nd year, G
        161: Apres une lecture du Dante; Sonetto del Petrarca. Laszlo
        Simon, pno. BIS LP 154
                +-HFN 12-80 p137
    Sonata, piano, op. 36, no. 2, G major. See no. 1108
    Sonata, piano, op. 37, no. 2, G major. See no. 1106
1109 Sonata, piano, 4 hands, op. 14, no. 3, E flat major. RESPIGHI:
        Pieces, piano, 4 hands (6). RIEGGER: Dance suite: Evocation, The
        cry, New dance. SCHUBERT: Rondo, D 608, D major. Frederick
        Schoettler, Theresa Dye, pno. Orion ORS 79337
                ++CL 2-80 p8   +-NR 1-80 p13
                +FF 11/12-79 p163
1110 Symphonies (4) (ed. Spada). PhO; Claudio Scimone. Erato STU 71174
        (2) (also Musical Heritage Society Tape (c) MHG 6150/1)
                ++Gr 2-79 p1415   +HFN 3-79 p123
                +HF 5-79 p73   +RR 2-79 p20
                ++HF 11-80 p88 tape
CLERAMBAULT, Louis Nicolas
    Largo on the G string. See no. 3964
1111 Medee. Orphee. Rachel Yakar, s; Reinhard Goebel, vln; Wilbert
        Hazelzet, flt; Charles Medlam, vla da gamba; Alan Curtis, hpd.
        DG 2533 442
                +Gr 8-80 p248   +RR 8-80 p80
                +HFN 8-80 p95
1112 La musette. MARAIS: Suite, viola da gamba and harpsichord, no. 2,
        D major. RAMEAU: L'Impatience. Pieces de clavecin en concert,
        no. 5, D minor. Ann Monoyios, s; Concert Royal; James Richman.
        Nonesuch H 71371
                +FF 7/8-80 p181   ++NR 5-80 p10
    Orphee. See no. 1111
1113 Suites, C major, C minor. JACQUET DE LA GUERRE: Suite, D minor.
        Kenneth Gilbert, hpd. Argo ZK 64
                +Gr 7-80 p153   ++RR 7-80 p79
                ++HFN 7-80 p106   +STL 9-14-80 p40
    Suite du 2nd ton. See no. 4040

CLERISSE, Robert
    Introduction et scherzo. See no. 2
CLONICK
    Be strong swift and brave. See no. 3922
COATES, Eric
    The dambusters. See no. 3619. See no. 3801
    Dancing nights. See no. 1114
    The enchanted garden. See no. 1114
    I heard you singing. See no. 3875
    London calling. See no. 1114
    The selfish giant. See no. 1114
    The seven seas march. See no. 1114. See no. 3619
    The three men suite. See no. 1114
1114 Works, selections: Dancing nights. The enchanted garden. London
       calling. The selfish giant. The seven seas march. The three
       men suite. Sydney Symphony Orchestra; John Lanchbery. HMV SQ
       ESD 7062 Tape (c) TC ESD 7062
             +ARG 9-80 p25   /-HFN 2-79 p117 tape
             +Gr 12-78 p1188   ++RR 12-78 p50
             +-HFN 1-79 p116
COCCIA
    Per la patria: Bella Italia. See no. 3978
COCHEREAU, Pierre
1115 Evocation des anciens instruments, des origines au XVII siecle.
       Forme libre. Une messe dominicale. Triptyque symphonique sur
       2 themes donnes. Variations sur un noel. Francois Carbou, org.
       FYO 59/60
             +MU 6-80 p8
       Forme libre. See no. 1115
       Une messe dominicale. See no. 1115
1116 Symphony, organ, in five movements. FRESCOBALDI: Ricercare. Toc-
       cata. GABRIELI, A.: Canzona. ZIPOLI: Aria. Pierre Cochereau,
       org. Klavier KS 529
             +FF 9/10-80 p270   +-St 10-74 p143
             +NR 8-74 p11
       Triptyque symphonique sur 2 themes donnes. See no. 1115
       Variations sur un noel. See no. 1115
COGAN, Robert
1117 Phrases from whirl...ds 1. DIDOMENICA: Concerto, violin. MCKINLEY:
       Paintings, no. 2. Eric Rosenblith, vln; Joan Heller, s; New
       England Conservatory Contemporary Music Ensemble; Gunther Schul-
       ler. Golden Crest NEC 119
             +-ARG 5-80 p50
COHAN, George
    Over there. See no. 3983
COLERIDGE-TAYLOR, Samuel
1118 Hiawatha's wedding feast. Richard Lewis, t; Royal Choral Society;
       PhO; Malcolm Sargent. Arabesque 8005
             +FF 11/12-80 p95   +St 7-80 p80
COLLICHIO
    Go-go. See no. 3679
COLONNA
    O lucidissima dies, motet. See no. 3716
CONGE, Michel
    La mort de Berenguer. See no. 3686

CONRADUS, Cornelius
    Canzon a 8. See no. 3818
CONYNGHAM, Barry
1119 To be alone. DUFAY: Nuper rosarum flores. FULKERSON: Music, brass
    instruments III. HAMES: Monody after Dufay. Victorian Time
    Machine; Richard Hames. Move MS 3028
        +–CL 4-80 p251
COOKE, Arnold
    Rondo, B flat major. See no. 3644
COOKE, Benjamin
    Songs: Deh dove; In paper case. see no. 3873
COOKE, John
    Fanfare. See no. 4051
1120 Stella coeli extirpavit. DAMETT: Beata Dei genitrix. DUNSTABLE:
    Gloria and credo; Salve scema sanctitatis, Salve salus servulor-
    um, Cantant celi agmina. POWER: Beata progenies; Ave regina
    coelorum. Gloria, 5 voices. Pro Cantione Antiqua, Collegium
    Aureum; Bruno Turner. Harmona Mundi 1C 065 99739
        +Audio 3-80 p44   +RR 7-79 p105
        +Gr 8-79 p363
COOLEY, Carlton
    Aria and dance. See no. 3606
COOPER, Paul
1121 Quartet, strings, no. 6. LANSKY: Quartet, strings. Shepherd Quar-
    tet, Pro Arte Quartet. CRI SD 402
        +ARG 11-79 p24   +NR 1-80 p6
        +FF 9/10-79 p71   ++SFC 1-13-80 p41
COPE, David
1122 Glassworks. Threshold and visions. David Cope, Ken Durling, pno;
    Santa Cruz Chamber Symphony; David Cope. Folkways FTS 33452
        +NR 4-80 p3
    Threshold and visions. See no. 1122
COPERARIO, John
    Al primo giorno. See no. 3675
    Fancie a 5. See no. 3675
    Fantasia, 6 viols, F major. See no. 4025
COPLAND, Aaron
1123 Appalachian spring (original version). Columbia Chamber Orchestra;
    Aaron Copland. CBS 61894 Tape (c) 40-61894 (also Columbia M
    32726 Tape (c) MT 32726 (ct) MA 32726)
        +Gr 6-80 p43   +HFN 9-80 p115 tape
        +Gr 9-80 p413 tape   +RR 7-80 p53
        +HFN 6-80 p106
1124 Appalachian spring. Billy the kid. Pittsburgh Symphony Orchestra;
    William Steinberg. Westminster MCA 1406
        /FF 11/12-80 p96   ++SFC 9-21-80 p21
        ++NR 6-80 p6
    Appalachian spring. See no. 910
    Billy the kid. See no. 1124
    Ceremonial fanfare. See no. 3566
1125 Dance symphony: Dance of the adolescent. Danza de Jalisco. MOSCH-
    ELES: Duo concertnat, op. 87b. VAUGHAN WILLIAMS: Introduction
    and fugue, 2 pianos. Evelinde Trenkner, Vladimir Pleshakov, pno.
    Orion ORS 79343
        +–ARG 9-80 p47   +–NR 4-80 p13
        +–FF 5/6-80 p167

Danza de Jalisco. See no. 1125
Down a country lane. See no. 1127
1126 Emblems. HANSON: Young composer's guide to the six-tone scale.
    SCHWANTNER: ...Amid the mountains rising nowhere. Eastman Wind
    Ensemble; Donald Hunsberger. Mercury SRI 75132
            +NR 12-80 p11   ++SFC 8-3-80 p33
            +NYT 9-28-80 pD31
Fanfare for the common man. See no. 3571. See no. 3623. See no.
    3660
Fantasy. See no. 1127
In evening air. See no. 1127
Midsummer nocturne. See no. 1127
Night thoughts. See no. 1127
Old American songs. See no. 1128. See no. 3776
Passacaglia. See no. 1127
Piano blues (4). See no. 1127
1127 Piano works: Down a country lane. Fantasy, piano. In evening air.
    Midsummer nocturne. Night thoughts (Homage to Ives). Piano
    blues (4). Passacaglia. Scherzo humoristique: The cat and the
    mouse. Sonata, piano. Sunday afternoon music. Variations,
    piano. The young pioneers. Leo Smit, pno. Columbia M2 35901
    (2)
            +ARG 7/8-80 p20   +NR 4-80 p13
            +FF 7/8-80 p72   +NYT 9-28-80 pD31
            +HF 5-80 p67   ++St 4-90 p87
1128 Poems of Emily Dickinson (12). Old American songs.* Adele Addison,
    s; William Warfield, bar; Aaron Copland, pno; CSO; Aaron Copland.
    CBS 61993 Tape (c) 40-61993 (*From SBRG 72218)
            +-Gr 9-80 p385   +-HFN 10-80 p117 tape
            +HFN 10-80 p115   ++STL 7-13-80 p38
Quiet city. See no. 3565
The red pony: Morning on the ranch. See no. 4046
Rodeo: Hoe-down. See no. 3785
Scherzo humoristique: The cat and the mouse. See no. 1127
Sonata, piano. See no. 1127
Sunday afternoon music. See no. 1127
1129 Symphony, no. 3. PhO; Aaron Copland. CBS 61869 Tape (c) 40-61869
    (also Columbia M 35113)
            +-ARG 10-79 p41   +-MT 4-80 p249
            +-FF 9/10-79 p72   +RR 9-79 p86
            +Gr 9-79 p467   +-RR 3-80 p105 tape
            +HF 2-80 p84   -SFC 7-29-79 p50
            +-HFN 9-79 p105   +St 11-79 p86
            +-HFN 11-79 p157 tape
Variations, piano. See no. 1127
1130 Vitebsk. MANZIARLY: Trilogue. TCHEREPNIN: Trio, op. 34, D major.
    TURINA: Trio, piano, no. 2, op. 74, B minor. Brian Hanly, vln;
    David Tomatz, vlc; Werner Rose, pno. Laurel LR 109
            ++Audio 12-80 p88   ++NR 4-80 p7
            +FF 9/10-80 p227   ++SFC 5-4-80 p42
The young pioneers. See no. 1127
CORDERO, Roque
1131 Duo 1954. INFANTE: Danzas andaluzas (3). PINTO: Scenas infantis.
    POULENC: Sonata, 2 pianos. Nelly and Jaime Ingram, pno. Inter-
    American Musical Editions OEA 003
            +LAMR Fall/Winter 1980 p291

Symphony, no. 2, in one movement. See no. 336
CORELLI, Arcangelo
    Christmas concerto: Pastorale. See no. 3943
    Concerto: Pastorale. See no. 3640
    Concerto, oboe: Prelude-gavotte. See no. 3526
1132 Concerti grossi, op. 6. I Musici. Philips 6770 023 (3) Tape (c)
    7650 023
                    +ARG 4-80 p20   +St 2-80 p122
                    +NYT 5-25-80 pD21
1133 Concerti grossi, op. 6, nos. 1-4. La Petite Bande; Sigiswald Kuij-
    ken. Harmonia Mundi 065 99613
                    +FF 1/2-80 p76   +HFN 9-78 p141
                    +Gr 1-79 p1284
1134 Concerto grosso, op. 6, no. 1, D major; no. 3, C minor. Sonata, op.
    1, no. 12, D major. Sonatas, op. 3, nos. 7-9. Collegium Aureum.
    Harmonia Mundi 065 99792
                    -HFN 7-80 p117   +RR 8-80 p40
                    +-MT 12-80 p784
1135 Concerti grossi, op. 6, nos. 5-8. La Petite Bande; Sigiswald Kuij-
    ken. Harmonia Mundi 065 99728
                    +FF 1/2-80 p76   ++RR 3-79 p64
                    +HFN 3-79 p123
1136 Concerto grosso, op. 6, no. 8, G minor. LOCATELLI: Concerto, op. 1,
    no. 8, F minor. MANFREDINI: Concerto grosso, op. 3, no. 12, C
    major. TORELLI: Concerto grosso, op. 8, no. 6, G minor. I Musi-
    ci. Philips 6570 179 Tape (c) 7310 179 (From 6580 121)
                    +Gr 11-80 p683   +HFN 11-80 p129
    Concerto grosso, op. 6, no. 8, C minor: Pastorale. See no. 4028
1137 Concerti grossi, op. 6, nos. 9-12. Sigiswald Kuijken, Lucy van
    Dael, vln; Wieland Kuijken, vlc; La Petite Bande. Harmona Mundi
    065 99803
                    ++Gr 4-80 p1553   +RR 11-79 p76
                    +FF 1/2-80 p76   +-ST 4-80 p927
                    ++HFN 11-79 p137
    Gigue, op. 5. See no. 3999
    Grave. See no. 3912
1138 Sarabande, gigue and badinerie (arr. Arbos). MOZART: Serenade, no.
    13, K 525, G major. PURCELL: Abdelazer: Suite. Slovak Chamber
    Orchestra; Bohdan Warchal. Musical Heritage Society MHS 4050
                    +ARG 2-80 p55   +FF 5/6-80 p198
    Sonata, op. 1, no. 12, D major. See no. 1134
    Sonata, op. 2, no. 12, G major: Ciacona. See no. 4016
    Sonatas, op. 3, nos. 7-9. See no. 1134
    Sonata, op. 5, no. 4, F major. See no. 3990
    Sonata, op. 5, no. 10, F major. See no. 3684
    Sonata, op. 5, no. 12, G minor. See no. 4020
    Trio sonata, op. 3, no. 8. See no. 3650
CORIGLIANO, John
    Concerto, piano. See no. 374
CORKINE, William
    Beauty sat bathing. See no. 3600
    Come live with me and be my love. See no. 1139
    Coranto (3). See no. 1139
    Galliard. See no. 1139
    If my complaints. See no. 1139

Mounsiers almaine. See no. 1139
Pavin. See no. 1139
The punches delight. See no. 1139
Songs: Fly swift my thoughts; We yet agree. See no. 3878
Walshingham. See no. 1139
Whoope doe me no harme good man. See no. 1139
1139 Works, selections: Come live with me and be my love. Coranto (3).
     Galliard. If my complaints. Mounsiers almaine. Pavin. The
     punches delight. Walshingham. Whoope doe me no harme good man.
     FERRABOSCO: Almain (2). Coranto (3). Galliard. ANON.: Kate of
     Bardie. The Lancashire pipes. Pipe of Rumsey. A pointe or
     preludium to be played before the Lancashire pipes. Jordi Savall,
     lyra and bass viols. Astree AS 51
               +RR 6-80 p79
CORNELIUS, Peter
     Der Barbier von Bagdad: Arias. See no. 3539
     Der Barbier von Bagdad: Ergreift den Alten...Heil diesem Haus denn
       du tratst ein Salam aleikum. See no. 3712
     Der Barbier von Bagdad: Heil sei der Schonen. See no. 3774
     Der Barbier von Bagdad: O holdes Bild in Engelschone. See no. 3646
     Der Barbier von Bagdad: Vor deinem Fenster die Blumen. See no. 3538
1140 Stabat mater. Reingard Didusch, s; Barbara Scherler, con; Manfred
     Schmidt, t; Siegmund Nimsgern, bs; Cologne Radio Orchestra and
     Chorus; Herbert Schernus. Schwann AMS 3524
               +ARG 2-80 p45   +FF 3/4-80 p76
CORNYSHE, William
     Ah Robin; Hoyda jolly Rutterkin. See no. 3744
     My love she moun'th. See no. 3768
CORONA
     Crown him with many crowns. See no. 3524
CORREA DE ARAUXO, Francisco
1141 Canto llano. Tiento lleno. Tiento pequeno. DANDRIEU: Cromorne en
     taille. Fugues, nos. 1 and 2. Magnificat. Offertoire. Plein
     jeu. Trio. FRESCOBALDI: Ricercare. Toccata avanti il ricer-
     care. LOPEZ: Versos (5). Francis Chapelet, org. Harmonia Mundi
     HM 1209
               +-FF 3/4-80 p192
1142 Tientos, nos. 10, 15-16, 28, 34, 37, 47, 52, 54. Gertrud Mersiov-
     sky, org. Harmonia Mundi 065 99679
               +RR 7-80 p77
     Tiento de medio registro. See no. 4021
     Tiento de medio registro de tiple de 7 tono. See no. 3756
     Tiento lleno. See no. 1141
     Tiento pequeno. See no. 1141
CORRETTE, Michel
     A la venue de Noel. See no. 4062
     Concerto, flute and harpsichord, op. 26, no. 6, D minor: Allegro.
       See no. 4028
1143 Laudate dominum. DESMARETS: Mysteres de Notre Seigneur Jesus-Christ.
     Lyon Vocal and Instrumental Ensemble; Guy Cornut. Musical Heri-
     tage Society MHS 4085 (From Erato STU 70914)
               +-FF 7/8-80 p73
     Magnificat du 3 and 4 ton. See no. 4064
     Sonata, viola d'amore, A major. See no. 47

COSTA, Michele
      Eli: I will extol thee. See no. 3770
      Songs: Napulitanata; Tu sei morta nella vita mia; Oili oila; Era de
         maggio. See no. 3981
COSTANZI, Giovanni
      Eupatra: Lusinga la speme. See no. 3669
COTEL, Morris
1144 August 12, 1952: The night of the murdered poets. Sonata, piano.
         Eli Wallach, narrator; Morris Moshe Costel, pno; Instrumental En-
         semble. Grenadilla GS 1051
                     +—ARG 3-80 p23   +NYT 9-16-79 pD24
                     +—FF 7/8-80 p74   +—St 4-80 p128
                     +—NR 5-80 p15
      Sonata, piano, no. 1144
COTTRAU, Teodoro
      Addio a Napoli. See no. 3900. See no. 3983
      Fenesta che lucive. See no. 3981
      Santa Lucia. See no. 3771
COULTER, Fred
      Concentric preludes (2). See no. 3994
COUPERIN, Francois
1145 L'Art de toucher de clavecin: Pieces. Suite, harpsichord, no. 8.
         COUPERIN, L.: Suite, D minor. Nicholas Jackson, hpd. Spectrum
         Tape (c) SC 204
                     +HF 6-80 p96 tape
1146 L'Art de toucher de clavecin: Preludes and allemande. Livres de
         clavecin, Bk II, Ordres nos. 6-12. Kenneth Gilbert, hpd. Har-
         monia Mundi HM 33558 (4)
                     ++FF 5/6-80 p70
      Chaconne en re mineur. See no. 3963
      Concerts royaux, excerpts. See no. 1151
      Dialogue sur les grands jeux. See no. 4047
1147 Lecons de tenebres. Motet pour le jour de Paques. Judith Nelson,
         Emma Kirkby, s; Jane Ryan, vla da gamba; Christopher Hogwood, org.
         L'Oiseau-Lyre DSLO 536
                     +FF 5/6-80 p71   +HFN 6-78 p121
                     +Gr 6-78 p95   ++RR 5/78 p60
1148 Livres de clavecin, Bk I. Kenneth Gilbert, hpd. Harmonia Mundi
         HMU 351/4
                     +FF 7/8-80 p74   +RR 3-78 p56
1149 Livres de clavecin, Bk I, Ordre no. 1. Blandine Verlet, hpd. Ast-
         ree AS 21
                     +—FF 9/10-80 p105
1150 Livres de clavecin, Bk I, Ordre no. 3: La tenebreuse. Livres de
         clavecin, Bk II, Ordre no. 6: Les moissonneurs; Les baricades
         misterieuses; Le moucheron; Ordre no. 8: Passacaille; Ordre no.
         11: L'Etincelante. Livres de clavecin, Bk III, Ordre no. 14:
         Le rossignol-en-amour; Le carillon de Cythere; Ordre, no. 15:
         L'Amour au berceau; Musete de Taverni; Ordre no. 17: Les petits
         moulins a vent; Ordre no. 18: Soeur Monique; Le tic-toc-choc.
         Livres de clavecin, Bk IV, Ordre no. 23: Les tricoteuses. Rob-
         ert Woolley, hpd. Meridian E 77012
                     +Gr 10-79 p675   +—RR 1-80 p100
                     +—HFN 9-79 p105
      Livres de clavecin, Bk II, Ordres nos. 6-12. See no. 1146

Livres de clavecin, Bk II, Ordre no. 9. See no. 330
1151 Livres de clavecin, Bk III, Ordres 13-19. Concerts royaux, excerpts.
Kenneth Gilbert, hpd. Harmonia Mundi HM 359/62 (4)
+FF 9/10-80 p105
Livres de clavecin, Ordre no. 15: Musete de choisi; Musete
de taverni. See no. 3795
Livres de clavecin, Bk IV, Ordre no. 17: Les petits Moulins a vent.
See no. 3964
1152 Livres de clavecin, Bk IV, Ordres nos. 20-27. Kenneth Gilbert, hpd;
Gian Lyman-Silbiger, vla da gamba. Musical Heritage Society MHS
4072/5 (4)
++FF 1/2-80 p76   +-HF 7-80 p66
1153 Livres de clavecin, Bk IV, Ordres nos. 20-27. Blandine Verlet, hpd.
Telefunken FK 6-35411 (3)
+FF 3/4-80 p77   +-NYT 1-27-80 pD20
-Gr 5-79 p1914   +-RR 3-79 p108
+-HF 7-80 p66   ++SFC 2-10-80 p41
+HFN 4-79 p119
1154 Messe pour les couvents. Messe pour les paroisses. Pierre Bardon,
org. Pierre Verany PV 1801/2 (2)
+FF 11/12-80 p97
1155 Messe pour les couvents. Messe pour les paroisses. Ton Koopman,
org. Telefunken 6-35415 (2)
+FF 3/4-80 p77
Messe pour les couvents: Elevation, Offertoire sur les grands jeux,
Cromorne en taille. See no. 95
Messe pour les paroisses. See no. 260. See no. 1154. See no. 1155
Messe pour les paroisses: Gloria; Kyrie. See no. 4038
Messe pour les paroisses: Tierce en taille, Kyrie couplet V. See
no. 95
Motet pour le jour de Paques. See no. 1147
Pieces en concert. See no. 80
Plein jeu. See no. 4055
Recit de tierce en taille. See no. 4055
Suite, harpsichord, no. 8. See no. 1145
1156 La Sultane, D minor. FARINA: Capriccio stravangante. MOZART: Eine
Musikalischer Spass, K 522, F major. TELEMANN: Quadro, B flat
major. Musica Holmiae. BIS LP 134
++FF 5/6-80 p195   +-RR 3-80 p78
+NR 4-80 p8   ++St 8-80 p96

COUPERIN, Louis
Carillon. See no. 3682
Chaconne. See no. 3661
Fantaisie. See no. 4061
1157 Pavane, F sharp minor. Suites, A minor, C major, F major. Gustav
Leonhardt, hpd. Harmonia Mundi 1C 065 99871
+Gr 10-80 p518   ++HFN 9-80 p101
Suites, A minor, C major, F major. See no. 1157
Suites, D minor. See no. 1145
1158 Suites, harpsichord, nos. 1 and 2. Jordi Savall, vla da gamba;
Arianne Maurette, bs gamba; Ton Koopman, hpd. Telefunken AW
6-42225
+FF 3/4-80 p78   +HFN 9-78 p141
+Gr 11-78 p916   +RR 10-78 p93
+HF 3-80 p77   ++SFC 2-10-80 p41

COURAGES,   de
      Fantasie. See no. 3852
COWAN
      At the mid-hour of night. See no. 3770
COWELL, Henry
      Exultation. See no. 3859
1159 Hymn and fuguing tune, no. 2. KOUSSEVITZKY: Concerto, double bass.
           PISTON: Concerto, string quartet, winds and percussion. Gary
           Karr, double bs; Oslo Philharmonic Orchestra, Emerson Quartet,
           Juilliard Orchestra, BSO; Alfredo Antonini, Sixten Ehrling, Serge
           Koussevitzky. CRI SD 248
                        +ARG 7-79 p50   +SFC 4-29-79 p53
                        -FF 5/6-80 p130   ++St 10-79 p142
                        +NR 4-79 p5
      Hymn and fuguing tune, no. 10. See no. 3565
      Piece, piano, Paris 1924. See no. 3727
CRECQUILLON, Thomas
      Toutes les nuictz. See no. 3683
CRESCENZO,   de
      Quanno a femmena vo. See no. 3900
      Tarantella sincera. See no. 3949
CRESHEVSKY, Noah
1160 Highway. Portrait of Rudy Perez. SCHUBEL: Paraplex. Ragwyrk.
           Andrew Violette, pno; Carla Scaletti, hp; Ensemble; David Oberg;
           Electronic tape. Opus One 50
                        ++ARG 12-80 p49
      Portrait of Rudy Perez. See no. 1160
CRESPO, Gomez
      Nortena, homage a Julian Aguirre. See no. 3634. See no. 3722.
           See no. 3798
CRESTON, Paul
      Choric dances, op. 17a. See no. 735
      A rumor. See no. 3565
      Toccata. See no. 4051
CROFT, William
      Psalm tune, no. 149. See no. 3848
      Suite, C minor. See n. 3751
CROSSAN, Jack
      Concertino, multiple keyboards. See no. 3737
      Prismatic rag. See no. 3737
CROUCH, Frederick
      Kathleen Mavourneen. See no. 4070
CRUMB, George
      Night music I. See no. 656
      Sonata, solo violoncello. See no. 304
CRUSELL, Bernhard
      Divertimento, op. 9. See no. 4
CUI, Cesar
      Prisoner of the Caucasus: The sun was brightly shining. See no.
           3774
CUNDICK, Robert
      Fanfare. See no. 3728
CURTIS, E. de
      Canta pe'me. See no. 3949
      Songs: Canta pe'me; Voce e notte. See no. 3900

Songs: Carmela; A surrentina. See no. 3981
Songs: Torna a Surriento; Tu ca nun chiagne. See no. 3667
Songs: Tu ca non chaigne; Senza nisciuno; Canta pe'me. See no. 3983
CURTIS-SMITH, Curtis
    Masquerades. See no. 1033
CUSTER, Arthur
1161 Found objects, no. 7. RUSH: Hexahedron. THORNE: Sonata, piano.
        Dwight Peltzer, pno. Serenus SRS 12071
                +-ARG 2-78 p38   +HF 5-78 p114
                +FF 3/4-80 p184   +NR 12-77 p12
CZERNY, Carl
    Divertissement de concert, op. 204. See no. 38
    Les heures du matin, op. 204. See no. 3628
    Kunst der Fingerfertigkeit, no. 4, B major; no. 6. See no. 3628
    Der Pianist im klassischen style, op. 856, nos. 1 and 2. See no.
        3628
    Schule der Gelaufigkeit, op. 299: Auswahl. See no. 3628
    Schule des Virtuosen, op. 365: Auswahl. See no. 3628
CZIBULKA, Alfons
    Stephanie gavotte. See no. 3870
DABROWSKI, Florian
1162 Concerto, violin, 2 pianos and percussion. MEYER: Concerto, violin,
        op. 12. Jadwiga Kaliszewska, vln; Polish Philharmonic Orchestra,
        Poznan Percussion Ensemble; Renard Czajkowski. Muza SX 1054
                +FF 7/8-80 p121   +NR 8-77 p6
DAETWYLER, Jean
    Marignan march. See no. 3627
DAHL, Ingolf
1163 Concerto, saxophone. ETLER: Concerto, clarinet. Donald Sinta, sax;
        David Shifrin, clt; University of Michigan Wind Ensemble; H. Rob-
        ert Reynolds. University of Michigan School of Music SM 0009
                +-ARG 7-79 p32   ++IN 7-79 p6
                +FF 1/2-80 p77
    Variations on a Swedish folktune. See no. 4006
DALLA CASA
    Ancor che col partire. See no. 3683
DALLAPICCOLA, Luigi
    Cori di Michelangelo Buonarroti di Giovane. See no. 3713
1164 Quarderno musicale di Annalibera. Sonatina canonica on Paganini
        caprices. MOEVS: Una collana musicale, nos. 2, 5-6, 10-12.
        Fantasia sopra un motivo. Phoenix. Wanda Maximilien, pno. CRI
        SD 404
                +ARG 1-80 p26   +NYT 9-16-79 pD24
                +FF 1/2-80 p77
    Sonatina canonica on Paganini caprices. See no. 1164
1165 Songs: Canti (5); Divertimento in quattro esercizi; Liriche de
        Antonio Machado; Rencesvals. Anna Carol Dudley, s; Tom Buckner,
        t; Instrumental accompaniments; Robert Hughes. 1750 Arch S 1782
                +NR 10-80 p11
1166 Songs: Sieben Goethe Lieder. SCHOENBERG: Herzgewachse, op. 20.
        STRAVINSKY: Elegy for J.F.K. Songs from Shakespeare (3). WEB-
        ERN: Lieder, opp. 14-18. Dorothy Dorow, s; Amsterdam Ensemble;
        Reinbert de Leeuw. Telefunken 6-42350
                +ARG 7/8-80 p49   +Op 3-8-80 p29
                +NYT 5-13-79 pD21   ++St 6-80 p125

DALZA, Joanambrosio
    Recercar. See no. 4042
    Tastar de corde. See no. 4042
DAMARE, Eugene
1167 Caprice, op. 174. Le merle blanc, op. 161. Piccolo polka, op. 157.
    Le tourbillon, op. 212. Le tourterelle, op. 119. GENIN: It is
    raining shepherdess, op. 3. DONJON: Bamboche. Jean-Louis Beau-
    madier, pic; Jean Koerner, pno. Calliope CAL 1867
            +HFN 6-80 p114   +RR 5-80 p40
    Le merle blanc, op. 161. See no. 1167
    Piccolo polka, op. 157. See no. 1167
    Le tourbillon, op. 212. See no. 1167
    Le tourterelle, op. 119. See no. 1167
DAMASE, Jean-Michel
    Sicilienne variee. See no. 3685
DAMETT, Thomas
    Beata Dei genitrix. See no. 1120
DANBY
    The nightingale who tunes her warbling notes. See no. 3873
DANDRIEU, Jean Francois
    Chanton de voix hautaine. See no. 3682
    Cromorne en taille. See no. 1141
    Fugues, nos. 1 and 2. See no. 1141
1168 Fugue sur l'Ave Maris stella. Offertoire. Recit de Nasard. GUIL-
    AIN: Suite du deuxieme ton. JULLIEN: Livre d'orgue, excerpts.
    RAISON: Livre d'orgue, 1st, excerpts. Pierre Bardon, org. Pier-
    re Verany PV 3791
            +FF 11/12-80 p209
    Fugue sur "Ave maris stella". See no. 4061
    Livre de noels: Noels pour l'amour de Marie; Sortons de nos chaumi-
    ers. See no. 165
    Magnificat. See no. 1141
1169 Magnificat and pieces, A minor. Magnificat and pieces, G minor.
    Gillian Weir, org. Argo ZK 84
            +Gr 8-80 p241   +-MT 12-80 p785
            +-HFN 7-80 p106   ++RR 7-80 p78
    Magnificat and pieces, G minor. See no. 1169
    La musette. See no. 3618
    Noels (3). See no. 3993
    Offertoire. See no. 1141. See no. 1168. See no. 3733
    Plein jeu. See no. 1141
    Recit de Nasard. See no. 1168
    Trio. See no. 1141
DANKS, Hart
    Silver threads among the gold. See no. 3874
DANOFF/NIVERT/DENVER
    Take me home country roads. See no. 3962
    DANSES ANCIENNES DE HONGRIE ET DE TRANSYLVANIE. See no. 3758
DANYEL, John
1170 Songs: Can doleful notes; Coy Daphne fled; Dost thou withdraw thy
    grace; Eyes look no more; Grief keep within; He whose desires
    are still abroad; I die when as I do not see; If I could shut
    the gate; Let not Cloris think; Like as the lute delights; Now
    the earth the skies the air; Stay cruel stay; Thou pretty bird;
    Time cruel time; What delight can they enjoy; Why canst thou not.

London Music Players; Martin Cole, lt. Aurora AUR 7001
     +Gr 8-79 p363   +-MT 1-80 p33
     +HFN 7-79 p104   +RR 7-79 p105
  Songs: Eyes look no more; Like as the lute delights; What delight
     can they enjoy. See no. 980
  Songs: Like as the lute delights. See no. 3877
DANZI, Franz
1171 Concerto, bassoon, F major. Sinfonia concertante, B flat major.
     Dieter Kocker, clt; Karl-Otto Hartmann, bsn; Concerto Amsterdam;
     Jaap Schroder. Acanta EA 23144
          +HFN 5-80 p119   +RR 4-80 p61
1172 Quintets, winds, op. 56, nos. 1-3. Danzi Quintet. Acanta EA 22070
          +-HFN 8-80 p95   +RR 8-80 p59
  Sinfonia concertante, B flat major. See no. 1171
DAQUIN, Louis
  Le coucou. See no. 4028
  Livres de noels: Noel etranger, Noel en trio et en dialogue, Noel
     grand jeu et duo. See no. 3591
  Noels, no. 6. See no. 4040
  Noels, no. 10, G major. See no. 3836
  Noel etranger. See no. 4062
  Noel suisse. See no. 4055
DARGOMYZKSHY, Alexander
1173 Le convive de Pierre. Tamara Milashkina, s; Vladimir Atlantov, t;
     Alexander Vedernikov, bar; Bolshoi Theatre Orchestra and Chorus;
     Mark Ermler. Chant du Monde LDX 78661/2 (2)
          +-HFN 8-80 p97
  The old corporal. See no. 3904
  Russalka: Miller's aria. See no. 3796
  The stone guest. See no. 3796
DARKE, Harold
  In the bleak midwinter. See no. 4066
DAUPRAT, Louis Francoise
1174 Sextets, horns, op. 10 (6). Cors d'Esprits; Christopher Leuba.
     Coronet LPS 3045
          ++NR 1-80 p5
DAVID, Johann Nepomuk
1175 Chaconne and fugue. Choralwerk II: Macht die Tur, die Tor Macht
     weit und Komm, heiliger Geist, Herr Gott. Choralwerk VIII: Es
     sungen drei Engel ein sussen Gesang. Prelude and fugue, G major.
     Graham Barber, org. Vista VPS 1048
          +Gr 8-77 p327   +RR 7-77 p80
          +HFN 6-77 p131   +St 7-78 p90
          +NR 3-80 p15
  Choralwerk II: Macht hoch die Tur, die Tor Macht weit und Komm,
     heiliger Geist, Herr Gott. See no. 1175
  Choralwerk VIII: Es sungen drei Engel ein sussen Gesang. See no.
     1175
  Prelude and fugue, G major. See no. 1175
DAVIE
  Songs: Come holy ghost; There is a balm. See no. 4060
DAVIES, Henry Walford
  God be in my head. See no. 3939
  Interlude, C major. See no. 3582. See no. 4054
  Magdalen at Michael's gate. See no. 3532

Psalm, no. 23. See no. 966
Psalm, no. 121. See no. 3567
Songs: A sacred cradle song; O little town of Bethlehem. See no.
   4066
Songs: Solemn melody; Tarry no longer. See no. 3534
Songs: Psalm, no. 121. See no. 3938
Tarry no longer. See no. 3533. See no. 3936

DAVIS, Chip
1176 Interlude, no. 6. DEBUSSY: Arabesque, no. 1. Preludes, Bk I:
   La catedrale engloutie. PERSICHETTI: Sonata, piano, no. 9.
   RACHMANINOFF: Prelude, op. 32, no. 12, G sharp minor. Jackson
   Berkey, pno. American Gramaphone AG 361
               +-FF 11/12-80 p207

DAVIS, Thomas
A nation once again. See no. 4070

DAVY, Richard
Joan is sick and ill at ease. See no. 3768

DAWSON, William
1177 Negro folk symphony. American Symphony Orchestra; Leopold Stokowski. Varese VC 81056
               +FF 5/6-79 p41   +RR 1-80 p70
               +HFN 1-80 p105

DE LA BARRE, Michel
Sarabande. See no. 3852
Suite, no. 9, G major. See no. 4020

DE LA SERNA, Estancio
Tiento, 6th tone. See no. 3708

DE LA VEGA, Aurelio
Para-tangents. See no. 3652

DE LARA, Isidore
Messaline: O nuit d'amour. See no. 3770

DE LEEUW, Ton
Men go their ways. See no. 955

DE MONFRED, Avenir H
In paradisum. See no. 4051

DE VERE, Stephen
The snow breasted pearl. See no. 4070

DEBUSSY, Claude
Arabesque, no. 1. See no. 1176. See no. 3685
1178 Berceuse heroique. D'un cahier de esquisses. Etudes, Bks I and II.
   Morceau de concours, no. 6. Livia Rev, pno. Saga 5475
               +HFN 9-80 p375   +HFN 10-80 p103
Berceuse heroique. See no. 1205
La boite a joujoux. See no. 3557
Chanson de Bilitis: La chevelure. See no. 3964
1179 Children's corner suite. Images. Theodore Paraskivesco, pno. Cal-
   liope CAL 1833
               +-Gr 12-80 p853   +-HFN 12-80 p137
Children's corner suite. See no. 3557
1180 Children's corner suite: Golliwog's cake walk; Doctor Gradus and
   Parnassum. Images: Hommage a Rameau. La plus que lente. Prelude, Bk I: La fille aux cheveux de lin. Pour le piano: Prelude.
   Suite bergamasque: Clair de lune. DOHANANYI: Rhapsody, op. 11,
   no. 3, C major. RACHMANINOFF: Polichinelle, op. 3, no. 4, F
   sharp minor. Prelude, op. 3, no. 2, C sharp minor. Preludes,
   op. 23, nos. 5 and 6. SCRIABIN: Poeme tragique, op. 34, B major.

Prelude, op. 11, no. 9, E major. Jean Carrington Cook, pno.
Golden Age 1016
+NR 10-80 p13
Children's corner suite: The little shepherd. See no. 3635
1181 Danses sacree et profane. RAVEL: Introduction and allegro. ROUS-
SEL: Impromptu, op. 21. SAINT-SAENS: Morceau de concert, op.
154. Lucile Johnson, Marcela Kozikova, hp. Desmar DSM 1018G
+FF 5/6-80 p186   +NR 10-79 p16
1182 Danses sacree et profane. DUSSEK: Sonata, violin, violoncello and
harp, B flat major. HANDEL: Concerto, harp, op. 4, no. 6, B
flat major. IBERT: Interludes, flute, violin and harp (2).
Entr'acte, flute and harp. Giselle Herbert, Joachim Starke, hp;
Jorg-Wolfgang Jahn, vln; Werner Jacksch, vlc; Heidelberg Chamber
Orchestra. Desto DC 7185
+-FF 11/12-80 p218
1183 Danses sacree et profane. Epigraphes antiques. Petite suite.
Lily Laskine, hp; Jean-Francois Paillard Chamber Orchestra; Jean-
Francois Paillard. Erato STU 70422
++FF 3/4-80 p79
D'un cahier d'esquisses. See no. 1178
Elegie. See no. 1204
En blanc et noir. See no. 1202
L'Enfant prodigue: Air de Lia. See no. 3367
L'Enfant prodigue: Cortege et air de danse. See no. 3799
L'Enfant prodigue: Prelude. See no. 3964
Epigraphes antiques. See no. 1183. See no. 1202
1184 Estampes. L'Isle joyeuse. Pour le piano. Preludes, Bk I: La cate-
drale engloutie. Berenice Lipson-Gruzen, pno. Desto DC 7182
Tape (c) 4-7182
+-ARG 6-80 p20   +HF 8-80 p70
+FF 9/10-80 p108
1185 Estampes. Images. Preludes, Bks I and II. Walter Gieseking, pno.
HMV RLS 752 (2) Tape (c) TC RLS 752 (From Columbia 33CX 1098,
33CX 1304, 33CX 1137)
+Gr 12-80 p889 tape   +Gr 9-80 p375
1186 Estampes. Images (1894). Images, Bks I and II. Paul Jacobs, pno.
Nonesuch H 71365 Tape (c) N 5-1365
/-FF 11/12-80 p98   ++RR 4-80 p93
+Gr 5-80 p1693   ++SFC 9-30-79 p45
++HF 2-80 p85   ++St 12-79 p137
+NR 12-79 p13
Estampes. See no. 1204
1187 Estampes: Jardins sous la pluie. Images: Reflets dans l'eau; Pois-
sons d'or. Preludes, Bk I: La catedrale engloutie. Preludes,
BK II: Ondine. GRIFFES: Roman sketches, op. 7: The fountain of
Acqua Paola. LISZT: Annees de pelerinage, 3rd year, G 163: Les
jeux d'eau a la Villa d'Este. RAVEL: Jeux d'eau. Gaspard de
nuit: Ondine. Carol Rosenberger, pno. Delos D/DMS 3006
+HF 8-80 p70   +-RR 4-80 p104
/-HFN 4-80 p116   ++St 7-80 p88
+-NR 4-80 p14
Etudes, Bks I and II. See no. 1178
Etudes, Bks I. See no. 3628
Etudes: Pour les arpeges composes. See no. 1203
Etude retrouvee. See no. 1203
Images. See no. 1179

Images. See no. 1185. See no. 1186. See no. 1204
Images, Bks I and II. See no. 1186. See no. 1203
Images: Hommage a Rameau. See no. 1180. See no. 3976
Images: Poissons d'or. See no. 3953. See no. 3954
Images: Reflets dans l'eau. See no. 3907
Images: Reflets dans l'eau; Poissons d'or. See no. 1187
Images: Reflets dans l'eau; Hommage a Rameau; Mouvement. See no.
    831
Images oubliees. See no. 1203
1188 Images pour orchestra. Prelude a l'apres-midi d'un faune. BSO;
    Michael Tilson Thomas. DG 2535 370 Tape (c) 3335 370 (From 2530
    145)

            ++Gr 11-79 p810   +RR 10-79 p86
            +-HFN 11-79 p153   ++RR 3-80 p105 tape
            +RR 11-79 p76

1189 Images pour orchestra. Prelude a l'apres-midi d'un faune. LSO;
    Andre Previn. HMV ASD 3804 Tape (c) TC ASD 3804 (also Angel DS
    37674)

          +-FF 9/10-80 p106   +-MUM 10-80 p34
          ++Gr 12-79 p1008   ++NR 4-80 p2
          ++Gr 3-80 p1446 tape   +RR 1-80 p70
          +-HF 8-80 p79   +SFC 3-23-80 p35
          +HFN 12-79 p159   ++St 6-80 p116
          +HFN 2-80 p107 tape   +STL 12-2-79 p37

Images pour orchestra: Gigues; Iberia; Rondes de printemps. See no.
    3556
1190 Images pour orchestra: Iberia. Jeux. Nocturnes. CO and Chorus;
    Lorin Maazel. London CS 7128 (also Decca SXL 6904 Tape (c)
    KSXC 6904)

          +FF 3/4-80 p79   +NR 3-80 p1
          ++Gr 3-80 p1386   +RR 3-80 p50
          ++HF 11-79 p92   +-St 10-79 p136
          -HFN 3-80 p87

L'Isle joyeuse. See no. 1184. See no. 1204. See no. 3820
1191 Jeux. Nocturnes (3). COA; Bernard Haitink. Philips 9500 674 Tape
    (c) 7300 769

          ++Gr 11-80 p665   ++NR 12-80 p2
          ++HFN 11-80 p117   +SFC 10-26-80 p20

Jeux. See no. 1190. See no. 3556
Jeux, excerpts. See no. 3604. See no. 3608
Lindaraja. See no. 1202
The little shepherd. See no. 3607
Marche ecossaise. See no. 1202
1192 Le martyrdom of Saint Sebastien: Symphonic fragments. Rhapsody,
    clarinet. Rhapsody, saxophone. ORTF; Guy Deplus, clt; Daniel
    Deffayet, sax; Marius Constant. Erato STU 70719

          +-ARG 10-79 p43   ++SFC 6-24-79 p57
          +-FF 9/10-80 p107

Le martyre de Saint Sebastien. See no. 3557
Masques. See no. 1204
1193 La mer. SCRIABIN: Poeme de l'extase, op. 54. CO; Lorin Maazel.
    Decca SXL 6905 Tape (c) KSXC 6095 (also London CS 7129)

          +-FF 7/8-80 p75   +-NR 5-80 p2
          +Gr 9-79 p468   +RR 9-79 p86
          +HF 4-80 p82   +RR 3-80 p105
          +-HFN 9-79 p105   ++St 1-80 p94

1194 La mer. Nocturnes, nos. 1-3. Orchestre and Chorus de Paris; Daniel
     Barenboim. DG 2531 056 Tape (c) 3301 056
                    +FF 9/10-79 p75   +-NYT 3-2-80 pD26
                    +-Gr 12-78 p1094   +RR 12-78 p55
                    +Gr 5-79 p1940 tape   +RR 8-79 p128 tape
                    -HF 11-79 p92   -SFC 6-24-79 p57
                    +HFN 1-79 p116   ++St 10-79 p136
                    +HFN 5-79 p134 tape
1195 La mer. RAVEL: Ma mere l'oye. Rapsodie espagnole. LAPO; Carlo
     Maria Giulini. DG 2531 264 Tape (c) 3301 264
                    +-Gr 6-80 p32   ++RR 6-80 p46
                    +HFN 6-80 p106   ++STL 5-11-80 p39
                    +HFN 8-80 p109 tape
     Morceau de concours. See no. 1203
     Morceau de concours, no. 6. See no. 1178
1196 Nocturnes (3). RAVEL: Ma mere l'oye. OSR; Ernest Ansermet. Lon-
     don STS 15488
                    +FF 9/10-80 p169
     Nocturnes, nos. 1-3. See no. 1194.
     Nocturnes. See no. 1190. See no. 1191.
     Nocturnes: Fetes. See no. 1002
     Noel des enfants qui n'ont plus de jouets. See no. 3965
     Page d'album. See no. 1204
1197 Pelleas et Melisande. Rachel Yakar, Collette Alliot-Lugaz, s;
     Jocelyne Taillon, ms; Eric Tappy, t; Philippe Huttenlocher, bar;
     Francois Loup, bs; Monte Carlo Opera Orchestra; Armin Jordan.
     Erato STU 71296
                    +Gr 10-80 p533
1198 Pelleas et Melisande. Frederica von Stade, Christine Barbaux, s;
     Nadine Denize, con; Richard Stilwell, Jose van Dam, bar; Ruggero
     Raimondi, Pascal Thomas, bs; German Opera Chorus; BPhO; Herbert
     von Karajan. HMV SLS 5172 (3) Tape (c) TC SLS 5172 (also Angel
     SZX 3885)
                    +ARG 7/8-80 p22   +NYT 12-23-79 pD28
                    ++FF 5/6-80 p72   +ON 3-15-80 p45
                    +Gr 12-79 p1040   +Op 5-80 p471
                    +-HF 4-80 p84   ++RR 1-80 p56
                    ++HFN 4-80 p121 tape   +-SFC 1-6-80 p43
                    ++HFN 2-80 p91   ++St 3-80 p100
                    ++NR 3-80 p12   +-STL 2-10-80 p40
1199 Pelleas et Melisande. Micheline Grancher, Camille Maurane,
     Jacques Mars, Andre Vessieres, Francoise Ogeas, Marie Luce
     Bellary, Jacques Vigneron; ORTF and Chorus; D. E. Inghelbrecht.
     Inedits ORTF 995014/16 (3)
                    +OC Winter 1980 p52
1200 Pelleas et Melisande. Irene Joachim, Leila Ben-Sedira, s; Germaine
     Cernay, ms; Jacques Jansen, t; H. Etcheverry, bar; Armand Narcon,
     Paul Cabanel, bs; Yvonne Gouvern Choeurs; Roger Desmormiere.
     Odeon 2C 153 12513/5 (3)
                    +ARSC Vol 12, no. 1-2   +HF 4-75 p76
                    1980 p119   +NYT 10-9-77 pD21
     Pelleas et Melisande: Je n'en dis rien. See no. 3631
     La petit negre. See no. 3568
1201 Petite piece. Prelude, Bk I: La fille aux cheveux de lin (arr.
     Leon Roques). HONEGGER: Sonatine. POULENC: Sonata, clarinet

and piano. SAINT-SAENS: Sonata, clarinet and piano, op. 167,
E flat major. Richard Stolzman, clt; Irma Vallecillo, pno. Desmar DSM 1014

    +-Audio 11-80 p84   +NYT 12-2-79 pD22
    +FF 11/12-78 p140   +RR 7-78 p80
    +Gr 9-78 p499   ++St 6-78 p161
    +HFN 7-78 p105

Petite piece. See no. 3650
Petite suite. See no. 1183. See no. 1202. See no. 3645
Petite suite: En bateau. See no. 3552. See no. 3788
1202 Piano works: En blanc et noir. Epigraphes antiques (6). Lindaraja.
    Marche ecossaise. Petite suite. Claude Helffer, Haakon Austbo,
    pno. Harmonia Mundi HM 957

    +HFN 1-80 p105   +-RR 11-79 p110

1203 Piano works: Images, Bks I and II. Images oubliees. Etude retrou-
    vee. Morceau de concours. Etudes: Pour les arpeges composes.
    Roy Howat, pno. Nimbus 2122

    +-HFN 9-80 p101   +RR 8-80 p70

1204 Piano works: Elegie. Estampes. Images. L'Isle joyeuse. Page
    d'album. Pour le piano. La plus que lente. Masques. Reverie.
    Suite bergamasque. Livia Rev, pno. Saga SAGA 5463 (2)

    +FF 11/12-80 p98   +HFN 5-79 p119
    +Gr 5-79 p1914   ++RR 3-79 p109
    +HF 8-80 p71

La plus que lente. See no. 1180. See no. 1204. See no. 3964
Pour le piano. See no. 1184. See no. 1204
Pour le piano: Prelude. See no. 1180
1205 Preludes, Bks I and II. Berceuse heroique. Theodore Paraskivesco,
    pno. Calliope CAL 1832/3

    +-Gr 12-80 p853   +-RR 7-77 p80
    +HFN 6-77 p121

1206 Preludes, Bks I and II. Dino Ciani, pno. DG 2535 260/1 Tape (c)
    3335 260/1

    +-FF 9/10-79 p76   +HFN 11-78 p187
    +Gr 9-78 p564 tape   +MJ 11/12-79 p49
    ++HF 2-80 p85   ++NR 12-79 p13
    +-HFN 9-78 p157 tape   +RR 11-78 p87

1207 Preludes, Bks I and II. Ernest Ulmer, pno. Protone PR 151/2 (2)
    +-FF 11/12-80 p98   ++HF 8-80 p71

Preludes, Bks I and II. See no. 1185
1208 Preludes, Bk I. Claudio Arrau, pno. Philips 9500 676 Tape (c)
    7300 771

    ++Gr 10-80 p518   ++SFC 9-21-80 p21
    +HFN 11-80 p117   ++St 12-80 p120
    +HFN 12-80 p159 tape +STL 11-9-80 p40
    ++NR 11-80 p9

1209 Preludes, Bk I. Livia Rev, pno. Saga 5391 Tape (c) CA 5391

    +-FF 7/8-80 p76   +HFN 4-79 p131
    +Gr 3-75 p1678   +-RR 4-75 p50
    +Gr 2-77 p1322 tape   +-RR 1-77 p88 tape
    ++HF 2-80 p85   ++RR 3-79 p109
    +HFN 12-76 p155 tape

Preludes, Bk I: La catedrale engloutie. See no. 1176. See no.
    1184. See no. 1187. See no. 3953. See no. 3954
Preludes, Bk I: La fille aux cheveux de lin. See no. 1180. See no.
    1201. See no. 3676. See no. 3883. See no. 3964

Preludes, Bk I: Le vent dans la plaine; Les colines d'Anecapri. See
    no. 999
1210 Preludes, Bk II. Livia Rev, pno. Saga 5442
                +–FF 7/8-80 p76   +HFN 4-79 p131
                ++Gr 12-77 p1106   +RR 11-77 p87
                +HF 8-80 p71   ++RR 3-79 p109
                +HFN 12-77 p168
Preludes, Bk II: La puerta del vino. See no. 3678
Preludes, Bk II: Les terrasses des audiences; Les tierces alternees.
    See no. 999
Preludes, Bk II: Ondine. See no. 1187
1211 Preludes a l'apres-midi d'un faune. DUKAS: L'Apprenti sorcier.
    FALLA: El sombrero de tres picos: Seguidillas; Farruca; Jota.
    RESPIGHI: Fountains of Rome. Budapest Philharmonic Orchestra;
    Janos Sandor. Hungaroton SLPX 12031
                +–FF 5/6-80 p199   ++SFC 3-23-80 p35
                +–NR 5-80 p2
1212 Prelude to the afternoon of a faun. RESPIGHI: Roman festivals.
    STRAUSS, R.: Till Eulenspiegel's merry pranks, op. 28. Czech
    Radio Orchestra, Bratislava; Ondrej Lenard. Musical Heritage
    Society MHS 4042
                /FF 1/2-80 p149
Prelude a l'apres-midi d'un faune. See no. 639. See no. 1002.
    See no. 1188. See no. 1189. See no. 3604. See no. 3608. See
    no. 3666. See no. 3799. See no. 3955. See no. 4069
1213 Printemps. DELIUS: On hearing the first cuckoo in spring. DVORAK:
    The golden spinning wheel, op. 109. MASSENET: La vierge: Le der-
    nier sommeil de la vierge. Orchestra; Thomas Beecham. World
    Records SH 1003
                +ARSC Vol 12, no. 3, 1980 p240
1214 Quartet, string, G minor. RAVEL: Quartet, strings, F major. Tokyo
    Quartet. Columbia M 35147 (also CBS 76824)
                +–FF 3/4-80 p80   +RR 7-79 p74
                +Gr 7-79 p215   ++SFC 5-13-79 p32
                +HF 9-79 p118   +St 8-79 p111
                +–HFN 7-79 p104   ++ST 11-79 p528
1215 Quartet, strings, G minor. RAVEL: Quartet, strings, F major. Mel-
    os Quartet. DG 2531 203 Tape (c) 3301 203
                +–FF 3/4-80 p80   +NYT 2-10-80 pD24
                +Gr 11-79 p861   +RR 11-79 p104
                +Gr 12-79 p1065 tape   ++RR 3-80 p104 tape
                ++HF 5-80 p68   +SFC 5-4-80 p42
                ++HFN 11-79 p137   ++St 3-80 p91
                ++NR 4-80 p8
1216 Quartet, strings, G minor. RAVEL: Quartet, strings, F major. New
    Hungarian Quartet. Turnabout Tape (c) CT 7001
                +HF 1-80 p91 tape
Reverie. See no. 1204
Rhapsody, clarinet. See no. 1192
Rhapsody, saxophone. See no. 1192
1217 Sonata, flute, viola and harp. Sonata, violin and piano, G minor.
    Sonata, violoncello and piano, D minor. Syrinx. Frans Vester,
    flt; Jaap Schroder, vln, vla; Edward Witsenburg, hp; Anner Byls-
    ma, vlc; Gerard van Blerk, pno. Acanta EA 21814
                +HFN 5-80 p119   +ST 7-80 p195
                +RR 4-80 p84

1218 Sonata, violin and piano, G minor. FAURE: Sonata, violin and piano,
     no. 1, op. 13, A major. Berceuse, op. 16. Pinchas Zukerman, vln,
     Marc Neikrug, pno. CBS 76813 (also Columbia M 35179)
   +ARG 9-80 p26   +NR 4-80 p8
   +FF 9/10-80 p120   +NYT 7-6-80 pD15
   +Gr 6-79 p66   +RR 6-79 p105
   +HFN 6-79 p105   +SFC 2-24-80 p39
1219 Sonata, violin and piano, G minor. FRANCK: Sonata, violin and piano,
     A major. Kyung Wha Chung, vln; Radu Lupu, pno. London CS 7171
     (also Decca SXL 6944 Tape (c) KSXC 6944)
   +Gr 9-80 p359   +HFN 9-80 p101
   +Gr 12-80 p889 tape   ++St 12-80 p124
     Sonata, violin and piano, G minor. See no. 1217. See no. 3772
1220 Sonata, violoncello and piano, D minor. RACHMANINOFF: Sonata, vio-
     loncello and piano, op. 19, G minor. Prelude, op. 2, no. 1.
     Danse orientale, op. 2, no. 2. Julian Lloyd Webber, vlc; Yitkin
     Seow, pno. Enigma K 53586
   +Gr 9-79 p483   +RR 9-79 p108
   +HFN 10-79 p151   +ST 1-80 p691
     Sonata, violoncello and piano, D minor. See no. 1217
1221 Songs: La damoiselle elui; Ballades de Francois Villon (3); Invoca-
     tion; Salut printemps. Barbara Hendricks, s; Jocelyne Taillon,
     ms; Dietrich Fischer-Dieskau, bar; Leonard Pezzini, t; L'Orches-
     tre and Chorus de Paris; Daniel Barenboim. DG 2531 263
   +Gr 8-80 p248   +NYT 12-14-80 pD38
   +-HFN 9-80 p101   +NYT 9-21-80 pD22
   +-NR 11-80 p7   +RR 8-80 p81
1222 Songs: Dans le jardin; Les Angelus; L'Echelonnement des haies;
     Fleur des bles; Mandoline; Nuit d'Etoiles; L'Ombre des arbres;
     Poemes de Baudelaire (5); Poemes de Stephane Mallarme (3); Rom-
     ance; Le son du cor. Hughes Cuenod, t; Martin Isepp, pno. Nim-
     bus 2127
   +Gr 9-80 p386   ++RR 8-80 p82
   +-HFN 9-80 p101   +STL 8-10-80 p30
1223 Songs: Aimons-nous et dormons; Angelus; Apparition; Ariettes oub-
     liees; Ballades de Francois Villon (3); Beau soir; La belle au
     bois dormant; Chanson de Bilitis; Chanson de France: Rondel; Le
     temps a laissee son manteau; Rondel: Pour ce que plaisance est
     monte; Claire de lune; Dans le jardin; Fetes galantes, Set 1 and
     2; Fleur des bles; Jane; Mandoline; Melodies (3); Noel des en-
     fants qui n'ont plus de maison; Nuit de'etoiles; Pantomime; Pay-
     sage sentimental; Pierrot; Poemes de Charles Baudelaire (5);
     Poemes de Stephane Mallarme (3); Le promenoir des deux amants;
     Proses lyriques; Romances: Romance, Les cloches; Rondeau; Ron-
     del chinois; Voici que le printemps; Zephyr. Elly Ameling, Mic-
     hele Command, Mady Mesple, s; Frederica von Stade, ms; Gerard
     Souzay, bar; Dalton Baldwin, pno. Pathe Marconi 2C 165 16371/4
     (4)
   +Gr 12-80 p860   +-HFN 12-80 p137
     Songs: Apparition; Clair de lune; Pantomime; Pierrot. See no. 3541
     Songs: Ariettes oubliees: Il pleure dans mon coeur. See no. 3964
     Songs: Ballade des femmes de Paris; C'est l'extase langoureuse.
     See no. 3738
     Suite bergamasque. See no. 1204
     Suite bergamasque: Clair de lune. See no. 1180. See no. 3605.
     See no. 3666. See no. 3677. See no. 4030

Syrinx, flute. See no. 1217. See no. 3714. See no. 3854

Valse romantique. See no. 3890

DE CALL, Leonard

1224 Trio, op. 26, C major. GRAGNANI: Trio, op. 12, D major. KUFFNER:
Polonaise, op. 168, A major. Thomatos Guitar Trio. Spectrum SR
109
+FF 7/8-80 p181

DEFAYE, Jean-Michel

Danses (2). See no. 3653

DEGHTYAROV

All nations have seen. See no. 775

DEL RIEGO Teresa

Homing. See no. 3831

O dry those tears. See no. 3774. See no. 3875

DELALANDE, Michel

Psallite domino. See no. 1006

DELANO

La bruja de Loiza: Fiesta en el pueblo; La novia desconsolada; Las
viejas chismosas. See no. 3645

DELIBES, Leo

1225 Coppelia. Rotterdam Philharmonic Orchestra; David Zinman. Philips
6769 035 (2) Tape (c) 7699 126
+–FF 7/8-80 p77   ++NR 6-80 p6
+Gr 5-80 p1660   +–RR 5-80 p57
+Gr 5-80 p1717 tape   +–RR 7-80 p96 tape
+HF 10-80 p74   +SFC 5-25-80 p41
+HFN 4-80 p121 tape   ++St 9-80 p77
+HFN 5-80 p119

Coppelia: Mazurka. See no. 3666

Coppelia: Prelude, Act 1, Mazurka, Valse, Ballade de Epi, Theme
slave varie, Valse de la poupee, Csardas. See no. 3557

Les filles de Cadiz. See no. 3872

Lakme: Air des clochettes; Blanche Dourga; D'ou viens tu...C'est la
Dieu; Les filles de Cadiz. See no. 3559

Lakme: Bell song. See no. 3625. See no. 3828

Lakme: Dove l'Indiana bruna. See no. 3789

Lakme: Fantasie aux divins mensonges. See no. 3770

Lakme: Weisse Durga; Duet; Bell song. See no. 3872

Sylvia: Pizzicato divertissement, Act 3. See no. 3605

Sylvia: Prelude; Les chasseresses; Intermezzo; Valse lente; Pizzicato;
Marche et cortege de Bacchus. See no. 3557

DELISLE, Rouget

La Marseillaise. See no. 3904

DELIUS, Frederick

1226 Air and dance. ELGAR: Serenade, op. 20, E minor. VAUGHAN WILLIAMS:
Concerto grosso. WARLOCK: Serenade for the 60th birthday of
Delius. Gerald Jarvis, vln; Bournemouth Symphony Orchestra; Nor-
man Del Mar. HMV ESD 7088 Tape (c) TC ESD 7088 (From ASD 2531)
+Gr 8-80 p234   +HFN 9-80 p115

Air and dance. See no. 1233. See no. 1235

Brigg Fair. See no. 1236

Concerto, piano. See no. 1236

Concerto, violin. See no. 1236

Dance. See no. 1235

Dance rhapsodies, nos. 1 and 2. See no. 1236

1227 Dance rhapsody, no. 2. Florida suite. Over the hills and far away.
       RPO; Thomas Beecham. HMV SXLP 30415 Tape (c) TC SXLP 30415 (From
       ASD 329)
                         +ARSC Vol 12, no. 3   +-HFN 4-80 p119
                            1980 p253   +-HFN 4-80 p121
                         ++Gr 1-80 p1142
       Fennimore and Gerda: Intermezzo. See no. 1233. See no. 1234
       Florida suite. See no. 1227
1228 Hassan: Incidental music. Ronald Thomas, vln; Martyn Hill, t; Brian
       Rayner Cook, bar; Bournemouth Sinfonietta and Chorus; Vernon Hand-
       ley. HMV ASD 3777 Tape (c) TC ASD 3777
                         +FF 9/10-80 p108   +HFN 2-80 p107 tape
                         +-Gr 11-79 p886   +MT 9-80 p566
                         +HFN 2-80 p91   +RR 11-79 p77
       Hassan: Intermezzo and serenade. See no. 1233. See no. 1236. See
         no. 3639
       Irmelin. See no. 396
       Irmelin: Prelude. See no. 1234. See no. 1236
       Koanga: La Calinda. See no. 1233. See no. 1234. See no. 1235
       Little pieces: Mazurka for a little girl; Waltz for a little girl;
         Waltz; Lullaby for a modern baby; Toccata. See no. 1235
1229 The magic fountain. Katherine Pring, ms; John Mitchinson, t; Nor-
       man Welsby, bar; Richard Angas, Francis Thomas, bs; BBC Singers;
       BBC Concerto Orchestra; Norman Del Mar. BBC Artium BBC 2001 (2)
                         +Gr 8-80 p265
       Marche caprice. See no. 1236. See no. 3801
1230 On hearing the first cuckoo in spring. Sleigh ride. ELGAR: Intro-
       duction and allegro, op. 47. VAUGHAN WILLIAMS: Fantasia on a
       theme by Thomas Tallis. WOOD: Fantasia on British sea songs
       (arr. & orch). RPO, PhO, London Sinfonia, Allegri Quartet, LSO;
       Thomas Beecham, Malcolm Sargent, John Barbirolli, Henry Wood.
       HMV STAMP 1 (From ALP 1586, SXLP 20007, ASD 521, Columbia DX 954/
       5)
                         +Gr 9-80 p354
       On hearing the first cuckoo in spring. See no. 1213. See no. 1233.
         See no. 1234. See no. 1236
       Over the hills and far away. See no. 1227
       Romeo and Juliet. See no. 1236
       Sleigh ride. See no. 1230. See no. 1234
       Sonata, string orchestra. See no. 1235
1231 Sonatas, violin and piano, nos. 1-3. Yehudi Menuhin, vln; Eric
       Fenby, pno. HMV ASD 3864
                         +Gr 6-80 p44   +RR 6-80 p76
                         /HFN 6-80 p106   ++ST 9-80 p344
                         +MT 12-80 p785
       A song before sunrise. See no. 1233. See no. 1234. See no. 1236
       A song of summer. See no. 346. See no. 396
       Songs: Heimkehr; Paa Vidderne; Songs of sunset; Song of the high
         hills; Summer evening; When twilight fancies; Whither; The vio-
         let. See no. 1236
1232 Songs of sunset. BORODIN: Prince Igor: Polovtsian dances. Maureen
       Forrester, con; John Cameron, bar; Beecham Choral Society; RPO;
       Thomas Beecham. Arabesque Recordings 8026 Tape (c) 9026
                         +-ARG 3-80 p23   +-MUM 11/12-80 p33
                         +FF 11/12-80 p99   +NYT 1-6-80 pD18
                         +HF 6-80 p96 tape   +St 4-80 p131

Summer night on the river. See no. 1233. See no. 1234. See no.
    1236
A village Romeo and Juliet: The walk to the paradise garden. See
    no. 396. See no. 1233. See no. 1234. See no. 3581
1233 Works, selections: Air and dance. Fennimore and Gerda: Intermezzo
    (arr. Beecham). Koanga: La Calinda (arr. Fenby). Hassan: Inter-
    mezzo; Serenade. On hearing the first cuckoo in spring. A song
    before sunrise. Summer night on the river. A village Romeo and
    Juliet: The walk to the paradise garden. AMF; Neville Marriner.
    Argo ZRG 875 Tape (c) KZRC 875
                +-FF 1/2-80 p79   +HF 12-79 p94
                +Gr 2-79 p1416   +HFN 2-79 p103
                +Gr 6-79 p109 tape   ++SFC 10-14-79 p61
1234 Works, selections: Fennimore and Gerda: Intermezzo. Irmelin: Pre-
    lude. Koanga: La Calinda (arr. Fenby). On hearing the first
    cuckoo in spring. Sleigh ride. A song before sunrise. Summer
    night on the river. A village Romeo and Juliet: The walk to the
    paradise garden (arr. Beecham). LPO; Vernon Handley. Classics
    for Pleasure CFP 40304 Tape (c) TC CFP 40304
                -FF 9/10-80 p109   +HFN 2-79 p103
                +Gr 2-79 p1416   +HFN 2-80 p107 tape
                +Gr 3-80 p1446 tape
1235 Works, selections: Air and dance. Koanga: La Calinda. Dance.
    Little pieces: Mazurka for a little girl; Waltz for a little
    girl; Waltz; Lullaby for a modern baby; Toccata. Sonata, string
    orchestra. (arr. Fenby). Bournemouth Sinfonietta; Elena Duran,
    flt; Eric Fenby. HMV ASD 3688 Tape (c) TC ASD 3688
                ++FF 1/2-80 p78   +HFN 7-79 p104
                +Gr 7-79 p198   +HFN 11-79 p157 tape
                +Gr 9-79 p533 tape   +RR 7-79 p51
1236 Works, selections: Brigg Fair. Concerto, piano. Concerto, violin.
    Dance rhapsodies, nos. 1 and 2. Hassan: Intermezzo and serenade.
    Irmelin: Prelude. Marche caprice. On hearing the first cuckoo
    in spring. Romeo and Juliet. A song before sunrise. Summer
    night on the river. Songs: Heimkehr; Paa Vidderne; Songs of
    sunset; Song of the high hills; Summer evening; When twilight
    fancies; Whither; The violet. Margaret Ritchie, Dorothy Bond,
    Lorely Dyer, Freda Hart, Elsie Suddaby, s; Nancy Evans, Marjorie
    Thomas, ms; Rene Soames, Leslie Jones, t; Denis Dowling, Freder-
    ick Sharp, Gordon Clinton, Redvers Llewellyn, bar; Jean Pougnet,
    vln; Betty Humby Beecham, pno; RPO; Thomas Beecham. World Rec-
    ords SHB 54 (6) (Reissues)
                +ARSC Vol 12, no. 3   +MT 5-80 p321
                   1980 p258   +RR 1-80 p71
                ++Gr 10-79 p697
DELL'ACQUA, Eva
    Villanelle. See no. 3872
DELLA JOIO, Norman
    Concertante, clarinet and piano. See no. 697
    Duo concertato. See no. 352
DEMANTIUS, Johann
    Polnischer Tanz und Galliarda. See no. 3754
1237 St. John Passion. LONGUEVAL: Passio Domini nostri Jesu Christi
    secundum Matthaeum. Cambridge University Chamber Choir; Richard
    Marlow. Cambridge CCRS 1001
                ++Gr 3-80 p1427   +RR 4-80 p113

St. John Passion. See no. 3765
DEMESSIEUX, Jeanne
1238 Te deum, op. 11. Tryptyque, op. 7. DUPRE: Vision, op. 44. LANG-
     LAIS: Fete. Graham Barber, org. Vista VPS 1032
                    +Gr 2-77 p1308   +RR 1-77 p71
                    ++NR 2-80 p13   +RR 2-77 p80
     Tryptyque, op. 7. See no. 1238
DEMPSTER, Stuart
1239 In the great abbey of Clement IV: Standing waves; Didjeridervish.
     Stuart Dempster, trom and plastic sewer pipe. 1750 Arch S 1775
                    +FF 7/8-80 p77   ++NR 7-80 p14
DENNIS, Robert
     Of a rose. See no. 3849
DENZI, Luigi
     Funiculi funicula. See no. 3667. See no. 3988
     Occhi di fata. See no. 3771. See no. 3981
     Songs: Culto; Occhi di fata. See no. 3978
1240 Vieni. LEONCAVALLO: I Pagliacci: Vesti la giubba; No Pagliccio
     non son. PUCCINI: Madama Butterfly: Addio fiorito asil. Tosca:
     Recondite armonia; E lucevan le stelle. VERDI: Rigoletto: Ella
     mi fu rapita. Il trovatore: Mal reggendo...Oh giusto cielo;
     Miserere; Ai nostri monti. Aureliano Pertile, t. Rubini GV 539
                    +-RR 4-80 p30
DERING, Richard
     The cryes of London. See no. 3941. See no. 3995
     Factum est silentium. See no. 3525. See n. 3894
     Pavan. See no. 3853
     Songs: Contristatus est Rex David; Quem vidistis pastores. See no.
     3530
DESMARETS, Henri
     Mysteres de Notre Seigneur Jesus-Christ. See no. 1143
DESSAUER, Josef
     Le retour des promis. See no. 3770
DESTOUCHES, Andre
1241 Suite des elements, no. 1. REBEL: Les elements. Academy of Ancient
     Music; Christopher Hogwood, hpd and cond. L'Oiseau-Lyre DSLO
     562
                    +Gr 9-80 p332   +HFN 9-80 p101
DEVIENNE, Francois
1242 Concerto, flute, no. 2, D major. LOEILLET: Concerto, flute and
     strings, D major. NAUDOT: Concerto, flute and strings, G major.
     Jean-Pierre Rampal, flt; Antiqua Musica Orchestra; Jacques Rous-
     sel. Quintessence PMC 7129
                    +FF 1/2-80 p173
DIA, Comtesse de
     A chanter; Vida. See no. 3749
DIABELLI, Anton
1243 Andante con espressione, G major. Marcia and allegro moderato, D
     major. Rondo and allegro, C major. MOSCHELES: Grand duo con-
     certante, op. 20, A major. WEBER: Divertimento, op. 38. Leo
     Witoszynski, gtr; Rosario Marciano, pno. Turnabout TV 34728
                    +FF 11/12-79 p165   ++NR 4-79 p8
                    +Gr 5-80 p1678   +-RR 4-80 p99
                    +-HFN 4-80 p116
     Marcia and allegro moderato, D major. See no. 1243
1244 Pieces, flute and guitar. GOEPPERT: Sonata, bassoon and guitar,

op. 13, D major. KREUTZER: Trio, flute, clarinet and guitar, op.
16. RUDOLF ERZHERZOG VON OSTERREICH: Serenade, B major. Consor-
tium Classicum. Telefunken 6-42171
   +FF 3/4-80 p194   ++St 4-80 p140
Rondo and allegro, C major. See no. 1243
Sonatina, piano, op. 168, no. 7, A major. See no. 3730
Wiener Tanz. See no. 3759

DIAMOND, David
 Night music. See no. 3651

DIAZ
 Le coupe du Roi de Thule: Ist est venu ce jour de lutte. See no.
  3774

DIBDIN, Charles
 Come away death. See no. 3840

DICKINSON, Peter
 Recorder music. See no. 3795

DIDOMENICA, Robert
 concerto, violin. See no. 1117

DIEPENBROCK, Alphons
 Im grossen Schweigen. See no. 3818

DINICU, Dimitri
 Hora staccato. See no. 3601. See no. 3772. See no. 3951. See no.
  3964. See no. 3998

DIRKSEN
 Christ our passover. See no. 4059
 Nativity. See no. 3993

DIRUTA, Giorlamo
 Ricercare del 7, 8, 11, 12 tuono. See no. 3813
 Toccata del 11 and 12 tuono. See no. 3813

DISTLER, Hugo
1245 Chorale motets: Ach Gott von Himmel sieh darein; Es ist das Heil
  uns kommen her; Ich wollt dass ich daheime war; Komm Heiliger
  Geist Herre Gott; Lobe den Herren den machtigen Konig der Ehren;
  Singet frisch und wohlgemut; Wachet auf ruft uns die Stimme.
  Rotraud Riedel-Pax, Esther Himmler, s; Frauke Hasseman, alto;
  Hans-Dieter Saretzki, t; Westphalian Kantorei; Wilhelm Ehmann.
  Musical Heritage Society MHS 4095
    +RR 9/10-80 p109
 Nun komm der Heiden Heiland, partita. See no. 153
1246 Partitas: Nun komm der Heiden Heiland, op. 8, no. 1; Christ der du
  bist der helle Tag, op. 8, no. 7; Wachet auf ruft uns die Stimme,
  op. 8, no. 2; Jesus Christus unser Heiland, op. 8, no. 3. Larry
  Palmer, org. Musical Heritage Society MHS 3943
    ++FF 3/4-80 p81   +-MU 7-79 p8
 Partita on "Wachet auf ruft uns die Stimme". See no. 3732
1247 Passion chorale, op. 7. Rottgen Chamber Choir and Soloists; Melchior von Borries. Aulos FSM 43515
    ++FF 3/4-80 p81

DITTERSDORF, Karl Ditters von
 Concerto, harp, op. 4, no. 6, B flat major. See no. 754

DLUGORAJ, Adalbert
 Fantasia. See no. 3966
 Finales (2). See no. 3966
 Vilanellas, nos. 1 and 2. See no. 3966

DLUGOSZEWSKI, Lucia
 Fire fragile flight. See no. 656

DOBROWOLSKI, Andrezej
    Music, strings, 2 groups of wind instruments, 2 loudspeakers. See
        no. 3857
DODGE, Charles
    Extensions. See no. 3652
DODGSON, Stephen
1248 Concerto, guitar. Duo concertante, harpsichord and guitar. Partita,
        no. 1. John Williams, gtr; Rafael Puyana, hpd; ECO; Charles
        Groves. CBS 61841 Tape (c) 40-61841 (From 72661, 72948, 72348)
                ++Gr 1-80 p1145   +HFN 3-80 p107 tape
                +HFN 2-80 p105   ++RR 2-80 p74
    Concerto, guitar, no. 2. See no. 55
    Duo concertante, harpsichord and guitar. See no. 1248
    Fantasy divisions. See no. 3634
    Partita, no. 1. See no. 1248
DOHNANYI, Ernest von
    Capriccio, op. 28, no. 6, F minor. See no. 1005
    Capriccio brillante, op. 2, no. 4. See no. 1005
    Cascades, op. 41, no. 4. See no. 3811
    A dedication, op. 13, no. 1. See no. 1005
    Humoresque, op. 17, no. 1. See no. 3811
    Pastorale. See no. 3811
    Postludium, op. 13, no. 10. See no. 1005
    Rhapsody, op. 11, no. 2, F sharp minor. See no. 1005. See no. 3811
    Rhapsody, op. 11, no. 3, C major. See no. 1180
1249 Ruralia Hungarica, op. 32. Variations on a nursery song, op. 25.
        Istvan Lantos, pno; Budapest Symphony Orchestra; Gyorgy Lehel.
        Hungaroton LSPX 12149
                +Gr 11-80 p665
    Ruralia Hungarica, op. 32: Gypsy andante. See no. 3964
    Serenade, op. 10, C major. See no. 617
    Symphonic minutes, op. 36. See no. 3898
1250 Variations on a nursery song, op. 25. LITOLFF: Concerto symphon-
        ique, no. 4, op. 102, D minor: Scherzo. STRAUSS, R.: Burleske,
        op. 11, D minor. Philippe Entremont, pno; National Philharmonic
        Orchestra; Okko Kamu. CBS 76910 Tape (c) 40-76910 (also Colum-
        bia M 35832 Tape (c) MT 35832)
                +FF 11/12-80 p100   +HFN 7-80 p113
                +-Gr 8-80 p215   +-RR 7-80 p54
                +HFN 9-80 p115 tape   +St 11-80 p84
    Variations on a nursery song, op. 25. See no. 1249
DOLLE, Charles
1251 Suite, no. 2, C minor. FORQUERAY: Suite, no. 3, D major. Wieland
        Kuijken, Sigiswald Kuijken, vla da gamba; Robert Kohnen, hpd.
        Accent ACC 7808
                +-FF 5/6-80 p195   +MT 11-79 p920
                +HFN 6-80 p101   +RR 6-80 p27
DOMANIC-ROLL-ALLMEDER
    Seht's Leut'in do war's anno dreissig in Wien. See no. 3711
DOMPIERRE, Francois
1252 Concerto, piano. Harmonica flash. Edith Boivin-Beluse, pno; Claude
        Garden, harm; Montreal Symphony Orchestra; Charles Dutoit. DG
        2531 265
                +Gr 8-80 p215   +MUM 7/8-80 p30
                +-HFN 11-80 p117

Harmonica flash. See no. 1252
DONAJOWSKY
   The Preobrajensky march. See no. 3617
DONATI, Ignatio
   Psalmus, no. 6. See no. 3546
DONATO DA FIRENZE
   Come in sul fonte. See no. 4032
DONAUDY, Stefano
   O bel nidi d'amore. See no. 3900
DONIZETTI, Gaetano
   Anna Bolena: Al dolce guidami. See no. 3596
   Anna Bolena: Pianget voi...Al dolce guidami castel natio. See no.
      629
1253 L'Assedio di Calais: Danza militare; Ballabile. Don Sebastiano:
      Passo a tre; Passo a due; Ballabile di Schiavi. La favorita:
      Introduzione delle danze; Passo a tre; Passo a sei; Finale delle
      danze. Les martyrs: Airs de danse, nos. 1-3. PhO; Antonio de
      Almeida. Philips 9500 673 Tape (c) 7300 768
                  +ARG 12-80 p24   +-HFN 9-80 p101
                +-FF 11/12-80 p100   /+HFN 10-80 p117
                +/Gr 9-80 p334   /NR 10-80 p3
                  +Gr 10-80 p548 tape   ++SFC 8-10-80 p29
1254 Concertino, clarinet, B flat major. concertino, flute, C major.
      Concertino, oboe, F major. Concertino, oboe d'amore, G major.
      Concertino, violin and violoncello, D minor. Karl-Bernhard Se-
      bon, flt; Gunther Passin, ob, ob d'amore; Jorg Fadle, clt; Hans
      Maile, vln; Rene Forest, vlc; RIAS Sinfonietta; Jiri Starek.
      Schwann VMS 2082
                  +/FF 11/12-80 p101
1255 Concertino, cor anglais, G major. HAYDN: Concerto, oboe, C major
      (attrib.). REICHA: Scene, cor anglais. ROSSINI: Introduction
      and variations, C major (arr.). Heinz Holliger, ob, cor anglais;
      COA; David Zinman. Philips 9500 564 Tape (c) 7300 713
                  +FF 3/4-80 p30   ++NR 1-80 p4
                  +Gr 7-79 p198   +NYT 12-2-79 pD22
                  +Gr 10-79 p727 tape   ++RR 7-79 p58
                  +HFN 7-79 p116   +RR 4-80 p128
                +-HFN 11-79 p157 tape
   Concertino, cor anglais, G major. See no. 625
   Concertino, flute, C major. See no. 1254
   Concertino, oboe, F major. See no. 1254
   Concertino, oboe d'amore, G major. See no. 1254
   Concertino, violin and violoncello, D minor. See no. 1254
   Il diluvio universale: Non mi tradir speranza...Ah non tacermi in
      core. See no. 1261
   Don Pasquale: Overture. See no. 1262
   Don Pasquale: Povero Ernesto...Cerchero lontana terra. See no. 3977
   Don Pasquale: Quel guardo il cavaliere. See no. 3766
   Don Pasquale: Quel guardo il cavaliere...So anch'io la virtu magica.
      See no. 3554. See no. 3774
   Don Pasquale: Va ben ma riflettete...Cheti, cheti immantinente. See
      no. 3770
   Don Sebastiano: Deserto in terra. See no. 3945. See no. 4008
   Don Sebastiano: Passo a tre; Passo a due; Ballabile di Schiavi.
      See no. 1253
   Don Sebastiano: Que faire ou cacher ma tristesse. See no. 1261

1256 L'Elisir d'amore. Joan Sutherland, s; Luciano Pavarotti, t; ECO;
        Richard Bonynge. London OSA 13101 (also Decca Tape (c) K154K32)
                +NYT 10-9-77 pD21   +RR 6-80 p94 tape
      L'Elisir d'amore: Arias. See no. 3539
      L'Elisir d'amore: Chiedi all'aura lusinghiera. See no. 3672
      L'Elisir d'amore: Come paride; Udite udite; Una furtiva lagrima.
        See no. 3770
      L'Elisir d'amore: Ecco il magico liquore...Obbligato obbligato. See
        no. 3981
      L'Elisir d'amore: La donna e un animale...Venti scudi. See no. 3771
      L'Elisir d'amore: Una furtiva lagrima. See no. 3633. See no. 3830.
        See no. 3949. See no. 3977. See no. 4008
      La favorita: A tanto amor. See no. 3770
      La favorita: A tanto amour; Vien Leonora. See no. 3982
      La favorita: Favorita del re...Spirto gentil. See no. 3672
      La favorita: Fernando dove mai lo trovero; A tanto amor. See no.
        3774
      La favorita: In questo suolo a lusinghar tua cara. See no. 3928
      La favorita: Introduzione delle danze; Passo a tre; Passo a sei;
        Finale delle danze. See no. 1253
      La favorita: Non sai tu; Splendon piu belle. See no. 3899
      La favorita: O mio Fernando. See no. 3903
      La favorita: Spirto gentil. See no. 3945. See no. 4008
      La favorita: Splendon piu belle. See no. 3927
      La favorita: Una vergine. See no. 3535. See no. 3981
      La favorita: Vien Leonora. See no. 3812
      La fille du regiment: Ah mes amis; Pour me rapprocher de Marie. See
        no. 3672
      La fille du regiment: Deciso e dunque. See no. 3886
      La fille du regiment: Par le rang...Salut a la France. See no. 3828
      Gianni di Parigi: Mira o bella il trovatore. See no. 1261
      The gypsy: Das Laub nur zum Lager. See no. 3872
      Imelda di Lambertazzi: Vincesti alfon...Amarti e nel martoro. See
        no. 1261
      Linda di Chamounix: Ah tardai troppo. See no. 3886
      Linda di Chamounix: Overture. See no. 1262
      Lucia di Lammermoor: Chi mi frena. See no. 3900. See no. 3945
      Lucia di Lammermoor: Chi mi frena; Tu che a Dio. See no. 3672
      Lucia di Lammermoor: Cruda funesta smania. See no. 3982
      Lucia di Lammermoor: Dalle stanze. See no. 3899
      Lucia di Lammermoor: Eccola...Il dolce suono. See no. 3918
      Lucia di Lammermoor: Fra poco a me; Tu che a Dio. See no. 3984
      Lucia di Lammermoor: Mad scene. See no. 3872
      Lucia di Lammermoor: O giusto cielo...Il dolce suono. See no. 3559
      Lucia di Lammermoor: Regnava nel silenzio; Mad scene. See no. 3723
      Lucia di Lammermoor: Regnava nel silenzio...Quando rapita in estasi.
        See no. 3770
      Lucia di Lammermoor: Sparsa e di rose...Il dolce suono...Spargi d'
        amaro pianto. See no. 3793
      Lucia di Lammermoor: Tombe degli ave miei...Fra poco a me. See
        no. 3977. See no. 4031
      Lucia di Lammermoor: Tombe degli...Fra poco; Tu che a Dio. See no.
        3988
1257 Lucrezia Borgia. Joan Sutherland, s; Marilyn Horne, ms; Giacomo
        Aragall, Graham Clark, Piero de Palma, Graeme Ewer, t; Ingvar
        Wixell, bar; Lieuwe Visser, John Brocheler, Richard Van Allan,

Nicholas Zaccaria, bs; London Opera Voices; National Philharmonic
Orchestra; Richard Bonynge. Decca D93D3 (3) Tape (c) K93K32 (also
London OSA 13129 Tape (c) OSA 5-13129)

+—ARG 10-79 p7   +NYT 9-30-79 pD22
+—FF 11/12-79 p62   ++OC Fall 1980 p46
+—Gr 3-79 p1611   +ON 1-19-80 p37
+—HF 10-79 p87   +—Op 7-79 pD681
++HFN 3-79 p123   +RR 4-79 p49
++HFN 8-79 p123 tape   ++SFC 8-12-79 p49
+—MT 4-80 p249   +—St 12-79 p138
+—NR 4-80 p10

Lucrezia Borgia: Com'e bello. See no. 3596
Lucrezia Borgia: Come e bello; M'odi ah m'odi; M'odi ah m'odi;
    Separati a l'alba...Vieni la mia vendetta. See no. 3770
Lucrezia Borgia: Hor mein Flehen. See no. 3774
Lucrezia Borgia: Il segreto. See no. 3560. See no. 3903
Lucrezia Borgia: Viena la mia vendetta. See no. 3904. See no. 3930
Maria di Rohan: Bella e di sol vestite. See no. 3980
Maria di Rohan: Overture. See no. 1262
Maria di Rudenz: Ah non avea piu. See no. 3980
Maria Stuarda: O nube che lieve per l'aria. See no. 3828
Marin Faliero: Les martyrs. See no. 1262
1258 Les martyrs. Leyla Gencer, s; Ottavio Garaventa, t; Renato Bruson,
    bar; Ferruccio Furlanetto, bs; Franco Signor, Iscar di Credico,
    Mario Guggia; La Fenice Teatro Orchestra and Chorus; Gianluigi
    Gelmetti. Voce 16 (3)
            -ARG 10-80 p12
Les martyrs: Airs de danse, nos. 1-3. See no. 1253
1259 Miserere. Il Pigmalione. Orianna Santunione, Margherita Rinaldi,
    Dora Carral, s; Giovanna Fioroni, ms; Ernesto Palacio, Carlo
    Gaifa, Doro Antonioli, t; Augostino Ferrin, Vito Maria Brunetti,
    bs; RAI Orchestra and Chorus, Teatro delle Novita Orchestra; Ar-
    mando Gatto, Fernando Previtali. Voce 15
            +FF 11/12-80 p102
1260 Miserere, D minor. Julia Paszthy, s; Zsolt Bende, bar; Slovak Phil-
    harmonic Orchestra and Chorus; Jozsef Maklari. Hungaroton SLPX
    12147
            +Gr 11-80 p717   -HFN 12-80 p137
1261 Ne m'oublez pas. Arias: Il diluvio universale: Non mi tradir sper-
    anza...Ah non tacermi in core. Don Sebastiano: Que faire ou
    cacher ma tristesse. Gianni di Parigi: Mira o bella il trova-
    tore. Imelda de Lambertazzi: Vincesti alfin...Amarti e nel mar-
    toro. Margreta Elkins, ms; Alexander Oliver, t; Christian du
    Plessis, bs; Geoffrey Mitchell Choir; PhO; James Judd. Opera
    Rara OR 4
            +—ARG 1-80 p27   +ON 8-80 p36
            +FF 1/2-80 p80   +—Op 3-80 p269
            +Gr 11-79 p903   +RR 11-79 p48
            +NYT 9-30-79 pD22
1262 Overtures: Don Pasquale. Linda di Chamounix. Marin Faliero: Les
    martyrs. Maria di Rohan. Monte Carlo Opera Orchestra; Claudio
    Scimone. Erato STU 71211
            +—Gr 1-80 p1145
Il Pigmalione. See no. 1259
Poliuto: Di quai soavi lacrime. See no. 3770
1263 Poliuto: Questo pianto favelli...Ah fuggi da morte. Roberto Dever-

eux: Tutto e silenzio. PUCCINI: Madama Butterfly: Bimba bimba
non piangere. VERDI: I Lombardi: Dove sola m'inoltro...Per dirupi e per foreste. Katia Ricciarelli, s; Jose Carreras, t; Linda
Finnie, ms; Ambrosian Opera Chorus; LSO; Lamberto Gardelli.
Philips 9500 750 Tape (c) 7300 835
        +Gr 11-80 p735   +HFN 11-80 p125

1264 Quartet, strings, D major. ROSSINI: Sonatas, strings, no. 2 and 4.
AMF; Neville Marriner. Argo ZRG 603 Tape (c) KRC 603 (r) E 506,
603
        +HF 5-80 p90   ++HFN 7-76 p104 tape

1265 Quartet, strings, D major (arr.). GLUCK: Don Juan: Movements (4).
GRIEG: Holberg suite, op. 40. SIBELIUS: Suite champetre, op.
98b. Southwest German Chamber Orchstra Strings; Paul Angerer.
Claves D 709
        +-HFN 5-80 p133

1266 Quartets, strings, nos. 1-6. Amati Quartet. Dischi Ricordi ARCL
327 002 (3)
        -Gr 11-80 p691

1267 Quartet, strings, no. 13, A major. PUCCINI: I crisantemi. VERDI:
Quartet, strings, E minor. Alberni Quartet. CRD CRD 1066 Tape
(c) CRDC 4066
        +Gr 3-80 p1403   +MT 5-80 p325
        +-HFN 3-80 p103   +RR 3-80 p76
        +HFN 12-80 p159 tape

Roberto Devereux: Tutto e silenzio. See no. 1263
Roberto Devereux: O Roberto tu che adoro. See no. 3774
Sonata, flute and piano, C major. See no. 3885
La Zingara: Fra l'erbe cosparse. See no. 3559

DONJON, Johannes
Bamboche. See no. 1167

DOPPLER, Albert Franz
Airs valaques, op. 10. See no. 1269
Berceuse, op. 15. See no. 1270
Chanson d'amour, op. 20. See no. 1270

1268 Concerto, 2 flutes, D minor. ROMBERG: Concerto, flute, op. 17.
Jean-Pierre Rampal, Andras Adorjan, flt; Monte Carlo Opera Orch-
estra; Claudio Scimone. Musical Heritage Society MHS 4117 (also
RCA ZL 30525)
        +FF 7/8-80 p81

Duettino, op. 36. See no. 1269
Fantaisie pastorale hongroise, op. 26. See no. 1269
Fantaisie pastorale hongroise, op. 26. See no. 3951
Mazurka de salon, op. 16. See no. 1270
Nocturnes, opp. 17 and 19. See no. 1270
L'Oiseau des bois, op. 21. See no. 1270. See no. 3782
Paraphrase on Schubert's "Die Verschworenen", op. 18. See no. 1269
Souvenir a Mme. Adelina Patti, op. 42. See no. 1270
Souvenir di Prague, op. 24. See no. 1269
Souvenir du Rigi, op. 34. See no. 1270

1269 Works, selections: Airs valaques, op. 10. Duettino, op. 36. Paraphrase on Schubert's "Die Verschworenen", op. 18. Fantaisie
pastorale hongroise, op. 26. Souvenir di Prague, op. 24. Per
Oien, Robert Aitken, flt; Geir Henning Braaten, pno. BIS LP 145
        +FF 7/8-80 p78   +NR 3-80 p6
        +HFN 3-80 p89   +RR 3-80 p79
        +MUM 11/12-80 p34

1270 Works, selections: Berceuse, op. 15. Chanson d'amour, op. 20. Maz-
     urka de salon, op. 16. Nocturnes, opp. 17 and 19. L'Oiseau des
     bois, op. 21. Souvenir du Rigi, op. 34. Souvenir a Mme. Adelina
     Patti, op. 42 (Paraphrase on "La sonnambula"). Per Oien, Robert
     Aitken, flt; Geir Henning Braaten, onp. BIS LP 146
                    +FF 7/8-80 p78   +NR 3-80 p6
                    +HFN 3-80 p89   +RR 3-80 p79
                    +MUM 11/12-80 p34

DOPPLER, Karl and Albert
1271 Andante te rondo, op. 25. Fantaisie sur des motifs Hongrois, op. 35.
     Rigoletto fantaisie, op. 38. Valse di bravura, op. 33. Per
     Oien, Robert Aitken, flt; Geir Henning Braaten, pno. BIS LP 128
                    +FF 7/8-80 p78   +NR 3-80 p6
                    +HFN 3-80 p89   +RR 3-80 p79
                    +MUM 11/12-80 p34   ++St 4-80 p131
     Fantaisie sur des motifs Hongrois, op. 35. See no. 1271
     Rigoletto fantaisie, op. 38. See no. 1271
     Valse di bravura, op. 33. See no. 1271

DORNEL, Louis Antoine
     Sonata, op. 3, no. 2, D major. See no. 4016
     Sonata, 3 recorders, B flat major. See no. 4018
     Sonate en quatuor, D minor. See no. 3547

DOSTAL, Nico
1272 The Hungarian wedding. Margit Schramm, Isy Oren, s; Anton de Rid-
     der, Willi Brokmeier, t; Cologne Civic Theatre Chorus; PH; Roman
     Dostal. Electrola 1C 061 28828
                    +FF 3/4-80 p82

DOWLAND, John
     Almain. See no. 1273
     Alman a 2. See no. 1277
     Aloe. See no. 1273
     Away with those self-loving lads. See no. 3997
     Can she excuse. See no. 1273. See no. 1277. See no. 3648. See
        no. 4044
     Captain Digorie Piper's galliard. See no. 1273. See no. 3647
     Captain Digorie Piper's pavan and galliard. See no. 1277
     Come away. See no. 1273
     Complaint. See no. 1273
     Coranto. See no. 1273
     A coy toy. See no. 1273
     Dowland's first galliard. See no. 1273. See no. 1277. See no.
        3577
     Dowland's galliard. See no. 1273
     Dr. Case's pavan. See no. 1273
     Dream almain. See no. 1273
     Earl of Derby's his galliard. See no. 1273
     Earl of Essex galliard. See no. 971. See no. 1273. See no. 1276.
        See no. 3883. See no. 4025
     A fancy. See no. 971. See no. 1273
     Fantasia (2). See no. 1273. See no. 3577. See no. 3966
     Farewell fancy. See no. 1273
     Farewell on "In nomine" theme. See no. 1273
     Fine knacks for ladies. See no. 3867
     Flow not so fast ye fountains. See no. 3719
     Forlorn hope fancy. See no. 971. See no. 1273. See no. 1276

Fortune. See no. 1273
Frog galliard. See no. 1273. See no. 1277. See no. 3577
Galliard. See no. 1273. See no. 3540
Galliard on Walsingham. See no. 1273
George Whitehead his almand. See no. 1276
Giles Hobie's galliard. See no. 1273. See no. 1276
Go crystal tears. See no. 1276
Go from my window. See no. 1273
Henry Noel his galliard. See no. 1276
Henry Umptons funerall. See no. 1276
I saw my lady weep. See no. 1276
In darkness let me dwell. See no. 1276. See no. 3997
Jig. See no. 1273
John Dowland's galliard. See no. 1273
John Langton's pavan. See no. 4025
John Langton's pavan and galliard. See no. 1277
Katherine Darcy's galliard. See no. 1277
King of Denmark's galliard. See no. 971. See no. 1273. See no.
     3577. See no. 3647
Lachrimae. See no. 1273
Lachrimae (Cozens version). See no. 1273
Lachrimae and galliard. See no. 1273
Lachrimae antiqua novae pavan and galliard. See no. 1277
Lachrimae pavan. See no. 1277. See no. 3593. See no. 3883
Lachrimae: Antiquae pavan. See no. 3540
Lady Clifton's spirit. See no. 1273
Lady Hunsdon's puffe. See no. 1273
Lady Laiton's almain. See no. 1273
Lady Rich her galliard. See no. 1273
Lady Russell's pavan. See no. 1273
Lasso vita mia. See no. 3997
Lord Strang's march. See no. 1273
Lord Viscount Lisle his galliard. See no. 1273
Loth to depart. See no. 1273
1273 Lute works: Almain (2). Aloe. Can she excuse (2). Captain Digo-
     rie Piper's galliard. Coranto. A coy toy. Complaint. Dowland's
     galliard. Dowland's first galliard. Dream almain. Dr. Case's
     pavan. Earl of Derby's his galliard. Earl of Essex his galliard.
     Fancy (3). Fantasia (2). Farewell fancy. Farewell on the "In
     nome" theme. Forlorne fancy. Fortune. Frog galliard (2). Gal-
     liard (6). Galliard on Walsingham. Giles Hobie's galliard. Go
     from my window. Jig. John Dowland's galliard. King of Denmark's
     galliard. La mia Barbara. Lachrimae. Lachrimae (Cozens version).
     Lachrimae and galliard. Lady Clifton's spirit. Lady Hunsdon's
     puffe. Lady Laiton's almain. Lady Russell's pavan. Lord Stra-
     ng's march. Lord Viscount Lisle his galliard. Lady Rich her
     galliard. Loth to depart. My Lord Willoughby's welcome home.
     Melancholy galliard. Mignarda. Queen Elizabeth her galliard.
     Mr. Dowland's midnight. Mr. Langton's galliard. Mr. Knight's
     galliard. Mrs. Clifton's almain. Mrs. Brigide Fleetwood's pav-
     an. Mrs. Norrish's delight. Mrs. Nicholas almain. Mrs. Vaux's
     galliard. Mrs. Vaux's jig. Mrs. Winter's jump. Mrs White's
     nothing. Mrs. White's thing. Orlando sleepeth. Pavan (2).
     Pavana Johan Douland. Pipers pavan. Preludium. The queen's
     galliard. Robin. Resolution. Semper Dowland semper dolens.

Sir John Langton's pavan. Sir John Smith his almain. Sir Henry
Umpton's funeral. Sir Henry Guilforde his almaine. Sir John
Souch's galliard. Solus cum sola. Tarleton's jig. Tarleton's
resurrection. Walsingham. What if a day. The shoemaker's wife.
Anthony Bailes, Jakob Lindberg, Nigel North, Anthony Rooley,
Christopher Wilson, lt. L'Oiseau-Lyre D187D5 (5)
        +Gr 12-80 p853   +HFN 12-80 p137
Melancholy galliard. See no. 1273. See no. 3997
La mia Barbara. See no. 1273
La mia Barbara pavan and galliard. See no. 1277
Mignarda galliard. See no. 971. See no. 1273
Mr. Dowland's midnight. See no. 1273
Mr. George Whitehead his almand. See no. 3997
Mr. John Langton's pavan. See no. 3577
Mr. Knight's galliard. See no. 1273
Mr. Langton's galliard. See no. 1273
Mrs. Brigide Fleetwood's pavan. See no. 1273
Mrs. Clifton's almain. See no. 1273
Mrs. Nicholas almain. See no. 1273
Mrs. Nichols alman a 2 a 5. See no. 1277
Mrs. Norrish's delight. See no. 1273
Mrs. Vaux's galliard. See no. 1273
Mrs. Vaux's jig. See no. 1273
Mrs. White's nothing. See no. 1273
Mrs. White's thing. See no. 1273
Mrs. Winter's jump. See no. 1273
My Lady Hunsdon's puffe. See no. 971
My Lord Willoughby's welcome home. See no. 1273
Nicholas Gryffith his galliard. See no. 1276
Now O now I needs must part. See no. 3997
Orlando sleepeth. See no. 1273
Pavan (2). See no. 1273
Pavan a 4. See no. 1277
Pavana. See no. 971
Pavana Johan Douland. See no. 1273
Piper's pavan. See no. 1273
Preludium. See no. 1273
Queen Elizabeth's galliard. See no. 1273. See no. 3577. See no.
  3966
The queen's galliard. See no. 1273
Resolution. See no. 1273
Robin. See no. 1273
Round battle galliard. See no. 1277
Semper Dowland semper dolens. See no. 1273. See no. 1276
The shoemaker's wife. See no. 1273
Sir Henry Gifford's almaine. See no. 971
Sir Henry Guilforde his almaine. See no. 1273
Sir Henry Umpton's funeral. See no. 1273
Sir John Langton's pavan. See no. 1273
Sir John Smith's almaine. See no. 1273. See no. 1276. See no.
  3577
Sir John Souch's galliard. See no. 1273
Solus cum sola pavan. See no. 1273
1274 Songs: All people that on earth do dwell; An heart that's broken;
    Behold and have regard; Lord consider my distress; Lord hear my

prayer; Lord in thy wrath; Lord to Thee I make my moan; Lord
turn not away; My soul praise the Lord; O Lord of whom I do depend; A prayer for the queen's most excellent majesty; Put me
not to rebuke O Lord; Sorrow come; I shame at mine unworthiness;
Where righteousness doth say. Consort of Musicke; Anthony Rooley.
L'Oiseau-Lyre DSLO 551 Tape (c) KDSLC 551

    +ARG 4-80 p21   +HFN 7-79 p119 tape
    +FF 7/8-80 p81   ++NYT 8-10-80 pD17
    +-Gr 5-79 p1921   +-RR 6-79 p112
    +-HFN 6-79 p105

1275 Songs: Awake sweet love thou art returned; Can she excuse my wrongs;
  Come again sweet love doth now invite; Fine knacks for ladies;
  Flow not so fast ye fountains; Go crystal tears; Me me and none
  but me; Shall I sue; Sorrow stay; What if I never speed; When
  Phoebus first did Daphne love. Lute lessons: Captain's Candish's
  galliard. Lady Laiton's almain. A musical banquet: Lady if you
  so spite me. A pilgrim's solace: Shall I strive with words to
  move; Tell me true love. Preludium and lachrimae pavan. Semper
  Dowland semper dolens. James Bowman, c-t; Robert Spencer, lt.
  Saga 5449

    +Gr 3-78 p1600   +MT 3-78 p242
    +HFN 1-78 p123   +-RR 1-78 p76
    +HFN 4-80 p119

 Songs: Can she excuse my wrongs. See no. 3600
 Songs: Come again. See no. 3778
 Songs: Die not before thy day; Mourne day is with darkness fled;
  Sorrow stay. See no. 3878
 Songs: Fortune my foe; Lady if you so spite me. See no. 1277
 Songs: I saw my lady weepe; In this trembling shadow. See no. 3877
 Songs: Mrs. White's nothing; Tarleton's resurrectione. See no.
  3941
 Sorrow stay. See no. 1276
 Susanna fair galliard. See no. 1277
 Tarleton's jig. See no. 1273. See no. 1277
 Tarleton's resurrection. See no. 1273. See no. 3577
 Thomas Collier his galliard. See no. 1276
 Volta. See no. 3675
 Volta a 4. See no. 1277
 Walsingham. See no. 1273
 Were every thought an eye. See no. 1277
 What if a day. See no. 1273

1276 Works, selections: Earl of Essex galliard. Forlorn hope fancy.
  George Whitehead his almand. Giles Hobies galliard. Go crystal
  tears. Henry Noel his galliard. Henry Umptons funerall. I
  saw my lady weep. In darkness let me dwell. Nicholas Gryffith
  his galliard. Semper Dowland semper dolens. Sir John Smith's
  almain. Sorrow stay. Thomas Collier his galliard. Le Collectif
  de Musique Ancienne de Paris. Calliope CAL 1627

    +-FF 11/12-80 p103   +HFN 9-80 p101

1277 Works, selctions: Alman a 2. Can she excuse galliard. Captain
  Piper's pavan and galliard. Dowland's first galliard. Frog
  galliard. John Langton pavan and galliard. Katherine Darcy's
  galliard. Lachrimae antiquae novae pavan and galliard. Lachrimae pavan. La mia Barbara pavan and galliard. Mrs. Nichols alman a 2 a 5. Pavan a 4. Round battle galliard. Susanna fair
  galliard. Tarleton's jigge. Volta a 4. Were every thought an

eye. Songs: Fortune my foe; Lady if you so spite me. Consorte
of Musicke; Anthony Rooley. L'Oiseau Lyre DSLO 533 Tape (c)
KDSLC 533

+–FF 3/4-79 p53	+–HFN 7-78 p111 tape
+Gr 4-78 p1743	+–MT 8-78 p688
+–Gr 9-78 p566 tape	+NR 1-80 p6
+HF 4-79 p49 tape	+RR 4-78 p51
+HFN 4-78 p113	+–RR 10-78 p117 tape

1278 Works, selections (Transcriptions): Byrd: Pavana lachrimae. Farna-
by: Lachrimae pavan. Morley: Pavana and gallarda. Peerson/Bull:
Piper's pavan and galliard. Siefert: Paduana. Schildt: Paduana
lachrymae. Wilbye: The frogge. Anon.: Can she; Frog's galliard;
Can she excuse; Pavion solus cum sola; Dowland's almayne. Colin
Tilney, hpd. L'Oiseau-Lyre DSLO 552

+ARG 4-80 p21	+–HFN 5-79 p119
+FF 1/2-80 p81	+–MT 11-79 p920
+Gr 4-79 p1917	

DOWNEY, John
1279 Quartet, strings. no. 2. JOHNSTON: Quartet, strings, no. 2.
SEEGER: Quartet, strings. Fine Arts Quartet. Gasparo GS
205

+FF 11/12-80 p103	+–St 12-80 p122
+–NR 12-80 p7	

DRAESEKE, Felix
1280 Symphony, no. 3, op. 40, C major. BeSO; Hermann Desser. Varese
VC 81092 (From Urania URLP 7162)

+ARG 1-80 p26	-HF 10-79 p104
+–FF 1/2-80 p81	

DRAGANSKI, Donald
The bestiary: Weathervane cock; Fish and the river; Fish eggs; Ic
ane geseah idese sittan; Book worm. See no. 3892
DRAGHI, Giovanni
Trio sonata, G minor. See no. 4015
DRECHSLER, Josef
Der Bauer als Millionar: Bruderlein fein. See no. 3952
DRIGO, Richard (Riccardo)
Airs de ballet, no. 2: Valse bluette. See no. 3964
Les millions d'Arlequin: Serenade. See no. 3951
DRING, Madeleine
American dance. See no. 1281
Caribbean dance. See no. 1281
Colour suite. See no. 1281
Danza gaya. See no. 1281
Valse francaise. See no. 1281
1281 Works, selections: Caribbean dance. Colour suite. American dance.
Danza gaya. Valse francaise. TAILLEFERRE: Fleurs de France.
Jeux de plein air. Pastorale, D major. Sicilienne. Valse
lente. Leigh Kaplan, Susan Pitts, pno. Cambria C 1014

+–ARG 9-79 p23	+NR 6-80 p12
+FF 3/4-80 p184	

DRUZECKY, Jiri
1282 Partita, no. 4, E flat major. HUMMEL: Septet, op. 114, C major.
Partita, E flat major. Bratislave Chamber Harmony; Justus Pavlik. United Artists UACL 10015 (From Opus 9111 0409)

+FF 9/10-80 p138	+–HFN 1-80 p121
+Gr 1-80 p1167	

DUARTE, John
     Variations on a Catalan folk song, op. 25.   See no. 3722
DUBEN
     Suite, no. 5, G minor.   See no. 3932
DUBOIS, Francois Theodore
     Fiat lux.   See no. 3618
     Toccata, G major.   See no. 4064
DUBOIS, Pierre
     Toccata, G major.   See no. 3664
DUBROVAY, Laszlo
1283 A², Oscillations, nos. 1-3.   Zsuzsanna Kiss, synthesizer; Laszlo
          Dubrovay, pno and org; Gyula Stuller, vln; Gabor Kosa, perc;
          Katalin Vas, vlc; Ilona Szeverenyi, cimb.   Hungaroton SLPX 12030
                    *ARG 1-80 p26
     Duets, violin and percussion.   See no. 3810
     Oscillations, nos. 1-3.   See no. 1283
DU FAULT, Francois
     Pavane, E minor.   See no. 1284
1284 Pieces, lute.   Pavane, E minor.   Suites, A minor, C major, C minor,
          G minor.   Hopkinson, Smith, lt.   Telefunken 6-42328 Tape (c) 4-
          42328
                    +ARG 2-80 p51   +HF 2-80 p102 tape
                    +FF 1/2-80 p170   ++HFN 2-80 p92
     Suites, A minor, C major, C minor, G minor.   See no. 1284
DUFAY, Guillaume
1285 Missa caput.   Clemencic Consort; Rene Clemencic.   Harmonia Mundi
          HMU 996 (also HNH 4009)
                    +ARG 1-80 p27   +RR 1-78 p77
                    +FF 7/8-79 p48
     Missa l'homme arme: Kyrie.   See no. 3910
     Nuper rosarum flores.   See no. 1119
1286 Songs (choral): Anima mea liquefacta est; Ave regina caelorum; Ec-
          clesie militantis; Gloria resurrexit dominus; Je me complains;
          Missa ecce ancilla domini; Navre je suy.   Pomerium Musices;
          Alexander Blachly. Nonesuch H 71367
                    ++FF 1/2-80 p16   +NYT 8-17-80 pD20
                    +Gr 4-80 p1575   +RR 4-80 p109
                    ++MQ 7-80 p449   ++St 12-79 p138
                    +NR 1-80 p11
     Songs: Dona gentile; Le serviteur hault guerdonne; Vostre bruit et
          vostre grant fame.   See no. 3880
     Vergine bella.   See no. 3864
DUFFERIN
     Irish emigrant.   See no. 3947
     Terence's farewell to Kathleen.   See no. 4070
DUFFY, Philip
     Sacerdos et pontifex.   See no. 3531
DUGGER, Edwin
1287 Abwesenheiten und Wiedersehen.   Intermezzi.   LERDAHL: Eros.   Beverly
          Morgan, ms; San Francisco Contemporary Music Players, Berkeley
          Contemporary Chamber Players, Collage; Fred Lerdahl, Jean-Louis
          Le Roux, Jonathan Khuner.   CRI SD 378
                    +ARG 1-79 p15   +NR 11-78 p7
                    +FF 3/4-80 p14   +NYT 2-25-79 pD21
     Intermezzi.   See no. 1287

DUKAS, Paul
1288 L'Apprenti sorcier. MUSSORGSKY: Night on the bare mountain. SAINT-
        SAENS: Danse macabre, op. 40. STRAUSS, R.: Till Eulenspiegels
        lustige Streiche, op. 28. David Nadien, vln; NYP; Leonard Bern-
        stein. CBS 61976 (From 72740)
                        +Gr 9-80 p414   +-HFN 10-80 p115
1289 L'Apprenti sorcier. OFFENBACH: Gaite parisienne, excerpts (arr.
        Rosenthal). SAINT-SAENS: Danse macabre, op. 40. French National
        Orchestra; Lorin Maazel. CBS 76909 Tape (c) 40-76909
                        +Gr 10-80 p496   +-HFN 12-80 p159 tape
                  +-HFN 10-80 p111
1290 L'Apprenti sorcier. La peri. La peri: Fanfare. Polyeucte. Rot-
        terdam Philharmonic Orchestra; David Zinman. Philips 9500 533
        Tape (c) 7300 677 (r) B-C G 9500 533
                        +Audio 12-79 p101   +HFN 7-79 p119 tape
                        +Gr 5-79 p1893   +MT 10-79 p837
                        ++HF 11-80 p88   +NR 3-79 p4
                        +HFN 4-79 p119   +RR 4-79 p71
        L'Apprenti sorcier. See no. 1000. See no. 1002. See no. 1211.
        See no. 3666. See no. 3797
1291 Ariane et Barbe-Bleue. Soloists; Orchestra and Chorus; Tony Aubin.
        MRF Records MRF 154 (2)
                        ++FF 11/12-80 p105
        La peri. See no. 1290
        La peri: Fanfare. See no. 1290
        Polyeucte. See no. 1290
        Villanelle. See no. 485
DUKE, John
1292 Songs: Chinese love lyrics (4); Poems. by e.e. cummings (4); Poems
        by Emily Dickinson, 1968 (6); 1975 (4); Songs on texts by Sara
        Teasdale (5); Stopping by woods on a snowy evening (Frost).
        Carol Bogard, s; John Duke, pno. Cambridge CRS 2776
                        +ARG 3-80 p24   +NR 4-80 p12
                        +FF 1/2-80 p83   ++St 4-80 p131
                        ++HF 8-80 p72
DU MONT
        Pavanne, D minor. See no. 3852
        Prelude, D minor. See no. 3852
DUNHILL, Thomas
        Cornucopia. See no. 3644
DUNN, Vivian
        The captain general. See no. 3619
        The Mountbatten march. See no. 3617
DUNSTABLE, John
        O rosa bella. See no. 3880. See no. 4042
        Songs: Gloria and credo; Salve scema sanctitatis, Salve salus
        servulorum Cantat celi agmina. See no. 1120
DUPARC, Henri
        Chanson triste, op. 2, no. 2. See no. 3985
1293 Songs: Au pays ou se fait la guerre; Elegie; Extase; Chanson triste;
        L'invitation au voyage; Lamento; Le manoir de Rosamonde; Phy-
        dile; Serenade florentine; Soupir; Testament; La vague et la
        cloche; La vie anterieure. Danielle Galland, s; Bernard Kruysen,
        bar; Noel Lee, pno. Telefunken AS 6-42113
                        +FF 3/4-80 p82   +RR 5-77 p80
                        +Gr 5-77 p1718   ++St 6-80 p113

Songs: Au pays ou se fait la guerre; L'invitation au voyage; La
    manoir. See no. 3611
Songs: Chanson triste. See no. 3774
Songs: Phidyle. See no. 3738
DUPONT, Gabriel
    Antar: Air de l'oasis. See no. 3774
DUPRE, Marcel
    Antiennes: Lumen ad revelationem. See no. 4061
    Ballade. See no. 4040
    Canzona. See no. 4040
    Lamento. See no. 4050
    Poeme heroique. See no. 3661
    Prelude and fugue, G minor. See no. 3658
1294 Preludes and fugues, op. 7, nos. 1 and 3. LEIGHTON: Paean. MOZART:
    Fantasia, K 594, F minor. Fantasia, K 608, F minor. Judith Han-
    cock, org. Hessound S 1003
                +NR 11-80 p10
    Preludes and fugues, op. 7, no. 1, B major. See no. 3725
    Preludes and fugues, op. 7, no. 3, G minor. See no. 3940
    Sortie. See no. 4040
    Variations on a noel, op. 20. See no. 3591
    Versets pour les Vepres du commun des fetes de la Sainte Vierge,
        op. 18: Antiphon; Magnificat, nos. 1 and 6. See no. 156
    Vision, op. 44. See no. 1238
DURAN DE LA MOTA, Antonio
    Laudate pueri. See no. 3707
DURANTE, Francesco
1295 Songs: Alme voi che provaste; Amor Metilde e morta; Dormono l'aure
    estive; Fiero acerbo destin; Metilde mio tesoro; Qualor tento
    scoprire; Son io barbara donna. Judith Nelson, s; Rene Jacobs,
    c-t; Wieland Kuijken, vlc; William Christie, hpd. Harmonia Mundi
    HM 1014
                +Gr 11-79 p891   +NYT 8-10-80 pD17
                +-HFN 1-80 p105   +-RR 9-79 p119
DURKO, Zsolt
1296 Colloids. Moses, excerpts. Turner illustrations. Sylvia Sass, s;
    Ferenc Szonyi, t; Csabo Otvos, bar; Endre Uto, bs; Erich Gruen-
    berg, vln; Attila Lajos, flt; Hungarian Radio and Television Fe-
    male Chamber Chorus; Hungarian State Opera Orchestra and Chorus;
    Budapest Chamber Ensemble, Budapest Symphony Orchestra; Andras
    Korodi, Gyorgy Lehel, Andras Mihaly. Hungaroton SLPX 11982
                +FF 9/10-80 p110
    Moses, excerpts. See no. 1296
    Turner illustations. See no. 1296
DURON, Sebastian
    Gaitilla de mano izquierda. See no. 3756
DURUFLE, Maurice
1297 Motets on Gregorian themes, op. 10. HOWELLS: Here is the little
    door; Long long ago. VICTORIA: The lamentations of Jeremiah
    for holy saturday: Lessons, 1-3. Exon Singers; Christopher Tol-
    ley. Alpha APS 309
                +Gr 10-80 p527   +HFN 10-80 p110
    Prelude et fugue sur le nom d'Alain, op. 7. See no. 4056. See no.
    4062
    Songs: Pange lingua; Tantum ergo. See no. 3531

1298 Suite, op. 5: Prelude et recitatif, E flat major. WIDOR: Symphonie,
     no. 5, op. 42, no. 1, F major: Variations. IMPROVISATION: Salve
     regina; Lux eterna; Victimae Paschali. Michael Estellet-Brun,
     org. Ursina Motette M 1031
                +FF 9/10-80 p269   +MU 10-80 p12
     Tota pulcra es Maria. See no. 3934
DUSSEK, Johann (also Dusik, Dessek)
     Rondo on "O dear what can the matter be". See no. 4011
1299 Sonata, piano, op. 10, no. 2, G minor; op. 35, no. 2, G major; op.
     75, E flat major. Frederick Marvin, pno. Genesis GS 1071
                +Audio 7-80 p81   ++FF 11/12-79 p63
                +CL 2-80 p8   ++St 2-80 p124
     Sonatas, piano, op. 35, no. 2, G major. See no. 1299
     Sonatas, piano, op. 75, E flat major. See no. 1299
     Sonatas, violin, violoncello and harp, B flat major. See no. 1182
     Sonatina, G major. See no. 3730
DUTILLEUX, Henri
1300 Sarabande et cortege. MOSCHELES: Grand duo concertante, piano and
     bassoon. SAINT-SAENS: Sonata, bassoon and piano, op. 168, G
     major. TCHAIKOVSKY: Nocturne, op. 19, no. 4. Eberhard Buschmann,
     bsn; Monica von Saalfeld, pno. Da Camera Magna SM 92920
                -FF 3/4-80 p188
1301 Sonatine, flute and piano. IBERT: Jeux. JOLIVET: Sonata,
     flute and piano. ROUSSEL: Joueuers de flute, op. 27. Gunther
     Pohl, flt; Wilfried Kassebaum, pno. Musicaphon BM SL 1920
                +RR 8-80 p74
1302 Symphony, no. 1. Lille Philharmonic Orchestra; Jean-Claude Casade-
     sus. Calliope CAL 1861
                +Gr 5-80 p1660   +HFN 8-80 p97
                +HFN 11-78 p168   +RR 6-80 p47
DVORAK, Anton
     Biblical songs, op. 99. See no. 3560
     Carnival overture, op. 92. See no. 1309. See no. 1328. See no.
     3621
1303 Concerto, piano, op. 33, G minor. Radoslav Kvapil, pno. Brno Phil-
     harmonic Orchestra; Frantisek Jilek. Supraphon 110 2373
                +Gr 10-80 p496   +-HFN 10-80 p103
     Concerto, piano, op. 33, G minor. See no. 1349
1304 Concerto, violin, op. 53, A minor. Romance, op. 11, F minor. Josef
     Suk, vln; CPhO; Karel Ancerl. Quintessence PMC 7112 (also Supra-
     phon 410 2423)
                +-FF 9/10-79 p79   ++SFC 7-1-79 p44
                +Gr 7-80 p136
1305 Concerto, violin, op. 53, A minor. Romance, op. 11, F minor. Josef
     Suk, vln; CPhO; Vaclav Neumann. Supraphon 410 2423
                +FF 9/10-80 p111   ++NR 8-80 p6
                +-HFN 8-80 p97   +RR 7-80 p55
     Concerto, violin, op. 53, A minor. See no. 1349
1306 Concerto, violoncello, no. 1, A major. Concerto, violoncello, op.
     104, B minor. Polonaise, A major. Rondo, op. 94, G minor.
     Silent woods, op. 68. Milos Sadlo, vlc; Alfred Holecek, pno;
     CPhO; Vaclav Neumann. Supraphon 110 2081/2 (2)
                +-ARG 9-79 p25   -MT 3-79 p225
                +FF 9/10-79 p78   /NR 10-79 p3
                +HF 1-80 p72

1307 Concerto, violoncello, op. 104, B minor. GRANADOS: Danzas espanolas,
     op. 37: Andaluza. HANDEL: Largo. SAINT-SAENS: Carnival of the
     animals: The swan. Gaspar Cassado, vlc; BPhO; Hans Schmidt-
     Isserstedt. Past Masters PM 29
                    +NR 10-80 p5
1308 Concerto, violoncello, op. 104, B minor. Rondo, op. 94, G minor.
     Silent woods, op. 68. Maurice Gendron, vlc; LPO; Bernard Hai-
     tink. Philips 6570 112 Tape (c) 7310 112 (From SAL 3675)
                    ++Gr 5-80 p1660   +HFN 9-80 p116 tape
                    ++HF 2-79 p72   +NR 11-78 p6
                    +HF 6-79 p96 tape   +RR 5-80 p58
                    +—HFN 6-80 p115 tape
1309 Concerto, violoncello, op. 104, B minor. Carnival overture, op. 92.
     Mstislav Rostropovich, vlc; CPhO; Vaclav Talich, Karel Ancerl.
     Quintessence PMC 7124
                    +FF 3/4-80 p83   +FU 5-80 p47
     Concerto, violoncello, op. 104, B minor. See no. 1306. See no.
     1349
1310 Czech suite, op. 39, D major. Serenade, op. 44, D minor. Musica
     Aeterna Orchestra; Frederick Waldman. Westminster MCA 1400
     (from Decca 710137)
                    +ARG 12-80 p25   +FF 7/8-80 p82
     The golden spinning wheel, op. 109. See no. 1213. See no. 1348
     Humoresque, op. 101. See no. 3998
     Husitska overture, op. 67. See no. 1348
1311 Hymnus, op. 30. FORSTER: May, op. 159. SMETANA: Czech song.
     Zdenek Otava, bar; Radovan Lukavsky, narrator; CPhO, Prague Sym-
     phony Orchestra; Zdenek Kosler. Supraphon 112 1437
                    +—HFN 9-79 p116   +NR 11-78 p9
                    /MT 2-80 p109   ++SFC 2-24-80 p39
                    +—RR 8-79 p120
1312 The Jacobin. Marcela Machotkova, Daniela Sounova, Ivana Mixova, s;
     Vilem Pribyl, Beno Blachut, t; Vaclav Zitek, Rene Tucek, bar;
     Karel Berman, bs-bar; Karel Prusa, bs; Brno PO; Kantilena Child-
     rens Chorus, Kuhn Chorus; Jiri Pinkas. Supraphon 110 2481/3
                    ++ARG 10-80 p12   +NR 8-80 p11
                    ++FF 9/10-80 p112   +Op 1-80 p63
                    +—Gr 2-80 p1293   +RR 1-80 p57
                    +HF 12-80 p75   ++SFC 8-24-80 p36
                    +—HFN 1-80 p105   +SR 9-80 p96
                    +MT 9-80 p566   +St 10-80 p112
     Mazurka, op. 49, E minor. See no. 1349
     Melodia, op. 55, no. 4. See no. 3694
     Nocturne, op. 40, B minor. See no. 3794
     The noonday witch, op. 108. See no. 1348
     Polonaise, A major. See no. 1306
1313 Quartet, strings, no. 11, op. 61, C major. Quartet, strings, no.
     12, op. 96, F major. Talich Quartet. Calliope CAL 1617
                    +HFN 6-80 p117   +RR 6-80 p66
1314 Quartet, strings, no. 12, op. 96, F major. HAYDN: Quartet, strings,
     op. 64, no. 5, D major. SCHUBERT: Quartet, strings, no. 12, D
     703, C minor. Panocha Quartet. Supraphon 111 1683
                    ++St 5-80 p81
     Quartet, strings, no. 12, op. 96, F major. See no. 1313
1315 Quintet, piano, op. 81, A major. Emanuel Ax, pno; Cleveland Quar-

tet. RCA RL 1-2240 Tape (c) ARK 1-2240
    +Gr 3-80 p1403   +-RR 4-80 p85
    +HFN 4-80 p103   ++ST 9-80 p339
1316 Requiem, op. 89. Maria Stader, s; Sieglinde Wagner, con; Ernst
    Hafliger, t; Kim Borg, bs; Czech Chorus; CPhO; Karel Ancerl.
    DG 2726 089 (2) (From SLPM 138026/7)
        +-Gr 5-80 p1700   +-RR 7-80 p87
        +HFN 7-80 p119
    Romance, op. 11, F minor. See no. 1304. See no. 1305. See no.
    1349
    Rondo, op. 94, G minor. See no. 1306. See no. 1308. See no. 1349
    Rusalka, op. 114: O silver moon. See no. 3695
    Rusalka, op. 114: Vidino divna, presladka. See no. 3633
1317 Scherzo capriccioso, op. 66, D flat major. GLINKA: Russlan and Lud-
    milla: Overture. MUSSORGSKY: Pictures at an exhibition. TCHAI-
    KOVSKY: Capriccio italien, op. 45. COA; Bernard Haitink. Phil-
    ips 6570 176 Tape (c) 7310 176 (From 6580 059, SAL 3462, 6833
    033)
        +Gr 7-80 p167   +RR 6-80 p57
        +-HFN 6-80 p115
    Scherzo capriccioso, op. 66, D flat major. See no. 1331. See no.
    1332. See no. 1338
1318 Serenade, op. 22, E major. PURCELL: Dido and Aeneas: Dido's lament.
    VAUGHAN WILLIAMS: Fantasia on a theme by Thomas Tallis. LPO;
    Leopold Stokowski. Desmar 1011 Tape Advent (c) E 1047 (4) B-C
    D 1011
        +-ARG 4-78 p37   +-HFN 3-78 p137
        +ARG 5-80 p45   ++NR 2-78 p4
        +Gr 2-78 p1400   ++RR 2-78 p60
        +HF 4-77 p121 tape   +SFC 12-18-77 p53
        +HF 10-78 p136   +St 1-78 p102
        +HF 12-78 p49 tape
1319 Serenade, op. 22, E major. Symphonic variations, op. 78. LSO;
    Loris Tjeknavorian. RCA RL 2-5230 Tape (c) RK 2-5230
        +Gr 7-80 p136   +-RR 6-80 p48
        +HFN 6-80 p107
    Serenade, op. 22, E major. See no. 3694
    Serenade, op. 44, D minor. See no. 1310
    Silent woods, op. 68. See no. 1306. See no. 1308. See no. 1349
1320 Slavonic dances, op. 46, nos. 1-8. Slavonic dances, op. 72, nos.
    1-8. CO; Georg Szell. CBS 30114 Tape (c) 40-30114
        +Gr 1-80 p1203   +RR 12-79 p53
        +-HFN 1-80 p119
    Slavonic dances, op. 46, nos. 1, 8. See no. 823
    Slavonic dances, op. 46, nos. 2, 4, 6. See no. 1334
    Slavonic dances, op. 46, no. 2, E minor. See no. 3964
1321 Slavonic dances, op. 46, no. 8, G minor. LISZT: Les preludes, G 97.
    SMETANA: Ma Vlast: The Moldau. PH; Zoltan Rozsnyai. M & K Real-
    time RT 205, PS 1006
        -HF 11-80 p86
    Slavonic dances, op. 46, no. 8, G minor. See no. 1333
    Slavonic dances, op. 72, nos. 1-8. See no. 1320
    Slavonic dances, op. 72, no. 2, E minor. See no. 3964
    Slavonic dances, op. 72, no. 8, A major. See no. 3964
1322 Slavonic rhapsody, op. 45, no. 3, A flat major. ENESCO: Roumanian

rhapsody, op. 11, no. 1, A major. LISZT: Hungarian rhapsody, no.
2, G 244, C harp minor (arr. Muller-Berghans). RAVEL: Rapsodie
espagnole. Detroit Symphony Orchestra; Antal Dorati. Decca SXL
6896 Tape (c) KSXC 6896 (also London CS 7119)
          -FF 1/2-80 p183   +NR 6-80 p6
          +Gr 7-79 p259   +-RR 7-79 p59
          +HFN 7-79 p117
Songs, op. 55: Songs my mother taught me. See no. 3738. See no.
     3774. See no. 3785
Symphonic variations, op. 78. See no. 1319
1323 Symphonies, nos. 1-9. BPhO; Rafael Kubelik. DG 2720 066 (9)
          +Gr 10-73 p681   ++RR 10-73 p62
          +HF 2-74 p82   ++SFC 12-7-80 p33
1324 Symphony, no. 7, op. 70, D minor. LPO; Mstislav Rostropovich. HMV
     ASD 3869 (also Angel SZ 37717 Tape (c) 4ZS 37717)
          +Gr 8-80 p216   +-NR 9-80 p3
          -HF 11-80 p62   +-RR 8-80 p40
          +HFN 9-80 p104   ++St 11-80 p82
1325 Symphony, no. 7, op. 70, D minor. CO; Georg Szell. Odyssey Y
     35931 (From Epic BC 1111)
          +FF 11/12-80 p106
1326 Symphony, no. 7, op. 70, D minor. CPhO; Zdenek Kosler. Quintes-
     sence PMC 7126 (From Supraphon SUA 50647, Crossroads 2216098)
          +ARG 4-80 p22   +-SFC 11-4-79 p40
          +-FF 3/4-80 p83
1327 Symphony, no. 7, op. 70, D minor. PO; Eugene Ormandy. RCA ARL 1-
     3555 Tape (c) ARK 1-3555
          +ARG 10-80 p42   +NR 7-80 p4
          -FF 11/12-80 p106   ++SFC 7-20-80 p34
          ++HF 11-80 p61   ++St 11-80 p84
1328 Symphony, no. 8, op. 88, G major. Carnival overture, op. 29. PhO;
     Andrew Davis. CBS 76393 (also Columbia M 35865)
          +ARG 12-80 p26   +HFN 1-80 p106
          -FF 11/12-80 p107   +-RR 2-80 p51
          +Gr 1-80 p1145   +St 11-80 p82
          +HF 11-80 p62
1329 Symphony, no. 8, op. 88, G major. CSO; Carlo Maria Giulini. DG
     2531 046 Tape (c) 3301 046
          ++FF 3/4-80 p84   ++NR 3-80 p3
          +Gr 10-79 p633   +NYT 12-9-79 pD25
          +HF 3-80 p78   +RR 11-79 p78
          ++HF 10-80 p98 tape   ++SFC 11-18-79 p47
          +HFN 11-79 p139   +St 4-80 p132
1330 Symphony, no. 8, op. 88, G major. BPhO; Rafael Kubelik. DG 2535
     397 Tape (c) 3335 397 (From 139181)
          +Gr 7-80 p136   +HFN 9-80 p116 tape
          ++Gr 9-80 p413 tape   +RR 7-80 p54
          +HFN 7-80 p115
1331 Symphony, no. 8, op. 88, G major. Scherzo capriccioso, op. 66, D
     flat major. PhO; Carlo Maria Giulini. EMI (Japan) EAC 30298
          +-ARSC Vol 12, nos. 1-2, 1980 p88
1332 Symphony, no. 8, op. 88, G major. Scherzo capriccioso, op. 66, D
     flat major. Halle Orchestra; John Barbirolli. Everest SDBR
     3449 (From Mercury MG 50162, Vanguard SRV 133)
          +-ARG 9-79 p44   +NR 7-79 p1
          +-FF 3/4080 p83

1333 Symphony, no. 8, op. 88, G major. Slavonic dances, op. 46, no. 8,
     G minor. BPhO; Herbert von Karajan. HMV ASD 3775 Tape (c) TC
     ASD 3775 (also Angel SZ 37686 Tape (c) 4ZS 37686)
          +–ARG 12-80 p26   +HFN 9-80 p116 tape
          +–FF 9/10-80 p113   +NR 8-80 p4
          +–Gr 5-80 p1660   ++RR 6-80 p47
          +–HF 11-80 p62   ++SFC 7-20-80 p34
          ++HFN 5-80 p121

1334 Symphony, no. 8, op. 88, G major. Slavonic dances, op. 46, nos. 2,
     4, 6. COA; Bernard Haitink. Philips 6570 078 Tape (c) 7310 078
     (From SAL 3451)
          +Gr 1-80 p1145   +HFN 1-80 p123 tape
          +HF 8-78 p98 tape   +–RR 12-79 p53
          +–HFN 1-80 p119

1335 Symphony, no. 8, op. 88, G major. COA; Colin Davis. Philips 9500
     317 Tape (c) 7300 611
          +FF 1/2-80 p84   ++HFN 12-79 p185 tape
          +Gr 10-79 p633   +NYT 12-9-79 pD25
          +HF 3-80 p78   +RR 10-79 p86
          ++HF 10-80 p98 tape   +St 4-80 p132
          ++HFN 10-79 p151

1336 Symphony, no. 8, op. 88, G major. CPhO; Vaclav Neumann. Quintes-
     sence PMC 7119 (From Supraphon 110 1203, Vanguard SU 2)
          ++ARG 9-79 p24   +FF 3/4-80 p85

1337 Symphony, no. 8, op. 88, G major. Sydney Symphony Orchestra; Jose
     Serebrier. RCA ARL 1-3550 Tape (c) ARK 1-3550
          -ARG 12-80 p26   -HF 11-80 p62
          -FF 9/10-80 p113   ++NR 7-80 p2

1338 Symphony, no. 9, op. 95, E minor. Scherzo capriccioso, op. 66, D
     flat major. RPO, BPhO; Rudolf Kempe. Arabesque 8019 Tape (c)
     9019 (From Seraphim S 60098)
          +–FF 11/12-80 p108   +HF 11-80 p62
          +HF 10-80 p98 tape

1339 Symphony, no. 9, op. 95, E minor. VPO; Kiril Kondrashin. Decca
     SXDL 7510 Tape (c) DSXDC 7510 (also London LSR L0011)
          +–FF 11/12-80 p107   +NR 10-80 p4
          +Gr 7-80 p136   ++RR 7-80 p55
          ++HF 11-80 p62   +SFC 7-20-80 p34
          +HFN 7-80 p107   ++St 11-80 p82

1340 Symphony, no. 9, op. 95, E minor. VPO; Karl Bohm. DG 2531 098 Tape
     (c) 3301 098
          +–ARG 4-80 p22   +–NR 1-80 p2
          +FF 5/6-80 p74   +NYT 12-9-79 pD25
          ++Gr 6-79 p42   +RR 8-79 p79
          +HF 3-80 p78   ++St 2-80 p124
          +HFN 7-79 p104

1341 Symphony, no. 9, op. 95, E minor. NPhO; Vernon Handley. Enigma
     K 23532
          +HFN 8-80 p113

1342 Symphony, no. 9, op. 95, E minor. LPO; Mstislav Rostropovich. HMV
     ASD 3786 Tape (c) TC ASD 3786 (also Angel SZ 37719)
          +–ARG 5-80 p21   +HFN 1-80 p123 tape
          ++FU 6-80 p43   -NR 3-80 p2
          +Gr 11-79 p817   +–NYT 12-9-79 pD25
          +–HF 3-80 p78   +–RR 11-79 p79
          +–HFN 1-80 p106   +St 5-80 p82

1343 Symphony, no. 9, op. 95, E minor. PhO; Carlo Maria Giulini. HMV
         SXLP 30163 Tape (c) TC SXLP 30163 (From Columbia SAX 2405)
                     +Gr 7-74 p201   +RR 2-74 p28
                     +-HFN 10-80 p117 tape
1344 Symphony, no. 9, op. 95, E minor. Slovak Philharmonic Orchestra;
         Zdenek Kosler. Musical Heritage Soicety MHS 4084
                     +ARG 5-80 p21   +St 5-80 p82
                     +-HF 3-80 p78
1345 Symphony, no. 9, op. 95, E minor. COA; Colin Davis. Philips 9500
         511 Tape (c) 7300 671
                     +Audio 6-79 p132   +-NR 12-78 p4
                     ++FF 1/2-79 p46   +RR 2-79 p61
                     ++Gr 2-79 p1421   +RR 4-79 p124 tape
                     +-HF 3-80 p78   +-SFC 10-8-78 p46
                     +HFN 3-79 p123   +St 1-79 p98
                     +HFN 4-79 p134 tape
     Symphony, no. 9, op. 95, E minor. See no. 3581
1346 Trio, piano, no. 3, op. 65, F minor. Raphael Trio. Sonar SD 180
                     +-FF 7/8-80 p82   ++St 2-80 p121
                     ++NR 12-80 p7
1347 Trio, piano, no. 4, op. 90, E minor. MENDELSSOHN: Trio, piano, no.
         1, op. 49, D minor. Beaux Arts Trio. Pearl SHE 553
                     +Gr 9-80 p359
     Trio, piano, no. 4, op. 90, E minor. See no. 744
     The water goblin, op. 107. See no. 1348
     The wood dove, op. 110. See no. 1348
1348 Works, selections: The golden spinning wheel, op. 109. Husitska
         overture, op. 67. The noonday witch, op. 108, The water goblin,
         op. 107. The wood dove, op. 110. CPhO; Vaclav Neuman. Supra-
         phon 410 2591/2 (2)
                     +Gr 1-80 p1145   +-MT 6-80 p382
                     +-HF 1-80 p72   +-RR 1-80 p72
                     +HFN 2-80 p92
1349 Works, selections: Concerto, piano, op. 33, G minor. Concerto,
         violoncello, op. 104, B minor. Concerto, violin, op. 53, A min-
         or. Mazurka, violin, op. 49, E minor. Romance, op. 11, F minor.
         Rondo, op. 94, G minor. Silent woods, op. 68. Ruggiero Ricci,
         vln; Rudolf Firkusny, pno; Zara Nelsova, vlc; St. Louis Symphony
         Orchestra; Walter Susskind. Vox (Q) QSVBX 5135 (3) Tape (c) CBX
         5135
                     +HF 5-76 p81 Quad   ++St 9-77 p119 Quad
                     ++NR 3-76 p3   +St 3-80 p107 tape
                     ++SFC 2-22-76 p29
DVORESKY
     O gentle light. See no. 776
DYKES
     The navy hymn. See no. 3970
DYKES, John
     Eternal father. See no. 3973
EADES
     A dream. See no. 3848
EAKIN, Charles
1350 Frames. HAMILTON: Palinodes. HUTCHESON: Faintaisie-Impromptu.
         MCLEAN: Dimensions II. David Burge, Louis Svard Burge, pno.
         CRI SD 407
                     +-FF 5/6-80 p79

EAST, Michael
    Magnificat: Nun dimittis. See no. 34
    Songs: O Lord of whom I do depend; When Israel came out of Egypt;
        When David heard that Absalom was slain. See no. 34
    Songs (madrigals): No haste but good, pt 2; Quick quick away, pt 1.
        See no. 3893
    When David heard that Absalom was slain. See no. 3530
    EASTER ON MOUNT ATHOS. See no. 3692
EATON, John
1351 Danton and Robespierre. Edith Vanerette, Nelda Nelson, Mary Shear-
        er, s; Debra Dominiak, Diane Coloton, ms; Paula Redd, alto; James
        Anderson, Randy Hansen, Gran Wilson, t; Tim Noble, bar; William
        Parcher, bs-bar; Kevin Langan, bs; Indiana University Opera
        Theater Orchestra and Chorus; Thomas Baldner. CRI IUS 421 (3)
                +-ARG 10-80 p14   +NR 7-80 p9
                ++FF 7/8-80 p83   +NYT 2-24-80 pD20
                +HF 7-80 p67   +SR 9-80 p96
EBEN, Petr
1352 Sonntagesmusik: Moto ostinato. JANACEK: Glagolitic mass: Postlude.
        KLICKA: Fantasie de concert, op. 65. WIEDERMANN: Impetuoso.
        Notturno. Jiri Ropek, org. Vista VPS 1062
                +FF 11/12-79 p161   +NR 6-80 p13
                +HFN 8-79 p117
ECCARD, Johann
    Songs: Over the mountains Mary goes; Von der Geburt Christi. See
        no. 3697
ECCLES, John
    Sonata, horn, G minor. See no. 3644
ECHEVERRIA
    Sonata de 6 tono. See no. 3871
ECKHARDT-GRAMATTE, Sonia (Sophie-Carmen)
1353 Concerto, trumpet, clarinet, bassoon and percussion. MOZART: Sym-
        phony, no. 38, K 504, D major. Philip Collins, tpt; James Morton,
        clt; Gerald Corey, bsn; National Arts Centre Orchestra; Mario
        Bernardi. Canadian Broadcasting Corporation SM 272
                +FF 7/8-80 p84
EDEN
    What's in the air today. See no. 3831
EDER, Helmut
    Sonatine. See no. 4017
EDLUND, Lars
    Elegie. See no. 3713
EDMUNDSON, Garth
    Gargoyles. See no. 4057
    Preludes on old chorales (2). See no. 3836
    Vom Himmel hoch. See no. 4054
EDWARDS, Richard
    Songs: When griping griefs. See no. 3877
EFFINGER, Cecil
    Nocturne. See no. 3651
EISLER, Hanns
1354 Songs: Andere die Welt sie braucht es (Brecht); Ballade vom Soldat-
        en (Brecht); Ballade von der Judenhure Marie Sanders (Brecht);
        Einigkeit und Recht und Freiheit (Tucholsky); Die Hollywood-
        Elegien (Brecht); Mutter Beimlein (Brecht); O Fallada da du
        hangest (Brecht); Ostersonntag (Brecht); Lieder uber der Liebe

(Brecht, Goethe, Altenberg, etc); Uber den Selbstmord (Brecht).
Sylvia Anders; Dietrich Justus Noll, pno, clt. Acanta DC 23259
+RR 4-80 p110

EKLUND, Hans
Quartet, strings, no. 4. See no. 332

ELGAR, Edward
The apostles: Prologue. See no. 4019. See no. 4060
Ave verum corpus, op. 2, no. 1. See no. 3528
La capricieuse, op. 17. See no. 3964
Caractacus, op. 35: Sword song. See no. 1383
Caractacus, op. 35: Woodland interlude; Triumphal march. See no.
1382
Chanson de matin, op. 15, no. 2. See no. 3639
Chanson de nuit, op. 15, no. 1. See no. 3639
Civic fanfare. See no. 3959

1355 Cockaigne overture, op. 40. Enigma variations, op. 36. Serenade,
strings, op. 20, E minor. RPO; Thomas Beecham. CBS 61878 (From
Philips ABL 3053)
                +ARSC Vol 12, no. 3,   +Gr 1-80 p1146
                1980 p251   +HFN 2-80 p105

1356 Cockaigne overture, op. 40. Falstaff, op. 68, C minor. LPO;
Daniel Barenboim. CBS 61883 Tape (c) 40-61883 (From 76284)
                +Gr 2-80 p1264   +-HFN 4-80 p121 tape
                +Gr 9-80 p413 tape   +RR 3-80 p50
                +HFN 2-80 p105

1357 Cockaigne overture, op. 40. Falstaff, op. 68, C minor. LPO;
Vernon Handley. Classics for Pleasure CFP 40313 Tape (c) TC
CFP 40313
                +-Gr 7-79 p198   +RR 7-79 p53
                +Gr 3-80 p1446 tape   +-RR 7-80 p97 tape
                +-HFN 7-79 p104   +STL 12-9-79 p41
                +HFN 2-80 p107 tape

1358 Cockaigne overture, op. 40. Enigma variations, op. 36. LSO; Colin
Davis. Philips 6570 188 Tape (c) 7310 188 (From SAL 3516)
                +FF 9/10-80 p114   +HFN 12-80 p153
                +-Gr 12-80 p832
Cockaigne overture, op. 40. See no. 3585

1359 Concerto, violin, op. 61, B minor. Hugh Bean, vln; Royal Liverpool
Philharmonic Orchestra; Charles Groves. Classics for Pleasure
CFP 40322 (From HMV ASD 2883)
                +Gr 1-80 p1145   +RR 12-79 p54
                +HFN 12-79 p179
Concerto, violin, op. 61, B minor. See no. 3964

1360 Concerto, violoncello, op. 85, E minor. WALTON: Concerto, violoncello. Ralph Kirschbaum, vlc; Scottish National Orchestra;
Alexander Gibson. Chandos ABR 1007
                ++HF 9-80 p87   -RR 2-80 p52
                +-HFN 2-80 p92   ++St 8-80 p93

1361 Concerto, violoncello, op. 85, E minor. Elegy, op. 58. In the
south overture, op. 50. Robert Cohen, vlc; LPO; Norman Del Mar.
Classics for Pleasure CFP 40342 Tape (c) TC CFP 40342
                +Gr 12-80 p831
Coronation march, op. 65. See no. 1382
Coronation ode, op. 44: Land of hope and glory. See no. 1383
Crown of India suite, op. 66. See no. 1370. See no. 1382

Crown of India suite, op. 66: March. See no. 1383
Doubt not thy father's care. See no. 3533
1362 The dream of Gerontius, op. 38. Alfreda Hodgson, con; Robert Tear,
     t; Benjamin Luxon, bar; Scottish National Orchestra and Chorus;
     Alexander Gibson. Vanguard VSD 71258/9 (2)
              +—FF 5/6-80 p74   +NR 3-80 p10
              +HF 9-80 p87
The dream of Gerontius, op. 38: Softly and gently. See no. 3560
Elegy, op. 58. See no. 1361
Empire march. See no. 1383
1363 Enigma variations, op. 36. Introduction and allegro, strings, op.
     47. LPO; Adrian Boult. Classics for Pleasure CFP 40022 (From
     World Records ST 158)
              +—FF 9/10-80 p116   +HFN 2-73 p347
              -Gr 2-73 p1501   /RR 2-73 p58
              +—Gr 11-78 p973
1364 Enigma variations, op. 36. VAUGHAN WILLIAMS: Fantasia on a theme
     by Tallis. The wasps. LSO; Andre Previn. HMV ASD 3857 Tape (c)
     TC ASD 3857 (also Angel SZ 37627 Tape (c) 4ZS 37627)
              +ARG 12-80 p27   +HFN 9-80 p116 tape
              +—FF 9/10-80 p116   ++NR 8-80 p5
              +Gr 4-80 p1554   +RR 4-80 p63
              ++HFN 4-80 p103   +St 11-80 p86
1365 Enigma variations, op. 36. Falstaff, op. 68, C minor. Royal Albert
     Hall Orchestra, LSO; Edward Elgar. World Records SH 162
              +ARG 7/8-80 p24
Enigma variations, op. 36. See no. 1355. See no. 1358
Enigma variations, op. 36: Nimrod. See no. 3526. See no. 3858
1366 Falstaff, op. 68, C minor. In the south, op. 50. LPO; Georg Solti.
     Decca SXL 6963 Tape (c) KSXC 6963 (also London 7193)
              +—Gr 11-80 p665   +HFN 10-80 p103
              +Gr 12-80 p889 tape
1367 Falstaff, op. 68, C minor. Sanguine fan, op. 81. Fantasia and
     fugue, op. 86, C minor (trans. from Bach). LPO; Adrian Boult.
     Mobile Fidelity MFSL 2-501 (2) (From HMV ASD 2970)
              ++Gr 12-80 p831   ++FF 11/12-80 p109
Falstaff, op. 68, C minor. See no. 1356. See no. 1357. See no.
     1365
Fantasia and fugue, op. 86, C minor. See no. 1367
Imperial march, op. 32. See no. 394. See no. 1370. See no. 1382
1386 In the south overture, op. 50. Sea pictures, op. 37. Yvonne Min-
     ton, ms; LPO; Daniel Barenboim. CBS 76579 Tape (c) 40-76579
     (also Columbia M 35880)
              +—FF 11/12-80 p110   +NR 12-80 p2
              +—Gr 8-77 p328   +—NYT 12-14-80 pD38
              +—Gr 1-78 p1307 tape   +RR 9-77 p87
              +HFN 9-77 p141   +—RR 12-77 p1145 tape
              +HFN 12-77 p187 tape   +RR 12-77 p94 tape
              +MT 12-77 p1014
In the south overture, op. 50. See no. 1361. See no. 1366. See
     no. 1370. See no. 3526.
In the south overture, op. 50, excerpt. See no. 1383
Introduction and allegro, op. 47. See no. 1230. See no. 1363
King Olaf, op. 30: And King Olaf heard the cry. See no. 1383
1369 The kingdom, op. 51. Prelude. Symphony, no. 1, op. 55, A flat
     major. LSO; Edward Elgar. World Record SH 139

+ARG 7/8-80 p24
Light of life, op. 29: Doubt not thy father's care. See no. 3936
Light of life, op. 29: Meditation. See no. 1382
1370 Pomp and circumstance marches, op. 39, nos. 1-5. Crown of India
     suite, op. 66. Imperial march, op. 32. In the south overture,
     op. 50. LPO; Daniel Barenboim. CBS 61892/3 Tape (c) 40-61892/3
     (From 76248, 76579)
                  +-HFN 6-80 p115   +MT 12-80 p785
                  +-HFN 9-80 p116 tape   +-RR 7-80 p55
Pomp and circumstance marches, op. 39, no. 1, D major. See no. 394
Prelude. See no. 1369
Sanguine fan, op. 8. See no. 1367
Sea pictures, op. 37. See no. 670. See no. 1368
Sea pictures, op. 37: Where corals lie. See no. 3560. See no. 3625
Serenade, op. 20, E minor. See no. 50. See no. 908. See no. 1226.
     See no. 1355
1371 Sonata, organ, op. 28, G major. REUBKE: Sonata on the 94th psalm,
     C minor. Nicolas Kynaston, org. Mitra OSM 16157
                  +-HFN 1-80 p106
1372 Sonata, organ, op. 28, G major. FRANCK: Prelude, fugue and vari-
     ations, op. 18. GADE: Three tone pieces, op. 22. Thomas Murray,
     org. Town Hall Records S 23
                  +CL 4-80 p14   +HF 6-80 p94
                  +FF 11/12-80 p111   ++MU 9-79 p14
1373 Sonata, violin and piano, op. 82, E minor. VAUGHAN WILLIAMS: Sonata,
     violin and piano, A minor. Yehudi Menuhin vln; Hephzibah Menuhin,
     pno. HMV ASD 3820
                  +Gr 3-80 p1403   ++RR 3-80 p80
                  +HFN 3-80 p89   +-ST 9-80 p340
                  ++MT 10-80 p634
1374 Sonata, violin and piano, op. 82, E minor. MESSIAEN: Theme and vari-
     ations. WALTON: Pieces, violin and piano (2). Michael Davis,
     vln; Rosemary Platt, pno. Orion ORS 79360
                  +FF 9/10-80 p117   +NR 8-80 p8
1375 Songs: Ave verum corpus; Ecce sacerdos magnus; Psalm, no. 48. LISZT:
     Via Crucis, G 53. Stephen Connolly, treble; Donald Holmes, bar;
     John Wheeler, bs; Tom Corfield, Francis Jackson, org; Leeds Par-
     ish Church Choir; Simon Lindley. Abbey LPB 813
                  +Gr 3-80 p1427   +HFN 11-80 p117
1376 Songs: After, op. 31, no. 1; As I laye a-thynkyinge; Come gentle
     night; In the dawn, op. 41, no. 1; Is she not passing fair;
     Language of flowers; Pipes of Pan; Pleading, op. 48, no. 1; Ron-
     del, op. 16, no. 3; Shepherd's song, op. 16, no. 1; Song of
     autumn; A song of flight, op. 31, no. 2; Speak music, op. 41,
     no. 2; Through the long days, op. 16, no. 2; The wind at dawn.
     Brian Rayner Cook, bar; Roger Vignoles, pno. RCA GL 2-5205 Tape
     (c) GK 2-5205 (From Pearl SHE 526)
                  +-Gr 6-79 p93   +-MT 2-80 p105
                  +-HFN 7-79 p118   +RR 6-79 p112
                  +-HFN 9-79 p123 tape   +STL 12-2-79 p37
Songs: From the Bavarian Highland, op. 27; The dance; Fly singing
     bird fly, op. 26, no. 2; I sing the birth; In the dawn, op. 41,
     no. 2; Like to the damask rose; Pipes of Pan; Pleading, op. 48,
     no. 1; The river, op. 60, no. 2; The snow, op. 26, no. 1. See
     no. 1383

Songs: Give unto the lord. See no. 4019
Songs: Land of hope and glory. See no. 3560
Songs: Pleading, op. 48, no. 1. See no. 3774
Songs: Pleading, op. 48, no. 1; Song cycle, op. 59; Songs, op. 60.
    See no. 962
Sospiri, op. 70. See no. 1383
1377 Symphony, no. 1, op. 55, A flat major. LPO; Daniel Barenboim. CBS
    61880 Tape (c) 40-61880 (From 77247)
        +-Gr 1-80 p1146   /-HFN 2-80 p107 tape
        +HFN 12-79 p177   +RR 1-80 p73
1378 Symphony, no. 1, op. 55, A flat major. LPO; Vernon Handley. Clas-
    sics for Pleasure CFP 40331
        +Gr 6-80 p32   +RR 6-80 p48
        +-HFN 5-80 p121
1379 Symphony, no. 1, op. 55, A flat major. VAUGHAN WILLIAMS: Fantasia
    on a theme by Thomas Tallis. LPO; Adrian Boult. Lyrita REAM 1
    (From SRCS 39, SRC 41)
        ++Gr 1-80 p1146   ++RR 12-79 p53
        +-HF 1-80 p119
Symphony, no. 1, op. 55, A flat major. See no. 1369
1380 Symphony, no. 2, op. 63, E flat major. LPO; Daniel Barenboim. CBS
    61988 Tape (c) 40-61988
        +-Gr 11-80 p666   +-HFN 12-80 p159 tape
        +-HFN 12-80 p153
1381 Symphony, no. 2, op. 63, E flat major. LPO; Adrian Boult. Lyrita
    REAM 2 (From SRCS 40)
        +-Gr 1-80 p1146   +-RR 11-79 p80
        +HFN 11-79 p153
1382 Works, selections: Caractacus, op. 35: Woodland interlude; Triumphal
    march. Crown of India suite, op. 66. Coronation march, op. 65.
    Imperial march, op. 32. Light of life, op. 29: Meditation. Roy-
    al Liverpool Orchestra; Charles Groves. Arabesque 8002
        +-FF 11/12-80 p108   +SFC 5-11-80 p35
        +HF 9-80 p90
1383 Works, selections: Caractacus, op. 35: Sword song. Coronation
    ode, op. 44: Land of hope and glory. Crown of India, op. 66:
    March. Empire march. In the south overture, op. 50, excerpt.
    King Olaf, op. 30: And King Olaf heard the cry. Sospiri, op. 70.
    Songs: From the Bavarian Highlands, op. 27; The dance; Fly sing-
    ing bird fly, op. 26, no. 2; I sing the birth; In the dawn, op.
    41, no. 2; Like to the damask rose; Pipes of Pan; Pleading, op.
    48, no. 1; The river, op. 60, no. 2; The snow, op. 26, no. 1.
    Rosina Buckman, s; Edna Thornton, con; Louise Kirkby Lunn, ms;
    John Coates Tudor Davies, t; George Baker, bar; Andrew Black, bs;
    Madame Adami, pno; Black Diamonds Band, La Scala Orchestra, BBC
    Radio Orchestra, BBC Symphony Orchestra, unnamed orchestras;
    Sheffield Choir, Royal Choral Society; Baraldi Trio; Carlo Sab-
    ajno, Percy Pitt, Adrian Boult, Henry Coward, Eugene Goossens,
    Georgy Byng, Malcolm Sargent. Elgar Society ELG 001
        +-Gr 8-80 p216
ELIASSON, Anders
    Designo, string quartet. See no. 332
ELLINGTON, Edward
    Solitude. See no. 3962

ELLIOTT
    Hybrius the Cretan. See no. 4007
ELLIS, John
    Satyric suite. See no. 3718
ELMAS, Stepan
    Nocturne. See no. 3850
ELUARD
    Nous deux. See no. 3760
ENCINA Juan del
    Ay triste que vengo. See no. 3864. See no. 4002
    Isi abra en este baldres. See no. 4002
    Mi libertad en sosiego. See no. 4002
    Oy comamos y bebamos. See no. 4002
    Pedro i bien te quiero. See no. 4002
    Qu'es de ti desconsolado. See no. 4002
    Tan buen ganadico. See no. 4002
    Vuestros amores e senora. See no. 4002
ENESCO, Georges
    Cantabile et presto. See no. 3854
    Rumanian rhapsody, op. 11, no. 1, A major. See no. 1000. See no.
        1322. See no. 3797. See no. 3915
    Sonata, piano, no. 3, op. 24, D major. See no. 357. See no. 3777
ENGLUND, Einar
    Passacaglia. See no. 3726
1384 Symphony, no. 1. Turku Philharmonic Orchestra; Pertti Pekkanen.
        Finlandia FA 304
                +FF 5/6-80 p76   +RR 2-80 p52
                +-NR 10-80 p2
EOTVOS, Peter
1385 Mese, excerpts. PATACHICH: Maganhangzok. Hangzo Fuggvenyek. PON-
        GRACZ: Mariphonia. The story of a chord, C sharp major. VIKTOR/
        WINKLER: Viscositas. Electronic music. Hungaroton SLPX 11851
                +-ARG 10-80 p54   +-NR 4-80 p15
EPSTEIN, David
1386 Night voices. WALTON: Facade. Janet Bookspan, speaker; Various
        instrumentalists; Boston Boys Choir; MIT Symphony Orchestra;
        David Epstein. Candide CE 31116 Tape (c) CT 2257
                +-ARG 11-80 p36   +-HF 6-80 p91
                +-FF 7/8-80 p153   ++St 8-80 p102
ERICKSON, Frank
1387 Concerto, alto saxophone and band. HUMMEL (arr. Corley): Concerto,
        trumpet and band. RIMSKY-KORSAKOV (arr. Piket & Fittelberg):
        Concerto, clarinet and band. Mark Taggart, sax; Rebecca Reese,
        tpt; Cornell University Wind Ensemble; Marice Stith. Cornell
        CUWE 25
                +FF 11/12-80 p223   -NR 2-80 p6
ERKEL, Ferenc
    Hunyadi Laszlo: Ah rebeges, a mi vadul. See no. 3770
ERKIN, Ulvi Cemal
    Kocekce. See no. 6
ERNST
    Concert variations on "The last rose of summer". See no. 3637
ERNST, Heinrich
1388 Fantasy on themes from Rossini's "Otello", op. 11. PAGANINI: Vari-
        ations on "Di tanti palpiti" from Rossini's "Trancredi", op. 13.

SARASATE: Carmen fantasy, op. 25. WIENIAWSKI: Fantasy on themes
from Gounod's "Faust", op. 20. Ruggiero Ricci, vln; Luxembourg
Radio Orchestra; Louis de Froment. Turnabout QTV 34720 Tape (c)
CT 2214, KTVC 34720
+Gr 2-80 p1302   +RR 3-80 p67
+-HFN 2-80 p103   +SFC 5-20-79 p49
+NYT 7-6-80 pD15   ++St 8-79 p122

ESCHER, Rudolf
    Univers de Rimbaud. See no. 3818
ESTEVE, Pablo
    Songs: Alma sintamos. See no. 3698
ETLER, Alvin
    Concerto, clarinet. See no. 1163
EUROPE, James
    Castles half and half. See no. 4045
EVETT
    Chaconne. See no. 3859
EYBLER, Joseph
    Omnes. See no. 3961
EYSLER, Edmund
    Die Schutzanliesel: Mutterl lieb's Mutterl. See no. 3711
FACOLI, Marco
    Aria della comedia nuovo. See no. 3590
    Hor ch'io son gionto quivi. See no. 3590
    Padoana terza dita la finetta. See no. 3590
    S'io m'accorgo ben mio. See no. 3590
FALCONIERI
    Perche piangi pastore. See no. 3878
FALIK, Yuri
1389 Concerto, orchestra. Elegiac music. Quartet, strings, no. 3.
    Leningrad Philharmonic Academic Symphony, Taneyev Quartet, Lenin-
    grad Chamber Orchestra; Gennady Rozhdestvensky. Melodiya S10
    10233-34
                +FF 5/6-80 p77
1390 Concerto, violin. TISHCHENKO: Concerto, violin. Victor Liberman,
    vln; Leningrad Orchestra of Old and New Music, Leningrad Phil-
    harmonic Orchestra Academic Symphony; Eduard Serov, Victor Fedo-
    tov. Melodiya S10 8787-88
                +FF 5/6-80 p77
    Elegiac music. See no. 1389
1391 Music, strings. SLOMINSKY: Dramatic song. TISHCHENKO: Sinfonia rob-
    usta. USPENSKY: Music, strings and percussion. Prague Symphony
    Orchestra; Petr Vronsky. Supraphon 110 2280
                +FF 9/10-80 p226   +-SFC 10-12-80 p21
                +NR 7-80 p3
    Quartet, strings, no. 3. See no. 1389
FALLA, Manuel de
    El amor brujo: Cancion de amor dolido; Cancion de fuego fatua; Danza
    del jungo de amor. See no. 3985
    El amor brujo: Danza del terror. See no. 3882
    El amor brujo: Pantomime. See no. 3964
    El amor brujo: Pantomime; Ritual fire dance. See no. 12
    El amor brujo: Ritual fire dance. See no. 3555. See no. 3825. See
    no. 3890. See no. 3953. See no. 3954
    El amor brujo: Ritual fire dance; Pantomime. See no. 3665

Homenaje. See no. 957
Homenaje a Debussy. See no. 3600
El sombrero de tres picos: Danza del molinero. See no. 3609
El sombrero de tres picos: Final dance. See no. 12
El sombrero de tres picos: The neighbours; The miller's dance;
    Final dance. See no. 3665. See no. 3797. See no. 3955
El sombrero de tres picos: Seguidillas; Farruca; Jota. See no. 1211
El sombrero de tres picos: Suites, nos. 1 and 2. See no. 1001
1392 Spanish popular songs (7). GRANADOS: Goyescas: La maja y el ruise-
    nor. Songs: Canco d'amor; Elegia eterna; L'Ocell profeta. TUR-
    INA: Songs: Anhelos, Cantares; Farruca; Si con mis deseos. Mont-
    serrat Caballe, s; Miguel Zanetti, pno. London OS 26575 (also
    SXL R 6888 Tape (c) KSXC R 6888)

+FF 5/6-79 p111	+-ON 3-3-79 p41
+Gr 6-79 p96	+RR 6-79 p113
+HFN 6-79 p111	++SFC 3-4-79 p41
+NR 1-80 p10	+St 8-79 p122
+NYT 3-4-79 pD23	

Spanish popular songs (5). See no. 957
Spanish popular songs: Jota. See no. 3928. See no. 3964
Spanish popular songs: Jota; Polo. See no. 3551
1393 Suite populaire espagnole (arr. Kochanski). GRANADOS: Spanish dance,
    op. 37: Andaluza (arr. Kreisler). HALFFTER: Danza de la gitana
    (arr. Heifetz). SARASATE: Caprice basque, op. 24. Spanish dan-
    ces, nos. 1 and 2, op. 21; no. 5, op. 23; no. 8, op. 26. Itzhak
    Perlman, vln; Samuel Sanders, pno. Angel SZ 37590 Tape (c) 4ZS
    37590 (also HMV ASD 3910 Tape (c) TC ASD 3910)

+-FF 9/10-80 p284	+NR 10-80 p8
+Gr 10-80 p512	+NYT 7-6-80 pD15
+-HFN 10-80 p112	++St 10-80 p120
+HFN 12-80 p159 tape	

La vida breve: Danse espagnole. See no. 3772
La vida breve: Danza, no. 1. See no. 3964
La vida breve: Interlude and Spanish dance. See no. 3665
La vida breve: Spanish dance, no. 1. See no. 12
La vida breve: Vivan los que rien; Alliesta riyenda junto a esa
    mujer. See no. 3668
FALVO, Rudolfo
    Dicitencello vuie. See no. 3771
FANTINI, Girolamo
    Ballet et caprice. See no. 165
1394 Caprices (2). Courante and sonata. FRESCOBALDI: Ave maris stella.
    Bergamasca. Mass of the virgin. TORELLI: Sinfonia, trumpet.
    TRABACI: Gaillarde. Abbey of Bec Hellouin Schola; Marie-Andree
    Morisset-Balier, org; Michel Morriset, tpt. Grande Orgue MBM
    790510

+FF 5/6-80 p190	+MU 3-80 p8

Courante and sonata. See no. 1394
Dances. See no. 3656
Sonatas, trumpet and organ, nos. 1-2, 7. See no. 3866
FARINA, Carlo
    Capriccio stravagante. See no. 1156
    Pavana. See no. 3956
    Sonata detta la Polacca. See no. 3690

FARKAS, Ferenc
      Antiche danze Ungheresi. See no. 400
      Antique dances. See no. 60
1395 Autumnalia. Correspondences. Quartet, strings. Klara Takacs, ms;
      Maria Zempleni, s; Jeno Jando, Ferenc Farkas, pno; Laszlo Bar-
      sony, vla; Bela Kovacs, clt; New Budapest Quartet. Hungaroton
      SLPX 12054
                  +FF 9/10-80 p118
      Correspondences. See no. 1395
      Quartet, strings. See no. 1395
      Songs: Butterflies reposed; Hark the sun whispers; Madrigal of the
      rose. See no. 3803
FARMER, John
      Songs: Fair Phyllis I saw sitting all alone. See no. 3893
      Songs: Fair Phyllis I saw sitting all alone; Sweet friend thy absen-
      ce. See no. 3719
FARNABY, Giles
      Construe my meaning. See no. 3893
      Fantasia. See no. 3755
      Fantasia, no. 9. See no. 1396
      The flatt pavan. See no. 1396
      Giles Farnaby's dream, his rest, Farnaby's conceit. See no. 1396
      Lachrymae pavan. See no. 1396
      Loath to depart. See no. 1396. See no. 3648. See no. 3855. See
      no. 4044
      Mal Sims. See no. 1396
      Maske. See no. 1396
      Muscadin. See no. 3648
      Muscadin or Kempe's morris. See no. 4044
      The old spagnoletta. See no. 1396
      Paul's warf. See no. 1396
      Pawles wharf. See no. 3755
      Quodling's delight. See no. 1396. See no. 3755
      Rosasolis. See no. 3745
      Songs: Carters now cast down your whips; Construe my meaning; Daphne
      on the rainbow. See no. 3719
      Tell me Daphne. See no. 1396
      Tower Hill. See no. 1396. See no. 3755
      A toye. See no. 1396. See no. 3855
      Up tails all. See no. 3755
      Woody-cock. See no. 1396
1396 Works, selections: Fantasia, no. 9, The flatt pavan. Giles Farna-
      by's dream, his rest, Farnaby's conceit. Lachrymae pavan. Loath
      to depart. Mal Sims. Maske. The old spagnoletta. Paul's warf.
      Quodling's delight. Tell me Daphne. Tower Hill. A toye. Woody-
      cock. Joseph Payne, hpd. Musical Heritage Society MHS 4091
                  +FF 9/10-80 p119
FARNON, Robert
      Colditz march. See no. 3786
FARRANT, Richard
      Lord for thy tender mercy's sake. See no. 3894
FARRENC, Louise
      Trio, op. 45, E minor. See no. 3822
FARWELL, Arthur
      Wa-Wan choral. See no. 4045

FASCH, Johann
    Concerto, bassoon, C major. See no. 3804
1397 Concerto, trumpet, D major. HANDEL: Suite, trumpet, D major. TELE-
    MANN: Concerto, trumpet, D major. TORELLI: Sonata a cinque, D
    major. Carole Dawn Reinhardt, tpt; German Bach Soloists; Helmut
    Winschermann. Acanta DC 23067
              +FF 5/6-79 p119   +HFN 7-80 p113
              ++Gr 8-80 p233   +RR 7-80 p56
1398 Concerto, trumpet, D major. Sinfonias, A major, G major. PACHEL-
    BEL: Canon. Suites, B major, G major. Maurice Andre, tpt; Jean-
    Francois Paillard Orchestra; Jean-Francois Paillard. Erato Tape
    (c) C 480 (also RCA ZL 3-0645)
              ++HFN 12-80 p159 tape
    Concerto, trumpet, D major. See no. 3563
    Sinfonias, A major, G major. See no. 1398
    Trio sonata, G major. See no. 310
FATTORINI, Gabriele
    Ricercare del 10 and 11 tuono. See no. 3813
FAURE, Gabriel
    Apres un reve, op. 7, no. 1. See no. 3596. See no. 3906. See no.
    3962
    Ave verum corpus, op. 65, no. 1. See no. 3531
1399 Ballade, op. 19. MOZART: Variations on a minuet by Duport, K 573,
    D major. POULENC: Theme varie. SCHUMANN: Fantasiestucke, op.
    111 (3). Grant Johannesen, pno. Golden Crest 4201 DD, 4201 DIG
              +Audio 5-80 p89   +-CL 9-80 p18
    Ballade, op. 19. See no. 1049
    Barcarolle, no. 1, op. 26, A minor. See no. 1403
    Barcarolle, no. 6, op. 70, E flat major. See no. 1403
    Berceuse, op. 16. See no. 1218
1400 Caligula, op. 52: Prologue, fanfares; March and chorus; Quasi-adagio;
    L'hiver s'enfuit; Air de danse; De roses vermeilles; Cesar a fer-
    me la paupiere. Prometheus, op. 82: Prelude; Air de Gaia; Pre-
    lude, Cortege de Pandora, Interlude, Air de Bia; Prelude, Choeurs
    des Oceanides. Danielle Galland, s; Maitrise Gabriel Faure, Mon-
    te Carlo Opera Orchestra; Roger Norrington. Peters PLE 037 Tape
    PCE 037 (also IPG 7466)
              +-FF 9/10-78 p51   +ON 2-3-79 p33
              +-Gr 8-80 p248
    Cantique de Jean Racine, op. 11. See no. 1405
    Crucifix. See no. 3949. See no. 3961
1401 Dolly suite, op. 56. FRANCK: Prelude, chorale et fugue. MENDELSSOHN:
    Allegro brillant, op. 92. Cyril Smith, P. Sellick, pno. Nimbus 212(
              +RR 8-80 p69
    Dolly suite, op. 56. See no. 3799
    Elegie, op. 24, C minor. See no. 751. See no. 3606
    Fantaisie, op. 79. See no. 3594. See no. 3714. See no. 3854
    Impromptu, no. 3, op. 34, A flat major. See no. 1403
    Madrigal. See no. 638
    Morceau de concours. See no. 3854
    Nocturnes, nos. 1, 3-4, 6, 13. See no. 1403
1402 Nocturnes, op. 33, nos. 1-3; op. 36; op. 37, op. 63; op. 74; op. 84,
    no. 8; op. 97; op. 99; op. 104; op. 107; op. 119. Theme and
    variations, op. 73, C minor. Jean-Philippe Collard, pno. Conno-
    isseur Society CS 2072 Tape (c) In Sync C 4027/8

    +HF 6-75 p94   ++SFC 4-6-75 p22
    +MJ 4-76 p30   ++St 7-75 p69
    ++NR 9-80 p11 tape
Nocturne, op. 33, no. 3, A flat major. See no. 3953. See no. 3954
Papillon, op. 77. See no. 751
Pavane. See no. 3715
Pavane, op. 50. See no. 1404. See no. 3666. See no. 3794. See
    no. 3799
1403 Piano works: Barcarolle, no. 1, no. 26, A minor. Barcarolle, no. 6,
    op. 70, E flat major. Impromptu, no. 3, op. 34, A flat major.
    Nocturnes, nos. 1, 3-4, 6, 13. Romance sans paroles, op. 17, no.
    3, A flat major. Albert Ferber, pno. Saga 5385
            +-FF 9/10-80 p119   +RR 12-79 p97
            +HFN 1-80 p121
    Prometheus, op. 82: Prelude; Air de Gaia; Prelude cortege de Pan-
    dora, Interlude; Air de Bia; Prelude, Choeurs des Oceanides. See
    no. 1400
1404 Requiem, op. 48. Pavane, op. 50. Lucia Popp, s; Siegmund Nimsgern,
    bar; Leslie Pearson, org; Ambrosian Singers; PhO; Andrew Davis.
    CBS 76734 Tape (c) 40-76734 (also Columbia M 35153 Tape (c) MT
    35153)
            +FF 1/2-80 p89   +-MM 2-79 p37
            +FU 2-80 p44   +MU 9-79 p17
            ++Gr 12-78 p1142   +MUM 3/4-80 p36
            ++Gr 5-79 p1940 tape   +NR 7-79 p11
            ++HF 10-79 p108   +-RR 12-78 p104
            +HFN 12-78 p155   ++SFC 6-17-79 p41
            +-HFN 3-79 p139 tape   ++St 10-79 p138
1405 Requiem, op. 48. Cantique de Jean Racine, op. 11. Bernard Kruy-
    sen, bar; Denis Thilliez, treble; Phillipe Caillard Chorale;
    Monte Carlo Opera Orchestra; Louis Fremaux; Henri Carol, org.
    RCA GL 2-5243 Tape (c) GK 2-5243 (From World Records SCM 51)
            +-Gr 11-79 p891   +-HFN 10-79 p169
            +-HFN 1-80 p123 tape
1406 Requiem, op. 48. Martina Arroyo, s; Hermann Prey, bar; Robert
    Arnold, org; Musica Aeterna Orchestra and Chorus; Frederic Wald-
    man. Westminster MCA 1411 (From Decca)
            -FF 11/12-80 p111
    Requiem, op. 48. See no. 3557
    Romance sans paroles, op. 17, no. 3, A flat major. See no. 1403
    Serenade, op. 98. See no. 751
    Serenade Toscane. See no. 3965
1407 Sonata, violin and piano, no. 1, op. 13, A major. Sonata, violin
    and piano, no. 2, op. 108, E minor. Pierre Amoyal, vln; Anne
    Queffelec, pno. Erato STU 71195
            +-Gr 10-79 p667   +-MT 4-80 p251
            +HFN 11-79 p139   +RR 11-79 p251
1408 Sonata, violin and piano, no. 1, op. 13, A major. Sonata, violin
    and piano, no. 2, op. 108, E minor. Arthur Grumiaux, vln; Paul
    Crossley, pno. Philips 9500 534
            +FF 9/10-79 p80   +NR 7-79 p10
            ++Gr 7-79 p215   +NYT 7-6-80 pD15
            ++HF 9-79 p118   +RR 7-79 p89
            ++HFN 7-79 p104   ++SFC 6-17-79 p41
            +-MT 12-79 p1007   +STL 12-2-79 p37
            +MUM 3/4-80 p33

Sonata, violin and piano, no. 1, op. 13, A major. See no. 1218.
   See no. 3964
Sonata, violin and piano, no. 2, op. 108, E minor. See no. 1407.
   See no. 1408

1409 Songs: Accompagnement, op. 85, no. 3; Arpege, op. 76, no. 2; La
     bonne chanson, op. 61; Dans la foret de septembre, op. 85, no.
     1; La fleur qui va sur l'eau, op. 85, no. 2; Le perfum imperis-
     sable, op. 76, no. 1; Le plus doux chemin, op. 87, no. 1; Prison,
     op. 83, no. 1; Le ramier, op. 87, no. 2; Serenade du bourgeois
     gentilhombre; Soir, op. 83, no. 2. Jacques Herbillon, bar; Theo-
     dore Paraskivesco, pno. Calliope CAL 1844
                    -Gr 5-76 p1794   +RR 8-80 p18
                    +MT 8-76 p660   +RR 3-76 p67
                    +RR 10-75 p24

1410 Songs: Chanson, op. 94. Le don silencieux, op. 92. L'horizon
     chimerique, op. 118: La mer est infinie; Je me suis embarque;
     Diane Selene; Vaisseaux, nous vous aurons aimes. Le jardin
     clos, op. 106: Exaucement; Quand tu plonges tes yeux; La messa-
     gere; Je me poserai sur ton coeur; Dans la nymphee; Dans la pen-
     ombre; Il m'est cher mon amour; Inscription sur le sable. Mir-
     ages, op. 113: Cynges sur l'eau; Reflets dans l'eau; Jardin noc-
     turne; Danseuse. Serenade toscane, op. 3, no. 2. Anne-Marie
     Rodde, s; Theodore Paraskivesco, pno. Calliope CAL 1845
                    +Gr 5-76 p1794   +RR 3-76 p67
                    +MT 8-76 p660   +RR 8-80 p19

1411 Songs: Puisqu'ici-bas, op. 10, no. 1. Tarantelle, op. 10, no. 2.
     La chanson d'Eve, op. 95: Paradis; Prima verba; Roses ardentes;
     Comme Dieu rayonne; L'aube blanche; Eau vivante; Veilles-tu ma
     senteur de soleil; Dans un parfum de roses blanches; Crepuscule;
     O mort poussieres d'etoiles. Melisande's song, op. posth.
     Notre amour, op. 23, no. 2. Pleurs d'or, op. 72. Seule, op. 3,
     no. 1. Vocalise, without opus. Anne-Marie Rodde, Sonia Nigog-
     hossian, s; Theodore Paraskivesco, pno. Calliope CAL 1846
                    +Gr 5-76 p1794   +RR 3-76 p67
                    +MT 8-76 p660   +RR 8-80 p19

Songs: Apres un reve, op. 7, no. 1; Nell, op. 18, no. 1. See no.
   3611
Songs: Apres un reve, op. 7, no. 1; Mirages, op. 113. See no. 3863
Tantum ergo, op. 65, no. 2. See no. 3528
Theme and variations, op. 73, C minor. See no. 1402
Trio, piano, op. 120, D minor. See no. 1024

FEHER
   Homo sapiens, no. 1. See no. 3803
FELDMAN, Morton
   Instruments (4). See no. 3739
   Piece, piano (To Philip Guston). See no. 3727
   Verticle thoughts IV. See no. 3727
FELLNER-SCHNEIDER
   's Nussdorfer Sterndl. See no. 3711
FENNELLY, Brian
1412 Scintilla prisca. GHEZZO: Aphorisms. GILBERT: Suonare. SAYLOR:
     Psalms (4). Constance Beavon, ms; Irene Simonsen, flt; Jack
     Kreiselman, clt; Roger Boardman, Brian Fennelly, pno; David Moore,
     vlc. Orion ORS 80368
                    +-FF 11/12-80 p221   +-NR 7-80 p15

FERGUSON, Barry
    Songs: Death and darkness get you packing; Psalm, no. 137, verses,
       no. 1-6; Reverie. See no. 3524
FERNANDES, Gaspar
    Eso rigor e repente. See no. 3707
FERNANDEZ HIDALGO, Gutierre
    Salve regina a 5. See no. 3707
FERNEYHOUGH, Brian
1413 Time and motion study, no. 2. KESSLER: Piano control. Smog. Wer-
      ner Taube, vlc; Vinko Globokar, trom; Jurg Wyttenbach, pno; Ex-
      perimental Studio of South West German Radio, Studio for Elec-
      tronic Music of the Basle Music Academy, Radio Symphony Orches-
      tra of the Basler Orchester-Gesellschaft; Jurg Wyttenbach.
      Musicaphon BM 30 SL 1715
           +-HFN 11-80 p117   +-RR 8-80 p41
1414 Transit. Rosemary Hardy, s; Linda Hurst, Elisabeth Harrison, ms;
      Peter Hall, t; Brian Etheridge, bar; Roderick Earle, bs; London
      Singfonietta; Elgar Howarth. Decca HEAD 18
           +-FF 3/4-80 p85   ++MM 3-79 p35
          ++Gr 12-78 p1142   +MT 6-79 p491
           +HF 4-80 p88   *RR 1-79 p58
          +HFN 12-78 p155   +STL 12-2-79 p37
FERNSTROM
1415 Trio, strings. ROSENBERG: Divertimento. Einar Sveinjornsson, vln;
      Ingvar Jonasson, vla; Guido Vecchi, vlc. Polydor 2474 101
          ++FF 7/8-80 p125
FERRABOSCO, Alfonso I
    Pavan. See no. 3966
FERRABOSCO, Alfonso II
    Almayne. See no. 3675
    Dovehouse pavan. See no. 3675
    Fantasy. See no. 4025
    Pavane. See no. 3593. See no. 3612
    Pieces for the lyra viol: Almaine; Coranto; Galliard. See no. 1139
    Songs: Fayre cruell nimph; Tell me o love. See no. 3879
FERRARI
    Pipele: Questa notte mentro a letto. See no. 3930
FERRARI, Benedetto
    Songs: Amar io ti consiglio; Amanti io vi so dire. See no. 3879
FESCH, Willem de
    Trio sonata, no. 4, G minor. See no. 310
    Tu fai la superbetta. See no. 3764
FESTA, Constanzo
    Quis dabit oculis nostris. See no. 3702
FESTING, Michael
    Largo, allegro, aria and 2 variations. See no. 3618
    FESTIVAL OF LESSONS AND CAROLS. See no. 3784
FEUERSTEIN, Robert
    Io. See no. 3642
    Philip and Eva. See no. 3642
    To thee. See no. 3642
    Transmutations, nos. 1 and 2. See no. 3642
FEVRIER
    Monna Vanna: Ce n'est pas un vieillard. See no. 3774
FIALA, Joseph
1416 Quartet, strings, no. 2, F major. STAMITZ: Quartet, strings, op. 8,

no. 4, E flat major. VANHAL: Sonata, op. 3, G major. VRANICKY:
Quartet, strings, no. 3, F major. Musica da Camera, Prague.
Supraphon 111 2470
    +NR 12-80 p7

FIBICH, Zdenek
Poeme. See no. 3601
Poeme, op. 41, no. 4. See no. 3694
Romance, op. 10, B flat major. See no. 4009
1417 Symphony, no. 2, op. 38, E flat major. Brno PO; Jiri Waldhans.
Supraphon SQ 410 2165
        +-ARG 1-80 p28   +-HFN 3-79 p123
        +FF 9/10-79 p82   +-MT 2-80 p106
        +FU 9-79 p52   +RR 3-79 p69
        +-Gr 4-79 p1706   +St 4-80 p133
        +-HF 9-79 p118

FIEBRICH
Das silberne Kanderln. See no. 3711
FIELD, John
1418 Duos, piano. HUMMEL: Sonata, 2 pianos, op. 51, E flat major. SPOHR:
Waltz, 4 hands, op. 89. David Branson, Andrew Davies, pno. RCA
GL 2-5227 Tape (c) GK 2-5227
        +Gr 10-79 p675   +HFN 1-80 p123 tape
        +HFN 10-79 p167   +-RR 2-80 p98 tape
Fantasie, op. 3. See no. 4011
FILTZ, Anton
Concerto, violoncello, G major. See no. 3703
FINCK, Heinrich
Greiner zanner. See no. 4004
Greiner zanner; Ich stund an einem morgen; Ich wird erlost; Der
Ludel und der Hensel. See no. 3805
Instrumental pieces (3). See no. 3805
FINE, Irving
1419 Quartet, strings. KIRCHNER: Quartet, strings, no. 1. American Art
Quartet, Juilliard Quartet. CRI SD 395 (From Columbia ML 4843)
        +FF 3/4-80 p110   ++NYT 2-25-79 pD21
        +NR 3-79 p10   +SFC 4-6-80 p31
FINZI, Gerald
1420 Concerto, clarinet, op. 31. STANFORD: Concerto, clarinet, op. 80,
A minor. Thea King, clt; PhO; Alun Francis. Hyperion A 66001
        +Gr 11-80 p666   ++HFN 11-80 p117
1421 Dies natalis, op. 8. For St. Cecilia, op. 30. Philip Langridge, t;
LSO and chorus; Richard Hickox. Argo ZRG 896
        ++FF 3/4-80 p86   +RR 5-79 p96
        +Gr 5-79 p1921   ++St 2-80 p124
        +HFN 5-79 p119
For St. Cecilia, op. 30. See no. 1421
1422 In terra pax, op. 36. Introit, op. 6. Lo the full final sacrifice.
Magnificat. Norma Burrowes, s; John Shirley-Quirk, bar; Simon
Standage, vln; Richard Hickox Singers; London Sinfonia; Richard
Hickox. Argo ZRG 909
        +Gr 12-79 p1034   ++RR 2-80 p86
        +HFN 2-80 p93   ++STL 4-13-80 p39
        +MT 7-80 p444
Introit, op. 6. See no. 1422
Lo the full final sacrifice. See no. 1422

Magnificat. See no. 1422
1423 Songs (choral): All this night, op. 33. Elegies, op. 5 (3). God
     is gone up, op. 27, no. 2. Lo the full final sacrifice. Mag-
     nificat, op. 36. Partsongs, op. 17 (7). Exultate Singers; Gar-
     rett O'Brien, cond; Timothy Farrell, org. L'Oiseau-Lyre DSLO 32
                 +Gr 8-80 p251   +-HFN 9-80 p104

FISCHER, Johann Caspar
1424 Chaconne. Le parnasse musical: Uranie, Euterpe. Praeludium, nos.
     6, 8. William Christie, hpd. Harmonia Mundi HM 1026
                 ++FF 7/8-80 p85   ++NR 5-80 p13
                 +Gr 5-80 p1693   ++RR 5-80 p85
                 +-HFN 5-80 p121   ++St 10-80 p113
                 +MT 11-80 p711   +STL 4-13-80 p39

     Musikalisches Blumenbuschlein: Suite, no. 6, D major. See no. 4022
     Le parnasse musical: Uranie, Euterpe. See no. 1424
     Praeludium, nos. 6, 8. See no. 1424
     Ricercare for Advent, Quadragesima, Easter and Pentecost. See no.
     3757
FISCHER, L.
     Amoroso. See no. 3601
FISER, Lubos
1425 Sonata, piano, no. 4. KILLMAYER: An John Field. SCRIABIN: Etudes,
     op. 65, nos. 1-3. Sonata, piano, no. 10, op. 70. Volker Ban-
     field, pno. Wergo 60081
                 ++FF 9/10-80 p141   +MUM 12-80 p34
     FITZWILLIAM VIRGINAL BOOK: Pieces. See no. 3855
FLAGELLO
     Symphony of winds. See no. 3643
     FLAMENCO. See no. 3657
FLEGIER, Ange
     Le cor. See no. 3631. See no. 3904
FLEMING, Robert
1426 Divertimento. MONNIKENDAM: Concerto, organ and brass. MOZART:
     Church sonata, no. 15, K 336. PISTON: Partita, organ. Gerald
     Wheeler, org; Chamber Ensembles. Canadian Broadcasting Corpora-
     tion SM 292
                 /FF 7/8-80 p171
FLETCHER
     Festival toccata. See no. 162. See no. 3858
FLEURY, Andre
     Variations sur un Noel Bourguignon. See no. 4036
FLOTHUIS, Marius
     Pour le tombeau d'Orphee. See no. 3564
FLOTOW, Friedrich
     Allesandro Stradella: Arias. See no. 3539
     Alessandro Stradella: Jungfrau Maria. See no. 3641
     Alessandro Stradella: Seid mener Wonne. See no. 3770
     Martha: Ach so fromm. See no. 4031
     Martha: Arias. See no. 3539
     Martha: Canzone del porter. See no. 3979
     Martha: Chi me dira; Ja seit fruhester Kindheit Tagen. See no. 3770
     Martha: Letze Rose...Mein Los mit Dir zu Teilen; Die Herrin rastet
        dort...Mag der Himmel Euch vergeben; Der Lenz ist gekommen...
        Diese Hand die sich gewendet. See no. 3584
     Martha: M'appari. See no. 3945

Martha: Siam giunti o giovinette; Questo cameo e per voi; Che vuol
    dir cio; Presto presto andiam; T'ho raggiunta sciagurata. See no.
    3949
Martha: Solo profugo reietto. See no. 3946
FLOYD, Monty
    Blues, horn and piano. See no. 3842
FO (15th century Italy)
    Tua voisi esser sempre mai. See no. 3864
FODERL-HOCHMT-WERNER
    In Grinzing gibt's a Himmelstrass'n. See no. 3711
FODOR, Carel
    Symphony, no. 4, op. 19, C minor. See no. 3818
FOLK
    Jungfru Maria till Betlehem gick. See no. 3934
FOLQUET DE MARSELHA
    Sitot me vol; Vida. See no. 3749
FONTANA, Giovanni
    Madonna mia pieta. See no. 3683
    Sonata, 3 violini. See no. 3690
FONTEI, Niccolo
    Dio ti salvi pastor. See no. 3879
FOOTE, Arthur
    A night piece. See no. 399
FORD, Thomas
1427 The baggepipes. Musicke of sundrie kindes: Why not here. Pavan
    and galliard. JENKINS: Fantasias, G minor, D minor. LOCKE:
    Duos, C major, C minor. SIMPSON, C.: Divisions on a ground, G
    major, F major, E minor. Wieland and Sigiswald Kuijken, bs
    viols, vln; Robert Kohnen, hpd. Accent ACC 8014
            +-Gr 11-80 p697   +HFN 11-80 p127
    Musicke of sundrie kindes: Why not here. See no. 1427
    Pavan and galliard. see no. 1427
    Shut not sweet breast. See no. 3879
FORQUERAY, Antoine
1428 Suite, no. 1, D minor. Suite, no. 2, G major. Jordi Savall, Chris-
    tophe Coin, vla da gamba; Ton Koopman, hpd. Telefunken AP 6-
    42366 Tape (c) 4-42366
            +ARG 2-80 p50   *HF 2-80 p102 tape
            +FF 1/2-80 p170   +HFN 4-79 p119
            +Gr 6-79 p71   ++RR 4-79 p98
    Suite, no. 2, G major. See no. 1428
    Suite, no. 3, D major. See no. 1251
FORSTER, Christoph
    Sonata, oboe, C minor. See no. 3542
FORSTER, Joseph
1429 Cyrano de Bergerac, op. 55. CPhO; Vaclav Smetacek. Supraphon 110
    2456
            +-Gr 10-80 p496   +-HFN 10-80 p103
1430 Sonata, violin and piano, op. 117. JANACEK: Dumka, C minor. Rom-
    ance, E major. Sonaa, violin and piano. NEDBAL: Sonata, violin
    and piano, op. 9, B minor. NOVAK: Sonata, violin and piano, D
    minor. Josef Suk, vln; Jan Panenka, pno. Supraphon 111 2341/2
            +Gr 8-80 p239   ++RR 7-80 p82
            +HFN 7-80 p113   +SFC 1-27-80 p44
            +NR 4-80 p7   ++St 4-80 p87

FOSS, Lukas
  Three airs on O'Hara's angels. See no. 914
FOSTER, Stephen
  Jeanie with the light brown hair. See no. 3552. See no. 3788. See
    no. 3874
FRANCAIX, Jean
1431 Concerto, piano, D major. Rhapsody, viola and chamber orchestra.
    Suite, violin and orchestra. Claude Paillard-Francaix, pno;
    Susanne Lautenbacher, vln; Ulrich Koch, vla; Luxembourg Radio
    Orchestra; Jean Francaix. Turnabout TVS 34552 Tape (c) KTVC
    34552
                +Gr 1-80 p1146   ++RR 12-79 p54
                +-HFN 1-80 p106
  Quartet, saxophones. See no. 3718
1432 Quintet, winds. TAFFANEL: Quintet, winds, G minor. Vienna Wind
    Soloists. Decca SDD 555
                +Gr 3-80 p1404   ++RR 3-90 p76
                ++HFN 6-80 p106
  Rhapsody, viola and chamber orchestra. See no. 1431
  Suite, violin and orchestra. See no. 1431
FRANCESCHINI, Petronio
  Sonata, 2 trumpets and strings, D major. See no. 3779
FRANCHETTI, Alberto
  Germania: Ascolta io moriro. See no. 3774
  Germania: Studenti udite; Ah vieni qui...No non chiuder gli occhi
    vaghi. See no. 3946
FRANCISQUE, Antoine
  Courante. See no. 3676
  Pavane et bransles. See no. 3676
FRANCK, Andrew
1433 Arcadia. Sonata da camera. OLAN: Composition, clarinet and tape.
    Sonata, violin and piano. Robert Miller, pno; Linda Quan, Rolf
    Schulte, vln; Paul Dunkel, flt; Laura Flax, clt. CRI SD 491
                +ARG 11-80 p51   +NR 7-80 p6
  Sonata da camera. See no. 1433
FRANCK, Cesar
  Andante cantabile. See no. 4061
1434 Cantabile. Chorales, nos. 1-3. Rene Saorgin, org. Harmonia Mundi
    HM 1213
                +-HFN 2-80 p93   +-RR 2-80 p75
  Cantabile. See no. 659. See no. 1437
  Le chasseur maudit. See no. 720. See no. 3556. See no. 3557
  Chorale, A minor. See no. 659
  Chorales, nos. 1-3. See no. 1434. See no. 1437
  Chorales, no. 2, B minor. See no. 4038. See no. 4062
  Chorales, no. 3, A minor. See no. 8. See no. 3940
1435 Les Djinns. Symphonic variations. GRIEG: Concerto, piano, op. 16,
    A minor. Cristina Ortiz, pno; PhO; Vladimir Ashkenazy. HMV ASD
    3970 Tape (c) TC ASD 3960
                +Gr 11-80 p666   +HFN 12-80 p159
                ++HFN 11-80 p120
  Les Djinns. See no. 3556
  Les Eolides. See no. 3556
  Fantasia, A major. See no. 156. See no. 1437. See no. 4058
  Fantasia, op. 16, C major. See no. 1437

Final, op. 21, B flat major. See no. 1437

1436 Grande piece symphonique, op. 17. POULENC: Concerto, organ, timpani
and strings, G minor. Roger Nyquist, org; Orchestra; Lynn Shurtleff. Orion ORS 79346

+-ARG 4-80 p38   +-MU 2-80 p10
+CL 4-80 p14   +-NR 2-80 p4
+-FF 5/6-80 p131

Grande piece symphonique, op. 17. See no. 1437

Interlude symphonique de redemption. See no. 1437

1437 Organ works: Chorales, nos. 1-3. Cantabile. Fantasia, A major.
Fantaisie, op. 16, C major. Final, op. 21, B flat major. Grande
piece symphonique, op. 17. Interlude symphonique de redemption
(trans. Dupre). Piece heroique. Priere, op. 20. Pastorale, op.
19, E major. Prelude, fugue et variation, op. 18. Graham Steed,
org. Decca D165D3 (3)

+-Gr 12-80 p854   +-HFN 12-80 p137

Panis angelicus. See no. 3531. See no. 3961

Pastorale, op. 19, E major. See no. 212. See no. 1437

Piece heroique. See no. 659. See no. 1437. See no. 3571. See no.
3658. See no. 3728. See no. 3973

Prelude, chorale et fugue. See no. 255. See no. 1401

Prelude, fugue and variations. See no. 3994

1438 Prelude, fugue and variations, op. 18. GIGOUT: Grand choeur dialogue.
MULET: Carillon sortie. VIERNE: Symphony, no. 3, op. 28, F sharp
minor. John Rose, org. Towerhill T 1001

+ARG 1-80 p50   +MU 2-80 p10
+FF 9/10-80 p266

Prelude, fugue and variations, op. 18. See no. 1372. See no. 1437

Priere, op. 20. See no. 1437

Psalm, no. 150. See no. 3970

Psyche. See no. 1448

Psyche: Le sommeil de Psyche, Psyche enlevee par les zephyrs, Le
jardin d'Eros, Psyche et Eros. See no. 3557

1439 Quartet, strings, D major. Fitzwilliam Quartet. L'Oiseau-Lyre
DSLO 46

+Gr 5-80 p1678   ++RR 5-80 p76
++HFN 5-80 p121   ++STL 6-8-80 p38

Redemption. See no. 3556. See no. 3557

1440 Sonata, violin and piano, A major. SAINT-SAENS: Sonata, violin
and piano, no. 1, op. 75, D minor. Elmar Oliveira, vln; Jonathan
Feldman, pno. Columbia MX 35829

+-ARG 10-80 p46   +NYT 7-6-80 pD15
+FF 9/10-80 p193   +-SFC 7-27-80 p34
+-HF 9-80 p96   ++St 6-80 p121
+NR 7-80 p7

1441 Sonata, violin and piano, A major. STRAUSS, R.: Sonata, violin
and piano, op. 18, E flat major. Ulf Hoelscher, vln; Michel
Beroff, pno. EMI 1C 065 02995

+FF 5/6-80 p156

1442 Sonata, violin and piano, A major. GRIEG: Sonata, violin and piano,
no. 3, op. 45, C minor. Arthur Grumiaux, vln; Gyorgy Sebok, pno.
Philips 9500 568

+-ARG 2-80 p27   +-Gr 10-80 p511
+-FF 9/10-80 p120   ++HFN 10-80 p103
+FU 2-80 p45   +NR 1-80 p5

1443 Sonata, violin and piano, A major. WEBER: Sonata, piano, no. 2, A
     flat major. Aurele Nicolet, flt; Boris Berman, pno. Tudor 73028
          +Gr 11-80 p692   +-HFN 12-80 p137
     Sonata, violin and piano, A major. See no. 849. See no. 850. See
     no. 1219
1444 Songs: L'Emir de Bengador; Le mariage des roses; Lied; Nocturne;
     La procession; S'il est un charmant gazon; Le vase brise. LEKEU:
     Chanson de Mai; Poems: Sur une tombe, Ronde, Nocturne; Les pavots.
     Bruno Laplante, bar; Janine Lachance, pno. Calliope CAL 1870
          +-HFN 10-80 p103   +RR 7-80 p80
          +RR 8-80 p18
1445 Symphonic variations. SCHUMANN: Concerto, piano, op. 54, A minor.
     Ivan Moravec, pno; CPhO; Vaclav Neumann. Supraphon 410 2073
     (also Quintessence PMC 7153)
          ++FF 3/4-79 p113   ++MUM 10-80 p32
          ++FF 11/12-80 p170   ++NR 8-78 p7
          +-Gr 10-78 p682   +RR 8-78 p68
          ++HF 8-78 p86   ++St 4-79 p93
          ++HFN 8-78 p103
1446 Symphonic variations. Symphony, D minor. Ilse von Alpenheim, pno;
     RPO; Antal Dorati. Turnabout TVS 34663 Tape Vox (c) CT 2125
          /ARG 6-77 p24   +-NR 5-77 p2
          +HF 8-77 p82   +-RR 3-80 p53
          +-HFN 4-80 p104   +-St 6-77 p127
          +MJ 7-77 p70
     Symphonic variations. See no. 1435. See no. 3557
1447 Symphony, D minor. BRSO; Lorin Maazel. DG 2535 156 Tape (c) 3335
     156 (From SLPM 138693)
          ++Gr 4-76 p1598   +HFN 9-80 p116 tape
          +Gr 7-80 p141   +-RR 3-76 p39
          +HFN 3-76 p109   -RR 2-77 p97 tape
          +HFN 7-80 p115   +RR 6-80 p48
1448 Symphony, D minor. Psyche. PhO; Carlo Maria Giuliani. EMI (Japan)
     EAC 30295
          +-ARSC Vol 12, nos. 1-2, 1980 p88
1449 Symphony, D minor. COA; Edo de Waart. Philips 9500 605 Tape (c)
     7300 727
          +FF 9/10-80 p120   +NR 3-80 p3
          +-Gr 2-80 p1264   +-RR 2-80 p52
          +HFN 2-80 p93   +RR 5-80 p106
          +HFN 4-80 p121 tape   -SFC 11-18-79 p47
1450 Symphony, D minor. NBC Symphony Orchestra; Guido Cantelli. World
     Records SH 376 (From HMV ALP 1219) (also RCA 1-3005)
          +ARSC Vol 12, nos. 1-2   +-HFN 8-80 p97
                1980 p117   +RR 8-80 p42
          ++Gr 9-80 p334
     Symphony, D minor. See no. 877. See no. 1446. See no. 3557
FRANCK, Melchior
     Intrada. See no. 3569
     Pavane et galliarde. See no. 3754
FRANCO, Hernando
     Salve regina. See no. 3849
FRANCOUER, Francois
     Concertino, G minor. See no. 3942
1451 Suites, nos. 2 and 4. Symphonies du festin royal de Monseigneur

le Comte d'Artois. Maurice Andre, tpt; Jean-Francois Paillard
Orchestra; Jean-Francois Paillard. Erato STU 70316
+FF 5/6-80 p78
Symphonies du festin royal de Monseigneur le Comte d'Artois. See
no. 1451

FRANZ
Delight of melancholy. See no. 3769

FREDERICK II, King
Sonata, flute, no. 48, E minor. See no. 90
Symphony, D major. See no. 91

FREEDMAN, Harry
Mono, solo horn. See no. 3842

FREIRE
Songs: ay ay ay; El nino perdido; Yo quisiera. See no. 3888

FRESCOBALDI, Girolamo
Air with variations. See no. 3825
Ave maris stella. See no. 1394
Bergamasca. See no. 1394
1452 Capricci, Bk 1, 1624. Harry van de Kamp, bar; Gustav Leonhardt,
hpd, org. Harmonia Mundi 157 99835/6 (2)
+HFN 5-80 p121   ++RR 5-80 p86
Galiarda. See no. 599
Mass of the virgin. See no. 1394
Ricarcare. See no. 1116. See no. 1141
Ricercar decimo on La, fa, sol, la, re. See no. 3762
Se l'aura spira. See no. 3997
Sonnetti spirituali: Ohime che fur che sono; Dove sparir si ratto i
di serani; Maddalena alla croce. See no. 3546
Toccata. See no. 145. See no. 1116
Toccatas, nos. 4, 6. See no. 3762
Toccata avanti il ricercare. See no. 1141

FREUNDT, Cornelius
Wie schon singt uns der Engel Schar. See no. 3697

FRICKER
A babe is born. See no. 3823

FRIDAY/TOUSSAINT/TYLER
Java. See no. 3962

FRIDERICI, Daniel
Ladilom. See no. 3814

FRIEDELL
The way to Jerusalem. See no. 4059

FROBERGER, Johann
1453 Fantasia, no. 3, E minor. Lamentations for Ferdinand III. Toccat-
as, nos. 3, 10, 12. Suites, nos. 1, 15, 20. Gustav Leonhardt,
hpd. Harmonia Mundi HM 20360 (also 1C 065 99819) (From RCA VICS
1494)
++FF 5/6-80 p78   +HFN 6-79 p107
++Gr 7-79 p229   +RR 5-79 p84
Gigue. See no. 3549. See no. 3775
Lamentation for Ferdinand III. See no. 1453
Suite, D major. See no. 3751
Suites, nos. 1, 15, 20. See no. 1453
Toccatas, nos. 3, 10, 12. See no. 1453

FROHNE, Vincent
Study, solo clarinet, op. 17. See no. 988

FRUMERIE, Gunnar de
1454 Chaconne. Lyric intermezzo. Suite, no. 1. ROSENBERG: Plastic
     scenes. Suite 1924. Rolf Lindblom, pno. Proprius 7820
          /FF 5/6-80 p142
     Lyric intermezzo. See no. 1454
1455 Musica per nove, op. 75. Puck. Trio, piano, no. 2, op. 45. Esther
     Bodin, Kerstin Hindart, pno; Mircea Saulesco, Bernt Lysell, vln;
     Leo Winland, Ake Olofsson, vlc; Torlief Lannerholm, ob; Ulf
     Nilsson, clt; Tore Ronneback, bsn; Mark Schrello, tpt; Gideon
     Roehr, vla; Thorsten Sjogren, double bs. Caprice CAP 1170
          +FF 11/12-80 p112   +NR 12-80 p7
     Suite, no. 1. See no. 1454
     Trio, piano, no. 2, op. 45. See no. 1455
FRYE, Wlater
     Tout a par moy. See no. 3880. See no. 4042
FUCIK, Julius
     Florentiner, op. 214. See no. 4012
FUCITO
     Scordame. See no. 3983
FUENTES,   de
     Tu habanera. See no. 3869
FUKAI, Shiro
1456 Parodic movements (4). KIYOSE: Japanese festival dances. OHKI:
     Night meditation. YAMADA: Mandara no hara. Takanori Kobayashi,
     pno; Yomiuri Nippon Symphony Orchestra; Shigenobu Yamaoka. Varese
     VX 81061
          +-ARG 12-78 p53   +HFN 1-80 p117
          +FF 11/12-78 p58   +RR 1-80 p74
FUKUSHIMA, Kazuo
     Chu-U Mei: 3 pieces. See no. 1457
     Ekagra. See no. 1457
     Kadha-Karuna, version no. 2. See no. 1457
     Mei. See no. 3629
     Requiem. See no. 1457
     Shun-San. See no. 1457
1457 Works, selections: Chu-U Mei: 3 pieces. Ekagra. Kadha-Karuna,
     version, no. 2. Requiem. Shun-San. Robert Aitken, flt; Yuji
     Takahashi, pno. Denon OX 7136
          +FF 1/2-80 p85
FULKERSON, James
     Music, brass instruments III. See no. 1119
FURSTENAU, Anton
     Rondo brillant, op. 38. See no. 3782
FUX, Johann
     Ad te domine levavi. See no. 3763
     Chaconne, D major. See no. 271
     Gli ossequi della notte: Caro mio ben. See no. 3729
     Harpeggio e fuga, G major. See no. 271
1458 Partie, G minor. KERLL: Toccata, nos. 1 and 3. Canzona, no. 1, D
     minor. Canzona, C major. PACHELBEL: Chaconne, C major. WAGEN-
     SEIL: Divertimento, F major. Bradford Tracey, hpd, org. Toccata
     FSM 53626
          +HFN 5-80 p131
1459 Partita, no. 7, F major. KIRNBERGER: Sonata, flute, G major.
     QUANTZ: Trio sonata, C major. TELEMANN: Sonata, flute, E minor.

Manfred Harras, rec; Konrad Hunteler, flt; Martha Gmunder, hpd;
Roswitha Friedrich, vla da gamba. Musicaphon BM 30 SL 1921
          +FF 9/10-80 p280   +HFN 7-80 p114
1460 Partita, harpsichord, A major. Partita, 2 violins, G minor. Sin-
       fonia, F major. Suite, G major. Jorg-Wolfgang Jahn, Gudrun
       Hehrmann, vln; Jurgen Wolf, vlc; Manfred Peters, rec; Adolf
       Meidhof, ob; Ernst Prappacher, bsn; Marga Scheurich, Hans Schmidt,
       hpd. Musical Heritage Society MHS 4046 (also Da Camera SM 192802.
       Impromptu 192802, CMS/Oryx 1717)
                   /FF 1/2-80 p85
    Partita, 2 violins, G minor. See no. 1460
    Sinfonia, F major. See no. 1460. See no. 3547
    Suite, A minor. See no. 271
    Suite, G major. See no. 1460
GABRIEL-MARIE
    La cinquantaine. See no. 3998
GABRIELI, Andrea
    Canzona. See no. 1116
    Canzona francese. See no. 3546. See no. 4021
    Ricercar del duodecimo tuono. See no. 4000
    Ricercar del sesto tuono. See no. 3675
    Toccata del 10 tuono. See no. 3813
GABRIELI, Domenico
    Sonata, trumpet and strings. See no. 3716
GABRIELI, Giovanni
    Benedixisti domine. See no. 3697
    Canzona. See no. 3813
    Canzona, no. 3. See no. 4000
    Canzona per sonare, no. 2. See no. 4001
    Canzona per sonare, nos. 4 and 5. See no. 3675
    Canzona per sonare "La spiritata". See no. 3675
    Canzona prima a cinque. See no. 4043
    Sonata, violini. See no. 3690
    Toccata del 2 tuono. See no. 3813
GADE, Niels
1461 A folk tale (Hartmann). Tivoli Symphony Orchestra; John Frandsen.
       EMI 6C 165 39320/1 (2)
                +-Gr 8-80 p216   +RR 7-80 p53
    Jalousie. See no. 3962
    Three tone pieces, op. 22. See no. 1372
GAGLIANO, Marco da
    Bel pastor. See no. 3879
    Pastor levate su. See no. 3546
GAGNEBIN, Henri
    Carillon. See no. 3734
    Psalm, no. 89. See no. 3734
GALILEI, Michelangelo
    Fantasia, lute. See no. 3997
GALILEI, Vincenzo
    Studies, guitar (6). See no. 355
GALINDO, Dimas Blas
    Sones de Mariachi. See no. 1025
GALLES, Jose
    Sonata, guitar, C major. See no. 3642
    Sonata, guitar, E major. See no. 3816

GALLON
1462 Cantabile. MARTINU: Sonatina. REGER: Sonata, clarinet and piano,
        op. 107, B flat major. John Norton, clt; Gary Wolf, pno. Golden
        Crest RE 7084
                  +ARG 10-80 p82   +Audio 11-80 p84
GALLOT, Jacques
        Le bout de l'an de M. Gaultier. See no. 4013
        Dauphine, gavotte. See no. 4013
        La divine, sarabande. See no. 4013
        Le Doge de Venice, chaconne sans chanterelle. See no. 4013
        Prelude. See no. 4013
        Tombeau de Madame, courante. See no. 4013
        Le tombeau de muses, allemande. See no. 4013
GALLUS, Jacobus
        Pueri concinite. See no. 3814
GALUPPI, Baldassare
1463 Magnificat, G major. VIVALDI: Gloria, D major. Ana-Maria Miranda,
        s; Ria Bollen, ms; Bern Chamber Choir; Southwest German Chamber
        Orchestra; Jorg Ewald Dahler. Claves D 801
                  +-Gr 7-80 p157
1464 Passatempo al cembalo: Sonatas, nos. 1-6. Jorg Ewald Dahler, hpd.
        Claves D 603
                  +Gr 7-80 p157   +-HFN 6-80 p106
        Trio sonata, G major. See no. 3543
GAMBARDELLA
        Nun me guardate chiu. See no. 3981
        O Marenariello. See no. 3667
GANNE
        Extase. See no. 3870
GANNE, Louis
        Marche Lorraine. See no. 4012
GARANT, Serge
1465 Works, selections: Anerca. Asymetries pour piano. Caprices. Cage
        d'oiseau. Circuits II. ...chants d'amour. Concerts sur terre.
        Et je prierai ta grace. Jeu a quatre. Offrande I, III. Piece
        pour piano, nos. 1 and 2. Phrases. Various performers. Radio
        Canada International unnumbered (4)
                  +-MUM 3/4-80 p32
GARCIA, Russ
1466 Variations, flugelhorn, string quartet, bass and drums. Chuck Find-
        ley, flugelhorn; Di Vinci Quartet; Bob Magnusson, double-bs;
        Steve Schaeffer, drums. Trend TR 522
                  +NR 11-80 p5
GARCIMUNOS
        Pues bien para esta. See no. 4002
GARDINER, Henry Balfour
        Evening hymn. See no. 4019
GARDNER, John
        Songs: Fight the good fight; Tomorrow shall be my dancing day. See
        no. 3527
GARSI DA PARMA, Santino
        La Lisfeltina. See no. 3956
GART, John
        Vivo. See no. 3651

GASPAR, Fernandes
     Songs. Motets.   See no. 3708
GASTALDON, Stanislao
     Musica proibita.   See no. 3771
GASTOLDI, Giovanni
     Amor in Nachen.   See no. 3662
GAUBERT, Philippe
     Madrigal.   See no. 3885
     Sonata, flute and piano, no. 1, A major.   See no. 3854
GAULTIER, Denis
     Le chevre, canaries.   See no. 4013
     Cleopatre amante, courante.   See no. 4013
     Tombeau de Mademoiselle Gaultier.   See no. 4013
GAULTIER, Ennemond
     Canaries.   See no. 4013
     Courante.   See no. 4013
     Prelude.   See no. 4013
     Testament de Mezangeau, gigue.   See no. 4013
     Tombeau de Mezangeau.   See no. 4013
GAUNTLETT
     Once in royal David's city.   See no. 3823
GAUTIER DE CHATILLON
     Ver pacis apperit.   See no. 3960
GAUTIER DE COINCY
1467 Les miracles de Notre-Dame.   Ensemble Guillaume de Machaut.   Arion
     ARN 38347
          +RR 3-80 p32
GAY, John and John Pepusch
1468 The beggar's opera.   Angela Jenkins, Shirley Minty, Margaret Cable,
     Elizabeth Lane, Patricia Clark, Nigel Rogers, Edgar Fleet, John
     Noble, Peter Hall, Vernon Midgley, soloists; Elisabeth Perry,
     vln; Sarah Francis, ob; Peter Vel, vlc; Leslie Pearson, hpd;
     Accademia Monteverdiana Orchestra and Chorus; Denis Stevens.
     Musical Heritage Society MHS 4011/2 (2) 9also ABC AX 67046/2)
          +-ARG 10-79 p10   +-HF 2-80 p85
          +-FF 9/10-79 p86   +NR 1-80 p8
          +FF 1/2-80 p86   +SFC 10-14-79 p41
1469 The beggar's opera (arr. Austin).   Sylvia Nelis, s; Violet Marques-
     ita, s; Kathleen Hilliard, ms; Nellie Walker, con; Frederic
     Austin, bar; Alfred Heather, t; Frederick Ranalow, bar; Hammer-
     smith Lyric Theatre Orchestra and Chorus.   WRC RTRM 501
          +HFN 12-80 p140
GAZAROSSIAN
     Prelude.   See no. 3851
GEBAUR
1470 Trio, bassoon, violin and violoncello, op. 33, no. 3.   MOZART: Son-
     ata, bassoon and violoncello, K 292, B flat major.   REICHA:
     Quintet, bassoon and strings.   VILLA-LOBOS: Ciranda das sete
     notas.   Arthur Grossman, bsn; Veda Reynolds, Irwin Eisenberg,
     vln; Alan Iglitzin, vla; Charles Brennard, vlc; James Harnett,
     bs.   Musical Heritage Society MHS 3862
          +FF 9/10-80 p282
GEEHL, Henry
     For you alone.   See no. 3946

GELALIAN
    Andantino. See no. 3851
GEMINIANI, Francesco
    Concerto grosso, D minor. See no. 3691
    Concerto grosso, op. 2, no. 4, D major. See no. 3547
1471 Sonatas, guitar, nos. 1-4, 6, 10. Laszlo Karper, gtr; Ede Banda,
        vlc; Janos Sebestyen, hpd. Hungaroton SXLP 12013
                    +ARG 4-80 p23   ++NR 4-80 p8
                    +FF 3/4-80 p87
    Sonata, oboe, no. 1, E minor. See no. 3542
GENIN, Paul Agricola
    It is raining shepherdess, op. 3. See no. 1167
GENTIAN (15th century France)
    Je suis Robert. See no. 3741
GEORGES, Alexandre
    Miarka: L'Eau qui nourt; Nuages. See no. 3632
GERHARD, Roberto
1472 Sketches (2). LAMONT DE GRIGNON: Preludes (3). MOMPOU: Song and
        dance, no. 3. ROSENBERG: Plastic scenes. Sonata, piano, no. 1.
        Jose Ribera, pno. Caprice 1172
                    +FF 5/6-80 p142
GERLE
    Ach Elslein liebes Elselein. See no. 3590
GERMAN, Edward
    Have you news of my boy Jack. See no. 4071
    My bonnie lass. See no. 3527
GERMANI, Fernando
    Toccata. See no. 4063
GERSHWIN, George
1473 An American in Paris. Rhapsody in blue. Josef Hala, pno; Slovak
        Philharmonic Orchestra; Dennis Burkh. Musical Heritage Society
        MHS 4158
                    +FF 9/10-80 p122
    An American in Paris. See no. 1476
    Bidin' my time. See no. 1479
    But not for me. See no. 1479
    Concerto, piano, F major. See no. 1476
    Concerto, piano, F major: Finale, excerpt. See no. 3882
    Cuban overture. See no. 1476
    Embraceable you. See no. 1479
1474 Fantasy on Porgy and Bess (arr. Grainger). Song fantasy: S' wonder-
        ful; I loves you Porgy; I got rhythm; Love walked in; Foggy day;
        Liza (arr. Phillips and Renzulli). Robert Phillips, Franco Ren-
        zulli, pno. Crystal Clear CCS 6002
                    +ARG 4-80 p50   +St 1-80 p95
                    -FF 11/12-79 p16
    Fascinatin' rhythm. See no. 1479
    Funnay face: Overture. See no. 1478
    Girl crazy: Overture. See no. 1475. See no. 1478
    I got rhythm. See no. 1479. See no. 3882
    Let em eat cake: Overture. See no. 1478
    Liza. See no. 1479
    Love is sweeping the country. See no. 1479
    Love walked in. See no. 1479
    Lullaby. See no. 1476

The man I love. See no. 1479
Of thee I sing: Overture. See no. 1475. See no. 1478
Oh Kay: Overture. See no. 1475. See no. 1478
Oh lady be good. See no. 1479
1475 Overtures: Girl crazy. Of the I sing (arr. Don Rose). Oh Kay. A
     portrait of George (arr. Frank Proto). Tiptoes. Cincinnati
     Pops Orchestra; Erich Kunzel. Turnabout TV 34749
                    -ARG 2-80 p28   +SFC 11-25-79 p46
                    +FF 3/4-80 p88
1476 Piano works: An American in Paris. Concerto, piano, F major. Cuban
     overture. Lullaby. Porgy and Bess: Suite. Promenade. Rhapsody
     in blue. Rhapsody, no. 2. Variations on "I got rhythm". Jef-
     fry Siegel, pno. St. Louis Symphony Orchestra; Leonard Slatkin.
     Vox SVBX 5132 Tape (c) CBX 5132, CT 2122 (also Turnabout TV
     37080/2)
                    +-Gr 7-75 p176   +-NR 12-74 p2
                    /HF 4-75 p85   +RR 6-75 p36
                    +HF 11-77 p138 tape   +SFC 10-27-74 p3
                    +HF 4-80 p104 tape   ++St 2-75 p110
                    +-HFN 6-75 p88   +St 3-80 p107 tape
Porgy and Bess: Suite. See no. 1476
Porgy and Bess: Summertime. See no. 3718
A portrait of George: Overture. See no. 1475
Preludes (3). See no. 1478
Promenade. See no. 1476
Rhapsody, no. 2. See no. 1476. See no. 1478
1477 Rhapsody in blue. Songs: Blue blue blue; But not for me; Do do do;
     Embraceable you; I've got a crush on you; He loves and she loves;
     Land of the gay caballero; Love is here to stay; Lady be good;
     Love is sweeping the country; Mine; S' wonderful; Someone to
     watch over me; Strike up the band; Sweet and low-down. Gary
     Graffmann, Dick Hyman, pno; NYP; Zubin Mehta. Columbia JS 36020
                    +ARG 1-80 p28
Rhapsody in blue. See no. 35. See no. 1473. See no. 1476. See
     no. 3790. See no. 3915. See no. 3962
S' wonderful. See no. 1479
Someone to watch over me. See no. 1479
Song fantasy: S' wonderful; I loves you Porgy; I got rhythm; Love
     walked in; Foggy day; Liza. See no. 1474
Songs: Blue blue blue; But not for me; Do do do; Embraceable you;
     I've got a crush on you; He loves and she loves; Land of the gay
     caballero; Love is here to stay; Lady be good; Love is sweeping
     the country; Mine; S' wonderful; Someone to watch over me;
     Strike up the band; Sweet and low-down. See no. 1477
Tiptoes: Overture. See no. 1475
Variations on "I got rhythm". See no. 1476. See no. 3962
Wintergreen for president. See no. 1478
1478 Works, selections: Girl crazy. Funny face: Overture. Oh Kay:
     Overture. Let 'em eat cake: Overture. Of thee I sing: Overture.
     Preludes (3). Rhapsody, no. 2. Wintergreen for president.
     Ralph Votapek, pno; BPO; Arthur Fiedler. London SPC 21185 Tape
     (c) 5-21185 (also Decca PFS 4438)
                    +-ARG 2-80 p28   +NR 6-80 p5
                    +FF 11/12-79 p71   +-RR 10-79 p87
                    +-Gr 10-79 p720   ++SFC 11-25-79 p46

++HF 12-79 p96   +St 11-79 p106
+HFN 10-79 p153

1479 Works, selections: Bidin' my time. But not for me. Embraceable
you. I got rhythm. Fascinating rhythm. Liza (All the clouds'll
roll away). Love is sweeping the country. Love walked in. The
man I love. Oh lady be good. 'S wonderful. Someone to watch
over me. Frederick Fennell and His Orchestra. Mercury SRI 75127
(From PPS 6006)
+FF 11/12-79 p72   +SFC 7-29-79 p49
+NR 6-80 p5

GERVAISE, Claude
Branle. See no. 3754
Renaissance dances, nos. 1-6. See no. 3566

GESUALDO, Carlo
Gagliarda. See no. 3597

1480 Responsoria for Holy Week. Montserrat Escolania; Ireneu Segarra.
DG 2710 028 (3) (also 2723 062)
++FF 7/8-80 p86   +NR 5-80 p8
+Gr 1-80 p1187   ++NYT 8-17-80 pD18
+HF 12-80 p79   +RR 2-80 p87
++HFN 2-80 p93   ++STL 3-9-80 p41

1481 Responsoria: Sabbato sancto. Deller Consort; Alfred Deller. Musical Heritage Society MHS 4132
+HF 12-80 p79

GHEZZO, Dinu
Aphorisms. See no. 1412

GHISELIN, Johannes
La Alfonsina. See no. 4000

GHIZEGHEM, Hayne van
De tous biens playne (2). See no. 3597

GHORGHANIAN, Guenarios
Bayati. See no. 3850

GIAMBERTI, Giuseppe
O belle lagrimette. See no. 3546

GIANELLA, Luigi
1482 Concerto, flute, no. 1, D minor. Concerto lugubre, C minor (attrib.)
Concerto militaire, D major. Jean-Pierre Rampal, flt; I Solisti
Veneti; Claudio Scimone. Erato STU 70849
+HFN 4-80 p104   +RR 9-79 p89
Concerto lugubre, C minor. See no. 1482
Concerto militaire, D major. See no. 1482

GIANELLI
Olga: E io sapevi. See no. 3770

GIBBONS, Orlando
Alman (2). See no. 1485
Coranto. See no. 1485
The cries of London. See no. 3744
The fairest nymph. See no. 1485. See no. 3648. See no. 4044
Fantasia, A minor. See no. 4014
Fantasias, nos. 3, 9. See no. 3583
Fantasia, no. 8. See no. 1485
1483 Fantasias, 3 parts, nos. 1-10, 12, 14-15. In nomine a 4. Jordi
Savall, Christophe Coin, Sergei Casademunt, viols; Johannes
Sonnleitner, org. Astree AS 43
+FF 9/10-80 p122   ++RR 6-80 p78
+Gr 5-80 p1678

Fantasia, 4 parts. See no. 4052
Fantasias, tone 1 (2). See no. 1485
French air. See no. 1485
French coranto. See no. 1485
Ground. See no. 1485. See no. 3595
Ground, A minor. See no. 4014
Hosanna to the son of David. See no. 3532
In nomine. See no. 4025
In nomine a 4. See no. 1483
Italian ground. See no. 1485
Lady Hatton's galliard. See no. 1485
Lord of Salisbury's pavan and galliard. See no. 3648
Lord Salisbury's pavan and galliard. See no. 4044
O clap your hands together. See no. 3783. See no. 3937
Pavan. See no. 3855
Pavan, tone 3. See no. 1485
Pavan and galliard, tone 1. See no. 1485
Preludes, tones 3 and 8. See no. 1485
The queen's command. See no. 3853
The secret sins. See no. 3525
The silver swan. See no. 3867

1484 Songs: Hosanna to the son of David; I am the resurrection; Lord we
     beseech thee; O clap your hands; O Lord in thy wrath; Praise the
     lord, O my soul; See see the word is incarnate. Hymns and songs
     of the church, nos. 1, 3-5, 9, 13, 18, 20, 22, 24, 31, 47, 67.
     Clerkes of Oxenford; David Wulstan. Nonesuch H 71374
                    +—ARG 10-80 p50   +NR 7-80 p11
                    +—FF 9/10-80 p123   +—NYT 8-10-80 pD17
     Songs (madrigals): Ah dear heart; O that the learned poets; The
     silver swan; What is our life. See no. 3893
     Songs (anthems): Hosanna to the son of David; O Lord in thy wrath
     rebuke me not. See no. 3894
     A voluntary. See no. 3595
     Welcome home, mask. See no. 1485
     When I was one and twenty. See no. 3837
     Whoop do me no harm good man. See no. 1485
     The woods so wild. See no. 1485. See no. 3648. See no. 4044

1485 Works, selections: Alman (2). Coranto. The fairest nymph, mask.
     Fantasias, tone 1 (2). Fantasia, no. 8. French air. French
     coranto. Ground. Italian ground. Lady Hatton's galliard.
     Pavan, tone 3. Pavan and galliard, tone 1. Preludes, tone 3
     and 8. Welcome home, mask. Whoop do me no harm good man. The
     woods so wild. Joseph Payne, hpd. Musical Heritage Society MHS
     4090
                    +FF 7/8-80 p87   +St 5-80 p94

GIBSON, Robert
     Quintet, winds. See no. 3731
GIDEON, Miriam
     Nocturnes. See no. 789
     The season of time. See no. 650
     Songs of youth and madness. See no. 789
GIGOUT, Eugene
     Grand choeur dialogue. See no. 1438. See no. 3618. See no. 3660.
     See no. 3735. See no. 3958
     Minuetto. See no. 752

Pieces, organ, no. 4, B minor: Toccata. See no. 4034
Rhapsodie sur des noels. See no. 3836
Toccata. See no. 3658
Toccata, B minor. See no. 3783
GILBERT, John
    Suonare. See no. 1412
GILBERT, Pia
    Interrupted suite. See no. 761
    Transmutations. See no. 761
GILES, Nathaniel
    Cease now vain thoughts. See no. 4025
GILLES, Jean
1486 Te deum. Jeunesses Musicales de France Chorale; Marie-Claire Alain,
    org; Francoise Petit, hpd; Pasdeloup Orchestra; Louis Martini.
    Musical Heritage Society MHS 554
                +MU 4-80 p10
GILLIS, Don
    En sueno. See no. 3841
    The joust. See no. 3841
GIMENEZ, Jeronimo
1487 El baile de Luis Alonso. MOLLEDA: Triptico. TORROBA: Estampas:
    Danza rapsodica (rev. Modina). Celedonio, Pepe, Angel and Celin
    Romero, gtr. Philips 9500 296
                +Gr 3-80 p1568   ++RR 4-80 p96
                +HFN 4-80 p116   +St 10-78 p170
                +-MJ 3/4-79 p46
GINASTERA, Alberto
    Cancion al arbol del Olvido. See no. 3717
    Estancia: Danza final. See no. 3955
1488 Estancia suite. RAVEL: Bolero. SHOSTAKOVICH: Festive overture, op.
    96. WEINBERGER: Schwanda the bagpiper: Polka and fugue. LSO;
    Morton Gould. ;Chalfont SDG 301
                +-ARG 11-79 p31   +St 10-79 p92
                +HF 11-79 p115   +-St 11-80 p94
                ++HFN 1-80 p115
    Panambi: Suite. See no. 666. See no. 3969
1489 Quartet, strings, no. 1, op. 20. TURINA: Quartet, piano, A minor.
    Philarte Quartet. Gasparo GS 201
                ++ARG 11-79 p26   ++FF 1/2-80 p86
1490 Quartet, strings, no. 1, op. 20. PROKOFIEV: Quartet, strings, no.
    1, B minor. Blair Quartet. QCA/Red Mark RM 3105
                +-NR 8-80 p8   ++St 11-80 p88
    Sonata, piano. See no. 3622
GIORDANO, Umberto
    Andrea Chenier: Colpito que m'avete...Un di all'azzurro spazio;
    Come un bel di di maggio; Si fui soldato. See no. 3671
    Andrea Chenier: Come un bel di di maggio. See no. 3827
    Andrea Chenier: Come un bel di di maggio; Un di all'azzurro spazio.
    See no. 3774
    Andrea Chenier: La mamma morta. See no. 3789
    Andrea Chenier: Nemico della patria. See no. 3771. See no. 3888.
    See no. 3925
1491 Andrea Chenier: Un di all'azzuro spazio. MEYERBEER: L'Africaine:
    O paradiso. PUCCINI: La fanciulla del West: Ch'ella mi creda.
    Madama Butterfly: Addio fiorita asil. Manon Lescaut: Ah non

v'avvicinate. Turandot: Nessun dorma. VERDI: Otello: Esultate;
Gia nella notte; Ora per sempre; Si per ciel; Dio mi potevi scag-
liar; Niun mi tema. Rigoletto: Parmi veder. Giacomo Lauri-
Volpi, t; Various Orchestras and Conductors. Preiser LV 260
        +FF 5/6-80 p172
Andrea Chenier: Un di all'azzuro spazio. See no. 3945
Andrea Chenier: Un di all'azzuro spazio; Un di m'era di gioia. See
    no. 3770
1492 La cena dell beffe. Soloists; RAI Symphony Orchestra; Nino Bona-
        volonta. MRF Records MRF 147 (2)
        +FF 11/12-80 p112
    Fedora: Amor ti vieta. See no. 3671. See no. 3770
    Fedora: Amor ti vieta; Mia madre la mia vecchia madre; Vedi io
        piangi. See no. 3981
    Fedora: La Donna Russa. See no. 3771
    Siberia: Nel suo amor. See no. 3770
    Songs: Caro mio ben. See no. 3669
    Songs: Crepuscolo triste. See no. 3928
GIOVANNI DA CASCIA
    De come dolcemente. See no. 4032
GIROUST, Francois
    Le deluge. See no. 3844
GIULIANI, Mauro
1493 Concerto, guitar, op. 30, A major. RODRIGO: Fantasia para un gentil-
        hombre. Narciso Yepes, gtr; ECO; Garcia Navarro. DG 2530 975
        Tape (c) 3300 975
                +-FF 11/12-79 p165   +HFN 2-79 p103
                ++Gr 2-79 p1421   +RR 2-79 p63
                +HF 4-80 p104 tape
    Concerto, guitar, op. 30, A major. See no. 3612
    Grand overture, op. 61. See no. 1496
    La melanconia, op. 147, no. 7. See no. 1496
    Quintet, guitar. See no. 743
1494 Le Rossiniane, opp. 119 and 122. Variations, op. 7 (6). Variations
        on a theme by Handel, op. 107. Angel Romero, gtr. Angel SZ
        37326 Tape (c) 4ZS 37326
                +FF 5/6-80 p139   ++St 2-80 p127
                +NR 8-80 p14
1495 Sonata, flute and guitar, op. 85. LOEILLET: Sonata, flute, op. 1,
        A minor. VISEE: Suite, guitar. Jean-Pierre Rampal, flt; Rene
        Bartoli, gtr. Harmonia Mundi HMU 711 Tape (c) HM 40711
                +-Gr 9-80 p359   -RR 12-75 p83
                +HFN 7-80 p117   +RR 8-80 p71
    Sonata, guitar, op. 150, A major. See no. 1496
    Sonata, violin and guitar, op. 25, E minor. See no. 355
    Variations, op. 7 (6). See no. 1494
    Variations on a theme by Handel, op. 107. See no. 1494. See no.
        1496
    Variations on "I bin a Kohlbauern Bub", op. 49. See no. 1496
1496 Works, selections: Grande overture, op. 61. La melanconia, op. 147,
        no. 7. Sonata, op. 150, A major. Variations on a theme by Han-
        del, op. 107. Variations on "I bin a Kohlbauern Bub", op. 49.
        Pepe Romero, gtr. Philips 9500 513 Tape (c) 7300 660
                ++ARG 3-79 p25   +HFN 8-80 p109 tape
                +FF 5/6-80 p139   +HFN 10-80 p117 tape

```
        +Gr 4-80 p1571              +NR 2-79 p15
        +Gr 8-80 p275 tape         +-RR 4-90 p95
        +HFN 4-80 p104             ++St 5-79 p99
```

GLASS, Philip
1497 Dances, nos. 1 and 3. Philip Glass Ensemble. Tomato TOM 8029
         +FF 11/12-80 p113
GLAZUNOV, Alexander
1498 Birthday offering, excerpts (arr. Irving). LECOCQ: Mam'zelle Angot
        (arr. Jacob). RPO; Robert Irving. HMV ESD 7080 Tape (c) TC ESD
        7080 (From CLP 1140, CSD 1252)
                ++Gr 11-79 p918   ++RR 11-79 p84
                +HFN 1-80 p121   +RR 7-80 p97 tape
                +HFN 2-80 p107 tape
    Carnival overture, op. 45. See no. 1502
1499 Concerto, piano, no. 2, op. 100, B major. Concerto, violin, op. 82,
        A minor. Meditation, violin. Ruggiero Ricci, vln; Michael Ponti,
        pno; PH, Westphalian Symphony Orchestra; Reinhard Peters, Sieg-
        fried Landau. Turnabout QTS S 34621
                +Audio 1-77 p84   +-RR 11-79 p80
                +Gr 11-79 p817   ++SFC 7-25-76 p29
                /-HFN 1-80 p106   +-ST 3-80 p837
                +-NR 5-76 p6
1500 Concerto, violin, op. 82, A minor. KHACHATURIAN: Concerto, violin.
        Eugene Fodor, vln; LSO; Eduardo Mata. RCA ARL 1-2954
                +FF 9/10-80 p123   +SFC 3-11-79 p49
                ++MJ 9/10-79 p51   +-St 10-79 p139
                +-NR 4-79 p5
    Concerto, violin, op. 82, A minor. See no. 918. See no. 1499.
        See no. 3964. See no. 3968
    Cortege solennel, op. 91, G major. See no. 342
1501 In memory of Gogol, op. 87. The Kremlin, op. 30. Stenka Razin,
        op. 13. Bamberg Symphony Orchestra; Aldo Ceccato. RCA RL 3-0323
                ++FF 9/10-80 p124
    The Kremlin, op. 30. See no. 1501
    Meditation. See no. 1499. See no. 3964
    Raymonda, op. 57: Valse grande adagio. See no. 3964
    Stenka Razin, op. 13. See no. 1501
1502 Symphony, no. 1, op. 5, E major. Carnival overture, op. 45. MRSO;
        S. Sherman, org; E. Akulov, Leo Ginzburg. Melodiya D 026137-38
                +-FF 1/2-80 p87
GLIERE, Reinhold
1503 Concerto, harp, op. 74, E flat major. REINECKE: Concerto, harp,
        op. 182, E minor. Catherine Michel, hp; Luxembourg Radio Orch-
        estra; Louis de Froment. Turnabout QTV 34721
                +-FF 5/6-79 p47   +NR 4-79 p6
                +Gr 4-80 p1554   +-RR 4-80 p63
                +-HFN 6-80 p106
    Intermezzo, op. 35, no. 11. See no. 3684
1504 The red poppy, op. 70. RIMSKY-KORSAKOV: The legend of Sadko, op. 5.
        SHOSTAKOVICH: The golden age, op. 22. Henry Siegl, vln; Seattle
        Symphony Orchestra; Milton Katims. Turanbout TVS 34644 Tape (c)
        KTVC 34644
                +Gr 3-80 p1386   +RR 3-80 p54
                +-HFN 4-80 p113
1505 The red poppy, op. 70, excerpts. Bolshoi Theatre Orchestra; Yuri
        Fayer. Musical Heritage Society MHS 4193

+FF 11/12-80 p113
1506 The red poppy, op. 70: Sailor's dance. IPPOLITOV-IVANOV: Caucasian
     sketches, op. 10. RIMSKY-KORSAKOV: Symphony, no. 2, op. 9.
     Orchestra; Maurice Abravanel. Vanguard C 10060 Tape (c) D 10060
          -+HF 2-80 p102 tape
     The red poppy, op. 70: Sailor's dance. See no. 3882
1507 Symphony, no. 3, op. 42, B minor. RPO; Harold Farberman. Unicorn
     PCM 500/1 (2) Tape (r) Barclay-Crocker UNC M 0500 (c) UKC 500-1
          +ARG 2-80 p29   +HF 1-80 p91 tape
          +ARG 4-80 p24 tape   +HFN 11-80 p131 tape
          +FF 5/6-80 p82   +NYT 9-7-80 pD29
          +FF 11/12-80 p114 tape   +St 3-80 p94
          +-Gr 12-80 p889 tape

GLINKA, Mikhail
     Jota aragonesa. See no. 1510
     A life for the Tsar: I do not grieve about that dear friends; I look
       into empty fields; They guess the truth. See no. 3770
     A life for the Tsar: Now I am alone; They guess the truth. See no.
       3904
     A life for the Tsar: Overture. See no. 337
1508 A life for the Tsar: Polonaise, Krakowiak, Pas de quatre. Prince
     Kholmsky: Overture, Entr'actes (4). Spanish overture, no. 2:
     Souvenir of a night in Madrid. Bamberg Symphony Orchestra; Aldo
     Ceccato. RCA RL 3-0320
          +ARG 4-80 p48   +NR 12-80 p3
     The midnight review. See no. 3905
1509 Nocturne. Variations on a theme by Mozart. LISZT: Etude de con-
     cert, no. 3, G 144, D flat major: Un sospiro (arr. Renie). The
     nightingale, G 250. RENIE: Contemplation. Legende. Piece sym-
     phonique. SPOHR: Fantasie, op. 35, A flat major. Susann Mc-
     Donald, hp. Klavier KS 543 (also DBS GS 2012)
          +ARG 5-80 p45   ++NR 10-75 p4
     Prince Kholmsky: Overture, Entr'actes (4). See no. 1508
     Russlan and Ludmila: Magic dances. See no. 337
     Russlan and Ludmila: O my Ratmir. See no. 3774
1510 Russlan and Ludmila: Overture. Waltz fantasie. Jota aragonesa.
     MUSSORGSKY: Khovanschina: Prelude; Dance of the Persian slaves.
     A night on the bare mountain. OSR; Ernest Ansermet. London STS
     15383
          +FF 9/10-80 p169
     Russlan and Ludmila: Overture. See no. 1317
     Russlan and Ludmila: Overture. See no. 3638
     Spanish overture, no. 2: Souvenir of a night in Madrid. See no.
       1508
     Variations on a theme by Mozart. See no. 1509
     Waltz fantasie. See no. 1510
GLUCK, Christoph
     Alceste: Divinites du Styx. See no. 3367. See no. 3931
     Alceste: J'enieve un tendre epoux. See no. 3770
     Begrogene Kadi: Arietta amorosa. See no. 3977
     Don Juan: Movements (4). See no. 1265
     Melodie Orpheus. See no. 3935
1511 Orfeo ed Euridice. Julia Hamari, Veronika Kincses, Maria Zempleni,
     s; HSOO and Chamber Chorus; Ervin Lukacs. Hungaroton SLPX
     12100/1 (2)
          +-Gr 12-80 p872

Orfeo ed Euridice: Away with mourning and crying. See no. 3770
Orfeo ed Euridice: Che faro senza Euridice. See no. 1512. See no.
3562
Orfeo ed Euridice: Dance; Minuet. See no. 3957
Orfeo ed Euridice: Dance of the blessed spirits. See no. 296. See
no. 3715. See no. 3951. See no. 4030
Orfeo ed Euridice: Malheureux qu'ai-je fait...J'ai perdu mon Euri-
dice. See no. 3926
Orfeo ed Euridice: Melodie. See no. 3772
Orfeo ed Euridice: Quest'asilo ameno e grato; Che fiero momento.
See no. 3584
Orfeo ed Euridice: Sposa Euridice...Che faro senza Euridice. See
no. 3560
1512 Paride ed Elena: O del mio dolce ardor. Orfeo ed Euridice: Che faro
senza Euridice. HANDEL: Alcina: Sta nell'ircana. MOZART: La
clemenza di Tito, K 621: Parto parto ma tu ben mio. Cosi fan
tutte, K 588: El parte...Per pieta. Le nozze di Figaro, K 492:
Voi che sapete. ROSSINI: Il barbiere di Siviglia: Una voce poco
fa. La cenerentola: Nacqui all affanno...Non piu mesta. L'
Italiana in Algeri: Cruda sorte; Amor tiranno. Teresa Berganza,
ms; ROHO, VSOO, LSO, Rossini Orchestra; Maggio Musicale Fioren-
tino; Alexander Gibson, Istvan Kertesz, John Pritchard, Richard
Bonynge, Silvio Varviso. Decca JB 98 Tape (c) KJBC 98
                +Gr 11-80 p736   +HFN 11-80 p129
Paride ed Elena: O del mio dolce ardor. See no. 3901
Paride ed Elena: Spiagge amate. See no. 3770. See no. 3774
1513 Symphonies, nos. 2, 4-5, 8. Cyril Diederich Instrumental Ensemble;
Cyril Diederich. Arion ARN 38445
                /-Gr 2-80 p1264   +RR 2-79 p63
GODARD, Banjamin
Jocelyn: Berceuse. See no. 3695. See no. 3770
Pieces, op. 116: Waltz. See no. 3951
Songs: Chanson d'Estelle; Embarquez-vous. See no. 3770
Songs: Embarquez-vous. See no. 3979
GODFREY, David
1514 A celebration. Character pieces (5). Trio, clarinet, viola and
horn. HERVIG: Sonata, clarinet and piano, no. 1. Quartet,
strings. Thomas Ayres, clt; James Avery, pno; William Preucil,
vla; Thomas Hundemer, hn; Stradivari Quartet. Orion ORS 79340
                +FF 1/2-80 p94
Character pieces. See no. 1514
Trio, clarinet, viola and horn. See no. 1514
GODOWSKY, Leopold
Alt Wien. See no. 3552. See no. 3788. See no. 3964
Studies on Chopin etudes, nos. 4, 13-15, 25-26, 33, 36, 45, 47-48.
See no. 1055
Symphonic metamorphosis on "Artist's life waltz". See no. 1055
Symphonic metamorphosis on themes from "Die Fledermaus". See no.
1055
Waltz, D major. See no. 3964
GOEDICKE
Etude, op. 28, no. 2. See no. 3650
GOEPPERT, Karl Andreas
Sonata, bassoon and guitar, op. 13, D major. See no. 1244

GOETZ, Hermann
    Francesca da Rimini. See no. 3824
    The taming of the shrew: Die Draft versagt. See no. 3931
GOLDBERG, Johann
    Trio, 2 violins and continuo, G minor. See no. 3845
GOLDMARK, Karl
    Concerto, violin, op. 28, A minor: Andante. See no. 3964
    Die Konigin von Saba: Magische Tone. See no. 3770. See no. 3946.
        See no. 4008
    Merlin: Overture. See no. 3824
1515 Symphony, no. 1, op. 26, E flat major (Rustic wedding). Pittsburgh
        Symphony Orchestra; Andre Previn. HMV ASD 3891 Tape (c) TC ASD
        3891 (also Angel SZ 37662 Tape (c) 4ZS 37662)
                    ++FF 11/12-80 p115   ++NR 11-80 p3
                    +Gr 8-80 p216   +NYT 9-7-80 pD29
                    +HFN 9-80 p104   ++RR 8-80 p42
                    +HFN 12-80 p159 tape   +St 12-80 p124
                    +MT 12-80 p785
    Ein Wintermarchen: O Menschengluck du gleischet der schwanken Blute.
        See no. 3774
GOLDSCHMIDT
    Im mai. See no. 3770
GOLDSTEIN, Malcolm
    A summoning of focus. See no. 993
GOLSON
    I remember Clifford. See no. 3626
GOMBERT, Nicolas
    Cantibus organicis; Fundite cantores; Servite domino; Venite filii.
        See no. 3806
GOMES, Antonio
    Lo schiavo: L'importuna insistenza; Quando nascesti tu. See no.
        3949
    Salvator Rosa: Die sposo. See no. 3930
GOODHART
    A fairy went a-marketing. See no. 3560
GOODWIN
    Frenzy. See no. 3786
GOOSSEN, Frederic
    Fantasy, aria and fugue. See no. 3859
GOOSSENS, Eugene
1516 Symphony, no. 1, op. 58. Adelaide Symphony Orchestra; David Meas-
        ham. Unicorn KP 8000
                    ++Gr 11-80 p666   ++HFN 11-80 p105
GORECKI, Henryk
    Ad matrem. See no. 3857
GORING-THOMAS, Arthur
    Esmeralda: O vision entrancing. See no. 3986
    Nadeshka: Dear love of mine. See no. 3903
    Nadeshka: My heart is weary. See no. 3774
    A summer night. See no. 3903
GORNER, Johann
    Songs: Der ordentliche Hausstand; Der Kuss. See no. 3764
GOSSEC, Francois
    Symphonie, 7 parties, F major. See no. 1517
1517 Symphony, op. 5, no. 1, F major. Symphony, op. 6, no. 5, G minor.

Symphonie, 7 parties, F major. Liege Symphony Orchestra; Jacques
Houtmann. Harmonia Mundi VMS 2076
+-FF 11/12-80 p116   +-FF 5/6-80 p85
Symphony, op. 6, no. 5, G minor. See no. 1517
GOSSWIN, Anton
Songs: Am Abend spat lieb Bruderlein. See no. 3536
GOTTSCHALK, Louis
Bamboula, op. 2. See no. 1519
La bananier, op. 5. See no. 1519. See no. 1520
The banjo, op. 15. See no. 1519
Berceuse, op. 47. See no. 1519
The dying poet. See no. 1519
La gallina, op. 53. See no. 1520
La jota aragonesa, op. 14. See no. 1520
Marche de nuit, op. 17. See no. 1520
Marche funebre, op. 61. See no. 1519
1518 Night in the tropics. HEINRICH: The ornithological combat of kings,
or The condor of the Andes and the eagle of the Cordilleras.
Anthony and Joseph Paratore, pno; Syracuse Symphony Orchestra;
Christopher Keene. New World Records NW 208
-ARG 3-79 p28   +NYT 1-14-79 pD19
+FF 3/4-80 p100   +St 4-79 p134
+MQ 4-79 p296
Ojos criollos, op. 37. See no. 1519. See no. 1520
Ouverture de Guillaume Tell (Rossini). See no. 1520
Pasquinade, op. 59. See no. 1519
1519 Piano works: Bamboula, op. 2. Le bananier, op. 5. The banjo, op.
15. Berceuse, op. 47. The dying poet. Marche funebre, op. 61.
Ojos criollos, op. 37. Pasquinade, op. 59. La scintilla, op.
20. Souvenir de Porto Rico. Tournament galop. Amiram Rigai,
pno. Folkways FSS 37485
+ARG 6-80 p20   +NR 3-80 p13
+FF 7/8-80 p87
1520 Piano works: La bananier, op. 5. La gallina, op. 53. La jota ara-
gonesa, op. 14. Marche de nuit, op. 17. Ojos criollas, op. 37.
Ouverture de Guillaume Tell (Rossini). Reponds-moi, op. 50.
Radieuse, op. 72. Ses yeux, op. 66. David and Deborah Apter,
pno. Musical Heritage Society MHS 3430
+ARG 7-77 p22   +CL 2-80 p9
+Audio 6-79 p125
Radieuse, op. 72. See no. 1520
Reponds-moi, op. 50. See no. 1520
La scintilla, op. 20. See no. 1519
Ses yeux, op. 66. See no. 1520
Souvenir de Porto Rico. See no. 1519
Tournament galop. See no. 1519
GOULD, Morton
Cotillion. See no. 1521
The curfew. See no. 4007
Fall River legend. See no. 1521
Festive music. See no. 1521
Latin American symphonette. See no. 1521
Latin American symphonette: Conga. See no. 3962
Philharmonic waltzes. See no. 1521. See no. 3860
Symphony on marching tunes, quickstep. See no. 1521

Windjammer: Main theme. See no. 4046
1521 Works, selections: Cotillion. Festive music. Fall River legend.
Latin American symphonette. Philharmonic waltzes. Symphony on
marching tunes, quickstep. LSO; Morton Gould. Varese VCDM
1000.10 DBX VCDM 1000.10

          ++FF 5/6-80 p83   ++St 2-80 p128
          +HFN 1-80 p106   +St 11-80 p94

GOUNOD, Charles
Ave Maria. See no. 3888. See no. 3938
Cinq-Mars: Sur les flots vous entraine. See no. 3770
1522 Faust. Mirella Freni, Michele Command, s; Jocelyne Taillon, ms;
Placido Domingo, t; Marc Vento, bs; Thomas Allen, bar; Nicolai
Ghiaurov, bs; Paris Opera Orchestra and Chorus; Georges Pretre.
HMV SLS 5170 (4) Tape (c) TC SLS 5170 (also Angel SZ DX 3868
Tape (c) 4Z4X 3868)

          ++ARG 1-80 p31   +NYT 9-30-79 pD22
          +FF 1/2-80 p88   +ON 3-15-80 p45
          +FU 2-80 p45   +Op 12-79 p1168
          +Gr 9-79 p508   +RR 9-79 p48
          +-HF 1-80 p79   +RR 6-80 p94 tape
          +HFN 10-79 p153   ++SFC 9-23-79 p37
          +HFN 12-79 p185 tape   +St 12-79 p142
          +HFN 2-80 p107 tape

1523 Faust: Ballet music. SAINT-SAENS: Samson et Delila: Ballet music.
VERDI: Aida: Ballet music. WAGNER: Tannhauser: Venusberg music.
Slovak Philharmonic Orchestra; Dennis Burkh. Opus 9110 0770
          +NR 10-80 p3
Faust: Ballet music. See no. 665. See no. 3666
Faust: C'est ici...Salut demeure chaste et pure. See no. 4031
Faust: Faites lui mes aveux; Ah je ris. See no. 3774
Faust: Gloire immortelle de nos adieux. See no. 3553
Faust: Il etait un Roi de Thule; Air des Bijoux. See no. 3985
Faust: Il se fait tard. See no. 3792
Faust: Le veau d'or; Ebben che ti pare...Io voglio il piacer. See
    no. 3899
Faust: Le veau d'or; Serenade. See no. 3927
Faust: O nuit d'amour. See no. 3830
Faust: O santa medaglia...Dio possente. See no. 3901
Faust: Rien...En vain j'interroge en mon ardente veille. See no.
    3926
Faust: Rien, En vain j'interroge; Allons amis point de vaines alar-
    mes...Le veau d'or; Nous nous retrouverons mes amis...Ainsi que
    la brise; Salut demeure chaste et pure; Il etait temps; Qu'
    attendezvous encore...Vous qui faites l'endormie. See no. 3773
Faust: Salut demeure chaste et pure. See no. 3535. See no. 3945
Faust: Salve dimora; Le parlate d'amor; Vous que faites l'endormie.
    See no. 3770
Faust: Seigneur Dieu que vois-je; Eh quoi toujours seule; Il se
    fait tard...Eternelle o nuit d'amour; O merveille; Que voulez-
    vous messieurs; Mon coeur est penetre d'epouvante; Attends;
    Voici la rue; Alerte ou vous etes perdus. See no. 3946
Faust: Siegneur daignes permettre; Quand du Seigneur. See no. 3904
Faust: Serenade; Le veau d'or. See no. 3979
Faust: Tardi si fa; Salve dimora casta e pura; Tardi si fa. See
    no. 3981

Faust: The calf of gold. See no. 4007
Faust: Walpurgisnacht. See no. 3807
Faust: When all was young. See no. 3903
1524 Mireille. Janette Vivalda, Madeleine Ignal, Christiane Jacquin, s;
     Christiane Gayraul, ms; Nicolai Gedda, t; Michel Dens, bar; Andre
     Vessieres, Marcello Cortis, Robert Tropin, bs; Aix-en-Provence
     Festival Chorus; OSCCP; Andre Cluytens. EMI C 153 10613/5 (3)
                +-ARSC Vol 12, nos. 1-2, 1980 p104
1525 Mireille. Mirella Freni, Christine Barbaux, Michele Command, s;
     Jane Rhodes, ms; Alain Vanzo, t; Jose van Dam, bar; Gabriel
     Bacquier, Marc Vento, bs-bar; Jean-Jacques Cubaynes, b; Toulouse
     Capitole Orchestra and Chorus; Michel Plasson. HMV SLS 5203 (3)
     (also Angel SX 3905)
                +Gr 12-80 p872   +HFN 12-80 p140
     Mireille: Oh d'amour messagerra. See no. 3770
     Mireille: Waltz. See no. 3872
     Mors et vita: Judex. See no. 3623
1526 Petite symphonie, B flat major. d'INDY: Chansons et danses, op. 50.
     Maurice Bourgue Wind Ensemble. Noneusch H 71382
                ++FF 9/10-80 p124   ++SFC 8-10-80 p29
                +St 10-80 p113
1527 Petite symphonie, B flat major. IBERT: Pieces breves, wind quartet
     (3). POULENC: Sextet, piano and wind instruments. Joan Clamp,
     ob; Donald Watson, clt; Peter Smith, hn; John Orford, bsn; Ian
     Brown, pno; Athena Ensemble. RCA RL 2-5278 Tape (c) RK 2-5278
                +-Gr 5-80 p1683   +RR 6-80 p67
                +-HFN 5-80 p133   +STL 5-11-80 p39
                +HFN 8-80 p107 tape
     Petite symphony, B flat major: 1st movement. See no. 3526
     Philemon et Baucis: Ecoutez ecoutez; C'est l'orage; Au bruit des
     lourds marteaux. See no. 3631
     Philemon and Baucis: Vulcan's song. See no. 3905
     La reine de Saba: How frail and weak...Lend me your aid. See no.
     3770
     La reine de Saba: Plus grand dans son obscurite; Sous les pieds.
     See no. 3774
     La reine de Saba: Sous les pieds d'une femme. See no. 3631
1428 Requiem (1893). Instrumental Ensemble et Choeurs de la Madeleine;
     Jaochim Harvard de la Montagne. Arion ARN 38443 (also Musical
     Heritage Society MHS 4068)
                +FF 5/6-80 p84   +RR 2-79 p90
                -Gr 3-80 p1427   +-St 5-80 p82
                ++MU 4-80 p10
     Romeo et Juliette, Act 2. See no. 2568
     Romeo et Juliette: Allons jeunes gens. See no. 3979
     Romeo et Juliette: Deh sorgi il luce in ciel. See no. 3981
     Romeo et Juliette: Le sommeil de Juliette. See no. 3799
     Romeo et Juliette: Qui fais-tu blanche tourterelle. See no. 3770
     Romeo et Juliette: Qui fais-tu blanche; Salut tombeau. See no. 3774
     Sapho: O ma lyre immortelle. See no. 3666. See no. 3770
1529 Songs: Au printemps; L'absent; Chanson de printemps; Envoi de fleurs;
     Le deux pigeons; Le lever; Ma belle amie est morte; Mignon; Ou
     voulez-vous aller; O ma belle rebelle; Le premier jour de mai;
     Priere; Serenade; Le vallon; Venise; Viens les gazons sont verts.
     Bruno Laplante, bar; Janine Lachance, pno. Calliope 1850
                +RR 8-80 p18

Songs: Aubade; Au rossignol; Boire a l'ombre; O ma belle rebelle;
Au bruit des lourdes marteaux; Madje; O ma belle rebelle; Le
premier jour de Mai; Venise. See no. 3863
Songs: Le vallon. See no. 3631
Sortie. See no. 3582
1530 Symphony, no. 1, D major. Seymphony, no. 2, E flat major. Toul-
ouse Capitole Theatre Orchestra; Michel Plasson. Angel SZ 37726
Tape (c) 4ZS 37726 (also HMV ESD 7093 Tape (c) TC ESD 7093

+-ARG 9-80 p27	++NR 5-80 p2
+FF 7/8-80 p88	++RR 8-80 p42
+Gr 8-80 p221	+SFC 5-25-80 p41
+-HF 7-80 p68	+-STL 9-14-80 p40
+-HFN 9-80 p104	

Symphony, no. 2, E flat major. See no. 1530
GOWERS, Patrick
1531 Chamber concerto, guitar. Rhapsody, guitar, electric guitars and
electric organ. John Williams, gtr; John Scott, sax, flt; Patrick Halling, vln; Stephen Shingles, vla; Denis Vigay, vlc; Herbie Flowers, bs guitar; Patrick Gowers, org; Tristan Fry, drum;
Godfrey Salmon. CBS 61790 Tape (c) 40-61790 (From 72979, 73350)
(also CBS M 35866 Tape (c) MT 35866)

+FF 9/10-80 p125	+-RR 8-77 p67
+-Gr 10-77 p628	+-RR 11-77 p119
+HFN 9-77 p151	+-St 11-80 p86
+HFN 10-77 p169 tape	

Rhapsody, guitar, electric guitars and electric organ. See no. 1531
GRABOVSKY (Hrabovsky), Leonid
1532 Trio, violin, double bass and piano. KOSENKO: Pieces, violin and
piano, op. 4: Dreams; Impromptu. LIATOSHINSKY: Sonata, violin
and piano, op. 19. STANKOVICH: Triptych: Lullaby; Wedding; Im-
provisation. Eugene Gratovich, vln; Virko Baley, pno; Bertram
Turetzky, double bs. Orion ORS 79331
+FF 5/6-80 p191
GRAFULLA
Washington greys. See no. 4012
GRAGNANI, Filippo
Trio, op. 12, D major. See no. 1224
GRAINGER, Percy
Danish folk-music. See no. 1534
The immovable "Do". See no. 1534
In a nutshell. See no. 1534
Irish tune from County Derry. See no. 1534
1533 Lincolnshire posy. SHOSTAKOVICH: Symphony, no. 9, op. 70, E flat
major: Mouvements, 1, 4-5. Cornell Univesity Wind Ensemble;
Marice Stith. Cornell CUWE 24
+FF 11/12-80 p223   +NR 2-80 p14
Lincolnshire posy. See no. 49
Molly on the shore. See no. 1534
Over the hills and far away. See no. 3801
Shepherd's hey. See no. 49
Songs: The jolly-sailor song; Six dukes went a'fishing. See no.
3776
1534 Works, selections: Danish folk-music. In a nutshell. Irish tune
from County Derry. The immovable "Do". Molly on the shore.
English Sinfonia; Neville Dilkes. HMV ASD 3651 Tape (c) TC ASD
3651

          +FF 1/2-80 p89   +HFN 9-79 p123 tape
        ++Gr 5-79 p1893   ++RR 5-79 p56
          +HFN 5-79 p123

GRANADOS, Enrique
1535 Danzas espanolas (Spanish dances), op. 37. Alicia de Larrocha, pno.
     RCA GL 2-5242 Tape (c) GK 2-5242 (From Erato EFM 8059)
          +Gr 11-79 p875   +-HFN 2-80 p107 tape
        +-HFN 10-79 p169   ++RR 10-79 p124
        +-HFN 1-80 p123 tape   +-RR 2-80 p98 tape
     Danza espanola, op. 37: Andaluza. See no. 1307. See no. 1393.
        See no. 3665. See no. 3964
     Danzas espanolas, op. 37: Andaluza, Danza triste. See no. 3549.
        See no. 3775
     Danzas espanolas, op. 37: Oriental. See no. 3609
     Goyescas: Intermezzo. See no. 12. See no. 3816
     Goyescas: La maja y el ruisenor. See no. 1392. See no. 3665. See
        no. 3668. See no. 3774. See no. 3825
     Songs: Canco d'amor; Elegia eterna; L'Ocell profeta. See no. 1392
     Tonadillas: La maja dolorosa; El majo discreto; El tra la la y el
        punteado; El majo timido. See no. 3698
     Tonadillas al estilo antiguo: El tra-la-la; El maja timido. See
        no. 3665
     Tonadillas al estilo antiguo: La maja de Goya. See no. 3883
     GRANDES HEURES LITURGIQUES. See no. 3673
GRANDI, Alessandro
     Cantabo domino. See no. 3546
     Surge propera. See no. 3878
GRANDJANY, Marcel
     Siciliana. See no. 3676
GRANT/ROSS
     The Lord's my shepherd. See no. 3939
GRANT-SCHAEFER
     The cuckoo clock. See no. 3831
GRAUN, Johann
     Das Tochterchen. See no. 3764
     Trio sonata, F major. See no. 91
GRAVES, Alfred
     Songs: The foggy dew; Trottin' to the fair. See no. 4070
GREAVES, Thomas
     Come away sweet love. See no. 3893
     GREEK ORTHODOX MUSIC. See no. 3689
GREEN
     Gortnamona. See no. 3875
GREFINGER, Wolfgang
     Songs: Ah Gott, Ich stel leicht ab; Wol kumbt der mey. See no. 3805
     GREGORIAN CHANTS. See no. 3574. See no. 3575. See no. 3576. See
        no. 3579. See no. 3580. See no. 3699. See no. 3700. See no.
        3704. See no. 3914
     GREGORIAN CHANTS: Alma redemptoris mater. See no. 3763
     GREGORIAN CHANTS: Elegies for kings and princes. See no. 3720
     GREGORIAN CHANTS: Good Friday tenebrae responsories. See no. 3911
     GREGORIAN CHANTS: Laudes Mariae. See no. 4005
     GREGORIAN CHANTS: Mass of the Annunciation; Mass of St. Joseph.
        See no. 3913
     GREGORIAN CHANTS: Prague Easter play. See no. 3746

GREGORIAN CHANTS: Prima missa in commemoratione omnium fidelium de-
   functorum. See no. 3701
GREGORIAN CHANTS: The wedding of Cana. See no. 3721
GREGORIAN CHANTS FROM HUNGARY. See no. 3802. See no. 3808. See
   no. 3809
GREGSON, Edward
   Connotations. See no. 3620
GRETCHANINOV, Alexander
1536 Children's songs, op. 89 (5). MUSSORGSKY: The nursery. PROKOFIEV:
   The ugly duckling, op. 18. Elisabeth Soderstrom, s; Vladimir
   Ashkenazy, pno. Decca SXL 6900 (also London OS 26579)
              +FF 7/8-80 p118   ++NYT 3-2-80 pD26
              +Gr 7-79 p238   +RR 7-79 p113
              ++HF 6-80 p80   ++St 6-80 p129
              +HFN 7-79 p115
   Dobrynia Nikitich: Flowers were blooming. See no. 3770
   Glory to God, Credo, Nunc dimittis. See no. 3973
1537 Symphony, no. 4, op. 102, C major. HUMMEL: Memory of friendship, op.
   99 (arr. Glinka). MRSO; Algis Zhuraitis. Melodiya S10 09269-70
   (also HMV ASD 3712)
              +ARG 11-79 p33   +HFN 9-79 p107
              -FF 9/10-79 p30   *MT 1-80 p34
              ++Gr 8-79 p331   +RR 8-79 p80
GRETRY, Andre
1538 Anacreon Chez Polycrate: Eprise d'un feu temeraire. Cephale et
   Procris: Plus d'ennemis dans mon empire. La Fausse magie: Comme
   un eclair, Je ne le dis qu'a vous. Richard Coeur de Leon: Je
   crains de lui parler. PHILIDOR: La belle esclave: O ciel se
   pourrait-il...Quel espoir est pour moi. Les femmes vengees: De
   la coquette volage. Melide ou le navigateur: Tout dormait. Tom
   Jones: Respirons un moment...O toi que ne peut m'entendre. Chris-
   tiane Eda-Pierre, s; AMF; Neville Marriner. Philips 9500 609
   Tape (c) 7300 800
              ++FF 5/6-80 p85   ++NR 4-80 p12
              +Gr 4-80 p1594   +NYT 6-15-80 pD31
              +HFN 4-80 p104   +Op 8-80 p843
              +HFN 6-80 p119 tape   ++RR 4-80 p46
              +-MT 11-80 p712   +-STL 4-13-80 p39
   Cephale et Procris: Plus d'ennmis dans mon empire. See no. 1538
   Concerto, flute, C major. See no. 3942
   Danse suite. See no. 3942
   La Fausse magie: Comme un eclair, Je ne le dis qu'a vous. See no.
      1538
   Richard Coeur de Leon: Je crains de lui parler. See no. 1538
   Richard Coeur de Leon: Una fievre brillante. See no. 3770
   Zemire et Azor: Air de ballet. See no. 4069
GRIEG, Edvard
1539 Albumblatter, op. 28. Ballade, op. 24, G minor. Scenes from peas-
   ant life, op. 19. Eva Knardahl, pno. BIS LP 110
              +FF 7/8-79 p54   +-RR 3-80 p81
              +Gr 8-80 p242   ++St 11-79 p86
              ++NR 5-79 p12
   Ballade, op. 24, G minor. See no. 1539
1540 Concerto, piano, op. 16, A minor. Norwegian dances, op. 35. Kjell
   Ingebretsen, Eva Knardahl, pno; RPO; Kjell Ingebretsen. BIS LP
   115

```
        +Gr  8-80  p247              +NR  3-80  p13
        +-HFN  3-80  p89             +-RR  3-80  p55
```

1541 Concerto, piano, op. 16, A minor. SCHUMANN: Concerto, piano, op.
     54, A minor. Solomon, pno; PhO; Herbert Menges. Classics for
     Pleasure CFP 40255 Tape (c) TC CFP 40255 (From HMV ASD 272)
```
        +Gr  12-76  p995             +-HFN  8-80  p107  tape
        +Gr  8-80  p247              +-RR  10-76  p50
        +-HFN  11-76  p171           +-RR  8-80  p95
```

1542 Concerto, piano, op. 16, A minor. SCHUMANN: Concerto, piano, op.
     54, A minor. Radu Lupu, pno; LSO; Andre Previn. Decca SXL 6624
     Tape (c) KSXC 6624 (also London CS 6840)
```
        +-Gr  2-74  p1552            ++NR  11-74  p5
        +Gr  8-80  p247              +RR  2-74  p33
        +HF  11-74  p122             ++RR  2-76  p71  tape
        +HFN  3-74  p105             +-SFC  8-11-74  p34
        +HFN  9-75  p110             +MJ  1-75  p48
```

1543 Concerto, piano, op. 16, A minor. SCHUMANN: Concerto, piano, op.
     54, A minor. Walter Gieseking, pno; BPhO; Wilhelm Furtwangler.
     Everest SDBR 3434
```
        ++ARG  6-79  p32             +-NR  6-79  p8
        -FF  7/8-80  p133
```

1544 Concerto, piano, op. 16, A minor. SCHUMANN: Concerto, piano, op.
     54, A minor. Dinu Lipatti, pno; PhO; Alceo Galliera, Herbert von
     Karajan. HMV HLM 7046 (From Columbia LX 1029/32, 1110/3)
```
        +Gr  12-74  p1134            +RR  11-74  p38
        +Gr  8-80  p247
```

1545 Concerto, piano, op. 16, A minor. Lyric pieces, op. 65: Wedding
     day at Troldhaugen. Norwegian dances, op. 35. Grant Johannesen,
     pno; Utah Symphony Orchestra; Maurice Abravanel. Turnabout (Q)
     QTV S 34624 Tape (c) KTVC 34624
```
        +Gr  3-80  p1386             +NR  8-76  p5
        +Gr  8-80  p247              -RR  2-80  p53
        +HF  11-76  p118          •  +St  12-76  p141
        -HFN  3-80  p53
```
     Concerto, piano, op. 16, A minor. See no. 1435

1546 Elegiac melodies, op. 34. NIELSEN: Little suite, op. 1, A minor.
     SIBELIUS: Rakastava, op. 14. Kuolema, op. 44: Valse triste.
     WIREN: Serenade, op. 11. AMF; Neville Marriner. Argo ZRG 877
     Tape (c) KZRC 877
```
        ++Gr  4-90  p1567            +RR  4-80  p80
        ++HFN  4-80  p113
```

1547 Elegiac melodies, op. 34. Holberg suite, op. 40. Lyric pieces, op.
     68: At the cradle. Norwegian melodies, op. 53 (2). Norwegian
     melodies, op. 63 (2). Norwegian Chamber Orchestra; Terje Tonne-
     sen. BIS LP 147
```
        ++ARG  11-80  p21            ++HFN  8-80  p97
        +FF  11/12-80  p117          +RR  8-80  p45
        ++Gr  11-80  p739            ++St  8-80  p72
        +HF  11-80  p68
```

1548 Elegiac melodies, op. 34 (2). Holberg suite, op. 40. TCHAIKOVSKY:
     Serenade, op. 48, C major. Polish Chamber Orchestra; Jerzy Mak-
     symiuk. HMV ESD 7084 Tape (c) TC ESD 7084
```
        +-Gr  3-80  p1386            +-RR  3-80  p64
        +HFN  3-80  p89              +-RR  7-80  p97  tape
        +HFN  6-80  p119  tape
```

Elegiac melodies, op. 34 (2). See no. 1561. See no. 1571. See no. 3794

Elegiac melodies, op. 34, no. 2. See no. 3843

Funeral march for Ricard Nordraak. See no. 1561

1549 Haugtussa, op. 67. Poems by Vilhelm Krag, op. 60. Ellen Westberg Andersen, s; Jens Harald Bratlie, pno. Simax PS 1011
+HFN 10-80 p105

1550 Holberg suite, op. 40. Lyric pieces, op. 54. Sigurd Jorsalfar, op. 56: Suite. ECO; Raymond Leppard. Philips 9500 748 Tape (c) 7300 833

/Gr 12-80 p832

Holberg suite, op. 40. See no. 1265. See no. 1547. See no. 1548. See no. 1565. See no. 1571

Holberg suite, op. 40: 1st movement. See no. 3715

Humoresques, op. 6. See no. 1561

I love thee. See no. 3831

1551 Improvisations on Norwegian folk songs, op. 29. Norwegian mountain melodies, op. 112. Norwegian songs and dances, op. 17. Eva Knardahl, pno. BIS LP 109
+FF 7/8-79 p54   ++NR 5-79 p12
+Gr 8-80 p247   +-RR 3-80 p81

In autumn, op. 11. See no. 1571

Landkjenning, op. 31. See no. 1555

1552 Lyric pieces, opp. 12, 38, 43, 47, 54, 57, 62, 65, 68, 71. Eva Knardahl, pno. BIS LP 104/7 (4)
+FF 9/10-78 p54   +RR 7-79 p91
+Gr 8-80 p247   +SFC 4-23-78 p49
+-HFN 7-79 p105   ++St 8-78 p91
++RR 6-78 p78

1553 Lyric pieces, op. 12, no. 1; op. 38, no. 1; op. 43, nos. 1-2; op. 47, nos. 2-4; op. 54, nos. 4-5; op. 57, no. 8; op. 62, nos. 4, 6; op. 65, no. 5; op. 68, nos. 2-3, 5; op. 71, nos. 1, 3, 6-7. Emil Gilels, pno. DG 2542 142 Tape (c) 3342 142 (From 2530 476)
++Gr 10-80 p518   +HFN 10-80 p113
+Gr 12-80 p889 tape   +STL 11-9-80 p40

Lyric pieces, op. 54. See no. 1550

Lyric pieces, op. 54: Nocturne, C major. See no. 3825

Lyric pieces, op. 54: Scherzo. See no. 3964

Lyric pieces, op. 54: Suite. See no. 1571

Lyric pieces, op. 65: Wedding day at Troldhaugen. See no. 1545

Lyric pieces, op. 68: At the cradle. See no. 1547

Lyric pieces, op. 68: Evening in the mountains; At the cradle. See no. 1571

Lyric pieces, op. 71: Puck. See no. 3964

Moods, op. 73. See no. 1561

Norwegian dance, no. 2. See no. 3555

Norwegian dance, no. 4. See no. 3883

Norwegian dances, op. 35. See no. 1540. See no. 1545

Norwegian folk melodies, op. 66 (19). See no. 1561

Norwegian melodies, op. 53. See no. 1547

Norwegian melodies, op. 63. See no. 1547

Norwegian mountain melodies, op. 112. See no. 1551

1554 Norwegian peasant dances (Slatter), op. 72. Eva Knardahl, pno. BIS LP 114
+Gr 8-80 p247   +RR 7-80 079

+—HFN 8-80 p97   ++St 6-80 p112
+—NR 7-80 p12
Norwegian songs and dances, op. 17. See no. 1551
1555 Olav Trygvason, op. 50, excerpts. Landkjenning (Recognition of the
    land), op. 31. Asbjorn Hansli, bar; Toril Carlsen, s; Vessa
    Hanssen, ms; Oslo Philharmonic Chorus; LSO; Per Dreier. Unicorn
    RHS 364 Tape (r) B-C M 0361
            +FF 7/8-80 p89   +—HFN 11-80 p131 tape
            +Gr 3-80 p1434   +ON 6-80 p45
            ++HF 6-80 p76   +RR 3-80 p93
            ++HF 11-80 p88 tape   +SFC 2-24-80 p39
            +HFN 3-80 p89   +St 6-80 p112
    Old Norwegian melody with variations, op. 51. See no. 1571
1556 Peer Gynt, op. 23. Toril Carlsen, s; Vessa Hanssen, ms; Kare Kjor-
    koy, t; Asbjorn Hansli, bar; Knud Buen, fiddle; Oslo Philharmonic
    Orchestra; Per Dreier. Unicorn UN 2-75030 (2) Tape (c) UKC 361
    (4) UNC M 0361 (also RHS 361/2)
            ++FF 9/10-79 p90   +NR 10-79 p9
            +FF 11/12-79 p18 tape   ++NYT 5-27-79 pD18
            +Gr 4-79 p1706   ++RR 3-79 p48
            ++HF 8-79 p53 tape   ++SFC 6-3-79 p48
            ++HFN 2-79 p99   ++St 8-79 p79
            ++HFN 11-80 p131 tape
1557 Peer Gynt, op. 23: Incidental music. Taru Valjakka, s; Edith
    Thallaug, ms; Leipzig Radio Chorus; Dresden State Orchestra; Her-
    bert Blomstedt. HMV ASD 3640 Tape (c) TC ASD 3640 (also Angel S
    37535)
            +FF 9/10-79 p90   ++NYT 5-27-79 pD18
            +Gr 5-79 p1894   +ON 6-80 p45
            +HFN 5-79 p123   +RR 5-79 p97
            +MT 12-79 p1008   ++SFC 4-15-79 p41
            ++NR 7-79 p3
    Peer Gynt, op. 46/55, excerpts. See no. 721. See no. 3909
    Peer Gynt, op. 46: Morning. See no. 3605
    Peer Gynt, op. 46: Solveig's song. See no. 3769. See no. 3774
1558 Peer Gynt, op. 46: Suite, no. 1. Peer Gynt, op. 55: Suite, no. 2.
    Sigurd Jorsalfar, op. 56: Incidental music. Eva Knardahl, pno.
    BIS 116
            +—HFN 8-80 p97   +RR 7-80 p79
1559 Peer Gynt, op. 46: Suite, no. 1. SIBELIUS: Finlandia, op. 26.
    Karelia suite, op. 11. Legends, op. 22: The swan of Tuonela.
    Debrecen Philharmonic Orchestra; Laszlo Szabo. Hungaroton SLPX
    12037
            -FF 5/6-80 p150   +NR 5-80 p2
    Peer Gynt, op. 46: Suite, no. 1. See no. 1571
1560 Peer Gynt, op. 46/55: Wedding march; Ingrid's lament; In the hall
    of the mountain king; Morning; Death of Aase; Arabian dance;
    Solveig's song; Anitra's dance; Return of Peer Gynt; Wiegenlied.
    Ilse Hollweg, s; Beecham Choral Society; RPO; Thomas Beecham.
    HMV SXLP 30423 Tape (c) TC SXLP 30423 (From ASD 258)
            +ARSC Vol 12, no. 3   +—HFN 2-80 p105
                 1980 p253   +—HFN 4-80 p121 tape
            +—Gr 2-80 p1269   +RR 2-80 p54
    Peer Gynt, op. 55: Suite, no. 2. See no. 1559. See no. 1571
1561 Piano works: Elegiac melodies, op. 34 (2). Funeral march for Rikard

Humoresques, op. 6. Moods, op. 73. Norwegian folk melodies, op.
66 (19). Pieces, piano, op. 1 (4). Poetic tone pictures, op. 3.
Songs, opp. 41 and 52 (arr. for piano). Eva Knardahl, pno. BIS
LP 111/3
+FF 11/12-79 p77   +-RR 3-80 p81
+Gr 8-80 p247   +St 1-80 p95
Pieces, piano, op. 1 (4). See no. 1561
Poems by Vilhelm Krag, op. 60. See no. 1549
1562 Poetic tone pictures, op. 3. Songs, opp. 41 and 52 (arr. for piano).
Eva Knardahl, pno. BIS LP 112
+Gr 8-80 p247   +St 1-80 p95
+FF 11/12-79 p77
Poetic tone pictures, op. 3. See no. 1561
Quartet, strings, F major. See no. 1563
1563 Quartet, strings, op. 27, G minor. Quartet, strings, F major. Hin-
dar Quartet. Philips 839 241
+-HFN 7-80 p107   +RR 7-80 p71
1564 Quartet, strings, op. 27, G minor. SIBELIUS: Quartet, strings, op.
56, D minor. Copenhagen Quartet. Turnabout TVC 37010 Tape (c)
CT 7010
+FF 5/6-80 p151
Scenes from peasant life, op. 19. See no. 1539
Scenes from peasant life, op. 19: Bridal procession passing by.
See no. 1571
Sigurd Jorsalfar, op. 56. See no. 1571
Sigurd Jorsalfar, op. 56: Incidental music. See no. 1558
Sigurd Jorsalfar, op. 56: Suite. See no. 1550
1565 Sonata, piano, op. 7, E minor. Holberg suite, op. 40. Eva Knar-
dahl, pno. BIS LP 108
+FF 7/8-79 p55   +-HFN 7-79 p105
+Gr 8-80 p247   +RR 7-79 p91
1566 Sonata, piano, op. 7, E minor. NIELSEN: Chaconne, op. 32. STEN-
HAMMAR: Fantasies, op. 11 (3). Little piano pieces (3). Jacob
Moscovicz, pno. Caprice CAP 1160
+-FF 9/10-79 p91   +RR 5-80 p87
+-Gr 5-80 p1693
1567 Sonata, violin and piano, no. 2, op. 13, G major. SAINT-SAENS: Son-
ata, violin and piano, no. 1, op. 75, D minor. Christiaan Bor,
vln; Jerome Lowenthal, pno. Pelican LP 2014
+-FF 3/4-80 p88   ++SFC 7-27-80 p34
+HF 9-80 p96   +-St 6-80 p121
1568 Sonata, violin and piano, no. 2, op. 13, G major. Sonata, violin
and piano, no. 3, op. 45, C minor. Arve Tellefsen, vln; Robert
Levin, pno. Philips 839240
+-Gr 9-80 p359   +RR 8-80 p70
+-HFN 7-80 p117
1569 Sonata, violin and piano, no. 2, op. 13, G minor. Sonata, violin
and piano, no. 3, op. 45, C minor. Joseph Silverstein, vln;
Harriet Shirvan, pno. Sound Environment TR 1011
+ARG 7/8-80 p26
Sonata, violin and piano, no. 2, op. 13, G minor. See no. 3964
Sonata, violin and piano, no. 3, op. 45, C minor. See no. 1442.
See no. 1568. See no. 1569. See no. 3964
Sonata, violoncello and piano, op. 36, A minor. See no. 1088
1570 Songs: A hope, op. 26, no. 1; Among the roses, op. 39, no. 4; The

first meeting, op. 21, no. 1; From Monte Pincio, op. 39, no. 1; I
give my song to the spring, op. 21, no. 3; I love thee, op. 5, no.
3; Two brown eyes, op. 5, no. 1; With a primrose, op. 26, no. 4;
With a water lily, op. 25, no. 4; While I wait, op. 60, no. 3.
STRADELLA: Salome: Overture; Arias, nos. 1-4; Recitatives, nos.
90 and 100; Recitative and ritornelle. Anita Soldh, s; Arnold
Ostman, pno; Vadstena Instrumental Ensemble; Arnold Ostman. Cap-
rice CAP 1114
            +Gr 5-80 p1700   +RR 5-80 p101
Songs: A swan. See no. 3769
Songs: Thanks for advice. See no. 3738
Songs, opp. 41 and 52 (arr. for piano). See no. 1561. See no.
    1562
Symphonic dances, op. 64. See no. 1571
Varen (Spring). See no. 3589

1571 Works, selections: Elegiac melodies, op. 34 (2). Holberg suite,
    op. 40. In autumn, op. 11. Lyric pieces, op. 54: Suite. Lyric
    pices, op. 68: Evening in the mountains; At the cradle. Old
    Norwegian melody with variations, op. 51. Peer Gynt, op. 46:
    Suite, no. 1. Peer Gynt, op. 55: Suite, no. 2. Scenes from
    peasant life, op. 19, no. 2: Bridal procession passing by. Sig-
    urd Jorsalfar, op. 56. Symphonic dances, op. 64. Utah Symphony
    Orchestra; Maurice Abravanel. Vox QSVBX 5140 (3) Tape (c) CBX
    5140
            +Audio 1-77 p85   ++NR 9-76 p3
            +HF 11-76 p118   ++SFC 8-15-76 p38
            +MJ 11-76 p45   +St 3-80 p107 tape

GRIFFES, Charles
    Roman sketches, op. 7. See no. 3887
    Roman sketches, op. 7: The fountain of Acqua Paola. See no. 1187
GRIGNY, Nicholas de
1572 Livre d'orgue: Mass; Hymns: Veni creator; Pange lingua; Verbum sup-
    ernum; Ave maris stella; A solis ortus. Marie-Claire Alain, org;
    Guillaume Bony Choir; Jean Teixeira. Erato STU 71380 (2)
            +-Gr 10-80 p527
    Veni creator. See no. 3994
GRISAR, Albert
    Les porcherons: Romance de la lettre. See no. 3630
GRISELLE/YOUNG
    The cuckoo clock. See no. 3831
GROSSI, Carlo
1573 Ebraica in dialogo. ROSSI: Les cantiques de Salomon. SALADIN:
    Canticum Hebraicum. Boston Camerata; Joel Cohen. Harmonia Mun-
    di 1021
            ++ARG 11-80 p51   ++NR 6-80 p6
            +FF 7/8-80 p180   +NYT 8-10-80 pD17
            +Gr 10-80 p527   +RR 6-80 p85
            +HFN 5-80 p127   ++St 9-80 p85
GROVE, Richard
1574 El Gamino. OGERMAN: Symphonic dances: 1st and 2nd movements.
    WILLIAMS: An American concerto, jazz quartet: 3rd movement. Or-
    chestra; Allyn Ferguson, Jack Elliott. Foundation for New Ameri-
    can Music FNAM 1
            +FF 7/8-80 p187
GRUBER, Franz
    Mei Mautterl war a Weanerin. See no. 3711

Stille Nacht heilige Nacht. See no. 3697. See no. 3933
GRUNENWALD, Jean-Jacques
1575 Diptyque liturgique. Hymne aux memoires heroiques. LANGLAIS: Pas-
        ticcio. Poems evangeliques: L'Annonciation; Nativite; Les ram-
        eaux. David Britton, org. Delos DEL 25443
                        ++MU 7-80 p10   ++St 6-80 p113
    Hymne aux memoires heroiques. See no. 1575
GUAMI, Gioseffo
    Canzona, no. 19. See no. 4000
    Ricercar. See no. 3597
    Toccata del 2 tuono. See no. 3813
GUARNIERI, Camargo
    Ave Maria. See no. 3934
    Declaracao. See no. 3965
1576 Sonata, violin and piano, no. 2. PORTER: Sonata, violin and piano,
        no. 2. STILL: Ennanga. VAUGHAN WILLIAMS: Concerto accademico,
        D minor. Louis Kaufman, vn; Arthur Balsam, pno; Winterthur
        String Orchestra; Ensemble; Clemens Dahinden, Louis Kaufman. Or-
        ion ORS 79359
                        +ARG 9-90 p51   +-NR 4-80 p9
                        +FF 11/12-80 p211
GUERRERO, Francisco
    Cancion del sembrador. See no. 3888
    Carols (3). See no. 3993
    El huesped del sevillano: Raquel. See no. 3919
GUIDO OF AREZZO
    Ut queant laxis resonare. See no. 3960
GUIGNON, Jean-Pierre
    Sonata, flute, op. 1, no. 8, A major. See no. 3544
GUILAIN, Jean
1577 Suites, nos. 1-4. Wolfgang Rubsam, org. Spectrum SR 102 Tape (c)
        D 102
                        +-FF 11/12-79 p78   +HF 7-80 p82 tape
    Suite du deuxieme ton. See no. 1168
    Suite in the 1st tone. See no. 3733
GUILHEM DE CABESTANH
    Vida. See no. 3749
GUILMANT, Felix Alexandre
    Grand choeur, D major. See no. 3663
    March on a theme by Handel, op. 15. See no. 3958
    Marche funebre et chant seraphique. See no. 4064
    Morceau symphonique, op. 88. See no. 3606
1578 Noel polonais et noel carcassonnais. Sonatas, organ, nos. 3-5, 7.
        Odile Pierre, org. RCA RL 3-7295
                        +MU 5-80 p12
    Sonata, organ, no. 1, op. 42, D minor: Pastorale. See no. 4061
    Sonatas, organ, nos. 3-5, 7. See no. 1578
    Sonata, organ, no. 3, op. 56, C minor. See no. 4048
    Sonata, organ, no. 5, op. 80, C minor. See no. 4049
GULIELMUS, M.
    Falla con misuras. See no. 3864
GUMPELZHAIMER, Adam
    Vom Himmel hoch. See no. 3697
GURIDI, Jesus
    Canciones castellanas: Llamale con el penuelo: No quiero tus avel-

lanas; Como quieres que adivine. See no. 3698
El caserio: Romanza. See no. 3919
Como quieres que adivine. See no. 3665
Viejo zortzico. See no. 3564
GURNEY, Ivor
    The fields are full. See no. 3778
    The western playland: Reveille; Loveliest of trees; Golden friends;
        Twice a week; The aspens; Is my team ploughing; The far country;
        March. See no. 3837
GWILT, David
    Sonatina. See no. 3644
HAAG, Jakob
1579 Albumblad. Andante. Sonata, violoncello, op. 1, E minor. SJOGREN:
        Sonata, violoncello, op. 58, A major. Guid Vecchi, Hilja Saarne,
        vlc. Gothenburg University GU 001
                    +MT 10-80 p634
    Andante. See no. 1579
    Sonata, violoncello, op. 1, E minor. See no. 1579
HAAS, Joseph
    Kirchen sonate on "In dulci jubilo". See no. 4066
HACKBARTH
1580 Double concerto. POWELL: Nocturnes. Daniel Perantoni, tuba; David
        Hickman, tpt; Illinois Contemporary Chamber Players. Crystal S
        394
                    +FF 9/10-80 p283   +NR 12-78 p9
                    +IN 10-79 p14
HACQUART, Carolus
    Sonata, op. 3, no. 2, F major. See no. 4016
HADJU
    Sketches in a sentimental mood (5). See no. 3739
HAGEMAN
    Do not go my love. See no. 3986
HAHN
    Invictus. See no. 3905
HAHN, Reynaldo
    Si mes vers avaient des ailes. See no. 3770
1581 Songs: A Chloris; D'une prison; L'enamouree; Etudes latines: Lydie,
        Neere, Salinum, Thaliarque, Lydie, Vile potabis, Tyndaris,
        Pholoe, A Phidyle, Phyllis; Fetes galantes; L'incredule; L'Off-
        rande; Quant je fus pris au pavillon; Paysage; Le rossignol des
        lilas; Si mes vers avaient des ailes; Infidelite. Bruno Laplante,
        bar; Janine Lachance, pno; Chorus; Jean-Pierre Guindon. Calli-
        ope CAL 1840
                    +-Gr 3-79 p1599   +RR 8-80 p18
    Songs: Infidelite; Le rossignol des lilas. See no. 3965
    Songs: The hour. See no. 3986
HAIEFF, Alexei
    Concerto, piano. See no. 1582
1582 Symphony, no. 2. Concerto, piano. Leo Smit, pno; BSO, VSO; Charles
        Munch, Walter Hendl. Serenus SRS 12086
                    +-FF 9/10-80 p126   ++St 12-79 p142
HALEVY, Jacques
    L'Eclair: Call me thine own. See no. 3774
1583 La juive: Dieu que ma voix tremblante; Rachel quand du Seigneur.
        MEYERBEER: L'Africaine: O paradis; Combien tu m'es chere; Erreur

fatal. Dinorah: Les bles sont beaux a faucher. Les Huguenots:
Plus blanche que la blanche hermine. Le Prophete: Roi du ciel;
Pour Bertha moi je souspire. REYER: Sigurd: Prince du Rhin;
J'ai garde mon ame ingenue; Oui Sigurd est vainqueur; Esprits
gardiens; Un souvenir poignant. Cesar Vezzani, t; Various orch-
estras and conductors. EMI 2C 051 16367
         +ARSC Vol 12, nos. 1-2, 1980 p101
La juive: Dieu que ma voix tremblante; Eudoxie's aria; Rachel quand
     du Seigneur; Voi che del Dio. See no. 3770
La juive: Il va venir. See no. 3630
La juive: Rachel quand du Seigneur. See no. 3535
La juive: Recha als Gott dich einst; Er kommt zuruck. See no. 3774
La juive: Se oppressi ognor; Voi che del Dio vivante. See no. 3899
La juive: Tho faithless men. See no. 3905
La juive: Wenn ew'ger Hass. See no. 3712
HALFFTER, Ernesto
Danza de la gitana. See no. 1393. See no. 3785. See no. 3964
Danza de la pastora. See no. 3609
HALFFTER, Rodolfo
Don Lindo de Almeria. See no. 1025
HALL
The new colonial. See no. 3617
HALSEY
Swedish love song. See no. 3774
HALVORSEN, Johan
1584 Fossegrimen, op. 21. Mascarade: Suite. Norwegian Broadcasting Or-
     chestra; Oivind Bergh; Sigbjorn Bernhoft Osa, hardingfele. Nor-
     way Kulturrads NKF 30029
         +FF 3/4-80 p89
Mascarade: Suite. See no. 1584
1585 Norwegian rhapsodies, nos. 1-2. Suite ancienne, op. 31. Bergen
     Symphony Orchestra; Karsten Andersen. Norway NFK 30030
         +Gr 1-80 p1167
Suite ancienne, op. 31. See no. 1585
HAMBRAEUS, Bengt
Mikrogram. See no. 3598
HAMES, Richard
Monody after Dufay. See no. 1119
HAMILTON, Iain
Palinodes. See no. 1350
HAMMERSCHMIDT, Andreas
Die Kunst des Kussens. See no. 3764
O ihr lieben Hirten. See no. 4068
HAMPTON
Doxology. See no. 3848
HANART
Le serviteur. See no. 3597
HANDEL, Georg Friedrich
Acis and Galatea: Lo hear...Love in her eyes sits playing. See no.
     3770
Acis and Galatea: O ruddier than the cherry. See no. 3795
1586 Admeto. Rachel Yakar, Jill Gomez, s; Rita Dams, alto; Rene Jacobs,
     James Bowman, c-t; Max van Egmond, bar; Ulrik Cold, bs; Il Com-
     plesso Barocco; Alan Curtis. EMI SQ 1C 163 30808/12 (5)
         +-Gr 11-79 p903   ++Op 1-80 p61

++NYT 5-20-79 pD26   +RR 11-79 p48
+ON 11-1-80 p44
Agrippina: Pur ritorno a rimirarvi.   See no. 1595
Air, A major.   See no. 1619
Air, B flat major.   See no. 1620
Air and variations.   See no. 3677
1587 Alceste: Incidental music.   Judith Nelson, Emma Kirkby, s; Margaret
     Cable, ms; Paul Elliot, t; David Thomas, bs; Academy of Ancient
     Music; Christopher Hogwood.   L'Oiseau-Lyre DSLO 581 Tape (c)
     KDSLC 581
              +Gr 12-80 p860
Alcina: Overture.   See no. 3766
1588 Alcina: Overture; Ballet; Sinfonia; Entree; Tamburino; Dream music.
     Ariodante: Overture; Sinfonia pastorale; Il ballo.   Il pastor
     Fido: Pour les Chasseurs I and II.   Colin Tilney, hpd; AMF;
     Neville Marriner.   Argo ZK 68 (From ZRG 686)
              ++Gr 1-80 p1146   +HFN 1-80 p121
Alcina: Sta nell'ircana.   See no. 1512
Alessandro: Ne trionfo d'Alessandro; Lusinghe piu care.   See no.
     3560.   See no. 3770
1589 Alexander's feast.   Helen Donath, Sally Burgess, s; Robert Tear, t;
     Thomas Allen, bar; King's College Chapel Choir; ECO; Philip Led-
     ger.   HMV SLS 5168 (2) Tape (c) TC SLS 5168 (also Angel SZB 3874)
              +-ARG 5-80 p23   +MT 6-80 p382
              ++FF 5/6-80 p86   +NR 3-80 p11
              +Gr 10-79 p689   +NYT 1-20-80 pD22
              +-HF 4-80 p90   +RR 10-79 p135
              +HFN 11-79 p139   +St 5-80 p83
              +HFN 2-80 p107 tape   +STL 12-2-79 p37
1590 Alexander's feast.   Overture, D major.   Royal fireworks music.
     AMF; Nveille Marriner.   Philips 9500 768 Tape (c) 7300 843
              +NR 12-80 p2
1591 Alexander's feast.   Felicity Palmer, s; Anthony Rolfe Johnson, t;
     Stephen Roberts, bs; Stockholm Bach Choir; VCM; Nikolaus Harnon-
     court.   Telefunken EK 6-35440 92) Tape (c) 4-35440 (r) B-C 0
     6-35440
              +ARG 5-80 p23   +HFN 11-78 p171
              +FF 5/6-79 p50   +-MT 11-79 p921
              +Gr 11-78 p938   ++NYT 5-20-79 pD26
              +HF 5-79 p84   +RR 10-78 p103
              +HF 7-80 p82 tape   +-St 7-79 p96
1592 Alexander's feast.   Honor Sheppard, s; Max Worthley, t; Maurice
     Bevan, bar; Oriana Concerto Orchestra and Choir; Alfred Deller.
     Vanguard Bach Guild HM 50/1 (2) (also Vanguard S 282/3)
              +ARG 11-76 p25   +-SFC 12-12-76 p55
              +-ARG 5-80 p23
Alexander's feast.   See no. 1610
Alexander's feast: Behold a ghastly band...Revenge Timotheus cries.
     See no. 4007
Alexander's feast: Revenge, Timotheus cries.   See no. 1595
1593 L'Allegro, el penseroso ed il moderato: pts 1 and 2.   Payrizia
     Kwella, Marie McLaughlin, Jennifer Smith, s; Michael Ginn, treble;
     Maldwyn Davies, Martyn Hill, t; Stephen Varcoe, bs; Monteverdi
     Choir, English Baroque Soloists; John Eliot Gardiner.   Erato STU
     71325 (2)
              ++Gr 11-80 p718

Aria. See no. 4001
Aria con variazioni, B flat major. See no. 1620
1594 Arias: Israel in Egypt: He spoke the word; He gave them hailstones.
     Jeptha: When his loud voice. Judas Maccabaeus: See the conquer-
     ing hero comes. Messiah: Hellelujah; For unto us a child is
     born; Worthy is the lamb; Amen. Solomon: May no rash intruder.
     Saul: Gird on thy sword. Zadok the priest. Handel Opera Society
     Orchestra and Chorus; Charles Farncombe. Decca SPA 567 Tape (c)
     KCSP 567 (From PFS 4295)
                    +Gr 11-80 p739
1595 Arias: Agrippina: Pur ritorno a rimirarvi. Alexander's feast: Re-
     venge, Timotheus cries. Belshazzar: Oppressed with never-
     ceasing grief. Berenice: Si tra i ceppi. Ottone: Dopo l'orrore.
     Samson: Honour and arms. Saul: With rage I shall burn. Solomon:
     When the sun o'er yonder hills. Susanna: Peace crown'd with
     roses. Serse: Ombra mai fu. Dietrich Fischer-Dieskau, bar; Hed-
     wig Bilgram, org; Munich Chamber Orchestra; Hans Stadlmair.
     DG 2530 979
                    +–Gr 8-80 p266   +RR 7-80 p88
                    +–HFN 8-80 p97   +–SFC 6-22-80 p36
                    +–NR 3-79 p12   +–St 4-79 p138
                    +ON 3-31-79 p40
1596 Ariodante. Edith Mathis, Norma Burrowes, s; Janet Baker, ms; James
     Bowman, c-t; David Rendall, t; Samuel Ramey, bs; Alexander Oliv-
     er, t; London Voices; ECO; Raymond Leppard. Philips 6769 025
     (4) Tape (c) 7699 112
                    +–ARG 10-80 p16   +NR 6-80 p10
                    +FF 7/8-80 p93   ++NYT 4-20-80 pD24
                    +–Gr 12-80 p889 tape   +–ON 11-1-80 p44
                    +–Gr 9-80 p391   +–Op 10-80 p1013
                    +HF 8-80 p72   ++SFC 4-20-80 p34
                    +HFN 9-80 p104   ++St 7-80 p71
                    +HFN 11-80 p131 tape
     Ariodante: Overture, Sinfonia pastorale, Il ballo. See no. 1588
1597 Armida abbandonata, no. 13. Figlio d'alte speranze, no. 15. Nel
     dolce dell'oblio, no. 17. Un'alma innamorata, no. 23. Mari-
     anne Kweksilber, s; Musica Antiqua Amsterdam; Ton Koopman.
     Telefunken AW 6-42367
                    +–ARG 6-80 p21   +–HFN 6-79 p108
                    +FF 3/4-80 p89   +–RR 6-79 p113
                    +–FU 2-80 p46
     Belshazzar: Oppressed with never-ceasing grief. See no. 1595
     Berenice: Minuet. See no. 298
1598 Berenice: Overture. Concerto a due cori, no. 3, F major. Royal
     fireworks music. NYP, Philharmonia Chamber Orchestra; Pierre
     Boulez. Columbia M 35833 Tape (c) MT 35833 (also CBS 76834 Tape
     (c) 40-76834)
                    +FF 11/12-80 p119   +HFN 9-80 p116 tape
                    +–Gr 7-80 p141   +–HFN 10-80 p117 tape
                    +HF 7-80 p68   +RR 7-80 p57
                    +HFN 7-80 p107
     Berenice: Si tra i ceppi. See no. 1595
1599 Cantate da camera: Beato in ver; Parti l'idolo mio; Sento la che
     ristretto; Tanti strali. Judith Nelson, s; Rene Jacobs, c-t;
     Wieland Kuijken, vlc; William Christi, hpd; Konrad Junghanel,

theorbo; Concerto Vocale. Harmonia Mundi HM 1004
>   +FF 5/6-80 p87
Capriccio, G minor. See no. 1619
1600 Chaconne, G major. Minuet, G minor. Suites, B flat major, G minor,
>   D minor, E minor. Robert Woolley, hpd. Saga 5476
>   +Gr 11-80 p703   +HFN 11-80 p105
1601 Chaconne, G major. Fantasia, C major. Lesson, no. 1, B flat major.
>   Suite, harpsichord, no. 16: Sarabande, G major. HAYDN: Sonata,
>   piano, E major: Presto. Sonata, piano, F major. MOZART: Sonata,
>   piano, no. 5, K 283, G major. SCARLATTI: Sonatas, harpsichord,
>   Kk 159, C major; Kk 3, A minor; Kk 215, E major. Robert Ald-
>   winckle, hpd. Sound News SM 188
>   +RR 4-80 p95
Concerto, harp, op. 4, no. 6, B flat major. See no. 1182
Concerto, harp, op. 4, no. 6, B flat major: Allegro. See no. 4028
Concerto, harpsichord, G major. See no. 1620
Concerto, 2 horns, F major. See no. 356
Concerto, oboe, G minor. See no. 3610
1602 Concerti, organ (16). Rudolf Ewerhart, org; Collegium Aureum;
>   Reinhard Peters, Franzjosef Maier. Harmonia Mundi 1C 197 99880/3
>   (4)
>   +FF 11/12-80 p117
Concerto, organ, op. 4, no. 1, G major: Finale. See no. 3858
1603 Concerti, organ, op. 4, nos. 2 and 4; op. 7, nos. 4 and 13. George
>   Malcolm, org; AMF; Neville Marriner. Argo ZRG 888 Tape (c) KZRC
>   888 (From D3D4)
>   +FF 5/6-80 p87   ++RR 9-79 p90
>   +Gr 10-79 p634   +RR 4-80 p127 tape
>   +HFN 9-79 p107
Concerto, organ, op. 4, no. 5, F major. See no. 187
1604 Concerto, organ, op. 4, no. 6, B flat major. MOZART: Concerto,
>   flute and harp, K 299, C major. Samuel Baron, flt; Marcel Grand-
>   jany, hp; Musica Aeterna Orchestra; Frederic Waldman. Westmin-
>   ster MCA 1403 (From Decca)
>   +FF 9/10-80 p166
1605 Concerti, organ, op. 4, no. 7; op. 7, nos. 9, 11 and 12. Eduard
>   Muller, org; Schola Cantorum Basiliensis; August Wenzinger. DG
>   2535 264 Tape (c) 3335 264 (From SKL 917/21)
>   +Gr 7-79 p199   ++RR 10-79 p151 tape
>   +HFN 9-79 p121   +RR 4-80 p127 tape
>   +RR 7-79 p56
Concerto, organ, op. 4, nos. 4 and 13. See no. 1603
Concerto, organ, op. 7, no. 4, D minor. See no. 187
Concerti, organ, op. 7, nos. 9, 11-12. See no. 1605
1606 Concerti, organ, op. 7, nos. 10-13. Daniel Chorzempa, org; Concerto
>   Amsterdam; Jaap Schroder. Philips 9502 022 Tape (c) 7313 022
>   (From 6709 009)
>   +Gr 4-80 p1554   +HFN 8-80 p109 tape
>   +HFN 4-80 p119   +-RR 4-80 p63
1607 Concerto, recorder, F major. SAMMARTINI: concerto, recorder, F maj-
>   or. TELEMANN: Concerto, recorder, C major. VIVALDI: Concerto,
>   recorder, RV 443, C major. Michala Petri, rec; AMF; Iona Brown.
>   Philips 9500 714 Tape (c) 7300 808
>   +Gr 11-80 p683   ++NR 11-80 p4
>   ++HFN 11-80 p127

1608 Concerti, recorder, G major, F major. TELEMANN: Concerto, recorder,
        C major. VIVALDI: Concerto, recorder, RV 445, C major. Bernard
        Krainis, rec; London Strings; Neville Marriner. Quintessence
        PMC 7146 (From Mercury SR 90443)
                    +ARG 11-80 p39   +FF 9/10-80 p278
1609 Concerti, a due cori, nos. 1-3. Various soloists; Leslie Pearson,
        hpd; ECO; Raymond Leppard. Philips 6570 114 Tape (c) 7310 014
        (From SAL 3707)
                    +Gr 1-80 p1146   ++NR 4-79 p5
                    +HFN 11-79 p157   ++RR 11-79 p83
                    +-HFN 1-80 p123 tape   ++SFC 1-14-79 p48
1610 Concerto, a due cori, no. 2, F major. Alexander's feast. Royal
        fireworks music. Schola Cantorum Basiliensis; Capella Colonien-
        sis; August Wenzinger. DG 2547 006 Tape (c) 3347 006 (From SAPM
        198146, 198017/8)
                    +-Gr 4-80 p1595   +-RR 6-80 p49
                    +-HFN 6-80 p117
1611 Concerti grossi, op. 3. Cappella Coloniensis; August Wenzinger.
        DG 2547 017 Tape (c) 3347 017 (from SAPM 198017/8)
                    +Gr 4-80 p1595   +RR 6-80 p49
                    +HFN 6-80 p117
1612 Concerti grossi, op. 3. PCO; Charles Mackerras. HMV ESD 7089 Tape
        (c) TC ESD 7089
                    +Gr 8-80 p221   +RR 8-80 p45
                    +HFN 9-80 p104
1613 Concerti grossi, op. 3. Northern Sinfonia; George Malcolm. None-
        such H 71376 (also Enigma VAR 1045 Tape (c) TC VAR 1045)
                    +-ARG 12-80 p28   +-RR 5-78 p30
                    +-FF 9/10-80 p126   +-RR 10-78 p117 tape
                    +-Gr 5-78 p1858   +SFC 6-15-80 p36
                    +-HF 10-80 p74   +St 7-80 p81
                    +-HFN 7-78 p95
1614 Concerti grossi, op. 3. Concerti grossi, op. 6, nos. 1-12. La
        Grande Ecurie et la Chambre du Roy; Jean-Claude Malgoire. Ody-
        ssey Y4 35234 (4)
                    +FF 3/4-80 p91   ++SFC 6-10-79 p45
                    +-FU 3-80 p45   +St 11-79 p88
                    +-HF 11-79 p96
     Concerti grossi, op. 6, nos. 1-12. See no. 1614
     Concerto grosso, op. 6, no. 12, B minor: Allegro. See no. 4028
     Concerto a 4, D minor. See no. 3543
1615 Coronation anthems: The king shall rejoice. Let thy hand be streng-
        thened. My heart is inditing. Zadok the priest. Huddersfield
        Choral Society; Northern Sinfonia; Keith Rhodes, org; John
        Pritchard. Enigma K 23533
                     +-HFN 9-80 p115
1616 Deborah. Soloists; St. Jacobi Kantorei Chorus; NDR Rundfunkorches-
        ter. Musicaphon BM 30 SK 1341/2
                    +HFN 10-80 p105
1617 Dixit dominus. Zadok the priest. Felicity Palmer, Margaret Mar-
        shall, s; John Angelo Messana, Charles Brett, c-t; Richard Mor-
        ton, Alastair Thompson, t; Monteverdi Orchestra and Choir; John
        Eliot Gardiner. Erato STU 71055 Tape (c) MCE 71055 (also Musi-
        cal Heritage Society MHS 4104)
                    +ARG 6-80 p21   +HFN 5-78 p131
                    ++FF 7/8-80 p93   +HFN 10-80 p117 tape

      ++Gr 3-78 p1605   +RR 3-78 p63

1618 Dixit dominus. Teresa Zylis-Gara, s; Janet Baker, ms; Martin Lane,
    alto; Robert Tear, t; John Shirley-Quirk, bar; John Langdon, org;
    Andrew Davis, hpd; King's College Choir; ECO; David Willcocks.
    HMV SXLP 30444 Tape (c) TC SXLP 30444 (From ASD 2262)
          +Gr 10-80 p527   +HFN 12-80 p159 tape
          +HFN 11-80 p129

Fantasia, C major. See no. 1601. See no. 1610
Figlia d'alte speranze, no. 15. See no. 1597
Forest music. See no. 3728
Fugue, A minor. See no. 1620
Fugue, no. 3, B flat major. See no. 1619
Giulio Cesare: V'adoro pupillo; Hercules, my father. See no. 147
Grand lesson on an air from "Rinaldo" (Babell). See no. 3745

1619 Harpsichord works: Air, A major. Capriccio, G minor. Fugue, no. 3,
    B flat major. Overture, B flat major. Preludes, D minor, F major.
    Sonata, harpsichord, G minor. Suite, no. 5, E major. Franzpeter
    Goebels, hpd. Musicaphon BM 30 SL 1922
          +HFN 10-80 p105

1620 Harpsichord works: Aria con variazioni, B flat major. Air, B flat
    major. Concerto, harpsichord, G major. Fantasia, C major.
    Fugue, A minor. Preludio and allegro, G minor. Sonatas, harpsi-
    chord, C major, G minor. Suites, G major, D minor, F major, B
    flat major. Zuzana Ruzickova, hpd. Supraphon 111 2491/2 (2)
          -Gr 10-80 p518   +NR 10-80 p14
          +-HFN 12-80 p140

1621 Israel in Egypt. Jean Knibbs, Marilyn Troth, Daryl Greene, Elisa-
    beth Priday, s; Christopher Royall, Ashley Stafford, Brian Gor-
    don, Julian Clarkson, c-t; Paul Elliott, William Kendall, t;
    Stephen Varcoe, Charles Stewart, bs; Marilyn Sansom, vlc; Mal-
    colm Hicks, org; Alastair Ross, hpd; Monteverdi Orchestra and
    Choir; John Eliot Gardiner. Erato STU 71245 (2)
          +Gr 1-80 p1187   +RR 2-80 p88

1622 Israel in Egypt: But as for his people; Moses and the children of
    Israel; The Lord is a man of war. MOZART: Die Zauberflote, K
    620: Schnelle Fusse. VERDI: Macbeth: Sleep walking scene. WAG-
    NER: Die Gotterdammerung: Ho ho. Tiana Lemnitz, Margherita
    Grandi, Vera Terry, s; Heinrich Tessmer, Helge Roswange, t; Her-
    bert Janssen, Ernest Frank, bar; Wilhelm Strienz, bs; Favres
    Solisten Vereinigung; BPhO, LPO, RPO; Thomas Beecham. World
    Records SH 1004
          +ARSC Vol 12, no. 3, 1980 p240

Israel in Egypt: He sent a thick darkness; He smote all the first-
    born of Egypt. See no. 262
Israel in Egypt: He spake the word; He gave them hailstones. See
    no. 1594
Israel in Egypt: The Lord is a man of war. See no. 3774

1623 Jeptha. Margaret Marshall, Emma Kirkby, s; Alfreda Hodgson, con;
    Paul Esswood, c-t; Anthony Rolfe-Johnson, t; Christopher Keyte,
    bs; Southend Boys choir; AMF and Chorus; Neville Marriner. Argo
    D181D4 (4) Tape (c) K181K44
          +Gr 2-80 p1287   +RR 1-80 p107
          +HFN 1-80 p119

1624 Jeptha. Lenys Linos, ms; Elizabeth Gale, s; Paul Esswood, c-t;
    Werner Hollweg, t; Thomas Thomaschke, bs; Arnold Schoenberg

Choir, Mozart Boys Choir; VCM; Nikolaus Harnoncourt. Telefunken
6-35499 (4)
       +Gr 1-80 p1188   +RR 11-79 p118
       +-HFN 12-79 p161   +-FF 3/4-80
       +-NYT 1-20-80 pD22
       +-SFC 4-20-80 p34
Jeptha: When his loud voice. See no. 1594
Judas Maccabaeus: See the conquering hero comes. See no. 262. See
    no. 1594. See no. 3858
Judas Maccabaeus: Sound an alarm. See no. 3986
Judas Maccabaeus: The Lord worketh wonders. See no. 3770
The king shall rejoice. See no. 1615. See no. 1654. See no. 3937
Largo. See no. 1307. See no. 3663
Lesson, no. 1, B flat major. See no. 1601
Let thy hand be strengthened. See no. 1615. See no. 1654
1625 Messiah. James Bowman, c-t; Robert Tear, t; Benjamin Luxon, bar;
    King's College Boys Choir, soprano solos; King's College Choir;
    AMF; David Willcocks. Arabesque 8030-3 (3)
           +FF 11/12-80 p118   +SFC 12-14-80 p20
1626 Messiah. Jennifer Smith, s; Charles Brett, t; Ulrik Cold, bs; Wor-
    cester Cathedral Choir; La Grande Ecurie et la Chambre du Roy;
    Jean-Claude Malgoire. CBS 76953 (3)
           ++HFN 12-80 p140
1627 Messiah. Jennifer Smith, s; Andrew King, Martyn Hill, t; Charles
    Brett, t; Ulrik Cold, bs; Worcester Cathedral Choir; La Grande
    Ecurie et la Chambre de Roy; Jean-Claude Malgoire. CBS 79336 (3)
           +-Gr 12-80 p860   ++STL 11-9-80 p40
           ++HFN 12-80 p140
1628 Messiah. Judith Nelson, Emma Kirkby, s; Carolyn Watkinson, con;
    Paul Elliott, t; David Thomas, bs; Christ Church Cathedral Choir;
    Academy of Ancient Music; Christopher Hogwood. Decca D189D3 (3)
    Tape (c) K189K33
           ++Gr 4-80 p1575   +NYT 10-19-80 pD24
           ++Gr 9-80 p413 tape   ++RR 4-80 p111
           ++HFN 4-80 p99   +-SFC 12-14-80 p20
           +MT 10-80 p634
1629 Messiah, excerpts. Adele Addison, s; David Lloyd, t; Russell Ober-
    lin, c-t; William Warfield, bar; Westminster Choir; NYP; Leonard
    Bernstein. CBS 30115 Tape (c) 40-30115
           +-Gr 1-80 p1203   +-RR 12-79 p110
           -HFN 1-80 p123
1630 Messiah, excerpts. Georgine Resick, s; Jeanne Haughn, con; William
    Livingston, t; Carl Gerbrandt, bs; James Dale, org; Hood College
    Choir, U.S. Naval Academy Choir; Orchestra; John Talley. Richard-
    son RRS 2
           +-RR 12-80 p8
Messiah: Hallelujah. See no. 262
Messiah: Hallelujah; For unto us a child is born; Worthy is the
    lamb; Amen. See no. 1594
Messiah: I know that my redeemer liveth. See no. 3938
Messiah: Rejoice greatly. See no. 3774
Minuet, G minor. See no. 1600
My heart is inditing. See no. 1615. See no. 1654
Nel dolce dell'oblio, no. 17. See no. 1597
1631 Ode for St. Cecilia's day. Felicity Palmer, s; Anthony Rolfe John-

son, t; Stockholm Bach Choir; VCM; Nikolaus Harnoncourt. Telefunken AW 6-42349 Tape (c) CX 4-42349 (r) 6-42349
    +ARG 3-80 p25   +HFN 4-79 p119
    ++FF 9/10-79 p92   ++RR 3-79 p118
    ++Gr 4-79 p1756   +St 10-79 p138
    +HF 7-80 p82 tape

The origin of design: Ballet suite. See no. 4072
Ottone: Dopo l'orrore. See no. 1595
Overture, B flat major. See no. 1619.
Overture, D major. See no. 1590

1632 Partenope. Krisztina Laky, s; Helga Muller Molinari, con; Rene
    Jacobs, John Skinner, c-t; Martyn Hill, t; Stephen Varcoe, bar;
    La Petite Bande; Sigiswald Kuijken. Harmonia Mundi 1C 157 99855/
    8 (4)
        +FF 9/10-80 p127   +NYT 4-20-80 pD24
        +Gr 12-79 p1047   +ON 11-1-80 p44
        +HFN 12-79 p161   +RR 12-79 p18
        +MT 4-80 p251   +STL 12-2-79 p37

Il Pastor Fido: Pour les Chasseurs I and II. See no. 1588
Preludes, D minor, F major. See no. 1619
Prelude and allegro, G minor. See no. 1620

1633 Psalms: Laudate pueri, D major; Nisi dominus; Salve regina. Deller
    Consort, The King's Music; Mark Deller. Harmonia Mundi HM 1054
    Tape (c) 1054
        +Gr 12-80 p865

Radamisto: Vanne sorella ingrata. See no. 3551
Rejoice daughter of Zion. See no. 3933
Riemuitse tytar Siionin. See no. 3592
Rigadoon. See no. 3895

1634 Royal fireworks music. Water music. New Koto Ensemble. Angel S
    37620 Tape (c) 4XS 37620
        +NR 5-80 p15   +NYT 5-20-79 pD26

1635 Royal fireworks music. Water music: Overture; Adagio e staccato;
    Allegro in 3/4; Air; Minuet; Bourree; Hornpipe; Andante, D minor;
    Allegro; Bourree; Alla hornpipe. ECO Wind Ensemble; Johannes
    Somary. Vanguard VSD 71176 Tape (c) ZCVSM 71176 (r) E 71176 (Q)
    VSQ 30020
        -HF 9-73 p106   -RR 3-75 p73 tape
        +HF 2-80 p102 tape   ++St 7-73 p104
        +RR 11-73 p37

Royal fireworks music. See no. 1590. See no. 1598. See no. 1610
Royal fireworks music: A royal firework. See no. 3841

1636 Royal fireworks music: Suite. Water music: Suite. (arr. Newman).
    Anthony Newman, org. Soundstream Digitech DIGI 103 Tape (c) 103D
        +-HF 7-80 p69

1637 Samson. Norma Burrowes, Felicity Lott, s; Janet Baker, ms; Helen
    Watts, alto; Robert Tear, Philip Langridge, Alexander Oliver, t;
    John Shirley-Quirk, bar; Benjamin Luxon, bs-bar; London Voices;
    ECO; Raymond Leppard. RCA ARL 4-3635 (4) Tape (c) ARK 3-3635
    (also Erato STU 71240)
        +Gr 9-80 p392   ++SFC 11-23-80 p21
        +NR 10-80 p9   +St 12-80 p124

Samson: Honour and arms. See no. 1595
Samson: Then round about the starry throne. See no. 262
Saul: Gird on thy sword. See no. 1594

Saul: Mourn Isreal mourn. See no. 262
Saul: With rage I shall burn. See no. 1595
Scipio: Hear me ye winds and waves. See no. 4007
Semele: Where'er you walk. See no. 3948
1638 Serse (Xerxes). Barbara Hendricks, Anne-Marie Rodde, s; Carolyn
     Watkinson, Ortrun Wenkel, con; Paul Esswood, c-t; Ulrik Cold,
     Ulrich Studer, bs; Jean Bridier Vocal Ensemble; La Grande Ecurie
     et la Chambre du Roy; Jean-Claude Malgoire. CBS 79325 (3)
                    +-Gr 10-79 p698   +-Op 11-79 p1070
                    +-HFN 10-79 p153   ++RR 10-79 p56
                    +-MT 3-80 p180
     Serse: Arias. See no. 3999
     Serse: Largo. See no. 3943. See no. 3961
     Serse: Ombra mai fu. See no. 1595. See no. 3903
     Serse: Va godendo. See no. 3770
     Silent worship. See no. 3874
1639 Solomon (edit. and rev. Beecham). Elsie Morison, Louis Marshall, s;
     Alexander Young, t; John Cameron, bar; Beecham Choral Society;
     RPO; Thomas Beecham. HMV SLS 5163 (2) Tape (c) TC SLS 5163 (From
     Columbia 33CS 1397/8)
                    ++ARSC Vol 12, no. 3   +-HFN 8-79 p123 tape
                       1980 p252   ++RR 7-79 p107
                    ++Gr 6-79 p93   +-RR 10-79 p157 tape
                    +-HFN 7-79 p118
     Solomon: Arrival of the Queen of Sheba. See no. 298. See no. 3639.
       See no. 3715. See no. 3916. See no. 4072
     Solomon: From the censer curling rise. See no. 1654
     Solomon: May no rash intruder. See no. 1594
     Solomon: When the sun o'er yonder hills. See no. 1595
1640 Sonatas, flute and harpsichord, op. 1 (10). Paula Robison, flt;
     Kenneth Cooper, hpd; Timothy Eddy, vlc. Vanguard VSD 71229/30
     (2)
                    +Audio 12-79 p123   +HF 7-79 p142
                    ++ARG 9-79 p28   ++NR 7-79 p8
                    +FF 7/8-79 p57   ++SFC 4-20-80 p34
                    +-FU 9-79 p52
1641 Sonatas, flute and harpsichord, op. 1, nos. 1-, 4-6. Ronald Roseman,
     Virginia Brewer, ob; Edward Brewer, hpd; Donald MacCourt, bsn.
     Nonesuch H 71380
                    +FF 7/8-80 p95   ++St 10-80 p114
                    ++HF 12-80 p80
     Sonata, flute and harpsichord, op. 1, no. 4, A minor. See no. 3717
     Sonatas, harpsichord, C major, G minor. See no. 1620
     Sonata, harpsichord, G minor. See no. 1619
     Sonata, oboe, E major. See no. 3542
     Sonata, oboe, op. 1, no. 6, G minor. See no. 269
1642 Sonatas, 2 oboes and harpsichord, nos. 1-6. Heinz Holliger, Maurice
     Bourgue, ob; Christiane Jaccottet, hpd; Manfred Sax, bsn. Phil-
     ips 9500 671 Tape (c) 7300 766
                    +FF 9/10-80 p128   ++NR 10-80 p8
     Sonata, recorder, A minor. See no. 3593
1643 Sonatas, violin and harpsichord, op. 1 (6). Arthur Grumiaux, vln;
     Robert Veyron-Lacroix, hpd. Philips 9502 023 (From SAL 3687)
                    +FF 7/8-80 p94   +HFN 5-80 p135
                    +Gr 5-80 p1683   ++NR 8-80 p9
                    +HF 7-80 p59   +-RR 5-80 p87

1644 Sonatas, violin and harpsichord, op. 1, nos. 3, 6, 10-11, 13-15.
     Josef Suk, vln; Zuzana Ruzickova, hpd. Supraphon 410 2321/2 (2)
                +FF 11/12-79 p80   -HFN 2-80 p93
                +-HF 11-79 p98   +RR 1-80 p103
1645 Sonatas, violin and harpsichord, op. 1, nos. 3, 10, 12. Susanne
     Lautenbacher, vln; Hugo Ruf, hpd; Johannes Koch, vla da gamba.
     Musicaphon BM 30 SL 3010
                +-HFN 12-80 p140   +RR 7-80 p80
     Sonatas, violin and harpsichord, op. 1, no. 13, D major. See no.
        3964
     Songs: O sleep why does thou leave me. See no. 3541
     Sosarme: Rend'il sereno. See no. 3367. See no. 3560
     Suites, D minor, E minor, G minor, B flat major. See no. 1600
     Suites, G major, D minor, F major, B flat major. See no. 1620
     Suite, harpsichord, D minor: Sarabande. See no. 3659
1646 Suites, harpsichord, nos. 1-8. Kenneth Gilbert, hpd. Harmonia
     Mundi HM 447/8 (2)
                +FF 1/2-80 p89   ++NYT 1-27-80 pD20
                ++Gr 3-78 p1597   +RR 3-78 p57
     Suite, harpsichord, no. 3, D minor. See no. 4022
     Suite, harpsichord, no. 5, E major. See no. 1619
     Suite, harpsichord, no. 16: Sarabande, G major. See no. 1601
     Suite, trumpet, D major. See no. 1397
     Susanna: Peace crown'd with roses. See no. 1595
     Trio sonata, op. 2, no. 6, G major. See no. 4016
     Un'alma innamorata, no. 23. See no. 1597
1647 Utrecht te deum and jubilate. Zadok the priest. Ilse Wolf, s;
     Helen Watts, con; Wilfred Brown, Edgar Fleet, t; Thomas Hemsley,
     bar; Geraint Jones Singers; Orchestra; Geraint Jones. DG 2547
     022 Tape (c) 3347 022 (From SAPM 198008)
                +Gr 4-80 p1595   +-RR 4-80 p111
                +HFN 6-80 p119
1648 Utrecht te deum and jubilate. Emma Kirkby, Judith Nelson, s; Char-
     les Brett, alto; Rogers Covey-Crump, Paul Elliott, t; David Thom-
     as, bs; Christ Church Cathedral Choir; Academy of Ancient Music;
     Simon Preston. L'Oiseau-Lyre DSLO 582 Tape (c) KDSLC 582
                +Gr 12-80 p865   +HFN 12-80 p140
     Verdi prati. See no. 3545
1649 Water music. ECO; Raymond Leppard. Philips 6570 018 Tape (c) 7310
     018 (From 6500 047)
                +Gr 1-80 p1146   +HFN 1-80 p107 tape
                +HFN 12-79 p177   ++RR 12-79 p56
1650 Water music. COA; Eduard van Beinum. Philips 6570 171 (From Epic
     BC 1016, Philips PHC 9016)
                ++ARG 1-80 p30
1651 Water music. AMF; Neville Marriner. Philips 9500 691 Tape (c) 7300
     779
                +ARG 12-80 p28   +HFN 9-80 p116 tape
                +FF 9/10-80 p128   +NR 8-80 p4
                +-Gr 8-80 p221   +RR 7-80 p57
                +-HF 10-80 p74   ++St 9-80 p79
                +HFN 7-80 p107
     Water music. See no. 1634
     Water music: Air. See no. 3942
     Water music: Air and hornpipe. See no. 298

Water music: Allegro. See no. 4028
Water music: Hornpipe. See no. 3663
Water msuic: Minuet; Air; Hornpipe; Allegro maestoso. See no. 145
Water music: Overture; Adagio e staccato; Allegro in 3/4; Air;
        Minuet; Bourree; Hornpipe; Andante, D minor; Allegro; Bourree;
        Alla hornpipe. See no. 1635
Water music: Suite. See no. 299. See no. 1636. See no. 1664
1652 Water music: Suites, F major, D major, G major. Jean-Francois Pail-
        lard Chamber Orchestra; Jean-Francois Paillard. RCA GL 2-5241
        Tape (c) GK 2-5241 (From World Records ST 474)
                    +-Gr 11-79 p817   +-HFN 1-80 p123 tape
                    +-HFN 10-79 p167   +-RR 4-80 p127 tape
Water music: Suite: Allegro. See no. 3640
1653 The ways of Zion do mourn (Funeral anthem for Queen Caroline).
        Norma Burrowes, s; Charles Brett, c-t; Martyn Hill, t; Stephen
        Varcoe, bs; Michael Lewin, theorbo; Malcolm Hicks, org; Monte-
        verdi Orchestra and Choir; John Eliot Gardiner. Erato STU 71173
        (also Musical Heritage Society MHS 4162)
                    +FF 9/10-80 p129   +Gr 5-79 p1922
1654 Works, selections: The king shall rejoice. Let thy hand be streng-
        thened. My heart is inditing. Solomon: From the censer curling
        rise. Zadok the priest. Ambrosian Singers; Susan Longfield, s;
        Alfreda Hodgson, con; Ian Partridge, t; Christopher Keyte, bs;
        Menuhin Festival Orchestra; Yehudi Menuhin. Classics for Pleas-
        ure CFP 40321 (From HMV ASD 2584)
                    +Gr 1-80 p1187   +RR 12-79 p110
                    +HFN 1-80 p121
        Zadok the priest. See no. 1594. See no. 1615. See no. 1617. See
        no. 1647. See no. 1654. See no. 3937
HANDL, Jacob
        Confirma hoc deus. See no. 3973
HANFF, Johann
        Chorale preludes, Ach Gott von Himmel sieh darein; Ein feste Burg
        ist unser Gott; Erbarm dich mein. See no. 953
HANLON, Kevin
1655 Electronic music. HOLMES: Nova. MCLEAN, B.: Night images. MC-
        CLEAN, P.: Invisible chariots. Folkways FPX 6050
                    +NR 11-80 p11
HANSON, Howard
        Young composer's guide to the six-tone scale. See no. 1126
HANUS, Jan
1656 Concertino, timpani and tape, op. 69: 2 movements. Little suite,
        op. 78. Sonata seria, violin and percussion, op. 80. Sonata
        variata, clarinet and piano, op. 87. Meyer Kupferman, clt; Kaz-
        uko Hayami, pno; Vaclav Snitil, vln; Oldrich Satava, perc; Petr
        Sprunk, timpani; Prague Chamber Orchestra Members. Serenus SRS
        12083
                    +-ARG 4-80 p24   +-FF 9/10-80 p130
        Little suite, op. 78. See no. 1656
        Sonata seria, violin and percussion, op. 80. See no. 1656
        Sonata variata, clarinet and piano, op. 87. See no. 1656
HARBISON, John
1657 The flower-fed buffaloes. RZEWSKI: Song and dance. Sepeculum Musi-
        cae. Nonesuch H 71366
                    +FF 3/4-80 p139   +NYT 9-16-76 pD24
                    +NR 2-80 p8   +St 1-80 p100

1658 Quintet. ROCHBERG: Slow fires of autumn. Aulos Wind Quintet; Carol
        Wincenc, flt; Nancy Allen, hp. CRI SD 436
                ++NR 11-80 p6
d'HARDELOT, Guy
     Roses of forgiveness. See no. 3774
HARPER, Edward
1659 Fanny Robin. Ricercari in memoriam Luigi Dallapiccola. Quintet,
        flute, clarinet, violin, violoncello and piano. Jane Manning, s;
        Nigel Waugh, bar; Scottish Opera Chorus; Scottish Chamber Orch-
        estra, New Music Group of Scotland; Edward Harper. Oxford OUP
        200
                +Gr 4-80 p1589   +—MT 5-80 p322
                +—HFN 3-80 p91   +RR 4-80 p47
     Quintet, flute, clarinet, violin and violoncello and piano. See no.
        1659
     Ricercari in memoriam Luigi Dallapiccola. See no. 1659
HARRIS, Albert
     Suite. See no. 3884
HARRIS, Roy
     Chorale, organ and brass. See no. 1661
     Cimarron. See no. 1660
1660 Concerto, piano. Cimarron. Symphony, band. Johana Harris, pno;
        UCLA Wind Ensemble, International String Congress Orchestra,
        1960; James Westbrook, Roy Harris. Varese VC 81100
                ++FF 7/8-80 p95   +NYT 9-28-80 pD31
                ++Gr 5-80 p1660   +RR 6-80 p49
                +HFN 5-80 p121
1661 Concerto, piano, brass, string bass and percussion. Fantasy, organ,
        brass and timpani. Toccata, organ and brass. Chorale, organ and
        brass. Johana Harris, pno; Thomas Harmon, org; U.S. Air Force
        Academy Band, UCLA Brass Ensemble; Roy Harris, James Westbrook.
        Varese VC 81085
                +FF 11/12-79 p80   +RR 1-80 p76
                +Gr 3-80 p1391   ++St 11-79 p88
                +HFN 1-80 p106
     Fantasy, organ, brass and timpani. See no. 1661
     Symphony, band. See no. 1660
     Toccata, organ and brass. See no. 1661
1662 When Johnny comes marching home. PISTON: Symphony, no. 1. WEIN-
        ZWEIG: Symphonic ode. Louisville Orchestra; Jorge Mester.
        Louisville LS 766
                +—FF 5/6-80 p130   +NYT 6-16-79 pD24
HARRIS, W.H.
     Behold the tabernacle. See no. 3992
     Come thou fount. See no. 3992
     Simple gifts. See no. 3992
     Vox ultima crucis. See no. 3992
HARRIS, William
     Fair is the heaven. See no. 4019
     Songs: Almighty and most merciful father; I was glad when they said
        unto me; Come down O lord divine; King of glory king of peace.
        See no. 34
HARRISON
     In the gloaming. See no. 3875

HARRISON, Lou
    Serenade. See no. 4026
HARTMANN, Karl Amadeus
1663 Concerto funebre. WEILL: Concerto, violin, op. 12. Susanne Lauten-
        bacher, vln; Detmold Wind Ensemble, Wurttemberg Chamber Orchestra;
        Jost Michaels, Jorg Faerber. Candide QCE 31105
                    ++FF 9/10-80 p1235
HARTY, Hamilton
1664 Concerto, violin. John Field suite. Londonderry air. Variations
        on a Dublin air. HANDEL (arr. Harty): Water music: Suite. Ralph
        Holmes, vln; Ulster Orchestra; Bryden Thomson. Chandos BDR 2001
        (2) Tape (c) DBT 2001
                    +Gr 1-80 p1151   +HFN 1-80 p93
    John Field suite. See no. 1664
    Londonderry air. See no. 1664
    Variations on a Dublin air. See no. 1664
HARWOOD, Basil
    Paean, op. 15, no. 2. See no. 4049
HASSLER, Hans
    Canzona, C major. See no. 4035
    Intradas (3). See no. 3754
    Intradas a 5. See no. 3569
    Laetentur coeli. See no. 3973
    Songs: Cantate domino; Alleluia, the lord is king; A-roving; Shenan-
        doah; Old man Noah; America the beautiful. See no. 3971
    Verbum caro factum est. See no. 3697
HATTON, John
    The enchantress. See no. 3560
    He that hath a pleasant face; The letter; The way to build a boat
        or Jack's opinion. See no. 3791
    Simon the cellarer. See no. 3770. See no. 3905
HAUG, Hans
    Alba. See no. 3975
HAVELKA, Svatopluk
    Hommage a Hieronymus Bosch. See no. 1017
HAYDN Josef
    Allegretto, flute clock. See no. 4067
1665 Allemandes (6). Concerto, trumpet, E flat major. HAYDN, M.: Con-
        certo, horn, D major. Minuets (6). Alan Stringer, tpt; Barry
        Tuckwell, hn; AMF; Neville Marriner. Argo ZRG 543 Tape (c) KZRC
        543 (r) E 543
                    +HF 5-80 p90 tape   +RR 6-76 p87
                    +HFN 7-76 p104 tape   +RR 4-80 p128 tape
    Andante and variations, F minor. See no. 404
1666 Armida. Jessye Norman, Norma Burrowes, s; Claes Ahnsjo, Robin
        Leggat, Anthony Rolfe Johnson, t; Samuel Ramey, bs; Lausanne
        Chamber Orchestra; Antal Dorati. Philips 6769 021 (3)
                    ++ARG 2-80 p34   +NR 1-80 p7
                    +FF 3/4-80 p93   ++Op 10-79 p972
                    ++FU 3-80 p45   +RR 9-79 p51
                    +Gr 9-79 p508   ++SFC 11-11-79 p45
                    +HF 3-80 p81   ++St 2-80 p127
                    ++HFN 10-79 p153   +STL 12-2-79 p37
1667 Cassation, G major. Concerto, violin and harpsichord, F major.
        Pina Carmirelli, vln; Maria Teresa Garatti, hpd; I Musici. Phil-

```
        ips 9500 602 Tape (c) 7300 724
                +FF 9/10-80 p132                    ++St 8-80 p96
                +NR 6-80 p7
```

1668 Concerto, horn, no. 1, D major. HOFFMANN: Concerto, flute, D major
     (attr. Haydn). Hans-Martin Linde, flt; Erich Penzel, hn; Col-
     legium Aureum. Harmonia Mundi 065 99650 (also Quintessence PMC
     7124 Tape (c) P4C 7124)
```
                +FF 9/10-80 p130                    +RR 9-78 p52
                +HFN 9-78 p153                      +St 1-80 p95
```

1669 Concerto, horn, no. 1, D major. Concerto, horn, no. 2, D major (ed.
     Steves). HAYDN, M.: Concertino, horn, D major. Barry Tuckwell,
     hn; John Constable, hpd; ECO; Barry Tuckwell. HMV ASD 3774 Tape
     (c) TC ASD 3774 (also Angel SZ 37569 Tape (c) 4SZ 37569)
```
                +Gr 10-79 p639                      +NYT 12-2-79 pD22
                +HF 4-80 p104 tape                  +RR 10-79 p88
                +HFN 10-79 p153                     +St 1-80 p95
                +-HFN 1-80 p123 tape
```
     Concerto, horn, no. 2, D major. See no. 1669
1670 Concerto, 2 horns, E flat major. Concerto, organ, C major. Concer-
     to, trumpet, E flat major. Maurice Andre, tpt; Marie-Claire
     Alain, org; Jean-Francois Paillard Orchestra. RCA GL 2-5238 Tape
     (c) GK 2-5238 (From World Records ST 651)
```
                +Gr 1-80 p1151                      +HFN 1-80 p123 tape
                +HFN 10-79 p167                     +-RR 4-80 p127 tape
```
1671 Concerti, 2 liras (5). Jean-Pierra Rampal, flt; Pierre Pierlot,
     ob; Collegium Musicum, Paris; Roland Douatte. Everest SDBR 3465
     Tape (c) 3465
```
                -FF 3/4-80 p93                      +-NR 4-80 p6
                +-HF 8-80 p87 tape
```
     Concerto, oboe, C major. See no. 1255
     Concerto, organ, C major. See no. 1670
     Concerti, organ, C major, F major. See no. 32
1672 Concerti, organ, nos. 1-3. Marie-Claire Alain, org; Bournemouth
     Symphony Orchestra; Theodor Guschlbauer. Musical Heritage Soci-
     ety MHS 4164
```
                +-FF 9/10-80 p131                   ++MU 11-80 p18
```
1673 Concerti, organ, nos. 1-3. Franz Lehrndorfer, org; Wurttemberg
     Chamber Orchestra; Jorg Faerber. Turnabout TVS 34694 Tape (c)
     KTVC 34694 (From TV 37103/5)
```
                +Gr 5-80 p1665                      +RR 3-80 p82
                +-HFN 4-80 p119
```
1674 Concerti, piano, D major, G major, F major. Christiane Jaccottet,
     hpd; Lausanne Instrumental Ensemble; Michel Corboz. Erato STU
     70989
```
                +-Gr 6-80 p37                       +RR 4-80 p65
                .+-HFN 4-80 p105
```
1675 Concerto, trumpet, C major. MOZART: Concerto, flute, no. 2, K 314,
     C major. Maurice Andre, tpt; Franz Liszt Chamber Orchestra;
     Frigyes Sandor. Erato STU 71148
```
                +-NR 1-80 p76
```
1676 Concerto, trumpet, E flat major. HUMMEL: Concerto, trumpet, E flat
     major. MOZART, L.: Concerto, trumpet, D major. Carole Dawn
     Reinhardt, tpt; Munich Philharmonic Orchestra; Marc Andreae.
     Acanta DC 22766
```
                +-HFN 5-80 p133                     +RR 5-80 p63
```

1677 Concerto, trumpet, E flat major. HUMMEL: Concerto, trumpet, E flat
     major. Gerard Schwarz, tpt; New York Y Chamber Symphony Orches-
     tra; Gerad Schwarz. Delos D DMS 3001
               +HF 2-80 p100   +NYT 5-18-80 pD32
               +HFN 4-80 p105   -RR 4-80 p60
               +NR 12-79 p5   ++St 2-80 p136
1678 Concerto, trumpet, E flat major. HAYDN, M.: Concerto, trumpet, C
     major. MOLTER: Concerto, trumept, D major. MOZART, L.: Concer-
     to, D major. Don Smithers, tpt; Berlin Chamber Orchestra; Wolf-
     Dieter Hauschild. Philips 6570 044 Tape (c) 7310 044
               +-Gr 4-80 p1567   ++HFN 6-80 p119 tape
               +-HFN 2-80 p103   +-RR 2-80 p54
1679 Concerto, trumpet, E flat major. MOZART, L.: Concerto, trumpet and
     horn, D major. PURCELL: Sonata, trumpet. TELEMANN: Concerto,
     trumpet, D major. Theo Mertens, tpt; Anneke Uittenbosch, Gustav
     Leonhardt, hpd; Concerto Amsterdam; Andre Rieu. Telefunken 6-
     41145
               +-FF 11/12-80 p213
1680 Concerto, trumpet, E flat major. HUMMEL: Concerto, trumpet, E flat
     major. NERUDA: Concerto, trumpet, E flat major. William Lang,
     tpt; Northern Sinfonia Orhcestra; Christopher Seaman. Unicorn
     RHS 337 Tape (c) UKC 354
               +Gr 12-80 p889 tape   +-HFN 11-80 p131 tape
     Concerto, trumpet, E flat major. See no. 29. See no. 298. See no.
     707. See no. 1102. See no. 1665. See no. 1670. See no. 3779
1681 Concerto, violin, no. 1, C major. Concerto, violin, no. 3, A major.
     Concerto, violin, no. 4, G major. Gerard Jarry, vln; Jean-Francois
     Paillard Chamber Orchestra; Jean-Francois Paillard. Erato STU
     70770
               +-HFN 4-80 p105   +-RR 10-79 p88
               +-RR 10-73 p66
     Concerto, violin, no. 3, A major. See no. 1681
     Concerto, violin, no. 4, G major. See no. 1681
     Concerto, violin and harpsichord, F major. See no. 1667
1682 Concerto, violoncello, C major. KOKKONEN: Concerto, violoncello.
     Arto Noras, vlc; Helsinki Philharmonic Orchestra, Helsinki Cham-
     ber Orchestra; Paul Freeman, Okko Kamu. Finnlevy SFX 36 (also
     Finlandia FA 310)
               +ARG 9-80 p43   +-NR 9-80 p4
               +-FF 7/8-80 p100   +-RR 4-80 p65
               +Gr 4-80 p1554   *Te 12-78 p48
               +HFN 6-80 p107
1683 Concerto, violoncello, C major. Symphony, no. 49, F minor. Roland
     Pidoux, vlc; Teatro Comunale Orchestra; Angelo Ephrikian. Har-
     monia Mundi HM 1030
               +-FF 9/10-80 p132   +-NR 6-80 p3
               +-HFN 3-80 p91   +-RR 4-80 p63
     Concerto, violoncello, C major. See no. 1684
1684 Concerto, violoncello, op. 101, D major. Concerto, violoncello, C
     major. Frederic Lodeon, vlc; Bournemouth Sinfonietta Orchestra;
     Theodor Guschlbauer. Erato STU 70869
               +Gr 3-75 p1650   +RR 10-79 p88
               /-HFN 4-80 p105
     German dances, nos. 4, 10-11. See no. 3989
     Divertimento. See no. 4003

Divertimento, no. 1, B flat major. See no. 3971

Divertimento, no. 8, C major. See no. 3626

1685 La fidelta premiata: Per te m'accese amore; Vanne...fuggi...tradi-
     tore; Barbaro conte...Dell'amor mio fedele. Il mondo della luna:
     Una donna come me; Se lo comando ci veniro. MOZART: La clemenza
     di Tito, K 621: Torna di Tito a lato; Tu fosti tradito. ROSSINI:
     Otello: Quanto son fieri i palpiti; Che smania...Oime che affanno;
     Assisa a pie d'un salice; Deh calma o ciel nel sonno. Frederica
     von Stade, ms; PhO, Lausanne Chamber Orchestra, ROHO; Jesus Lopez
     Cobos, Antal Dorati, Colin Davis. Philips 9500 716 Tape (c) 7300
     807 (From 6769 023, 6707 028, 6769 003, 6703 079)
                    +FF 9/10-80 p239   +NR 7-80 p9
                    +Gr 8-80 p270   +RR 8-80 p32
                    +HFN 10-80 p117 tape   ++St 9-80 p82

1686 L'Incontro improviso (The unexpected meeting). Linda Zoghby, Marg-
     aret Marshall, s; Della Jones, ms; Claes Ahnsjo, t; Domenico
     Trimarchi, Benjamin Luxon, bar; Lausanne Chamber Orchestra; Antal
     Dorati. Philips 6769 040 (3) (also Philips 9500 705/7)
                    +Gr 9-80 p392   +Op 10-80 p1013
                    +HFN 9-80 p105   ++STL 9-14-80 p40

1687 De Jahreszeiten (The seasons). Ileana Cotrubas, s; Werner Krenn, t;
     Hans Sotin, bs; Brighton Festival Chorus; RPO; Antal Dorati. Dec-
     ca D88D3 (3) Tape (c) K88K32 (also London OSA 13128 Tape (c) OSA
     5-13128)
                    +-ARG 2-80 p34   +HFN 4-79 p133 tape
                    +-FF 5/6-80 p89   +MT 3-79 p227
                    ++FU 12-79 p41   ++NR 2-80 p9
                    +-Gr 1-79 p1315   +-RR 12-78 p106
                    +HF 6-79 p84   ++St 6-79 p1320
                    +HFN 12-78 p147

1688 Die Jahreszeiten. Maria Stader, s; Ernst Hafliger, t; Josef Greindl,
     bs; St. Hedwig's Cathedral Choir; Orchestra; Ferenc Fricsay. DG
     2721 170
                    +-ARSC Vol 12, nos. 1-2, 1980 p124

1689 Die Jahreszeiten, excerpts. Gundula Janowitz, s; Peter Schreier, t;
     Martti Talvela, bs; Vienna Singverein, VSO; Karl Bohm. DG Tape
     (c) 3335 368
                    +-RR 5-80 p127 tape

1690 Die Jahreszeiten. Elsie Morison, s; Alexander Young, t; Michael
     Langdon, bs; Beecham Choral Society; RPO; Thomas Beecham. HMV
     SLS 5158 (3) Tape (c) TC SLS 5158 (From ALP 1606/8)
                    +-ARSC Vol 12, no. 3   +HFN 6-79 p117
                       1980 p252   +HFN 8-79 p123 tape
                    +-FF 7/8-80 p98   +MT 9-79 p747
                    +Gr 5-79 p1944   +RR 6-79 p114

1691 Die Jahreszeiten. Heather Harper, s; Ryland Davies, t; John Shirley-
     Quirk, bar; BBC Symphony Orchestra and Chorus; Maurits Sillem,
     fortepiano; Colin Davis. Philips 6770 035 (3) Tape (c) 7650 035
     (From SAL 3689-3700)
                    +Gr 11-80 p718   +HFN 11-80 p129

Die Jahreszeiten, excerpts. See no. 1761

Die Jahreszeiten: Come gentle spring. See no. 262

1692 Mass, no. 2, E flat major. Judith Nelson, s; Carolyn Watkinson,
     con; Martyn Hill, t; David Thomas, bs; Christ Church Cathedral
     Choir; Academy of Ancient Music; Simon Preston. L'Oiseau-Lyre
     DSLO 563

           +Gr 11-79 p892   ++MT 8-80 p504
           +HFN 12-79 p161   +RR 12-79 p111

1693 Mass, no. 5, B flat major. Mass, no. 8, C major. Pieces, musical
    clock, nos. 3, 6-8. Jennifer Smith, s; Helen Watts, con; Robert
    Tear, t; Benjamin Luxon, bar; John Scott, org; St. John's College
    Chapel Choir; AMF; George Guest. Argo ZRG 867
           ++ARG 3/4-80 p93   +NYT 2-3-80 pD22
           +Gr 10-78 p721   +RR 10-78 p104
           +HFN 10-78 p125

    Mass, no. 8, C major. See no. 1693
1694 Mass, no. 9, D minor. Julie Kennard, s; Ashley Stafford, alto; Alan
    Green, t; Maurice Bevan, bar; St. Paul's Cathedral Choir; London
    Bach Orchestra; Barry Rose. Bach Guild GRSP 7015
           +-Gr 11-80 p718   +-MT 12-80 p785
           +HFN 9-80 p105

    Mass, no. 9, D minor: Gloria. See no. 1761
1695 Mass, no. 10, B flat major. Uta Spreckelsen, s; Hanna Schaer, con;
    Gervase Elwes, t; Lausanne Vocal Ensemble; Lausanne Chamber Or-
    chestra; Michel Corboz. Erato STU 71058
           +HFN 4-80 p104   +-RR 10-79 p136

    Minuets, nos. 1-2, 5, 7, 9-11. See no. 1696
    Il mondo della luna: Una donna come me; Se lo comando ci veniro.
    See no. 1685
1696 Piano works: Minuets, nos. 1-2, 5, 7, 9-11. The seven last words of
    Christ, op. 51. Sonatas, piano, nos. 8, 12, 14-15, 28-29, 37,
    61-62. Variations, D major, E flat major. SCHWANENBERG (formerly
    attrib. Haydn): Sonata, piano, B flat major. ANON.(formerly at-
    trib. Haydn): Sonata, piano, E flat major. John McCabe, pno.
    London STS 15428/31 (4)
           +FF 1/2-80 p91   ++St 10-79 p132

    Pieces, musical clock, nos. 3, 6-8. See no. 1693
    Pieces, musical clock: March. See no. 3895
1697 Quartets, flute, op. 5 (6). Trios, flute, op. 100 (6). Wolfgang
    Schulz, flt; Gerhard Schulz, vln; Ulla Schulz, vla; Walther
    Schulz, vlc. Telefunken 6-35395 (2)
           +-FF 1/2-80 p92   ++SFC 8-31-80 p31
           +NYT 2-3-80 pD22

1698 Quartets, strings, op. 3. The seven last words of Christ, op. 51.
    Peter Pears, narrator; Aeolian Quartet. Argo HDNV 82/4 (3) (also
    London STS 15459/61)
           +FF 11/12-79 p32   +-NR 3-80 p6
           +Gr 9-77 p444   +RR 9-77 p75
           +HFN 9-77 p143   +SFC 12-23-79 p40

    Quartets, strings, op. 3, no. 5, F major: Andante cantabile. See
    no. 3998
1699 Quartets, strings, op. 20, nos. 1-6. Juilliard Quartet. CBS 79305
    (3) (also Columbia M 34593)
           +ARG 1-80 p31   +-MT 3-79 p228
           ++FF 3/4-80 p95   +RR 12-78 p84
           ++Gr 1-79 p1296   +St 11-79 p92
           +HFN 12-78 p155

1700 Quartets, strings, op. 20, nos. 1-6. Quartets, strings, op. 64,
    nos. 1-6. Aeolian Quartet. London STS 15447/52 (6)
           ++NR 3-80 p8   +NYT 12-3-78 pD19

1701 Quartets, strings, op. 20, no. 4, D major. Quartets, strings, op.

74, no. 3, G minor. Guarneri Quartet. RCA ARL 1-3485 Tape (c)
ARK 1-3485
   +–ARG 12-80 p33   +St 10-80 p114
   ++NR 7-80 p7
1702 Quartets, strings, op. 33. Tatrai Quartet. Hungaroton SLPX 11887/9
 (3)
   +–ARG 1-80 p31   -NR 7-79 p10
   +FF 11/12-79 p82
1703 Quartets, strings, op. 54, nos. 1-3; op. 55, nos. 1-3. Aeolian Quar-
 tet. London STS 15346/8
   ++NR 3-80 p8
 Quartets, strings, op. 64, nos. 1-6. See no. 1700
 Quartets, strings, op. 64, no. 5, D major. See no. 1314
 Quartets, strings, op. 64, no. 5, D major: Vivace. See no. 3964
1704 Quartets, strings, op. 71, nos. 1-3, op. 74, nos. 1-3. Amadeus
 Quartet. DG 2709 090 (3)
   +–FF 7/8-80 p97   +–NYT 2-10-80 pD24
   +Gr 11-79 p861   +NYT 2-3-80 pD22
   +HF 5-80 p73   +RR 12-79 p87
   +HFN 12-79 p161   +St 6-80 p115
   +NR 3-80 p6
 Quartets, strings, op. 74, no. 3, G minor. See no. 1701
1705 Quartets, strings, op. 76, no. 2, D minor. Quartets, strings, op.
 76, no. 3, C major. Concord Quartet. Turnabout 37003 Tape (c)
 CT 7003
   +HF 1-80 p71 tape
1706 Quartets, strings, op. 76, no. 3, C major. MOZART: Quartet, strings,
 no. 17, K 458, B flat major. Amadeus Quartet. DG 2542 123 Tape
 (c) 3342 123 (From SLPM 138886)
   ++Gr 10-79 p862   -RR 11-79 p105
   +–HFN 11-79 p153   +RR 4-80 p127 tape
1707 Quartets, strings, op. 76, no. 3, C major. MOZART: Quartet, strings,
 no. 17, K 458, B flat major. Quartetto Italiano. Philips 9500
 662 Tape (c) 7300 762 (From 9500 157, SAL 3633)
   +Gr 8-80 p234   +HFN 9-80 p116 tape
   ++Gr 9-80 p413 tape ++NR 3-80 p6
   +HF 5-80 p73   +RR 7-80 p60
   +HFN 8-80 p98
 Quartets, strings, op. 76, no. 3, C major. See no. 1705. See no.
 1761
 Quartets, strings, op. 103, B flat major: Minuet. See no. 471
1708 Salve regina, E flat major. Stabat mater, G minor. Arleen Auger,
 s; Alfreda Hodgson, con; Anthony Rolf Johnson, t; Gwynne Howell,
 bs; London Chamber Choir; Argo Chamber Orchestra; Laszlo Heltay.
 Argo ZRG 917/8 (2) Tape (c) K215K22
   ++Gr 5-80 p1705   +–RR 6-80 p85
   +–HFN 5-80 p121   +STL 7-13-80 p38
1709 Salve regina, G minor. MOZART: Litaniae lauretanae, K 109, B major.
 Church sonatas, K 278, C major; K 379, C major. Ursula Buckel,
 s; Maureen Lehane, alto; Richard van Vrooman, t; Eduard Wollitz,
 bs; Tolzer Knabenchor; Collegium Aureum; Rolf Reinhardt. Har-
 monia Mundi 1C 065 99826
   +FF 5/6-80 p88
 Salve regina, G minor. See no. 1711
1710 Die Schopfund (The creation). Heather Harper, s; Robert Tear, t;
 John Shirley-Quirk, bs; King's College Chapel Choir; AMF; David

Willcocks. Arabesque 8039-2 (2) Tape (c) 9039
    +ARG 7/8-80 p26   +-HF 6-80 p96 tape
    +FF 11/12-80 p120   +NYT 1-6-80 pD18
    +HF 5-80 p72   +St 5-80 p83
Die Schopfung, excerpts. See no. 1761
Die Schopfung: The heavens are telling the glory of God. See no. 262
Schottische und Walisische Lieder. See no. 546
1711 The seven last words of Christ, op. 71. Salve regina, G minor.
    Veronika Kincses, s; Klara Takacs, con; Gyorgy Korondy, t; Jozsef Gregor, bs; Istvan Lantos, org; Budapest Chorus; Hungarian State Symphony Orchestra; Janos Ferencsik. Hungaroton SLPX 12199/200 (2)
              /Gr 12-80 p865
The seven last words of Christ, op. 51. See no. 1696. See no. 1698
Sonatas, piano, B major, D major. See no. 82
Sonata, piano, E flat major. See no. 3887
Sonata, piano, E major: Presto. See no. 1601
Sonata, piano, F major. See no. 1601
1712 Sonatas, piano, nos. 1-18. Ilse von Alpenheim, pno. Vox SVBX 5490 (3)
           ++ARG 5-79 p26   +NYT 7-1-79 pD22
           +FF 9/10-80 p131   ++SFC 7-15-79 p47
           +NR 4-79 p13
Sonatas, piano, nos. 8, 12, 14-15, 28-29, 37, 61-62. See no. 1696
1713 Sonatas, piano, nos. 20, 23, 26, 32, 34, 43, 46. Malcolm Bilson, pno. Titanic 51/2 Tape (c) Advent E 1068
        +HF 8-79 p53 tape   +NYT 10-19-80 pD24
1714 Sonatas, piano, nos. 25, 41, 60-61. Richard Burnett, fortepiano. Amon Ra SAR 5
        +HFN 3-80 p91   ++RR 2-80 p76
1715 Sonatas, piano, nos. 29, 42, 45, 60. Gilbert Kalish, pno. Nonesuch H 71379
        +ARG 12-80 p33   +-FF 11/12-80 p120
1716 Sonatas, piano, nos. 31-33 (nos. 22, 24, 26). Charles Rosen, pno. Vanguard VCS 10131 Tape (r) BCD 10131 (From CBS 61112)
        +FF 1/2-80 p93   +-NYT 4-23-78 pD20
        +HF 2-80 p102 tape   ++SFC 6-25-78 p61
        -MJ 7-78 p57   +St 9-78 p104
        +NR 10-78 p11
1717 Sonatas, piano, nos. 33, 38, 54. Variations, E flat major. Gilbert Kalish, pno. Nonesuch H 71362 Tape (c) 51362
        +FF 9/10-80 p131   +NYT 4-22-79 pD25
        +Gr 1-80 p1171   +RR 11-79 p111
        +HF 10-79 p126 tape   ++St 10-79 p132
        +HFN 12-79 p161
Sonata, piano, no. 33, C minor. See no. 3622
Sonata, piano, no. 50, D major. See no. 615
1718 Sonata, piano, no. 52, E flat major. MUSSORGSKY: Pictures at an exhibition. Vladimir Horowitz, pno. RCA ARM 1-3263 Tape (c) ARK 1-3263 (From LM 1957, 1249, 1014)
        +ARG 3-80 p26   ++NR 1-80 p14
        +-FF 1/2-80 p119   +NYT 2-3-80 pD22
        +HF 1-80 p63   ++SFC 10-28-79 p53
Sonata, piano, no. 58, C major: Rondo. See no. 1761

1719 Sonata, piano, no. 62, E flat major. PROKOFIEV: Pieces, piano, op.
       4, no. 4: Suggestion diabolique. Sonata, piano, no. 6, op. 82,
       A major. Viktor Friedman, pno. Orion ORS 79341
                     -HF 7-80 p72
1720 Songs (quartets and trios): Abendlied zu Gott; An den Vetter; An die
       Frauen; Alles hat seine Zeit; Der Augenblick; Aus dem Dankliede
       zu Gott; Die Beredsamkeit; Betrachtung des Todes; Daphnens ein-
       ziger Fehler; Der Greis; Die Harmonie in der Ehe; Die Warnung;
       Wider den Ubermuth. Lieder Quartet; Brigitte Haudebourg, hpd.
       Arion ARN 38403
                     +Gr 1-80 p1188   ++RR 2-80 p89
1721 Lo speziale (The apothecary). Magda Kalmar, Veronika Kincses, s;
       Attila Fulop, Istvan Rozsos, t; Liszt Chamber Orchestra; Gyorgy
       Lehel. Hungaroton SLPX 11926/7 (2)
             +ARG 6-79 p20   +HFN 3-79 p124
             +-FF 3/4-80 p94   +NR 6-79 p11
             -FU 4-80 p46   ++RR 3-79 p50
             +-Gr 5-79 p1929   +SFC 4-22-79 p57
             +HF 11-79 p98
       Stabat mater, G minor. See no. 1708
1722 Symphony, no. 31, D major. Symphony, no. 73, D major. AMF; Neville
       Marriner. Philips 9500 518 Tape (c) 7300 674
             ++ARG 5-80 p25   +NYT 2-3-80 pD22
             +Audio 12-79 p101   +ON 3-80 p4
             +Gr 7-79 p199   +RR 7-79 p57
             +Gr 9-79 p534 tape   ++SFC 8-31-80 p31
             +HFN 7-79 p105   +St 3-80 p95
             +HFN 9-79 p123 tape
1723 Symphony, no. 40, F major. Symphonies, nos. 93-98. RPO; Thomas
       Beecham. Arabesque 8024/3 (3)
             +NR 12-80 p4
       Symphony, no. 40, F major. See no. 4072
1724 Symphony, no. 43, E flat major. Symphony, no. 44, E minor. PH;
       Antal Dorati. Decca SDD 546 Tape (c) KSDC 546 (From HDNC 13/18)
             +Gr 1-80 p1151   +-RR 12-79 p56
             +HFN 12-79 p177
1725 Symphony, no. 44, E minor. Symphony, no. 45, F sharp minor. Zagreb
       Radio Orchestra; Antonio Janigro. Vanguard HM 59SD
             -FF 3/4-80 p96   +FU 11-79 p43
       Symphony, no. 44, E minor. See no. 1724
1726 Symphony, no. 45, F sharp minor. Symphony, no. 48, C major. ECO;
       Daniel Barenboim. DG 2531 091 Tape (c) 3301 091
             +FF 3/4-80 p96   -NR 1-80 p3
             +-Gr 7-79 p200   +NYT 2-3-80 pD22
             +HF 2-80 p86   +RR 7-79 p57
             +HFN 7-79 p105   ++RR 9-79 p134 tape
             +HFN 8-79 p123 tape   ++St 3-80 p95
1727 Symphony, no. 45, F sharp minor. Symphony, no. 101, D major. AMF;
       Neville Marriner. Philips 9500 520 Tape (c) 7300 676
             +-ARG 11-79 p27   +HFN 6-79 p108
             +-FF 11/12-79 p85   +HFN 9-79 p123 tape
             +Gr 6-79 p48   +NYT 2-3-80 pD22
             +-Gr 9-79 p534 tape   +RR 6-79 p79
       Symphony, no. 45, F sharp minor. See no. 1725
1728 Symphony, no. 46, B minor. Symphony, no. 47, G major. Zagreb Radio

Orchestra; Antonio Janigro. Vanguard HM 60SD
+FF 3/4-80 p96   +FU 11-79 p43
Symphony, no. 47, G major. See no. 1728
1729 Symphony, no. 48, C major. Symphony, no. 49, F minor. PH; Antal
Dorati. Decca SDD 547 Tape (c) KSDC 547 (From HDND 19/22, KHNC
13/18)
+Gr 1-80 p1151   +-RR 12-79 p56
+HFN 12-79 p179
1730 Symphony, no. 48, C major. Symphony, no. 49, F minor. Zagreb
Radio Orchestra; Antonio Janigro. Vanguard HM 61SD
+FF 3/4-80 p96   +FU 11-79 p43
Symphony, no. 48, C major. See no. 1726
Symphony, no. 49, F minor. See no. 1683. See no. 1729. See no.
1730
1731 Symphony, no. 57, D major. Symphony, no. 86, D major. Cincinnati
Symphony Orchestra; Max Rudolf. Westminster MCA 1405 (From Decca
DL 10107)
-FF 9/10-80 p133   +HF 10-80 p76
1732 Symphony, no. 59, A major. Symphony, no. 70, D major. Orchestra;
David Blum. Vanguard Tape (r) 71161
+HF 2-80 p102 tape
Symphony, no. 70, D major. See no. 1732
1733 Symphony, no. 73, D major. Symphony, no. 74, E flat major. PH;
Antal Dorati. London STS 15445
+FF 3/4-80 p98
Symphony, no. 73, D major. See no. 1722
Symphony, no. 74, E flat major. See no. 1733
1734 Symphonies, nos. 82-87. Naples Orchestra; Denis Vaughan. Arabes-
que 8047-3 (3) Tape (c) 9047-3
+-ARG 12-80 p29   +HF 10-80 p76
+FF 9/10-80 p133
1735 Symphony, no. 82, C major. Symphony, no. 83, G minor. Collegium
Aureum; Franzjosef Maier. Harmonia Mundi 1C 065 99762
/Gr 5-80 p1665   +-RR 4-80 p64
+-HFN 3-80 p91
1736 Symphony, no. 82, C major. Symphony, no. 83, G minor. AMF; Neville
Marriner. Philips 9500 519 Tape (c) 7300 675
++ARG 2-80 p33   +HFN 2-80 p88
+FF 1/2-80 p93   ++NR 1-80 p3
++Gr 5-79 p1894   +NYT 2-3-80 pD22
+HFN 5-79 p123   +RR 5-79 p58
+HFN 7-79 p119 tape   +-RR 9-79 p134 tape
Symphony, no. 83, G minor. See no. 1735. See no. 1736
1737 Symphony, no. 86, D major. Symphony, no. 98, B flat major. COA;
Colin Davis. Philips 9500 678 Tape (c) 7300 773
++Gr 12-80 p832   +-NR 12-80 p3
+HFN 12-80 p140   ++St 12-80 p126
Symphony, no. 86, D major. See no. 1731
1738 Symphony, no. 88, G major. Symphony, no. 104, D major. Bourne-
mouth Sinfonietta; Ronald Thomas. CRD 1070 Tape (c) CRDC 4070
+Gr 8-80 p222   +HFN 12-80 p159 tape
+HFN 8-80 p98   +RR 8-80 p46
1739 Symphony, no. 88, G major. Symphony, no. 100, G major. Columbia
Symphony Orchestra; Bruno Walter. Odyssey Y 35932 (From Columbia
MS 6486)
+-FF 9/10-80 p133   +HF 10-80 p76

1740 Symphony, no. 92, G major. Symphony, no. 103, E flat major. BRSO;
     Lorin Maazel. Quintessence PMC 7157 Tape (c) 7157
                    -FF 11/12-80 p121
     Symphonies, nos. 93-98. See no. 1723
1741 Symphonies, nos. 93-104. RPO; Thomas Beecham. EMI 1C 137 52038/43
     (3)
                    +-ARSC Vol 12, no. 3, 1980 p256
1742 Symphony, no. 93, D major. Symphony, no. 94, G major. RPO; Thomas
     Beecham. HMV SXLP 30285 Tape (c) TC SXLP 30285 (From ALP 1624)
              +-ARSC Vol 12, no. 3,   +-HFN 6-79 p115
                 1980 p252   +MT 9-79 p747
              +-Gr 5-79 p1899   -RR 9-79 p134 tape
              +HFN 6-79 p117 tape
1743 Symphony, no. 93, D major. Symphony, no. 103, E flat major. HSOO;
     Miklos Erdelyi. Hungaroton SLPX 11923
                    +Audio 2-80 p42   +-NR 4-79 p2
                    +-FF 11/12-79 p85
     Symphony, no. 93, D major. See no. 562
1744 Symphony, no. 94, G major. Symphony, no. 104, D major. Pitts-
     burgh Symphony Orchestra; Andre Previn. Angel SZ 37575 (also
     HMV ASD 3839 Tape (c) TC ASD 3839)
                    +-ARG 12-80 p32   +NR 6-80 p3
                    +Gr 4-80 p1557   +-RR 4-80 p64
                    +-HF 10-80 p76   +St 9-80 p79
                    +-HFN 4-80 p104
1745 Symphony, no. 94, G major. SCHUBERT: Symphony, no. 8, D 759, B
     minor. PhO; Carlo Maria Giulini. EMI (Japan) EAC 30290
                    +-ARSC Vol 12, nos. 1-2, 1980 p88
1746 Symphony, no. 94, G major. Symphony, no. 103, E flat major. Col-
     legium Aureum. Harmonia Mundi 1C 065 99873
                    +FF 11/12-80 p122
     Symphony, no. 94, G major. See no. 1742. See no. 1761
1747 Symphony, no. 96, D major. Symphony, no. 99, E flat major. COA;
     Bernard Haitink. Philips 6570 083 Tape (c) 7310 083 (From SAL
     3721)
                    +Gr 11-80 p671   +HFN 12-80 p159 tape
                    +-HFN 11-80 p129   +SFC 5-28-78 p41
1748 Symphony, no. 97, C major. Symphony, no. 98, B flat major. NYP;
     Leonard Bernstein. CBS M 35844 Tape (c) MT 35844
                    +FF 9/10-80 p134   +St 10-80 p114
                    ++HF 10-80 p76
     Symphony, no. 98, B flat major. See no. 1737. See no. 1748
     Symphony, no. 99, E flat major. See no. 562. See no. 1747
1749 Symphony, no. 100, G major. Mostly Mozart Orchestra; Johannes Som-
     ary. Vanguard VA 25000
                    +FF 11/12-80 p122   +St 10-80 p116
                    +-NR 8-80 p4
     Symphony, no. 100, G major. See no. 1739. See no. 1761
1750 Symphony, no. 101, D major. Symphony, no. 104, D major. National
     Arts Centre Orchestra; Mario Bernardi. CBC SM 5001
                    +-MUM 12-80 p33
1751 Symphony, no. 101, D major. Symphony, no. 102, B flat major. COA;
     Colin Davis. Philips 9500 679 Tape (c) 7300 774
                    ++NR 12-80 p2
     Symphony, no. 101, D major. See no. 1727. See no. 1761

1752 Symphony, no. 102, B flat major. Symphony, no. 103, E flat major.
     MOZART: Concerto, flute, no. 2, K 314, D major. Symphony, no.
     39, K 543, E flat major. Severino Gazzelloni, flt; Orchestra;
     Sergiu Celibidache. Rococo 2140
          +–NR 5-80 p3
     Symphony, no. 102, B flat major. See no. 1751
     Symphony, no. 103, E flat major. See no. 1740. See no. 1743. See
     no. 1746. See no. 1752
     Symphony, no. 104, D major. See no. 562. See no. 1738. See no.
     1744. See no. 1750
1753 Trios, baryton, D major (2), D minor, C major, B minor. Munich
     Baryton Trio. DG 2533 405 Tape (c) 3310 405
          +ARG 7-79 p34   +HFN 4-79 p123
          ++FF 9/10-79 p94   ++NR 7-79 p10
          +Gr 4-79 p1735   ++RR 5-79 p76
          +–HF 4-80 tape   +SFC 7-15-79 p47
1754 Trios, baryton, nos. 37, 48, 70-71, 85, 96-97, 109, 113, 117, 121.
     Esterhazy Baryton Trio. HMV SQ SLS 5095 (2) (also Seraphim STB
     6116)
          ++FF 1/2-80 p92   +MT 1-78 p47
          +Gr 9-77 p451   +RR 10-77 p66
          +HFN 11-77 p172   +RR 1-78 p15
1755 Trios, baryton, nos. 51, 70, 107, 113, 117. Munich Baryton Trio.
     DG 2533 444
          +Gr 8-80 p234   ++RR 8-80 p60
          +HFN 8-80 p98
1756 Trios, baryton, nos. 63-64, 82, 87, 88, 107, 110. Esterhazy Bary-
     ton Trio. HMV HQS 1424
          ++Gr 9-80 p359   +HFN 10-80 p105
1757 Trios, flute, op. 38 (6). Barthold Kuijken, flt; Sigiswald Kuijken,
     vln; Wieland Kuijken, vlc. Accent ACC 7807
          +FF 3/4-80 p98   +RR 6-80 p27
          +HFN 6-80 p101
     Trios, flute, op. 100 (6). See no. 1697
1758 Trios, piano, nos. 1, 6, 37, 39. Beaux Arts Trio. Philips 9500 657
          +FF 3/4-80 p99   +NYT 2-3-80 pD22
          ++HFN 4-80 p119   +–RR 4-80 p85
          +–NR 2-80 p7   ++SFC 12-23-79 p40
1759 Trios, piano, no. 1, C major; no. 4, G major. Beaux Arts Trio.
     Philips 9500 658
          ++FF 7/8-80 p99   ++NR 5-80 p7
          +HFN 12-80 p153   ++SFC 8-31-80 p31
1760 Trio, piano, no. 16, D major. Trio, piano, no. 27, C major. Emil
     Gilels, pno; Leonid Kogan, vln; Mstislav Rostropovich, vlc.
     Saga STXID 5311 (Reissue)
          +–HFN 7-80 p117   ++RR 7-80 p72
          +–RR 5-73 p75
     Trio, piano, no. 27, C major. See no. 1760
     Variations, D major, E flat major. See no. 1696
     Variations, E flat major. See no. 1717
     Variations, F minor. See no. 618
1761 Works, selections: Die Jahreszeiten, excerpts. Mass, no. 9, D min-
     or: Gloria. Quartet, op. 76, no. 3, C major. Die Schopfung, ex-
     cerpts. Sonata, piano, no. 58, C major: Rondo. Symphony, no.
     94, G major. Symphony, no. 100, G major. Symphony, no. 101, D

major. Various orchestras and conductors. Decca SPA 577 Tape
    (c) KCSP 577
                    +-Gr 11-80 p740   +-HFN 11-80 p131
HAYDN, Michael
    Concertino, horn, D major. See no. 1669
1762 Concerto, horn, D major. STAMITZ: Concerto, horn, E major. TEYBER:
        Concerto, horn, E flat major. Hermann Baumann, hn; PH; Yoav
        Talmi. Telefunken 6-42418
                    +-FF 11/12-80 p214
    Concerto, horn, D major. See no. 1665
    Concerto, organ and viola, C major. See no. 32
    Concerto, trumpet, C major. See no. 1678
    Lauft ihr Hirten. See no. 4068
    Minuets (6). See no. 1665
    Nocturne, F major. See no. 3957
    Pieces, glockenspiel (3). See no. 3682
1763 Der Traum. Dolores Aldea, s; Karin Kuster-Jordan, s; Ingrid Mayr,
        alto; Walter Raninger, bs; Salzburg Camerata Academica; Ernst
        Hinreiner. Schwann VMS 2036
                    +ARG 8-78 p36   +NR 9-80 p7
                    +FF 3/4-79 p64
HAYNE
    Loving shepherd of thy sheep. See no. 3527
HAYS, Doris
    Sunday nights. See no. 3727
HAZELL, Chris
    Black Sam. See no. 3568
    Borage. See no. 3568
    Kraken. See no. 3568
    Mr. Jums. See no. 3568
HEALEY, Derek
1764 Arctic images. HETU: concerto, piano, op. 15. Irma Vallecillo,
        pno; Louisville Orchestra; Pierre Hetu. Louisville LS 769
                    ++FF 11/12-80 p125   +-NR 9-80 p4
HEATH, John
    Verse service: Magnificat. See no. 3524
HEIDEN, Bernard
1765 Quintet, horn and string quartet. MOZART: Quintet, horn, K 407, E
        flat major. Mason Jones, Fr hn; Philarte Quartet. Gasparo GS
        207
                    +-FF 11/12-80 p140   +NR 8-80 p10
HEIFETZ, Robin Julian
1766 Flykt, computer and piano. For Anders Lundberg: Mardrom 29-30-10.
        Susurrus, 2 channel tape. Wasteland, computer. Performed by
        Robin Julian Heifetz. Orion ORS 80366
                    -FF 11/12-80 p123   +-NR 7-80 p15
    For Anders Lundberg: Mardrom 29-30-10. See no. 1766
    Susurrus, 2 channel tape. See no. 1766
    Wasteland, computer. See no. 1766
HEILLER, Anton
1767 Ecce lignum crucis. Fantasia on "Salve regina". In festo corporis
        Christi. Tanz toccata. Victimae paschali laudes. Thomas Froe-
        licht, org. Musical Heritage Society MHS 4106
                    +FF 7/8-80 p99   ++MU 9-80 p10
    Fantasia on "Salve regina". See no. 1767

Improvisation, no. 1, on a twelve-tone theme by Nikolas Fheodoroff.
    See no. 167
Improvisation, no. 2, on the hymn "Ach wie fluchtig ach wie nichtig".
    See no. 167
In festo corporis Christi. See no. 1767
Tanz toccata. See no. 1767
Victimae Paschali aludes. See no. 1767
HEILMANN, Harald
    Passacaglia. See no. 4035
HEINRICH, Anthony
    The minstrel's catch. See no. 3741
    The ornithological combat of kings, or The condor of the Andes and
        the eagle of the Cordilleras. See no. 1518
HEISE, Peter
    Twelfth night: Den gang jeg var kun saa stor saa. See no. 3774
HELFMAN
    Odon Olam. See no. 3922
HELLENDAAL, Pieter
    Concerto, harpsichord, op. 3, no. 4, E flat major. See no. 3691
    Concerto grosso, op. 3, no. 1, G minor. See no. 3818
HELPS, Robert
1768 Saccade. MOORE: Metamorphosis. PLESKOW: Pieces, piano, 4 hands
        (3). SHEPHERD: Capriccio II. Exotic dances (2). Eclogue, no.
        4. Gigue fantasque. In modo ostinato. Lento amabile. Gene-
        vieve Chinn, Allen Brings, Vivien Slater, pno. CRI SD 383
                +-CL 10-78 p10   +NR 11-78 p13
                +-FF 3/4-80 p14
1769 Symphony, no. 1. THOMSON: Symphony, no. 3. New Hampshire Symphony
        Orchestra, Columbia Symphony Orchestra; James Bolle, Zolton Roz-
        snyai. CRI SD 411 (From Columbia MS 6801)
                +FF 9/10-80 p223   +NYT 9-28-80 pD31
                /HF 10-80 p91   +SFC 6-1-80 p35
                +-NR 8-80 p3
HELSTED, Eduard
1770 Flower festival at Genzano: Pas de deux. LOVENSKJOLD: La sylphide.
        PAULLI: The Kermesse in Bruges. Copenhagen Philharmonic Orches-
        tra; Ole Schmidt. EMI 6C 165 39262/3 (2)
                +-Gr 8-80 p221   +RR 7-80 p53
HEMBERG, Eskil
    Zona rosa. See no. 332
HENRY, Pierre
1771 Le microphone bien tempere. Electronic sound. Harmonia Mundi INA
        GRM AM 00608
                +FF 7/8-80 p35
HENRY VIII, King
    Songs: Adieu madame et ma maistresse; Alas what shall I do for love;
        Helas madame; O my heart is sore. See no. 3768
HENSCHEL, Georg
    Morning hymn. See no. 3774
HENSELT, Adolph von
    Berceuse, F sharp major. See no. 3902
HENZE, Hans Werner
    Kammermusik, 1958: Tentos (3). See no. 3967
    Sonatina. See no. 3652
1772 Tristan. Homero Francesch, pno; Cologne Radio Orchestra; Hans Wer-

ner Henze. DG 2530 834
               +FF 11/12-80 p124   +MT 12-77 p1014
               +Gr 8-77 p305   +RR 9-77 p62
               +HFN 10-77 p156
HEPPENER, Robert
1773 Del jubilo del core che esce in voice. Nachklange. PORCELIJN:
     Sound poem in Shikara Tala. SCHAT: The fall, op. 9. STRAESSER:
     Blossom songs. Pool for Modern Music, Netherlands Chamber Choir,
     Netherlands Vocal Ensemble, Radio Chamber Choir; Frans Muller,
     Jos Leussink, Kuub Kerstens, Hans van den Hombergh. Composers
     Voice VC 7902
               +FF 9/10-80 p247
     Nachklange. See no. 1773
HERBERT
     Kiss me again. See no. 3831
     Prince Arianias: Ah Cupid. See no. 1101
HERMANN
     Es steht ein Lind. See no. 3662
HERRMANN, Bernard
1774 North by Northwest. London Studio Symphony Orchestra; Lauri John-
     son. Unicorn DKP 9000 (also Varese SV 95001)
               +-FF 7/8-80 p12   +Gr 6-80 p37
HERMANN, Ralph
     Quintet, brass, no. 1. See no. 3740
HERMANSON, Ake
     Stadier, op. 5. See no. 3598
HEROLD, Louis Joseph Ferdinand
     Zampa: Overture. See no. 3638
     Zampa: Perche tremar. See no. 3901. See no. 3978
HERTEL, Johann
     Concerto, trumpet and oboe, a 6. See no. 24
     Concerto, a cinque, D major. See no. 3563
HERVE (Florimond Ronger)
1775 Le petit Faust. Lina Dachary, ms; Aime Doniat, bar; Liliane Ber-
     ton, s; Jean-Christoph Benoit, bar; Orchestra; Jean Doussard.
     Rare Recorded Editions RRE 176/7 (2)
               +ARG 4-80 p10
HERVIG, Richard
     Quartet, strings. See no. 1514
     Sonata, clarinet and piano, no. 1. See no. 1514
HERZ, Henri
     Contradanses: Le pantalon, La poule, La trenise, Valse. See no.
     4011
HERZOGENBERG, Heinrich von
1776 Trio, op. 61, D major. REINECKE: Trio, op. 188, A minor. Ingo
     Goritzki, ob; Barry Tuckwell, hn; Ricardo Requejo, pno. Claves
     D 803
               +HFN 6-80 p107   +RR 8-80 p23
               +RR 4-80 p88
HESPE
     King o' the clouds. See no. 3619
HETU, Jacques
     Concerto, piano, op. 15. See no. 1764
HEUBERGER, Richard
1777 Opernball. Soloists; Biedermeyer Concert Orchestra; Otto Schulz.

Vienna Light Music Society Tape (c) BDRS 220/1
+—HF 1-80 p91 tape
Der Opernball: Overture. See no. 3897
HEWITT-JONES, Tony
Fanfare. See no. 4052
HILLEMACHER
Gavotte tendre. See no. 3906
HILTON, John
Fair Oriana, beauty's queen. See no. 3995
Fantasies, nos. 1-3. See no. 4015
HIMMEL, Friedrich
Maurerlied. See no. 3844
HINDEMITH, Paul
1778 Concert music, op. 50. Symphonic metamorphoses on themes by Carl
Maria von Weber. PO; Eugene Ormandy. HMV ASD 3743 Tape (c) TC
ASD 3743 (also Angel SZ 37536 Tape (c) 4ZS 37536)
++ARG 3-80 p27   +NR 3-80 p4
++Gr 11-79 p818   ++RR 12-79 p59
++HFN 11-79 p139   ++SFC 12-16-79 p60
++HFN 2-80 p107 tape   ++St 2-80 p127
1779 Concerto, organ. Trios, 3 trautoniums (7). Konzertstuck, trauton-
ium and strings. Anton Heiller, org; Oskar Sala, trautonium;
ORTF, Munich Chamber Orchestra; Milan Horvat, Hans Stadlmair.
Telefunken 6-42529
+—FF 9/10-80 p135
1780 Concerto, violoncello, op. 3, E flat major. JENNER: Serenade, A
major. Angelica May, vlc; Kassel State Theatre Orchestra; James
Lockhart. Barenreiter Musicaphon BM 30 SL 1711/12
+FF 1/2-79 p54   +RR 11-78 p64
+—HFN 12-80 p141
Easy pieces. See no. 3654
1781 Four temperaments. PISTON: Concertino, piano. Walter Gieseking,
pno; Frankfurt Radio Orchestra; Kurt Schroeder. Past Masters 28
++ARG 11-80 p21   +NR 10-80 p12
1782 Kleine Kammermusik, op. 24, no. 2. MILHAUD: La cheminee de Roi
Rene, op. 205. NIELSEN: Quintet, op. 43. Danish Wind Quintet.
Unicorn RHS 366
++Gr 1-80 p1167   +SFC 1-27-80 p44
+HFN 12-79 p177   ++St 4-80 p136
+RR 12-79 p38
Konzertstuck, trautonium and strings. See no. 1779
1783 Ludus tonalis: Interlude and fugue. JANACEK: Sonatas, piano, nos.
1 and 10. PROKOFIEV: Love for three oranges, op. 33: March.
Symphony, no. 1, op. 25, D major: Gavotte. Sonata, piano, no.
3, op. 28, A minor. SCRIABIN: Poemes, op. 32 (2). John Briggs,
pno. Look Records LK 6464
+—RR 3-80 p89
1784 Das Marienleben, op. 27. Erna Berger, s; Gerhard Puchelt, pno.
Acanta DD 22504 (also BASF 10 22504-6)
+FF 9/10-79 p95   +—RR 4-80 p113
+HFN 3-80 p91
1785 Mathis der Maler. Rose Wagemann, Ursula Koszut, s; James King,
William Cochran, t; Dietrich Fischer-Dieskau, bar; Bavarian
Radio Orchestra and Chorus; Rafael Kubelik. Angel SZCX 3869 (3)
(also HMV SLS 5182, 1C 65 035151/7)

++ARG 4-80 p26	+NYT 11-18-79 pD24
++FF 3/4-80 p100	+ON 12-29-79 p34
+Gr 12-79 p1047	+Op 12-80 p1215
+-HF 2-80 p78	+RR 1-80 p58
+HFN 12-79 p162	++SFC 11-11-79 p44
+-NR 2-80 p11	++St 1-80 p86

1786 Mathis der Maler. Nobilissima visione. Philharmonic concerto.
    Symphonic metamorphoses on themes by Carl Maria von Weber.
    BPhO, Hamburg Philharmonic Orchestra; Paul Hindemith, Joseph
    Keilberth. Telefunken 6-48019 (2)
        +-FF 1/2-80 p94

1787 Mathis der Maler. STRAUSS, R.: Tod und Verklarung, op. 24. LSO;
    Jascha Horenstein. Unicorn UN 1-75024 (also RHS 312 Tape (c)
    UKC 312)

+-FF 3/4-79 p65	+NR 6-79 p3
+-HFN 11-79 p153	+RR 12-79 p59
+-HFN 11-80 p131 tape	

Nobilissima visione. See no. 1786

1788 Nobilissima visione: Meditation. Sonata, solo viola, op. 11, no. 5.
    Sonata, solo viola, op. 25, no. 1. Sonata, viola and piano,
    op. 11, no. 4. Karel Spelina, Josef Kodousek, vla; Karel Friesl,
    Jan Novotny, pno. Supraphon 111 2271/2 (2)

+Gr 6-80 p44	+NR 4-80 p7
+-HFN 7-80 p107	+RR 7-80 p80

Philharmonic concerto. See no. 1786
Pieces, flute (8). See no. 4006

1789 Pieces, string orchestra, op. 44, no. 4. SCHONBERG: Verklarte Nacht,
    op. 4. WEBERN: Movements, op. 5 (5). AMF; Neville Marriner. Ar-
    go ZRG 763 Tape (r) E 763

++Gr 1-75 p1342	++NR 6-75 p2
+-HF 9-75 p90	+RR 1-75 p33
++HF 5-80 p90	+St 9-75 p120

1790 Quartet, strings, no. 3, op. 22. Quartet, strings, no. 4, op. 32.
    Los Angeles String Quartet. GSC 10
        ++FF 9/10-80 p136

1791 Quartet, strings, no. 3, op. 22. JANACEK: Quartet, strings, no. 1.
    Alard Quartet. Golden Crest CRS 4184

+ARG 6-80 p22	+IN 11-80 p62
+FF 3/4-80 p103	

Quartet, strings, no. 4, op. 32. See no. 1790

1792 Requiem (When lilacs last in the dooryard bloom's). Louise Parker,
    con; George London, bs-bar; Schola Cantorum New York, NYP; Paul
    Hindemith. CBS 61890

+Gr 4-90 p1576	+-RR 5-80 p96
+-HFN 4-80 p105	

1793 Requiem. REDEL: Konfrontationen. LUTOSLAWSKI: Concerto, orchestra.
    Das Landesjungendorchester Nordhein-Westfalen; Martin Stephani.
    Da Camera Magna SM 91604
        +-FF 5/6-80 p90

1794 Der Schwanandreher. WALTON: Concerto, viola. William Primrose,
    vla; RPO, Columbia Symphony Orchestra; Malcolm Sargent, John
    Pritchard. Odyssey Y 35922 (From Columbia ML 4905)

++ARG 7/8-80 p46	+SFC 1-27-80 p44
+FF 3/4-80 p178	

Der Schwanendreher. See no. 370

Sine musica nulla disciplina. See no. 3741
Sonata, bassoon and piano. See no. 3588
Sonata, oboe and piano. See no. 765
Sonata, organ, no. 1. See no. 3732
Sonata, trumpet and piano. See no. 35
Sonata, solo viola, op. 11, no. 5. See no. 1788
Sonata, solo viola, op. 25, no. 1. See no. 1788
Sonata, viola and piano, op. 11, no. 4. See no. 1788
Sonata, solo violoncello, op. 25, no. 3. See no. 304
Songs: La belle dans sans merci; Chansons (6). See no. 638
1795 Suite, 1922. SCHOENBERG: Suite, op. 25. STRAVINSKY: Sonata, piano.
    Franzpeter Goebels, pno. Musicaphon BM 30 SL 1524
              +-HFN 10-80 p113
    Symphonic metamorphoses on a theme by Carl Maria von Weber. See
    no. 1778. See no. 1786
    Trios, 3 trautoniums (7). See no. 1779
    Trio for soprano and 2 alto recorders. See no. 3795
HINE, William
    A flute piece. See no. 4055
HOBBS
    Phyllis is my only joy. See no. 3791
HODKINSON, Sydney
1796 The edge of the olde one. PERSICHETTI: Concerto, English horn, op.
    137. Thomas Stacy, hn; New York String Orchestra, Eastman Musi-
    ca Nova; Vincent Persichetti, Paul Phillips. Grenadilla GS 1048
              +-FF 9/10-80 p178   +-NR 7-80 p4
              +HF 11-80 p72
HOFFMANN, Ernst
1797 Miserere, B minor. Krisztina Laky, Hildegard Laurich, s; Gwendolyn
    Killebrew, alto; Aldo Baldin, t; Nikolaus Hillebrand, bs; Cologne
    Radio Orchestra and Chorus; Roland Bader. Schwann AMS 3525
              +-FF 11/12-80 p125
HOFFMANN, Leopold
    Concerto, flute, D major. See no. 1668
HOFFMEISTER, Franz
1798 Concerto, clarinet, B flat major. SCHACHT: Concerto, clarinet, B
    flat major. Dieter Klocker, clt; Concerto Amsterdam; Jaap Schrod-
    er. Acanta EA 23145
              +HFN 5-80 p121   +STL 5-11-80 p39
              ++RR 4-80 p61
1799 Concerto, flute, G major. TELEMANN: Suite, A minor. Ingrid Ding-
    felder, flt; ECO; Lawrence Leonard. Enigma K 23534
              +-HFN 10-80 p113
    Concerto, flute, no. 6, D major. See no. 74
1800 Concerto, viola, D major. PAGANINI: Sonata, viola, op. 35, C minor.
    STAMITZ: Concerto, viola, D major. Atar Arad, vla; PH; Reinhard
    Peters. Telefunken AW 6-42007 Tape (c) 4-42007
              ++Gr 11-76 p792   +NR 1-77 p6
              +HF 4-80 p104 tape
HOFHAIMER, Paul
    Ach lieb mit leyd. See no. 4004
    Ain frewlich Wesenn. See no. 4004
    Greyner zanner. See no. 4004
    Songs: Carmen in re; Carmen magistri Pauli; Cupido; Der Hundt; Man
    hat bisher; Greiner zanner; Nach willen dein. See no. 3805

Tandernaken. See no. 3702

HOLBORNE, Anthony
1801 Almayne. As it fell on holie eve. Ecce quam bonum. The funerals.
       Galliard (3). Heres paternus. Heigh ho holiday. The honey-
       suckle. The image of melancholly. Infernum. Muylinda. Para-
       dizo. Pavan. Pavana ploravit. Sic semper soleo. The sighes.
       Consort of Musicke, Guildhall Waits; Anthony Rooley, Trevor Jones.
       L'Oiseau-Lyre DSLO 569
                    +-Gr 10-80 p511   +HFN 9-80 p105
     As it fell upon a holy eve. See no. 1801
     The choise. See no. 3795. See no. 4001
     Coranto, heigh ho holiday. See no. 3853
     The Countess of Pembroke's paradise. See no. 1803
     The cradle pavan and galliard "The woods so wild". See no. 1803
     Ecce quam bonum. See no. 1801
     The fairy round. See no. 4000
     The funerals. See no. 1801
     Gallairds. See no. 1801. See no. 1803. See no. 4043
     Heigh ho holiday. See no. 1801. See no. 1803
     Heres paternus. See no. 1801. See no. 1803
     The honeysuckle. See no. 1801. See no. 4000
     The image of melancholly. See no. 1801. See no. 4000
     Infernum. See no. 1801
     Last will and testament. See no. 4001
     Maire-Golde. See no. 4001
     Muylinda. See no. 1801. See no. 1803. See no. 3795. See no. 4043
     The new yeres gift. See no. 4001
     The nightwatch. See no. 980
     Noel's galliard. See no. 1803
     Paradizo. See no. 1801
     Patienca. See no. 4001
     Pavan. See no. 1801
     Pavan and galliard. See no. 980. See no. 1803. See no. 3795
     Pavana ploravit. See no. 1801. See no. 3853
     Quadro pavan and galliard. See no. 1803
1802 Short airs both grave and light. LAMBRANZI: Dances: Bolognesa, Nar-
       cisin, Dimo Jesu and genio, Ruberto, La disamecitia and entree,
       Logi and hurlo Bacho. PRAETORIUS: Terpsichore: Dances. Prae-
       torius Consort; Christopher Ball. Classics for Pleasure CFP
       40335 Tape (c) TC CFP 40335
                    +Gr 12-80 p334   +HFN 11-80 p131 tape
                    +HFN 9-80 p114
     Sic semper soleo. See no. 1801. See no. 3795
     The sighes. See no. 1801
     Suite: Holborne's almain. See no. 1803
     The wanton. See no. 1803. See no. 4000
     When daffodils begin to peere. See no. 3840
     The widowes myte. See no. 3675. See no. 4000
1803 Works, selections: The cradle pavan and galliard, "The woods so
       wild". Muylinda. Pavan and galliard (2). Quadro pavan and
       galliard. Suite: Holborne's almain. The Countess of Pembroke's
       paradise. Noel's galliard. Galliard. Heres paternus. Heigh
       ho holiday. The wanton. Extempore String Ensemble; George Wei-
       gand. Meridian E 77027
                    +Gr 5-80 p1683   +RR 4-80 p86
                    +HFN 4-80 p105

HOLBROOKE, Josef
    Concerto, piano, no. 1. See no. 348
HOLDEN
    The Lord is good to all. See no. 3848
HOLLIGER, Heinz
    Sequenzen uber Johannes. See no. 3564
HOLLINS, Alfred
    Trumpet minuet. See no. 3838. See no. 4049
HOLMBOE, Vagn
    Benedic domino, op. 59. See no. 3587
HOLMES
    Quartet, tubas. See no. 4033
HOLMES, Reed
    Nova. See no. 1655
HOLST, Gustav
1804 Hammersmith, op. 52. Suite, no. 1, op. 28, no. 1, E flat major.
        Suite, no. 2, op. 28, no. 2, F major. VAUGHAN WILLIAMS: Eng-
        lisfh folk song suite. Toccata marziale. London Wind Orchestra;
        Denis Wick. Enigma K 53565 (also Noneusch H 78002)
                    +-Gr 12-78 p1117   ++SFC 9-21-80 p21
    Lullay my liking. See no. 3823
    The perfect fool, op. 39. See no. 3797
1805 The planets, op. 32. NYP; Leonard Bernstein. CBS 61932 Tape (c)
        40-61932 (From 73001)
                    +-Gr 10-79 p639   +-RR 9-79 p94
                    +-HFN 9-79 p121   +RR 3-80 p104 tape
                    +-HFN 11-79 p157 tape
1806 The planets, op. 32. Scottish National Orchestra and Chorus; Alex-
        ander Gibson. Chandos ABRD 1010 Tape (c) ABTD 1010
                    +Gr 11-80 p671   ++HFN 11-80 p120
1807 The planets, op. 32. LPO and Chorus, Women's voices; Georg Solti.
        Decca SET 628 Tape (c) KCET 628 (also London CS 7110 Tape (c)
        CS 5-7110)
                    +Audio 12-79 p101   +HFN 6-79 p117
                    +-FF 9/10-80 p136   ++NR 5-80 p3
                    +Gr 3-79 p1565   +RR 3-79 p75
                    +-HF 12-79 p98   -SFC 9-30-79 p45
                    +HFN 3-79 p125   +St 12-79 p144
1808 The planets, op. 32. LPO; Adrian Boult. Everest 3443 Tape (c)
        3443
                    +-FF 5/6-80 p91   +-HF 8-80 p87 tape
1809 The planets, op. 32. Ambrosian Singers; COA; Neville Marriner.
        Philips 9500 425 Tape (c) 7300 643 (r) G 9500 425
                    ++ARG 2-79 p18   +-HFN 8-78 p103
                    ++FF 1/2-79 p57   +HFN 10-78 p139 tape
                    +Gr 8-78 p331   +MJ 12-78 p45
                    +-Gr 11-78 p963 tape   +-NR 10-78 p2
                    +HF 2-79 p76   +RR 8-78 p59
                    ++HF 11-80 p88   +RR 11-78 p113 tape
                    +SFC 7-16-78 p50
    St. Paul's suite, op. 29, no. 2. See no. 3996
1810 Songs: Ave Maria; Bring us in good ale; Canons, nos. 1-4, 7-8;
        Choral folk songs, no. 4; Choruses, H 186, nos. 1-6; Evening
        watch; Of one that is so fair and bright; Old English carols,
        no. 2; Part songs, nos. 1-7; Pastoral; The song of the black-

smith; Songs, H 174 (12); Songs, voice and violin (4); The swal-
low leaves her nest; Terly terlow; This have I done for my true
love; A welcome song; Welsh folk snongs, nos. 3, 9, 12. Purcell
Singers; Benjamin Britten, pno; Norbert Brainin, vln; Peter
Pears, t; ECO; Imogen Holst. Argo ZK 74/5 (2) (From ZRG 5497,
512, 5495)
         ++Gr 1-80 p1188   +RR 12-79 p112

Songs: Chrissemas day in the morning; Jesu sweet; I sing of a
maiden. See no. 4066

Songs: Evening on the Moselle; If t'were the time of lilies. See
no. 3741

Suite, no. 1, op. 28, no. 1, E flat major. See no. 1804

Suite, no. 1, op. 28, no. 1, E flat major: 1st movement march. See
no. 3801

Suite, no. 2, op. 28, no. 2, F major. See no. 1804

HOLZBAUER, Ignaz
Sinfonia, op. 4, no. 3, E flat major. See no. 3703
Sinfonia concertante, A major. See no. 3703

HOLZGRAF, Lloyd
Mormon hymns: Come come ye saints; Oh my father. See no. 162
Variations on "Londonderry air". See no. 162

HONEGGER, Arthur
Danse de la chevre. See no. 3854

1811 Jeanne d'Arc au Bucher. Nelly Borgeaud, Michel Favory, narrators;
CPhO and Chorus; Serge Baudo. Supraphon 112 1651/2 (2) (Q)
412 1651/2 Tape (c) KSUP 1651/2
              ++ARG 6-78 p35   +NR 2-78 p9
              ++FF 3/4-78 p39   +RR 2-78 p84
              +Gr 1-78 p1277   +-RR 3-80 p105 tape
              +HFN 12-77 p172   ++SFC 2-19-78 p49
              +HFN 10-79 p171 tape +St 4-78 p84

Prelude arioso fughette sur le nom de Bach. See no. 989
Sonatine, clarinet and piano. See no. 1201
Songs: Salute de Bartas. See no. 3861

HOOD
The Nelson touch. See no. 3619

d'HOOGHE, Clement
The little Geisha. See no. 3889

HOOPER, Ralph
Psalm, no. 96, Responsorial psalm for midnight mass. See no. 3993

HOOVER, Katherine
Divertimento. See no. 399
On the betrothal of Princess Isabelle of France, aged six. See no.
3822
Sinfonia. See no. 3821
Trio, violin, violoncello and piano. See no. 1103

HOPKINS
Sonatina. See no. 3730

HOPKINSON
The toast. See no. 3971

HORN
I've been roaming. See no. 3774

HORNE
I know a bank. See no. 3774

HOTTETERRE, Jacques
Sonata, oboe, op. 5, no. 3, D major. See no. 3753

HOVHANESS, Alan
    Achtamar. See no. 3851
    Farewell to the mountains. See no. 3851
    Mystic flute. See no. 3851
    Prayer of St. Gregory. See no. 3545
    Sharagan and fugue, op. 58. See no. 3740
1812 Symphony, no. 38, op. 314. Hinako Fugihara, s; Verne Nocodemus,
        tpt; Linda Orr, flt; Linda Melsted, vln; Northwest Chamber Or-
        chestra; Alan Hovhaness. Pandora PAN 3001
               +-FF 1/2-80 p96   -NR 7-79 p4
    Vanadour. See no. 3851
HOVLAND, Egil
    Og ordet ble kjod. See no. 3527
HOWARTH, Elgar
    Processional fanfares. See no. 3566
HOWELLS, Herbert
    Gloucester service: Magnificat. See no. 3528
    Here is the little door. See no. 4066
    Jubilate Deo. See no. 3530
    Like as the hart. See no. 3992. See no. 4019
    Master Tallis' testament. See no. 4055
    Procession, op. 38. See no. 3801
    Psalm prelude, op. 32, no. 1. See no. 4052
    Rhapsody, op. 17, no. 3. See no. 4050
1813 Songs: Alas alack; Come sing and dance; The dunce; King David; Lady
        Caroline; Merry Margaret; Miss T; On the merry first of May; The
        three cherry trees. ORR: Along the field; Bahnhofstrasse; Fare-
        well to barn and stack and tree; In valleys green and still; Is
        my team ploughing; The lads in their hundreds; When I watch the
        living meet; When smoke stood up from Ludlow; With rue my heart
        is laden; While summer on is stealing. Philip Langridge, t;
        Bruce Ogston, bar; Eric Parkin, pno. Unicorn RHS 369
               +-Gr 12-80 p866   +HFN 11-80 p120
    Songs: All my hope on God is founded. See no. 3528
    Songs: Here is the little door; Long long ago. See no. 1297
HOWETT, Gregory
    Fantasia. See no. 3966
HUBER, Paul
    Symphonic music. See no. 3620
HUDSON, Joseph
    Fantasy/refrain. See no. 1016
HUGHES, Robert
    Sonitudes. See no. 376
HULLAH, John Pike
    Three fishers went sailing. See no. 3560
HUME, Tobias
    Songs: Touch me lightly; Death; Life. See no. 3853
    Tobacco, tobacco. See no. 3876
HUMFREY, Pelham
    A hymn to God the Father. See no. 3938
    O Lord my god. See no. 738
HUMMEL, Johann
    Concerto, bassoon, F major. See no. 102
1814 Concerto, mandolin, G major. Introduction, theme and variations,
        op. 102, F major. Rondo de societe, op. 117. Andre Saint-
        Clivier, mand; Jacques Chambon, ob; Anne Queffelec, pno; Jean-

Francois Paillard Chamber Orchestra; Jean-Francois Paillard.
Erato STU 70700
    +-Gr 3-73 p1688   +-RR 3-73 p50
    +HFN 4-73 p782   +RR 10-79 p91
    +HFN 4-80 p105
Concerto, trumpet, E flat major. See no. 24. See no. 707. See
    no. 1676. See no. 1677. See no. 1680. See no. 3563
Concerto, trumpet and band. See no. 1387
1815 Etudes, op. 125, nos. 1-24. Mary Louise Boehm, pno. Turanbout TVS
    34562
    +-Gr 3-80 p1417   +-MT 10-80 p634
    +-HFN 2-80 p93   +RR 12-79 p99
Introduction, theme and variations, op. 102, F major. See no. 624.
    See no. 1814
Memory of friendship, op. 99. See no. 1537
Partita, E flat major. See no. 1282
Rondo, op. 11, E flat major. See no. 3964
Rondo de societe, op. 117. See no. 1814
Septet, op. 74, D minor. See no. 701. See no. 748
Septet, op. 114, C major. See no. 1282
Sonata, mandolin, C major. See no. 403
Sonata, 2 pianos, op. 51, E flat major. See no. 1418
HUMPERDINCK, Engelbert
1816 Hansel und Gretel. Ileana Cotrubas, Kiri Te Kanawa, Ruth Welting,
    Elisabeth Soderstrom, s; Frederica von Stade, Christa Ludwig, ms;
    Siegmund Nimsgern, bar; Cologne Opera Children's Chorus; Cologne
    Gurzenich Orchestra; John Pritchard. CBS 79217 (2) Tape (c) 40-
    79217 (also Columbia M2 35898)
    ++ARG 3-80 p28   +ON 12-29-79 p34
    ++FF 5/6-80 p91   ++Op 10-79 p975
    +-Gr 10-79 p703   +RR 10-79 p57
    +Gr 2-80 p1302 tape   +RR 6-80 p94 tape
    +HFN 10-79 p157   ++SFC 11-25-79 p46
    ++HFN 2-80 p107 tape +St 12-79 p92
    +NR 12-79 p9   +STL 12-2-79 p37
    ++NYT 9-30-79 pD22
1817 Hansel und Gretel. Lucia Popp, Norma Burrowes, Edita Gruberova, s;
    Brigitte Fassbaender, Julia Hamari, Anny Schlemm, ms; Walter
    Berry, bar; Vienna Boys Choir; VPO; Georg Solti. Decca D131D2
    (2) Tape (c) K132K22 (also London OSA 12112 Tape (c) OSA 5-12112)
    +-ARG 6-79 p22   ++HFN 4-79 p133 tape
    +Audio 6-79 p132   +NR 2-80 p12
    +-FF 7/8-79 p61   +ON 3-3-79 p41
    +-Gr 12-78 p1165   +Op 2-79 p147
    +Gr 5-79 p1940 tape ++RR 1-79 p51
    +-HF 3-79 p96   ++SFC 12-17-78 p64
    ++HFN 12-78 p155   +-St 5-79 p99
1818 Hansel und Gretel, excerpts. MOZART, L.: Cassation, G major: Toy
    symphony. OCHS: 's kommt ein Vogerl geflogen. Berlin State Op-
    era Orchestra, Berlin Chamber Orchestra; Hans von Benda, Richard
    Muller-Lampertz, Wolfgang Martin. Telefunken AG 6-41334
    -ARG 3-80 p56   +RR 11-75 p46
1819 Hansel und Gretel: Ach wir armen armen Luet. Konigskinder: Verdor-
    ben gestorben. LORTZING: Zar und Zimmermann: Auf Gesellen greift
    zur Axt...Sonst spielt ich mit Zepter. MOZART: Don Giovanni, K

527: La ci darem la mano. Le nozze di Figaro, K 492: Non piu
andrai...Hai gia vinta la causa...Vedro mentr'io sospiro. Die
Zauberflote, K 620: Bei Mannern. WAGNER: Tannhauser: Als du in
kuhnem Sange...Blick ich umher...Wohl wusst ich hier; Wie Todesahnung...O du mein holder Abendstern. Gerhard Husch, bar; Berlin State Opera Orchestra; Hans Udo Muller. Arabesque 8022 Tape
(c) 8022

+ARG 11-80 p47   +MUM 12-80 p35
+-FF 11/12-80 p197

1820 Hansel und Gretel: Overture; Witch's ride; Dream pantomime; The
gingerbread house; Finale. Lucia Popp, Norma Burrowes, Edita
Gruberova, s; Brigitte Fassbaender, Julia Hamari, ms; Walter
Berry, bar; Vienna Boys Choir; VPO; Georg Solti. Decca SET 633
(From D131D2)

+-Gr 12-80 p876   +HFN 12-80 p153

Hansel und Gretel: Suse, liebe Suse...Bruderchen komm tanz mit mir.
See no. 3584
Konigskinder: Verdorben gestorben. See no. 1819

HUNDLEY, Richard
Songs: Ballad on Queen Anne's death; Some sheep are loving; Spring;
Wild plum. See no. 650

HUNT, Jerry
1821 Lattice. KRUMM: Sound machine. WILLINGHAM: T'Chu. Jerry Hunt,
pno; Sabrina Bennett, flt; Kat Huffman, bsn; Tom Sleeper, trom;
Jeff Solomon, hn; LeAnn Stafford, marimba; Electronic tape.
Irida 0026

+-ARG 12-80 p49

HURFORD, Peter
Fanfare on "Old 100th". See no. 3895

HURLSTONE, William
1822 Concerto, piano. Fantasie-variations on a Swedish air. Eric Parkin, pno; LPO; Nicholas Braithwaite. Lyrita SRCS 100

+Gr 2-80 p1269   ++RR 12-79 p60
+HFN 12-79 p162

Fantasie-variations on a Swedish air. See no. 1822

HUSA, Karel
1823 Al fresco. Concerto, percussion and wind ensemble. Concerto, alto
saxophone and concert band. James Forger, sax; Michigan State
Wind Symphony Orchestra, The Symphony Band; Karel Husa, Stanley
DeRusha. Golden Crest ATH 5066

+FF 5/6-80 p92

Concerto, percussion and wind ensemble. See no. 1823
Concerto, alto saxophone and concert band. See no. 1823

HUTCHESON, Jere
Fantaisie-Impromptu. See no. 1350

HUWET
Fantasie. See no. 3612

HUYBRECHTS, Albert
Sicilienne. See no. 3889

HUYGENS, Constantin
1824 Pathodia sacra et profana (Latin psalms): Multi dicunt animae meae;
Domine ne in furore; Usquequo Domine; Domine Deus meus; Avertis-
ti faciem; Dilataverunt super me; Ab omnibus iniquitatibus; Sit-
ivit anima mea; Quare tristis es anima mea; Domine spes mea; In
quo corriget adolescentior; Cognovi domine; Quomodo dilexi;

Erravi domine; Laetatus sum; De profundus clamavi; Confitebor
tibi domine; Proba me meus; Memor fui dierum. (Italian airs):
Morte dolce; Sospiro della sua donna; Amor secreto; Neo di bel
volto; Errori de bella chioma; Caccia amorosa; Gia ti chiesi un
sospir; A dispetto de venti; Riposta dalla rinestra; Deh s'a
tanta belta; Va donna ingrata. (French airs): Que ferons nous;
Graves temoins des mes delices; Vous me l'aviez bien dit; Quoy
Clorinde tu pars; Tu te trompes Philis; Le reveil de calliste;
Ne crains le serein. Elly Ameling, s; Max van Egmond, bar;
Toyohiko Satoh, lt; Jaap Ter Linden, vla da gamba; Anneke Uitten-
bosch, hpd, org. EMI 5N 165 25634/5 (2)
                ++Gr 12-80 p866   +HFN 10-80 p105
HYMNS. See no. 3529
IANNACONNE, Anthony
    Parodies. See no. 3731
IBERT, Jacques
    Aria (Vocalise). See no. 3892
1825 Concerto, violoncello and winds. NELHYBEL: Concertino da camera.
    RIEGGER: Introduction and fugue. STEVENS: Rhapsody, violoncello
    and winds. University of South Florida Winds; James Croft. Gol-
    den Crest GC 4189
                +IN 11-80 p62
    Entr'acte. See no. 1182. See no. 3717
    Interludes, flute, violin and harp (2). See no. 1182
    Jeux. See no. 1301
    Little white donkey. See no. 3887
    Lyric aria. See no. 3891
    Piece, flute. See no. 3714
    Pieces breves (3). See no. 60. See no. 1527
    Steles orientees: Mon amant a la vertus dans l'eau; On me dit. See
    no. 3892
IMBRIE
    Tell me where is fancy bred. See no. 4026
    IMPROVISATIONS. See no. 4037
d'INDIA, Sigismondo
    Da l'onde del mio pianto. See no. 3879
1826 Songs: Amico hai vinto; Ancidetemi pur dogliosi affanni; Chi nudris-
    ce tua spema; Giunto a la tomba; Langue al vostro languir; O
    leggiedr'occhi; Quella vermiglia rosa; Son gli accenti che ascol-
    ta. Concerto Vocale. Harmonia Mundi HM 1011
                +FF 5/6-80 p93   ++SFC 5-18-80 p38
                +NYT 8-10-80 pD17
    Songs: Che farai Meliseo; Odi quel rossignuolo; Qual fiera si cru-
    del. See no. 3878
d'INDY, Vincent
    Chansons et danses, op. 50. See no. 1526
1827 La foret enchantee, op. 8. Jour d'ete a la Montagne, op. 61. Tab-
    leaux de voyage, op. 36. Orchestre Philharmonique des Pays de
    Loire; Pierre Dervaux. Pathe Marconi C 069 16301
                +ARG 9-80 p45
    Jour d'ete a la Montagne, op. 61. See no. 1827
    Symphony on a French mountain air, op. 25. See no. 3557
    Tableaux de voyage, op. 36. See no. 1827
INFANTE, Manuel
    Danzas andaluzas (3). See no. 1131

INGLOTT
  The leaves be greene. See no. 3719
IPPOLITOV-IVANOV, Mikhail
  Bless the Lord o my soul. See no. 3970
  Caucasian sketches, op. 10. See no. 1506
  Evening in Georgia, op. 69a. See no. 7
IRELAND, John
  The almond trees. See no. 1829
  April. See no. 1829
  The boys are up in the woods all day. See no. 3837
  Columbine. See no. 1829
  Concertino pastorale. See no. 658
  Dances: Gypsy dance, Country dance, Reapers dance. See no. 1829
  Decorations, nos. 1-3. See no. 1829
  Down the Salley gardens. See no. 3778
1828 Epic march. The overlanders (arr. Mackerras). VAUGHAN WILLIAMS:
      On Wenlock edge (orch. composer). Gerald English, t; West Aust-
      ralian Symphony Orchestra; David Measham. Unicorn KP 8001
                   +Gr 11-80 p723   +-HFN 11-80 p123
  Greater love. See no. 3992
  The holy boy. See no. 1829
  Intermezzo. See no. 3786
  A London overture. See no. 396
  The overlanders. See no. 1828. See no. 3786
1829 Piano works: The almond trees. April. Columbine. Dances: Gypsy
      dance, Country dance, Reapers dance. Decorations, nos. 1-3.
      The holy boy. Prelude, no. 3. Sarnia, nos. 1-3. Daniel Adni,
      pno. HMV HQS 1414
                   +FF 1/2-80 p97   +HFN 7-79 p105
                   +Gr 7-79 p229   ++RR 7-79 p92
  Prelude, no. 3. See no. 1829
  Romance. See no. 3786
  Sarnia, nos. 1-3. See no. 1829
  Songs: I have twelve oxen; Love and friendship; My fair; The Sally
      gardens; Sea fever. See no. 3991
ISAAC
  Warship theme. See no. 3619
ISAAC, Heinrich
  Es het ein Bauer ein Tochterlein. See no. 4004
  Innsbruck. See no. 4004
  Innsbruck ich muss dich lassen. See no. 3864. See no. 3957
  Instrumental piece without title. See no. 4000
  La la ho ho. See no. 4004
  La martinella. See no. 4004
  Maudit seyt. See no. 4000
  L'Ombre. See no. 4004
  Songs: A la bataglia; An buos; Carmen in fa; Fortuna in mi; Imperii
      proceres; Innsbruck ich muss dich lassen; J'ay pris amours; La
      morra; San Sancti spiritus assit nobis gratia. See no. 3702
  Der Welte fundt. See no. 4000
  Wolauff. See no. 3597
ISAACSON, Michael
  Sh'nayhem, B'amkom. See no. 3922
ISOUARD, Nicolo
  Le billet de lotterie: Non je ne veux pas chanter. See no. 3886

La Joconde: Dans un delire extreme. See no. 3770

IVANCIC, Amando (Amandus)
1830 Mass, D major. Soloists; RTV Zagreb Choir; Zagreb Symphony Orches-
     tra. Jugoton/Fonoars LSY 68064
                    +CL 7-80 p445

IVANOVICI, Iosif
     Waves of the Danube. See no. 3962

IVANOVS, Janis
1831 Andante, violoncello ensemble. Concerto, violin, E minor. Concer-
     to, violoncello, B minor. Juris Svolkoskis, vln; Ernst Bertovsky,
     vlc; Latvian Radio Orchestra, Latvian S.S.R. Philharmonic Cello
     Ensemble; E. Tons, Ernst Bertovsky. Melodiya 33S 01475-76
                    +FF 3/4-80 p105
     Concerto, violin, E minor. See no. 1831
     Concerto, violoncello, B minor. See no. 1831

IVES, Charles
     A Christmas carol. See no. 3849
     Symphony, no. 3. See no. 3565
     The unanswered question. See no. 3781

JACKSON
     The Archbishop's fanfare. See no. 3895
     The dear little shamrock. See no. 4070

JACOB, Gordon
     Concertino, clarinet: 34d and 4th movements. See no. 4030
     Music for a festival: Interludes for trumpets and trombones, Intra-
     da, Round of seven parts, Interlude, Saraband, Madrigal. See no.
     3959
     Sonata, oboe and piano. See no. 56

JACOB DE SENLECHES
     En ce gracieux. See no. 766
     Fuions de ci. See no. 766

JACOPO DA BOLOGNA
     I'Sent'za. See no. 4032
     Vola el bel sparver. See no. 4032

JACOTIN, Jacques
     Voyant souffrir. See no. 3795

JACQUET DE LA GUERRE, Elizabeth
     Rondeau, G minor. See no. 4024
     Suite, D minor. See no. 1113

JANACEK, Leos
     Chorale preludes: Auf Fels gebaut; O Jesu Christ. See no. 4056
     The cunning little vixen: Suite. See no. 3781
1832 The diary of a young man who disappeared. Libuse Marova, con; Vil-
     em Pribyl, t; Kuhn Female Choir; Josef Palenicek, pno. Supra-
     phon 112 2414
                    +Gr 8-80 p251   +NR 10-80 p11
                    +HF 11-80 p68   +RR 7-80 p88
                    +HFN 7-80 p107
     Dumka, C minor. See no. 1430
1833 Fate. Magdalena Hajossyova, s; Jarmila Palivcova, ms; Vilem Pribyl,
     t; Brno State Theatre Opera Orchestra and Chorus; Frantisek Jil-
     ek. Supraphon SUP 112 2011/2 (2)
                    +ARG 10-80 p18   +NR 8-80 p10
                    +-FF 9/10-80 p139   +RR 2-80 p38
                    +Gr 3-80 p1437   ++SFC 9-21-80 p21
                    +-HF 10-80 p66   +STL 12-2-79 p37

+HFN 1-80 p106
1834 From the house of the dead. Jaroslava Janska, s; Eva Zikmundova, ms;
    Jiri Zahradnicek, Vladimir Krejcik, Beno Blachut, Ivo Zidek, t;
    Dalibor Jedlicka, bar; Antonin Svorc, bs-bar; Richard Novak, bs;
    VSOO Chorus; VPO; Charles Mackerras. Decca D224D2 Tape (c) K224
    K22
            ++Gr 11-80 p731   ++HFN 11-80 p120
    Glagolitic mass: Postlude. See no. 1352
1835 Jenufa. Prague National Orchestra; Bohumil Gregor. Supraphon Tape
    (c) KSUP 0711/2
            +-RR 3-80 p105 tape
    Jenufa: Mutter un habe den Kopf schwer. See no. 3774
    Lachian dances, no. 1. See no. 3897
1836 The Makropoulos affair. Elisabeth Soderstrom, s; Anna Czakova, ms;
    Peter Dvorsky, Vladimir Krejcik, Benno Blachut, Zdenek Svehla, t;
    Vaclav Zitek, bar; Dalibor Jedlicka, bs; Vienna State Opera Chor-
    us; VPO; Charles Mackerras. Decca D144D2 (2) Tape (c) K144K22
    (also London OSA 12116 Tape (c) OSA 5-12116)
            +ARG 5-80 p26   ++NYT 12-16-79 pD21
            +FF 3/4-80 p107   +ON 3-8-80 p29
            ++Gr 10-79 p703   +Op 3-80 p270
            *Gr 2-80 p1302 tape   +RR 10-79 p59
            +HF 5-80 p75   +RR 6-80 p94 tape
            +HF 8-80 p87 tape   ++SFC 1-27-80 p44
            ++HFN 10-79 p157   +-St 4-80 p126
            ++MT 4-80 p252   +STL 12-2-79 p37
1837 Quartet, strings, no. 1. Quartet, strings, no. 2. Gabrieli Quar-
    tet. Decca SDD 527 Tape (c) KSDC 527 (also London STS 15432)
            +ARG 2-80 p36   ++NR 4-80 p7
            +-FF 1/2-80 p98   +RR 2-78 p72
            +Gr 2-78 p1420   ++RR 5-78 p77 tape
            +-HF 10-79 p110   +SFC 1-27-80 p44
            +HFN 3-78 p139   ++St 12-79 p144
            +-MT 1-79 p43
    Quartet, strings, no. 1. See no. 1791
    Quartet, strings, no. 2. See no. 1837
    Romance, E major. See no. 1430
1838 Sinfonietta. Taras Bulba. CSO, RPO; Seiji Ozawa, Rafael Kubelik.
    HMV SXLP 30420 Tape (c) TC SXLP 30420 (From ASD 2652, ALP 1675)
            +Gr 1-80 p1151   +RR 1-80 p76
            +HFN 1-80 p121   ++RR 5-80 p106 tape
            +HFN 4-80 p121 tape
1839 Sinfonietta. Taras Bulba. CPhO; Karel Ancerl. Supraphon SUAST
    50380 Tape (c) 045 380   (From Parliament PLP 166)
            ++FF 1/2-80 p207   +RR 2-74 p71 tape
            +NR 10-74 p4
1840 Sinfonietta. Taras Bulba. CPhO; Zdenek Kosler. Supraphon 410 2167
            +-ARG 10-79 p43   +-NR 7-79 p4
            -FF 1/2-80 p98   +-RR 10-79 p93
            +-Gr 11-79 p818   ++SFC 8-12-79 p49
            +-HFN 12-79 p162
    Sinfonietta: Allegretto. See no. 3571
    Sonatas, piano, nos. 1 and 10. See no. 1783
    Sonata, violin and piano. See no. 1430
1841 Suite, strings. STRAUSS, R.: Capriccio, op. 85: Sextet (arr. for

string orchestra). SUK: Serenade, strings, op. 6, E flat major.
Los Angeles Chamber Orchestra; Neville Marriner. Argo ZRG 792
Tape (r) E 792

+Gr 3-75 p1653	+NR 7-75 p5
+HF 9-75 p92	+-RR 3-75 p36
+HF 5-80 p90 tape	++St 11-75 p139
+MJ 4-77 p33	

  Taras Bulba. See no. 1838. See no. 1839. See no. 1840

JANITSCH, Johann
  Quartet, F major. See no. 3543

JANOWSKI
  Sim shalom, Kol nidre, Sh'ma Koleynu, Avinu Malkeynu. See no. 3922

JANSSEN, Guus
  Dans van de Melic Matrijzen. See no. 3818

JAUFRE RUDEL
1842 Lanquan li jorn. MARCABRUN: L'autrier jost una sebissa. RAIMON DE
  MIRAVAL: Selh que non vul. ANON.: Novel amor. Clemencic Consort; Rene Clemencic. Harmonia Mundi HM 398
      +FF 11/12-80 p203

JAVALOYES
  El abanico. See no. 3921

JELIC, Vinko
1843 Vesperae beatae Mariae virginis. Zagreb Symphonists; Zagreb RTV
  Choir. Jugoton/Fonoars LSY 68065
      +-CL 6-80 p383

JENKINS, John
  Almain, no. 9, D major. See no. 1845
  Fancy-air sett, no. 6, G minor. See no. 1845
  Fantasia. See no. 4025
  Fantasia, D minor. See no. 1845
  Fantasias, G minor, D minor. See no. 1427
  Four-part ayres, nos. 51 and 27. See no. 1845
  Lady Katherine Audley's bells. See no. 1845
  A New Year's gift to TC. See no. 1845
  Pavane, G minor. See no. 1845
  Suite, D minor. See no. 1845
  Suite of three-part ayres, nos. 53-55, C major. See no. 1845
1844 Why in this shade of night. LAWES, H.: Cease o cease ye jolly shep-
  herds; Psalm, no. 22. LAWES, W.: Dialogues, psalmes and elegies:
  The catts as other creatures doe; Charon O Charon; Charon O gen-
  tle Charon, let me wooe thee; Come heavy heart; How like a widow;
  The master of thy art is dead; Musicke; Orpheus O Orpheus gently
  touch thy Lesbyan lyre; Tis not boy thy amorous looke; When death
  shall snatch us from these kidds. Consort of Musicke; Anthony
  Rooley. L'Oiseau-Lyre DSLO 574

+-Gr 10-80 p527	+HFN 10-80 p106

1845 Works, selections: Almain, no. 9, D major. Fantasia, D minor.
  Four-part ayres, nos. 51 and 27. Fancy-air sett, no. 6, G minor.
  Lady Katherine Audley's bells. A New Year's gift to TC. Pavane,
  G minor. Suite, D minor. Suite of three-part ayres, nos. 53-55,
  C major. Ars Nova; Peter Holman. Meridian E 77020

+Gr 2-79 p1436	+MT 1-80 p34
+HFN 2-79 p105	+RR 2-79 p40

JENNER, Gustav
  Serenade, A major. See no. 1780

JENSEN
    Press thy cheek against my own. See no. 3769
    Row gently here my gondolier. See no. 3769
JEPPESEN, Knug
    Fjorden. See no. 3587
JERSILD, Jorgen
    Kaerlighedsrosen. See no. 3587
JESSELL, Leon
1846 Schwarzwaldmadel (Girl of the Black Forest). Marianne Schubart,
        Gretl Schorg, Gitta Lind, s; Rene Kollo, Franz Fehringer, Willy
        Hofmann, t; Benno Kusche, bs-bar; Cologne Radio Orchestra and
        Chorus; Franz Marszalek. RCA VL 3-0406
                +FF 11/12-80 p182
JEZEK, Jaroslav
1847 Concerto, violin and wind orchestra. Quartet, strings. Suk Quar-
        tet; Petr Messieureur, vln; Prague Symphony Orchestra Wind En-
        semble; Jiri Belohlavek. Panton 110 681
                +FF 3/4-80 p107
1848 Fantasia. Nerves. MARTINU: Concerto, piano, no. 2. Jan Novotny,
        pno; Musici di Praga; Eduard Fischer. Panton 110 336
                +FF 3/4-80 p107
    Quartet, strings. See no. 1847
    Rhapsody. See no. 1849
1849 Sonata. Sonatina. Rhapsody. Toccata. Jan Novotny, pno. Panton
        110 455
                +FF 3/4-80 p107
    Sonatina. see no. 1849
    Toccata. See no. 1849
JOACHIM, Joseph
    Hebrew melodies, op. 9, nos. 1 and 3. See no. 2752
JOHANSON, Sven-Eric
1850 Concerto, keyed fiddle. NYSTROEM: Song by the sea. RANGSTROM:
        Divertimento elegiaco. Marianne Johansson, s; Mats Kuoppala,
        keyed fiddle; Goteborg Symphony Orchestra, Musica Sveciae; Ser-
        giu Comissiona, Carl von Garaguly, Sven Verde. Caprice CAP 1109
                ++ARG 11-80 p46
JOHNSON
    Oh let us howle. See no. 3876
    When you and I were young Maggie. See no. 3874
JOHNSON, Bengt Emil
1851 Escaping. In time. Vittringar. Kerstin Stahl, voice; Goran Ryd-
        berg, perc; Kjell-Inge Stevensson, clt; Peter Schuback, vlc;
        Mats Persson, Kristine Scholz, keyboard; Lars-Gunnar Bodin, syn-
        thesizer; Bengt Emil Johnson, tape delay. Caprice CAP 1174
                +FF 7/8-80 p100
    In time. See no. 1851
    Vittringar. See no. 1851
JOHNSON, Edward
    Eliza is the fairest queen. See no. 3995. See no. 3997
JOHNSON, Laurie
    Vivat Regina, suite. See no. 4029
JOHNSON, Robert
    Benedicam domino. See no. 3995
    Care-charming sleep. See no. 3744
    Songs: As I walked forth; Charon O Charon; Tis late and cold. See

no. 3878
    Songs: Defiled is my name. See no. 3719
    Songs: Full fathom five; Where the bee sucks. See no. 3997
    Where the bee sucks. See no. 3853
JOHNSON, Tom
1852 An hour for piano. Frederick Rzewski, pno. Lovely Music/Vital
    Records VR 1081
              +FF 9/10-80 p140
JOHNSTON, Ben
    Quartet, strings, no. 2. See no. 1279
JOLIVET, Andre
1853 Arioso barocco. Hymne a l'univers. Mandala. Songs: Hymne a Saint-
    Andre. Dany Barraud, s; Rene Perinelli, tpt; Daniel Roth, org.
    Arion ARN 38530
              +RR 7-80 p88
1854 Concerto, bassoon. WOLF-FERRARI: Suite concertino, op. 16, F
    major. Valery Popov, bsn; Soloists Ensemble; Gennady Rozhdest-
    vensky. Melodiya 33S 10 08495-96
              +-FF 5/6-80 p171
    Empithaleme. See no. 3713
    Fanfares pour Britannicus: Prelude. See no. 3566
    Hymne a l'univers. See no. 1853
    Mandala. See no. 1853
    Sonata, flute and piano. See no. 1301
    Songs: Hymne a Saint-Andre. See no. 1853
    Suite en concert. See no. 4017
JONES, Daniel
    Dance fantasy. See no. 1855
1855 Symphonies, nos. 8 and 9. Dance fantasy. BBC Welsh Symphony Orch-
    estra; Bryden Thomson. BBC Artium REGL 359
              +-FF 3/4-80 p109   +RR 11-79 p90
              ++Gr 11-79 p818
JONES, Kenneth
1856 Dialysis. A gay psaltery. Remembrance of an inward eye. Serpen-
    tine dances. Ruth Dyson, Carol Cooper, hpd; Duo Antiqua. Weal-
    den WS 189
              +Gr 7-80 p148   +RR 4-80 p96
    A gay psaltery. See no. 1856
    Remembrance of an inward eye. See no. 1856
    Serpentine dances. See no. 1856
JONES, Robert
    If in this flesh. See no. 3877
    Whither runneth my sweetheart. See no. 3878
JONGEN, Joseph
    Chant de mai, op. 53. See no. 3528
    Impromptu-Caprice, op. 37, no. 2. See no. 4056
    Sonata eroica, op. 94. See no. 752
    Symphonie concertante: Toccata. See no. 3658
JOPLIN, Scott
    Bethena. See no. 4045
    Easy winners. See no. 1857. See no. 3568
    The entertainer. See no. 1857
    Eugenia. See no. 3679
    The favorite. See no. 4043
    Gladiolus rag. See no. 1857. See no. 3679

Heliotrope bouquet. See no. 1857. See no. 3679
Magnetic rag. See no. 1857. See no. 3718
Maple leaf rag. See no. 1857. See no. 3626
Paragon rag. See no. 1857
1857 Piano works: Easy winners. The entertainer. Gladiolus rag. Helio-
       trope bouquet. Magnetic rag. Maple leaf rag. Paragon rag.
       Pineapple rag. Solace. Joshua Rifkin, pno. Angel DS 37331 Tape
       (c) 4ZS 37331
                    +NR 9-80 p11
Pineapple rag. See no. 1857
Pleasant moments. See no. 4043
Ragtime dance. See no. 3568
Solace. See no. 1857. See no. 4045
1858 Treemonisha. Marion Lowe and Cast; Chorus; Adrian Davis, pno;
       Anthony Watts. Rare Recorded Editions SRRE 183/3 (2)
                    +HFN 3-80 p91
JOSQUIN DES PRES
       Faulte d'argent. See no. 3806
       Fortuna desperata missa. See no. 959
       Heth sold ein meiskin. See no. 4001
       Mater patris et filia missa. See no. 956
       Motets: In principio erat verbum. See no. 959
       Motets: O Domine Jesu Christe. See no. 956
       Royal fanfare. See no. 4043
1859 Songs: Adieu mes amours; Basiez-moy; De tous bien plaine; La ber-
       nardina; Mille regrets; Missa de veata vergine; La plus de plus.
       West Virginia University Collegium Musicum; Harry Elzinga.
       Spectrum SR 114
                    +FF 5/6-80 p93
       Songs: Comment peult. See no. 3702
       Tu solus qui facis mirabilia. See no. 3763
JOUBERT
       Prelude on "Picardy". See no. 3618
JUDE
       The mighty deep. See no. 4007
JULIAN, Joseph
       Wave canon. See no. 3649
JULLIEN
       Livre d'orgue, excerpts. See no. 1168
JUON, Paul
       Berceuse. See no. 3964
JUROVSKY, Simon
1860 Symphony, no. 2. SUCHON: Symphonic fantasy on B-A-C-H. Ferdinand
       Klinda, org; Slovak Philharmonic Orchestra; Ludovic Rajter.
       RCA PRL 1-9055
                    ++FF 7/8-80 p139
KABALEVSKY, Dmitri
1861 The comedians. KHACHATURIAN: Gayaneh: Suite. VSOO; Vladimir Golsch-
       mann. Vanguard SRV 207 Tape (r) D 0207
                    +HF 2-80 p102   /RR 1-73 p43
                    +HFN 1-73 p117
KALAJIAN
       Songs. See no. 3851
KALKBRENNER, Friedrich
       Nocturne, op. 129. See no. 4011

KALLIWODA, Johan Wenzel (also Kalivoda, Jan Vaclav)
    Introduction and rondo, op. 51, F major. See no. 3839
KALMAN, Emmerich
1862 Countess Maritza, excerpts. Gretel Hartung, Christine Gorner, s;
        Fritz Wunderlich, Willy Hofmann, t; Benno Kusche, bs-bar; Col-
        ogne Radio Orchestra and Chorus; Franz Marszalek. RCA GL 3-0315
        Tape (c) GK 3-0315
                +−Gr 2-80 p1305   +RR 8-80 p15
                +−HFN 8-80 p109 tape
1863 Countess Maritza: Maritza's entrance; Sag ja. LEHAR: Giuditta:
        Meine Lippen sie Kussen so heiss. The Count of Luxembourg:
        Waltz. The merry widow: Waltz; Vilia. Schon ist die Welt: Ich
        bin verliebt. SIECYNSKI: Wien, Wien nur du allein. STRAUSS, J.
        II: The beautiful blue Danube, op. 314. Die Fledermaus, op. 363:
        Czardas. Tritsch Tratsch, op. 214. Carole Farley, s; Columbia
        Symphony Orchestra; Andre Kostelanetz. Columbia M 35167 Tape
        (c) MT 35167
                +ARG 2-80 p48   +NR 4-80 p13
                +FF 3/4-80 p179   +−St 2-80 p137
1864 Die Csardasfurstin. Erika Koth, Hedda Heusser, s; Philipp Gehly,
        Willy Hofmann, Franz Fehringer, t; Benno Kusche, bar; Cologne
        Radio Orchestra and Chorus; Franz Marszalek. RCA VL 3-0363
                +FF 9/10-80 p141
1865 Die Czardasfurstin, excerpts. Agnes Berger, Johann Feicht, Chris-
        tine Urfer; Linz City Theater Operetta Ensemble; Franz Werfel.
        Summit SUM 5001
                +ARG 7/8-80 p51
1866 Grafin Mariza. Anneliese Rothenberger, Olivera Miljakovic, Edda
        Moser, s; Nicolai Gedda, Willi Brokmeier, t; Kurt Bohme, bs;
        Bavarian State Opera Chorus; Graunke Symphony Orchestra; Willi
        Mattes. Arabesque 8057-2 (2)
                +FF 9/10-80 p14   +SFC 12-7-80 p33
                +NYT 7-13-80 pD20
    Komm Zigany. See no. 3738
KALMAR
    Anera. See no. 3810
KALNINS, Imants
1867 Symphony, no. 4. Latvian Radio and Television Orchestra; Leonids
        Vigners. Melodiya 33S 04503-4
                +FF 1/2-80 p100
KAPSBERGER, Giovanni
    Nigra sum. See no. 3546
KARAMANUK
    Admiration. See no. 3851
KARG-ELERT, Siegfried
    Chorale improvisation, op. 65, no. 5. See no. 4054
    Clair de lune, op. 72, no. 2. See no. 3728
    Harmonies du soir. See no. 659
    In dulci jubilo, op. 75, no. 2. See no. 3836
    Jerusalem du hochgebaute Stadt, op. 65. See no. 4047
1868 Kaleidoscope, op. 144. Pastels from Lake Constance, op. 96: The
        reed-grown waters. Sonatina, no. 1, op. 47, A minor. Triptych,
        op. 141: Legend. Michael Austin, org. Chalfont C 77014
                ++ARG 1-80 p33   ++MU 5-79 p8
                +FF 11/12-79 p90   +NR 10-78 p14

Marche triomphale. See no. 4067
1869 Passacaglia, op. 25, E flat minor. Pastel, op. 92, no. 1, B major.
   Symphonic chorales, no. 1, op. 87, no. 1, E flat major; no. 2,
   op. 87, no. 2, C minor. Robert Husson, org. Wealden WS 180
             ++Gr 8-80 p241   +RR 6-79 p107
   Pastel, op. 92, no. 1, B minor. See no. 1869
   Pastels from Lake Constance, op. 96: Pastel. See no. 156
   Pastels from Lake Constance, op. 96: The reed-grown waters. See
      no. 1868
   Rondo alla campanella, op. 156. See no. 156
   Sonata appassionata, op. 140, F sharp minor. See no. 3629
   Sonatina, no. 1, op. 74, A minor. See no. 1868
   Symphonic chorales, no. 1, op. 87, no. 1, E flat major; no. 2, op.
      87, no. 2, C minor. See no. 1869
   Tryptych, op. 141: Legend. See no. 1868
   Valse mignonne, op. 142, no. 2. See no. 4063
KARGES, Wilhelm
   O Mensch bewein. See no. 4057
KAROLYI, Pal
1870 Consolatio. Epilogus. Triphtongus 3a and 3b. Liszt Academy Cham-
   ber Choir; Ilona Szeverenyi, Tunde Enzsol, cimb; Gabor Lehotka,
   org; Ferenc Tarjani, hn; Janos Rolla, vln; Szombathely Symphony
   Orchestra; Janos Petro. Hungaroton SLPX 11969
             +FF 1/2-80 p100   +-NR 7-80 p14
   Epilogus. See no. 1870
   Triptongus 3a and 3b. See no. 1870
KAUFMAN, Jeffrey
   A solemn music. See no. 3740
KEE, PIet
   Choral prelude "Aus tiefer Not schrei ich zu Dir". See no. 3742
   Fantasia on "Wachet auf ruft uns die Stimme". See no. 3742
KEEBLE, John
   Double fugue, C major. See no. 3595
KEEL, Frederick
   Salt water ballads: Trade winds. See no. 3991
KEENEY, Wendell
   Sonatina. See no. 3859
KEFALIDI, Igor
   Trio a quattro. See no. 3834
KELLNER, Johann
   Jesu meine Zuversicht. See no. 4039
   Prelude, C major. See no. 4039
   Was Gott tut das ist wohlgetan. See no. 4049
KELTERBORN, Rudolf
1871 Chamber music, 5 wind instruments. Music, piano and 8 wind instru-
   ments. Phantasms. Symphony, no. 3. Basle Symphony Orchestra,
   Stalder Quintet, Stuttgart Radio Orchestra, Sudwestfunk Wind
   Players; Charles Dobler, pno; Moshe Atzmon, Rudolf Kelterborn.
   Musicaphon BM 30 SL 1716
             +HFN 12-80 p141
   Music, piano and 8 wind instruments. See no. 1871
   Phantasms. See no. 1871
   Symphony, no. 3. See no. 1871
KERCKHOVEN, Abraham von den
   Fantasias (3). See no. 95

Fantasias, D minor, C minor, G major, E minor, F major. See no.
1872
Fugues, A minor, C major. See no. 1872
1872 Organ works: Fantasias, D minor, C minor, G major, E minor, F major.
Fugues, A minor, C major. Prelude and fugue, G major. Versus,
no. 5, B major. Versus, no. 7, E major. Jozef Sluys, org.
Zephyr ZO 3
+-Gr 7-80 p153
Prelude and fugue, G major. See no. 1872
Versus, no. 5, B major; no. 7, E major. See no. 1872
KERLL, Johann
Canzona, C major. See no. 1458
Canzona, no. 1, D minor. See no. 1458
Capriccio "Cucu". See no. 3682
Toccatas, nos. 1 and 3. See no. 1458
KERN, Jerome
All the things you are. See no. 3882
KESSLER, Thomas
1873 Lost paradise. Violon control. LEVINAS: Appels. Arsis et Thesis
ou la chanson du souffle. Froissements d'ailes. Voix dans un
vaisseau d'airain, chants en escalier. J. J. Dussert, clt; J.
P. Seguin, bsn; L. Roquin, tpt; Charles Marchand, trom; Tristan
Murail, pno and perc; P. Labadie, P. Guise, perc; J. Leandre,
bs; P. Y. Artaud, flt; N. Froget, s; A. Cazalet, hn; P. Bocquil-
lon, flt; Michael Levinas, pno; G. Renon-McLaughlin, vla; D.
Sapin, hn; S. Beltrando, hp; Janos Negyesy, vln; Charles Bruck,
Michael Levinas, Thomas Kessler, cond. Harmonia Mundi INA GRM
AM 82110
+FF 7/8-80 p16
Piano control. See no. 1413
Smog. See no. 1413
Violon control. See no. 1873
KETELBY, Albert
In a Persian market. See no. 3843
KETTING, Otto
1874 Symphony, no. 1. Symphony, saxophones. Netherlands Saxophone Quar-
tet, COA; Bernard Haitink, Hans Rosbaud. Composers Voice VC 8001
+FF 11/12-80 p127
Symphony, saxophones. See no. 1874
KHACHATURIAN, Aram
Concerto, violin. See no. 1500
1875 Concerto, violin, D major. Jean-Pierre Rampal, flt; French National
Radio and Television Orchestra; Jean Martinon. Erato STU 70586
+HFN 4-80 p105   +RR 10-79 p93
Gayaneh: Lesginka; Dance of the rose maidens; Dance of the Kurds;
Sabre dance. See no. 3955
Gayaneh: Suite. See no. 1861
1876 Masquerade: Ballet suite. Spartacus: Ballet suite. LSO; John Geor-
giadis, vln; Stanley Black. Decca PFS 4434 Taep (c) KPFC 4434
(also London SPC 21184)
+Gr 5-79 p1945   +NR 4-80 p3
+HFN 5-79 p123   +-RR 7-79 p59
Masquerade: Mazurka; Galop. See no. 3962
Sonata, solo violin. See no. 1877
1877 Sonata, solo violoncello. Sonata, solo violin. Trio, clarinet,

violin and piano. Victor Pikaizen, vln; Natalia Shakhovskaya,
vlc; Rafael Bagdasarian, clt; Arnold Kaplan, pno. Melodiya 33S
10 08783-84
+FF 3/4-80 p109
Sonatina, C major. See no. 3730
Spartacus: Adagio of Spartacus and Phrygia. See no. 3623
Spartacus: Ballet suite. See no. 1876
1878 Symphony, no. 3. RIMSKY-KORSAKOV: Russian Easter festival overture,
op. 36. RACHMANINOFF: Vocalise, op. 34, no. 14. Anna Moffo, s;
CSO, American Symphony Orchestra; Leopold Stokowski. RCA GL 4-
2923 Tape (c) GK 4-2923 (From SB 6804)
+Gr 8-80 p222   +HFN 10-80 p117 tape
+Gr 9-80 p413 tape   +–RR 8-80 p46
+HFN 8-80 p107
Trio, clarinet, violin and piano. See no. 1877
KHANDOSHKIN, Ivan
Sentimental aria. See no. 3601
KIENZL, Wilhelm
Der Evangelimann: O schone Jugendtage. See no. 3770
Der Evangelimann: Selig sind die Verfolgung leiden. See no. 3961
KILAR, Wojciech
Dipthongos. See no. 3857
1879 Krzesany. LUTOSLAWSKI: Livre pour orchestra. Warsaw Philharmonic
Orchestra; Witold Rowicki. Aurora AUR 7002
+Gr 1-80 p1151   +–RR 12-79 p62
+HFN 12-79 p162
KILLMAYER, Wilhelm
An John Field. See no. 1425
KILPINEN, Yrjo
1880 Songs: Elegia satakielelle; Ihme; Kuutamolla; Lehdokki; Kesayo; Ran-
nalta I and II. MERIKANTO: 'Songs: Laula tytto; Liknelse; Tule.
NUMMI: Songs: Mietteliaat vainiot; Mutta kun olen runoniekka;
Rakastunut. SIBELIUS: Diamanten pa marssnon; Svarta Rosor.
Matti Juhani Pilponnen, t; Ute Starke, pno. Da Camera Magna SM
90007
+ARG 1-80 p49
KING
Barnum and Bailey's favorite. See no. 4012
KING, Larry
Fanfare to the tongue of fires. See no. 4058
KINGSLEY
Popcorn. See no. 3962
KIRCHNER, Leon
Quartet, strings, no. 1. See no. 1419
1881 Trio, violin, violoncello and piano. VILLA-LOBOS: Trio, strings,
no. 2. Philhadelphia Trio. Centaur CRC 1004
+–FF 9/10-80 p142
KIRKBYE, George
See what a maze of error. See no. 3893
KIRNBERGER, Johann
Cembalostucke. See no. 3845
Sonata, flute, G major. See no. 1459
KITSON, Charles
communion on an Irish air "Alone with none but thee my God". See
no. 3743

KIYOSE, Yasuji
    Japanese festival dances. See no. 1456
KLAMI, Uuno
1882 Cheremissian fantasy, op. 19. Kalevala suite, op. 23. Arto Noras,
    vlc; Helsinki Philharmonic Orchestra; Jorma Panula. Finlandia
    FA 302 (also Finnlevy SFX 4)
           +ARG 4-80 p50   +-RR 8-77 p56
           +FF 11/12-79 p91   +RR 11-78 p28
           +-NR 10-80 p2   +RR 1-80 p77
    Kalevala suite, op. 23. See no. 1882
KLEBER, Leonard
    Die Brunnlein die da fliessen. See no. 3590
    Zucht Ehr und Lob. See no. 3590
KLICKA, Josef
    Fantasie de concert, op. 65. See no. 1352
    Fantasie de concert, op. 65: Final. See no. 4067
KNEUBUHL, John
    Variations on a pretty bird. See no. 3884
KNIGHT
    Rocked in the cradle of the deep. See no. 3905
KODALY, Zoltan
1883 Chromatic fantasia (Bach). SCHUMANN: Marchenbilder, op. 113. STRA-
    VINSKY: Elegie. VIEUXTEMPS: Capriccio, op. post. Sonata, viola
    and piano, op. 36. Atar Arad, vla; Evelyne Brancart, pno. Tele-
    funken 6-42075 Tape (c) 4-42075
           ++HF 4-80 p104 tape
1884 Concerto, orchestra. Hary Janos: Suite. Hungarian State Symphony
    Orchestra; Janos Ferencsik. Hungaroton LSPX 12190
           +HFN 12-80 p141
1885 Dances of Galanta. Dances of Marosszek. Hary Janos: Suite. PO;
    Eugene Ormandy. CBS 61930 Tape (c) 40-61930 (From SBRG 72362,
    72627)
           ++Gr 10-79 p639   +RR 11-79 p83
           +-HFN 9-79 p121   +RR 3-80 p105
           +-HFN 11-79 p157 tape
    Dances of Galanta. See no. 1887
    Dances of Marosszek. See no. 1885. See no. 1887
1886 Duo, violin and violoncello, op. 7.* Sonata, solo violoncello, op.
    8. Arnold Eidus, vln; Janos Starker, vlc. Saga 5386 (*From
    Nixa PLP 510)
           ++Gr 10-74 p727   ++RR 8-74 p52
           ++HFN 6-80 p117   ++RR 7-80 p80
           ++MT 12-80 p785
1887 Hary Janos: Suite. Dances of Marosszek. Dances of Galanta. Orch-
    estra; Ferenc Fricasy. DG 2535 706
           +ARSC Vol 12, nos. 1-2, 1980 p124
    Hary Janos: Suite. See no. 1884. See no. 1885
    Praeludium. See no. 3742
1888 Quartet, strings, no. 2, op. 10. SUK: Quartet, strings, no. 1, op.
    1, B flat major. WOLF: Italian serenade, G major. Musikverein
    Quartet. Decca SDD 543
           +Gr 10-79 p667   +RR 10-79 p115
           ++HFN 10-79 p167   +ST 4-80 p927
    Sonata, solo violoncello, op. 4. See no. 352
    Sonata, solo violoncello, op. 8. See no. 1886

Songs: Esti dal; Egyetem-Begyetem; Zold erdoben. See no. 3814
KOECHLIN, Charles
1889 Les heures persanes, op. 65, no. 4: Matin frais, dans la haute val-
      lee. Pastorales, op. 77. Paysages et marines, op. 63. Boaz
      Sharon, pno. Orion ORS 79332

+ARG 2-80 p36	++MQ 1-80 p155
+CL 3-80 p15	+MT 1-80 p34
++FF 11/12-79 p91	+-NR 1-80 p13
+-HF 6-80 p80	+RR 1-80 p103

    Pastorales, op. 77. See no. 1889
    Paysages et marines, op. 63. See no. 1889
KOENEMANN
    When the king went forth to war. See no. 3904
KOHS, Ellis
    Variations, piano. See no. 3737
KOKKONEN, Joonas
    Concerto, violoncello. See no. 1682
    Lux aeterna. See no. 3726
    Songs: Evenings. See no. 3586
1890 Symphony, no. 3. SIBELIUS: Tapiola, op. 112. Finnish Radio Orches-
      tra; Paavo Berglund. Finlandia FA 311 (From Decca SXL 6432)

+ARG 9-80 p43	+HFN 11-80 p129
+FF 7/8-80 p101	+NR 11-80 p4

KOLB, Barbara
    The sentences. See no. 4026
KOLLO, Walter and Willi
1891 One day in May (Wie einst im Mai). Angela Muthel, Wolfgang Ziffer,
      Harry Wustenhagen, Iska Geri, Kurt Waitzmann, Volker Brandt,
      Margot Rothweiler; Theatre des Westens, Berlin; Wolfgang Peters.
      RCA VL 3-0413
                    +FF 11/12-80 p183
KOMITAS
    Dances. See no. 3850
KOPYTMAN, Mark
    About an old tune. See no. 3739
KORNGOLD, Erich
1892 Much ado about nothing, op. 11. WEILL: Quodlibet, op. 9. West-
      phalian Symphony Orchestra; Siegfried Landau. Candide CE 31091
      (also Turnabout TVS 37124)

+-Gr 1-80 p1151	+-MT 4-80 p253
+HFN 1-80 p107	+-NR 8-76 p4
+MJ 5-77 p32	/RR 12-79 p82
+-MQ 7-77 p446	+STL 12-9-79 p41

    Much ado about nothing, op. 11: Holzapfel und Schlehwein, Garden
      scene. See no. 3964
1893 Symphony, op. 40, F sharp major. Munich Philharmonic Orchestra;
      Rudolf Kempe. RCA GL 4-2919 Tape (c) GK 4-2919 (From ARL 1-
      0443)

++Gr 8-80 p222	+HFN 9-80 p116 tape
+Gr 9-90 p413 tape	

    Die tote Stadt, op. 12: Mein sehen mein Wahnen. See no. 3774
1894 Violanta. Eva Marton, Getraut Stocklassa, s; Ruth Hesse, ms; Sieg-
      fried Jerusalem, Horst Laubenthal, Manfred Schmidt, Heinrich
      Weber, t; Walter Berry, Paul Hansen, bs; Bavarian Radio Chorus;
      Munich Radio Orchestra; Marek Janowski. CBS 79229 (2)

+Gr 12-80 p876   +STL 12-14-80 p38
+-HFN 12-80 p141
KOSA, Gyorgy
    Divertimento. See no. 3810
1895 Miniatures, harp trio (12). Orpheus, Eurydike, Hermes. Sonata,
    violoncello and piano. Katalin Szokelfalvi-Nagy, s; Klara Tak-
    acs, ms; Gabriella Zsigmond, con; Attila Fulop, t; Gabor Nemeth,
    bar; Peter Kovacs, bs; Peter Lukacs, vla; Arpad Szasz, Ede Banda,
    vlc; Laszlo Som, double-bs; Henrik Prohle, alto flt; Hedy Lubik,
    hp; Andras Gartner, timpani; Gyorgy Kosa, pno; Hungarian Harp
    Trio; Miklos Erdelyi. Hungaroton SLPX 11628
            +Gr 7-75 p182   +RR 4-75 p60
            +NR 5-75 p9   ++SFC 8-17-80 p36
    Orpheus, Eurydike, Hermes. See no. 1895
    Sonata, violoncello and piano. See no. 1895
    Two. See no. 3810
KOSENKO, Viktor
    Pieces, violon and piano, op. 4: Dreams; Impromptu. See no. 1532
KOSTIAINEN, Pekka
1896 Fantasia. Mass, organ. SIBELIUS: Pieces, op. 111: Funeral; Intra-
    da. Hymn, op. 113, no. 1. Impromptu, op. 5, no. 1. Marche
    funebre, op. 113, no. 8. Mati Vainio, org. Finlandia FA 318
            +FF 11/12-80 p210   +-HFN 12-80 p151
    Mass, organ. See no. 1896
KOTONSKI, Wlodzimierz
    Mikrostriktury. See no. 3857
KOUSSEVITZKY, Serge
    Concerto, double bass. See no. 1159
KOVEN, Reginald
    O promise me. See no. 3875
KOZELUH, Leopold
1897 Concerto, piano duet, E flat major. Sinfonia concertante, E flat
    major. Bonifacio Bianchi, mand; Jean-Paul Leroy, tpt; Franco
    Angeleri, Michaela Mingardo Angeleri, pno; I Solisti Veneti;
    Claudio Scimone. Erato STU 71305
            +-Gr 10-80 p498   +-HFN 10-80 p105
    Sinfonia concertante, E flat major. See no. 1897
KOZLOVSKY, Alexei
1898 Festivity. Lola. Karakalpak suite. Tanavar. USSR Radio Orches-
    tra, Uzbek Philharmonic Orchestra; Alexei Kozlovsky. Melodiya
    33 D 02969-60
            +-FF 7/8-80 p102
    Karakalpak suite. See no. 1898
    Lola. See no. 1898
    Tanavar. See no. 1898
KRAFT, William
1899 Requiescat. LESEMAN: Nataraja. SUBOTNICK: Liquid strata. Ralph
    Grierson, pno. Town Hall S 24
            +ARG 2-80 p49   +-FF 11/12-80 p208
    Suite for brass. See no. 3740
KRAKAUER
    Du gauter Himmelvater. See no. 3711
KRAMAR-KROMMER, Frantisek
1900 Concerto, clarinet, op. 36, E flat major. Concerto, oboe, op. 37,
    F major. Bohuslav Zahradnik, clt; Jiri Mihule, ob; PCO; Franti-

sek Vajnar. Supraphon 110 2458

    +—FF 9/10-80 p143   +HFN 11-80 p120

    +Gr 11-80 p671   +NR 8-80 p6

Concerto, oboe, op. 37, F major. See no. 1900

1901 Octet partitas, opp. 57, 69, 79. NWE. Philips 9500 437 Tape (c)
    7300 659

    +ARG 1-79 p14   +NR 12-78 p15

    +Gr 3-80 p1404   ++SFC 11-12-78 p49

KRATZL-BICZO

Das Gluck is' a Vogerl. See no. 3711

KRAUS, Joseph

1902 Sonata, piano, no. 1, E major. Sonata, piano, no. 2, E flat major.
    Lucia Negro, fortepiano. Caprice 1173

        ++FF 5/6-80 p94

Sonata, piano, no. 2, E flat major. See no. 1902

KRCEK, Jaroslav

Symphony, no. 1. See no. 994

KREBS, Johann

Chorale preludes, no. 2, Wachet auf; no. 5, Komm heiliger Geist,
    Herre Gott. See no. 3866

Fantasia, F major. See no. 4039

Mein Gott das Herze bring ich dir. See no. 4039

Prelude, B flat major. See no. 84

Trio, C minor. See no. 4039

Trio sonata, flute and violin, D major. See no. 3845

Wachet auf ruft uns die Stimme. See no. 3545

KREISLER, Fritz

Allegretto in the style of Boccherini. See no. 1904

Canzonetta. See no. 1904

Caprice Viennois, op. 2. See no. 1904

Cavatina. See no. 1904

Chanson Lous XIII and pavane (Couperin). See no. 1904

La gitana. See no. 1904

Liebesfreud. See no. 1904

Liebesleid. See no. 1904

Madrigal. See no. 1904

March miniature Viennoise. See no. 3601

Minuet in the style of Niccolo Porpora. See no. 3964

Polichinelle serenade. See no. 1904

Praeludium and allegro in the style of Pugnani. See no. 1904

1903 Quartet, strings, A minor. PAGANINI: Quartet, strings, E minor.
    Stuyvesant Quartet. Odyssey Y 35933 Tape (c) YT 35933

        ++FF 9/10-80 p177   +St 9-80 p86

Recitative and scherzo. See no. 3637

Recitative and scherzo capriccio, op. 6. See no. 1904

Romance. See no. 1904

Rondino on a theme by Beethoven. See no. 1904

Schon Rosmarin. See no. 1904. See no. 3998

Sicilienne and rigaudon. See no. 3964

Toy soldiers march. See no. 1904

1904 Works, selections: Allegretto (Boccherini). Canzonetta. Caprice
    Viennois, op. 2. Cavatina. Chanson Louis VIII and pavane (L.
    Couperin). La gitana. Liebesfreud. Liebesleid. Madrigal.
    Polichinelle serenade. Praeludium and allegro (Pugnani). Reci-
    tative and scherzo caprice, op. 6. Romanze. Rondino on a theme

by Beethoven. Schon Rosmarin. Toy soldiers march. Miklos Szen-
    thelyi, vln; Judith Szenthelyi, pno. Hungaroton SLPX 12141
        +FF 9/10-80 p143   ++SFC 7-27-80 p34
        ++NR 7-80 p13   +St 10-80 p128
KRENEK, Ernst
1905 Acco-music, solo accordian. NORDHIEM: Dinosaurus. PENTLAND: Inter-
    play. SCHAFER: La testa d'Adriane. Joseph Macerollo, accord;
    Mary Morrison, s; Purcell String Quartet. Melbourne MSLP 4034
        ++FF 11/12-80 p218
1906 Capriccio. The dissembler. MOSS: Symphonies. Evelyn Elsing, vln;
    Michael Ingham, bar; Annapolis Brass Quintet. Orion ORS 79362
        +ARG 7/8-80 p27   +NR 5-80 p15
        ++FF 5/6-80 p95
    The dissembler. See no. 1906
1907 Kitharaulos, op. 213. Static and ecstatic, op. 214. James Ostry-
    niec, ob; Karen Lindquist, hp; Los Angeles Chamber Orchestra;
    Ernst Krenek. Varese VR 81200
        +NR 8-80 p8
    Quintina, op. 191. See no. 1910
    Sonata, piano, no. 4. See no. 782
1908 Songs: Songs, op. 30a (3); Songs, op. 112 (4); Zeitlieder, op. 215
    (2). NORDENSTROM: Zeit XXIV. Neva Pilgrim, s; Dennis Helmrich,
    pno; Madison Quartet; William Nichols, clt. Orion ORS 79348
        +-ARG 2-80 p38   ++RR 1/2-80 p101
        +NR 4-80 p12
1909 Songs: Durch die Nacht, op. 69; Gemischte Choere, op. 61 (3); Die
    Jahreszeiten, op. 35; Lessons, op. 210 (3); O holy ghost, op. 186a;
    Sacred pieces, op. 210 (3); Settings to poems by William Blake,
    op. 226 (2). College of the Desert Vocal Ensemble; Anne Marie
    Ketchum, s; George Calusdian, pno; John Norman. Orion ORS 80377
        ++ARG 12-80 p35   +NR 8-80 p12
    Static and ecstatic, op. 214. See no. 1907
    Suite, solo guitar. See no. 3884
1910 They knew what they wanted, op. 227. Quintina, op. 191. Rheda Bec-
    ker, narrator; Constance Navratil, s; James Ostryniec, ob; Paul
    Hoffmann, pno; Carol Winterbourne, flt; Carrie Holzman, vla; John
    Kneubuhl, gtr; Fred Lee, vibraphone; Joseph Kucera, Sue Hopkins,
    Mark Goldstein, perc; Ernst Krenek. Orion ORS 80380
        -NR 12-80 p11
KREUTZER, Conradin
1911 Quintet, piano, flute, clarinet, viola and violoncello. WITT: Quin-
    tet, op. 6, E flat major. Werner Genuit, pno; Frans Vester, flt;
    Gernot Schmalfuss, ob; Dieter Klocker, clt; Jurgen Kussmaul, vla;
    Anner Bylsma, vlc; Werner Meyendorf, hn; Karl-Otto Hartmann, bsn.
    Acanta EA 23139
        +ARG 5-80 p51
1912 Rondo, piano, A flat major. Sonata, flute and piano, op. 35, G
    major. Trio, op. 23, no. 1, B flat major. Konrad Richter, pno;
    Karl Zoller, flt; Wolfgang Boettcher, vlc. Preiser PSR 3285
        +RR 3-80 p73
    Sonata, flute and piano, op. 35, G major. See no. 1912
    Trio, op. 23, no. 1, B flat major. See no. 1912
KREUTZER, Joseph
    Trio, flute, clarinet and guitar, op. 16. See no. 1244

KRIEGER, Johann
    Songs: Coridon in Noten; Ein Kussgen in Ehren; Im Dunkeln ist gut
        munkeln; Die schlimmen Manner. See no. 3764
KROTKOV
    The poet: I have long despised all women. See no. 3774
KRUMM, Philip
    Sound machine. See no. 1821
KUFFNER
    Polonaise, op. 168, A major. See no. 1224
KUBIK, Ladislav
    Inventions (2). See no. 4010
KUHLAU, Friedrich
    Fantasia. See no. 4006
    Fantasia, D major. See no. 3629
    Sonatina, op. 20, no. 2, G major. See no. 3730
KUHNAU, Johann
    Der Gerechte kommt um. See no. 230
KUHNEL, August
    Sonata, 2 violas da gamba, E minor. See no. 3767
    Suite, A major. See no. 3686
KUMMER, Gaspard
    Divertissement op. 13. See no. 3782
KUNZE
    Refuge. See no. 3760
KUPFERMAN, Meyer
    Abracadabra. See no. 3739
1913 Atto (2 versions). Good friends duo. Premeditation. WALKER: Anti-
        fonys. Sonata, violoncello and piano. Italo Babino, David
        Moore, vlc; Meyer Kupferman, clt; David Starobin, gtr; George
        Walker, pno; RPO; Paul Freeman. Serenus SRS 12081
                +−ARG 1-80 p43   +NR 10-79 p6
                +−FF 9/10-80 p233
    Good friends duo. See no. 1913
1914 Infinities 15. PERSICHETTI: Concerto, piano, 4 hands. STARER:
        Fantasia concertante. Jean and Kenneth Wentworth, pno. Grena-
        dilla GS 1050
                +−FF 9/10-80 p178   ++NR 10-80 p14
    Premeditation. See no. 1913
    Three ideas. See no. 3652
KURZ, Ivan
    Sonata, violin and piano. See no. 4010
KUULA, Toivo
1915 Songs (choral): Auringon Noustessa, op. 11, no. 3; Hautalaulu, op.
        11, no. 5; Karavaanik oro, op. 21, no. 1; Kevatlaulu, op. 11,
        no. 7; Keinutan Kaikua, op. 11, no. 6; Meren Virsi, op. 11, no.
        2; Rukous, op. 34b, no. 1; Savel, op. 29b, no. 1; Siell on Kauan
        Jo Kukkinette Omenapuut, op. 11, no. 1; Venelaulu, op. 21, no. 2;
        Virta Venhetta Vic, op. 4, no. 5. Klementti Institute Chamber
        Chorus; Harald Andersen. Finlandia FA 306
                +FF 5/6-80 p95   +NR 10-80 p9
                +HFN 10-80 p106
KUUSISTO, Taneli
    Finnish husbandry. See no. 3586
    Ramus virens olivarum, op. 55, no. 1. See no. 3726

LA BARRE, Michel de
1916 Suite, no. 2, G major. Suite, no. 5, D minor. Suite, no. 9, G maj-
     or. Stephen Preston, transverse flt; Jordi Savall, vla da gamba;
     Blandine Verlet, hpd; Hopkinson Smith, theorbo. Telefunken AP
     6-42325
                    +ARG 2-80 p50   +HFN 2-79 p113
                    +FF 1/2-80 p170   +RR 3-79 p96
                    +Gr 4-79 p1730
     Suite, no. 5, D minor. See no. 1916
     Suite, no. 9, G major. See no. 1916
LACHNER, Franz
     Fugue, D minor. See no. 3834
1917 Nonet, F minor. Danzi Quintet; Jaap Schroder, vln; Wiel Peeters,
     vla; Anner Bylsma, vlc; Anthony Woodrow, bs. Acanta EA 23143
     (From BASF)
                    +ARG 5-80 p51   +FF 1/2-80 p102
LALO, Edouard
1918 Namouna: Ballet suites, nos. 1 and 2. Luxembourg Radio Orchestra;
     Louis de Froment. Turanbout QRV 34724
                    /FU 9-79 p52   +MUM 7/8-80 p32
     Rapsodie norvegienne. See no. 3915
     Le Roy d'Ys: Chanson de l'epousee. See no. 3770
     Le Roi d'Ys: Vainement ma bien-aimee. See no. 3774. See no. 3926
1919 Symphonie espagnole, op. 21, D minor. SAINT-SAENS: Introduction
     and rondo capriccioso, op. 28. Havanaise, op. 83. Arthur Grum-
     iaux, vln; Lamoureux Concerts Orchestra; Manuel Rosenthal. Phil-
     ips 6570 192 Tape (c) 7310 192
                    +FF 9/10-80 p144
1920 Symphonie espagnole, op. 21, D minor. SAINT-SAENS: Introduction
     and rondo capriccioso, op. 28. Konstanty Kulka, vln; Polish
     Radio Orchestra; Kazimierz Kord. Telefunken 6-41027
                    +FF 9/10-80 p123
     Symphonie espagnole, op. 21, D minor. See no. 917
     Symphonie espagnole, op. 21, D minor: Andante. See no. 3964
1921 Trio, no. 1, op. 7, C minor. SAINT-SAENS: Trio, piano, no. 1, op.
     18, F major. Caecilian Trio. Turnabout TVC 37002 Tape (c) CT
     7002
                    +FF 9/10-79 p130   +HF 1-80 p91 tape
                    +HF 11-79 p100   ++SFC 6-17-79 p41
LAMBERT, Constant
1922 Pomona. Romeo and Juliet. ECO; Norman Del Mar. Lyrita SRCS 110
                    +Gr 1-80 p1152   ++RR 12-79 p62
                    +HFN 12-79 p162
     Romeo and Juliet. See no. 1922
LAMBRANZI, Gregorio
     Dances: Bolognesa, Narcisin, Dimo Jesu and genio, Ruberto, La disa-
     mecitia and entree, Logi and hurlo Bacho. See no. 1802
LAMONT DE GRIGNON, Ricard
     Preludes (3). See no. 1472
LA MONTAINE, John
1923 Conversations, op. 42. Sonnets of Shakespeare, op. 12. Polly Jo
     Baker, s; Thomas Tatton, vla; John La Montaine, pno. Fredonia
     FD 8
                    +NR 11-80 p7
1924 Dance preludes, op. 18 (6). Incantation, op. 39. Pieces, piano.

John La Montaine, pno; Eastman Jazz Ensemble; Rayburn Wright.
Fredonia FD 3
        +FF 7/8-78 p47   *NR 5-80 p15
Incantation, op. 39. See no. 1924
1925 The nine lessons of Christmas, op. 44. Polly Jo Baker, s; David
    Griffith, t; Fredonia Singers; Carol Baum, hp; John La Montaine.
    Fredonia FD 6
        +MU 3-80 p8   +NR 12-79 p2
Pieces, piano. See no. 1924
Sonnets of Shakespeare, op. 12. See no. 1923
LANDGRAVE DE HESSE
Pavan. See no. 3966
LANDINI, Francesco
Caro signor pales. See no. 4032
Donna i prego. See no. 4032
In somm' alteca. See no. 4032
Ochi dolenti mie. See no. 4032
LANG
Das Lieben bringt. See no. 3662
Prelude and fugue, C major. See no. 3651
LANG, Craig
Tuba tune, D major. See no. 3527
Tuba tune, op. 15, D major. See no. 3743. See no. 4054. See no.
    4048
LANGFORD, Gordon
Famous British marches. See no. 3617
Marching with Sousa. See no. 3617
Prince of Wales march. See no. 3617
Rhapsody. See no. 3627
LANGLAIS, Jean
1926 Aus tiefer Not. Jesu meine Freude. In dulci jubilo. Piece pour
    trompette. Psalm, no. 140. Sonatina. Freddy Grin, tpt; Dick
    Klomp, org. Ursina Motette M 2004
        +FF 9/10-80 p271   ++MU 11-80 p17
Ave mundi gloria. See no. 3934
Chants de Bretagne, op. 161. See no. 1928
Chants de paix. See no. 3970. See no. 4023
Fete. See no. 1238
Hymne d'actions de graces: Te deum. See no. 3994
1927 Improvisation on Conditor alme siderum. Improvisation on Salve
    Regina. Incantation pour un jour saint, op. 46. Te deum.
    VIERNE: Fantasiestucke, op. 54: Carillon de Westminster; Sur le
    Rhin. Jean Langlais, org. Ursina Motette M 1023
        ++FF 1/2-80 p102   +MU 2-80 p12
Improvisation on Salve Regina. See no. 1927
In dulci jubilo. See no. 1926
Incantation pour un jour saint, op. 46. See no. 1927. See no.
    1928. See no. 4034
Jesu meine Freude. See no. 1926
Mors et resurrection, op. 5, no. 1. See no. 161
1928 Organ works: Chants de Bretagne, op. 161 (huit). Incantation pour
    un jour saint, op. 46. Paraphrases gregoriennes, op. 5 (3).
    Poemes evangeliques, op. 2 (3). Pieces, op. 28 (9). Suite
    breve, op. 38. Suite folklorique, op. 61. Ann Labounsky, org.
    Musical Heritage Society MHS 4127/9 (3)

+HF 7-80 p70   +MJ 10-80 p12

Paraphrases gregoriennes, op. 5. See no. 1928
Paraphrases gregoriennes, op. 5: Te deum. See no. 3838. See no.
    4034
Pasticcio. See no. 1575
Piece pour trompette. See no. 1926
Pieces, organ, op. 28. See no. 1928
Poemes evangeliques, op. 2. See no. 1928
Poemes evangeliques, op. 2: L'Annonciation; Nativite; Les rameaux.
    See no. 1575
Poemes evangeliques, op. 2: La nativite. See no. 3973
Psalm, no. 140. See no. 1926
Sonatina. See no. 1926
Suite breve, op. 38. See no. 1928
Suite folklorique, op. 61. See no. 1928
Te deum. See no. 1927

LANNER, Joseph
    Huntsman's pleasure galop. op. 82. See no. 3826
    Neue Wiener Landler, op. 1. See no. 3759
    The parting of the ways. See no. 3989
    Pesther-Walzer, op. 93. See no. 3826
    Summer night's dream, op. 90. See no. 3989
    Die Werber, op. 103. See no. 3759

LANSING
    The darkie'd dream. See no. 3679

LANSKY, Paul
    Quartet, strings. See no. 1121

LAPPI, Pietro
    Fanfare. See no. 3597
    La serafina. See no. 3597

LARRANAGA
    Sonata de 5 tono. See no. 3871

LARSSON, Lars-Erik
    Concertino, trombone and strings. See no. 33
1929 Forkladd Gud (The disguised god), op. 24. Symphony, no. 3, op. 34,
    C minor. Birgit Nordin, s; Hakan Hagegard, bar; Per Jonsson, re-
    citer; Helsingborg Concert House Chorus; Helsingborg Symphony
    Orchestra; Sten Frykberg. BIS LP 96
                +FF 11/12-79 p95   +RR 3-30 p55
                +NR 5-79 p2
1930 Pastoral suite. LUNDQUIST: Concerto, violin. SODERMAN: Swedish
    festival music. Karel Sneberger, vln; Orebro Symphony Orchestra;
    Goran Nilson. Bluebell 101
                +-FF 3/4-80 p110
    Symphony, no. 3, op. 34, C minor. See no. 1929

LASSUS, Roland de
    Bonjour mon coeur. See no. 3683
1931 Lagrime de San Pietro. Psalmus poenitentialis, no. 2. Motets: Tim-
    or et tremor; Pronuba Juno; Cum rides mihi. Liszt Chamber Choir;
    Istvan Parkai. Hungaroton LSPX 12081/2 (2)
                +-Gr 11-80 p723
1932 Motets: Angelus Domini locutus est; Emendemus in melius; Multarum
    hic resonat concors; Pater Abraham miserere miei; Pater noster;
    Quid prodest constantia; Quid prodest homini si mundum; Si bona
    suscepimus; Stabunt iusti in magna constantia; Veni dilecte mi;

Verba mea auribus. Collegium Vocale, Hanover Boys Choir Members;
    Philippe Herreweghe. Astree AS 44
            +Gr 5-80 p1705   +RR 5-80 p96
1933 Motets: Lauda Sion salvatorem; Musica Dei donum. Puisque j'ay per-
    du, mass. Pro Cantione Antiqua; Bruno Turner. Harmonia Mundi
    1C 065 99741 (also BASF EA 226174)
            +FF 3/4-80 p111
    Motets: Timor et remor; Pronuba Juno; Cum rides mihi. See no. 1931
    La nuit groide et sombre. See no. 3683
    Psalmus poenitentialis, no. 2. See no. 1931
    Puisque j'ay perdu, mass. See no. 1933
1934 Sacrae lectiones ex propheta Job. Raphael Passaque Vocal Ensemble;
    Raphael Passaquet. Harmonia Mundi HMU 771/2 (also HM 2479)
            ++HFN 2-80 p105   +-RR 2-80 p89
            +-RR 5-76 p70
    Songs: A voi Guglielmo; Am Abend spat beim kuhlen Wein; Bicinium;
        Die fasstnacht ist ein schone Zeit; Im Mayen hort man die hanen
        Krayen; Matona mia cara; La nuict froide et sombre; O fugace
        dolcezza; Sybilla Europea; Der Tag ist so freudenreich; Vedi
        l'aurora. See no. 3536
    Susanne un jour. See no. 4014
    Tui sunt coeli. See no. 3763
    Unnepelni jojjeted. See no. 3814
    Veni in hortum meum. See no. 3806
LASZLO
    Ma come bali bella bimba. See no. 3814
LAURO, Antonio
    Prelude. See no. 3614
    Valse. See no. 3706
    Valses, nos. 2 and 3. See no. 3614
    Valse angostura. See no. 3614
    Valse criollo. See no. 3634. See no. 4030
LAVIGNE, Philibert de
    Sonata, oboe. See no. 3753
LAWES, Henry
    Songs: Among thy fancies; Aged man that moves these fields. See
        no. 3879
    Songs: Cease o cease ye jolly shepherds; Psalm, no. 22. See no.
        1844
LAWES, William
    Dialogues, psalmes and elegies: The catts as other creatures doe;
        Charon O Charon; Charon O gentle Charon, let me wooe thee; Come
        heavy heart; How like a widow; The master of thy art is dead;
        Musicke; Orpheus O Orpheus gently touch thy Lesbyan lyre; Tis
        not boy thy amorous looke; When death shall snatch us from these
        kidds. See no. 1844
1935 Sett, 3 lyra viols. Setts, 2 violins, 2 bass viols, 2 theorbos,
        nos. 1, 7-8. Consorte of Musicke; Anthony Rooley. L'Oiseau-Lyre
    DSLO 573
            ++Gr 12-80 p846   +HFN 12-80 p141
1936 Setts, 2 violins, nos. 2-3, 8. Consorte of Musicke. L'Oiseau-Lyre
    DSLO 564
            +GR 1-80 p1168   +-MT 8-80 p504
            +HFN 12-79 p162   +RR 12-79 p89
    Setts, 2 violins, 2 bass viols, 2 theorbos, nos. 1, 7-8. See no.
        1935

Songs: Daphne and Strephon; Venus and Vulcan. See no. 3878
LAZAROF, Henri
1937 Cadence V. RUSH: Quartet, strings, C sharp minor. STREET: Quintet,
    strings. Concord Quartet, San Francisco Contemporary Music Play-
    ers; Jean-Louis LeRoux; James Galway, flt. CRI SD 381
              +ARG 9-78 p51   +NR 7-78 p6
              +-FF 3/4-80 p14
Concertazioni. See no. 3652
LEBEGUE, Nicolas de
Les cloches. See no. 3682
LEBRUN, Ludwig
Concerto, oboe, D minor. See no. 3703
LECHNER, Leonhard
Allein zu dir Herr Jesu Christ. See no. 3765
Magnificat primi toni. See no. 3934
Nach meiner Lieb viel hundert Knaben trachten. See no. 3536
LECLAIR, Jean-Marie
1938 Concerti, violin, op. 7, nos. 1-6. Concerti, violin, op. 10, nos.
    1-6. Gerard Jarry, vln; Christian Larde, flt; Jean-Francois
    Paillard Chamber Orchestra; Jean-Francois Paillard. Erato STU
    71093 (3)
              +Gr 11-79 p818   ++RR 10-79 p42
              +HFN 1-80 p107   +ST 7-80 p197
              +-MT 9-80 p567
1939 Concerto, violin, op. 7, no. 3, C major. NARDINI: Concerto, violin,
    E minor. VIVALDI: Concerto, violin, RV 199, C minor. Concerto,
    op. 3, no. 6, A minor. Pinchas Zukerman, vln; LAPO; Pinchas
    Zukerman. CBS 76678 (also Columbia M 34571)
              +FF 3/4-79 p143   +-NR 10-78 p3
              +Gr 9-79 p470   +-RR 8-79 p97
              +-HFN 9-79 p117   +-ST 1-80 p692
Concerto, violin, op. 7, no. 3, C major. See no. 25
Concerti, violin, op. 10, nos. 1-6. See no. 1938
Sonata, flute, op. 9, no. 7, G major. See no. 3544
LECLERC, Michel
Par monts et par vaux. See no. 99
LECOCQ, Alexandre Charles
1940 La Camargo. Lina Dachary, ms; Monique Stiot, Janine Capderou; Jean-
    Christophe Benoit, bar; Aime Doniat, bar; Joseph Peyron, t.
    Rare Recorded Editions RRE 166/7 (2)
              +ARG 4-80 p10
Mam'zelle Angot. See no. 1498
LEE, Noel
1941 Caprices on the name Schoenberg. Convergences. Dialogues. Noel
    Lee, hpd and pno; Andras Adorjan, flt; Ole Bohn, vln; Nouvel
    Philharmonic Orchestra; Jean-Pierre Marty. CRI SD 408
              +ARG 3-80 p28   +FU 2-80 p47
              +Audio 8-80 p72   ++NR 12-79 p6
              +FF 3/4-80 p14
Convergences. See no. 1941
Dialogues. See no. 1941
LEEMANS, Pierre
Belgian paratroopers march. See no. 4012. See no. 3643
LEES, Benjamin
Sonata, piano, no. 4. See no. 390

LEETHERLAND, Thomas
     Pavan. See no. 4025
LEGRAND, Michel
1942 The go-between: Theme and variations. The umbrellas of Cherbourg.
     Michel Legrand, Robert Noble, pnp; LSO; Michel Legrand. CBS
     73886 Tape (c) 40-73886 (also Columbia M 35175 Tape (c) MT 35175)
               +FF 1/2-80 p185   +HFN 2-80 p107 tape
               +Gr 1-80 p1203   +-NR 3-80 p5
               +HFN 12-79 p162   +St 4-80 p133
     The umbrellas of Cherbourg. See no. 1942
LEGRANT, Guillaume
     Entre vous nouviaux maries. See no. 3864
LEHAR, Franz
     Alone at last: Waltz entrancing. See no. 3774
     The Count of Luxembourg: Waltz. See no. 1863
1943 Frasquita: Hab ein blaues Himmelbett. Paganini: Schones Italien;
     Was ich denke was ich fuhle; Gern hab ich die Frau'n gekusst;
     Einmal mocht ich was Narrisches tun; Niemand liebt dich so
     wiech ich; Wenn eine schone Frau befiehlt; Erste Liebe; Ging da
     nicht eben das Gluck. Der Zarewitsch: Wolgalied; Hab nur dich
     allein; Warum hat jeder Fruhling; Willst du. Richard Tauber, t;
     Various Orchestras and Conductors. HMV HLM 7172 Tape (c) HLM
     7172 (Reissues)
               +ARSC Vol 12, no. 1-2,   +HFN 1-80 p115
                 1980 p99   +HFN 2-80 p107 tape
               +Gr 11-79 p921   +RR 11-79 p49
     Giuditta: Du bist meine Sonne; Freunde das Leben ist lebenswert.
     See no. 3558
     Giuditta: Meine Lippen sie kussen so heiss. See no. 1863
1944 Gold and silver waltz, op. 79. Das Land des Lachelns: Overture.
     Die lustige Witwe, excerpts. STRAUSS, J. II: Die Fledermaus, op.
     363: Overture. The beautiful blue Danube, op. 314. Kaiserwalz-
     er, op. 437. Grosses Wiener Rundfunkorchestra; Robert Stolz.
     Acanta BB 23240
               +Gr 5-80 p1718   +-RR 5-80 p72
               +-HFN 6-80 p107
1945 Das Land des Lachelns (The land of smiles). Anneliese Rothenberger,
     Renate Holm, s; Nicolai Gedda, Harry Friedauer, t; Jobst Moeller,
     bs; Bavarian Radio Chorus; Graunke Symphony Orchestra; Willy
     Mattes. Arabesque 8055-2 Tape (c) 9055-2
               +FF 7/8-80 p102   +ON 12-20-80 p52
               *HF 6-80 p96 tape   +SFC 12-7-80 p33
               +NYT 1-6-80 pD18   +St 9-80 p80
     Das Land des Lachelns: Als Gott die Welt erschuf...Meine Liebe deine
     Liebe. See no. 3711
     Das Land des Lachelns: Overture. See no. 1944
1946 Die lustige Witwe (The merry widow). Elizabeth Harwood, s; Rene
     Kollo, Werner Hollweg, Donald Grobe, Werner Krenn, t; Zoltan
     Kelemen, bar; Karl Renar, bs; German Opera Chorus; BPhO; Herbert
     von Karajan. DG 2725 102 (2) Tape (c) 3374 102 (From 2707 070)
               +-Gr 5-80 p1711   +-HFN 8-80 p109 tape
               +-HFN 5-80 p135   +RR 6-80 p34
1947 Die lustige Witwe. Helen Donath, Edda Moser, s; Siegfried Jerusa-
     lem, Norbert Orth, Friedrich Lenz, t; Benno Kusche, Hermann Prey,
     bar; Bavarian Radio Chorus; Munich Radio Orchestra; Heinz Wall-

berg. HMV SLS 5202 (2) Tape (c) TC SLS 5202
    +Gr 10-80 p534
Die lustige Witwe, excerpts. See no. 1944
Die lustige Witwe: O Vaterland...Da geh ich zu Maxim. See no. 3711
1948 The merry widow: Overture (arr. Gamley); A highly respectable wife;
    Gentlemen no more; I'm off to Chez Maxim; Proceed one girl has al-
    mond eyes; Ladies choice; Let's all now waken memories...Vilia;
    Such a silly soldier boy; Love in my heart was dying; This match
    should last at least a year; The cake walk; I was born by cruel
    fate; We're the famous Maxim playgirls; Love unspoken. Joan
    Sutherland, Valerie Masterson, s; Regina Resnik, ms; Werner Krenn,
    John Brecknock, John Fryatt, Francis Egerton, Graeme Ewer, t;
    Ambrosian Singers; NPhO; Richard Bonynge. Decca SET 629 Tape (c)
    KCET 629 (also London OSA 1172 Tape (c) OSA 5-1172)

+–ARG 8-79 p72	*NR 4-80 p13
+–FF 11/12-79 p96	+–ON 12-1-79 p44
+–Gr 2-79 p1474	+–Op 5-79 p506
+–HFN 1-79 p119	+–RR 2-79 p48
+–HFN 2-79 p118 tape	+St 10-79 p142

Die lustige Witwe: Vilia. See no. 3870
Die lustige Witwe: Waltz; Vilia. See no. 1863
Paganini: Liebe du Himmel Erden. See no. 3774
Paganini: Schones Italien; Was ich denke was ich fuhle; Gern hab
    ich die Frau'n gekusst; Einmal mocht ich was Narrisches tun;
    Niemand liebt dich so wiech ich; Wenn eine schone Frau befiehlt;
    Erste Liebe; Ging da nicht eben das Gluck. See no. 1943
Schon ist die Welt: Ich bin verliebt. See no. 1863
Der Zarewitsch: Wolgalied; Hab nur dich allein; Warum hat jeder
    Fruhling; Willst du. See no. 1943
LE HEURTEUR, Guillaume
    Troys jeunes bourgeoises. See no. 3795
LEHMANN
    Myself when young. See no. 4007
LEIFS, Jon
1949 Saga symphony, no. 26. Iceland Symphony Orchestra; Jussi Jalas.
    Iceland Music Information Centre ITM 2
        +RR 6-77 p58   +RR 4-80 p67
LEIGH, Walter
    Agincourt. See no. 3829
LEIGHTON, Kenneth
    Festival fanfare. See no. 4048
    Lully lulla thou little tiny child. See no. 4066
    Paean. See no. 1294
LEISRING
    O sons and daughters. See no. 4059
LEJEUNE, Claude
    Revecy venir du printemps. See no. 4043
1950 Parages. Harmonia Mundi GRM AM 70906
        +FF 7/8-80 p16
LEKEU, Guillaume
1951 Poems (3). Quartet, piano. Sonata, violoncello and piano: Lento
    assai. Kay McCracken, s; Natalie Ryshna, Vernon Duke, pno;
    William Van den Berg, vlc; Baker Quartet. SFM S 2008
        ++FF 7/8-80 p207
Quartet, piano. See no. 1951

Sonata, violoncello and piano: Lento assai. See no. 1951

Songs: Chanson de Mai; Poems: Sur une tombe, Ronde, Nocturne; Les pavots. See no. 1444

1952 Trio, piano and strings, C minor. Natalie Ryshna, pno; Israel Baker, vln; Armand Kaproff, vlc. SFM S 7023
++FF 7/8-80 p207

LEMMENS, Jaak-Nicolaas

Cantabile, B minor. See no. 1953

Creator alma siderum. See no. 1953

1953 Organ works: Cantabile, B minor. Creator alma siderum. Pater superni. Pastorale, F major. Prelude a cinque, E flat major. Prier, E major. Sonate pascale. Sonate pontificale: Fanfare. Jozef Sluys, org. Zephyr ZO 4
+-Gr 7-80 p153

Pastorale, F major. See no. 1953

Pater superni. See no. 1953

Prelude a cinque, E flat major. See no. 1953

Priere, E major. See no. 1953

Sonate pascale. See no. 1953

Sonate pontificale: Fanfare. See no. 1953

LENDVAY, Kamillo

The feller. See no. 3803

1954 The respectful prostitute. Julia Paszthy, s; Denes Gulyas, t; Laszlo Polgar, bs; Istvan Gati, bar; Janos Csanyi, Tamas Kertesz, t; Budapest Symphony Orchestra Members; Tamas Breitner. Hungaroton SLPX 12132

+ARG 12-79 p43	+NR 12-79 p10
+FF 1/2-80 p103	+SFC 12-16-79 p60

LENNON/MCCARTNEY

Songs: And I love her; I want to hold your hand. See no. 3962

LENTZ, Johan

Concerto, harpsichord, no. 2, C major. See no. 3818

LEO, Leonardo

Concerto, violoncello, F minor. See no. 740

LEONCAVALLO, Ruggiero

La boheme: E destin. See no. 3636

La boheme: Mimi Pinson. See no. 3770

La boheme: Musette; O gioia della mia dimora; Io non ho che una povera stanzetta; Testa dorata. See no. 3949

1955 I Pagliacci. MASCAGNI: Cavalleria rusticana. Montserrat Caballe, Renata Scotto, s; Jose Carreras, Ugo Benelli, t; Julia Hamari, Astrid Varnay, ms; Kari Nurmela, Thomas Allen, bar; Ambrosian Opera Chorus; PhO; Riccardo Muti. Angel SZCX 3895 Tape (c) 4Z3X 3895 (also HMV SLS 5187 Tape (c) TC SLS 5187)

+-ARG 10-80 p21	+NR 6-80 p10
+FF 9/10-80 p144	+NYT 5-11-80 pD24
+Gr 4-80 p1589	+-ON 10-80 p42
+-HF 9-80 p79	+Op 6-80 p620
+HFN 5-80 p121	+RR 5-80 p44
+HFN 10-80 p117 tape	+-St 9-80 p80

1956 I Pagliacci. MASCAGNI: Cavalleria rusticana. Julia Varady, Mirella Freni, s; Ida Bormida, con; Carmen Gonzales, ms; Luciano Pavarotti, Vincenzo Bello, t; Piero Cappuccilli, Lorenzo Saccomano, Ingvar Wixell, bar; London Voices; National Philharmonic Orchestra; Gianandrea Gavazzeni, Giuseppe Patane. London OSAD 13125 (3) (also Decca D83D3 Tape (c) K83K32)

+–ARG 10-79 p12
+FF 7/8-79 p63
+FU 9-79 p54
++Gr 4-79 p1767
+HF 6-79 p66
+HFN 8-79 p123 tape
+–NR 1-80 p7

+NYT 3-4-79 pD23
+OC Winter, 1979 p51
+–ON 5-79 p52
+–RR 4-79 p50
+RR 6-80 p94 tape
++SFC 2-11-79 p47
++St 5-79 p102

I Pagliacci: Arias. See no. 3539
I Pagliacci: E fra quest'ansie...Decido il mio destino. See no. 3792
I Pagliacci: Intermezzo. See no. 3847
I Pagliacci: No Pagliaccio non son. See no. 3946
I Pagliacci: Prologue. See no. 3962
I Pagliacci: Qual fiamma avea nel guardo...Stridono lassu. See no. 3948
I Pagliacci: Recitar...Vesti la giubba. See no. 3945
I Pagliacci: Vesti la giubba. See no. 3633
I Pagliacci: Vesti la giubba; No Pagliaccio non son. See no. 1240
I Pagliacci: Vesti la giubba: Si pio. See no. 3774
I Pagliacci: Warum denn hielst du mich. See no. 3770
Songs: Lasciata amar; Mattinata. See no. 3983
Songs: Notte ha steso il gran vel. See no. 3770
Zaza: Buono Zaza: E un riso gentil. See no. 3770
Zaza: Buono Zaza; Zaza piccola zingara. See no. 3771
Zaza: O mio piccolo tavolo. See no. 3774

LERDAHL, Fred
Eros. See no. 1287

LE ROUX, Gaspard
1957 Pieces de clavecin: Suites, nos. 2-3, 5-6. William Christie, Arthur Haas, hpd. Harmonia Mundi HM 339
+FF 1/2-80 p137
++Gr 10-78 p711

+HFN 1-79 p121
+RR 11-78 p92

Suite, F major. See no. 3751

LE ROY, Adrian
Branle de Poitou. See no. 3613
Passemezze. See no. 3613
Si je m'en vais. See no. 3613

LESEMANN, Frederick
Nataraja. See no. 1899

LESLIE
Charm me asleep. See no. 3791

LESUR, Daniel
A kecske. See no. 3814

LEVINAS, Michael
Appels. See no. 1873
Arsis et Thesis ou la chanson du souffle. See no. 1873
Foissements d'ailes. See no. 1873
Voix dans un vaisseau d'airain, chants en escalier. See no. 1873

LEVITIN, Yuriy
1958 Quartet, strings, no. 9, op. 66. Quartet, strings, no. 10, op. 73. Glinka Quartet. Melodiya S10 07307-8
+FF 5/6-80 p96
Quartet, strings, no. 10, op. 73. See no. 1958

LEVY
Russian fantasie. See no. 1101

LEWIN, Frank
1959 Innocence and experience. Music for the new family of violins:
         Dramatic suite; Introduction on a psalm tune; L'Homme arme mass:
         Sanctus; Pleni sunt coeli. Susan Davenny Wyner, s; Yehudi Wyner.
         Musical Heritage Society MHS 4102
                 +-ARG 11-80 p22
      Music for the new family of violins: Dramatic suite; Introduction
         on a psalm tune; L'Homme arme mass: Sanctus; Pleni sunt coeli.
         See no. 1959
LEWIS, Peter Tod
1960 Quartet, strings, no. 21 Signs and circuits. ROVICS: Events.
         Piece, violoncello, piano and electronic tape. Songs: Echo;
         Look friend at me; What Grandma knew. Lee Dougherty, s; Anne
         Chamberlain, pno; David Wells, vlc; Sylvia Alexander, flt; Col-
         umbia String Quartet. CRI SD 392
                 +ARG 10-79 p43   ++NR 1-80 p15
      Signs and circuits. See no. 1960
LEWIS, Robert Hall
1961 Combinazioni: I, violin, violoncello, clarinet and piano; II, per-
         cussion ensemble and piano; IV, violoncello and piano. Penn
         Contemporary Players, Eastman Percussion Ensemble; Stephen Kates,
         vlc; Ellen Mack Senofsky, pno. Orion ORS 79363
                 ++FF 7/8-80 p103   +NR 6-80 p8
      Nuances II. See no. 5
LEWKOVITCH, Bernhard
      Songs: Madrigali di Torquato Tasso, op. 13; Tidligt forar. See no.
         3587
LIADOV, Anatol
      Musical snuff box, op. 32. See no. 3622
      Prelude, op. 11, no. 1, B minor. See no. 3832
      Russian folksongs, op. 58 (8). See no. 3257
LIATOSHINSKY, Boris
      Sonata, violin and piano, op. 19. See no. 1532
LIDHOLM, Ingvar
1962 Pieces, violoncello and piano (4). MARTINU: Sonata, violoncello
         and piano, no. 1. STRAUSS, R.: Sonata, violoncello and piano,
         op. 6, F major. Elemer Lavotha, vlc; Kerstin Aberg, pno. BIS
         LP 121
                 +FF 7/8-79 p93   +HFN 4-80 p115
                 ++FU 3-80 p48   +RR 5-80 p92
      Ritornello. See no. 702
LIDL
      Trio, violin, violoncello and viola da gamba, E major. See no. 3729
LIDON, Jose
      Sonata con trompeta real. See no. 3528
      Sonata de primo tono. See no. 4023
LIEB, Richard
      Feature suite. See no. 3740
LIGETI, Gyorgy
1963 Concerto, flute, oboe and orchestra. Concerto, 13 instrumentalists.
         Melodien, orchestra. London Sinfonietta; Aurele Nicolet, flt;
         Heinz Holliger, ob; David Atherton. Decca HEAD 12
                 +FF 5/6-80 p97   +MM 4-77 p40
                 ++Gr 8-76 p286   ++MT 8-77 p651
                 +Gr 9-77 p499   ++RR 7-76 p54

        +HF 5-80 p75   ++SFC 1-20-80 p47
        +—HFN 7-76 p89   +—Te 12-76 p32
    Concerto, 13 instrumentalists. See no. 1963
    Melodien, orchestra. See no. 1963
1964 Pieces, 2 pianos. ZIMMERMANN: Monologue. Perspectives. Alfons
     and Aloys Kontarsky. DG 2531 102
            +Gr 9-80 p376   +STL 8-10-80 p30
            +—HFN 11-80 p120

LINEK, Georg
    Concerto, organ, D major. See no. 3752
    Fanfares, nos. 1-3, 5-6, 13-14. See no. 3752
LINLEY, Thomas
    Let me care less. See no. 3873
LINN, Robert
    Saxifrage blue. See no. 755
LINTON
    I give thanks to you. See no. 3874
LISZT, Franz
    (G refers to Grove's number, 5th editon)
1965 Ad nos ad salutarem undam, G 259. Orpheus, G 98 (trans. Guillou).
     MOZART: Fantasia, K 608, F minor. Jean Guillou, org. Festivo
     501
            ++Gr 11-80 p704
    Adagio, G 263, D flat major. See no. 3735
1966 Annees de pelerinage, 1st year, G 160: Au bord d'une source. An-
     nees de pelerinage, 2nd year, G 161: Petrarch sonnet. Etudes
     d'execution transcendente, no. 10, G 139, F minor. Mephisto
     waltz, no. 1, G 514. Sonata, piano, G 178, B minor. Horacio
     Gutierrez, pno. HMV HQS 1427 (also Angel SZ 37477)
            +ARG 3-80 p29   +—HF 6-80 p80
            +—CL 12-79 p10   +HFN 8-79 p107
            +—FF 7/8-80 p105   +RR 8-79 p110
            +—FU 4-80 p47   ++St 12-79 p147
            +—Gr 7-79 p230
    Annees de pelerinage, 1st year, G 160: Au bord d'une source. See
        no. 1993. See no. 3678
    Annees de pelerinage, 2nd year, G 161: Apres une lecture du Dante;
        Sonetto del Petrarca. See no. 1108
    Annees de pelerinage, 2nd year, G 161: Dante sonata. See no. 3550
    Annees de pelerinage, 2nd year, G 161: Il penseroso. See no. 528
    Annees de pelerinage, 2nd year, G 161: Sonetto del Petrarca. See
        no. 1966. See no. 3777
    Annees de pelerinage, 2nd year, G 161: Sposalizio; Supplement, G
        162. See no. 3622
1967 Annees de pelerinage, 2nd year, G 162: Venezia e Napoli. Harmonies
     poetiques et religieuses, G 173: Funerailles; Invocation. Leg-
     endes, G 175. Aldo Ciccolini, pno. Seraphim S 60343
            +FF 9/10-80 p145   +NR 5-80 p11
    Annees de pelerinage, 2nd year, G 162: Venezia e Napoli. See no.
        3897
    Annees de pelerinage, 3rd year, G 163: Aux cypres de la Villa d'Este.
        See no. 1187. See no. 1992. See no. 3622. See no. 3678
    Apparition, no. 1, G 185. See no. 1991
    Bagatelle without tonality. See no. 1992
    The battle of the Huns. See no. 2414

1968 Concerto, piano, no. 1, G 124, E flat major. concerto, piano, no. 2,
     G 125, A major. Philippe Entremont, pno; Zurich Radio Orchestra;
     Walter Goehr. Everest SDBR 3433
                    -FF 5/6-80 p98   /NR 7-79 p7
1969 Concerto, piano, no. 2, G 125, A major. Fantasia on Hungarian folk-
     tunes, G 123. Hungarian rhapsody, no. 8, G 244. Jeno Jando,
     pno; HSO; Janos Ferencsik. Hungaroton SLPX 12024 Tape (c) MK
     12024
                    +-FF 7/8-79 p64   +NR 7-79 p7
                    ++FU 3-80 p46   ++SFC 6-17-79 p41
                    +HF 5-80 p90 tape
     Concerto, piano, no. 2, G 125, A major. See no. 1968
     Concerto pathetique, G 258, E minor. See no. 3645
1970 Consolation, no. 3, G 172, D flat major. Mephisto waltz, no. 1, G
     514. RACHMANINOFF: Barcarolle, op. 10, no. 3, G minor. Humor-
     esque, op. 10, no. 5, G major. SCHUMANN: Humoreske, op. 20,
     B flat major. Vladimir Horowitz, pno. RCA ARL 1-3433 Tape (c)
     ARK 1-3433
                    +-ARG 6-80 p50   +-HFN 11-80 p131 tape
                    +CL 12-79 p10   ++NR 1-80 p14
                    ++FF 1/2-80 p208   +-RR 5-80 p90
                    ++Gr 4-80 p1571   +-SFC 10-28-79 p53
                    ++HF 1-80 p63   +-St 2-80 p133
                    ++HF 2-80 p102 tape   +STL 6-8-80 p38
                    +-HFN 4-80 p116
     Consolation, no. 3, G 172, D flat major. See no. 3811
1971 Csardas macabre, G 244. La lugubre gondola, G 200. Nuages gris,
     G 199. Richard Wagner: Venezia, G 201. BULOW: Ballade, op. 11.
     WAGNER: Albumblatt for Frau Betty Schott, E flat major. Zurich-
     er Vielliebchen. Fantasia, F sharp minor. In das album der
     Furstin M. Sonata, piano, B flat major. Werner Genuit, pno.
     Acanta EB 23049 (2)
                    +MT 1-80 p37   +RR 11-79 p116
1972 Don Sanche, G 1. Soloists; Orchestra and Chorus; Guy Wolfenden.
     Unique Opera Records UORC 365 (2)
                    +-FF 11/12-80 p128
     Duo, violin and piano, G 127. See no. 1980
1973 Episodes from Lenau's "Faust". A Faust symphony, G 108. Gyorgy
     Korondy, t; Hungarian People's Army Male Chorus; HSO; Janos
     Ferencsik. Hungaroton SLPX 12022/3 (2) Tape (c) MK 12022/3
                    +ARG 10-80 p43   +HF 10-80 p98 tape
                    +-FF 7/8-80 p104   ++NR 4-80 p2
                    +HF 7-80 p70   +SFC 2-3-80 p45
1974 Epithalam, G 129. Grand duo concertant, G 128. SAINT-SAENS: Son-
     ata, violin, no. 1, op. 75, D minor. Igor Oistrakh, vln; Nat-
     alia Zertsalova, pno. United Artists UACL 10017
                    +Gr 11-79 p862   ++RR 12-79 p101
                    +HFN 3-80 p93
     Epithalam, G 129. See no. 1980
1975 Etudes, G 136. Etudes d'execution transcendente, G 139. Thomas
     Rajna, pno. CRD CRD 1058/9 (2)
                    +Gr 9-80 p376   +RR 6-80 p15
                    +HFN 5-80 p122
1976 Etudes de concert, nos. 1-3, G 144. Etudes de concert, nos. 1-2,
     G 145. Etudes d'execution transcendente d'apres Paganini, G 140.

Valerie Tryon, pno. Educo 3086
          ++CL 9-80 p14
1977 Etudes de concert, nos. 1-3, G 144; nos. 1-2, G 145. Paraphrases
     (reminiscences) de Don Juan (Mozart), G 418. Jorge Bolet, pno.
     L'Oiseau-Lyre DSLO 41 Tape (c) KDSLC 41
               ++ARG 11-80 p23   +HF 6-80 p80
                +FF 5/6-80 p98   ++St 5-80 p83
                +Gr 5-80 p1717 tape
     Etude de concert, no. 2, G 144, F minor: La leggierezza. See no.
        3678
     Etude de concert, no. 3, G 144: Un sospiro. See no. 1509.
     Etudes de concert, nos. 1-2, G 145: Waldesrauschen; Gnomenreigen.
        See no. 1976. See no. 3935
     Etudes d'execution transcendente, G 139. See no. 1975
     Etudes d'execution transcendente, G 139: Chasse neige. See no. 1992
     Etudes d'execution transcendente, G 139: Prelude. See no. 3628
     Etudes d'execution transcendente, G 139, no. 10, F minor. See no.
        1966
1978 Etudes d'execution transcendente d'apres Paganini, G 140 (Busoni).
     MOSCHELES: Etudes, op. 111 (4). Vladimir Pleshakov, pno. Orion
     ORS 80376
               +-ARG 11-80 p24   -NR 7-80 p12
               +-FF 9/10-80 p145
     Etudes d'execution transcendente d'apres Paganini, G 140. See no.
        1976
     Etudes d'execution transcendente d'apres Paganini, nos. 1-2, 5-6,
        G 140. See no. 3678
1979 Etudes d'execution transcendente d'apres Paganini, nos. 5 and 6, G
     140. Rhapsodie espagnole, G 254. Paraphrases: Schubert: Auf
     dem Wasser zu singen; Gretchen am Spinnrade; Hark hark the lark;
     Standchen; Der Wanderer. Oxana Yablonskaya, pno. Orion Tape
     (c) In Sync C 4033
               +HFN 9-80 p105 tape   +NR 9-80 p10 tape
     Etudes d'execution transcendente d'apres Paganini, G 140: La cam-
        panella. See no. 3856
     Fantasia and fugue on the name B-A-C-H, G 529. See no. 989
     Fantasia on Hungarian folktunes, G 123. See no. 1969
     A Faust symphony, G 108. See no. 1973
     Gaudeamus igitur. See no. 1991
1980 Grand duo concertante, G 128. Duo, violin and piano, G 127. Epi-
     thalam, G 129. Romance oubliee, G 132. Jean-Jacques Kantorow,
     vln; Henri Barda, pno. Arion ARN 38466
               ++Gr 8-80 p239   +RR 7-80 p80
                +HFN 8-80 p98
     Grand duo concertant, G 128. See no. 1974
     Grand galop chromatique, G 219. See no. 1991
     Grand valse di bravura, op. 6. See no. 339
     Harmonies poetiques et religieuses, G 173: Funerailles. See no.
        1993
     Harmonies poetiques et religieuses, G 173: Funerailles; Invocation.
        See no. 1967
     Hungarian fantasia, G 123. See no. 825
     Hungarian portraits: Michael Mosonyi. See no. 1992
     Hungarian rhapsodies, nos. 2 and 3, G 244. See no. 1996
1981 Hungarian rhapsodies, nos. 2-4, 6, G 244. Szeged Symphony Orchestra;

Tamas Pal. Hungaroton SLPX 12062 Tape (c) MK 12062
     +FF 9/10-80 p145   +HF 10-80 p98 tape
1982 Hungarian rhapsodies, nos. 2, 5, 9, 14-15, 19, G 244. Robert Szi-
     don, pno. DG 2535 420 Tape (c) 3335 420 (From 2720 072)
     +Gr 10-80 p523   +HFN 10-80 p113
     +Gr 12-80 p889 tape   +HFN 11-80 p131 tape
1983 Hungarian rhapsodies, nos. 2, 6, 11-15, G 244. Solomon, Ignaz
     Friedman, Mischa Levitzki, Alfred Cortot, Gina Bachauer, Ferruc-
     cio Busoni, Mark Hambourg, pno. Arabesque AR 8011 Tape (c) 9011
     (From various Columbia and HMV originals)
     +-FF 11/12-80 p128   +NR 10-80 p12
     +HF 12-80 p81   ++St 11-80 p92
     Hungarian rhapsody, no. 2, G 244, C sharp minor. See no. 1322.
     See no. 3909
     Hungarian rhapsody, no. 4, G 244, E flat major. See no. 825. See
     no. 3915
     Hungarian rhapsody, no. 5, G 244, E minor. See no. 825
     Hungarian rhapsody, no. 8, G 244. See no. 1969
     Hungarian rhapsody, no. 11, G 244, A minor. See no. 1993. See no.
     3622
     Hungarian rhapsody, no. 14, G 244, F minor. See no. 1993
1984 Hungarian rhapsodies, G 359. LSO; Antal Dorati. Philips 6570 140
     Tape (c) 7310 140 (From EMI AMS 16101, Philips SGL 5789)
     +Gr 6-80 p69   +HFN 9-80 p116 tape
     +HFN 6-80 p115   +RR 6-80 p53
     Impromptu, F major. See no. 1991
     Legends, G 175. See no. 1967
     Die Lorelei, G 369. See no. 1993
     La lugubre gondola, S 200. See no. 1971. See no. 3601
     Malediction, G 121. See no. 38. See no. 39
     Mazeppa. See no. 1992
     Mephisto waltz, no. 1, G 514. See no. 1966. See no. 1970. See
     no. 1993
     The nightingale, G 250. See no. 1509
     Nuages gris, G 199. See no. 1971
     Orpheus, G 98. See no. 1965
1985 Paraphrases: Schubert: Auf dem Wasser zu singen; Aufenthalt; Erl-
     konig; Die Forelle; Liebesbotschaft; Der Lindenbaum; Die Post;
     Standchen; Standchen von Shakespeare; Der Wanderer. Klaus Hell-
     wig, pno. Audite FSM 53185
               -FF 11/12-80 p129
1986 Paraphrases (transcriptions): Bach: Ich hatte viel Bekummernis; Aus
     tiefer not; Adagio. Chopin: Preludes, op. 28, nos. 4 and 9.
     Lassus: Regina coeli. Mozart: Ave verum. Verdi: Agnus Dei.
     Wagner: Pilgrim's chorus. Francois-Henri Houbart, org. Harmonia
     Mundi HM 1210
     /Gr 3-80 p1418   +-HFN 2-80 p95
     +HFN 12-79 p163   -RR 8-79 p110
1987 Paraphrases (transcriptions): Der Doppelganger, G 560, no. 12; Erl-
     konig, G 558, no. 4; Die Forelle, G 563, no. 6; Der Lindenbaum,
     G 561, no. 7; Des Madchens Klage, G 563, no. 2; Morgenstandchen,
     G 588, no. 9; Der Muller und der Bach, G 565, no. 2; Rastlose
     Liebe, G 558, no. 10; Das Sterbeglocklein, G 563, no. 3; Die
     Taubenpost, G 560, no. 13 (Schubert). John Bingham, pno. Meri-
     dian E 77019
     +Gr 9-79 p487   ++MT 2-80 p106

1988 Paraphrases (transcriptions): Ave Maria, op. 52, no. 4; Erlkonig,
     op. 1; Die junge Nonne, op. 43, no. 1; Der Leiermann, op. 89,
     no. 24; Trauschung, op. 89, no. 19; Wohin, op. 25, no 2. SCHU-
     MANN: Fantasiestucke, op. 12: Warum; Grillen. Sonata, piano,
     no. 2, op. 22, G minor. Lazar Berman, pno. Musical Heritage
     Society MHS 4066 (From Columbia M 34528)
                 +ARG 4-80 p44   +St 5-80 p89
                 +FF 3/4-80 p151
1989 Paraphrases (transcriptions): Beethoven: Fantasy on themes from
     "The ruins of Athens". Adelaide. Schubert: Marche, no. 2, B
     minor. Soiree de Vienne, no. 7. Joseph Villa, pno. Spectrum
     SR 115
                 ++ARG 9-80 p28   ++FF 7/8-80 p105
1990 Paraphrases (transcriptions): Beethoven: Fantasy on themes from
     "Ruins of Athens", G 649. Schubert: Fantasy on Wanderer, D 760,
     D major. Weber: Polonaise brillante on "L'Hilarite", op. 72,
     no. 3. Jerome Rose, pno; PH; Richard Kapp. Turanbout QTV 34708
                 +-FF 1/2-79 p64   +HFN 6-80 p107
                 +-Gr 9-80 p334   +NR 7-79 p14
                 +HF 4-80 p95   +-RR 6-80 p54
     Paraphrases: Chopin: My joys; The maiden's wish. See no. 3935
     Paraphrases (reminiscences): Mozart: Don Juan, G 418. See no. 1977
     Paraphrases (reminiscences): Mozart: Don Juan, G 656. See no. 1994
     Paraphrases: Schubert: Auf dem Wasser zu singen; Gretchen am Spinn-
     rade; Hark hark the lark; Standchen; Der Wanderer. See no. 1979
     Paraphrases: Schubert; Ave Maria, op. 52, no. 4; Der Erlkonig, op.
     1; Die junge Nonne, op. 43, no. 1; Der Leiermann, op. 89, no. 24;
     Tauschung, no. 89, no. 19; Wohin, op. 25, no. 2. See no. 2938
1991 Piano works: Apparition, no. 1, G 185. Gaudeamus igitur. Grand
     galop chromatique, G 219. Impromptu, F major. Scherzo and
     march. Die Zelle in Nonnenwerth. Gregor Weichert, pno. FSM
     Records 53203
                 ++ARG 7/8-80 p28   +-FF 9/10-79 p104
1992 Piano works: Annees de pelerinage, 3rd year, G 163: Aux cypres de
     la Villa d'Este. Bagatelle without tonality. Etudes d'execution
     transcendente, G 139: Chasse neige. Hungarian portraits: Michael
     Mosonyi. Von der Wiege bis zum Grabe, G 107. Mazeppa. Loretta
     Goldberg, pno. Orion ORS 79365
                 +-ARG 10-80 p45   +-NR 5-80 p11
                 -FF 9/10-80 p145
1993 Piano works: Annees de pelerinage, 1st year, G 160: Au bord d'une
     source. Harmonies poetiques et religieuses, G 173: Funerailles.
     Hungarian rhapsody, no. 11, G 244, G minor. Hungarian rhapsody,
     no. 14, G 244, G minor. Die Lorelei, G 369. Mephisto waltz, no.
     1, G 514. Schwanengesang, G 560: Liebesbotschaft. Mischa Dich-
     ter, pno. Philips 9500 401 Tape (c) 7300 639
                 -FF 9/10-78 p106   /MJ 7-78 p56
                 +Gr 3-80 p1418   +NR 11-78 p13
                 +HF 11-78 p116   +-RR 3-80 p83
                 +HF 5-79 p103 tape   ++SFC 7-30-78 p49
                 +HFN 3-80 p91   +-St 8-78 p129
1994 Polonaise, no. 2, G 223, E major. Paraphrases (reminiscences):
     Mozart: Don Juan, G 656. Sonata, piano, G 178, B minor. Tamas
     Vasary, pno. DG 2535 270 Tape (c) 3335 270 (From SLPEM 136258)
                 +FF 9/10-79 p104   +HFN 1-79 p127
                 +Gr 11-78 p928   +RR 2-79 p81

                +HF 2-80 p102 tape   +SFC 4-1-79 p44
                +-RR 5-79 p124 tape
1995 Les preludes, G 97. Tasso, lamento e trionfo, G 96. RIMSKY-KORSAKOV:
        May night. PhO; Constantin Silvestri. HMV SXLP 30447
                +-HFN 11-80 p129
        Les preludes, G 97. See no. 449. See no. 450. See no. 823. See
        no. 1321
        Prelude and fugue on the name of B-A-C-H, G 260. See no. 3735. See
        no. 3858
1996 Rakoczy march (Hungarian battle march). Hungarian rhapsodies, nos.
        2 and 3, G 244. LPO, PH; Willi Boskovsky. Angel SS 45014
                +ARG 2-80 p55
        Rhapsodie espagnole, G 254. See no. 1979. See no. 3678
        Richard Wagner: Venezia, G 201. See no. 1971
        Romance oubliee, G 132. See no. 1980
        Scherzo and march. See no. 1991
        Schwanengesang, G 560: Liebesbotschart. See no. 1993
1997 Sonata, piano, G 178, B minor. SCHUMANN: Fantasia, op. 17, C major.
        Dag Achatz, pno. BIS LP 144
                +-FF 11/12-80 p172   +-RR 7-80 p84
                +HFN 8-80 p98
1998 Sonata, piano, G 178, B minor. SCHUMANN: Fantasia, op. 17, C major.
        David Wilde, pno. Saga 5460
                +Gr 7-78 p225   +-MT 1-79 p44
                +Gr 3-80 p1449   +RR 6-78 p30
                +HFN 6-78 p124   +RR 2-80 p77
                +HFN 2-80 p105
        Sonata, piano, G 178, B minor. See no. 528. See no. 1057. See
        no. 1966. See no. 1994
1999 Songs: Anfangs wollt ich fast verzagen, G 311; Wer nie sein Brot
        mit Tranen ass, G 297; Blume und Duft, G 324; Der du von dem
        Himmel bist, G 279; Drei Sonette von Petrarca, G 270; Die drei
        Zigeuner, G 320; Es muss ein Wunderbares sein, G 314; Ein Ficht-
        enbaum steht einsam, G 309; Die Fischerstochter, G 325; Lasst
        mich ruhen, G 317; Morgens steh ich auf und frage, G 290; Nimm
        einen Strahl der Sonne, G 310; Uber allen Gipfeln ist Ruh, G 306;
        Die Vatergruft. Hermann Prey, bar; Alexis Weissenberg, pno.
        EMI 1C 065 30845
                +Gr 10-80 p528   +HFN 11-80 p120
2000 Songs: Der du von dem Himmel bist, G 279; Die drei Zigeuner, G 320;
        Du bist wie eine Blume, G 287; Es war ein Konig in Thule, G 278;
        Fischerstochter, G 325; Freudvoll and Leidvoll, G 280; Im Rhein
        im schonen Strome; Die Lorelei, G 273; S'il est un charmant gaz-
        on, G 284; Uber allen Gipfeln ist Ruh, G 306; Die Vatergruft,
        G 281; Das Veilchen, G 316, no. 1. Janet Baker, ms; Geoffrey
        Parsons, pno. HMV ASD 3965 Tape (c) TC ASD 3965
                +Gr 11-80 p723
        Songs: Die drei Zigeuner, G 320. See no. 3573
        Songs: Ihr Glocken von Marling; Himm einem Strahl der Sonne; Oh
        quand je dors. See no. 3965
        Songs: Oh quand je dors. See no. 3770
        Tarantelle. See no. 3897
        Tasso, lamento e trionfo, G 96. See no. 661. See no. 1995
        Totentanz. See no. 1035
        Valse oubliee, no. 1, G 215, F sharp minor. See no. 3953. See no.
        3954

2001 Variations on Bach's "Weinen, Klagen, Sorgen, Zagen", G 673. REUBKE:
      Sonata on the 94th spalm. SANDVOLD: Introduction and passacaglia.
      Bjorn Boysen, org. Simax PS 1001
                   +—HFN 11-80 p125
    Via crucis, G 53. See no. 1375
    Von der Wiege bis zum Grabe (From the cradle to the grave), G 107.
      See no. 1992
2002 Weihnachtsbaum, G 186. Rhondda Gillespie, pno. Chandos ABR 1006
      Tape (c) ABT 1006
                   +Gr 2-80 p1281   +RR 2-80 p77
                   +GR 8-80 p275 tape   +RR 8-80 p95 tape
                   +HFN 2-80 p95
    Die Zelle in Nonnenwerth. See no. 1991
LITOLFF, Henry
    Concerto symphonique, no. 4, op. 102, D minor: Scherzo. See no.
      1250
    Scherzo. See no. 3962
LLOYD, C. H.
    Allegretto. See no. 4064
LOCATELLI, Pietro
    Concerto, violin, op. 3, no. 2: Andante capriccio. See no. 4028
    Concerto grosso, op. 1, no. 8, F minor. See no. 1136
2003 Introduzione teatrale, op. 4, no. 5. RICCIOTTI: Concertino, no.
      4, F minor. VAN BREE: Allegro. VIVALDI: Concerto grosso, P 444,
      D major. AMF; Neville Marriner. Philips 9500 171
                   +Gr 8-80 p222   +RR 7-80 p47
                   +HFN 7-80 p114
2004 Sonatas, flute, op. 2 (12). Stephen Preston, Nicholas McGegan, flt;
      Anthony Pleeth, vlc; Christopher Hogwood, hpd. L'Oiseau-Lyre
      DSLO 578/9 (2)
                   +—Gr 5-80 p1683   +RR 5-80 p20
                   +—HFN 5-80 p122
LOCKE, Matthew
    Duos, C major, C minor. See no. 1427
    How doth the city sit solitary. See no. 738
    Music for His Majesty's sackbutts and cornetts. See no. 4000
    Suite, C major. See no. 3745
    Suites, nos. 1 and 2. See no. 4015
    The tempest: Lilk and curtain tune. See no. 3715
LOCKWOOD, Norman
    Sonata fantasy. See no. 3651
LOEB, David
2005 Fantasia e due scherzi. Sonata, viola da gamba. SCHAFFRATH: Duet-
      to, 2 bass viols, D minor. SCHENCK: Sonata, 2 viols, op. 8, no.
      10, G major. August Wenzinger, Hannelore Muller, vla da gamba.
      Gasparo GS 210
                   ++NR 10-80 p7
    Sonata, viola da gamba. See no. 2005
LOEILLET, Jacques
    Concerto, flute and strings, D major. See no. 1242
LOEILLET, Jean-Baptiste
2006 Sonatas, op. 1, nos. 1-3. Sonata, op. 3, no. 9, B flat major. Son-
      ata, op. 4, no. 11, F minor. Ferdinand Conrad, rec; Hugo Ruf,
      hpe; Johannes Koch, vla da gamba. Musicaphon BM 30 SL 1905
                   +HFN 10-80 p106   +RR 8-80 p71

Sonata, op. 1, A minor. See no. 1495
Sonata, op. 3, no. 4, A minor. See no. 4020
Sonata, op. 3, no. 9, B flat major. See no. 2006
Sonata, op. 4, no. 11, F minor. See no. 2006
Sonata, op. 5, no. 1, E minor. See no. 3753
Trio, oboe, violin and violoncello, B minor. See no. 3583
LOEVENDIE, Theo
    Turkish folk poems (6). See no. 3818
LOEWE, Karl
    Edward. See no. 3905
    Quem pastores laudavere. See no. 3697
2007 Songs: Der Feind, op. 145, no. 2; Der Rauber, op. 34, no. 2; Der
        Nock, op. 129, no. 2; Heinrich der Vogler, op. 56, no. 1; Hink-
        enden Jamben, op. 65, no. 2; Kleiner Hauschalt, op. 71; Nacht-
        liche Heerschau, op. 23; Spirito santo, op. 143; Susses Begrab-
        nis, op. 62, no. 4; Die Uhr, op. 123, no. 3; Die verfallene Muh-
        le, op. 109. Hermann Prey, bar; Karl Engel, pno. Acanta DC
        22598
                    +FF 11-79 p119   +HFN 3-80 p93
                    ++Gr 1-80 p1193
    Songs: Ballad, op. 123, no. 2; Lieder, op. 9, no. 5; Odins Meeres-
        ritt. See no. 852
    Songs: Edward, op. 1, no. 1. See no. 3573
    Songs: Fredericus Rex, op. 61, no. 1; Canzonetta; Der Mummelsee.
        See no. 3774
LOFFELHOLTZ, Christoph
    Es het ein Baur sein freylein vorlohren. See no. 3590
    Die kleine Schacht. See no. 3590
LOFFLER
    Ad astra. See no. 3619
LOGAN, Wendel
2008 Duo exchanges. Pieces, piano (5). Pieces, violin and electric
        piano (3). Proportions, 9 players. Frances Walker, Sanford
        Margolis, pno; Lawrence McDonald, clt; Michael Rosen, perc; En-
        semble; Kenneth Moore. Orion ORS 80373
                    +-FF 7/8-80 p106   +NR 7-80 p2
    Pieces, piano (5). See no. 2008
    Pieces, violin and electric piano (3). See no. 2008
    Proportions, 9 players. See no. 2008
LONGUEVAL
    Passio Domini nostri Jesu Christi secundum Matthaeum. See no. 1237
LONQUE, George
    Sonatina, op. 36, G major. See no. 3889
LOPE
    Gallito. See no. 3921
    Gerona. See no. 3921
LOPEZ, Miguel
    Versos (5). See no. 1141
LOPEZ CAPILLAS, Francisco
    Gloria laud et honor. See no. 3707
LORTZING, Gustav
    Undine: Ballet music. See no. 3709
    Der Waffenschmied. See no. 3696
    Der Waffenschmied: Auch ich war ein Jungling. See no. 3711. See
        no. 3712. See no. 3770

Wildschutz: Funftausend Taler. See no. 3711. See no. 3712
2009 Zar und Zimmermann. Lucia Popp, s; Werner Krenn, Adalbert Kraus, t;
      Hermann Prey, Karl Ridderbusch, bs; Bavarian Radio Orchestra;
      Heinz Wallberg. Columbia M2 35904 (2) (also Acanta JB 22424)
                +FF 11/12-80 p130   +ON 12-20-80 p52
                +Gr 10-80 p534   +NYT 6-1-80 pD20
                +HFN 9-80 p105

      Zar und Zimmermann: Auf Gesellen greift zur Axt...Sonst spielt ich
        mit zepter. See no. 1819
      Zar und Zimmermann: Dance. See no. 3709
      Zar und Zimmermann: O sancta justitia. See no. 3711
      Zar und Zimmermann: O sancta justitia...Den hohen Herrscher wurdig
        zu empfangen...Heil sei dem Tag. See no. 3712
LOSY VON LOSINTHAL, Johann
      Pieces, guitar (6). See no. 3540
LOTTI, Antonio
      Crucifixus. See no. 762
      Ecce panis angelorum. See no. 3814
      Songs: Pur dicesti. See no. 3669
LOUGHBOROUGH
      Ireland mother Ireland. See no. 3947
LOVELOCK
      Concerto, organ: Toccata. See no. 4067
LOVENSKJOLD, Hermann
      La sylphide. See no. 1770
LUALDI
      La canzone di Fraciscio. See no. 3928
LUBLIN, Johannes de
      Dances. See no. 3805
      Danse, no. 8. See no. 3963
      Mon mary. See no. 3805
LUCCHINETTI
2010 Concerti, 2 organs, D major, B flat major. PIAZZA: Sonata, 2 org-
      ans, F major. TERRINI: Sonata, 2 organs, D major. ANON.: In-
      tradas, D major. Rudolf Ewerhart, Mathias Siede, org; Walter
      Holy, Ingus Schmidt, tpt; Erich Penzel, Gerd Seifert, hn; Chris-
      toph Caskel, timpani. DG 2535 362
                +-FF 5/6-80 p195   ++NR 4-80 p8
LUCHINETTI, Giovanni
      Sonata, 2 organs, D major. See no. 4027
LUKE, Ray
2011 Symphony, no. 2. ROCHBERG: Symphony, no. 1. Louisville Orchestra;
      Robert Whitney. Louisville LOU 634
                +FF 5/6-80 p224
LULLY, Jean
2012 Alcidiane et Polexandre: Ballet. La Follia Ensemble; Miguel de la
      Fuente, vln and cond. Arion ARN 38454 (also Musical Heritage
      Society MHS 4194)
                +-FF 11/12-80 p131   +RR 6-79 p96
                +-Gr 8-79 p348   +-RR 10-79 p151

      Amadis: Bois epais. See no. 3774
2013 Te deum. Jennifer Smith, Francine Bessac, s; Zeger Vandersteene,
      c-t; Louis Devos, t; Philippe Huttenlocher, bs; A Coeur Joi
      Vocal Ensemble of Valence; Jean-Francois Paillard Chamber Orches-
      tra; Jean-Francois Paillard. Erato STU 70927 (also Musical Heri-
      tage Society MHS 4145)

```
          +FF 9/10-80 p149              ++MU 10-80 p10
          -Gr 6-76 p71                  -RR 6-76 p79
          +-HF 3-79 p92
```

LUNA, Pablo
    La picara molinera: Paxarin tu que vuelas. See no. 3919
LUNDQUIST, Torbjorn
    Concerto, violin. See no. 1930
LUPI, Johannes (Lupus, Johannes)
2014 Ergo ne conticuit. OCKEGHEM: Missa prolationem. Capella Nova;
        Richard Tarushkin. Musical Heritage Society MHS 4026
              +ARG 1-80 p38   +-FF 3/4-80 p129
LUPO, Thomas
    Fantasia. See no. 3853
LUTHER, Martin
    Ein feste Burg ist unser Gott. See no. 3961
LUTOSLAWSKI, Witold
    Concerto, orchestra. See no. 1793
    Dance preludes. See no. 909
    Livre. See no. 3857
    Livre pour orchestra. See no. 1879
LUZZASCHI, Luzzasco
    Ricercare del 1 and 2 tuono. See no. 3813
    Toccata del 4 tuono. See no. 3813
MACCUNN, Hamish
    Land of the mountain and the flood. See no. 3623
MACHAUT, Guillaume de
2015 La fontaine amoureuse: Poetry and music. Music for a While; Tom
        Klunis, narrator. 1750 Arch S 1773
              ++AR 11-79 p124   +NR 11-80 p12
              +ARG 7-79 p39   ++St 7-79 p73
MACHY, Sieur de
2016 Suites, viola da gamba, nos. 1, 3-4. Jordi Savall, vla da gamba.
        Telefunken AW 6-42329
              +FF 3/4-80 p79   +HFN 11-78 p172
              +-Gr 12-78 p1130   +RR 11-78 p87
              +HF 3-80 p77
MACKEBEN
    Warum. See no. 3872
MACKENZIE, Alexander
    The little minister overture, op. 57. See no. 348
MACMURROUGH
    Eileen Aroon. See no. 4070
MACY, J. C.
    Jenk's vegetable compound. See no. 3791
MADERNA, Bruno
2017 Aura. Biogramma. Quadrivium. North German Radio Orchestra; Gius-
        eppe Sinopoli. Dg 2531 272
              +Gr 9-80 p334   ++NR 12-80 p3
              +HFN 11-80 p120
    Biogramma. See no. 2017
    Quadrivium. See no. 2017
MADETOJA, Leevi
    Comedy overture. See no. 2018
    Songs: Come with me, op. 9, no. 3; Dark herbs, op. 9, no. 1; Since
        you left me, op. 2, no. 1; Swing swing, op. 60, no. 1; You
        thought I was watching you, op. 68, no. 3. See no. 3586
```
```

2018 Symphony, no. 3. Comedy overture. Helsinki Philharmonic Orchestra;
     Jorma Panula. Finnlevy SFX 20 (also FA 307)
                    /FF 11-77 p35   +NR 11-80 p4
                    +FF 5/6-80 p99   +-RR 7-76 p54
                    +HFN 10-80 p106   +RR 11-78 p28
MAHLER, Gustav
2019 Kindertotenlieder. Ruckert Lieder. Christa Ludwig, ms; BPhO; Her-
     bert von Karajan. DG 2531 147 Tape (c) 3301 147 (From 2707 081,
     2707 082)
                    +Gr 11-79 p892   +RR 2-80 p90 tape
                    +HFN 11-79 p155   +RR 3-80 p104 tape
2020 Des Knaben Wunderhorn. Lieder eines fahrenden Gesellen. Lieder und
     Gesange aus der Jugendzeit. Ruckert Lieder. Dietrich Fischer-
     Fieskau, bar; Daniel Barenboim, pno. HMV SLS 5173 (3) (also EMI
     1C 165 03446/8)
                    +Gr 6-80 p54   +NYT 9-21-80 pD22
                    +HFN 6-80 p107   ++RR 8-80 p83
                    ++MT 12-80 p786   ++STL 7-13-80 p38
     Des Knaben Wunderhorn: Lob des honen Verstandes. See no. 3573
     Des Knaben Wunderhorn: Revelge. See no. 2048
2021 Des Knaben Wunderhorn: Wer hat dies Liedlein erdacht; Rheinlegend-
     chen. Lieder eines fahrenden Gesellen. Ruckert Lieder. Freder-
     ica von Stade, s; LPO; Andrew Davis. CBS 76828 Tape (c) 40-76828
     (also Columbia M 35863 Tape (c) MT 35863)
                    -FF 11/12-80 p132   +HFN 11-79 p141
                    ++FU 5-80 p47   +NYT 6-15-80 pD29
                    +-Gr 11-79 p392   +RR 12-79 p112
                    -HF 12-80 p82   +RR 3-80 p104 tape
                    ++HFN 1-80 p123 tape   ++St 10-80 p116
2022 Das Lied von der Erde. Lili Chookasian, con; Richard Cassilly, t;
     Cincinnati Symphony Orchestra; Walter Susskind. Candide QCE
     31117 Tape (c) CT 2258
                    +-ARG 12-80 p36   +-HF 10-80 p80
                    +-FF 7/8-80 p106
2023 Das Lied von der Erde. Christa Ludwig, ms; Rene Kollo, t; Israel
     Philharmonic Orchestra; Leonard Bernstein. CBS 61884 Tape (c)
     40-61884 (also Comumbia M 31919)
                    +Gr 4-80 p1576   -HFN 4-80 p121
                    -HFN 2-80 p105   +-RR 3-80 p93
2024 Das Lied von der Erde. Nan Merriman, con; Ernst Hafliger, t; COA;
     Eugen Jochum. DG 2535 184 Tape (c) 3335 184
                    +FF 11/12-78 p84   +RR 9/76 p94 tape
                    +-MUM 1/2-80 p36   +SFC 5-28-78 p41
                    +NYT 5-28-78 pD13
2025 Das Lied von der Erde. Mildred Miller, con; Ernst Hafliger, t;
     NYP; Bruno Walter. Odyssey Y 30043 (From Columbia MS 6426)
                    +HF 12-70 p137   +-MUM 1/2-80 p36
2026 Das Lied von der Erde. Nan Merriman, alto; Ernst Hafliger, t; COA;
     Eduard van Beinum. Philips 6570 193 Tape (c) 7310 193 (From
     Epic SC 6023)
                    +ARG 12-80 p36   +HF 10-80 p82
                    +FF 9/10-80 p149
2027 Das Lied von der Erde. Kathleen Ferrier, alto, Julius Patzak, t;
     VPO; Bruno Walter. Richmond R 23182 (From London A 4212)
                    ++HF 4-71 p65   ++MUM 1/2-80 p36
                    ++HF 12-73 p106   ++SFC 5-19-74 p30

2028 Das Lied von der Erde. Kerstin Thorborg, con; Charles Kullmann, t;
       VPO; Bruno Walter. Seraphim 60191 (also Parnassus 2004, Peren-
       nial 2004) (From Columbia M 300)
                +HF 6-71 p98   +NR 6-71 p11
                ++LJ 4-15-71 p1346   +NYT 4-18-71 pD26
                +MUM 1/2-80 p36   +St 5-71 p86
2029 Das Lied von der Erde. Dietrich Fischer-Dieskau, bar; Murray Dic-
       kie, t; PhO; Paul Kletzki. Seraphim S 60260
                +MUM 1/2-80 p36   +NR 5-76 p12
2030 Lieder eines fahrenden Gesellen. Ruckert Lieder. Marilyn Horne,
       ms; LAPO; Zubin Mehta. Decca SXL 6898 Tape (c) KSXC 6898 (also
       London OS 26578)
                ++ARG 5-80 p10   +-HFN 12-79 p163
                +-FF 3/4-80 p112   +-NYT 6-15-80 pD29
                +-Gr 11-79 p892   +RR 12-79 p112
                +-HF 4-80 p71   ++SFC 12-2-79 p53
     Lieder eines fahrenden Gesellen. See no. 2020. See no. 2021. See
       no. 2049
     Lieder und Gesange aus der Jugendzeit. See no. 2020
2031 Quartet, piano, A minor. SCHNITTKE: Quintet, piano. Gidon Kremer,
       vln; Yuri Bashmet, vla; Karine Georgina, Dmitri Ferschtmann, vlc;
       Yuri Smirnov, Alexei Lyubimov, pno. Ariola Eurodisc 24384
                +FF 1/2-80 p141
     Ruckert Lieder. See no. 2019. See no. 2020. See no. 2021. See
       no. 2030
     Ruckert Lieder: Blicke mir nicht in die Lieder; Ich bin der Welt
       abhanden gekommen; Um Mitternacht. See no. 2048
2032 Symphonies, nos. 1-9. Symphony, no. 10, F sharp major: Adagio.
       Edith Mathis, Elsie Morison, Martina Arroyo, Erna Spoorenberg,
       s; Norma Procter, Marjorie Thomas, Julia Hamari, con; Donald
       Grobe, t; Dietrich Fischer-Dieskau, bar; Franz Crass, bs; Bavar-
       ian Radio Chorus, Tolzer Boys Choir, North German Radio and West
       German Radio Chorus, Munich Motet Choir, Women's voices; Eberhard
       Kraus, org; Bavarian Radio Orchestra; Rafael Kubelik. DG 2720
       090 (14). (From 139331, 139332/3, 2707 036, 139339, 2720 033,
       2707 037, 2707 038)
                +Gr 10-79 p640   +-RR 2-80 p57
                +-HFN 12-79 p177
2033 Symphony, no. 1, D major. LPO; Klaus Tennstedt. Angel SSB 4501 (2)
                -ARG 5-80 p10
2034 Symphony, no. 1, D major. LPO; Gaetano Delogu. Clssics for Pleas-
       ure CFP 40264
                +FF 9/10-80 p150   +-HFN 8-77 p85
                +Gr 11-77 p838   +-RR 8-77 p57
2035 Symphony, no. 1, D major. LSO; Jascha Horenstein. Noneusch 71240
       Tape (c) D 1019 (also Unicorn RHS 301 Tape (r) F 0301)
                +HF 12-74 p146 tape   ++NR 8-75 p5
                +HF 11-80 p-8 tape   ++SFC 4-24-71 p32
                +HFN 11-80 p131 tape
2036 Symphony, no. 1, D major. Symphony, no. 10, F sharp major: Adagio.
       CPhO; Karel Ancerl, Vaclav Neumann. Quintessence PMC 2700 (2)
                -FF 1/2-80 p104
2037 Symphony, no. 1, D major. MPO; Kiril Kondrashin. Quintessence PMC
       7144
                +FF 7/8-80 p107   /SFC 5-25-80 p41

2038 Symphony, no. 2, C minor. Edith Mathis, s; Norma Procter, con;
     Bavarian Radio Orchestra and Chorus; Rafael Kubelik. DG 2726 026
     (2) (From 139332/3)
               +FF 9/10-80 p150   +HFN 8-77 p93
               +-Gr 3-77 p1396   +-RR 3-77 p50
2039 Symphony, no. 3, D minor. Ortrun Wenkel, con; Southend Boys Choir,
     LPO and Chorus; Klaus Tennstedt. HMV SLS 5195 (2) Tape (c) TC
     SLS 5195 (also Angel DS 3902 Tape (c) 4Z2S 3902)
               +Gr 11-80 p671
2040 Symphony, no. 3, D minor. LAPO; Zubin Mehta. London CSA 2449 (2)
     (also Decca D117D2 Tape (c) K117K22)
               +ARG 5-80 p10   +NR 6-80 p4
               +-FF 3/4-80 p113   ++NYT 12-9-79 pD25
               +-Gr 5-80 p1665   ++RR 5-80 p64
               -HF 4-80 p71   ++SFC 5-11-80 p35
               +-HFN 5-80 p122   ++St 2-80 p128
2041 Symphony, no. 3, D minor. Orchestra; Dmitri Mitropoulos. Rococo
     2055 (2)
               +-NR 5-80 p3
2042 Symphony, no. 3, D minor. Norma Procter, con; Wandsworth School
     Boys Choir, Ambrosian Singers; LSO; Jascha Horenstein. Unicorn
     UN 2-75004 Tape (r) N 302 (From CZUN 302/3)
               +FF 3/4-79 p76   +NR 6-79 p5
               +HF 11-80 p88 tape   ++SFC 4-15-79 p41
2043 Symphony, no. 4, G major. Barbara Hendricks, s; Israel Philharmonic
     Orchestra; Zubin Mehta. Decca SXDL 7501 Tape (c) KSXDC 7501 (al-
     so London LDR 10004 Tape (c) LDR 5-10004)
               +Audio 12-79 p99   +-NR 4-80 p2
               +-FF 11/12-79 p15   +NYT 12-9-79 pD25
               +Gr 7-79 p205   ++RR 8-79 p84
               ++Gr 12-79 p1065 tape   +-RR 3-80 p104 tape
               +-HF 11-79 p102   ++SFC 6-24-79 p57
               +-HF 10-80 p98 tape   +St 10-79 p142
               +HFN 7-79 p107
2044 Symphony, no. 4, G major. Edith Mathis, s; BPhO; Herbert von Kara-
     jan. DG 2531 205 Tape (c) 3301 205
               +-ARG 5-80 p10   ++HFN 12-79 p163
               +FF 5/6-80 p100   +-NR 6-80 p4
               ++Gr 11-79 p827   ++RR 1-80 p77
               +HF 4-80 p71   ++SFC 2-3-80 p45
               +HF 7-80 p82 tape   ++St 5-80 p83
2045 Symphony, no. 4, G major. Elly Ameling, s; Pittsburgh Symphony
     Orchestra; Andre Previn. HMV ASD 3783 Tape (c) TC ASD 3783
     (also Angel SZ 37576 Tape (c) 4ZS 37576)
               +-ARG 5-80 p10   +-MT 4-80 p252
               +-FF 3/4-80 p115   +NR 2-80 p2
               +Gr 9-79 p469   +NYT 12-9-79 pD25
               +-HF 4-80 p71   +RR 11-79 p84
               +-HFN 10-79 p157   +SFC 11-18-79 p47
               +-HFN 12-79 p185 tape   ++St 2-80 p81
2046 Symphony, no. 5, C sharp minor. Symphony, no. 10, F sharp major:
     Adagio. LPO; Klaus Tennstedt. HMV SLS 5169 (2) Tape (c) TC
     SLS 5169 (also Angel SZB 3883 Tape (c) 4Z2S 3883)
               +-ARG 5-80 p10   ++NR 3-80 p3
               +-FF 3/4-80 p114   +NYT 12-9-79 pD25
               +-Gr 10-79 p640   +RR 11-79 p84

        +HF 4-80 p71   +RR 3-80 p104 tape
        ++HFN 12-79 p163   +SFC 12-2-79 p53
        +HFN 1-80 p123 tape   +St 4-80 p134

2047 Symphony, no. 5, C sharp minor. Symphony, no. 10, F sharp major.
    MRSO, MRSO Large Symphony Orchestra; Kiril Kondrashin, Gennady
    Rozhdestvensky. Musical Heritage Society MHS 3991/2 (2)
        +-FF 9/10-80 p151

2048 Symphony, no. 5, C sharp minor. Des Knaben Wunderhorn: Revelge.
    Ruckert Lieder: Blicke mir nicht in die Lieder; Ich bin der Welt
    abahanden Gekommen; Um Mitternacht. Karel Berman, bs; CPhO;
    Vaclav Neumann. Supraphon 410 2511/2 (2)
        +-ARG 5-80 p10   -HF 4-80 p71
        -FF 9/10-80 p151   +-NR 9-80 p3

2049 Symphony, no. 5, C sharp minor. Lieder eines fahrenden Gesellen.
    Roland Hermann, bar; Symphonica of London; Wyn Morris. Symphon-
    ica SYMR 3/4 (2) Tape (c) CSYM 3/4 (also Peters PLE 100/1) (From
    Independent World Releases SYM 3/4)
        +ARG 5-80 p10   +-HF 4-80 p71
        +-FU 9-79 p52   +HFN 9-78 p143
        +-Gr 8-78 p331   +-HFN 9-78 p159 tape
        +-Gr 11-78 p964 tape   +-RR 11-78 p66
        +Gr 9-79 p499   +-RR 1-79 p91 tape

2050 Symphony, no. 6, A minor. CSO; Claudio Abbado. DG 2707 117 (2)
    Tape (c) 3370 031
        ++Gr 11-80 p672   ++STL 11-9-80 p40
        +HFN 11-80 p120

2051 Symphony, no. 6, A minor. LSO; James Levine. RCA ARL 2-3213 (2)
    Tape (c) ARK 2-3213
        +ARG 11-79 p28   +HF 7-80 p82 tape
        +-FF 7/8-79 p66   ++HFN 6-80 p107
        +-Gr 5-80 p1665   +SFC 8-5-79 p53
        +-HF 10-79 p114

2052 Symphony, no. 6, A minor. Stockholm Philharmonic Orchestra; Jascha
    Horenstein. Unicorn RHS 320/1 (2) (also UN 2-75025)
        +FF 9/10-80 p151   +-MT 1-76 p41
        ++Gr 9-75 p465   +RR 9-75 p40
        +HFN 9-75 p100   +RR 6-78 p60
        +HFN 8-78 p113   +SFC 8-5-79 p53

2053 Symphony, no. 7, E minor. CPhO; Vaclav Neumann. Supraphon 410
    2721/2 (2)
        +-ARG 5-80 p10   +NR 9-80 p3
        +-FF 9/10-80 p151   ++SFC 6-8-80 p36
        +-HF 4-80 p71

2054 Symphony, no. 8, E major. Symphony, no. 10, F sharp major: Adagio.
    Bavarian Radio Orchestra; Rafael Kubelik. DG 2726 053 Tape (c)
    3372 053
        +-FF 9/10-80 p152   +-HF 7-80 p82 tape

2055 Symphony, no. 8, E flat major. Mimi Coertse, Hilde Zadek, Lucretia
    West, s; Ira Malaniuk, con; Giuseppe Zampiere, t; Hermann Prey,
    bar; Otto Edelmann, bs; Vienna Festival Orchestra and Choirs;
    Dimitri Mitropoulus. Everest SDBR 3441
        +ARG 9-79 p44   +-NR 6-79 p6
        -FF 3/4-80 p115

2056 Symphony, no. 9, D major. LPO; Klaus Tennstedt. HMV SLS 5188 (2)
    Tape (c) TC SLS 5188 (also Angel SZ 3899 Tape (c) 4Z2S 3899)

            +ARG 11-80 p24   +MUM 11/12-80 p34
          +-FF 9/10-80 p153   ++NR 9-80 p3
            +Gr 3-80 p1391   +RR 4-80 p66
            +Gr 7-80 p166 tape   ++SFC 6-8-80 p36
          ++HF 10-80 p80   ++St 10-80 p110
            +HFN 3-80 p93   ++STL 4-13-80 p39
            +HFN 8-80 p109 tape
2057 Symphony, no. 9, D major. PO; James Levine. RCA ARL 2-3461 (2)
        Tape (c) ARK 2-3461
            ++ARG 5-80 p10   ++HFN 6-80 p107
            +FF 3/4-80 p116   +NR 3-80 p3
            ++Gr 7-80 p141   +RR 7-80 p47
            ++HF 4-80 p71   ++St 5-80 p84
            +HF 7-80 p82 tape
2058 Symphony, no. 9, D major. London Symphonica; Wyn Morris. Symphon-
        ica SYMR 14/5 (2) (also Peters PLE 116/7)
            ++ARG 5-80 p10   +-HFN 10-78 p127
            +-FF 3/4-80 p116   +RR 11-78 p66
            +Gr 12-78 p1103   +SFC 11-4-79 p40
            +-HF 4-80 p71   ++St 1-80 p96
2059 Symphony, no. 10, F sharp major (rev. ed Deryck Cooke). Bourne-
        mouth Symphony Orchestra; Simon Rattle. HMV SLS 5206 (2) Tape
        (c) TC SLS 5206
            +Gr 12-80 p832
        Symphony, no. 10, F sharp major. See no. 2047
        Symphony, no. 10, F sharp major: Adagio. See no. 2032. See no.
        2036. See no. 2046. See no. 2054
MAHU, Stefan
        Es gieng. See no. 4004
MAILLART, Louis-Aime
        Les dragons de Villars: Chanson a boire. See no. 3770
        Das Glockchen des Eremiten: O schweige still o lasse dich erbitten.
        See no. 3539
MAILMAN, Martin
2060 Decorations, op. 54. Geometrics, nos. 1 and 4. Hymns and praises,
        op. 52. Capital University Symphony Wind Ensemble; Richard Sud-
        dendorf. Golden Crest 5056
            +-FF 9/10-80 p154   +IN 5-79 p105
        Geometrics, nos. 1 and 4. See no. 2060
        Hymns and praises, op. 52. See no. 2060
MAIS, Chester
        Fantasy on Jewish tunes. See no. 3643
MALASHKIN
        O could I in song tell my sorrow. See no. 3774
MALATS, Joaquin
        Serenata. See no. 3549. See no. 3775
MALAWSKI, Arthur
        Overture. See no. 3857
        Symphonic etudes. See no. 70
MALDONADO, Raoul
        Air de huella. See no. 3706
MALEC, Ivo
2061 Bizarra. Triola. Harmonia Mundi INA GRM AM 83011
            +FF 7/8-80 p16
        Triola. See no. 2061

MALIPIERO, Gian-Francesco
Dialogue, no. 4. See nu. 485
MALOTTE, Albert
The Lord's prayer. See no. 30
MALVEZZI, Cristofano
Canzone on the 2nd tone. See no. 3762
MANAS, Edgar
Petite suite. See no. 3850
MANCINI, Henry
Moon river. See no. 3962
MANFREDINI, Francesco
Concerto grosso, op. 3, no. 12, C major. See no. 1136
Concerto grosso, op. 3, no. 12, G major: Pastorale; Allegro. See no. 4028
MANGON, Johannes
Salve regina. See no. 3763
MANNEKE, Daan
2062 A quatre mains. Diaphony for Geoffrey. En passant. Madrigaal.
    Psalmen (4). Three times. Geoffrey Madge, Theo Bles, Herman
    Uhlhorn, pno; Ad Ros, tpt; Harry Dieterman, trom; Peter Hoekmey-
    er, hn; Amsterdam University Chorus; Free University Chamber
    Chorus; Oosterhout Chamber Choir, Capella Amsterdam; USKO Orches-
    tra; Sweelinck Conservatory Students; Huub Kerstens, Jaap Hillen,
    Huub Bartz, Daan Manneke. Composers Voice 1978/1
                    +-FF 9/10-80 p155
    Diaphony for Geoffrey. See no. 2062
    En passant. See no. 2062
    Madrigaal. See no. 2062
    Psalmen (4). See no. 2062
    Three times. See no. 2062
MANSFIELD
    The red cloak. See no. 3617
MANZIARLY, Marcelle de
    Fables de la Fontaine: La cigale et la fourmi; L'Oiseau blesse d'un
    fleche; La grenoulliere. See no. 3862
    Trilogue. See no. 1130
MARAIS, Marin
    Le basque. See no. 485
2063 Chaconne, G major. Suites, D minor, G major. Tombeau de Monsieur
    Meliton. Jordi Savall, Christophe Coin, vla da gamba; Ton
    Koopman, hpd; Hopkinson Smith, theorbo. Astree AS 39
                    ++FF 9/10-80 p156
2064 Folies d'Espagne. Suite, B minor. Les voix humaines. Jorde Sav-
    all, vla da gamba; Anne Gallet, hpd; Hopkinson Smith, theorbo.
    Telefunken AW 6-42121
                    *FF 1/2-80 p105   +HFN 1-79 p119
                    +Gr 3-79 p1580   ++RR 12-78 p27
    Les folies d'Espagne. See no. 4006
2065 Pieces a trois violes, G major. Pieces de viole d'un gout etrang-
    er. Pieces en trio, no. 1. Sonnerie de Sainte-Genevieve du
    Mont de Paris. Oberlin Baroque Ensemble; James Weaver, August
    Wenzinger. Gasparo GS 202
                    +ARG 12-79 p6   +FF 1/2-80 p104
                    +AR 2-80 p175   +IN 11-80 p62
                ++Audio 11-79 p128

Pieces de viole d'un gout etranger. See no. 2065
Pieces en trio, no. 1. See no. 2065
La sonnerie de Sainte Genevieve du Mont de Paris. See no. 2065
2066 Suites, B minor, E minor, F major. Jean-Claude Veilhan, flt and
     rec; Ellen Maserati, hpd; Guy Roberts, lt and theorbo; Elizabeth
     Matiffa, vla da gamba. Arion ARN 38531
                 +Gr 8-80 p239   ++RR 7-80 p72
                 +-HFN 8-80 p98
Suite, B minor. See no. 2064
Suite, D minor, G major. See no. 2063
2067 Suites, recorder, F major, E minor. Hotteterre Quartet. Telefunken
     AW 6-42035
                 +ARG 12-79 p6   +HFN 11-77 p173
                 -FF 1/2-80 p105   -MM 9-78 p30
                 +Gr 11-77 p859   +RR 11-77 p80
2068 Suites, recorder, G minor, C major. Hotteterre Quartet. Telefun-
     ken AW 6-42192
                 -FF 1/2-80 p105   +HFN 11-78 p172
                 +ARG 12-79 p6   +RR 11-78 p83
                 +Gr 1-79 p1301
Suite, viola da gamba and harpsichord, no. 2, D major. See no. 1112
2069 Suite d'un gout etranger: La tartarine et double; Les fetes cham-
     petres; Le tourbillon; Le labyrinthe; L'Arabesque; Allemande la
     superbe; La reveuse; Marche; Gigue; La badinage. Jordi Savall,
     vla da gamba; Ton Koopman, hpd; Hopkinson Smith, gtr and theorbo.
     Telefunken 6-42341
                 +ARG 6-80 p24
Tombeau de Monsieur Meliton. See no. 2063
Les voix humaines. See no. 2064
MARCABRUN
     L'Autrier jost una sebissa. See no. 1842
MARCELLO, Alessandro
     Concerto, guitar, D minor. See no. 17. See no. 3602
     Concerto, oboe, C minor: Adagio. See no. 4028
     Concerto, oboe, C minor: Adagio. See no. 3640. See no 3943. See
     no. 4028
     Concerto, trumpet, C minor. See no. 29
2070 Sonatas, flute, nos. 1-12. Arrigo Tassinari, flt; Riccardo Tora,
     hpd. Ricordi ARCL 227 001 (2)
                 +-RR 8-80 p72
MARCELLO, Benedetto
2071 Concerti, op. 1, nos. 1, 4, 6. Concerto, oboe, C minor. Lucien
     Debray, ob; Musiciens de Paris; Catherine Bodet. Arion ARN 30A
     115
                 +RR 1-80 p78
Concerto, oboe, C minor. See no. 2071
2072 Sonatas, flute, op. 2 (12). Rene Clemencic, rec; Christiane Jaccot-
     tet, hpd; Alexandra Bachtiar, vlc; Peter Widensky, positiv
     organ; Vilmos Stadler, bs rec; Walter Stiftner, bsn; Andras Kecs-
     kes, lt. Harmonia Mundi HM 974/6 (3) (also HNH 3-4075, also HNH
     4083, 4086, 4089)
                 +AR 5-80 p35   +NR 7-79 p11
                 +FF 7/8-79 p67   +RR 1-78 p70
                 /-Gr 1-78 p1264   ++SFC 7-30-78 p49
                 +-HF 8-78 p80

Sonata, organ, no. 2, G major. See no. 3762
Sonata, recorder, op. 2, no. 2, D minor. See no. 3990
2073 Sonatas, violoncello, nos. 1-6. Anthony Pleeth, Richard Webb, vlc;
    Christopher Hogwood, hpd. L'Oiseau-Lyre DSLO 546
              +Gr 7-80 p148   +MT 12-80 p786
              +HFN 7-80 p107   +RR 8-80 p72
Songs: Quella fiamma che m'accende. See no. 3669
MARCHETTI, Filippo
Ruy Blas: Ai miei rivale cedere. See no. 3980
MARENZIO, Luca
Innocentes por Christo infantes. See no. 391
MARINI, Biagio
Balletto, no. 1. See no. 2074
Capriccio. See no. 3690
Corrente, no. 9. See no. 2074
Eco, 3 violini. See no. 3690
Gagliarda, no. 1. See no. 2074
Le lagrime d'Erminia. See no. 2074
Passacaglia a 4. See no. 3690
Sinfonie, nos. 2 and 5. See no. 2074
Sonatas, violin, op. 8, nos. 1-2, 58-59. See no. 2074
Sonata sopra la Monica. See no. 3690
2074 Works, selections: Balletto, no. 1. Corrente, no. 9. Gagliarda,
    no. 1. Le lagrime d'Erminia. Sinfonie, nos. 2 and 5. Sonatas,
    violin, op. 8, nos. 1-2, 58-59. Emma Kirkby, s; Nigel Rogers, t;
    Consort of Musicke; Anthony Rooley, Trevor Jones. L'Oiseau-Lyre
    DSLO 570
              +Gr 6-80 p54   +STL 7-13-80 p38
              +HFN 6-80 p107   +RR 6-80 p87
MARIO
Santa Lucia luntana. See no. 3900
MAROS, Miklos
Distances. See no. 3803
Oolit. See no. 3598
MARQUINA
Espana cani. See no. 3921
MARSCHNER, Heinrich
2075 Hans Heiling: An jenem Tag has du mir Treue versprochen. ROSSINI:
    Il barbiere di Siviglia: Die Verleumdung sie ist ein Luftchen.
    VERDI: Aida: Er ists er ists...Ich hab gekampft; Zu dir fuhrt
    mich ein ernster Grund. Falstaff: Die Ehre Gauner; Es verzehrt
    uns heisse Reue...Meine Ehrfurcht. Otello: Zur Nachtzeit war es.
    WAGNER: Der fliegende Hollander: Erfahre das Geschick; Die Frist
    ist um; Wie aus der Ferne langst vergangner Zeiten. Die Meister-
    singer von Nurnberg: Wahn Wahn uberall Wahn; Was duftet doch der
    Flieder. Die Walkure: Leb wohl du kuhnes herrliches Kind. Hilde
    Scheppan, Viorica Ursuleac, s; Margarete Klose, Wilma Fichtmuller,
    con; Helge Roswange, Karl Ostertag, t; Hans Hotter, bar; Wilhelm
    Lang, Wilhelm Schirp, Georg Hann, bs; Various Orchestras; Artur
    Rother, Hans Weisbach, Heinrich Hollreiser, Clemens Krauss. Ac-
    anta DE 22017 (2)
              +HFN 4-80 p112   +-RR 3-80 p43
MARSHALL, Charles
I hear you calling me. See no. 3874
MARTIN
Let maids be false so wine be true. See no. 3791

Mass. See no. 3713
MARTIN, Frank
Ballade, piano. See no. 3713. See no. 4017
Chants de Noel (3). See no. 4066
Concerto, violoncello. See no. 53
2076 Mass, 2 4-part choirs. Cologne Kantorei; Volker Hempfling. Can-
tate 657 617
+RR 7-80 p89
Petite symphonie concertante. See no. 734
Pieces breves (4). See no. 3967
2077 Preludes, piano (8). PROKOFIEV: Sonata, piano, no. 6, op. 82, A
major. Robert Silverman, pno. Orion ORS 79328
+ARG 11-79 p40   +Gr 9-79 p94
+-CL 12-79 p11   +HF 7-80 p72
+FF 11/12-79 p112

MARTINI, Giovanni Battista
2078 Duetti da camera. Anna Gabrieli, s; Joan Caplan, Valerie Walters,
ms; Ray DeVoll, t; Peter Elvins, bs; Martin Pearlman, hpd; Ruth
Rubinow, vlc. Orion ORS 79356
+-ARG 3-80 p31   +NR 7-80 p11
+-FF 7/8-80 p107
Largo, E major. See no. 4041
Pastorale, G major. See no. 3682
MARTINI IL TEDESCO, Johann
Plaisir d'amour. See no. 3640
MARTINO, Donald
Concerto, clarinet, bass clarinet and contrabass clarinet. See no.
67
MARTINU, Bohuslav
2079 Concertino, piano trio. Sinfonietta giocosa. Josef Suk, vln; Josef
Chuchro, vlc; Jan Panenka, pno; CPhO; Vaclav Neumann, Zdenek
Kosler. Supraphon 410 2198
+ARG 11-79 p41   +HFN 3-79 p125
++FF 9/10-80 p157   ++RR 1-79 p62
+Gr 10-79 p640   ++SFC 5-4-80 p42
+HF 9-79 p106   ++St 10-79 p94
Concerto, piano, no. 2. See no. 1848
2080 Concerto, piano, no. 5, B flat major. Concerto, 2 pianos. Ales
Bilek, Vera Lejskova, Vlastimil Lejsek, pno; PSO, Brno PO;
Jindrich Rohan, Jiri Waldhans. Supraphon 110 2338
+-FF 11/12-80 p132   +NR 9-80 p5
Concerto, 2 pianos. See no. 2080
2081 The epic of Gilgamesh. Marceal Machotkova, s; Jiri Zahradnicek, t;
Vaclav Zitek, bar; Karel Prusa, bs; CPhO Chorus; PSO; Jiri Bel-
ohlavek. Supraphon 112 1808
++ARG 7/8-80 p30   +-HFN 7-80 p107
++FF 11/12-80 p133   +NR 2-80 p8
+Gr 6-80 p59   +-RR 6-80 p86
+-HF 8-80 p77   +-St 4-80 p134
2082 Inventions. Symphony, no. 1. CPhO; Vaclav Neumann. Supraphon 410
2166
++ARG 6-79 p27   +-HFN 1-80 p107
++FF 9/10-79 p106   ++NR 7-79 p5
++Gr 5-80 p1666   +RR 1-80 p78
+HF 9-79 p106   +STL 12-2-79 p37

2083 Madrigal sonata. Sonata, flute and piano. Trio sonata, flute,
　　　　violin and piano. Alexandre Magnin, flt; Philipp Naegele, vln;
　　　　Ralf Gothoni, pno. Da Camera Magna SM 92918
　　　　　　　　　+FF 7/8-80 p108
　　Sinfonietta giocosa. See no. 2079
　　Sinfonietta La Jolla. See no. 2087
　　Sonata, flute and piano. See no. 2083
2084 Sonatas, violoncello and piano, nos. 1-3. Philippe Muller, vlc;
　　　　Ralf Gothoni, pno. Da Camera Magna SM 93714
　　　　　　　　　++ARG 1-80 p35　　　　　　　　　+++FF 7/8-80 p108
　　Sonatas, violoncello and piano, no. 1. See no. 1962
　　Sonatina. See no. 35. See no. 1462
　　Symphony, no. 1. See no. 2082
2085 Symphony, no. 2. Symphony, no. 6. CPhO; Vaclav Neumann. Supraphon
　　　　SUP 110 2096
　　　　　　　　　+FF 9/10-80 p157　　　　　　　+NR 8-80 p4
　　　　　　　　　++Gr 5-80 p1666　　　　　　　+RR 1-80 p78
　　　　　　　　　+HF 6-80 p80　　　　　　　　　+St 10-80 p83
　　　　　　　　　+-HF 1-80 p107　　　　　　　　+STL 12-2-79 p37
2086 Symphonies, nos. 3-5. CPhO; Vaclav Neumann. Supraphon SUP 410
　　　　2771/2
　　　　　　　　　++Gr 5-80 p1666　　　　　　　+RR 1-80 p78
　　　　　　　　　+-HFN 1-80 p107　　　　　　　+STL 12-2-79 p37
　　　　　　　　　+MT 10-80 p635
2087 Symphony, no. 41 Sinfonietta La Jolla. Royal Liverpool Orchestra;
　　　　Walter Weller. HMV ASD 3888 Tape (c) TC ASD 3888
　　　　　　　　　+Gr 7-80 p107　　　　　　　　+HFN 9-80 p116
　　　　　　　　　+HFN 6-80 p107　　　　　　　+RR 8-80 p48
　　Symphony, no. 6. See no. 2085
　　Trio sonata, flute, violin and piano. See no. 2083
MARX, Josef
　　Songs: Der bescheidene Schafer; Hat dich die Liebe beruhrt; Und
　　　　gestern hat er mir Rosen gebracht; Valse de Chopin; Windrader.
　　　　See no. 859
MASCAGNI, Pietro
　　L'Amico Fritz: Intermezzo, Act 3. See no. 3847
2088 L'Amico Fritz: Son pochi fiori. MOZART: Le nozze di Figaro, K 492:
　　　　E Susanna non vien...Dove sono. PUCCINI: La boheme: Si mi chia-
　　　　mano Mimi. Gianni Schicchi: O mio babbino caro. Madama Butter-
　　　　fly: Piangi perche...Un bel di vedremo. La rondine: Chi il bel
　　　　sogno di Doretta. Turandot: Tu che di gel sei cinta. ROSSINI:
　　　　Guillaume Tell: Ils s'eloignent enfin...Sombre foret. VERDI:
　　　　Ernani: Surta e la notte...Ernani involami...Tutto sprezzo che
　　　　d'Ernani. Leona Mitchell, s; National Philharmonic Orchestra;
　　　　Kurt Herbert Adler. London OS 62591
　　　　　　　　　+-HF 12-80 p73
　　L'Amico Fritz: Son pochi fiori. See no. 3670
　　L'Amico Fritz: Suzel buon di. See no. 3792
2089 Cavalleria rusticana. Renata Scotto, s; Isola Jones, ms; Placido
　　　　Domingo, t; Pablo Elvira, bar; Ambrosian Opera Chorus; National
　　　　Philharmonic Orchestra; James Levine. RCA CRL 1-3091 Tape (c)
　　　　CRK 1-3091
　　　　　　　　　+ARG 1-80 p35　　　　　　　　+NYT 9-30-79 pD22
　　　　　　　　　+FF 5/6-80 p101　　　　　　　+OC Spring 1980 p73
　　　　　　　　　+FU 5-80 p48　　　　　　　　　+ON 1-5-80 p57

                    +Gr 2-80 p1293   ++Op 4-80 p409
                    +Gr 9-80 p413 tape   +RR 1-80 p59
                    +HFN 3-80 p93   ++SFC 9-23-79 p37
                    +HFN 9-80 p116 tape   +St 1-80 p96
                    +NR 12-79 p9   +STL 5-11-80 p39

Cavalleria rusticana. See no. 1955. See no. 1956
Cavalleria rusticana: Arias. See no. 3539
Cavalleria rusticana: Ave Maria. See no. 3831
Cavalleria rusticana: Intermezzo. See no. 3555. See no. 3843.
     See no. 3847
Cavalleria rusticana: O Lola ch' hai di latti. See no. 3981
Cavalleria rusticana: Siciliana. See no. 3770. See no. 3946.
     See no. 3984
Cavalleria rusticana: Voi lo sapete. See no. 3538. See no. 3924
Cavalleria rusticana: Voi lo sapete; Tu qui Santuzza. See no. 3929
Iris: Apri la tua finestra. See no. 3671. See no. 3984
Isabeau: Gia per terra e castella. See no. 3925
Isabeau: Questo mio biano manto. See no. 3774
Lodoletta: Ah il suo nome...Flammen perdonami. See no. 3774
MASCHERONI, Eduardo
     Eternamente. See no. 3949
MASEK, Vaclav
2090 Andante, A major. Moderato e cantabile, C major. Partitas, A maj-
     or, E flat major, D major. Serenata, E flat major. Variations
     (6). Bruno Hoffmann, glass hp; Josef Hala, hpd; Collegium Musi-
     cum, Prague; Frantisek Vajnar. Supraphon 111 2424
                    +FF 3/4-80 p117   +MT 2-80 p106
                    ++FU 12-79 p44   +RR 3-79 p77
                    +HFN 3-79 p125
     Moderato e cantabile, C major. See no. 2090
     Partitas, A major, E flat major, D major. See no. 2090
     Serenata, E flat major. See no. 2090
     Variations (6). See no. 2090
MASINI
     I mulatieri. See no. 3770
MASSE, Victor
     Variations on "Carnival of Venice". See no. 3774
MASSENET, Jules
     Annee passee, Bks 1-4. See no. 2098
     Ariane: La fine grace. See no. 3774
     Berceuse (2). See no. 2098
2091 Cendrillon. Ruth Welting, Jane Berbie, s; Frederica von Stade, ms;
     Nicolai Gedda, t; Jules Bastin, bs; Ambrosian Opera Chorus; PO;
     Julius Rudel. Columbia M3 35194 (3) (also CBS 79323)
                    +-ARG 10-79 p15   +NYT 5-6-79 pD21
                    +Audio 2-80 p43   ++OC Vol XX, no. 3, p55
                    +FF 7/8-79 p67   +ON 6-79 p44
                    +Gr 7-79 p255   +Op 9-79 p880
                    ++HF 8-79 p81   +RR 7-79 p34
                    +HFN 7-79 p107   /-SFC 5-20-79 p49
                    +-MT 8-80 p504   ++St 9-79 p89
                    +-NR 7-79 p13
     Cendrillon: Ma pauvre enfant cherie...Nous quitterons cette ville.
          See no. 3774
     Le Cid: Air de l'infante; C'est vous que l'on benit; Pleurez mes
          yeux. See no. 3770

Le Cid: Alleluia. See no. 3632
2092 Le Cid: Ballet msuic. Suite, orchestra: Scenes pittoresques. La
     vierge: The last sleep of the virgin. Birmingham Symphony Orch-
     estra; Vivian Dunn, Louis Fremaux. Klavier KS 522 (also DBS
     2011)
                        +ARG 5-80 p45   +-NR 12-73 p4
                        -HF 7-74 p113   +St 5-74 p104
     Le Cid: Il a fait noblement. See no. 3631
2093 Cigale. Valse tres lente. National Philharmonic Orchestra; Richard
     Bonynge. London CS 7163 (also Decca SXL 6932)
                        +Gr 10-80 p498   +NYT 10-12-80 pD28
                        ++HFN 9-80 p105   +SFC 10-26-80 p20
     Concerto, piano, E flat major. See no. 2098
     Danses (6). See no. 2098
     Devant la Madone. See no. 2098
2094 Don Quichotte. Michele Command, Annick Dutertre, s; Regine Crespin,
     ms; Peyo Garazzi, t; Jean-Marie Fremeau, Gabriel Bacquier, bar;
     Nicolai Ghiaurov, bs; ORS and Chorus; Kazimierz Kord. Decca D
     156D3 (3) Tape (c) K156K32 (also London OSA 13134 Tape (c) OSA
     5-13134)
                        +-ARG 6-80 p25   +OC Summer 1980 p47
                        +FF 3/4-80 p118   +-ON 6-80 p45
                        +Gr 11-79 p907   +NYT 12-16-79 pD21
                        +Gr 2-80 p1302 tape   ++SFC 1-6-80 p43
                        +HF 4-80 p67   +St 3-80 p98
                        +HF 8-80 p87 tape   +STL 12-2-79 p37
                        +HFN 12-79 p163   +RR 11-79 p50
                        +-MT 8-80 p504
2095 Don Quichotte: Interludes, nos. 1 and 2. Suites, orchestra, nos.
     3-4, 6-7. La vierge: Le dernier sommeil de la vierge. Monte
     Carlo Opera Orchestra; John Eliot Gardiner. Musical Heritage
     Society MHS 4212/3 (2)
                        +St 12-80 p134
     Don Quichotte: Interludes, nos. 1 and 2. See no. 2104
     Eau courante. See no. 2098
     Eau dormante. See no. 2098
     Elegie. See no. 3769
     Elegie. op. 10. See no. 3684
     Les Erinnyes: Incidental music. See no. 3557
     Esclarmonde: Esprits de l'air. See no. 3828
2096 Espada: Dances (3). Paris Opera Orchestra; Georges Sebastian. Var-
     ese VC 81110 (From Urania)
                        +NYT 10-12-80 pD28
     Griselidis: Je suis l'oiseau; La mer et sur les flots toujours
        bleue...Il partit au printemps. See no. 3774
     Herodiade: Astres etincelants. See no. 3631
     Herodiade: Celui dont la parole...Il est doux, il est bon; Vision
        fugitive. See no. 3770
     Herodiade: Il est doux. See no. 3632. See no. 3985
     Herodiade: Pour moi tout autre est le destin. See no. 3630
     Herodiade: Salome...Demande au prisonnier. See no. 3774
     Herodiade: Visione fuggitiva. See no. 3901
     Improvisations (7). See no. 2098
2097 Le jongleur de Notre Dame. Alain Vanzo, Tibere Raffalli, t; Marc
     Vento, Jules Bastin, bs; Jean-Marie Fremeau, Michel Carey, bar;

Monte Carlo Opera Orchestra and Chorus; Roger Boutry. Angel SBLX
3877 (2) Tape (c) 4X2X 3877 (also EMI 2C 167 16275/6)

+ARG 8-79 p24	+NYT 5-6-79 pD21
+FF 7/8-79 p70	+ON 6-79 p44
+-Gr 9-80 p397	++SFC 3-18-79 p44
+HF 6-79 p84	++St 7-79 p100
+HF 9-79 p131 tape	+NR 5-79 p9
+HFN 11-80 p121	

Le jongleur de Notre Dame: Fleurissait une rose au bord du chemin.
See no. 3925
Le jongleur de Notre Dame: Liberte. See no. 3770
Manon: Act 2. See no. 1099
Manon: Ah fuyez douce image. See no. 3535
Manon: Arias. See no. 3539
Manon: Chiudo gli occhi. See no. 3981
Manon: En fermant les yieux; Ah fuyez douce image. See no. 3926
Manon: Gavotte. See no. 3632
Manon: Helas helas...N'est-ce plus ma main; Je suis encore tout
etourdie. See no. 3770
Manon: Je ne suis que faiblesse...Adieu notre petite table; Ah rands-
moi ton amour...N'est-ce plus ma main. See no. 3774
Manon: Je suis seul...Ah fuyez douce image. See no. 3949
Manon: Restons ici; Je suis encore tout etourdie. See no. 3886
Marches (3). See no. 2098
Marie Magdeleine: C'est ici meme; O bien-aime. See no. 3630
Marie Magdeleine: O mes soeurs...C'est ici meme a cette. See no.
3774
Musique pour bercer les petits enfants. See no. 2098
Papillons blancs. See no. 2098
Papillons noirs. See no. 2098
Phedre: Overture. See no. 3557
2098 Piano works: Annee passee, Bks 1-4. Berceuse (2). Concerto, piano,
E flat major. Danses (6). Devant la Madone. Eau courante.
Eau dormante. Improvisations (7). Marches (3). Musique pour
bercer les petits enfants. Papillons blancs. Papillons noirs.
Pieces de genre, op. 10. Suite, orchestra, no. 1, op. 11. Toc-
cata. Valse folle. Valse tres lente. La vierge: Danse galili-
enne. Aldo Ciccolini, pno; Monte Carlo Opera Orchestra; Sylvain
Camberling. Pathe Marconi 2C 167 73005/7 (3)
+Gr 12-80 p835
Pieces de genre, op. 10. See no. 2098
2099 Le Roi de Lahore. Joan Sutherland, Huguette Tourangeau, s; Sherrill
Milnes, bar; James Morris, Nicolai Ghiaurov, bs; Louis Lima, t;
London Voices; National Philharmonic Orchestra; Richard Bonynge.
London 3RLD 10025 (3) (also Decca D210D3 Tape (c) K210K3)

+Gr 11-80 p732	+-NYT 10-12-80 pD28
+HFN 11-80 p121	+SFC 10-12-80 p21

Le Roi de Lahore: O casto fior. See no. 3980
2100 Sapho. Renee Doria, Elya Waisman, s; Gisele Ory, ms; Christian
Baudean, t; Rene Gamboa, bar; Jacques Doumene, bs; Paris Radio
Orchestra; Roger Boutry. Peters PLE 129/31 (3) (also HMV 2C 167
16203/5)

-ARG 5-80 p28	-NYT 12-16-79 pD21
/FF 5/6-80 p102	+ON 6-80 p45
-HF 4-80 p67	+-SFC 1-6-80 p43
+HFN 10-80 p106	+-St 4-80 p134

2101 Songs: A Colombine; Automne; Elegie; Fleuramye; Madrigal; Oh si les
     fleurs avaient des yeux; Ouvre tes yeux bleus; Pensee d'automne;
     Poeme d'Avril; Nuit d'Espagne; Roses d'Octobre; Serenade de Zan-
     etto; Si tu veux Mignonne; Souvenir de Venise. Bruno Laplante,
     bar; Janine Lachance, pno. Calliope CAL 1830
                    +Gr 12-76 p1033   +-RR 11-76 p97
                    +NYT 10-12-80 pD28   +RR 8-80 p19
     Songs: Marquise; Chant provencal. See no. 3770
     Songs: O si les fleurs avaient des yeux; Pensee d'automne; Crepus-
     cule. See no. 3774
     Suite, orchestra, no. 1, op. 11. See no. 2098
     Suites, orchestra, nos. 3-4, 6-7. See no. 2095
     Suites, orchestra: Scenes alsaciennes; Scenes dramatiques; Scenes
     de feerie; Scenes pittoresques. See no. 2104
     Suites, orchestra: Scenes alsaciennes; Scenes pittoresques. See
     no. 3557
     Suites, orchestra: Scenes pittoresques. See no. 2092
     Thais: Ah je suis seule enfin...Dismoi que je suis belle...Ah tais-
     toi voix impitovable. See no. 3554
     Thais: Helas enfant encore; Voila donc la terrible cite. See no.
     3925
     Thais: L'Amour est une vertu rare; Voila donc la terrible cite. See
     no. 3774
     Thais: Meditation. See no. 3623. See no. 3847
     Thais: Mirror aria; L'Amour est une vertu rare; Scene de l'Oasis.
     See no. 3632
     Thais: Te souvient-il. See no. 3987
     Therese: Jour de juin. See no. 3774
     Toccata. See no. 2098
     Valse folle. See no. 2098
     Valse tres lente. See no. 2093. See no. 2098
     La vierge: Danse galilienne. See no. 2098
     La vierge: Le dernier sommeil de la verge. See no. 1213. See no.
     2092. See no. 2095. See no. 2104
2102 Werther. Tatiana Troyanos, ms; Christine Barbaux, s; Alfredo Kraus,
     Philip Langridge, t; Jean-Philippe Lafont, Matteo Manuguerra,
     bar; Jules Bastin, bs; LPO; Michel Plasson. Angel SZCX 3894 (3)
     Tape (c) 4Z3X 3894 (also HMV SLS 5183)
                    +ARG 9-80 p29   +ON 3-29-80 p36
                    +FF 5/6-80 p103   ++Op 4-80 p376
                    +Gr 2-80 p1293   ++RR 2-80 p39
                    +HF 4-80 p67   ++SFC 1-20-80 p47
                    +HFN 2-80 p95   +St 6-80 p121
                    +-NR 4-80 p11   +STL 2-10-80 p40
                    +OC Spring 1980 p73
2103 Werther. Arleen Auger, s; Elena Obraztsova, Gertrud von Ottenthal,
     ms; Placido Domingo, Alejandro Vasquez, Wolfgang Vater, t; Lasz-
     lo Anderko, bar; Franz Grundheber, Kurt Moll, bs; Cologne Child-
     ren's Chorus; Cologne Radio Orchestra; Riccardo Chailly. DG
     2709 091 (3) Tape (c) 3371 048
                    +ARG 9-80 p29   +-OC Spring 1980 p73
                    +-FF 5/6-80 p102   +ON 3-29-80 p36
                    +Gr 11-79 p904   +-Op 12-79 p1168
                    +-HF 4-80 p67   +RR 11-79 p56
                    +-HF 8-80 p87 tape   +-RR 6-80 p94 tape
                    +-HFN 11-79 p141   ++SFC 11-25-79 p46

```
    ++MT 8-80 p504                    +St 4-80 p135
    +-NR 1-80 p9                      +STL 12-2-79 p37
    +-NYT 12-23-79 pD28
```
Werther, excerpts (3). See no. 1099
Werther: Ah non mi ridestar. See no. 3901. See no. 3980. See no.
    3981. See no. 4008
Werther: Air des larmes. See no. 3774
Werther: C'est moi...J'aurais sur ma poitrine; Pourquoi me reveil-
    ler. See no. 3770
Werther: Letter scene. See no. 3928
Werther: O nautre pleine de grace; Lorsque l'enfant revient d'un
    voyage avant l'heure; Pourquoi me reveiller. See no. 3926
Werther: Pourquoi me reveiller. See no. 3671. See no. 4031
2104 Works, selections: Don Quichotte: Interludes, nos. 1 and 2. Suites,
    orchestra: Scenes dramatiques; Scenes de feerie; Scenes alsacien-
    nes; Scenes pittoresques. La vierge: Last sleep of the virgin.
    Monte Carlo Opera Orchestra; John Eliot Gardiner. Erato STU 71208
    (2)
```
                +Gr 1-80 p1152                    +RR 1-80 p80
                +NYT 10-12-80 pD28
```

MATHIAS, William
2105 This worlde's joie. Janet Price, s; Kenneth Bowen, t; Michael Rip-
    pon, bar; Bach Choir, St. George's Chapel Choir; NPhO; David
    Willcocks. HMV ASD 3301
```
                ++FF 3/4-80 p38                   +HFN 1-77 p111
                ++Gr 12-76 p1033                  +RR 1-77 p82
```
Toccata giocosa, op. 36, no. 2. See no. 3528
Wassail. See no. 3823
MATT
    Fame and glory. See no. 3617
MATTEIS, Nicola
    Ayres with divisions. See no. 3990
MATTHESON, Johann
    Sonata, op. 1, no. 3, G minor. See no. 4018
MATTHEWS
    Pastime rag, no. 5. See no. 3679
MATTHEWS, William
    Summer is icumen in: Lhude sing. See no. 710
MAW, Nicholas
2106 Life studies, nos. 1-8. AMF; Neville Marriner. Argo ZRG 899
```
                ++Gr 1-80 p1152                   +ST 8-80 p267
                +HFN 12-79 p165                   +STL 12-2-79 p37
                ++MT 3-80 p180                    ++Te 3-80 p29
                ++RR 12-79 p62
```
MAXWELL DAVIES, Peter
    St. Thomas wake. See no. 43
2107 Songs for a mad king (8). Julius Eastman; Soloists; Fires of Lon-
    don; Peter Maxwell Davies. Unicorn UNS 261 (From RHS 261)
```
                +-Gr 6-80 p59                     +RR 8-80 p80
                ++HFN 7-80 p119
```
2108 Symphony. PhO; Simon Rattle. Decca HEAD 21
```
                ++Gr 11-79 p827                   +STL 12-2-79 p37
                +HFN 12-79 p165                   +Te 3-80 p27
                ++RR 12-79 p63
```
MAYER, Johann
    Schnofler Tanz. See no. 3759
```
```

MAYNARD, John
>The twelve wonders of the world: The courtier; Divine; The souldiour; The lawyer; The marchant; The countrey genteman; The marryed man; The batchelar; The wife; The widow; The maid. See no. 3876

MAYONE
>Toccata no. 5. See no. 3846

MAYUZIMI, Toshiro
>2109 Mandala. Nirvana. NHK Symphony Orchestra; Japan Chorus Union; Kazua Yamada. Philips 5900 762 Tape (c) 7300 841
>>++FF 9/10-80 p158   +SFC 9-28-80 p21
>>+NR 11-80 p3   +St 11-80 p92
>
>Nirvana. See no. 2109

MAZZA
>Campanone: Senorita amigos mios. See no. 3774

MCCABE, John
>2110 The Chagall windows. Variations on a theme by Karl Amadeus Hartmann. Halle Orchestra; James Loughran. HMV Q ASD 3096
>>+Audio 3-76 p63   +MM 7-76 p37
>>+FF 9/10-80 p159   +MT 2-76 p143
>>+Gr 10-75 p621   ++RR 9-75 p39
>>++HFN 10-75 p144   *Te 3-76 p31
>
>Variations on a theme by Karl Amadeus Hartmann. See no. 2110

MCCAULEY
>Miniature overture. See no. 4043

MCDOWELL, Edward
>Woodland sketches, op. 51: To a wild rose. See no. 4045

MCFREDERICK, Michael
>2111 Duo, alto flute and piano. Rhapsody, solo piano. Sextet, woodwinds, strings and piano. Trio, piano, bass and drums. New City Ensemble. Golden Age 1015
>>-NR 6-80 p8
>
>Rhapsody, solo piano. See no. 2111
>Sextet, woodwinds, strings and piano. See no. 2111
>Trio, piano, bass and drums. See no. 2111

MCKINLEY, William
>Paintings, no. 2. See no. 1117

MCLEAN, Barton
>Dimensions II. See no. 1350
>Night images. See no. 1655

MCLEAN, Priscilla
>Invisible chariots. See no. 1655

MCPHEE, Colin
>Tabuh-Tabuhan. See no. 737

MEDER, Jean
>Symphony, op. 3, no. 1, C major. See no. 3818
>MEDIAEVAL AND RENAISSANCE SOUNDS. See no. 3680. No. 3861. No 3896

MEDTNER, Nikolai
>2112 Concerto, piano, no. 2, op. 50, C minor. A. Shatskes, pno; USSR Symphony Orchestra; Yevgeny Svetlanov. Melodiya D 5080
>>+-RR 1-80 p80
>2113 Concerto, piano, no. 3, op. 60, E minor. Tatyana Nikolayeva, pno; MRSO; Yevgeny Svetlanov. Melodiya C 229
>>++RR 1-80 p81
>
>Skazkhi (Fairy tale), B flat minor. See no. 3964
>2114 Skazkhi, op. 8, nos. 1, 2; op. 20, nos. 1, 2; op. 26, nos. 1-4. Sonata, piano, op. 53, no. 1, G minor. Daniel Graham, pno. MHS 3976
>>+FF 9/10-80 p160   +-St 11-79 p98

2115 Skazki, opp. 20 and 26. Sonata Orageuse, op. 53, no. 2, F minor.
     Antony Rolle, pno. Finnadar SR 9026
                +ARG 12-80 p37   ++NR 7-80 p11
                +FF 9/10-80 p160   +St 7-80 p88
                +HF 10-80 p82
     Sonata, piano, op. 53, no. 1, B flat minor. See no. 2114
     Sonata Orageuse, op. 53, no. 2, F minor. See no. 2115
     Sonata reminiscenza, op. 38, A minor. See no. 3944
2116 Songs: The flower, op. 36, no. 2; Gone are my desires, op. 29, no.
     6; The rose, op. 29, no. 6; To a dreamer, op. 32, no. 6; Winter
     evening, op. 13, no. 1. TANEYEV: Songs: Fountains, op. 26, no.
     7; In a magic haze, op. 17, no. 8; Music, op. 26, no. 4; My rest-
     less heart, op. 17, no. 9; My heart like a brook, op. 34, no. 7;
     People sleep, op. 17, no. 10; Serenade, op. 9, no. 2; Stalactit-
     es, op. 26, no. 6; Tis not the wind, op. 17, no. 5; Venice at
     night, op. 9, no. 1; When autumn leaves circle, op. 17, no. 6.
     Irina Arkhipova, ms; Igor Glusel'nikov, pno; A. Sobolev, mand.
     Melodiya S10 08229-30
                +FF 3/4-80 p163
MEESTER, Louis de
     Toccata. See no. 3889

MEKEEL, Joyce
2117 Vigil. SCHICKELE: Pentangle. THORNE: Elegy. Kenneth Albrecht, Fr
     hn; Louisville Orchestra; Jorge Mester. Louisville LS 768
                +FF 9/10-80 p196   +-NR 8-80 p5
MELII DA REGGIO, Pietro
     Capriccio cromatico. See no. 3577
     Capriccio detto "Il gran Matias". See no. 3577
MELLO JESUS, Caetano
     Se o canto enfraquecido. See no. 3708
MENALT (16th century Spain)
     Tiento de falsas de sexto tono. See no. 3756
MENASCE, Jacques
     Lettres d'enfants (2). See no. 3861
MENDELSSOHN, Felix
     Allegro brillant, op. 92. See no. 1401
     Andante con variazioni, op. 82, E flat major. See no. 893
     Athalia, op. 74: March of the priests. See no. 2151
     Auf Flugeln des Gesanges, op. 34, no. 2. See no. 3684
     Calm sea and prosperous voyage, op. 27. See no. 2154. See no. 2155
2118 Capriccio, E minor. Fugue, E flat major. Quartets, strings, no. 2,
     op. 13, E flat major; no. 4, op. 44, E minor. Bartholdy Quartet.
     Acanta HA 21815 (2)
                +ST 1-80 p690
     Capriccio brillante, op. 22, B minor. See no. 1035
2119 Concerto, piano, no. 1, op. 25, G minor. Concerto, piano, no. 2,
     op. 40, D minor. Valentin Gheorghiu, pno; Liverpool Radio Orch-
     estra; Herbert Kegel. DG Tape (c) 3335 416
                +-HFN 11-80 p131 tape
2120 Concerto, piano, no. 1, op. 25, G minor. Concerto, piano, no. 2,
     op. 40, D minor. James Johnson, pno; RPO; Paul Freeman. Musi-
     cal Heritage Society MHS 4057
                -ARG 3-80 p32   -FF 5/6-80 p104
     Concerto, piano, no. 2, op. 40, D minor. See no. 2119. See no.
     2120

2121 Concerti, 2 pianos, A minor, E flat major. John Ogdon, Brenda Lucas, pno; AMF; Neville Marriner. Argo Tape (r) B-C E 605
        *HF 1-80 p91 tape
2122 Concerto, violin, D minor. Symphony, strings, no. 12, G minor.
    Yehudi Menuhin, vln; Hephzibah Menuhin, pno; Menuhin Festival
    Orchestra; Yehudi Menuhin. HMV ASD 3628
        ++Gr 4-79 p1712   ++RR 4-79 p74
        ++HFN 4-79 p123   ++RR 5-80 p85
    Concerto, violin, op. 64, E minor. See no. 428. See no. 489. See
        no. 3968
    Concerto, violin, op. 64, E minor: Finale. See no. 3964
    Consolation. See no. 3769
    Elijah, op. 70: It is enough. See no. 4007
    Elijah, op. 70: Then shall the righteous shine forth. See no. 3770
2123 Die erste Walpurgisnacht, op. 60. Symphony, no. 2, op. 52, B flat
    major. Sona Ghazarian, Edita Gruberova, s; Margarita Lilowa,
    con; Horst Laubenthal, Werner Krenn, t; Tom Krause, bar; Alfred
    Sramek, bs; Vienna Singverein, Vienna State Opera Chorus; VPO;
    Christoph von Dohnanyi. London CSA 2250 (2) (also Decca D133D2)
        ++ARG 9-80 p33   +MT 4-80 p252
        +FF 7/8-80 p109   +St 5-80 p84
2124 Die erste Walpurgisnacht, op. 60. Hebrides, op. 26. Rose Taylor,
    ms; Jerold Norman, t; Simon Estes, bs-bar; Mendelssohn Club of
    Philadelphia; PO; Eugene Ormandy. RCA ARL 1-3460 Tape (c) ARK
    1-3460
        ++ARG 2-80 p39   +HFN 9-80 p116 tape
        -FF 5/6-80 p105   +NR 2-80 p9
        +-Gr 8-80 p251   +-RR 7-80 p89
        +HFN 8-80 p98
    Fantasies, op. 16 (3). See no. 893
    Fugue, E flat minor. See no. 2118
    Hark the herald angels sing. See no. 3823
    Hear my prayer, op. 39, no. 1. See no. 3534. See no. 3835
    Hebrides overture, op. 26. See no. 2124. See no. 2150. See no.
        2152. See no. 2153. See no. 2155. See no. 2158. See no. 2162.
        See no. 3950
    Introduction and rondo capriccioso, op. 14, E flat major. See no.
        3902
    Laudate pueri dominum. See no. 3525
2125 A midsummer night's dream, opp. 21/61: Incidental music. Elizabeth
    Gale, Ann Murray, s; Female Vocal Ensemble; LPO; Raymond Leppard.
    Erato STU 71090 (also Musical Heritage Society MHS 3967)
        ++FF 1/2-80 p107   +MM 12-78 p28
        +Gr 5-78 p1865   +-MT 2-79 p134
        +HFN 5-78 p135   +RR 7-78 p53
    A midsummer night's dream, opp. 21/61: Overture. See no. 2158. See
        no. 3688
2126 A midsummer night's dream, opp. 21/61: Overture; Scherzo; March of
    the fairies; Ye spotted snakes; Intermezzo; Nocturne; Wedding
    march; Funeral march; Dance of the clowns; Finale. Edith Mathis,
    s; Ursula Boese, con; Bavarian Radio Orchestra and Chorus; Rafael
    Kubelik. DG 2535 393 Tape (c) 3334 393
        +-HFN 6-80 p115   /RR 6-80 p55
        +HFN 9-80 p116 tape
    A midsummer night's dream, op. 21/61: Overture; Scherzo; Wedding
    march. See no. 2899

A midsummer night's dream, opp. 21/61: Scherzo. See no. 3860

2127 Motets (3). Psalms (2). Bernius Stuttgart Chamber Choir. Spectrum
    Tape (r) B-C D 103
          +HF 7-80 p82 tape

2128 Octet, op. 20, E flat major. SPOHR: Quartet, op. 65, D minor.
    Melos Ensemble. Arabesque 8017
          +FF 11/12-80 p135   +-NR 10-80 p7

2129 Octet, op. 20, E flat major. Israel Philharmonic Orchestra Strings;
    Zubin Mehta. Decca SXDL 7506 Tape (c) KSXDC 7506 (also London
    LDR 10009)
          +-Gr 9-80 p334   +HFN 9-80 p105
          +Gr 12-80 p889 tape

2130 Octet, op. 20, E flat major. Quintet, strings, no. 2, op. 87, B
    flat major. AMF Chamber Ensemble. Philips 9500 616
          +-FF 7/8-80 p110   +-NR 8-80 p9
          +Gr 3-80 p1404   +RR 2-80 p64
          +HFN 2-80 p95   ++St 7-80 p81
          +-MT 5-80 p322   +STL 3-9-80 p41
          +-MT 7-80 p445

2131 Octet, op. 20, E flat major.* SCHUBERT: Trio, strings, no. 2, D
    581, B flat major. Trio, strings, no. 1, D 471, B flat major.
    Bamberg Symphony Chamber Music Ensemble, Bell'Arte String Trio.
    Turnabout TVC 37011 Tape (c) CT 7011 (*From 34403)
          +-FF 3/4-80 p119

On wings of song, op. 34, no. 2. See no. 3785. See no. 3964

Pieces, string quartet, op. 81 (4). See no. 2135

Prelude and fugue, D minor. See no. 153

Prelude and fugue, op. 35, E minor. See no. 893

Preludes and fugues, op. 37, C minor, G major, D minor. See no. 4023

2132 Preludes and fugues, op. 37, nos. 1-3. REUBKE: Sonata on the 94th
    psalm. Martin Hasselbock, org. Pape 203
          +-FF 7/8-80 p169

Psalms (2). See no. 2127

2133 Quartets, strings, nos. 1, 4-6. Bartholdy Quartet. Acanta HA
    21966 (2)
          +Gr 10-80 p511   +-RR 4-80 p87
          +-HFN 6-80 p108

Quartet, strings, no. 1, op. 12, E flat major: Canzonetta. See no.
    3549. See no. 3775

Quartet, strings, no. 2, op. 13, E flat major. See no. 2118

2134 Quartet, strings, no. 3, op. 44, D major. Quartet, strings, no. 6,
    op. 80, F minor. Bartholdy Quartet. Acanta DC 229 130
          ++HFN 8-80 p98   ++RR 8-80 p63

2135 Quartet, strings, no. 4, op. 44, no. 2, E minor. Pieces, string
    quartet, op. 81 (4). Gabrieli Quartet. London STS 15397
          ++FF 1/2-80 p106

Quartet, strings, no. 4, op. 44, E minor. See no. 2118

Quartet, strings, no. 6, op. 80, F minor. See no. 985. See no.
    2134

2136 Quintet, strings, no. 1, op. 18, A major. Quintet, strings, no. 2,
    op. 87, B flat major. Vienna Philharmonia Quintet. Decca SDD
    562
          +-Gr 10-80 p512   +HFN 10-80 p106

Quintet, strings, no. 2, op. 87, B flat major. See no. 488. See
    no. 2130. See no. 2136

Romanze. See no. 2169

Rondo capriccioso, op. 14, E major. See no. 893

Ruy Blas overture, op. 95. See no. 2149. See no. 2158

Sextet, op. 110, D major. See no. 773

2137 Sonata, clarinet and piano. REGER: Sonata, clarinet and piano, op.
49, no. 2, F sharp minor. John Russo, clt; Lydia Walton Ignacio,
pno. Crystal S 334

     +—Audio 11-80 p85   +NYT 12-2-79 pD22

     +FF 1/2-80 p107   +SFC 8-5-79 p53

     +—NR 6-79 p9

2138 Sonata, organ, op. 65, no. 1, F major. MOZART: Fantasia, K 608, F
minor. SCHUMANN: Sketches, op. 58. Thomas Murray, org. Vista
VPS 1069

     +MT 11-80 p712   +—RR 4-80 p99

Sonata, organ, op. 65, no. 2, C minor. See no. 3735. See no. 3742

2139 Sonata, violin and piano, no. 1, op. 4, F minor. Sonata, violin
and piano, no. 2, F major. Oliver Steiner, vln; Barry Snyder,
pno. Orion ORS 79339

     +FF 1/2-80 p107   +—HF 9-80 p96

Sonata, violin and piano, no. 2, F major. See no. 2139

2140 Sonata, violoncello and piano, no. 1, op. 45, B flat major. Sonata,
violoncello and piano, no. 2, op. 58, D major. Frederic Lodeon,
vlc; Daria Hovora, pno. Erato STU 70967

     +—HFN 10-79 p157   +RR 4-80 p98

Sonata, violoncello and piano, no. 2, op. 58, D major. See no. 2140

2141 Songs: Psalms, no. 42, op. 42, Wie der Hirsch schreit; no. 95, op.
46, Kommt lasst uns anbeten. Christiane Baumann, Joana Silva, s;
Pierre-Andre Blaser, t; Gulbenkian Foundation Symphony Orchestra
and Chorus; Michel Corboz. Erato STU 71101 (also Musical Heritage Society MHS 4185)

     ++ARG 10-79 p44   +HFN 7-78 p97

     ++FF 9/10-79 p106   −MT 2-79 p134

     +—FF 11/12-80 p136   +NYT 10-7-79 pD24

     +Gr 7-78 p236   +RR 7-78 p87

     +HF 11-79 p102

2142 Songs: Psalm, no. 115, op. 31, Nicht unsern Namen Herr; Psalm, no.
98, op. 91, Singet dem Herrn ein neues Lied; Lauda Sion, op. 73.
Evelyn Brunner, s; Naoko Ihara, con; Alejandro Ramirez, t; Philippe Huttenlocher, bar; Gulbenkian Foundation Symphony Orchestra
and Chorus; Michel Corboz. Erato STU 71223

     +Gr 10-79 p689   +—MT 6-80 p383

     +HFN 10-79 p157   +RR 10-79 p137

2143 Songs: Allnachtlich im Traume seh ich dich, op. 86, no. 4; Auf Flugeln des Gesanges, op. 34, no. 2; Bei der Wiege, op. 47, no. 6;
Das erste Veilchen, op. 19, no. 2; Fruhlingslied, op. 47, no. 3;
Herbstlied, op. 84, no. 2; Die Liebende schreibt, op. 86, no. 3;
Des Madchens Klage; Neue Liebe, op. 19, no. 4; Der Mond, op. 86,
no. 5; Romanze, op. 8, no. 10; Schilflied, op. 71, no. 4; Suleika,
op. 34, no. 4; Venetianisches Gondellied, op. 57, no. 5; Songs
without words, op. 30, no. 6; op. 53, no. 2; op. 62, no. 1; op.
67, no. 5. Annette Celine, s; Felicja Blumenthal, pno. Everest
3458

     −FF 5/6-80 p106

Songs, op. 48 (6). See no. 854

Songs: Allnachtlich in Traume, op. 86, no. 4; Auf Flugeln des Ge-

sanges, op. 34, no. 2; Bei der Wiege, op. 47, no. 6; Das erste
Veilchen, op. 19a, no. 2; Fruhlingslied; Herbstlied, op. 63, no.
4; Die Liebende schreibt, op. 86, no. 3; Madchens Klage; Der
Mond, op. 86, no. 5; Neue Liebe, op. 19a, no. 4; Schilflied, op.
71, no. 4; Songs without words, no. 4, F sharp minor; Suleika,
op. 57, no. 3; Venezianisches Gondolied, op. 57, no. 5. See no.
See no. 2169
Songs: Auf Flugeln des Gesanges, op. 34, no. 2. See no. 3573
Songs: Hear my prayer, op. 39, no. 1; O for the wings of a dove.
See no. 3938
Songs (choral): Lauda Sion, op. 73. See no. 970
2144 Songs without words, op. 19, nos. 1, 5-6; op. 30, nos. 3-4, 6; op.
38, nos. 2-3, 5; op. 53, nos. 2-3; op. 62, nos. 1, 5-6; op. 67,
nos. 2, 4-6; op. 85, nos. 3, 6; op. 102, nos. 1, 4, 6. Daniel
Barenboim, pno. DG 2531 260

> +Gr 8-80 p242   ++RR 7-80 p81
> +-HFN 7-80 p117   +St 12-80 p129
> ++NR 11-80 p9   +STL 7-13-80 p38

Songs without words, op. 30, E flat major. See no. 2169
Songs without words, op. 30, no. 1; op. 38, no. 2; op. 53, no. 4;
op. 85, no. 3. See no. 624
Songs without words, op. 30, no. 6, F minor. See no. 3626
Songs without words, op. 30, no. 6; op. 53, no. 2; op. 62, no. 1;
op. 67, no. 5. See no. 2143
Songs without words, op. 67, no. 4, C major: Spinning song. See
no. 519
Sweet remembrance. See no. 3964
2145 Symphonies, nos. 1-5. Celestina Casapietra, Adele Stolte, s; Peter
Schreier, t; Leipzig Radio Chorus; Leipzig Gwandhaus Orchestra;
Kurt Masur. Vanguard VCS 10133/6 (4) Tape (r) Z 10133

> +-ARG 10-78 p31   ++HF 2-79 p92 tape
> +Audio 12-78 p128   +MJ 11-78 p27
> +-Audio 6-80 p43   +NR 6-78 p2
> +FF 9/10-78 p75   ++SFC 4-23-78 p50
> +HF 10-78 p98   +St 11-78 p124

2146 Symphony, no. 1, op. 11, C minor. Symphony, no. 2, op. 52, B flat
major. Helen Donath, Rotraud Hansmann, s; Waldemar Kmentt, t;
NPhO and Chorus; Wolfgang Sawallisch. Philips 6768 030 (3)
(From AXS 4004)

> +Gr 10-79 p643   +-MT 4-80 p252
> +HFN 10-79 p169   +RR 10-79 p93

2147 Symphony, no. 1, op. 11, C minor. Symphony, no. 4, op. 90, A major.
LPO; Bernard Haitink. Philips 9500 708 Tape (c) 7300 803

> +-ARG 10-80 p45   +HFN 9-80 p116
> /FF 9/10-80 p161   +-NR 7-80 p4
> /Gr 6-80 p37   +-RR 6-80 p54
> +HF 9-80 p91   +SFC 7-6-80 p27
> +HFN 6-80 p108   +St 10-80 p117

2148 Symphony, no. 2, op. 52, B flat major. Symphony, no. 3, op. 56, A
minor. Margaret Price, Sally Burgess, s; Siegfried Jerusalem, t;
LPO and Chorus, LSO; Riccardo Chailly. Philips 6769 042 (2)
Tape (c) 7699 128

> +-Gr 12-80 p835   +HFN 12-80 p141

Symphony, no. 2, op. 52, B flat major. See no. 2123. See no. 2146
2149 Symphonies, nos. 3-5. Ruy Blas overture, op. 95. NPhO; Wolfgang

Sawallisch. Philips 6768 031 (2) (From AXS 4004) (also Philips
6770 027 Tape (c) 7650 027)

+-ARG 9-80 p32   +HFN 11-79 p153
++FF 7/8-80 p110   +-NR 4-80 p4
+-Gr 11-79 p827   +-RR 11-79 p85

2150 Symphony, no. 3, op. 56, A minor. Hebrides overture, op. 26. Scot-
    tish National Orchestra; Alexander Gibson. Classics for Pleasure
    CFP 40270 Tape (c) TC CFP 40270

+-Gr 10-77 p636   +RR 10-77 p48
/-HFN 10-77 p157   +RR 2-78 p50
+HFN 8-80 p109 tape

2151 Symphony, no. 3, op. 56, A minor. Athalia, op. 74: War march of
    the priests. VPO; Christoph von Dohnanyi. Decca SXL 6954 Tape
    (c) KSXC 6954

+-Gr 7-80 p141   +-RR 7-80 p57
+HFN 7-80 p109

2152 Symphony, no. 3, op. 56, A minor. Hebrides overture, op. 26. Is-
    rael Philharmonic Orchestra; Leonard Bernstein. DG 2531 256
    Tape (c) 3301 256

+Gr 9-80 p335   +-HFN 10-80 p106
+Gr 12-80 p889 tape   +-HFN 11-80 p131 tape

2153 Symphony, no. 3, op. 56, A minor. Hebrides overture, op. 26. St.
    John's Orchestra; John Lubbock. Enigma K 53588

+-Gr 1-80 p1152   -HFN 5-80 p122

2154 Symphony, no. 3, op. 56, A minor. Clam sea and prosperous voyage,
    op. 27. LPO; Bernard Haitink. Philips 9500 535 Tape (c) 7300
    678   +ARG 9-80 p32   +-NR 6-80 p5
             +HF 9-80 p91   ++SFC 3-2-80 p41

    Symphony, no. 3, op. 56, A minor. See no. 2148

2155 Symphony, no. 4, op. 90, A major. Overtures: Calm sea and prosper-
    ous voyage, op. 27. Hebrides, op. 26. VPO; Christoph von Doh-
    nanyi. Decca SXDL 7500 Tape (c) KSXDC 7500 (also London LDR
    10003)

+Audio 12-79 p99   +HFN 7-79 p107
+-FF 11/12-79 p15   +HFN 10-79 p171 tape
+-FU 6-80 p45   +NR 4-80 p2
+Gr 7-79 p206   +RR 8-79 p85
+-Gr 10-79 p727 tape   ++SFC 7-29-79 p49
+HF 10-79 p98 tape   ++St 10-79 p142

2156 Symphony, no. 4, op. 90, A major. Symphony, no. 5, op. 107, D minor.
    Israel Philharmonic Orchestra; Leonard Bernstein. DG 2531 097
    Tape (c) 3301 097

+FF 9/10-80 p161   +NR 4-80 p5
++Gr 11-79 p828   +NYT 12-9-79 pD25
+-HF 4-80 p91   +RR 11-79 p85
++HFN 11-79 p141   +St 4-80 p132

2157 Symphony, no. 4, op. 90, A major. SCHUBERT: Symphony, no. 8, D 759,
    B minor. BPhO; Herbert von Karajan. DG 2531 291 Tape (c) 3301
    291

+-HFN 9-80 p115

2158 Symphony, no. 4, op. 90, A major. Overtures: Hebrides, op. 26. A
    midsummer night's dream, opp. 21/61. Ruy Blas, op. 95. LSO;
    Andre Previn. HMV ASD 3763 Tape (c) TC ASD 3763 (also Angel SZ
    37614)

+ARG 9-80 p32   +NR 3-80 p3
+-HF 9-80 p91   ++SFC 2-24-80 p39

+HFN 1-80 p123 tape   +St 4-80 p132
2159 Symphony, no. 4, op. 90, A major. Symphony, no. 5, op. 107, D min-
     or. CPhO; Gaetano Delogu. Quintessence PMC 7121 (also Supraphon
     110 2430)
                    -ARG 1-80 p36   +-NR 3-80 p3
                    +-FF 9/10-80 p162   +St 4-80 p132
2160 Symphony, no. 4, op. 90, A major.* SCHUBERT: Symphony, no. 8, D
     759, B minor. PhO; Guido Cantelli. World Records SH 290 (*From
     ALP 1325)
                    ++ARSC Vol 12, no. 1-2, 1980 p117
                    +Gr 6-79 p48
     Symphony, no. 4, op. 90, A major. See no. 2147
2161 Symphony, no. 5, op. 107, D major. SCHUMANN: Symphony, no. 1, op.
     38, B flat major. PhO; Riccardo Muti. HMV SQ ASD 3781 Tape (c)
     TC ASD 3781 (also Angel SZ 37601)
                    +-Gr 10-79 p643   +-NYT 5-11-80 pD24
                    +-HFN 11-79 p141   +RR 10-79 p104
                    +-HFN 1-80 p123 tape   ++SFC 7-20-80 p34
                    +NR 7-80 p3   +St 11-80 p94
2162 Symphony, no. 5, op. 107, D minor. Hebrides overture, op. 26. LPO;
     Bernard Haitink. Philips 9500 713 Tape (c) 7300 804
                    ++FF 11/12-80 p136   ++St 11-80 p94
                    +NR 9-80 p2
     Symphony, no. 5, op. 107, D minor. See no. 2156. See no. 2159
2163 Symphonies, strings, nos. 6-7, 10. Baden Baden Ensemble 13; Manfred
     Reichert. Harmonia Mundi 1C 065 99823
                    +-Gr 4-80 p1557   +-RR 4-80 p68
                    +HFN 3-80 p93   +-ST 6-80 p118
     Symphony, strings, no. 12, G minor. See no. 2122
2164 Trio, piano, no. 1, op. 49, D minor. Trio, piano, no. 2, op. 66,
     C minor. Anne Quéffelec, pno; Pierre Amoyal, vln; Frederic
     Lodeon, vlc. Erato STU 71025
                    +HFN 9-79 p108   +RR 4-80 p87
2165 Trio, piano, no. 1, op. 49, D minor. SCHUMANN: Trio, piano, no. 1,
     op. 63, D minor. Kyung-Wha Chung, vln; Paul Tortelier, vlc;
     Andre Previn, pno. HMV ASD 3894 Tape (c) TC ASD 3894
                    +Gr 9-80 p360   +STL 11-9-80 p40
                    +HFN 9-80 p105
2166 Trio, piano, no. 1, op. 49, D minor. Trio, piano, no. 2, op. 66,
     C minor. Ravel Trio. Musical Heritage Society MHS 4094
                    ++FF 5/6-80 p106
2167 Trio, piano, no. 1, op. 49, D minor. Trio, piano, no. 2, op. 66,
     C minor. Beaux Arts Trio. Philips 6570 075 Tape (c) 7310 075
     (From SAL 3646)
                    ++Gr 3-80 p1404   +HFN 10-80 p117 tape
                    +HFN 2-80 p105   ++RR 3-80 p74
2168 Trio, piano, no. 1, op. 49, D minor. Trio, piano, no. 2, op. 66, C
     minor. Haydn Trio, Vienna. Telefunken 6-42351
                    +FF 9/10-80 p162
     Trio, piano, no. 1, op. 49, D minor. See no. 1347
     Trio, piano, no. 1, op. 49, D minor: Scherzo. See no. 3964
     Trio, piano, no. 2, op. 66, C minor. See no. 2164. See no. 2166.
     See no. 2167. See no. 2168
     Variations serieuses, op. 54, D minor. See no. 618
     Wedding march. See no. 3624. See no. 3663

2169 Works, selections: Romanze. Songs without words, op. 30, E flat
        major. Songs: Allnachtlich in Traume, op. 86, no. 4; Auf Flu-
        geln des Gesanges, op. 34, no. 2; Bei der Wiege, op. 47, no. 6;
        Das erste Veilchen, op. 19a, no. 2; Fruhlingslied; Herbstlied,
        op. 63, no. 4; Die Liebende schreibt, op. 86, no. 3; Madchens
        Klage; Der Mond, op. 86, no. 5; Neue Liebe, op. 19a, no. 4;
        Schilflied, op. 71, no. 4; Songs with words, no. 4, F sharp min-
        or; Suleika, op. 57, no. 3; Venezianisches Gondolied, op. 57,
        no. 5. Annette Celine, s; Felicja Blumenthal, pno. Everest SDBR
        3456
                +NR 6-80 p11
MENDELSSOHN-HENSEL, Fanny
    Prelude, E minor. See no. 4024
    Trio, op. 11, D minor. See no. 4065
MENDEZ
    La virgin de la macarena. See no. 4043
MENOTTI, Giancarlo
2170 The medium. The telephone. Marie Powers, Evelyn Keller, Beverly
        Dame, Marilyn Cotlow; Frank Rogier; Orchestra; Emanuel Balaban.
        Odyssey Y2 35239 (2)
                +FF 5/6-80 p107   +SFC 1-6-80 p43
2171 The old maid and the thief. Judith Blegen, Margaret Baker, s; Anna
        Reynolds, ms; John Reardon, bar; Trieste Teatro Verdi Orchestra;
        Jorge Mester. Turnabout TV 34745 Tape (c) CT 2256
                ++FU 4-80 p47
2172 The telephone. THEMMEN: Shelter this candle from the wind. Paula
        Seibel, s; Robert Orth, bar; Louisville Orchestra; Jorge Mester.
        Louisville LS 767
                +FF 5/6-80 p107   +St 4-80 p135
    The telephone. See no. 2170
2173 The unicorn, the gorgon and the manticore. Michigan University
        Chamber Choir; Instrumental Ensemble; Thomas Hilbish. University
        of Michigan School of Music SM 0012
                +ARG 11-80 p26   +St 8-80 p96
                +FF 7/8-80 p111
MERCADANTE, Guiseppe Saverio
2174 Concerto, clarinet, op. 101, B flat major. MOLTER: Concerto, clari-
        net, D major. PLEYEL: Concerto, clarinet, C major. Thomas
        Friedli, clt; Southwest German Symphony Orchestra; Paul Angerer.
        Claves D 813
                +HFN 11-79 p149   ++RR 4-80 p75
    Concerto, clarinet, op. 101, B major. See no. 777
    Concerto, flute, E minor. See no. 739
    Sinfonia on themes from Rossini's "Stabat mater". See no. 758
MERCURE, Pierre
    Kaleidoscope. See no. 449
MERIKANTO, Oskar
    Passacaglia, op. 80. See no. 3726
    Songs: Laula tytto; Liknelse; Tule. See no. 1880
MERILAINEN, Usko
    Concerto, piano, no. 2. See no. 2175
2175 Symphony, no. 3. Concerto, piano, no. 2. Rhondda Gillespie, pno;
        Finnish Radio Orchestra, Helsinki Philharmonic Orchestra; Jiri
        Belohlavek, Ulf Soderblom. Finlandia FA 305
                +ARG 11-80 p27   +-NR 10-80 p2
                +FF 5/6-80 p108   +-RR 2-80 p58

MERULA, Tarquinio
    Canzona IV. See no. 3846
    Capriccio. See no. 3846
    No ch'io non mi fido. See no. 3878
    Sonata cromatica. See no. 3846
    Toccata on the 2nd tone. See no. 3762
MERULO, Claudio
    Toccata quarta del 6 tono. See no. 4021
MESSAGER, Andre
    Fortunio: J'aimais le vieille maison grise; Si vous croyez. See
       no. 3774
    Songs: Si j'avais vos ailes. See no. 3770
    Veronique: Adieu je pars. See no. 3770
MESSIAEN, Oliver
    Les corps glorieux: Joie et clarte des corps glorieux. See no.
       3940
    Diptyque. See no. 4063
    La merle noir. See no. 765. See no. 3594. See no. 3714. See no.
       4017
    La nativite du Seigneur: Les anges; Dieu parmi nous. See no. 3836
    La nativite du Seigneur: Desseins eternels. See no. 4061
    La nativite du Seigneur: Dieu parmi nous. See no. 4047
2176 Quartet for the end of time. Ruben Yordanoff, vln; Albert Tetard,
      vlc; Claude Desurmont, clt; Daniel Barenboim, pno. DG 2531 093

+-ARG 6-80 p24	++HFN 8-79 p107
+FF 7/8-80 p111	+-MM 8-79 p30
+FU 12-79 p46	+MT 1-80 p35
+-Gr 8-79 p348	++NR 3-80 p7
+-HF 4-80 p92	+RR 8-79 p26

    Rechants (5). See no. 3713
    Theme and variations. See no. 1374
MEYER, Hannes
    Schanfigger Bauernhochzeit. See no. 3626
    Zu Ehren d'Alphorns. See no. 3626
MEYER, Krzysztof
    Concerto, violin, op. 12. See no. 1162
    Quartettino. See no. 3857
MEYERBEER, Giacomo
    L'Africaine: Adieu mon beau rivage; Pays merveilleux...O paradis;
      Wie hat mein Herz amato; Von hier seh ich das Meer. See no.
      3774
    L'Africaine: Adieu mon doux rivage; Sur mes genoix; O grand St. Dom-
      inique. See no. 3630
    L'Africaine: Figlia di regi. See no. 3982
    L'Africaine: Figlia di regi; Quando amor accende; Schlummer aire.
      See no. 3770
    L'Africaine: Land so wunderbar. See no. 3641
    L'Africaine: Mi batte il cor...O paradiso. See no. 3671. See no.
      3945
    L'Africaine: O paradiso. See no. 1491. See no. 3827. See no.
      3900. See no. 4008
    L'Africaine: O paradiso; Combien tu m'es chere; Erreur fatal. See
      no. 1583
2177 Dinorah. Deborah Cook, s; Della Jones, ms; Alexander Oliver, t;

Christian du Plessis, bar; PhO; James Judd.   Opera Rara OR 5 (3)
            +ARG 10-80 p23   +ON 8-80 p36
            +FF 9/10-80 p163   +–Op 9-80 p911
            +–Gr 8-80 p266   +RR 7-80 p20
            +NYT 6-29-80 pD20   +STL 6-8-80 p38
Dinorah: En chasse. See no. 3872
Dinorah: Les bles sont beaux a faucher. See no. 1583
Dinorah: Ombra leggiera. See no. 3695. See no. 3789. See no. 3886
Dinorah: Schattentanz. See no. 3770
Dinorah: Sei vendicata assai; Scena e canzonetta del capraio. See
    no. 3774
L'Etoile du nord: Cadenza. See no. 3770
L'Etoile du nord: O jours heureux. See no. 3631. See no. 3979
L'Etoile du nord: Peter's romance. See no. 3930
Les Huguenots: Ah qual soave vision...Bianca al par di neve alpina.
    See no. 3946
Les Huguenots: Bianca al par. See no. 4008
Les Huguenots: No no giammai; Plus blanche que la blanche ermine.
    See no. 3770
Les Huguenots: Nobles seigneurs salut. See no. 3886
Les Huguenots: Nobles seigneurs; Ihr Wagenpaar. See no. 3774
Les Huguenots: Plus blanche que la blanche hermine. See no. 1583
Les Huguenots: Seigneur rampart et seul soutine; Piff paff. See
    no. 3631
Le prophete: Ach mein Sohn; Sopra Berta. See no. 3770
Le prophete: Donnez donnez pour un pauvre ame; Non non...O toi que
    m'abandonnes; Air de Baal; Church scene. See no. 3774
Le prophete: Roi du ciel; Pour Bertha moi je souspire. See no. 1583
Robert le diable: Evocazione; Sicilienne; Valse infernale. See no.
    3770
Robert le diable: Invocation. See no. 3774. See no. 3979
Robert le diable: Le rovine son queste...Suore che riposte. See
    no. 3899
Robert le diable: Nonnes qui reposez. See no. 3631
Robert le diable: Va dit-elle va mon enfant; Robert toi que j'aime.
    See no. 3630
MIASKOVSKY, Nikolai
    Pieces, piano, op. 36 (2). See no. 2178
2178 Symphony, no. 11, op. 34, B flat minor. Pieces, piano, op. 36 (2).
     MSO; Veronika Dudarova. Melodiya 33C 10 09483/4 (also HMV ASD
     3879)
                +ARG 12-79 p33   +–RR 8-80 p48
                +–FF 1/2-80 p108   +–HFN 8-80 p98
                +Gr 9-80 p335
2179 Symphony, no. 15, op. 38, D minor. MPO; Kiril Kondrashin. Melo-
     diya 33S 08010-2
                +–FF 7/8-80 p112
2180 Symphony, no. 22, op. 54, B minor. SVETLANOV: Festive poem, op. 9.
     USSR Symphony Orchestra; Yevgeny Svetlanov. HMV ASD 3062 (also
     Melodiya 33CM 03157-58)
                +FF 3/4-80 p119   +MT 9-75 p799
                +–Gr 4-75 p1808   +–RR 4-75 p28
MIDDLETON, John
    Fantasie. See no. 4052

MIKULI, Karol
    Etude. See no. 3850
    Lied. See no. 3850
MILAN, Luis de
    Fantasia. See no. 3917
    Fantasias, nos. 1-3. See no. 3540
2181 Fantasias, nos. 7, 9, 16, 22. Pavanas, nos. 1, 4-6. Tiento, no. 1.
       NARVAEZ: Los seys libros del Delphin de musica, Bk 1: Fantasia,
       no. 5; Bk 2: Fantasias, nos. 5-6; Bk 3: La cancion del Empera-
       dor; Bk 4: O glorioso domina: Variations (6); Bk 5: Arde coracon
       arde ya se asiente el Rey Ramiro; Bk 6: Conde claros, Guardame
       las vacas, Tres diferencias por otra parte, Baxa de contrapunto.
       Julian Bream, lt. RCA ARL 1-3435 Tape (c) RK 1-3435
               +ARG 6-80 p49   ++HF 4-80 p104 tape
               +FF 1/2-80 p109   ++HFN 1-80 p117
               +FF 9/10-80 p272   +NR 8-80 p15
               +Gr 1-80 p1172
    Fantasia de redobles. See no. 3577
    Pavanas. See no. 3917. See no. 3975
    Pavanas, no. 1. See no. 3600
    Pavanas, nos. 1, 4-6. See no. 2181
    Tiento, no. 1. See no. 2181
    Tiento, no. 4. See no. 3577
MILANDRE, L.
    Andantino and menuetto, D major. See no. 47
MILANO, Francesco da
    Fantasia. See no. 3683
    Pescatore que va cantando. See no. 3612
    Ricercare. See no. 3593. See no. 3683
    Ricercare, nos. 1 and 2. See no. 3577
    Ricercare "La campagna". See no. 3577. See no. 3612
MILCHBERG/ROBLES/SIMON
    El candor pasa. See no. 3909
MILHAUD, Darius
2182 Carnaval a la Nouvelle Orleans. Concerto, 2 pianos. Scaramouche,
       op. 165b. Joan Yarbrough, Robert Cowan, pno; RPO; Paul Freeman.
       Orion ORS 78297 Tape (c) OC 820
               +ARG 11-78 p29   +NR 11-78 p6
               +FF 11/12-78 p88   +NR 9-80 p7 tape
    Catalogue de fleurs. See no. 3862
2183 La cheminee de Roi Rene, op. 205. Divertissement en trois parties,
       op. 299b. Pastorale, op. 147. Sketches, op. 227b (2). Suite
       d'apres Corette, op. 161b. Athena Ensemble. Chandos ABR 1012
       Tape (c) ABT 1012
               ++Gr 8-80 p239   +HFN 11-80 p121
               +Gr 12-80 p889 tape   +RR 8-80 p63
               +HFN 10-80 p117 tape
    La cheminee de Roi Rene, op. 205. See no. 1782
    Concerto, 2 pianos. See no. 2182
    La creation du monde. See no. 3955
    Divertissement en trois parties, op. 299b. See no. 2183
    Pastorale, op. 147. See no. 2183
    Poemes de Leo Latil (4). See no. 3862
    Saudades do Brasil: Corcovado. See no. 3964
    Saudades do Brasil: Sumare. See no. 3964

Scaramouche, op. 165b. See no. 2182
Sketches, op. 227b. See no. 2183
Suite d'apres Corrette, op. 161b. See no. 2183
Le train bleu. See no. 64. See no. 3908
MILLER
When I survey the wondrous cross. See no. 3531
MILLOCKER, Carl
2184 Der Bettelstudent. Rita Streich, Renate Holm, s; Nicolai Gedda, t;
     Gerhard Unger, t; Hermann Prey, bar; Bavarian Radio Orchestra;
     Franz Allers. Arabesque 8065-2 (2)
                    +NR 12-80 p9   +SFC 12-7-80 p33
                    +ON 12-20-80 p52
MILNER, Anthony
Love is his word. See no. 3531
MILVEDEN
Barn av Guds karlek. See no. 3934
MIMAROGLU, Ilhan
Rosa. See no. 3727
MISSA, Edmond de
Muguette: Entr'acte. See no. 4071
MIYAGI, Michio
Haru no umi. See no. 3951
MODERNE, Jacques
Branles de Bourgogne (3). See no. 3754
Branles gay nouveau. See no. 3754
MOERAN, Ernest
Ludlow town: When smoke stood up from Ludlow; Farewell to barn and
     stack and tree; Say lad have you things to do; The lads in their
     hundreds. See no. 3837
Songs: Tis time I think by Wenlock town. See no. 3837
MOEVS, Robert
Una collana musicale, nos. 2, 5-6, 10-12. See no. 1164
Fantasia sopra un motivo. See no. 1164
Phoenix. See no. 1164
MOLINARO, Simone
Ballo detto "Il Conte Orlando". See no. 3966
Fantasia. See no. 3966
Saltarellos (2). See no. 3966
MOLLEDA, Jose Munoz
Triptico. See no. 1487
MOLLOY
The Kerry dance. See no. 3875
MOLTER, Johann
Concerto, clarinet, D major. See no. 2174
2185 Concerto, clarinet, no. 4, A major. STAMITZ, C.: Concerto, clari-
     net, E flat major. STAMITZ, J.: Concerto, clarinet and 2 horns,
     B flat major. Laszlo Horvath, clt; Liszt Ferenc Chamber Orchest-
     ra; Janos Rolla. Hungaroton SLPX 11954
                    ++ARG 6-79 p44   +NR 7-79 p6
                    +FF 1/2-80 p109
Concerto, trumpet, D major. See no. 1678
MOMPOU, Federico
Cancion y danza, no. 1. See no. 3976
Song and dance, no. 3. See no. 1472

MONCAYO, Jose
    Huapango. See no. 1025
MONDONVILLE, Jean-Joseph Cassanea de
2186 Songs: Benefac Domine; Domino laudabitur; Cantate Deo; In decachordo
    psalterio; In Domino laudabitur; Laudate Dominum; Paratum cor
    meum; Protector meus; Quare tristis es; Regna terrae; Spera in
    Deo. Judith Nelson, s; William Christie, hpd; Stanley Ritchie,
    vln; Harmonia Mundi HM 1045
             +FF 11/12-80 p136   /-HFN 8-80 p99
             +-Gr 7-80 p158
    Tambourikne. See no. 3642
MONIUSZKO, Stanislaw
    The haunted castle: The clock scene. See no. 3774
    The haunted castle: Polonaise. See no. 3770
MONK, Meredith
2187 Songs frm the hill. Tablet. Meredith Monk, Monica Solem, Susan
    Kampe, Andrea Goodman, vocals; Meredith Monk, pno; Andrea Good-
    man, recorder. Wergo SM 1022
             +FF 9/10-80 p165
    Tablet. See no. 2187
    MONKS AND TROUBADORS. See no. 3750
MONNIKENDAM, Marius
    Concerto, organ and brass. See no. 1426
MONRO, George
    My lovely Celia. See no. 3778
MONTECLAIR, Michel Pignolet de
    Concerto, flute, no. 12. See no. 3544
MONTEVERDI, Claudio
    Baci soavi e cari. See no. 3744
    Bel pastor. See no. 3879
    Lagrime d'amante al sepolcro dell'amata. See no. 3713
    Lamento della Ninfa. See no. 3744
2188 Madrigals: Ah dolente partita; Al lume delle stelle; Amor che deggio
    far; Chiome d'oro; Damigella tutta bella; Dolci miei sospiri; Ec-
    comi pronta ai baci; Lamento della Ninfa; Non vedro mai le stel-
    le; O come sei gentile; La piaga ch'ho nel core; Sfogava con le
    stelle; Si ch'io vorrei morire. Purcell Consort of Voices; Ray-
    mond Kennlyside, Sydney Humphries, vln; Dennis Nesbitt, vla da
    gamba; James Tyler, flt and chitarrone; Adam Skeaping, violone;
    Andrew Davis, hpd; Grayston Burgess. Argo ZK 66 (From ZRG 668)
             +Gr 5-80 p1705   +-RR 7-80 p91
             +HFN 5-80 p122
2189 Madrigals: Alcun non mi consigli; Ardo e scoprir; Bel pastor; Eccomi
    pronta ai baci; Eri gia tutta mia; Una donna fra l'altre; Lamento
    d'Arianna; Lamento della Ninfa; Ohime ch'io cado; Tu dormi. Mari-
    anne Kweksilber, s; Rene Jacobs, c-t; Marius van Altena, Michiel
    ten Houte de Lange, t; Floris Rommerts, bs; Gustav Leonhardt, hpd
    and cond. RCA RL 3-0390
             +FF 9/10-80 p165
2190 Madrigals, Bk 3. Vocal Ensemble; Raymond Leppard. Philips 9502 008
             ++FF 11/12-79 p101   +-RR 5-80 p96
             +-Gr 3-80 p1427   ++SFC 6-10-79 p45
             +HFN 3-80 p107
2191 Madrigals, Bk 4. Sheila Armstrong, Wendy Eathorne, Lillian Watson,
    s; Alfreda Hodgson, ms; Helen Watts, con; Bernard Dickerson,
    Robert Tear, t; Stafford Dean, Christopher Keyte, bs; Glyndebourne

Opera Chorus; Raymond Leppard. Philips 9502 024 (From 6703 035)
+—HFN 7-80 p109   +RR 7-80 p91
2192 Il ritorno d'Ulisse in patria. Frederica von Stade, s; Ann Murray,
ms; Richard Lewis, Alexander Oliver, t; Richard Stilwell, bar;
Glyndebourne Festival Chorus; LPO; Raymond Leppard. CBS 79332
(2). (also M 35910)
+—Gr 12-80 p878   +Op 12-80 p1214
+HFN 12-80 p141   +SFC 12-7-80 p33
Il ritorno d'Ulisse in patria: Torna torna. See no. 3636
2193 Songs (sacred monodies and motets): Cantate domino; Confitibor tibi
domine; Duo seraphim; Ecce sacrum paratum; Ego flos campi; Exulta
filia Sion; Fugge fugge anima mea; Jubilet; Laudate dominum; Nig-
ra sum; O beatae viae; O bone Jesu; O quam pulchra; Pianto della
Madonna sopra il "Lamento d'Arianna"; Pulchra es; Salve o regina;
Salve regina. Concerto Vocale. Harmonia Mundi HM 1032/3
+FF 9/10-80 p165   +—HFN 5-80 p122
+HF 8-80 p77   +RR 8-80 p84
+Gr 5-80 p1705
Songs: Ahi troppo duro; Quel sguardo sdegnosetto. See no. 631
Songs: Maledetto sia l'aspetto; Ohime Ch'io cado ohime. See no.
3551
MONTGOMERY
Chaser, 2 horns and electronics. See no. 3842
MONTI
Czardas. See no. 3568. See no. 3909. See no. 3998
MONTSALVATGE, Bassols Xavier
2194 Canciones negras (5). STRAUSS, R.: Als mir dein Lied erklang, op.
68, no. 4; Des Dichters Abendgang, op. 47, no. 2; Freundliche
Vision, op. 48, no. 1; Heimliche Aufforderung, op. 27, no. 3;
Ich schwebe, op. 48, no. 2; Ich trage meine Minne, op. 32, no. 1;
Die Nacht, op. 10, no. 3; Ruhe meine Seele, op. 27, no. 1; Schle-
chtes Wetter, op. 69, no. 5; Standchen, op. 17, no. 2; Traum
durch die Dammerung, op. 29, no. 1; Waldseligkeit, op. 49, no. 1;
Wie sollten wir geheim sie halten, op. 19, no. 4; Wiegenlied, op.
41, no. 1; Zueignung, op. 10, no. 1. TURINA: Canto a Sevilla,
op. 37. Montserrat Caballe, s; Alexis Weissenberg, pno. Angel
SZB 3903 (2)
+—ARG 11-80 p48   ++NR 6-80 p11
++FF 7/8-80 p146   +—NYT 3-23-80 pD25
+—HF 8-80 p85   +—ON 9-80 p68
Canciones negras: Punto de habanera. See no. 3551
Songs: Canciones negras. See no. 3698
MOORE, Thomas
Metamorphosis. See no. 1768
MORALES, Cristobal de
2195 Lamentations a 4, 5 and 6. Ensemble A Sei Voci. Le Chant du Monde
LDX 78680
+HFN 8-80 p99   +RR 8-80 p85
Motette Exaltata est Sancta Dei Genetrix. See no. 2196
2196 Quaeramus cum pastoribus. Motette Exaltata est Sancta Dei Genetrix.
Montserrat Capella and Escolania der Benediktirnerabtei; Ireneu
Segarra. Harmonia Mundi 065 99740
+—HFN 7-80 p119   +RR 8-80 p85
+—MT 12-80 p786

MORATH, Max
    Polyragmic. See no. 3679
MOREL, Francois
    Me duele Espana. See no. 637
MORENO, Salvador
    Aztec songs (4). See no. 14
MORGAN, Robert
    Trio, flute, violoncello and harpsichord. See no. 1016
MORLEY, Thomas
    Blow shepherds blow your pipes. See no. 3995
    I saw my ladye weeping. See no. 3877
    Joyne hands. See no. 3675
    Lachrymae pavane and galliard. See no. 4014
    Nolo mortem peccatoris. See no. 3533. See no. 3936
    Now is the month of maying. See no. 3971
    Nun strahlt der Mai den Herzen. See no. 3662
    O mistress mine. See no. 3997
    Songs: April is in my mistress face; Daemon and Phyllis; Fire fire;
       I love alas; Leave this tormenting; My bonny lass; Now is the
       month of maying; O grief; Those dainty daffadillies; Though Phil-
       omela lost her love. See no. 3867
    Songs (madrigals): Fyer fyer April is my mistress face; My bonny
       lass she smileth; Now is the month of maying; Sing we and chant
       it. See no. 3893
    Songs: I go before my darling; My bonny lass she smileth; Sweet
       nymph come to thy lover. See no. 3941
    Thyrsis and Milla. See no. 3719
    Ti edes majus-Fenyek. See no. 3814
2197 The triumps of Oriana. Deller Consort, Morley Consort; Alfred Del-
      ler, David Munrow. Musical Heritage Society MHS 4137 (From Har-
      monia Mundi HMU 4137)
               +FF 7/8-80 p112
    La volta. See no. 3648
    Watership down: Kehaars theme. See no. 3786
    Who is it that this dark night. See no. 3879
    Will ye buy a fine dog. See no. 3995
MOROI, Saburo
2198 Symphony, no. 2. Yomiuri Nippon Symphony Orchestra; Shigenobu Yam-
      aoka. Varese VX 81062
        +-ARG 12-78 p53   +RR 1-80 p81
         +FF 11/12-78 p58   +-St 1-79 p106
         ++HFN 1-80 p107
MOROSS, Jerome
    The big country: Main theme. See no. 4046
2199 Concerto, flute and string quartet. Sonata, piano duet and string
      quartet. Frances Zlotkin, flt; Sahan Arzruni, Ron Gianattosio,
      pno; Richard Sortomme, Benjamin Hudson, vln; Toby Appel, vla;
      Frederick Zlotkin, vlc. Varese VC 81101
        ++ARG 2-80 p40   +HFN 5-80 p122
         +FF 1/2-80 p110   +NR 2-80 p4
         +-Gr 5-80 p1683   +-RR 6-80 p67
         +HF 3-80 p82   +SFC 3-9-80 p39
    Sonata, piano duet and string quartet. See no. 2199
MORTARI, Virgilio
    Canzone. See no. 3892

MORTARO, Antonio
    Canzone. See no. 3813
MORTELMANS, Lodewijk
    Like a singing bird. See no. 3889
MORTENSEN, Finn
    Sonata, flute, op. 6. See no. 2450
MORTON, Robert
    Il sera pour vous conbatu, L'ome arme. See no. 4042
    Songs: N'aray je jamais mieulx; Le souvenir de vous me tue. See
        no. 3880
MORYL, Richard
2200 Das Lied.   THORNE: Set pieces for 13 players (7). Jan DeGaetani,
      ms; New England Contemporary Ensemble; University of Chicago Con-
      temporary Chamber Players; Gerard Schwarz, Ralph Shapey. CRI SD
      397
            +-ARG 10-79 p48   +NR 1-80 p6
            +FF 9/10-79 p108
MOSCHELES, Ignaz
    Duo concertant, op. 87b. See no. 1125
    Etudes, op. 111 (4). See no. 1978
    Grand duo concertante, piano and bassoon. See no. 1300
    Grand duo concertante, op. 20, A major. See no. 1243
MOSS, Katie
    Songs: The floral dance. See no. 3562
MOSS, Lawrence
    Symphonies. See no. 1906
MOSZKOWSKI, Moritz
    En automne, op. 36, no. 4. See no. 2201
    Etincelles, op. 36, no. 6. See no. 2201
2201 Piano works: En automne, op. 36, no. 4. Etincelles, op. 36, no. 6.
      Siciliano, op. 42, no. 2. Stucke, op. 45, no. 2: Guitarre. Val-
      se brillante, A flat major. Virtuoso etudes, op. 72. Ilana
      Vered, pno. Connoisseur Society CS 2023 Tape (c) In Sync C 4040
            +-ARG 5-71 p586   ++SFC 2-13-72 p34
             +Ha 11-71 p145   +SR 3-27-71 p71
            +-MJ 2-72 p14   ++St 6-71 p92
            ++NR 6-71 p11   +NR 9-80 p2
            ++RR 3-75 p50
    Serenade, no. 15. See no. 3872
    Siciliano, op. 42, no. 2. See no. 2201
    Spanish dances, op. 12, no. 2, G minor. See no. 3962
    Stucke, op. 45, no. 2: Guitarre. See no. 2201. See no. 3964
2202 Suite, op. 71, G minor. PROKOFIEV: Sonata, 2 violins, op. 56, C
      major. SHOSTAKOVICH: Duets, violin (3). Itzhak Perlman, Pinchas
      Zukerman, vln; Samuel Sanders, pno. HMV ASD 3861 (also Angel SZ
      37668)
            +-FF 11/12-80 p210   ++NR 8-80 p8
            ++Gr 7-80 p153   +SFC 7-6-80 pD15
            +HFN 7-80 p114   +St 11-80 p97
    Valse brillante, A flat major. See no. 2201
    Virtuoso etudes, op. 72. See no. 2201
MOURET, Jean-Joseph
    Rondeau. See no. 3661
    Sinfonies de fanfares. See no. 3545
    Suite en re. See no. 3736

Symphonies de chasse. See no. 3610

MOUTON, Charles
    Les cabrioles, courante. See no. 4013
    Canarie. See no. 4013
    Gavotte. See no. 4013
    Prelude. See no. 4013
    La princesse, sarabande. See no. 4013
    Tombeau de Gogo, allemande. See no. 4013
    Tombeau de Madame, pavanne. See no. 4013

MOZART, Franz Xavier
    Rondo, E minor. See no. 3885

MOZART, Leopold
2203 Cassation, G major: Toy symphony. PROKOFIEV: Peter and the wolf,
    op. 67. Jacqueline du Pre, narrator; ECO; Daniel Barenboim.
    DG 2531 275 Tape (c) 3371 275
           +-Gr 10-80 p498   +NR 12-80 p2
           +HFN 10-80 p107   +-NYT 12-14-80 pD38
           +-HFN 11-80 p131 tape
2204 Cassation, G major: Toy symphony. MOZART, W.A.: German dances, K
    605 (3). POULENC: The story of Babar the little elephant. Ang-
    ela Rippon, narrator; David Parkhouse, pno; St. John's Orchestra;
    John Lubbock. Enigma 53598
           +Gr 1-80 p1158   +RR 1-80 p84
           +-HFN 1-80 p113
    Cassation, G major: Toy symphony. See no. 1818
2205 Concerto, 2 horns, E flat major. POKORNY: Concerto, 2 horns, F
    major. WITT: Concerto, 2 horns, F major. Hermann Baumann, Mahir
    Cakar, Christoph Kohler, hn; Concerto Amsterdam; Jaap Schroder.
    Acanta DC 22433
           +HFN 5-80 p133   ++RR 3-80 p56
    Concerto, trumpet, D major. See no. 33. See no. 1676. See no.
    1678. See no. 3563
    Concerto, trumpet and horns, D major. See no. 1679
    Sinfonia da caccia, G major. See no. 42
    Sinfonia da camera, D major. See no. 42
    Sinfonia pastorella, A major. See no. 3610

MOZART, Wolfgang Amadeus
2206 Adagio, K 261, E major. Concerto, violin, no. 1, K 207, B flat maj-
    or. Concerto, violin, no. 4, K 218, D major. Rondo, violin,
    K 269, B flat major. Henryk Szeryng, vln; NPhO; Alexander Gib-
    son. Philips 6570 109 Tape (c) 7310 109 (From 6707 011)
           +-Audio 1-80 p116   +HFN 9-80 p116 tape
           /FF 3/4-79 p82   ++NR 2-79 p6
           +-Gr 7-80 p142   ++RR 6-80 p56
           +HFN 7-80 p117
2207 Adagio, K 540, B minor. Adagio and fugue, K 546, C minor. Fantas-
    ias, K 594, K 608, F minor. Eine kleine Gigue, K 574, G major.
    Nicolas Kynaston, org. Mitra OSM 16155
           +HFN 2-80 p95
    Adagio, K 540, B minor. See no. 2323
2208 Adagio and fugue, K 546, C minor. Divertimenti, K 136-138. Sere-
    nade, no. 13, K 525, G major. Scottish Baroque Ensemble; Leonard
    Friedman. Abbey ABY 809
           +Gr 10-79 p644   +MT 2-80 p106
           +HFN 9-79 p108   +-RR 9-79 p94

Adagio and fugue, K 546, C minor. See no. 2207

Alleluja, K 553. See no. 2397

Alma Dei creatoris, K 277. See no. 2397

2209 Andante, K 315, C major. Concerto, flute, no. 1, K 313, G major.
Concerto, flute, no. 2, K 314, D major. Richard Adeney, flt;
ECO; Raymond Leppard. Classics for Pleasure CFP 40072 Tape (c)
CFP 40072
+Gr 7-74 p213   +RR 8-74 p39
+HFN 8-80 p109 tape

2210 Andante, K 315, C major. Concerto, flute, no. 1, K 313, G major.
Concerto, flute, no. 2, K 314, D major. Chang-Kook Kim, flt;
Heidelberg Chamber Orchestra; Bernhard Usedruuf. Da Camera Mag-
na SM 91046
-FF 5/6-80 p111

2211 Andante, K 315, C major. Concerto, flute, no. 1, K 313, G major.
Concerto, flute, no. 2, K 314, D major. Andras Adorjan, flt;
Munich Chamber Orchestra; Hans Stadlmair. Denon OX 7180
+FF 11/12-80 p137   +St 11-80 p96

2212 Andante, K 315, C major. Concerto, flute, no. 1, K 313, G major.
Concerto, flute, no. 2, K 314, D major. Jean-Pierre Rampal, flt;
VSO; Theodor Guschlbauer. Erato STU 70330
+-HFN 4-80 p107   ++RR 10-79 p98

2213 Andante, K 315, C major. Concerto, flute, no. 1, K 313, G major.
Concerto, flute, no. 2, D 314, D major. Jean-Pierre Rampal, flt;
Israel Music Centre Chamber Orchestra; Isaac Stern. Erato STU
71144
+HFN 4-80 p107

2214 Andante, K 315, C major. Concerto, flute, no. 1, K 313, G major.
Concerto, flute, no. 2, K 314, D major. Hubert Barwahser, flt;
LSO; Colin Davis. Philips Tape (c) 7317 195 (also Philips 6570
691 Tape (c) 7310 091. From SAL 3499)
+Gr 10-78 p748   +-HFN 1-80 p123 tape
+Gr 12-79 p1017   +RR 10-78 p117 tape
+HFN 11-79 p157   +RR 11-79 p88

2215 Andante, K 315, C major. Concerto, flute, no. 1, K 313, G major.
Concerto, flute, no. 2, K 314, D major. Aurele Nicolet, flt;
COA; Davis Zinman. Philips 9500 392 Tape (c) 7300 748
+NYT 9-23-79 pD28   ++St 2-80 p128

2216 Andante, K 315, C major. Concerto, flute, no. 1, K 313, G major.
Concerto, flute, no. 2, K 314, D major. Jean-Pierre Rampal, flt;
Jerusalem Music Center Chamber Orchestra; Isaac Stern. RCA ARL
1-3084 (also Erato STU 71144)
+ARG 7-79 p41   +-NR 6-79 p8
+-FF 1/2-80 p112   +-RR 4-80 p68
+Gr 2-80 p1269   +HFN 4-80 p107

Andante, K 315, C major. See no. 25. See no. 2398. See no. 2399.
See no. 3589

Andante, K 616. See no. 2397

Andante with variations, K 501, G major. See no. 2324

2217 Arias: La betulia liberata, K 118: Quel nocchier che in gran procella. Exsultate jubilate, K 165. Grabmusik, K 42: Betracht
dies Herz. Die Schuldigkeit des ersten Gebots, K 35: Ein ergrimmter Lowe brullet; Hat der Schopfer dieses Leben. Vesperae solennes de Dominica, K 321: Laudate Dominum. Vesperae solennes de
Confessore, K 339, E major: Laudate Dominum. Edith Mathis, s;

Hans Otto, org, hpd; Dresden Boys Choir; Dresden State Orchestra;
Bernhard Klee. DG 2530 978 Tape (c) 3300 978
   ++ARG 3-80 p32   +ON 12-13-80 p44
   ++FF 1/2-80 p116   ++RR 8-79 p117
   +Gr 8-79 p367   ++St 1-80 p92
   +HFN 8-79 p107
2218 Arias: Ch'io mi scordi di te...Non temer amato bene, K 505; Vorrei
   spiegarvi o Dio, K 418. Exsultate jubilate, K 165: Alleluia.
   Le nozze di Figaro, K 492: Porgi amor; Voi che sapete; E Susanna
   non vien...Dove sono; Diunse alfin il moment...Deh vieni non
   tardar. Il Re pastore, K 208: L'amero saro costante. Die Zauber-
   erflote, K 620: Ach ich fuhl's. Joan Sutherland, s; National
   Philharmonic Orchestra; Richard Bonynge. London OS 26613 (also
   Decca SXL 6933 Tape (c) KSXC 6933)
   +-FF 11/12-80 p142   +-HFN 11-80 p121
   +-Gr 11-80 p732   +-NYT 6-15-80 pD29
   -HF 9-80 p102   -ON 12-13-80 p44
   Arias: Ich mochte wohl der Kaiser sein, K 539; Manner suchen stets
   zu naschen, K 433; Musst ich auch durch tausend Drachen, K 435;
   Schon lacht der holde Fruhling, K 580; Welch angstliches Beben,
   K 389. See no. 2300
   Arias (concert): Non temer amato bene, K 490; Vorrei spiegarvi oh
   Dio, K 418. See no. 2302
   Ave Maria, K 554. See no. 2397
   Ave verum corpus, K 618. See no. 2310. See no. 2397. See no.
   3524. See no. 3528. See no. 3835. See no. 3938
2219 Bastien and Bastienne, K 50. Brigitte Linder, s; Adolf Dallapozza,
   t; Kurt Moll, bs; Bavarian Symphony Orchestra; Eberhard Schoener.
   Arabesque 8064
   +NR 12-80 p8   +SFC 10-5-80 p21
   La betulia liberata, K 118: Quel nocchier che in gran procella. See
   no. 2217
   Canons. See no. 3741
2220 Cantata, K 619. Songs: Abendempfidung, K 23; An die Freude, K 53;
   An die Freundschaft, K 125; Dans un bois solitaire, K 308; Das
   Lied der Trennung, K 510; Oiseaux si tous les ans, K 307; Riden-
   te la calma, K 152; Sehnsucht nach dem Fruhling, K 596; Das
   Traumbild, K 530; Das Veilchen, K 496; Warnung, K 433; Der Zaub-
   erer, K 472. Gerda Hartman, s; John Whitelaw, fortepiano.
   Pavane ADW 7019
   +HFN 3-80 p95   +RR 4-80 p115
2221 Cassation, no. 2, K 99, B flat major. Divertimento, no. 1, K 63, G
   major. Vienna Mozart Ensemble; Willi Boskovsky. Decca JB 66
   Tape (c) KJBC 66 (From SXL 6500)
   +Gr 11-80 p674   +HFN 10-80 p115
   Ch'io mi scordi di te...Non temer amato bene, K 505. See no. 2218
   Church sonatas, nos. 1-9. See no. 2397
   Church sonatas, no. 14, K 287, C major; K 379, C major. See no.
   1709
   Church sonatas, no. 17, K 336, C major. See no. 1426
2222 La clemenza di Tito, K 621. Julia Varady, Edith Mathis, s; Marga
   Schiml, con; Teresa Berganza, ms; Peter Schreier, t; Theo Adam,
   bs-bar; Leipzig Radio Chorus; Dresden State Orchestra; Karl Bohm.
   DG 2709 092 (3) Tape (c) 3371 049
   +ARG 10-80 p25   +NYT 3-2-80 pD26

++FF 5/6-80 p109
+Gr 9-79 p513
+Gr 9-79 p534 tape
+-HF 8-80 p87 tape
+-HF 10-80 p84
+HFN 11-79 p141
+MT 8-80 p87 tape
++NR 3-80 p11

+OC Fall 1980 p47
+ON 7-90 p37
+Op 1-80 p62
+RR 8-79 p16
++RR 11-79 p58
+RR 6-80 p95 tape
+SFC 2-18-80 p44
+St 5-80 p85

2223 La clemenza di Tito, K 621. Lucia Popp, s; Janet Baker, Yvonne Minton, Frederica von Stade, ms; Stuart Burrows, t; Robert Lloyd, bs; ROHO and Chorus; Colin Davis. Philips 6703 079 (3) Tape (c) 7699 038

+ARG 8-78 p18
++FF 5/6-78 p62
+Gr 11-77 p886
+-Gr 4-78 p1179 tape
+HF 5-78 p83
++HF 6-78 p114 tape
++HF 8-80 p87 tape
+HFN 11-77 p175
+HFN 6-78 p139 tape
++MJ 5-78 p28

+MT 3-78 p246
++NYT 2-19-78 pD17
+-ON 3-18-78 p60
+-Op 3-78 p286
+RR 11-77 p38
+RR 4-78 p107 tape
+RR 7-78 p95 tape
++SFC 2-12-78 p47
++St 5-78 p88

La clemenza di Tito, K 621: Parto parto ma tu ben mio. See no. 1512
La clemenza di Tito, K 621: Torna di Tito a lato; Tu fosti tradito. See no. 1685

2224 Concerto, bassoon, K 191, B flat major. Concerto, clarinet, K 622, A major. Harold Wright, clt; Sherman Walt, bsn; BSO; Seiji Ozawa. DG 2531 254 Tape (c) 3301 254

+ARG 12-80 p39
+-FF 11/12-80 p137
+HFN 5-80 p122
+-NR 6-80 p7

+-NYT 5-4-80 pD24
+RR 6-80 p55
++SFC 8-31-80 p31
++St 7-80 p82

2225 Concerto, bassoon, K 191, B flat major. Concerto, clarinet, K 622, A major. March, K 249, D major. Thamos, King of Egypt, K 345: Entr'acte, no. w. Jack Brymer, clt; Gwydion Brooke, bsn; RPO; Thomas Beecham. HMV SXLP 30246 Tape (c) TC SXLP 30246 (also EMI 1C 037 00176) (From ASD 344, 423, 259)

+ARSC Vol 12, no. 3 1980 p256
++Gr 9-77 p429

+-Gr 11-77 p899 tape
+-HFN 10-77 p167
+RR 9-77 p64

Concerto, bassoon, K 191, B flat major. See no. 2396
Concerto, bassoon, K 191, B flat major: 1st movement, excerpt. See no. 2398

2226 Concerto, clarinet, K 622, A major. Concerto, horn, no. 3, K 447, E flat major. Hans Deinzer, clt; Hubert Cruts, hn; Collegium Aureum; Franzjosef Maier. Harmonia Mundi 1C 065 99829

+FF 5/6-80 p111
+HFN 4-80 p119

+-RR 5-80 p66

2227 Concerto, clarinet, K 622, A major. ROSSINI: Introduction and variations, C major. WEBER: Concertino, clarinet, op. 26, C minor. Bela Kovacs, clt; Budapest Philharmonic Orchestra; Andras Korodi. Hungaroton SLPX 12046

++ARG 3-80 p49
+FF 5/6-80 p111

++NR 2-80 p6

2228 Concerto, clarinet, K 622, A major. SPOHR: Concerto, clarinet, no. 4, E minor. Thea King, clt; ECO; Alun Francis. Meridian E

77022
+Gr 1-80 p1157   +—RR 12-79 p65
+HFN 12-79 p166   +STL 3-9-80 p41
+—MT 4-80 p252

2229 Concerto, clarinet, K 622, A major (edit. Galway). Concerto, flute
   and harp, K 299, C major. James Galway, flt; Marisa Robles, hp;
   LSO; Eduardo Mata. RCA RL 2-5171 Tape (c) RK 2-5171 (also RCA
   1-3353 Tape (c) ARK 1-3353)
                +—FF 1/2-80 p111   +NYT 9-23-79 pD28
                +—Gr 12-78 p1103   +—NYT 5-4-80 pD24
                +Gr 5-79 p1940 tape   ++RR 12-78 p62
                +HF 12-79 p110 tape   ++SFC 11-11-79 p45
                +HFN 3-79 p127   +St 12-79 p154
   Concerto, clarinet, K 622, A major. See no. 2224. See no. 2225.
   See no. 2396
2230 Concerto, flute, no. 1, K 313, G major. Concerto, flute, no. 2, K
   314, D major. Hans-Martin Linde, flt; Heinz Holliger, ob; Munich Chamber Orchestra; Hans Stadlmair. DG 2547 015 Tape (c)
   3347 015 (From 198342)
                +Gr 8-80 p258   +—HFN 9-80 p116 tape
                +Gr 9-80 p413 tape   ++RR 6-80 p56
                +—HFN 7-80 p117
2231 Concerto, flute, no. 1, K 313, G major. Concerto, flute, no. 2, K
   314, D major. Lorant Kovacs, flt; HSO; Ervin Lukacs. Hungaroton SLPX 11974
                +—FF 1/2-80 p112   +—NR 7-79 p6
2232 Concerto, flute, no. 1, K 313, C major. Concerto, flute, no. 2, K
   314, D major. James Galway, flt; New Irish Chamber Orchestra;
   Andre Prieur. New Irish Recording Company NIR 010 (also Quintessence SHM 3010A)
                +—Audio 6-80 p47   ++Gr 1-76 p1198
2233 Concerto, flute, no. 1, K 313, G major. Concerto, flute, no. 2, K
   314, D major. James Galway, flt; New Irish Chamber Orchestra;
   Andre Prieur. Pickwick NR 3010 Tape (c) HSC 3010 (From New
   Irish Recording NIR 010)
                +—ARG 9-80 p33   +HF 7-80 p82 tape
                +FF 3/4-80 p120   ++SFC 12-30-79 p33
                +—Gr 11-79 p833   ++St 2-80 p129
                +HF 2-80 p90
   Concerto, flute, no. 1, K 313, G major. See no. 2209. See no.
   2210. See no. 2211. See no. 2212. See no. 2213. See no. 2214.
   See no. 2215. See no. 2216. See no. 2396. See no. 2399
   Concerto, flute, no. 2, K 314, D major. See no. 296. See no. 1675.
   See no. 1752. See no. 2209. See no. 2210. See no. 2211. See
   no. 2212. See no. 2213. See no. 2214. See no. 2215. See no.
   2216. See no. 2230. See no. 2231. See no. 2232. See no. 2233.
   See no. 2235. See no. 2396. See no. 2399
2234 Concerto, flute and harp, K 299, C major. Concertone, 2 violins, K
   190, C major (arr. Adorjan). Rondo, flute, K Anh 184, D major.
   Andras Adorjan, flt; Susanna Mildonia, hp; Jean-Jacques Kantorow,
   vln; Diethelm Jonas, ob; Emmerich Bunemann, vlc; Munich Chamber
   Orchestra; Hans Stadlmair. Denon OX 7181
                +FF 11/12-80 p137   +St 11-80 p96
2235 Concerto, flute and harp, K 299, C major. Concerto, flute, no. 2,
   K 314, D major. Rondo, violin, K 373b, D major (arr.). Jean-

Pierre Rampal, flt; Pierre Pierlot, ob; Marielle Nordmann, hp;
ECO; Jean-Pierre Rampal. ERato STU 71321
+-Gr 10-80 p500
2236 Concerto, flute and harp, K 299, C major. Divertimento, no. 2, K
131, D major. Rene le Roy, flt; Lili Laskine, hp; RPO; Thomas
Beecham. World Records SH 316 (From HMV DB 6485/7, DB 6649/51)
+ARSC Vol 12, no. 3   +HFN 6-80 p108
1980 p247   +RR 6-80 p55
++Gr 5-80 p1666
Concerto, flute and harp, K 299, C major. See no. 1604. See no.
2229. See no. 2396
2237 Concerti, horn, nos. 1-4, K 412, 417, 447, 495. Concerto, horn, K
App 98a, E major, fragment. Barry Tuckwell, hn; LSO; Peter Maag.
Decca JB 70 Tape (c) KJBC 70 (From SXL 2238, SWL 8011, SXL 6108)
+Gr 11-79 p833   +RR 10-79 p99
+HFN 10-79 p169   +RR 4-80 p127
2238 Concerti, horn, nos. 1-4, K 412, 417, 447, 495. Hermann Baumann,
hn; Salzburg Mozarteum Orchestra; Leopold Hager. Telefunken AW
6-42360 Tape (c) 4-42360
+-Gr 10-79 p643   +RR 8-79 p87
+HFN 8-79 p109   +St 12-80 p129
Concerti, horn, nos. 1-4, K 412, 417, 447, 495. See no. 2396
Concerto, horn, no. 1, K 412, D major. See no. 127
Concerto, horn, no. 3, K 447, E flat major. See no. 421. See no.
2226
Concerto, horn, K App 98a, E major, fragment. See no. 2237
2239 Concerto, piano, no. 5, K 175, D major. Concerto, piano, no. 9, K
271, E flat major. Daniel Barenboim, pno; ECO; Daniel Baren-
boim. HMV SXLP 30418 Tape (c) TC SXLP 30418 (From ASD 2484)
+Gr 1-80 p1157   +-HFN 4-80 p121 tape
+-HFN 4-80 p119   +-RR 8-80 p93 tape
2240 Concerto, piano, no. 8, K 246, C major. Concerto, piano, no. 22,
K 482, E flat major. Murray Perahia, pno; ECO; Murray Perahia.
CBS M 35869 Tape (c) MT 35869
++St 11-80 p76
2241 Concerto, piano, no. 8, K 246, C major. Concerto, piano, no. 12, K
414, A major. Ferenc Rados, pno; Liszt Chamber Orchestra; Frig-
yes Sandor. Hungaroton SLPX 11912
++ARG 7-79 p41   /NR 6-79 p8
+FF 7/8-80 p112
2242 Concerto, piano, no. 9, K 271, E flat major. Concerto, piano, no.
21, K 467, C major. Alexis Weissenberg, pno; VSO; Carlo Maria
Giulini. Angel S 37567 Tape (c) 4XS 37567
+-FF 1/2-80 p112   ++SFC 9-9-79 p45
+-FU 3-80 p47   ++St 11-79 p98
2243 Concerto, piano, no. 9, K 271, E flat major. Concerto, piano, no.
27, K 595, B flat major. Christoph Eschenbach, pno; LPO; Chris-
toph Eschenbach. HMV ASD 3776 Tape (c) TC ASD 3776
+-Gr 11-79 p833   +HFN 2-80 p107 tape
+HFN 1-80 p109   +RR 12-79 p65
2244 Concerto, piano, no. 9, K 271, E flat major. Concerto, piano, no.
14, K 449, E flat major. Dezso Ranki, pno; Liszt Chamber Orchestra; Frigyes Sandor. Hungaroton SLPX 11942 Tape (c) MK 11942
+-ARG 2-79 p24   +-HFN 4-79 p124
+FF 1/2-79 p79   +-NR 4-79 p5

+FU 3-80 p47   +-RR 5-79 p66
+HF 5-80 p90 tape   ++SFC 9-9-79 p45

2245 Concerto, piano, no. 9, K 271, E flat major. Concerto, 2 pianos,
     K 365, E flat major.* Alfred Brendel, Imogen Cooper, pno; AMF;
     Neville Marriner. Philips 9500 408 Tape (c) 7300 616 (*From
     6768 096)
             +-CL 7/8-80 p8   +HFN 4-80 p121
             +FF 5/6-80 p112   ++NR 5-80 p5
             +Gr 1-80 p1157   +NYT 5-4-80 pD24
             +Gr 3-80 p1446 tape   +RR 1-80 p82
             +HFN 2-80 p95   ++SFC 2-17-80 p44
            ++HFN 2-80 p107 tape   +St 6-80 p118
     Concerto, piano, no. 9, K 271, E flat major. See no. 2239
2246 Concerto, piano, no. 11, K 413, F major. Concerto, piano, no. 20,
     K 466, D minor. Murray Perahia, pno; ECO; Murray Perahia. CBS
     76651 Tape (c) 40-76651 (also Columbia M 35134 Tape (c) MT 35134)
            ++CL 11-79 p8   +HFN 5-78 p146 tape
            ++FF 1/2-80 p113   ++NYT 7-15-79 pD22
             +-FU 3-80 p47   +-RR 4-78 p61
             +-Gr 4-78 p1726   +RR 6-78 p95
             +Gr 6-78 p107 tape   +-St 10-79 p144
             +HFN 4-78 p119
2247 Concerto, piano, no. 11, K 413, F major. Concerto, piano, no. 12,
     K 414, A major. Michael Studer, pno; Cologne Chamber Orchestra;
     Helmut Muller-Bruhl. Claves P 710
             +-HFN 6-80 p108
2248 Concerto, piano, no. 12, K 414, A major. Concerto, piano, no. 27,
     K 595, B flat major. Murray Perahia, pno; ECO; Murray Perahia.
     CBS 76731 Tape (c) 40-76731 (also Columbia M 35828 Tape (c) MT
     35828)
             +-FF 9/10-80 p166   +NYT 5-4-80 pD24
             +-Gr 5-80 p1666   ++RR 5-80 p67
             +HFN 4-80 p107   +RR 8-80 p93 tape
             +HFN 8-80 p109 tape   +St 9-80 p81
2249 Concerto, piano, no. 12, K 414, A major. Concerto, piano, no. 19,
     K 459, F major. Maria-Joao Pires, pno; Lausanne Chamber Orches-
     tra; Armin Jordan. Erato STU 71057
             +-HFN 4-80 p107   +-RR 10-79 p95
2250 Concerto, piano, no. 12, K 414, A major. Concerto, piano, no. 27,
     K 595, B flat major. Jorg Demus, fortepiano; Collegium Aureum;
     Franzjosef Maier. Harmonia Mundi 1C 056 99767 (From BASF 3066)
             +FF 5/6-80 p112   +-NYT 7-27-80 pD20
             +-Gr 3-79 p1566   +RR 9-78 p63
     Concerto, piano, no. 12, K 414, A major. See no. 2241. See no.
     2247
2251 Concerto, piano, no. 13, K 415, C major. Sonata, piano, no. 2,
     K 280, F major. Variations on "Ah vous dirai-je Maman", K 265,
     C major (12). Clara Haskil, pno. DG 2535 115 Tape (c) 3335 115
            ++FF 1/2-80 p114   +MUM 7/8-80 p33
             +HF 2-80 p102 tape   ++NYT 8-5-79 pD19
2252 Concerto, piano, no. 13, K 415, C major. Concerto, piano, no. 14,
     K 449, E flat major. Alfred Brendel, pno; AMF; Neville Marriner.
     Philips 9500 565 Tape (c) 7300 714 (From 6768 096)
             +CL 2-80 p6   ++NR 2-80 p4
             +-FF 3/4-80 p121   +NYT 5-4-80 pD24
             +Gr 3-80 p1391   ++RR 2-80 p58

                    +HFN 3-80 p105   +RR 8-80 p93 tape
                    ++MUM 5/6-80 p32

2253 Concerto, piano, no. 14, K 449, E flat major. Concerto, piano, no.
      26, K 537, D major. Tamas Vasary, pno. BPhO; Tamas Vasary. DG
      2531 207 Tape (c) 3301 207
                    ++CL 9-80 p16   +NR 6-80 p7
                    +-FF 7/8-80 p113   +NYT 5-4-80 pD24
                    ++Gr 1-80 p1157   +RR 2-80 p59
                    +HFN 3-80 p95   ++St 6-80 p77

2254 Concerto, piano, no. 14, K 449, E flat major. Concerto, piano, no.
      23, K 488, A major. Ivan Moravec, pno; Czech Chamber Orchestra;
      Josef Vlach. Quintessence PMC 7107 (From Supraphon)
                    +ARG 7-79 p43   +NYT 7-15-79 pD22
                    +FF 9/10-79 p110   ++SFC 9-9-79 p45
                    ++MUM 1/2-80 p32   +-St 9-79 p98

     Concerto, piano, no. 14, K 449, E flat major. See no. 2244. See
      no. 2252

2255 Concerto, piano, no. 15, K 450, B flat major. Concerto, piano, no.
      26, K 537, D major. Ingrid Haebler, pno; LSO; Witold Rowicki,
      Colin Davis. Philips 6570 144 Tape (c) 7310 144
                    +FF 3/4-80 p121

2256 Concerto, piano, no. 17, K 453, G major. Concerto, piano, no. 21,
      K 467, C major. Vladimir Ashkenazy, pno; PhO; Vladimir Ashke-
      nazy. London CS 7104 Tape (c) CS 5-7104 (also Decca SXL 6881
      Tape (c) KSXC 6881)
                    +FF 11/12-79 p103   +NYT 7-15-79 pD22
                    ++FU 9-79 p56   +RR 5-79 p66
                    ++Gr 5-79 p1899   +-RR 9-79 p134 tape
                    ++HFN 5-79 p124   ++SFC 4-22-79 p57
                    +-MT 1-80 p35   ++St 8-79 p111
                    +NR 2-80 p5

2257 Concerto, piano, no. 19, K 459, F major. Concerto, piano, no. 21,
      K 467, C major. Ingrid Haebler, pno; LSO; Witold Rowicki.
      Philips 6570 077 Tape (c) 7310 077 (From AXS 12000)
                    +Gr 11-79 p833   +RR 11-79 p88
                    +HFN 11-79 p157 tape   +RR 2-80 p97 tape
                    +HFN 11-79 p157   +STL 12-9-79 p41

2258 Concerto, piano, no. 19, K 459, F major. Concerto, piano, no. 20,
      K 466, D minor. Clara Haskil, pno; RIAS Symphony Orchestra, BSO;
      Ferenc Fricsay, Charles Munch. Rococo 2086
                    +-NR 2-80 p5

     Concerto, piano, no. 19, K 459, F major. See no. 2249
     Concerto, piano, no. 20, K 466, D minor. See no. 2246. See no.
      2258
     Concerto, piano, no. 20, K 466, D minor: 1st movement, excerpt. See
      no. 3950

2259 Concerto, piano, no. 21, K 467, C major. Concerto, piano, no. 22,
      K 482, E flat major. Geza Anda, pno; Salzburg Mozarteum Camerata
      Academica; Geza Anda. DG 2535 317 Tape (c) 3335 317 (From SLPM
      138783, 138824)
                    +Gr 6-80 p38   +HFN 9-80 p116 tape
                    +HFN 8-80 p107   ++RR 7-80 p58

2260 Concerto, piano, no. 21, K 467, C major. Concerto, 2 pianos, K 365,
      E flat major. Andor Foldes, Carl Seeman, pno; BPhO; Paul Schmitz,
      Fritz Lehmann. DG 2535 744
                    +-FF 11/12-80 p139

2261 Concerto, piano, no. 21, K 467, C major. Concerto, piano, no. 24,
     K 491, C major. Paul Badura-Skoda, pno; Prague Chamber Orches-
     tra; Paul Badura-Skoda. Quintessence PMC 7123 (From Supraphon
     1972)
                   +—ARG 4-80 p28   +FU 3-80 p47
                   /FF 11/12-80 p138   +HF 7-80 p71
     Concerto, piano, no. 21, K 467, C major. See no. 194. See no.
     2242. See no. 2256. See no. 2257. See no. 3777
     Concerto, piano, no. 21, K 467, C major: 2nd movement. See no. 2398
2262 Concerto, piano, no. 22, K 482, E flat major. Concerto, 2 pianos,
     K 365, E flat major. Paul Badura-Skoda, Dagmar Bella, pno; VPO;
     Wilhelm Furtwangler. Audax 765
                   +—FF 7/8-80 p113
     Concerto, piano, no. 22, K 482, E flat major. See no. 2240. See
     no. 2259
     Concerto, piano, no. 23, K 488, A major. See no. 425. See no.
     2254
     Concerto, piano, no. 24, K 491, C minor. See no. 2261
2263 Concerto, piano, no. 25, K 503, C major. Serenade, no. 13, K 525,
     G major. Leonard Bernstein, pno; Israel Philharmonic Orchestra,
     NYP; Leonard Bernstein. Columbia M 34574 (also CBS 61896 Tape
     (c) 40-61896)
                   +ARG 11-78 p30   +MJ 12-78 p45
                   -FF 11/12-78 p90   +NR 8-78 p4
                   +—Gr 8-80 p225   +—RR 7-80 p59
                   +—HFN 7-80 p109   +St 11-78 p114
                   +HFN 9-80 p116 tape
2264 Concerto, piano, no. 25, K 503, C major. Concerto, piano, no. 27,
     K 595, B flat major. Alicia de Larrocha, pno; LPO; Georg Solti.
     London CS 7109 (also Decca SXL 6887)
                   +—Audio 5-80 p90   +HFN 9-79 p108
                   +—FF 5/6-79 p68   +NYT 3-11-79 pD23
                   +FU 9-79 p56   ++RR 9-79 p94
                   +—Gr 9-79 p469   ++SFC 2-25-79 p41
                   +—Gr 9-79 p534 tape   +—St 6-79 p136
2265 Concerto, piano, no. 25, K 503, C major. Fantasia, K 475, C minor.
     Ivan Moravec, pno; CPhO; Joseph Vlach. Quintessence PMC 7108
     (From Supraphon)
                   +—FF 9/10-79 p109   +NYT 7-15-79 pD22
                   ++MUM 1/2-80 p32
     Concerto, piano, no. 26, K 537, D major. See no. 2253. See no.
     2255
     Concerto, piano, no. 27, K 595, B flat major. See no. 2243. See
     no. 2248. See no. 2250. See no. 2264
     Concerto, 2 pianos, K 365, E flat major. See no. 2245. See no.
     2260. See no. 2262
     Concerto, 2 pianos, K 365, E flat major: 3rd movement, excerpt. See
     no. 2398
2266 Concerto, violin, no. 1, K 207, B flat major.* Concerto, violin,
     no. 3, K 216, G major.* Rondos, violin, K 269, B flat major;
     K 373, C major. Josef Suk, vln; PCO; Josef Suk. RCA GL 2-5288
     Tape (c) GK 2-5288 (*From LR 1-5084, 1-5046)
                   +—Gr 10-80 p498   +HFN 11-80 p129
2267 Concerto, violin, no. 1, K 207, B flat major. Serenade, no. 3, K
     167a (185), D major. Thomas Zehetmair, vln; Salzburg Mozarteum

Orchestra; Leopold Hager. Telefunken 6-42537 Tape (c) 4-42537
    +FF 7/8-80 p114   +St 5-80 p88
Concerto, violin, no. 1, K 207, B flat major. See no. 2206
2268 Concerto, violin, no. 2, K 211, D major. Il re pastore, K 208:
    L'Amero saro costante. Symphony, no. 32, K 318, G major. Sym-
    phony, no. 38, K 504, D major. Edith Mathis, s; Annagret Died-
    richsen, vln; Salzburg Mozarteum Orchestra; Leopold Hager. Ac-
    anta DC 22471
        +-HFN 8-80 p99   /-RR 8-80 p49
2269 Concerto, violin, no. 2, K 211, D major. Concerto, violin, no. 5,
    K 219, A major. ECO; Valdimir Spivakov, vln. HMV ASD 3639 (also
    Angel SZ 37511)
        +ARG 1-80 p51   +MUM 7/8-80 p30
        +FF 11/12-79 p104   ++NR 10-79 p3
        +-FU 1-79 p43   +NYT 7-15-79 pD22
        +Gr 7-79 p206   ++RR 7-79 p63
        ++HF 11-79 p106   -SFC 10-14-79 p61
        +HFN 7-79 p109   +ST 11-79 p528
        +HFN 9-79 p123 tape   ++St 12-79 p88
2270 Concerto, violin, no. 2, K 211, D major. Sinfonia concertante, K
    364, E flat major.* Josef Suk, Josef Kodousek, vln; PCO. RCA
    GL 2-5284 Tape (c) GK 2-5284 (*From LRL 1-5084)
        +-Gr 8-80 p222   +RR 7-80 p49
        +-HFN 8-80 p107   ++STL 7-13-80 p38
        +HFN 9-80 p116 tape
2271 Concerto, violin, no. 3, K 216, G major. Concertone, 2 violins,
    K 190 (K166b), C major. Alan Loveday, Ioan Brown, Carmel Caine,
    vln; Kenneth Heath, vlc; Tess Miller, ob; AMF; Neville Marriner.
    Argo ZRG 729 Tape (f) E 729
        ++Audio 3-79 p97   ++NR 6-73 p6
        +Gr 1-73 p1331   ++RR 1-73 p45
        ++HF 11-73 p112   ++SFC 7-8-73 p32
        +HF 5-80 p90 tape   ++St 9-73 p122
        ++HFN 1-73 p119
2272 Concerto, violin, no. 3, K 216, G major. Concerto, violin, no. 4,
    K 218, D major. Iona Brown, vln; AMF; Iona Brown. Argo ZRG
    880 Tape (c) KZRC 880
        +Gr 7-80 p142   +RR 7-80 p59
        +HFN 7-80 p109
2273 Concerto, violin, no. 3, K 216, G major. Sinfonia concertante, K
    364, E flat major. Vladimir Spivakov, vln; Yuri Bashmet, vla;
    ECO; Vladimir Spivakov. HMV ASD 3859 Tape (c) TC ASD 3859
        +Gr 6-80 p37   +RR 6-80 p56
        +-HFN 6-80 p108
Concerto, violin, no. 3, K 216, G major. See no. 490. See no. 2266
Concerto, violin, no. 4, K 218, D major. See no. 2206. See no.
    2272
Concerto, violin, no. 5, K 219, A major. See no. 421. See no. 804.
    See no. 2269. See no. 3964. See no. 3968
Concertone, 2 violins, K 190, C major. See no. 2234. See no. 2271
2274 Contredanse, K 609 (5). Galimathias musicum, K 32. Ein musicalis-
    cher Spass, K 522, F major. Collegium Aureum. Harmonia Mundi
    065 99874
        +HFN 9-80 p109
2275 Cosi fan tutte, K 588, excerpts. Montserrat Caballe, Janet Baker,

s; Nicolai Gedda, t; Richard Van Allen, bs; Wladimiro Ganzarolli,
bar; Orchestra; Colin Davis. Philips 6570 099 Tape (c) 7310 099
     +Gr 10-80 p548 tape   +HFN 10-80 p117 tape
     +HFN 8-80 p107
Cosi fan tutte, K 588: Amore e un ladroncello. See no. 147
Cosi fan tutte, K 588: Arias. See no. 3539
Cosi fan tutte, K 588: Come scoglio. See no. 3793. See no. 3918
Cosi fan tutte, K 588: El parte...Per pieta. See no. 1512
Cosi fan tutte, K 588: In aura amorosa. See no. 3977
Cosi fan tutte, K 588: Overture. See no. 3860
Cosi fan tutte, K 588: Questa piccola offerta...Il core vi dono
   bell'idole mio. See no. 3711
Cosi fan tutte, K 588: Un'aura amorosa. See no. 3770
2276 Davidde penitente, K 469. Eva Csapo, Gisela Koban, s; Aldo Baldin,
   t; Wurttemberg Chamber Orchestra; Dieter Kurz. Candide CE 31107
   (also Turnabout TVS 37141 Tape (c) KTVC 37141)
        +-ARG 5-79 p30   +HFN 3-80 p93
        +Audio 8-79 p97   +NR 4-79 p8
        -FF 9/10-79 p111   -NYT 7-15-79 pD22
        +Gr 3-80 p1428   +RR 3-80 p95
        +-HF 7-79 p144   /SFC 2-17-80 p44
Deutsche Tanze (German dances), K 509 (6). See no. 2395
Deutsche Tanze, K 605. See no. 2204
Dir Seele des Weltalls, K 429. See no. 3844
2277 Divertimenti, K 136-138. Serenade, no. 6, K 239, D major. AMF;
   Neville Marriner. Argo ZRG 554 Tape (r) B-C E 554
     +HF 5-80 p90 tape
Divertimenti, K 136-138. See no. 2208
2278 Divertimento, K 136, D major. Serenade, no. 5, K 213a (K204), D
   major. Serenade, no. 6, K 239, D major. Rainer Kuchl, vln;
   Vienna Mozart Ensemble; Willi Boskovsky. Decca JB 88 Tape (c)
   KJBC 88
        ++Gr 4-80 p1559   +RR 4-80 p69
        +HFN 4-80 p107
2279 Divertimento, K 136, D major. Divertimento, K 137, B flat major.
   Berlin Philharmonic Octet Members. HMV HQS 1432
     +Gr 9-80 p360
Divertimento, K 136, D major. See no. 2338. See no. 2385
2280 Divertimento, K 137, B flat major. Divertimento, no. 15, K 287, B
   flat major. Vienna Mozart Ensemble; Willi Boskovsky. Decca JB
   90 Tape (c) KJBC 90
        +Gr 12-80 p836   +HFN 11-80 p121
Divertimento, K 137, B flat major. See no. 2279
2281 Divertimento, K 138, F major. Divertimento, no. 10, K 247, F major.
   Serenade, no. 8, K 286, D major. Vienna Mozart Ensemble; Willi
   Boskovsky. Decca JB 89 Tape (c) KJBC 89
        +Gr 6-80 p37   +-RR 6-80 p56
        +HFN 6-80 p108
Divertimento, no. 1, K 63, G major. See no. 2221
Divertimento, no. 2, K 131, D major. See no. 2236
2282 Divertimento, no. 7, K 205, D major. Divertimento, no. 11, K 251,
   D major. Vienna Mozart Ensemble; Willi Boskovsky. Decca SXL
   6670 (also London STS 15416)
        +FF 1/2-80 p115   +NYT 7-15-79 pD15
        +-Gr 12-74 p1138   +RR 12-74 p34

2283 Divertimenti, no. 8, K 213, F major; no. 9, K 240, B major; no. 13,
     K 253, F major; no. 14, K 270, B flat major. VPO Wind Soloists.
     DG 2531 296
                    ++Gr 12-80 p846   +HFN 12-80 p143
     Divertimento, no. 9, K 240, B flat major. See no. 2283
     Divertimento, no. 10, K 247, F major. See no. 2281
2284 Divertimento, no. 11, K 251, D major. Serenade, no. 7, K 205, D
     major. Vienna Mozart Ensemble; Willi Boskovsky. Decca JB 65
                    ++RR 1-80 p82
     Divertimento, no. 11, K 251, D major. See no. 375. See no. 2282
     Divertimento, no. 13, K 253, F major. See no. 2283
     Divertimento, no. 14, K 270, B flat major. See no. 2283
2285 Divertimento, no. 15, K 287, B flat major. Collegium Aureum Mem-
     bers. Harmonia Mundi 1C 065 99696
                    +Gr 5-80 p1671   ++RR 5-80 p65
                    +HFN 6-80 p108
2286 Divertimento, no. 15, K 287, B flat major. Liszt Chamber Orchestra;
     Janos Rolla. Hungaroton SLPX 12026
                    +-FF 1/2-80 p115   +NR 10-79 p3
     Divertimento, no. 15, K 287, B flat major. See no. 2280
2287 Divertimento, no. 17, K 334, D major. Vienna Mozart Ensemble; Willi
     Boskovsky. Decca SXL 6724 (also London STS 15417)
                    +FF 1/2-80 p115   +NYT 7-15-79 pD22
                    +-Gr 11-75 p819   ++RR 10-75 p45
                    ++HFN 10-75 p144
2288 Divertimento, no. 17, K 334, D major. Jean-Francois Paillard Cham-
     ber Orchestra; Jean-Francois Paillard. Erato STU 71069
                    +-FF 3/4-80 p121   +RR 10-79 p99
                    +-HFN 9-79 p108
2289 Divertimento, no. 17, K 334, D major. Liszt Chamber Orchestra; Jan-
     os Rolla. Hungaroton SLPX 12027
                    +NR 7-80 p7
     Divertimento, no. 17, K 334, D major: Minuet. See no. 298. See
     no. 3964
     Divertimento, no. 17, K 334, D major: 3rd movement, excerpt. See
     no. 2398
2290 Divertimenti, K 439b, B flat major. Kalman Berkes, Istvan Mali,
     clt; Gyorgy Hortobagyi, bsn. Hungaroton SLPX 11985/6 (2)
                    +ARG 2-80 p40
     Divertimento, K 439b, B flat major. See no. 3890
2291 Divertimento, K 563, E flat major. Franzjosef Maier, vln; Heinz
     Otto Graf, vla; Horst Beckedor, vlc. Harmonia Mundi 065 99726
                    +Gr 9-80 p360   ++RR 8-80 p63
                    +HFN 8-80 p99
2292 Don Giovanni, K 527. Edda Moser, Kiri Te Kanawa, s; Teresa Bergan-
     za, ms; Kenneth Riegel, t; Jose van Dam, bar; Ruggiero Raimondi,
     Malcolm King, John Macurdy, bs; Paris Opera Orchestra and Chorus;
     Lorin Maazel. CBS 79321 (3) Tape (c) 40-79321 (also Columbia M3
     35192)
                    +-ARG 4-80 p32   +-NR 1-80 p9
                    +FF 5/6-80 p113   +-NYT 12-23-79 pD28
                    +-FU 4-80 p48   +-ON 4-12-80 p37
                    +-Gr 10-79 p704   +Op 10-79 p973
                    +-HF 2-80 p75   +RR 10-79 p59
                    +-HFN 10-79 p159   +-RR 6-80 p94 tape
                    +HFN 2-80 p107 tape   +-SFC 11-11-79 p45

2293 Don Giovanni, K 527. Margaret Price, Sylvia Sass, Lucia Popp, s;
     Bernd Weikl, Gabriel Bacquier, Alfred Sramek, bar; Stuart Bur-
     rows, t; Kurt Moll, bs; London Opera Chorus; LPO; Georg Solti.
     Decca D162D4 (4) Tape (c) K162K42 (also London OSA 1444 Tape (c)
     OSA 5-1444)

          +—ARG 4-80 p32   +—NYT 12-23-79 pD28
          +—FF 5/6-80 p113   +—ON 4-12-80 p37
          +Gr 9-79 p514   +—Op 10-79 p973
          +—HF 2-80 p75   +RR 9-79 p52
          +—HF 8-80 p87 tape   +—SFC 12-30-79 p33
          +HFN 10-79 p157   +STL 12-2-79 p37

2294 Don Giovanni, K 527. Sena Jurinac, Maria Stader, Irmgard Seefried,
     s; Ernst Hafliger, t; Dietrich Fischer-Dieskau, bar; Karl Kohn,
     Walter Kreppel, Ivan Sardi, bs; RIAS Chamber Chorus; BRSO; Fer-
     enc Fricsay. DG 2728 033 (2) Tape (c) 3373 003 (From SLPM 138
     050/3)

          +—FF 5/6-80 p113   +—NYT 12-23-79 pD28
          +—Gr 2-73 p1556   +—ON 4-12-80 p3
          +HF 8-80 p87 tape   +Op 6-73 p527
          +—HFN 4-73 p783   /RR 2-73 p46

2295 Don Giovanni, K 527, excerpts. Edda Moser, Kiri Te Kanawa, s; Ken-
     neth Riegel, t; Ruggero Raimondi, John Macurdy, Jose Van Dam,
     Malcolm King, bs; Teresa Berganza, ms; Paris Opera Orchestra and
     Chorus; Lorin Maazel. Columbia M 35859 Tape (c) MT 35859 (also
     CBS 73888)

          +—HFN 11-80 p129   -NR 4-80 p10

     Don Giovanni, K 527: Arias. See no. 3539
     Don Giovanni, K 527: Bravo bravo archibravo...Finch han dal vano;
     Deh vieni alla finestra; Don Ottavio son morta...Or sai chi l'
     onore; Non mi dir; In quali eccessi...Mi tradi. See no. 3770
     Don Giovanni, K 527: Catalogue aria. See no. 3927
     Don Giovanni, K 527: Dalla sua pace. See no. 3977
     Don Giovanni, K 527: Dalla sua pace; Il mio tesoro. See no. 3981
     Don Giovanni, K 527: Deh vieni alla finestra. See no. 3899
     Don Giovanni, K 527: Don Ottavio son morta...Or sai chi l'onore.
     See no. 3668
     Don Giovanni, K 527: Duet, Act 1; Il mio tesoro. See no. 1099
     Don Giovanni, K 527: Finch'han dal vino. See no. 3980
     Don Giovanni, K 527: Finch'han dal vino; Deh vieni alla finestra.
     See no. 3901
     Don Giovanni, K 527: La ci darem la mano. See no. 1819
     Don Giovanni, K 527: Madamina il catalogo. See no. 3711

2296 Don Giovanni, K 527: Madamina il catalogo e questo; La ci darem la
     mano; Don Ottavio son morta...Or sai chi l'onore; Dalla sua pace;
     Finch'han dal vino; Batti batti; Ah taci ingiusto core; Deh vieni
     alla finestra; Vedrai carino; Sola sola in buio loco; Il mio
     tesoro intanto; O statua gentilissima. Martina Arroyo, Kiri Te
     Kanawa, Mirella Freni, s; Stuart Burrows, t; Ingvar Wisell, bar;
     Luigi Roni, Wladimiro Ganzarolli, Richard van Allan, bs; ROHO;
     Colin Davis. Philips 6570 097 Tape (c) 7310 097 (From 6707 022)

          +Gr 7-80 p161   +HFN 9-80 p116 tape
          +HFN 7-80 p119   /RR 6-80 p35

     Don Givanni, K 527: Mi tradi. See no. 147
     Don Givoanni, K 527: On her contentment; To her I love. See no.
     3986
     Don Giovanni, K 527: Schmale tobe aus; Wenn du fein fromm bist.

See no. 3774

Don Giovanni, K 527: Troppo mi spiace...Non mi dir. See no. 3793

2297 Duo, violin and viola, no. 1, K 423, G major. Sinfonia concertante,
     K 364, E flat major. Igor Oistrakh, vln; David Oistrakh, vla;
     MPO; Kiril Kondrashin. London STS 15482 (From Decca SXL 6088,
     London CS 6377)
                    +-FF 3/4-80 p127

2298 Duo, violin and viola, no. 1, K 423, G major. Duo, violin and viola,
     no. 2, K 424, B flat major. Joseph Fuchs, vln; Lillian Fuchs,
     vla. Odyssey Y 35228 (From Columbia ML 5692, MS 6292)
                    /FF 1/2-80 p116

Duo, violin and viola, no. 2, K 424, B flat major. See no. 2298

2299 Die Entfuhrung aus dem Serail, K 384. Lois Marshall, Ilse Hollweg,
     s; Leopold Simoneau, Gerhard Unger, t; Gottlob Frick, bs; Beecham
     Choral Society; RPO; Thomas Beecham. HMV SLS 5153 (2) Tape (c)
     TC SLS 5153 (From Columbia 33CS 1462/3) (also Angel SBL 3555)
         ++ARSC Vol 13, no. 3   +MT 9-79 p747
            1980 p252   +-Op 8-79 p780
         +Gr 4-79 p1767   +RR 4-79 p54
         +-HFN 4-79 p133   +RR 11-79 p126 tape
         +-HFN 6-79 p117 tape

2300 Die Entfuhrung aus dem Serail, K 384. Arias: Ich mochte wohl der
     Kaiser sein, K 539; Manner suchen stets zu naschen, K 433; Musst
     ich auch durch tausend Drachen, K 435; Schon lacht der holde
     Fruhling, K 580; Welch angstliches Beben, K 389. Christiane Eda-
     Pierre, Norma Burrowes, s; Stuart Burrows, Robert Tear, t; Robert
     Lloyd, bs; AMF; Colin Davis. Philips 6769 026 (3)
         +-Gr 9-80 p397   ++NYT 10-19-80 pD24
         +HFN 9-80 p109   +-ON 12-13-80 p44
         +HFN 11-80 p131 tape   +Op 9-80 p910
         +NR 11-80 p7   ++SFC 10-5-80 p21

2301 Die Entfuhrung aus dem Serail, K 384, excerpts. Fritz Wunderlich,
     t; Erika Koth, Lotte Schadle, s; Friedrich Lenz, t; Kurt Bohme,
     bs; Bavarian State Opera Orchestra and Chorus; Eugen Jochum. DG
     2535 277
         +RR 8-80 p14

Die Entfuhrung aus dem Serail, K 384: Arias. See no. 3539

Die Entfuhrung aus dem Serail, K 384: Hier soll ich dich denn sehen.
     See no. 3558

Die Entfuhrung aus dem Serail, K 384: Martern aller Arten. See no.
     3538. See no. 3872

Die Entfuhrung aus dem Serail, K 384: Martern aller Arten; Welch
     ein Geschick. See no. 147. See no. 3646

Die Entfuhrung aus dem Serail, K 384: O wie angstlich. See no.
     3977

Die Entfuhrung aus dem Serail, K 384: O wie will ich triumphieren.
     See no. 3770

Die Entfuhrung aus dem Serail, K 384: Welcher Kummer herrscht in
     meiner Selle...Traurigkeit ward mir zum Lose; Martern aller Arten.
     See no. 3584

Die Entfuhrung aus dem Serail, K 384: Wer ein Liebchen hat gefunden;
     Ho wie will ich triumphieren. See no. 3712

2302 Exsultate jubilate, K 165. Arias: Non temer, amato bene, K 490;
     Vorrei spiegarvi oh Dio, K 418. Il re pastore, K 208: L'amero
     saro costante. Judith Blegen, s; Mostly Mozart Orchestra; Pin-
     chas Zukerman. CBS 76814 (also Columbia M 35142 Tape (c) 35142)

+ARG 6-79 p29   +MJ 9/10-79 p50
+-FF 5/6-79 p68   +NYT 7-15-79 pD22
+Gr 4-79 p1761   +ON 12-13-80 p44
+HFN 4-79 p124   +RR 5-79 p100

2303 Exsultate jubilate, K 165. Edith Mathis, s; Staatskapelle Orches-
     tra; Bernhard Klee. DG 2530 978
          +NYT 5-4-80 pD24   +SFC 6-15-80 p36
     Exsultate jubilate, K 165. See no. 2217. See no. 2397. See no.
     3541
     Exsultate jubilate, K 165: Alleluja. See no. 2218. See no. 2398
     Fantasia, K 397, D minor. See no. 83. See no. 2323. See no. 2360.
     See no. 3677. See no. 3825

2304 Fantasia, K 475, C minor. Sonata, piano, no. 14, K 457, C minor.
     Variations on an allegretto, K 500, B flat major (12). David
     Ward, pno. Meridian E 77030
          +-Gr 2-80 p1282   +-RR 2-80 p78
          +HFN 2-80 p95
     Fantasia, K 475, C minor. See no. 2265. See no. 2360
     Fantasia, K 594, F minor. See no. 1294. See no. 2207. See no.
     2397
     Fantasia, K 608, F minor. See no. 1294. See no. 1965. See no.
     2138. See no. 2207. See no. 2397. See no. 3615. See no. 3616
     Fugue, K 426, C minor. See no. 2324. See no. 4035
     Galithmathias Musicum, K 32. See no. 2274
     Grabmusik, K 42: Betracht dies Herz. See no. 2217

2305 Harmoniemusiken: Excerpts from Le nozze di Figaro and Entfuhrung
     Aus dem Serail, arranged for wind octet. Collegium Aureum Mem-
     bers. Harmonia Mundi 1C 065 99838
          +HFN 8-80 p99   +-FF 11/12-80 p139

2306 Idomeneo, Re di Creta, K 366. Edda Moser, Anneliese Rothenberger,
     s; Nicolai Gedda, Adolf Dallapozza, Peter Schreier, t; Theo Adam,
     bs-bar; Leipzig Radio Chorus; Dresden Staatskapelle; Hans Schmidt-
     Isserstedt. Arabesque 8054-4 Tape (c) 9054-4
          +-ARG 7/8-80 p31   +NYT 1-6-80 pD18
          ++FF 5/6-80 p116   +ON 7-80 p37
          +-HF 10-80 p84   +-St 6-80 p117
          +HF 6-80 p96 tape   +SFC 8-31-80 p31
          +NR 4-80 p9
     Idomeneo, Re di Creta, K 366: Noch tont mir ein Meer in Busen. See
     no. 3774

2307 Idomeneo, Re di Creta, K 366: Overture; Quando avran fine omai,
     Padre germani addio; Vedrommi intorno l'ombra dolente; Se il
     padre perdei; Duor del mar; March; Sidonie sponde; Placido e il
     mar; Qual nuovo terrore; Eccoti in me; Corriamo fuggiamo; Sef-
     fretti lusinghieri; Andro ramingo e solo; O voto tremendo; March;
     Accogli o re del mar. Sena Jurinac, Dorothy McNeil, s; Alexander
     Young, Richard Lewis, t; Glyndebourne Festival Orchestra and
     Chorus; Fritz Busch) World Records SH 294 (From DB 21525, 21526,
     21527, 21528, 21529)
          +-ARSC Vol 12, no. 1-2   +Op 1-80 p62
          1980 p107   +RR 12-79 p165
          +Gr 11-79 p907   ++RR 1-80 p60
     Inter natas mulierum, K 72. See no. 2397
     Eine kleine Gigue, K 574, G major. See no. 404. See no. 2207.
     See no. 2323
     Kleiner Trauermarsch, K 453, C minor. See no. 2323

Kryie, K 89, K 341. See no. 2397
Landler, K 606 (6). See no. 3989
Litaniae Laurentanae, K 109, B major. See no. 1709
2308 Lucia Silla, K 135. Arleen Auger, Julia Varady, Edith Mathis, Hel-
     en Donath, s; Peter Schreier, Werner Krenn, t; Salzburg Radio
     and Mozarteum Chorus; Salzburg Mozarteum Orchestra; Leopold Hag-
     er. DG 2740 183 (From BASF 78 22472/4 (4)
                  +–Gr 1-76 p1236   +–MT 7-76 p577
                  +Gr 9-80 p398   ++RR 1-76 p25
                  ++HFN 2-76 p107   +STL 1-11-76 p36
                  +HFN 10-80 p115
     March, K 249, D major. See no. 2225
     Marches, K 408 (3). See no. 2395
     Masonic songs, K 148, K 468, K Anh 623. See no. 3844
     Mass, no. 4, K 139, C minor. See no. 2397
     Mass, no. 6, K 192, F major. See no. 2397
2309 Mass, no. 7, K 167, C major. Mass, no. 11, K 257, C major. Kurt
     Equiluz, t; Max van Egmond, bs; Vienna Boys Choir; Josef Bock,
     org; Chorus Viennensis; VCM; Hans Gillesberger. RCA RL 3-0455
                  +ARG 1-80 p45
2310 Mass, no. 10, K 220, C major. Mass, no. 13, K 259, C major. Motet:
     Ave verum corpus, K 618. Soloists; Vienna Boys Choir; Dom Orch-
     estra; Ferdinand Grossman. Philips 6570 079 Tape (c) 7310 079
                  +–HFN 3-80 p107   +–RR 3-80 p95
                  +–HFN 6-80 p119 tape
     Mass, no. 10, K 220, C minor. See no. 2397
2311 Mass, no. 11, K 257, C major. Mass, no. 16, K 317, C major. Helen
     Donath, s; Gillian Knight, con; Ryland Davies, t; Clifford Grant,
     Stafford Dean, bs; John Alldis Choir; LSO; Colin Davis; John
     Constable, org. Philips 6570 025 Tape (c) 7310 025 (From 6707
     016)
                  +–Gr 2-80 p1287   +–HFN 4-80 p121 tape
                  +–HFN 2-80 p105   +–RR 3-80 p96
     Mass, no. 11, K 257, C major. See no. 2309. See no. 2397
     Mass, no. 13, K 259, C major. See no. 2310. See no. 2397
2312 Mass, no. 16, K 317, C major. Vesperae solennes de confessore, K
     339, C major. Hans Buchhierl, boy soprano; Andreas Stein, boy
     contralto; Theo Altmeyer, t; Michael Schopper, bs; Tolzer Boys
     Choir; Collegium Aureum; Gerhard Schmidt-Gaden. Harmonia Mundi
     C 065 99763
                  +–ARG 1-80 p45   +HFN 8-80 p99
                  +–Gr 8-80 p251   +–RR 7-80 p92
     Mass, no. 16, K 317, C major. See no. 2311. See no. 2397
     Mass, no. 16, K 317, C major: Kyrie. See no. 2398
2313 Mass, no. 18, K 427, C minor. Margaret Marshall, Felicity Palmer,
     s; Anthony Rolfe Johnson, t; Gwynne Howell, bs; AMF and Chorus;
     Neville Marriner. Philips 9500 680 Tape (c) 7300 775
                  ++ARG 12-80 p38   +HFN 10-80 p117
                  +–FF 11/12-80 p140   ++NR 6-80 p9
                  ++Gr 7-80 p158   +RR 8-80 p87
                  +Gr 10-80 p548 tape   +SFC 6-15-80 p36
                  +HFN 7-80 p109   +St 11-80 p96
     Mass, no. 18, K 427, C minor. See no. 2397
2314 Mass, no. 19, K 626, D minor. Helen Donath, s; Christa Ludwig, ms;
     Robert Tear, t; Robert Lloyd, bs; PhO and Chorus; Carlo Maria
     Giulini. HMV ASD 3723 Tape (c) TC ASD 3723 (also Angel SZ 37600

Tape (c) 4ZS 37600)

++ARG 9-80 p34	+HFN 1-80 p123 tape
+FF 3/4-80 p127	+NR 2-80 p9
++Gr 10-79 p690	+NYT 5-4-80 pD24
+-HF 4-80 p92	++RR 10-79 p139
++HFN 1-80 p107	++St 4-80 p123

2315 Mass, no. 19, K 626, D minor. Magda Kalmar, Klara Takacs, s; Gyorgy
     Korondy, t; Jozsef Gregor, bs; Sandor Margittay, org; HRT Choir;
     Hungarian State Orchestra; Janos Ferencsik. Hungaroton LSPX
     12038

++ARG 9-80 p34	+NR 5-80 p8
+FF 5/6-80 p117	

2316 Mass, no. 19, K 626, D minor. Irmgard Seefried, s; Jennie Tourel,
     alto; Leopold Simoneau, t; William Warfield, bs; Westminster
     Choir; NYP; Bruno Walter. Odyssey Y 34619

+-ARSC Vol 12, nos. 1-2	+FF 7/8-78 p58
1980 p109	

2317 Mass, no. 19, K 626, D minor. Margareta Hallin, s; Anne-Marie Muh-
     le, alto; Brian Burrows, t; Magnus Linden, bs; St. Jacob Choir,
     Stockholm; Stockholm Conservatory Musicians; Stefa Skold. Pro-
     prius PROP 7815

     +FF 5/6-80 p117

Mass, no. 19, K 626, D minor. See no. 2397
Minuet, K 355, D major. See no. 2323
Minuet, K 409, C major. See no. 2395
Minuets, K 599 (6). See no. 2395
Misericordias Domini, K 222. See no. 2397

2318 Ein Musikalischer Spass, K 522, F major. Serenade, no. 13, K 525,
     G major. Rainer Zepperitz, bs; Gerd Seifert, Manfred Klier, hn;
     Amadeus Quartet. DG 2531 253 Tape (c) 3301 253

+ARG 12-80 p38	+NR 8-80 p9
++Gr 4-80 p1567	+NYT 5-4-80 pD24
+HF 12-80 p83	+-RR 5-80 p66
++HFN 5-80 p123	+-St 8-80 p96

Ein Musikalischer Spass, K 522, F major. See no. 1156. See no.
     2274

2319 Le nozze di Figaro, K 492 (sung in German). Margarete Teschemacher,
     Maria Cebotari, Angela Kolniak, Hannerle Frank, s; Elisabeth
     Waldenau, ms; Karl Wessely, Hubert Buchta, t; Matthieu Ahlers-
     meyer, Paul Schoffler, bar; Kurt Bohme, Hans Herbert Fiedler, bs;
     Stuttgart Radio Orchestra and Chorus; Karl Bohm. Acanta DE
     23133/4

+-Gr 9-80 p408	/RR 7-80 p45
+HFN 8-80 p99	

2320 Le nozze di Figaro, K 492. Anna Tomova-Sintow, Ileana Cotrubas,
     Jane Berbie, s; Frederica von Stade, ms; Heinz Zednik, Kurt Equi-
     luz, t; Tom Krause, Jose van Dam, bar; Jules Bastin, bs; Vienna
     State Opera Chorus; VPO; Herbert von Karajan. Decca D132D4 (4)
     Tape (c) K132K42 (also London OSA 1443 Tape (c) OSA 5-1443)

+-ARG 6-80 p27	+-NYT 12-23-79 pD28
+-FF 3/4-80 p122	++OC Spring 1980 p74
+-Gr 9-79 p513	+-ON 4-12-80 p37
+Gr 12-79 p1065 tape	+-Op 10-79 p974
+-HF 8-80 p87 tape	+-RR 8-79 p61
+-HF 1-80 p82	+-RR 6-80 p95 tape

                    +HFN 9-79 p108   ++SFC 10-14-79 p41
                    -NR 5-80 p10   ++St 12-79 p87
2321 Le nozze di Figaro, K 492. Maria Stader, Irmgard Seefried, Lilian
     Benningsen, s; Hertha Topper, con; Paul Kuen, Friedrich Lenz, t;
     Dietrich Fischer-Dieskau, Renato Capecchi, bar; Ivan Sardi, bs;
     RIAS Chamber Chorus; BRSO; Ferenc Fricsay. DG 2728 004 (3) Tape
     (c) 3373 004 (From SLPM 138697/9)
                    +ARG 5-79 p29   +-NYT 8-5-79 pD19
                    -FF 9/10-79 p114   +ON 4-12-80 037
                    +-Gr 2-73 p1557   +-Op 6-73 p527
                    +-HF 10-79 p126 tape   /RR 2-73 p46
                    +-HFN 4-73 p783   ++SFC 2-25-79 p41
2322 Le nozze di Figaro, K 492. Elisabeth Rethberg, Licia Albanese,
     Jarmila Novotna, s; Alessio de Paolis, t; Ezio Pinza, Salvatore
     Baccaloni, bs; Metropolitan Opera Orchestra; Ettore Panizza.
     MET 1 (3)
                    +-ON 4-12-80 p37
     Le nozze di Figaro, K 492: Aprite un po quegli'occhi. See no. 3771
     Le nozze di Figaro, K 492: De viene non tardar. See no. 147. See
         no. 3766
     Le nozze di Figaro, K 492: Dove sono. See no. 3670
     Le nozze di Figaro, K 492: E Susanna non viene...Dove sono. See no.
         2088
     Le nozze di Figaro, K 492: Eh capitano...Non piu andrai; Sull'aria
         ...Che soave zeffiretto. See no. 3770
     Le nozze di Figaro, K 492: Non piu andrai...Hai gia vinta la causa
         ...Vedro mentr'io sospiro. See no. 1819
     Le nozze di Figaro, K 492: Non so piu; Voi che sapete. See no.
         3923. See no. 3928
     Le nozze di Figaro, K 492: Overture. See no. 3638. See no. 3688.
         See no. 4033
     Le nozze di Figaro, K 492: Porgi amor; Dovo sono. See no. 3561
     Le nozze di Figaro, K 492: Porgi amor; Voi che sapete; E Susanna
         non vien...Dove sono; Giunse alfin il momento...Deh vieni non
         tardar. See no. 2218
     Le nozze di Figaro, K 492: Se vuol ballare; Non piu andrai. See
         no. 3711. See no. 3812
     Le nozze di Figaro, K 492: Susse Rache ja susse Rache. See no. 3712
     Le nozze di Figaro, K 492: Voi che sapete. See no. 1512
     Le nozze di Figaro, K 492: Wedding march. See no. 3895
2323 Piano works: Adagio, K 540, B minor. Fantasia, K 397, D minor.
     Eine kleine Gigue, K 574, G major. Kleiner Trauermarsch, K 453a,
     C minor. Minuet, K 355, D major. Prelude and fugue, K 394, C
     major. Rondo, K 511, A minor. Trio, G major (attrib.). Vari-
     ations on "Ah vous dirai'je Maman", K 265, C major (12). Paul
     Badura-Skoda, fortepiano. Telefunken AP 6-42425 Tape (c) 4-42425
                    ++ARG 2-80 p51   *HF 2-80 p102 tape
                    +FF 1/2-80 p170   +HFN 4-79 p124
                    +Gr 8-79 p357   +RR 4-79 p102
                    +-FU 9-79 p54   ++St 1-80 p96
2324 Piano works (4 hands): Andante with variations, K 501, G major.
     Fugue, K 426, C minor. Sonatas, piano, 4 hands, K 19d, C major;
     K 357, G major; K 358, B flat major; K 381, D major; K 497, F
     major; K 521, C major. Sonata, 2 pianos, K 448, D major. Ingrid
     Haebler, Ludwig Hoffmann, pno. Philips 6703 088 (3)
                    +ARG 11-79 p42   +FF 11/12-79 p105

           ++CL 1-80 p9   +−NYT 6-3-79 pD22
Prelude and fugue, K 394, C major. See no. 2323
2325 Quartets, flute, K 285, K 298 (4). Richard Adeney, flt; Hugh Ma-
     guire, vln; Cecil Aronowitz, vla; Terence Weil, vlc. Enigma K
     23535
           +HFN 10-80 p115
2326 Quartets, flute, K 285, K 298 (4). Samuel Baron, flt; Fine Arts
     Quartet Members. Saga 5474 (Nos. 1, 4 from SID 5172)
           +−Gr 9-80 p360   +−HFN 10-80 p107
2327 Quartets, flute, K 285, K 298 (4). Paul Robison, flt; Tokyo Quar-
     tet Members. Vanguard VSD 71228 Tape (r) B−C D 71228
           +FF 11/12-78 p92   +NR 6-78 p7
           *HF 1-80 p91 tape   ++SFC 8-20-78 p62
           −MJ 1-79 p46   ++St 8-78 p133
     Quartets, flute, K 285, K 298 (4). See no. 2399
2328 Quartet, oboe, D 370, F major. Quintet, horn, K 407, E flat major.
     Michel Piguet, ob; Hermann Baumann, hn; Esterhazy Quartet. Tele-
     funken AW 6-42173 Tape (c) 4-42173
           +FF 3/4-80 p125   +HFN 5-78 p135
           +−Gr 5-78 p1889   +−NYT 5-4-80 pD24
           +−HF 5-80 p76   +RR 5-78 p45
2329 Quartet, oboe, K 370, F major. Quintet, clarinet, K 581, A major.
     Charles Draper, clt; Leon Goossens, ob; Lener String Quartet.
     World Records SH 318 (From Columbia L 2252/5, CAX 6738/41, LX
     256/7)
           +Gr 9-79 p483   +RR 1-80 p94
           +HFN 12-79 p166   +STL 12-2-79 p37
     Quartet, oboe, K 370, F major. See no. 4
2330 Quartet, piano, K 478, G minor. Quintet, piano, K 452, E flat maj-
     or. James Levine, pno; Ravinia Festival Orchestra Members. RCA
     ARL 1-3376 Tape (c) ARK 1-3376
           −ARG 3-80 p33   ++NYT 10-14-79 pD24
           +FF 3/4-80 p126
2331 Quartet, piano, K 478, G minor. Quartet, piano, K 493, E flat major.
     Dezso Ranki, pno; Pal Eder, vln; Zoltan Toth, vla; Gyorgy Eder,
     vlc. Telefunken 6-42523
           ++FF 11/12-80 p141
     Quartet, piano, K 493, E flat major. See no. 2331
2332 Quartet, strings, nos. 14-19. Chilingirian Quartet. CRD CRD 1062/4
     (3)
           +Gr 12-80 p846   ++HFN 12-80 p143
2333 Quartets, strings, nos. 14-23. Alban Berg Quartet. Telefunken 6-
     35485 (5)
           +−FF 5/6-80 p118   +NYT 2-10-80 pD24
2334 Quartets, strings, no. 14, K 387, G major. Quartets, strings, no.
     15, K 421, D minor. Dimov Quartet. United Artists UACL 10013
           +HFN 3-80 p95   +−RR 1-80 p95
     Quartets, strings, no. 15, K 421, D minor. See no. 2334
2335 Quartets, strings, no. 16, K 428, E flat major. Quartets, strings,
     no. 17, K 458, B flat major. Musikverein Quartet. Decca SDD
     559 Tape (c) KSDC 559
           +Gr 6-80 p44   ++RR 6-80 p69
           +HFN 6-80 p109   ++STL 7-13-80 p38
2336 Quartets, strings, no. 16, K 428, E flat major. Quartets, strings,
     no. 17, K 458, B flat major. Alban Berg Quartet. Telefunken AW
     6-42348

              +FF 5/6-80 p118   +HFN 8-79 p109
              ++Gr 11-79 p866   ++RR 8-79 p99
              +-HF 12-79 p100
Quartets, strings, no. 17, K 458, B flat major. See no. 466. See
     no. 1706. See no. 1707. See no. 2335. See no. 2336
Quartets, strings, no. 17, K 458, B flat major: 1st movement. See
     no. 2398
Quartets, strings, no. 19, K 465, C major. See no. 466
Quartets, strings, no. 23, K 590, F major. See no. 466
2337 Quintets, clarinet, K 581, A major. Trio, clarinet, K 498, E flat
     major. Peter Schmidl, clt; Heinz Medjimorec, pno; New Vienna
     Octet Members. Decca SDD 558 Tape (c) KSDC 558
              +Gr 3-80 p1411   +RR 3-80 p74
              +-HFN 3-80 p95
2338 Quintets, clarinet, K 581, A major. Divertimento, K 136, D major.
     Thea King, clt; Aeolian Quartet. Saga SAGA 5291
              +Gr 3-80 p1449   +RR 2-80 p67
              +HFN 3-80 p107
2339 Quintets, clarinet, K 581, A major. Quintets, piano, K 452, E
     flat major. George Silfies, clt; Walter Klien, pno; Peter Bow-
     man, ob; George Berry, bsn; Roland Pandolfi, hn; Giovanni String
     Quartet. Turnabout TVC 37013 Tape (c) 70013
              ++ARG 11-80 p27   +NYT 5-4-80 pD24
              ++FF 7/8-80 p115   ++St 9-80 p81
Quintets, clarinet, K 581, A major. See no. 2329. See no. 3650
Quintets, clarinet, K 581, A major: 1st movement, excerpt. See no.
     2398
Quintets, horn, K 407, E flat major. See no. 127. See no. 1765.
     See no. 2328
Quintets, piano, K 452, E flat major. See no. 486. See no. 2330.
     See no. 2339
2340 Quintets, strings, nos. 1-6. Juilliard Quartet; John Graham, vla.
     CBS 79322 (3) (also Columbia M3 35896)
              +FF 1/2-80 p117   +NR 12-79 p8
              ++FU 5-80 p46   +NYT 2-10-80 pD24
              ++Gr 11-79 p865   +RR 11-79 p106
              +HF 2-80 p89   +-St 3-80 p99
              +HFN 11-79 p143   +-ST 1-90 p690
2341 Quintets, strings, nos. 1-6. Bulgarian Quartet. Harmonia Mundi
     HM 146/8 (3)
              +-Gr 11-79 p865   +-RR 11-79 p106
              +-HFN 9-79 p121   +-ST 1-80 p690
              +-HFN 12-79 p166
2342 Quintets, strings, nos. 1-6. Budapest Quartet; Milton Katims, Wal-
     ter Trampler, vla. Odyssey Y3 35233 (3) (From Columbia originals
     1942-57)
              +FF 11/12-78 p92   -MJ 1-79 p46
              +HF 2-80 p89
Il Re pastore, K 208: L'amero saro costante. See no. 2218. See no.
     2268. See no. 2302. See no. 3766
Regina coeli, K 276, C major. See no. 2397
Rondo, flute, K Anh 184, D major. See no. 2234. See no. 2399
Rondo, flute, K 485, D major. See no. 514. See no. 2360. See no.
     3825
Rondo, piano, K 511, A minor. See no. 255. See no. 404. See no.
     514. See no. 2323

Rondo, violin, K 269, B flat major. See no. 2206. See no. 2266
Rondo, violin, K 373b, C major. See no. 2235. See no. 2266. See
   no. 3957
Sancta Maria, K 273. See no. 2397
Der Schauspieldirektor, K 486: Overture. See no. 2398
Die Schuldigkeit des ersten Gebots, K 35: Ein ergrimmter Lowe brul-
   let; Hat der Schopfer dieses Leben. See no. 2217
Serenade, no. 3, K 167a (K 185), D major. See no. 2267
2343 Serenades, nos. 4, 6-7, 9. Philharmonia Virtuosi; Richard Kapp.
   Vox SVBX 5107 (3)
           +-Audio 4-80 p48   +NYT 7-15-79 pD22
Serenade, no. 5, K 213a (K 204), D major. See no. 2278
Serenade, no. 6, K 239, D major. See no. 2277
Serenade, no. 7, K 250, D major. See no. 2284
Serenade, no. 7, K 250, D major: Rondo. See no. 3964
Serenade, no. 8, K 286, D major. See no. 2281
2344 Serenade, no. 9, K 320, D major. Serenade, no. 13, K 525, G major.
   VPO; Karl Bohm. DG 2531 191 Tape (c) 3301 191 (From DG 2530 082)
        ++FF 7/8-80 p116   ++SFC 8-31-80 p31
         +HF 12-80 p83   +St 8-80 p97
        ++NR 3-80 p5
Serenade, no. 9, K 320, D major: 6th movement. See no. 2398
2345 Serenades, nos. 10-12. London Wind Ensemble; NPhO Wind Ensemble;
   Otto Klemperer. HMV 3050 Tape (c) RC SXDW 3050
        ++HFN 1-80 p123 tape
2346 Serenade, no. 10, K 361, B flat major. London Sinfonetta; David
   Atherton. Argo ZRG 919
        +-Gr 11-80 p672   +HFN 11-80 p121
2347 Serenade, no. 10, K 361, B flat major.* Serenade, no. 11, K 375,
   E flat major. Serenade, no. 12, K 388, C minor.* London Wind
   Quintet and Ensemble, New Philharmonia Wind Ensemble; Otto Klemperer. HMV SXDW 3050 (2) Tape (c) TC SXDW 3050 (*From Columbia
   SAX 5259, 5290)
        +Gr 10-79 p649   +HFN 1-80 p109
        +HFN 11-79 p155   +-RR 10-79 p97
2348 Serenade, no. 10, K 361, B flat major. CPhO Ensemble. Musicaphon
   BM 30 SL 4115
        +HFN 10-80 p107
2349 Serenade, no. 10, K 361, B flat major. Collegium Aureum. Quintessence PMC 7125 (From Harmonia Mundi, 1972)
        +-Audio 2-80 p42   ++SFC 10-14-79 p61
        +-FF 1/2-80 p118
2350 Serenade, no. 11, K 375, E flat major. Serenade, no. 12, K 388,
   C minor. London Sinfonietta; Antony Pay. Argo ZRG 911 Tape (c)
   KZRG 911
        +-Gr 5-80 p1684   +RR 4-80 p69
        +HFN 4-80 p107   ++STL 5-11-80 p39
2351 Serenade, no. 11, K 375, E flat major. Serenade, no. 13, K 525, G
   major. The Music Party; Alan Hacker. L'Oiseau-Lyre DSLO 549
        +-Gr 5-80 p1684   +RR 5-80 p65
        +-HFN 5-80 p123
Serenade, no. 11, K 375, E flat major. See no. 2347
Serenade, no. 12, K 388, C minor. See no. 2347. See no. 2350
2352 Serenade, no. 13, K 525, G major. Symphony, no. 32, K 318, G major.
   Sinfonia concertante, K 364, E flat major. Alan Loveday, vln;

Stephen Shingles, vla; AMF; Neville Marriner. Argo ARG 679 Tape
(c) KZRG 679 (r) E 679
    ++ARG 9-72 p663   ++HFN 3-72 p513
    ++HF 11-72 p88   +NR 5-72 p663
    ++HF 12-76 p147 tape   ++St 1-73 p110
    +HF 5-80 p90 tape

2353 Serenade, no. 13, K 525, G major. Symphony, no. 29, K 201, A major.
  Bologna Teatro Comunale Orchestra; Angelo Ephrikian. Harmonia
  Mundi HM 1022
    +HFN 3-80 p95   +-RR 3-80 p55
 Serenade, no. 13, K 525, G major. See no. 298. See no. 421. See
  no. 450. See no. 706. See no. 1138. See no. 2208. See no.
  2263. See no. 2318. See no. 2344. See no. 2351
 Serenade, no. 13, K 525, G major: 1st movement. See no. 3715
 Serenade, no. 13, K 525, G major: Tuba serenade. See no. 3568

2354 Sinfonia concertante, KA 9 (K297b), E flat major. Sinfonia concertante, K 364, E flat major. Collegium Aureum. Harmonia Mundi
  065 99801
    +FF 9/10-80 p64   +-RR 11-79 p87
    +HFN 12-79 p166
 Sinfonia concertante, K 297b, E flat major. See no. 2396
 Sinfonia concertante, K 364, E flat major. See no. 2270. See no.
  2273. See no. 2297. See no. 2352. See no. 2354

2355 Il sogno di Scipione, K 126. Lucia Popp, Edita Gruberova, Edith
  Mathis, s; Peter Schreier, Claes Ahnsjo, Thomas Moser, t; Salz-
  burg Chamber Choir; Salzburg Mozarteum; Leopold Hager. DG 2709
  098 (3) (also DG 2740 218)
    +-ARG 10-80 p26   +NR 7-80 p9
    +-Gr 3-80 p1437   +-NYT 5-4-80 pD23
    +-HF 10-80 p84   +RR 4-80 p48
    +HFN 3-80 p93   +-SFC 4-27-80 p35
    +-MT 12-80 p787   +-SR 11-80 p94
    +-MUM 11/12-80 p34   ++St 8-80 p100
 Sonata, bassoon and violoncello, K 292, B flat major. See no. 1470
 Sonatas, flute and harpsichord, nos. 1-6. See no. 2399
 Sonata, piano, C major. See no. 108

2356 Sonatas, piano, nos. 1-17. Walter Gieseking, pno. Seraphim 4ID
  6047/9
    +MUM 7/8-80 p33

2357 Sonatas, piano, nos. 1-17. Glenn Gould, pno. Columbia D5S 35899
  (5) (Reissues)
    +FF 3/4-80 p123   +-MUM 7/8-80 p33

2358 Sonatas, piano, nos. 1-17. Walter Klien, pno. Turnabout SVBX 5428/
  29
    +MUM 7/8-80 p33

2359 Sonatas, piano, nos. 1-10. Lili Kraus, pno. Odyssey Y 33220 (3)
    +HF 8-75 p92   ++NR 3-75 p11
    +MUM 7/8-80 p33   +St 10-75 p112
 Sonata, piano, no. 2, K 280, F major. See no. 2251
 Sonata, piano, no. 5, K 283, G major. See no. 1601
 Sonata, piano, no. 8, K 310, A minor. See no. 408. See no. 3777

2360 Sonatas, piano, nos. 11-17. Fantasia, K 397, D minor. Fantasia,
  K 475, C minor. Rondo, piano, K 485, D major. Lili Kraus, pno.
  Odyssey 33224 (3)
    +HF 8-75 p92   ++NR 3-75 p11
    +MUM 7/8-80 p33   +St 10-75 p112

Sonata, piano, no. 11, K 331, A major. See no. 3811
Sonata, piano, no. 11, K 331, A major: Rondo alla turca. See no.
   3677. See no. 3825
Sonata, piano, no. 11, K 331, A major: 3rd movement. See no. 2398
Sonata, piano, no. 14, K 457, C minor. See no. 2304
Sonata, piano, no. 15, K 545, C major. See no. 182
Sonata, piano, 4 hands, K 19d, C major. See no. 2324
Sonata, piano, 4 hands, K 357, G major. See no. 2324
Sonata, piano, 4 hands, K 358, B flat major. See no. 2324
Sonata, piano, 4 hands, K 381, D major. See no. 2324
Sonata, piano, 4 hands, K 497, F major. See no. 537. See no. 2324
Sonata, piano, 4 hands, K 521, C major. See no. 2324
Sonata, 2 pianos, K 448, D major. See no. 2324

2361 Sonatas, violin and piano, KV 6-9, 26-31. Esmond Wright, hammerflugel; Annegret Diedrichsen, vln. Acanta HA 23005 (2)
                +-Gr 4-80 p1567   +RR 8-79 p110
                +-HFN 9-79 p108   -ST 11-79 p528
                +-MT 12-79 p1009

2362 Sonatas, violin and piano, K 301-306, K 396. Annegret Diedrichsen,
   vln; Desmond Wright, fortepiano. Acanta HA 22478 (2)
                +-HFN 3-80 p95   +ST 8-80 p267
                +RR 3-80 p83

2363 Sonata, violin and piano, K 306, D major. Sonata, violin and piano,
   no. 25, K 377, F major. Sonata, violin and piano, no. 32, K 454,
   B flat major. Sonata, violin and piano, no. 33, K 481, E flat
   major. David Oistrakh, vln; Paul Badura-Skoda, pno. Audax 763
   (2)
                +-FF 9/10-80 p167

2364 Sonatas, violin and piano, nos. 24-28, K 376-380. Variations, K
   359, K 360. Annegret Diedrichsen, vln; Desmond Wright, forte-
   piano. Acanta HA 22638 (2)
                +-HFN 6-80 p109   +ST 8-80 p267
Sonata, violin and piano, no. 25, K 377, F major. See no. 2363
Sonata, violin and piano, no. 32, K 454, B flat major. See no. 2363
Sonata, violin and piano, no. 33, K 481, E flat major. See no. 2363

2365 Songs:Abendempfidung, K 523; Als Luise die Briefe, K 520; Die Alte,
   K 517; An Chloe, K 524; Dans un bois solitaire, K 308; Das Kinder-
   spiel, K 598; Das Traumbild, K 530; Das Veilchen, K 476; Im Fruh-
   lingsanfange, K 597; Die kleine Spinnerin, K 531; Das Lied der
   Trennung, K 519; Oiseaux si tous les ans, K 307; Ridente la calma, K 152; Sehnsucht nach dem Fruhling, K 596; Der Zauberer, K
   492; Die Zufriedenheit, K 349. Elizabeth Schwarzkopf, s; Walter
   Gieseking, pno. HMV ASD 3858 Tape (c) TD ASD 3858 (From 33CX
   1321)
                +Gr 5-80 p1706   +HFN 6-80 p119
                +Gr 9-80 p413 tape   +HFN 9-80 p116 tape

2366 Songs: Abendempfidung, K 523; Als Luise die Briefe Verbrannte, K
   520; Die Alte, K 517; An Chloe, K 524; Dans un bois solitaire, K
   308; Das Lied der Trennung, K 519; Die Kleine Spinnerin, K 531;
   Komm liebe Zither komm, K 351; Un moto di gioia, K 579; Oiseau
   si tous les ans, K 307; Ridente la calma, K 152; Sehnsucht nach
   dem Fruhling, K 596; Sei du mein Trost, K 391; Das Traumbild, K
   530; Das Veilchen, K 476; Die Verschweignung, K 518; Warnung, K
   433; Der Zauberer, K 472; Die Zufriedenheit, K 473. Elly Ameling, s; Jorg Demus, fortepiano; Willi Rosenthal, mand. Seraphim
   S 60334

+NR 9-80 p8   +St 11-80 p79
+ON 12-13-80 p44

2367 Songs: Abendempfidung an Laura, K 523; An Chloe, K 524; Die Betrog-
ene Welt, K 474; Die Kleine Friedrichs Geburtstag, K 529; Der
Fruhling, K 597; Ich wurd auf meinen Pfad, K 340; Das Kinder-
spiel, K 598; Komm Liebe Zither komm, K 351; Das Lied der Trennung, K 519; Lied der Freiheit, K 506; Sehnsucht nach dem Fruhling, K 596; Sei du mein Trost, K 391; Das Traumbild, K 530; Das
Veilchen, K 476; Wie Unglucklich bin ich, K 147; Die Zufriedenheit, K 369.   Peter Schreier, t; Jorg Demus, pno; Erhard Fietz,
mand. Vangaurd VSD 71246
            +ARG 11-79 p44   +ON 12-13-80 p44
            ++FF 11/12-79 p107   ++St 10-79 p144
    Songs: Abendempfidung, K 523; An die Freude, K 53; An die Freund-
schaft, K 125; Dans un bois solitaire, K 308; Das Lied der
Trennung, K 510; Oiseau si tous les ans, K 307; Ridente la calma,
K 152; Sehnsucht nach dem Fruhling, K 596; Das Traumbild, K 530;
Das Veilchen, K 496; Warnung, K 433; Der Zauberer, K 472.   See
no. 2220
    Songs: An Chloe, K 524.   See no. 3537
    Songs: Due pupille amabile, K 439; Luci care luci belle, K 346; Mi
lagnero tacendo, K 437; Piu non si trovano, K 459.   See no. 3952
    Suite, K 399, C minor: Allemande.   See no. 404
2368 Symphonies (Salzburg).   Academy of Ancient Music; Christopher Hogwood.   L'Oiseau-Lyre D170D3 (3) Tape (c) K170D3
            +Gr 9-80 p338   +STL 11-9-80 p40
            +HFN 9-80 p109
2369 Symphonies, nos. 18-27.   Academy of Ancient Music; Jaap Schroder,
vln; Christopher Hogwood, hp.   O'Oiseau-Lyre D169D3 (3) Tape (c)
K169K33
            ++FF 5/6-80 p120   +RR 12-79 p63
            +Gr 12-79 p1008   +SFC 6-1-80 p34
            +Gr 5-80 p1717 tape   +SR 11-80 p94
            +-HF 5-80 p61   ++St 5-80 p72
            +-HFN 1-80 p107   +STL 2-10-80 p40
2370 Symphonies, nos. 21-41.   AMF; Neville Marriner.   Philips 6769 043
(8)
            +Gr 9-80 p338   ++HFN 11-80 p106
2371 Symphonies, no. 23, K 181, D major.   Symphonies, no. 24, K 182, B
flat major.   Symphonies, no. 29, K 201, A major.   Baden Baden
Ensemble 13; Manfred Reichert.   Harmonia Mundi 065 99822
            +HFN 7-80 p109   +-RR 8-80 p49
    Symphonies, no. 24, K 182, B flat major.   See no. 2371
2372 Symphonies, nos. 25, 29, 31-32, 34-36, 38-41.   COA; Josef Krips.
Philips Tape (c) 7699 046
            +-HFN 11-79 p157 tape   +-RR 4-80 p127 tape
2373 Symphonies, no. 25, K 183, G major.   Symphonies, no. 29, K 201, A
major.   BRSO; Lorin Maazel.   Quintessence PMC 7149
            +SFC 8-31-80 p31
2374 Symphonies, nos. 26, 31, 38.   BPhO; Karl Bohm.   DG 2542 127 Tape (c)
3342 127 (From SLPM 139159, 139112)
            +-Gr 9-80 p339   +RR 5-80 p106 tape
2375 Symphonies, no. 26, K 184, E flat major.   Symphonies, no. 31, K 297,
D major.   Symphonies, no. 38, K 504, D major.   BPhO; Karl Bohm.
DG 2542 127

+–HFN 8-80 p107

Symphonies, no. 29, K 201, A major. See no. 2353. See no. 2371.
See no. 2373

2376 Symphonies, nos. 30-41. VPO, ECO, Israel Philharmonic Orchestra,
AMF; Istvan Kertesz, Leonard Bernstein, Robert von Karajan, Ben-
jamin Britten, Zubin Mehta, Neville Marriner, Colin Davis, Carlo
Maria Giulini. Time Life Records unnumbered
+IN 10-80 p12

2377 Symphonies, no. 31, K 297, D major. Symphonies, no. 35, K 385, D
major. Bamberg Symphony Orchestra; Hans Schmidt-Isserstedt.
Acanta DC 21983
+RR 7-80 p58

2378 Symphonies, no. 31, K 297, D major. Symphonies, no. 32, K 318, G
major. Symphonies, no. 35, K 385, D major. Stuttgart Philharmonic Orchestra; Karl Munchinger. London STS 15529
+NR 12-80 p4

2379 Symphonies, no. 31, K 297, D major. Symphonies, no. 35, K 385, D
major. Bamberg Symphony Orchestra; Hans Schmidt-Isserstedt.
Odyssey Y 35921
++FF 5/6-80 p124   +NR 3-80 p4
+FU 6-80 p43   ++SFC 12-30-79 p33

Symphonies, no. 31, K 297, D major. See no. 2375

2380 Symphonies, no. 32, 35-36, 38-41. BPhO; Herbert von Karajan. DG
Tape (c) 3371 038
+HF 7-80 p82 tape

2381 Symphonies, no. 32, K 318, G major. Symphonies, no. 35, K 385, D
major. Symphonies, no. 36, K 425, C major. BPhO; Karl Bohm.
DG 2542 119 Tape (c) 3342 119 (From SLPM 138112, 139160)
+Gr 10-79 p649   +–RR 11-79 p88
+–HFN 11-79 p153   *RR 4-80 p127 tape

Symphonies, no. 32, K 318, G major. See no. 2268. See no. 2352.
See no. 2378

2382 Symphonies, no. 33, K 319, B flat major. Symphonies, no. 40, K 550,
G minor. Collegium Aureum; Franzjosef Maier. Quintessence PMC
7159 Tape (c) 7159
+FF 11/12-80 p142   ++SFC 10-5-80 p21

Symphonies, no. 35, K 385, D major. See no. 2377. See no. 2378.
See no. 2379. See no. 2381

2383 Symphonies, no. 36, K 425, C major. Symphonies, no. 38, K 504, D
major. Mostly Mozart Orchestra; Jean-Pierre Rampal. CBS M 35840
+–FF 11/12-80 p142   -SFC 10-19-80 p20

2384 Symphonies, no. 36, K 425, C major. Symphonies, no. 38, K 504, D
major. Maurits Sillem, hpd; LPO; Charles Mackerras. Classics
for Pleasure CFP 40336 (From CFP 40079)
+Gr 9-80 p335   +–HFN 9-80 p115

2385 Symphonies, no. 36, K 425, C major. Divertimento, K 136, D major.
Mozart Festival Orchestra; George Cleve. Sonic Arts LS 19
+SFC 12-9-80 p33

Symphonies, no. 36, K 425, C major. See no. 2381. See no. 3585

2386 Symphonies, no. 38, K 504, D major. Symphonies, no. 39, K 543, E
flat major. VPO; Karl Bohm. DG 2531 206 Tape (c) 3301 206
+FF 7/8-80 p116   +NR 6-80 p3
++Gr 11-79 p833   +RR 11-79 p88
+HFN 12-79 p166   +–RR 4-80 p127 tape

Symphonies, no. 38, K 504, D major. See no. 1353. See no. 2268.

See no. 2375. See no. 2383. See no. 2384
2387 Symphonies, no. 39, K 543, E flat major. Symphonies, no. 40, K 550,
     G minor. LSO; Colin Davis. Philips 6570 143 Tape (c) 7310 143
     (From 835113)
               +Gr 11-80 p672   +-HFN 12-80 p153
     Symphonies, no. 39, K 543, E flat major. See no. 1752. See no.
     2386
2388 Symphonies, no. 39, K 543, E flat major: 3rd movement. Symphonies,
     no. 41, K 551, C major: 1st movement. ANON.: God save the Queen.
     Beecham lecture highlights "Mozart and his music"; "The changing
     world of music". RPO; Thomas Beecham. World Records SH 1008
               +ARSC Vol 12, no. 3, 1980 p241
2389 Symphonies, no. 40, K 550, G minor. Symphonies, no. 41, K 551, C
     major. BPhO; Herbert von Karajan. DG 2531 138 Tape (c) 3301 138
     (From 2740 189)
               -FF 7/8-80 p117   +-HFN 5-79 p131
               ++Gr 4-79 p1712   +RR 5-79 p65
               +Gr 5-79 p1940 tape
2390 Symphonies, no. 40, K 550, G minor. Symphonies, no. 41, K 551, C
     major. LSO; Claudio Abbado. DG 2531 273 Tape (c) 3301 273
               +-Gr 11-80 p672   +HFN 11-80 p121
               +Gr 12-80 p889   +HFN 12-80 p159 tape
               +-NR 12-80 p4
2391 Symphonies, no. 40, K 550, G minor. Symphonies, no. 41, K 551, C
     major. LSO, BBC Symphony Orchestra; Colin Davis. Philips 6539
     004
               +-HFN 10-80 p106
2392 Symphonies, no. 40, K 550, G minor. Symphonies, no. 41, K 551, C
     major. Salzburg Mozarteum Orchestra; Leopold Hager. Turnabout
     QTVS 34563 Tape (c) KTVC 34563
               -Audio 1-77 p86   /HFN 6-80 p108
               -Gr 4-80 p1557   -RR 4-80 p68
     Symphonies, no. 40, K 550, G minor. See no. 2382. See no. 2387
     Symphonies, no. 40, K 550, G minor: Finale. See no. 2398
2393 Symphonies, no. 41, K 551, C major. SCHUBERT: Symphonies, no. 6,
     D 589, C major. RPO; Thomas Beecham. HMV SXLP 30443 Tape (c)
     SXLP 30443
               +-HFN 10-80 p117 tape   +-RR 8-80 p52
     Symphonies, no. 41, K 551, C major. See no. 2389. See no. 2390.
     See no. 2391. See no. 2392
     Symphonies, no. 41, K 551, C major: 1st movement. See no. 2388
     Symphonies, no. 41, K 551, C major: 1st movement, excerpt. See no.
     2398
     Thamos, King of Egypt, K 345: Entr'acte, no. 2. See no. 2225
     Trio, G major (attrib.). See no. 2323
     Trio, clarinet, K 498, E flat major. See no. 2337
2394 Trios, piano (6). Beaux Arts Trio. Philips 6768 032 (2) (From SAL
     3681/2)
               +-Gr 7-80 p148   ++SFC 9-9-79 p45
               +HFN 8-80 p107   +STL 7-13-80 p38
               ++RR 7-80 p18
     Variations, K 359, K 360. See no. 2364
     Variations on a minuet by Duport, K 573, D major. See no. 1399
     Variations on "Ah vous dirai-je Maman", K 265, C major. See no.
     2251. See no. 2323

Variations on an allegretto, K 500, B flat major. See no. 2304
Variations on "Unser Dummer Pobel", K 455. See no. 618
Veni sancte spiritus, K 47. See no. 2397
Venite populi, K 260. See no. 2397
Vesperae solennes de confessore, K 339, C major. See no. 2312. See
    no. 2397
Vesperae solennes de confessore, K 339, C major: Laudate Dominum.
    See no. 2217
Vesperae solennes de Dominica, K 321: Laudate Dominum. See no. 2217.
    See no. 2397
Vorrei spiegarvi o Dio, K 418. See no. 2218
2395 Works, selections: German dances, K 509 (6). Marches, K 408 (3).
    Minuet, K 409, C major. Minuets, K 599 (6). Die Zauberflote,
    K 620: March of the priests. LSO; Erich Leinsdorf. CBS 76473
    Tape (c) 40-76473 (also Columbia M 35154)
            +-FF 1/2-80 p117   -HFN 5-76 p117 tape
            +Gr 4-76 p1604   +-RR 2-76 p32
            +-HFN 2-76 p105   +-RR 7-76 p83 tape
2396 Works, selections: Concerto, bassoon, K 191, B flat major. Concer-
    to, clarinet, K 622, A major. concerto, flute, no. 1, K 313, G
    major. Concerto, flute, no. 2, K 314, C major. Concerto, flute
    and harp, K 299, C major. Concerti, horn, nos. 1-4. Sinfonia
    concertante, K 297b, E flat major. Alfred Prinz, clt; Dietmar
    Zeman, Peter Schmidl, clt; Fritz Faltl, bsn; Werner Tripp, Wolf-
    gang Schulz, flt; Gerhard Turetschek, Walter Lehmayer, ob; Nica-
    nor Zabaleta, hp; Gunther Hogner, h; VPO; Karl Bohm. DG 2740
    231 (4) (From 2530 441, 2530 527, 5230 715)
            +-Gr 12-80 p836   +-HFN 11-80 p121
2397 Works, selections: Alleluja, K 553. Alma Dei creatoris, K 277.
    Ave Maria, K 554. Ave verum corpus, K 618. Andante, K 616.
    Church sonatas, nos. 1-9. Exsultate jubilate, K 165. Fantasias,
    K 594, K 608. Inter natas mulierum, K 72. Kyrie, K 89, K 341.
    Masses, no. 4, K 139, C minor; no. 6, K 192, F major; no. 10, K
    220, C major; no. 11, K 257, C major; no. 13, K 259, C major; no.
    16, K 317, C major; no. 18, K 427, C minor; no. 19, K 626, D
    minor. Misericordias Domini, K 222. Regina coeli, K 276, C
    major. Sancta Maria, K 273. Veni sancte spiritus, K 47. Ven-
    ite populi, K 260. Vesperae solennes de confessore, K 339, C major.
    Vesperae solennes de Dominica, K 321: Laudate dominum. Elly Am-
    eling, s; Daniel Chorzempa, org; Leipzig Radio Orchestra and
    Chorus, Vienna Boys Choir; Dom Orchestra, ECO, John Alldis Choir,
    LSO and Chorus, BBC Symphony Orchestra, German Bach Soloists;
    Herbert Kegel, Ferdinand Grossman, Raymond Leppard, Colin Davis,
    Helmut Winschermann. Philips 6747 384 (10) (also 6570 079 Tape
    7310 079)
            +-Gr 9-77 p490   +HFN 9-77 p153
            +-Gr 3-80 p1449   +-RR 9-77 p28
2398 Works, selections: Andante, K 315, C major. Concerto, bassoon, K
    191, B flat major: 1st movement, excerpt. Concerto, piano, no.
    21, K 487, C major: 2nd movement. Concerto, 2 pianos, K 365, E
    flat major: 3rd movement, excerpt. Divertimento, no. 17, K 334,
    D major: 3rd movement, excerpt. Exsultate jubilate, K 165: Al-
    leluia. Der Schauspieldirektor, K 486: Overture. Mass, no. 16,
    K 317, C major: Kyrie. Quartet, strings, no. 17, K 458, B flat
    major: 1st movement. Quintet, clarinet, K 581, A major: 1st

movement, excerpt. Serenade, no. 9, K 320, D major: 6th movement.
Sonata, piano, no. 11, K 331, A major: 3rd movement. Symphony,
no. 40, K 550, G minor: Finale. Symphony, no. 41, K 551, C
major: 1st movement, excerpt. Various soloists and orchestras.
Turnabout TV 34802
+NR 2-80 p4

2399 Works, selections: Andante, K 315, C major. concerto, flute, no. 1,
K 313, G major. concerto, flute, no. 2, K 314, D major. Quar-
tets, flute, K 285, K 298 (4). Rondo, flute, K Anh 184, D major.
Sonatas, flute and harpsichord, nos. 1-6. Renee Siebert, flt;
Rodney Friend, vln; Walter Trampler, vla; George Neikrug, vlc;
Judith Norell, hpd; Wurttemberg Chamber Orchestra; Jorg Faerber.
Vox SVBX 5153
++ARG 1-80 p36   ++SFC 7-22-79 p53
+NYT 7-15-79 pD22

Zaide, K 344: Ruhe sanft. See no. 3774

2400 Die Zauberflote, K 620. Rita Streich, Maria Stader, Marianne
Schech, Liselotte Losch, Lisa Otto, s; Margarete Klose, con;
Ernst Hafliger, Howard Vandenburg, Martin Vantin, t; Dietrich
Fischer-Dieskau, bar Josef Greindl, Kim Borg, bs; RIAS Chamber
Choirs, Berlin Motet Choir; RIAS Symphony Orchestra; Ferenc Fric-
say. DG 2701 015 (3) (also DG 2728 009, DG 2701 003) (From DG
18267-9)
+ARSC Vol 12, no. 1-2   +HFN 2-79 p117
      1980 p124   +ON 12-13-80 p44
+-Gr 1-79 p1324   +RR 2-79 p49

2401 Die Zauberflote, K 620. Edith Mathis, Karen Ott, Janet Perry, s;
Francisco Araiza, t; Gottfried Hornik, bar; Jose van Dam, bs;
Deutsch Oper Chorus; BPhO; Herbert von Karajan. DG 2741 001 (3)
Tape (c) 3382 001
+Gr 10-80 p534   +Op 11-80 p1109
+HF 12-80 p76   ++SFC 10-19-80 p20
+HFN 11-80 p121   +St 11-80 p71
+NYT 10-26-80 pB33   +STL 12-14-80 p38
+-ON 12-13-80 p44

Die Zauberflote, K 620: Ach ich fuhl's. See no. 2218
Die Zauberflote, K 620: Ach ich fuhl's; Dies Bildnis ist bezaubernd
schon. See no. 3774
Die Zauberflote, K 620: Arias. See no. 3539
Die Zauberflote, K 620: Bei Mannern. See no. 1819
Die Zauberflote, K 620: Der Vogelfanger bin ich ja...Ein Madchen
oder Weibchen...Papagena Papagena. See no. 3711
Die Zauberflote, K 620: Dies Bildnis ist bezaubernd schon. See no.
3641
Die Zauberflote, K 620: Die Holle rache kocht in meinem Herzen.
See no. 3584. See no. 3872
Die Zauberflote, K 620: March of the priests. See no. 2395
Die Zauberflote, K 620: O loveliness beyond compare; O voice of
magic melody. See no. 3986
Die Zauberflote, K 620: O Isis and Osiris. See no. 3930
Die Zauberflote, K 620: O Isis und Osiris; In diesen heil'gen Hal-
len. See no. 3712
Die Zauberflote, K 620: O zittre nicht mein lieber Sohn. See no.
3646
Die Zauberflote, K 620: Possenti numi. See no. 3899

Die Zauberflote, K 620: Schnelle Fusse. See no. 1622
Die Zauberflote, K 620: Within this hallowed dwelling. See no.
    3905
MUCZYNSKI, Robert
    Dance movements, op. 17. See no. 735
    Serenade for summer, op. 38. See no. 735
MUDARRA, Alonso de
    Diferencies sobre El Conde claros. See no. 3577
    Fantasia. See no. 3665. See no. 3966
    Fantasia que contrahaza la harpa en la manera de Ludovico. See no.
        3577
    Gallarda. See no. 3917
    Pavana. See no. 3577
    Pavana de Alexandre y gallarda. See no. 3577
MUFFAT, George
    Concerto, D minor. See no. 705
    Nova cyclopeias harmonica. See no. 3682
    Passacaglia en sol mineur. See no. 3963
    Suite, E minor. See no. 705
    Toccata, no. 1, D minor. See no. 95
2402 Toccatas, nos. 2-3, 7, 9-10, 12. Rene Saorgin, org. Harmonia Mun-
        di HM 966
                    +Gr 9-80 p376   +HFN 9-80 p109
MUGUERZA
    Tristes amores. See no. 3930
MULET, Henri
    Carillon sortie. See no. 1438. See no. 3725. See no. 3838
    Tu es Petra. See no. 752. See no. 3664. See no. 4056
MULLER
    The girl from Biberach: Jetz gang i ans Brunnele. See no. 3872
MUNDY, John
    Robin. See no. 3755
MUNDY, William
    O Lord the maker of all things. See no. 3894
    Vox patris caelestis. See no. 40
    Were I a king. See no. 3867
MURRAY
    I'll walk beside you. See no. 3875
MURRAY, Bain
    Songs. See no. 3655
MURRELLS
    Sitting by the window. See no. 3875
MURRILL
    Nunc dimittis. See no. 3527
MURSCHHAUSER, Franz
    Aria pastoralis variata. See no. 163
    Lasst uns das Kindelein wiegen. See no. 3682
MUSET, Colin
    Quant je voy yver. See no. 3864
MUSGRAVE, Thea
2403 A Christmas carol. Soloists; Virginia Opera Orchestra; Peter Mark.
        Moss Music Group MMG 302 (3)
                    +-ON 11-22-80 p44
2404 Concerto, horn. Concerto, orchestra. Barry Tuckwell, hn; Keith
        Pearson, clt; Scottish National Orchestra; Thea Musgrave, Alex-

ander Gibson. Decca HEAD 8 (also London HEAD 8)

+FF 7/8-80 p117	++NR 2-76 p6
+Gr 6-75 p46	++RR 5-75 p36
+-HFN 6-75 p89	++SFC 2-26-78 p56
++MJ 3-76 p24	+SR 1-24-76 p53
+MQ 10-77 p570	++STL 6-8-76 p36
++MT 10-75 p886	++Te 3-76 p31

Concerto, orchestra. See no. 2404

2405 Mary Queen of Scots. Ashley Putnam, s; Jon Garrison, Barry Busse, t; Jake Gardner, bar; Kenneth Bell, bs-bar; Virginia Opera Orchestra; Peter Mark. Moss Music Group MMG 301 (3) (also Vox MMG 301)

+ARG 7/8-80 p32	+NR 3-80 p11
+FF 5/6-80 p125	+-ON 11-79 p58
+-Gr 4-80 p1590	++RR 6-80 p35
+-HF 1-80 p83	++St 1-80 p100

MUSHEL, George

Toccata. See no. 4055

MUSSORGSKY, Modest

Boris Godunov: Coronation scene; And you my son; Ouf I suffocate; Well shall we vote; Leave us alone. See no. 3773

Boris Godunov: Yet one more tale. See no. 3904

2406 Ceremonial march. Intermezzo in modo classico. Pictures at an exhibition (orch. Toushmalov). Scherzo, B flat major. Munich Philharmonic Orchestra; Marc Andreae. BASF 20 22128-8 (also Acanta DC 22128)

++FF 3/4-79 p87	+HFN 5-80 p123
++Gr 9-80 p335	++RR 4-80 p69

Fair at Sorochinsk: Gopak. See no. 3860

Intermezzo in modo classico. See no. 2406

Khovanschina: Dance of the Persian slaves. See no. 3807

Khovanschina: Entr'acte, Act 4; Dance of the Persian slaves. See no. 770

Khovanschina: Prelude; Dance of the Persian slaves. See no. 1510

2407 A night on the bare mountain. Pictures at an exhibition. LSO; Georg Richter. CMS/Summit 1021 Tape (c) X 41021

-HF 6-80 p96 tape

2408 A night on the bare mountain (arr. Rimsky-Korsakov). Pictures at an exhibition (arr. Ravel). CO; Lorin Maazel. Telarc 10042

+ARG 11-79 p31	+-RR 12-79 p71
+-FF 11/12-79 p14	++SFC 10-12-80 p21
+HF 11-79 p107	++St 11-79 p81
++HFN 12-79 p166	

A night on the bare mountain. See no. 767. See no. 769. See no. 1288. See no. 1510. See no. 2630. See no. 3254

The nursery. See no. 1536

2409 Pictures at an exhibition (orch. Ravel). PROKOFIEV: Symphony, no. 1, op. 25, D major. LPO; John Pritchard, Arthur Davison. Classics for Pleasure CFP 40319 (From CFP 106)

+Gr 10-79 p649	+-RR 10-79 p101
-HFN 10-79 p159	+RR 7-80 p97 tape
+HFN 1-80 p123 tape	

2410 Pictures at an exhibition (orch. Ravel). RAVEL: La valse. NYP; Zubin Mehta. Columbia M 35165 Tape (c) MT 35165 (also CBS 76880)

+-ARG 9-80 p35	+-HF 8-80 p66

        +—FF 11/12-80 p143   +HFN 9-80 p109
        +—Gr 9-80 p335
2411 Pictures at an exhibition. SHOSTAKOVICH: Preludes, op. 34, no. 1,
     4, 12, 12, 14-16, 19, 22, 24. Lazar Berman, pno. DG 2531 096
     Tape (c) 3301 096
             +—CL 3-80 p12   +—HFN 5-79 p134 tape
             +FF 7/8-79 p72   +—MJ 11/12-79 p49
             +Gr 3-79 p1590   +MM 5-79 p34
             ++Gr 7-79 p256 tape   +RR 3-79 p113
             +HF 7-79 p145   ++St 9-79 p94
             +—HFN 4-79 p124
2412 Pictures at an exhibition (trans. Wills). Arthur Wills, org. Hyp-
     erion AS 66006
             +Gr 12-80 p854   +HFN 11-80 p143
2413 Pictures at an exhibition. RAVEL: Le tombeau de Couperin. CSO;
     Georg Solti. London LDR 10040 (also Decca SXDL 7520 Tape (c)
     KSXDC 7520)
             +Gr 12-80 p836   ++SFC 11-23-80 p21
             +—HFN 12-80 p143
2414 Pictures at an exhibition. LISZT: The battle of the Huns. OSR;
     Ernest Ansermet. London STS 15475
             +—FF 1/2-80 p119
2415 Pictures at an exhibition. PROKOFIEV: Sonata, piano, no. 3, op. 28,
     A minor. Visions fugitives, op. 22, nos. 1, 3, 5-6, 8, 10, 14,
     16-18. Oxana Yablonskaya, pno. Orion Tape (c) In Sync C 4034
             +HFN 9-80 p105 tape   +NR 9-80 p10 tape
2416 Pictures at an exhibition. STRAVINSKY: The firebird: Suite (Agosti).
     Robin McCabe, pno. Vanguard VSD 71264
             +—ARG 3-80 p43   +HF 2-80 p90
             +—Audio 2-80 p94   ++SFC 10-28-79 p53
             +—FF 3/4-80 p159   +—St 2-80 p133
             +FU 6-80 p47
2417 Pictures at an exhibition. SCHUMANN: Carnival, op. 9. Benno Mois-
     ievitsch, pno. Westminster MCA 1408
             +ARG 12-80 p40   -FF 9/10-80 p169
     Pictures at an exhibition. See no. 770. See no. 1317. See no.
     1718. See no. 2406. See no. 2407. See no. 2408
     Pictures at an exhibition: The great gate at Kiev. See no. 3555
     Scherzo, B flat major. See no. 2406
2418 Songs: Sunless cycle. SHOSTAKOVICH: King Lear: Songs of the fool.
     Songs: Preface to the complete collection of my works and brief
     reflections, op. 123; Romance to words from "Krokodil", op. 121;
     Verses of Captain Lebyadkin, op. 146. Yevgeny Nesterenko, bs;
     Vladimir Krainev, Yevgeny Shenderovich, pno. HMV ASD 3700
             +FF 3/4-80 p152   ++MM 11-79 p29
             +Gr 9-79 p496   +RR 8-79 p118
             +HFN 9-79 p108   +STL 12-2-79 p37
     Songs and dances of death: Trepak. See no. 3601. See no. 3904
MUTHEL, Johann
     O traurigkeit. See no. 4039
     Sonata, flute. See no. 3845
MUZIO
     Mazurka. See no. 3769
MYSLIVECEK, Josef
     Suite, strings. See no. 3752

2419 Quintets, strings, nos. 1-4, 6.   Czech Chamber Soloists; Miroslav
        Matyas.   Supraphon 110 1880
                    +Gr 7-77 p197   +-RR 6-77 p61
                    +HFN 8-77 p147   ++SFC 2-17-80 p44
                    +NR 10-77 p7
NAKADA
        A behavazott verosban.   See no. 3814
NANA-ZUCCA
        The big brown bear.   See no. 3831
NANCARROW, Conlon
2420 Studies, player piano, nos. 4-6, 14, 22, 26, 31-32, 35, 37, 40a-40b.
        Recorded in composer's studio, Mexico City.   1750 Arch S 1777
                    ++FF 9/10-80 p170   +Te 9-80 p85
                    +NR 8-80 p12
NAPRAVNIK, Eduard
        Dubrovsky: Oh give me oblivion.   See no. 3774
        Dubrovsky: Vladimir's recitative and romance.   See no. 3796
2421 Sonata, violin and piano, op. 52, G major.   Grigori Feigin, vln;
        Viktor Poltoratsky, pno.   Melodiya S10 09699-700
                    +FF 1/2-80 p174
NARDINI, Pietro
2422 Concerto, violin, E flat major.   TARTINI: Concerto, violin, D major.
        Eduard Melkus, vln; Vienna Cappella Academica; August Wenzinger.
        DG 2547 027 Tape (c) 3347 027 (From 198370)
                    +-Gr 9-80 p413 tape   +HFN 10-80 p117 tape
                    +-HFN 6-80 p117   +RR 8-80 p265
        Concerto, violin, E minor.   See no. 1939
        Sonata, violin, no. 1, B flat major.   See no. 998
NARVAEZ, Luis de
        Baxa de contrapunto.   See no. 3577
        Cancion de Emperador.   See no. 3577
        Diferencias sobre "El Conde claros".   See no. 3577
        Diferencias sobre "Guardame las vacas".   See no. 3577.   See no. 3917
        Los seys libros del Delphin de musica, Bk 1: Fantasia, no. 5; Bk 2:
            Fantasias, nos. 5-6; Bk 3: La cancion del emperador; Bk 4: O
            glorioso domina: Variations (6); Bk 5: Arde corazon arde, ya se
            asiente el Rey Ramiro; Bk 6: Conde claros, Guardame las vacas,
            Tres diferencias por otra parte, Baxa de contrapounto.   See no.
            2181
NAUDOT, Jacques-Christophe
        Concerto, flute and strings, G major.   See no. 1242
NEAR, Gerald
        O magnum mysterium.   See no. 3992
NEDBAL, Oskar
        Sonata, violin and piano, op. 9, B minor.   See no. 1430
NEEDHAM
        My dark Rosaleen.   See no. 4070
NEGRI, Cesare
        La nizzarda.   See no. 3956
NELHYBEL, Vaclav
        Concert etudes.   See no. 3821
        Concertino da camera.   See no. 1825
NERUDA, Jan Krtitel
        Concerto, trumpet, E flat major.   See no. 1680

NESTICO, Sammy
    A study in contrasts. See no. 3718
NEUSIDLER, Hans
    Danse washa mesa. See no. 3612
    Hie folget ein welscher Tantz. See no. 3966
    Ich klag den Tag. See no. 3966
    Der Judentanz. See no. 3966
    Mein Herz hat sich mit Lieb verpflicht. See no. 3966
    Mon coeur s'est d'amour rempli. See no. 3612
    Preambule et danse du plectre. See no. 3612
NEVIN, Ethelbert
    Ein Liedchen. See no. 4045
NEWMAN
    Airport: Main theme. See no. 4046
NICHELMANN, Christoph
    Cembalostucke. See no. 3845
NICOLAI, Otto Karl
    Die lustigen Weiber von Windsor (The merry wives of Windsor): Als
        Bublein klein. See no. 3712
    Die lustigen Weiber von Windsor: Overture. See no. 3688. See no.
        3847
    Die lustigen Weiber von Windsor: Verfuhrer warum; Wie freu ich mich.
        See no. 3770
    The temple knight. See no. 3824
NIEDERMEYER
    Pieta signore. See no. 3983
NIELSEN, Carl
2423 At a young artist's bier (Andante lamentoso). The mother, op. 41:
        Incidental music (3). Quintet, woodwinds, op. 43. Serenata in
        vano. West Jutland Chamber Ensemble. DG 2530 515
            +-Gr 11-80 p692   +NR 2-76 p5
            +HF 4-76 p118   +St 5-76 p119
2424 Canto serioso. Fantasias, op. 2. The mother, op. 41. Quintet,
        winds, op. 43. Serenata in vano. Athena Ensemble. Chandos ABR
        1003
            +Gr 3-80 p1411   +RR 2-80 p67
            +HFN 2-80 p97
    Chaconne, op. 32. See no. 1566
2425 Commotio, op. 58. Preludes, op. 51 (31). Elisabeth Westenholz,
        org. BIS LP 131
            +HFN 6-80 p109   +-RR 3-80 p84
            +NR 2-80 p13
2426 Concerto, flute. NORBY: Illuminations. Jean-Pierre Rampal, flt;
        Sjaellands Symphony Orchestra; John Frandsen. Erato STU 71273
            +Audio 2-80 p47   +HFN 9-79 p109
            +-Gr 11-79 p834   +-RR 10-79 p101
    Fantasias, op. 2. See no. 2424
    An imaginary journey to the Faroe Islands. See no. 2431
    Little suite, op. 1, A minor. See no. 1546
2427 Maskarade. Edith Brodersen, Tove Hyldgaard, s; Gurli Plesner, con;
        Tonny Landy, Christian Sorensen, t; Mogens Schmidt Johansen,
        Gert Bastian, Ove Verner Hansen, bar; Ib Hansen, bs-bar; Aage
        Haugland, Jergen Klint, bs; Danish Radio Orchestra and Chorus;
        John Frandsen. Unicorn RHS 350/2 (3) Tape (r) B-C W 0350 (also
        UN 3-75006)

                +ARG 12-78 p34   +NR 8-78 p12
                +FF 7/8-78 p60   +ON 6-78 p48
                +Gr 4-78 p1762   ++Op 5-78 p492
                +HF 7-78 p92   +RR 4-78 p22
                +HF 7-80 p82 tape   ++SFC 6-18-78 p43
                ++HFN 5-78 p123   ++St 6-78 p150
                +MT 9-78 p770

    The mother, op. 41. See no. 2424
    The mother, op. 41: Incidental music. See no. 2423
    Motets, op. 55. See no. 3587
    Pan and syrinx, op. 49. See no. 2431
    Preludes, op. 51 (31). See no. 2425
2428 Quartet, strings, no. 2, op. 5, F minor. Quartet, strings, no. 3,
        op. 14, E flat major. Nielsen Quartet. DG 2531 135
                ++ARG 4-80 p35   +-NR 1-80 p6
                +FF 3/4-80 p128   +NYT 2-10-80 pD24
    Quartet, strings, no. 3, op. 14, E flat major. See no. 2428
    Quintet, op. 43. See no. 60. See no. 1782. See no. 2423. See
        no. 2424
    Saul and David: Prelude, Act 2. See no. 2430
    Serenato in vano. See no. 2423. See no. 2424
    Sonata, violin and piano, no. 2, op. 35. See no. 699
2429 Symphonies, nos. 1-3. Jill Gomez, s; Brian Rayner Cook, bar; LSO;
        Ole Schmidt. Unicorn KPM 7001/3 (From RHS 324/330)
                +-Gr 11-80 p674   +HFN 11-80 p129
2430 Symphony, no. 1, op. 7, G minor. Saul and David: Prelude, Act 2.
        LSO; Andre Previn. RCA GL 4-2872 Tape (c) GK 4-2872 (From SB
        6714)
                ++Gr 8-80 p225   +HFN 9-80 p116 tape
                +Gr 9-80 p413 tape   +ST 8-80 p344
2431 Symphony, no. 4, op. 29. An imaginary journey to the Faroe Islands.
        Pan and Syrinx, op. 49. Scottish National Orchestra; Alexander
        Gibson. RCA RL 2-5226 Tape (c) RK 2-5226
                +Gr 1-80 p1158   +RR 1-80 p84
                +HFN 1-80 p109

NIEMAN, Alfred
2432 Canzona for quintet. Chromotempera. Rohan de Saram, vlc; Yitkin
        Seow, pno; New Cavendish Quintet. Serenus SRS 12079
                +-ARG 5-80 p28   +NR 10-79 p6
                +-FF 11/12-80 p144
    Chromotempera. See no. 2432
NILSSON, Torsten
2433 Nos angustiae. Marianne Mellnas, s; Karl-Erik Welin, org; Oscar's
        Motet Choir; Torsten Nilsson. BIS LP 123
                +FF 9/10-79 p118   +-RR 4-80 p115
                +-HFN 3-80 p95
NIN-CULMELL, Joaquin
    Cantilena asturiana. See no. 3964
    Songs: Pano murciano; Asturiana. See no. 3551
NIXON
    By-by-baby. See no. 3993
NIXON, Roger
2434 Fiesta del Pacifico. REED: la fiesta mexicana. SURINACH: Paeans
        and dances of heathen Iberia. Eastman Wind Ensemble; Donald
        Hunsberger. Westminster MCA 1409 (From Decca DL 10157)
                +FF 9/10-80 p185

NOBLE
    Magnificat and nunc dimittis. See no. 966
NOBRE, Marlos
    Ago lona. See no. 3849
2435 In memoriam. SANTORO: Interacoes assintoticas. VILLA-LOBOS: Bach-
    ianas brasileiras, no. 1. Orquesta Sinfonica del Brasil; Isaac
    Karabtchevsky. Inter-American Musical Editions OEA 002
                +LAMR Fall/Winter 1980 p291
NOLA, Gian Domenico da
    Chi la gagliarda. See no. 3683
NONO, Luigi
    Como una ola de fuerza y luz. See no. 3705
    Sofferte onde serene. See no. 3705
NOON, David
    Motets and monodies. See no. 710
NORBY, Erik
    Illuminations. See no. 2426
NORDENSTROM, Gladys
    Zeit XXIV. See no. 1908
NORDHEIM, Arne
    Dinosaurus. See no. 1905
2436 Songs: Doria; Epitaffio; Greening. Peter Pears, t; RPO; Per Dreier.
    Decca HEAD 23
            +Gr 1-80 p1158   +-MT 4-80 p252
           ++HFN 12-79 p166   +RR 2-80 p59
2437 The tempest: Suite. Susan Campbell, s; Christopher Keyte, bar;
    South German Radio Orchestra and Chorus; Charles Darden; Elec-
    tronic realisation by Bohdan Mazurek. Philips 9598 043
            +Gr 8-80 p225   +HFN 8-80 p99
NORMAN, Theodore
    Moods in 12 tone. See no. 3884
    Samba. See no. 3884
    Toccata. See no. 3884
NORMIGER, August
    Tantz Adelich und from. See no. 3590
    Viel Freuden mit sich bringet. See no. 3590
    Von Gott will ich nicht lassen. See no. 3590
NOUGES, Jean
    Quo Vadis: Amica l'ora. See no. 3978
    Quo Vadis: Errar sull'ampio mar. See no. 3980
    Quo Vadis: Viens pres de moi. See no. 3774
NOVA, Sayat
    Songs (2). See no. 3850
NOVACEK, Ottokar
2438 Perpetuum mobile, op. 5, no. 4. SIBELIUS: Concerto, violin, op. 47,
    D minor. SINDING: Suite, op. 10, A minor. Ruggiero Ricci, vln;
    Bochum Symphony Orchestra, Luxembourg Radio Orchestra; Matthias
    Kuntzsch, Louis de Froment. Turnabout QTV 34722
            +ARG 6-79 p46   +-NYT 7-6-80 pD15
            +-FF 1/2-80 p148   ++SFC 8-12-79 p49
            +NR 3-79 p7   +-St 7-79 p102
NOVAK
    Prelude on a Wallachian love song. See no. 4067
NOVAK, Vitezslav
    Sonata, violin and piano, D minor. See no. 1430

NUMMI, Seppo
    Songs: Mietteliaat vainiot; Mutta kun olen runoniekka; Rakastunut.
        See no. 1880
NUNES GARCIA, Jose Mauricio
    Lauda Sion salvatorem. See no. 3707
NUTILE
    Mamma mia che vo sapete. See no. 3946
NYSTEDT
    Velsignet vaere han. See no. 3527
NYSTROEM, Gosta
    Songs by the sea. See no. 1850
OBRECHT, Jacob
2439 Missa fortuna desperata. ANON.: Fortuna desperata (chanson).
        Clemencic Consort; Rene Clemencic. Harmonia Mundi HM 998 (also
        Musical Heritage Society MHS 4122)
                    +-Gr 8-78 p366   +-HFN 6-78 p125
                    +FF 11/12-80 p145
    Vavilment. See no. 3702
O'BRIEN
    The fair tree. See no. 3947
O'BRIEN, Eugene
    Lingual. See no. 3655
OCHS, Siegfried
    's kommt ein Vogerl geflogen. See no. 1818
OCKEGHEM, Johannes
    Deploration sur la mort de Binchois. See no. 3910
    Missa "Cuiusivis toni". See no. 3910
2440 Missa prolationem. Capella Nova. Musical Heritage Society MHS
        4026
                    +NYT 8-10-80 pD17
    Missa prolationem. See no. 2014
2441 Motets: Alma redemptoris mater; Ave Maria; Celeste beneficium;
        Gaude Maria; Intemerata dei mater; Salve regina I and II. BUS-
        NOIS: In hydraulis. Capella Nova. Musical Heritage Society
        MHS 4179
                    +FF 9/10-80 p171   ++NYT 8-10-80 pD17
2442 Requiem. Clemencic Consort; Rene Clemencic. Harmonia Mundi HM 999
        (also HNH 1013)
                    +ARG 1-80 p27   ++RR 1-78 p78
    Songs: L'Autre d'antan l'autrier passa; Ma bouche rit. See no.
        3880
O'CONNOR
    The old house. See no. 3947
OFFENBACH, Jacques
2443 Arias: Barbe-bleue: Y'a des bergers; Faut'il y aller...V'la d'encor
        de droi's de jeunesses. La belle Helene: C'est le devoir des
        jeunes filles; Amours divins ardentes flammes; On me nomme Helene
        la blonde. La grande Duchesse de Gerolstein: Vous aimez le dan-
        ger...Ah que j'aime les militaires; Voici le sabre de mon pere;
        Dites-lui qu'on l'a remarque; Il etait des mes aieux. La Peri-
        chole: Ah quel diner je viens de faire; Oh mon cher amant je te
        jure; Que veulent dire ces coleres...Ah que les hommes sont bet-
        es; Tu n'est pas beau tu n'es pas riche. La vie parisienne:
        Vous souvient'il ma belle; C'est ici l'endroit redoute. Jane
        Rhodes, ms; Ellane Lavall Acquitaine Vocal Ensemble; Brodeau

Aquitaine Orchestra; Roberto Benzi. EMI 2C 069 16386
        +Gr 9-80 p398   +-HFN 11-80 p122
Barbe-bleu: Wedding scene and polonaise. See no. 2449
Barbe-bleu: Y'a des bergers; Faut-il y aller...V'la d'encor de droi's
    de jeunesses. See no. 2443
La belle Helene: C'est le devoir des jeunes filles; Amours divins
    ardentes flammes; On me nomme Helene la blonde. See no. 2443
La belle Helene: Dis-moi Venus. See no. 3774
2444 La belle Helene: Overture. Les belles Americaines: Waltz. Gene-
    vieve de Brabant: Galop. Grand Duchess of Gerolstein: Overture.
    Musette: Air de ballet. Orpheus in the underworld: Overture.
    La perichole: Potpourri. The tales of Hoffmann: Intermezzo, In-
    troduction, Minuet, Barcarolle. Samuel Mayes, vlc; BPO; Arthur
    Fiedler. RCA GL 4-3193 Tape (c) GK 4-3193 (From HMV CLP 1101,
    RCA VICS 1466)
            +Gr 8-80 p225   +RR 8-80 p50
        +-HFN 9-80 p116
La belle Helene: Overture. See no. 2449. See no. 3962
Les belles Americaines: Waltz. See no. 2444
La chanson de fortunio: La chanson de fortunio. See no. 3770
La chanson de fortunio: Overture. See no. 2449
Les contes de Hoffmann (The tales of Hoffmann): Doll's song. See
    no. 3559. See no. 3828. See no. 3872. See no. 4071
Les contes de Hoffmann: Epilogue; Barcarolle; Entr'acte; Duet, Giu-
    lietta and Hoffmann; Intermezzo, Act 1. See no. 4069
Les contes de Hoffmann: Intermezzo, Introduction, Minuet, Barcarol-
    le. See no. 2444
Les contes de Hoffmann: Legend of Kleinsack. See no. 3986
Les contes de Hoffmann: Sie entfloh die Taube so minnig Hoffmann;
    Antonia...Ich wusst es ja Du liebest mich noch. See no. 3584
Les deux aveugles: Overture. See no. 2449
2445 Duos, violoncello, op. 54: Suites, nos. 1 and 2. Roland Pidoux,
    Etienne Peclard, vlc. Harmonia Mundi HM 1043 Tape (c) HM 40-1043
            ++FF 9/10-80 p175   +HF 11-80 p70
        +Gr 6-80 p44
2446 Gaite parisienne (arr. Rosenthal). STRAUSS, J. II: Graduation
    ball, op. 97 (arr. Dorati). PhO; Charles Mackerras. Arabesque
    8020
            +FF 11/12-80 p149   +St 7-80 p82
Gaite parisienne, excerpts. See no. 1289
Genevieve de Brabant: Galop. See no. 2444. See no. 3962
Grande Duchesse de Gerolstein: Overture. See no. 2444
Grande Duchesse de Gerolstein: Vous aimez le danger...Ah que j'aime
    les militaires; Voici le sabre de mon pere; Dites-lui qu'on l'a
    remarque; Il etait de mes aieux. See no. 2443
2447 Madame Favart. Lina Dachary, s; Linda Felder; Aime Doniat, bar;
    Gerard Chapuis, bs; Bernard Plantey, bar; Orchestra; Jean Dous-
    sard. Rare Recorded Editions RRE 159/60 (2)
            +ARG 4-80 p10
Un mari a la porte: Overture. See no. 2449
Musette: Air de ballet. See no. 2444
2448 Orfee au enfers (Orpheus in the underworld). Jane Rhodes, Mady
    Mesple, Michele Pena, Michele Command, s; Jane Berbie, ms; Mic-
    hel Senechal, Charles Burles, Andre Mallabrera, Bruce Brewer, t;
    Michel Trempont, bar; Toulouse Capitole Orchestra and Chorus;

Michel Plasson.   Angel SZCX 3886 (3) Tape (c) 4Z3X 3886 (also
HMV SLS 5175)

+-ARG 12-79 p46   +NYT 9-30-79 pD22
+FF 1/2-80 p120   +Op 6-80 p620
+Gr 3-80 p1437   +RR 3-80 p41
+HFN 3-80 p95   +-SFC 11-25-79 p46
++MT 10-80 p635   ++St 12-79 p147
++NR 12-79 p9   +STL 3-9-80 p41

Orfee au enfers: Overture.   See no. 2444.   See no. 2449.   See no.
    3638
La perichole: Ah quel diner je viens de faire; Oh mon cher amant
    je te jure; Que veulent dire ces coleres...Ah que les hommes ont
    betes; Tu n'est pas beau tu n'es pas riche.   See no. 2443
La perichole: O mon cher amant.   See no. 3770
La perichole: Potpourri.   See no. 2444
La permission de dix heures: Overture.   See no. 2449
La vie parisienne: Vous souvient-il ma belle; C'est ici l'endroit
    redoute.   See no. 2443
2449 Works, selections: Barbe-bleu: Wedding scene and polonaise.   La
    belle Helene: Overture.   La chanson de fortunio: Overture.   Les
    deux aveugles: Overture.   Orfee au enfers: Overture.   La permis-
    sion de dix heures: Overture.   Un mari a la porte: Overture.
    Raphaele Concert Orchestra; Peter Walden.   Raphaele RRS 103
                    +Gr 11-80 p674

OGERMAN
    Symphonic dances: 1st and 2nd movements.   See no. 1574
O'HARA, Geoffrey
    The perfect melody.   See no. 4045
OHKI, Masao
    Night meditation.   See no. 1456
OLAGUE, Bartolomeo
    Sonata de 8 tono.   See no. 3871
OLAN, David
    Composition, clarinet and tape.   See no. 1433
    Sonata, violin and piano.   See no. 1433
OLIVER
    Yonder.   See no. 3903
OLIVIERI
    Canzona a due voci: Menia d'amore.   See no. 3771
    Garibaldi hymn.   See no. 3983
OLSEN, Sparre
2450 Serenade, op. 46.   ORBECK: Pastorale and allegro.   MORTENSEN: Son-
    ata, flute, op. 6.   SOMMERFELT: Varlater (Spring tunes), op. 44.
    Per Oien, flt; Norwegian Chamber Orchestra.   BIS LP 103
                    +-RR 4-80 p70
OLSSON
    Songs: Advent; Christmas.   See no. 3933
OLSSON, Otto
    Ave maris stella, op. 42.   See no. 2451.   See no. 3934
    Berceuse, op. 45.   See no. 2451
    Fantasia cromatica.   See no. 2451
2451 Organ works: Ave maris stella, op. 42.   Berceuse, op. 45.   Fantasia
    cromatica.   Sestetto.   Sonata, organ, op. 38, E major.   Hans
    Fagius, org.   BIS LP 85
                    +FF 3/4-80 p129   +RR 3-80 p85
                    +HFN 6-80 p109

Sestetto. See no. 2451

Sonata, organ, op. 38, E major. See no. 2451

ONSLOW, George

Sonata, piano, op. 7, E minor. See no. 339

ORBECK, Anne-Marie

Pastorale and allegro. See no. 2450

ORD HUME

The royal marine. See no. 3619

ORFF, Carl

2452 Antigone. Inge Borkh, Claudia Hellmann, s; Hetty Plumacher, con;
Gerhard Stolze, Fritz Uhl, Ernst Hafliger, t; Carlos Alexander,
bar; Kim Borg, Keith Engen, bs; Bavarian Radio Orchestra and
Chorus; Ferdinand Leitner. DG 2740 226 (3) (From SLPM 138717)
+Gr 8-80 p266   +-HFN 11-80 p129

2453 Astutuli. Carl Orff, speaker. Harmonia Mundi 1C 065 99869
*FF 11/12-80 p149

2454 Carmina burana. Arleen Auger, s; John van Kesteren, t; Jonathan
Summers, bar; PhO and Chorus; Riccardo Muti. Angel SZ 37666
Tape (c) 4ZS 37666 (also HMV ASD 3900 Tape (c) TC ASD 3900)
+-FF 11/12-80 p150   +NR 10-80 p9
++Gr 8-80 p251   +-NYT 9-7-80 pD29
+Gr 10-80 p548 tape   +-RR 8-80 p87
+-HFN 8-80 p101   -SFC 8-17-80 p36
+-HFN 9-80 p116 tape   ++St 12-80 p130

2255 Carmina burana. Virginia Babikian, s; Clyde Hager, t; Guy Gardner,
bar; Houston Chorale, Houston Youth Symphony Boys Choir; Houston
Symphony Orchestra; Leopold Stokowski. Classics for Pleasure
CFP 40311 Tape (c) TC CFP 40311 (From Capitol SP 8470)
+-Gr 9-79 p496   +HFN 2-80 p107 tape
+HFN 7-79 p109   +-RR 8-79 p119

2456 Carmina burana. Milada Subrtova, s; Jaroslav Tomanek, t; Teodor
Srubar, bar; CPhO; Vaclav Smetacek. Quintessence PMC 7122
+-ARG 2-80 p41

2457 Carmina burana. Lucia Popp, s; John van Kesteren, Karl Kreil, t;
Anton Rosner, bar; Heinrich Weber, t; Hermann Prey, bar; Paul
Hansen, Gunter Haussler, Josef Weber, bs; Bavarian Radio Orches-
tra and Chorus; Kurt Eichhorn. RCA GL 2-5196 Tape (c) GK 2-5196
+-Gr 11-79 p895   +-RR 10-79 p142
-HFN 10-79 p171   +-RR 3-80 p104 tape
+-HFN 1-80 p123 tape

2458 Catulla carmina. Arleen Auger, s; Wieslaw Ochman, t; German Opera
Chorus; Eugen Jochum. DG 2535 403 Tape (c) 3335 403 (From 2530
074)
++Gr 6-80 p59   +HFN 9-80 p116 tape
++HFN 6-80 p119   +RR 6-80 p88
+-HFN 8-80 p107

2459 Gassenhauer (Street song). Tolzer Boys Choir; Instrumental Ensem-
ble; Carl Orff. Quintessence PMC 7127 Tape (c) P4C 7127 (From
BASF HC 25122)
+ARG 4-80 p36   +St 4-80 p137
++SFC 10-21-79 p57

2460 Die Kluge (The wise woman). Elisabeth Schwarzkopf, s; Rudolf Christ,
Paul Kuen, t; Gottlob Frick, Georg Weiter, Hermann Prey, bar;
Benno Kusche, Marcel Cordes, Gustav Neidlinger, bs-bar; PhO;
Wolfgang Sawallisch. Arabesque 8021-2 (2) From Angel 3551)

+ARG 10-80 p27   +NYT 7-13-80 pD20
++FF 9/10-80 p177
2461 Lamenti. Lucia Popp, s; Hanna Schwarz, con; Rose Wagemann, ms; Her-
mann Prey, bar; Karl Ridderbusch, bs; Carl Orff, speaker; Bavar-
ian Radio Chorus; Munich Radio Orchestra; Kurt Eichhorn. BASF
22458/9 (2) (also Acanta HC 22458)
+-FF 11-77 p42   ++NR 3-77 p11
+HFN 5-80 p123   +-RR 4-80 p115
2462 Oedipus Tyrannus. Hubert Buchta, Heinz Cramer, speakers; Astrid
Varnay, s; Gerhard Stolze, James Harper, t; Hans Gunter Nocker,
Carlos Alexander, bs-bar; Karl Christian Kohn, Keith Engen, bs;
Bavarian Radio Orchestra and Chorus; Rafael Kubelik. DG 2740
227 (3) (From SLPM 139251/3)
+Gr 8-80 p266   ++RR 8-80 p88
+HFN 8-80 p107
2463 Schulwerk: Street song. Tolzer Boys Choir; Instrumental Ensemble;
Carl Orff. Quintessence PMC 7127 (From BASF HC 25122)
+-FF 3/4-80 p130   ++SFC 10-21-79 p57
+ARG 4-80 p36   +St 4-80 p137
+HFN 12-80 p143
2464 Trionfo di Afrodite. Enriqueta Tarres, Brigitte Durrlers, Hannel-
ore Bode, Carol Malone, s; Donald Grobe, Horst Laubenthal, Andre
Peysang, Toni Maxen, t; Werner Becker, bar; Hans Gunter, bs; Col-
ogne Radio Orchestra and Chorus; Ferdinand Leitner. Acanta DC
22454
+HFN 3-80 p107   ++RR 4-80 p70
ORGAD, Ben-Zion
Shaar Shaar. See no. 3739
ORNSTEIN, Leo
2465 A biography in sonata form. Michael Sellers, pno. Orion ORS 78285
+FF 3/4-80 p184   -FU 9-79 p56
Impressions de Notre Dame. See no. 3727
ORR, Charles
Songs: Along the field; The lent lily; Oh when I was in love with
you. See no. 3837
Songs: Along the field; Bahnhofstrasse; Farewell to barn and stack
and tree; In valleys green and still; Is my team ploughing; The
lads in their hundreds; When I watch the living meet; When smoke
stood up from Ludlow; With rue my heart is laden; While summer
on is stealing. See no. 1813
ORTELLI
The glass mountain: Song of the mountains. See no. 3771
ORTIZ, Alfredo
La guabina. See no. 3676
Llanos. See no. 3676
Recercadas, no. 2. See no. 158
Recercadas, nos. 2 and 4. See no. 3593
Recercadas felici occhi mei. See no. 3593
Recercadas primera y segunda. See no. 3864
OSNOWYCZ, Anne
Impro mi. See no. 3760
OSSEWAARDE
Fanfare for Easter Day. See no. 4059
OTHMAYR, Kaspar
Mir ist ein feins Brauns Maidelein. See no. 4042

OUSELEY, Frederick
    Songs: It came even to pass; When all thy mercies o my God.   See no.
        3525
OXINAGA
    Sonata de 5 tono.   See no. 3871
PACHELBEL, Charles
    Magnificat.   See no. 4068
PACHELBEL, Johann
    Canon, D major.   See no. 18.   See no. 145.   See no. 299.   See no.
        1398.   See no. 3715.   See no. 3943.   See no. 3957.   See no. 3998.
        See no. 3999
    Canon sur une basse obstinee.   See no. 1027
    Chaconne, C major.   See no. 1458
2466 Chaconne, F minor.   Fantasia, G minor.   Partitas: Werde munter mein
        Gemute, Was Gott tut das ist wohlgetan.   Ricercare, C minor.   Toc-
        cata pastorale, F major.   Helmut Winter, org.   Harmonia Mundi HM
        582
                        +FF 7/8-80 p119
    Chaconne, F minor.   See no. 164.   See no. 167.   See no. 3957
    Ciacona, D minor.   See no. 4050
    Fantasia, G minor.   See no. 2466
    Fughetta.   See no. 3883
    Partitas: Werde munter mein Gemute, Was Gott tut das ist wohlgetan.
        See no. 2466
    Ricercare, C minor.   See no. 2466.   See no. 3757
    Suites, B flat major, G major.   See no. 1027.   See no. 1398
    Suites, lute.   See no. 286
    Toccata pastorale, F major.   See no. 2466
    Vom Himmel hoch.   See no. 3993
PADEREWSKI, Jan
    Minuet, op. 14, no. 1, G major.   See no. 3856.   See no. 3907
2467 Sonata, piano, op. 21, E flat minor.   Variations and fugue, op. 23,
        E flat major.   Antonin Kubalek, pno.   Citadel CT 7001 (also Mus-
        ical Heritage Society MHS 4103)
                    ++FF 7/8-80 p119   +NR 3-79 p15
                    +HF 10-79 p103   +-RR 12-78 p97
    Variations and fugue, op. 23, E flat minor.   See no. 2467
PAER, Ferdinando
2468 Leonora.   Ursula Koszut, Edita Gruberova, s; Siegfried Jerusalem,
        Norbert Orth, John van Kesteren, t; Wolfgang Brendel, bar; Gior-
        gio Tadeo, bs; Bavarian Symphony Orchestra; Peter Maag.   Decca
        D130D3 (3) Tape (c) K130K33 (also London OSA 13133)
                    +-ARG 3-80 p34   +-MM 9-79 p32
                    +-FF 1/2-80 p121   +-MT 1-80 p35
                    +-FU 2-80 p47   +-NR 6-80 p10
                    +-Gr 8-79 p368   +NYT 9-30-79 pD22
                    +Gr 11-79 p924 tape   +-ON 2-2-80 p28
                    +-HF 1-80 p84   +-Op 1-80 p62
                    +HFN 7-79 p99   +-RR 7-79 p37
                    +HFN 10-79 p171 tape   /SFC 9-23-79 p37
    La maitre de Chapelle: Pour limiter.   See no. 3770
    O dolce concento: Variations.   See no. 3770
PAGANINI, Niccolo
    Cantabile, op. 17, D major.   See no. 824
2469 Caprices, op. 1, nos. 1-24.   Caprice, no. 25.   Duo, solo violin.

Ruggiero Ricci, vln.   Ultra Fi ULDD 11 (2)
          ++MUM 1/2-80 p35
Caprices, op. 1, nos. 9, 11.   See no. 957
Caprices, op. 1, nos. 13, 20.   See no. 3964
Caprices, op. 1, nos. 13, 20, 24.   See no. 3964
Caprices, op. 1, no. 14, E flat major. See no. 3601
Caprices, no. 25.   See no. 2469
2470 Centone di sonate, op. 64, nos. 1, 3-4, 6.   Grand sonata, violin
     and guitar, A major.   Sonata, violin, A major.   Sonatas, violin
     and guitar, op. 6 (6).   Sonja Prunnbauer, gtr; Gyorgy Terebesi,
     vln.   Telefunken 6-41300 Tape (c) 4-41300 (r) 6-41300
          ++HF 2-78 p104 tape   +HF 1-80 p91 tape
2471 Concerto, violin, no. 1, op. 6, D major.   Concerto, violin, no. 2,
     op. 7, B minor.   Shmuel Ashkenasi, vln; VSO; Herbert Esser.   DG
     2535 207 Tape (c) 3335 207 (From SLPM 139424)
          ++Audio 6-80 p43   +RR 12-76 p63
          +Gr 12-76 p1001   +-RR 2-77 p98 tape
          +HFN 12-76 p151
2472 Concerto, violin, no. 1, op. 6, D major.   Victor Tretyakov, vln;
     MPO; Neimye Yarvy.   Musical Heritage Society MHS 4181
          +-FF 11/12-80 p151
2473 Concerto, violin, no. 2, op. 7, B minor.   SAINT-SAENS: Concerto,
     violin, no. 1, op. 20, A major.   Ruggiero Ricci, vln; Cincinnati
     Symphony Orchestra; Max Rudolf.   Westminster MCA 1402 (From Dec-
     ca DL 10106)
          +FF 9/10-80 p177   ++SFC 3-23-80 p35
Concerto, violin, no. 2, op. 7, B minor.   See no. 2471
Concerto, violin, no. 2, op. 7, B minor: La clochette.   See no.
     3785
2474 Concerto, violin, no. 6, op. posth., E minor.   Salvatore Accardo,
     vln; LPO; Charles Dutoit.   DG Tape (c) 3335 421
          +HFN 11-80 p131 tape
Duo, solo violin.   See no. 2469
Grand sonata, violin and guitar, A major.   See no. 2470
Moto perpetuo, op. 11.   See no. 3964
Moto perpetuo, op. 11, no. 2.   See no. 3951
Quartet, strings, E minor.   See no. 1903
Sonata, viola, op. 35, C minor.   See no. 1800
Sonata, violin, A major.   See no. 2470
Sonatas, violin and guitar, op. 6 (6).   See no. 2470
Sonatas, violin and guitar, nos. 1, 4.   See no. 957
Le Streghe, variations on a theme by Sussmayr, op. 8.   See no. 824
Variations on "Di tanti palpiti" from Rossini's "Trancredi", op. 13.
     See no. 1388
Variations on "Nel cor piu non mi sento".   See no. 3637
PAINE, John
     Concert variations on "Austria", op. 3.   See no. 4062
PAISIELLO, Giovanni
2475 Il barbiere di Siviglia.   Graziella Sciutti, s; Nicola Monti, Flor-
     indo Andreolli, t; Rolando Panerai, bar; Mario Petri, Renato
     Capecchi, Leonardo Monreale, bs; Collegium Musicum Italicum; I
     Virtuosi di Roma; Renato Fasano.   Dischi Ricordi AOCL 216001 (2)
     (From Delyse D 56079/80)
          /Gr 1-80 p1194
Nina: Il mio ben quando vera.   See no. 3636

Songs: Nel cor piu non mi sento.   See no. 3669
PAIX, Jacob
   Der Keyserin Tantz.   See no. 3590
PALADILHE, Emile
   Psyche.   See no. 3770
PALESTRINA, Giovanni de
   Adoramus te.   See no. 599
   Dies santificatus.   See no. 3993
   Haec dies.   See no. 3528
   Hodie Christus natus est.   See no. 3697
   Missa Papae Marcelli.   See no. 40
   Missa Sine Nomine: Kyrie.   See no. 3531
   Motets: Cantabo domino; Dextera domini; Exaltabo te; Improperium ex-
      spectavit; Paucitas dierum; Tota pulchra es; Vox dilecti mei;
      Vulnerasti cor meum.   See no. 391
   Ricercare del primo tuono.   See no. 4001
2476 The song of songs. CPhO Chorus; Josef Veselka. Supraphon 412 2141/
      2 (2)
               ++ARG 6-80 p33   +-HFN 4-80 p101
                +FF 5/6-80 p126   +NR 3-80 p10
                +Gr 8-80 p252   +-RR 6-80 p89
               ++HF 9-80 p95
2477 Songs: Alma redemptoris mater; Ave Maria; Ave regina caelorum; Mis-
      sa sine nomine (Mantua); Regina caeli; Salve regina. Schola
      Cantorum Sankt Foillan, Aachen; Wilhelm Eschweiler. Da Camera
      Magna SM 94054
                +FF 5/6-80 p126
   Songs: Anyai sziv; Jesu rex admirabilis.   See no. 3814
   Terra tremuit.   See no. 3763
PALIASHVILI, Zachary
2478 Absalom and Etery. Lamara Chkoniya, Zisana Tatishvili, s; Liana
      Tatishvili, Olga Kuszenova, ms; Surab Sotkilava, Abrek Pirzcha-
      lava, Aedischer Gelashvili, t; Shota Kiknadze, bar; Irakli Shus-
      haniya, Nikolay Kapanadze, bs; USSR Radio Orchestra and Chorus;
      Didim Mirzchulava. DG 2709 094 (3) (also Melodiya 33 CM 02831-
      36)
               +ARG 6-80 p28   +NR 2-80 p10
               +FF 5/6-80 p127   +NYT 12-16-79 pD21
               +FF 7/8-80 p120   +RR 12-79 p41
               +Gr 11-79 p908   +-SFC 1-6-80 p43
               +HFN 11-79 p143   +St 4-80 p137
PALMER, Rudolph
   Contrasts.   See no. 3821
PANUFNIK, Andrzej
2479 Autumn music. Heroic overture. Nocturne. Tragic overture. LSO;
      Jascha Horenstein. Unicorn RHS 306
                +FF 11/12-80 p152   +RR 3-80 p57
               ++NR 8-75 p5
   Heroic overture.   See no. 2479
   Homage to Chopin.   See no. 3781
2480 Invocation for peace. Thames pagaent. John Amis, narrator; King's
      House School Choir; Thames Youth Ensemble; Michael Stuckey.
      Unicorn UNS 264
                +Gr 3-80 p1428   +RR 5-80 p98
               +-HFN 3-80 p97   +Te 9-80 p86

Nocturne. See no. 2479
2481 Sinfonia di Sfere. Sinfonia mistica. LSO; David Atherton. Decca
     HEAD 22
                    +Gr 6-79 p54   +RR 5-79 p34
                    ++HFN 6-79 p109   +Te 9-80 p86
     Sinfonia mistica. See no. 2481
     Thames pagaent. See no. 2480
     Tragic overture. See no. 2479
PAPELYAN, Stepan
     La fin d'un reve. See no. 3850
PARADIS, Maria Theresia von
     Sicilienne. See no. 3552. See no. 3772. See no. 3788. See no.
        4030
PARCHAM, Andrew
     Solo, G major. See no. 986
PARISH-ALVARS, Elias
2482 Nocturne, E flat major. Reveries, op. 82. Romances sans paroles,
        nos. 4-6. Serenade. Giselle Herbert, hp. Da Camera Magna SM
        93002
                    +FF 1/2-80 p122
     Reveries, op. 82. See no. 2482
     Romances sans paroles, nos. 4-6. See no. 2482
     Serenade. See no. 2482
PARKER
     Love is come again. See no. 4059
PARMEGIANI, Bernard
2483 De natura sonorum. Harmonia Mundi INA GRM AM 71401
                    +FF 7/8-80 p16
2484 Dedans dehors. Pour en finir avec le pouvoir d'Orphee. Harmonia
        Mundi INA Gramme 9102
                    +FF 7/8-80 p16
     Pour en finir avec le pouvoir d'Orphee. See no. 2484
PARRY, Charles Hubert
     The birds: Bridal march. See no. 3801
     Chorale prelude, no. 4: The old 104th. See no. 4050
2485 Chorale preludes, op. 205: Martyrdom; St. Thomas; Croft's 136th;
        St. Cross. Fantasia and fugue, op. 188, G major. Little organ
        book. Toccata and fugue, op. 222. Roy Massey, org. Vista VPS
        1086
                    +Gr 11-79 p876   +MT 11-80 p712
                    +HFN 1-80 p109   +RR 4-80 p100
     Chorale prelude on "St. Thomas". See no. 4053
     Dear Lord and father of mankind. See no. 3527
2486 Elegy to Johannes Brahms. Symphonic variations. Symphony, no. 5,
        B minor. LPO; Adrian Boult. HMV ASD 3725 Tape (c) TC ASD 3725
                    +FF 5/6-80 p128   +HFN 2-80 p107 tape
                    ++Gr 11-79 p834   +-MT 11-80 p711
                    +Gr 3-80 p1446 tape   ++RR 11-79 p89
                    +HFN 11-79 p143   +-Te 3-80 p30
     English suite. See no. 3996
     Fantasia and fugue, op. 188, G major. See no. 2485
     Fantasia on the old 104th. See no. 4064
     I was glad when they said unto me. See no. 3815. See no. 3835.
        See no. 3937
     Jerusalem, op. 208. See no. 3939

Little organ book. See no. 2485
Love is a bable. See no. 3562
2487 Songs: And yet I love her till I die; Blow blow thou winter wind;
    Bright star; From a city window; Looking backward; Love is a
    bable; Marian; No longer mourn for me; O mistress mine; On a
    time the amorous Silvy; Take o take those lips away; There be
    none of beauty's daughters; There; Thine eyes still shine for
    me; Weep you no more; A Welsh lullaby; When icicles hang by the
    wall; When come my Gwen; When lovers meet again; When we two par-
    ted. Robert Tear, t; Philips Ledger, pno. Argo ZK 44
            +-Gr 10-79 p690   ++RR 10-79 p142
            ++HFN 10-79 p159   +STL 12-2-79 p37
            +MT 5-80 p322

    Songs: O mistress mine; Proud Maisie. See no. 3778
    Symphonic variations. See no. 2485
    Symphony, no. 5, B minor. See no. 2485
    Toccata and fugue (The wanderer). See no. 4048
    Toccata and fugue, op. 222. See no. 2485
    When I survey the wondrous cross, chorale fantasia. See no. 4050
PARSCH, Arnost
2488 The bird flew above the clouds. REZAC: Sinfonietta. Jiri Kaniak,
    ob; PSO, Brno PO; Jindrich Rohan, Jiri Belohlavek. Supraphon
    110 2339
            ++NR 8-80 p3
PARSONS, Robert
    Ave Maria. See no. 3894
    Joan quoth John. See no. 3876
    Pandolpho. See no. 3941
PARTOS, Oedoen
    Quartet, piano. See no. 3739
PARVIAINEN, Jarmo
    Toccata and fugue. See no. 3726
PASADAS
    Noche feliz. See no. 3983
PASQUINI, Bernardo
    Partita sopra al Aria della Folia da Espagna. See no. 4021
    Partita sopra la Aria della Folia de Espagna. See no. 4023
PASSEREAU, Pierre
    Il est bel et bon. See no. 3971
PATACHICH, Ivan
    Hangzo Fuggvenyek. See no. 1385
    Maganhangzok. See no. 1385
    Metamorphoses. See no. 3810
PAUER, Jiri
    Quintet, winds. See no. 400
PAULLI, Holger
    The Kermesse in Bruges. See no. 1770
PAYET
    Cabellos de oro. See no. 3607. See no. 3635
    Lejania. See no. 3607. See no. 3635
PAYNE
    Quartet, tubas. See no. 4033
PEARSALL
    Songs: Light of my soul; Waters of Elle. See no. 3791

PECK, Russell
  Suspended sentence. See no. 3727
PEEL, Graham
  Songs: In summertime on Bredon; Reveille; When the lad for longing
    sighs. See no. 3837
PEERSON, Martin
  The fall of the leaf. See no. 3590
  The primrose. See no. 3590
  Upon my lap. See no. 3941
PEETERS, Flor
  Ave maris stella, op. 28. See no. 4057
  Chorale prelude, O God thou faithful God. See no. 4067
  Chorale prelude on "How brightly shines the morning star", op. 68,
    no. 7. See no. 3836. See no. 4056
2489 Concerto, organ and piano, op. 74. STANFORD: Fantasia and toccata,
    op. 57, D minor. Short preludes and postludes, op. 101, Set II.
    SANTLEY: Voluntary, E minor (arr. Campbell). Ronald Perrin, org.
    Vista VPS 1040
            +−Gr 3-77 p1444   +NR 1-80 p12
            +−HF 7-77 p95   /-RR 3-77 p83
            +MU 7-77 p14
  Konzertstuck, op. 52a. See no. 4047
  Suite modale, op. 43: Adagio. See no. 3838
PEIROL (13th century France)
  Quant amors trobet partit. See no. 3748
PELUSI
  Concert piece, baritone, saxophone, brass quintet and percussion.
    See no. 755
PENKERECKI, Krzysztof
2490 Anaklasis. De natura sonoris II. Fluorescences. Kosmogonia.
    Stefania Woytowicz, s; Kazimierz Pustelak, t; Bernard Ladysz, bs;
    Warsaw Philharmonic Orchestra and Chorus; Andrzej Markowski.
    Philips 6500 683
            +Gr 3-90 p1428   ++SFC 12-8-74 p36
            ++HF 1-75 p84   +St 5-75 p98
            *NR 11-74 p7
  Cantata in honor of the Jagellonian University on the 600th anniver-
    sary of its founding. See no. 2491
2491 Canticum canticorum Salomonis. Cantata in honor of the Jagellonian
    University on the 600th anniversary of its founding. Strophes.
    Stefania Woytowicz, s; Andrzej Szalawski, narrator; Cracow Phil-
    harmonic Orchestra and Chorus; Jerzy Katlewicz. Muza SX 1151
            +FF 7/8-80 p121
2492 Concerto, violin. Isaac Stern, vln; Minnesota Orchestra; Stanislaw
    Skrowaczewski. Columbia M 35150 (also CBS 76739)
            +ARG 9-79 p34   +MT 9-80 p567
            ++FF 7/8-79 p77   ++NR 6-79 p7
            +FU 9-79 p58   +NYT 4-18-79 pD28
            ++Gr 7-80 p142   ++RR 4-80 p75
            +HF 9-79 p123   +SFC 4-1-79 p44
            ++HFN 4-80 p107   +St 7-79 p103
  De natura sonoris II. See no. 2490
  Fluorescences. See no. 2490
  Kosmogonia. See no. 2490
2493 Saint Luke Passion. Stefania Woytowicz, s; Andrzej Hiolsi, bar;

Bernard Ladysz, bs; Rudolf Jurgen Bartsch, speaker; Tolzer Boys
Choir; Cologne Radio Orchestra and Chorus; Henryk Czyz. Harmonia
Mundi 1C 156 99660/1 (2)
      +FF 5/6-80 p128   +HFN 11-78 p173
      +Gr 1-79 p1316   ++RR 9-78 p90

Stabat mater. See no. 3857
Strophes. See no. 2491
Threnody to the victims of Hiroshima. See no. 70. See no. 3857

2494 Utrenja. Delfina Ambroziak, Stefania Woytowicz, s; Krystyna Szczepanska, ms; Kazimierz Pustelak, t; Wiodzimierz Denysenko, Bernard Ladysz, bar; Boris Carmeli, Peter Lagger, bs; Pioneer Choir;
Warsaw Orchestra and Chorus; Andrzej Markowski. Philips 6700 065
(2) (also Philips 6500 557/8. Also Muza 889 890)
      +FF 7/8-80 p121   +NR 3-74 p8
      +Gr 3-74 p1729   ++RR 2-74 p57
      ++HF 5-74 p91   ++SFC 4-14-74 p26
      +HFN 2-74 p343   ++St 6-74 p122
      +MJ 2-74 p9

PENN
    Smiling through. See no. 3875
PENNINO
    Pecche. See no. 3667. See no. 4008
PENTLAND, Barbara
    Interplay. See no. 1905
PEPPING, Ernst
    Bearbeitungen uber Vom Himmel hoch da komm ich her. See no. 3591
    Sollt ich meinem Gott ich singen. See no. 4036
PEPUSH, John
    Sonata, guitar. See no. 3717
    Sonata, recorder, no. 4, F major. See no. 986
PERGOLESI, Giovanni
    Concerto, flute, G major. See no. 25
    Concerto armonico, no. 2, G major. See no. 2498
2495 Miserere, no. 2, C minor. Ilse Wolf, s; David James, alto; Roger
Covey-Crump, t; Richard Stuart, bs; Magdalen College Choir; Wren
Orchestra; Bernard Rose. Argo ZRG 915
      +Gr 8-80 p252   +HFN 8-80 p101
2496 La serva padrona. Maddalena Bonifaccio, s; Siegmund Nimsgern, bs-
bar; Collegium Aureum. Harmonia Mindu 1C 065 99749
      +Gr 3-80 p1438   +RR 3-80 p42
      +-HFN 3-80 p107
2497 La serva padrona. La Scala Orchestra; Carlo Maria Giulini. Seraphim 60333
      ++ARG 7/8-80 p35   +-NYT 7-13-80 pD20
    La serva padrona: Stizzoso mio stizzoso; A serpina penserete. See
no. 3723
    Songs: Se tu m'ami. See no. 3669
    Songs: Se tu m'ami; Aria di Martia. See no. 3687
2498 Stabat mater. Concerto armonico, no. 2, G major (attrib. Ricciotti).
Felicity Palmer, s; Alfreda Hodgson, con; David Hill, org; St.
John's College Choir; Argo Chamber Orchestra; George Guest.
Argo ZRG 913 Tape (c) KZRC 913
      /-Gr 11-80 p724   +HFN 11-80 p107

PERI, Jacopo
    Al fonte al prato. See no. 3878

PERKIN, Helen
    Carnival suite: Burlesque. See no. 3621
PERKOWSKI, Piotr
    Nocturne. See no. 3857
PERLE, George
    Etudes (6). See no. 3859
    Quintet, woodwinds, no. 3. See no. 3731
2499 Songs: Dickinson songs (13); Rilke songs (2). Bethany Beardslee,
       s; Morey Ritt, George Perle, pno. CRI SD 403

+—ARG 1-80 p39	+MT 12-79 p1010
+FF 3/4-80 p14	+HF 12-79 p100
+—FU 2-80 p48	++St 12-79 p148

PERNAMBUCO, Joao
    Sons de carrilhoes. See no. 3614
PEROTINUS LE GRAND
    Organum "Virgo". See no. 3910
2500 Songs: Alleluja nativitas; Sederunt omnes; Viderunt omnes. ANON.:
      Alleluja Christus resurgens with the clausula "Mors"; Dic Christi
      veritas; Pater Noster commiserans. Alfred Deller, c-t; Deller
      Consort. Harmonia Mundi 065 99634

+Gr 3-80 p1433	+RR 10-79 p139
+HFN 9-79 p123	

PERSICHETTI, Vincent
    Concerto, English horn, op. 137. See no. 1796
    Concerto, piano, 4 hands. See no. 1914
2501 Parable, solo oboe. SCHMIDT: The sparrow and the amazing Mr. Avaunt.
      STILL: Miniatures, flute, oboe and piano. THOMPSON: Suite, oboe,
      clarinet and viola. Peter Christ, ob; Alan de Veritch, vla;
      David Atkins, clt; Gretel Shanley, flt; Sharon Davis, pno. Cry-
      stal S 321

+ARG 9-80 p51	+NR 4-80 p9
-FF 5/6-80 p129	++St 4-80 p140

    Parable II. See no. 99
    Sonata, piano, no. 9. See no. 1176
PERTI
    Aestuat mundi mare, motet. See no. 3716
    Quando si belle, aria. See no. 3716
PERTIS
    Unfaithful girl. See no. 3803
PERUGIA, Matteo de
    Belle sans per. See no. 2502
    Dame d'onour. See no. 2502
    Dame que j'aym. See no. 2502
    Dame souvrayne. See no. 2502
    Gia da rete d'amor. See no. 2502
    Helas merci. See no. 2502
    Ne me chaut. See no. 2502
    Pour bel accueil. See no. 2502
    Pres du soleil. See no. 2502
    Se je me plaing. See no. 2502
    Sera quel zorno mai. See no. 2502
    Trover ne puis. See no. 2502
2502 Works, selections: Belle sans per. Dame d'onour. Dame que j'aym.
      Dame souvrayne. Gia da rete d'amor. Helas merci. Ne me chaut.
      Pour bel accueil. Pres du soleil. Se je me plaing. Sera

quel zorno mai. Trover ne puis. Medieval Ensemble of London.
L'Oiseau-Lyre DSLO 577
+Gr 4-80 p1579   +RR 4-80 p114
+-HFN 4-80 p108
PESCETTI, Giovanni
    Sonata, harp, C minor. See no. 3890
PETERSEN, Wilhelm
2503 Quartet, piano, op. 42, C minor. Sinfonietta, op. 5. Variations,
    string orchestra, op. posth. Mainz Chamber Orchestra; Jacque-
    line Eymar, pno; Kehr Trio; Gunther Kehr. Da Camera Magna SM
    92412/3 (2)
                /ARG 6-80 p36
    Sinfonietta, op. 5. See no. 2503
    Variations, string orchestra, op. posth. See no. 2503
PETERSON, Wayne
    Capriccios (42). See no. 376
PETERSON-BERGER, Olof Wilhelm
2504 Songs, op. 11 (8). A walk in the mountains, op. 6. Malmo Kammar-
    kor; Lunds Studentsangare; Dan-Olof Stenlund. BIS LP 139
                ++FF 11/12-80 p153
    A walk in the mountains, op. 6. See no. 2504
PETRALLI, Vincenzo
    Versets (2). See no. 3762
PETRASSI, Goffredo
2505 Concerti, orchestra, nos. 1 and 2. BBC Symphony Orchestra; Zoltan
    Pesko. Italia ITL 70005
                +Gr 3-80 p1391
PETRICH
    Ah holy Jesus. See no. 4059
PETRIE, Henry
    Roll on thou deep and dark blue ocean. See no. 3905
PETROVICS, Emil
    Hungarian children's songs (15). See no. 3885
    Slow dancing tune. See no. 3803
PETTERSSON, Gustaf Allen
2506 Sonatas, 2 violins, nos. 1-2, 4-6. Josef Grunfarb, Karl-Ove Mann-
    berg, vln. Caprice CAP 1138
                ++ARG 4-80 p36   +RR 5-80 p89
                +FF 1/2-80 p123
2507 Symphony, no. 8. Baltimore Symphony Orchestra; Sergiu Comissiona.
    DG 2531 176
                +FF 11/12-80 p153   ++SFC 6-1-80 p35
                +HF 11-80 p73   ++St 8-80 p74
                ++NR 7-80 p2
2508 Symphony, no. 8. Baltimore Symphony Orchestra; Sergiu Comissiona.
    Polar POLS 289
                +-ARG 7-79 p10   +-FF 1/2-80 p123
2509 Symphony, no. 9. Gothenburg Symphony Orchestra; Sergiu Comissiona.
    Philips 6767 951 (2)
                +FF 1/2-80 p123
PETTMAN
    O babe divine. See no. 3823
PEUERL, Paul
    Intrade, sarabande and bal. See no. 4001

PEZEL, Johann
    Intradas, nos. 1, 3, 8, 10. See no. 4043
    Sarabande. See no. 4043
    Sonata hora decima, no. 22. See no. 4000
    Sonatinas, 2 trumpets and violoncello, nos. 4 and 5, C major. See
      no. 3866
PFITZNER, Hans
2510 Der arme Heinrich: Dietrichs Erzahlung. Songs: An den Mond, op. 18;
    An die Mark, op. 15, no. 3; Herr Oluf, op. 12; Lethe, op. 37; Sie
    haben heut abend Gesellschaft, op. 4, no. 2; Zorn, op. 15, no. 2.
    Dietrich Fischer-Dieskau, bar; Bavarian Radio Orchestra; Wolf-
    gang Sawallisch. EMI 1C 065 45616
         +—Gr 5-80 p1706   +RR 7-80 p93
2511 Das Christelfein. Soloists; Vienna Boys Choir; ORTF Orchestra and
    Chorus; Ernst Maerzendorfer. MRF Records MRF 159 (2)
         ++FF 11/12-80 p155
    Concerto, piano, op. 31. See no. 425
2512 Quartet, strings, no. 1, op. 13, D major. Quartet, strings, D
    minor. Sinnhoffer Quartet. Musical Heritage Society MHS 4101
         +FF 11/12-80 p155
    Quartet, strings, D minor. See no. 2512
2513 Die Rose vom Liebesgarten. Soloists; Symphony Orchestra and Chorus;
    Robert Heger. Rococo 1020 (2)
         /NR 2-80 p12
2514 Songs: Abschied, op. 9, no. 5; Das Alter, op. 41, no. 4; Der Bote,
    op. 5, no. 3; Die Einsame, op. 9, no. 2; Der Gartner, op. 9, no.
    1; Im Herbst, op. 9, no. 3; In Danzig, op. 21, no. 1; Klage op.
    25, no. 2; Der Kuhne, op. 9, no. 4; Lockung, op. 7, no. 4; Die
    Nachtigallen, op. 21, no. 2; Nachts, op. 26, no. 2; Nachtwander-
    er, op. 7, no. 2; Neue Liebe, op. 26, no. 3; Sonst, op. 15, no.
    4; Studentenfahrt, op. 11, no. 3; Der Vespatete Wanderer, op.
    41, no. 2; Der Weckruf, op. 40, no. 6; Zorn, op. 15, no. 2; Zum
    Abschied meiner Tochter, op. 10, no. 3. Wolfgang Annheisser,
    bar; Julius Severin, pno. Acanta DC 21087
         +Gr 8-80 p252   +RR 7-80 p93
         +HFN 6-80 p109
    Songs: An den Mond, op. 18; An die Mark, op. 15, no. 3; Herr Oluf,
    op. 12; Lethe, op. 37; Sie haben heut abend Gesellschaft, op. 4,
    no. 2; Zorn, op. 15, no. 2. See no. 2510
    Symphony, op. 46, C major. See no. 3710
PHALESE, Pierre
    L'Arboscello ballo furlano. See no. 3754
PHILE
    The president's march. See no. 3971
PHILIDOR, Francois
    La belle esclave: O ciel se pourrait-il...Quel espoir est pour moi.
    See no. 1538
    Les femmes vengees: De la coquette volage. See no. 1538
    Melide ou le navigateur: Tout dormait. See no. 1538
    Tom Jones: Respirons un moment...O toi que ne peut m'entendre. See
    no. 1538
PHILIPPE DE CHANCELIER
    Mundus a munditia. See no. 3960
PHILIPS, Peter
    Amarilli di Julio Romano. See no. 3719

Ascendit Deus. See no. 3783. See no. 3894
Galliard and chromatic pavan. See no. 3966
Songs: Ecce tu pulchra es; O beatum et sacrosanctum diem. See no.
      3530
PIATIGORSKY, Gregor
      Variations on a theme by Paganini (14). See no. 4003
PIAZZA, Gaetano
      Sonata, 2 organs, F major. See no. 2010. See no. 4027
PICCHI, Giovanni
      Ballo alla Polacha. See no. 2515
      Ballo detto il Picchi. See no. 2515
      Ballo ditto il Stefanin. See no. 2515
      Ballo Ongaro. See no. 2515
2515 Harpsichord works: Ballo alla Polacha. Ballo detto il Picchi.
      Ballo ditto il Stefanin. Ballo Ongaro. Padoana ditta la Ong-
      ara. Pass'e mezzo antico di sei parti. Saltarello del ditto
      pass'e mezzo. Todesca. Toccata. Ton Koopman, hpd. Telefunken
      AP 6-42212 Tape (c) 4-42212
                  +-ARG 2-80 p50   +HF 2-80 p102 tape
                  +FF 1/2-80 p170   +HFN 11-78 p181
                  +Gr 9-78 p507   +RR 9-78 p83
      Padoana ditta la Ongara. See no. 2515
      Pass'e mezzo antico di sei parti. See no. 2515
      Saltarello del ditto pass'e mezzo. See no. 2515
      Toccata. See no. 2515
      Todesca. See no. 2515
PICK
      Fiakerlied. See no. 3711
PICKER, Tobias
2516 Rhapsody. Romance. Sextet, no. 3. When soft voices die. Specu-
      lum Musicae Members. CRI SD 427
                  +NR 10-80 p6
      Romance. See no. 2516
      Sextet, no. 3. See no. 2516
      When soft voices die. See no. 2516
PIERACCINI
      Beppino rubacori. See no. 3928
PIERCE, Edward
      The queen's galliard. See no. 3997
PIERNE, Gabriel
2517 Les cathedrales: Prelude. Images, op. 49. Paysages Franciscains,
      op. 43. Orchestre Philharmonique des Pays de Loire; Pierre Der-
      vaux. Pathe Marconi C 069 16302
                  +ARG 9-80 p45
      Images, op. 49. See no. 2517
      Introduction et variations sur une ronde populaire. See no. 2
      Pastorale. See no. 4067
      Paysages Franciscains, op. 43. See no. 2517
      Pieces, organ, op. 29. See no. 4055
      Scherzando. See no. 3615. See no. 3616
      Serenade. See no. 3769
      Trois conversations. See no. 2
PIETRAGRUA, Carlo
      Tortorella. See no. 3997

PIKET
    Shomeir Yisraeil. See no. 3922
PILKINGTON, Francis
    Songs: Come all ye; Musick deare solace; Rest sweet nimphs. See no.
        3877
PINO
    Concertino. See no. 3651
PINSUTI
    Goodnight beloved. See no. 3791
    Queen of the earth. See no. 3774
PINTO, George
    Sonata, op. 3, no. 2: Romance. See no. 4011
PINTO, Octavio
    Scenas infantis. See no. 1131
PISADOR, Diego
    Pavana. See no. 3917
PISTON, Walter
    Concertino, piano. See no. 1781
    Concerto, string quartet, winds and percussion. See no. 1159
    Partita, organ. See no. 1426
2518 Quartet, strings, no. 2. SESSIONS: Quartet, strings, no. 1, E min-
        or. Budapest Quartet, Pro Arte Quartet. New World Records NW
        302
                +-ARG 4-80 p37   +NYT 9-28-80 pD31
    Symphony, no. 1. See no. 1662
PITONI
    Boldog Aki-Enekel. See no. 3814
PITONI, Giuseppe
    Cantate domino. See no. 3970
PIZZETTI
    Songs: Levommi il mio pensier; Donna Lombarda; La pesca dell'anello;
        La prigioniera; Quel rosignuol. See no. 631
PIZZETTI, Ildebrando
    Composizioni corali (3). See no. 3713
PLANQUETTE, Robert
    Le regiment de Sambre et meuse. See no. 4029
    THE PLAY OF DANIEL. See no. 3570. See no. 3868
PLAYFORD, John
2519 The English dancing master: Hyde Park; Jenny pluck pears; Bobbing
        Joe; Mayden Lane; Halfe Hannikin; Rufty tuffty; The fine compan-
        ion; Hearts ease; Confesse; The maid peept out at the window; An
        old man is a bed full of bones; Boate man; Petticoat wag; Grim-
        stock; Stingo; Jack pudding; Kettle drum; Lulle me beyond thee;
        Dissembling love; The beggar boy; The glory of the west; Parsons
        farewell. John Wright, vln; Jew's harp, vocal; Denis Gasser,
        hpd; Janine Rubinlicht, vln; Yvonne Guicher, rec, tin whistle,
        3-holed flute, bodhran; Dominique Paris, Northumbrian pipes. Le
        Chant du Monde LDX 74690
                +HFN 8-80 p101   +RR 8-80 p65
PLESKOW, Raoul
    Pentimento. See no. 704
    Pieces, piano, 4 hands (3). See no. 1768
PLEYEL, Ignaz
    Concerto, clarinet, C major. See no. 2174

POKORNY, Franz Xavier
      Concerto, 2 horns, F major. See no. 2205
POLDOWSKI, Irene
      Tango. See no. 3964
POLIN, Claire
      Margo'a. See no. 697
      Synaulia II. See no. 697
PONCE, Manuel
      Andantino. See no. 3642
      Balletto. See no. 2520
      Estrellita. See no. 3964
      Folies d'Espagne: Theme, variations and fugue. See no. 3775
      Hace oche meses. See no. 2520
      Marchita el alma. See no. 2520
      Mazurka. See no. 3549. See no. 3775
      Mexican folksongs (3). See no. 2520
      Mexican popular songs (3). See no. 3722
      Petite valse. See no. 3549. See no. 3775
      Preludio. See no. 2520
      Sonata, guitar, no. 3. See no. 3549
      Sonata, guitar, no. 3: 1st movement; 2nd movement: Cancion; Post-
         lude. See no. 3775
      Sonatina meridional. See no. 3634. See no. 3798
      Suite, A minor. See no. 3549
      Suite, A major. See no. 3775
      La valse. See no. 2520. See no. 3706
      Variations and fugue on "Folia de Espana". See no. 2520. See no.
         3549
2520 Works, selections: Balletto. Hace ocho meses. Marchita el alma.
         Mexican folksongs (3). Preludio. Variations and fugue on
         "Folia de Espana". La valse. Yo adoro a mi madre. John Wil-
         liams, gtr. CBS 76730 Tape (c) 40-76730 (also CBS M 35820)
                  +FF 9/10-80 p275   ++HFN 5-79 p134 tape
                  ++Gr 4-79 p1749   ++NR 7-80 p14
                  ++HFN 4-79 p125   +-RR 5-79 p86
      Yo adoro a mi madre. See no. 2520
PONCHIELLI, Amilcare
2521 La gioconda. Maria Callas, s; Fiorenza Cossotto, Pier Ferraro, t;
         Irene Campaneez, con; Piero Cappuccilli, bar; Carlo Forti, Ivo
         Vinco, Leonardo Monreale, bs; La Scala Orchestra and Chorus;
         Antonino Votto. HMV SLS 5176 (3) Tape (c) TC SLS 5176 (From
         Columbia SAX 2359/61) (also Seraphim SIC 6031)
                  +Gr 11-79 p908   +Op 2-80 p166
                  +-HFN 11-79 p155   +-RR 12-79 p42
                  +HFN 8-80 p109 tape   +SFC 8-26-79 p52
      La gioconda: Bella cosi madonna. See no. 3927
      La gioconda: Cielo e mar. See no. 3946. See no. 3984. See no.
         4008
      La gioconda: Dance of the hours. See no. 3807
      La gioconda: Ebbrezza delirio. See no. 3901
      La gioconda: Enzo Grimaldo. See no. 3988
      La gioconda: Enzo Grimaldo...Principe di Santafior...O grido di
         quest'anima. See no. 3770
      La gioconda: Suicidio. See no. 628. See no. 3869
      La gioconda: Suicidio; L'amo come il fulgor. See no. 3929

La gioconda: Voce di donna. See no. 3774
PONGRACZ, Zoltan
    Mariphonia. See no. 1385
    The story of a chord, C sharp major. See no. 1385
POPP, Wilhelm
    Scherzo fantastique, op. 423. See no. 3782
POPPER, David
    Duet, violoncello. See no. 3583
    POPULAR TUNES IN 17TH CENTURY ENGLAND. See no. 3761
PORCELIJN, David
    Sound poem in Shikara Tala. See no. 1773
PORRINO, Ennio
    Gli Orazi: Io per l'amico diritto. See no. 3927
PORTER, Quincy
    Sonata, violin and piano, no. 2. See no. 1576
POSTON, Elizabeth
    Jesus Christ the apple tree. See no. 3527. See no. 3531. See no.
        4066
POULENC, Francis
    Aubade. See no. 1092
2522 Les biches. SAUGUET: La chatte. Monte Carlo Opera Orchestra and
        Chorus; Igor Markevitch. Varese VC 81096
                +-ARG 3-80 p53   +FF 11/12-80 p156
    Les biches. See no. 3908
    Chansons (9). See no. 3713
2523 Concert champetre. Concerto, organ, strings and timpani, G minor.
        George Malcolm, org, hpd; AMF; Iona Brown. Argo ZRG 878 Tape (c)
        KZRC 878
                    +ARG 4-80 p38   +HFN 7-79 p109
                    +-FF 5/6-80 p131   +HFN 8-79 p123 tape
                    +-Gr 7-79 p209   +-RR 7-79 p65
                    +-Gr 10-79 p727 tape   ++SFC 6-1-80 p35
2524 Concerto, organ, timpani and strings, G minor. Simon Preston, org;
        LSO; Andre Previn. Angel SS 45006
                    +ARG 2-80 p55
    Concerto, organ, timpani and strings, G minor. See no. 9. See no.
        1436. See no. 2523
    Gloria, G major. See no. 730
    Intermezzo, A flat major. See no. 3953. See no. 3954
    Motets: O magnum mysterium. See no. 3993
    Mouvements perpetuels. See no. 3953. See no. 3954
    Mouvements perpetuels, no. 1. See no. 3964
    Sextet, piano and wind instruments. See no. 1527
    Sonata, clarinet and piano. See no. 1201
    Sonata, flute and piano. See no. 3594. See no. 3714. See no. 3854
    Sonata, oboe and piano. See no. 56
    Sonata, 2 pianos. See no. 1131
2525 Sonata, violin and piano. RAVEL: Berceuse sur le nom de Gabriel
        Faure. Sonata, violin and piano. Gerald Tarack, vln; David
        Hancock, pno. Sine Qua Non SA 2016 Tape (c) C 2016
                +-FF 11/12-80 p157   +St 10-78 p160
                +SFC 7-6-80 p27
    Songs: Bluet; C; A sa guitare; Priez pour paix; La grenoullere.
        See no. 3862
    The story of Babar the little elephant. See no. 2204

Theme varie. See no. 1399
2526 Trio, oboe, bassoon and piano. SAINT-SAENS: Sonata, bassoon and
     piano, op. 168. SCHUMANN: Romances, op. 94 (3). TANSMAN: Sona-
     tina, bassoon and piano. Ray Still, ob; Milan Turkovic, bsn;
     John Perry, pno. Telefunken 6-42081
                    +FF 5/6-80 p194

POWELL
     Nocturnes. See no. 1580
POWELL, Baden
     Valsa sem nome. See no. 3706
POWER, Leonel
     Gloria, 5 voices. See no. 1120
     Songs: Beata progenies; Ave regina coelorum. See no. 1120
PRADO, Almeida
     Magnificat. See no. 3849
PRAETORIUS, Michael
     Es ist ein Ros entsprungen. See no. 3697
     In dulci jubilo. See no. 4068
     O vos omnes. See no. 3765
     Peasant dances. See no. 3647
2527 Terpsichore: Dances. SCHEIN: Banchetto musicale: Suites, nos. 3-5.
     WIDMANN: Daentze und Galliarden. Collegium Terpsichore; Fritz
     Neumeyer. DG 2547 005 Tape (c) 3347 005 (From SAPM 198166)
                    +Gr 4-80 p1595   +RR 5-80 p67
                    +HFN 6-80 p117
     Terpsichore: Dances. See no. 1802
     Terpsichore: Fire dance; Stepping dance; Windmills; Village dance;
          Sailor's dance; Fisherman's dance; Festive march. See no. 3647
     Veisatkaa. See no. 3592
PREMRU, Raymond
     Le bateau sur Leman. See no. 3568
     Blues march. See no. 3568
     Music for Harter Fell. See no. 59
     Of nights and castles. See no. 3568
PRIOLI, Giovanni
     Canzona seconda a b. See no. 4001
PROCH, Heinrich
     Air and variations. See no. 3559
     Variations on "Torno mio bene". See no. 3872
PROKOFIEV, Serge
2528 Alexander Nevsky, op. 78. Claudine Carlson, ms; St. Louis Symphony
     Orchestra and Chorus; Leonard Slatkin. Candide QCE 31098 (also
     Turnabout TVS 37135 Tape (c) KTVC 37135)
                    +-FF 9/10-78 p93   +RR 12-79 p115
                    +-Gr 1-80 p1193   +SFC 5-7-78 p46
                    +-HF 8-78 p83   ++SFC 1-14-79 p48
                    +-HFN 1-80 p109   +St 8-78 p142
                    /NR 6-78 p10
2529 Alexander Nevsky, op. 78. Elena Obraztsova, ms; LSO and Chorus;
     Claudio ABbado. DG 2531 202 Tape (c) 3301 202
                    +FF 9/10-80 p180   +-NR 7-80 p9
                    +Gr 4-80 p1579   +RR 4-80 p116
                    +HF 7-80 p71   +RR 7-80 p98 tape
                    ++HFN 4-80 p108   +SFC 6-22-80 p36
2530 Alexander Nevsky, op. 78. Larissa Avdeyeva, ms; RSFSR Russian

Chorus; USSR Symphony Orchestra; Yevgeny Svetlanov. HMV SXLP
30427 Tape (c) TC SXLP 30427 (From ASD 2521)
+Gr 4-80 p1579   +RR 2-80 p91
+-HFN 2-80 p105   +RR 7-80 p98 tape
+-HFN 4-80 p121 tape
2531 Concerto, piano, no. 1, op. 10, D flat major. Sinfonia concertante,
op. 125. Laszlo Varga, vlc; Gabriel Tacchino, pno; Luxembourg
Radio Orchestra; Louis de Froment. Turnabout TVS 34585
+-Gr 5-80 p1671   +RR 6-80 p57
+HFN 6-80 p109 tape
2532 Concerto, piano, no. 2, op. 16, G minor. Concerto, piano, no. 3,
op. 26, C major. Dmitri Alexeev, pno; RPO; Yuri Temirkanov. HMV
ASD 3871
+Gr 9-80 p339
Concerto, piano, no. 3, op. 26, C major. See no. 2532
2533 Concerto, violin, no. 2, op. 63, G minor. SIBELIUS: Concerto, violin, op. 47, D minor. Henryk Szeryng, vln; LSO; Gennady Rozhdes-
tvensky. Quintessence PMC 7150
+FF 9/10-80 p206
Concerto, violin, no. 2, op. 63, G minor. See no. 3964. See no.
3968
2534 Eugene Onegin, op. 71. Moscow State Musical Theatre Chorus; Moscow
Radio and TV Symphony Orchestra; Kemal Abdullayev. Melodiya 33S
10 11911-4 (2)
+-FF 1/2-80 p125
2535 Fantasia, op. 127. Waltzes, op. 100. BALAKIREV: Overture on 3
Russian themes. Kansas City Philharmonic Orchestra; Hans Sch-
weiger. Varese VC 81091 (From Urania, 1959)
+FF 5/6-80 p132
Gavotte. See no. 3964
Lietuenant Kije, op. 60: Troika. See no. 3605. See no. 3625
The love for three oranges, op. 33. See no. 2547. See no. 2552
The love for three oranges, op. 33: March. See no. 1783. See no.
3882. See no. 3953. See no. 3954
The love for three oranges, op. 33: March; Scherzo. See no. 3944
2536 The love for three oranges, op. 33: Suite. STRAVINSKY: Petrouchka.
Minnesota Orchestra; Stanislaw Skrowaczewski. Candide QCE 31103
+HF 12-80 p42
March, F minor. See no. 3964
2537 Le pas d'Acier, op. 41: Suite. RAVEL: La valse. STRAVINSKY: Pe-
trouchka (1911 version). LSO; Albert Coates. Encore E 302
(From HMV/Victor originals)
+ARG 2-80 p52   +HF 3-80 p90
+FF 11/12-79 p115   /NR 1-80 p3
Peter and the wolf, op. 67. See no. 2203
Pieces, piano, op. 4, no. 4: Suggestion diabolique. See no. 1719.
See no. 3622
Quartet, strings, no. 1, B minor. See no. 1490
2538 Quartet, strings, no. 2, op. 92, G major. SHOSTAKOVICH: Quartet,
strings, no. 3, op. 73, F major. Fine Arts Quartet. Gasparo G
203
+ARG 4-80 p45   ++IN 11-80 p63
+FF 3/4-80 p153   ++NR 2-80 p7
2539 Quintet, op. 39. STRAVINSKY: L'Histoire du soldat. Ensembles;
Gennady Rozhdestvensky. Quintessence PMC 7158 Tape (c) 7158

(From Melodiya/Angel)
          +—FF 11/12-80 p181   +SFC 8-3-80 p33
Quintet, op. 39, G minor. See no. 909
Romeo and Juliet, op. 64, excerpts. See no. 674. See no. 2540
Romeo and Juliet, op. 64: Ballet suites, excerpts. See no. 675
Romeo and Juliet, op. 64: Pieces. See no. 2542
Romeo and Juliet, op. 64: Suite, no. 2. See no. 3140
Sinfonia concertante, op. 125. See no. 2531
2540 Sonata, piano, no. 2, op. 14, D minor. Romeo and Juliet, op. 64,
        excerpts. Lazar Berman, pno. DG 2531 095 Tape (c) 3301 095
              +ARG 1-80 p39   +HFN 8-79 p123 tape
              +—FF 1/2-80 p125   +RR 7-79 p96
              +Gr 6-79 p85   +—St 1-80 p100
              +HFN 7-79 p109
Sonata, piano, no. 2, op. 14, D minor. See no. 390
2541 Sonata, piano, no. 3, op. 28, A minor. RAVEL: Valses nobles et
        sentimentales. SZYMANOWSKI: Sonata, piano, no. 3, op. 36. Phil-
        ips Jenkins, pno. Gaudeamus KRS 37
              +—Gr 9-80 p376
Sonata, piano, no. 3, op. 28, A minor. See no. 1783. See no. 2415
Sonata, piano, no. 6, op. 82, A major. See no. 1719. See no. 2077
Sonata, piano, no. 7, op. 83, B flat minor. See no. 1087. See no.
        3705
2542 Sonata, piano, no. 8, op. 84, B flat major. Romeo and Juliet, op.
        64: Pieces (10). Andrei Gavrilov, pno. HMV ASD 3802 Tape (c)
        TC ASD 3802
              +Gr 7-80 p154   +HFN 9-80 p116 tape
              +Gr 9-80 p413 tape   +—RR 6-80 p89
              +—HFN 6-80 p109
2543 Sonata, 2 violins, op. 56, C major. SCHNITTKE: Prelude to the mem-
        ory of Dmitri Shostakovich. SHOSTAKOVICH: Sonata, violin and
        piano, op. 134. Gidon Kremer, Tatiana Gridenko, vln; Andrei
        Gavrilov, pno. HMV ASD 3547
              +FF 11/12-80 p220   +HFN 8-78 p99
              +Gr 9-78 p492   +RR 12-78 p98
Sonata, 2 violins, op. 56, C major. See no. 2202
2544 Sonata, violoncello and piano, op. 119, C major. SHOSTAKOVICH:
        Sonata, violoncello and piano, op. 40, D minor. Erkki Rautio,
        vlc; Ralf Gothoni, pno. Da Camera Magna SM 93716
              -FF 3/4-80 p152
2545 Suite of waltzes (Schubert). SCRIABIN: Etudes, op. 8. TANEYEV:
        Prelude and fugue, op. 29, G sharp minor. Vladimir Leyetchkiss,
        pno. Orion ORS 80378
              +NR 11-80 p10
2546 Symphony, no. 1, op. 25, D major. RACHMANINOFF: Concerto, piano,
        no. 2, op. 18, C minor. Nicolai Petrov, pno; USSR Symphony Or-
        chestra; Yevgeny Svetlanov. HMV ASD 3872
              +—Gr 6-80 p38   +—RR 7-80 p63
              +—HFN 6-80 p109
2547 Symphony, no. 1, op. 25, D major. Symphony, no. 7, op. 131, C
        sharp minor. Love for three oranges, op. 33. PhO; Nicolai Mal-
        ko. HMV SXLP 30437 Tape (c) TC SXLP 30437 (From CLP 1060, 1044)
              +—Gr 5-80 p1671   +—HFN 9-80 p116 tape
              +HFN 5-80 p135   +RR 6-80 p57
2548 Symphony, no. 1, op. 25, D major. Symphony, no. 7, op. 131, C

sharp minor. MRSO; Gennady Rozhdestvensky. Quintessence PMC 7138
+FF 9/10-80 p181

2549 Symphony, no. 1, op. 25, D major. Symphony, no. 5, op. 100, B flat major. Orchestra, Bavarian Radio Orchestra; Sergiu Celibidache, Dimitri Mitropoulos. Rococo 2082
+NR 5-80 p3

2550 Symphony, no. 1, op. 25, D major. SHOSTAKOVICH: Symphony, no. 1, op. 10, F major. PhO; Efrem Kurtz. Seraphim S 60330
++ARG 4-80 p45

2551 Symphony, no. 1, op. 25, D major. Symphony, no. 7, op. 131, C sharp minor. CPhO; Zdenek Kosler. Supraphon 110 2457
-FF 11/12-80 p157   +NR 7-80 p2

Symphony, no. 1, op. 25, D major. See no. 2409
Symphony, no. 1, op. 25, D major: Gavotte. See no. 1783

2552 Symphony, no. 2, op. 40, D minor. Love for three oranges, op. 33. LPO; Walter Weller. Decca SXL 6945
+Gr 3-80 p1392   +RR 4-80 p76
++HFN 3-80 p97

2553 Symphonies, nos. 4-6. MRSO; Gennady Rozhdestvensky. Musical Heritage Society MHS 3981/3 (3)
+-FF 1/2-80 p127

2554 Symphony, no. 5, op. 100, B flat major. Israel Philharmonic Orchestra; Leonard Bernstein. CBS IM 35877 Tape (c) HMT 35877 (also CBS 35877 Tape (c) 40-35877)
-FF 11/12-80 p157   +-HFN 12-80 p143
+Gr 12-80 p836   +-St 12-80 p118

2555 Symphony, no. 5, op. 100, B flat major. LSO; Andre Previn. HMV SXLP 30315 Tape (c) TC SXLP 30315 (From ASD 3115)
+Gr 2-80 p1269   +HFN 6-80 p115
+HFN 4-80 p121 tape   +RR 5-80 p106 tape

2556 Symphony, no. 5, op. 100, B flat major. CO; Lorin Maazel. London CS 7099 (also Decca SXL 6875 Tape (c) KSXC 6875)
++FF 5/6-79 p76   +HFN 8-79 p123 tape
++Gr 5-79 p1900   +NR 2-80 p3
+-Gr 10-79 p727 tape   ++NYT 3-25-79 pD20
+-HF 7-79 p146   +-RR 5-79 p68
+HFN 5-79 p124   +-St 5-79 p106

2557 Symphony, no. 5, op. 100, B flat major. CO; Georg Szell. Odyssey Y 35923 (From Epic LC 3688, BC 1079)
++ARG 6-80 p36   ++SFC 1-20-80 p47
+FF 3/4-80 p130

Symphony, no. 5, op. 100, B flat major. See no. 2549

2558 Symphony, no. 6, op. 111, E flat minor. LPO; Walter Weller. Decca SXL 6777 (also London CS 7003)
+-FF 1/2-80 p124   +RR 9-76 p58
+-Gr 9-76 p423   +SFC 4-15-79 p41
++HFN 9-76 p126

Symphony, no. 7, op. 131, C sharp minor. See no. 2551. See no. 2547. See no. 2548

The ugly duckling, op. 18. See no. 1536

2559 Visions fugitives, op. 22. RACHMANINOFF: Sonata, piano, no. 2, op. 36, B flat minor. Rainer Klaas, pno. Integral IL 2791 KS
+CL 1-80 p10

Visions fugitives, op. 22, nos. 1, 3, 5-6, 8, 14, 16, 18. See no. 2415

Waltzes, op. 100. See no. 2535
War and peace, op. 91: Waltz. See no. 3694
PRYOR, Arthur
Love's enchantment. See no. 3627
PUCCINI, Giacomo
2560 Aida. Soloists; VPO; Herbert von Karajan. Angel SZCX 3888 (3)
        ++NYT 12-26-80 pD33
2561 Arias: La boheme: Si mi chiamano Mimi; Donde lieta usci. Gianni
     Schicchi: O mio babbino caro. Madama Butterfly: Un bel di ved-
     remo; Con onor muore. Manon Lescaut: In quelle trine morbide;
     Sola perduta abbandonata. Suor Angelica: Senza mamma. Turandot:
     Signore ascolta; In questa reggia; Tu che di gel sei cinta. Maria
     Callas, s; PhO; Tullio Serafin. HMV ALP 3799 Tape (c) TC ALP
     3799 (From Columbia 33CX 1204)
             +Gr 10-79 p709   +-Op 7-80 p686
             +-HFN 11-79 p155   ++RR 10-79 p64
             +-HFN 1-80 p123 tape
2562 La boheme. Renata Scotto, Jolanda Meneguzzer, s; Gianna Poggi, t;
     Tito Gobbi, Giorgio Giorgetti, bar; Giuseppe Modesti, bs; Maggio
     Musicale Orchestra and Chorus; Antonino Votto. DG 2726 086 Tape
     (c) 3372 086 (From 138764/5)
             +-FF 5/6-80 p132   +-ON 3-29-80 p36
             +-NYT 6-29-80 pD18   +SFC 1-20-80 p47
2563 La boheme. Renata Scotto, Carol Neblett, s; Alfredo Kraus, Paul
     Crook, t; Sherrill Milnes, Matteo Manuguerra, bar; Paul Plishka,
     Renato Capecchi, Italo Tajo, bs; Trinity Boys Choir, Ambrosian
     Opera Chorus; National Philharmonic Orchestra; James Levine.
     HMV SLS 5192 (2) Tape (c) TC SLS 5192 (also Angel SZBX 3900 Tape
     (4) 4Z2X 3900)
             +-Gr 7-80 p162   +ON 9-80 p68
             +-HF 11-80 p57   +-Op 10-80 p1015
             +HFN 9-80 p109   +-RR 8-80 p29
             +HFN 10-80 p117 tape   +SFC 7-27-80 p34
             +-NR 9-80 p7   +-St 11-80 p98
             +NYT 6-29-80 pD18
2564 La boheme. Katia Ricciarelli, Ashley Putnam, s; Jose Carreras,
     Francis Egerton, t; Ingvar Wixell, Hakan Hagegard, bar; Robert
     Lloyd, Giovanni de Angelis, bs; ROHO and Chorus; Colin Davis.
     Philips 6769 031 (2) Tape (c) 7699 116
             +-ARG 10-80 p28   +OC Winter 1980 p51
             ++FF 5/6-80 p133   +-ON 3-29-80 p36
             +Gr 12-79 p1048   +Op 2-80 p167
             +-HF 9-80 p95   ++RR 1-80 p61
             +HFN 12-79 p167   ++RR 2-80 p40
             +HFN 3-80 p107 tape   +-RR 6-80 p95 tape
             +NR 4-80 p11   ++SFC 1-27-80 p44
             +-NYT 3-2-80 pD26   +St 6-80 p118
     La boheme, excerpts. See no. 3696
     La boheme: Che gelida manina. See no. 3535. See no. 3625. See no.
     3774. See no. 3984. See no. 4031
     La boheme: Che gelida manina; O Mimi tu piu non torni; O soave fan-
     ciulla; Addio dolce svegliare. See no. 3945
     La boheme: Che gelida manina...Si mi chiamano Mimi...O soave fanci-
     ulla. See no. 3830
     La boheme: Gioventu mia; Dormo; Ripose; Entrate...C'e Rodolfo; Don-
     de lieta usci; Addio dolce svegliare all mattina. See no. 3773

La boheme: In un coupe; O Mimi tu piu non torni. See no. 3672.
See no. 3988
La boheme: Leb wohl denn und ohne Hass. See no. 3646
La boheme: Mi chiamano Mimi; Musetta' waltz. See no. 3869
La boheme: O Mimi tu piu non torni. See no. 724
La boheme: Si mi chiamano Mimi. See no. 2088. See no. 3670. See
no. 3770. See no. 3780. See no. 3793. See no. 3929
La boheme: Si mi chiamano Mimi; Addio senza rancor. See no. 3923
La boheme: Si mi chiamano Mimi; Donde lieta usci. See no. 2561
Capriccio sinfonico. See no. 758
I crisantemi (The chrysanthemums). See no. 1267
Edgar: Prelude. See no. 758
La fanciulla del West (Girl of the golden west): Arias. See no.
3539
2565 La fanciulla del West: Ch'ella mi creda. Madama Butterfly: Bimba
dagl'occhi. Tosca: E lucevan le stelle; Recondita armonia; Vis-
si d'arte. Turandot: Tu che di gel sei cinta. VERDI: Don Carlo:
Morte di Rodrigo. Macbeth: Pieta rispetto amore. Rigoletto:
Cortigiani vil razza danata. La traviata: Addio del passato.
Mirella Freni, Raina Kabaiwanska, Katia Ricciarelli, s; Gianni
Raimondi, t; Renato Bruson, bar; Verona Arena Orchestra; Bruno
Martinotti, Armando Gatto. Ars Nova ANC 25003
        +Gr 3-80 p1438
La fanciulla del West: Ch'ella mi creda. See no. 1491. See no.
3671. See no. 3774
La fanciulla del West: Minnie dalla mia casa. See no. 3771. See
no. 3925
Gianni Schicchi: Firenze e come un albero. See no. 3535
Gianni Schicchi: O mio babbino caro. See no. 2088. See no. 2561.
See no. 3670. See no. 3774. See no. 3780
2566 Madama Butterfly. National Philharmonic Orchestra; Salvador Cama-
rata. Decca PFS 4437 (also London SPC 21186)
        +Gr 8-79 p379   +NR 10-80 p3
        +HFN 7-79 p109   +RR 7-79 p65
Madama Butterfly: Addio fiorita asil. See no. 1491. See no. 4008
Madama Butterfly: Amore or grillo; Non ve l'avevo detto. See no.
3946
Madama Butterfly: Ancora un passo; Ieri son salita; Un po di vero;
Un bel di vedremo; Ora a noi; Sai cos'ebbe cuore...Che tua madre;
Tutti i fior; Con anor muore...Tu tu piccolo addio. See no. 3987
Madama Butterfly: Bimba bimba non piangere. See no. 1263
Madama Butterfly: Bimba dagli'occhi. See no. 2565
Madama Butterfly: Finale, Act 1. See no. 3830
Madama Butterfly: Humming chorus. See no. 3553
Madama Butterfly: Piangi perche...Un bel di vedremo. See no. 2088
Madama Butterfly: Tu tu piccolo addio. See no. 3668
Madama Butterfly: Un bel di vedremo. See no. 3670. See no. 3774.
See no. 3793. See no. 3924
Madama Butterfly: Un bel di vedremo; Con onor muore. See no. 2561
Madama Butterfly: Un po di vero c'e. See no. 3945
2567 Manon Lescaut. Maria Callas, s; Giuseppe di Stefano, t; Fiorenza
Cossotto, ms; Giulio Fioraventi, bar; Franco Calabrese, bs; La
Scala Orchestra and Chorus; Tullio Serafin. Seraphim IC 6089
(3) (also HMV RLS 737 Tape (c) TC RLS 737. From Columbia 33CS
1583-5)

```
        +FF 1/2-79 p88                  +-HFN 8-80 p109 tape
        +Gr 4-80 p1593                  +-NR 1-79 p11
        +-HF 1-79 p67                   +Op 12-80 p1215
        +-HFN 4-80 p121                 +SFC 12-17-78 p64
```
2568 Manon Lescaut, abridged. GOUNOD: Romeo et Juliette, Act 2. Elisa-
     betta Barbato, Adrianna Guerrini, s; Mafalda Favero, ; Beniamino
     Gigli, t; Silvio Viera, Guilherme Damiano; Orchestra; Antonino
     Votto. MDP Collectors Limited Edition 101 (2)
                 +ARG 2-80 p41
     Manon Lescaut: Ah Manon mi tradisce; Presto in fila...Non pazzo son.
     See no. 724
     Manon Lescaut: Ah non v'avvicinate. See no. 1491
     Manon Lescaut: Arias. See no. 3539
     Manon Lescaut: Donna non vidi mai. See no. 3535. See no. 3827
     Manon Lescaut: In quelle trine morbide. See no. 3770. See no. 3869
     Manon Lescaut: In quelle trine morbide; Sola perduta abbandonata.
     See no. 2561
     Manon Lescaut: Intermezzo, Act 3. See no. 3847
     Manon Lescaut: Ma se vi talenta...Tra voi belle; Donna non vidi mai;
       Ah non v'avvicinate...No no pazzo son. See no. 3671
     Manon Lescaut: Sola perduta abbandonata. See no. 3668
     Minuet, no. 1, A major. See no. 777
     Minuet, no. 2, A major. See no. 777
     Preludio sinfonico, A major. See no. 758
     La rondine: Chi il bel sogno di Doretta. See no. 2088. See no.
       3596. See no. 3670
2569 Suor Angelica. Joan Sutherland, Isobel Buchanan, Marie McLaughlin,
     Janet Price, s; Christa Ludwig, Anne Collins, Elizabeth Connell,
     Enid Hartle, Della Jones, ms; London Opera Chorus, Finchley Chil-
     dren's Group, National Philharmonic Orchestra; Richard Bonynge.
     Decca SET 627 Tape (c) KCET 627 (also London OSA 1173 Tape (c)
     OSA 5-1173)
```
            +-ARG 7/8-80 p35                +-NYT 3-23-80 pD25
            ++FF 7/8-80 p122                +-ON 3-29-80 p36
             +Gr 12-79 p1048                +-Op 7-80 p686
             +Gr 5-80 p1717 tape            +-RR 12-79 p43
             +-HF 6-80 p82                  ++SFC 3-30-80 p39
             ++HFN 12-79 p167               +St 5-80 p88
```
2570 Suor Angelica. Katia Ricciarelli, Rosanna Lippe, s; Fiorenza Cos-
     sotto, Maria Grazia Allegri, Anna di Stasio, ms; Polyphonic
     Chorus; Santa Cecilia Orchestra; Bruno Bartoletti. RCA ARL 1-
     2712 Tape (c) ARK 1-2712
```
             +-ARG 10-78 p38                +MJ 11-78 p30
              +Audio 5-80 p48               +NR 7-78 p9
             +-FF 11/12-78 p102             +RR 9-79 p53
             +-Gr 10-79 p704                +SFC 6-18-78 p43
             +-HF 10-78 p132                +St 8-78 p135
             +HFN 9-79 p109
```
     Suor Angelica: Senza mamma. See no. 2561. See no. 3668. See no.
     3774
2571 Tosca. Katia Ricciarelli, s; Jose Carreras, Heinz Zednik, t; Rug-
     gero Raimondi, Gottfried Hornik, Fernando Corena, Victor von
     Halem, bs; Berlin Opera Chorus; BPhO; Herbert von Karajan. DG
     2707 121 Tape (c) 3370 033
```
             ++Gr 7-80 p162                 +-NYT 9-14-80 pD26
```

        ++Gr 10-80 p548 tape   +-Op 9-80 p953
        +-HF 11-80 p57   +-RR 8-80 p31
        ++HFN 9-80 p109   ++SFC 8-24-80 p36
        +++HFN 10-80 p111 tape   +-St 12-80 p130
        +NR 10-80 p10

2572 Tosca. Magda Olivero, s; Luciano Pavarotti, Andrea Velis, t; Cornell MacNeil, Italo Tajo, bar; John Cheek, bs; Orchestra and Conductor. Historical Recording Enterprises HRE 312 (2)
        +FF 11/12-80 p158

2573 Tosca. Mirella Freni, s; Luciano Pavarotti, Michel Senechal, t; Sherrill Milnes, Paul Hudson, bar; Italo Tajo, Richard Van Allan, John Tomlinson, bs; Wandsworth School Boys Choir, London Opera Chorus; National Philharmonic Orchestra; Nicola Rescigno. London OSAD 12113 (2) (Also Decca D134D2 Tape (c) K134K22
        +-ARG 10-79 p19   +-NR 1-80 p10
        +-FF 9/10-79 p122   +-NYT 4-29-79 pD26
        +-Gr 5-80 p1711   +ON 7-79 p37
        ++Gr 12-80 p889 tape   +-Op 9-80 p953
        +-HF 7-79 p146   +-RR 5-80 p47
        +HFN 5-80 p123   ++St 8-79 p112

    Tosca: Arias. See no. 3539
    Tosca, excerpts. See no. 3696

2574 Tosca: Act 1. Claudia Muzio, s; Dino Borgioli, t; Alfred Gandolfi, bar; San Francisco Opera Orchestra; Gaetano Merola. MDP Records 028
        +-FF 5/6-80 p176

    Tosca: E lucevan le stelle. See no. 3672. See no. 4031
    Tosca: E lucevan le stelle; Recondita armonia; Vissi d'arte. See no. 2565
    Tosca: Ella vera...Ha piu forte sapore; Gia mi dicon venal. See no. 3925
    Tosca: Non la sospiri; Vissi d'arte. See no. 3632
    Tosca: Ora stammi a sentir. See no. 3924
    Tosca: Recondita armonia. See no. 3538. See no. 3981
    Tosca: Recondita armonia; E lucevan le stelle. See no. 3827. See no. 3830. See no. 3945
    Tosca: Recondita armonia; E lucevan le stelle; O dolci mani. See no. 4008
    Tosca: Recondita armonia; Vissi d'arte; E lucevan le stelle. See no. 1240
    Tosca: Se la guirata fede; Vissi d'arte; Nur der Schonheit. See no. 3774
    Tosca: Tu di tua mano...O dolci mani. See no. 3988
    Tosca: Vissi d'arte. See no. 3596. See no. 3668. See no. 3770. See no. 3828. See no. 3869. See no. 3918. See no. 3929. See 3987

2575 Turandot. Maria Callas, Elisabeth Schwarzkopf, s; Giuseppe Nessi, Renato Ercolani, Piero de Palma, t; Mario Boriello, bar; Nicolas Zaccaria, Giulio Mauri, bs; La Scala Orchestra and Chorus; Tullio Serafin. HMV RLS 741 Tape (c) TC RLS 741 (From Columbia 33CX 1555/7)
        +Gr 9-79 p517   +-Op 11-79 p1071
        +HFN 10-79 p171   ++RR 9-79 p53
        +-HFN 1-80 p123 tape

    Turandot: Arias. See no. 3539

Turandot: In questa reggia. See no. 3828
Turandot: Nessun dorma. See no. 1491. See no. 3535
Turandot: Non piangere liu. See no. 3672
Turandot: Perche tarda la luna. See no. 3553
Turandot: Signore ascolta; In questa reggia; Tu che di gel sei cinta.
    See no. 2561
Turandot: Tu che di gel sei cinta. See no. 2088. See no. 2565.
    See no. 3596. See no. 3670
2576 Le Villi. Renata Scotto, s; Placido Domingo, t; Tito Gobbi, speak-
    er; National Philharmonic Orchestra; Lorin Maazel. CBS M 36669
                +SFC 12-7-80 p33
Le Villi: Anima santa. See no. 3774
PUJOL VILLARRUBI, Emilio
Evocation cubaine. See no. 3706
Guajira. See no. 3603
PURCELL, Edward
Passing by. See no. 3875
PURCELL, Henry
Abdelazer: Incidental music. See no. 2602
Abdelazer: Rondeau. See no. 3715. See no. 3916
Abdelazer: Suite. See no. 1138
Air. See no. 2586
2577 Amphitryon. The old bachelor. The virtuous wife. Judith Nelson,
    s; Martyn Hill, t; Christopher Keyte, bs; Academy of Ancient
    Music; Christopher Hogwood. L'Oiseau-Lyre DSLO 550
                ++ARG 9-80 p35   +MT 9-80 p567
                ++FF 7/8-80 p123   +NYT 11-25-79 pD15
                +-Gr 12-79 p1034   +ON 4-19-80 p28
                +HFN 2-80 p97   +RR 10-79 p143
Arise my muse: Hail gracious Gloriana hail. See no. 2601
2578 Bonduca, excerpts. Circe, excerpts. Sir Anthony Love, excerpts.
    Singers; Taverner Choir; Academy of Ancient Music; Christopher
    Hogwood. L'Oiseau-Lyre DSLO 527 Tape (c) KDSLC 527
                +ARG 11-78 p36   +MT 6-78 p516
                +FF 3/4-79 p96   +NYT 11-25-79 pD15
                +Gr 2-78 p1460   +ON 4-19-80 p28
                +Gr 5-78 p1939 tape   +RR 2-78 p87
                +HFN 2-78 p113   ++RR 4-78 p108 tape
Canary. See no. 2586
Chaconne. See no. 2586
Chaconne, F major. See no. 4018
Chaconne "Two in one upon a ground". See no. 4015
2579 Chacony, G minor. Fantasia, 3 parts to a ground, D major. Pavans,
    nos. 1-5. Sonata, violin, bass viol and organ. Songs: Elegy on
    the death of John Playford; Elegy on the death of Thomas Farmer;
    Elegy on the death of Matthew Locke. Martyn Hill, t; Christopher
    Keyte, bs; Academy of Ancient Music; Christopher Hogwood. L'
    Oiseau-Lyre DSLO 514
                +-FF 3/4-80 p131   ++NR 4-80 p6
                +Gr 10-77 p678   +ON 4-19-80 p28
                +HFN 10-77 p161   +RR 10-77 p84
                +MT 11-78 p965   +SFC 1-13-80 p40
Chacony, G minor. See no. 3639. See no. 3998
Circe, excerpts. See no. 2578
Come ye sons of art: Sound the trumpet. See no. 2601. See no. 3625

2580 Concerto, trumpet, D major, excerpts. The Gordian knot untied, ex-
      cerpts. Sonata, trumpet, D major. VIVALDI: Concerti, mandolins,
      C major (2). Concerto, 2 mandolins, G major. Scott Kuney, mand;
      Frederick Hand, gtr; New York Sinfonietta, ECO; Max Goberman,
      Raymond Leppard. CBS M 35873
                        -ARG 12-80 p52
    Deliciae musicae, Bk 2: If music be the food of love. See no. 2601
2581 Dido and Aeneas. Tatiana Troyanos, Sheila Armstrong, Margaret Baker-
      Genovesi, s; Patricia Johnson, Margaret Lensky, con; Paul Esswood,
      alto; Nigel Rogers, t; Barry McDaniel, bar; Hamburg Monteverdi
      Choir; North German Radio Chamber Orchestra; Charles Mackerras.
      DG 2547 032 Tape (c) 3347 032 (from SAPM 198424)
                        +-Gr 11-80 p735
2582 Dido and Aeneas. Kirsten Flagstad, Elisabeth Schwazrkopf, Eilidh
      McNab, Sheila Rex, Anna Pollack, s; Arda Mandikian, ms; David
      Lloyd, t; Thomas Hemsley, bar; Mermaid Singers and Orchestra;
      Geraint Jones. EMI 2C 051 03613
                        +ARSC Vol 12, nos. 1-2, 1980 p107
2583 Dido and Aeneas. Nancy Armstrong, Susan Klebanow, Roberta Anderson,
      s; D'Anna Fortunato, ms; Bruce Fithian, t; Mark Baker, bs; Bos-
      ton Camerata; Joel Cohen. Harmonia Mundi HM 10067
                  -FF 11/12-80 p158   +HFN 8-80 p101
                  +Gr 7-80 p162   +NYT 8-10-80 pD17
    Dido and Aeneas: Dido's lament. See no. 1318
    Dido and Aeneas: Suite. See no. 3639
    Distressed innocence: Incidental music. See no. 2602
    Diverse pieces. See no. 2598
2584 Don Quixote. Emma Kirkby, Judith Nelson, s; James Bowman, c-t;
      Martyn Hill, t; David Thomas, bs; Academy of Ancient Music;
      Christopher Hogwood, hpd and cond. L'Oiseau-Lyre DSLO 534 Tape
      (c) DSLC 534
                  +FF 3/4-80 p131   +NYT 11-25-79 pD15
                  +Gr 11-78 p944   +ON 4-19-80 p28
                  ++Gr 5-79 p1940 tape   +RR 11-78 p104
                  +HFN 11-78 p173   ++SFC 1-13-80 p40
                  +MT 3-79 p228   ++St 10-79 p144
    The fairy queen: Let the fires and the clarions; Hark the ech'ing
      air; One charming night. See no. 2601
    Fantasias, C minor. See no. 3583
    Fantasias, D minor, G major. See no. 4025
    Fantasia, 3 parts on a ground, D major. See no. 96. See no. 2579
    Fantasia upon one note. See no. 3583
2585 Fantasias, viola da gamba (15). Ulsamer Collegium. DG 2533 366
                  +ARG 10-78 p39   ++NR 8-78 p9
                  +FF 11/12-78 p103   ++RR 1-78 p64 tape
                  ++Gr 2-78 p1425   +RR 1-78 p15
                  +HFN 2-78 p115   ++SFC 1-13-80 p40
                  +MT 12-78 p1053   +St 8-78 p135
    Fantasia, no. 13, F major. See no. 3776
    Fly bold rebellion: Be welcome then great sir. See no. 2601
    Funeral music for Queen Mary. See no. 141. See no. 2591
    Gavotte. See no. 2586
    The Gordian knot untied, excerpts. See no. 2580
    The Gordian knot untied: Incidental music. See no. 2602
    Ground. See no. 2586

Ground, C minor. See no. 2586
Ground in gamut. See no. 2586
Hail bright Cecilia: In vain the am'rous flute. See no. 2601
2586 Harpsichord works: Air. Canary. Chaconne. Ground. Ground, C min-
      or (2). Ground in gamut. Gavotte. Hornpipe. Jig. Marches
      (3). Minuet. A new ground. A new Irish tune. New minuet. A
      new Scotch tune. Prelude. Prelude, G minor. The queen's dol-
      our. Rigadoon. Round O. Saraband with division. Sefauchi's
      farewell, D minor. Suites, nos. 1-8. A suite of lessons. Trum-
      pet tune. Robert Woolley, hpd. Saga 5458/9 (2)
                  +ARG 12-80 p40   +MT 12-78 p1053
                  +-Gr 7-78 p226   +RR 9-78 p83
                  +HFN 9-78 p147   ++St 8-80 p100
                  +HFN 12-79 p167
Hear my prayer. See no. 3939
Hornpipe. See no. 2586
If ever I more riches did desire: Here let my life; Me o ye Gods.
      See no. 2601
2587 In guilty night. Man that is born of a woman. Te deum and jubi-
      late Deo, D major. Honor Sheppard, Christina Clarke, s; Neil
      Jenkins, t; Maurice Bevan, bar; Robert Elliott, org; Stour Music
      Festival Orchestra and Choir; Alfred Deller, c-t and cond. Har-
      monia Mundi HM 207
                  +-Gr 4-80 p1580   +RR 5-80 p98
                  +-HFN 4-80 p121
In nomine. See no. 4025
2588 The Indian Queen. Jennifer Smith, s; Martyn Hill, John Elwes, t;
      Stephen Varcoe, bar; David Thomas, bs; Monteverdi Choir; English
      Baroque Soloists; John Eliot Gardiner. Erato STU 71275 Tape (c)
      71275
                  +Gr 9-80 p398   +HFN 10-80 p117 tape
                  +HFN 8-80 p101
The Indian Queen: Trumpet tune. See no. 3916
Jehova quam multi sunt hostes mei. See no. 3530
Jig. See no. 2586
2589 King Arthur. Deller Consort, King's Musik; Alfred Deller. Harmon-
      ia Mundi HM 252/3 (2) (also Musical Heritage Society MHS 4188/9)
                  +FF 1/2-80 p128   +NYT 11-25-79 pD15
                  +FF 11/12-80 p159   +-ON 4-19-80 p28
                  ++Gr 5-79 p1925   +-RR 5-79 p44
                  +-HFN 5-79 p124   +-St 12-80 p132
King Arthur: Allegro and air. See no. 4001
King Arthur: Trumpet tune. See no. 3895
Let mine eyes. See no. 3532
Love's goddess sure: Sweetness by nature; Many many such days. See
      no. 2601
Man that is born of a woman. See no. 2587
Marches (3). See no. 2586
The married beau: Incidental music. See no. 2602
Minuet. See no. 2586. See no. 2596
Motets and anthems. See no. 738
Musick's hand-maid: March; Song tune; Air; Minuet; New minuet; New
      Scotch tune; Minuet; Sefauchi's farewell; Minuet rigadoon; A
      new ground; Minuet; A new Irish tune; Suite, G minor; Toccata;
      Hornpipe; Air. See no. 3855

A new ground. See no. 2586. See no. 2596
A new Irish tune. See no. 2586
New minuet. See no. 2586
A new Scotch tune. See no. 2586
Nymphs and shepherds. See no. 3971
The old bachelor. See no. 2577
Pavans, nos. 1-5. See no. 2579
Pleasant musical companion, Bk 3: Saccarissa's grown old. See no.
    2601
Prelude. See no. 2586
Prelude, G minor. See no. 2586
The queen's dolour. See no. 2586
The queen's epicedium. See no. 3776
Rejoice in the Lord alway. See no. 3835
Rigadoon. See no. 2586
Round O. See no. 2586. See no. 2596
Saraband with division. See no. 2586
Sefauchi's farewell, D minor. See no. 2586
Sir Anthony Love, excerpts. See no. 2578
Sonatas, trumpet. See no. 1679
Sonatas, trumpet, D major. See no. 1102. See no. 2580. See no.
    3912
Sonata, violin, bass viol and organ. See no. 2579
Songs (3). See no. 3932
2590 Songs: Ah cruel nymph; As Amoret and Thirsis lay; I lov'd fair
    Celia; Incassum Lesbia; The fatal hour comes on a pace; Musick
    for a while; Pious Celinda goes to prayers; Retir'd from any
    mortal's sight; Since from my dear Astrea's sight; Sweeter than
    roses; Tis nature's voice; Young Thirsis fate. Rene Jacobs, c-t;
    Wieland Kuijken, vla da gamba; Konrad Junghanel, theorbo. Ac-
    cent 7802
                +FF 3/4-80 p132   +RR 6-80 p31
                +HFN 6-80 p101
2591 Songs: Come ye sons of art (Birthday ode for Queen Mary). Funeral
    music for Queen Mary. Felicity Lott, s; Charles Brett, John
    Williams, c-t; Thomas Allen, bs; Monteverdi Orchestra and Choir,
    Equale Brass Ensemble; John Eliot Gardiner. Erato STU 70911
    Tape (c) MCE 70911
                +ARG 11-79 p46   ++HFN 10-80 p117 tape
                ++FF 1/2-80 p128   +-MM 4-78 p40
                +-Gr 8-77 p331   ++NR 10-79 p7
                +-HF 8-78 p84   +RR 8-77 p77
2592 Songs: Blow up the trumpet in Sion; Hear my prayer; My song shall
    be alway; O give thanks; O Lord God of hosts; O solitude. Del-
    ler Consort and Choir; Alfred Deller. Harmonia Mundi HM 247
                +FF 1/2-80 p128   +HFN 8-78 p106
                +Gr 9-78 p24   +RR 7-78 p87
2593 Songs: Evening hymn; Fairest isle; From rosy bowr's; I attempt from
    love's sickness to fly; If music be the food of love; Music for
    a while; Not all my torments; The plaint; O lead me to some
    peaceful gloom; Retired from any mortal's sight; Since from my
    dear Astrea's sight; Sweeter than roses; Thrice happy lovers.
    Alfred Deller, c-t; Wieland Kuijken, bs-viol; William Christie,
    hpd; Roderick Skeaping, baroque vln. Harmonia Mundi HM 249
                +ARG 10-80 p45   +-MT 3-80 p181

+FF 5/6-80 p135   +-NR 5-80 p10
+-Gr 8-79 p364   +ON 4-19-80 p28
+HFN 12-79 p167   ++RR 12-79 p115
2594 Songs, nos. 240, 245, 256, 263, 265, 272, 273, 277, 281, 286. Del-
     ler Consort; Alfred Deller. HNH 4046
              +ARG 1-80 p40   +FF 3/4-80 p131
2595 Songs: Come let us drink; A health to the nut brown lass; I gave
     her cakes and I gave her ale; If ever I more riches did desire;
     Laudate ceciliam; The miller's daughter; Of all the instruments;
     Once twice thirce I Julia tried; Prithee ben't so sad and ser-
     ious; Since time so kind to us does prove; Sir Walter enjoying
     his damsel; Tis woman makes us love; Under this stone; Young
     John the gard'ner. Deller Consort; Alfred Deller. Musical Her-
     itage Society MHS 4124
              +ARG 7/8-80 p36   ++FF 9/10-80 p181
2596 Songs: An evening hymn on a ground; Bess of Bedlam; The fatal hour;
     I attempt from love's sickness to fly; If music be the food of
     love; More love or more disdain; Not all my torments; A song on
     a ground; Solitude; Sweeter than roses; Urge me no more. Grounds:
     Minuet. A new ground. Round O. Anna Carol Dudley, s; Laurette
     Goldberg, hpd. 1750 Arch Records S 1766
              ++ARG 12-80 p42   +-FF 11/12-80 p158
     Songs: Elegy on the death of John Playford; Elegy on the death of
     Thomas Farmer; Elegy on the death of Matthew Locke. See no. 2579
     Songs: Lord what is man. See no. 2601
     Songs: Lord what is man; Sleep Adam sleep. See no. 3778
     Songs: Lucinda is bewitching fair; See where repenting Celia lies.
     See no. 2602
     A suite of lessons. See no. 2586
     Suites, harpsichord, G major. See no. 3659
2597 Suites, harpsichord, nos. 1-8. Colin Tilney, hpd. DG 2533 415
              +Gr 11-79 p876   +NYT 1-27-80 pD20
              ++HFN 11-79 p143   ++RR 11-79 p112
              ++MT 11-79 p923
2598 Suites, harpsichord, nos. 1-8. Diverse pieces. Laurence Boulay,
     hpd, virginal. Erato STU 71162
              +-FU 3-80 p48   +RR 4-80 p100
              +-HFN 4-80 p108
     Suites, harpsichord, nos. 1-8. See no. 2586
     Symphonies, nos. 1 and 2. See no. 4015
2599 Te deum et jubilate Deo, D major. Yorkshire Feast song. Pro Can-
     tione Antiqua Soloists; St. Mary of Warwick Choir; La Grande
     Ecurie et Chambre du Roy; Jean-Claude Malgoire. CBS 76925 Tape
     (c) 40-76925
              +Gr 10-80 p528   +-HFN 12-80 p159
              -HFN 10-80 p107   +STL 9-14-80 p40
     Te deum and jubilate Deo, D major. See no. 2587
2600 The tempest. Jennifer Smith, Rosemary Hardy, s; Carol Hall, ms;
     John Elwes, t; Stephen Varcoe, bar; David Thomas, Roderick Earle,
     bs; Monteverdi Orchestra and Choir; John Eliot Gardiner. Erato
     STU 71274 Tape (c) MCE 71274
              ++Gr 4-80 p1579   +RR 5-80 p48
              +HFN 4-80 p108   +STL 4-13-80 p39
              +HFN 10-80 p117 tape
     Thesaurus musicus, Bk 5: Lovely Albina's come ashore. See no. 2601

Three parts upon a ground: Fantasia. See no. 3795
Trumpet tune. See no. 212. See no. 2586. See no. 3545. See no. 3566
Trumpet tune and air. See no. 3582
Trumpet tune and air, D major. See no. 1102
Trumpet tune and almand. See no. 3895
The virtuous wife. See no. 2577
Voluntary, G major. See no. 4052
Voluntary, 2 trumpets, C major. See no. 1102
Voluntary on the old 100th. See no. 3595
Welcome to all the pleasures: Beauty thus scene of love. See no. 2601

2601 Works, selections: Come ye sons of art: Sound the trumpet. Deliciae musicae, Bk 2: If music be the food of love. Arise my muse: Hail gracious Gloriana, hail. The fairy queen: Let the fires and the clarions; Hark the ech'ing air; One charming night. Fly bold rebellion: Be welcome then great sir. Hail bright Cecilia: In vain the am'rous flute. If ever I more riches did desire: Here let my life; Me o ye Gods. Love's goddess sure: Sweetness by nature; Many many such days. Pleasant musical companion, Bk 3: Saccarissa's grown old. Thesaurus musicus, Bk 5: Lovely Albina's come ashore. Welcome to all the pleasures: Beauty thus scene of love. Songs: Lord what is man. Jeffrey Dooley, c-t; Howard Crook, t; David Carp, rec; Dennis Godburn, rec and bsn; Louis Shulman, Daniel Reed, vln; Mary Springfels, vla da gamba; Edward Brewer, hpd. Nonesuch H 71343

+ARG 4-78 p27	+NR 7-78 p10
+FF 5/6-78 p73	+ON 4-19-80 p28
+Gr 4-78 p1756	+-RR 4-78 p90
+HF 7-78 p96	+St 5-78 p93
+-HFN 4-78 p119	+STL 10-8-78 p38

2602 Works, selections: Abdelazer: Incidental music. Distressed innocence: Incidental music. The Gordian knot untied: Incidental music. The married beau: Incidental music. Songs: Lucinda is bewitching fair; See where repenting Celia lies. Joy Roberts, s; Academy of Ancient Music; Christopher Hogwood. L'Oiseau-Lyre DSLO 504

+-Gr 6-76 p51	+NYT 11-25-79 pD15
+-HF 3-77 p106	+ON 4-19-80 p28
+HFN 6-76 p95	+RR 6-76 p51
+MJ 1-77 p26	+SFC 12-12-76 p55
++NR 1-77 p8	

Yorkshire feast song. See no. 2599

PYLKKANEN, Tauno
The swan of death, op. 21. See no. 3586

QUAGLIATI, Paolo
Toccata del 8 tuono. See no. 3813

QUANTZ, Johann
2603 Concerto, flute, G major. STAMITZ: Concerto, flute, G major. Peter Lukas Graf, flt; Zurich Chamber Orchestra; Edmond de Stoutz. Claves P 808

+HFN 6-80 p111	++RR 4-80 p76

Concerto, flute, G major. See no. 91
Sonata, flute, op. 1, no. 1, A minor. See no. 90
Trio sonata, C major. See no. 1459

QUARANTA
    O ma charmante. See no. 3978
QUILTER, Roger
    Love's philosophy, op. 3, no. 1. See no. 3778
RABAUD, Henri
2604 Divertissement sur des chansons russes, op. 2. Eglogue, op. 7.
    Marouf, Savetier du Caire: Ballet music. La procession nocturne,
    op. 6. Orchestre Philharmonique des Pays de Loire; Pierre Der-
    vaux. Pathe Marconi C 069 16303
                +ARG 9-80 p45
    Eglogue, op. 7. See no. 2604
    Marouf, Savetier du Caire: Ballet music. See no. 2604
    Marouf, Savetier du Caire: A travers le desert. See no. 3774
    La procession nocturne, op. 6. See no. 2604
RABBATH, Francois
2605 Briez. Embruns. Equation. Incantation pour Junon. L'Odysee d'
    eau. Horda. Mutants d'eau pale. Poucha-dass. Papa Georges.
    Thyossane. Francois Rabbath, double-bs; with percussion. QCA
    RM 394
                +-NR 8-80 p8
    Embruns. See no. 2605
    Equation. See no. 2605
    Horda. See no. 2605
    Incantation pour Junon. See no. 2605
    Mutants d'eau pale. See no. 2605
    L'Odysee d'eau. See no. 2605
    Papa Georges. See no. 2605
    Poucha-dass. See no. 2605
    Thyossane. See no. 2605
RACHMANONOFF, Sergei
2606 Aleko. Blagovesta Karnobatlova-Dobreva, s; Tony Khristova, con;
    Pavel Kurshumov, t; Nikola Gyuzelev, Dimiter Petkov, bs; Bul-
    garian Radio and Television Vocal Ensemble; Plovdiv Symphony
    Orchestra; Russlan Raychev. Balkaton BOA 1530 (2) (also Monitor
    HS 90102/3. Also Harmonia Mundi HMU 135. Also Musical Heritage
    Society MHS 4036/7)
                +-FF 3/4-80 p133   +ON 3-6-76 p42
                +Gr 9-74 p578   +RR 11-75 p34
                +-HF 1-76 p93   +SFC 11-9-75 p22
                +HFN 1-76 p117   /St 10-75 p116
                +-NR 8-75 p11
    Barcarolle, op. 10, no. 3. G minor. See no. 1970. See no. 3833
2607 Concerti, piano, nos. 1-4. Rhapsody on a theme by Paganini, op. 43.
    Abbey Simon, pno; St. Louis Symphony Orchestra; Leonard Slatkin.
    Vox QSVBX 5149 (3) Tape (c) CBS 5149
                +-ARG 2-79 p28   +-NR 2-79 p7
                +-CL 4-79 p10   +NYT 8-6-78 pD13
                +-FF 3/4-79 p99   ++SFC 11-5-78 p57
                +HF 1-79 p83   +St 3-80 p107 tape
2608 Concerto, piano, no. 1, op. 1, F sharp minor. Rhapsody on a theme
    by Paganini, op. 43. Daniel Wayneberg, Malcolm Binns, pno; PhO,
    LPO; Christoph von Dohnanyi, Alexander Gibson. Classics for
    Pleasure CFP 40267 Tape (c) TC CFP 40267 (From World Records ST
    459, 672)
                +Gr 1-78 p1257   +-HFN 8-80 p109 tape
                +-HFN 11-77 p179   +-RR 11-77 p67

2609 Concerto, piano, no. 1, op. 1, F sharp major. Concerto, piano, no. 2, op. 18, C minor. Earl Wild, pno; RPO; Jascha Horenstein. RCA GL 2-5291 Tape (c) GK 2-5291 (From Reader's Digest RDS 6251/ 4)
    +Gr 10-80 p500   +HFN 11-80 p122
2610 Concerto, piano, no. 2, op. 18, C minor. Rhapsody on a theme by Paganini, op. 43. Benno Moisewitsch, pno; PhO; Hugo Rignold. World Records SH 380
    +-HFN 12-80 p153
    Concerto, piano, no. 2, op. 18, C minor. See no. 2546. See no. 2609
2611 Concerto, piano, no. 3, op. 30, D minor. Andre Laplante, pno; MPO; Alexander Lazarev. Canadian Broadcasting Corporation SM 352
    +FF 9/10-80 p182
2612 Concerto, piano, no. 4, op. 40, G minor. RAVEL: Concerto, piano, G major. Arturo Benedetti Michelangeli, pno; PhO; Ettore Gracis. HMV SXL 30169 Tape (c) TC SXL 30169, TC EXE 111 (ct) 8X EXE 111 (From ASD 255) (also Angel S 35567)
    ++Gr 9-74 p512   ++RR 8-74 p40
    +-HFN 10-80 p117 tape
    Daisies, op. 38, no. 3. See no. 3964
    Danse orientale, op. 2, no. 2. See no. 1220
    Etudes-Tableaux, op. 33, nos. 3 and 6. See no. 2614
    Etudes-Tableaux, op. 39, no. 2. See no. 3964
    Floods of spring, op. 14, no. 11. See no. 3887
    Humoreske, op. 10, no. 5, G major. See no. 1970
    The isle of the dead, op. 29. See no. 2625
2613 Moments musicaux, op. 16. Pieces, piano, op. 10 (7). Ruth Laredo, pno. CBS M 35836 Tape (c) MT 35836
    +-ARG 9-80 p36
    Moments musicaux, op. 16, no. 6. See no. 2614
    Oriental sketch. See no. 3964
2614 Piano works: Etudes Tableaux, op. 33, nos. 3 and 6. Pieces, piano, op. 3, no. 3: Melodiya. Moments musicaux, op. 16, no. 6. Polichinelle, op. 3, no. 4, F sharp minor. Romanza, op. 10, no. 6, F minor. Polka de V. R. TCHAIKOVSKY: Chanson triste, op. 40, no. 2. Minuetto scherzoso, op. 51, no. 3. L'Espiegle, op. 72, no. 12. Un poco di Chopin, op. 72, no. 15. Romanza, op. 51, no. 5, F major. Salon valse, op. 51, no. 1, A flat major. Reverie soir, op. 19, no. 1. Sviatoslav Richter, pno. Rococo 2120
    +NR 3-80 p14
    Pieces, piano, op. 3, no. 3: Melodiya. See no. 2614
    Pieces, piano, op. 10. See no. 2613
    Pieces, piano, op. 11: Barcarolle; Waltz. See no. 3645
    Polichinelle. See no. 3935
    Polichinelle, op. 3, no. 4, F sharp minor. See no. 1180. See no. 2614
    Polka de V. R. See no. 2614
    Prelude, op. 2, no. 1. See no. 1220
2615 Preludes, op. 3, no. 2, C sharp minor; op. 23, no. 1, F sharp minor; op. 23, no. 4, D major; op. 32, no. 12, G sharp minor; op. 32, no. 10, B minor; op. 23, no. 2, B flat major. Variations on a theme by Corelli, op. 42. Lazar Berman, pno. DG 2531 276
    +Gr 11-80 p703   +-HFN 11-80 p122
2616 Preludes, op. 3, no. 2, C sharp minor. Preludes, op. 23. Preludes,

op. 32. Peter Katin, pno. Unicorn 230/1 (2)

    +–FF 11/12–80 p159   +RR 7–80 p82

    +HFN 7–80 p117   ++SFC 9–21–80 p21

Prelude, op. 3, no. 2, C sharp minor. See no. 1180

Preludes, op. 23. See no. 2616

Preludes, op. 23, nos. 1, 2, 4. See no. 2615

Preludes, op. 23, nos. 3, 7. See no. 3820

Preludes, op. 23, nos. 5, 6. See no. 1180

Preludes, op. 32. See no. 2616

Preludes, op. 32, nos. 5, 12. See no. 3820

Preludes, op. 32, no. 10, B minor. See no. 3615

Preludes, op. 32, no. 12, G sharp minor. See no. 1176. See no. 2615

Rhapsody on a theme by Paganini, op. 43. See no. 2607. See no. 2608. See no. 2610. See no. 3915

The rock, op. 7. See no. 2624. See no. 2625

Romanza, op. 10, no. 6, F minor. See no. 2614

2617 Russian folk songs, op. 41. Spring cantata, op. 20. TCHAIKOVSKY: Overture, the year 1812, op. 49. John Shaw, bar; Ambrosian Singers; NPhO; Igor Buketoff. RCA GL 4–2924 Tape (c) GK 4–2924 (From SB 6763)

    +Gr 8–80 p257   +–HFN 11–80 p131 tape

    +–HFN 8–80 p107   +–RR 8–80 p55

Russian folk songs, op. 41. See no. 2623

2618 Russian rhapsody, E minor. Symphonic dances, op. 45. Vladimir Ashkenazy, Andre Previn, pno. Decca SXL 6926 Tape (c) KSXC 6926 (also London 7159)

    ++FF 11/12–80 p160   +NYT 9–21–80 pD22

    ++Gr 4–80 p1568   +RR 4–80 p101

    +–HFN 4–80 p108   ++St 11–80 p98

2619 Sonata, piano, no. 1, op. 28, D minor. Sonata, piano, no. 2, op. 36, B flat minor. John Ogdon, pno. RCA GL 4–2867 Tape (c) GK 4–2867 (From SB 6793)

    +Gr 4–80 p1571   +–HFN 8–80 p109 tape

2620 Sonata, piano, no. 2, op. 36, B flat minor. SCRIABIN: Sonata, piano, no. 5, op. 53, F sharp minor. Vers la flamme, op. 72. Marta Deyanova, pno. Nimbus DC 905

    +–HFN 9–80 p110   +RR 3–80 p85

Sonata, piano, no. 2, op. 36, B flat minor. See no. 2559. See no. 2619

Sonata, violoncello and piano, op. 19, G minor. See no. 1220

2621 Songs: All once I gladly owned, op. 26, no. 2; April a spring festive day; Beloved let us fly, op. 26, no. 5; Brooding, op. 8, no. 3; Christ is risen, op. 26, no. 6; Come let us rest, op. 26, no. 3; Daisies, op. 38, no. 3 (solo piano); Dusk descending; The heart's secret, op. 26, no. 1; How few the joys, op. 14, no. 3; I came to her, op. 14, no. 4; I will tell you nothing; Like blossom dew-freshen'd to gladness, op. 8, no. 2; Morning, op. 4, no. 2; My heartbeat quickened; Oh stay my love forsake me not, op. 4, no. 1; A prayer, op. 8, no. 6; Reeds on the river, op. 8, no. 1; The water lily; Two partings, op. 26, no. 4. Elisabeth Soderstrom, s; John Shirley-Quirk, bar; Vladimir Ashkenazy, pno. Decca SXL 6869 (also London 26559)

    ++ARG 12–79 p50   +NR 3–80 p13

    +FF 11/12–79 p1114   +ON 12–8–79 p28

+Gr 2-79 p1453   ++RR 4-79 p115
+HFN 2-79 p105

2622 Songs: All things depart, op. 26, no. 15; As fair as day in blaze
     of noon, op. 14, no. 9; By the gates of the holy dwelling; Did
     you hiccough; Do you remember the evening; A flower fell; From
     St. John's gospel; Let me rest here alone, op. 26, no. 9; Letter
     to S. Stanislavsky from S. Rachmaninoff; Lilacs, op. 21, no. 5
     (piano solo); Love's flame, op. 14, no. 2; Night; O do not grieve,
     op. 14, no. 8; Song of disappointment; The soul's concealment, op.
     34, no. 2; Thy pity I implore, op. 26, no. 8; Tis time, op. 14,
     no. 12; When yesterday we met, op. 26, no. 13; With holy banner
     firmly held, op. 34, no. 11.   Elisabeth Soderstrom, s; Vladimir
     Ashkenazy, pno. Decca SXL 6940
                    +Gr 10-80 p528   +HFN 9-80 p110
     Songs: A passing breeze; The answer; Christ is risen; How long since
     love; The harvest of sorrow; Lilacs; Oh do not grieve; To the
     children. See no. 1023
     Songs: Before my window, op. 26, no. 10. See no. 3774
     Songs: My love; O stay; When yesterday we met. See no. 3965
     Spring cantata, op. 20. See no. 2617
2623 Symphonic dances, op. 45. Russian songs, op. 41 (3). MPO; Bolshoi
     Theatre Orchestra and Chorus; Kiril Kondrashin, Yevgeny Svetla-
     nov. Quintessence PMC 7136 (From Angel SR 40093)
                    -FF 3/4-80 p133   +SFC 11-25-79 p46
     Symphonic dances, op. 45. See no. 2618
2624 Symphonies, nos. 1-3. The rock, op. 7. OSR, LPO; Walter Weller.
     Decca JB 91/3 Tape (c) KJBC 91/3 (From SXL 6583, 6623, 6720)
                    +Gr 10-80 p500   +HFN 10-80 p113
2625 Symphonies, nos. 1-3.* Isle of the dead, op. 29. The rock, op. 7.*
     Rotterdam Philharmonic Orchestra; Edo de Waart. Philips 6768 148
     (4) (*From 9500 445, 9500 309, 9500 302)
                    +Gr 9-80 p339   +HFN 9-80 p115
2626 Symphony, no. 1, op. 13, D minor. PO; Eugene Ormandy. CBS 61991
     Tape (c) 40-61991 (From 72571)
                    +Gr 8-80 p225   +-HFN 9-80 p115
2627 Symphony, no. 1, op. 13, D minor. Rotterdam Philharmonic Orchestra;
     Edo de Waart. Philips 9500 445 Tape (c) 7300 616
                    ++FF 3/4-80 p135   +NR 12-79 p4
                    +Gr 12-79 p1018   +RR 1-80 p84
                    ++HFN 1-80 p109   +RR 5-80 p107 tape
                    ++HFN 6-80 p119 tape
2628 Symphony, no. 2, op. 27, E minor. OSR; Paul Kletzki. Decca ECS
     837 (From SXL 6342) (also London STS 15500)
                    +FF 7/8-80 p123   +-HFN 3-80 p105
                    +-Gr 8-80 p225   ++RR 4-80 p77
2629 Symphony, no. 2, op. 27, E minor. LPO; Walter Weller. Decca SXL
     6623 (also London CS 6839)
                    ++Gr 11-73 p936   +-RR 12-73 p47
                    +NR 2-80 p3
     Symphony, no. 2, op. 27, E minor. See no. 3581
2630 Symphony, no. 3, op. 44, A minor. MUSSORGSKY: A night on the bare
     mountain. OSR; Paul Kletzki. Decca ECS 838 (From SXL 6399)
                    +-Gr 8-80 p225   +-RR 4-80 p77
                    +-HFN 3-80 p105
     Variations on a theme by Corelli, op. 42. See no. 2615

Vocalise, op. 34, no. 14. See no. 1878. See no. 3589. See no.
    3605. See no. 3694
RACQUET
    Fantasie. See no. 3852
RADESCA, Enrico
    Non miri io mio bel sole. See no. 3878
RAFF, Joachim
    Cavatina. See no. 3788
    Cavatina, A flat major. See no. 3552
RAIMON DE MIRAVAL
    Selh que non vol. See no. 1842
RAISON, Andre
    Livre d'orgue, 1st, excerpts. See no. 1168
    Trio en passacaille. See no. 4061
RALPH-DRIFFILL, W.
    Toccata. See no. 3725
RAMEAU, Jean
2631 Le berger fidele. Hippolyte et Aricie: Air du rossignol. Orphee.
    Colette Herzog, s; I Solisti Veneti; Claudio Scimone. Eratu STU
    71214
                +-HFN 4-80 p108   +-RR 5-80 p99
2632 La dauphine. Pieces de clavecin en concert. Suite, harpsichord,
    A minor. Trevor Pinnock, hpd. Vanguard VSD 71271
                +FF 9/100-80 p182   +NR 10-80 p15
    Les fetes d'Hebe. See no. 3659
2633 Les fetes d'Hebe: La danse, Act 3. Jill Gomez, Anne-Marie Rodde, s;
    Jean-Claude Orliac, t; Marilyn Sansom, vlc; Nicholas Kramer, hpd;
    Monteverdi Orchestra and Choir; John Eliot Gardiner. Eratu STU
    71089
                +Gr 5-79 p1925   +RR 3-79 p52
                ++MT 1-80 p35
    Hippolyte et Aricie: Air du rossignol. See no. 2631
2634 Hippolyte et Aricie: Suite. La Petite Bande; Sigiswald Kuijken.
    Harmonia Mundi 1C 065 99837
                ++Gr 5-80 p1671   ++RR 5-80 p68
                +-HFN 6-80 p111   +STL 6-8-80 p38
    L'Impatience. See no. 1112
2635 Les Indes galantes: Airs and dances. Kenneth Gilbert, hpd. Har-
    monia Mundi HM 1028
                +FF 5/6-80 p135   +HFN 3-80 p97
                +Gr 2-80 p1282   +St 6-80 p119
2636 Les Indes galantes: Ballet suite. Collegium Aureum. Harmonia Mun-
    di 1C 065 99864
                +FF 11/12-80 p122
    Orphee. See no. 2631
    Pieces de clavecin en concert: Suite, A minor. See no. 2632
2637 Pieces de clavecin: Suite, D minor, G major. Trevor Pinnock, hpd.
    Vanguard VSD 71270
                +FF 9/10-80 p182   +NR 10-80 p15
2638 Pieces de clavecin en concert, nos. 1-5. Boston Museum Trio. Tit-
    anic TI 28
                ++ARG 6-80 p37   +FF 5/6-80 p136
    Pieces de clavecin en concert, no. 5, D minor. See no. 1112
    La poule, G minor. See no. 3916
2639 Suites, harpsichord, A minor, E minor. Trevor Pinnock, hpd. Van-

guard VSD 71256
+-Audio 4-80 p95   ++SFC 2-10-80 p41
+-NR 3-80 p15
Suite, harpsichord, E major: Musette; Tambourin. See no. 3659
Suite en concert. See no. 3942
Tambourin. See no. 3970

RAMSEY, Gordon
2640 Descriptive pieces, violin and viola (4). Quartet, flute. Quartet,
     strings. Harold Wolf, Karon Jones, vln; Arthur Hoberman, flt;
     Harry Rumpler, vla; Irit Assayas, vlc. Orion ORS 79354
                +-ARG 5-80 p30   +-NR 2-80 p7
                +-FF 5/6-80 p136
2641 Movements, flute and piano (3). La petite collection, piano. Son-
     ata, violin and piano. Harold Wolf, vln; Arthur Hoberman, flt;
     Martha Gustetto, pno. Orion ORS 79353
                +-FF 5/6-80 p136   +-NR 2-80 p7
     La petite collection, piano. See no. 2641
     Quartet, flute. See no. 2640
     Quartet, strings. See no. 2640
     Sonata, violin and piano. See no. 2641

RAMSEY, Robert
     Sleep fleshly birth. See no. 3893

RANGSTROM, Anders Johan Ture
     Divertimento elegiaco. See no. 1850
2642 Symphony, no. 1, C sharp minor. Swedish Radio Orchestra; Leif Seg-
     erstam. EMI 7C 061 35712
                +Gr 9-80 p339   +RR 8-80 p50

RASBACH
     Trees. See no. 3875

RATHGEBER, Johann
     Von den Weibsbildern. See no. 3764

RAUTAVAARA, Einojuhani
     A requiem for our time. See no. 3009

RAVEL, Maurice
     A la maniere de Borodine. See no. 2658
     A la maniere de Chabrier. See no. 2658
2643 Berceuse sur le nom de Faure. Sonata, violin and piano. Sonate
     posthume. Tzigane. Charles Libove, vln; Nina Lugovoy, pno.
     Finnadar SR 9028
                +NR 10-80 p8
     Berceuse sur le nom de Faure. See no. 2525
2644 Bolero. Daphnis et Chloe: Suite, no. 2. Pavane for a dead princess.
     LSO; Andre Previn. Angel SZ 37670 Tape (c) 4ZS 37670 (also HMV
     ASD 3912 Tape (c) TC ASD 3912)
                ++Gr 11-80 p674   ++SFC 11-30-80 p21
                ++HFN 11-80 p122
2645 Bolero. French National Orchestra; Leonard Bernstein; Moog synth-
     esizer. CBS MX 35860
                -FF 11/12-80 p161
2646 Bolero. Daphnis et Chloe: Suite, no. 2. La valse. Halle Orchestra;
     John Barbirolli. Everest SDBR 3471
                *NR 12-80 p5
2647 Bolero. Ma mere l'oye. La valse. LSO; Pierre Monteux. Philips
     6570 092 Tape (c) 7310 092 (From SAL 3500)
                +Gr 10-79 p650   ++RR 11-79 p90

+–HFN 11-79 p157   +RR 3-80 p104 tape
+HFN 2-80 p107 tape   ++SFC 5-28-78 p41
+NYT 5-28-78 pD13

2648 Bolero. Daphnis et Chloe: Suite, no. 2. Ma mere l'oye. Pavane
     for a dead princess. Isao Tomita, electronics. RCA ARL 1-3412
     Tape (c) RK 1-3412
                    -FF 7/8-80 p124   +NR 5-80 p15
          +–HFN 10-80 p117

2649 Bolero. Miroirs: Alborada del gracioso. Rapsodie espagnole. Dal-
     las Symphony Orchestra; Eduardo Mata. RCA ARC 1-3686 Tape (c)
     ARK 1-3686
              ++NR 11-80 p2   ++SFC 10-26-80 p20
     Bolero. See no. 1488. See no. 2662. See no. 3556. See no. 3557
2650 Concerto, piano, G major. Concerto, piano, for the left hand, D
     major. Jean-Philippe Collard, pno; French National Orchestra;
     Lorin Maazel. HMV ASD 3845 Tape (c) TC ASD 3845 (also Angel SZ
     37730)
                  +Gr 6-80 p38   +RR 6-80 p58
                 ++Gr 9-80 p413   ++SFC 11-30-80 p21
                  +HFN 6-80 p111   +STL 7-13-80 p38
                 ++HFN 9-80 p116 tape
     Concerto, piano, G major. See no. 369. See no. 2612
     Concerto, piano, for the left hand, D major. See no. 2650
2651 Daphnis et Chloe. Rene Duclos Choir; OSCCP; Andre Cluytens. Clas-
     sics for Pleasure CFP 40323 (From Columbia SAX 2476)
                  +Gr 1-80 p1158   +RR 12-79 p73
                  +–HFN 1-80 p121
2652 Daphnis et Chloe. ROHO Chorus; LSO; Pierre Monteux. Decca JB 69
     Tape (c) KJBC 69 (From SXL 2164)
                  +Gr 1-80 p1158   ++RR 12-79 p73
                  +HFN 1-80 p121
2653 Daphnis et Chloe. Dallas Symphony Orchestra and Chorus; Eduardo
     Mata. RCA ARC 1-3458
                 ++ARG 9-80 p38   +–HFN 7-80 p109
                  +–FF 7/8-80 p135   ++NR 5-80 p2
                  +Gr 7-80 p142   +–RR 7-80 p63
                  +HF 8-80 p79   +SFC 3-23-80 p35
     Daphnis et Chloe: Ballet. See no. 3556
     Daphnis et Chloe: Suites, nos. 1 and 2. See no. 2662. See no.
     3557
2654 Daphnis et Chloe: Suite, no. 2. Pavane pour une infante defunte.
     Songs: Melodies hebraiques. Nadine Denize, s; Lille Philharmon-
     ic Orchestra; Jean-Claude Casadesus. Harmonia Mundi HM 10064
                 ++FF 9/10-80 p183   +–HFN 6-80 p111
                  +–Gr 5-80 p1672   +RR 5-80 p69
     Daphnis et Chloe: Suite, no. 2. See no. 2644. See no. 2646. See
     no. 2648
     Fanfare for "L'Eventail de Jeanne". See no. 2662
2655 Gaspard de la nuit. Jeux d'eau. Pavane pour une infante defunte.
     Sonatine. Pascal Devoyon, pno. Erato STU 71385
                  +–Gr 12-80 p854
2656 Gaspard de la nuit. SCRIABIN: Preludes, op. 11 (24). Walter Gies-
     eking, pno. Rococo 2090
                 ++NR 3-80 p14
     Gaspard de la nuit. See no. 2658. See no. 2659

Gaspard de nuit: Ondine. See no. 1187

L'Heure espagnole. See no. 3557

Introduction and allegro. See no. 372. See no. 1181

Jeux d'eau. See no. 1187. See no. 2655. See no. 2658. See no.
2659. See no. 3944

Ma mere l'oye. See no. 722. See no. 1195. See no. 1196. See no.
2647. See no. 2648. See no. 2658. See no. 2662. See no. 3556.
See no. 3883

Ma mere l'oye: Suite. See no. 3557

Menuet antique. See no. 2658. See no. 2662. See no. 3556. See
no. 3557

Menuet sur le nom de Haydn. See no. 2658. See no. 2659

Miroirs. See no. 2658

2657 Miroirs: Alborada del gracioso. Rapsodie espagnole. Le tombeau de
Couperin. La valse. Orchestre de Paris; Herbert von Karajan.
HMV SXLP 30446 Tape (c) TC SXLP 30446 (From ASD 2766)
      ++Gr 9-80 p339   ++HFN 10-80 p113

Miroirs: Alborada del gracioso. See no. 2649. See no. 3557. See
no. 3777

Miroirs: Alborada del gracioso; Une barque sur l'ocean. See no.
2662. See no. 3556

Miroirs: Noctuelles; Oiseaux tristes; La vallee des cloches. See
no. 3622

Miroirs: La vallee des cloches. See no. 3953. See no. 3954

Pavane de la belle a bois dormant. See no. 3883

Pavane pour une infante defunte. See no. 2644. See no. 2648. See
no. 2654. See no. 2655. See no. 2658. See no. 2662. See no.
3556. See no. 3557. See no. 3666. See no. 3685. See no. 3883.
See no. 3944

2658 Piano works: A la maniera de Borodine. A la maniere de Chabrier.
Gaspard de la nuit. Jeux d'eau. Menuet sur le nom de Haydn.
Ma mere l'oye. Menuet antique. Pavane pour une infante defunte.
Prelude. Miroirs. Les sites auriculaires: Habanera. Le tombeau
de Couperin. Valses nobles et sentimentales. Robert Casadesus,
Gaby Casadesus, pno. CBS 77346 (3)
      +Gr 11-80 p703

2659 Piano works: Gaspard de la nuit. Jeux d'eau. Menuet sur le nom de
Haydn. Prelude. Sonatine. Paul Badura-Skoda, pno. Musical
Heritage Society MHS 4148
      +FF 9/10-80 p184   +HF 8-80 p71

Piece en forme de habanera. See no. 3772. See no. 3785. See no.
3882. See no. 3885

Prelude. See no. 2658. See no. 2659

Quartet, strings, F major. See no. 381. See no. 1214. See no.
1215. See no. 1216

Rapsodie espagnole. See no. 1001. See no. 1195. See no. 1322.
See no. 2649. See no. 2657. See no. 2662. See no. 3556. See
no. 3557

Les sites auriculaires: Habanera. See no. 2658

2660 Sonata, violin and piano, G major. Trio, piano, A minor.* Tzigane.
Beaux Arts Trio; Arthur Grumiaux, vln; Istvan Hajdu, pno. Philips 6570 177 (*From SAL 3619)
      +Gr 10-80 p512   +HFN 11-80 p129

Sonata, violin and piano. See no. 2525. See no. 2643

Sonate posthume. See no. 2643

Sonatine, piano. See no. 2655. See no. 2659

Songs: Melodies hebraiques. See no. 2654

Le tombeau de Couperin. See no. 2413. See no. 2657. See no. 2658.
    See no. 2662. See no. 3556. See no. 3557

2661 Trio, piano, A minor. SAINT-SAENS: Trio, piano, no. 1, op. 18, F
    major. Maria de la Pau, pno; Yan Pascal Tortelier, vln; Paul
    Tortelier, vlc. HMV ASD 3729
                    +Gr 3-80 p1411   ++RR 3-80 p75
                    +HFN 3-80 p97   +ST 7-80 p197
                    +MT 9-80 p567

Trio, piano, A minor. See no. 2660

Tzigane. See no. 1019. See no. 1021. See no. 2643. See no. 2660.
    See no. 3772. See no. 3964

La valse. See no. 2410. See no. 2537. See no. 2646. See no.
    2647. See no. 2657. See no. 2662. See no. 3556. See no. 3557.
    See no. 3666. See no. 3955

Valses nobles et sentimentales. See no. 2541. See no. 2658. See
    no. 2662. See no. 3556. See no. 3557

Valses nobles et sentimentales, nos. 6 and 7. See no. 3964

Vocalise en forme de habanera. See no. 3596

2662 Works, selections: Bolero. Daphnis et Chloe: Suites, nos. 1 and 2.
    Fanfare for "L'Eventail de Jeanne". Ma mere l'oye. Menuet an-
    tique. Miroirs: Alborada del gracioso; Une barque sur l'ocean.
    Pavane pour une infante defunte. Rapsodie espagnole. Le tom-
    beau de Couperin. La valse. Valses nobles et sentimentales.
    Minnesota Orchestra; Stanislaw Skrowaczewski. Vox SVBX 5133 (4)
    (Q) QSVBX 5133 Tape (c) CBX 5133
                    ++Audio 1-77 p83   ++NR 6-75 p1
                    ++HF 7-75 p66   +St 8-75 p102 Quad
                    +HF 4-80 p104 tape   +St 3-80 p107 tape

RAVENSCROFT, Thomas

A bellman's song. See no. 3719

Fantasia, no. 4. See no. 3853

Hornpipe. See no. 3895

Maids to be and cover coal. See no. 3995

Where are you fair maids. See no. 3995

Yonder comes a courteous knight. See no. 3876

RAWSTHORNE, Alan

Street corner. See no. 3829

RAY

The sunshine of your smile. See no. 3874

READ, Daniel

Songs: Expression; He is king of kings; I believe this is Jesus;
    Star in the East; Rise up shepherd and follow; Sherburne. See
    no. 3849

REBEL, Jean-Fery

Les elements. See no. 1241

RECK, David

Studies for tuba alone (4). See no. 3654

REDEL, Martin

Konfrontationen. See no. 1793

REED, Alfred

The music makers. See no. 4029

REED, Herbert Owen

La fiesta mexicana. See no. 2434

REEVE
    I am a friar of orders gray. See no. 3774
REGER, Max
2663 Allegretto grazioso, A major. Serenade, op. 141a, G major. Sonata,
        clarinet and piano, op. 107, B flat major. Werner Richter, flt;
        Wendelin Gartner, clt; Sandor Karolyi, vln; Hans Eurich, vla;
        Richard Laugs, pno. Da Camera Magna SM 92710 (also Musical Her-
        itage Society MHS 1329)
                +—ARG 5-80 p31
2664 Canons and fugues in the old style, op. 131b (3). Serenades, op.
        77a, D major; op. 141a, G minor. Aurele Nicolet, flt; Susanne
        Lautenbacher, vln; Ulrich Koch, vla; Georg Egger, vln. FSM Rec-
        ords 53002
                +FF 3/4-80 p136
    Choral fantasies, op. 67, nos. 3 and 41. See no. 258
2665 Chorale preludes, op. 67, nos. 4, 13, 24, 28, 47. Monologues, op.
        63, nos. 1-2, 4, 11-12. Wolfgang Rubsam, org. Da Camera Magna
        SM 93254
                +FF 11/12-80 p162
2666 Comedy overture, op. 120. Concerto in the old style, op. 123, F
        major. Jeunesses Musicales Nordrhein-Westfalen Orchestra; Karl-
        Heinz Cloemeke. Da Camera Magna SM 91606
                +—FF 7/8-80 p124
    Concerto in the old style, op. 123, F major. See no. 2666
2667 Fantasia, op. 40, no. 1. Fantasias, op. 52, nos. 2 and 3. Hans
        Klotz, Richard Voge, org. SDG 610 701
                +—HFN 12-80 p143
2668 Fantasia and fugue, op. 135b, D minor. Sonata, organ, no. 2, op.
        60, D minor. Toccata, op. 80b, no. 11, A minor. Josef Serafin,
        org. Muza SX 0549
                +FF 7/8-80 p121
2669 Fantasia on Wachet auf ruft uns die Stimme, op. 52, no. 2. Vari-
        ations and fugue on an original theme, op. 73, F sharp minor.
        Martin Haselbock, org. Preiser SPR 3286
                ++MU 10-78 p10   +RR 2-80 p79
    Fantasias, op. 52, nos. 2 and 3. See no. 2667
    Maria's Wiegenlied. See no. 3831
    Monologues, op. 63, nos. 1-2, 4, 11-12. See no. 2665
    Pieces, organ, op. 59: Benedictus. See no. 3624
    Pieces, organ, op. 59: Pastorale. See no. 4063
    Pieces, organ, op. 59: Toccata. See no. 3858
2670 Pieces, organ, op. 65 (12). Andreas Schroder, org. Da Camera
        Magna SM 93253
                +FF 11/12-80 p162
    Pieces, organ, op. 65: Scherzo. See no. 4063
    Pieces, organ, op. 80: Perpetuum mobile. See no. 4063
    Pieces, organ, op. 145: Weihnachten. See no. 3591
    Praise the Lord, chorale. See no. 3618
    Prelude, op. 85, no. 4, E minor. See no. 2670
2671 Psalm, op. 106, C major. Prelude, op. 85, no. 4, E minor. Te deum,
        op. 85. Werner Jacob, org; Nurnberg Teachers Choral Society;
        Nurnberg Symphony Orchestra; Wolfram Rohrig. MPS Records 168
        020
                -FF 3/4-80 p135
2672 Quartet, strings, no. 3, op. 74, D minor. Zagreb Quartet. Da

Camera Magna SM 92730
/ARG 6-80 p37
2673 Quartet, strings, no. 5, op. 121, F sharp minor. Tel Aviv Quartet.
Da Camera Magna SM 92731
+ARG 1-80 p40
Scherzino. See no. 3839
Serenade, op. 77a, D major. See no. 2664
Serenade, op. 141a, G major. See no. 2663. See no. 2664
Sonata, clarinet and piano, op. 49, no. 1, A major. See no. 3891
Sonata, clarinet and piano, op. 49, no. 2, F sharp minor. See no.
2137
Sonata, clarinet and piano, op. 107, B flat major. See no. 1462.
See no. 2663
Sonata, organ, no. 2, op. 60, D minor. See no. 2668
Songs: Es waren zwei Konigskinder; Ich hab heut Nacht getraumet.
See no. 854
Songs: Mary's cradle song. See no. 3933
Songs: Valet will ich dir geben; Wunderbarer Konig. See no. 4036
Te deum, op. 85. See no. 2670
Toccata, op. 80b, no. 11, A minor. See no. 2668
2674 Toccata and fugue. REUBKE: Sonata, organ. Brent Hylton, org. Wes-
tern Maryland College Bookstore unnumbered
+MU 2-80 p10
Toccata and fugue, op. 59, no. 5. See no. 4058
Toccata and fugue, op. 59, nos. 5 and 6. See no. 3664
2675 Trio, strings, op. 77b, A minor. Trio, strings, op. 141b, D min-
or. New String Trio. Acanta EA 21642
+-Gr 11-80 p692   +RR 7-80 p73
+HFN 8-80 p101
Trio, strings, op. 141b, D minor. See no. 2675
Variations and fugue on a theme by Mozart, op. 132, A major. See
no. 3710
Variations and fugue on an original theme, op. 73, F sharp minor.
See no. 2669
REGIS
S'il vous plaist que vostre je soye. See no. 3880
REGNART, Jacob
Megbabonaz Sok Szivet. See no. 3814
REIBEL, Guy
2676 Etudes aux modulations (2). Suite pour Edgar Poe. Variations en
toile. Jean-Pierre Drouet, perc; Laurent Terzieff, voice. Har-
monia Mundi INA Gramme 9103
+FF 7/8-80 p16
2677 Franges du signe. Granulations sillages. Harmonia Mundi INA GRM
AM 77102
+FF 7/8-80 p16
Granulations sillages. See no. 2677
Suite pour Edgar Poe. See no. 2676
Variations en toile. See no. 2676
REICHA, Anton
Quintet, bassoon and strings. See no. 1470
2678 Quintets, winds, op. 88, nos. 1 and 2. Ars Nova Woodwind Quintet.
Musical Heritage Society MHS 4120
+FF 5/6-80 p137
Scene, cor anglais. See no. 1255

2679 Trios, horn, op. 82. Bedrich Tylsar, Emanuel Hrdina, Zdenek Tylsar,
      hn. Supraphon 111 2617
                    ·+HFN 10-80 p107   +STL 9-14-80 p40
REICHA, Joseph
      Duo, violin and violoncello, no. 2, op. 84, F major. See no. 753
REICHARDT, Johann
      Heilige Nacht. See no. 3697
REICHEL, Bernard
      Pastorale, G major. See no. 3734
REIMANN, Aribert
2680 Lear. Helga Dernesch, Colette Lorand, Julia Varady, s; Karl Helm,
      George Paskuda, Richard Holm, t; Dietrich Fischer-Dieskau, bar;
      Hans Wilbrink, Hans Gunter Nocker, bs-bar; Bavarian State Opera
      Orchestra and Chorus; Gerd Albrecht. DG 2709 089 (3)
                    +ARG 12-79 p52   +NR 12-79 p9
                    ++FF 1/2-80 p130   ++ON 12-1-79 p44
                    +FU 2-80 p50   +Op 10-79 p976
                    +Gr 9-79 p518   ++RR 9-79 p29
                    +HFN 9-79 p109   ++St 1-80 p108
                    +MM 12-79 p28   +STL 12-2-79 p37
                    +MT 2-80 p107
REINAGLE
      Gavotte. See no. 3971
REINECKE, Carl
      Concerto, harp, op. 182, E minor. See no. 1503
      Trio, op. 188, A minor. See no. 1776
REINER, Jacob
      Schone newe Teutsche Lieder: Behut euch Gott zu aller Zeit. See
      no. 3536
REISSIGER, Karl
      A favourite waltz by Weber. See no. 4011
REIZENSTEIN, Franz
2681 Partita, op. 13. Quintet, piano, op. 23, D major. Sonatina, oboe
      and piano, op. 11. Melos Ensemble. L'Oiseau-Lyre SOL 344
                    +AR 8-80 p85   +MT 12-75 p1071
                    +Gr 7-75 p206   ++NR 10-75 p4
                    +HF 11-75 p110   +-RR 7-75 p43
                    +HFN 12-75 p163
      Quintet piano, op. 23, D major. See no. 2681
      Sonatina, oboe and piano, op. 11. See no. 2681
RENIE, Henriette
      Contemplation. See no. 1509
      Legende. See no. 1509
      Piece symphonique. See no. 1509
RESPIGHI, Ottorino
2682 Ancient airs and dances. LPO; Jesus Lopez-Cobos. Decca SXL 6846
      Tape (c) KSXC 6846
                    +-Gr 4-80 p1558   +RR 4-80 p77
                    +HFN 4-80 p108
2683 Ancient airs and dances, nos. 1-3. BSO; Seiji Ozawa. DG 2530 891
      Tape (c) 3300 891
                    ++ARG 4-80 p39   +NR 3-80 p4
                    +FF 1/2-80 p132   ++RR 6-79 p83
                    +-Gr 6-79 p55   ++SFC 12-23-79 p40
                    +HFN 7-79 p111   ++St 4-80 p137

Ancient airs and dances: Suite, no. 3. See no. 351
2684 La bella addormentata nel bosco. Emilia Ravaglia, Cannarile Berdini, Ennio Buoso, Lino Puglisi, Wilma de Eusebio; Orchestra
and Chorus. A.N.N.A. Record Company ANNA 1023
                ++FF 11/12-80 p162
Concerto gregoriano. See no. 657
2685 Feste romane. The pines of Rome. Vancouver Symphony Orchestra;
Kazuyoshi Akiyama. Canadian Broadcasting Corporation SM 335
          +FF 5/6-80 p137   +MUM 2-80 p33
2686 Fest romane. Fountains of Rome. LAPO; Michael Tilson Thomas.
Columbia M 35846
          +NR 11-80 p2   +NYT 9-7-80 pD26
Fest romane. See no. 1212. See no. 2687
2687 Fountains of Rome. Pines of Rome. Roman festivals. BSO; Seiji
Ozawa. DG 2530 890 Tape (c) 3300 890
          +-ARG 4-80 p39   ++NR 3-80 p1
          +FF 3/4-80 p136   +RR 7-79 p68
          ++Gr 6-79 p55   ++SFC 12-23-79 p40
          ++HFN 8-79 p109   +STL 12-2-79 p37
2688 Fountains of Rome. Pines of Rome. Zagreb Philharmonic Orchestra;
Milan Horvat. Everest 3436
          -FF 3/4-80 p136
Fountains of Rome. See no. 1211. See no. 2686
Pieces, piano, 4 hands (6). See no. 1109
Pines of Rome. See no. 2685. See no. 2687. See no. 2688
2689 Songs: Deita silvane; Lauda per la nativita del Signore. Trittico
Botticelliano. Jill Gomez, s; Meriel Dickinson, ms; Robert Tear,
t; London Chamber Orchestra, Argo Chamber Orchestra; Laszlo Hel-
tay. Argo ZRG 904
          +Gr 2-80 p1287   ++MT 12-80 p787
          +HFN 12-79 p167   ++RR 11-79 p90
Songs: Nebbie. See no. 3771
Trittico Botticelliano. See no. 2689
REUBKE, Julius
Sonata, organ. See no. 2674
Sonata on the 94th psalm, C minor. See no. 209. See no. 1371.
    See no. 2001. See no. 2132. See no. 3895. See no. 4051
REUSNER, Esaias
Sonatina. See no. 3540
REYER, Ernest
Sigurd: La bruit des chants...Esprits gardiens. See no. 3774
Sigurd: Prince du Rhin; J'ai garde mon ame ingenue; Oui Sigurd est
    vainqueur; Esprits gardiens; Un souvenir poignant. See no. 1583
REYNOLDS, Roger
The emperor of ice cream. See no. 914
REZAC, Ivan
Sinfonietta. See no. 2488
REZNICEK, Emil
Donna Diana: Overture. See no. 3847. See no. 3897
RHEINBERGER, Joseph
2690 Nonet, op. 139, E flat major. Jaap Schroder, vln; Wiel Peeters,
vla; Anner Bylsma, vlc; Anthony Woodrow, contrabass; Danzi Quin-
tet. Acanta EA 23045
          +FF 1/2-79 p94   +HFN 11-79 p155
          +Gr 1-80 p1168   +RR 12-79 p31

2691 Pieces, organ (6). Suite, op. 149. Trevor Williams, vln; Christo-
      pher Green, vlc; Simon Lindley, org. Vista VPS 1050
                  +Gr 10-78 p702   +NR 3-80 p15
                  +HFN 7-78 p93   +RR 7-78 p71
      Suite, op. 149. See no. 2691
      Suite, op. 166, C major. See no. 1020
RHENE-BATON
      Passacaille, op. 35. See no. 3594
RHODES, Philip
      Visions of remembrance. See no. 393
RIBARI, Antal
      Concerto grosso, flute, clarinet and harp. See no. 2692
2692 Duo concertante, violins (12). Concerto grosso, flute, clarinet
      and harp. Quartet, strings, no. 5. Sonata, violin and piano,
      no. 4. Songs on poems of Michelangelo (2). Gabor Vida, flt;
      Bela Kovacs, clt; Hedy Lubik, hp; Norbert Szelecsenyi, Antal
      Ribari, pno; Mihaly Barta, Maria Balint, vln; Erika Sziklay, s;
      Tatrai Quartet, Budapest Philharmonia Orchestra; Ervin Lukacs.
      Serenus SRS 12084
                  +-FF 9/10-80 p185
      Quartet, strings, no. 5. See no. 2692
      Sonata, violin and piano, no. 4. See no. 2692
      Songs on poems of Michelangelo (2). See no. 2692
RICCI, Federico
      La prigione d'Edimburgo: Sulla poppa. See no. 3774
RICCIARDI
      Amor mio. See no. 3983
      Luna'lu. See no. 3770. See no. 3981
RICCIO, Giovanni
      La rosignola. See no. 4018
      Sonata a 4, A minor. See no. 4018
RICCIOTTI, Carlo
      Concertino, no. 4, F minor. See no. 2003. See no. 3916
RICHARD
      Prelude, D minor. See no. 3852
RICHARD I, King
      Je nus hons pris. See no. 3
RICHARDS, Eric
      Though under medium... See no. 914
RICHTER, Franz (Frantisek)
      Concerto, flute, D major. See no. 635
      Concerto, flute, E minor. See no. 3703
      Symphony, B flat major. See no. 3703
RICO
      Stella. See no. 3770
RIDOUT, Alan
      I turn the corner. See no. 3532
      Let us with a gladsome mind. See no. 4060
RIEDLBAUCH, Vaclav
      Allegri e pastorali. See no. 4010
RIEGGER, Wallingford
      Dance suite: Evocation, The cry, New dance. See no. 1109
      Evil shall not prevail. See no. 3973
      Introduction and fugue. See no. 1825

RIETI, Vittorio
    Poemes de Max Jacob (4). See no. 650
RIFFARD
    A la cambrousse. See no. 3760
RIISAGER, Knudage
    Snevind. See no. 3587
RILEY, Terry
2693 Shri camel. Terry Riley, org. CBS M 35164 Tape (c) MT 35164
                +FF 9/10-80 p185
RIMMER
    Extro-Intro, horn and electronics. See no. 3842
RIMSKY-KORSAKOV, Nikolai
2694 Capriccio espagnol, op. 34. TCHAIKOVSKY: Capriccio italien, op. 45.
        BPO; Arthur Fiedler. Crystal Clear CCS 7003
                +ARG 5-80 p40   +NR 12-78 p2
                +-FF 3/4-79 p14   +SFC 6-3-79 p49
                +-Gr 7-78 p259   ++St 10-79 p131
                +HF 6-79 p94
2695 Capriccio espagnol, op. 34. The golden cockerel: Suite. Russian
        Easter festival overture, op. 36. CO; Lorin Maazel. Decca SXL
        6966 Tape (c) KSXC 6966 (also London 7196)
                ++Gr 11-80 p674   +-HFN 11-80 p122
2696 Capriccio espagnol, op. 34. Scheherazade, op. 35. LSO; Igor Mar-
        kevitch. Philips 6570 148 Tape (c) 7310 148 (From SAL 3437)
                +FF 3/4-80 p137   +HFN 6-80 p119 tape
                +-Gr 3-80 p1449   +-RR 4-80 p80
                +-HFN 3-80 p105
    Concerto, clarinet and band. See no. 1387
2697 Le coq d'or. The legend of Sadko, op. 5: Aria and scene of Lyubava;
        Song of the Venetia merchant. The legend of the invisible city
        of Kitezh: Fevronia's aria, Act 1. The snow maiden: Fair spring
        aria; Second song of Lel, Act 1; Third song of Lel, Act 1. Nina
        Polyskova, Tamara Milashkina, Klara Kadinskaya, s; Antonina
        Klescheva, Larissa Avedeyeva, Irina Arkhipova, ms; Yuri Yelnikov,
        Gennady Pishchayev, t; Yuri Mazurok, bar; Leonid Ktitorov, bs-
        bar; Aleksei Korolyov, Aleksander Polyakov, bs; MRSO and Chorus,
        Bolshoi Theatre Orchestra; Alexei Kovalyov, Yevgeni Akulov, Al-
        exander Melik-Pashayev, Yevgeny Svetlanov, Asen Naidenov, Mark
        Ermler. Musical Heritage Society MHS 4142/4 (3)
                +ARG 10-80 p29   +FF 9/10-80 p186
    Le coq d'or: Hymne au soleil. See no. 3770. See no. 3872
    Le coq d'or: Suite. See no. 2695
    The legend of Sadko, op. 5. See no. 1504
    The legend of Sadko, op. 5: Aria and scene of Lyubava; Song of the
        Venetian merchant. See no. 2697
    The legend of Sadko, op. 5: Song of India. See no. 3872
2698 The legend of the invisible city of Kitezh. Nadia Rozhdestvenskaya,
        s; Vladimir Ivanovsky, D. Tarkhov, t; Ivan Petrov, bs; USSR
        Radio Orchestra and Chorus; Vasili Nebolsin. Melodiya D 06489-
        92 (4)
                +FF 9/10-80 p187
    The legend of the invisible city of Kitezh: Frevonia's aria. See
        no. 2697
    May night. See no. 1995
    May night: Levko's aria. See no. 3926

Mlada: Procession of the nobles. See no. 3969

2699 Mozart and Salieri, op. 48. Thomas Moser, t; Robert Holl, bs; Harald Himmel, vln; Walter Groppenberger, pno; Graz Concert Choir;
Graz Mozart Ensemble; Alois Hochstrasser. Preiser SPR 3283
                +-ARG 11-78 p37   +RR 2-80 p41
                /FF 7/8-78 p75

Quintet, B flat major. See no. 7

2700 Quintet, op. posth., B flat major. RUBINSTEIN: Quintet, op. 55, F
major. Felicja Blumenthal, pno; New Philharmonia Wind Ensemble.
Everest SDBR 3466 (From Turnabout TVS 34477)
                +FF 5/6-80 p138   +-NR 5-80 p6

Russian Easter festival overture, op. 36. See no. 772. See no.
1878. See no. 2695

2701 Scheherazade, op. 35. Irvine Arditti, vln; LSO; Loris Tjeknavorian.
Chalfont SDG 304
                +-Gr 11-80 p677   +HFN 10-80 p107
                +HF 12-80 p84

2702 Scheherazade, op. 35. TCHAIKOVSKY: Capriccio italien, op. 45. Hugh
Bean, vln; PhO; Paul Kletzki. Classics for Pleasure CFP 40341
Tape (c) TC CFP 40341 (From SXLP 20026, ASD 343)
                +-Gr 11-80 p677   +-HFN 12-80 p159 tape
                +-HFN 11-80 p129

2703 Scheherazade, op. 35. LSO; Pierre Monteux. Decca SPA 89 Tape (c)
KCSP 89
                +-Gr 3-80 p1449

2704 Scheherazade, op. 35. John Georgiadis, vln; LSO; Yevgeny Svetlanov.
HMV ASD 3779 Tape (c) TC ASD 3779 (also Angel SZ 37555 Tape (c)
4ZS 37555)
                +-ARG 7/8-80 p37   +HFN 12-79 p169
                +-Gr 10-79 p650   -NR 7-80 p4
                +HF 6-80 p83   +-RR 11-79 p92

2705 Scheherazade, op. 35. RPO; Thomas Beecham. HMV SXLP 30253 Tape
(c) SXLP 30253 (From ASD 251)
                ++Gr 10-77 p638   +-HFN 10-77 p165
                ++Gr 11-77 p899   ++RR 10-77 p58
                +Gr 3-80 p1447 tape

2706 Scheherazade, op. 35. Henrik Fridheim, vln; USSR Symphony Orchestra; Yevgeny Svetlanov. Musical Heritage Society MHS 4096 (From
Melodiya/Angel SR 40112)
                +-ARG 7/8-80 p37   +-HF 6-80 p83
                +FF 7/8-80 p125

2707 Scheherazade, op. 35. LSO; Igor Markevitch. Philips 6570 148 Tape
(c) 7310 148
                +RR 7-80 p97 tape

2708 Scheherazade, op. 35. COA; Kiril Kondrashin. Philips 9500 681
Tape (c) 7300 776
                +-Gr 11-80 p677   +-NR 12-80 p3
                +-HF 12-80 p84   +NYT 9-7-80 pD29
                ++HFN 11-80 p122   +St 12-80 p133

2709 Scheherazade, op. 35. Norman Carol, vln; PO; Eugene Ormandy. RCA
Q ARD 1-0028 Tape (ct) ART 1-0028
                +-ARG 7/8-80 p37   +MJ 5-73 p37
                +-FF 3/4-80 p137   -NR 5-73 p4
                -Gr 6-73 p57   ++RR 7-73 p56
                -HF 1-74 p84   *St 8-73 p111
                +HFN 6-73 p1182

2710 Scheherazade, op. 35. The tale of the Tsar Sultan, op. 57: March;
     Flight of the bumblebee. LSO; Andre Previn. RCA GL 4-2703 Tape
     (c) GK 4-2703 (From SB 6774)
                    +Gr 1-79 p1289   +HFN 1-79 p128 tape
                    +Gr 3-79 p1614 tape   +RR 8-79 p129 tape
                    +Gr 3-80 p1449
2711 Scheherazade, op. 35. Concert Arts Orchestra; Erich Leinsdorf.
     Seraphim S 60329 Tape (c) 4XG 60329 (From Capitol SP 8538)
                    *ARG 7/8-80 p37   -HF 6-80 p83
     Scheherazade, op. 35. See no. 2696
     Scheherazade, op. 35, excerpt. See no. 3604. See no. 3608
     Servilia: Servilia's aria. See no. 3796
     Snow maiden (Snegourotchka): Chanson de Lehl. See no. 3985
     Snow maiden: Fair spring aria; Second and third songs of Lel, Act
        1. See no. 2697
     Songs: O fearful crags; Ariosos, op. 49: The prophet. See no. 3904
     Symphony, no. 2, op. 9 (Antar). See no. 769. See no. 1506
     The tale of the Tsar Sultan, op. 57: Flight of the bumblebee. See
        no. 3694. See no. 3769. See no. 3891. See no. 3951. See no.
        3964
     The tale of the Tsar Sultan, op. 57: March; Flight of the bumblebee.
        See no. 2710
     The tale of the Tsar Sultan, op. 57: Suite. See no. 774
     The Tsar's bride: I bade farewell to my only true love. See no.
        3774
     The Tsar's bride: Marfa's aria. See no. 3872
RISSET, Jean-Claude
2712 Dialogues. Inharmonique. Moments newtoniens. Mutations. R. Fran-
        cois, flt; M. Arrignon, clt; Carlos Roque-Alsina, pno; Jean-
        Pierre Drouet, perc; I. Jarsky, s; Nouvel Orchestra Philharmon-
        ique; Michel Decoust, Michel Philippot. Harmonia Mundi INA GRM
        AM 56409
                    +FF 7/8-80 p16
     Inharmonique. See no. 2712
     Moments newtoniens. See no. 2712
     Mutations. See no. 2712
RITTER VON HERBECK, Johann
     Songs: Adeste fideles; Pueri concinite. See no. 3961
ROBB, John
2713 Songs: Better banditree; The drivers; Good night my love; I am very
        old tonight; Requiem; Richmond Hill; The shepherdess; Snowy
        mountain; Tears; Tecolote; To Elecktra; Tragedy; What is this
        glory. Donna McRae, s; Eugene Ives, bar; George Robert, pno;
        Darrel Randall, ob. Opus One 48
                    +HF 6-80 p84
ROBERDAY, Francois
     Fugues, nos. 10, 12. See no. 3852
     Fugue and caprice, nos. 1 and 3. See no. 3852
ROBERTS
     Pierrot. See no. 3774
ROBINSON, Thomas
     Bonny sweet Robin or Robin is to the greenwode gone. See no. 3840
     A gigue. See no. 3577
     Religious songs (4). See no. 3686
     A toye. See no. 3577

ROCHBERG, George
    La bocca della verita. See no. 3649
2714 Concerto, violin. Isaac Stern, vln; Pittsburg Symphony Orchestra;
        Andre Previn. Columbia M 35149 (also CBS 76797)
                        +ARG 9-79 p34   ++NR 6-79 p7
                        +FF 7/8-79 p80   +NYT 4-18-79 pD28
                        +Gr 3-80 p1392   +RR 3-80 p57
                        +HF 9-79 p123   +SFC 4-1-79 p44
                        +HFN 2-80 p97   +St 7-79 p103
                        ++MJ 5/6-79 p47
    Slow fires of autumn. See no. 1658
    Symphony, no. 1. See no. 2011
RODGERS, Richard
    South Pacific: Medley. See no. 3962
RODRIGO, Joaquin
    Canciones espanoles (3). See no. 3600
2715 Concierto andaluz. Concierto de Aranjuez. Pepe Romero, gtr; Romero
        Guitar Quartet, AMF; Neville Marriner. Philips 9500 563 Tape (c)
        7300 705
                        +FF 5/6-80 p139   ++HFN 9-79 p109
                        +Gr 9-79 p470   ++HFN 10-79 p171 tape
                        +-Gr 9-79 p534 tape   ++NR 2-80 p4
                        +HF 4-80 p104 tape   +RR 8-79 p88
2716 Concierto de Aranjuez. Concierto madrigal. Narciso Yepes, Gode-
        lieve Monden, gtr; PhO; Garcia Navarro. DG 2531 208 Tape (c)
        3301 208
                        +-Gr 6-80 p38   +-HFN 9-80 p116 tape
                        +Gr 8-80 p275 tape   +-RR 7-80 p63
                        +-HFN 7-80 p109
    Concierto de Aranjuez. See no. 2715. See no. 3612
    Concierto madrigal. See no. 2716
2717 Concierto pastoral. Fantasia para un gentilhombre (arr. Galway).
        James Galway, flt; PhO; Eduardo Mata. RCA RL 2-5193 Tape (c)
        RK 2-5193 (also RCA ARL 1-3416 Tape (c) ARK 1-3416)
                        +ARG 2-80 p42   +HFN 3-79 p129
                        -FF 1/2-80 p133   +NYT 9-23-79 pD28
                        +FU 11-79 p43   +-RR 4-79 p79
                        +Gr 4-79 p1719   +SFC 9-30-79 p45
                        +HF 2-80 p90   +-St 12-79 p154
                        +-HF 4-80 p104 tape
    Elogio de la guitarra. See no. 15
    Fantasia para un gentilhombre. See no. 1493. See no. 2717. See
        no. 3612
    Nocturne. See no. 3603
    Pequenas piezas (3). See no. 3599
    Prelude. See no. 3603
    Scherzino. See no. 3603
    Sephardic songs (4). See no. 14
    Songs: Cancion del Grumete; De los alamos vengo madre; Trovadores-
        ca. See no. 3551
    Songs: Verde verderol; Pajaro del agua. See no. 3892
ROGERS
    Hears not my Phyllis. See no. 3791
ROIG
    La gracia de Dios. See no. 3921

ROLAND-MANUEL, Alexis
     Elegies: Charmant rossignol; Chanson. See no. 3892
ROLDAN, Amadeo
2718 Small poems (3). VALDES: Cuban suite. VILLA-LOBOS: Choros, no. 10.
     MRSO; Boris Khaikin, Enrique Gonzalez Mantichi. Melodiya 33D
     014563-64
               +FF 3/4-80 p169
ROMAN, Johan
     Swedish mass, excerpt. See no. 3932
     Symphony, E minor. See no. 702
     ROMAN DE FAUVEL. See no. 3800
ROMBERG, Bernhard
     Concerto, flute, op. 17. See no. 1268
ROMERO, Celedonio
     Preludes (2). See no. 15
RONALD, Landon
     Rosy morn. See no. 3770
RONTANI
     Or ch'io non seguo piu. See no. 3738
ROQUELAY
     Ta bonne grace. See no. 3683
RORE, Cipriano de
     Anchor che col partire. See no. 3683. See no. 3956
ROREM, Ned
2719 Miss Julie, excerpts. Judith James, s; Veronica August, ms; Ronald
     Madden, bar; Orchestra; Peter Leonard. Painted Smiles PS 1388
               +-ARG 10-80 p35   +St 6-80 p120
     A Quaker reader: First-day thoughts; Mary Dyer did hang as a flag;
          Evidence of things not seen; There is a spirit that delights to
          do no evil...; A secret power; The world of silence. See no.
          3732
2720 Serenade on five English poems. STARER: Quartet, piano. Elaine
     Bonazzi, ms; The Cantilena Chamber Players. Grenadilla GS 1031
               +-ARG 3-80 p36   +NR 1-80 p6
               ++FF 9/10-79 p126
ROSA
     To be near thee. See no. 3738
ROSENBERG, Hilding
     Divertimento. See no. 1415
     Fantasie e fuga. See no. 2721
2721 Hymnus: Lover gud i himmelshod. Fantasie e fuga. Preludium e
     fuga. Toccata, aria pastorale, ciaconna. Alf Linder, org. Cap-
     rice CAP 1064
               +FF 11/12-80 p163   ++NR 9-80 p9
     Plastic scenes. See no. 1454. See no. 1472
     Preludium e fuga. See no. 2721
     Sonata, piano, no. 1. See no. 1472
     Suite 1924. See no. 1454
     Toccata, aria pastorale, ciaconna. See no. 2721
ROSENBOOM, David
2722 And out come the night ears. How much better if Plymouth Rock had
     landed on the Pilgrims, Section V. David Rosenboom, pno, syn-
     thesizer; Donald Buchla, synthesizer. 1750 Arch S 1774
               +-FF 9/10-80 p301   +St 10-79 p146
               *NR 1-80 p15

ROSENMULLER, Johann
    Sonata, 2 violins, no. 2, E minor. See no. 3767
ROSETTI, Francesco Antonio (Franz Anton Rossler)
    Concerto, horn, F major. See no. 42
ROSIER, Carel
    Sonata, C major. See no. 3818
ROSS, Walter
    Divertimento. See no. 3731
ROSSETER, Philip
    Prelude, galliard and almain. See no. 980
    Songs: No grave for woe; Shall I come if I swim; Sweet come again;
       What then is love but mourning; Whether men do laugh or weep.
       See no. 980
    Songs: When Laura smiles. See no. 3600. See no. 3719
ROSSI, Luigi
    Erminia sventurata. See no. 2723
    Gelosia. See no. 2723
    Lamento della Regina di Svezia. See no. 2723
    Lamento di Zaida mora. See no. 2723
    Mentre sorge dal mar. See no. 2723
    Quando spiega la notte. See no. 2723
    Sopra conca d'argenta. See no. 2723
2723 Works, selections: Erminia sventurata. Gelosia. Lamento della
    Regina di Svezia. Lamento di Zaida mora. Mentre sorge dal mar.
    Quando spiega la notte. Sopra conca d'argento. Judith Nelson,
    s; Wieland Kuijken, bs viol; William Christie, hpd, org; Concer-
    to Vocale. Harmonia Mundi HM 1010
             +ARG 12-80 p42   +HFN 6-80 p111
             ++FF 7/8-80 p157   +NR 5-80 p10
             ++Gr 5-80 p1706   +NYT 8-10-80 pD17
             +HF 8-80 p78   +RR 5-80 p100
ROSSI, Michelangelo
    Toccata settima. See no. 3751
    Toccatas, nos. 6, 14. See no. 3846
ROSSI, Salomone de
    Les cantiques de Salomon. See no. 1573
    Sonata sopra l'aria di Ruggiero. See no. 3690
ROSSINI, Gioacchino
    Armida: Overture. See no. 2737
    Assez de memento. See no. 2741
2724 Il barbiere di Siviglia. Mercedes Capsir, Cesira Ferrari, s; Dino
    Borgioli, t; Riccardo Stracciari, bar; Salvatore Baccaloni, bs-
    bar; Vincenzo Bettoni, bs; La Scala Orchestra and Chorus; Loren-
    zo Molajoli. Arabesque 8029-3 (3) Tape (c) 8029
             +ARG 10-80 p30   +NYT 7-13-80 pD20
             +-FF 9/10-80 p188   +ON 8-80 p36
    Il barbiere di Siviglia, excerpts. See no. 3696
    Il barbiere di Siviglia: Ah se e ver...L'innocenza di Lindoro. See
       no. 3554
    Il barbiere di Siviglia: Die Verleumdung sie ist ein Luftchen. See
       no. 2075
    Il barbiere di Siviglia: Die Verleumdung sie ist ein Luftchen...
       Einen Doktor meinesgleichen. See no. 3712
    Il barbiere di Siviglia: Dunque io son. See no. 3770
    Il barbiere di Siviglia: Frag ich mein beklomnen Herz. See no. 3646
    Il barbiere di Siviglia: La calunnia e un venticello. See no. 3538

Il barbiere di Siviglia: La calunnia. See no. 3899
Il barbiere di Siviglia: Largo al factotum. See no. 3812. See no.
3980. See no. 3982
2725 Il barbiere di Siviglia: Overture. La gazza ladra. Guillaume Tell:
Overture. SUPPE: Light cavalry: Overture. Pique dame. Poet and
peasant: Overture. BPhO; Herbert von Karajan. DG Tape (c) 3335
629
+—HFN 10-80 p117 tape
Il barbiere di Siviglia: Overture. See no. 667. See no. 2735.
See no. 2736. See no. 2737. See no. 3638
Il barbiere di Siviglia: Se il mio nome. See no. 3977
Il barbiere di Siviglia: Si il mio nome; All'idea di quel metallo;
Una voce poco fa. See no. 3774
Il barbiere di Siviglia: Se il mio nome; Ecco ridente in cielo;
Numbero quindici; All'idea di quel metallo; Ah qual colpo; Se il
mio nome; Ah qual colpo; Ecco ridente in cielo. See no. 3981
Il barbiere di Siviglia: Una voce poco fa. See no. 1512. See no.
3559. See no. 3766. See no. 3769. See no. 3789. See no. 3793.
See no. 3872
Barcarolle. See no. 2741
Bianca e Falliero: Overture. See no. 2737
2726 La boutique fantasque (arr. Respighi). LSO; Lamberto Gardelli.
HMV ASD 7077 Tape (c) TC ESD 7077 (also Angel SZ 37570)
++FF 1/2-80 p134	+NR 12-79 p3
+Gr 11-79 p918	+—RR 11-79 p92
+—HFN 11-79 p143	+RR 7-80 p96 tape
+HFN 2-80 p107 tape	+SFC 11-4-79 p40
+MUM 5/6-80 p35	++St 12-79 p153
2727 La boutique fantasque (arr. Respighi). Suite Rossiniana (arr.
Respighi). RPO; Antal Dorati. London SPC 21172 Tape (c) 5-
21172 (also Decca JB 79 Tape (c) KJBC 79) From PFS 4407)
++FF 11/12-79 p118	++HFN 3-80 p105
++Gr 3-80 p1392	++NR 8-78 p1
++HF 9-79 p131 tape	++RR 3-80 p58
La boutique fantasque: Tarantella. See no. 3962
Cambiale di matrimonio: Overture. See no. 2737
2728 La cenerentola. Bianca Casoni, ms; Ugo Benelli, t; Sesto Bruscantini, bar; Alfredo Mariotti, bs; Giovanna Di Rocca, Teresa Rocc-
hino, Federico Davia; Berlin State Opera Chorus; Berlin Radio
Orchestra; Piero Bellugi. Acanta JB 23271/3 (3)
        +—FF 9/10-80 p187   +—ON 8-80 p36
2729 La cenerentola (sung in Russian). Zara Dolukhanova, ms; Orchestra;
Chorus. Eclat EC 1003
        -FF 11/12-80 p165
La cenerentola: Nacqui all affanno...Non piu mesta. See no. 1512
La cenerentola: Overture. See no. 2737. See no. 3581
2730 Le Comte Ory. Jeannette Sinclair, Sari Barabas, s; Cora Canne-Meijer,
ms; Monica Sinclair, con; Juan Oncina, Dermot Troy, t; Ian Wal-
lace, bar; Michel Roux, bs; Glyndebourne Festival Orchestra and
Chorus; Vittorio Gui. HMV RLS 744 (2) (From ALP 1473/4)
+Gr 5-80 p1712	+RR 5-80 p49
+—HFN 5-80 p135	+STL 7-13-80 p38
++Op 8-80 p799	
Demetrio e Polibio: Overture. See no. 2737
Edipo a Colona: Overture. See no. 2737

Edoardo e Cristina: Overture. See no. 2737
Elisabetta, Regina d'Inghilterra: Indegno; Fellon la pena avrai.
   See no. 3918
Ermione: Overture. See no. 2737
La gazza ladra: Overture. See no. 667. See no. 2725. See no.
   2735. See no. 2736. See no. 2737
2731 Guillaume Tell (William Tell). Mirella Freni, s; Elizabeth Connell,
   ms; Luciano Pavarotti, t; Sherrill Milnes, bar; Nicolai Ghiaurov,
   Richard van Allan, bs; NPhO; Riccardo Chailly. London OSA 1446
   (4)
           ++SFC 11-30-80 p21
Guillaume Tell: Ils s'eloignent enfin...Sombre foret. See no. 2088
Guillaume Tell: Overture. See no. 667. See no. 2725. See no.
   2735. See no. 2736. See no. 2737. See no. 3638
Guillaume Tell: Resta immobile. See no. 3771. See no. 3812
Guillaume Tell: Selva opaca. See no. 3670. See no. 3886. See no.
   3929
Guillaume Tell: Sombres forets. See no. 3630. See no. 3632
L'Inganno felice: Overture. See no. 2737
Introduction and variations, C major. See no. 1255. See no. 2227
2732 L'Italiana in Algeri. Graziella Sciutti, s; Mafalda Masini, Giuli-
   etta Simionato, ms; Cesare Valletti, t; Marcello Cortis, bar;
   Mario Petri, Enrico Campi, bs; La Scala Orchestra and Chorus;
   Carlo Maria Giulini. HMV RLS 747 (2) (From Columbia 33CX 1215/6)
   (also Seraphim IB 6119)
           +-Gr 8-80 p269   +NYT 10-26-80 pB33
           +-HFN 7-80 p119   +RR 7-80 p46
L'Italiana in Algeri: Cruda sorte; Amor tiranno. See no. 1512
L'Italiana in Algeri: Languir per una bella. See no. 3977
L'Italiana in Algeri: Overture. See no. 2735. See no. 2736. See
   no. 2737
Maometto II: Overture. See no. 2737
Marche et reminiscences pour mon dernier voyage. See no. 2741
Melodie candide. See no. 2741
Memento homo. See no. 2741
Mon prelude hygienique du matin. See no. 2741
2733 Mose. Caterina Mancini, Bruna Rizzoli, s; Lucia Danieli, ms; Ago-
   stino Lazzari, Mario Filippeschi, Piero de Palma, t; Giuseppe
   Taddei, bar; Plinio Clabassi, Nicola Rossi-Lemani, bs; San Carlo
   Opera Orchestra and Chorus; Tullio Serafin. Philips 5670 001/3
   (3) (From ABL 3201/3)
           +-Gr 7-80 p165   +-HFN 7-80 p119
           +-RR 7-80 p47
2734 Otello, op. 11. Nucci Condo, s; Frederica von Stade, ms; Jose Carreras, Gianfranco Pastine, Keith Lewis, Alfonso Leoz, t; Samuel
   Ramey, bs; Ambrosian Opera Chorus; PhO; Jesus Lopez-Cobos.
   Philips 6769 023 (3) Tape (c) 7699 110
           +-ARG 4-80 p41   +NR 1-80 p7
           ++FF 1/2-80 p135   ++NYT 9-30-79 pD22
           +Gr 9-79 p518   +OC Spring 1980 p73
           +Gr 11-79 p924 tape   +-ON 2-9-80 p37
           +HF 5-80 p77   +Op 12-79 p1167
           +HFN 9-79 p111   +-RR 9-79 p58
           ++HFN 11-79 p157 tape   +St 12-79 p150
           +MT 5-80 p323   +STL 12-2-79 p37

Otello: Overture. See no. 2737
Otello: Quanto son fieri i palpiti; Che smania...Oime che affanno;
   Assisa a pie d'un salice; Deh calma o ciel nel sonno. See no.
   1685
Ouf les petits pois. See no. 2741
2735 Overtures: Il barbiere di Siviglia. La gazza ladra. Guillaume
   Tell. L'Italiana in Algeri. La scala di seta. Semiramide.
   PhO; Herbert von Karajan. HMV SXLP 30203 Tape (c) TC SXLP 30203,
   TC EXE 194 (From Columbia SAX 2378)
            ++Gr 5-76 p1807   +HFN 10-80 p117 tape
            +-HFN 7-76 p103   +-RR 6-76 p52
            +HFN 8-76 p95
2736 Overtures: Il barbiere di Siviglia. La gazza ladra. Guillaume
   Tell. L'Italian in Algeri. Semiramide. Il Signor Bruschino.
   Budapest Symphony Orchestra; Adam Fischer. Hungaroton SLPX
   11932 Tape (c) MK 11932
            -FF 3/4-79 p107   /NR 12-78 p3
            +HF 5-80 p90 tape
2737 Overtures: Armida. Il barbiere di Siviglia.* Bianca e Falliero.
   La cambiale di matrimonio.* La cenerentola. Demetrio e Polibio.
   Edipo a Colona. Edoardo e Cristina. Ermione. La gazza ladra.
   Guillaume Tell.* L'Inganno felice.* L'Italiana in Algeri.*
   Maometto II. Otello. Ricciardo e Zoraide. La scala di seta.*
   Semiramide.* Il Signor Bruschino.* Le siege de Corinth.* Sin-
   fonia di Bologna. Sinfonia al conventello. Trancredi.* Torval-
   do e Dorliska. Il Turco in Italia. Il viaggio a Reims.* AMF;
   Neville Marriner. Philips 6768 064 (4) Tape (c) 7699 136 (*From
   9500 349, 16500)
            +Gr 10-80 p500   +HFN 11-80 p131 tape
            ++HFN 11-80 p122
Les peches de vieillesse: Une caresse a ma femme; Prelude inoffen-
   sif; L'innocence italienne; La candeur francaise; Tarantelle pur
   sang; Specimen de l'ancien regime. See no. 2741
La pesarese. See no. 2741
Petit caprice. See no. 2741
Un petit train de plaisir. See no. 2741
2738 Petite messe solennelle. Margaret Marshall, s; Alfreda Hodgson,
   con; Robert Tear, t; Malcolm King, bs; London Chamber Choir;
   Sylvia Holford, John Constable, pno; John Birch, harm; Laszlo
   Heltay. Argo ZRG 893/4 (2) Tape (c) K118K22
            +FF 5/6-80 p143   +ON 2-9-80 p37
            +-Gr 12-78 p1150   ++RR 1-79 p81
            +HFN 12-78 p159   ++RR 8-79 p129 tape
            +NYT 10-7-79 pD24
2739 Petite messe solennelle. Mirella Freni, s; Lucia Valentini, ms;
   Luciano Pavarotti, t; Ruggero Raimondi, bs; La Scala Coro Polifonico; Leone Magiera, pno; Vittorio Rosetta, harm; Romano Gandolfo. London Cime Ars Nova C3S 134 (2)
            +-FF 3/4-79 p106   +-ON 2-9-80 p37
            +-Gr 3-80 p1428   +SFC 10-22-78 p53
            -HF 3-79 p100   +St 12-78 p162
2740 Petite messe solennelle. Kari Lovaas, s; Brigitte Fassbaender, con;
   Peter Schreier, t; Dietrich Fischer-Dieskau, bar; Munchner Vokalisten; Hans Ludwig Hirsch, Wolfgang Sawallisch, pno; Reinhard
   Raffalt, harm; Wolfgang Sawallisch. RCA SER 5693/4 (2) (also

Eurodisc 86321 XGK (2), RCA ARL 2-2626 Tape (c) ARK 2-2626)
        +-ARG 8-78 p42   +-ON 2-9-80 p37
        +-FF 7/8-78 p77   +-RR 10-73 p114
        +Gr 10-73 p714   +SFC 8-16-78 p48
        -HF 6-73 p98   ++St 5-73 p120
Petite messe solennelle: Crucifixus. See no. 3723. See no. 3983
2741 Piano works: Assez de memento. Barcarolle. Les peches de vieil-
       lesse: Une caresse a ma femme; Prelude inoffensif; L'innocence
       italienne; La candeur francaise; Tarantelle pur sang; Specimen
       de l'ancien regime. Marche et reminiscences pour mon dernier
       voyage. Melodie candide. Memento homo. Mon prelude hygienique
       du matin. Ouf les petits pois. La pesarese. Petit caprice.
       Un petit train de plaisir. Prelude pretentieux. Un reve. Bruno
       Mezzena, pno. Dischi Ricordi ARCL 327 003 (3)
               +-Gr 11-80 p704
Prelude pretentieux. See no. 2741
Prelude, theme and variations. See no. 3684
Un reve. See no. 2741
Ricciardo e Zoraide: Overture. See no. 2737
La scala di seta: Overture. See no. 2735. See no. 2737
Semiramide: Bel raggio lusinghier. See no. 3770
Semiramide: Overture. See no. 2735. See no. 2736. See no. 2737
Semiramide: Wie glanzte so freundlich mir. See no. 3636
2742 Le siege de Corinth. Renata Tebaldi, s; Miriam Pirazzini, ms;
       Mirto Picchi, t; Mario Petri, Augusto Romani, bs; RAI Orchestra
       and Chorus; Gabriele Santini. Historical Recordings Enterprises
       HRE 298 (2)
               +FF 11/12-80 p163
Siege de Corinth: Giusto ciel, In tal pergiglio...Parmi vederlo ahi
       misero. See no. 3554
Siege de Corinth: Overture. See no. 2737
Il Signor Bruschino: Overture. See no. 2736. See no. 2737
Sinfonia al conventello. See no. 2737
Sinfonia di Bologna: Overture. See no. 2737
Soirees musicales: March. See no. 3801
Sonata, harp, E flat major. See no. 3819
Sonatas, strings, nos. 2 and 4. See no. 1264
Songs: Pieta signore. See no. 3981
2743 Stabat mater. Sung-Sook Lee, s; Florence Quivar, ms; Kenneth Rieg-
       el, Paul Plishka, bs; Cincinnati May Festival Chorus; CnSO;
       Thomas Schippers. Turnabout Q QTV S 34634 Tape (c) KTVC 34634
               /-Gr 3-80 p1428   ++RR 4-80 p117
               +-HFN 2-80 p97   ++SFC 6-27-76 p29
               +MJ 3-77 p74   ++St 12-76 p146
               /NR 10-76 p9   +STL 3-9-80 p41
               +-NYT 11-27-77 pD15
Stabat mater: Inflammatus. See no. 3630
Stabat mater: Pro peccatis. See no. 3930. See no. 3979
Suite Rossiniana. See no. 2727
Tancredi: Di tanto palpiti. See no. 3636
Tancredi: Overture. See no. 2737
Torvaldo e Dorliska: Overture. See no. 2737
Il Turco di Italia: Overture. See no. 2737
Il viaggio a Reims. See no. 2737

ROTA
     The glass mountain: Take the sun.   See no. 3771
ROTOLI
     Songs: La gondola nera; Mia sposa sara la mia bandiera.   See no.
          3978
ROUSSEAU, Jean-Jacques
     Echo.   See no. 3764
     Pastoral variations on an old Christmas carol.   See no. 3685
     Tarass Bulba: Non je n'ai pas.   See no. 3774
ROUSSEL, Albert
2744 Aeneas, op. 54.   ORTF; Jean Martinon.   Erato STU 70578 (also Musi-
          cal Heritage Society MHS 3374)
                         *Gr 4-71 p1626   +SFC 9-16-79 p61
                         +NR 10-79 p9   +St 1-80 p100
     Bacchus et Ariane, op. 43: Suite, no. 2.   See no. 3556
2745 Evocations, op. 15.   CPhO and Chorus; Zdenek Kosler.   Supraphon 112
          2454
                         +-Gr 10-80 p528   +STL 9-14-80 p40
                         +HFN 12-80 p143
     Le festin de l'araignee, op. 17.   See no. 3556
2746 Impromptu, op. 21.   Serenade, op. 30.   Trio, op. 40.   Marie-Claire
          Jamet Quintet.   Harmonia Mundi HM 735
                         +Gr 6-79 p71   +RR 9-78 p71
                         +HFN 6-80 p111
     Impromptu, op. 21.   See no. 1181.   See no. 3685
     Joueuers de flute, op. 27.   See no. 1301.   See no. 3594.   See no.
          3714
     Poemes de Ronsard.   See no. 638
     Poemes de Ronsard: Rossignol mon mignon; Ciel aer et vens.   See no.
          3892
     Prelude and fugue, op. 41.   See no. 3735
     Serenade, op. 30.   See no. 2746
     Sinfonietta, op. 52.   See no. 3556
     Songs: Le bachelier de Salamanque; Coeur en peril; Jazz dans la
          nuit.   See no. 3862
     Symphony, no. 3, op. 42, G minor.   See no. 3556
     Symphony, no. 4, op. 53, A major.   See no. 3556
     Trio, op. 40.   See no. 2746
ROVETTA, Giovanni
     Uccidetemi pur bella.   See no. 3878
ROVICS, Howard
     Events.   See no. 1960
     Piece, violoncello, piano and electronic tape.   See no. 1960
     Songs: Echo; Look friend at me; What Grandma knew.   See no. 1960
ROZSA, Miklos
     Spellbound: Spellbound concerto.   See no. 3790
     That Hamilton woman: Love theme.   See no. 4046
2747 Time after time.   RPO; Miklos Rozsa.   Entr'Acte ERS 6517
                         +-NR 8-80 p3
     Tribute to a bad man: Suite.   See no. 4046
RUBBRA, Edmund
     Fanfare for Europe, op. 142.   See no. 3959
     Magnificat and nunc dimittis, op. 65, A flat major.   See no. 3783
     Soliloquy, op. 57.   See no. 2748
2748 Symphony, no. 7, op. 88, C major.   Soliloquy, op. 57.   Rohan de

Saram, vlc; LPO, LSO; Adrian Boult, Vernon Handley. Lyrita SRCS
119 (From SRCS 41)
                    +—Gr 1-80 p1158   +RR 12-79 p74
                    +HFN 12-79 p169
RUBINSTEIN, Anton
2749 Concerto, piano, no. 1, op. 25, E minor. Michael Fardink, pno; RPO;
        Paul Freeman. Orion ORS 79347
                    +ARG 6-80 p38   +NR 5-80 p6
                    +FF 5/6-80 p144
2750 Concerto, piano, no. 4, op. 70, D minor. SCRIABIN: Concerto, piano,
        op. 20, F sharp minor. Victor Bunin, Igor Zhukov, pno; MRSO,
        Estonian State Symphony Orchestra; Edward Serov, Neimi Jarvi.
        HMV ASD 3707
                    +—Gr 8-79 p332   +—MT 4-80 p253
                    +HFN 9-79 p111   +—RR 8-79 p89
                    +—MM 11-79 p29
    The demon: Accursed world; On desire's soft fleeing wing. See no.
        3770
    The demon: In the quiet of the night. See no. 3774
    The demon: Tamara's song. See no. 3796
    Impromptu, op. 16, no. 1, F major. See no. 3832
    Kamennoi ostrow, op. 10. See no. 3870
    Melancholy, op. 51, no. 1, G minor. See no. 3833
    Melody, op. 3, no. 1, F major. See no. 3694
    Nero: Epitalamium. See no. 3770. See no. 3774
    Prelude, op. 75, no. 9, D minor. See no. 3833
    Quintet, op. 55, F major. See no. 2700
    Reve angelique. See no. 3902
    Serenade, D minor. See no. 3902
2751 Sonata, violin and piano, op. 13, no. 1, G major. Grigori Feigin,
        vln; Viktor Poltoratsky, pno. Melodiya S10 09501-2
                    +FF 1/2-80 p176
2752 Sonata, violin and piano, op. 49, F minor. JOACHIM: Hebrew melod-
        ies, op. 9, nos. 1 and 3. Lubomir Maly, vla; Libuse Krepelova,
        pno. Supraphon 111 2475
                    +—NR 11-80 p5   +—St 11-80 p99
RUDHYAR, Dane
2753 Advent. Crisis and overcoming. Kronos String Quartet. CRI SD 418
                    +—FF 7/8-80 p126   +NYT 2-24-80 pD20
                    +NR 5-80 p8
    Crisis and overcoming. See no. 2753
2754 Tetragram, nos. 1-3. WEIGL: Night fantasies. Dwight Peltzer, pno.
        Serenus SRS 12072
                    +FF 3/4-80 p184   +St 1-78 p94
                    +NR 11-77 p13
RUDIGER
    Songs: Still o Himmel; Es bluhen die Maien. See no. 3697
RUDOLF ERZHERZOG VON OSTERREICH
    Serenade, B major. See no. 1244
RUDZINSKI, Zbigniew
    Contra fidem. See no. 3857
RUDZINSKI, Witold
    The dismissal of the Grecian envoys: Recitative and duet. See no.
        3857

RUE, Pierre de la
    Fors seulement. See no. 3702
RUFFO, Vincenzo
    La disparata. See no. 3597
    La gamba. See no. 3597
RUGGLES, Carl
    Angels. See no. 2755
    Evocations. See no. 2755
    Exaltation. See no. 2755
    Men. See no. 2755
    Men and mountains. See no. 2755
    Organum. See no. 2755
    Portals. See no. 2755
    Sun-treader. See no. 2755
    Toys. See no. 2755
    Vox clemens in deserto. See no. 2755
2755 Works, selections: Angels (2 versions). Evocations (2). Exaltation.
    Men. Men and mountains. Organum. Portals. Sun-treader. Toys.
    Vox clemens in deserto. Judith Blegen, s; Beverly Morgan, ms;
    Michael Tilson Thomas, John Kirkpatrick, pno; Leonard Raver, org;
    Gerard Schwarz Brass Ensemble; Gregg Smith Singers; Speculum
    Musicae, Buffalo Philharmonic Orchestra; Michael Tilson Thomas.
    Columbia M2 34591 (2)
           +-ARG 12-80 p43   +-NYT 8-17-80 pD15
           +-FF 9/10-80 p189   ++SFC 8-3-80 p33
           -HF 10-80 p69   +St 10-80 p80
           +MQ 10-80 p604
RUIFROK, Henri
    Minuet, op. 4, no. 1. See no. 4045
    Song without words, op. 5, no. 2. See no. 4045
RUPE
    Gentle words. See no. 3848
RUSAGER, Knudage
    Concertino, op. 29. See no. 3606
RUSH, Loren
    Hexahedron. See no. 1161
2756 A little traveling music. Oh Susanna. Soft music, hard music.
    Dwight Peltzer, pno. Serenus SRS 12070
           +-ARG 2-78 p38   +NR 12-77 p12
           +FF 3/4-80 p184   +NYT 3-12-78 pD19
           +HF 5-78 p114
    Oh Susanna. See no. 2756
    Quartet, strings, C sharp minor. See no. 1937
    Soft music, hard music. See no. 2756
RUSSELL
    The bells of Saint Anne de Beaupre. See no. 309
    Millenial praise. See no. 3848
    RUSSIAN ORTHODOX CHURCH MUSIC: Vespers of Good Friday. See no. 3817
    RUSSIAN ORTHODOX MUSIC: Liturgy for All Saints Day. See no. 3693
RUSSO, John
    Studies, clarinet and piano (2). See no. 697
    Songs (3). See no. 3891
RUTTER
    Il est ne le divin enfant. See no. 3933
RUYNEMAN, Daniel
    Hieroglyphen. See no. 3818

RYBAR, Jaroslav
    Elementi continuali (7). See no. 4010
RZEWSKI, Frederic
    Song and dance. See no. 1657
SABOLI, Nicolas
    Noels (Tomasi). See no. 3318
SADERO
    Songs: Gondoliera Veneziana: Amuri amuri. See no. 3771
SAINT-LUBIN
    Fantasy on the sextet from Donizetti's "Lucia di Lammermoor". See
        no. 3637
SAINT-SAENS, Camille
2757 Africa, op. 89. Concerto, piano, no. 3, op. 29, E flat major. Rap-
        sodie d'Auvergne, op. 73. Wedding cake, op. 76. Philippe Entre-
        monte, pno; Toulouse Capitole Orchestra; Michel Plasson. Colum-
        bia M 35162
                    +FF 1/2-80 p138   +SFC 9-30-79 p45
                    +NR 12-79 p5
2758 Allegro appassionata, op. 43. Concerto, violoncello, no. 1, op. 33,
        A minor. Le carnival de animaux: The swan. TCHAIKOVSKY: Vari-
        ations on a Rococo theme, op. 33. Pezzo capriccioso, op. 62.
        Paul Tortelier, vlc; Birmingham Symphony Orchestra, Northern
        Sinfonia Orchestra; Louis Femaux, Yan Pascal Tortelier. Arabes-
        que 8038 Tape (c) 8038
                    ++ARG 9-80 p39   ++FF 7/8-80 p145
    Allegro appassionato, op. 43. See no. 751
    Ascanio: Ballet music, Adagio and variations. See no. 3951
    Il canto del cigno. See no. 3988
    Caprice andalous, op. 122. See no. 2770
2759 Le carnaval des animaux (Carnival of the animals). Polonaise, op.
        77. Variations on a theme by Beethoven, op. 35. Philippe Entre-
        mont, Gaby Casadesus, pno; Ensemble; Philippe Entremont. CBS
        76735 Tape (c) 40-76735 (also CBS M 35851)
                    +FF 11/12-80 p165   +HFN 4-79 p134 tape
                    +-Gr 3-79 p1571   +RR 3-79 p83
                    +HFN 3-79 p129
    Le carnaval des animaux. See no. 722. See no. 1004
    Le carnaval des animaux: Le cygne. See no. 751. See no. 1307.
        See no. 2758. See no. 3906. See no. 3935. See no. 4030
    Le carnaval des animaux: Suite. See no. 3621
2760 Cavatine, op. 114. Romance, op. 36. Sonata, clarinet and piano,
        op. 167, E flat major. Sonata, bassoon and piano, op. 168, G
        major. Sonata, oboe and piano, op. 166, D major. Maurice Bour-
        gue, ob; Maurice Allard, Gilbert Coursier, Jacques Toulon, trom;
        Maurice Gabai, clt; Annie d'Arco, pno. Calliope CAL 1819
                    +-Gr 9-80 p367   +RR 7-80 p83
    Concerto, piano, no. 3, op. 29, E flat major. See no. 2757
    Concerti, violin, nos. 1-3. See no. 2770
    Concerto, violin, no. 1, op. 20, A major. See no. 2473
2761 Concerto, violin, no. 3, op. 61, B minor. Havanaise, op. 83. In-
        troduction and rondo capriccioso, op. 28. Pierre Amoyal, vln;
        NPhO; Vernan Handley. Musical Heritage Society MHS 3738 (also
        Erato STU 70985)
                    +-FF 3/4-78 p66   +RR 10-79 p103
                    +-HFN 4-80 p108   -St 5-78 p98

Concerto, violoncello, no. 1, op. 33, A minor. See no. 816. See
    no. 2758
Danse macabre, op. 40. See no. 449. See no. 1288. See no. 1289.
    See no. 3666
Le deluge, op. 45: Prelude. See no. 2770
Etudes, op. 52, no. 6. See no. 999. See no. 2770
Etudes, op. 111: Toccata. See no. 999
Fantaisie, E flat major. See no. 3725. See no. 3958
Havanaise, op. 83. See no. 1019. See no. 1021. See no. 1919. See
    no. 2761. See no. 2770. See no. 3964
Improvisation. See no. 4061
Introduction and rondo capriccioso, op. 28. See no. 1019. See no.
    1021. See no. 1919. See no. 1920. See no. 2761. See no. 2770.
    See no. 3964
Marche heroique, op. 34. See no. 2766
2762 Mass, no. 4. Simon Colston, treble; Anthony de Rivaz, Jon Vickers,
    c-t; Trevor Owen, t; Brian Harvey, bs; Worcester Cathedral Choir;
    Roy Massey, Paul Trepte, org; Donald Hunt. Argo ZRG 889
                    ++FF 5/6-80 p144   +NYT 10-7-79 pD24
                    +-Gr 9-78 p527   +-ON 3-15-80 p45
                    +HFN 9-78 p147   +RR 9-78 p90
                    +MT 3-79 p228   +-St 1-80 p102
Morceau de concert, op. 62. See no. 2770
Morceau de concert, op. 94. See no. 3606
Morceau de concert, op. 154. See no. 1181
La muse et le poete, op. 132. See no. 2770
Le pas d'armes du Roi Jean. See no. 3631
Phaeton, op. 39. See no. 2766
Polonaise, op. 77. See no. 2759
Rapsodie d'Auvergne, op. 73. See no. 2757
Rapsodies sur des cantiques bretons, op. 7, no. 3 (3). See no.
    3838
Romance, op. 36. See no. 2760. See no. 3684
Romance, op. 37, D flat major. See no. 2770. See no. 3782
Romance, op. 48, C major. See no. 2770
Le rossignol et la rose. See no. 3695
Le rouet d'Omphale, op. 31. See no. 3799
2763 Samson et Dalila. Elena Obraztsova, ms; Placido Domingo, t; Renato
    Bruson, bar; Pierre Thau, Robert Lloyd, bs; Orchestre and Choir
    de Paris; Daniel Barenboim. DG 2531 167/9 (3) Tape (c) 3371 050
    (also DG 2709 095 Tape (c) 3371 050)
                    +ARG 5-80 p32   +-NYT 12-23-79 pD28
                    ++FF 3/4-80 p139   +OC Summer 1980 p47
                    +-FU 5-80 p49   +-ON 3-15-80 p45
                    +Gr 10-79 p710   +Op 2-80 p167
                    +Gr 12-79 p1065 tape   ++RR 11-79 p59
                    +HF 4-80 p93   +-RR 6-80 p94 tape
                    +-HF 8-80 p87 tape   +-SFC 11-25-79 p46
                    -NR 1-80 p10   +St 2-80 p130
2764 Samson et Dalila. Helene Bouvier, ms; Jose Luccioni, t; Paul Caba-
    nel, Henri Medus, bs; Charles Chambon, bar; Paris Opera Chorus;
    Orchestre National de l'Opera; Louis Fourestier. EMI 2C 153
    10619-19 (3) (From Pathe PDT 116/30, Columbia MPO 28, Columbia
    SL 107, Vox PL 8323, Pathe 5007/9)
                    +-ARSC Vol 12, nos. 1-2, 1980 p103

Samson et Dalila, excerpts. See no. 3909

Samson et Dalila: Arretez o mes freres; Mon coeur s'ouvre a ta voix.
See no. 3770

Samson et Dalila: Ballet music. See no. 1523

Samson et Dalila: Danse des pretresses de Dagon; Bacchanale. See
no. 3799

Samson et Dalila: J'ai gravi la montagne. See no. 3899

Samson et Dalila: Maudita a jamais soit la race des enfants d'Israel. See no. 3925

Samson et Dalila: Mon coeur s'ouvre a ta voix. See no. 3903

Sonata, bassoon and piano, op. 168, G major. See no. 1300. See no.
2526. See no. 2760

Sonata, clarinet and piano, op. 167, E flat major. See no. 1201.
See no. 2760

Sonata, oboe and piano, op. 166, D major. See no. 56. See no. 2760

Sonata, violin and piano, no. 1, op. 75, D minor. See no. 1440.
See no. 1567. See no. 1974. See no. 3964

2765 Sonata, violoncello and piano, no. 1, op. 32, C minor. Sonata,
violoncello and piano, no. 2, op. 123, D major. Andre Navarra,
vlc; Annie d'Arco, pno. Calliope CAL 1818
          +-HFN 8-80 p102   +RR 7-80 p83
          +-RR 3-77 p84

Sonata, violoncello and piano, no. 2, op. 123, D major. See no.
2765

Songs: Sabre en main; Au cimitiere. See no. 3770

Suite Algerienne, op. 60: Marche militaire francaise. See no. 3582

2766 Symphony, no. 1, op. 2, E flat major. Phaeton, op. 39. Marche
heroique, op. 34. Luxembourg Radio Orchestra; Louis de Froment.
Turnabout TVS 37117 Tape (c) KTVC 37117
          +Gr 7-79 p210   +-MT 2-80 p107
          +-HFN 7-79 p111   +RR 6-79 p84

2767 Symphony, no. 3, op. 78, C minor. Bernard Gavoty, org; French National Radio Orchestra; Jean Martinon. HMV ASD 3674 Tape (c) TC
ASD 3674 (From SLS 5035)
          +Gr 10-79 p653   +HFN 2-80 p107 tape
          +HFN 10-79 p169   +RR 7-80 p97 tape
          ++RR 10-79 p103

2768 Symphony, no. 3, op. 78, C minor. Alexandre Cellier, org; Denise
Herbrecht, Lucien Petijean, pno; L'Orchestre Symphonique de
Gramophone; Piero Coppola. Past Masters 21
          +-FF 1/2-80 p138

2769 Symphony, no. 3, op. 78, C minor. Michael Murray, org; PO; Eugene
Ormandy. Telarc 10051
          +FF 9/10-80 p194   +-RR 8-80 p51
          +-Gr 9-80 p349   +SFC 8-17-80 p36
          +HF 8-80 p81   ++St 8-80 p73
          +HFN 8-80 p101

Symphony, no. 3, op. 78, C minor. See no. 3557

Le timbre d'Argent: Le bonheur est une chose legere. See no. 3985

Trio, piano, no. 1, op. 18, F major. See no. 1921. See no. 2661

Variations on a theme by Beethoven, op. 35. See no. 2759

Wedding cake, op. 76. See no. 2757

2770 Works, selections: Concerti, violin, nos. 1-3. Caprice andalous,
op. 122. Le deluge, op. 45: Prelude. Etude, op. 52, no. 6.
Havanaise, op. 83. Introduction and rondo capriccioso, op. 28.

La muse et le poete, op. 132. Morceau de concert, op. 62. Romance, op. 37, D flat major. Romance, op. 48, C major. Ulf Hoelscher, vln; Ralph Kirschbaum, vlc; NPhO; Pierre Vervaux. Seraphim SIC 6111 (3) Tape (c) 4XG 6111

+-ARG 7-79 p46   ++NR 5-79 p6
+-FF 7/8-79 p83   +NYT 7-6-80 pD15
+HF 5-79 p85   ++St 7-79 p101

SAINZ DE LA MAZA, Eduardo
    Campanas del alba. See no. 13
SAJNSZKIJ
    Kiszamolo. See no. 3814
SALADIN, Louis
    Canticum Hebraicum. See no. 1573
SALIERI, Antonio
    Concerto, flute and oboe, C major. See no. 105. See no. 625
    Sinfonia, D major. See no. 105
SALLINEN, Aulis
    Dream songs (4). See no. 3586
2771 The horseman (Ratsumies). Taru Valjakka, s; Tuula Nieminen, ms; Anita Valkki, alto; Eero Erkkila, t; Matti Salminen, Usko Viitanen, bar; Heikki Toivanen, Martti Wallen, bs; Savonlinna Opera Festival Orchestra and Chorus; Ulf Soderblom. Finnlevy SFX 101 (3) (From Finnlevy SFX 41/3)
                +ARG 10-80 p31   +FF 5/6-80 p145
    Simpati. See no. 3814
SALOME, Theodore
    Grand choeur. See no. 4047
SALONEN, Sulo
    Frukta icke Maria. See no. 3934
    Sen suuven suloisuutta. See no. 3726
SALVATORE
    Canzona frances, no. 3. See no. 3846
    Toccata, no. 1. See no. 3846
SALZEDO, Carlos
    Piece concertante. See no. 3653
    Song in the night. See no. 3676
SALZEDO, Leonard
    Capriccio, op. 90. See no. 59
    Chanson de la nuit. See no. 3685
SAMMARTINI, Guiseppe
    Concerto, recorder, F major. See no. 1607
SAMUEL, Gerhard
    What of my music. See no. 896
SANDERS, John
    Toccata. See no. 4064
SANDERSON
    My dear soul. See no. 3903
SANDERSON, Wilfred
    As I sit here. See no. 3874
SANDIG
    A kis ponilo. See no. 3814
SANDOVAL
    Ave Maria. See no. 3831
SANDSTROM, Sven-David
    Out of. See no. 3598

SANDVOLD
     Introduction and passacaglia. See no. 2001
SANTORO, Claudio
     Interacoes assintoticas, See no. 2435
SANZ, Gaspar
     La cavalleria de Napoles con dos clarines. See no. 3577
     Folias. See no. 3577
     Fuga al ayre de giga. See no. 3577
     Fuga del primer tono. See no. 3577
     La esfachata de Napoles. See no. 3577
     Gallardas. See no. 3577
     Giga al ayre ingles. See no. 3577
     Maricapalos. See no. 3577
     La minona de Cataluna. See no. 3577
     Paradetas. See no. 3577
     Passacalles por la C, por cruzado y por quinto tono punto alto.
          See no. 3577
     Passacalles por la L, por el 2 bemolado y por primer tono punto
          bajo. See no. 3577
     Pavana. See no. 3577
     Preludio o capricho arpeado por la cruz. See no. 3577
     Rujero. See no. 3577
     Sesquialtera. See no. 3577
     Suite espanola. See no. 3917
SARASATE, Pablo
2772 Caprice basque, op. 24. Introduction and tarantella, op. 43. Span-
          ish dances, nos. 1-8. Serenade andalouse, op. 28. Ruggiero
          Ricci, vln; Brooks Smith, pno. Westminster MCA 1410
                    +FF 11/12-80 p166   ++St 10-80 p120
     Caprice basque, op. 24. See no. 1393
     Carmen fantasy, op. 25. See no. 1388. See no. 3964
     Danzas espanolas, nos. 1-8. See no. 2772
     Danzas espanolas, nos. 1 and 2, op. 21; nos. 5, op. 23; no. 8, op.
          26. See no. 1393
     Danzas espanolas, op. 21: Malaguena; Habanera. See no. 3964
     Danzas espanolas, op. 23: Zapateado. See no. 3665. See no. 3785.
          See no. 3964
     Introduction and tarantella, op. 43. See no. 2772. See no. 3606.
          See no. 3964
     Serenade andalouse, op. 28. See no. 2772
     Zigeunerweisen, op. 20, no. 1. See no. 3964
SARGENT
     Silent night. See no. 3993
SARGENT, Malcolm
     Songs: Lullaby; Zither carol. See no. 3933
SARJEANT
     Blow blow thou winter wind. See no. 4007
SARY, Laszlo
     Lied to Lyd. See no. 3803
     Sonata, percussion, no. 2. See no. 3810
SATIE, Erik
     Avant-dernieres pensees. See no. 2780
     Can-can grand mondain. See no. 3642
     Chapitres tournes en tous sens. See no. 2778. See no. 2780
     Croquis et agaceries d'un gros bon homme en bois. See no. 2778

2773 En habit de cheval. Petit pieces montees (3). Parade. Socrate,
     Pt 3. French Radio and Televison Orchestra; Maurice Rosenthal.
     Everest 3234 Tape (c) 3234
                     -Gr 11-70 p799   +-HF 8-80 p87 tape
     Le fils des etoiles. See no. 2780
2774 Genevieve de Brabant. Mass for the poor, op. posth. Songs: Le
     Chapelier; La diva de l'empire; Dapheneo; Three songs of 1886;
     Three other songs. Mady Mesple, s; Jean-Christoph Benoit, bar;
     Rene Duclos Choir; Gaston Litaize, org; Aldo Ciccolini, pno;
     National Theater Opera Chorus; Orchestre de Paris; Pierre Dervaux.
     Arabesque 8053 Tape (c) 9053
                     +HF 10-80 p98 tape   +St 6-80 p124
                     +NYT 1-6-80 pD18
     Gnossienne. See no. 3642
     Gnossiennes, nos. 1, 4-5. See no. 2779
     Gnossiennes, no. 2 and 3. See no. 2780
     Gnossiennes, nos. 2 and 4. See no. 2778
     Grimaces (5). See no. 2780
2775 Gymnopedies. Ogives. Sarabandes. Reinbert de Leeuw, pno. Tele-
     funken 6-42224
                     +FF 9/10-80 p195
     Gymnopedies (3). See no. 999. See no. 2778
     Gymnopedies, nos. 1-3. See no. 2779
2776 Gymnopedies, nos. 1 and 3 (arr. Debussy). Parade. Relache. RPO;
     Philippe Entremont. CBS 61992 Tape (c) 40-61992 (From 72915)
                     +Gr 8-80 p226   +-HFN 9-80 p115
                     ++Gr 12-80 p889 tape   +RR 8-80 p51
                     +-HFN 10-80 p117 tape
     Gymnopedies, nos. 1 and 3. See no. 3555. See no. 3623. See no.
     3625
     Gymnopedies, no. 1. See no. 3607. See no. 3635. See no. 3666.
     See no. 3718. See no. 3841. See no. 3998
     Heures seculaires et instantanees. See no. 2778
2777 Jack in the box (orch. Milhaud). Monotones (orch. Lanchbery, Deb-
     ussy, Roland-Manuel). Morceaux en forme de poire (3). Preludes,
     nos. 1 and 3. ROHO; John Lanchbery. HMV ESD 7069 Tape (c) TC
     ESD 7069 (also Angel S 37580 Tape (c) 4XS 37580)
                     +ARG 8-79 p34   +HFN 5-79 p124
                     +FF 7/8-79 p84   +HFN 5-79 p134 tape
                     +Gr 3-79 p1572   ++NYT 7-22-79 pD21
                     +HF 10-80 p98 tape
     Jack in the box. See no. 64. See no. 3908
     Je te veux. See no. 2780
     Mass for the poor, op. posth. See no. 2774
     Monotones. See no. 2777
     Morecaux en forme de poire (3). See no. 2777
     Nocturnes, no. 1. See no. 2779
     Nocturnes, nos. 2 and 4. See no. 2778
     Nocturnes, nos. 3 and 5. See no. 2780
     Nouvelles pieces froides. See no. 2778
     Ogives (2). See no. 2775
     Le pantins dansent. See no. 2780
     Parade. See no. 2773. See no. 2776
     Parade: Rag-time. See no. 2779
     Passacaille. See no. 2778. See no. 2779

Pensee Rose et Croix, no. 1. See no. 2780
Petites pieces monees. See no. 2773
2778 Piano works: Chapitres tournes en tous sens. Croquis et agaceries
     d'un gros bonhomme en bois. Gnossiennes, nos. 2 and 4. Gymn-
     opedies (3). Heures seculaires et instantanees. Nocturnes,
     nos. 2 and 4. Nouvelles pieces froides. Passacaille. Le piege
     de Meduse. Prelude, no. 2. Sonatina bureaucratique. Peter Law-
     son, pno. Classics for Pleasure CFP 40329 Tape (c) TC CFP 40329
                    +Gr 6-80 p54   +RR 6-80 p82
                    +HFN 6-80 p111   +RR 8-80 p95 tape
                    +HFN 8-80 p109 tape
2779 Piano works: Gnossiennes, nos. 1, 4-5. Gymnopedies, nos. 1-3. Noc-
     turnes, no. 1. Parade: Rag-time (arr. Ourdine). Passacaille.
     Pieces: Desespoir agreable; Effronterie; Poesie; Prelude canin;
     Profondeur; Songe creux. Sarabandes, nos. 1, 3. Sonatine bur-
     eaucratique. Sports et divertissments. Veritable preludes
     flasques. Vieux sequins et vieilles cuirasses. John McCabe,
     pno. Saga 5387 Tape (c) CA 5387
                    +-FF 9/10-80 p195   +HFN 4-79 p131
                    +-Gr 12-74 p1182   +RR 12-74 p63
                    +-Gr 2-77 p1322 tape   +RR 1-77 p91 tape
                    +-HFN 10-76 p185 tape   ++RR 3-79 p114
2780 Piano works: Avant dernieres pensees. Chapitres tournes en tous
     sens. Le fils des etoiles. Gnossiennes, nos. 2 and 3. Grim-
     aces (5). Je te veux. Nocturnes, nos. 3 and 5. Le pantins
     dansent. Pensee Rose et Croix, no. 1. Pieces froides. Piege
     de Meduse. Prelude de la porte heroique du ciel. Reverie du
     pauvre. Reveries nocturnes (2). Valses du precieux degoute (3).
     Valse ballet. John McCabe, pno. Saga 5472
                    +Gr 6-80 p54   +RR 6-80 p81
                    +HFN 7-80 p109   +STL 6-8-80 p38
     Pieces: Desespoir agreable; Effronterie; Poesie; Prelude canin;
       Profondeur; Songe creux. See no. 2779
     Pieces froides. See no. 2780
     Piege de Meduse. See no. 2778. See no. 2780
     Preludes, nos. 1 and 3. See no. 2777
     Preludes, no. 2. See no. 2778
     Prelude de la porte heroique du ciel. See no. 2780
     Relache. See no. 2776
     Reverie du pauvre. See no. 2780
     Reveries nocturnes (2). See no. 2780
     Sarabandes (3). See no. 2775
     Sarabandes, nos. 1, 3. See no. 2779
     Socrate, Pt 3. See no. 2773
     Sonatine bureaucratique. See no. 2778. See no. 2779
     Songs: Le Chapelier; La diva de l'empire; Dapheneo; Three songs of
       1886; Three other songs. See no. 2774
     Songs: Ludions; Melodies (3). See no. 3861
     Sports et divertissements. See no. 2779
     Valse ballet. See no. 2780
     Valses distinguees du precieux degoute (3). See no. 2780
     Veritable preludes flasques. See no. 2779
     Vieux sequins et vieilles cuirasses. See no. 2779
SAUGUET, Henri
     La chatte. See no. 2522. See no. 3908

SAVIO
  Nesta rua. See no. 3614
SAVOURET, Alain
2781 L'arbre et caetera. Selon. Gerard Fremy, pno; Alain Savouret, org
     and hpd. Harmonia Mundi INA GRM AM 64707
              +FF 7/8-80 p16
  Selon. See no. 2781
SAYGUN, A. Adnan
  Bes halk Turkusu. See no. 6
SAYLOR, Bruce
  Psalms (4) . See no. 1412
SCARLATESCU
  Bagatelle. See no. 3772
SCARLATTI, Alessandro
2782 Concerti grossi, nos. 1-6. Scarlatti Orchestra; Ettore Gracis. DG
     2547 020 Tape (c) 3347 020 (From 198442)
              +-Gr 8-80 p258   +-HFN 9-80 p115
              +Gr 9-80 p413 tape   +HFN 9-80 p116 tape
              -HFN 6-80 p119
2783 Concerti gorssi, nos. 1-6. I Musici. Philips 9500 603 Tape (c)
     7300 725
              +FF 5/6-80 p145   +HFN 10-80 p107
              ++Gr 9-80 p349   ++NR 5-80 p5
              +HFN 5-80 p123   +NYT 5-25-80 pD21
  La donna ancora e fedele: Se Florindo e fedele. See no. 3687
  Flavio: Canzonetta. See no. 3687
  Gavotte. See no. 3722
2784 Il giardino di amore. Catherine Gayer, s; Brigitte Fassbaender, con;
     Munich Chamber Orchestra; Hans Stadlmair. DG 2535 361 Tape (c)
     3335 361 (From DG 73244) (also DG 2547 033 Tape (c) 3347 033.
     From SAPM 198344)
              +ARG 6-80 p39   +Gr 11-80 p724
              +FF 5/6-80 p145   ++NR 4-80 p12
2785 Partita, D minor. SCARLATTI, D.: Sonatas, harpsichord, K 175, A
     minor; K 213, D minor; K 217, A minor; K 218, A minor; K 298, D
     major; K 517, D minor; K 519, F minor. Judith Norell, hpd.
     Sine Qua Non Superba SA 2018 Tape (c) C 2018
              +ARG 7-79 p46   +NYT 1-27-80 pD20
              +FF 9/10-79 p130   +-St 1-80 p102
              +-HF 7-79 p148
  Pirro e Demetrio: Le violette. See no. 3687
  Il Pompeo: O cessate di piagarmi. See no. 3774
2786 St. Cecilia mass. Elizabeth Harwood, Wendy Eathorne, s; Margaret
     Cable, con; Wynford Evans, t; Christopher Keyte, bs; St. John's
     College Chapel Choir; Wren Orchestra; George Guest. Argo ZRG
     903 Tape (c) KZRC 903
              +Gr 7-80 p161   +RR 8-80 p88
              +HFN 7-80 p110   ++STL 9-14-80 p40
2787 St. Cecilia mass. Heidi Klebl, Catherine Aks, s; Judith Malafronte,
     ms; Peter Becker, c-t; Paul Solem, Gordon Shannon, t; Matthew
     Murray, bs; Edward Brewer, org; Schola Cantorum of Church of St.
     Mary the Virgin; McNeil Robinson. Musical Heritage Society MHS
     4076
              +FF 3/4-80 p140
  Sonata, 3 recorders, F major. See no. 4018

Songs: Se delitto e l'adorarti. See no. 3687
SCARLATTI, Domenico
2788 Le quattro stagioni. Kari Lovaas, s; Ria Bollen, ms; Regina Mar-
    heineke, s; Heiner Hopfner, t; Munich Vokalsolisten; Munich Cham-
    ber Orchestra; Hans Hirsch. Tudor 73014
                  -HFN 12-80 p145
Sonatas, guitar (5). See no. 256
Sonatas, guitar, K 9, E minor. See no. 3816
Sonatas, guitar, K 380, A major. See no. 3816
Sonatas, harpsichord, E major, D minor. See no. 3777
Sonatas, harpsichord (2). See no. 3976
2789 Sonatas, harpsichord (30). Blandine Verlet, hpd. Philips 6770 650
    (2) Tape (c) 7650 650
                  +NR 11-80 p11
2790 Sonatas, harpsichord, K 1-30. Scott Ross, hpd. Telefunken 6-35487
    (2) Tape (c) 4-35487
                  +FF 5/6-80 p146   ++NYT 1-27-80 pD20
                  +-HF 7-80 p52   ++St 5-80 p74
                  +HF 11-80 p88 tape
2791 Sonatas, harpsichord, Kk 1/L366; Kk 8/L488; Kk 9/L413; Kk 11/L352;
    Kk 19/L383; Kk 45/L265; Kk 49/L301; Kk 63/L84; Kk 70/L50; Kk 84/
    L10; Kk 87/L33; Kk 113/L345; Kk 125/L487; Kk 123/L111; Kk 244/
    L348; Kk 278/L515; Kk 322/L283; Kk 375/L389/ Kk 386/L171; Kk 388/
    L414; Kk 406/L5; Kk 426/L128; Kk 446/L433; Kk 461/L8; Kk 519/
    L475. Zuzana Ruzickova, hpd. Supraphon 111 2261/2
                  +ARG 11-79 p47   +HFN 8-79 p109
                  ++Audio 6-80 p49   +-NR 10-79 p12
                  ++FF 9/10-79 p130   +RR 7-79 p98
                  +-Gr 10-79 p675
2792 Sonatas, harpsichord, Kk 3, A minor; Kk 184/5, F minor; Kk 227, B
    minor; Kk 238/9, F minor; Kk 52, D minor; Kk 192/3, E flat major;
    Kk 208/9, A major; Kk 252/3, E flat major; Kk 191, D minor.
    Gustav Leonhardt, hpd. RCA RL 3-0334
                  +Gr 4-80 p1572   +-RR 5-80 p89
                  +HFN 4-80 p109
Sonatas, harpsichord, nos. 9, 132-133, 146, 419. See no. 3659
2793 Sonatas, harpsichord, Longo Kirkpatrick, nos. 21/162, 483/322, 449/
    27, 465/96, 275/394, 384/17, 2/420, 116/518, 475/519, 238/208,
    286/427, 164/491. Andras Schiff, pno. Hungaroton SLPX 11806
                  ++CL 1-80 p10   +-FF 9-77 p45
                  +ARG 9-77 p46   +-NR 10-78 p14
Sonatas, harpsichord, Kk 39, A major. See no. 3622
2794 Sonatas, harpsichord, Kk 65, 79, 83, 113, 284, 394, 404, 425, 470,
    476, 491, 495. Maria Tipo, pno. Dischi Ricordi RCL 27038
                  +Gr 9-80 p379
2795 Sonatas, harpsichord, Kk 109, 110, 127, 130, 170, 189, 190, 390,
    391, 343, 435, 436. Gilbert Rowland, hpd. Keyboard KGR 1011
                  +-HFN 12-80 p145
2796 Sonatas, harpsichord, Kk 111, 142, 148-149, 160-161, 170, 176, 183-
    184, 199-200, 213-214, 225-226, 266-267, 274-276, 279-280, 283-
    284, 310-311, 322-325, 331-332, 335-336, 343-344, 352-353, 370-
    371, 376-377, 380-381, 424-425, 462, 463, 474-475, 485-487, 503-
    504, 507-508, 514-515, 536-537, 540-541. Luciano Sgrizzi, hpd.
    Erato ERA 9222 (4)
                  +-Gr 11-80 p704   ++HFN 12-80 p145

2797 Sonatas, harpsichord, K 142, 162-163, 167-168, 183-184, 227, 258,
      304-305, 484. Gilbert Rowland, hpd. Keyboard KGR 1010
               +-HFN 5-80 p123   +RR 7-80 p84
2798 Sonatas, harpsichord, K 146, G major; K 204a, F minor, K 204b, F
      minor, K 205, F minor, K 513, C major, K 87, B minor, K 322, A
      major, K 323, A major, K 337, G major, K 338, G major, K 443, D
      major, K 444, D minor/major. Igor Kipnis, cld, hpd. Angel SZ
      37310 Tape (c) 4ZS 37310
               ++ARG 2-80 p42   ++HF 11-80 p88 tape
               ++FF 3/4-80 p141   +NR 10-79 p12
               +-FU 4-80 p50   +NYT 1-27-80 pD20
               ++HF 7-80 p52   ++St 12-79 p148
     Sonatas, harpsichord, Kk 159, C major; Kk 3, A minor; Kk 215, E
        major. See no. 1601
     Sonatas, harpsichord, K 175, A minor; K 213, D minor; K 217, A min-
        or; K 218, A minor; K 298, D major; K 517, D minor; K 519, F
        minor. See no. 2785
     Sonatas, harpsichord, K 288, D major. See no. 3762
     Sonatas, harpsichord, Kk 380, 430, 443. See no. 3569
     Stabat mater. See no. 141
SCHACHT, Theodor von
     Concerto, clarinet, B flat major. See no. 1798
SCHAFER, R. Murray
     The crown of Ariadne. See no. 912
SCHAFER, R. Murray
2799 Loving: Music for the morning of the world. Mary Lou Fallis, Susan
      Gudgeon, s; Jean MacPhail, Kathy Terrell, ms; Trulie MacLeod,
      Gilles Savard, speakers; Chamber Orchestra; Robert Aitken. Mel-
      bourne WRC 6-784 (2) (also SMLP 4035/6)
               +FU 6-80 p42   +MUM 7/8-80 p31
     Quartet, strings, no. 2. See no. 401
     La testa d'Adriane. See no. 1905
SCHAFFRATH, Christoph
     Duetto, 2 bass viols, D minor. See no. 2005
SCHAT
     Anathema, op. 19. See no. 955
SCHAT, Peter
     The fall, op. 9. See no. 1773
2800 Houdini. Soloists; Netherlands Choir; Netherlands National Ballet;
      Amsterdam Electric Circus, Studio Silver Strings, Steelband Cir-
      cle Ensemble; COA; Hans Vonk. Donemus CVS 19771/3
               +FF 1/2-80 p139   *Te 6-78 p38
               +RR 5-78 p24
     Septet, op. 3. See no. 2801
2801 Symphony, no. 1, op. 27. Septet, op. 3. COA, Radio Wind Ensemble;
      Colin Davis, Huub Kerstens. Composers Voice VC 7901
               +-HF 3-80 p82
SCHEIDEMANN, Heinrich
     Chorales: Ach Gott von Himmel sieh darein; Durch Adams fall ist
        ganz verderbt; Es ist das Heil uns kommen her. See no. 3757
     Es ist gewisslich an der Zeit. See no. 4036
SCHEIDLER, Christian
     Sonata, flute and guitar, D major. See no. 355
     Sonata, guitar, D major. See no. 3717

SCHEIDT, Samuel
    Battle suite. See no. 3675
    Bergamasca. See no. 4014
    Canzona a 10. See no. 3569
    Canzona Aechiopicam. See no. 4043
    Canzona bergamasca. See no. 4001
    Canzona on a French theme. See no. 4000
    Echo ad manuale duplex, forte et lene. See no. 3682
    Galliard battaglia. See no. 4043
    Hymnus de Sancto spiritu: Veni creator spiritus. See no. 4021
2802 Motets: Herr unser Herrscher; Jauchzet Gott; Duo seraphim clamabant;
      Richte mich Gott; Sende dein Licht. Spandauer Kantorei; Helmuth
      Rilling, Musical Heritage Society MHS 4021
            +–FF 3/4-80 p141   +MU 9-79 p16
    O Jesulein zart. See no. 3697
    Paduan a 4, D minor. See no. 4018
    Passamezzo. See no. 954
    Suite, strings. See no. 3932
    Variations on "Von der fortuna". See no. 3757
SCHEIN, Johann
    Banchetto musicale: Suites, nos. 3-5. See no. 2527
    Ebreszto. See no. 3814
    Intrada. See no. 4059
    Paduana and galliard. See no. 4001
    Vom Himmel hoch. See no. 4068
SCHELLING
    Nocturne a Raguze. See no. 3907
SCHENCK, Johann
    L'Echo du Danube: Sonata, no. 2. See no. 3729
    La nymphe di Rheno, op. 8: Chaconne, G major. See no. 3767
    Sonata, 2 viols, op. 8, no. 10, G major. See no. 2005
    Suite, A minor. See no. 3540
SCHICKELE, Peter
    Diversions. See no. 3731
2803 Elegies. The knight of the buring pestle: Songs (9). Summer trio.
      Lucy Shelton, s; Margot Rose, alto; Frank Hoffmeister, t; Robert
      Kuehn, bar; Richard Stoltzman, clt; Peter Schickele, pno; In-
      strumental Ensemble, Walden Trio; Peter Schickele. Vanguard VSD
      71269
            ++FF 11/12-80 p166   +HF 4-80 p76
    The knight of the burning pestle: Songs. See no. 2803
    Last tango in Bayreuth. See no. 3821
    Pentangle. See no. 2117
    Summer trio. See no. 2803
SCHICKHART, Johann
    La tricoteuse. Ee no. 4067
SCHILLINGS, Max von
2804 Glockenlieder, op. 22: Die Fruhglocke; Die Nachzugler; Ein Bildchen;
      Mittagskonig und Glockenherzog. STRAUSS, R.: Songs: Morgen, op.
      27, no. 4; Standchen, op. 17, no. 2; Traum durch die Dammerung,
      op. 29, no. 1; Verfuhrung, op. 33, no. 1; Waldseligkeit, op. 49,
      no. 1. Peter Anders, t; Orchestra; Joseph Keilberth, Artur Rother,
      Arthur Gruber, Robert Heger. Acanta BB 23185
            +–ARG 12-80 p45

SCHMELZER, Johann
    Sonata a 7 flauti. See no. 3795
SCHMID, Bernard
    Alemando novelle: Ein guter neuer Dantz. See no. 3590
    Der Imperial: Ein Furtlicher Hofdantz; Ein schoner Englischer Dantz;
       Wie schon Bluet uns der Maye. See no. 3590
SCHMIDT
    Im Tiefsten Walde, op. 34. See no. 3684
SCHMIDT, Franz
2805 Fugue, F major. Prelude and fugue, E flat major. Kurt Rapf, org.
       Musical Heritage Society MHS 4093 (From Amadeo AVRS 6468)
           +FF 3/4-80 p142
    Prelude and fugue, E flat major. See no. 2805
SCHMIDT, William
    The sparrow and the amazing Mr. Avaunt. See no. 2501
SCHMIDT-MANNHEIM
    Songs: Die Hexen; Waldfreuden; Der verirrte Jager. See no. 3662
SCHNABEL, Josef Ignaz
    Quintet, guitar, C major. See no. 745
SCHNEIDER, Johann Christian
    Fantasia and fugue, D minor. See no. 84
SCHNITTKE, Alfred
2806 Concerto grosso. SIBELIUS: Concerto, violin, op. 47, D minor.
       Gidon Kremer, Tatiana Gridenko, vln; LSO; Gennady Rozhdestvensky.
       Vanguard VSD 71255 (also Eurodisc SQ 25099)
           +ARG 5-80 p39   +-NYT 11-30-80 p35B
           +FF 11/12-79 p120   +SFC 12-30-79 p33
           +HF 7-80 p85   +-St 2-80 p133
    Prelude to the memory of Dmitri Shostakovich. See no. 2543
    Quintet, piano. See no. 2031
SCHOECK, Othmar
2807 Concerto, horn, op. 65, D minor. SCHUMANN: Konzertstuck, op. 86, F
       major. WEBER: Concertino, op. 45, E minor. Hermann Baumann,
       Mahir Cakar, Werner Meyerdorf, Johannes Ritzkowsky, Jean-Pierre
       Lepetit, hn; VSO; Dietfried Bernet. Metronome MPS 168 015
           +HFN 7-80 p114   ++RR 7-80 p64
2808 Songs: Agnes; An einem heitern Morgen; Es ist bestimmt im Gottes
       Rat; Im Kreuzgang von St. Stegano; Marienlied; Mit einem gemal-
       ten Band; Nur zu; Peregrina III; Der Postillon, op. 18; 's Seeli;
       Sapphische Strophe; Sehnsucht; Septembermorgen; Ein Voglein singt
       im Walde; Waldvogelein; Zimmerspruch. Ernst Hafliger, t; Wet-
       tinger College Choir; Tonhalle Orchestra Brass Players; Karl
       Grenacher, pno and cond. Jecklin Disco 504
           +Gr 12-80 p866
SCHOENBERG, Arnold
    Canons (2). See no. 3741
    Chamber symphony, no. 1, op. 9, E major. See no. 639
2809 Concerto, piano, op. 42, C major. STRAVINSKY: Concerto, piano and
       wind instruments. Movements, piano and orchestra. Adam Fellegi,
       pno; Budapest Symphony Orchestra; Ivan Fischer. Hungaroton SLPX
       12021
           +-RR 7-80 p67
2810 Fantasy, op. 47. Suite, op. 29. BSO Chamber Players; Joseph Sil-
       verstein, vln; Gilbert Kalish, pno. DG 2531 277
           +Gr 9-80 p367   +HFN 9-80 p110

2811 Gurrelieder. Jessye Norman, s; Tatiana Troyanos, con; James McCrac-
     ken, t; Tanglewood Chorus; BSO; Seiji Ozawa. Philips 6769 038
     Tape (c) 7699 124

+—ARG 6-80 p13   +—MT 3-80 p181
+FF 3/4-80 p142   +NR 2-80 p8
++FU 4-80 p44   +NYT 11-18-79 pD24
+Gr 1-80 p1193   +ON 2-9-80 p37
+—HF 3-80 p84   ++RR 1-80 p108
+—HF 5-80 p90 tape   +RR 3-80 p105 tape
+—HFN 1-80 p109   ++SFC 12-2-79 p53
+—HFN 2-80 p107 tape   ++SR 1-5-80 p39
+—MUM 7/8-80 p32   ++St 3-80 p83
+STL 12-2-79 p37

     Herzgewachse, op. 20. See no. 1166
2812 Music for a cinematographic scene, op. 34. Pieces, orchestra, op.
     16 (5). A survivor from Warsaw, op. 46. Variations, op. 31.
     BBC Symphony Orchestra; Pierre Boulez. CBS 35882
          +FF 11/12-80 p167   +SFC 11-30-80 p21
     Pieces, orchestra, op. 16. See no. 2812
     Pieces, piano, op. 11 (3); op. 19 (6); op. 23 (5); op. 33 (2). See
     no. 3705
     Pieces, piano, 4 hands (6). See no. 3834
     Suite, op. 25. See no. 1795. See no. 3705
     Suite, op. 29. See no. 2810
     A survivor from Warsaw, op. 46. See no. 2812
     Variations, op. 31. See no. 2812
     Verklarte Nacht, op. 4. See no. 646. See no. 647. See no. 1780
SCHOFFER, Nicolas
2813 Hommage a Bartok. Chronosonor, 1-2, 3, 5. Percussonor, 1-2. Hun-
     garoton SLPX 12084
          -ARG 10-80 p54   -NR 4-80 p15
     Chronosonor, 1-2, 3, 5. See no. 2813
     Percussonor, 1-2. See no. 2813
SCHOLEFIELD, C. C.
     The day thou gavest. See no. 4019
SCHONHERR
     Die sieben Sprunge. See no. 3962
SCHRAMM
     Ein edler Jager wohlgemut. See no. 3662
SCHREKER, Franz
     Die Gezeichneten. See no. 3824
SCHROEDER, Hermann
     Gott heilger Schopfer aller Stern. See no. 4036
SCHUBEL, Max
     Paraplex. See no. 1160
     Ragwyrk. See no. 1160
SCHUBERT, Franz
     Adagio, D 612, E major. See no. 2839
2814 Allegretto, D 915, C minor. Andante, D 604, A major. Klavierstucke,
     D 946 (3). Sonata, piano, no. 3, D 459, E major. Variations on
     a waltz by Diabelli, D 718, C minor. Edmund Battersby, pno.
     Musical Heritage Society MHS 4024
          +FF 9/10-79 p133   +HF 11-80 p73
     Allegretto, D 915, C minor. See no. 2839
     Andante, D 604, A major. See no. 902. See no. 2814

2815 Andantino varie, D 823, B minor. Ecossaises, D 145 (6). Fantasia,
     op. 103, D 940, F minor.   Grand rondeau, K 951, A major.   Emil
     and Elena Gilels, pno. DG 2531 079
        +-ARG 10-79 p47   +MT 5-79 p407
        ++CL 4-80 p10   +NYT 6-3-79 pD22
        +FF 9/10-79 p132   +-RR 6-79 p110
        +Gr 2-79 p1439   ++SFC 10-14-79 p61
        +HFN 2-79 p107   ++St 8-79 p115

Andantino varie, D 823, B minor. See no. 2841
Ave Maria, D 839. See no. 113. See no. 3785. See no. 3961. See
     no. 3964
Cotillon, D 976, E flat major. See no. 2838
Deutsche Tanze (German dances). See no. 2837.
Deutsche Tanze (6). See no. 383
Deutsche Tanze, D 366. See no. 2913
2816 Deutsche Tanze, D 618, G major. Grand duo sonata, op. 140, D 812,
     C major. Landler, G 681, E major (2). Landler, D 814 (4).
     Christoph Eschenbach, Justus Frantz, pno. HMV ASD 3814 Tape (c)
     TC ASD 3814
        +-Gr 7-80 p154   +HFN 9-80 p116 tape
        +HFN 7-80 p110   +RR 7-80 p84

Deutsche Tanze, D 643, C sharp minor. See no. 2838
Deutsche Tanze, D 783 (16). See no. 2838
Deutsche Tanze with coda and 7 trios. See no. 3989
Divertissement, D 818, G minor. See no. 2840
Divertissement a la francaise, D 823, F minor. See no. 2879
2817 Divertissement a la hongroise, D 818, G major. Sonata, piano, 4
     hands, op. 140, D 812, C major. Variations on an original theme,
     op. 35, D 813, A flat major. Jorg Demus, Paul Badura-Skoda,
     hammerflugel. Harmonia Mundi HM 2900 (2)
        +HFN 3-80 p107   +-RR 4-80 p102

Duo, D 947, A minor. See no. 2841
Ecossaises (6). See no. 3826
Ecossaises, D 145 (6). See no. 2815
Der Erlkonig, D 328. See no. 3601
2818 Fantasia, op. 15, D 760, C major. Impromptus, op. 142, nos. 1-4,
     D 935. Clifford Curzon, pno. Decca ECS 804 (From LS 3059, LXT
     2781)
        ++Gr 3-80 p1418   +-HFN 3-80 p107

2819 Fantasia, op. 15, D 760, C major. Sonata, piano, no. 13, K 664, A
     major. Sviatoslav Richter, pno. HMV SXLP 30297 Tape (c) TC SXLP
     30297 (From ASD 561)
        +Gr 1-80 p1171   +-HFN 4-80 p121 tape
        ++HFN 1-80 p121   +-RR 1-80 p104

2820 Fantasia, op. 15, D 760, B major (arr. Liszt). SCHUMANN: Concerto,
     piano, op. 54, A minor. Ilan Rogoff, pno; PhO; Kurt Sanderling.
     Unicorn RHS 367 Tape (c) UKC 367
        +-FF 3/4-80 p149   +-HFN 11-80 p131 tape
        +-HF 4-80 p95   +-RR 12-79 p75
        +-HFN 12-79 p170   +SFC 3-23-80 p35

Fantasia, op. 15, D 760, C major. See no. 525. See no. 2839. See
     no. 3678
Fantasia, op. 103, D 940, F minor. See no. 2815. See no. 2840.
     See no. 2841. See no. 2871
2821 Fantasia, op. 159, D 934, C major. Rondo brillant, op. 70, D 895,

B minor. Sonatina, violin and piano, no. 1, op. 137, D 384, D major. Sergiu Luca, vln; Joseph Kalichstein, pno. Nonesuch H 71370

> +ARG 9-80 p39   +NR 5-80 p6
> ++HF 9-80 p96   +-SFC 6-15-80 p36
> +FF 7/8-80 p129   ++St 6-80 p122

Fantasia, D 993, C minor. See no. 2837

Fierrabras, K 796: Overture. See no. 2836. See no. 2901

Die Freunde von Salamanka, D 326: Overture. See no. 2836

Fugue, D 952, E minor. See no. 3834

Galopp, D 735, G major. See no. 2913

2822 Gesang des Geister uber den Wassem, D 714. Eine kleine Trauermusik, D 79. Mass, D 961, C major. Minuet and finale, D 72, F major. Phyllis Bryn Julson, s; Jan deGaetani, con; Anthony Rolfe Johnson, t; Malcolm King, bs; London Sinfonietta and Chorus; David Atherton. Argo ZRG 916

> +Gr 6-80 p59   ++RR 7-80 p93
> +HFN 7-90 p110

Grand duo sonata, op. 140, D 812, C major. See no. 2816. See no. 2841

Grand rondeau, D 951, A major. See no. 2815. See no. 2840. See no. 2841

Gute Nacht (arr. Godowsky). See no. 3902

Hark hark the lark. See no. 3678. See no. 3902

2823 Impromptus, op. 90, D 899 and op. 142, D 935. Wilhelm Kempff, pno. DG 2542 111 Tape (c) 3342 111 (From 139149)

> +Gr 12-79 p1028   +-RR 12-79 p102
> ++HFN 12-79 p179   +RR 2-80 p97 tape

2824 Impromptus, op. 90, D 899 and op. 142, D 935. Moments musicaux, op. 94, D 780. Klavierstucke, D 946 (3). Rudolf Buchbinder, pno. Telefunken 6-48132 (2) Tape (c) 4-48132

> +-HF 11-80 p75

Impromptus, op. 90, D 899. See no. 2839

2825 Impromptus, op. 90, nos. 3 and 4, D 899. Sonata, piano, no. 17, op. 53, D 850, D major. Clifford Curzon, pno. Decca SXL 6135 Tape (c) KSXC 6135 (also London STS 15483)

> +FF 1/2-80 p144   +HFN 6-78 p139 tape
> +Gr 2-78 p1472 tape

Impromptus, op. 90, no. 3, D 899, G flat major. See no. 2913. See no. 3953. See no. 3954. See no. 3964

2826 Impromptus, op. 90, no. 4, D 899, A flat major. Sonata, piano, no. 12, D 784, A major. SCHUMANN: Carnival, op. 9. Alicia de Larrocha, pno. Decca SXL 6910 Tape (c) KSXC 6910 (also London CS 7134 Tape (c) CS 5-7134)

> +-FF 11/12-80 p170   +-RR 2-80 p80
> +Gr 2-80 p1282   +-St 10-80 p121
> +-HFN 2-80 p97   +STL 3-9-80 p41

Impromptus, op. 90, no. 4, D 899, A flat major. See no. 2838

2827 Impromptus, op. 142, D 935. Rudolf Serkin, pno. Columbia M 35178.

> +-ARG 6-80 p39   +HF 7-80 p72
> ++CL 4-80 p8   +-SFC 12-30-79 p33
> +FU 6-80 p49   +-SFC 7-20-80 p34
> +-NR 4-80 p14   +St 6-80 p122

Impromptus, op. 142, D 935. See no. 2839

Impromptus, op. 142, nos. 1-4, D 935. See no. 2818

Impromptus, op. 142, nos. 2-3, D 935. See no. 519
Impromptus, op. 142, no. 2, D 935, A flat major. See no. 2868. See
   no. 3907
Impromptus, op. 142, no. 3, D 935, B flat major. See no. 1044. See
   no. 2838
Klavierstucke, D 946. See no. 2814. See no. 2824. See no. 2839.
   See no. 2867
Klavierstucke, no. 2, D 946, E flat major: Allegretto. See no. 404
Eine kleine Trauermusik, D 79. See no. 2822
2828 Konzertstuck, D 345, D major. SCHUMANN: Concerto, violin, D minor.
   Vaclav Snitil, vln; PSO; Libor Hlavacek. Supraphon 110 2288
              +FF 11/12-80 p171   +-NR 10-80 p5
              +-HF 11-80 p78
2829 Konzertstuck, D 345, D major. Minuets, D 89. Polonaise, D 580, B
   major. Rondo, D 438, A major. Susanne Lautenbacher, vln; Wurt-
   temberg Chamber Orhcestra; Jorg Faerber. Turnabout QTV 34729
              +-ARG 6-79 p31   +RR 12-79 p75
              +-FF 7/8-79 p87   ++SFC 4-11-79 p44
              +Gr 11-79 p840   +-St 9-79 p100
              +-HFN 2-80 p97   +ST 4-80 p927
              +NR 10-79 p13
Konzertstuck, D 345, D major. See no. 410. See no. 489
Kupelwieser Walzer, G major. See no. 404
Kupelwieser Walzer, D 893a. See no. 2837
Landler. See no. 2840
Landler, D 366 (4). See no. 902
Landler, D 681, E major (2). See no. 2816
Landler, no. 3, D 790. See no. 404. See no. 2878
Landler, D 814 (4). See no. 2816
Landler, D 820. See no. 2837
2830 Magnificat, D 486, C major. Offertorium, D 963. Stabat mater, D
   383, F minor. Sheila Armstrong, s; Hanna Schaer, ms; Alejandro
   Ramierez, t; Philippe Huttenlocher, bar; Lausanne Vocal Ensemble;
   Lausanne Orchestra; Michel Corboz. Erato STU 71262
              +Gr 4-80 p1580   +RR 5-80 p100
              +-HFN 4-80 p109
2831 Marches, D 818, nos. 2-4, 6. Marches, D 602 (3). Karl-Heinz and Mic-
   hael Schluter, pno. Da Camera Magna SM 93145
              +FF 3/4-80 p144
Marches, D 602 (3). See no. 2831
Marches, D 606, E major. See no. 2839
Marches, D 886, C major. See no. 2840
Marches militaire. See no. 3902
Marches militaires, D 733 (3). See no. 2841
Marches militaires, no. 1, op. 51, D 733, D major. See no. 2840.
   See no. 3709
Mass, no. 2, D 167, G major: Gloria. See no. 3531
Mass, no. 2, D 167, G major: Kyrie. See no. 3527
2832 Mass, no. 4, op. 48, D 452, C major. Salve regina, D 386; D 811.
   Delcina Stevenson, s; Nina Hinson, ms; Keith Wyatt, t; Richard
   Wagner, bar; Los Angeles Camerata; H. Vincent Mitzelfelt. Grand
   Prix GP 9004
              +-ARG 11-80 p28   -FF 7/8-80 p127
Mass, D 961, C major. See no. 2822
Minuet, F major. See no. 2837

Minuets, D 89. See no. 2829
Minuet and finale, D 72, F major. See no. 2822
Moments musicaux, F minor. See no. 3906
2833 Moments musicaux, op. 94, D 780. SCHUMANN: Carnival, op. 9. Lee
    Luvisi, pno. Rivergate Recordings
                +–CL 3-80 p15
Moments musicaux, op. 94, D 780. See no. 2824
Moments musicaux, op. 94, D 780 (6). See no. 2839
Moments musicaux, op. 94, nos. 2 and 3, D 780. See no. 2838
Moments musicaux, op. 94, no. 2, D 780, A flat major. See no. 2913
    See no. 3856
Moments musicaux, op. 94, no. 3, D 780, F minor. See no. 3677.
    See no. 3935. See no. 3998
Moments musicaux, op. 94, no. 4, D 780, C sharp minor. See no. 3832
Morgengruss (arr. Godowsky). See no. 3902
My peace thou art. See no. 3769
Nocturne, op. 148, D 897, E flat major. See no. 2860
2834 Octet, op. 166, D 803, F major. Munchner Nonett Members. Da Camera
    Magna SM 92811
                +FF 5/6-80 p146
2835 Octet, op. 166, D 803, F major. Music Group of London. Enigma K
    53590
                +–Gr 9-80 p367   +HFN 9-80 p110
Offertorium, D 963. See no. 2830
Overture, D 470, B flat major. See no. 2836
Overture in the Italian style, D 590, D major. See no. 2836
Overture in the Italian style, D 591, C major. See no. 2901
2836 Overtures: Fierrabras, D 796. Die Freunde von Salamanka, D 326.
    Overture, D 470, B flat major. Overture in the Italian style,
    D 590, D major. Der vierjahrige Posten, D 190. Die Zauberharfe,
    D 644. Die Zwillingsbruder, D 647. Bournemouth Symphony Orches-
    tra; Rudolf Schwarz. HMV ESD 7086 Tape (c) TC ESD 7086
                +–Gr 4-80 p1558   +–HFN 8-80 p109 tape
                +–ARG 9-80 p44   +RR 5-80 p70
                +–HFN 5-80 p123
2837 Piano works: Fantasia, D 993, C minor. German dances (5). Kupel-
    wieser Walzer, D 893a. Landler, D 820. Minuet, F major. Son-
    ata, piano, no. 6, D 566, E minor. Variations on a waltz by
    Diabelli, D 718, C minor. Rosario Marciano, pno. Musical Heri-
    tage Society MHS 4065
                +–FF 3/4-80 p148   +HF 11-80 p75
2838 Piano works: Cotillon, D 976, E flat major. German dances, D 643,
    C sharp minor. Germand dances, D 783 (16). Impromptus, op. 142,
    no. 3, D 935, B flat major. Moments musicaux, op. 94, D 780,
    nos. 2 and 3. Rosamunde, op. 26, D 979, excerpts. Impromptus,
    op. 90, no. 4, D 899, A flat major. Sonata, piano, no. 13, D
    664, A major: 1st movement. Gilbert Schuchter, pno. RCA GL 3-
    0307 Tape (c) GK 3-0307
                /Gr 10-79 p675   +–RR 10-79 p128
                –HFN 10-79 p161   +RR 2-80 p98 tape
                /–HFN 1-80 p123 tape
2839 Piano works: Allegretto, D 915, C minor. Adagio, D 612, E major.
    Fantasia, op. 15, D 760, C major. Impromptus, op. 90, D 899 and
    op. 142, D 935. March, D 606, E major. Moments musicaux, op.
    94, D 780. Klavierstucke, D 946. Scherzi, D 593. Variations

on a waltz by Diabelli, D 718, C minor. Peter Frankl, pno. Vox
SVBX 5487 Tape (c) CBX 5487
　　　　+—FF 1/2-79 p98　　　　　　　++SFC 10-22-78 p53
　　　　+—HF 10-79 p118　　　　　　　+St 3-80 p107 tape
　　　　+—NR 11-78 p13
2840 Piano works (4 hands): Divertissement, D 818, G minor. Grand rond-
　　　eau, D 951, A major. Fantasia, op. 103, D 904, F minor. Landler
　　　(arr. Brahms). Marches militaires, no. 1, D 733, D major. Mar-
　　　ches, D 886, C major. Rondo, D 608, D major. Variations on an
　　　original theme, op. 35, D 813, A flat major. Paul Badura-Skoda,
　　　Jorg Demus, pno. Audax 766 (2)
　　　　+—FF 7/8-80 p128　　　　　　+—NR 2-80 p14
2841 Piano works (4 hands): Andantino varie, D 823, B minor. Duo, D 947,
　　　A minor. Fantasia, op. 103, D 940, F minor. Grand duo sonata,
　　　op. 140, D 812, C major. Marches militaires, D 733 (3). Polo-
　　　naise, D 824 (6). Grand rondeau, D 951, A major. Variations
　　　on an original theme, op. 35, K 813, A flat major. Anne Queffel-
　　　ec, Imogen Cooper, pno. Erato STU 71044 (3)
　　　　+Gr 5-79 p1911　　　　　　　++RR 10-79 p130
　　　　+HFN 4-80 p109　　　　　　　+STL 12-2-79 p37
　　Polonaise, D 580, B major. See no. 410. See no. 2829
　　Polonaise, D 824 (6). See no. 2841
　　Quartet, strings, no. 8, D 112, B flat major: Minuet and trio. See
　　　no. 902
2842 Quartet, strings, no. 10, D 87, E flat major. Quartet, strings, no.
　　　14, D 810, D minor. Vienna Philharmonic Quartet. London STS
　　　15410 (From London 6384)
　　　　+—FF 3/4-80 p145
　　Quartet, strings, no. 10, K 87, E flat major: Finale. See no. 2848
2843 Quartet, strings, no. 12, D 703, C minor. Quartet, strings, no. 13,
　　　D 804, A minor. Collegium Aureum Quartet. Harmonia Mundi 065
　　　99732
　　　　+—FF 1/2-80 p143　　　　　　+—ST 9-79 p357
　　　　+RR 9-79 p103
2844 Quartet, strings, no. 12, D 703, C minor. Quartet, strings, no. 14,
　　　D 810, D minor. New Budapest Quartet. Hungaroton SLPX 12042
　　　　+—FF 1/2-80 p143　　　　　　+NR 1-80 p4
2845 Quartet, strings, no. 12, D 703, C minor. Quartet, strings, no. 15,
　　　D 887, G major. Gabrieli Quartet. London STS 15418
　　　　+RR 3/4-80 p145
2846 Quartet, strings, no. 12, D 703, C minor. Quartet, strings, no. 14,
　　　D 810, D minor. Prague Quartet. Supraphon 111 1997
　　　　+—Gr 11-80 p697　　　　　　+—NR 7-80 p7
　　　　+—HFN 10-80 p107　　　　　　++SFC 6-15-80 p36
　　Quartet, strings, no. 12, D 703, C minor. See no. 902. See no.
　　　1314
　　Quartet, strings, no. 13, D 804, A minor. See no. 2843
2847 Quartet, strings, no. 14, D 810, D minor. Allegri Quartet. Argo
　　　ZK 77 Tape (c) KZKC 77
　　　　+ST 1-80 p692
2848 Quartet, strings, no. 14, D 810, D minor. Quartet, strings, no. 10,
　　　D 87, E flat major: Finale. Smetana Quartet. Denon OX 7151
　　　　+FU 4-80 p50
　　Quartet, strings, no. 14, D 810, D minor. See no. 2842. See no.
　　　2844. See no. 2846

2849 Quartet, strings, no. 15, D 887, G major. Allegri Quartet. Argo
     ZK 78 Tape (c) KZKC 78
                    +-Gr 5-80 p1684   -RR 5-80 p78
                    +HFN 5-80 p123
2850 Quartet, strings, no. 15, D 887, G major. Juilliard Quartet. Col-
     umbia M 35827 Tape (c) MT 35827 (also CBS 76908)
                    +-FF 9/10-80 p198   ++NR 5-80 p6
                    +Gr 12-80 p847   +-SFC 3-23-80 p35
                    ++HF 6-80 p85   ++St 7-80 p84
     Quartet, strings, no. 15, D 887, G major. See no. 2845
2851 Quintet, piano, op. 114, D 667, A major. Sonatina, violin and
     piano, no. 2, op. 137, D 385, A minor. Jorg Demus, Walter Klien,
     pno; Wolfgang Schneiderhan, vln; Schubert Quartet. DG 2535 225
     Tape (c) 3335 225 (From 136038, 136101)
                    +-FF 3/4-80 p145
     Quintet, piano, op. 114, D 667, A major: Theme and variations; Fin-
     ale. See no. 902
2852 Quintet, strings, op. 163, D 956, C major. Allegri Quartet; Moray
     Welsh, vlc. Argo ZK 83
                    +-Gr 10-80 p512   +HFN 9-80 p110
2853 Quintet, strings, op. 163, D 956, C major. LaSalle Quartet. DG
     2531 209
                    ++FF 7/8-80 p127   +-NR 5-80 p6
                    +Gr 11-79 p866   +-RR 1-80 p95
                    +HF 6-80 p85   ++SFC 7-6-80 p27
                    +HFN 12-79 p169
2854 Quintet, strings, op. 163, D 956, C major. Amadeus Quartet; William
     Pleeth, vlc. DG 2542 139 Tape (c) 3342 139 (From SLPM 139105)
                    ++Gr 12-80 p847   +HFN 12-80 p159 tape
2855 Quintet, strings, op. 163, D 956, C major. Bulgarian Quartet; Rol-
     and Pidoux, vlc. Musical Heritage Society MHS 4118
                    +-FF 9/10-80 p197   /HF 6-80 p85
     Quintet, strings, op. 163, D 956, C major: Adagio and scherzo. See
     no. 902
     Rondo, D 438, A major. See no. 410. See no. 2829
     Rondo, D 608, D major. See no. 1109. See no. 2840
     Rondo brillant, op. 70, D 895, B minor. See no. 2821
     Rosamunde, op. 26, D 797, excerpts. See no. 2838
2856 Rosamunde, op. 26, D 797: Incidental music. Ileana Cotrubas, s;
     Leipzig Radio Chorus; Dresden Staatskapelle; Willi Boskovsky.
     Seraphim S 60338
                    -NR 11-80 p8
     Rosamunde, op. 26, D 797: Incidental music. See no. 2893. See no.
     2902
     Rosamunde, op. 26, D 797: Overture. See no. 664
     Rosamunde, op. 26, D 797: Overture and incidental music. See no.
     2897
     Rosamunde, op. 26, D 797: Overture; Ballets, B minor, G minor. See
     no. 2895
     Rosamunde, op. 26, D 797: Overture; Ballets, B minor, G major. See
     no. 2900
     Rosamunde, op. 26, D 797: Overture; Ballet music, nos. 1 and 2.
     See no. 2883
     Salve regina, D 386; D 811. See no. 2832
     Scherzi, D 593 (2). See no. 2839

Scherzo, no. 1, D 593, B flat major. See no. 182
Scherzo, no. 2, D 593, D flat major. See no. 902
2857 Die schone Mullerin, op. 25, D 795. Thomas Pfeiffer, bar; Dieter
      Hornung, pno. Musical Heritage Society MHS 2097
                +—ARG 6-80 p40   +St 8-80 p101
                +—FF 9/10-80 p198
2858 Schwanengesang, D 957. Peter Schreier, t; Walter Olbertz, pno. DG
      2542 144 Tape (c) 3342 144 (From 2530 469)
                +Gr 12-80 p866   +HFN 12-80 p153
      Schwanengesang, D 957. See no. 3863
      Schwanengesang, D 957: Abschied; Am Meer. See no. 3770
      Serenade. See no. 3769. See no. 3870
      Soiree de Vienne, no. 6. See no. 3550
2859 Sonata, arpeggione and piano, D 821, A minor. SHOSTAKOVICH: Sonata,
      violoncello and piano, op. 40, D minor. Arto Noras, vlc; Tap-
      ani Valsta, pno. Finnlevy SFX 5 (also Finlandia FA 303)
                +FF 3/4-80 p152   ++RR 1-78 p73
                +NR 11-80 p5   +RR 12-79 p104
2860 Sonata, arpeggione and piano, D 821, A minor. Nocturne, op. 148, D
      897, E flat major. Trio di Milano. Ricordi RCL 27032
                +RR 8-80 p64
2861 Sonatas, piano, complete. Wilhelm Kempff, pno. DG 2740 132 (9)
      (From 2720 024)
                +Gr 4-76 p1640   ++NYT 10-5-80 pD24
                +—HFN 12-75 p171   +RR 2-76 p53
2862 Sonata, piano, no. 1, D 157, E major. Sonata, piano, no. 16, D 845,
      A minor. Radu Lupu, pno. Decca SXL 6931
                +Gr 12-79 p1028   +RR 1-80 p104
                +HFN 12-79 p169
      Sonata, piano, no. 3, D 459, E major. See no. 2814
      Sonata, piano, no. 6, D 566, E minor. See no. 2837
2863 Sonata, piano, no. 8, D 571, F sharp minor. Sonata, piano, no. 11,
      D 625, F minor. Martino Tirimo, pno. Saga 5469
                +ARG 10-80 p47   +HFN 12-79 p169
                +FF 9/10-80 p199   +RR 11-79 p114
                +HF 11-80 p75
      Sonata, piano, no. 11, D 625, F minor. See no. 2863
      Sonata, piano, no. 12, D 784, A major. See no. 2826
2864 Sonata, piano, no. 13, D 664, A minor. Sonata, piano, no. 16, D
      845, A minor. Lili Kraus, pno. Vanguard VCS 10074 Tape (r) D
      10074
                +HF 2-71 p86   +NR 2-71 p12
                +HF 2-80 p102 tape   +SFC 4-18-71 p32
      Sonata, piano, no. 13, D 664, A major. See no. 2819
      Sonata, piano, no. 13, D 664, A major: 1st movement. See no. 2838
2865 Sonata, piano, no. 14, D 784, A minor. Sonata, piano, no. 19, D
      958, C minor. Hans Richter-Haaser, pno. Harmonia Mundi HM 10063
                +Gr 12-80 p846
2866 Sonata, piano, no. 15, D 840, C major. Sonata, piano, no. 17, D
      850, D major. Michel Dalberto, pno. Erato STU 71309
                +Gr 9-80 p379   +HFN 9-80 p110
2867 Sonata, piano, no. 15, D 840, C major. Klavierstucke, D 946 (3).
      Gilbert Kalish, pno. Nonesuch H 71386
                +FF 11/12-80 p168   ++St 11-80 p100
                +HF 11-80 p73

Sonata, piano, no. 16, op. 42, D 845, A minor. See no. 2862. See
   no. 2864
Sonata, piano, no. 17, D 850, D major. See no. 2825. See no. 2866
Sonata, piano, no. 18, D 894, G major: Minuet and trio. See no. 902
2868 Sonata, piano, no. 19, D 958, C minor. Impromptu, op. 142, no. 2,
     D 935, A flat major. Sviatoslav Richter, pno. Columbia M 35161
        +–ARG 3–80 p37
Sonata, piano, no. 19, D 958, C minor. See no. 2865
2869 Sonata, piano, no. 20, D 959, A major. Alan Weiss, pno. Pavane
     ADW 7008
        +HFN 3–80 p97   +–RR 4–80 p102
2870 Sonata, piano, no. 21, D 960, B flat major. Lili Kraus, pno. Van-
     guard VSD 71267
        ++ARG 6–80 p40   +–HF 4–80 p95
        +Audio 10–80 p136   ++NR 4–80 p14
        ++CL 4–80 p8   +–St 4–80 p138
        ++FF 3/4–80 p146
2871 Sonata, piano, 4 hands, op. 140, D 812, C major. Fantasia, op. 103,
     D 940, F minor. Alfons and Aloys Kontarsky, pno. DG 2531 050
        +Gr 6–80 p53   +–NYT 9–21–80 pD22
        +HFN 6–80 p112   +RR 6–80 p81
        –NR 11–80 p9
Sonata, piano, 4 hands, op. 140, D 812, C major. See no. 2817
Sonata, piano trio, D 28, B flat major. See no. 2910
2872 Sonatas, violin and piano, nos. 1–3. Jaap Schroder, vln; Christop-
     her Hogwood, fortepiano. L'Oiseau-Lyre DSLO 565
        ++Gr 11–80 p697
2873 Sonatinas, nos. 1–3. Bohuslav Matousek, vln; Petr Adamec, pno.
     Supraphon 111 2619
        +NR 12–80 p7
Sonatina, violin and piano, no. 1, op. 137, D 384, D major. See
   no. 990. See no. 2821
Sonatina, violin and piano, no. 1, op. 137, D 384, D major: Rondo.
   See no. 3964
Sonatina, violin and piano, no. 2, op. 137, D 385, A minor. See
   no. 824. See no. 2851
Sonatina, violin and piano, no. 3, op. 137, K 408, G minor. See
   no. 3964
2874 Songs: Als ich erroten sah, D 153; An die Apfelbaume, D 197; An die
     Nachtigall, D 497; Drang in die Ferne, D 770; Im Walde, D 834;
     Stimme der Liebe, D 412; Uber Wildemann, D 884. Schwanengesang,
     D 957: Abchied. Die schone Mullerin, D 795: Ungeduld. STRAUSS,
     R.: Freundlich Vision, op. 48, no. 1; Heimliche Aufforderung, op.
     27, no. 3; Ich trage meine Minne, op. 32, no. 1; Morgen, op. 27,
     no. 4; Standchen, op. 17, no. 2. Julius Patzak, t; Orchestra;
     Richard Strauss, Clemens Krauss. Acanta BB 22055
        +Gr 10–79 p693   +RR 8–79 p120
        +HFN 8–79 p111   +STL 4–13–80 p39
2875 Songs: Ave Maria, D 839; Die Allmacht, D 852; Gretchen am Spinnrade,
     D 118; Die junge Nonne, D 828; Liebesbotschaft, D 957; Mignons
     Lied II, D 877, So lasst mich scheinen; Nacht und Traume, D
     827. STRAUSS, R.: Als mir dein Lied erklang, op. 68, no. 4; Be-
     freit, op. 39, no. 4; Breit uber mein Haupt, op. 19, no. 2; Cac-
     ilie, op. 27, no. 2; Heimkehr, op. 15, no. 5; Morgen, op. 27,
     no. 4; Seitdem dein Aug, op. 17, no. 1; Wasserrose, op. 22, no.

4. Leontyne Price, s; David Garvey, pno. Angel SZ 37631
          -ARG 3-80 p42   +-NYT 10-28-79 pD24
     +-FU 5-80 p47   +-ON 1-5-80 p37
     -NR 12-79 p11   +St 2-80 p138

2876 Songs: An die Musik, D 547; An Sylvia, D 891; Auf dem Wasser zu
     singen, D 774; Ganymed, D 544; Im Fruhling, D 882; Die junge
     Nonne, D 828; Gretchen am Spinnrade, D 118; Das Lied im Grunen,
     D 917; Der Musensohn, D 764; Nachtviolen, D 752; Nahe des Ge-
     liebten, D 162; Wehmut, D 772. Elisabeth Schwarzkopf, s; Edwin
     Fischer, pno. HMV ASL 4843 (From Columbia 33CX 1040)
          +Gr 4-80 p1580   +-HFN 4-80 p121

2877 Songs: Auf dem Strom, D 943; Der Hirt auf dem Felsen, D 965; Italian
     songs (4); Songs of the season (4). Elly Ameling, s; Irwin Gage,
     pno; Guy Deplus, clt; Julia Studebaker, hn. Peters PLE 123 Tape
     (c) PCE 123
          +NYT 10-28-79 pD24   ++St 2-80 p136
          ++SFC 10-7-79 p49

2878 Songs: Du liebst mich nicht, D 756; Gretchen am Spinnrade, D 118;
     Heimliches lieben, D 922; Der Hirt auf dem Felsen, D 965; Im
     Fruhling, D 882; Der Jungling an der Quelle, D 300; Der Musen-
     sohn, D 764; Seligkeit, D 433; Der Vogel, D 691. Landler, D
     790 (12). Elly Ameling, s; Jorg Demus, pno. Hans Deinzer, clt.
     Quintessence PMC 7099 (From Victor 1405)
          +ARG 8-79 p35   ++SFC 3-4-79 p41
          +HFN 7-79 p119 tape   ++St 2-80 p136
          +NYT 3-4-79 pD23

2879 Songs: Alinde, D 904; Der Einsame, D 800; Nachtstuck, D 672; Der
     Schiffer, D 536; Totengrabers Heimweh, D 842; Der Wanderer an
     den Mond, D 870. Divertissement a la francaise, D 823, E minor.
     Theo Altmeyer, t; Fritz Neumeyer, Rolf Junghanns, hammerklavier.
     Toccata FSM 53620
          +HFN 6-80 p112

2880 Songs: Gesang der Geister uber den Wassern, D 714; Miriam's Sieges-
     gesang, D 942; Nachtgesang im Walde, D 913. Ursula Buckel, s;
     Gerd Lohmeyer, pno; South German Madrigal Choir; Wolfgang Gonnen-
     wein. Turnabout TVS 37116 Tape (c) KTVC 37116
          ++Gr 6-79 p94   +RR 6-79 p116
          +HFN 7-79 p112   +STL 12-9-79 p41
          +-MT 2-80 p107

     Songs: Abendstern, D 806; Ach um deine feuchten Schwingen, D 717;
     Auf dem Strom, D 943; Auflosung, D 807; Ave Maria, D 839; Die
     Forelle, D 550; Dass sie hier gewesen, D 775; Fruhlingsglaube,
     D 686; Heidenroslein, D 257; Der Hirt auf dem Felsen, D 965; Im
     Fruhling, D 882; Jager Ruhe, D 838; Lachen und Weinen, D 777;
     Liebesbotschaft, D 957; Lob der Tranen, D 711; Nachtviolen, D
     752; Raste Krieger, D 837; Seligkeit, D 433; Was Bedeutet die
     Bewegnung, D 720. See no. 2913

     Songs: Amalia, D 195; Der Fluchtling, D 402; Der Jungling am Bache,
     D 30; Licht und Liebe, D 352; Nur wer die Sehnsucht kennt, D
     887; Sehnsucht, D 636; Der Ungluckliche, D 713. See no. 902

     Songs: An den Mond; An die Musik, D 547; Du bist die Ruh, D 776;
     Die Forelle, D 550; Der Jungling am Bache, D 30; Gruppe aus dem
     Tartarus, D 583; Im Fruhling, D 882; An Silvia, D 891; Fischer-
     weise, D 881; Litanei, D 343; Meeres Stille, D 216; Der Tod und
     das Madchen, D 531; Der Wanderer an dem Mond, D 870. See no.
     3863

Songs: An die Dioskuren; An die Laute, D 905; Die Forelle, D 550; Im Abendrot, D 799; Der Musensohn, D 764. See no. 543

Songs: An die Dioskuren; An die Laute, D 905; An die Musik, D 547; An Sylvia, D 891; Der Einsame, D 800; Fruhlingsglaube, D 868; Heidenroslein, D 257; Die Forelle, D 550; Im Abendrot, D 799; Der Musensohn, D 764; Standchen, D 889. See no. 544

Songs: An die Nachtigall, D 947; Lachen und Weinen, D 777. See no. 3541

Songs: Auf der Bruck, D 853; Im Fruhling, D 882. See no. 3776

Songs: Auf der Bruck, D 853; Bei dir allein, D 866; Die liebe Farbe, D 795; Mio ben ricordatei, D 688; Morgengruss, D 795; Non t'ac-costar all'urna, D 688; Schafers Klagelied, D 121; Willkommen und Abschied, D 767. See on. 3537

Songs: Death and the maiden, D 531; The organ grinder, D 911. See no. 3905

Songs: Die abgebluhte Linde, D 514; Heimliches Lieben, D 922; Minne-lied, D 429; Der Musensohn, D 764. See no. 858

Songs: Erlkonig, D 328; Wanderers Nachtlied, D 768. See no. 3573

Songs: Gott meine Zuversicht, D 706; Die Nachtigall, D 724; La Pas-torella, D 513; Standchen, D 921; Widerspruch, D 865. See no. 3952

Songs: Greisengesang, D 778; Die Liebe hat gelogen, D 755; Orest auf Tauris, D 548; Die Schafer und der Reiter, D 517; Schiffers Scheidelied, D 910; Totengrabers Heimweh, D 842. See no. 852

Songs: Gretchen am Spinnrade, D 118; Hark hark the lark; Wohin, D 795. See no. 3770

Songs: Gretchen am Spinnrade, D 118; Nacht und Traume, D 827; Rast-lose, D 138. See no. 3611

Songs: Im Walde, D 834. See no. 859

Songs: Lachen und Weinen, D 777; Mein. See no. 3551

Songs: Rastlose Liebe, D 138; Wasserfluth. See no. 3562

Songs: Sei mir gegrusset. See no. 3774

2881 Stabat mater, D 383, F minor. Gerti Zeumer, s; Dieter Ellenbeck, t; Ernst Schramm, bs; RIAS Chamber Chorus; BRSO; Roland Bader. Schwann AMS 3523
          +ARG 2-80 p45

Stabat mater, D 383, F minor. See no. 2830

2882 Symphonies, nos. 1-4. Die Zauberharfe, D 644, excerpts. Naples Orchestra and Chorus; Denis Vaughan. Arabesque 8045-3 Tape (c) 9045-3
          +ARG 5-80 p33   +HF 7-80 p82 tape
          +FF 9/10-80 p200   +NYT 1-6-80 pD18

2883 Symphonies, nos. 1-6, 8-9. Rosamunde, op. 26, D 797: Overture; Ballet music, nos. 1 and 2. BPhO; Karl Bohm. DG 2740 127 (5) Tape (c) 3378 082 (also DG 2720 097)
          +Gr 1-76 p1204   +RR 10-75 p49
          +Gr 6-79 p109 tape   ++SFC 12-9-80 p33
          +HFN 10-75 p152

2884 Symphony, no. 1, D 82, D major. Symphony, no. 2, D 125, B flat major. Israel Philharmonic Orchestra; Zubin Mehta. Decca SXL 6892 Tape (c) KSX 6892 (also London CS 7114 Tape (c) CS 5-7114)
          +ARG 12-79 p55   +HFN 4-79 p125
          +Audio 12-79 p101   +NR 4-80 p4
          +FF 1/2-80 p144   +RR 4-79 p80
          +Gr 4-79 p1718   +St 1-80 p104
          +HF 11-79 p112

2885 Symphony, no. 1, D 82, D major. Symphony, no. 2, D 125, B flat maj-
        or. VPO; Istvan Kertesz. London STS 15473 (also Decca JB 73
        Tape (c) KJBC 73. From SXL 6552)
                    +FF 11/12-79 p123   +-HFN 3-80 p105
                    +Gr 3-80 p1392   ++RR 3-80 p58
                    +Gr 9-80 p413 tape
        Symphony, no. 2, D 125, B flat major. See no. 2884. See no. 2885
2886 Symphony, no. 3, D 200, D major. Symphony, no. 6, D 589, G major.
        VPO; Istvan Kertesz. Decca JB 74 Tape (c) KJBC 74
                    +Gr 9-80 p413 tape
2887 Symphony, no. 3, D 200, D major. Symphony, no. 8, D 759, B minor.
        VPO; Carlos Kleiber. DG 2531 124 Tape (c) 3301 124
                    +FF 7/8-80 p130   -NR 6-80 p5
                    +-FU 6-80 p43   +RR 11-79 p93
                    +-Gr 11-79 p839   ++SFC 7-20-80 p34
                    +HF 8-80 p68   +St 6-80 p122
                    +HFN 12-79 p169   +STL 12-2-79 p37
                    +-MT 6-80 p383
2888 Symphony, no. 3, D 200, D major. Symphony, no. 5, D 485, B flat
        major. BPhO; Herbert von Karajan. HMV ASD 3860 Tape (c) TC ASD
        3860 (From SLS 5127) (also Angel SZ 37754)
                    +Gr 7-80 p142   +-HFN 6-80 p115
                    +Gr 9-80 p413 tape   ++NR 9-80 p2
2889 Symphony, no. 3, D 200, D major. Symphony, no. 5, D 485, B flat
        major. RPO; Thomas Beecham. HMV SXLP 30204 Tape (c) TC SXLP
        30204, TC EXE 184 (From ASD 345)
                    ++Gr 2-76 p1346   +-HFN 10-80 p117 tape
                    +HFN 2-76 p115   +RR 2-76 p41
                    +HFN 5-76 p117 tape   +RR 4-76 p80 tape
2890 Symphony, no. 3, D 200, D major. Symphony, no. 6, D 589, C major.
        VPO; Karl Munchinger. London STS 15499
                    +-FF 7/8-80 p129
2891 Symphony, no. 4, D 417, C minor. Symphony, no. 5, D 485, B flat
        major. VPO; Istvan Kertesz. Decca JB 75 Tape (c) KJBC 75
                    +Gr 9-80 p413 tape   ++RR 6-80 p58
                    +HFN 6-80 p117
2892 Symphony, no. 4, D 417, C minor. Symphony, no. 8, D 759, B minor.
        CSO; Carlo Maria Giulini. DG 2531 047 Tape (c) 3301 047
                    +-FF 1/2-80 p145   +NYT 12-9-79 pD25
                    ++Gr 11-78 p890   +RR 12-78 p68
                    +-HF 5-79 p92   +RR 5-79 p110 tape
                    +-HFN 12-78 p159   +-SFC 6-17-79 p41
                    +HFN 2-79 p118 tape   ++St 9-79 p100
                    +-MJ 7/8-79 p57
2893 Symphony, no. 5, D 485, B flat major. Symphony, no. 6, D 589, C
        major. Symphony, no. 8, D 759, B minor. Symphony, no. 9, D 944,
        C major. Rosamunde, op. 26, D 797: Incidental music. Lucia Popp,
        s; Naples Orchestra; Denis Vaughan. Arabesque 8046/3 (3) Tape
        (c) 9046
                    +-NR 12-80 p4
2894 Symphony, no. 5, D 485, B flat major. SCHUMANN: Symphony, no. 4,
        op. 120, D minor. VPO; Karl Bohm. DG 2531 279 Tape (c) 3301
        279
                    ++Gr 11-80 p677   +-HFN 12-80 p145
2895 Symphony, no. 5, D 485, B flat major. Rosamunde, op. 26, D 797:

Overture; Ballets, B minor, G major. BPhO; Lorin Maazel, Karl
   Bohm. DG 2535 398 Tape (c) 3335 398 (From SLPM 138685, 2720 062)
     +–Gr 7-80 p142   +HFN 9-80 p116 tape
     +Gr 9-80 p413 tape   +–RR 6-80 p58
     +–HFN 6-80 p117
2896 Symphony, no. 5, K 485, B flat major. Symphony, no. 8, D 759, B
   minor. HSO; Janos Ferencsik. Hungaroton SLPX 12039
     +–FF 3/4-80 p147   +NR 4-80 p5
   Symphony, no. 5, D 485, B flat major. See no. 877. See no. 2888.
   See no. 2889. See no. 2891
2897 Symphony, no. 6, D 589, C major. Rosamunde, op. 26, D 797: Overture
   and incidental music. Israel Philharmonic Orchestra; Zubin Mehta. London CS 7115 Tape (c) CS 5-7115 (also Decca SXL 6891 Tape
   (c) KSX 6891)
     +ARG 12-79 p55   +–HFN 9-79 p111
     +FF 1/2-80 p146   +–NR 4-80 p4
     +–Gr 10-79 p653   +–RR 9-79 p96
     +–HF 11-79 p112   ++SFC 12-30-79 p33
   Symphony, no. 6, D 589, C major. See no. 2393. See no. 2886. See
   no. 2890. See no. 2893
2898 Symphony, no. 7, D 729, E major (arr. Weingartner). BRSO; Heinz
   Rogner. Spectrum SR 116 Tape (c) SC 216
     +FF 9/10-80 p201   +HF 10-80 p98 tape
     ++HF 8-80 p68
2899 Symphony, no. 8, D 759, B minor. MENDELSSOHN: A midsummer night's
   dream, opp. 21/61: Overture, Scherzo, Wedding march. Cincinnati
   Symphony Orchestra; Thomas Schippers, Walter Susskind. Candide
   QCE 31114
     -FF 3/4-80 p147
2900 Symphony, no. 8, D 759, B minor. Symphony, no. 9, D 944, C major.
   Rosamunde, op. 26, D 797: Overture; Ballet, B minor, G major.
   BPhO; Karl Bohm. DG 2725 103 Tape (c) 3374 103 (From SLPM 138
   685, 2720 062)
     +Gr 7-80 p147   +HFN 8-80 p107 tape
     +Gr 9-80 p413 tape   ++RR 7-80 p65
     +HFN 7-80 p115
2901 Symphony, no. 8, D 759, B minor. Fierrabras, D 796: Overture.
   Overture in the Italian style, D 591, C major. Des Teufels
   Lustschloss, D 84. VPO; Istvan Kertesz. London STS 15476 (also Decca JB 76 Tape (c) KJBC 76. From SXL 6090)
     +–FF 3/4-80 p148   +HFN 3-80 p105
     +Gr 2-80 p1269   +RR 3-80 p58
     +Gr 9-80 p413 tape
2902 Symphony, no. 8, D 759, B minor. Rosamunde, op. 26, D 797: Incidental music. Moscow Academic Philharmonic Orchestra; Veronica Dudarova. Musical Heritage Society MHS 4035
     +FF 1/2-80 p149
2903 Symphony, no. 8, D 759, B minor. BRAHMS: Variations on a theme by
   Haydn, op. 56a. PhO; Carlo Maria Giulini. Seraphim S 60335
   Tape (c) 4SX 60335
     +HF 8-80 p68   +SFC 5-18-80 p38
     ++NR 6-80 p5
   Symphony, no. 8, D 759, B minor. See no. 877. See no. 1745. See
   no. 2157. See no. 2160. See no. 2887. See no. 2892. See no.
   2893. See no. 2896

2904 Symphony, no. 9, D 944, C major. BPhO; Herbert von Karajan. Angel
     SZ 37545 Tape (c) 4XS 37545
            ++FF 11/12-80 p168   +-NR 12-80 p3
2905 Symphony, no. 9, D 944, C major. VPO; Istvan Kertesz. Decca JB 77
     Tape (c) KJBC 77 (From SXL 6089) (also London STS 15505)
            +FF 11/12-80 p177   +HFN 11-79 p153
            +Gr 11-79 p840   +RR 11-79 p93
2906 Symphony, no. 9, D 944, C major. Berlin Radio Symphony Orchestra;
     Heinz Rogner. Denon PCM OB 7350 51 (2)
            +St 2-80 p132
2907 Symphony, no. 9, D 944, C major. CO; Georg Szell. Odyssey Y 30669
     Tape (c) YT 30669
            ++FF 7/8-80 p207
     Symphony, no. 9, D 944, C major. See no. 2893. See no. 2900
2908 Symphony, C major (based on Grand duo, D 812) (orch. Joachim). Mun-
     ich Philharmonic Orchestra; Marc Andreae. Acanta DC 22123
            +Gr 5-80 p1672   +HFN 3-80 p97
            +-Gr 8-80 p226   +-RR 3-80 p97
     Des Teufels Lustschloss, D 84: Overture. See no. 2901
2909 Trio, piano, no. 1, op. 99, D 898, B flat major. Trio, piano, no.
     2, op. 100, D 929, E flat major. Regis Pasquier, vln; Roland
     Pidoux, vlc; Jean Claude Pennetier, pno. Harmonia Mundi HM 1047/
     8 (2)
            +-Gr 12-80 p846
2910 Trio, piano, no. 1, op. 99, D 898, B flat major. Sonata, piano
     trio, D 28, B flat major. Trio di Milano. Ricordi RCL 27031
            +RR 8-80 p64
     Trio, piano, no. 2, op. 100, D 929, E flat major. See no. 2909
     Trio, strings, no. 1, D 471, B flat major. See no. 2131
     Trio, strings, no. 2, D 581, B flat major. See no. 2131
     Valses (Waltzes) (3). See no. 3890
     Valses (12). See no. 3826
     Valses, D 145, no. 2, B major. See no. 2913
     Valses nobles, op. 77, D 969. See no. 3737. See no. 3811
     Variations on a waltz by Diabelli, D 718, C minor. See no. 2814.
     See no. 2837. See no. 2839
     Variations on an original theme, op. 35, D 813, A flat major. See
     no. 2817. See no. 2840. See no. 2841
2911 Die Verschworenen (The conspirators or the domestic war), D 787.
     Ilona Steingruber, Elizabeth Roon, Laurence Duotit, s; Walton
     Anton, t; Walter Berry, bs; Vienna Academy Chamber Chorus; VSO;
     Ferdinand Grossman. Musical Heritage Society MHS 4176 (From
     Lyrichord LLST 7207)
            -FF 11/12-80 p169
     Der Vierjahrige Posten, D 190: Overture. See no. 2836
     Where thou reignest. See no. 3533. See no. 3936
2912 Winterreise, op. 89, D 911. Dietrich Fischer-Dieskau, bar; Daniel
     Barenboim. DG 2707 118 (2) Tape (c) 3301 237
            +Gr 11-80 p724   ++HFN 12-80 p159 tape
            ++HFN 11-80 p122   +NYT 12-14-80 pD38
     Die Winterreise, op. 89, D 911: Die Wetterfahne; Erstarrung; Die
     Krahe; Der Wegweiser; Die Post. See no. 902
2913 Works, selections: Deutsche Tanze, D 366 (6). Galopp, D 735, G
     major. Impromptus, op. 90, no. 3, D 899, G flat major. Moment
     musicaux, op. 94, no. 2, D 780, A flat major. Songs: Abendstern,

D 806; Ach um deine feuchten Schwingen, D 717; Auf dem Strom, D
943; Auflosung, D 807; Ave Maria, D 839; Die Forelle, D 550; Dass
sie hier gewesen, D 775; Fruhlingsglaube, D 686; Heidenroslein,
D 257; Der Hirt auf dem Felsen, D 965; Im Fruhling, D 882; Jager
Ruhe, D 838; Lachen und Weinen, D 777; Liebesbotschaft, D 957;
Lob der Tranen, D 711; Nachtviolen, D 752; Raste Krieger, D 837;
Seligkeit, D 433; Was Bedeutet die Bewegnung, D 702. Valse,
D 145, no. 2, B major. Judith Nelson, s; Jorg Demus, pno; Alfred
Prinz, clt; Franz Sollner, hn. Harmonia Mundi HM 1023/4 (2)
        +—FF 12-79 p116   ++NR 6-80 p11
        -FU 5-80 p49
Die Zauberharfe, D 644, excerpts. See no. 2882
Die Zauberharfe, D 644: Overture. See no. 2836
Die Zwillingsbruder, D 647: Overture. See no. 2836

SCHUBIGER, Anselm
    Cacilien march. See no. 3626

SCHULLER, Gunther
    Studies on themes of Paul Klee (7). See no. 737
    Suite. See no. 400
    Trio. See no. 3649

SCHULTZ, Svend
    Songs: Dansevise; Midsommervise. See no. 3587

SCHUMAN, William
    New England triptych: Chester. See no. 3962
    Orpheus and his lute. See no. 4026

SCHUMANN, Clara
2914 Trio, op. 17, G minor. SCHUMANN, R.: Trios, piano, nos. 1-3.
      Beaux Arts Trio. Philips 6700 051 (2)
           +—Gr 10-80 p512   +—HFN 10-80 p107
    Trio, op. 17, G minor. See no. 4065
    Variations on a theme by Robert Schumann, op. 20. See no. 4024

SCHUMANN, Robert
    Adagio and allegro, op. 70, A flat major. See no. 2960. See no.
      3839
2915 Album fur die Jugend, op. 68. Jorg Demus, pno. Harmonia Mundi 1C
      151 99775/6 (2)
           +Gr 4-80 p1572   +—NYT 7-27-80 pD20
           +HFN 4-80 p119   +RR 5-80 p90
2916 Album fur die Jugend, op. 68. Liederkreis, op. 39. Elly Ameling,
      s; Jorg Demus, pno. Philips 6769 037 (2)
           +Gr 8-80 p257   +NYT 9-21-80 pD22
           +HFN 8-80 p102   ++St 12-80 p86
           +NR 11-80 p8   +STL 8-10-80 p30
2917 Arabesque, op. 18, C major. Fantasia, op. 17, C major. Kinderscen-
      en, op. 15. Daniel Barenboim, pno. DG 2531 089 Tape (c) 3301
      089
           +Gr 6-79 p85   +RR 7-79 p99
           +—HF 5-80 p81   +St 6-80 p123
           +HFN 7-79 p112   +STL 12-2-79 p37
2918 Arabesque, op. 18, C major. Fantasia, op. 17, C major. Youri Eg-
      orov, pno. Peters PLE 122 Tape (c) PCE 122
           +FF 3/4-80 p151   +HF 5-80 p81
    Arabesque, op. 18, C major. See no. 1044. See no. 2953. See no.
      3550. See no. 3954
    Bilder aus Osten (Pictures from the East), op. 66. See no. 2989

Blumenstuck, op. 19, D major. See no. 1044

Die Braut von Messina (The bride of Messina), op. 100. See no. 2948. See no. 2955

Canons, op. 56, no. 6, B major. See no. 161

2919 Carnaval, op. 9. Kinderscenen, op. 15. Inger Sodergren, pno. Calliope CAL 1650

      +—HFN 7-80 p110   -RR 7-80 p84

2920 Carnaval, op. 9. Faschingsschwank aus Wien, op. 26. Daniel Barenboim, pno. DG 2531 090 Tape (c) 3301 090

      +—ARG 5-80 p37   +HFN 10-79 p161
      +—CL 3-80 p14   +NR 3-80 p13
      +FF 3/4-80 p149   +RR 8-79 p112
      +Gr 7-79 p233   +St 3-80 p99
      +—HF 5-80 p81

2921 Carnaval, op. 9. Humoresque, op. 20, B flat major. Bella Davidovich, pno. Philips 9500 667 Tape (c) 7300 765

      +—CL 9-80 p14   +—NR 7-80 p12
      +FF 7/8-80 p132   ++St 10-80 p121
      +—HF 5-80 p81

Carnaval, op. 9. See no. 1058. See no. 2417. See no. 2826. See no. 2833

Carnaval, op. 9, excerpt. See no. 3604. See no. 3608

2922 Concerto, piano, op. 54, A minor. Annie Fischer, pno; Orchestra; Otto Klemperer. Columbia SAX 4285

      +Gr 12-80 p881

2923 Concerto, piano, op. 54, A minor. Introduction and allegro, op. 92, G major. Introduction and allegro, op. 134, D minor. Vladimir Ashkenazy, pno; LSO; Uri Segal, Vladimir Ashkenazy. London CS 7082 Tape (c) CS 5-7082 (also Decca SXL 6861 Tape (c) KSXC 6861)

      ++Gr 3-79 p1572   +NR 10-79 p4
      +HF 3-79 p102   ++RR 3-79 p85
      ++HFN 4-79 p125   -RR 9-79 p134 tape
      ++HFN 7-79 p119 tape   +SFC 8-5-79 p53
      +MM 6-79 p34   ++St 5-79 p109
      +—MT 2-80 p108

2924 Concerto, piano, op. 54, A minor. WEBER: Konzertstuck, op. 79, F minor. Alfred Brendel, pno; LSO; Claudio Abbado. Philips 9500 677 Tape (c) 7300 772

      +—Gr 11-80 p677   +HFN 12-80 p159 tape
      +—HFN 10-80 p109   +—NR 12-80 p6

Concerto, piano, op. 54, A minor. See no. 425. See no. 1050. See no. 1445. See no. 1541. See no. 1542. See no. 1543. See no. 1544. See no. 2820. See no. 3709. See no. 3976

Concerto, violin, D minor. See no. 2828

Dedication. See no. 3769

Les deux grenadiers. See no. 3797

2925 Dichterliebe, op. 48. Liederkreis, op. 39. Dietrich Fischer-Dieskau, bar; Christoph Eschenbach, pno. DG 2531 290 Tape (c) 3301 290 (From 2740 185, 2740 167)

      ++Gr 11-80 p724   +HFN 12-80 p145

2926 Dichterliebe, op. 48. TCHAIKOVSKY: Trio, piano, op. 50, A minor: Pezzo elegaico. Ivan Kozlovsky, t; David Oistrakh, vln; Sviatoslav Knushevitzky, vlc; Konstantin Igumnov, pno. Melodiya S10 05525/6 (4)

      +ARSC Vol 12, nos. 1-2, 1980 p110

Dichterliebe, op. 48. See no. 543. See no. 2944. See no. 3863
Dichterliebe, op. 48: Ich grolle nicht. See no. 548. See no. 3770
Dichterliebe, op. 48: Songs (6). See no. 544

2927 Fantasia, op. 17, C major. Fantasiestucke, op. 12. Martha Argerich,
     pno. CBS 76713 (Also Columbia M 35168)

+Audio 6-79 p131	++MM 6-79 p34
+-CL 3-80 p12	+MT 8-79 p659
-FF 3/4-80 p150	+NR 3-80 p13
+-Gr 2-79 p1447	-RR 2-79 p85
+-HF 5-80 p81	+STL 12-2-79 p37
+HFN 1-79 p123	

2928 Fantasia, op. 17, C major. Symphonic etudes, op. 13. Misha Dichter,
     pno. Philips 9500 318 Tape (c) 7300 590

+-FF 9/10-78 p106	++MJ 7-78 p56
+-Gr 8-80 p242	+NR 7-78 p12
+-HF 5-78 p110	+RR 8-80 p75
+HFN 8-80 p102	+St 5-78 p102
+HFN 12-80 p159 tape	

2929 Fantasie, op. 17, C major. Noveletten, op. 21, nos. 1 and 2. Ar-
     tur Rubinstein, pno. RCA ARL 1-3427 Tape (c) ARK 1-3427 (From
     SB 6747)

+-ARG 5-80 p37	+NR 3-80 p13
++FF 9/10-80 p202	++SFC 2-3-80 p45
+Gr 12-80 p854	-St 6-80 p123
+-HF 5-80 p81	

Fantasia, op. 17, C major. See no. 1997. See no. 1998. See no.
     2917. See no. 2918. See no. 2937

2930 Fantasiestucke, op. 12. Intermezzi, op. 4. Imre Rohmann, pno.
     Hungaroton SLPX 11799

+-FF 9/10-78 p107	-NR 10-78 p14
++HF 5-80 p81	

2931 Fantasiestucke, op. 12. Sonata, piano, no. 2, op. 22, G minor.
     Susan Starr, pno. Orion ORS 77284 Tape (c) OC 825

+-ARG 8-79 p40	+-HF 8-80 p87 tape
+-CL 3-80 p12	+NR 9-80 p1 tape
+-FU 5-80 p50	+St 10-79 p146
+-HF 5-80 p81	

Fantasiestucke, op. 12. See no. 2927
Fantasiestucke, op. 12: Warum; Grillen. See no. 1988. See no.
     2938
Fantasiestucke, op. 12: Warum, Fabel, Traumeswirren, In der Nacht,
     Des Abends. See no. 1044
Fantasiestucke, op. 73. See no. 2960. See no. 3684
Fantasiestucke, op. 88. See no. 2960
Fantasiestucke, op. 111 (3). See no. 1399
Faschingsschwank aus Wien, op. 26. See no. 535. See no. 536. See
     no. 2920. See no. 3976
Faschingsschwank aus Wien, op. 26: Intermezzo. See no. 1044
Frauenliebe und Leben, op. 42. See no. 858. See no. 2942
Gedichte und Requiem, op. 90. See no. 2935
Gesange der Fruhe, op. 133. See no. 2937
Hermann and Dorothea overture, op. 136, B minor. See no. 2948.
     See no. 2953
Humoresque, op. 20, B flat major. See no. 1970. See no. 2921

2932 Intermezzi, op. 4. Kinderscenen, op. 15. Variations on ABEGG, op.

   1. Waldscenen, op. 82: Solitary flowers; The prophet bird; The
departure. Christoph Eschenbach, pno. DG 2535 224 Tape (c)
3335 224
        +ARG 4-80 p43   +CL 3-80 p14

Intermezzi, op. 4. See no. 2930
Introduction and allegro, op. 92, G major. See no. 2923.
Introduction and allegro, op. 134, D minor. See no. 2923
Kinderscenen, op. 15. See no. 2917. See no. 2919. See no. 2932
Kinderscenen, op. 15: Traumerei. See no. 3677. See no. 3870
Klavierstucke in Fughettenform, op. 126. See no. 2937
Konzertstuck, op. 86, F major. See no. 2807. See no. 2956
2933 Kreisleriana, op. 16. Nachtstucke, op. 23. Papillons, op. 2.
    Marina Horak, pno. Pavane ADW 7020
        +-Gr 3-80 p1418   +-RR 6-80 p81
2934 Kreisleriana, op. 16. Noveletten, op. 21, nos. 1, 8. Youri Egorov,
    pno. Peters PLE 113 (also HMV HQS 1428)
        +-FF 9/10-79 p137   +-MT 2-80 p108
        +Gr 7-79 p233   ++RR 7-79 p99
        +HF 5-80 p81   -SFC 7-1-79 p44
        +-HFN 7-79 p112   ++St 5-79 p93
        +HFN 8-79 p111

Kreisleriana, op. 16. See no. 832. See no. 3833
Lieder, op. 40. See no. 2935
2935 Liederkreis, op. 39. Gedichte und Requiem, op. 90. Lieder, op. 40.
    Peter Pears, t; Murray Perahia, pno. CBS 76815 Tape (c) 40-76815
        +Gr 2-80 p1288   +RR 2-80 p91
        +Gr 8-80 p275 tape   +RR 8-80 p95 tape
        +HFN 2-80 p97   +-STL 3-9-80 p41
        +HFN 8-80 p109 tape

Liederkreis, op. 39. See no. 2916. See no. 2925. See no. 2942
2936 Liederkreis, op. 39: Die Lotosblume; Was will die Einsame Trane;
    Du bist wie ene Blume; Dein Angesicht; Lehn deine Wang an meine
    Wang; Mein Wagne rollet Langsam; An den Sonnenschein; Ich wand're
    Nicht; Der frohe Wandersmann; Der Einsiedler; Der Nussbaum. Peter
    Schreier, t; Norman Shetler, pno. Musical Heritage Society MHS
    4062
        +FF 5/6-80 p147   +St 7-80 p74

Liederkreis, op. 24: Schone Wiege meine Leiden. See no. 548
Manfred overture, op. 115. See no. 2947. See no. 2949. See no.
    2954. See no. 2958. See no. 3688
Marchenbilder, op. 113. See no. 1883. See no. 2960
Marchenerzahlungen, op. 132. See no. 922. See no. 2960
Myrthen, op. 25: Du bist wie eine Blume. See no. 3611
Myrthen, op. 25: Widmung. See no. 3964
Nachtstucke, op. 23. See no. 2933
Nachtstucke, op. 23, no. 4. See no. 1044
Noveletten, op. 21. See no. 2937
Noveletten, op. 21, nos. 1 and 2. See no. 2929
Noveletten, op. 21, nos. 1 and 8. See no. 2934
Noveletten, op. 21, no. 8. See no. 3825
Overture, scherzo and finale, op. 52, E major. See no. 2951. See
    no. 2952. See no. 2959
Papillons, op. 2. See no. 2933
2937 Piano works: Fantasia, op. 17, C major. Gesange der Fruhe, op. 133.
    Noveletten, op. 21. Klavierstucke in the form of fughettas, op.

126 (7). Sonata, piano, no. 1, op. 11, F sharp minor. Waldscen-
en, op. 82. Theme and variations, E flat major. Peter Frankl,
pno. Turnabout TVS 37131/3
    +—HFN 2-80 p99   +—RR 12-79 p103
Quartet, piano, op. 47, E flat major. See no. 2960
Quartets, strings, nos. 1-3. See no. 2960
Quintet, op. 44, E flat major. See no. 2960
Romance, op. 28, no. 2, F sharp major. See no. 3677
Romances, op. 94. See no. 2526. See no. 2960. See no. 3885
Sketches, op. 58. See no. 2138
Sketches, op. 58, no. 2, C major. See no. 4054
Sketches, op. 58, no. 4, D flat major. See no. 3728
Sonata, piano, no. 1, op. 11, F sharp minor. See no. 2937
2938 Sonata, piano, no. 2, op. 22, G minor. Fantasiestucke, op. 12:
Warum; Grillen. LISZT: Paraphrases: Schubert: Ave Maria, op. 52,
no. 4; Der Erlkonig, op. 1; Die junge Nonne, op. 43, no. 1; Der
Leiermann, op. 89, no. 24; Tauschung, op. 89, no. 19; Wohin, op.
25, no. 2. Lazar Berman, pno. Quintessence PMC 7155
    +—FF 11/12-80 p173
Sonata, piano, no. 2, op. 22, G minor. See no. 1988. See no. 2931
Sonata, violin and piano: Intermezzo (F.A.E.). See no. 2939
2939 Sonata, violin and piano, op. 105, A minor. Sonata, violin and
piano, no. 2, op. 121, D minor. Sonata, violin and piano: Intermezzo (F.A.E.). Jaime Laredo, vln; Ruth Laredo, pno. Desto DC
6442 Tape (c) DCX 46442
    +ARG 7/8-80 p39   +SFC 3-2-80 p41
    +—FF 7/8-80 p134   +St 4-80 p138
    -HF 9-80 p96
2940 Sonata, violin and piano, no. 1, op. 105, A minor. Sonata, violin
and piano, no. 2, op. 121, D minor. Raphael Oleg, vln; Yves
Rault, pno. Harmonia Mundi HM 489
    +Gr 10-79 p668   +RR 8-79 p113
    -HFN 8-79 p111   +—ST 11-79 p529
    +—MT 2-80 p107
Sonata, violin and piano, no. 1, op. 105, A minor. See no. 2960
Sonata, violin and piano, no. 2, op. 121, D minor. See no. 2939.
See no. 2940. See no. 2960
2941 Songs, op. 141. WOLF: Geistliche Lieder. Vokalensemble Marburg.
Musicaphon BM 30 SL 1335
    +HFN 7-80 p110
2942 Songs: Der frohe Wandersmann, op. 77, no. 1. Frauenliebe und Leben,
op. 42. Liederkreis, op. 39. Evelyn Lear, s; Roger Vignoles,
pno. Chandos ABR 1009 Tape (c) ABT 1009
    -Gr 8-80 257   +HFN 8-80 p102
2943 Songs: Bedeckt mich mit Blumen, op. 138, no. 4; Blaue Augen hat
das Madchen, op. 138, no. 9; Duette, op. 34 (4); Duette op. 78
(4); Fruhlingslied, op. 79, no. 19; Das Gluck, op. 79, no. 16;
Ich bin dein Baum, op. 101, no. 3; In der Nacht, op. 74, no. 4;
Intermezzo, op. 74, no. 2; Landliches Lied, op. 29, no. 1; Liebes-
gram, op. 74, no. 3; Die Lotosblume, op. 33; Mailied, op. 79, no.
10; Schon ist das Fest des Lenzes, op. 37, no. 7; Die Schwalben,
op. 79, no. 21; So wahr die Sonne scheinet, op. 37, no. 12; Som-
merruh; Die tausend Grusse, op. 101, no. 7; Zweistimmige Lieder,
op. 43 (3). Julia Varady, s; Peter Schreier, t; Dietrich Fischer-
Dieskau, bar; Christoph Eschenbach, pno. DG 2531 204

++Gr 8-80 p257   +NYT 9-21-80 pD22
+HFN 8-80 p102   +STL 8-10-80 p30
+—MT 12-80 p787

2944 Songs: Abends am Strand, op. 45, no. 3; Auf dem Rhein, op. 51, no.
     4; Auftrage, op. 77, no. 5; Aus dem Zyklus "Spanisches Lieder-
     spiel", op. 74; Belsatzer, op. 57; Dichterliebe, op. 48; Lied-
     eralbum fur die Jugend, op. 79, excerpts; Liederkreis, op. 24;
     Gedichte, op. 35 (12); Romanzen und Balladen, opp. 49 and 53;
     Tragodie, op. 64, no. 3. Dietrich Fischer-Dieskau, bar; Chris-
     toph Eschenbach. DG 2709 079 (3)
              +ARG 3-80 p38   +NR 12-79 p10
              +—HF 2-80 p92

2945 Songs: Minnespiel, op. 101, no. 4; Spanische Liebeslieder, op. 138,
     nos., 2-3, 5, 7; Balladen, op. 122; Fruhe Lieder, WoO 21 (6);
     Gesange (6), nos. 1-5; Gesange, op. 83, nos. 1, 3; Gesange,
     op. 95, op. 2; Gesange, op. 107, nos. 3, 6; Gesange, op. 125,
     nos. 1-3; Gesange, op. 142, nos. 1-2, 4; Gedichte, op. 119, no. 2;
     Gedichte, op. 90 (6); Der Handschuh, op. 87; Husarenlieder, op.
     117, nos, 1-4; Lieder und Gesange, op. 96, nos. 1-3; Lieder und
     Gesange, op. 98a, nos. 2, 4, 6, 8; Lieder und Gesange, op. 127,
     nos. 2-3; Provencalisches Lied, op. 139, no. 4. Dietrich Fischer-
     Dieskau, bar; Christoph Eschenbach, pno. DG 2709 088
              +—ARG 9-80 p40   ++NR 4-80 p13
              +—FF 7/8-80 p133

2946 Songs: Abends am Strand, op. 43, no. 5; Auf dem Rhein, op. 51, no.
     4; Auftrage, op. 77, no. 5; Die beiden Grenadiere, op. 49, no. 1;
     Belsazar, op. 57; Blondels Lied, op. 53, no. 1; Der arme Peter,
     op. 53, no. 3; Dichterliebe, op. 48; Die feindlichen Bruder,
     op. 49, no. 2; Kerner Lieder, op. 35; Liederalbum fur die Jugend,
     op. 79, nos. 7-8, 14, 18, 23-24, 27-28; Liederkreis, op. 24;*
     Lorelei, op. 53, no. 2; Spanisches Liederspiel, op. 74: Melan-
     cholie; Gestandnis; Der Kontrabandiste; Tragoedie I-II, op. 64.
     Dietrich Fischer-Dieskau, bar; Christoph Eschenbach, pno. DG
     2740 200 (3) (*From 2530 543)
              +FF 1/2-80 p147   ++HFN 9-79 p112
              ++Gr 9-79 p501   +RR 9-79 p127
              ++Gr 11-79 p896   +STL 3-9-80 p41

     Songs: Belsazar, op. 57; Die beiden Grenadiere, op. 49, no. 1; Dich-
       terliebe, op. 48: Ich grolle nicht; Liederkreis, op. 24: Schone
       Wiege meine Leiden; Lotusblume, op. 25, no. 7; Widmung, op. 25,
       no. 1. See no. 548
     Songs: Der Konig von Thule, op. 67, no. 1; Im Walde, op. 75, no. 2.
       See no. 854
     Songs: Die beiden Grenadiere, op. 49, no. 1; Die Lotosblume, op. 25,
       no. 7. See no. 3573
     Songs: Gedichte, op. 35: Stille Tranen; Soldatenbraut. See no. 3611
     Songs: Gedichte, op. 90, no. 2: Meine Rose. See no. 3774
     Songs: Lied eines Schiedes. See no. 3770
     Songs: The two grenadiers, op. 49, no. 1. See no. 3904
     Songs: Zigeunerleben, op. 29. See no. 3952
     Stucke im Volkston, op. 102 (5). See no. 2960
     Symphonic etudes, op. 13. See no. 2928
2947 Symphonies, nos. 1-4. Manfred overture, op. 115. Bavarian Radio
     Orchestra; Rafael Kubelik. CBS 79324 (3) (also Columbia M3
     35199)

                    +ARG 5-80 p34   +HFN 11-79 p143
                    +-FF 5/6-80 p147   ++NR 12-79 p5
                    +-Gr 10-79 p653   +RR 10-79 p103
                    ++HF 1-80 p88   /SFC 11-4-79 p40
2948 Symphonies, nos. 1-4. Hermann and Dorothea overture, op. 136, B
     minor. The bride of Messina, op. 100. PhO; Riccardo Muti. HMV
     SLS 5199 (3) (From ASD 3781, 3365, 3648, 3696)
                    +-Gr 8-80 p226
2949 Symphonies, nos. 1-4. Manfred overture, op. 115. St. Louis Symph-
     ony Orchestra; Jerzy Semkov. Vox QSVBX 5146 (3) Tape (c) CBX
     5146
                    +ARG 5-78 p39   +-NR 1-78 p2
                    +Audio 5-78 p109   +NYT 11-27-77 pD15
                    -FF 7/8-78 p83   +SFC 12-11-77 p61
                    +-HF 9-78 p95   +St 3-80 p107 tape
                    -MJ 9-78 p35
2950 Symphony, no. 1, op. 38, B flat major. Symphony, no. 4, op. 120,
     D minor. NPhO; Eliahu Inbal. Philips 6570 151 Tape (c) 7310
     151 (From 6500 134)
                    +-FF 11/12-79 p127   +HFN 8-80 p109 tape
                    +Gr 4-80 p1558   +-RR 4-80 p78
                    +HFN 4-80 p119
2951 Symphony, no. 1, op. 38, B flat major. Overture, scherzo and
     finale, op. 52, E major. Leipzig Gewandhaus Orchestra; Kurt
     Masur. RCA GL 2-5285 Tape (c) GK 2-5285
                    -Gr 8-80 p226   -HFN 10-80 p117 tape
                    -HFN 8-80 p107   -RR 8-80 p52
     Symphony, no. 1, op, 38, B flat major. See no. 383. See no. 2161
     Symphony, no. 1, op. 38, B flat major: 1st movement. See no. 3950
2952 Symphony, no. 2, op. 61, C major. Overture, scherzo and finale,
     op. 52, E major. NPhO; Eliahu Inbal. Philips 6570 090 Tape (c)
     7310 090 (From 6580 269)
                    +-Gr 12-79 p1018   +-RR 1-80 p85
                    +-HFN 1-80 p121   +RR 5-80 p107 tape
                    /-HFN 3-80 p107
2953 Symphony, no. 2, op. 61, C major. Hermann and Dorothea overture,
     op. 136, B minor. Leipzig Gewandhaus Orchestra; Kurt Masur.
     RCA GL 2-5286 Tape (c) GK 2-5286
                    /Gr 10-80 p500   +-HFN 10-80 p113
2954 Symphony, no. 3, op. 97, E flat major (orch. Mahler). Manfred over-
     ture, op. 115. PhO; Carlo Maria Giulini. EMI (Japan) EAC 30291
                    -ARSC Vol 12, nos. 1-2, 1980 p88
2955 Symphony, no. 3, op. 97, E flat major. The bride of Messina, op.
     100. PhO; Riccardo Muti. HMV SQ ASD 3696 Tape (c) TC ASD 3696
     (also Angel SZ 37603)
                    +ARG 5-80 p34   +-MT 2-80 p108
                    ++Gr 6-79 p55   ++NR 12-79 p3
                    +Gr 10-79 p727 tape   +NYT 12-9-79 pD25
                    +HFN 9-79 p112   +-RR 7-79 p70
                    ++HFN 9-79 p123 tape   +St 2-80 p133
2956 Symphony, no. 3, op. 97, E flat major. Konzertstuck, op. 86, F
     major. Gerd Seifert, Norbert Hauptmann, Christoph Kohler, Man-
     fred Klier, hn; BPhO; Klaus Tennstedt. HMV ASD 3724 Tape (c) TC
     ASD 3724 (also Angel SZ 37655)
                    +-ARG 4-80 p43   +RR 2-80 p60

+–FF 5/6-80 p147   +RR 5-80 p107
+–Gr 12-79 p1018   +SFC 3-23-80 p35
+–HFN 2-80 p97   ++St 5-80 p92
+–HFN 3-80 p107 tape   ++STL 2-10-80 p40
++NR 4-80 p4

2957 Symphony, no. 3, op. 97, E flat major. Symphony, G minor. NPhO;
Eliahu Inbal. Philips 6570 152 Tape (c) 7310 152
+Gr 4-80 p1558   +–RR 4-80 p78
+–HFN 4-80 p105   +–STL 6-8-80 p38
+HFN 8-80 p109 tape

2958 Symphony, no. 4, op. 120, D minor.* Manfred overture, op. 115.
WEBER: Euryanthe: Overture. BPhO; Wilhelm Furtwangler. DG 2535
805 (*From 16063)
+–FF 5/6-80 p149   +NR 8-80 p6
+Gr 7-78 p199   +RR 6-78 p60
+HFN 6-78 p121

Symphony, no. 4, op. 120, D minor. See no. 883. See no. 2894.
See no. 2950

2959 Symphony, G minor (rev Marc Andreae). Overture, scherzo and finale,
op. 52, E major. Munich Philharmonic Orchestra; Marc Andreae.
Acanta DC 21421
+ARG 11-80 p45   +–RR 5-80 p70
+Gr 8-80 p226   +/ST 9-80 p344
/HFN 5-80 p125

Symphony, G minor. See no. 2957
Theme and variations, E flat major. See no. 2937
Trios, piano, no. 1, op. 63, D minor. See no. 2165
Trios, piano, nos. 1-3. See no. 2914
Variations on ABEGG, op. 1. See no. 2932
Waldscenen, op. 82. See no. 2937
Waldscenen, op. 82: Entrance, Solitary flowers, The prophet bird,
The departure. See no. 2932
Waldscenen, op. 82: The prophet bird. See no. 3907. See no. 2953.
See no. 3954

2960 Works, selections: Adagio and allegro, op. 70, A flat major. Fantasiestucke, op. 73. Fantasiestucke, op. 88. Marchenbilder, op.
113. Marchenerzahlungen, op. 132. Quartet, piano, op. 47, E
flat major. Quartets, strings, nos. 1-3. Quintet, piano, op.
44, E flat major. Romances, op. 94 (3). Sonatas, violin and
piano, no. 1, op. 105, A minor; no. 2, op. 121, D minor. Stucke
im Volkston, op. 102. Trios, piano, nos. 1-3. Jean Jubeau,
Daria Hovora, pno; Jean Mouillere, Jean-Pierre Sabouret, vln;
Claude Naveau, Gerard Causse, vla; Jean-Marie Gamard, Frederic
Lodeon, vlc; Pierre del Vescova, hn; Pierre Pierot, ob; Walter
Boeykens, clt; Via Nova Quartet. Erato STU 71252 (7)
+Gr 11-80 p692

SCHURMANN, Gerard
2961 Studies of Francis Bacon (6). Variants. BBC Symphony Orchestra;
Gerard Schurmann. Chandos ABR 1011 Tape (c) ABT 1011
++Gr 8-80 p229   +MT 11-80 p711
+–HFN 10-80 p117 tape   +RR 8-80 p53
+HFN 10-80 p122

Variants. See no. 2961

SCHUTZ, Heinrich
Christ to thee be glory. See no. 3970

2962 Geistliche Chormusik, 1648. Gundula Bernat-Klein, Annemarie Topler-
       Marizy, Herrad Wehrung, s; Frauke Hasseman, Maureen Lehane, con;
       Theo Altmeyer, Hans-Dieter Ellenbeck, Johannes Hoefflin, Fried-
       reich Melzer, Hans-Dieter Saretzki, Gert Spiering, t; Wilhelm
       Pommerien, bs; Westphalian Choir; Wilhelm Ehmann. Cantata 660
       503/5 (3)
                    +HFN 8-80 p103
       Die Himmel erzahlen. See no. 3528
2963 Songs (choral): Domini est terra, S 476 (from Psalm 24); Erbarm dich
       mein, S 447; Heute ist Christus der Herr geboren, S 439; O bone
       Jesu, S 471; Song of Simeon, S 433; Vater Abraham, S 477. Ars
       Europea Choeur National; Jacques Grimbert. Harmonia Mundi HMU
       958
                    +-HFN 5-76 p109   +RR 3-76 p71
                    +-HFN 9-80 p110
       Die Wort der Einsetzung des heiligen Abandmahls. See no. 3765
SCHWANENBERG
       Sonata, piano, B flat major (attrib. Haydn). See no. 1696
SCHWANTNER, Joseph
       ...Amid the mountains rising nowhere. See no. 1126
SCHWARTZ, Elliott
       Extended oboe. See no. 993
SCHWARZ, Jean
2964 Erda. Symphonie. Harmonia Mundi INA GRM AM 71503
                    +FF 7/8-80 p16
       Symphonie. See no. 2964
SCOTT
       The gentle maiden. See no. 3964
       Tallahassee suite. See no. 3964
SCOTTO (15th century Italy)
       O fallace speranza. See no. 3864
SCRIABIN, Alexander
       Caresse dansee, op. 57, no. 2. See no. 2966
       Concerto, piano, op. 20, F sharp minor. See no. 2750
       Dances, op. 73 (2). See no. 2967
       Danse languide, op. 51, no. 4. See no. 2966
       Day dreams, op. 24. See no. 337
       Desir, op. 57, no. 1. See no. 2966
       Etude, op. 2, no. 1, C sharp minor. See no. 2966
2965 Etudes, op. 8. Sonata, piano, no. 2, op. 19, G sharp minor. Angela
       Brownridge, pno. Meridian E 77035
                    +Gr 12-80 p854   +-HFN 12-80 p145
       Etudes, op. 8. See no. 2545
       Etudes, op. 8, no. 12, D sharp minor. See no. 2966
       Etudes, op. 42, no. 3. See no. 2966
       Etudes, op. 65, nos. 1-3. See no. 1425
       Feuillet d'album, op. 45, no. 1, E flat major. See no. 2966
       Mazurka, op. 3, no. 3, D minor. See no. 2966
       Mazurka, op. 25, no. 7, F sharp minor. See no. 3833
       Nuances, op. 56, no. 3. See no. 2966
2966 Piano works: Caresse dansee, op. 57, no. 2. Danse languide, op.
       51, no. 4. Desir, op. 57, no. 1. Etudes, op. 2, no. 1, C sharp
       minor; op. 8, no. 12, D sharp minor; op. 42, no. 3. Feuillet d'
       album, op. 45, no. 1, E flat major. Mazurka, op. 3, no. 3, G
       minor. Nuances, op. 56, no. 3. Poemes, op. 69 (2). Preludes,

op. 16, no. 4; op. 27, no. 2; op. 48, no. 4. Sonatas, no. 5,
op. 53, F sharp minor; no. 10, op. 70, C major. Vers la flamme,
op. 72. Dag Achatz, pno. BIS LP 119
    +-HFN 3-80 p97   +-RR 3-80 p87
2967 Piano works: Dances, op. 73 (2). Pieces, piano, op. 56 (4). Poemes, op. 32 (2). Sonatas, piano, nos. 2, 7, 10. Vladimir Ashkenazy, pno. Decca SXL 6868 (also Dondon CS 7087)
      +-FF 3/4-79 p113   ++NR 1-80 p14
      +Gr 9-78 p508   +RR 7-78 p32
      +HFN 7-78 p103   ++SFC 8-5-79 p53
      +HFN 12-78 p161   ++St 2-79 p135
      +MM 5-79 p34
Pieces, piano, op. 56 (4). See no. 2967
2968 Poeme de l'extase, op. 54. Prometheus, poem of fire, op. 60. Gil-
bert Johnson, tpt; Vladimir Sokoloff, pno; Mendelssohn Club of
Philadelphia; PO; Eugene Ormandy. RCA GL 4-2870 Tape (c) GK 4-
2870 (From SB 6854)
      +Gr 10-79 p653   +RR 11-79 p94
      -HFN 10-79 p169   +-RR 3-80 p105 tape
      -HFN 1-80 p123 tape
Poeme de l'extase, op. 54. See no. 1193. See no. 2969
Poeme tragique, op. 34. B major. See no. 1180
Poemes, op. 32. See no. 2967. See no. 1783
Poemes, op. 32, no. 2, F sharp major. See no. 3833
Poemes, op. 69 (2). See no. 2966
Preludes, op. 11. See no. 2656
Preludes, op. 11, no. 9, E major. See no. 1180
Preludes, op. 16, no. 4. See no. 2966
Preludes, op. 27, no. 2. See no. 2966
Preludes, op. 48, no. 4. See no. 2966
Prometheus, poem of fire, op. 60. See no. 2968. See no. 2969
Sonatas, piano, nos. 2, 7, 10. See no. 2967
Sonatas, piano, no. 2, op. 19, G sharp minor. See no. 2965
Sonatas, piano, no. 5, op. 53, F sharp major. See no. 2620. See
no. 2966. See no. 3820
Sonatas, piano, no. 10, op. 70, C major. See no. 1425. See no.
2966
2969 Symphonies, nos. 1-3. Poeme de l'extase, op. 54. Prometheus,
poem of fire, op. 60. Frankfurt Radio Orchestra; Eliahu Inbal.
Philips 6769 041 (4)
      +Gr 9-80 p349   +-HFN 9-80 p111
Vers la flamme, op. 72. See no. 2620. See no. 2966
SCRONX, Gherardus
Echo, C major. See no. 3682
Echo, F major, C major. See no. 68
SEEGER, Ruth Crawford
Diaphonic suite, no. 1. See no. 3649
Quartet, strings. See no. 1279
SEGERSTAM, Leif
2970 Concerto serioso, violin, Patria. Skizzen aus "Pandora". Hannele
Segerstam, vln; Austrian Radio Orchestra; Leif Segerstam. BIS
LP 84
      +FF 9/10-79 p138   +-RR 4-80 p79
Patria. See no. 2970
Skizzen aus "Pandora". See no. 2970

Songs of experience. See no. 648
SEGOND, Pierre
    Psalm, no. 24. See no. 3734
SEIBER, Matyas
    Introduction and allegro. See no. 3651
SEITZ
    University of Pennsylvania march. See no. 4012
SELBY, Luard
    Psalm, no. 67. See no. 3567
SEMENZATO, Domingo
    Divagando. See no. 3706
SENFL, Ludwig
    Ach Elslein liebe Elselein. See no. 4004
    Es taget vor dem Walde. See no. 4042
    Fortuna ad voces musicales. See no. 4004
    Ich armes Kauzlein Klein. See no. 4004
    Im Maien. See no. 4004
    Mit Lust tat ich ausreiten. See no. 3626
    Nun wollt ihr horen neue Mar. See no. 3864
    Songs: Carmen in la; Carmen in re; Nasci pati mori. See no. 3702
    Songs: Das Gelaut zu Speyer; Es taget vor dem Walde; Es wollt ein
        Frau zum Weine gahn; Fortuna Nasci pati mori; Ich armes Kauzlein
        kleine; Patienca muss ich han. See no. 3536
SENNY, Edouard
    Plain chant pour une cathedrale. See no. 165
    Vitrail pour Jeanne d'Arc. See no. 3736
SERMILA
    Monody, horn and percussion. See no. 3842
SERMISY, Claude de
    A douce amour. See no. 3683
    Allez souspirs. See no. 3795
    Amour me voyant. See no. 3795
    Dont vient cela. See no. 4042
    Tant que vivray. See no. 3744. See no. 3805
SEROCKI, Kazimierz
    Fantasia elegiaca. See no. 3857
SEROV, Alexander
    Judith: I put on my garments. See no. 3770
    The power of evil: Yeromka's song. See no. 3796
SERRADELL
    La golondrina. See no. 3831
SERRANO, Jose
    La alegria del batallon. See no. 3930
    La alegria del batallon: Cancion guijira. See no. 3919
    Alma de Dios. See no. 3888
    Alma de Dios: Cancion hungara. See no. 3919
    Los de Aragon: Cuantas veces solo. See no. 3919
    El principe carneval: Cancion espanola. See no. 3774
SESSIONS, Roger
    Quartet, no. 1, E minor. See no. 2518
    Sonata, piano, no. 2. See no. 781
SEVERAC, Deodat de
    Le soldat de plomb. See no. 1004
SHAKESPEARE, William
    Sonnets and plays, excerpts. See no. 3853

SHAPERO, Harold
2971 Symphony, classical orchestra. Columbia Symphony Orchestra; Leonard
        Bernstein. CRI SRD 424
                    +ARG 7/8-80 p39   +NYT 2-24-80 pD20
                    +FF 5/6-80 p150
SHAPEY, Ralph
        Rhapsodie. See no. 3649
SHARP
        Dearest of all. See no. 3875
SHARPE, Trevor
        Ceremonial occasion. See no. 4029
        Nulli secundus. See no. 4029
        Royal jubilee. See no. 4029
        Soldiers: Fantasia (arr. Sharpe). See no. 4029
SHAW, Martin
        The greater light. See no. 3533. See no. 3936
SHEPHERD, Arthur
        Capriccio II. See no. 1768
        Eclogue, no. 4. See no. 1768
        Exotic dances (2). See no. 1768
        Gigue fantasque. See no. 1768
        In modo ostinato. See no. 1768
        Lento amabile. See no. 1768
SHERIFF, Noam
        Mai ko mashma lan. See no. 3564
SHOSTAKOVICH, Dmitri
        The age of gold, op. 22. See no. 2986
        Christopher Columbus, op. 19, no. 1: Overture. See no. 3781
2972 Concerto, piano, no. 1, op. 35, C minor. STRAVINSKY: Capriccio.
        John Ogdon, pno; John Wilbraham, tpt; AMF; Neville Marriner.
        Argo ZRG 674 Tape (r) E 674
                        ++Audio 3-79 p97   ++MJ 12-72 p64
                        ++HF 12-72 p108   ++NR 10-72 p5
                        +HF 5-80 p90 tape   +-St 1-73 p117
                        ++HFN 2-72 p315
        Concerto, piano, no. 2, op. 101, F major: 2nd movement. See no.
        3605
        Duets, violin (3). See no. 2202
        Festive overture, op. 96. See no. 1488. See no. 2982. See no.
        2987
        The gadfly, op. 97a: Romance. See no. 2987. See no. 3694
2973 The gamblers. Boris Tarkhov, Nikolai Kurpe, t; Yaroslav Radivonik,
        bar; Vladimir Ribassenko, Valerii Byelikh, Ashot Sarkissov, bs;
        Leningrad Philharmonic Orchestra; Gennady Rozhdestvensky. Melo-
        diya/Eurodisc 200 370405 (also HMV ASD 3880)
                        +FF 9/10-80 p204   ++Gr 9-80 p399
        The golden age, op. 22. See no. 1504
        King Lear: Songs of the fool. See no. 2418
2974 Lady Macbeth of Mtsensk, op. 29. Galina Vishnevskaya, Taru Valjak-
        ka, s; Birgit Finnila, ms; Nicolai Gedda, Werner Krenn, Robert
        Tear, Martyn Hill, Alexander Malta, t; Dimiter Petkov, Leonard
        Mroz, Aage Haugland, bs; Ambrosian Opera Chorus; LPO; Mstislav
        Rostropovich. HMV SLS 5157 (3) (also Angel SDLX 3866)
                        +ARG 10-79 p21   +ON 12-8-79 p28
                        ++Audio 3-80 p44   +-RR 6-79 p62

++FF 9/10-79 p140   ++SFC 7-8-79 p43
+Gr 5-79 p1930   ++SR 8-79 p47
++HF 9-79 p103   +St 10-79 p93
++HFN 6-79 p101   +STL 12-2-79 p37
+MM 11-79 p26

Preludes, op. 34, nos. 1, 4, 10, 12, 14-16, 19, 22, 24. See no.
    2411
Preludes, op. 34, no. 17, A flat amjor. See no. 3601
2975 Quartet, strings, no. 1, op. 49, C major. Quartet, strings, no. 2,
    op. 68, A major. Fitzwilliam Quartet. L'Oiseau-Lyre DSLO 31
        ++ARG 6-80 p41   +-HFN 3-79 p131
        +FF 3/4-80 p152   ++MT 6-79 p491
        +Gr 3-79 p1583   ++RR 4-79 p91
        +HF 1-80 p89   ++ST 9-79 p362
    Quartet, strings, no. 2, op. 68, A major. See no. 2975
    Quartet, strings, no. 3, op. 73, F major. See no. 2538
    Quartet, strings, no. 7, op. 108, F sharp major. See no. 382
2976 Quintet, piano, op. 57, G minor. Trio, piano, op. 67, E minor.
    Roger Woodward, pno; Edinburgh Quartet. RCA RL 2-5224 Tape (c)
    RK 2-5224
        +-Gr 1-80 p1168   +-RR 1-80 p95
        /HFN 1-80 p109   +-ST 9-80 p340
2977 Sonata, viola and piano, op. 147. Sonata, violin and piano, op.
    134. Gidon Kremer, vln; Andrei Gavrilov, pno; Fyodor Druzhinin,
    vla; Michael Muntyan, pno. Columbia M 35109
        +-FF 3/4-80 p152   ++SFC 7-8-79 p43
        +FU 12-79 p49   ++St 12-79 p152
    Sonata, violin and piano, op. 134. See no. 2543. See no. 2977
    Sonata, violoncello and piano, op. 40, D minor. See no. 2544. See
    no. 2859
2978 Songs: (Burns) In the fields, Jeannie, MacPherson before his exe-
    cution; (Michelangelo) Truth, Morning, Love, Parting, Rage,
    Dante, To the exile, Creativity, Night, Death, Immortality;
    (Raleigh) To a son; (Shakespeare) Sonnet, no. 66; (Tsvetayeva)
    Hamlet's dialogue with his conscience; My poems; No the drumbeat,
    Poet and Tsar, To Anna Akhmatova, Whence such tenderness; (Trad.)
    King's procession. Irina Bogacheva, ms; Yevgeny Nesterenko, bs;
    MCO, MRSO; Maxim Shostakovich, Rudolf Barshai. Columbia M3 34594
    (2)
        +ARG 5-80 p38   +-NR 12-79 p11
        +-FF 3/4-80 p152   +ON 12-8-79 p28
        ++HF 4-80 p96   ++St 3-80 p84
    Songs: Preface to the complete collection of my works and brief re-
    flections, op. 123; Romance to words from "Krokodil", op. 121;
    Verses of Captain Lebyadkin, op. 146. See no. 2418
    Symphony, no. 1, op. 10, F minor. See no. 2550
2979 Symphony, no. 4, op. 43, C minor. LPO; Bernard Haitink. Decca SXL
    6927 Tape (c) KSXC 6927 (also London CS 7160)
        +FF 9/10-80 p204   +-HFN 12-79 p170
        +-Gr 11-79 p840   ++RR 12-79 p75
        +HF 11-80 p79   +STL 12-2-79 p37
2980 Symphony, no. 5, op. 47, D minor. NY: Leonard Bernstein. CBS IM
    35854 Tape (c) HMT 35854 (also CBS 35854 Tape (c) 40-35854)
        ++FF 11/12-80 p173   +HFN 12-80 p145
        +Gr 12-80 p836   ++SFC 10-26-80 p20
        +-HF 9-80 p78

2981 Symphony, no. 5, op. 47, D minor. Bournemouth Symphony Orchestra;
       Paavo Berglund. Classics for Pleasure CFP 40330 Tape (c) TC CFP
       40330 (From HMV SLS 5044)
                         ++Gr 6-80 p38   ++RR 6-80 p58
                         +HFN 5-80 p135
2982 Symphony, no. 5, op. 47, D minor. Festive overture, op. 96. USSR
       Symphony Orchestra; Yevgeny Svetlanov. HMV ASD 3855 Tape (c)
       TC ASD 3855
                         +Gr 5-80 p1672   +RR 5-80 p71
                         +-HFN 5-80 p125
2983 Symphony, no. 5, op. 47, D minor. OSR; Istvan Kertesz. London STS
       15492
                         +-FF 3/4-80 p152
2984 Symphony, no. 5, op. 47, D minor. MPO; Kiril Kondrashin. Quintes-
       sence PMC 7156 (also Melodiya/Angel 4004)
                         +-FF 11/12-80 p174
2985 Symphony, no. 6, op. 54, B minor. Symphony, no. 11, op. 103, G min-
       or. Bournemouth Symphony Orchestra; Paavo Berglund. HMV SLS
       5177 (2)
                    ++Gr 2-80 p1270   +RR 4-80 p79
                    +HFN 3-80 p99   ++STL 2-10-80 p40
                    ++MT 10-80 p635
2986 Symphony, no. 7, op. 60. The age of gold, op. 22. LPO; Bernard
       Haitink. Decca D213D2 (2)
                         +Gr 11-80 p678
2987 Symphony, no. 7, op. 70, E flat major. Festive overture, op. 96.
       The gadfly, op. 97a: Romance. Tahiti trot, op. 16. USSR State
       Academic Symphony Orchestra; Yevgeny Svetlanov. Melodiya 33S 10
       10339/400
                    +ARG 7/8-80 p54
     Symphony, no. 9, op. 70, E flat major: Movements, nos. 1, 4-5. See
       no. 1533
     Symphony, no. 11, op. 103, G minor. See no. 2985
2988 Symphony, no. 15, op. 141, A major. LPO; Bernard Haitink. Decca
       SXL 6906 Tape (c) KSXC 6906 (also London CS 7130)
                    +Audio 6-79 p131   +NR 4-80 p3
                    ++FF 3/4-80 p152   +NYT 11-18-79 pD24
                    +Gr 3-79 p1572   +RR 3-79 p89
                    +Gr 6-79 p109 tape   +SFC 2-3-80 p45
                    +HFN 2-79 p107   ++St 10-79 p147
                    ++HFN 4-79 p134 tape   ++STL 2-10-80 p40
                    +MT 7-79 p582
     Tahiti trot, op. 16. See no. 2987
2989 Trio, piano, op. 67, E minor. SCHUMANN: Bilder aus Osten, op. 66.
       Valeria Volker, vln; Beth Pearson, vlc; Eric Stumacher, Robert
       Merfeld, pno. Sine Qua Non SAS 2039
                    +-FF 3/4-80 p152
     Trio, piano, op. 67, E minor. See no. 490. See no. 2976
SIBELIUS, Jean
     Belshazzar's feast, op. 51. See no. 3008
2990 Concerto, violin, op. 47, D minor. SINDING: Suite, op. 10, A min-
       or. Itzhak Perlman, vln; Pittsburgh Symphony Orchestra; Andre
       Previn. Angel SZ 37663 (also HMV ASD 3933 Tape (c) TC ASD 3933)
                    +Gr 10-80 p502   +HFN 12-80 p159 tape
                    +NYT 11-30-80 p35B   +HFN 12-80 p146

2991 Concerto, violin, op. 47, D minor. Scenes historiques, op. 25: Fes-
     tivo. Scenes historiques, op. 66: The chase; Love song; At the
     drawbridge. Isaac Stern, vln; RPO; Thomas Beecham. CBS 61876
              +ARSC Vol 12, no. 3, 1980 p251
2992 Concerto, violin, op. 47, D minor. Melodies, op. 77 (2). Serenad-
     es, op. 69 (2). Boris Belkin, vln; PhO; Vladimir Ashkenazy.
     Decca SXL 6953 Tape (c) KSXC 6953 (also London CS 7181)
              +Gr 6-80 p43   +NYT 11-30-80 p35B
              +-HF 10-80 p86   +RR 8-80 p65
              ++HFN 6-80 p112
2993 Concerto, violin, op. 47, D minor. Humoresques (6). Pierre Amoyal,
     vln; PhO; Charles Dutoit. Erato STU 71324
              +HFN 12-80 p145
2994 Concerto, violin, op. 47, D minor. Scenes historiques, op. 25: Fes-
     tivo. Scenes historiques, op. 66. Isaac Stern, vln; RPO; Thomas
     Beecham. Odyssey Y 35200 (From Columbia ML 4550) (also CBS 61876.
     From Columbia LX 8947/50, 33C 1018)
              +ARSC Vol 12, no. 3   +-HFN 1-80 p121
                 1980 p251   +-FF 9/10-79 p143
              +-FF 9/10-79 p143   ++ST 3-80 p837
              +-Gr 1-80 p1158   ++NYT 4-18-79 pD28
2995 Concerto, violin, op. 47, D minor. Humoresques (6). Salvatore
     Accardo, vln; LSO; Colin Davis. Philips 9500 675 Tape (c) 7300
     770
              ++FF 9/10-80 p206   ++MUM 10-80 p32
              ++FF 11/12-80 p174 tape   +NR 9-80 p5
              +Gr 10-80 p502   +NYT 7-6-80 pD15
              +HF 10-80 p86   +-NYT 11-30-80 p35B
              +-HFN 11-80 p123   +SFC 7-27-80 p34
              +-HFN 12-80 p159 tape   +St 11-80 p100
     Concerto, violin, op. 47, D minor. See no. 2438. See no. 2533.
        See no. 2806. See no. 3772. See no. 3968
2996 Finlandia, op. 26. SMETANA: Ma Vlast: The Moldau. BPhO; Herbert
     von Karajan. Angel SS 45017
              +ARG 2-80 p55
2997 Finlandia, op. 26. Karelia suite, op. 11. Legends, op. 22: The
     swan of Tuonela. En saga, op. 9. PO; Eugene Ormandy; Morman
     Tabernacle Choir. CBS 61938 Tape (c) 40-61938
              +Gr 1-80 p1203   +-HFN 2-80 p107 tape
              +-HFN 1-80 p121   +RR 1-80 p86
2998 Finlandia, op. 26. Karelia suite, op. 11. Legends, op. 22: The
     swan of Tuonela. Kuolema, op. 44: Valse triste. Tapiola, op.
     112. NPhO, OSR; Kazimierz Kord, Ernest Ansermet. Decca SPA
     549 (From PFS 4378)
              +Gr 10-79 p723   +RR 12-79 p66
              +HFN 10-79 p169   ++STL 12-9-79 p41
              +-HFN 1-80 p121
     Finlandia, op. 26. See no. 651. See no. 1560. See no. 3000
     Humoresques. See no. 2993. See no. 2995
     Hymn, op. 113, no. 1. See no. 1896
     Impromptu, op. 5, no. 1. See no. 1896
     Karelia suite, op. 11. See no. 1560. See no. 2997. See no. 2998
     Kuolema, op. 44: Valse triste. See no. 1546. See no. 2998
2999 Legends, op. 22. PO; Eugene Ormandy. Angel S 37537 Tape (c) 4XS
     37537 (also HMV ASD 3644 Tape (c) TC ASD 3644)

++ARG 7-79 p15   +–HFN 1-80 p121
-FF 7/8-79 p90   +NR 5-79 p2
+–FU 9-79 p59   +NYT 4-1-79 pD26
++Gr 4-79 p1719   ++RR 5-79 p69
++HF 7-79 p148   ++SFC 4-1-79 p44
++HFN 5-79 p125   ++St 8-79 p116
++HFN 6-79 p117 tape

Legends, op. 22: Lemminkainen and the maidens of Saari. See no. 651
Legends, op. 22: The swan of Tuonela. See no. 1560. See no. 2997.
    See no. 2998. See no. 3007
Marche funebre, op. 113, no. 8. See no. 1896
Melodies, op. 77. See no. 2992
Night ride and sunrise, op. 55. See no. 3585
The oceanides, op. 73. See no. 3013
On hangel korkeat nietokset, op. 1, no. 5. See no. 3592
Pieces, organ, op. 111: Funeral; Intrada. See no. 1896
Pieces, violin and piano, op. 78, nos. 1-4. See no. 3014
Pieces, violin and piano, op. 81, nos. 1-3, 5. See no. 3014
Pieces, violin and piano, op. 115, nos. 1-4. See no. 3014
Pieces, violin and piano, op. 116, nos. 1-2. See no. 3014
Quartet, strings, op. 56, D minor. See no. 1564
Rakastava, op. 14. See no. 1546
Romance, op. 24, no. 9, D flat major. See no. 3677
Romance, op. 42, C major. See no. 3008
En saga, op. 9. See no. 2997
Scenes historiques, op. 25: Festivo. See no. 2991. See no. 2994
Scenes historiques, op. 66. See no. 2994
Scenes historiques, op. 66: The chase; Love song; At the drawbridge.
    See no. 2991
Serenades, op. 69. See no. 2992
Songs: Diamanten pa marssnon; Svarta rosor. See no. 1880
Suite champetre, op. 98b. See no. 1265
3000 Symphony, no. 1, op. 39, E minor. Finlandia, op. 26. BSO; Colin
     Davis. Philips 9500 140 Tape (c) 7300 517 (r) G 9500 140
                  +–Audio 11-77 p126   ++HFN 5-77 p138 tape
                  +Gr 3-77 p1409   +NR 3-77 p4
                  +Gr 8-77 p349 tape   +RR 3-77 p61
                  ++HF 6-77 p100   +RR 7-77 p100
                  +HF 9-77 p119 tape   +SFC 1-23-77 p37
                  +HF 11-80 p88   ++St 7-77 p124
                  +HFN 3-77 p111
3001 Symphony, no. 2, op. 43, D major. BBC Symphony Orchestra; Thomas
     Beecham. Arabesque 8023 Tape (c) 9023 (also World SH 1007)
                  +ARG 11-80 p32   +HF 9-80 p98
                  +–ARSC Vol 12, no. 3   +–NYT 11-30-80 p35B
                     1980 p241   +St 11-80 p100
                  +FF 9/10-80 p207
3002 Symphony, no. 2, op. 43, D major. Sinfonia of London; Tauno Hanni-
     kainen. Classics for Pleasure CFP 40315 Tape (c) TC CFP 40315
     (From World Records ST 33)
                  +Gr 11-79 p840   +RR 12-79 p76
                  -HFN 10-79 p169   +RR 5-80 p107 tape
                  -HFN 1-80 p123 tape
3003 Symphony, no. 2, op. 43, D major. PhO; Herbert von Karajan. HMV
     SXLP 30414 Tape (c) TC SXLP 30414 (From Columbia SAX 2379)

```
                ++Gr 1-80 p1161                  +RR 3-80 p59
                +HFN 1-80 p121                   +RR 5-80 p106 tape
                +HFN 4-80 p121 tape
```

3004 Symphony, no. 2, op. 43, D major. PhO; Vladimir Ashkenazy. London
     LDR 10014 (also Decca SXDL 7513 Tape (c) KSXDC 7513)
```
                ++Gr 11-80 p678                  +HFN 11-80 p123
                +-Gr 12-80 p889 tape             +NYT 11-30-80 p35B
```

3005 Symphony, no. 2, op. 43, D major. PO; Eugene Ormandy. RCA GL 4-
     2868 Tape (c) GK 4-2868 (From ARD 1-0018)
```
                +Gr 4-80 p1558                   -HFN 8-80 p109 tape
                -HFN 4-80 p119                   +-RR 4-80 p80
```

3006 Symphony, no. 3, op. 52, C major. Symphony, no. 7, op. 105, C maj-
     or. MRSO; Gennady Rozhdestvensky. HMV ASD 3671 (From Melodiya
     C10 05639/40, C 10 05643/4)
```
                +Gr 8-79 p343                    +-MT 1-80 p36
                +-HFN 7-79 p112
```

3007 Symphony, no. 4, op. 63, A minor. Legends, op. 22: The swan of
     Tuonela. Gerard Stempnik, cor anglais; BPhO; Herbert von Kara-
     jan. DG 2542 128 Tape (c) 3342 128 (From SLPM 138974)
```
                ++Gr 8-80 p229                   +HFN 9-80 p116 tape
                ++Gr 9-80 p413 tape              +RR 8-80 p54
                +HFN 8-80 p107
```

3008 Symphony, no. 4, op. 63, A minor. Belshazzar's feast, op. 51. Rom-
     ance, op. 42, C major. MRSO, Leningrad Philharmonic Orchestra;
     Gennady Rozhdestvensky. HMV ASD 3699 (From CM 03189/90, ASD
     2407)
```
                +Gr 8-79 p343                    +MT 1-80 p36
                +-HFN 9-79 p112                  +-RR 9-79 p97
```

3009 Symphony, no. 5, op. 82, E flat major. RAUTAVAARA: A requiem for
     our time. Helsinki Philharmonic Orchestra; Jorma Panula. Fin-
     landia FA 313
```
                -FF 11/12-80 p175
```

3010 Symphony, no. 5, op. 82, E flat major. Symphony, no. 6, op. 104,
     D minor. MRSO; Gennady Rozhdestvensky. HMV ASD 3780 (From
     Melodiya C10 05639-40, C10 05643-4)
```
                +-Gr 4-80 p1558                  +-RR 5-80 p71
                +-HFN 4-80 p109
```

3011 Symphony, no. 5, op. 82, E flat major. Symphony, no. 7, op. 105,
     C major. PhO; Herbert von Karajan. HMV SXLP 30430 Tape (c) TC
     SXLP 30430 (From Columbia SAX 2392, 33CX 1341)
```
                +Gr 7-80 p147                    +HFN 10-80 p117 tape
                +-HFN 7-80 p115                  +-RR 7-80 p65
```

3012 Symphony, no. 6, op. 104, D minor. Symphony, no. 7, op. 105, C
     major. BPhO; Herbert von Karajan. DG Tape (c) 3342 137
```
                +HFN 12-80 p159 tape
```
     Symphony, no. 6, op. 104, D minor. See no. 3010
3013 Symphony, no. 7, op. 105, C major. The oceanides, op. 73. Tapiola,
     op. 112. RPO; Thomas Beecham. HMV SXLP 30290 Tape (c) TC SXLP
     30290 (From ALP 1480, ASD 518)
```
                +-Gr 6-79 p56                    +-HFN 7-79 p119 tape
                ++ARSC Vol 12, no. 3,
                  1980 p252
```
     Symphony, no. 7, op. 105, C major. See no. 3006. See no. 3011.
     See no. 3012
     Tapiola, op. 112. See no. 1890. See no. 2998. See no. 3013

3014 Works, selections: Pieces, violin and piano, op. 78, nos. 1-4.
     Pieces, violin and piano, op. 81, nos. 1-3, 5. Pieces, violin
     and piano, op. 115, nos. 1-4. Pieces, violin and piano, op. 116,
     nos. 1-2. Yuval Yaron, vln; Rena Stepelman, pno. Finlandia FA
     301
                    +ARG 7/8-80 p55   +HFN 8-79 p111
                    +FF 1/2-80 p147   +-NR 11-80 p5
                    +Gr 10-79 p671   +-RR 8-79 p113
SIECZYNSKI
     Wien, Wien nur du allein. See no. 1863
SIEGMEISTER, Elie
3015 Quartet, strings, no. 3. Songs: The face of war; Madam to you.
     Esther Hinds, s; Alan Mandel, pno; Primavera String Quartet.
     CRI SD 416
                    +ARG 10-80 p48   +NR 5-80 p11
                    +FF 5/6-80 p152   +NYT 2-24-80 pD20
                    +HF 6-80 p84
     Songs: The face of war; Madam to you. See no. 3015
     Songs of experience. See no. 3739
SIFLER, Paul
     The despair and agony of Dachau. See no. 4058
3016 The seven last words of Christ. St. John's Episcopal Church, Los
     Angeles; Paul Sifler, org. Fredonia FD 7
                    +MU 3-80 p8   +NR 9-80 p9
SIKORSKI, Tomasz
     Prologues. See no. 3857
SIMPSON
     Allemande. See no. 3675
SIMPSON, Christopher
     Divisions on a ground, G major, F major, E minor. See no. 1427
SIMPSON, Robert
     Canzona for brass. See no. 3959
3017 Symphony, no. 3. LSO; Jascha Horenstein. Unicorn UNS 262 (From
     UNS 225, 234)
                    +Gr 7-80 p147   +RR 7-80 p65
                    +HFN 7-80 p115
     Volcano. See no. 3620
SIMPSON, Thomas
     Bonny sweet robin. See no. 3853
SIMS, Ezra
3018 Elegie. Quartet, strings, no. 2. Elsa Charlston, s; Boston Musica
     Viva; Richard Pittman. CRI SD 377
                    -ARG 7-78 p27   +NR 7-78 p6
                    +-Audio 8-78 p98   +SFC 9-2-79 p49
                    +-FF 3/4-80 p14
     Quartet, strings, no. 2. See no. 3018
SINDING, Christian
3019 Concerto, piano, op. 6, D flat major. STAVENHAGEN: Concerto, piano,
     op. 4, B minor. Roland Keller, pno; BeSO; Jorg Faerber. Can-
     dide QCE 31110
                    +-ARG 9-79 p40   +-MUM 3/4-80 p34
                    +FF 7/8-79 p91   +SFC 8-12-79 p49
                    +-FU 9-79 p47   +St 10-79 p147
3020 Concerto, piano, op. 6, D flat major. Eva Knardahl, pno; Oslo Phil-
     harmonic Orchestra; Oivin Fjeldstad. NKF 30017

+–FF 3/4-79 p117   +–Gr 1-80 p1167
3021 Pieces, violoncello and piano, op. 66, nos. 1, 3-5. Romances, op.
     9 (3); op. 30; op. 79, no. 1. Kalman Dobos, vlc; Verena Shaw,
     vln; Rosario Marciano, pno. Musical Heritage Society MHS 4108
     +FF 5/6-80 p152
     Romances, op. 9 (3); op. 30; op. 79, no. 1. See no. 3021
     Rondo infinito, op. 42. See no. 3023
     Suite, op. 10, A minor. See no. 2438. See no. 2990
3022 Symphony, no. 1, op. 21, D major. Oslo Philharmonic Orchestra;
     Oivin Fjeldstad. Polydor Norway NKF 30011
                    +–FF 3/4-79 p117   +RR 1-77 p63
                    +–Gr 1-80 p1167   +–RR 1-77 p75
                    +HFN 3-77 p109
3023 Symphony, no. 2, op. 83, D major. Rondo infinito, op. 42. Oslo
     Philharmonic Orchestra; Kjell Ingebretsen. NKF 30025
                    +FF 5/6-79 p92   +HFN 7-80 p110
                    +–Gr 9-80 p408

SINGER
     Work. See no. 3649
SINIGAGLIA, Leone
     Adagio tragico, op. 21. See no. 777
     Romanze, op. 3. See no. 624
SJOGREN, Emil
     Sonata, violoncello, op. 58, A major. See no. 1579
SKEATS, H.
     Psalm, no. 139. See no. 3567
SLATER
     From Oberon in fairyland. See no. 4007
SLAVICKY, Milan
     Brightening I. See no. 4010
SLOMINSKY, Sergei
     Dramatic song. See no. 1391
3024 Icarus. Bolshoi Theatre Orchestra and Chorus; Eri Klas. Melodiya
     C10 08867/8 (2)
                    +–FF 9/10-80 p224
SMAREGLIA, Antonio
3025 Nozze istriane. Renata Mattioli, Franco Pugliese, Guido Mazzini,
     Luigi Rumbo, Nestore Catalani, Dora Minarchi; Teatro Giuseppe
     Verdi Orchestra and Chorus; Sergio Amadi. A.N.N.A. Recording
     Company ANNA 1003 (2)
                    +–FF 11/12-80 p175
SMETANA, Bedrich
     The bartered bride (Die verkaufte Braut): Arias. See no. 3539
     The bartered bride: Endlich allein; Wie fremd und tot. See no. 3780
     The bartered bride: Hans aria, Act 2. See no. 3641
     The bartered bride: Marenka-Jenik duets; Jenik's aria, Act 2. See
        no. 3633
     The bartered bride: Overture. See no. 3638
     Czech song. See no. 1311
     Dalibor: Blickst du mein Freund; Jakje mi. See no. 3770
     Dalibor: Slysel's to priteli. See no. 3774
     The devil's wall: Where can I flee. See no. 3633
3026 Dreams, excerpts. Sketches, opp. 4 and 5 (8). Frantisek Rauch,
     pno. Supraphon 111 2587
                    +–FF 9/10-80 p208   ++SFC 7-20-80 p34
                    +NR 8-80 p13

Equisses. See no. 1058
The kiss: If I knew how to redeem my guilt. See no. 3633
3027 Ma Vlast. BSO; Rafael Kubelik. DG 2726 111 (2) (From 2707 054)
                    +Gr 6-80 p43   ++RR 7-80 p66
                    +HFN 7-80 p117
     Ma Vlast: Vltava (The Moldau). See no. 450. See no. 823. See no.
        1321. See no. 2996
3028 Quartet, strings, no. 1, E minor. Quartet, strings, no. 2, D minor.
        Smetana Quartet. Supraphon 410 2130
                    ++ARG 1-80 p41   +HFN 2-80 p99
                    ++FF 9/10-79 p144   +RR 1-80 p96
                    +Gr 3-80 p1411   +St 11-79 p102
                    +HF 1-80 p72
     Quartet, strings, no. 2, D minor. See no. 3028
     Reves. See no. 1058
     The secret: You cast down your sweet eyes. See no. 3633
     Sketches, opp. 4 and 5. See no. 3026
     Trio, piano, op. 15, G minor. See no. 1091
3029 The two widows. Nada Sormova, Daniela Sounova, Marcela Machotkova,
        s; Jiri Zahradnicek, Zdenek Svehla, t; Jaroslav Horacek, bs;
        Prague National Theatre Orchestra and Chorus; Frantisek Jilek.
        Supraphon 112 2041/3
                    +FF 11/12-78 p115   +RR 6-78 p39
                    +Gr 9-78 p544   +SFC 10-15-78 p43
                    +-HFN 7-78 p105   +St 11-78 p137
                    +NR 9-78 p12   ++STL 1-27-80 p39
     The two widows: Ladislav's aria. See no. 3633
SMITH, Claude
     Anthem, winds and percussion. See no. 3030
     Dance prelude. See no. 3030
     Jubilant prelude. See no. 3030
     March on an Irish air. See no. 3030
     Overture on an early American folk hymn. See no. 3030
     Symphony, band, no. 1. See no. 3030
3030 Works, selections: Anthem, winds and percussion. Dance prelude.
        Jubilant Prelude. March on an Irish air. Overture on an early
        American folk hymn. Symphony, band, no. 1. Southwestern State
        University Wind Symphony; James Jurrens. Golden Crest ATH 5064
                    +ARG 5-80 p40
SMITH, Gregg
     Steps. See no. 4026
SMITH, Robert Edward
3031 Variations on an American folktune. John Rose, org. Towerhill T
        1004
                    +Audio 6-80 p112   +FF 9/10-80 p266
SMITH-BRINDLE, Reginald
     El polifemo de oro. See no. 3599
SODERMAN
     Swedish festival music. See no. 1930
SOJO, Vicente
     Pieces from Venezuela (5). See no. 3634
SOKOLA, Milos
     Passacaglia quasi toccata on B-A-C-H. See no. 3732
SOLA, Andres de
     Medio registro de mano derecho. See no. 3756

Tiento, no. 1, de 1 tono. See no. 3871
SOLER Y RAMOS, Antonio
3032 Concerto, 2 harpsichords, no. 3, G major. Fandango. Sonatas, harp-
     sichord, F sharp major, C sharp minor, D major, D flat major, D
     minor, C minor. Rafael Puyana, Genoveva Galvez, hpd. Mercury
     SRI 7513 (From SR 90459)
                    +FF 9/10-80 p209   +HF 12-80 p60
     Concerto, 2 harpsichords, no. 3, G major. See no. 330
3033 Concerti, 2 organs, C major, A major, G major, F major, A minor, D
     major. Kenneth Gilbert, Trevor Pinnock, hpd, fortepianos. DG
     2533 445
                +-FF 9/10-80 p209   +MT 11-80 p711
                +Gr 5-80 p1693   +NR 10-80 p14
                +HF 12-80 p60   ++RR 5-80 p91
                ++HFN 5-80 p125   +St 11-80 p101
     Fandango. See no. 3032
3034 Sonatas, harpsichord, B minor, F minor, G major, E minor, F major,
     D minor (2), F sharp minor, D major, A minor. Gilbert Rowland,
     hpd. Nimbus 2123
                    +-Gr 3-80 p1418   ++RR 2-80 p80
3035 Sonatas, harpsichord, C major (2), A minor, D major (2), C minor
     (2), D flat major, G minor, B flat major. Gilbert Rowland, hpd.
     Nimbus 2128
                    +HFN 9-80 p111   +-STL 8-10-80 p30
                    ++RR 8-80 p75
3036 Sonatas, harpsichord, D minor, E minor, D major, A major, G major.
     Bernard Brauchli, cld. Titantic TI 42
                    +-ARG 11-80 p32   +-HF 12-80 p60
                    +-FF 9/10-80 p208
3037 Sonatas, harpsichord, F sharp major, C sharp minor, G minor. D
     flat major, D minor, D major, F sharp minor, F major. Alicia
     de Larrocha, pno. Turnabout TV 34753 (From Epic BC 1389)
                    +FF 9/10-80 p208   +HF 12-80 p60
     Sonatas, harpsichord, F sharp major, C sharp minor, D major, D flat
     major, D minor, C minor. See no. 3032
     Sonatas, harpsichord, G major. See no. 3659
SOMERVELL, Arthur
     A Shropshire lad: Loveliest of trees; When I was one and twenty;
     There pass the careless people; In summertime on Bredon; The
     street sounds to the soldiers tread; On the idle hill of summer;
     White in the moon the long road lies; Think no more lad laugh
     be jolly; Into my heart an air that kills; The lads in their
     hundreds. See no. 3837
SOMMERFELDT, Oistein
     Varlater (Spring tunes), op. 44. See no. 2450. See no. 2589
SOPRONI, Jozsef
3038 Concerto, violoncello. Eklypsis. Quartet, strings, no. 4. Sonata,
     flute and piano. Laszlo Mezo, vlc; Erzsebet Csik, flt; Zoltan
     Kocsis, pno; Hungarian Radio and Television Orchestra; Gyorgy
     Lehel. Hungaroton SLPX 11743
                    +FF 3/4-80 p158   +NR 9-76 p14
     Concerta da camera. See no. 3039
     Eklypsis. See no. 3038
     Intermezzi. See no. 3039
     Musica da camera, no. 2. See no. 3039

Pieces, flute and cimbalom. See no. 3039
Quartet, strings, no. 4. See no. 3038
Sonata, flute and piano. See no. 3038
Sonata, horn and piano. See no. 3039
3039 Works, selections: Concerta da camera. Intermezzi (4). Pieces,
     flute and cimbalom (3). Musica da camera, no. 2. Sonata, horn
     and piano. Gellert Tihanyi, clt; Eszter Perenyi, vln; Miklos
     Perenyi, vlc; Klara Kormendi, pno; Istvan Matuz, flt; Marta
     Fabian, cimb; Ferenc Tarjani, hn; Budapest Chamber Ensemble; An-
     dras Mihaly. Hungaroton SLPX 12061
              +FF 3/4-80 p158   +-NR 3-80 p8
SOR, Fernando
     Les deux amis, op. 41. See no. 3042
     Divertimento, op. 62: Andante cantabile. See no. 3042
     Divertissement, no. 1. See no. 3609
     Fantaisie, op. 38: Introduction; Andantino. See no. 3042
     Fantaisie, op. 54. See no. 216
     Fantaisie on "Ye banks and braes", op. 40. See no. 3040
     Fantaisie villageoise. See no. 3686
3040 Guitar works: Sonata, guitar, op. 14, D major. Sonata, guitar, op.
     15, C major. Theme and variations, without op. number. Vari-
     ations on a theme by Mozart, op. 9. Variations on "Malbrouk
     s'en vat'en guerre", op. 28. Variations on "Ye banks and braes",
     op. 40. Diego Blanco, gtr. BIS LP 133
              +FF 9/10-80 p275   +RR 3-80 p88
              +-HFN 6-80 p112   ++St 8-80 p101
              +NR 7-80 p14
     Minuets, op. 5, no. 3, C major. See no. 3600
     Minuets, op. 24, no. 1, C minor. See no. 3600
     Le premier pas vers moi, op. 53: Andantino; Allegretto. See no.
     3042
     Sonata, guitar, op. 14, D major. See no. 3040
     Sonata, guitar, op. 15, C major. See no. 216. See no. 3040
3041 Sonata, guitar, op. 22, C major. Sonata, guitar, op. 25, C major.
     Pepe Romero, gtr. Philips 9500 586 Tape (c) 7300 709
              +FF 5/6-80 p139   +NYT 6-1-80 pD19
              +NR 7-80 p14   ++St 8-80 p101
     Sonata, guitar, op. 25, C major. See no. 3041
     Souvenie de Russie, op. 63. See no. 3042
     Theme and variations, without op. number. See no. 3040
     Theme varie, op. 9. See no. 3775
     Variations on a theme by Mozart, op. 9. See no. 3040. See no.
     3549
     Variations on "Malbrouk s'en vat'en guerre", op. 28. See no. 3040
     Waltzes, nos. 1-3. See no. 3607. See no. 3635
3042 Works, selections: Les deux amis, op. 41. Divertimento, op. 62:
     Andante cantabile. Fantaisie, op. 38: Introduction; Andantino.
     Le premier pas vers moi, op. 53: Andantino; Allegretto. Souve-
     nie de Russie, op. 63. Philippe Lemaigre, Guy Lukowski, gtr.
     Pavane ADW 7016
              +Gr 1-80 p1172   +RR 3-80 p88
              +-HFN 3-80 p99
SORENSON
     Barn av Guds karlek. See no. 3934

SORIANO, Perez
    Regina caeli. See no. 3934
SOTHCOTT, John
    Fanfare. See no. 3647
SOUSA, John
    Cubaland suite: Under the Spanish flag. See no. 3643
    High school cadets. See no. 3962
    Liberty bell. See no. 3619
    Stars and stripes forever. See no. 3962. See no. 4012. See no.
      4029
SOUTULLO, Reveriano
    Puenteareas. See no. 3921
    El ultimo romantico: Noche de amor noche misteriosa. See no. 3919
SOWERBY, Leo
    Passacaglia. See no. 4058
SPEER, Daniel
    Sonatas, brass ensemble, nos. 1-4. See no. 3569
    Sonatas, brass quintet (2). See no. 3675
SPENTIARIAN, Alexandre
    Enzeli. See no. 3850
    Lullaby. See no. 3850
SPERONTES (Scholze, Johann)
    Songs: Blaustrumpflied; Liebe mich redlich. See no. 3764
    SPIRITUALS. See no. 2930
SPOHR, Ludwig (Louis)
    Concertante, harp and violin. See no. 3044
    Concerto, clarinet, no. 4, E minor. See no. 2228
3043 Concerto, violin, no. 8, op. 47, A minor. VIEUXTEMPS: Concerto,
      violin, no. 5, op. 37, A minor. Thomas Christian, vln; VSO;
      Dietfried Bernet. Acanta DC 21102
                +—Gr 7-80 p147   +RR 8-80 p54
                +—HFN 8-80 p102
3044 Concerto, violin, no. 8, op. 47, A major. Concertante, harp and
      violin. Pierre Amoyal, vln; Marielle Nordmann, hp; Lausanne
      Chamber Orchestra; Armin Jordan. Erato STU 71318
                +—HFN 12-80 p146
    Fantasie, op. 35, A flat major. See no. 1503
3045 Nonet, op. 31, F major. Octet, op. 32, E minor. Nash Ensemble.
      CRD CRD 1054 Tape (c) CRDC 4054
                +Gr 7-79 p216   +MT 8-79 p659
                +HFN 6-79 p109   +RR 6-79 p98
                +HFN 2-80 p107 tape
3046 Nonet, op. 31, F major. Octet, op. 32, E minor. Quintet, op. 52,
      C minor. Septet, op. 147, A minor. Consortium Classicum, Danzi
      Quintet Members; Werner Genuit, pno; Anner Bylsma, vlc; Jaap
      Schroder, vln. MPS 88014 (From BASF 23132)
                +Gr 11-80 p697   +FF 5/6-78 p87
    Octet, op. 32, E minor. See no. 3045. See no. 3046
    Overture to "Faust", op. 60. See no. 919
    Quartet, op. 65, D minor. See no. 2128
    Quintet, op. 52, C minor. See no. 3046
    Septet, op. 147, A minor. See no. 3046
3047 Sonata, violin and harp, op. 113, E flat major. Sonata, violin and
      harp, op. 115, A flat major. Philipp Naegele, vln; Giselle Her-
      bert, hp. Da Camera Magna SM 92915
                +FF 1/2-80 p148

Sonata, violin and harp, op. 115, A flat major. See no. 3047
Waltz, 4 hands, op. 89. See no. 1418
SPONTINI, Gasparo
La vestale: Tu che invoco. See no. 3774
STAIGERS
Carnival of Venice. See no. 3627
STAINER, John
The crucifixion: God so loved the world. See no. 3525
Evening canticles, B flat major. See no. 3815
STAMITZ, Anton (Jan Antonin)
3048 Concerto, violin, B flat major. STAMITZ, C.: Sinfonia concertante,
    D major. Josef Suk, vln; Josef Kodousek, vla; Suk Chamber Or-
    chestra; Hynek Farkac. Supraphon 110 2626
              +Gr 11-80 p678   +HFN 10-80 p109
STAMITZ, Carl
Capriccio sonata, A major. See no. 3629
Concerto, clarinet, E flat major. See no. 2185
Concerti, flute, D major, G major. See no. 89
Concerto, flute, op. 29, G minor. See no. 72
Concerto, horn, E major. See no. 1762
Concerto, viola, D major. See no. 1800
Concerto, viola d'amore, no. 1, D major. See no. 1026
Quartet, strings, op. 8, no. 4, E flat major. See no. 1416
Quartet, strings, op. 19, no. 6, F major. See no. 3804
3049 Sinfonia concertante, D major. Symphony, E flat major. Ulrich
    Grehling, vln; Ulrich Koch, vla; Collegium Aureum; Rolf Rein-
    hardt. Harmonia Mundi 065 99863
              +HFN 7-80 p117   ++RR 7-80 p66
Sinfonia concertante, D major. See no. 3048
Sonata, viola d'amore, D major. See no. 47
Symphony, E flat major. See no. 3049
Trio sonata, G major. See no. 310
STAMITZ, Johann
Concerto, clarinet and 2 horns, B flat major. See no. 2185
Concerto, flute, G major. See no. 2603
Concerto, violin, C major. See no. 3703
Trio, op. 1, no. 5, B flat major. See no. 3703
STANFORD, Charles
Beati quorum via, op. 51, no. 3. See no. 3939
Becket: The martyrdom. See no. 3801
La belle dame sans merci. See no. 3778
Concerto, clarinet, op. 80, A mionr. See no. 1420
Drake's drum. See no. 3991
Evening canticles, G major. See no. 3815
Fantasia and toccata, op. 57, D minor. See no. 2489
Father O'Flynn. See no. 3905
Gloria in excelsis. See no. 3937
The Lord is my shepherd. See no. 3532
Magnificat and nunc dimittis, G major. See no. 3939. See no. 4019
Postlude, D minor. See no. 4052. See no. 4053
Psalms, nos. 95 and 150. See no. 3567
Short preludes and postludes, op. 101, Set II. See no. 2489
Sonata, organ, no. 4, op. 153. See no. 3743
Sonata britannica, op. 152, D minor: Benedictus. See no. 4050

STANKOVICH, Yevgenii
    Triptych: Lullaby; Wedding; Improvisation. See no. 1532
STANLEY, John
3050 Concerti, op. 2, nos. 1-6. Leslie Jones, org; Harold Lester, hpd;
       LOL; Leslie Jones. Desto DC 7189 Tape (c) 47189
            +FF 9/10-80 p210
    Concerto, op. 2, no. 3, G major. See no. 3691
3051 Concerti, organ, op. 10 (6). Gerald Gifford, org; Northern Sinfonia
       Orchestra; Gerald Gifford. CRD CRD 1065 Tape (c) CRDC 4065
              +-Gr 3-80 p1392   +-HFN 4-80 p121 tape
              +-Gr 5-80 p1717 tape   +RR 3-80 p59
              +HFN 3-80 p99
    Concerti, organ, nos. 4 and 6. See no. 3534
    The contemptibles. See no. 3617
    Introduction and trumpet tune. See no. 3582
    Minuet, D major. See no. 3618
    Trumpet tune. See no. 3618
    Trumpet tune and airs: Voluntaries (3). See no. 3661
    Trumpet voluntary . See no. 3895. See no. 3970
    Voluntary, D major. See no. 3545. See no. 4064
    Voluntary, E minor. See no. 2489
    Voluntary, op. 5, no. 1, C major. See no. 4052
STARER, Robert
    Fantasia concertante. See no. 1914
    Quartet, piano. See no. 2720
STARKE, Herman
    With sword and lance. See no. 4029
STAROBIN, David
    Song for David. See no. 4026
STAVENHAGEN, Bernhard
    Concerto, piano, op. 4, B minor. See no. 3019
STEFANI, Giovanni
    Pargoletta che non sai. See no. 3956
STEINBERG
    Shalom Rav. See no. 3922
STELZMULLER, Vincenz
    Stelzmuller Tanz. See no. 3759
STENHAMMAR, Wilhelm
    Fantasies, op. 11 (3). See no. 1566
3052 Florez och Blanzeflor, op. 3. Serenade, op. 31, F major. Swedish
       Radio Orchestra; Ingvar Wixell, bar; Stig Westerberg. HMV 4E
       061 35148
            ++Gr 12-75 p1061   +RR 7-80 p67
            +Gr 8-80 p229
    Little piano pieces (3). See no. 1566
    Serenade, op. 31, F major. See no. 3052
3053 Symphony, no. 2, op. 34, G minor. Stockholm Philharmonic Orchestra;
       Stig Westerberg. Caprice CAP 1151
            ++FF 11/12-79 p128   +RR 12-79 p78
            ++Gr 4-80 p1563
STERN
    Songs: Coquette. See no. 3770
STERNHOLD AND HOPKINS PSALTER
    Psalms, nos. 7, 85, 115. See no. 3848

STEVENS
    All my sense thy sweetness gained. See no. 3791
    Manhattan suite. See no. 4033
STEVENS, John
    Dances. See no. 3654
STEVENS, Noel
    Rhapsody, violoncello and winds. See no. 1825
STEVENSON
    Tell me where if fancy bred. See no. 3774
STEWART
    Crown him with many crowns. See no. 3524
STEWART, Charles Hylton
    Psalms, nos. 23, 39, 69, 90, 130. See no. 3567
STILL
    Ennanga. See no. 1576
STILL, William
    Miniatures, flute, oboe and piano. See no. 2501
STIRLING, Ian
    Horncore. See no. 3644
    Variations on a Tyrolean theme. See no. 3644
STOCKHAUSEN, Karlheinz
3054 Formel. Inori. Suzanne Stephens, Japanese rin; Maria Bergmann,
    pno; Southwest German Radio Orchestra; Karlheinz Stockhausen.
    DG 2707 111 (2)
           +Gr 4-80 p1563   +HFN 5-80 p125
3055 Harlekin. Der kleine Harlekin. Suzanne Stephens, clt. DG 2531
    006
           +Gr 8-80 p229
3056 Indianerlieder. Helga Hamm-Albrecht, ms; Karl Barkey, t; Karlheinz
    Stockhausen. DG 2530 876
           +Gr 8-80 p229
    Inori. See no. 3054
    Der kleine Harlekin. See no. 3055
3057 Musik im Bauch. Tierkreis. Les Percussions de Strasbourg. DG
    2530 913
           +Gr 8-80 p229
3058 Sirius. Markus Stockhausen, tpt; Annette Meriweather, s; Boris
    Carmeli, bs; Suzanne Stephens, clt; Electronic tape; Karlheinz
    Stockhausen. DG 2707 122 (2)
           +Gr 9-80 p367   +HFN 11-80 p123
    Sonatina, violin and piano. See no. 3059
    Songs, alto and chamber orchestra. See no. 3059
3059 Spiel (Game), orchestra. Sonatina, violin and piano. Songs, alto
    and chamber orchestra. Trio, piano and timpani. Sylvia Ander-
    son, alto; Saschko Gawriloff, vln; Aloys Kontarsky, pno; Jean
    Batigne, Georges van Gucht, timpani; Southwest German Radio Or-
    chestra; Karlheinz Stockhausen. DG 2530 827
           +FF 3/4-78 p75   +NR 6-78 p15
           +Gr 8-80 p229   +St 6-78 p152
           +HF 3-78 p107
    Spiral. See no. 993
3060 Sternklang. Various artists; Karlheinz Stockhausen. DG 2707 123
    (2) (From Polydor 2612 031)
           +Gr 8-80 p230   +HFN 11-80 p123
    Tierkreis. See no. 3057

Trio, piano and timpani. See no. 3059

STOJOWSKI
Chant d'amour, op. 26, no. 3: By the brookside. See no. 3907

STOKER, Richard
3061 Aspects of flight, op. 48. Concerto, 2 guitars and tape, op. 56.
Sonata, guitar duo, op. 55. Variations, op. 45. Carolyn Maia,
ms; Richard Stoker, pno; English Guitar Duo. Gaudeamus KRS 33
+-RR 3-80 p88

Concerto, 2 guitars and tape, op. 56. See no. 3061
Sonata, guitar duo, op. 55. See no. 3061
Variations, op. 45. See no. 3061

STOLTZER, Thomas
Ich klag den Tag. See no. 4004
Ricercar. See no. 4004
Songs: Es mut vil leut; Ich klag den tag; Man sicht nun wol. See
no. 3805

STOLZ, Robert
Songs: Im Prater bluh'n wieder die Baume. See no. 3738

STOLZEL, Gottfried
Bist du bei mir. See no. 3545

STONE
Mexican shuffle. See no. 3627

STORACE, Bernardo
Ballo della battaglia. See no. 3682
Toccata a canzona. See no. 3846

STORL
Sonata, brass quintet. See no. 3675

STOVIN
Flying stations. See no. 3619

STRADELLA, Alessandro
Pieta Signore. See no. 3888
Salome: Overture; Arias, nos. 1-4; Recitatives, nos. 90 and 100;
Recitative and ritornelle. See no. 1570

STRAESSER, Joep
Blossom songs. See no. 1773

STRATEGIER, Herman
Inventions: Entree. See no. 4040

STRAUBE, Rudolf
Minuet. See no. 3642

STRAUSS
Orchesterlieder. See no. 546

STRAUSS, Eduard
Bahn frei, op. 45. See no. 3068

STRAUSS, Johann I
Exeter polka, op. 249. See no. 3826
Indians galop, op. 111. See no. 3826
Ketternbrucke Walzer, op. 4. See no. 3062
3062 Lorelei Rheinklange, op. 154. Ketternbrucke Walzer, op. 4. Radetzky march, op. 228. Sperl galopp, op. 42. STRAUSS, J. II: Accelerationen, op. 234. Champagne polka, op. 211. Pesther Csardas, op. 23. Tritsch Tratsch, op. 214. Unter Donner und Blitz,
op. 324. Wiener Blut, op. 354. STRAUSS, J. II/Josef: Pizzicato
polka. London Concert Orchestra; John Georgiadis. Polydor 2460
266 Tape (c) 3170 288 (also Chalfont C 77011)
+FF 9/10-80 p211   +Gr 2-77 p1330

Radetzky march, op. 228. See no. 3062. See no. 3070. See no.
    3526. See no. 4012
Sperl galopp, op. 42. See no. 3062
Sperl polka, op. 133. See no. 3759
Tivoli slide waltz, op. 39. See no. 3826
Vienna carnival, op. 3. See no. 3989
Youthful fire galop, op. 90. See no. 3826
STRAUSS, Johann II
Accelerationen, op. 234. See no. 3062. See no. 3071
An der schonen blauen Donau (The beautiful blue Danube), op. 314.
    See no. 1863. See no. 1944. See no. 3071. See no. 3831
Annen Polka, op. 117. See no. 3069
Auf der Jagd, op. 373. See no. 3069
Banditen, op. 378. See no. 3068
Champagne polka, op. 211. See no. 3062
Czechen polka. See no. 3070
Demolirer, op. 269. See no. 3071
Egyptischer Marsch, op. 335. See no. 3068. See no. 3072
Eljen a Magyar, op. 332. See no. 3072
Die Fledermaus, op. 363: Czardas. See no. 1863
3063 Die Fledermaus, op. 363: I'll be at the ball tonight; Ah woe is me;
    Drown the truth in wine; What a feast; Chacun a son gout; Laugh-
    ing song; The watch duet; Brother mine and sister mine; I have
    a suspicion; Forgive him and forget. Victoria Elliott, Marion
    Studholme, s; Anna Pollak, con; Alexander Young, Rowland Jones,
    t; John Heddle Nash, Frederick Sharp, bar; Sadler's Wells Opera
    Orchestra and Chorus; Vilem Tausky. HMV ESD 7083 Tape (c) TC
    ESD 7083 (From CSD 1266)
                +Gr 12-79 p1061   +HFN 1-80 p123
Die Fledermaus, op. 363: Kommt mit mir zum Souper. See no. 3711
Die Fledermaus, op. 363: Mein Herr Marquis; Spiel ich die unschuld
    vom Lande. See no. 3695
Die Fledermaus, op. 363: Overture. See no. 1944. See no. 3069.
    See no. 3638. See no. 3897. See no. 4071
Freikugeln, op. 326. See no. 3072
Freut euch des Lebens, op. 340. See no. 3072
Fruhlingstimmen (Voices of spring), op. 410. See no. 3695. See
    no. 3872
Geschichten aus dem Wienerwald (Tales from the Vienna Woods), op.
    325. See no. 3068. See no. 3069. See no. 3072. See no. 3695
Graduation ball, op. 97. See no. 2446
Im Krapfenwald, op. 336. See no. 3068
Indigo Marsch, op. 349. See no. 3072
3064 Kaiserwalzer, op. 437. Rosen aus dem Suden, op. 388 (arr. Schoen-
    berg). Wein, Weib und Gesang, op. 333 (arr. Berg). Der Zigeun-
    erbaron, op. 420: Treasure waltz (arr. Webern). Boston Symphony
    Chamber Players. DG 2530 977 Tape (c) 3300 997
                +ARG 3-80 p40   +HF 2-80 p102 tape
Kaiserwalzer, op. 437. See no. 1944. See no. 3070
Kunstlerleben (Artist's life), op. 316. See no. 3071. See no.
    3962
Lovesong waltz, op. 114. See no. 3826
3065 Der lustige Krieg (The merry war), excerpts. Soloists; Salzburg
    City Theatre Operetta Ensemble; Rudolf Eisler. Summit SUM 5003
                +ARG 7/8-80 p51
Der lustige Krieg: Nur fur Natur. See no. 3711

Morgenblatter, op. 279. See no. 3068. See no. 3071

3066 Eine Nacht in Venedig. Jeanette Scovotti, Elisabeth Steiner, s; Elke Schary, ms; Carlo Bini, t; Karl Donch, t; Wolfgang Brendel, bar; Frieder Stricker, bs; HRT Orchestra and Chorus; Ernst Maerzendorfer. BASF EB 225 275 (2) (also Qualiton LSPX 16592/4, Acanta EB 22527, CBS M2 35908)

+ARG 3-78 p27	+HFN 9-79 p113
+FF 1/2-79 p106	/NYT 7-13-80 pD20
+-FF 11/12-80 p176	+-RR 11-79 p66
+-Gr 11-79 p921	+St 11-80 p101

3067 Eine Nacht in Venedig (rev. Korngold). Elisabeth Schwarzkopf, Emmy Loose, Hanna Ludwig, s; Nicolai Gedda, Peter Klein, t; Erich Kunz, Karl Donch, bar; PhO and Chorus; Otto Ackerman. HMV SXDWS 3043 (2) Tape (c) TC SXDWS 3043 (also Electrola 149 03171/2) (From Columbia 33CXS 1224/5)

+Gr 5-78 p1953	++NYT 7-13-80 pD20
+Gr 11-78 p970 tape	+RR 6-78 p40
+-HFN 8-78 p113	+-RR 11-79 p126 tape
+-HFN 9-78 p159 tape	

Eine Nacht in Venedig: Komm in die Gondel...Ach wie so herrlich zu schau'm. See no. 3711

Neue pizzicato polka, op. 449. See no. 3759

Perpetuum Mobile, op. 257. See no. 3071

Persische Marsch, op. 289. See no. 3071

Pesther Csardas, op. 23. See no. 3062

Ritter Pasman, op. 441: Polka. See no. 3962

Rosen aus dem Suden (Roses from the South), op. 388. See no. 3064. See no. 3068. See no. 3070

Sangerlust, op. 328. See no. 3070

Tausend und eine Nacht, op. 346 (A thousand and one nights). See no. 3072. See no. 3872

Tritsch Tratsch, op. 214. See no. 863. See no. 3062

Unter Donner und Blitz, op. 324. See no. 3062

Vergnugungszug, op. 281. See no. 3071

Wein, Weib und Gesang, op. 333. See no. 3064

Wiener Blut (Vienna blood), op. 354. See no. 3062. See no. 3070. See no. 3072

Wiener Blut, op. 354: Wunsch gut'n Morgen Herr von Pepi. See no. 3711

Wiener Bonbons (Vienna bonbons), op. 307. See no. 3070. See no. 3071

3068 Works, selections: Banditen, op. 378. Egyptian march, op. 335. Geschichten aus dem Wienerwald, op. 325. Im Krapfenwald, op. 336. Morgenblatter, op. 279. Rosen aus dem Suden, op. 388. Der Zigeunerbaron, op. 420: March. STRAUSS, J. II/Josef: Pizzicato polka. STRAUSS, Josef: Eingesendent, op. 240. STRAUSS, Eduard: Bahnfrei, op. 45. Halle Orchestra; James Loughran. Classics for Pleasure CFP 40256 Tape (c) TC CFP 40256

+Gr 11-76 p894	+HFN 8-80 p109 tape
+HFN 7-76 p101	+-RR 7-76 p63
+RR 7-80 p97 tape	

3069 Works, selections: Annen polka, op. 117. Auf der Jagd, op. 373. Die Fledermaus, op. 363: Overture. The gypsy baron, op. 420: Overture. Tales from the Vienna woods, op. 325. STRAUSS, Josef: Delirien, op. 212. VPO; Herbert von Karajan. Decca JB 68 Tape

(c) KJBC 68 (From RCA SB 2091)
+Gr 1-80 p1203   +-HFN 12-79 p177

3070 Works, selections: Czechen polka. Kaiserwalzer, op. 437. Rosen aus
dem Suden, op. 388. Sangerlust, op. 328. Wiener Blut, op. 354.
Wiener Bonbons, op. 307. STRAUSS, J. I: Radetzky march, op. 228.
STRAUSS, J. II/Josef: Pizzicato polka. STRAUSS, Josef: Feuer-
fest, op. 269. Ohne Sorgen, op. 271. LSO; John Georgiadis.
Enigma K 53577
++Gr 1-80 p1203   +RR 12-79 p51
+HFN 12-79 p175

3071 Works, selections: Accelerationen, op. 234. An der schonen blauen
Donau, op. 314. Demolirer, op. 269. Kunstlerleben, op. 316.
Morgenblatter, op. 279. Perpetuum mobile, op. 257. Persian
march, op. 289. Vergnugungszug, op. 281. Wiener Bonbons, op.
307. BeSO, VSO; Robert Stolz. RCA GL 2-5263 Tape (c) GK 2-5263
+Gr 7-80 p167   +HFN 9-80 p116 tape
+HFN 8-80 p107   +RR 8-80 p56

3072 Works, selections: Egyptischer Marsch, op. 335. Eljen a Magyar, op.
332. Freut euch des Lebens, op. 340. Freikugeln, op. 326. Ge-
schichten aus dem Wienerwald, op. 325. Indigo Marsch, op. 349.
Ein Tausend und eine Nacht, op. 346. Wiener Blut, op. 354.
BeSO, VSO; Robert Stolz. RCA GL 2-5264 Tape (c) GK 2-5264 (From
World Records SM 113/8)
+Gr 11-80 p739   +HFN 11-80 p131

Der Zigeunerbaron (The gypsy baron), op. 420: Ja das Schreiben und
das Lesen. See no. 3711

Der Zigeunerbaron, op. 420: March. See no. 3068

Der Zigeunerbaron, op. 420: Overture. See no. 3069

Der Zigeunerbaron, op. 420: Treasure waltz. See no. 3064

Der Zigeunerbaron, op. 420: Waltz song. See no. 3830

STRAUSS, J. II/Josef
Pizzicato polka. See no. 3062. See no. 3068. See no. 3070

STRAUSS, Josef
Delirien, op. 212. See no. 3069
Eingesendent, op. 240. See no. 3068
Feuerfest, op. 269. See no. 3070
Fireproof polka. See no. 3962
The good old days waltz, op. 26. See no. 3826
Ohne Sorgen, op. 271. See no. 3070

STRAUSS, Oscar
The chocolate soldier: My hero. See no. 3831

3073 Ein Walzertraum. Anneliese Rothenberger, Edda Moser, s; Brigitte
Fassbaender, ms; Nicolai Gedda, Willi Brokmeier, t; Wolfgang
Annheisser, bar; Bavarian State Opera Chorus; Graunke Symphony
Orchestra Willy Mattes. Arabesque 8063/2
+NR 12-80 p9

STRAUSS, Richard
3074 Die Aegyptische Helena, op. 75. Gwyneth Jones, Dinah Bryant, Barbara Hendricks, s; Matti Kastu, Curtis Rayam, t; Willard White,
bs; Kenneth Jewell Chorale; Detroit Symphony Orchestra; Antal
Dorati. Decca D176D3 (3) Tape (c) K176K33 (also London OSA
13135)
+-ARG 10-80 p31   +ON 5-80 p44
+FF 5/6-80 p153   +-Op 5-80 p472
+Gr 12-79 p1052   +RR 11-79 p18

                    +Gr 5-80 p1717 tape   +-SFC 3-2-80 p41
                    +-HF 6-80 p86   +-St 5-80 p123
                    +HFN 12-79 p170   +STL 12-2-79 p37
                    +-MT 4-80 p253
3075 Alpine symphony, op. 64. Saxon State Orchestra; Karl Bohm. DG
        2548 175 Tape (c) 3348 175 (From 18476)
                    ++Gr 3-80 p1397   +-RR 2-80 p61
                    +-HFN 4-80 p119
3076 Alpine symphony, op. 64. Bavarian Radio Orchestra; Georg Solti.
        London CS 7189 (also Decca SXL 6959 Tape (c) KSXC 6959)
                    +Gr 9-80 p349   +HFN 10-80 p109
                    +Gr 12-80 p889 tape   ++SFC 10-5-80 p21
3077 Also sprach Zarathustra, op. 30. PO; Eugene Ormandy. HMV ASD 3897
        Tape (c) TC ASD 3897 (also Angel DS 37744)
                    +-Gr 12-80 p841   +SFC 12-7-80 p33
                    +-HFN 12-80 p146
3078 Also sprach Zarathustra, op. 30. Schlagobers, op. 70: Waltz. VPO;
        Richard Strauss. Saphir INT 120928
                    +-Gr 9-80 p350   ++RR 6-80 p59
        Also sprach Zarathustra, op. 30: Opening fanfare. See no. 3661
3079 Arabella, op. 79: Du sollst mein Gebieter sein; Er ist der Richtige
        nicht...Aber der Richtige. Ariadne auf Naxos, op. 60: Quer-
        schnitt. Capriccio, op. 85: Du Spiegelbild der verliebten Made-
        leine; Holla ihr Streiter in Apoll. Daphne, op. 82: Gotter
        Bruder im hohen Olympos; O wie gern blieb ich bei dir. Die Frau
        ohne Schatten, op. 65: Intermezzo, Act 1; Falke du wiedergefund-
        ener; Sie haben es mir gesagt. Salome, op. 54: Salomes Tanz.
        Soloists; Staatskapelle, VSOO; Karl Bohm. Acanta DE 23280/1 (2)
                    +-HFN 6-80 p112   +-RR 5-80 p49
                    +Op 8-80 p800
3080 Arabella, op. 79: Ich danke Fraulein; Welko das Bild; Mein Elemer;
        Sie wolln mich heiraten; Und jetzt sag ich adieu; Das war sehr
        gut. Capriccio, op. 85: Morgen mittag um elf. Vier letzte
        Lieder, op. posth. Elisabeth Schwarzkopf, s; PhO; Otto Acker-
        mann, Lovro von Matacic. HMV RLS 751 (2) (From Columbia 33CS
        1107, 33CX 1226)
                    +Gr 11-80 p735   +-HFN 11-80 p131
        Arabella, op. 79: Ich mochte meinen fremden Mann; So wie Sie sind.
        See no. 3561
3081 Ariadne auf Naxos, op. 60. Maria Reining, Irmgard Seefried, Alda
        Noni, s; Max Lorenz, t; Paul Schoffler, Erich Kunz, bar; Vienna
        State Opera Orchestra; Karl Bohm. Acanta DE 23309/10 (2)
                    ++HFN 6-80 p112   +RR 4-80 p49
3082 Ariadne auf Naxos, op. 60. Leontyne Price, Deborah Cook, Norma
        Burrowes, Edita Gruberova, s; Enid Hartle, con; Tatiana Troyanos,
        ms; Rene Kollo, Kurt Equiluz, t; Walter Berry, bar; Manfred
        Jungwirth, bs; LPO; Georg Solti. London OSA 13131 (3)
                    +NR 2-80 p9
        Ariadne auf Naxos, op. 60: Es gibt ein Reich. See no. 3774
        Ariadne auf Naxos, op. 60: Grossmachtige Prinzessin. See no. 3584
3083 Ariadne auf Naxos, op. 60: Overture; Final scene. Elektra, op. 58:
        Final scene.* Maria Cebotari, Margaret Field-Hyde, Erna Schlut-
        er, Ljuba Welitsch, s; Gwladys Garside, con; Karl Friedrich,
        Walter Widdop, t; Paul Schoffler, bar; Ernst Erbach, bs; RPO and
        Chorus; Thomas Beecham. RCA RL 4-2821 (From DB 9393/6)

```
        +ARSC vol 12, no. 3          ++Op 6-79 p575
           1980 p248                 ++RR 8-79 p41
        +-Gr 6-79 p102               +STL 12-2-79 p37
        +-MT 9-79 p747
```
Ariadne auf Naxos, op. 60: Querschnitt. See no. 3079

3084 Le bourgeois gentilhomme, op. 60. Concerto, oboe, D major. Peter
     Frankl, pno; Neil Black, ob; ECO; Daniel Barenboim. CBS 76826
     Tape (c) 40-76826 (also CBS M 35160 Tape (c) MT 35160)
```
        +-FF 11/12-80 p177           +NYT 12-14-80 pD38
        +Gr 11-79 p841               +RR 11-79 p95
        +HFN 11-79 p143              +RR 3-80 p106 tape
        ++HFN 1-80 p123 tape         +St 12-80 p133
        ++MT 5-80 p325               +STL 12-2-79 p37
```

3085 Le bourgeois gentilhomme, op. 60. Don Juan, op. 20. VPO; Clemens
     Krauss. London STS 15504 (From LL 233, 684)
```
        -FF 11/12-80 p177
```

3086 Le bourgeois gentilhomme, op. 60, excerpts. Feuersnot, op. 50:
     Love scene. Intermezzo, op. 22: Interlude. RPO; Thomas Beecham.
     World Records SH 378
```
        +Gr 12-80 p880               +HFN 12-80 p146
```
Burleske, op. 11, D minor. See no. 1250
Capriccio, op. 85: Du Spiegelbild der verliebten Madeleine; Holla
     ihr Streiter in Apoll. See no. 3079
Capriccio, op. 85: Morgen mittag um elf. See no. 3080
Capriccio, op. 85: Sextet. See no. 1841
Concerto, oboe, D major. See no. 3084
Daphne, op. 82: Gotter Bruder im hohen Olympos; O wie gern blieb
     ich bei dir. See no. 3079

3087 Don Juan, op. 20. Till Eulenspiegels lustige Streiche, op. 28. Tod
     und Verklarung, op. 24. CO; Lorin Maazel. CBS IM 35826 Tape (c)
     HMT 35826
```
        +FF 11/12-80 p178            ++SFC 8-24-80 p36
        +Gr 12-80 p841               +St 12-80 p118
        +HFN 12-80 p146
```

3088 Don Juan, op. 20. Festival prelude, op. 61. Salome, op. 54: Sal-
     ome's dance. Till Eulenspiegels lustige Streiche, op. 28. BPhO;
     Karl Bohm. DG 2535 208 (From SLPM 138866)
```
        +-FF 11/12-80 p178           +HFN 12-76 p151
        +Gr 12-76 p1002              +-RR 12-76 p65
```

3089 Don Juan, op. 20. Vier letzte Lieder, op. posth. Montserrat Cab-
     alle, s; Strasbourg Philharmonic Orchestra; Alain Lombard.
     Erato STU 71054
```
        +-FF 5/6-80 p155             -ON 3-3-79 p41
```

3090 Don Juan, op. 20. Ein Heldenleben, op. 40. Till Eulenspiegels lus-
     tige Streiche, op. 28. VPO; Richard Strauss. Everest SDBR 3435
     (From Vanguard SRV 325/9)
```
        +-ARG 9-79 p44               +NR 5-79 p5
        +-FF 5/6-80 p157
```

3091 Don Juan, op. 20. Salome, op. 54: Dance of the seven veils. Till
     Eulenspiegels lustige Streiche, op. 28. PhO; Otto Klemperer.
     HMV SXLP 30298 Tape (c) TC SXLP 30298 (From SAX 2367)
```
        +-Gr 5-80 p1672              +RR 5-80 p72
        +-HFN 6-80 p117
```

3092 Don Juan, op. 20. Munchen commemorative waltz. Der Rosenkavalier,
     op. 59: Suite. LSO; Andre Previn. RCA AGL 1-2940 (also GL 4-

2871 Tape (c) GK 4-2871. From SB 6838)
      +FF 3/4-79 p119   +HFN 1-80 p123 tape
      +-Gr 10-79 p654   +RR 3-80 p106 tape
      +HFN 10-79 p169

Don Juan, op. 20. See no. 664. See no. 3085. See no. 3710

3093 Don Quixote, op. 35. WAGNER: A Faust overture. Rene Pollain, vla;
    Alfred Wallenstein, vlc; NYP, LPO; Thomas Beecham. HMV HLM 7154
    (From Columbia LX 186/90, CAX 7508/10, LX 481/2)
        +ARSC vol 12, no. 3   +HFN 4-79 p125
            1980 p247   +MT 9-79 p747
        ++FF 9/10-80 p211   +RR 4-79 p80
        +Gr 4-79 p1719

3094 Don Quixote, op. 35. Der Rosenkavalier, op. 59: Waltzes. Paul
    Tortelier, vlc; Max Rostal, vla; Dresden State Orchestra; Rudolf
    Kempe. HMV SXLP 30428 Tape (c) TC SXLP 30428 (From SLS 880)
        +Gr 4-80 p1563   +HFN 8-80 p109 tape
        +HFN 6-80 p117   +RR 6-80 p59

Elektra, op. 58: Allein Weh ganz allein. See no. 3931
Elektra, op. 58: Final scene. See no. 3083
Fanfare. See no. 3116
Fanfare fur die Wiener Philharmoniker. See no. 3116
Feierlicher Einzug der Titter des Johanniterordens. See no. 3116
Festival prelude, op. 61. See no. 3088
Festmusik der Stadt Wien. See no. 3116. See no. 3571

3095 Feuersnot, op. 50: Love scene. Der Rosenkavalier, op. 59: Intro-
    duction, Act 1; Letter scene and waltz; Introduction and waltzes,
    Act 3. Schlogobers, op. 70: Waltz. Munchen commemorative waltz.
    LPO; Norman Del Mar. Classics for Pleasure CFP 40327
        +Gr 3-80 p1397   +RR 3-80 p62
        ++HFN 3-80 p99

Feuersnot, op. 50: Love scene. See no. 3086

3096 Die Frau ohne Schatten, op. 65. Leonie Rysanek, Christel Goltz, s;
    Hans Hopf, t; Paul Schoffler, bs; VPO; Karl Bohm. Richmond 64503
        +NYT 10-9-77 pD21   +SFC 9-2-80 p28

Die Frau ohne Schatten, op. 65: Intermezzo, Act 1; Falke du wieder-
    gefundener; Sie haben es mir gesagt. See no. 3079

Hamlet: Ophelia Lieder (3). See no. 3541

3097 Ein Heldenleben, op. 40. LSO; John Barbirolli. Classics for Pleas-
    ure CFP 40325 (From HMV ASD 2613)
        /-Gr 3-80 p1449   +RR 3-80 p63
        ++HFN 3-80 p105

3098 Ein Heldenleben, op. 40. VPO; Rainer Kuchl, vln; Georg Solti.
    Decca SET 601 Tape (c) KCET 601 (also London 7083 Tape (c) 5-
    7083)
          -FF 9/10-79 p147   +MM 5-79 p33
          ++Gr 3-79 p1577   +-MT 6-79 p492
          +-Gr 6-79 p109 tape +NR 3-80 p1
          +-HF 9-79 p124   ++RR 3-79 p84
          +-HFN 2-79 p109   ++SFC 6-17-79 p41
          +-HFN 4-79 p134 tape +St 9-79 p90

3099 Ein Heldenleben, op. 40. RPO; Thomas Beecham; Steven Staryk, vln.
    HMV SXLP 30293 Tape (c) TC SXLP 30293 (From ASD 421)
        +ARSC Vol 12, no. 3   +Gr 3-80 p1449
            1980 p252   +-HFN 6-79 p115
        ++Gr 6-79 p56   +-HFN 8-79 p123 tape
        +-Gr 9-79 p533 tape   ++RR 6-79 p86

3100 Ein Heldenleben, op. 40. PO; Eugene Ormandy. RCA ARL 1-3581 Tape
     (c) ARK 1-3581
                  /FF 11/12-80 p179   ++SFC 8-24-80 p36
                  +NR 9-80 p3   +St 12-80 p135
                  +NYT 9-7-80 pD29
3101 Ein Heldenleben, op. 40. RPO; Oscar Lampe, vln; Thomas Beecham.
     World Records SH 1006
                  +ARSC Vol 12, no. 3, 1980 p241
     Ein Heldenleben, op. 40. See no. 3090
3102 Intermezzo, op. 72. Lucia Popp, Gabriele Fuchs, Gudrun Greindl-
     Rosner, s; Adolf Dallapozza, Martin Finke, t; Dietrich Fischer-
     Dieskau, Klaus Hirte, Raimund Grumbach, bar; Kurt Moll, bs; Phil-
     ipp Brammer, speaker; Bavarian Radio Orchestra; Wolfgang Sawal-
     lisch. HMV SLS 5204 (3)
                  +Gr 11-80 p735   +STL 12-14-80 p38
     Intermezzo, op. 72: Interlude. See no. 3086
3103 Josephslegende, op. 63. Bavarian State Opera Orchestra; Robert
     Heger. Audax 764
                  +-FF 7/8-80 p134
     München commemorative waltz. See no. 3902. See no. 3095
     Olympische hymne. See no. 3116
     Parade marches, nos. 1 and 2. See no. 3116
     Der Rosenkavalier, op. 59: Arias. See no. 3539
     Der Rosenkavalier, op. 59: Di rigori armato. See no. 3558. See
        no. 3672. See no. 3774
3104 Der Rosenkavalier, op. 59: Introduction and opening scene; Marschal-
     lin's monologue; Duet and closing scene; Presentation of the
     silver rose and duet; Marschallin's meeting with Sophie; Trio
     and final duet. Regine Crespin, Elisabeth Soderstrom, Hilde
     Gueden, s; Heinz Holecek, bar; VSOO Chorus; VPO; Silvio Varviso.
     Decca JB 57 Tape (c) KJBC 57 (From SXL 6146)
                  +Gr 2-80 p1294   +RR 2-80 p42
                  +HFN 3-80 p107
     Der Rosenkavalier, op. 59: Introduction, Act 1; Letter scene and
     waltz; Introduction and waltzes, Act 3. See no. 3095
     Der Rosenkavalier, op. 59: Ist ein Traum. See no. 3538. See no.
        3584
     Der Rosenkavalier, op. 59: Suite. See no. 3092
     Der Rosenkavalier, op. 59: Waltzes. See no. 3094. See no. 3882
3105 Der Rosenkavalier, op. 59: Wie Du warst, wie Du bist, da; Weiss
     keiner; Da gent er hin, der aufgeblas 'ns schlechte Kerl; Mir
     ist die Ehre widerfahren das lieg ich; Hab mir's gelobt ihn
     liebzuhaben; Ist ein Traum kann nicht wirklich sein. Viorica
     Ursuleac, Adele Kern, s; Georgine von Milinkovic, ms; Luise Wil-
     ler, con; Ludwig Weber, Georg Hann, bs; Bavarian State Opera
     Orchestra and Chorus; Clemens Krauss. BASF 10 22322/1 (also Ac-
     anta BB 22322)
                  -Gr 12-75 p1094   +-RR 4-80 p50
                  +HFN 5-80 p125
     Salome, op. 54: Ah du wolltest mich nicht deinen Mund kussen lassen.
     See no. 3924
     Salome, op. 54: Dance of the seven veils. See no. 3091. See no.
        3079. See no. 3088
     Schlagobers, op. 70: Waltz. See no. 3078. See no. 3095
3106 Serenade, op. 7. Sonatina, no. 1, F major. Sonatina, no. 2, E

flat major. Suite, op. 4, B flat major. Harmonia de Chambre de
la Musique des Gardiens de la Paix; Desire Dondeyne. Arion 336
019 (3)
+-Gr 2-80 p1270   +RR 12-79 p90
3107 Sinfonia domestica, op. 53. VPO; Richard Strauss. Saphir INT 120
929
+-Gr 9-80 p350   ++RR 6-80 p59
Sinfonia domestica, op. 53. See no. 433
3108 Sonata, violin and piano, op. 18, E major. Sonata, violoncello and
piano, op. 6, F major. Rudolf Koeckert, vln; Gerhard Mantel,
vlc; Erika Frieser, pno. Da Camera Magna SM 93709
+-ST 12-80 p575
3109 Sonata, violin and piano, op. 18, E flat major. SZYMANOWSKI: Caprices after Paganini, op. 40. Romance, op. 23. Vincent Skowronski, vln; Donald Isaak, pno. Eb-Sko 1006
+-ARG 3-80 p41   +-HF 12-79 p103
+FF 5/6-80 p156
Sonata, violin and piano, op. 18, E flat major. See no. 1441. See
no. 3772. See no. 3964
Sonata, violoncello and piano, op. 6, F major. See no. 1962. See
no. 3108
3110 Sonatina, no. 1, F major. Suite, op. 4, B flat major. London Symphony Winds; Gervase de Peyer. Arabesque 8015 Tape (c) 9015
+ARG 11-80 p33   +SFC 8-24-80 p36
+FF 11/12-80 p179
Sonatina, no. 1, F major. See no. 3106
Sonatina, no. 2, E flat major. See no. 3106
3111 Songs: All mein Gedanken Ach Lieb ich muss nun scheiden; Du meines
Kerzens Kronelein, op. 21; Freundliche Vision, op. 48; Gluckes
genug Meinem Kinde, op. 37; Heimkehr, op. 15; Mit deinen blauen
Augen Gefunden, op. 56; Schlagende Herzen, op. 29; Sehnsucht, op.
32; Standchen, op. 17; Wiegenlied, op. 41; Die Zeitlose Allerseelen; Die Nacht, op. 10. Ingeborg Hallstein, s; Erik Werba,
pno. Acanta DC 21965
+-HFN 10-79 p171   +STL 4-13-80 p39
++RR 9-79 p129
3112 Songs: Befreit, op. 39, no. 4; Morgen, op. 27, no. 4; Muttertande-
lei, op. 43, no. 2; Ruhe meine Seele, op. 27, no. 1; Wiegenlied,
op. 41, no. 1; Zueignung, op. 10, no. 1. Vier letzte Lieder,
op. posth. Kiri Te Kanawa, s; LSO; Andrew Davis. CBS 76794 Tape
(c) 40-76794 (also Columbia M 35140 Tape (c) MT 35140)
+-ARG 3-80 p42   +MUM 5/6-80 p37
+FF 5/6-80 p155   +NR 12-79 p11
+FU 5-80 p50   +NYT 10-28-79 pD24
+-Gr 5-79 p1925   +-ON 1-5-80 p37
+-HF 2-80 p94   +Op 8-79 p782
+-HFN 5-79 p127   +-RR 6-79 p117
+-HFN 9-79 p123 tape   +SFC 12-9-79 p43
+MM 8-79 p29   +SR 1-5-80 p39
+MT 8-79 p659   +-St 1-80 p104
3113 Songs: Am Ufer, op. 41, no. 3; Befreit, op. 39, no. 4; Breit uber
mein Haupt, op. 19, no. 2; Freundliche Vision, op. 48, no. 1;
Heimliche Aufforderung, op. 27, no. 3; Ich Schwebe, op. 48, no.
2; Lieder der Orphelia aus Hamlet (3); Nichts, op. 10, no. 2;
Schlechtes Wetter, op. 69, no. 5; Standchen, op. 17, no. 2; Wie

sollten wir gehiem, op. 19, no. 4; Wiegenlied, op. 41, no. 1;
Wozu noch Madchen, op. 19, no. 1; Die Zeitlose. Helen-Kay Eberly, s; Donald Isaak, pno. Eb-Sko 1005
       +—Audio 11-80 p85   +FF 11/12-80 p180

3114 Songs: Ach Liebe ich muss nun scheiden, op. 21, no. 3; Ach weh mir
ungluckhaftem Mann, op. 21, no. 4; All mein Gedanken Gluckes genug, op. 21, no. 1; Blick vom oberen Belvedere, op. 88, no. 2;
Du meines Herzens Kronelein, op. 21, no. 2; Heimkehr, op. 15, no.
5; Heimliche Aufforderung, op. 27, no. 3; In goldener Fulle, op.
49, no. 2; Das Rosenband, op. 36, no. 1; Ruhe meine Seele, op.
27, no. 1; Sehnsucht, op. 32, no. 2; Schlechtes Wetter, op. 69,
no. 5; Seitdem dein Aug in meines schaute, op. 17, no. 1; Winter-
liebe, op. 48, no. 5; Wozu noch Madchen soll es frommen, op. 19,
no. 1. Hilde Konetzni, s; Anton Dermota, t; Alfred Poell, bar;
Richard Strauss, pno. Preiser PR 3261
       +ARG 3-80 p55   +RR 2-79 p25

Songs: Allerseelen, op. 10, no. 8. See no. 3573
Songs: Als mir dein Lied erklang, op. 68, no. 2; Des Dichters Abendgang, op. 47, no. 2; Freundliche Vision, op. 48, no. 1; Heimliche Aufforderung, op. 27, no. 3; Ich schwebe, op. 48, no. 2;
Ich trage meine Minne, op. 32, no. 1; Die Nacht, op. 10, no. 3;
Ruhe meine Seele, op. 27, no. 1; Schlechtes Wetter, op. 69, no.
5; Standchen, op. 17, no. 2; Traum durch die Dammerung, op. 29,
no. 1; Waldseligkeit, op. 49, no. 1; Wie sollten wir geheim sie
halten, op. 19, no. 4; Wiegenlied, op. 41, no. 1; Zueignung, op.
10, no. 1. See no. 2194
Songs: Als mir dein Lied erklang, op. 68, no. 4; Befreit, op. 39,
no. 4; Breit uber mein Haupt, op. 19, no. 2; Cacilie, op. 27, no.
2; Heimkehr, op. 15, no. 5; Morgen, op. 27, no. 4; Seitdem dein
Aug, op. 17, no. 1; Wasserrose, op. 22, no. 4. See no. 2875
Songs: Das Geheimnis, op. 17, no. 3. See no. 3537
Songs: Der Abend; Die Gottin im Putzzimer. See no. 3713
Songs: Freundliche Vision, op. 48, no. 1; Heimliche Aufforderung,
op. 27, no. 3; Ich trage meine Minne, op. 32, no. 1; Morgen, op.
27, no. 4; Standchen, op. 17, no. 2. See no. 2874
Songs: Morgen, op. 27, no. 4; Standchen, op. 17, no. 2. See no.
3738
Songs: Morgen, op. 27, no. 4; Standchen, op. 17, no. 2; Traum durch
die Dammerung, op. 29, no. 1; Verfuhrung, op. 33, no. 1; Wald-
seligkeit, op. 49, no. 1. See no. 2804
Songs: Standchen, op. 17, no. 2. See no. 3928
Songs: Traum durch die Dammerung, op. 29, no. 1; Wiegenlied; Freundliche Vision, op. 48, no. 1. See no. 3774
Stimmungsbilder, op. 9: An einsamer Quelle. See no. 3964
Suite, op. 4, B flat major. See no. 3106. See no. 3110
Till Eulenspiegels lustige Streiche, op. 28. See no. 1212. See
no. 1288. See no. 3087. See no. 3088. See no. 3090. See no.
3091. See no. 3710
3115 Tod und Verklarung, op. 24. VPO; Richard Strauss. Saphir INT 120
927
       ++RR 6-80 p59
Tod und Verklarung, op. 24. See no. 1787. See no. 3087
Vier letzte Lieder, op. posth. See no. 3080. See no. 3089. See
no. 3112
3116 Works, selections: Fanfare. Fanfare fur die Wiener Philharmoniker.

Feierlicher Einzug der Titter des Johanniterordens. Festmusik
der Stadt Wien (original version). Olympische hymne. Parade
marches, nos. 1 and 2 (arr. Locke). Locke Brass Consort; James
Stobart. Chandos ABR 1002 Tape (c) ABT 1002
                +Gr 2-80 p1270   +RR 2-80 p61
                +Gr 8-80 p275 tape

STRAVINSKY, Igor
3117 Agon. Canticum sacrum.   Los Angeles Festival Orchestra and Chor-
     us; Igor Stravinsky. Odyssey Y 35227
                +FF 1/2-80 p149   ++SFC 10-21-79 p57
3118 Apollon musagete (Apollo). Symphony of psalms. Utah Chorale;
     Utah Symphony Orchestra; Maurice Abravanel. Angel S 37316 Tape
     (c) 4XS 37316
                +-ARG 6-79 p32   +-MJ 5/6-79 p48
                +-FF 9/10-80 p212   +NR 4-79 p3
3119 Apollon musagete. Orpheus. St. John's Orchestra; John Lubbock.
     Enigma K 53585
                +Gr 1-80 p1161   +RR 12-79 p77
                -HFN 1-80 p111
3120 Apollon musagete. Concerto, orchestra, D major. Septet. Baden
     Baden Ensemble 13; Manfred Reichert. Harmonia Mundi 065 99730
                +FF 9/10-80 p212   +-RR 5-79 p78
                +-HFN 4-79 p123   +-ST 8-79 p275
     Apollon musagete. See no. 379
     Canticum sacrum. See no. 3117
     Cantique. See no. 3148
     Capriccio. See no. 2972
     Chanson russe. See no. 3788
3121 Chant du rossignol. The firebird: Suite. PhO; Constantin Silvest-
     ri, Josef Krips. Classics for Pleasure CFP 40328 (From HMV ASD
     401, 654)
                +Gr 3-80 p1449   ++RR 3-80 p63
                +-HFN 3-80 p105
3122 Chant du rossignol. L'Oiseau de feu: Suite. BRSO; Lorin Maazel.
     DG 2535 405 Tape (c) 3335 405
                +ARG 12-80 p46   /-FF 9/10-80 p212
     Les cinq doigts. See no. 3137
     Circus polka. See no. 3137
     Concertino. See no. 3137
     Concerto, orchestra. See no. 3120
3123 Concerto, piano and wind instruments. Serenade, A major. Sonata,
     piano, C major. Zdenek Kozina, pno; Dvorak Chamber Orchestra;
     Vladimir Valek. Supraphon 110 2419
                +-Gr 10-80 p504   +NR 9-80 p5
                +HFN 10-80 p109
     Concerto, piano and wind instruments. See no. 2809
     Concerto, 2 pianos. See no. 3137
3124 Concerto, 16 instruments, E flat major. Danses concertantes. Rag-
     time. Tango. London Sinfonietta; Riccardo Chailly. Dischi
     Ricordi RCL 27037
                +-Gr 7-80 p147   +RR 7-80 p68
3125 Concerto, 16 wind instruments, E flat major. L'Histoire du soldat:
     Suite. Octet, wind instruments. Nash Ensemble; Elgar Howarth.
     Sine Qua Non SA 2011
                +-FF 1-78 p51   +-FU 2-80 p33

Concerto, violin, D major. See no. 640
Danses concertantes. See no. 3124
Dirge canons. See no. 3148
Double canon. See no. 3148
Dumbarton Oaks concerto. See no. 3137
Easy pieces. See no. 3148
Elegy. See no. 1883
Elegy for J.F.K. See no. 1166. See no. 3148
Epitaphium fur das Grabmal des Prinzen Max Egon zu Furstenberg.
     See no. 3148
Etudes, op. 7 (4). See no. 1041. See no. 3137
Fireworks. See no. 3897
Five easy pieces. See no. 3137
3126 L'Histoire du soldat. Japanese lyrics (3). Renard. Adrienne
     Csengery, s; Denes Gulyas, Boldizsar Keonch, bs; Laszlo Polgar,
     t; Gyorgy Bordas, bar; Budapest Chamber Ensemble; Andras Mihaly.
     Hungaroton SLPX 12020
          +ARG 7/8-80 p42   +-NR 4-80 p7
          +-FF 7/8-80 p136   ++SFC 3-9-80 p39
3127 L'Histoire du soldat. Les noces. Ravinia Festival Performers;
     James Levine. RCA ARL 1-3375 Tape (c) ARK 1-3375
          +-ARG 4-80 p46   +NR 3-80 p2
          +FF 7/8-80 p136   +St 4-80 p138
          +-HF 3-80 p86
L'Histoire du soldat. See no. 2539
L'Histoire du soldat: Suite. See no. 3125
L'Histoire du soldat: Valse. See no. 3137
Japanese lyrics (3). See no. 3126
Lullaby. See no. 3148
Madrid. See no. 3137
Mavra: Chanson Russe. See no. 3552
Movements, piano and orchestra. See no. 2809
3128 Les noces. Ragtime. Renard (rev. version). Mildred Allen, s;
     Regina Sarfaty, ms; George Shirley, Loren Driscoll, t; William
     Murphy, bar; Donald Gramm, Robert Oliver, bs; Toni Koves, cimb;
     Samuel Barber, Aaron Copland, Lukas Foss, Roger Sessions, pno;
     American Concert Choir; Columbia Percussion Ensemble, Columbia
     Chamber Ensemble; Igor Stravinsky. CBS 61975 Tape (c) 40-61975
     (From SBRG 72071)
          +Gr 9-80 p385   +Gr 12-80 p889 tape
3129 Les noces. Renard. Ragtime. Basia Retchitzka, s; Arlette Chedel,
     alto; Eric Tappy, Pierre-Andre Blazer, t; Philippe Huttenlocher,
     bar; Jules Bastin, bs; Lausanne University Chorus; Instrumental
     Ensemble; Charles Dutoit. Erato STU 70737
          +FF 7/8-80 p136
Les noces. See no. 3127
Norwegian moods (4). See no. 3860
Octet, wind instruments. See no. 3125
3130 L'Oiseau de feu (The firebird). VPO; Christoph von Dohnanyi. Decca
     SXDL 7511 Tape (c) KSXDC 7511
          +-Gr 11-80 p678   +HFN 11-80 p123
L'Oiseau de feu. See no. 771
L'Oiseau de feu: Berceuse and finale. See no. 3148
L'Oiseau de feu: Dance of the firebird; Scherzo; Infernal dance.
     See no. 4071

3131 L'Oiseau de feu: Suite. COA; Colin Davis. Philips 9500 637 Tape (c)
     7300 742
                    +-FF 3/4-80 p160   ++NYT 3-2-80 pD26
                    ++Gr 10-79 p654   ++RR 11-79 p96
                    ++HFN 10-79 p161   +RR 3-80 p105
                    +HFN 1-80 p123 tape   ++SFC 12-16-79 p60
                    +NR 3-80 p4
3132 L'Oiseau de feu: Suite. Symphony in 3 movements. Dallas Symphony
     Orchestra; Eduardo Mata. RCA ARL 1-3459
                    +-ARG 7/8-80 p41   +-HFN 7-80 p110
                    +-FF 7/8-80 p135   +NR 5-80 p3
                    +Gr 7-80 p148   +RR 7-80 p68
                    +HF 8-80 p79   +St 7-80 p84
     L'Oiseau de feu: Suite. See no. 2416. See no. 3121. See no. 3122.
        See no. 3955
     Orpheus. See no. 3119
     Pastorale. See no. 3148
3133 Petrouchka. NYP; Zubin Mehta. CBS IM 35823 Tape (c) HMT 35823
                    ++FF 11/12-80 p121   ++HFN 12-80 p146
                    +Gr 12-80 p841   ++SFC 8-17-80 p36
                    +-HF 9-80 p78   ++St 12-80 p118
                    +HF 10-80 p98 tape
3134 Petrouchka. VPO; Horst Gobel, pno; Christoph von Dohnanyi. Decca
     SXL 6883 Tape (c) KSXC 6883 (also London CS 7106)
                    +Audio 4-79 p83   +HFN 11-78 p187
                    +-FF 11/12-79 p129   -NR 3-80 p2
                    +Gr 10-78 p695   -NYT 7-27-79 pD24
                    +-Gr 12-78 p1177 tape   +RR 10-78 p79
                    -HF 6-79 p88   ++RR 1-79 p92 tape
                    +-HFN 10-78 p131
3135 Petrouchka. LSO; Charles Dutoit. DG 2535 419 Tape (c) 3335 419
     (From 2530 711)
                    +Gr 10-80 p504   +-HFN 11-80 p131 tape
                    +-HFN 11-80 p129
3136 Petrouchka. Leningrad Philharmonic Orchestra; Yuri Temirkanov.
     Quintessence PMC 7147 Tape (c) P4C 7147
                    +-ARG 9-80 p41   +HF 7-80 p82 tape
                    ++FF 7/8-80 p138   +-SFC 5-4-80 p42
     Petrouchka. See no. 2536. See no. 2537
     Petrouchka, excerpts. See no. 3604. See no. 3608
     Petrouchka: Danse Russe. See no. 3678
     Petrouchka: Movements (3). See no. 3137. See no. 3138. See no.
        3705
     Petrouchka: Scenes (3). See no. 1041
     Piano rag music. See no. 3137. See no. 3138
3137 Piano works: Les cinq doigts. Circus polka. Concertino. Concerto,
     2 pianos. Dumbarton Oaks concerto. Etudes, op. 7 (4). Five
     easy pieces. L'Histoire du soldat: Valse. Madrid. Petrouchka:
     3 movements. Piano rag music. Pulcinella: 2 movements. Rag-
     time. Serenade, A major. Sonata, piano (1903-4). Sonata, pi-
     ano (1924). Sonata, 2 pianos. Tango. Three easy pieces. Valse
     pour les enfants. Bernard Ringeissen, Andre Gorog, pno. Disques
     Ades 7074 (4)
                    ++ARG 1-80 p42   /FF 3/4-80 p161
3138 Piano works: Petrouchka: 3 movements. Piano rag music. Serenade,

A major. Sonata, piano. Tango. Dezso Ranki, pno. Telefunken
   6-42358 Tape (c) 4-42358
                +-FF 7/8-80 p138   +-St 10-80 p121
Pieces, string quartet (3). See no. 382
3139 Pulcinella (revised version). Teresa Berganza, ms; Ryland Davies,
   t; John Shirley-Quirk, bar; LSO; Claudio Abbado. DG 2531 087
   Tape (c) 3301 087
                ++ARG 2-80 p43   +HFN 8-79 p123 tape
                +FF 3/4-80 p162   ++NR 12-79 p4
                +Gr 6-79 p59   ++RR 6-79 p87
                +HF 2-80 p98   ++SFC 10-21-79 p57
                +HF 11-80 p88 tape   +St 1-80 p104
                +HFN 7-79 p112
Pulcinella: Movements (2). See no. 3137
Ragtime. See no. 3124. See no. 3128. See no. 3129. See no. 3137
Renard. See no. 3126. See no. 3128. See no. 3129
3140 Le sacre du printemps. PROKOFIEV: Romeo and Juliet, op. 64: Suite,
   no. 2. Minnesota Orchestra; Stanislaw Skrowaczewski. Candide
   QCE 31108
                +-FU 2-80 p51   +HF 8-80 p81
3141 Le sacre du printemps. Orchestra; Ferenc Fricsay. DG 2535 721
                +-ARSC Vol 12, nos. 1-2, 1980 p124
3142 Le sacre du printemps. Bruno Canino, Antonio Ballista, pno. Dischi
   Ricordi RCL 27036
                +Gr 8-80 p242   +RR 7-80 p85
3143 Le sacre du printemps. PO; Riccardo Muti. HMV ASD 3807 Tape (c)
   TC ASD 3807 (also Angel SZ 37646)
                +ARG 7/8-80 p40   ++NR 3-80 p2
                +FF 5/6-80 p158   +NYT 3-2-80 pD26
                +Gr 11-79 p841   +RR 11-79 p96
                +-HF 8-80 p81   +RR 7-80 p97 tape
                +HFN 12-79 p170   +-SFC 3-9-80 p39
                +HFN 2-80 p107 tape   +St 8-80 p101
3144 Le sacre du printemps. BSO; Seiji Ozawa. Philips 9500 781 Tape
   (c) 7300 855
                +Gr 12-80 p841   +-HFN 12-80 p146
3145 Le sacre du printemps. Dickran Atamian, pno. RCA ARC 1-3636
                +NR 11-80 p10   -SFC 11-30-80 p21
                +NYT 10-19-80 pD24
3146 Le sacre du printemps. CO; Lorin Maazel. Telarc DG 10054
                ++SFC 11-30-80 p21
Le sacre du printemps, excerpts. See no. 3604. See no. 3608
Septet. See no. 3120
Serenade, A major. See no. 3123. See no. 3137. See no. 3138
Sonata, piano. See no. 1795. See no. 3138
Sonata, piano (1903-4). See no. 3137
Sonata, piano (1924). See no. 3137
Sonata, piano, C major. See no. 3123
Sonata, 2 pianos. See no. 3137
Songs (4). See no. 4026
Songs from Shakespeare (3). See no. 1166
Suites, nos. 1 and 2. See no. 3950
3147 Symphony, C major. Symphony in 3 movements. OSR; Ernest Ansermet.
   London STS 15490 (From CS 6190)
                +-FF 5/6-80 p159

Symphonies, wind instruments. See no. 3148
Symphony in 3 movements. See no. 3132. See no. 3147
Symphony of psalms. See no. 226. See no. 3118
Tango. See no. 3124. See no. 3137. See no. 3138. See no. 3148
Three easy pieces. See no. 3137
Valse pour les enfants. See no. 3137

3148 Works, selections: Cantique. Dirge canons. Double canon. Easy
pieces. Elegy for J.F.K. Epitaphium fur das Grabmal des Prinzen
Max Egon zu Furstenberg. Lullaby. L'Oiseau de feu: Berceuse
et final. Pastorale. Symphonies, wind instruments. Tango. Oskar Gottlieb Blarr, org. Schwann VMS 2047
          +-NR 9-80 p8

STRAVINSKY, Soulima
Sonatina. See no. 3884

STREET, Tison
Quintet, strings. See no. 1937

STROHMAYER, Alois
Schone Ida. See no. 3759
Die Tanzlustigen. See no. 3759

SUBOTNIK, Morton
3149 After the butterfly. A sky of cloudless sulphur. Mario Guarneri,
tpt; Twentieth Century Players; Morton Subotnik. Nonesuch N
78001
          +FF 11/12-80 p181   +HF 11-80 p80
Liquid strata. See no. 1899
A sky of cloudless sulphur. See no. 3149

SUCHON, Eugen
3150 Balladic suite. Metamorphoses. Klara Havlikova, pno.   RCA PRL 1-
9056
          +FF 7/8-80 p139
Metamorphoses. See no. 3150
Symphonic fantasy on B-A-C-H. See no. 1860

SUK, Josef
About mother, op. 28. See no. 3151
3151 Piano works: About mother, op. 28. Pieces, piano, op. 7, no. 1.
Slumber songs, op. 33, nos. 2 and 6. Spring, op. 22a. Things
lived and dreamed, op. 30. Pavel Stepan, pno. Supraphon 111
2471/2 (2)
          +ARG 11-79 p52   +-MT 2-80 p109
          +FF 9/10-79 p147   +RR 1-79 p76
          ++FU 4-80 p52   +RR 5-79 p89
          +-Gr 4-79 p1749   +SFC 7-20-80 p34
          +-HFN 1-79 p123   +SFC 12-30-79 p33
Pieces, op. 17. See no. 3772
Pieces, piano, op. 7, no. 1. See no. 3151
Quartet, strings, no. 1, op. 11, B flat major. See no. 1888
Serenade, strings, op. 6, E flat major. See no. 1841
Slumber songs, op. 33, nos. 2 and 6. See no. 3151
Spring, op. 22a. See no. 3151
Things lived and dreamed, op. 30. See no. 3151

SULLIVAN, Arthur
3152 Cox and box. The zoo. Julia Goss, Jane Metcalfe, s; Geoffrey
Shovelton, Meston Reid, t; Gareth Jones, Michael Rayner, Kenneth
Sandford, John Ayldon, bar; RPO; D'Oyly Carte Opera Chorus; Roy-
ton Nash. Decca TXS 128 Tape (c) KTXC 128 (also London OSA 1171
Tape (c) CS 4-1171)

+ARG 7-79 p48   +NR 1-80 p11
+-FF 9/10-79 p148   +-NYT 12-16-79 pD21
+FU 5-80 p50   +SFC 1-20-80 p47
+Gr 12-78 p1191   +St 7-79 p107
++HFN 12-78 p161

The gondoliers, excerpts. See no. 3164

3153 The gondoliers: From the sunny Spanish shore; In enterprise of
     martial kind; Take a pair of sparkling eyes; On the day when I
     was wedded; Small titles and orders; Finale. H.M.S. Pinafore:
     Hail men-o-wars-men; I'm called little buttercup; When I was a
     lad; Never mind the why and wherefore. The Mikado: A wand'ring
     minstrel; As some day it may happen; The sun whose rays; Here's
     a how-de-do; On a tree by a river; There is a beauty in the bel-
     low; Finale. The pirates of Penzance: Poor wandring one; When
     a felon's not engaged; Stay Frederic stay. Marion Studholm, s;
     Jean Allister, con, Edmund Bohan, t; Ian Wallace, bar; English
     Chorale; London Concert Orchestra; Marcus Dods. Chalfont C 77003
            +ARG 2-80 p47   +St 1-79 p98
            +-FF 11/12-79 p73

The gondoliers: Listen and learn; When a merry maiden marries; Then
     one of us. See no. 3163

3154 H.M.S. Pinafore. Trial by jury. Winifred Lawson, Elsie Griffin, s;
     Nellie Briercliffe, ms; Bertha Lewis, con; Derek Oldham, Charles
     Goulding, t; Arthur Hosking, George Baker, Henry Lytton, bar; Leo
     Sheffield, Sydney Granville, bs-bar; Darrel Fancourt, Stuart Rob-
     ertson, bs; Orchestra and Chorus; Harry Norris, Malcolm Sargent.
     Arabesque 8052-2L (2) Tape (c) 9052-2L (From HMV originals)
            +-HF 5-80 p68   +NYT 1-6-80 pD18

3155 H.M.S. Pinafore, excerpts. Valerie Masterson, Helen Landis, s;
     Thomas Round, t; John Carter, Michael Wakeham, bar; Festival
     Orchestra and Chorus; Peter Murray. Everest SDBR 3454
            +FF 5/6-80 p81   +-NR 6-80 p12

H.M.S. Pinafore: Hail men-o-wars-men; I'm called little buttercup;
     When I was a lad; Never mind the why and wherefore. See no. 3153

H.M.S. Pinafore: I am the monarch of the sea; When I was a lad I
     served a term; Never mind the why and wherefore. See no. 3163

3156 Iolanthe. Nellie Briercliffe, Winifred Lawson, s; Bertha Lewis,
     Nellie Walker, con; George Baker, Derek Oldham, Sydney Granville,
     bar; Darrell Fancourt, Leslie Rands, bs; D'Oyly Carte Opera Orch-
     estra and Chorus; Malcolm Sargent. Arabesque 8066/2 (2)
            +NR 12-80 p9

3157 Iolanthe (without dialogue). Trial by jury. Nellie Briercliffe,
     Alice Moxon, Winifred Lawson, Beatrice Elburn, s; Nellie Walker,
     Bertha Lewis, con; Derek Oldham, t; George Baker, Leslie Rands,
     Arthur Hosking, bar; Sydney Granville, Leo Sheffield, bs; Orches-
     tra and Chorus; D'Oyle Carte Opera Chorus; Harry Norris. World
     Records SHB 64 (2) (From HMV D 1785/95)
            +-ARSC Vol 12, nos. 1-2   +-HFN 5-80 p125
               1980 p108   ++RR 4-80 p50
            +Gr 4-80 p1596

Iolanthe, excerpts. See no. 3164
The long day closes. See no. 3791

3158 The Mikado. Brenda Bennett, Marjorie Eyre, Elizabeth Nickell-Lean,
     s; Josephine Curtis, Radley Flynn, bar; Darrell Fancourt, bs;
     Derek Oldham, Martyn Green, Sydney Granville, bar; Leslie Rands,

bs; D'Oyly Carte Orchestra and Chorus; Isidore Godfrey. Arabesque 8051/2 (2)
> +NR 10-80 p12

The Mikado, excerpts. See no. 3164

The Mikado: A wand'ring minstrel; As someday it may happen; The sun
whose rays; Here's a how-de-do; On a tree by a river; There is a
beauty in the bellow; Finale. See no. 3153

The Mikado: Our great Mikado: Here's a how-de-do; The flowers that
bloom in the spring; On a tree by the river a little tom-tit.
See no. 3163

Patience: Prithee pretty maiden; A magnet hung in a hardware shop;
If Saphir I choose to marry; When I go out of door. See no. 3163

3159 Pineapple Poll: Ballet, excerpt. VERDI: The lady and the fool:
Ballet, excerpts. LPO; Charles Mackerras. Classics for Pleasure CFP 40293
> +FF 5/6-80 p159   +HFN 10-78 p131
> +Gr 11-78 p973

3160 The pirates of Penzance (without dialogue). Elsie Griffin, Nellie
Briercliffe, s; Nellie Walker, Dorothy Gill, con; Derek Oldham,
t; George Baker, Stuart Robertson, bar; Peter Dawson, bs-bar;
Leo Sheffield, bs; Orchestra and Chorus; Malcolm Sargent. Pearl
GEMM 171/2 (2) (From HMV D 1678/8)
> +Gr 4-80 p1596   +-RR 5-80 p49
> +-HFN 6-80 p112

3161 The pirates of Penzance, excerpts. Valerie Masterson, s; John
Carter, bar; Donald Adams, bs; Thomas Round, t; Festival Orchestra and Chorus; Peter Murray. Everest SDBR 3467
> +FF 5/6-80 p81   +-NR 6-80 p12

The pirates of Penzance, excerpts. See no. 3164

The pirates of Penzance: Poor wandring one; When a felon's not en-
gaged; Stay Frederic stay. See no. 3153

3162 Ruddigore. Margaret Mitchell, Deidree Thurlow, s; Ella Halman, Ann
Drummond-Grant, con; Leonard Osborn, t; Martyn Green, Radley
Flynn, bar; Richard Watson, Darrell Fancourt, bs; D'Oyly Carte
Opera Orchestra and Chorus; Isidore Godfrey. Decca DAP 3061/2
(2) (From LK 4027/8)
> +Gr 2-80 p1305

Ruddigore, excerpts. See no. 3164

Ruddigore: Fair is Rose; If somebody there chanced to be. See no.
3163

Songs: God shall wipe away all tears. See no. 3560

Songs: The willow song. See no. 3903

The sorcerer: Time was when love and I. See no. 3770

Trial by jury. See no. 3154. See no. 3157

Trial by jury, excerpts. See no. 3164

Victoria and merrie England: Suite, no. 1. See no. 3165

3163 Works, selections: The gondoliers: Listen and learn; When a merry
maiden marries; Then one of us. H.M.S. Pinafore: I am the monarch of the sea; When I was a lad I served a term; Never mind
the why and wherefore. The Mikado: Our great Mikado; Here's a
how-de-do; The flowers that bloom in the spring; On a tree by
the river a little tom-tit. Patience: Prithee pretty maiden; A
magnet hung in a hardware shop; If Saphir I choose to marry;
When I go out of door. Ruddigore: Fair is Rose; If somebody
there chanced to be. The Yeoman of the guard: Is life a boon;

Were I thy bride; Here upon were both agreed; When a wooer goes
a'wooing. Glyndebourne Chorus; Pro Arte Orchestra; Malcolm Sargent. Classics for Pleasure CFP 40282 Tape (c) TC CFP 40282
+HFN 5-78 p145   +RR 5-78 p24
+HFN 8-80 p109 tape
3164 Works, selections: The gondoliers, excerpts. Iolanthe, excerpts.
The Mikado, excerpts. The pirantes of Panzance, excerpts. Rud-
digore, excerpts. Trial by jury, excerpts. Glyndebourne Chorus;
Pro Arte Orchestra; Malcolm Sargent. Classics for Pleasure CFP
40338 Tape (c) CFP 40338
+-HFN 10-80 p115   +HFN 12-80 p159 tape
3165 The yeomen of the guard. Victoria and merrie England: Suite, no. 1.
Barbara Lilley, Jane Metcalfe, s; Patricia Leonard, Suzanne O'
Keefe, ms; Geoffrey Shovelton, Meston Reid, Barry Clark, t;
Michael Rayner, John Ayldon, John Reed, Kenneth Sandford, Gareth
Jones, bar; D'Oyly Carte Opera Chorus; RPO; Royston Nash. Decca
SKL 5307/8 (2) Tape (c) K157K22 (also London OSA 12117 Tape (c)
OSA 5-12117)
+-Gr 11-79 p921   +St 11-80 p87
The yeomen of the guard: Is life a boon; Were I thy bride; Hereupon
were both agreed; When a wooer goes a-wooing. See no. 3163
The zoo. See no. 3152
SUNDERLAND, Raymond
Fanfare, march and fugue. See no. 4057
SUPPE, Franz von
3166 Boccaccio. Edda Moser, Kari Lovaas, Anneliese Rothenberger, s; Gis-
ela Litz, con; Willi Brokmeier, Adolf Dallapozza, Friedrich Lenz,
t; Hermann Prey, bar; Kurt Bohme, Walter Berry, bs; Bavarian
State Opera Orchestra and Chorus; Willi Boskovsky. EMI 1C 157
30216/7 (2)
+Gr 12-80 p878   +HFN 10-80 p109
3167 Boccaccio. Rita Streich, Lisa Jungkind, s; Rupert Glawitsch, Otto
Albrecht, t; Kurt Marschner, Horst Gunter, bar; Gustav Neidlinger,
bs; Hans-Herbert Fiedler, bs-bar; North German Radio Chorus; Ham-
burg Radio Orchestra; Wilhelm Schuchter. RCA VL 3-0404
+FF 11/12-80 p182
Boccaccio: Hab ich nur deine Liebe. See no. 3695
Light cavalry: Overture. See no. 2725. See no. 3638. See no. 3843
Pique Dame: Overture. See no. 2725
Poet and peasant: Overture. See no. 2725. See no. 3638
3168 Die schone Galatea. Renate Holm, s; Reinhold Bartel, Ferry Gruber,
t; Kurt Grosskurth; Cologne Radio Orchestra and Chorus; Franz
Marszalek. RCA VL 3-0352
+FF 9/10-80 p213
SURINACH, Carlos
Paeans and dances of heathen Iberia. See no. 2434
SUSATO, Tielman
Bergerette. See no. 3597
Il estoit une fillette, ronde. See no. 3754
Gaillarde. See no. 3597
Hoboecken tanz. See no. 3597. See no. 3754
Mille regretz, pavane. See no. 3754
Mon amy, ronde. See no. 3597
Pavane. See no. 3597
Ronde. See no. 3754

Ronde and saltarelle. See no. 3754
Si pas souffrir. See no. 3754
SUTERMEISTER, Heinrich
Romeo and Juliet: Balcony scene. See no. 3931
SUTTON, Tom
Come sweet Marguerite. See no. 3791
SVEINSSON, Atli
Aria. See no. 3598
3169 Concerto, flute. THORARINSSON: Concerto, violin. Robert Aitken,
flt; Einar Sveinbjornsson, vln; Iceland Symphony Orchestra; Pall
Palsson, Karsten Andersen. Iceland Music Information Centre ITM
3
+RR 4-80 p67
SVENDSEN, Johan
3170 Andante funebre. Carnival in Paris, op. 9. Icelandic melodies (2).
Polonaise, no. 2, op. 28. Romance, op. 26, G major. Ornulf
Boye Hansen, vn; Oslo Philharmonic Orchestra; Kjell Ingebretsen,
Oivin Fjeldstad. Norsk Kulturrads NFK 30028
+—FF 5/6-79 p93   +Gr 9-80 p408
+Gr 1-80 p1167
Carnival in Paris, op. 9. See no. 3170
3171 Concerto, violin, op. 6. Concerto, violoncello, op. 7. Norwegian
rhapsodies, nos. 1-4. Symphony, no. 1, op. 4, D major. Arve
Tellefsen, vln; Hege Waldeland, vlc; Oslo Philharmonic Orchestra,
Bergen Symphony Orchestra; Miltiades Caridis, Karsten Andersen.
Polydor Norway NKF 30001/2, 30006
+Gr 3-77 p1457   +HFN 3-77 p109
+—Gr 1-80 p1167   +—HFN 7-80 p110
+Gr 9-8 p408   +RR 1-77 p64
Concerto, violoncello, op. 7. See no. 3171
3172 Festival polonaise, op. 12. Norwegian artists carnival, op. 16.
Romeo and Juliet, op. 18. Zorahayda, op. 11. Bergen Symphony
Orchestra; Karsten Andersen. Polydor NKF 30016
+FF 11/12-78 p123   +HFN 7-80 p111
+Gr 9-80 p408   +RR 8-77 p63
+HFN 8-77 p89
Icelandic melodies (2). See no. 3170
Norwegian artists carnival, op. 16. See no. 3172
Norwegian rhapsodies, nos. 1-4. See no. 3171
Polonaise, no. 2, op. 28. See no. 3170
3173 Quartet, strings, op. 1, A minor. Quintet, strings, op. 5, C major.
Hindar Quartet; Asbjorn Lilleslatten, vla. NKF 30010
+FF 11/12-78 p123   +HFN 7-80 p111
+Gr 9-80 p408
Quintet, strings, op. 5, C major. See no. 3173
Romance, op. 26, G major. See no. 3170. See no. 4009
Romeo and Juliet, op. 18. See no. 3172
Symphony, no. 1, op. 4, D major. See no. 3171
3174 Symphony, no. 2, op. 15, B flat major. Oslo Philharmonic Orchestra;
Oivin Fjeldstad. Norsk Kulturrads NFK 30009
/FF 11-77 p54   +HFN 7-80 p110
+Gr 9-80 p408
Zorahayda, op. 11. See no. 3172
SVETLANOV
Aria. See no. 3694

SVETLANOV, Yevgeny
    Festive poem, op. 9. See no. 2180
SWEELINCK, Jan
    Ballet of the Grand Duke. See no. 3757. See np. 4049
    Chorale and variations. See no. 3942
    Da pacem Domine in diebus nostris. See no. 3175
    Durch Adams fall. See no. 3176
    Erbarm dich. See no. 3176
    Fantasia, D minor. See no. 260
    Fantasias, nos. 3-4, 9, 14. See no. 3176
    Fantasias, no. 4, D major. See no. 3175
    Fantasias, no. 5. See no. 3175
    Fantasias, no. 12, A minor. See no. 3175
    Fantasia chromatica. See no. 3757
    Fantasia en echo, no. 15. See no. 3176
    Mein junges Leben hat ein End. See no. 4021
3175 Organ works: Da pacem Domine in diebus nostris. Fantasia, no. 12,
    A minor. Fantasia, no. 4, D major. Fantasia, no. 5. Puer nob-
    is nascitur. Toccata, no. 17, A minor. Gustav Leonhardt, org.
    Harmonia Mundi 065 99608
            +Gr 9-80 p379   ++RR 8-80 p75
3176 Organ works: Durch Adams fall. Erbarm dich. Fantasias, nos. 3-4,
    9, 14. Fantasia en echo, no. 15. Psalm, no. 116, J'ayme mon
    Dieu. Louis Thiry, org. Musical Heritage Society MHS 4069
            +FF 3/4-80 p162
    Praeludium toccata. See no. 4014
    Psalms, no. 36. See no. 4021
    Psalm, no. 116, J'ayme mon Dieu. See no. 3176
    Puer nobis nascitur. See no. 3175
    Toccata, no. 17, A minor. See no. 3175
    Unter der Linden grune. See no. 163
    Von der fortuna, variations. See no. 3757
SWIFT, Richard
3177 Great praises. Summer notes. Carol Ann Dudley, s; Marin Tartak,
    Paul Hersh, pno. CRI SD 412
            +SFC 1-13-80 p41
    Great praises. See no. 698
    Summer notes. See no. 698. See no. 3177
SZABELSKI, Boleslaw
    Aphorisms "9". See no. 3857
SZALONEK, Witold
    Improvisations sonoristiques. See no. 3857
SZOKOLAY
    Revelation. See no. 3803
SZYMANOWSKI, Karol
    La berceuse d'Aitacho Enia, op. 52. See no. 3183
    Caprices after Paganini, op. 40. See no. 3109
    Chant de Roxanne, op. 46. See no. 3183
    Concerto, violin, no. 1, op. 35. See no. 3182
3178 Etude, op. 4, no. 3, B flat minor. King Roger, op. 46: Roxanne's
    song. Symphony, no. 2, op. 19, B flat major. Lodz Philharmonic
    Orchestra; Henryk Czyz. Musicaphon BM 30 SL 1408
            ++ARG 3-80 p55
3179 Etude, op. 4, no. 3, B flat minor. Masques, op. 34 (ed. Feder).
    Sonata, piano, no. 3, op. 36 (rev. Feder). Valse romantique.

Donn-Alexandre Feder, pno. Protone PR 149
     +FF 11/12-80 p183   +NR 11-80 p10
Harnasie, op. 55: Dance. See no. 3183
King Roger, op. 46: Roxane's song. See no. 3178. See no. 3964
Masques, op. 34. See no. 3179
Mazurkas, op. 50, nos. 1-3, 5-6, 9-11, 13-14, 18. See no. 3182
3180 Mythes, op. 30. Quartet, strings, op. 56, no. 2. Wilanow Quartet;
    Konstanty Kulka, vln; J. Marchwinski, pno. Aurora AUR 7004
        +-Gr 1-80 p1168   +-RR 12-79 p90
        +-HFN 12-79 p177
Mythes, op. 30. See no. 3183
Notturno et tarantella, op. 28. See no. 3183
Quartet, strings, op. 56, no. 2. See no. 3180. See no. 3182
Romance, op. 23. See no. 3109. See no. 3183
Sonata, piano, no. 3, op. 36. See no. 2541. See no. 3179
Sonata, violin and piano, op. 9, D minor. See no. 1089
Songs (4). See no. 3182
Stabat mater, op. 53. See no. 3181. See no. 3182
Symphonies, nos. 2-4. See no. 3182
Symphony, no. 2, op. 19, B flat major. See no. 3178
3181 Symphony, no. 3, op. 27. Stabat mater, op. 53. Warsaw Philharmonic
    Orchestra and Chorus; Witold Rowicki. Aurora AUR 7003 (From Muza
    XLO 149)
        +Gr 1-80 p1193   +-RR 12-79 p116
        +-HFN 12-79 p177
Valse romantique. See no. 3179
Variations on a Polish folk tune, op. 10. See no. 960
3182 Works, selections: Concerto, violin, no. 1, op. 35. Mazurkas, op.
    50, nos. 1, 3, 5-6, 9-11, 13-14, 18. Quartet, strings, op. 56,
    no. 2. Songs (4). Stabat mater, op. 53. Symphonies, nos. 2-4.
    Barbara Hesse, Jan Ekier, pno; Borodin Quartet; Stefania Woyto-
    wicz, s; Krystyna Szczepanska, alto; Andrzej Hiolski, bar; Chorus;
    Warsaw Philharmonic Orchestra, Polish Radio Orchestra; Witold
    Rowicki, Grzegorz Fitelberg. (add. disc Szymanowski speech and
    playing mazurkas, op. 50, no. 13; op. 62, no. 1). Muza SX 0116,
    0120, 0126, 0149 (4)
        +FF 7/8-80 p121
3183 Works, selections: La berceuse d'Aitacho Enia, op. 52. Chant de
    Roxanne, op. 46. Harnasie, op. 55: Dance. Mythes, op. 30.
    Notturno e tarantella, op. 28. Romance, op. 23. Hanna Lachert,
    vln. Telarc S 5025
        ++NR 11-77 p15   +NYT 3-30-80 pD24
TAFFANEL, Paul
    Quintet, winds, G minor. See no. 1432
TAGLIAFERRI, E.
    Piscatore e pusilleco. See no. 3667
TAILLEFERRE, Germaine
    Fleurs de France. See no. 1281
    Jeux de plein air. See no. 1281
    Pastorale. See no. 3822
    Pastorale, D major. See no. 1281
    Sicilienne. See no. 1281. See no. 4024
    Sonata, harp. See no. 912. See no. 3685
    Sonata, violin and piano, C sharp minor. See no. 4065
    Valse lente. See no. 1281

TAKEMITSU, Toru
3184 A flock descends into the pentagonal garden. Quatrain. Tashi, BSO;
      Seiji Ozawa. DG 2531 210
                  +Gr 8-80 p230   ++NR 12-80 p3
      Quatrain. See no. 3184
3185 Quatrain II. Water ways. Waves. Tashi. RCA ARL 1-3843 Tape (c)
      ARK 1-3843
                  ++FF 11/12-80 p184   +SFC 9-28-80 p21
                  +NR 10-80 p6   ++St 11-80 p102
      Water ways. See no. 3185
      Waves. See no. 3185
TAKTAKISHVILI, Otar
3186 Concerto, piano, no. 1, C minor. Concerto, violin, F minor. Liana
      Isakadze, vln; Marina Mdivani, pno; USSR Radio and Television
      Large Orchestra; Otar Taktakishvili. Melodiya 33C10 10115/6
                  +ARG 1-80 p46   +FF 3/4-80 p163
      Concerto, violin, F minor. See no. 3186
TALLIS, Thomas
      Fantasia. See no. 3595
      If ye love me. See no. 3970
      In jejunio et fletu. See no. 3530
      Lamentations of Jeremiah. See no. 967
      Motets: Salvator mundi; Suscipe quaeso domine. See no. 3187
      O nata lux de lumine. See no. 3531
      O ye tenderest babes. See no. 3648. See no. 4044
3187 Puer natus est, mass. Motets: Salvator mundi; Suscipe quaeso dom-
      ine. Clerkes of Oxenford; David Wulstan. Nonesuch H 71378 (al-
      so Calliope CAL 1623)
                  +ARG 12-80 p46   ++Gr 2-79 p1454
                  ++FF 9/10-80 p213   +-NYT 8-10-80 pD17
                  +FU 6-80 p50   +St 10-80 p122
      Salvator mundi. See no. 3894. See no. 3941
3188 Songs (choral): Audivi vocem de caelo; Honor virtus et potestas; O
      sacrum convivium; Salvator mundi; Sancte Deus. TAVERNER: Mater
      Christi. Western wind mass. New College Choir, Oxford; Edward
      Higginbottom. CRD CRD 1072
                  +-Gr 3-80 p1433   +-MT 10-80 p638
                  +-HFN 3-80 p99   ++RR 3-80 p97
      Songs (hymns): Es more docti mistico; Iam lucis orto sidere. See
      no. 3595
      Spem in alium. See no. 3713
TANEYEV, Sergei
3189 The Oresteia (The temple of Apollo in Delphi). Nelly Tkachenko,
      Lyudmila Ganestova, Tamara Shimko, s; Lidiya Galushkina, con;
      Ivan Dubrovin, t; Anatoly Bokov, Arkady Savchenko, bar; Victor
      Chernobayev, bs; Belorussian State Opera and Ballet Theatre Orch-
      estra and Chorus; Tatyana Kolomyzeva. DG 2709 097 (3)
                  +-ARG 6-80 p29   +NR 3-80 p12
                  +Gr 11-79 p911   +NYT 12-16-79 pD21
                  +HF 5-80 p83   +-Op 4-80 p375
                  +HFN 11-79 p143   ++RR 11-79 p61
                  +MT 2-80 p109   +-St 4-80 p139
      The Oresteia: Entr'acte. See no. 3192
      Prelude and fugue, op. 29, G sharp minor. See no. 2545
3190 Quartet, strings, no. 3, op. 7, D minor. Quartet, strings, no. 5,

op. 13, A major. Taneyev Quartet. Melodiya S10 09929-30
+FF 1/2-80 p150
Quartet, strings, no. 5, op. 13, A major. See no. 3190
3191 Quartet, strings, no. 7, E flat major. Taneyev Quartet. Melodiya
S10 10225-26
+FF 1/2-80 p150
3192 Symphony, no. 2, B flat major. The Oresteia: Entr'acte. Moscow
Radio and Television Symphony Orchestra; Vladimir Fedoseyev.
Melodiya 33S10 08045-46
+ARG 9-80 p44				+FF 9/10-78 p118
3193 Symphony, no. 4, op. 12, C minor. LSO; Yuri Ahronovitch. RCA RL
3-0372
+FF 9/10-80 p214
3194 Trio, op. 22, D major. Vladimir Ovcharek, vln; Iosif Levinzon, vlc;
Tamara Fidler, pno. Melodiya S 10 10203-4
+FF 1/2-80 p150
3195 Trio, op. 22, D major. TCHEREPNIN, A.: Trio, op. 39, D major. Od-
eon Trio. RCA RL 3-0324
++ARG 4-80 p48				+FF 9/10-79 p149
TANG, Jordan Cho-Tung
A little suite. See no. 3731
TANNER, Jerre
3196 Boy with goldfish. Leon Siu, Malia Elliott, vocals; Leon Siu, gtr;
Timothy Farrell, org; Nigel Brooks Chorale; LSO; Lee Holdridge.
Varese VCDM 1000 30
+-FF 11/12-80 p184				+HFN 11-80 p123
TANSMAN, Alexandre
Mouvement perpetuel. See no. 3964
Sonatina, bassoon and piano. See no. 2526. See no. 3588
TANS'UR
Westerham tune (Psalm, no. 81). See no. 3848
TARR, Edward
Suite of trumpet voluntaries, C major. See no. 3866
TARREGA, Francisco
La alborada. See no. 3665
Capricho arabe. See no. 3197
Danza mora. See no. 3197
Estudio brillante, A major. See no. 3549
Etude (Dream). See no. 3603
Etude, A major. See no. 3775
Grand waltz. See no. 3603
Introduction and variations on the theme "Carnival in Venice". See
no. 3603
Lagrima. See no. 3665
Maria. See no. 3197
Mazurka en sol. See no. 3197
Recuerdos de la Alhambra. See no. 3197. See no. 3549. See no.
3607. See no. 3635. See no. 3637. See no. 3665. See no. 3775
Tango. See no. 3197
Transcriptions: Handel: Chorale, Minuet. Haydn: Andante, Minuet.
Mendelssohn: Barcarolle, Canzonet. Schubert: Minuet. See no.
3197
Two little sisters. See no. 3603
Variations on "The carnival of Venice". See no. 3197
Waltz. See no. 3603

3197 Works, selections: Capricho arabe. Danza mora. Maria. Mazurca en
       sol. Recuerdos de la Alhambra. Tango. Variations on "Carnival
       of Venice". Transcriptions: Handel: Chorale, Minuet. Haydn:
       Andante, Minuet. Mendelssohn: Barcarolle, Canzonet. Schubert:
       Minuet. Alice Artzt, gtr. Meridian E 77026
                    +Gr 10-79 p676   +NYT 6-1-80 pD19
                    +HFN 9-79 p113   ++RR 10-79 p132
TARTINI, Giuseppe
3198 Concerto. flute, G major. Concerto, violin, A minor. Concerto,
       violoncello, D major. Sonata, strings, G major. Jean-Pierre
       Rampal, flt; Piero Toso, vln; Severino Zannerini, vlc; I Solisti
       Veneti; Claudio Scimone. Erato STU 70626
                    +HFN 4-80 p109   +RR 10-79 p107
     Concerto, flute, G major. See no. 739
     Concerto, violin, A minor. See no. 3198
     Concerto, violin, D major. See no. 2422
3199 Concerti, violin, D minor, D major. Concerto, violoncello, A major.
       Sonata, strings, A major. Piero Toso, vln; Severino Zannerini,
       vlc; I Solisti Veneti; Claudio Scimone. Erato STU 70970
                    +-Gr 8-80 p230   +RR 8-80 p54
                    +-HFN 8-80 p95   +ST 12-80 p575
     Concerto, violoncello, A major. See no. 3199
     Concerto, violoncello, D major. See no. 740. See no. 3198
     Sonata, strings, A major. See no. 3199
     Sonata, strings, G major. See no. 3198
     Sonata, violin, G minor. See no. 998
     Variations on a theme by Corelli. See no. 3772
TASKIN, Henri Joseph
     Masonic funeral march. See no. 3844
TAVERNER, John
     Mater Christi. See no. 3188
TCHAIKOVSKY, Peter
     Aveu passione, E minor. See no. 3832
     Berceuse, op. 16, no. 1, A flat minor. See no. 3832
3200 Capriccio italien, op. 45. The nutcracker, op. 71: Ballet suite.
       Quartet, strings, no. 1, op. 11, D minor: Andante cantabile.
       BPhO; Mstislav Rostropovich, vlc and cond. DG 2531 112 Tape (c)
       3301 112
                    +-FF 5/6-80 p160   +HFN 8-79 p113
                    +Gr 8-79 p344   +-NR 1-80 p2
                    +Gr 9-79 p534 tape   +RR 8-79 p95
3201 Capriccio italien, op. 45. Serenade, op. 48, C major. USSR
       Symphony Orchestra; Evgenyi Svetlanov. Quintessence PMC 7137
                    ++FF 3/4-80 p165
3202 Capriccio italien, op. 45. Mazeppa: Cossack dance. Overture, the
       year 1812, op. 49. Cincinnati Symphony Orchestra; Erich Kunzel.
       Telarc DG 10041
                    -ARG 5-80 p40   +-NR 10-80 p2
                    +Gr 4-80 p1597   +RR 4-80 p82
                    +-HFN 4-80 p111   +SFC 12-7-80 p33
                    +FF 3/4-80 p164   +St 1-80 p96
     Capriccio italien, op. 45. See no. 1317. See no. 2694. See no.
       2702
     Capriccio italien, op. 45, abridged. See no. 3709
     Chanson triste, op. 40, no. 2. See no. 2614

3203 Concerto, piano, no. 1, op. 23, B flat minor. Andrei Gavrilov, pno;
     PhO; Riccardo Muti. Angel SZ 37679 (also HMV ASD 3818 Tape (c)
     TC ASD 3818)

+Gr 5-80 p1677	+-NYT 5-11-80 pD24
+-HF 9-80 p99	++RR 6-80 p60
+-HFN 7-80 p111	+RR 8-80 p95 tape
+HFN 10-80 p117	+St 10-80 p122
+NR 6-80 p7	

3204 Concerto, piano, no. 1, op. 23, B flat minor. Martha Argerich, pno;
     RPO; Charles Dutoit. DG 2535 295 Tape (c) 3335 295 (From 2530
     112)

++Gr 10-78 p695	+RR 12-78 p75
+HFN 12-78 p167	+St 10-80 p122
+HFN 2-79 p118 tape	

3205 Concerto, piano, no. 1, op. 23, B flat minor. Clifford Curzon, pno;
     VPO; Georg Solti. London STS 15471 (From CS 6100)

                +-FF 1/2-80 p151

3206 Concerto, piano, no. 1, op. 23, B flat minor. Claudio Arrau, pno;
     BSO; Colin Davis. Philips 9500 695 Tape (c) 7300 783

-CL 4-80 p10	+HFN 10-80 p117
++FF 7/8-80 p141	+-NR 6-80 p7
+Gr 5-80 p1677	+-RR 5-80 p73
+-Gr 8-80 p27 tape	+St 10-80 p122
+-HF 9-80 p99	+-SFC 2-24-80 p39
++HFN 5-80 p125	

3207 Concerto, piano, no. 2, op. 44, G major. Concerto, piano, no. 3,
     op. 75, E flat major. Gary Graffman, pno; PO; Eugene Ormandy.
     CBS 61990 Tape (c) 40-61990 (From SBRG 72385)

+-Gr 10-80 p502	+-HFN 11-80 p129
+-HFN 10-80 p117 tape	

     Concerto, piano, no. 3, op. 75, E flat major. See no. 3207
3208 Concerto, violin, op. 35, D major. Souvenir d'un lieu cher, op. 42:
     Meditation. Isaac Stern, vln; National Symphony Orchestra;
     Mstislav Rostropovich. Columbia M 35126 Tape (c) MT 35126 (also
     CBS 76725 Tape (c) 40-76725)

+ARG 3-80 p43	+-HFN 6-79 p117 tape
+FF 11/12-79 p131	++NR 6-79 p7
+Gr 3-79 p1579	+-NYT 4-18-79 pD28
+Gr 6-79 p109 tape	+-RR 3-79 p91
+-HF 9-79 p112	+SFC 4-1-79 p44
+-HFN 3-79 p131	++St 7-79 p103

3209 Concerto, violin, op. 35, D major. Serenade melancolique, op. 26,
     B minor. Gidon Kremer, vln; BPhO; Lorin Maazel. DG 2532 001
     Tape (c) 3302 001

                +Gr 12-80 p841   +HFN 12-80 p146

3210 Concerto, violin, op. 35, D major. Serenade melancolique, op. 26,
     B flat minor. Itzhak Perlman, vln; PO; Eugene Ormandy. HMV
     ASD 3726 Tape (c) TC ASD 3726 (also Angel SZ 37640 Tape (c) 4ZS
     37640)

+-ARG 3-80 p43	++NR 4-80 p5
++Gr 12-79 p1018	++NYT 7-6-80 pD15
++HF 3-80 p87	+St 5-80 p93
+-HFN 12-79 p171	+RR 2-80 p62
+-HFN 2-80 p107 tape	

3211 Concerto, violin, op. 35, D major. Serenade, op. 48, C major: Waltz.

Erik Friedman, vln; Sofia Philharmonic Orchestra; Sofia Soloists;
Dimiter Manolov, Vassil Kasandjiev.   Monitor MCS 2162
    +-FF 9/10-80 p215   ++SFC 5-11-80 p35
    +NR 6-80 p7
3212 Concerto, violin, op. 35, D major.   Igor Oistrakh, vln; MPO; David
    Oistrakh.   Musical Heritage Society MHS 4049
        +ARG 3-80 p43   +-FF 7/8-80 p141
3213 Concerto, violin, op. 35, D major.   Serenade melancolique, op. 26,
    B minor.   Shizuka Ishikawa, vln; CPhO; Zdenek Kosler.   Supraphon
    110 2460
        ++NR 12-80 p5
    Concerto, violin, op. 35, D major.   See no. 804.   See no. 3964.   See
    no. 3968
    Concerto, violin, op. 35, D major: Canzonetta.   See no. 3964
    L'Espiegle, op. 72, no. 12.   See no. 2614
3214 Eugene Onegin, op. 24.   Tamara Milashkina, s; Tatiana Tugarinova,
    Tamara Sinyavskaya, Larissa Avdeyeva, ms; Vladimir Atlantov, Lev
    Kuznetsov, t; Yuri Mazurok, bar; Anton Japridze, Evgeny Nester-
    enko, Valeri Yaroslavstev, bs; Bolshoi Theatre Orchestra and
    Chorus; Mark Ermler.   HMV SLS 5191 (3) Tape (c) TC SLS 5191
        +-Gr 2-80 p1294   +-Op 4-80 p375
        +-HFN 3-80 p99   +RR 2-80 p43
3215 Eugen Onegin, op. 24, excerpts.   Fritz Wunderlich, t; Evelyn Lear,
    Brigitte Fassbaender, s; Dietrich Fischer-Dieskau, bar; Martti
    Talvela, bs; Bavarian State Opera Orchestra and Chorus; Otto
    Gerdes.   DG 2535 323
        +RR 8-80 p14
    Eugene Onegin, op. 24: Arias.   See no. 3539
    Eugene Onegin: Ein jeder kennt die Lieb auf Erden.   See no. 3712
    Eugene Onegin, op. 24: Faint echo of my youth.   See no. 3558
    Eugene Onegin, op. 24: Gremins aria.   See no. 3774
    Eugene Onegin, op. 24: Lensky's aria.   See no. 3633.   See no. 3641
    Eugene Onegin, op. 24: Polonaise.   See no. 3807
    Eugene Onegin, op. 24: Tatiana's letter scene.   See no. 3780
3216 Francesca da Rimini, op. 32.   Romeo and Juliet: Fantasy overture.
    Israel Philharmonic Orchestra; Leonard Bernstein.   DG 2531 211
    Tape (c) 3301 211
        +FF 7/8-80 p142   +RR 4-80 p81
        +-Gr 2-80 p1275   +RR 7-80 p97 tape
        ++HFN 3-80 p99   +SFC 7-6-80 p27
        +MUM 10-80 p35   ++St 7-80 p77
        +NR 6-80 p2
    Francesca da Rimini, op. 32.   See no. 3259
    Hamlet, op. 67a.   See no. 3259
    Humoresque, op. 10, no. 2, G major.   See no. 3232
    Impromptu, A flat major.   See no. 3232
    Impromptu caprice, G major.   See no. 3232
    Iolanthe, op. 69: My Lord if I offend.   See no. 3770
    Iolanthe, op. 69: Why did I not know before.   See no. 3774
3217 Liturgy of St. John Chrysostom, op. 41.   Songs (Hymns): Blessed are
    they whom thou has chosen; Hymn of the cherubim, no. 5; It is
    meet; Now the angels are with us; Our father; To thee we sing.
    Bulgarian A Capella Choir; Georgi Robev.   Angel SZB 3876 (2)
        +FF 1/2-80 p151   +NYT 11-4-79 pD28
        ++NR 12-79 p8   +ON 12-8-79 p28

The maid of Orleans (Jeanne d'Arc): Adieu forets. See no. 3774

3218 Manfred symphony, op. 58.   NPhO; Vladimir Ashkenazy. Decca SXL
  6853 Tape (c) KSXC 6853 (also London CS 7075 Tape (c) 5-7075)

  /ARG 4-79 p40
  +Audio 1-80 p117
  +-FF 3/4-79 p122
  +Gr 9-78 p487
  +Gr 12-78 p1178 tape
  +HF 12-79 p110 tape
  /HFN 9-78 p147
  +HFN 9-78 p159 tape
  -RR 9-78 p67
  +-RR 11-78 p114 tape
  ++SFC 3-11-79 p49
  ++St 3-79 p102

3219 Manfred symphony, op. 58. LPO; Mstislav Rostropovich. HMV ASD
  3730 Tape (c) TC ASD 3730 (From SLS 5099)

  +Gr 4-80 p1563
  ++HFN 4-80 p119
  +HFN 8-80 p109 tape
  +-MT 11-80 p711
  ++RR 4-80 p81

3220 Marche slav, op. 31. Mozartiana, op. 61. Romeo and Juliet: Fantasy
  overture. N. Y. Stadium Orchestra, VSO; Leopold Stokowski, Jonel
  Perlea. Everest SDBR 3463 (From Vox)

  -FF 9/10-80 p218   -NR 4-80 p4

3221 Marche slav, op. 31. Overture, the year 1812, op. 49. Romeo and
  Juliet: Overture. LSO; Andre Previn. Mobile Fidelity MFSL 1-
  502 (From Angel 36890)

  ++FF 11/12-80 p185

Marche slav, op. 31. See no. 3250
Mazeppa: Cossack dance. See no. 3202
Melodie. See no. 3788
Melodie, op. 42, no. 3. See no. 3601
Minuetto scherzoso, op. 51, no. 3. See no. 2614
Momento lirico. See no. 3232

3222 The months (The seasons). Konstantin Igumnov, pno. Melodiya S10
  05523/4

  +ARSC Vol 12, nos. 1-3, 1980 p110

The months, op. 37: January. See no. 3622
Morceau, op. 19: Reverie du soir. See no. 3832
Morceau, op. 51: Valse sentimentale. See no. 4003
Mozartiana, op. 61. See no. 3220
Nocturne, op. 10, no. 1. See no. 3232
Nocturne, op. 19, no. 4. See no. 1300

3223 The nutcracker, op. 71. Toronto Children's Chorus; Toronto Symphony
  Orchestra; Andrew Davis. CBS 79222 (2) (also Columbia M 35196
  Tape (c) M2T 35196)

  +-ARG 12-79 p16
  +FF 1/2-80 p153
  +-FU 4-80 p52
  +Gr 10-79 p661
  +-HF 12-79 p103
  -HFN 10-79 p163
  -MUM 5/6-80 p35
  -NR 10-79 p3
  +-RR 11-79 p108
  +SFC 9-23-79 p37

3224 The nutcracker, op. 71. OSR; Ernest Ansermet. Decca DPA 569/70
  (From SXL 2092/3) (also London STS 15433/4)

  +-Gr 2-77 p1326
  +HFN 3-77 p117
  +-MUM 10-80 p35
  +RR 2-77 p62
  ++SFC 12-11-77 p61

3225 The nutcracker, op. 71. National Philharmonic Orchestra; Richard
  Bonynge. London CSA 2239 (2) (Also Decca SXL 6688/9 Tape (c)
  KSXC 6688/9, KSXC 2-7059)

  ++Audio 2-80 p42
  +Gr 11-75 p833
  +HFN 12-78 p171 tape
  ++NR 2-75 p2

+-Gr 12-78 p1178 tape   ++NYT 3-9-75 pD23
+HF 3-75 p71   +RR 11-75 p55
+HFN 11-75 p169   +-RR 11-78 p114 tape
+HFN 1-76 p125 tape   +St 3-75 p109

3226 The nutcracker, op. 71, excerpts. Baltimore Symphony Orchestra;
     Sergiu Comissiona. Turnabout TV 34752
                +FF 9/10-80 p218
     The nutcracker, op. 71: Ballet suite. See no. 3200
3227 The nutcracker, op. 71: Suite. Swan Lake, op. 20: Valse; Scene;
     Dance of the swans; Scene Pas d'action; Hungarian dance; La
     Czardas; Scene. Israel Philharmonic Orchestra; Zubin Mehta.
     Decca SXDL 7505 Tape (c) KSXDC 7505 (also London LDR 10008)
                +-Gr 12-80 p842   +SFC 12-14-80 p20
                +-HFN 12-80 p146
3228 The nutcracker, op. 71: Suite. PO; Eugene Ormandy. RCA GL 4-2869
     Tape (c) GK 4-2869 (From LRL 3-7519)
                +Gr 10-79 p720   -HFN 1-80 p123 tape
                -HFN 10-79 p169
     The nutcracker, op. 71: Suite. See no. 3252
3229 The nutcracker, op. 71: Suite, no. 2. St. Bavo Cathedral Boys
     Choir; COA; Antal Dorati. Philips 9500 697 Tape (c) 7300 788
     (From 6747 364)
                +Gr 11-80 p683   +HFN 11-80 p129
3230 The nutcracker, op. 71: Suite, excerpts. Romeo and Juliet: Fantasy
     overture. PH; Zoltan Rozsnyai. M & K RT 201
                +ARG 5-80 p45   +-FF 9/10-80 p38
     The Opritchnik: As before God and thee. See no. 3770
3231 Overture, the year 1812, op. 49. Romeo and Juliet: Fantasy overture.
     LAPO; Zubin Mehta. Decca JB 96
                +-HFN 11-80 p129
     Overture, the year 1812, op. 49. See no. 767. See no. 772. See
     no. 2617. See no. 3202. See no. 3221
     Pezzo capriccioso, op. 62. See no. 2758
3232 Piano works: Humoresque, op. 10, no. 2, G major. Impromptu, A
     flat major. Impromptu caprice, G major. Momento lirico. Noc-
     turne, op. 10, no. 1. Russian volunteer fleet march. Six piec-
     es on a single theme, op. 21: Prelude; Fugue; Impromptu; Funeral
     march; Mazurka; Scherzo. Valse-Scherzo, no. 2. Tatiana Nikola-
     yeva, pno. United Artists UACL 10012
                +-Gr 11-79 p885   +RR 1-80 p105
                +-HFN 2-80 p99
     Pieces, piano, op. 9, no. 6, F major: Theme and variations. See
     no. 3622
     Pique dame, op. 68: Hermann's arias. See no. 3926
     Pique dame, op. 68: It is midnight. See no. 3770
     Pique dame, op. 68: Je crains de lui parler la nuit. See no. 3774
     Un poco di Chopin, op. 72, no. 15. See no. 2614
3233 Quartets, strings, nos. 1-3. Gabrieli Quartet. Decca SDD 524/5 (2)
     (also London STS 15424/5)
                +-FF 7/8-79 p96   +NR 3-80 p9
                +-HFN 11-77 p181   +-RR 10-77 p68
                +Gr 10-77 p654   +SFC 12-23-79 p40
                +HF 8-79 p90   ++St 4-79 p150
                +MM 6-78 p40
3234 Quartet, strings, no. 1, op. 11, D major. VERDI: Quartet, strings,

E minor. Amadeus Quartet. DG 2531 283 Tape (c) 3301 283
+Gr 9-80 p367   +HFN 10-80 p117 tape
+HFN 9-80 p111
Quartet, strings, no. 1, op. 11, D major: Andante cantabile. See
no. 3200. See no. 3794. See no. 3998
Reverie soir, op. 19, no. 1. See no. 2614
Romanza, op. 51, no. 5, F major. See no. 2614
Romeo and Juliet, excerpts. See no. 674
3235 Romeo and Juliet: Fantasy overture. WAGNER: Siegfried Idyll. PhO;
Guido Cantelli. World Records SH 287 Tape (c) TC SH 287 (From
HMV DG 1373/75, 9746/7)
++ARSC Vol 12, nos. 1-2   +HFN 4-79 p131
1980 p117   +RR 4-79 p83
++Gr 5-79 p1900
Romeo and Juliet: Fantasy overture. See no. 662. See no. 675.
See no. 3216. See no. 3220. See no. 3230. See no. 3231
Romeo and Juliet: Overture. See no. 3221
Russian volunteer fleet march. See no. 3232
Salon valse, op. 51, no. 1, A flat major. See no. 2614
3236 Serenade, op. 48, C major. Suite, no. 3, op. 55, G major: Theme
and variations. LPO; Norman Del Mar. Classics for Pleasure
CFP 40300 Tape (c) TC CFP 40300
+-Gr 2-80 p1275   +RR 3-79 p90
+-HFN 4-79 p128
Serenade, op. 48, C major. See no. 1548. See no. 3201
Serenade, op. 48, C major: Waltz. See no. 3211. See no. 3964
Serenade melancolique, op. 26. See no. 3209. See no. 3210. See
no. 3213. See no. 3964. See no. 4009
Six pieces on a single theme, op. 21: Prelude; Fugue; Impromptu;
Funeral march; Mazurka; Scherzo. See no. 3232
3237 The sleeping beauty, op. 66. BBC Symphony Orchestra; Gennady Rozh-
destvensky. BBC Artium 3001 (3) Tape (c) ZCBC 3001
++Gr 9-80 p350   +RR 8-80 p56
3238 The sleeping beauty, op. 66. National Philharmonic Orchestra; Ric-
hard Bonynge. Decca D78D3 (3) (also London CSA 2316 Tape (c)
CSA 5-2316)
+Audio 2-80 p42   ++NR 1-80 p2
/FF 5/6-79 p95   ++NYT 7-29-79 pD24
+-Gr 10-78 p752   -RR 10-78 p81
+HFN 10-78 p131 .   ++SFC 3-4-79 p41
+HF 5-79 p100
3239 The sleeping beauty, op. 66. OSR; Ernest Ansermet. London STS
15496/8 (3)
+FF 7/8-80 p143
3240 The sleeping beauty, op. 66: Ballet suite. Swan Lake, op. 20: Bal-
let suite. BPhO; Mstislav Rostropovich. DG 2531 111 Tape (c)
3301 111
+-FF 5/6-80 p160   ++HFN 9-79 p113
++FU 4-80 p52   ++NR 1-80 p2
+Gr 8-79 p334   ++RR 8-79 p96
+Gr 9-79 p534 tape   +-RR 7-80 p96 tape
The sleeping beauty, op. 66: Rose adagio, Act 1. See no. 3605
Sonata, piano, op. 37, G major: Andante non troppo quasi moderato.
See no. 3832
Songs: At the ball; Don Juan's serenade. See no. 3965

Songs: Autumn song; At evening; Romance; Waltz of the flowers. See
   no. 3870
Songs (hymns): Blessed are they whom thou has chosen; Hymn of the
   cherubim, no. 5; It is meet; Now the angels are with us; Our
   father; To thee we sing. See no. 3217
Songs: Lullaby. See no. 3774
3241 The sorceress (The enchantress). Rimma Glushkova, Galina Molodtsova, s; Lyudmila Simonova, Nina Derbina, ms; Lev Kuznetsov,
   Vladimir Mahkhov, t; Boris Doerin, bs-bar; Oleg Klenov, bar;
   Yevgeny Vladimirov, bs; MRSO and Chorus; Gennady Provatorov.
   HMV SLS 5167 (3) (also CBS M4X 35182)

+—FF 9/10-80 p215	+NYT 6-29-80 pD20
+Gr 9-79 p521	+Op 11-79 p1072
+—HF 10-80 p87	+RR 9-79 p60
+HFN 8-79 p113	+—St 11-80 p102
+—MT 2-80 p109	+STL 12-2-79 p37

The sorceress: Mein los ist seltsam. See no. 3561
Souvenir d'un lieu cher, op. 42: Meditation. See no. 3208
Souvenir d'un lieu cher, op. 42: Melodie. See no. 3552
Souvenir d'un lieu cher, op. 42: Scherzo. See no. 3964
3242 Suite, no. 3, op. 55, G major. LAPO; Michael Tilson Thomas. CBS
   76733 Tape (c) 40-76733 (also Columbia M 35124)

+FF 9/10-79 p151	+HFN 4-79 p134 tape
+—Gr 2-79 p1428	+—MUM 5/6-80 p36
+—Gr 6-79 p109 tape	+RR 3-79 p90
+HFN 2-79 p109	+—RR 8-79 p129 tape

Suite, no. 3, op. 55, G major: Theme and variations. See no. 3236
3243 Swan Lake, op. 20. BSO; Seiji Ozawa. DG 2709 099 (3) Tape (c)
   3371 051

+ARG 7/8-80 p43	+NR 5-80 p4
+—FF 7/8-80 p143	+RR 1-80 p90
+Gr 12-79 p1018	+RR 7-80 p96 tape
+HFN 2-80 p99	++SFC 2-24-80 p39

3244 Swan Lake, op. 20, excerpts. Yehudi Menuhin, vln; PhO; Efrem Kurtz.
   Classics for Pleasure CFP 40296 Tape (c) TC CFP 40296 (From HMV
   ALP 1644)

+Gr 1-79 p1333	++RR 12-78 p76
+HFN 1-79 p127	+—RR 7-80 p96 tape
+—HFN 8-80 p109 tape	

3245 Swan Lake, op. 20, excerpts. Hugh Maguire, vln; LSO; Pierre Mon-
   teux. Philips 6570 187 (From Philips 900089)
               -FF 11/12-80 p186
Swan Lake, op. 20, excerpts. See no. 3909
Swan Lake, op. 20: Ballet suite. See no. 3240
Swan Lake, op. 20: Valse; Scene; Dance of the swans; Scene pas d'
   action; Hungarian dance: La Czardas; Scene. See no. 3227
3246 Symphonies, nos. 1-3. BPhO; Herbert von Karajan. DG 2709 101 (3)
   Tape (c) 3371 053 (also DG 2531 284/5 Tape (c) 3301 284/6)

+FF 3/4-80 p166	+—HFN 12-80 p153
+Gr 10-80 p502	+—NR 2-80 p2
+Gr 12-80 p889 tape	++NYT 12-9-79 pD25
+HF 2-80 p98	+—St 5-80 p92
+—HF 11-80 p82 tape	+STL 11-9-80 p40

3247 Symphonies, nos. 1-6. LAPO; Zubin Mehta. Decca D95D6 (6) (also
   London CSP 10 Tape (c) CSP 5-10)

+—FF 9/10-79 p152	+—NR 6-80 p4

          +Gr 12-78 p1109   -RR 12-78 p75
          +-HF 8-79 p91   +-SFC 3-11-79 p49
          +HFN 12-78 p161
3248 Symphonies, nos. 1-6. BPhO; Herbert von Karajan. DG 2740 219 (6)
     Tape (c) 3378 084 (Nos. 4-6 from 2530 883, 2530 699, 2530 774)
          +Gr 11-79 p841   ++HFN 2-80 p99
          +Gr 12-79 p1065 tape   +RR 1-80 p88
3249 Symphony, no. 1, op. 13, G minor. BPhO; Herbert von Karajan. DG
     2531 284 Tape (c) 3301 284
          +HFN 11-80 p131
3250 Symphony, no. 1, op. 13, G minor. Marche slav, op. 31. LAPO; Zubin
     Mehta. London CS 7148 (also Decca SXL 6913. From D95D5)
          +FF 9/10-80 p218   +-NR 6-80 p4
          +Gr 5-80 p1677   +-RR 5-80 p72
          +-HFN 3-80 p135   +-St 5-80 p92
3251 Symphony, no. 1, op. 13, G minor. USSR Symphony Orchestra; Yevgeni
     Svetlanov. Melodiya 33C 01543-44 (also Quintessence PMC 7091.
     From Angel SR 40057)
          +ARG 11-80 p34   +RR 8-78 p71
          +FF 9/10-80 p219
3252 Symphony, no. 2, op. 17, C minor. The nutcracker, op. 71: Suite.
     RPO; Thomas Beecham. CBS 61875 (From Philips SBR 6213, ABL 3015)
          +ARSC Vol 12, no. 3,   +HFN 1-80 p121
           1980 p250   +RR 2-80 p90
          +Gr 1-80 p1161
3253 Symphony, no. 2, op. 17, C minor. BPhO; Herbert von Karajan. DG
     2531 285 Tape (c) 3301 285
          +HFN 12-80 p159 tape
3254 Symphony, no. 2, op. 17, C minor. MUSSORGSKY: A night on the bare
     mountain. PhO; Carlo Maria Giulini. EMI (Japan) EAC 30296
          +-ARSC Vol 12, nos. 1-2, 1980 p88
3255 Symphony, no. 2, op. 17, C minor. USSR Symphony Orchestra; Yevgeny
     Svetlanov. Quintessence PMC 7090 Tape (c) 7090 (From Angel SR
     40058)
          +-FF 11/12-80 p186
3256 Symphony, no. 2, op. 17, C minor. PO; Eugene Ormandy. RCA ARL 1-
     3352 Tape (c) ARK 1-3352
          ++ARG 11-80 p34   ++SFC 5-11-80 p35
          +FF 9/10-80 p219   +St 10-80 p124
          +-NR 6-80 p2
3257 Symphony, no. 2, op. 17, C minor. LIADOV: Russian folksongs, op.
     58 (8). LSO; Andre Previn. RCA GL 4-2960 Tape (c) GK 4-2960
     (From SB 6670)
          +-Gr 9-80 p413 tape   +-HFN 10-80 p117 tape
          +Gr 8-80 p222
3258 Symphony, no. 3, op. 29, D major. BPhO; Herbert von Karajan. DG
     2531 286 Tape (c) 3301 286
          +HFN 12-80 p159 tape
3259 Symphony, no. 3, op. 29, D major. Francesca da Rimini, op. 32.
     Hamlet, op. 67a. LSO; Albert Coates. Encore E 301 (From HMV/
     Victor originals)
          +ARG 2-80 p52   +HF 3-80 p90
          +FF 7/8-79 p99   +-NR 1-80 p3
3260 Symphony, no. 3, op. 29, D major. LAPO; Zubin Mehta. London CS
     7154
          +NR 6-80 p4

3261 Symphony, no. 3, op. 29, D major. USSR Symphony Orchestra; Yevgeny
       Svetlanov. Quintessence PMC 7164 Tape (c) 7164 (From Angel SR
       40059)
              +-FF 11/12-80 p186
3262 Symphony, no. 4, op. 36, F minor. PhO; Riccardo Muti. Angel S
       37624 (also HMV ASD 3816 Tape (c) TC ASD 3816)
              +-ARG 11-80 p34   +-NR 6-80 p2
              +-FF 11/12-80 p187   +-NYT 5-11-80 pD24
              +Gr 3-80 p1397   ++RR 4-80 p82
              +HF 8-80 p32   ++RR 4-80 p107 tape
              +HFN 4-80 p101   ++St 9-80 p82
              +HFN 4-80 p121
3263 Symphony, no. 4, op. 36, F minor. PhO; Vladimir Ashkenazy. Decca
       SXL 6919 Tape (c) KSXC 6919 (also London CS 7144 Tape (c) CS 5-
       7144)
              +-ARG 11-80 p34   +HFN 12-79 p171
              +-FF 9/10-80 p220   +NYT 3-2-80 pD26
              +Gr 12-79 p1023   ++RR 12-79 p78
              +-HF 7-80 p76   ++St 5-80 p93
3264 Symphony, no. 4, op. 36, F minor. LSO; Karl Bohm. DG 2531 078 Tape
       (c) 3301 078
              ++FF 1/2-80 p154   +HFN 5-79 p134 tape
              ++Gr 1-79 p1290   +-NR 12-79 p4
              ++Gr 6-79 p109 tape   ++RR 5-79 p74
              +HF 3-80 p88   +SFC 11-18-79 p47
              +HFN 2-79 p109
3265 Symphony, no. 4, op. 36, F minor. BPhO; Herbert von Karajan. HMV
       SXLP 30433 Tape (c) TC SXLP 30433 (From Columbia SAX 2357)
              +Gr 7-80 p148   +RR 7-80 p68
              +-HFN 7-80 p117
3266 Symphony, no. 4, op. 36, F minor. COA; Bernard Haitink. Philips
       9500 622 Tape (c) 7300 738
              +ARG 2-80 p44   ++HFN 1-80 p111
              +-FF 5/6-80 p161   ++HFN 1-80 p123 tape
              ++Gr 11-79 p842   ++NR 2-80 p2
              +-HF 3-80 p88   +RR 11-79 p99
3267 Symphony, no. 4, op. 36, F minor. USSR Symphony Orchestra; Yevgeny
       Svetlanov. Quintessence PMC 7134
              -FF 1/2-80 p155
3268 Symphony, no. 4, op. 36, F minor. National Philharmonic Orchestra;
       Loris Tjeknavorian. RCA RL 2-5050 Tape (c) RK 2-5050
              +-Gr 4-80 p1563   +-HFN 10-80 p117
              -HFN 4-80 p109   ++RR 5-80 p72
3269 Symphony, no. 4, op. 36, F minor. CO; Lorin Maazel. Telarc 10047
              +ARG 2-80 p44   ++HFN 12-79 p171
              ++FF 3/4-80 p164   +NR 10-80 p2
              ++HF 3-80 p88   +RR 1-80 p88
     Symphony, no. 4, op. 36, F minor: Finale. See no. 3581
3270 Symphony, no. 5, op. 64, E minor. International Festival Youth
       Orchestras; Leopold Stokowski. Cameo GOCL 9007
              +Gr 10-79 p654   -RR 1-80 p89
              -HFN 1-80 p111
3271 Symphony, no. 5, op. 64, E minor. LPO; Norman Del Mar. Classics
       for Pleasure CFP 40317 Tape (c) TC CFP 40317
              +Gr 12-79 p1065   +HFN 1-80 p123 tape

                    +Gr 1-80 p1161   ++RR 10-79 p108
                    +HFN 11-79 p145   +RR 5-80 p107 tape
3272 Symphony, no. 5, op. 64, E minor. Bamberg Symphony Orchestra; Horst
     Stein. Entracte ERS 6511
                    +FF 3/4-80 p167
3273 Symphony, no. 5, op. 64, E minor. PhO; Riccardo Muti. HMV SQ ASD
     3717 Tape (c) TC ASD 3717 (also Angel SZ 37625)
                    -ARG 11-80 p34   ++HFN 9-79 p123 tape
                    +-Audio 12-79 p101   +-NR 6-80 p2
                    ++FF 9/10-80 p220   +-NYT 5-11-80 pD24
                    +Gr 6-79 p60   +RR 8-79 p94
                    +-HF 8-80 p82   +St 9-80 p82
                    ++HFN 7-79 p112
3274 Symphony, no. 5, op. 64, E minor. LPO; Loris Tjeknavorian. RCA
     RL 2-5221 Tape (c) RK 2-5221
                    +Gr 8-80 p230   +-HFN 10-80 p117 tape
                    +HFN 8-80 p102
3275 Symphony, no. 5, op. 64, E minor. Symphony, no. 6, op. 74, B minor.
     La Scala Orchestra, PhO; Guido Cantelli. World Records SHB 52
     (2) Tape (c) TC 2-SHB 52 (From DB 21187/91, ALP 1042)
                    +ARSC Vol 12, no. 1-2   ++Gr 4-79 p1720
                       1980 p117   ++Gr 6-79 p109 tape
     Symphony, no. 5, op. 64, E minor. See no. 877
3276 Symphony, no. 6, op. 74, B minor. PhO; Paul Kletzki. Classics for
     Pleasure CFP 40220 Tape (c) TC CFP 40220
                    ++HFN 12-76 p151   -RR 12-76 p66
                    +-HFN 8-80 p109 tape
3277 Symphony, no. 6, op. 74, Bminor. BeSO; Kurt Sanderling. Denon
     PCM OX 7183
                    -FF 11/12-80 p188
3278 Symphony, no. 6, op. 74, B minor. LSO; Karl Bohm. DG 2531 212 Tape
     (c) 3301 212
                    +-ARG 9-80 p41   +HF 7-80 p76
                    +-FF 7/8-80 p144   +-HFN 12-79 p171
                    +FU 6-80 p51   +-NR 6-80 p4
                    +Gr 11-79 p842   +-NYT 3-2-80 pD26
                    +Gr 12-79 p1065 tape   +RR 12-79 p81
3279 Symphony, no. 6, op. 74, B minor. BPhO; Wilhelm Furtwangler. DG
     2535 164
                    +-FF 5/6-80 p161   +NR 8-80 p6
                    +-Gr 5-76 p177   +RR 5-76 p22
                    +HF 7-80 p76   +STL 1-9-77 p35
3280 Symphony, no. 6, op. 74, B minor. PhO; Carl Maria Giulini. EMI
     (Japan) EAC 30297
                    +ARSC Vol 12, nos. 1-2, 1980 p88
3281 Symphony, no. 6, op. 74, B minor. PhO; Riccardo Muti. HMV ASD 3901
     Tape (c) TC ASD 3901 (also Angel SZ 37626)
                    +Gr 11-80 p683   +HFN 11-80 p123
3282 Symphony, no. 6, op. 74, B minor. LAPO; Zubin Mehta. London CS
     7166
                    +FU 6-80 p51   +NR 6-80 p4
3283 Symphony, no. 6, op. 74, B minor. COA; Bernard Haitink. Philips
     9500 610 Tape (c) 7300 739
                    +-ARG 9-80 p41   ++HFN 6-80 p119 tape
                    ++FF 9/10-80 p218   ++NR 4-80 p4

      +Gr 4-80 p1564   +RR 4-80 p82
      +HF 7-80 p76   +RR 5-80 p107 tape
      ++HFN 4-80 p111

3284 Symphony, no. 6, op. 74, B minor. CPhO; Lovro von Matacic. Quintessence PMC 7102 (From Supraphon 110 0485)
      +-Audio 6-80 p51   +-FF 11/12-79 p134

3285 Symphony, no. 6, op. 74, B minor. LSO; Leopold Stokowski. RCA GL
4-2920 Tape (c) GK 4-2920 (From ARL 1-0426)
      +-Gr 10-80 p502   +-HFN 10-80 p113

Symphony, no. 6, op. 74, B minor. See no. 3275

3286 Trio, piano, op. 50, A minor. Yehudi Menuhin, vln; Maurice Gendron,
vlc; Hephzibah Menuhin, pno. Arabesque 8014 Tape (c) 9014
      ++FF 9/10-80 p221   ++SFC 7-27-80 p34

Trio, piano, op. 50, A minor: Pezzo elegiaco. See no. 2926

Valse-Scherzo, no. 2. See no. 3232

Variations on a Rococo theme, op. 33. See no. 2758

TCHEREPNIN, Alexander

3287 Andante, op. 64. Fanfares, trumpet and piano. Quintet, brass, op.
105. TCHEREPNIN, N.: Enchantement. Melodie d'amour. Pieces, 4
horns (6). Une oraison. Netherlands Horn Quartet; Albert Zuyderduin, trom; John Taber, tpt; Mel Culbertson, tuba; Michael
Krist, pno; John Moore, trom; Rodney Miller, tpt. RCA RL 3-0321
      +-ARG 4-80 p48   +-FF 9/10-79 p155

Fanfares, trumpet and piano. See no. 3287

Preludes, op. 38. See no. 3288

Quintet, brass, op. 105. See no. 3287

3288 Sonatas, violoncello and piano, nos. 1, 3. Preludes, op. 38 (12).
Esther Nyffenegger, vlc; Annette Weisbrod, pno. Da Camera Magna
SM 93718
      +FF 5/6-80 p163

Trio, op. 34, D major. See no. 1130

Trio, op. 39, D major. See no. 3195

TCHEREPNIN, Nikolai

Enchantement. See no. 3287

Melodie d'amour. See no. 3287

Pieces, 4 horns (6). See no. 3287

Une oraison. See no. 3287

TEIXIDOR

Amparito roca. See no. 3921

TELEMANN, Georg Philipp

Ach Herr strafe mich nicht. See no. 101

Air de trompette. See no. 3545

Air de trompette, C major. See no. 4041

Allein Gott in der Hoh sei Ehr. See no. 4041

Concert suite, sopranino recorder. See no. 1026

Concerti, flute, C major, D major. See no. 203

3289 Concerti, flute, G major, C major. Suite, flute, A minor. James
Galway, flt; I Solisti di Zagreb. RCA ARL 1-3488 Tape (c) ARK
1-3488
      +-ARG 9-80 p33   +NR 4-80 p6
      +FF 3/4-80 p167   +-St 4-80 p139
      +HF 4-80 p104 tape

3290 Concerto, flute and recorder, E minor. Suites, G minor, D major.
Banchetto Musicale; Martin Pearlman. Titanic TI 36
      +-AR 2-80 p175

3291 Concerti, flute and strings, B minor, E major. Concerto, 2 flutes
     and strings, E minor. Concerto, 2 flutes, oboe and violin, B
     flat major. Jean-Michel Tanguy, Jerry Felmlee, flt; Enrico
     Raphaelis, ob; Peter Rundel, vln; Heidelberg Chamber Orchestra.
     Da Camera SM 91044
                    +FF 5/6-80 p164
     Concerto, flute, violin and violoncello. See no. 18
     Concerto, 2 flutes and strings, E minor. See no. 3291
     Concerto, 2 flutes, oboe and violin, B flat major. See no. 3291
3292 Concerto, horn, D major. Concerto, 3 horns, D major. Suite, 2
     horns, 2 oboes and bassoon, D major. Suite, 4 horns, 2 oboes
     and bassoon, F major. Paul Klecka, Bodo Knuth, Siegfried Macha-
     ta, Gottfried Roth, hn; Enrico Raphaelis, Iris Kienzler, ob;
     Georg Franzen, bsn; Heidelberg Chamber Orchestra. Da Camera Mag-
     na SM 91039
                    /-FF 1/2-80 p155
3293 Concerto, horn, D major. Concerto, 3 horns and violin, D major.
     Suite, 2 horns, 2 oboes and bassoon, D major. Suite, 4 horns,
     2 oboes and bassoon, F major. Paul Klecka, Bodo Knuth, Siegfried
     Machata, Gottfried Roth, hn; Enrico Raphaelis, Iris Kienzler, ob;
     Georg Franzen, bsn; Marjan Karuza, vln; Heidelberg Chamber Orch-
     estra. Spectrum SR 111 (From SM 91039)
                    /FF 5/6-80 p164
     Concerto, horn, D major. See no. 356
     Concerto, 3 horns, D major. See no. 356. See no. 3292. See no.
     3293
     Concerto, oboe d'amore, D major. See no. 1026
     Concerto, recorder, C major. See no. 1607. See no. 1608
     Concerto, recorder and violins, G minor. See no. 3295
3294 Concerto, recorder, bassoon and strings, F major. Suite, A minor.
     Laszlo Czidra, rec; Jozsef Vajda, bsn; Ferenc Liszt Chamber Or-
     chestra; Frigyes Sandor. Hungaroton SLPX 12119
                    +FF 9/10-80 p223
3295 Concerto, recorder, viola da gamba and strings, A minor. Concerto,
     recorder and violins, G minor. Concerto, 2 violins, A major.
     Concerti, 4 violins, C major, D major. Musica Antiqua Cologne.
     DG 2533 421
                    +Gr 1-80 p1161   +-RR 1-80 p91
                    +HFN 1-80 p111
3296 Concerto, recorder, 2 violins, harpsichord, violoncello and double-
     bass, G minor. Suite, A minor. Trio, recorder and viola da
     gamba, F major. Michel Sanvoisin, rec; Elisabeth Matiffa, vla
     da gamba; Daniele Salzer, hpd; Herve Le Floc, Alain Moglia, vln;
     Etienne Peclard, vlc; Jean-Paul Celea, double bs. Arion ARN
     38418
                    +-Gr 5-80 p1689   +RR 5-80 p78
     Concerto, trumpet, D major. See no. 1397. See no. 1679. See no.
     3563. See no. 3674. See no. 3779
     Concerto, trumpet, F minor. See no. 29
3297 Concerto, trumpet, violin and strings, D major. Concerto, 3 trum-
     pets, timpani and strings, D major. Overture, D major. Friede-
     mann Immer, Albrecht Mugdan, Kalus Osterloh, tpt; Rolf Schaude,
     timpani; Philipp Naegele, vln; Heidelberg Chamber Orchestra;
     Bernhard Usedruuf. Da Camera SM 91045
                    +-FF 5/6-80 p164

Concerto, 3 trumpets, timpani and strings, D major. See no. 3297
Concerto, viola: Allegro. See no. 4028
3298 Concerto, viola, G major. Concerto, 3 violins, F major. Suite,
     flute, A minor. Severino Gazzelloni, flt; Cino Ghedin, vla;
     Felix Ayo, Arnoldo Apostoli, Italo Colandrea, vln; I Musici.
     Philips 9502 011 Tape (c) 7313 011

+FF 5/6-80 p164	+NR 8-80 p7
-Gr 6-80 p53	/RR 6-80 p63
+HFN 6-80 p112	+St 4-80 p139
+HFN 10-80 p117 tape	

Concerto, 2 violins, A major. See no. 3295
Concerto, 3 violins, F major. See no. 3298
Concerti, 4 violins, C major, D major. See no. 3295
Du aber Daniel gehe hin, funeral cantata. See no. 139
3299 Essercizii musici: Sonatas, A minor, D minor. Der Getreue Musik-
     Meister: Duet, B flat major; Sonata, F minor. Trio sonatas,
     recorder, F major, A minor, G minor, D minor, F major, C major.
     Kees Boeke, rec; Alice Harnoncourt, vln, pardessus de viole,
     violino, piccolo; Bob van Asperen, hpd. Telefunken EK 6-35451
     (2)

+FF 3/4-80 p168	++HFN 5-79 p127
++Gr 11-79 p866	++RR 4-79 p105
+HF 6-80 p88	+St 2-80 p134

Fantasia, C minor. See no. 3654
3300 Fantasias, solo flute, nos. 1-12. Barthold Kuijken, flt. Accent
     ACC 7803

++FF 5/6-80 p163	++RR 6-80 p27
+HFN 6-80 p101	++STL 8-10-80 p30

3301 Fantasias, solo flute, nos. 1-12. Arthur Grumiaux, vln. Philips
     9502 010

+Gr 3-80 p1423	+-RR 3-80 p88
+HFN 3-80 p101	++ST 9-80 p340
++MT 8-80 p505	

Fantasias, flute, no. 7, D major; no. 12, G minor. See no. 3629
Der Getreue Musik-Meister: Duet, B flat major; Sonata, F minor.
     See no. 3299
Heidenmusik. See no. 30
Introductione a tre, C major. See no. 3310
3302 Lukas-Passion 1744. Uta Spreckelsen, s; Theo Altmeyer, Adalbert
     Kraus, Gerd Beusker, t; Gerhard Faulstich, bar; Frankfurt Cham-
     ber Orchestra and Madrigal Ensemble. Cantate 658 203/4 (2)

              +HFN 10-80 p109

Marches (4). See no. 4041
Minuet, G minor. See no. 3957
3303 Musique de table: Concerti, A major, F major, E flat major. Schola
     Cantorum Basiliensis; August Wenzinger. DG 2547 013 Tape (c)
     3347 013 (From SAPM 198334/5, 198336/7, 198338/9)

              +Gr 4-80 p1595

Overture, C minor: Sommeille. See no. 3943
Overture, D major. See no. 3297
3304 Partita, no. 2, G major. Sonatas, B flat major, G minor. Suite, G
     minor. Paul Dombrecht, ob; Wieland Kuijken, vlc; Robert Kohnen,
     hpd. Accent ACC 8013

+Gr 8-80 p239	++RR 8-80 p76
+HFN 9-80 p111	

3305 Partita, no. 4, G minor. Sonata, oboe, E minor, G major. Sonata,
      oboe, harpsichord and violoncello, E flat major. Heinz Holliger,
      ob; Christiane Jaccottet, hpd; Nicole Hostettler, spinet; Manfred
      Sax, bsn; Philippe Mermoud, vlc. Philips 9500 441
                    +FF 11/12-78 p128   +MT 2-79 p43
                    +-Gr 5-80 p1684   ++NR 12-78 p9
                    ++HF 1-79 p89   +-RR 5-80 p92
                    ++HFN 5-80 p127   ++St 12-78 p103
      Partita, no. 6: Air, Allemande, Air. See no. 3626
      Quadro, B flat major. See no. 1156
3306 Quartet, bassoon, flute, oboe and harpsichord, D minor. Sonata,
      bassoon and harpsichord, F minor. Sonata, flute and harpsichord,
      C minor. Trio sonata, oboe and harpsichord, E flat major. Sam-
      uel Baron, flt; Ronald Roseman, ob; Arthur Weisberg, bsn; Tim-
      othy Eddy, vlc; Edward Brewer, hpd. Nonesuch H 71352
                    +AR 5-80 p34   ++NR 2-79 p8
                    ++FF 1/2-79 p112   +NYT 4-22-79 pD25
                    ++Gr 2-79 p1439   ++RR 3-79 p102
                    ++HF 1-79 p89   +St 2-79 p103
                    +-HFN 3-79 p131
3307 Quartet, flute, oboe, violin, bassoon and harpsichord, G major.
      Quartet, flute, violin, bassoon and harpsichord, E minor. Quar-
      tet, flute, violin, oboe, bassoon and harpsichord, D minor. Son-
      ata, flute, oboe and harpsichord, A major. Trio, flute and vio-
      lin, E major. Baroque Ensemble of Paris. Musical Heritage Soci-
      ety MHS 4041
                    +FF 1/2-80 p156
      Quartet, flute, violin, bassoon and harpsichord, E minor. See no.
      3307
      Quartet, flute, violin, oboe, bassoon and harpsichord, D minor.
      See no. 3307
      Scherzo, 2 flutes, E major. See no. 3310
      Sonatas, B flat major, G minor. See no. 3304
      Sonata, bassoon and harpsichord, F minor. See no. 3306
      Sonata, flute, E minor. See no. 1457
      Sonata, flute and harpsichord, C minor. See no. 3306
      Sonata, flute, oboe and harpsichord, A major. See no. 3307
      Sonata, oboe, A minor. See no. 3753
      Sonatas, oboe, E minor, G major. See no. 3305
      Sonata, oboe and harpsichord, E flat major. See no. 3306
      Sonata, oboe, harpsichord and violoncello, E flat major. See no.
      3305
      Sonatas, recorder, F major, A minor, G minor, D minor, F major, C
      major. See no. 3299
      Sonata, recorder, C major. See no. 3593
      Sonata, recorder, D minor. See no. 4020
      Sonata en re. See no. 3736
      Songs: Ein reiches Weib; Geld; Das Frauenzimmer; Die Lieb und auch
      die Floh; Ein reiches Weib; Die ungekammte Phillis. See no. 3764
      Suite, A minor. See no. 1799. See no. 3294. See no. 3296
      Suites, C minor, D major. See no. 3290
      Suite, G minor. See no. 3304
      Suite, flute, A minor. See no. 294. See no. 3289. See no. 3298
      Suite, 2 horns, F major. See no. 356
      Suite, 2 horns, 2 oboes and bassoon, D major. See no. 3292

Suite, 2 horns, 2 oboes and bassoon, D major. See no. 3293
Suite, 4 horns, 2 oboes and bassoon, F major. See no. 3292
Suite, 4 horns, 2 oboes and bassoon, F major. See no. 3293
3308 Suite, recorder, A minor. Suite, viola da gamba and strings, D
     major. Hans-Martin Linde, rec; Johannes Koch, vla da gamba;
     Collegium Aureum; Rolf Reinhardt. Harmonia Mundi 1C 065 99825
     (From RCA VICS 1272)
              +-HFN 12-80 p147   +FF 5/6-80 p164
     Suite, viola da gamba and strings, D major. See no. 3308
3309 Tafelmusik: Concerto, flute and violin, A major. Concerto, 3 vio-
     lins, F major. Concerto, 2 horns, E flat major. Schola Cantorum
     Basiliensis; August Wenzinger. DG 2547 013
              +-HFN 6-80 p119   +-RR 6-80 p63
     Trio, flute and harpsichord, A major. See no. 3310
     Trio, flute and oboe, D minor. See no. 3310
     Trio, flute and violin, E major. See no. 3307
     Trio, recorder and harpsichord, B flat major. See no. 3310
     Trio, recorder and oboe, C minor. See no. 3310
     Trio, recorder and pardessus de viole, D minor. See no. 3310
     Trio, recorder and viola da gamba, F major. See no. 3296. See no.
     3310
     Trios, recorder and violin, A minor, A major. See no. 3310
     Trio sonata, A minor. See no. 3547
     Trio sonata, G minor. See no. 3543
     Vater unser im Himmelreich. See no. 4040. See no. 4041
3310 Works, selections: Introductione a tre, C major. Scherzo, 2 flutes,
     E major. Trio, recorder and viola da gamba, F major. Trio,
     flute and harpsichord, A major. Trio, flute and oboe, D minor.
     Trio, recorder and harpsichord, B flat major. Trio, recorder and
     oboe, C minor. Trio, recorder and pardessus de viole, D minor.
     Trio, recorder and violin, E major, A minor. Frans Bruggen, rec
     and flt; Walter van Hauwe, rec; Berthold Kuijken, flt; Paul Dom-
     brecht, ob; Wieland Kuijken, vla da gamba, pardessus de viole;
     Bob van Asperen, Gustav Leonhardt, hpd; Anner Bylsma, vlc; An-
     thony Woodrow, double bs; Brian Pollard, bsn. RCA RL 3-0343 (2)
              +Gr 5-80 p1689   +RR 5-80 p79
              +HFN 6-80 p112
TERRINI
     Sonata, 2 organs, D major. See no. 2010
TERRY, R. R.
     Myn liking. See no. 4066
TERZIAN, Alicia
     Danza criolla. See no. 3851
     Jeugos para Diana. See no. 3851
     Toccata. See no. 3851
TESCHEMACHER-GARTNER
     Love is mine. See no. 3949
TEYBER, Anton
     Concerto, horn, E flat major. See no. 1762
THALBEN-BALL, George
     Birmingham pieces: Poema; Toccata Beorma. See no. 4054
     Elegy. See no. 4054
     Elegy, B flat major. See no. 3533. See no. 3936
     Gloria patria, E flat major. See no. 3936
     Jubilate Deo, B flat major. See no. 3533. See no. 3936

The Lord God omnipotent reigneth. See no. 3533. See no. 3936
Psalm, no. 48: Chant, E flat major. See no. 3936
Psalm, no. 130: Chant, D minor. See no. 3936
Psalm chants. See no. 3533
Songs: Sursum corda; Comfort ye. See no. 3534
Tune, E major. See no. 4051
Variations on a theme by Paganini. See no. 4054

THEMMEN, Ivana
Shelter this candle from the wind. See no. 2172

THIBAUT DE NAVARRE
3311 Amors me fet commencier. Au tens plain de felonnie. Ausi comme
unicorne sui. L'autre nuit. L'autrier par la matinee. Bons
Rois Thibaut. Chancon ferai. Contre le tens. Coustume est
bien. Dame ensi est. Dame est votre fins amis. De bone amour.
Dex est ensi comme le pelicans. Empereres ne rois. Fueille no
flor. J'aloi l'autrier. Je mi cuidoie partir. Je n'os chanter.
Le douz pensers. Per Dieu, sire de Champagne. Por conforter.
Por froidure. Por mau tens. Quant fine amor me prie. Robert
veez de perron. Rois Thibaut. Seigneurs sachiez qui or ne s'en
ira. Sire nel me celez demant. Sires fer faites me jugement.
Tout autresi. Une dolor enossee. Atrium Musicae of Madrid;
Gregorio Paniagua. Harmonia Mundi HM 1016
        +FF 5/6-80 p165   -RR 2-80 p82
        +HFN 2-80 p99

THIEL, Carl
Songs: Adeste fideles; Freu dich Erd und Sternenzelt. See no. 3697

THOMAS, Ambroise
Le Caid: Air du Tombour-major. See no. 3899. See no. 3979
Le Caid: Air du Tambour-major; Vive le mariage. See no. 3770
Le Caid: L'amour de dieu profane. See no. 3631
Hamlet: A voux veux mes amis...Partagez vous mes fleurs; Et mainte-
nant ecoutez ma chanson. See no. 629
Hamlet: Brindisi. See no. 3770
Hamlet: Come romito fior. See no. 3982
Hamlet: Doute de la lumiere. See no. 3774
Mignon: Adieu, Mignon. See no. 3538
Mignon: Adieu, Mignon; Ah non credevi tu. See no. 3900
Mignon: Adieu, Mignon; Elle ne croyait pas; Dort bein ihm ist sie
jetz. See no. 3774
Mignon: Ah non credevi tu; La tua alma; Addio Mignon. See no. 3981
Mignon: Connais-tu le pays; Elle est aimee. See no. 3985
Mignon: Del suo cor calmai. See no. 3899
Mignon: Entr'acte. See no. 3847
Mignon: Ihr Schwalben in den Luften. See no. 3770
Mignon: Je suis Titania. See no. 3886
Mignon: Legeres hirondelles; Styrienne. See no. 3987
Mignon: Overture. See no. 63
Mignon: Rondo gavotte. See no. 3769
Raymond: Overture. See no. 3860
Songe d'une nuit d'ete. See no. 3770
Songe d'une nuit d'ete: Ou suis-je. See no. 3774

THOMAS, Edward
3312 Concerto, clarinet. Quartet, strings. Sidney Fell, clt; London
Master Virtuosi, Highgate String Quartet; Gene Forrell. Musical
Heritage Society MHS 4063
        /FF 3/4-80 p168

      Quartet, strings. See no. 3312
THOMELIN
      Duo. See no. 3852
THOMPSON, Randall
      Suite, oboe, clarinet and viola. See no. 2501
3313 Symphony, no. 1. The testament of freedom. Utah Chorale; Alexander
         Schreiner, org; Utah Symphony Orchestra; Maurice Abravanel. An-
         gel S 37315
                     +–ARG 4-79 p41   +NYT 9-28-80 pD31
                     +–FF 5/6-79 p98   +–St 4-79 p152
                     +NR 2-79 p2
      The testament of freedom. See no. 3313
THOMSON, Virgil
3314 Etudes. Portraits: Cantabile; Catalan waltz; Bugles and birds; An
         old song; In a bird cage; Alternation. Arthur Tollefson, pno.
         Finnadar SR 9027
                     +FF 11/12-80 p188   +NR 12-80 p10
                     +HF 10-80 p91
3315 Pictures, orchestra (3). Portraits (3). Songs from William Blake
         (4). Mack Harrell, bar; PO; Eugene Ormandy, Virgil Thomson.
         CRI SRD 398 (From Columbia ML 2087, 4919)
                     ++ARG 12-79 p58   +HF 12-79 p100
                     +FF 3/4-80 p14   +SFC 5-4-80 p42
      Portraits (3). See no. 3315
      Portraits: Cantabile; Catalan waltz; Bugles and birds; An old song;
         In a bird cage; Alternation. See no. 3314
      Songs from William Blake (4). See no. 3315
      Symphony, no. 3. See no. 1769
THORARINSSON, Leifur
      Concerto, violin. See no. 3169
THORNE, Francis
      Elegy. See no. 2117
      Set pieces for 13 players (7). See no. 2200
      Sonata, piano. See no. 1161
TIGRANIAN
      Et-Arhaj. See no. 3850
TILLIS, Frederick
      Music for violin, violoncello and piano. See no. 3316
3316 Niger symphony. Music for violin, violoncello and piano. RPO;
         David Sackson, vln; Maurice Bialkin, vlc; Dwight Peltzer, pno;
         Paul Freeman. Serenus SRS 12087
                     +ARG 11-79 p53   +–FF 9/10-80 p224
TIPPETT, Michael
      Fanfare, brass. See no. 3566
      Fanfare, brass, no. 1. See no. 3959
TISCHENKO, Boris
3317 Concerto, harp, op. 69. Irina Donskaya, hp; Tatiana Melenteva, s;
         Leningrad Orchestra for Old and New Music; Eduard Serov. Melo-
         diya C10 12401/2
                     +–FF 9/10-80 p224
      Concerto, violin. See no. 1390
      Sinfonia robusta. See no. 1391
TISDALE, William
      Coranto. See no. 4014
TJEKNAVORIAN, Loris
      Armenian dance, no. 2. See no. 3851

TOCH, Ernst
  Burlesken, op. 31. See no. 960
TOMASI, Henri
3318 Divertissement pastoral. SABOLI: Noels (Tomasi) (12). RTF Boys
       Choir; Instrumentalists; Masseta Maiaenco Tambourine Players;
       Jacques Joineau. DG 2535 375 (From DG 136374)
                +FF 11/12-80 p189
  Fanfares liturgiques: Procession du Vendredi-Saint. See no. 3571
  To be or not to be. See no. 3654
TOMKINS, Thomas
  Alman. See no. 3853
  Barafostus dream. See no. 3648. See no. 3853. See no. 4044
3319 Musica Deo sacra: Blessed by the Lord God of Israel; The heavens
       declare; A verse of three parts (organ solo); O Lord graciously
       accept; Put me not to rebuke; Then David mourned; Glory be to
       God; Withdraw not thou thy mercy; Merciful Lord; Deal with me O
       Lord; O Lord grant the king; Blessed is he; A fancy (organ solo);
       O God the proud are risen. Magdalen College Choir; Geoffrey Mor-
       gan, org; Bernard Rose. Argo ZRG 897
                ++ARG 5-80 p41   +HFN 5-79 p127
                +FF 7/8-80 p146   ++RR 5-79 p101
                ++Gr 5-79 p1926
  A short verse. See no. 3755
  Songs (madrigals): Music divine; O oyez has any found a lad; Too
       much I once lamented. See no. 3893
  When David heard. See no. 3894
TORELLI, Giuseppe
  Concerto a 4, 2 violins and strings. See no. 3716
  Concerto grosso, op. 8, no. 6, G minor. See no. 1136
  Sinfonia, trumpet. See no. 1394
  Sonata, no. 1, G major. See no. 3674
  Sonata a 5, D major. See no. 1397. See no. 3916
  Suite, no. 7, a cinque, D major. See no. 3779
TORRE, Francisco de la
  Songs: Pampano verde. See no. 3698
TORROBA, Federico
  Burgalesa. See no. 15
3320 Concierto iberico. Dialogos. Los Romeros; AMF; Neville Marriner.
       Philips 9500 749 Tape (c) 7300 834
                ++Gr 12-80 p842   +HFN 12-80 p147
  Dialogos. See no. 3320
  Estampas: Danza rapsodica. See no. 1487
  Fandanguillo. See no. 15
  Luisa Fernanda: De este apacible rincon de Madrid. See no. 3919
  Nocturne. See no. 3549. See no. 3775
  Piezas caracteristicas. See no. 15
  Preludio. See no. 3549. See no. 3775
  Sonatine, A major: Allegretto. See no. 3549. See no. 3775
  Suite castellana: Arada and fandanguillo. See no. 3798
  Suite castellana: Fandanguillo. See no. 3549. See no. 3775
  Torija. See no. 3603
TOSTI, Francesco
  L'alba separa dalla luce l'ombra. See no. 3983
  Parted. See no. 3875
3321 Songs: A vucchella; Aprile; Chanson de l'adieu; Good-bye; Ideale;

L'alba separa della luce l'ombra; L'ultima canzone; Malia; Marechiare; Non t'amo piu; Segreto; La serenata; Sogno; Vorrei morire.
Jose Carreras, t; ECO; Edoardo Muller. Philips 9500 743 Tape (c)
7300 828
              +Gr 12-80 p871   +HFN 12-80 p147
    Songs: A vucchella; Marechiare. See no. 3667
    Songs: A vucchella; Marechiare; Malia; Donna vorrei morir; Ideale.
        See no. 3771
    Songs: Addio. See no. 3949
    Songs: Amour; Aprile; Invano; Mattinata. See no. 3770
    Songs: Ideale. See no. 4008
    Songs: Ideale; Marechiare; La serenata. See no. 3981
    Songs: Ideale; Pour un baiser. See no. 3945
    Songs: Malia; Non t'amo piu. See no. 3980
    Songs: Mattinata. See no. 3774
    Songs: Non ti ricordi piu; L'ultimo baccio. See no. 3869
    Songs: L'ultima canzone; Marechiare. See no. 3831
TOURNEMIRE, Charles
    Improvisation on "Te deum". See no. 3994
    L'Orgue mystique: Fantaisie sur le Te Deum; Guilandes alleluiatiques.
        See no. 4061
TOURNIER, Marcel
    Christmas songs, op. 32 (6). See no. 3685
    Etude de concert. See no. 3676
TOURS, Frank
    Mother o' mine. See no. 3874
TRABACI, Giovanni
    Canto fermo, no. 2. See no. 3846
    Canzona francese. See no. 3846
    Durezze e legature. See no. 3846
    Gaillarde. See no. 1394
TRAVIS, Roy
3322 Passion of Oediups, excerpts. Symphonic allegro. Sappho song set-
        tings (5). Harold Enns, bs-bar; RPO and Chorus; Jan Popper.
        Orion Tape (c) OC 830S
                    +HF 8-80 p87 tape   +NR 9-80 p1 tape
    Sappho song settings. See no. 3322
    Symphonic allegro. See no. 3322
TREBOR
    Quant joyne euer. See no. 766
    Se Alixandre et Hector. See no. 766
TREDINNICK, Noel
    Brief encounters. See no. 4051
TRENET
    I wish you love. See no. 3627
TRENKNER, Werner
    Arabesques, op. 28. See no. 357
TRUAX
    Sonic landscape, no. 1. See no. 3842
TUCAPSKY, Antonin
3323 In honorem vitae; Lauds I and II; The time of Christemas. Beryl
        Tucapsky, s; Philip Snowden, bar; London Chorale; Antonin Tucap-
        sky, Roy Wales. Bedivere Records BVR 301
                    +RR 1-80 p110

TUFTS
Psalm tune, no. 100. See no. 3848
TUFTS, Paul
3324 Sonata, viola and piano. Suite. Donald McInnes, vla; Bela Siki,
pno. Laurel LR 107
+—FF 5/6-80 p166   +NR 4-78 p7
Suite. See no. 3324
TULOU, Jean Louis
L'Angelus, op. 46. See no. 3782
TUMA, Frantisek
Parthia, D major. See no. 3752
TURINA, Joaquin
Cantares, op. 19, no. 3. See no. 3596
Canto a Sevilla. See no. 2194
Canto a Sevilla: El fatasma; Poema en forma de canciones; Cantares;
Saeta en forma de Salve a la virgen de la esperanza. See no.
3698
Danzas fantasticas, op. 22. See no. 3665
Danzas fantasticas, op. 22: Orgia. See no. 12
Fandanguillo. See no. 3549. See no. 3775
Fandanguillo, op. 36. See no. 13. See no. 3798
Quartet, piano, A minor. See no. 1489
Songs: Anhelos, Cantares; Farruca; Si con mis deseos. See no. 1392
Trio, piano, no. 2, op. 74, B minor. See no. 1130
TUZIN, Ferit
Esintiler. See no. 6
TYE, Christopher
In Nomine "Crye". See no. 3995
Songs: Laudate nomen Domini; Praise ye the Lord ye children. See
no. 3527
UCCELLINI, Marco
Sonata, op. 5, B flat major. See no. 4016
UHL, Alfred
Festfanfare. See no. 3571
ULEHLA, Ludmilla
Elegy for a whale. See no. 3822
UPENSKY, Vladislav
Music, strings and percussion. See no. 1391
URBANNER, Erich
3325 Concerto, double bass and chamber orchestra. VANHAL: Concerto,
double bass and chamber orchestra. Ludwig Streicher, double bs;
Innsbruck Chamber Orchestra; Erich Urbanner, Othmar Costa.
Telefunken AW 6-42045
+ARG 7/8-80 p55   +RR 5-77 p61
-Gr 7-77 p188
VALDERRABANO, Enriquez de
Sonata, no. 1. See no. 3917
VALDES, Gilberto
Cuban suite. See no. 2718
VALENTE, Antonio
Romanesca. See no. 4021
La Romanesca con cinque mutanze. See no. 4023
Torna. See no. 3771
VALERIA
Jalo jalo. See no. 3814

VALLS, Francisco
3326 Scala Aretina, mass. Mavis Beattie, Valerie Hill, Nancy Long, s;
       Christopher Robson, Ashley Stafford, alto; Edgar Fleet, t; Ant-
       hony Shelley, bar; London Oratory Choir; Thames Chamber Orchestra;
       John Hoban. CRD CRD 1071 Tape (c) CRDC 4071
                    +-Gr 11-80 p724   +-HFN 11-80 p123
VALVERDE, Joaquin
       Clavelitos. See no. 3551. See no. 3770. See no. 3831
VAN, Jeffrey
       Elegy (Homage to Falla). See no. 3599
VAN BAAREN, Kees
       Septet. See no. 3818
       Sonatina, piano. See no. 955
VAN BREE, Johannes Bernardus
       Allegro. See no. 2003
       Allegro moderato. See no. 3818
VAN DER HORST, Anthon
       La nuit, op. 67. See no. 3818
VAN EYCK, Jacob
       Amarilli mia bella. See no. 3593
       Doen Daphne. See no. 986
       Engels Nachtegaeltje. See no. 986. See no. 3593
       Pavane lachrymae. See no. 986
       Variations on "De-Lof-Zangh Marie". See no. 3593
VAN GHIZEGHEM, Hayne
       De tous biens plaine. See no. 3880
VAN OPSTAL, A.
       Scherzo. See no. 3725
VAN VLIJMEN, Jan
       Sonata, piano and 3 groups of instruments. See no. 3818
VANHAL, Johann (Jan)
       Concerto, double bass, E major: Allegro moderato. See no. 3606
       Concerto, double bass and chamber orchestra. See no. 3325
       Sonata, op. 3, G major. See no. 1416
VAQUEIRAS, Raimbault de
       Kalenda meia. See no. 3. See no. 4042
       Kalenda meia; Vida. See no. 3748
VARESE, Edgard
       Density 21.5. See no. 3327
       Deserts: Interpolations. See no. 3327
       Integrales. See no. 3327
       Ionisation. See no. 3327
       Octandre. See no. 910. See no. 3327
3327 Works, selections: Density 21.5. Deserts: Interpolations. Inte-
       grales. Ionisation. Octandre. New York Wind Ensemble, Juil-
       liard Percussion Orchestra; Rene Le Roy, flt; Frederic Waldman.
       Finnadar SR 9018
                    +-ARSC Vol 12, nos. 1-2   +NR 6-78 p15
                        1980 p123
VARNEY, Louis
       L'Amour mouille: Valse d'oiseau. See no. 3770
3328 Les mousquetaires au couvent. Mady Mesple, Christiane Chateau,
       Michele Command, s; Charles Burles, t; Michel Trempont, bar;
       Jules Bastin, bs; Theatre Royal de Monnaie Chorus; Belgian Radio-
       Television Orchestra and Chorus; Edgar Doneux. EMI 2C 167 16361/
       2 (2)

+Gr 9-80 p399
VAUGHAN WILLIAMS, Ralph
    The call. See no. 3992
3329 Concerto, oboe, A minor. Concerto grosso. WARLOCK: Capriol suite.
    Serenade, strings. Celia Nicklin, ob; AMF: Neville Marriner.
    Argo ZRG 881 Tape (c) KZRC 881

+FF 5/6-80 p166	++RR 9-79 p98
+Gr 9-79 p473	+-RR 3-80 p104 tape
+HFN 9-79 p115	+ST 1-80 p692

3330 Concerto, oboe, A minor. Concerto, tuba, F minor. Variants of
    "Dives and Lazarus" (5). The wasps. Evelyn Rothwell Barbirolli,
    ob; Philip Catelinet, tuba; LSO, Halle Orchestra; John Barbirolli.
    Barbirolli Society SJB 102
        +ARG 2-80 p46
Concerto, tuba, F minor. See no. 3330. See no. 3331
3331 Concerto, violin, D minor. Concerto, tuba, F minor. The England
    of Elizabeth: Suite. The wasps: Overture. John Fletcher, tuba;
    James Oliver Buswell, vln; LSO; Andre Previn. RCA GL 4-2953
    Tape (c) GK 4-2953 (From SB 6856, 6842, 6861, 6801)

+Gr 10-80 p504	+-HFN 8-80 p109 tape
+-HFN 4-80 p119	+RR 4-80 p82

Concerto accademico, D minor. See no. 1576
Concerto grosso. See no. 1226. See no. 3329
England of Elizabeth: Suite. See no. 3331
English folk song suite. See no. 49. See no. 1804
Fantasia on a theme by Thomas Tallis. See no. 913. See no. 1230.
    See no. 1318. See no. 1364. See no. 1379. See no. 3585
Fantasia on "Greensleeves". See no. 3639. See no. 3797. See no.
    4030
3332 Fantasy quintet. Sonata, violin and piano, A minor. Studies in
    English folk song (6). Hugh Bean, Frances Mason, vln; Christoph-
    er Wellington, Ian Jewel, vla; Eileen Croxford, vlc; David Park-
    house, pno. HMV HQS 1327
        ++ARG 9-80 p42
Fantasy quintet. See no. 3583
Festival Te deum. See no. 4060
The 49th parallel: Prelude and fugue. See no 4046
3333 The house of life. Songs of travel. Anthony Rolfe Johnson, t;
    David Willison, pno. Chalfont C 77017
        +St 1-80 p106
3334 Hugh the drover. Sally Burgess, Lynda Richardson, Sheila Armstrong,
    s; Shirley Minty, Helen Watts, con; Robert Tear, Leslie Fyson,
    David Johnston, Neil Jenkins, t; Bruce Ogston, bar; Oliver Broome,
    Robert Lloyd, Michael Rippon, bs; Choristers of St. Paul's Cath-
    edral Choir, Ambrosian Opera Chorus; RPO; Charles Groves. HMV
    SLS 5162 (3) (also Angel SZX 3879)

+-ARG 10-79 p25	++MT 12-79 p1011
+FF 11/12-79 p138	+-NYT 8-19-79 pD20
+FU 11-79 p48	+-ON 11-79 p58
+Gr 6-79 p102	+Op 9-79 p914
+-HF 12-79 p104	+RR 6-79 p63
+HFN 6-79 p111	+SFC 1-27-80 p44
+MM 12-79 p29	+St 12-79 p154
++MUM 2-80 p35	

Introduction and fugue, 2 pianos. See no. 1125

Let all the world. See no. 3524
Lord thou hast been our refuge. See no. 4019
Mystical songs: Come my way. See no. 3524
3335 On Wenlock edge. WARLOCK: The curlew. Ian Partridge, t; London
      Music Group. Arabesque 8018
                     +NR 11-80 p7
On Wenlock edge. See no. 962. See no. 1828
Prelude and fugue, C minor. See no. 3338
Preludes on Welsh hymn tunes: Rhosymedre. See no. 4052
Sea songs. See no. 4012
Sonata, violin and piano, A minor. See no. 1373. See no. 3332
3336 Songs (choral): English folksongs: The dark-eyed sailor, The spring-
      time of the year, Just as the tide was flowing, The lover's
      ghost, Wassail song; Heart's music; Prayer to the father of heav-
      en; Souls of the righteous; Te deum, G major; Valiant for truth;
      A vision of aeroplanes. Gillian Weir, org; BBC Northern Singers;
      Stephen Wilkinson. Abbey LPB 799
             ++Gr 6-79 p95   +-MT 1-80 p36
             +HFN 7-79 p112   +RR 6-79 p117
Songs (hymns): Dear lord and father of mankind. See no. 4019
Songs: Linden Lea. See no. 3778
Songs: Linden Lea; Silent noon; Songs of travel. See no. 3991
Songs: O how amiable are thy dwellings; Linden Lea. See no. 3527
Songs: O taste and see; The old hundredth. See no. 3937
Songs: The roadside fire. See no. 3551
Songs of travel. See no. 3333
Studies in English folk song. See no. 3332
Suite, viola and piano. See no. 732
3337 Symphony, no. 2. Halle Orchestra; John Barbirolli. Everest SDBR
      3446 (also Pye GSGC 15035) (From Vanguard SRV 134)
             +ARG 9-79 p44   +-HFN 1-79 p127
             +-FF 11/12-80 p189   +-NR 6-79 p5
3338 Symphony, no. 6, E minor. Prelude and fugue, C minor. David Ball,
      org; LPO; Vernon Handley. Classics for Pleasure CFP 40334
             +-Gr 9-80 p350   +HFN 9-80 p111
Toccata marziale. See no. 49. See no. 1804
Variants on "Dives and Lazarus". See no. 3330
The wasps. See no. 3330
The wasps: March past of the kitchen utensils. See no. 3801
The wasps: Overture. See no. 1364. See no. 3331
VAUTOR, Thomas
Mother I will have a husband. See no. 3744
Sweet Suffolk owl. See no. 3866. See no. 3893
VECCHI, Orazio
3339 L'Amfiparnaso. Deller Consort; Collegium Aureum; Alfred Deller.
      Harmonia Muni 1C 065 99816 (From Harmonis Mundi HM 30628/9)
             +FF 5/6-80 p168   +RR 4-80 p119
             +-HFN 4-80 p121
Neked zeng ez a dal. See no. 3814
So ben mio chi ha bon tempo. See no. 3956. See no. 3997
VEDAL
Today the master of the creation is crucified. See no. 775
VELLONES
Le posson volant. See no. 3738

VENTO, Ivo de
     Songs: Frisch ist mein Sinn; Ich weiss ein Maidlein; So wunsch ich
     ihr ein gute Nacht. See no. 3536
VERDI, Giuseppe
3340 Aida. Mirella Freni, Katia Ricciarelli, s; Agnes Baltsa, ms; Jose
     Carreras, t; Piero Cappuccilli, bar; Ruggero Raimondi, Jose van
     Dam, bs; VSOO Chorus; VPO; Herbert von Karajan. HMV SLS 5205
     (3) Tape (c) TC SLS 5205 (also Angel SZ 3888)
                    ++Gr 9-80 p399   +-HFN 11-80 p124
                    ++Gr 12-80 p889 tape
     Aida: Bald kommt Radames...Azurne Balaue; Fuggiam gli adori inos-
     piti...La tra foreste vergini; O patria mia. See no. 3774
     Aida: Ballet music. See no. 1523
     Aida: Celeste Aida. See no. 3535. See no. 3827. See no. 3945
     Aida: Er ists er ists...Ich hab gekampft; Zu dir fuhrt mich ein
     ernster Grund. See no. 2075
     Aida: Gia i sacerdoti. See no. 3770
     Aida: Gia i sacerdote adunansi; Misero appien mi festi; Se quel
     guerrier io fossi; Celeste Aida. See no. 3949
     Aida: Gloria all'egitto. See no. 3553
     Aida: La fatal pietra...O terra addio. See no. 3792. See no. 3946
     Aida: Mortal diletto ai numi; Nume custode e vindice. See no. 3899
     Aida: O cieli azzuri. See no. 3929
     Aida: O patria mia. See no. 3342. See no. 3869
     Aida: Pur ti riveggo. See no. 3343
     Aida: Quest assisa. See no. 3982
     Aida: Qui Radames verra...O patria mia. See no. 3793
     Aida: Ritorna vincitor. See no. 3632
     Aida: Ritorna vincitor; O patria mia. See no. 3931
3341 Aida: Se quel guerrier io fossi...Celeste Aida; Or di vulcano al
     tempio muovi...Ritorna vincitor; Gloria all'egitto; Que Radames
     verra...O patria mia...Rivedrai le foreste; Gia i sacerdoti adun-
     ansi; Presago il core. Leontyne Price, Mietta Sighele, s; Rita
     Gorr, ms; Franco Ricciardi, Jon Vickers, t; Robert Merrill, bar;
     Giorgio Tozzi, Plinio Clabassi, bs; Rome Opera Orchestra and Cho-
     rus; Georg Solti. Decca JB 81 Tape (c) KJBC 81 (From RCA SER
     4538/40)
                    +-Gr 6-80 p65   +RR 6-80 p37
                    +HFN 6-80 p119
     Aida: Triumphal march. See no. 3909
     Aida: Tu amonasro. See no. 724
3342 Arias: Aida: O patria mia. Il Corsaro: Non so le tetre imagini.
     Falstaff: Sul fil d'un suffio etesio. La forza del destino:
     Pace pace mio Dio. I Lombardi: La mia letizia infondere. Mac-
     beth: Ah la paterna mano. Otello: Gia nella notte densa. La
     traviata: De miei bollenti spiriti. Katia Ricciarelli, s; Luci-
     ano Pavarotti, t; Teatro Regio di Parma Orchestra; Giuseppe Pat-
     ane. Ars Nova ANC 25001
                    +Gr 4-80 p1593   +-ON 11-78 p82
                    +NR 10-79 p9   ++St 12-78 p162
                    +OC Vol XX, no. 1, 1979
                    p42
3343 Arias: Aida: Pur ti riveggo. Un ballo in maschera: Teco io sto;
     Non sai tu. Don Carlo: Io venga a domandar. Otello: Gia nella
     notte. Simon Boccanegra: Vieni a mirar. Eileen Farrell, s;
     Richard Tucker, t; Columbia Symphony Orchestra; Fausto Cleva.

Odyssey Y 35935 (From Columbia MS 6296)
        +ARG 10-80 p36
3344 Aroldo. Montserrat Caballe, s; Gianfranco Cecchele, t; Juan Pons,
     bar; Louis Lebherz, bs; New York Opera Orchestra; Eve Queler.
     CBS 79328 (3)
        +Gr 9-80 p400   +Op 10-80 p1014
        +HFN 10-80 p109   -RR 8-80 p32
        +MT 12-80 p788   +STL 8-10-80 p30
3345 Un ballo in maschera. Montserrat Caballe, s; Patricia Payne, con;
     Jose Carreras, t; Ingvar Wixell, bar; ROHO and Chorus; Colin
     Davis. Philips 6769 020 (3) Tape (c) 7699 108
        +ARG 10-79 p31   +MT 12-80 p788
        +FF 11/12-79 p140   +NR 7-79 p12
        +Gr 9-79 p521   +OC Winter 1979 p51
        +Gr 10-79 p727 tape   +ON 9-79 p68
        +HF 8-79 p93   -Op 10-79 p975
        +HFN 9-79 p115   +RR 9-79 p63
        +HFN 10-79 p171 tape   +RR 6-80 p95 tape
        +MJ 11/12-79 p54   +SFC 5-20-79 p49
        +MM 12-79 p29   +St 11-79 p102
     Un ballo in maschera: Alzati la tuo figlio...Eri tu. See no. 3771
     Un ballo in maschera: Di tu se fedele. See no. 4008
     Un ballo in maschera: Di tu se fedele; Forse la soglia attinse;
     Ma se m'e forza perderti. See no. 3949
     Un ballo in maschera: E scherzo; La rivedra. See no. 3984
     Un ballo in maschera: Ja du warst's; Wenn das Kraut wie hier ward.
     See no. 3774
     Un ballo in maschera: La rivedra nell'estasi; E scherzo ed e follia.
     See no. 3672
     Un ballo in maschera: Ma dall'arido stelo; Morro ma prima in grazia.
     See no. 3929
     Un ballo in maschera: Ma se m'e forza perderti. See no. 3827
3346 Un ballo in maschera: Posa in pace...Sire...Che leggo, il bando ad
     una donna; Ecco l'ordo campo; Alzati la tuo figlio...Eri tu; Ah
     perche qui fuggite. Cristina Deutekom, Patricia Hay, s; John
     Robertson, Charles Craig, t; Jan Derksen, bar; William McCue,
     Pieter van den Berg, bs; Scottish Opera Chorus; Scottish Nation-
     al Orchestra; Alexander Gibson. Classics for Pleasure CFP 40252
        +FF 9/10-80 p227   +HFN 12-76 p149
        +Gr 1-77 p1174   +RR 1-77 p40
     Un ballo in maschera: Saper vorreste. See no. 3770
     Un ballo in maschera: Teco io sto; Non sai tu. See no. 3343
3347 La battaglia di Legnano. Katia Ricciarelli, s; Ann Murray, ms;
     Jose Carreras, t; Matteo Manuguerra, Jonathan Summers, bar; Niko-
     lai Ghiuselev, Hannes Lichtenberger, Dimitri Kavrakos, bs; ORF
     Symphony Orchestra and Chorus; Lamberto Gardelli. Philips 6700
     120 (2) Tape (c) 7699 081 (r) 6700 120
        +ARG 4-79 p42   +MT 8-79 p660
        +FF 3/4-79 p126   +NR 4-79 p11
        +Gr 4-79 p1768   +NYT 12-3-78 pD19
        +Gr 11-79 p924 tape   +ON 1-27-79 p64
        +HF 4-79 p96   +Op 6-79 p574
        +HF 9-79 p131 tape   +RR 4-79 p56
        +HF 11-80 p88 tape   +RR 11-79 p126 tape
        +HFN 4-79 p128   +SFC 12-17-78 p64

        +HFN 7-79 p119   ++St 4-79 p91
        +MJ 5/6-79 p53   +STL 12-2-79 p37
La battaglia di Legnano: Overture. See no. 758
Il Corsaro: Ne sulla terra. See no. 3918
Il Corsaro: Non so le tetre immagini. See no. 3342
3348 Don Carlo (4 act version). Edita Gruberova, Mirella Freni, s; Agnes
     Baltsa, ms; Jose Carreras, Horst Nitsche, t; Jose Van Dam, Piero
     Cappuccilli, bar; Nicolai Ghiaurov, Ruggero Raimondi, bs; German
     Opera Chorus; BPhO; Herbert von Karajan. HMV SLS 5154 (7) Tape
     (c) TC SLS 5154 (also Angel SCLX 3875 Tape (C) 4Z4X 3875)
              +–ARG 6-80 p30   +NYT 12-23-79 pD28
              +–FF 1/2-80 p169   +–ON 12-15-79 p36
               +Gr 10-79 p711   +–Op 2-80 p165
              ++Gr 3-80 p1446 tape   +–RR 10-79 p66
              +–HF 4-80 p97   +RR 6-80 p95 tape
              +HFN 12-79 p17   ++SFC 1-20-80 p47
              +HFN 1-80 p123 tape   +–St 4-80 p136
              +–NR 2-80 p10
     Don Carlo, excerpts. See no. 3696
     Don Carlo: Dio che nell'alma infondere. See no. 3774. See no. 3792
     Don Carlo: Dormiro sol. See no. 3899
     Don Carlo: Io l'ho perduta...Qual pallor. See no. 724
     Don Carlo: Io venga a domandar. See no. 3343
     Don Carlo: Monologue of Philip. See no. 3979
     Don Carlo: Morte di Rodrigo. See no. 2565
     Don Carlo: O Carlo ascolta...Io morro. See no. 3771
     Don Carlo: O don fatale. See no. 3903
     Don Carlo: Per me giunto; Morro ma lieta in corre. See no. 3978
     Don Carlo: Sie hat mich nie geliebt. See no. 3712
3349 Don Carlo: Tu che le vanita. Ernani: Sorta e la notte...Ernani Er-
     nani involami. Macbeth: Nel di della vittoria...Vieni t'affretta;
     La luce langue; Una macchia e que tuttora. Nabucco: Ben io t'
     invenni; Anch'io diachiuso un giorno. Maria Callas, s; PhO;
     Nicola Rescigno. HMV ASD 3817 Tape (c) TC ASD 3817 (From Colum-
     bia SAX 2293)
              +–Gr 2-80 p1301   ++Op 7-80 p686
              +HFN 3-80 p107   ++RR 1-80 p44
              +–HFN 4-80 p121 tape
     Don Carlo: Tu che le vanita. See no. 3668
     I due Foscari: O vecchio cor. See no. 3982
     I due Foscari: Questa dunque. See no. 3770
     I due Foscari: Tace il vento e questa l'onda. See no. 3374
3350 Ernani. Leontyne Price, s; Julia Hamari, ms; Carlo Bergonzi, Fer-
     nando Iacopucci, t; Mario Sereni, bar; Ezio Flagello, Hartje
     Muller, bs; RCA Italiana Opera Orchestra and Chorus; Thomas
     Schippers. RCA RL 4-2866 (3) (From SER 5572/4)
              +–Gr 10-79 p712   +–Op 2-80 p164
              +–HFN 10-79 p171   +RR 10-79 p68
     Ernani: Che mai vegg'io...Infelice. See no. 3899. See no. 3904
     Ernani: Come rugiada al cespite; Ernani involami. See no. 3774
     Ernani: Da quel di. See no. 3929
     Ernani: Ernani involami. See no. 3670. See no. 3872
     Ernani: Eviva...beviam beviam; Un patto un giuramento; Si ridesti
        il Leon de Castiglia. See no. 3374
     Ernani: O dei verd'anni miei. See no. 3770

Ernani: O dei verd'anni miei; O sommo Carlo. See no. 3901
Ernani: O de verd'anni miei; Lo vedremo o veglio audace. See no.
　3982
Ernani: Surta e la notte...Ernani Ernani involami. See no. 3349
Ernani: Surta e la notte...Ernani Ernani involami...Tutto sprezzo che
　d'Ernani. See no. 2088
2351 Falstaff. Elisabeth Schwarzkopf, Anna Moffo, s; Nan Merriman, Fed-
　ora Barbieri, ms; Luigi Alva, t; Tito Gobbi, Rolando Panerai, bar;
　PhO and Chorus; Herbert von Karajan. HMV SLS 5211 (2) Tape (c)
　TC SLS 5211 (From Columbia 33CX 1410-2, SAX 2254/6)
　　　　　+Gr 12-80 p880
Falstaff: Dal labbro il canto. See no. 3774
Falstaff: Die Ehre Gauner; Es verzehert uns heisse Reue...Meine
　Ehrfurcht. See no. 2075
Falstaff: Sul fil d'un suffio etesio. See no. 3342
3352 La forza del destino, excerpts. Il trovatore, excerpts. Giovanni
　Martinelli, t; Orchestra and conductor. Pearl GEMM 181/2
　　　　　++Gr 11-80 p736
La forza del destino: Al suon del tamburo; Rataplan. See no. 3928
La forza del destino: Dalla natal sua terra...O tu che in seno ang-
　eli. See no. 3946
La forza del destino: Egli e salvo. See no. 3901
La forza del destino: Il santo nome di Dio. See no. 3368
La forza del destino: Invano Alvaro; Le minaccie i fieri accenti.
　See no. 3949
La forza del destino: Madre pietosa vergine; Pace pace mio Dio.
　See no. 3924
La forza del destino: Madre pietosa vergine; La vergine degl angeli.
　See no. 3774
La forza del destino: O tu che in seno agli angeli. See no. 3827
La forza del destino: Overture. See no. 662. See no. 3898
La forza del destino: Pace pace mio Dio. See no. 3342. See no.
　3596. See no. 3770. See no. 3869. See no. 3962
La forza del destino: Solenne in quest'ora. See no. 724. See no.
　3538. See no. 3792. See no. 3945. See no. 3988. See no. 4008
La forza del destino: Urna fatale del mio destino. See no. 3771.
　See no. 3812. See no. 3980
The lady and the fool: Ballet, excerpts. See no. 3159
I Lombardi: Dove sola m'inoltro...Per dirupi e per foreste. See
　no. 1263
I Lombardi: Gerusalem...La grande la promessa citta. See no. 3374
I Lombardi: La mia letizia infondere. See no. 3342
I Lombardi: Qual vo'uta transcorrere. See no. 3949
3353 Luisa Miller. Katie Ricciarelli, s; Elena Obraztsova, Audrey Mich-
　ael, ms; Placido Domingo, Luigi de Corato, t; Gwynne Howell,
　Wladimiro Ganzarolli, Renato Bruson, bar; ROHO and Chorus; Lorin
　Maazel. DG 2709 096 (3) Tape (c) 3370 035 (also DG 2531 229/31)
　　　　　+-ARG 10-80 p33　　　　　　++NR 7-80 p8
　　　　　+-FF 9/10-80 p229　　　　　+NYT 6-29-80 pD20
　　　　　+Gr 6-80 p65　　　　　　　+-ON 9-80 p68
　　　　　+Gr 8-80 p275 tape　　　　+-Op 7-80 p685
　　　　　+-HF 10-80 p92　　　　　　+-RR 6-80 p37
　　　　　++HFN 7-80 p111　　　　　+St 9-80 p73
　　　　　+HFN 8-80 p109 tape　　　+-STL 5-11-80 p39
　　　　　+MT 12-80 p788

Luisa Miller: Arias. See no. 3539
Luisa Miller: Il mio sangue. See no. 3927
Luisa Miller: O fede negar potessi...Quando le sere al placido. See no. 3672
Luisa Miller: O fedelta...Quando le sere. See no. 3977
Luisa Miller: Quando le sere al placido. See no. 3535. See no. 3770. See no. 3827. See no. 3981
Luisa Miller: Ti desta Luisa. See no. 3374
3354 Macbeth, abridged. Else Bottcher; Elisabeth Hongen, ms; Josef Witt, t; Mathieu Ahlersmeyer, bar; Herbert Alsen, bs; VSOO and Chorus; Karl Bohm. Acanta DE 23277/8 (2)
        +-HFN 6-80 p113   +-RR 4-80 p51
Macbeth: Ah la paterna mano. See no. 3342
Macbeth: Nel di della vittoria...Vieni t'affretta; La luce langue; Una macchia e que tuttora. See no. 3349
Macbeth: Nel di della vittoria...Vieni t'affretta...Or tutti sorgete; La luce langue. See no. 628
Macbeth: Patria oppressa; Che faceste dite su. See no. 3374
Macbeth: Perfidi; All'anglo contro me v'unite...Pieta rispetto amore. See no. 3812
Macbeth: Perfidi...Pieta rispetto amore. See no. 3771
Macbeth: Pieta rispetto amore. See no. 2565. See no. 3980
Macbeth: Sleep walking scene. See no. 1622
Macbeth: Tre volte miagola. See no. 3553
I Masnadieri: Venerabile o padre...Lo sguardo; Oh ma la pace...Tu del mio Carlo. See no. 3918
Nabucco: Ah prigioniero io sono...Dio di Giuda. See no. 3771
Nabucco: Ben io t'invenni; Anch'io diachiuso un giorno. See no. 3349
Nabucco: O chi piange...Del futuro nel buio. See no. 3774
Nabucco: Sperate o figli. See no. 4007
Nabucco: Sperate o figli...D'egitto la sui lidi; Oh chi piange... Del futuro nel bujo. See no. 3368
Nabucco: Tu sul labbro. See no. 3927
Nabucco: Tu sul labbro; Del futuro nel buio discerno. See no. 3930
Nabucco: Va pensiero. See no. 3553
Nabucco: Va pensiero; Gli arredi festivi giu cadano in fanti. See no. 3374
Nabucco: Warum klagt ihr und seid so verzweifelt. See no. 3712
O lass uns fliehen. See no. 3646
3355 Otello, excerpts (sung in German). Elena Nicolai, ms; Hilde Konetzni, s; Torsten Ralf, t; Paul Schoffler, bs; VSOO and Chorus; Karl Bohm. Acanta BB 23058
            +-Gr 9-80 p408   +-RR 8-80 p34
        +-HFN 8-80 p103
Otello: Credo. See no. 3888
Otello: Credo in un Dio crudel. See no. 3925
Otello: Emilia te ne prego...Piangea cantando. See no. 3780
Otello: Era la notte; Esultate; Niun mi tema; Nium ti tema; Ora e per sempre addio. See no. 3770
Otello: Esultate; Gia nella notte; Ora per sempre; Si pel ciel; Dio mi potevi scagliar; Niun mi tema. See no. 1491
Otello: Esultate; Ora e per sempre addio; Stilled by the gathering darkness; Du neigst dich zum Gebet. See no. 3774
Otello: Fuoco di gioia. See no. 3553

Otello: Gia nella notte densa. See no. 3342. See no. 3343
Otello: Nell'ara arcane...Ora e per sempre addio. See no. 3946
Otello: Piangea cantando...Ave Maria; Inaffia l'ugola; Mio Signore...
   che brani; Atroce...Ora e per sempre addio; Ah mille vite...Si
   pel ciel mormoreo; Dio mio potevi scaliar; Niun mi tema. See no.
   3773
Otello: Salce. See no. 3923
Otello: Si pel ciel marmoreo giuro. See no. 724
Otello: Vanne...Credo in un Dio crudel; Era la notte. See no. 3771
Otello: Zur Nachtzeit war es. See no. 2075

3356 Opera paraphrases: Aida: Grande fantaisie (Alder). Don Carlo: Fantasia elegante, op. 82 (Gariboldi). Macbeth: Fantasia brillante
   (Silvi). Rigoletto: Capriccio (Cunio/Pizzi). La traviata: Souvenir, op. 24 (Casaretto). Il trovatore: Divertimento, op. 23
   (Casaretto). Severino Gazzelloni, flt; Bruno Canino, pno. Dischi Ricordi RCL 27049
                  +–Gr 9-80 p368

3357 Pezzi sacre (4). Jo Ann Pickens, s; CSO and Chorus; Georg Solti.
   Decca SET 602 Tape (c) KCET 602 (also London OS 26610 Tape (c)
   OS 5-26610)
              +–ARG 6-80 p41   +–HF 11-80 p84
              +FF 7/8-80 p147   +HFN 5-79 p127
              +–FU 3-80 p50   ++NR 7-80 p8
              +Gr 5-79 p1926   +–ON 2-23-80 p45
              +Gr 7-79 p259 tape   +RR 5-79 p101

3358 Pezzi sacre (4). Leipzig Radio Orchestra and Chorus; Herbert Kegel.
   Philips 6570 111 Tape (c) 7310 111 (From 6580 213)
              +Gr 1-80 p1194   +HFN 1-80 p123 tape

3359 Pezzi sacri (4). Kvetoslava Nemeckova, s; CPhO and Chorus; Gaetano
   Delogu. Supraphon 112 2433
              +ARG 12-80 p47   ++NR 7-80 p8
              +FF 9/10-80 p84   ++SFC 6-22-80 p36
              +–HF 11-80 p84

Pezzi sacri: Te deum. See no. 757
Quartet, strings, E minor. See no. 1267. See no. 3234

3360 Requiem. Maria Stader, s; Mariana Radev, ms; Helmut Krebs, t; Kim
   Borg, bs; RIAS Chamber Chorus, St. Hedwig's Cathedral Choir;
   RIAS Symphony Orchestra; Ferenc Fricsay. DG 2700 113 (2) (From
   DG 18155-6)
              +–ARSC Vol 12, nos. 1-2   +–HFN 2-79 p117
                 1980 p124   +–RR 2-79 p94
              ++Gr 1-79 p1316

3361 Requiem. Katia Ricciarelli, s; Shirley Verrett, ms; Placido Domingo, t; Nicolai Ghiaurov, bar; La Scala Orchestra and Chorus;
   Claudio Abbado. DG 2707 120 Tape (c) 3370 032
              +–Gr 11-80 p727   ++NR 12-80 p8
              +HFN 11-80 p124   ++STL 11-9-80 p40

3362 Requiem. Maria Stader, s; Oralia Dominguez, alto; Gabor Carrelli,
   t; Ivan Sardi, bs; St. Hedwig's Cathedral Choir; Orchestra;
   Ferenc Fricsay. DG 2721 171 (2)
              +–ARSC Vol 12, nos. 1-2, 1980 p124

3363 Requiem. Renata Scotto, s; Agnes Baltsa, ms; Veriano Luchetti, t;
   Yevgeny Nesterenko, bs; Ambrosian Chorus; PhO; Riccardo Muti.
   HMV SLS 5185 (2) Tape (c) TC SLS 5185 (also Angel SZB 3858 Tape
   (c) 4Z2S 3858)

                    +ARG 7/8-80 p45   +–MUM 10-80 p36
                   ++FF 7/8-80 p148   +–NR 5-80 p8
                   ++Gr 12-79 p1034   +NYT 3-2-80 pD26
                    +–HF 12-80 p85   +–ON 7-80 p37
                    +–HFN 2-80 p99   +RR 12-79 p116
                    +HFN 4-80 p121 tape   +SFC 3-30-80 p39
                    +MT 9-80 p567   ++STL 2-10-80 p40

Requiem: Confutatis maledictis. See no. 3899. See no. 3930
Requiem: Ingemisco. See no. 3672. See no. 3770

3364 Rigoletto. Margherita Rinaldi, s; Viorica Cortez, ms; Franco Boni-
     solli, t; Rolando Panerai, bar; Bengt Rundgren, bs; Dresden
     Staatsoper Chorus; Dresden Staatskapelle; Francesco Molinari-
     Pradelli. Acanta HA 21474 (3)
                    +–FF 9/10-78 p121   +–HFN 3-80 p101
                    -Gr 12-79 p1052   +–ON 7-78 p37
                    +HF 1-79 p83   +–RR 11-79 p62

3365 Rigoletto. Beverly Sills, s; Mignon Dunn, ms; Sherrill Milnes, bar;
     Alfredo Kraus, t; Samuel Ramey, bs; Ambrosian Opera Chorus; PhO;
     Julius Rudel. Angel SZCX 3872 (3) Tape (c) 4Z3X 3872 (also HMV
     SLS 5193)
                    /ARG 5-80 p42   +–Op 6-80 p576
                    +–FF 3/4-80 p172   +RR 5-80 p50
                    +–Gr 4-80 p1593   /–SFC 12-9-79 p43
                    +–HFN 4-80 p111   +St 2-80 p79
                    +–NR 1-80 p9   +–STL 4-13-80 p39
                    +ON 1-19-80 p37

3366 Rigoletto. Elena Obreztsova, Ileana Cotrubas, s; Placido Domingo,
     t; Kurt Moll, Piero Cappuccilli, bar; Nicolai Ghiaurov, bs; VPO;
     Carlo Maria Giulini. DG 2740 225 (3) Tape (c) 3371 054
                    +Gr 12-80 p889 tape   +–ON 11-22-80 p44
                    +Gr 10-80 p541   ++SFC 9-21-80 p21
                   ++HFN 10-80 p109   ++SFC 11-2-80 p22
                    +HFN 11-80 p131 tape   +STL 11-9-80 p40
                    /NYT 10-26-80 pB33

Rigoletto, excerpts. See no. 3696
Rigoletto: Bella figlia dell'amore. See no. 3900
Rigoletto: Bella figlia dell'amore; La donna e mobile; Questa o
     quella. See no. 3945
Rigoletto: Caro nome. See no. 3770
Rigoletto: Caro nome; Tutte le feste. See no. 3723
Rigoletto: Complunto...Si vendetta tremenda vendetta. See no. 3538
Rigoletto: Cortigiani vil razza danata. See no. 2565. See no.
     3812. See no. 3888
Rigoletto: Duet and caro nome. See no. 3872
Rigoletto: Ella mi fu rapita. See no. 1240
Rigoletto: Ella mi fu rapita...Parmi veder le lagrime; La donna e
     mobile...Bella figlia dell'amore. See no. 3672
Rigoletto: Figlia mio padre; Tutte le feste. See no. 3632
Rigoletto: Gualtier Malde...Caro nome. See no. 3554. See no. 3948
Rigoletto: La donna e mobile. See no. 3830. See no. 3977
Rigoletto: La donna e mobile; E il sol dell anima. See no. 3981
Rigoletto: Pari siamo; Cortigiani vil razza dannata. See no. 3982
Rigoletto: Pari siamo; Figlia mio padre...Deh non parlare al misero;
     Cortigiani vil razza dannata. See no. 3925
Rigoletto: Parmi veder. See no. 1491

Rigoletto: Quel vecchio maledicami. See no. 3927
Rigoletto: Questa o quella; Bella figlia dell'amore. See no. 724
Rigoletto: Questa o quella; Ella mi fu rapita...Parmi veder le lag-
    rime. See no. 4031
Rigoletto: Tuerer Name dessen Klang. See no. 3646. See no. 3774
Rigoletto: Tochter...Mein Vater; Gualtier Malde...Teurer Name dessen
    Klang; Wer ist statt seiner hier im Sacke. See no. 3584
3367 Simon Boccanegra. Arias: BEETHOVEN: Ah perfido, op. 65. DEBUSSY:
    L'Enfant prodigue: Air de Lia. GLUCK: Alceste: Divinites du
    Styx. HANDEL: Sosarme: Rend'il sereno. Elisabeth Rethberg, s;
    Giovanni Martinelli, t; Lawrence Tibbett, Leonard Warren, bar;
    Instrumental Accompaniment; Ettore Panizza. Rococo 1017
            ++NR 1-80 p8
3368 Simon Boccanegra. Arias: BELLINI: Norma: Ite sul colle. VERDI:
    La forza del destino: Il santo nome di Dio. Nabucco: Sperate O
    figli...D'egitto la sui lidi; Oh chi piange...Del futuro nel bujo.
    Victoria de los Angeles, Silvia Bertona, s; Giuseppe Campora,
    Paolo Caroli, t; Tito Gobbi, Walter Monachesi, Paolo Dari, bar;
    Boris Christoff, bs; Rome Opera Orchestra and Chorus; Gabriele
    Santini, Vittorio Gui. Seraphim 1C 6115
            +ARG 3-80 p44
Simon Boccanegra: A te l'estremo addio...Il lacerato spirito. See
    no. 3899
Simon Boccanegra: Il lacerato spirito. See no. 3925
Simon Boccanegra: Leb wohl auf ewig...Palast der Vater. See no.
    3712
Simon Boccanegra: Vieni a mirar. See no. 3343
3369 Songs: Album di sei romanze; L'Esule; Il poveretto; La seduzione;
    Sei romanze. Klara Takacs, ms; Sandor Falvai, pno. Hungaroton
    SLPX 12197
            +-FF 9/10-80 p230   +HFN 12-80 p147
            +Gr 12-80 p871   ++NR 10-80 p11
            +HF 12-80 p86   +SFC 8-10-80 p29
Songs: Lo spazzocamino. See no. 3695
3370 Stiffelio. Sylvia Sass, s; Jose Carreras, t; ORTF; Vienna Chorus;
    Lamberto Gardelli. Philips 6769 039 (2) Tape (c) 7699 127
            +-Gr 10-80 p542   ++ON 10-80 p42
            +HFN 10-80 p109   +Op 10-80 p1014
            +-NR 10-80 p10   +-SFC 9-7-80 p32
            ++NYT 9-14-80 pD42   ++St 12-80 p135
3371 La traviata. Maria Callas, s; Mario Sereni, bar; Alfredo Kraus, t;
    San Carlo Opera Orchestra and Chorus; Franco Ghione. HMV RLS
    757 (2) (also Angel ZBX 3910 Tape (c) 4Z2X 3910)
            +Gr 10-80 p541   +St 12-80 p117
            +NYT 9-4-80 pD26   +STL 11-9-80 p40
3372 La traviata. Maria Caniglia, s; Beniamino Gigli, t; Mario Basiola,
    bar; Orchestra; Pietro Cimara. MDP Records 009 (2)
            +-FF 1/2-80 p156
3373 La traviata, excerpts. Hilde Gueden, s; Fritz Wunderlich, t; Diet-
    rich Fischer-Dieskau, bar; Bavarian Radio Orchestra and Chorus;
    Bruno Bartoletti. DG 2535 322
            +RR 8-80 p14
La traviata: Addio del passato. See no. 2565. See no. 3869
La traviata: Ah si da un anno...Un di felice eterea; Parigi o cara;
    De miei bollenti spiriti. See no. 3981

La traviata: Brindisi; Un di felice. See no. 3672
La traviata: De miei bollenti spiriti. See no. 3342
La traviata: Di provenza il mar. See no. 3925. See no. 3982
La traviata: E strano...Ah fors e lui; Parigi o cara. See no. 3774
La traviata: E strano...Ah fors'e lui che l'anima...Sempre libera.
   See no. 628
La traviata: Lunge dei lei...De miei bollenti spiriti. See no.
   3538. See no. 3977. See no. 4031
La traviata: Prelude, Cat 1. See no. 3847
La traviata: 'S ist seltsam...Er ist es... 'S est Torheit...Von der
   Freude Blumenkranzen. See no. 3646
La traviata: Tenesta la promessa...Addio del passato. See no. 3554
Il trovatore, excerpts. See no. 3352
Il trovatore: Ah si ben mio. See no. 3827
Il trovatore: Ah si ben mio; Di quella pira. See no. 3984
Il trovatore: Ah si ben mio; Se m'ami ancor; Ai nostri monti; Di
   quella pira. See no. 3945
Il trovatore: Arias. See no. 3539
Il trovatore: D'amor sull'ali rosee...Tu vedrai. See no. 3828
Il trovatore: Dass nur fur dich; Il balen del suo sorriso. See no.
   3770
Il trovatore: Deserto sulla terra; De qual tetra luce; Ah si ben
   mio; Di quella pira. See no. 724
Il trovatore: Di due figli...Abietta zingara. See no. 3899
Il trovatore: Di quella pira. See no. 3535. See no. 3538
Il trovatore: Loderne Flammen. See no. 3774
Il trovatore: Mal reggendo...Oh giusto cielo; Miserere; Ai nostri
   monti. See no. 1240
Il trovatore: Mal reggendo; Se m'ami ancor; Ai nostri monti. See
   no. 3949
Il trovatore: Mira d'acerbe; Vivra contende. See no. 3978
Il trovatore: Miserere. See no. 3946
Il trovatore: Qual voce...Come tu donna; Conte...Ne cessi. See no.
   3901
Il trovatore: Se m'ami ancor...Ai nostri monti. See no. 3672
Il trovatore: Tacea la notte; D'amor sull'ali rosee. See no. 3561.
   See no. 3929
Il trovatore: Vanne; Lasciami...D'amor sull'ali rosee. See no. 628
Il trovatore: Vedi le fosche. See no. 3553
Il trovatore: Vedi le fosche notturne; Squilli echeggi la trombe
   guerriera. See no. 3374
I vespri siciliani: Merce dilette amiche. See no. 3789
I vespri siciliani: O Heimat...O main Palermo. See no. 3712
I vespri siciliani: O patria...O tu Palermo. See no. 3899
I vespri siciliani: O tu Palermo. See no. 3930. See no. 4007
I vespri siciliani: Overture. See no. 3555
I vespri siciliani: Si celebri alfine tra canti tra fior. See no.
   3374
I vespri siciliani: Siciliani. See no. 3872
3374 Works, selections: I due Foscari: Tace il vento e questa l'onda.
   Ernani: Eviva...beviam beviam; Un patto un giuramento; Si ridesti
   il Leon de Castiglia. I Lombardi: Gerusalem...La grande la promessa citta. Luisa Miller: Ti desta Luisa. Macbeth: Patria
   opressa; Che faceste dite su. Nabucco: Va pensiero; Gli arredi
   festivi giu cadano in fanti. Il trovatore: Vedi le fosche not-

turne; Squilli echeggi la trombe guerriera. I vespri siciliani:
Si celebri alfine tra canti tra fior. Welsh National Opera Or-
chestra and Chorus; Richard Armstrong. HMV ASD 3811 Tape (c)
TC ASD 3811

          +-FF 9/10-80 p228   +HFN 2-80 p107 tape
          +Gr 1-80 p1195   +Op 5-80 p471
        ++Gr 3-80 p1446 tape   +RR 1-80 p61
         +HFN 1-80 p111

VERDIER, Pierre
    Lamento. See no. 3932
VERHEY, Theodoor
    Concerto, flute, no. 1, op. 43, D minor. See no. 3818
VERMEIREN, Jef
    Polytonal study. See no. 3889
VERMEULEN, Matthijs
    Symphony, no. 3. See no. 3818
VERNON
    When that I was a tiny boy. See no. 3840
VERSCHRAEGEN, Gabriel
    Partita octavi toni super Veni Creator. See no. 4055
VERSTOVSKY, Alexis
    Askold's tomb: Strangers aria and chorus. See no. 3796
VERT
    La leyenda del beso: Brindisi. See no. 3888
VICTORIA, Tomas de
    Ave Maria vidi speciosam. See no. 3763
    The lamentations of Jeremiah for holy Saturday: Lessons, 1-3. See
       no. 1297
3375 Lessons of Tenebrae and the responsories of matins. Officium Heb-
       domadea sanctae. Stephane Caillat Chorale, Ensemble Per Cantar
       et Sonar, Groupe Choral Gregorien; Stephane Caillat, Jean Bihan.
       Arion ARN 336016 (3)
          +-Gr 2-80 p1288   +RR 12-79 p118
    Litaniae de beata virgine. See no. 3376
    Magnificat primi toni. See no. 3376
    Marian antiphon, excerpts. See no. 3707
    Motets: Ave Maria; Ascendens Christus; Estote fortes in bello; Hic
       vic despiciens mundum; Guadent in coelis; Iste sanctus pro lege
       Dei; O magnum mysterium; O quam gloriosum est regnum; Veni sponsa
       Christi. See no. 3376
    O quam gloriosum, mass. See no. 3376
    Officium Hebdomadea sanctae. See no. 3375
    Requiem mass. See no. 3376
    Songs (choral): Lauda Sion; O sacrum convivium; Tantum ergo. See
       no. 970
3376 Works, selections: Litaniae de beata virgine. Magnificat primi
       toni. O quam gloriosum est regnum, mass. Requiem mass. Motets:
       Ave Maria; Ascendens Christus; Estote fortes in bello; Hic vir
       despiciens mundum; Guadent in coelis; Iste sanctus pro lege Dei;
       O magnum mysterium; O quam gloriosum est regnum; Veni sponsa
       Christi. St. John's College Choir; George Guest. Argo ZK 70/1
       (2)(From ZRG 570, 620)
          +Gr 1-80 p1194   ++RR 2-80 p92
VIDAL, Peire
    Songs: Vida et razos; Baros de mon dan convit. See no. 3748

VIERLING, Johann
    Melodia. See no. 4067
    Trio, C major. See no. 4039
VIERNE, Louis
    Berceuse. See no. 3728. See no. 4023
    Fantasiestucke, op. 51, A minor: Andantino. See no. 4034
    Fantasiestucke, op. 53: Clair de lune. See no. 3958
    Fantasiestucke, op. 53: Toccata. See no. 4034
    Fantasiestucke, op. 54: Carillon de Westminster. See no. 212. See
       no. 3381. See no. 3525. See no. 3958. See no. 4050. See no.
       4057
    Fantasiestucke, op. 54: Carillon de Westminster; Sur le Rhin. See
       no. 1927
    Fantasiestucke, op. 54: Impromptu. See no. 3994
3377 Fantasiestucke, op. 54: Sur la Rhin; Carillon de Westminster. Fan-
       tasiestucke, op. 55: Aubade; Resignation; Cathedrales; Naiades;
       Gargouilles et chimeres; Les cloches de Hinckley. Pierre Lab-
       ric, org. Grand Orgue LVM 791003
             +Gr 9-80 p379   +MU 3-80 p8
             +FF 5/6-80 p168
    Fantasiestucke, op. 55: Aubade; Resignation; Cathedrales; Naiades;
       Gargouilles et chimeres; Les cloches de Hinckley. See no. 3377
    Improvisations (3). See no. 3735
    Pieces en style libre, op. 31: Berceuse; Carillon de Longport. See
       no. 3582
    Pieces en style libre, op. 31: Prelude. See no. 4048
3378 Pieces en style libre, op. 31: Prelude, Scherzetto, Carillon de
       Longport, Berceuse. Symphony, no. 3, op. 28, F sharp minor.
       David Sanger, org. Meridian E 77024
             +Gr 10-79 p676   ++MT 4-80 p253
            ++HFN 10-79 p163   ++RR 9-79 p109
3379 Suite, no. 1, op. 51: Prelude, Andantino, Caprice, Intermezzo, Re-
       quiem aeternam, Marche nuptiale. Suite, no. 2, op. 53: Lamento,
       Sicilienne. Pierre Labric, org. Grand Orgue LVM 771101
             +-FF 1/2-80 p157   +-MU 2-79 p12
             +Gr 9-80 p379
3380 Suite, no. 2, op. 53: Hymne au soleil, Feux-follets, Clair de lune,
       Toccata. Suite, no. 3, op. 54: Dedicace, Impromptu, Etoile du
       soir; Fantomes. Pierre Labric, org. Grand Orgue LVM 780120
             +-FF 1/2-80 p157   +MU 6-79 p9
             +Gr 9-80 p379
    Suite, no. 2, op. 53: Lamento, Sicilienne. See no. 3379
    Suite, no. 3, op. 54: Dedicace, Impromptu, Etoile du soir, Fantomes.
       See no. 3380
    Symphony, no. 2, op. 20, E minor: Allegro. See no. 3582
    Symphony, no. 2, op. 20, E major: Choral. See no. 3733
    Symphony, no. 3, op. 28, F sharp minor. See no. 1438. See no.
       3378. See no. 4053
3381 Symphony, no. 6, op. 59, B major. Fantasiestucke, op. 54: Carillon
       de Westminster. Nicolas Kynaston, org. Mitra OSM 16156
             +Gr 6-80 p54   +-HFN 12-79 p171
    Symphony, no. 6, op. 59, B major: Finale. See no. 3658. See no.
       3970
VIEUXTEMPS, Henri
    Capriccio, op. posth. See no. 1883

Concerto, violin, no. 4, op. 31, D minor. See no. 3964
Concerto, violin, no. 5, op. 37, A minor. See no. 3964. See no.
    4043
Romance, op. 7, no. 2. See no. 3601
Sonata, viola and piano, op. 36. See no. 1883
Souvenir d'Amerique, op. 7, no. 3. See no. 3552. See no. 3788

VIKTOR/WINKLER
    Viscositas. See no. 1385

VILLA-LOBOS, Heitor
    A prole do bebe: Polichinelle. See no. 3953. See no. 3954
    Assobio a jato. See no. 376
3382 Bachianas brasileiras, nos. 2, 5-6, 9. Victoria de los Angeles, s;
        Fernand Benedetti, vlc; Fernand Dufrene, flt; Rene Plessier, bsn;
        French National Radio Orchestra; Heitor Villa-Lobos. HMV ALP 3803
        Tape (c) TC ALP 3803 (From ALP 1603)
                    +Gr 11-79 p896   +-HFN 2-80 p107 tape
                    +-HFN 11-79 p145   +RR 12-79 p81
    Bachianas brasileiras, no. 4. See no. 2435
    Bachianas brasileiras, no. 5: Aria. See no. 3600
    Choros, no. 1, E major. See no. 3384. See no. 3634
    Choros, no. 1, E minor: Prelude, no. 1. See no. 3614
    Choros, no. 10. See no. 2718
    Ciranda des sete notas. See no. 710. See no. 1470
    Concerto, guitar. See no. 3612
    Concerto, harmonica. See no. 52
    Distribuicao de flores. See no. 3717
    Etudes, guitar (2). See no. 3798
3383 Etudes, guitar, nos. 1, 3, 5-8, 11-12. Preludes (5). Suite popu-
        lar brasileira. Eric Hill, gtr. Saga 5453 Tape (c) CA 5453
                    -FF 9/10-80 p275   +-HFN 5-78 p147 tape
                    +-Gr 1-78 p1270   +HFN 11-79 p155
                    +Gr 7-78 p255 tape   +-RR 11-77 p97
                    +HFN 1-78 p135   +RR 9-78 p102 tape
    Etudes, guitar, no. 5, 7-8, 11. See no. 3384
    Etudes, guitar, no. 5, C major. See no. 3967
    Etudes, guitar, no. 7, E major. See no. 3967
    Etudes, guitar, nos. 11-12. See no. 3599
    Modinha. See no. 3600
    Preludes (5). See no. 3383
    Preludes, nos. 1-5. See no. 3384
    Preludes, no. 3. See no. 3975
    Schottisch choro. See no. 3384
    Serenata. See no. 3965
    Suite populaire brasileira. See no. 3383
    Trio, strings, no. 2. See no. 1881
    Valsa choro. See no. 3384
3384 Works, selections: Choros, no. 1, E major. Etudes, nos. 5, 7-8,
        11. Preludes, nos. 1-5. Schottisch choro. Valsa choro. Jos-
        eph Bacon, gtr. 1750 Arch S 1771
                    +-ARG 6-80 p42   +NR 8-80 p14
                    +-FF 3/4-80 p173

VINCENET
    Fortune par tu cruaulte. See no. 3880

VINCENT, Thomas
    Sonata, oboe, op. 1, no. 2, A minor. See no. 3542

VINTER, Gilbert
    John O'Gaunt. See no. 3620
    Hunter's moon. See no. 3644
    Lisbon carnival. See no. 3621
VIOTTI, Giovanni
    Sonata, harp, B flat major. See no. 3819
VISEE, Robert de
    Bourree. See no. 3549. See no. 3775
    Courante. See no. 4013
3385 Entree des espagnols de Mr. de Lully. La muzette. Suites, D major,
      C minor, D minor. Les sylvains de Mr. Couperin. Hopkinson
      Smith, theorbo. Astree AS 38
          ++FF 9/10-80 p231   ++RR 6-80 p77
    Gigue grave. See no. 4013
    Menuet. See no. 3549. See no. 3775
    La Montsermeil, rondeau. See no. 4013
    La muzette. See no. 3385
    La muzette de M. Forqueray. See no. 4013
    Passacaille. See no. 3600
3386 Prelude. Suites, A minor, G major, F sharp minor. Tombeau de Mr.
      Mouton. Transcriptions from Lully and Couperin. Nigel North,
      theorbo, lt, gtr. L'Oiseau-Lyre DSLO 542
             -FF 9/10-80 p272   +-HFN 12-78 p163
             +-Gr 1-79 p1309   +-RR 12-78 p94
    Prelude. See no. 4013
    Rondeau. See no. 4013
    Sarabande. See no. 3549. See no. 3775
    Suites, A minor, G major, F sharp minor. See no. 3386
    Suites, D major, C minor, D minor. See no. 3385
    Suites, D minor. See no. 3540
    Suites, guitar. See no. 1495
    Les sylvains de Mr. Couperin. See no. 3385
    Tombeau de du But, allemande. See no. 4013
    Tombeau de Mr. Mouton. See no. 3386. See no. 4013
    Tombeau de Tonty, allemande. See no. 4013
    Tombeau de vieux Gallot, allemande. See no. 4013
    Transcriptions from Lully and Couperin. See no. 3386
    Variations sur les Folies d'Espagne. See no. 3577
    La Venitienne de M. Fourqueray. See no. 4013
VITALI, Tommaso
    Chaconne, G minor. See no. 1020
    Sinfonia, 2 trumpets, 2 oboes and strings (attrib.). See no. 3716
VIVALDI, Antonio
    Armida al campo d'egitto: Overture. See no. 3438
    Arsilda Regina di Ponto: Overture. See no. 3438
    L'Ateneide: Un certo non so che. See no. 3669
    Bajazet: Overture. See no. 3438
    Bajazet: Sposa son disprezzata. See no. 3669
3387 Beatus vir. Dixit dominus. Magnificat. Songs (Psaumes et motets)
      (6). Lausanne Chamber Orchestra and Vocal Ensemble; Michel Cor-
      boz. Erato STU 71003 (3)
          +HFN 4-80 p111   +RR 10-79 p144
3388 Beatus vir, RV 598. Canta in prato, RV 623. In furore, RV 626.
      Magnificat, RV 610. Verena Schweizer, Uta Spreckelsen, s; Hanna
      Schaer, alto; Jean-Pierre Maurer, t; Lausanne Vocal Ensemble and

Chamber Orchestra; Michel Corboz. Musical Heritage Society MHS
4081
    +HF 3-80 p89   ++St 3-80 p102
Canta in prato, RV 623. See no. 3388
3389 Concerti, strings (8). I Musici. Philips Tape (c) 7300 569
    ++HFN 10-80 p117 tape
Concerti, op. 3. See no. 3443
3390 Concerti, op. 3. BPhO; Thomas Brandis, Leon Spierer, vln and cond.
DG 2709 100 (3) Tape (c) 3370 034, 3371 052
    +-FF 7/8-80 p150   +NR 6-80 p8
    +-Gr 3-80 p1397   ++NYT 5-25-80 pD21
    +HF 7-80 p77   +-RR 3-80 p66
    +HFN 3-80 p101   ++SFC 5-18-80 p38
    +HFN 10-80 p117 tape   +-ST 7-80 p196
    +MT 11-80 p712
3391 Concerti, op. 3, nos. 1, 3-6, 9. Lucerne Festival Strings; Rudolf
Baumgartner. DG 2547 012 Tape (c) 3347 012 (From SAPM 198469/71)
    +Gr 8-80 p258   +HFN 10-80 p117 tape
    +Gr 9-80 p413 tape   +-RR 6-80 p63
    +-HFN 6-80 p119
3392 Concerti, op. 3, nos. 2 and 11. Concerto, flute, RV 439, G minor.
Concerti, strings, RV 120, C major; RV 129, D minor. Concerto,
oboe, RV 461, A minor. Richard Chester, flt; Susan Tyte, ob;
Angus Anderson, Andrew Martin, vln; Adrian Shepherd, vlc; Canti-
lena; Adrian Shepherd. Chandos ABR 1008 Tape (c) ABT 1008
    +-Gr 8-80 p233   +HFN 10-80 p117 tape
    +-HFN 8-80 p103   -RR 8-80 p58
3393 Concerto, op. 3, no. 6, A minor. Concerto, bassoon, P 70, A minor.
Concerto, lute, P 209, D major. Sonata, violoncello, op. 14, no.
5, E minor. Oslo Chamber Orchestra; Ornulf Boye Hansen, vln;
Erik Stenstadvold, gtr; Aage Kvalbein, vlc; Terje Boye Hansen,
bsn. Simax PS 1002
    -HFN 10-80 p110
Concerto, op. 3, no. 6, A minor. See no. 1939
Concerto, op. 3, no. 8, A minor. See no. 199
Concerto, op. 3, no. 11, D minor. See no. 199
3394 Concerti, op. 4. Felix Ayo, vln; I Musici. Philips 6779 029 (2)
Tape (c) 7650 029 (From Philips 2-940)
    +FF 5/6-80 p168   +NYT 5-25-80 pD21
    +-HF 7-80 p77
Concerti, op. 4. See no. 3443
Concerto, op. 4: Largo. See no. 3640
3395 Concerti, op. 8. Franzjosef Maier, vln; Helmut Hucke, ob; Collegium Aureum. Harmonia Mundi 1C 065 99666, 1C 065 99727, 1C 065
99802
    +-FF 1/2-80 p158
3396 Concerti, op. 8, nos. 1-4. Ronald Thomas, vln; Linnhe Robertson,
hpd; Bournemouth Sinfonietta; Ronald Thomas. Chandos ABR 1004
    +Gr 12-79 p1023   +-RR 1-80 p92
    +-HFN 3-80 p101
3397 Concerti, op. 8, nos. 1-4. Kenneth Sillito, vln; Virtuosi of England; Arthur Davison. Classics for Pleasure CFP 40016
    +-FF 9/10-80 p231   +HFN 6-73 p1184
    +-Gr 6-73 p61   +MM 10-78 p34
3398 Concerti, op. 8, nos. 1-4. Simon Standage, baroque violin; English

Concert; Trevor Pinnock, hpd and cond. CRD CRD 1025 Tape (c)
CRD 4025 (also Vanguard VSD 71257)

+ARG 7-77 p36	+MM 10-78 p38
+Audio 7-80 p81	++NR 11-77 p7
+FF 3/4-80 p173	+RR 10-76 p75
+Gr 11-76 p823	+RR 7-78 p94 tape
+Gr 8-78 p380 tape	++SFC 1-13-80 p40
+HF 5-80 p86	++ST 1-77 p81
-HFN 9-78 p159 tape	++NR 2-80 p5

3399 Concerti, op. 8, nos. 1-4. Stuttgart Chamber Orchestra; Konstanty
Kulka, vln; Igor Kipnis, hpd; Karl Munchinger. Decca JG 63 Tape
(c) KJBC 63 (From SXL 6557)

+Gr 9-79 p474	+-RR 9-79 p100
+HFN 8-79 p121	++ST 1-80 p692

3400 Concerto, op. 8, nos. 1-4. Gunars Larsens, vln; Lucerne Festival
Strings; Rudolf Baumgartner. Denon OX 7174
+FF 5/6-80 p168

3401 Concerti, op. 8, nos. 1-4. Luigi Ferro, Guido Mozzato, vln; Virtuosi di Roma; Renato Fasano. HMV SXLP 30419 Tape (c) SXLP 30419
(From ASD 367)

+Gr 4-80 p1564	+HFN 8-80 p109 tape
+HFN 4-80 p119	+RR 4-80 p84

3402 Concerti, op. 8, nos. 1-4. John Holloway, vln; Grand Ecurie et
Chambre du Roy; Jean-Claude Malgoire. Odyssey Y 35930

+-FF 9/10-80 p231	+NYT 5-25-80 pD21
+-HF 7-80 p77	

3403 Concerti, op. 8, nos. 1-4. Felix Ayo, vln; I Musici. Philips 6500
877

+HFN 7-80 p117	+-RR 7-80 p68

3404 Concerti, op. 8, nos. 1-4. Henryk Szeryng, vln; ECO; Henryk Szeryng.
Philips 6570 061 Tape (c) 7310 061 (From 6580 082)

+Gr 12-79 p1023	+HFN 2-80 p107 tape
+HFN 12-79 p179	+RR 12-79 p82

3405 Concerti, op. 8, nos. 1-4. Arthur Grumiaux, vln; Solistes Romands;
Arpad Gerecz. Philips 9500 613 Tape (c) 7300 730

+FF 9/10-80 p231	++NR 7-80 p3
+-HF 7-80 p77	+NYT 5-25-80 pD21

3406 Concerti, op. 8, nos. 1-4. Iona Brown, vln; AMF; Iona Brown. Philips 9500 717 Tape (c) 7300 809

+-Gr 12-80 p842	++NR 12-80 p5
+HFN 12-80 p147	

3407 Concerti, op. 8, nos. 1-4. Shigeru Toyama, vln; Vivaldi Ensemble;
Masaaki Hayakawa. RCA RDCE 501/2 (2)

+Audio 1-80 p116	+RR 7/8-79 p12
++ARG 6-79 p51	+-St 9-79 p104

Concerti, op. 8, nos. 1-4. See no. 3443
Concerto, op. 8: Spring: Allegro. See no. 4028
Concerto, op. 8: Winter. See no. 4030
Concerto, op. 8: Winter largo. See no. 3943

3408 Concerti, op. 8, nos. 5-10. Simon Standage, vln; English Concert;
Trevor Pinnock, hpd. Vanguard VSD 71273
++NR 12-80 p5

3409 Concerti, op. 8, nos. 9-12. Helmut Hucke, ob; Werner Neuhaus, vln;
Collegium Aureum; Franzjosef Maier. Harmonia Mundi 065 99802

+HFN 3-80 p105	+RR 2-80 p63

3410 Concerti, op. 8, nos. 11 and 12. Concerto, flute, RV 429, D major.
     Concerto, violoncello, RV 424, B minor. Simon Standage, vln;
     Stephen Preston, flt; Anthony Pleeth, vlc; English Concert; Trev-
     or Pinnock, hpd. Vanguard VSD 71274
                    ++NR 12-80 p5
Concerti, op. 9. See no. 3443
3411 Concerti, op. 10 (6). PCO; Luc Urbain, flt; Alain Boulfroy. Cal-
     liope CAL 1620
                    +Audio 2-80 p51
3412 Concerti, op. 10 (6). Concerti, flute, RV 436, G major; RV 427, D
     major; RV 440, A minor; RV 429, D major; RV 441, C minor; RV 438,
     G major; RV 108, A minor; RV 533, C major; RV 445, A minor. Sev-
     erino Gazzelloni, Marja Steinberg, flt; I Musici. Philips 6768
     147 (3) (From 6500830, 6500707, SAL 3705)
                    +Gr 9-80 p350   +HFN 9-80 p115
3413 Concerto, op. 10, no. 1, F major. Concerti, flutes, RV 438, G maj-
     or; RV 441, C minor; RV 108, A minor. Concerto, 2 flutes, RV
     533, C major. I Musici; Severino Gazzelloni, flt. Philips 6570
     186 Tape (c) 7310 186 (Reissue)
                    +ARG 12-80 p48
Concerto, op. 10, no. 2, G minor. See no. 706
3414 Concerti, op. 11 (6). Piero Toso, Giuliano Carmignola, Juan Carlos
     Rybin, vln; Pierre Pierlot, ob; I solisti Veneti; Claudio Sci-
     mone. Musical Heritage Society MHS 4105
                    +HF 7-80 p77
Concerto, op. 11, no. 6. See no. 20
Concerti, P 74, C major; P 86, D minor; P 42, A minor; P 118, G
     major; P 119, E minor; P 208, D major. See no. 3639
Concerto, P 77, A minor. See no. 3795
Concerto, RV 93, D major. See no. 3602
3415 Concerti, RV 114, C major; RV 120, C minor; RV 128, D minor; RV 133,
     E minor; RV 152, G major; RV 157, G minor; RV 151, G major; RV
     158, A major; RV 163, B flat major; RV 167, B flat major. Sin-
     fonie, RV 132, E major; RV 134, E minor; RV 140, F major; RV 146,
     G major; RV 168, B minor. I Solisti Veneti; Claudio Scimone.
     Erato STU 71052/3 (2) (also Musical Heritage Society MHS 4058/9)
                    +FF 3/4-80 p175   +-MT 11-78 p967
                    +Gr 2-78 p1416   +-RR 4-78 p72
                    +HFN 4-78 p125
3416 Concerti, RV 114, 119, 126, 138, 141, 154, 157. Sinfonia, RV 149,
     G major. I Musici. Philips 9500 300
                    +-Gr 5-80 p1677   +NR 3-78 p7
                    +-HFN 5-80 p135   +RR 5-80 p74
                    ++MJ 2-79 p43
3417 Concerti, RV 129, D major; RV 151, G major; RV 159, A major; RV 169,
     B minor; RV 537, C major; RV 538, F major. Gerd Zapf, Miroslav
     Kejmar, tpt; Olfa Klamand, Otto Schmitz, hn; Jorg Ewald Dahler,
     hpd; Monteverdi Instrumental Academy; Hans Ludwig Hirsch. Claves
     D 602
                    ++Gr 7-80 p157
Concerto, bassoon, RV 501. See no. 20
3418 Concerto, bassoon, G minor. Concerto, flute and bassoon, G minor.
     Concerto, 2 mandolins and organ, P 133, G major. Concerto,
     harpsichord and strings, A major. Concerto, violin, 2 harpsi-
     chords and strings, C major. Anton Ganoci, Ferdo Pavlinek, mand;

Julius Baker, flt; Karl Hoffmann, Rudolf Klepac, bsn; Jelka Stanic, vln; Herbert Tachezi, Daniel Thune, hpd; I solisti di Zagreb;
Antonio Janigro. Vanguard HM 16SD (From Philips Vanguard VSL
11031)
        ++FF 9/10-80 p335   +RR 6-73 p64
        +Gr 6-73 p102

Concerto, bassoon, A minor. See no. 3443
Concerto, bassoon, P 70, A minor. See no. 3393

3419 Concerti, flute, C minor, G major, A minor, G major. Christopher
     Taylor, flt; London Philomusica; Carl Pini. Merlin MRF 78101
        +ARG 6-80 p16   +HFN 7-79 p113
        +-FF 7/8-80 p149   +RR 8-79 p97
        +Gr 6-78 p75

3420 Concerto, flute, RV 108, A minor. Concerti, piccolo, RV 443, C
     major; RV 444, C major; RV 445, A minor. Jean-Louis Beaumadier,
     pic, flt; French National Orchestra; Jean-Pierre Rampal. Calli-
     ope CAL 1630
        +-Gr 10-80 p504   +HFN 9-80 p111

3421 Concerti, flute, RV 108, A minor; RV 438, G major; RV 431, E minor;
     RV 432, E minor. Concerto, 2 flutes, RV 533, C major. Concerti,
     piccolo, RV 443, C major; RV 444, C major. Pean-Pierre Rampal,
     flt and pic; Joseph Rampal, flt; I Solisti Veneti; Claudio Sci-
     mone. Musical Heritage Society MHS 4190
        +FF 11/12-80 p190

Concerto, flute, RV 428, D major. See no. 72
Concerto, flute, RV 429, D major. See no. 3410
Concerti, flute, RV 436, G major; RV 427, D major; RV 440, A minor;
     RV 429, D major; RV 441, C minor; RV 438, G major; RV 108, A
     minor; RV 533, C major; RV 445, A minor. See no. 3412
Concerti, flute, RV 438, G major; RV 441, C minor; RV 108, A minor.
     See no. 3413
Concerto, flute, RV 439, G minor. See no. 3392
Concerto, flute, C minor. See no. 3443
Concerto, 2 flutes, RV 533, C major. See no. 3413. See no. 3421
Concerto, flute and bassoon, G minor. See no. 3418
Concerto, guitar, D major. See no. 17
Concerti, guitar, D major, A major. See no. 3612
Concerto, harpsichord and strings, A major. See no. 3418
Concerto, 2 horns, F major. See no. 3443
Concerto, lute, P 209, D major. See no. 3393
Concerto, mandolin: Allegro. See no. 4028
Concerti, mandolin, C major (2). See no. 2580
Concerto, 2 mandolins, G major. See no. 2580
Concerto, 2 mandolins and organ, P 133, G major. See no. 3418

3422 Concerti, oboe, A minor, C major, D major, D minor, F major, C major.
     Han de Vries, ob; I Solisti di Zagreb. Angel SZ 37741
        +NR 9-80 p6

3423 Concerti, oboe, C major, D minor, F major, A minor (2). Heinz Hol-
     liger, Maurice Bourgue, ob; I Musici. Philips 9500 742 Tape (c)
     7300 827
        +NR 12-80 p5

Concerto, oboe, F major. See no. 3443

3424 Concerti, oboe, RV 448, C major; RV 449, C major; RV 451, C major;
     RV 456, F major; RV 455, F major; RV 465, B flat major. Pierre
     Pierlot, ob; I Solisti Veneti; Claudio Scimone. Erato STU 70404
        +-HFN 4-80 p111   +RR 10-79 p108

3425 Concerti, oboe, RV 448, RV 449, RV 456, RV 543, RV 548. Heinz Hol-
      liger, ob; I Musici. Philips 9500 604 Tape (c) 7300 726
            ++FF 3/4-80 p34   +NR 4-80 p6
            ++HF 5-80 p85   +NYT 12-2-79 pD22
            ++HF 4-80 p104 tape
   Concerto, oboe, RV 461, A minor. See no. 3329
   Concerto, oboe and harpsichord, RV 461, A minor. See no. 3444
   Concerto, oboe, violin and harpsichord, RV Anh 17, C minor. See
      no. 3444
   Concerto, 2 oboes, D minor. See no. 3443
   Concerto, 2 oboes, bassoon, 2 horns and violin, F major. See no.
      3443
   Concerto, orchestra. See no. 20
3426 Concerti, orchestra, RV 120, C minor; RV 123, D major; RV 124, D
      major; RV 129, D minor; RV 152, G minor; RV 155, G minor. Bolog-
      na Teatro Comunale Orchestra; Angelo Ephrikian. Harmonia Mundi
      HM 1012
            ++FF 5/6-80 p168   -RR 6-79 p89
            /HFN 8-79 p113
3427 Concerto, orchestra, RV 556. Gloria, D major. Emanuele di Pare-
      ira's Neapolitan Singers and Orchestra. CMS/Summit 5069 Tape
      (c) X 45069
            +HF 6-80 p96 tape
   Concerto, organ, D minor. See no. 309
   Concerto, piccolo, C major. See no. 3443
   Concerti, piccolo, RV 443, C major; RV 444, C major. See no. 3421
   Concerti, piccolo, RV 443, C major; RV 444, C major; RV 445, A
      minor. See no. 3420
   Concerto, piccolo, RV 444/P 78, C minor. See no. 3589
   Concerto, recorder, RV 443, C major. See no. 1607
   Concerto, recorder, RV 445, C major. See no. 1608
   Concerto, strings, RV 120, C major; RV 129, D minor. See no. 3392
   Concerto, trumpet, C major. See no. 3674
   Concerto, 2 trumpets. See no. 295
   Concerto, 2 trumpets: Allegro. See no. 3640. See no. 4028
   Concerto, 2 trumpets, C major. See no. 1102
   Concerto, trumpet and organ, G minor (after Thilde's arrangement of
      op. 13, no. 6, Movements, 1, 3-4). See no. 3912
   Concerto, viola d'amore, PV 166. See no. 3431
3428 Concerti, violin, RV 199, C major; RV 208, D major; RV 270, E major;
      RV 271, E major; RV 208, D major; RV 363, B flat major. Piero
      Toso, Marco Fronaciari, vln; I Solisti Veneti; Claudio Scimone.
      Erato STU 71304
            ++Gr 9-80 p352   +HFN 9-80 p111
   Concerto, violin, RV 199, C minor. See no. 1939
3429 Concerti, violin, RV 212, D major; RV 286, F major; RV 581, C major;
      RV 579, B flat major. Piero Toso, Juan Carlos Rybin, vln; I
      Solisti Veneti; Claudio Scimone. Erato STU 70968
            +-HFN 4-80 p111   +RR 9-79 p101
3430 Concerto, violin, RV 271, E major. Concerti, 2 violins, RV 523, A
      minor. Concerto, violin and violoncello, RV 547, B flat major.
      Concerto, violoncello, RV 401, C minor. Pina Carmirelli, Anna
      Maria Cotogni, vln; Francesco Strano, Mario Centurione, vlc; I
      Musici. Philips 9500 301 (From 6768 014)
            ++Audio 5-78 p108   ++NR 4-78 p5

+Gr 4-80 p1564   ++RR 4-80 p83
+HFN 4-80 p111

Concerto, violin and harpsichord, RV 208, D major. See no. 3444
Concerto, violin and violoncello, RV 547, B flat major. See no. 3430
Concerto, violin, 2 harpsichords and strings, C major. See no. 3418
3431 Concerto, 2 violins, PV 423. Concerto, 2 violoncelli, PV 411, G
    minor. Concerto, viola d'amore, PV 166. Collegium Aureum. Har-
    monia Mundi 065 99747
                +HFN 3-80 p105   +RR 4-80 p83
Concerto, 2 violins, RV 523, A minor. See no. 3430
Concerti, violoncello, G minor, G major. See no. 80
Concerto, violoncello, RV 401, C minor. See no. 740. See no. 3430
3432 Concerti, violoncello, RV 415, G major; RV 416, G minor. Sonata, 2
    violins and violoncello, RV 60, C major. Sonata, violoncello, RV
    42, G minor. Anner Bylsma, vlc; Franzjosef Maier, Sigiswald
    Kuijken, vln; Collegium Aureum. Harmonia Mundi 1C 065 99748
    Tape (c) 1C 265 99748
                ++Gr 5-80 p1677   +RR 5-80 p75
                +HFN 5-80 p135
Concerto, violoncello, RV 424, B minor. See no. 3410
Concerto, 2 violoncelli, P 411, G minor. See no. 3431
Concerto, violoncello and harpsichord, RV 424. See no. 3444
Concerto grosso, P 444, D major. See no. 2003
Concerto grosso, RV 562a, D major. See no. 3916
Credo, RV 591, E minor. See no. 3436
3433 Dixit dominus. Stabat mater. Marilyn Hill Smith, Anna Bernardin,
    s; Helen Watts, con; Ian Partridge, t; Ian Caddy, bs; John Tall,
    org; English Bach Festival Orchestra and Chorus; Jean-Claude Mal-
    goire. CBS 76682 (also CBS M 35847 Tape (c) MT 35847)
                +-Gr 8-78 p367   +-RR 8-78 p96
                +HFN 8-78 p107   ++St 10-80 p124
                +MT 1-79 p45
3434 Dixit dominus. O qui coeli, RV 631. Uta Spreckelsen, s; Hanna
    Schaer, alto; Jean-Pierre Maurer, t; Michel Brodard, bs; Daniel
    Grosgurin, vlc; Christiane Jaccottet, hpd; Philippe Corboz, org;
    Lausanne Vocal Ensemble and Chamber Orchestra; Michel Corboz.
    Musical Heritage Society MHS 4112
                ++FF 7/8-80 p151
Dixit dominus. See no. 3387
Dorilla in tempe: Overture. See no. 3438
Ercole sul Termodonte: Onde chiare. See no. 3669
Farnace: Overture. See no. 3438
Giustino: Overture. See no. 3438
3435 Gloria, D major. Motets: Nulla in mundo pax sincera. Emma Kirkby,
    Judith Nelson, s; Carolyn Watkinson, alto; Christ Church Cathed-
    ral Choir; Academy of Ancient Music; Simon Preston. L'Oiseau-
    Lyre DSLO 554
                ++FF 3/4-80 p174   +NYT 1-20-80 pD22
                ++GR 1-79 p1323   +RR 12-78 p110
                +HFN 12-78 p163   +RR 10-79 p151 tape
                +-MT 5-79 p409   +SFC 12-23-79 p40
Gloria, D major. See no. 1463. See no. 3427
Griselda: Agitata da due venti; Da due venti. See no. 3669
Griselda: Overture. See no. 3438

In furore, RV 626. See no. 3388
L'Incoronazione di Dario: Overture. See no. 3438
Largo, D minor. See no. 3957
Magnificat. See no. 3387
Magnificat, RV 610. See no. 3388
3436 Mass, RV 586, C major. Credo, RV 591, E minor. Jeanne Marie Bima,
     s; Lucia Rizzi, con; Franco Sai, t; Franco Turicchi, bs; Italian
     Radio-Television Chamber Choir; I Solisti Veneti; Claudio Scimone.
     Italia ITL 70071
              +–Gr 9-80 p385
     Motets: Nulla in mundo pax sincera. See no. 3435
     O qui coeli, RV 631. See no. 3431
3437 L'Olimpiade. Maria Zempleni, s; Klara Takacs, ms; Jozsef Horvath,
     Gyorgy Kaplan, t; Lajos Miller, ba; Kolos Kovats, Istvan Gati,
     bs; Orchestra; Ferenc Szekeres. Hungaroton SLPX 11901/3 (3)
              +–ARG 5-79 p42   +NR 5-79 p10
              +–FF 3/4-79 p128   +NYT 12-17-78 pD25
              +–Gr 8-79 p371   +–ON 11-22-80 p44
              +HF 7-79 p151   +–RR 3-79 p53
              +HFN 5-79 p128   +SFC 1-28-79 p43
     L'Olimpiade: Overture. See no. 3438
     Ottone in Villa: Overture. See no. 3438
     Ottone in Villa: Vieni vieni o mio diletto. See no. 3669
3438 Overtures: Armida al campo d'egitto. Arsilda Regina di Ponto.
     Bajazet. Dorilla in tempe. Farnace. Giustino. Griselda. L'
     Incoronazione di Dario. L'Olimpiade. Ottone in Villa. La ver-
     ita in cimento. I solisti Veneti; Claudio Scimone. Erato STU
     71215
              +–Gr 4-80 p1564
3439 Il pastor fido, op. 13: Sonata, no. 6, G minor. Sonata, oboe, RV
     53, C major. Sonata, violoncello, RV 43, A minor; RV 46, B flat
     major. Ingo Goritzki, ob; Manfred Sax, bsn; Johannes Goritzki,
     vla; Jorg Ewald Dahler, hpd. Claves D 901
              +–Gr 7-80 p157   +–MT 12-80 p788
              +–HFN 5-80 p127   \
     Sinfonias, RV 132, E major; RV 134, E minor; RV 140, F major; RV
     146, G major; RV 168, B minor. See no. 3415
     Sinfonia, RV 149, G major. See no. 3416
     Sinfonia, RV 169, B minor. See no. 3444
     Sonata, flute, oboe, bassoon and harpsichord, RV 103, G minor. See
     no. 765
     Sonata, guitar, G major. See no. 3642
     Sonata, oboe, RV 53, C major. See no. 269. See no. 3439
     Sonata, recorder, op. 13, no. 6, G minor. See no. 3990
     Sonata, violin, op. 2, no. 2, A major. See no. 3964
     Sonata, 2 violins and viola, RV 130, E flat major. See no. 3444
     Sonata, 2 violins and violoncello, RV 60, C major. See no. 3432
     Sonata, violoncello, op. 14, no. 5, E minor. See no. 3393
     Sonata, violoncello, RV 42, G minor. See no. 3432
     Sonata, violoncello, RV 43, A minor. See no. 3439
     Sonata, violoncello, RV 46, B flat major. See no. 3439
3440 Songs (choral): Beatus vir, RV 597/598; Credidi propter quod, RV
     605; Credo, RV 591/592; Dixit dominus, RV 594/595; Domine ad adiu-
     vandum me, RV 593; Gloria, RV 588/589; In exitu Israel, RV 604;
     Introduction to Dixit Dominus, RV 635/636; Introduction to Gloria,

RV 639/642; Kyrie, RV 587; Lauda Jerusalem, RV 609; Laudate Dominum, RV 606; Laudate pueri, RV 602; Laetatus sum, RV 607; Magnificat, RV 610/611; Mass, RV 586, C major. Margaret Marshall,
Felicity Lott, Sally Burgess, s; Ann Murray, Susan Daniel, ms;
Anne Collins, Birgit Finnila, Linda Finnie, con; Anthony Rolfe
Johnson, t; Robert Holl, Thomas Thomaschke, bs; Jeffrey Tate,
Alastair Ross, John Constable, org; John Alldis Choir; ECO; Vittorio Negri. Philips 6768 149 (7) (Some reissues from 6768 016,
6769 032)

/+Gr 9-80 p385   +-HFN 10-80 p115

3441 Songs (choral works): Gloria, RV 589, D major; Credo, RV 591, E
minor; Mass, RV 586, C major; Psalms, no. 113, In exitu Israel,
C major; no. 115, Credidi propter quad, RV 605, C major; no. 116,
Laudate Dominum, RV 606, D minor; no. 121, Laetatus sum, RV 607,
F major. Margaret Marshall, s; Ann Murray, ms; Birgit Finnila,
Anne Collins, con; Anthony Rolfe Johnson, t; Robert Holl, bs;
John Alldis Choir; ECO; Vittorio Negri. Philips 6769 032 (2)
Tape (c) 7699 118

+-ARG 5-80 p43   ++NR 2-80 p8
++FF 3/4-80 p174   +NYT 1-20-80 pD22
+Gr 12-79 p1039   +ON 11-22-80 p44
+HF 3-80 p88   +RR 1-80 p110
++HF 5-80 p90 tape   +SFC 12-9-79 p42
+-MT 5-80 p325   ++St 3-80 p102

3442 Songs (choral): Beatus vir, RV 598; Credo, RV 592; Gloria, RV 588;
Dixit dominus, RV 595; Introduction to Gloria, RV 639; Introduc-
tion to Dixit dominus, RV 635; Laudate pueri, RV 602; Magnificat,
RV 610/611. Margaret Marshall, Felicity Lott, Sally Burgess, s;
Susan Daniel, ms; Linda Finnie, Anne Collins, con; Anthony Rolf
Johnson, t; Thomas Tomaschke, bs; John Constable, org; John All-
dis Choir; ECO; Vittorio Negri. Philips 6769 046 (3) (From 6768
149)

+Gr 12-80 p871   +HFN 12-80 p147

Songs (Psaumes et motets) (6). See no. 3387
Stabat mater. See no. 3433
Trio, flute and bassoon, A minor. See no. 3804
La verita in cimento: Overture. See no. 3438

3443 Works, selections: Concerti, op. 3. Concerti, op. 4. Concerti, op.
8, nos. 1-4. Concerti, op. 9. Concerto, bassoon, A minor. Concerto, flute, C minor. Concerto, 2 horns, F major. Concerto,
oboe, F major. Concerto, 2 oboes, D minor. Concerto, 2 oboes,
bassoon, 2 horns and violin, F major. Concerto, piccolo, C major.
Christopher Hogwood, Colin Tilney, hpd and org; Alan Loveday,
Iona Brown, Malcolm Latchem, vln; Robert Spencer, chitarrone;
Neil Black, Celia Nicklin, ob; Martin Gatt, bsn; Timothy Brown,
Robin Davis, hn; William Bennett, flt, pic; AMF; Neville Marriner, Iona Brown. Argo D101D10 (10) (From Argo ZRG 654, 733/4,
800/1, D 93D3, ZRG 834, 840)

++FF 1/2-80 p207   +NYT 12-17-78 pD25
+-Gr 10-78 p696   ++RR 10-78 p83
++HFN 10-78 p137   ++SFC 5-6-79 p61

3444 Works, selections: Concerto, oboe and harpsichord, RV 461, A minor.
Concerto, oboe, violin and harpsichord, RV Anh 17, C minor. Concerto, violin and harpsichord, RV 208, D major. Concerto, violoncello and harpsichord, RV 424. Sinfonia, RV 169, B minor. Son-

ata, 2 violins and viola, RV 130, E flat major. Wouter Muller,
vlc; Michel Piguet, ob; Concerto Amsterdam; Jaap Schroder, vln
and cond. Telefunken AW 6-42355 Tape (c) CX 4-42355 (From GK 6-
35416)

+FF 1/2-80 p159   ++HFN 5-79 p134 tape
+Gr 6-79 p65   ++RR 3-79 p94
+HFN 5-79 p128   ++RR 10-79 p151 tpae

VIVES, Amadeo
    Dona Francisquita: Por el humo. See no. 3919
VIVIANI, Giovanni
    Sonatas, trumpet, nos. 1 and 2. See no. 3656
    Sonata, trumpet, no. 1, D major. See no. 3779
    Sonata, trumpet, no. 2, D major. See no. 3779
    Sonata, trumpet, op. 4, no. 1, C major. See no. 3912
    Sonata, trumpet and organ. See no. 3545
VOGEL, Johann
3445 Quartet, clarinet, B flat major. Sinfonia concertante, no. 1, B
    flat major. Dieter Klocker, clt; Karl-Otto Harmann, bsn; Con-
    certo Amsterdam; Jaap Schroder. Acanta EA 23140
            +-HFN 10-80 p110
    Sinfonia concertante, no. 1, B flat major. See no. 3445
VOLGER
    Songs: Hosanna son of David; Rejoice you bride of Christ; Korean
    folksong, arr. See no. 3933
VOLPI, Adamo
    Preludio, op. 31. See no. 3651
VON BLON
    Die Wacht am Rhein. See no. 3643
VON BRONSART, Ingebord
    Valse caprice. See no. 4024
VON BULOW, Hans
    Ballade, op. 11. See no. 1971
VON KOCH, Erland
    Cantilena, op. 78. See no. 3589
    Monolog, no. 5. See no. 3588
VON PARADIS, Maria Theresia
    Sicilienne, E flat major. See no. 4024
VRANGEL
    O what a glorious night. See no. 3770
VRANICKY, Paul
    Quartet, strings, no. 3, F major. See no. 1416
VULPIUS, Melchior
    The strife is o'er. See no. 3533. See no. 3936
WAGENAAR, Johan
    Cyrano de Bergerac, op. 23. See no. 3818
WAGENSEIL, Georg
    Divertimento, F major. See no. 1458
WAGNER, Richard
    Albumblatt, C major. See no. 3898
    Albumblatt, for Betty Schott, E flat major. See no. 1971
3446 Arias: Gotterdammerung: Siegfried schlimmes wissen wir; Brunnhilde
    heilge Braut. Rienzi: Erstehe hohe Roma; Allmachtger Vater.
    Tannhauser: Auch ich das mich zum Heil den Sundigen; Inbrunst
    im Herzen. Tristan und Isolde: Alte Weise; Schiff. Die Walkure:
    Friedmund darf ich nich heiszen; Ein Schwert verheiss; Die sel-

que Frau; Wintersturme wichen. Paula Buchner, Maria Reining,
Hilde Scheppan, Margarete Teschemacher, s; Margarete Klose, alto;
Max Lorenz, Walther Ludwig, t; Jaro Prohaska, Karl Schmitt-Walter,
bar; Kurt Bohme, Ludwig Hofmann, bs; Berlin Rundfunk Orchestra and
Staatsoper Orchestra, Dresden Staatsoper Orchestra; Karl Elmendorff, Robert Hager, Artur Rother, Johannes Schuler. Acanta DE
22120

+HFN 5-80 p129	+-RR 3-80 p43

3447 Arias: Der fliegende Hollander: Senta's ballad. Lohengrin: Elsa's
dream. Die Meistersinger von Nurnberg: O Sachs mein Freund.
Rienzi: Gerechter Gott so ist's entschieden schon. Tannhauser:
Dich teure Halle; Elisabeth's prayer. Tristan und Isolde: Liebestod. Die Walkure: Du bist der Lenz. Joan Sutherland, s; National Philharmonic Orchestra; Richard Bonynge. London OS 26612
(also Decca SXL 6930 Tape(c) KSXC 6930)

+-ARG 5-80 p44	+NYT 10-28-79 pD24
+-FF 3/4-80 p177	+-ON 4-5-80 p29
+-Gr 3-80 p1438	+-Op 7-80 p687
+-HF 2-80 p99	+SFC 12-9-79 p43
+HFN 3-80 p103	+St 2-80 p135

Bridal chorus. See no. 3663
Fantasia, F sharp minor. See no. 1971
A Faust overture. See no. 3093
3448 Der fliegende Hollander. Viorica Ursuleac, s; Franz Klarwein, t;
Luise Willer, alt; Hans Hotter, bar; Goerge Hann, bs; Karl Oster-
tag; Bavarian State Opera Orchestra and Chorus; Clemens Krauss.
Acanta HA 23135/7 (3)

+-FF 7/8-80 p152	+ON 4-5-80 p29
+Gr 6-80 p66	+-Op 8-80 p799
+-HFN 5-80 p127	+-RR 7-80 p39

3449 Der fliegende Hollander. Gwyneth Jones, s; Sieglinde Wagner, ms;
Hermin Esser, Harald Ek, t; Thomas Stewart, bar; Karl Ridder-
busch, bs; Bayreuth Festival Orchestra and Chorus; Karl Bohm.
DG 2709 040 (3) Tape (r) 47040 (also DG 2520 052)

+-Gr 10-72 p747	+-ON 3-24-73 p36
+-HF 11-72 p106	+-Op 11-72 p1000
+-HFN 10-72 p1919	+-RR 10-72 p52
+LJ 4-75 p70 tape	+-RR 7-80 p39
+-NR 11-72 p12	+-SR 7-24-76 p36
+OC Fall 1980 p46	+-St 12-72 p141

3450 Der fliegende Hollander. Anja Silja, s; Fritz Uhl, Georg Paskuda,
t; Josef Greindl, Franz Crass, bar; Bayreuth Festival Orchestra
and Chorus; Wolfgang Sawallisch. Philips 6770 032 (3) Tape (c)
7650 032 (Also 6747 248)

+OC Fall 1980 p46	+-ON 4-5-80 p29
+-FF 5/6-80 p169	+RR 7-80 p39

3451 Der fliegende Hollander, excerpts. Kirsten Flagstad, s; Mary Jarred, ms; Max Lorenz, t; Herbert Janssen, bar; Ludwig Weber, bs;
ROHO; Fritz Reiner. Bruno Walter Society RR 469 (2)

++FF 11/12-80 p190	+NR 3-79 p11

3452 Der fliegende Hollander, excerpts. Anja Silja, s; Franz Crass, Josef Greindl, bs; Bayreuth Festival Orchestra and Chorus; Wolfgang
Sawallisch. Philips 6570 081 Tape (c) 7310 081

+-HFN 11-80 p131 tape	+RR 7-80 p39

Der fliegende Hollander: Erfahre das Geschick; Die Frist ist um;

Wie aus der Ferne Langst vergangner Zeiten. See no. 2075

3453 Der fliegende Hollander: Overture. Die Meistersinger von Nurnberg:
     Overture. Rienzi: Overture. Tannhauser: Overture. PhO; Lorin
     Maazel. CBS 76883 Tape (c) 40-76883
                    +Gr 3-80 p1398   +RR 7-80 p97 tape
                    +HFN 3-80 p107 tape

3454 Der fliegende Hollander: Overture. The Meistersingers von Nurnberg:
     Prelude, Act 3; Dance of the apprentices; Entry of the masters.
     Rienzi: Overture. Siegfried Idyll. LPO; Edward Downes. Clas-
     sics for Pleasure CFP 40287 Tape (c) TC CFP 40287
                    +Gr 12-78 p1117   +HFN 11-78 p177
                    +HFN 8-80 p109 tape   /RR 11-78 p77

3455 Der fliegende Hollander: Overture. Lohengrin: Prelude, Act 1.
     Rienzi: Overture. Tannhauser: Overture. PhO; Otto Klemperer.
     HMV SXLP 30436 Tape (c) SXLP 30436 (From Columbia SAX 2347)
                    ++Gr 8-80 p233   +HFN 10-80 p117 tape
                    +Gr 10-80 p548 tape

3456 Der fliegende Hollander: Overture. Rienzi: Overture. Tannhauser:
     Overture. Tristan und Isolde: Prelude and Liebestod. Munich
     Philharmonic Orchestra; Hans Knappertsbusch. Westminster MCA
     1413
                    +-FF 9/10-80 p233

Der fliegende Hollander: Overture. See no. 3860
Der fliegende Hollander: Senta's ballade. See no. 3447. See no.
     3770

3457 Gotterdammerung. Birgit Nilsson, Ludmilla Dvorakova, Dorothea Sie-
     bert, Helga Dernesch, Anja Silja, s; Martha Modl, Annelies Bur-
     meister, ms; Sieglinde Wagner, Marga Hoffgen, con; Wolfgang
     Windgassen, t; Thomas Stewart, bar; Gustav Neidlinger, Josef
     Greindl, bs; Bayreuth Festival Orchestra and Chorus; Karl Bohm.
     Philips 6747 049 (5)
                    +RR 5-80 p37

Gotterdammerung: Hagen's watch; Hagen's call. See no. 3905
Gotterdammerung: Hier sitz ich zur Wacht. See no. 3773
Gotterdammerung: Ho ho. See no. 1622
Gotterdammerung: Hoiho Hoiho; Ihr Gibischmannen machet euch auf.
     See no. 3712

3458 Gotterdammerung: Siegfried's funeral mausic. Lohengrin: Prelude,
     Act 1. Die Meistersinger von Nurnberg: Prelude. Parsifal:
     Prelude; Good Friday music. OSR; Ernest Ansermet. London STS
     15507
                    -FF 11/12-80 p191

Gotterdammerung: Siegfried schlimmes wissen wir; Brunnhilde heilge
     Braut. See no. 3446
In das album der Furstin M. See no. 1971

3459 Lohengrin. Gundula Janowitz, s; James King, t; Thomas Stewart, bar;
     Karl Ridderbusch, Gerd Nienstedt, bs; Bavarian Radio Orchestra
     and Chorus; Rafael Kubelik. DG 2740 141 (5) (From 2720 036)
                    +-Gr 7-80 p165   +RR 8-80 p34
                    +-HFN 8-80 p107

Lohengrin: Cessaro i canti alfin; Deh non t'incanten; Euch Luften
     die mein Klagen; Dass; In fernam land; Mein lieber Schwan. See
     no. 3770
Lohengrin: Dass susse Lied erhalt. See no. 3561

3460 Lohengrin: Einsam in truben Tagen. Parsifal: Ich sah das Kind.

Wesendonck Lieder. Die Walkure: Der Manner Sippe; Du bist der
Lenz. Kirsten Flagstad, s; VPO; Hans Knappertsbusch. Decca ECS
826 (From LXT 5249)
     +Gr 4-80 p1590   +HFN 3-80 p107

Lohengrin: Einsam in truben Tagen. See no. 3668
Lohengrin: Einsam in truben Tagen; Euch Luften die mein Klagen. See
no. 3780. See no. 3923
Lohengrin: Elsas Traum. See no. 3447
Lohengrin: Hochstes Vertrau'n hast du mir schon zu danken; Nun sei
bedankt; Einsam in truben Tagen. See no. 3774
Lohengrin: In fernem Land; Mein lieber Schwan. See no. 3558. See
no. 3641
Lohengrin: King Henry's prayer. See no. 3927
Lohengrin: Mein Herr und Gott. See no. 3712
Lohengrin: Merce merce cigno gentil; Di non t'incanta; S'el torna
alfin; Cessaro i canti alfin; Mio salvatore...Mai devi domandar-
mi; Merce merce cigno gentil. See no. 3981
Lohengrin: Prelude, Act 1. See no. 3455. See no. 3458
3461 Lohengrin: Prelude, Act 3. Die Meistersinger von Nurnberg: Prelude,
Act 1. Tannhauser: Grand march. Die Walkure: Ride of the Valkyries. LPO, NPhO; Adrian Boult. HMV 10
     ++HFN 5-80 p135   +RR 5-80 p75

Lohengrin: Treulich bewacht...Das susse Lied verhallt. See no. 3538
3462 Die Meistersinger von Nurnberg. Elisabeth Grummer, s; Marga Hoffgen,
con; Rudolf Schock, Gerhard Unger, Manfred Schmidt, t; Ferdinand
Frantz, Horst Wilhelm, bar; Gottlob Frick, Gustav Neidlinger,
Walter Stoll, bs; Benno Kusche, Herman Prey, bs-bar; St. Hedwig's
Cathedral Choir; BPhO; Rudolf Kempe. EMI RLS 740 Tape (c) TC RLS
740 (From Angel 3572)
     +ARSC Vol 12, no. 1-2   +HFN 1-80 p123 tape
     1980 p105   +Op 2-80 p166

Die Meistersinger von Nurnberg: Da zu dir der Heiland kam; Wach auf
es nahet gen der Tag; Morgenlich leuchtend. See no. 3773
Die Meistersinger von Nurnberg: Das schone Fest Johannistag. See
no. 3712
Die Meistersinger von Nurnberg: Ein Werbelied; Von Sachs; Ist's
wahr. See no. 3711
Die Meistersinger von Nurnberg: O Sachs mein Freund. See no. 3447.
See no. 3923
3463 Die Meistersinger von Nurnberg: Overture; Da zu dir der Heiland kam;
Prelude, Act 3; Dance of the apprentices...Entry of the masters;
Wach auf. Tannhauser: Overture; Naht euch dem Strande; Begluckt
darf nun dich. Vienna State Opera Chorus; VPO; Georg Solti.
Decca SXL 6860 Tape (c) KSXC 6860 (From SET 506/9, D13D5)
     +Gr 12-79 p1055   +RR 12-79 p44
     +HFN 1-80 p123
3464 Die Meistersinger von Nurnberg: Overture. Parsifal: Prelude. Rienzi: Overture. Tannhauser: Overture. VPO; Karl Bohm. DG 2531
214 Tape (c) 3301 214
     -FF 3/4-80 p176   +NR 2-80 p2
     +Gr 9-79 p474   +RR 10-79 p113
     +HFN 10-79 p163

Die Meistersinger von Nurnberg: Overture. See no. 3453
Die Meistersinger von Nurnberg: Preizlied. See no. 3641
Die Meistersinger von Nurnberg: Prelude. See no. 664. See no. 3458

Die Meistersinger von Nurnberg: Prelude, Act 1. See no. 3461
Die Meistersinger von Nurnberg: Prelude, Act 3; Dance of the apprentices; Entry of the masters. See no. 3454
Die Meistersinger von Nurnberg: Wahn Wahn uberall Wahn; Was duftet
  doch der Flieder. See no. 2075
3465 Parsifal, excerpts. Irene Dalis, s; Jess Thomas, t; Hans Hotter,
  bar; Gustav Neidlinger, bs; Bayreuth Festival Orchestra; Hans
  Knappertsbusch. Philips 6570 082 Tape (c) 7310 082
            +HFN 11-80 p131 tape   ++RR 8-80 p35
3466 Parsifal, Act 3, abridged. Gotthelf Pistor, t; Cornelis Bronsgeest,
  bar; Ludwig Hofmann, bs; Berlin State Opera Orchestra and Chorus;
  Karl Muck. Preiser LV 100 (From HMV 78s)
            +HF 8-73 p69   +RR 8-80 p12
Parsifal: Ich sah das Kind. See no. 3460
Parsifal: Ich sah das Kind an seiner Mutter Brust; Seit Ewigkeiten
  harre ich deiner. See no. 3924
Parsifal: Nur eine Waffe taugt. See no. 3774
Parsifal: Prelude. See no. 3464
Parsifal: Prelude; Good Friday music. See no. 3458
Polonaise, D major. See no. 339
3467 Das Rheingold. Anja Silja, Dorothea Siebert, Helga Dernesch, s;
  Annelies Burmeister, Vera Soukupova, Ruth Hesse, ms; Wolfgang
  Windgassen, Gustav Neidlinger, Erwin Wohlfahrt, t; Theo Adam,
  Gerd Nienstedt, Hermin Esser, Martti Talvela, Kurt Bohme, bs;
  Bayreuth Festival Orchestra; Karl Bohm. Philips 6747 046 (3)
            +RR 5-80 p37
Das Rheingold: Halt du Gieriger...Gonne mir auch was. See no. 3712
3468 Rienzi, excerpts. Hilde Scheppan, s; Margarete Klose, con; Max
  Lorenz, Jaro Prohaska, bar; Robert von der Linde, bs; Gustav
  Rodin, t; Berlin Radio Symphony Orchestra; Johannes Schuler, Rob-
  ert Heger. Acanta DE 23035 (2)
            +ON 4-5-80 p29
Rienzi: Erstehe hohe Roma; Allmachtger Vater. See no. 3446
Rienzi: Erstehe hohe Roma; Gerechter Gott...In seiner Bluthe bleicht.
  See no. 3770
Rienzi: Gerechter Gott so ist's entschieden schon. See no. 3447
Rienzi: Overture. See no. 865. See no. 3453. See no. 3454. See
  no. 3455. See no. 3456. See no. 3464
3469 Siegfried. Astrid Varnay, Wilma Lipp, s; Bernd Aldenhoff, Paul
  Kuen, Sigurd Bjorling, g; Frederick Dalberg; Bayreuth Festival
  Orchestra and Chorus; Herbert von Karajan. Foyer 1004 (4)
            ++Op 8-80 p800
3470 Siegfried. Birgit Nilsson, Erika Koth, s; Vera Soukupova, ms; Wolf-
  gang Windgassen, Erwin Wohlfahrt, Gustav Neidlinger, t; Kurt
  Bohme, bs; Bayreuth Festival Orchestra; Karl Bohm. Philips 6747
  048 (4)
            +RR 5-80 p37
Siegfried: Heil dir Sonne. See no. 3770
Siegfried Idyll. See no. 39. See no. 814. See no. 843. See no.
  942. See no. 3235. See no. 3454. See no. 3476. See no. 3794
Sonata, piano, B flat major. See no. 1971
3471 Tannhauser. Anja Silja, s; Grace Bumbry, con; Wolfgang Windgassen,
  Georg Paskuda, Gerhard Stolze, t; Eberhard Wachter, bar; Josef
  Greindl, Franz Crass, Gerd Nienstedt, bs; Bayreuther Festspiele;
  Wolfgang Sawallisch. Philips 6770 026 (3) Tape(c) 7605 026 (also

6747 249)

        +ARG 3-80 p45   +RR 8-80 p35
        +-FF 3/4-80 p176

3472 Tannahsuer, excerpts. Anja Silja, s; Grace Bumbry, con; Wolfgang
    Windgassen, t; Eberhard Wachter, bar; Bayreuth Festival Orchestra
    and Chorus; Wolfgang Sawallisch. Philips 6570 080 Tape (c) 7310
    080

        +-HFN 11-80 p131 tape   +RR 8-80 p35

Tannhauser: Allmachtge Jungfrau. See no. 3987

Tannhauser: Allor che tu coll'estro. See no. 3901

Tannhauser: Als du in kuhnem Sange; Blick ich umher. See no. 3774

Tannhauser: Als du in kuhnem Sange...Blick ich umher...Wohl wusst
    ich hier; Wie Todesahnung...O du mein holder Abendstern. See
    no. 1819

Tannhauser: Als du in kuhnem Sange; Dich teure Halle. See no. 3770

Tannhauser: Auch ich das mich zum Heil den Sundigen; Inbrunst im
    Herzen. See no. 3446

Tannhauser: Dich teure Halle. See no. 3923

Tannhauser: Dich teure Halle; Allmacht'ge Jungfrau. See no. 3780

Tannhauser: Dich teure Halle; Elisabeth's prayer. See no. 3447

Tannhauser: Freudig bergrussen. See no. 3553

Tannhauser: Grand march. See no. 309. See no. 3461

3473 Tannhauser: Overture; Dich teure Halle; Allmacht'ge Jungfrau. Tris-
    tan und Isolde: Prelude and Liebestod. Montserrat Caballe, s;
    Strasbourg Philharmonic Orchestra; Alain Lombard. RCA ARL 1-3551
    Tape (c) ARK 1-3351

              -Audio 3-80 p50   +-NYT 10-28-79 pD24
             +-FF 11/12-79 p144   +-ON 4-5-80 p29
             -HF 12-79 p106   ++SFC 7-29-79 p49
             +NR 10-79 p9   +St 2-80 p135

Tannhauser: Overture. See no. 3453. See no. 3455. See no. 3456.
    See no. 3464

Tannhauser: Overture; Naht euch dem Strande; Begluckt darf nun
    dich. See no. 3463

Tannhauser: Venusberg music. See no. 1523

Tannhauser: Wie Todesahnung...O du mein holder Abendstern. See no.
    3812

Traume. See no. 3898

Tristan und Isolde: Alte Weise; Schiff. See no. 3446

Tristan und Isolde: Dein Werk; O thorich'ge Magd; Wohin nun Tris-
    tan scheidet. See no. 3770

Tristan und Isolde: Die Wunde; Wo; Lasst sich mich heilen; Milde
    und leise. See no. 3924

Tristan und Isolde: Liebstod. See no. 3447. See no. 3948

Tristan und Isolde: Prelude and Liebestod. See no. 3456. See no.
    3473

3474 Tristan und Isolde: Prelude; Weh ach Wehe dies zu dulden; Mild und
    leise. Birgit Nilsson, s; VPO; Hans Knappertsbusch. Decca JB
    58 Tape (c) KJBC 58 (From SXL 2184)

             +Gr 12-79 p1052   +-Op 3-80 p270
             +-HFN 12-79 p179   +RR 12-79 p44

Tristan und Isolde: Wohin nun Tristan scheidet. See no. 3538

3475 Die Walkure. Leonie Rysanek, Birgit Nilsson, Daniza Mastilovic,
    Helge Dernesch, s; Annelies Burmeister, Gertraud Hopf, Sona
    Cervena, ms; Sieglinde Wagner, Elisabeth Schartel, con; James

King, t; Theo Adam, bs; Bayreuth Festival Orchestra; Karl Bohm.
Philips 6747 047 (4)
+RR 5-80 p37
3476 Die Walkure, Act 2, Scenes 3 and 5. Siegfried Idyll. Ella Flesch,
Lotte Lehmann, s; Lauritz Melchior, t; Alfred Jerger, bar; Emmanuel List, bs; VPO; Bruno Walter. Turnabout THS 65163 (From HMV
originals, 1935)
+ARG 4-79 p45   +NR 4-79 p12
++FF 7/8-79 p105   +NYT 6-17-79 pD32
+-HF 7-79 p152   +SFC 1-6-80 p43
Die Walkure: Der Manner Sippe. See no. 3923
Die Walkure: Der Manner Sippe; Du bist der Lenz. See no. 3460
Die Walkure: Du bist der Lenz. See no. 3447
Die Walkure: Du bist der Lenz; Ho-jo-to-ho; Leb wohl du kuhnes,
herrliches Kind; Siegmund heiss ich. See no. 3770
Die Walkure: Friedmund darf ich nich heiszen; Ein Schwert verheiss;
Die selque Frau; Wintersturme wichen. See no. 3446
Die Walkure: Leb wohl du kuhnes herrliches Kind. See no. 2075. See
no. 3812
Die Walkure: Mit acht Schwestern zog ich dich auf; Wintersturme;
Ho jo to ho. See no. 3774
Die Walkure: Mud am Herd fand ich den Mann. See no. 3712
Die Walkure: Nicht straf ich dich erst. See no. 3538
Die Walkure: Ride of the Valkyries. See no. 3461
Die Walkure: Wotan's farewell. See no. 3925
Wesendonk Lieder. See no. 3460
Zuricher Vielliebchen. See no. 1971
WALDTEUFEL, Emile
Estudiantina, op. 191. See no. 3477
Je t'aime. See no. 3477
Mon reve, op. 151. See no. 3477
Les patineurs, op. 183. See no. 3477
Pluie de diamants. See no. 3477
Les sirenes. See no. 3477
Songs: Barcarolle. See no. 3870
3477 Works, selections: Estudiantina, op. 191. Mon reve, op. 151. Les
patineurs, op. 183. Pluie de iamants. Les sirenes. BeSO; Robert Stolz. RCA GL 2-5281 Tape (c) GK 2-5281
+Gr 11-80 p739   +HFN 10-80 p113
WALKER, Goerge
Antifonys. See no. 1913
3478 Music for brass. Sonata, piano, no. 1. Perimeters. Variations.
Meyer Kupferman, clt; Kazuko Hayami, George Walker, pno; NPhO,
American Brass Quintet. Paul Freeman. Serenus SRS 12077
+-ARG 5-78 p45   +NR 6-78 p15
+-FF 9/10-80 p233   +NYT 9-16-79 pD24
Perimeters. See no. 3478
Sonata, piano, no. 1. See no. 3478
Sonata, violoncello and piano. See no. 1913
Variations. See no. 3478
WALLACE, William Vincent
Lurline: Oh thou to whom this heart...Sweet spirit hear my prayer.
See no. 3774
Maritana: Hear me gentle Maritana...The mariner in his baruqe. See
no. 4007

Maritana: Scenes that are brightest; Hear me gentle Maritana...The
     mariner and his barque. See no. 3774
Maritana: Yes let me like a soldier fall. See no. 3986

WALMISLEY, Thomas
Music all powerful. See no. 3873
Psalm, no. 49. See no. 3567

WALOND, William
Voluntary, D major. See no. 3565
Voluntary, D minor. See no. 4041
Voluntary, no. 1. See no. 3728
Voluntary, no. 5, G major. See no. 3595. See no. 3940

WALTHER, Johann
Concerto, organ, A major. See no. 3933
Lobe den Herren den machtigen Konig der Ehren. See no. 4040

WALTON, William
Bagatelles (5). See no. 637
Battle of Britain: Battle in the air. See no. 3786

3479 Belshazzar's feast. Te deum. Benjamin Luxon, bar; Salisbury, Win-
     chester and Chichester Cathedral Choirs, LPO and Chorus; Ralph
     Downes, org; Georg Solti. Decca SET 618 Tape (c) KCET 618 (also
     London S 26525 Tape (c) OSA 5-26525)

+—ARG 9-78 p47	/HFN 6-78 p139
+—Audio 6-78 p126	+—MJ 10-78 p24
+—FF 5/6-78 p102	+—NR 6-78 p10
+Gr 11-77 p879	+—ON 4-19-80 p28
+Gr 4-78 p1779 tape	+—RR 11-77 p110
+—HF 6-78 p105	+RR 4-78 p110 tape
+—HFN 11-77 p183	++SFC 2-19-78 p49
+—HFN 4-78 p131 tape	+St 4-78 p140

Concerto, viola. See no. 1794
Concerto, violin, B minor. See no. 3964
Concerto, violoncello. See no. 1360
Crown imperial. See no. 394

3480 Facade. Hermione Gingold, Russell Oberlin, speakers; Various in-
     strumentalists; Thomas Dunn. Westminster MCA 1401 Tape (c)
     MCAC 1401 (From Decca DL 10097)

+ARG 11-80 p36	++SFC 5-4-80 p42
+FF 7/8-80 p153	+St 8-80 p101
+HF 6-80 p91	

Facade. See no. 1386

3481 Facade I and II. Cathy Berberian, Robert Tear, speakers; Various
     instrumentalists; Steuart Bedford. Peters PLE 135 Tape (c)
     PCE 135 (also Oxford OUP 201)

+—FF 9/10-80 p234	+RR 1-80 p111
+—Gr 1-80 p1194	+SFC 6-8-80 p36
+HF 6-80 p91	++St 8-80 p102
+HFN 1-80 p111	+STL 5-11-80 p39

Fanfare "Hamlet". See no. 3959
Hamlet: Funeral march. See no. 3801
Orb and sceptre. See no. 394
Pieces, violin and piano (2). See no. 1374
A queen's fanfare. See no. 3937. See no. 3959
Songs: Daphne; Old Sir Faulk; Through gilded trellises. See no.
     3611
The spitfire. See no. 3566

Spitfire: Prelude and futue. See no. 4046
3482 Symphony, no. 1, B flat minor. LPO; Adrian Boult. Everest SDBR
     3448
                    +—ARG 9-79 p44   +—NR 6-79 p5
                    +FF 5/6-80 p170
     Te deum. See no. 3479
3483 Troilus and Cressida. Janet Baker, s; Richard Cassilly, Gerald
     English, t; Benjamin Luxon, bar; ROHO and Chorus; Lawrence Fos-
     ter. HMV SLS 997 (3) (also Capitol SLS 997)
                    +—FF 9/10-78 p123   +MT 10-77 p827
                    +Gr 4-77 p1599   +ON 4-19-80 p28
                    +—HF 1-78 p106   +—RR 4-17 p20
                    +HFN 6-77 p115   +ST 1-78 p843
                    +MM 11-77 p45

WARD, John
     Out from the vale. See no. 3941
     Songs (madrigals): Come sable night; Out from the vale. See no.
     3893
WARLOCK, Peter
     Capriol suite. See no. 908. See no. 3329. See no. 3639. See no.
     3996
     Captain Stratton's fancy. See no. 3991
     The curlew. See no. 3335
     Serenade, strings. See no. 3329
     Serenade on the 60th birthday of Delius. See no. 1226
     Songs: Pretty ring time. See no. 3778
WATKINS, David
     Fire dance. See no. 3676
WATSON, Walter
     Recital suite. See no. 3655
WATTS, John
3484 Elegy to a chimney: In memoriam. Mots d'heures: Gousses, Rames.
     Piano for te. Robert Levy, tpt; John Watts, Robert Levy, syn-
     thesizer, electronics, tape; Wesleyan Singers; Neely Bruce.
     Serenus SRS 12080
                    +—ARG 1-80 p43   +NR 10-79 p6
     Mots d'heures: Gousses, Rames. See no. 3484
     Piano for te. See no. 3484
     Sonata, piano. See no. 704
WAYDITCH, Gabriel von
3485 Jesus before Herod. Eileen Moss, Pauline Tweed, s; Michael Best,
     t; Christopher Lindbloom, bar; Stephen Scot-Shepherd, bs; San
     Diego Master Chorale; San Diego Symphony Orchestra; Peter Eros.
     Musical Heritage Society MHS 4167
                    +—HF 9-80 p100
WEBBE, Samuel
     Songs: When winds breathe soft; You gave me your heart. See no.
     3873
WEBER, Carl Maria von
3486 Abu Hassan. Elisabeth Schwarzkopf, s; Erich Witte, t; Michael Boh-
     nen, bs; Berlin Radio Orchestra and Chorus; Leopold Ludwig.
     Varese VC 81093 (From URLP 7029)
                    +—FF 5/6-80 p171   +—St 7-80 p84
                    +NYT 7-13-80 pD20
     Adagio and rondo. See no. 4003

Air russe and rondo. See no. 3785
Aufforderung zum Tanz, op. 65. See no. 960
Concertino, op. 26, C minor. See no. 2227
Concertino, op. 45, E minor. See no. 2807
Concerto, clarinet, no. 2, op. 74, E flat major. See no. 3581
3487 Concerti, piano, nos. 1 and 2. Konzertstuck, op. 79, F minor. Rol-
     and Keller, pno; BeSO; Siegfried Kohler. Turnabout QTV 34746
               +—ARG 1-80 p44   ++SFC 7-29-79 p49
               +CL 2-80 p8   +St 1-80 p110
               -FF 1/2-80 p159
Divertimento, op. 38. See no. 1243
Die drei pintos: Intermezzo. See no. 3824
Euryanthe: Arias. See no. 3539
Euryanthe: Overture. See no. 2958
The freeshooter: Through the forest. See no. 3986
3488 Der Freischutz. Irma Beilke, Elfriede Trotschel, s; Bernd Alden-
     hoff, t; Kurt Bohme; Dresden Staatsoper Orchestra and Chorus;
     Rudolf Kempe. Acanta DE 29268 (2)
               +HFN 2-80 p99   /-RR 2-80 p44
3489 Der Freischutz. Elisabeth Grummer, Rita Streich, s; Hans Hopf, t;
     Alfred Poell, Karl Donch, bar; Oscar Czerwenka, Kurt Bohme,
     Otto Edelmann, bs; Vienna State Opera Chorus; VPO; Wilhelm Furt-
     wangler. Turnabout THS 65148/50 (3)
               +—Audio 10-80 p136   +NR 4-79 p11
               +FF 5/6-79 p107   +SFC 2-11-79 p47
Der Freischutz: Nein langer trag ich nicht...Durch die Walder. See
     no. 3558
Der Freischutz: Trube Augen. See no. 3774
Der Freischutz: Un ob die Wolke. See no. 3923
Der Freischutz: Was gleicht wohl auf Erden. See no. 3553
Der Freischutz: Wie nahte mir der Schlummer...Leise leise fromme
     Weise; Un ob die Wolke. See no. 3561. See no. 3780
Invitation to the dance, op. 65. See no. 3556. See no. 3604. See
     no. 3608. See no. 3872. See no. 3955
Invitation to the dance, op. 65: Rondo brillant, D flat major. See
     no. 3688
Konzertstuck, op. 79, F minor. See no. 2924. See no. 3487
3490 Oberon. Irmgard Boas, s; Gunter Neumann, Rainer Goldberg, t; Paul
     Neis, Kathe Koch, speakers; Leipzig Radio Orchestra; Herbert
     Kegel. Bruno Walter Society IGI 362 (2)
               -NR 2-80 p11
3491 Oberon. Birgit Nilsson, Marga Schiml, Arleen Auger, s; Julia Ham-
     ari, ms; Donald Grobe, Placido Domingo, t; Hermann Prey, bar;
     Bavarian Radio Orchestra and Chorus; Rafael Kubelik. DG 2726
     052 (2) Tape (c) 3372 052 (From 2709 035)
               ++ARG 10-79 p33   +HFN 10-76 p179
               +FF 1/2-80 p160   +NYT 8-5-79 pD19
               +Gr 11-76 p874   ++RR 12-76 p50
               +HF 10-79 p126 tape
Oberon: Huon's recitative and aria, Act 1; Huons prayer, Act 2.
     See no. 3641
Oberon: Oh to the glorious night. See no. 3986
Oberon: Overture. See no. 3688. See no. 4072
Oberon: Ozean du Ungeheuer. See no 3770. See no. 3793. See no.
     3931. See no. 3948

Oberon: Ozean du Ungeheuer; Vater Hor mein Fieh'n zu dir. See no.
   3774
Oberon: Seit fruhster Jugend; Du der diese Profung schickt. See no.
   3558
Pieces, piano, op. 3 (6). See no. 537
Silvana: So soll den dieses Herz. See no. 3774
Sonata, piano, no. 1, op. 24, C major: Perpetuum mobile. See no.
   3737
Sonata, piano, no. 2, A flat major. See no. 1443
3492 Songs: An sie, op. 80, no. 5; Elfenlied, op. 80, no. 3; Est sturmt
   auf der Flur, op. 30, no. 2; Die gefangenen Sanger, op. 47, no.
   1; The four temperaments, op. 46; Die freien Sanger, op. 47, no.
   2; Ich denke dein, op. 66, no. 3; Ich sah ein Roschen, op. 15,
   no. 5; Klage; Der kleine Fritz an seine jungen Freunde; Mein
   Schatzerl is hubsch, op. 64, no. 1; Meine Farben, op. 23, no. 3;
   Meine Lieder, meine Sange, op. 15, no. 1; Minnelied, op. 30, no.
   4; Reigen, op. 30, no. 5; Sind es Schmerzen, sind es Freuden, op.
   30, no. 6; Uber die Berge mit Ungestum, op. 25, no. 2; Unbefang-
   enheit, op. 30, no. 3; Das Veilchen im Thale, op. 66, no. 1; Was
   zieht zu deinem Zauberkreise, op. 15, no. 4; Wiedersehen, op.
   30, no. 1; Die Zeit, op. 13, no. 5. Martyn Hill, t; Christopher
   Hogwood, fortepiano. L'Oiseau-Lyre DSLO 523
              +FF 7/8-80 p154   +RR 5-77 p85
             +Gr 1-77 p1168   ++St 9-80 p83
             +-HFN 1-77 p118
Turandot: Overture. See no. 661
WEBERN, Anton
   Das Augenlicht, op. 26. See no. 3495
   Bagatelles, op. 9 (6). See no. 382
   Entflieht auf leichten Kuhnen, op. 2. See no. 3495
   Lieder, opp. 14-18. See no. 1166
   Movements, op. 5 (5). See no. 1780
   Passacaglia, op. 1. See no. 3493. See no. 3495
   Pieces, orchestra, op. 6 (6). See no. 3493. See no. 3495
   Pieces, orchestra, op. 10 (5). See no. 3493. See no. 3781
   Symphony, op. 21. See no. 3493. See no. 3495
   Variations, op. 27. See no. 384. See no. 3705
   Variations, op. 30. See no. 3493
3493 Works, selections: Passacaglia, op. 1. Pieces, orchestra, op. 6
   (6). Pieces, orchestra, op. 10 (5). Symphony, op. 21. Vari-
   ations, op. 30. BACH: Ein musikalische Opfer, S 1079, C minor:
   Fugue (orch. Webern). LSO; Pierre Boulez. CBS 76911 Tape (c)
   40-76911 (From 79402)
              +Gr 11-80 p233   ++HFN 10-80 p117 tape
             +Gr 10-80 p548 tape   +HFN 11-80 p129
3494 Works, selections, opp. 1-31. Heather Harper, Halina Lukomska, s;
   Barry McDaniel, bar; Gregor Piatigorsky, vlc; Isaac Stern, vln;
   Charles Rosen, pno; John Alldis Choir; Juilliard Quartet, LSO;
   Pierre Boulez. Columbia M4 35193 (4) (also CBS 79402)
              ++ARG 12-79 p18   ++MM 4-79 p41
             ++FF 9/10-79 p159   ++NYT 5-13-79 pD21
             ++FU 11-79 p40   *ON 3-8-80 p29
             +HF 9-79 p124   +St 10-79 p148
             +MJ 11/12-79 p48
3495 Works, selections: Das Augenlicht, op. 26. Entflieht auf leichten

Kuhnen, op. 2. Passacaglia, op. 1. Pieces, orchestra, op. 6
(6). Symphony, op. 21. Cologne Radio Orchestra and Chorus;
Hiroshi Wakasugi. Harmonia Mundi 065 99849
   +FF 9/10-80 p234   +RR 7-80 p69
   +-Gr 8-80 p258

WECK (15th century Germany)
 Spanyoler Tanz and Hopper dancz. See no. 3864

WEELKES, Thomas
 Fantasy a 6, viols. See no. 3496
 Give ear O Lord. See no. 3532
 Hark I hear some dancing. See no. 3675
 In nomine a 5, viols. See no. 3496
 Lachrimae a 5, viols. See no. 3496
 The nightingale, the organ of delight. See no. 3941

3496 Songs (choral): All laud and praise; The Andalusian merchant; The
 cries of London; Hence care thou art too cruel; O care thou wilt
 despatch me; O Lord arise into thy resting place; Thule the per-
 iod of cosmography; To shorten winter's sadness; When David heard
 that Absalom was slain. Fantasy a 6, viols. In nomine a 5,
 viols. Lachrimae a 5, viols. Deller Consort; Jaye Consort of
 Viols; Afred Deller. Harmonia Mundi HM 224
   +FF 11/12-80 p191   +-RR 2-78 p27
   +HFN 1-80 p111   +RR 2-80 p92

 Songs: Cease sorrows now. See no. 3744
 Songs: Cease sorrows now; Come sirrah Jack ho; Since Robin Hood.
  See no. 3867
 Songs (madrigals): Hark all ye lovely saints; Hence care thou art
  too cruel, pt 2; Sing we at pleasure; O care thou wilt despatch
  me, pt 1; Thus sing my dearest jewel. See no. 3893
 Songs (anthems): Hosanna to the son of David; When David heard.
  See no. 3894
 Though my carriage be but careless. See no. 3971
 Why are you ladies staying. See no. 3675

WEIDENAAR, Reynold
 The tinsel chicken coop. See no. 3655

WEIGAND
 Farewell dear love. See no. 3840

WEIGL, Karl
 Night fantasies. See no. 2754

WEILL, Kurt
 Concerto, violin, op. 12. See no. 1663
 Kiddush. See no. 3922
 Quodlibet, op. 9. See no. 1892

3497 Silverlake. Elizabeth Hynes, Elaine Bonazzi, Joel Grey, William
 Neill, Jack Harrold; New York City Opera Orchestra; Julius Rudel.
 Nonesuch DB 79003 (2)
   +ON 12-20-80 p52

WEINBERGER, Jaromir
 Schwanda the bagpiper: Fantasia. See no. 3935
 Schwanda the bagpiper: Polka and fugue. See no. 1488

WEINGARTNER, Felix
 Thou art a child. See no. 3774

WEINZWEIG, John
 Concerto, harp and chamber orchestra. See no. 3498
 Concerto, violin. See no. 3498

Divertimenti, nos. 1-2, 5. See no. 3498
Interlude in an artist's life. See no. 3498
Of time, rain and the world. See no. 3498
Quartet, strings. See no. 3498
Quintet, woodwinds. See no. 3498
Sonata, violoncello. See no. 3498
Symphonic ode. See no. 1662
Wine of peace. See no. 3498
3498 Works, selections: Concerto, harp and chamber orchestra. Concerto,
    violin. Divertimenti, nos. 1-2, 5. Interlude in an artist's
    life. Quartet, strings. Quintet, woodwinds. Of time, rain and
    the world. Sonata, violoncello. Wine of peace. Various per-
    formers. Radio Canada International unnumbered (5)
        +-MUM 3/4-80 p32
WEISGALL, Hugo
3499 The golden peacock. Translations. Judith Raskin, s; Morey Ritt,
    pno. CRI SD 417
        +ARG 11-80 p37   +NYT 2-24-80 pD20
        +NR 5-80 p11   +St 9-80 p84
Translations. See no. 3499
WEISMANN, Julius
Concertino, op. 118, E flat major. See no. 3839
WEISS, Sylvius
Fantasie. See no. 3577
3500 Prelude and fugue, C major. Suites, C minor, G minor. Konrad
    Junghanel, lt. Accent 7910
        -FF 9/10-80 p273   +RR 6-80 p31
        +HFN 6-80 p101
Sonata, lute, D minor. See no. 215
Sonata, piano, op. 8, no. 1, D major. See no. 3730
Suites, C minor, G minor. See no. 3500
Tombeau sur la mort de M. Cajetan, Baron d'Hartig. See no. 215
WEITZ, Guy
Grand choeur. See no. 4052
Symphony, no. 1: Ave maris stella, final movement. See no. 4054
WESLEY
Air and gavotte. See no. 3663
Holsworthy church bells. See no. 3618
WESLEY, Samuel
Ascribe unto the Lord. See no. 3939
Behold how good and joyful. See no. 3524
Exultate deo. See no. 3815
Pieces, organ, nos. 6, 8-9, 11-12. See no. 3595
Psalm, no. 42. See no. 3567
WESLEY, Samuel Sebastian
An air composed for Holsworthy church bells with variations. See
    no. 4064
Andante cantabile. See no. 3858
Ascribe unto the Lord. See no. 966
Blessed be the God and father. See no. 3815. See no. 3938
Choral song and fugue, C major. See no. 3595
Songs: Blessed be the God and father. See no. 3835
Thou wilt keep him in perfect peace. See no. 3527. See no. 3937
WEYRAUCH
Songs: all mein gedanken; Weiss mir ein Blumlein blaue. See no.
    3662

WHITE
    Songs: A youth once loved a maiden; The tears that night. See no.
      3770
WHITE/JAI
    Utazo muzsikusok. See no. 3814
WHITE, L. J.
    Prayer of St. Richard at Chichester. See no. 3524
WHITLOCK, Percy
    Extemporisations, no. 4: Fanfare. See no. 3501
    Jesu grant me this I pray. See no. 3524
    Plymouth suite: Salix. See no. 4053
3501 Sonata, organ, C minor. Extemporisations, no. 4: Fanfare. Graham
      Barber, org. Vista VPS 1058
               ++ARG 2-80 p44   ++HFN 7-79 p113
               +FF 11/12-79 p145   +MT 7-79 p582
               +Gr 3-79 p1593   +NR 5-80 p14
WHITTAKER, William
3502 Among the Northumbrian hills. I said in the noontide of my days,
      anthem. Quintet, winds. Amphion Wind Ensemble; London Soloists
      Vocal Ensemble; Ensemble; Roderick Spencer, org; John Bate.
      Viking VRSS 001
               +-FF 9/10-80 p236   +MU 3-79 p16
               +Gr 4-80 p1580   ++RR 4-77 p84
               +HFN 2-77 p133
    I said in the noontide of my days, anthem. See no. 3502
3503 Northumbrian songs and pipe tunes: Billy boy; Blow the wind south-
      erly; Bobby Shaftoe; Bonny at morn; The bonny fisher lad; Ca'
      Hawkie; Chevy Chase; Derwentwater's farewell; Dollia; Doon the
      waggon way; Felton Lonnen; Gan to the kye wi' me; The Hexham-
      shire lass; The keel row; King Arthur's servants; Ma bonny lad;
      Madam I will buy you; The miller and his sons; Newburn lads;
      Noble Squire Dacre; O I hae seen the roses blaw; Sir John Fen-
      wick's the flower amang the mall; The shoemakker; The water of
      Tyne; The willow tree. Marian Aitchison, s; Denis Weatherley,
      bs-bar; Marion Senior, Eleanor Weatherley, pno; Richard Butler,
      Northumbrian pipes; Sinfonia Chorus; Alan Fearon. Viking VRW 002
               +Gr 4-80 p1580
    Quintet, winds. See no. 3502
WHYTHORNE, Thomas
    Buy a new broom. See no. 3995
WIDMAN, Erasmus
    Daentze und Galliarden. See no. 2527
WIDOR, Charles
3504 Nouvelles pieces, op. 87 (3). Suite latine. Jane Parker-Smith,
      org. L'Oiseau-Lyre SOL 352
               +-Gr 8-80 p242   -RR 7-80 p85
               +HFN 7-80 p111
    Suite latine. See no. 3504
3505 Symphony, organ, no. 3, op. 13, no. 3, F minor: Prelude; Adagio;
      Finale. Symphony, no. 4, op. 13, no. 4, F major. Symphony, no.
      6, op. 42, no. 2, B major. Symphony, no. 9, op. 70, C minor.
      Marie-Claire Alain, org. Erato STU 71165 (2)
               ++Gr 5-80 p1693   +RR 4-80 p104
               +-HFN 4-80 p112
    Symphony, organ, no. 4, op. 13, no. 4, F major. See no. 3505
    Symphony, organ, no. 4, op. 13, no. 4, F major: Andante cantabile;

Final. See no. 3725
3506 Symphony, organ, no. 5, op. 42, no. 1, F major. Symphony, organ,
     no. 6, op. 42, no. 2, G major: Allegro. Symphony, no. 8, op. 42,
     no. 4, B major: Prelude. David Sanger, org. Saga 5439 Tape (c)
     CA 5439

      ++ARG 6-80 p42   +HFN 4-79 p131
      +-FF 9/10-80 p237   ++MT 8-77 p653
      +Gr 1-77 p1161   +-RR 2-77 p82
      +HFN 2-77 p133   +RR 4-79 p106
      +-HFN 11-77 p187 tape

Symphony, organ, no. 5, op. 42, no. 1, F minor: Toccata. See no.
3615. See no. 3616. See no. 3624. See no. 3658. See no. 3661.
See no. 3663. See no. 3664. See no. 3743. See no. 3838. See
no. 3938. See no. 4034. See no. 4056
Symphony organ, no. 5, op. 42, no. 1, F major: Variations. See no.
1297
Symphony, organ, no. 6, op. 42, no. 2, B major. See no. 3505
Symphony, organ, no. 6, op. 42, no. 2, B major: Adagio. See no.
3733
Symphony, organ, no. 6, op. 42, no. 2, G major: Allegro. See no.
3506. See no. 4055
Symphony, organ, no. 6, op. 42, no. 2, G major: Finale. See no.
3615. See no. 3616. See no. 4057
Symphony, no. 8, op. 42, no. 4, B major: Finale. See no. 3624
Symphony, organ, no. 8, op. 42, no. 4, B major: Prelude. See no.
3506
Symphony, organ, no. 9, op. 70, C minor. See no. 3505
Symphony, organ, no. 73: Final. See no. 4061
WIEDERMANN, Bedrich
    Impetuoso. See no. 1352
    Notturno. See no. 1352
WIENIAWSKI, Henryk
    La cadenza. See no. 3637
    Capriccio valse, op. 7. See no. 3507
    Concerto, violin, no. 2, op. 22, D minor. See no. 3964
    Concerto, violin, no. 2, op. 22, D minor: Romance. See no. 4009
    Dudziarz, op. 19, no. 2. See no. 3507
    Fantasy on themes from Gounod's "Faust", op. 20. See no. 1388
    Legende, op. 17. See no. 3507
    Mazurka, op. 19, no. 1. See no. 3552. See no. 3788
    Obertass, op. 19, no. 1. See no. 3507
    Polonaise, op. 4, D major. See no. 3507. See no. 3964
    Polonaise brilliante, op. 21, no. 2. See no. 3507. See no. 3552.
    See no. 3788
    Romance, op. 22. See no. 3507
    Scherzo tarantelle, op. 16, G minor. See no. 3507. See no. 3964
    Souvenir de Moscou, op. 6. See no. 3507
3507 Works, selections: Capriccio valse, op. 7. Dudziarz, op. 19, no. 2.
     Legende, op. 17. Polonaise brilliante, op. 21, no. 2, A major.
     Polonaise, op. 4, D major. Obertass, op. 19, no. 1. Romance,
     op. 22. Scherzo tarantella, op. 16, G minor. Souvenir de Moscou,
     op. 6. Alfredo Campoli, vln; Daphne Ibbott, pno. L'Oiseau-Lyre
     DSLO 45

      ++Gr 9-80 p368   +HFN 10-80 p110

WIKLUND, Adolf
3508 Concerto, piano, op. 17, B flat minor. Pieces, strings and harp:
         Sang til varen. Greta Erikson, pno; Swedish Radio Orchestra;
         Stig Westerberg. Caprice CAP 1165
                        +NR 9-80 p4   +RR 8-80 p58
      Pieces, strings and harp: Sang til varen. See no. 3508
WIKMANSON, Johann
      Quartet, strings, op. 1, no. 2, E minor. See no. 700
WILBYE, John
      Songs: Adieu sweet Amarillis; Thus saith my Cloris bright. See
         no. 3867
      Songs (madrigals): Adieu sweet Amaryllis; Draw on sweet night;
         Flora gave me fairest flowers; Sweet honey-sucking bees, pt 1;
         Weep weep mine eyes; Yet sweet take heed, pt 2. See no. 3893
      Songs: Draw on sweet night; Sweet honey-sucking bees. See no. 3941
      Songs: Lady when I behold the roses. See no. 3744
WILDER, Alec
3509 Sextet, marimba and wind quartet. Suite, flute and marimba. Suite,
         trumpet and marimba. Gordon Stout, marimba; Virginia Nanzetta,
         flt; Robert Levy, tpt; Clarion Wind Quintet. Golden Crest CRS
         4190
                        ++St 9-80 p84
      Suite, flute and marimba. See no. 3509
      Suite, trumpet and marimba. See no. 3509
WILLAERT, Adrian
      O magnum mysterium. See no. 3763
      Songs: A quand; Allons allons gay; Ricercari (2); Villanelle. See
         3805
WILLAN, Healey
      Elegy and chaconne. See no. 4057
      Introduction, passacaglia and fugue, E flat minor. See no. 4047
      O sacred feast. See no. 3992
WILLCOCKS
      Adeste fideles. See no. 3993
      Fanfare on "Gopsal". See no. 3895
WILLIAMS
      Blue devil. See no. 3617
WILLIAMS, Charles
      While I live: The dream of Olwen. See no. 3790
WILLIAMS, Grace
      Ballads. See no. 3510
3510 Symphony, no. 2. Ballads. BBC Welsh Symphony Orchestra; Vernon
         Handley. BBC REGL 381
                        +Gr 6-80 p43   ++RR 6-80 p64
WILLIAMS, John
      Star wars: Main theme. See no. 4046
WILLIAMS, Pat
      An American concerto, jazz quartet: 3rd movement. See no. 1574
WILLIAMS, William
      Sonata, recorder, no. 4, A minor. See no. 4015
WILLIAMSON, Malcolm
      English lyrics (6). See no. 908
      Kerygma. See no. 3534
3511 Songs: Agnus Dei; The morning of the day of days; Procession of
         psalms; The world at the manger. Hazel Holt, s; Alastair Thomp-

son, t; Christopher Keyte, bs; Worcester Cathedral Choir and
Festival Choral Society; Paul Trepte, org; Donald Hunt. Abbey
LPB 805

    +Gr 11-79 p896   -MT L-80 p36
    +HFN 9-79 p115   +-RR 9-79 p131

Wrestling Jacob. See no. 3532

WILLINGHAM, Jerry
    T'Chu. See no. 1821

WILLS, Arthur
    Piece, organ: Processional. See no. 4047

WILSON, John
    Take o take those lisp away. See no. 3997

WINDSOR
    Alpine echoes. See no. 3627

WIREN, Dag
    Serenade, op. 11. See no. 1546

WISHART
    Alleluya. See no. 3823

WISZNIEWSKI, Zbigniew
    Pezzi della tradizione (3). See no. 3857

WITT, Friedrich
    Concerto, 2 horns, F major. See no. 2205
    Quintet, op. 6, E flat major. See no. 1911

WOELFL, Josef
    Grand duo, op. 31, D minor. See no. 492

WOLF, Hugo
3512 Der Corregidor. Marta Fuchs, Margarete Teschemacher, s; Karl Erb,
    Karl Wesseley, t; Josef Herrmann, bar; Kurt Bohme, Gottlob Frick,
    George Hann, bs; Dresden State Opera Chorus; Dresden State Orch-
    estra; Kurt Striegler. Acanta FA 21408 (3)

      +-Gr 3-80 p1441   +-RR 3-80 p44
      +HFN 5-80 p127   +STL 3-9-80 p41

    Der Corregidor: Overture. See no. 3824
    Geistliche Lieder. See no. 2941
    Italian serenade, G major. See no. 924. See no. 1888

3513 Italienisches Liederbuch. Christa Ludwig, ms; Dietrich Fischer-
    Dieskau, bar; Daniel Barenboim, pno. DG 2707 114 (2)

      +-FF 11/12-80 p191   +NYT 3-2-80 pD26
      +-Gr 12-79 p1039   ++RR 12-79 p120
      +-HF 8-80 p83   ++SFC 8-10-80 p2?
      +HFN 1-80 p113   +-St 10-80 p124
      +NR 5-80 p11

    Italianisches Liederbuch, no. 5. See no. 852
    Italianisches Liederbuch: Und willst du deinen Liebsten sterben
      sehen. See no. 3774
    Morike Lieder: Fussreise. See no. 852
    Morike Lieder: Gebet; Fussreise. See nol 3573

3514 Quartet, strings, D minor. Keller Quartet. Da Camera Magna SM
    92709

      +ST 12-80 p574

3515 Songs: Als ich auf dem Euphrat schiffte; Anakreons Grab; Blumengruss;
    Du milchunger Knabe; Epiphanias; Fruhling ubers Jahr; Ganymed;
    Hoch begluckt in deiner Liebe; Das Kohlerweib ist trunken; Kennst
    du das Land; Maufallenspruchlein; Mignon, 1-3; Morgentau; Nimmer
    will ich dich verlieren; Philine; St. Nepomuks Vorabend; Singt

mein Schatz; Die Spinnerin; Sonne der Schlummerlosen; Tretet ein
Krieger; Das Voglein; Wandl ich in dem Morgentau; Wie glantz
der Helle Mond; Wiegenlied in Sommer; Wiegenlied in Winter.
Elisabeth Schwarzkopf, s; Gerald Moore, pno. HMV SLS 5197 (2)
    ++Gr 9-80 p386   +STL 11-9-80 p40
Songs: Abschied; Bei einer Trauung; Jagerlied. See no. 3537
Songs: An eine Aeolsharfe; Bei einer Trauung; Im Fruhling; Jager-
lied; Lied eines Verliebten; Denk es o Seele; Heimweh. See no.
911
Songs: Auch kleine Dinge; Ihr jungen Leute; Heb auf dein blondes
Haupt; Mein Liebster singt; Mein Liebster hat zu Tische; Wir
haben lange Zeit. See no. 3541
Songs: Blumengruss. See no. 3611
3516 Spanisches Liederbuch. Elisabeth Schwarzkopf, s; Dietrich Fischer-
Dieskau, bar; Gerald Moore, pno. DG 2726 071 (2) (From SLPM
139329/30)
    +ARG 8-79 p45   +HFN 4-79 p133
    +-FF 1/2-80 p160   ++NYT 8-5-79 pD19
    +Gr 4-79 p1762   +RR 5-79 p92

WOLF-FERRARI, Ermanno
I gioiella della madonna: Aprile o bella. See no. 3771
I gioiella della madonna: Dance of the Camorristi. See no. 3962
Il segreto di Susanna: Oh gioia nube. See no. 3774
Il segreto di Susanna: Overture. See no. 3962
Songs: Se gli alberi; Serenata; Commiato. See no. 3771
Suite concertino, op. 16, F major. See no. 1854

WOOD, Charles
O thou the central orb. See no. 3815
Oculi omnium. See no. 3527

WOOD, Haydn
Roses of Picardy. See no. 3874

WOOD, Henry
Fantasia on British sea songs. See no. 1230

WOOD, Hugh
3517 Concerto, violin, op. 17. Concerto, violoncello, op. 12. Manoug
Parikian, vln; Moray Welsh, vlc; Royal Liverpool Philharmonic
Orchestra; David Atherton. Unicorn RHS 363
    +FF 5/6-80 p172   +RR 1-80 p94
    +Gr 11-79 p853   +STL 12-2-79 p37
    ++HFN 11-79 p145
Concerto, violoncello, op. 12. See no. 3517

WOTJA
Introduzione et aria. See no. 3752

WRIGHTON
Her bright smile haunts me still. See no. 3774

WUORINEN, Charles
Two-part symphony. See no. 976

WYTON
Palm Sunday. See no. 4059
This joyful Eastertide. See no. 4059

XENAKIS, Iannis
3518 Eonta, piano and 5 brass instruments. Evryali, piano. Herma,
piano. Geoffrey Madge, pno; Jeugden Muziek Middleburg; Peter
Eotvos. VBHAAST 007
    +FU 6-80 p52

Evryali, piano. See no. 3518
Herma, piano. See no. 3518
XIMENO, Fabian
    Ay ay galeguinos. See no. 3849
YAMADA, Kohsaku
    Mandara no hara. See no. 1456
YARDUMIAN, Richard
    Preludes (2). See no. 3851
YOCOH (Yoko), Yuquijiro
    Theme and variations on "Sakura". See no. 3634
YON, Pietro
    Toccatina, flute. See no. 4048
YOULL
    Majusi viragok. See no. 3814
YOUNG
    Kneller Hall slow march. See no. 4029
    Mother Machree. See no. 3875
YRADIER, Sebastian
    La paloma. See no. 3869
    La perla di trianna. See no. 3774
ZABEL
    La source. See no. 3676
ZACH, Johan
    Sonata a tre, A major. See no. 3752
ZACHAU (Zachow), Friedrich
    Suite, B minor. See no. 4022
    Trio, flute and bassoon, F major. See no. 3804
ZAIMONT, Judith
3519 A calendar set. Chansons nobles et sentimentales. La fin de siec-
        le. Charles Bressler, t; Gary Steigerwalt, Judith Zaimont, pno.
        Leonarda LPI 101
                    +ARG 3-80 p52   +NR 4-80 p12
                    +-FF 9/10-80 p237
    Chansons nobles et sentimentales. See no. 3519
    La fin de siecle. See no. 3519
ZANNETTI, Gasparo
    Songs: Fuggi fuggi fuggi; La Montovana. See no. 3956
ZAVALA
    Viva el rumbo. See no. 3921
ZEHLE
    Army and Marine. See no. 3619
    Trafalgar. See no. 3619
ZEHM, Friedrich
    Choralbearbeitung: Erschienen ist der herrliche Tag. See no. 4036
ZEITLIN, Denny
3520 Soundings. Denny Zeitlin, pno. 1750 Arch 1770
                    +NR 5-80 p12
ZELENKA, Johann
3521 Trio sonatas, nos. 1-6. Heinz Holliger, Maurice Bourgue, ob; Sasch-
        ko Gawriloff, vln; Klaus Thunemann, bsn; Lucio Buccarella, double
        bs; Christiane Jaccottet, hpd. DG 2708 027 (2)
                    +FF 9/10-80 p238   ++NR 8-80 p7
                    ++Gr 10-74 p718   ++RR 10-74 p72
                    +-HF 9-80 p101   ++St 10-80 p120
ZELLER, Karl
    Der Vogelhandler: Wie mein Ahnl zwanzig Jahr. See no. 3711

ZEMLINSKY, Alexander
3522 Quartet, strings, no. 2, op. 15. LaSalle Quartet. DG 2530 982
                    ++ARG 10-80 p48   +NYT 2-10-80 pD24
                     +FF 7/8-80 p155   ++RR 4-79 p91
                    ++Gr 4-79 p1736   ++St 5-80 p94
                    ++HF 6-80 p92   +STL 12-2-79 p37
                     +HFN 4-79 p128   +Te 6-79 p45
                    ++NR 4-80 p7
ZESSO (15th century Italy)
     E quando andarete al monte. See no. 3864
ZIMMERMAN
     Anchors aweigh. See no. 4012
ZIMMERMANN, Heinz
     Monologue. See no. 1964
     Perspectives. See no. 1964
ZIPOLI, Domenico
     Aria. See no. 1116
     Elevazione. See no. 3762
     Mass: Gloria. See no. 3707
     Pastorale, C major. See no. 4041
ZITO
     La cumparsita. See no. 3637
ZOSSO, Rene
     Une maison. See no. 3760
ZUPKO, Ramon
3523 Fluxus II. Nocturnes. Masques. Abraham Stokman, Arlene Stokman,
        pno; Western Brass Quintet. CRI SD 425
                    +FF 11/12-80 p193   +NR 7-80 p6
     Masques. See no. 3523
     Nocturnes. See no. 3523
ZWEERS, Bernard
     Symphony, no. 3. See no. 3818

Section II

MUSIC IN COLLECTIONS

ABBEY

APR 302
3524 ASHFIELD: The fair chivalry. BACH: Toccata, S 540, F major. BRID-
GE: God's goodness. CORONA: Crown him with many crowns, hymn.
FERGUSON: Death and darkness get you packing; Psalm, no. 137,
verses 1-6; Reverie. HEATH: Verse service: Magnificat. MOZART:
Ave verum corpus, K 618. STEWART: Crown him with many crowns.
VAUGHAN WILLIAMS: Mystical songs: Come my way. Let all the world.
WESLEY, S.: Behold how good and joyful. WHITE: Prayer of St.
Richard at Chichester. WHITLOCK: Jesu grant me this I pray.
Richard Paul, bar; David Poulter, org; Rochester Cathedral Choir;
Barry Ferguson.
       +Gr 5-80 p1706   +MT 10-80 p638
       +HFN 5-80 p129   +RR 7-80 p92

APR 303
3525 BRITTEN: Antiphon. BYRD: From virgin's womb this day did spring
Laudibus in sanctis. DERING: Factum est silentium. GIBBONS:
The secret sins. MENDELSSOHN: Laudate pueri dominum. OUSELEY:
It came even to pass; When all thy mercies o my God. STAINER:
The crucifixion: God so loved the world. VIERNE: Fantasiestucke,
op. 54: Carillon de Westminster. St. Michael's College Choir;
Andrew Millington, org. Roger Judd.
       +Gr 5-80 p1711   +MT 10-80 p638
       +HFN 5-80 p129   ++RR 5-80 p94

APR 304
3526 BACH: Brandenburg concerto, no. 3, S 1048, G major: 1st movement.
CORELLI (Barbirolli): Concerto, oboe: Prelude-gavotte. ELGAR:
Enigma variations, op. 36: Nimrod. In the south overture, op.
50. GOUNOD: Petite symphony, B flat major: 1st movement.
STRAUSS, J. I: Radetzky march, op. 222. Soloists; Lancashire
Schools Symphony Orchestra; Malcolm Doley
       +-HFN 5-80 p133   +RR 8-80 p47

APR 305
3527 BAIRSTOW: Let all mortal flesh keep silence. BRITTEN: Jubilate Deo,
C major. GARDNER: Fight the good fight; Tomorrow shall be my
dancing day. GERMAN: My bonnie lass. HAYNE: Loving shepherd of
thy sheep. HOVLAND: Og ordet ble kjod. MURRILL: Nunc dimittis.
NYSTEDT: Velsignet vaere han. PARRY: Dear Lord and father of
mankind. POSTON: Jesus Christ the apple tree. SCHUBERT: Mass,
no. 2, D 167, G major: Kyrie. TYE: Laudate nomen Domini; Praise
ye the Lord ye children. VAUGHAN WILLIAMS: O how amiable are
thy dwellings; Linden Lea (arr. Somervell). WESLEY, S.S.: Thou
wilt keep him in perfect peace. WOOD, C.: Oculi omnium. TRAD.:

De battle ob Jerico. De virgin Mary. I will give my love an
apple. King Edward VI School Choir; Jeremy Blandford, org; Eric
Merriman.
                -Gr 5-80 p1706   +-HFN 5-80 p127
APR 306
3528 BAIRSTOW: Though I speak with the tongues of men. BRITTEN: Hymn to
the virgin. BRUCKNER: Locus iste. BULLOCK: Give us the wings of
faith. ELGAR: Ave verum corpus, no. 2, no. 1. FAURE: Tantum
ergo, op. 65, no. 2. FRESCOBALDI: Aria with variations. HOWELLS:
Gloucester service: Magnificat. All my hope on God is founded.
JONGEN: Chant de mai, op. 53. LANG: Tuba tune, D major. LIDON:
Sonata para trompeta real. MATHIAS: Toccata giocosa, op. 36, no.
2. MOZART: Ave verum corpus, K 618. PALESTRINA: Haec dies.
SCHUTZ: Die Himmel erzahlen. Jonathan Newell, Keith Rhodes, org;
Bradford Cathedral Choirs; Keith Rhodes.
                +Gr 5-80 p1706   +MT 10-80 p638
                +HFN 4-80 p112   +RR 6-80 p84
MVP 808
3529 Hymns: All my hope on God is founded; Blessed city heavenly Salem;
Come down O love divine; The day thou gavest; Dear Lord and father of mankind; For all the saints; Glorious things of thee are
spoken; God be in my head; He who would valiant be; Immortal invisible God only wise; The king of love; Mine eyes have seen the
glory; My song is love unknown; O praise ye the Lord; O thou who
camest from above; Praise my soul the king of heaven; Praise to
the Lord the almighty. Worcester Cathedral Choir; Paul Trepte,
org; Donald Hunt.
                +-HFN 2-80 p101   +RR 3-80 p96
ABY 814
3530 BLOW: Salvator mundi. BRITTEN: Festival Te deum, op. 32. BYRD:
Sing joyfully unto God. DERING: Contristatus est Rex David:
Quem vidistis pastores. EAST: When David heard that Absalom
was slain. HOWELLS: Jubilate Deo. PHILIPS: Ecce tu pulchra es;
O beatum et sacrosanctum diem. PURCELL: Jehova quam multi sunt
hostes mei. TALLIS: In jejunio et fletu. TRAD. (Italian): Once
as I remember (C. Wood arr. Williams). St. Peter ad Vincula
Choir; John Williams, Joseph Sentance, org.
                +Gr 8-80 p258   +-HFN 8-80 p103
LPB 816
3531 BACH: Cantata, no. 147, Jesu joy of man's desiring. BRAHMS: Songs
of Mary, op. 22: A cry to Mary. BALFOUR-GARDINER: Evening hymn.
BRUCKNER: Christus factus est. CHAPMAN: Christ is the flower
within my heart. DUFFY: Sacerdos et pontifex. DURUFLE: Plainsong: Pange lingua; Tantum ergo. FAURE: Ave verum corpus, op.
65, no. 1. FRANCK: Panis angelicus. MILLER: When I survey the
wondrous cross. MILNER: Love is his word. PALESTRINA: Missa
sine nomine: Kyre. POSTON: Jesus Christ the apple tree. SCHU-
BERT: Mass, no. 2, D 167, G major: Gloria. TALLIS: O nata lux
de lumine. Terence Duffy, org; Liverpool Cathedral Choir; Philip Duffy.
                +Gr 5-80 p1706   +MT 10-80 p638
                +-HFN 5-80 p129   +RR 6-80 p86
ABY 817
3532 BROWN: Laudate dominum. BYRD: Laudibus in sanctis. DAVIES: Magdalen at Michael's gate. GIBBONS: Hosanna to the son of David.

PURCELL: Let mine eyes. RIDOUT: I turn the corner. STANFORD:
The Lord is my shepherd. WEELKES: Give ear O Lord. WILLIAMSON:
Wrestling Jacob. ANON.: Doxology (arr. Ridout). Canterbury
Cathedral Choir; David Flood, org; Allan Wicks.
+Gr 8-80 p258   +-HFN 8-80 p103

HMP 2280
3533 BACH: Flocks in pastures green abiding (arr. Roper). BULLIVANT: Te
deum, E flat major. ELGAR: Doubt not thy father's care. MORLEY:
Nolo mortem peccatoris. SCHUBERT: Where thou reignest. SHAW:
The greater light. THALBEN-BALL: Elegy, B flat major. Jubilate
Deo, B flat major. The Lord God omnipotent reigneth. Psalm
chants. VULPIUS: The strife is o'er. DAVIES: Tarry no longer.
George Thalben-Ball, org.
+RR 8-80 p87

HMP 2280
3534 MENDELSSOHN: Hear my prayer, op. 39, no. 1. STANLEY: Concerti, org-
an, nos. 4 and 6. THALBEN-BALL: Sursum corda; Comfort ye. DAV-
IES: Solemn melody; Tarry no longer. WILLIAMSON: Kerygma. Tem-
ple Church Choir; William Johannes, bs; Caroline Dearnley, vlc;
Ian le Grice, org; Royal College of Music Orchestra; George
Thalben-Ball, David Willcocks.
++Gr 6-80 p59   +RR 8-80 p87

ACANTA

DC 21723
3535 DONIZETTI: La favorita: Una vergine. GOUNOD: Faust: Salute demeure
chaste et pure. HALEVY: La juive: Rachel quand du seigneur.
MASSENET: Manon: Ay fuyez. PUCCINI: La boheme: Che gelida manina. Gianna Schicchi: Firenze e come un albero. Manon Lescaut:
Donna non vidi mai. Turandot: Nessun dorma. VERDI: Aida: Celeste Aida. Luisa Miller; Quando le sere placido. Il trovatore:
Di quella pira. Franco Bonisolli, t; Hamburg Philharmonic Orchestra; Leone Magiera.
+Gr 8-80 p270   +-RR 7-80 p46
+HFN 7-80 p111

DC 23034
3536 GOSSWIN: Am Abend spat lieb Bruderlein. LASSUS: A voi Gugliemo; Am
Abend spat beim kuhlen Wein; Bicinium; Die fasstnacht ist ein
schone Zeit; Im Mayen hort man die hanen krayen; Matona mia cara;
La nuict froide et sombre; O fugace dolcezza; Sybilla Europea;
Der Tag ist so freudenreich; Vedi l'aurora. LECHNER: Nach meiner Lieb viel hundert Knaben trachten. REINER: Schone newe Teut-
sche lieder: Behut euch Gott zu aller Zeit. SENFL: Das Gelaut
zu Speyer; Es taget vor dem Walde; Es wollt ein Frau zum Weine
gahn; Fortuna Nasci pati mori; Ich armes Kauzlein kleine; Patienca muss ich han. VENTO: Frisch ist mein Sinn; Ich weiss ein
Maidlein; So wunsch ich ihr ein gute Nacht. Munich Capella Antiqua; Konrad Ruhland.
+Gr 8-80 p258   ++HFN 7-80 p111

BB 23101
3537 BRAHMS: An die Nachtigall, op. 46, no. 4; An die Tauben, op. 63, no.
4; Nachtigallen schwingen, op. 6, no. 6. MOZART: An Chloe, K
524. SCHUBERT: Auf der Bruck, D 853; Bei dir allein, D 866; Die

liebe Farbe, D 795; Mio ben ricordati, D 688; Morgengruss, D 795;
Non t'accostar all'urna, D 688; Schafers Klagelied, D 121; Willkommen und Abschied, D 767. STRAUSS, R.: Das Geheimnis, op. 17,
no. 3. WOLF: Abschied; Bei einer Trauung; Jagerlied. Julius
Patzak, t; Michael Raucheisen, pno.
      +HFN 5-80 p129   ++RR 4-80 p117

BB 23119
3538 BEETHOVEN: Fidelio, op. 72: Jetzt Schatzchen jetz sind wir allein.
BIZET: Les pecheurs de perles: Au fond du temple saint. CORNEL-
IUS: Der Barbier von Bagdad: Vor deinem Fenster die Blumen. MAS-
CAGNI: Cavalleria rusticana: Voi lo sapete. MOZART: Die Entfuhrung aus dem Serail, K 384: Martern aller Arten. PUCCINI: Tosca:
Recondita armonia. ROSSINI: Il barbiere di Siviglia: La calunnia
e un venticello. STRAUSS, R.: Der Rosenkavalier, op. 59: Ist ein
Traum. THOMAS: Mignon: Adieu Mignon. VERDI: La forza del destino: Solenne in quest'ora. Rigoletto: Complunto...Si vendetta
tremenda vendetta. La traviata: Lunge dei lei...De miei bollenti
spiriti. Il trovatore: Di quella pira. WAGNER: Lohengren: Treulich bewacht...Das susse Lied verhallt. Tristan und Isolde: Wohin nun Tristan scheidet. Die Walkure: Nicht straf ich dich erst.
Maria Cebotari, Astrid Varnay, Erna Berger, Tiana Lemnitz, Elisabeth Schwarzkopf, Irmgard Seefried, Maria Muller, Kirsten Flagstad, s; Hans Hopf, Helge Roswaenge, Marcel Wittrisch, Peter Anders, Walther Ludwig, Richard Tauber, Anton Dermota, Peter Klein,
Max Lorenz, Franz Volker, t; Heinrich Schlusnus, Willi Domgraf-
Fassbaender, Hans Hotter, Karl Schmitt-Walter, Rudolf Bockelmann,
bar; Various accompaniments.
      +-Gr 3-80 p1441   +-HFN 11-79 p149

DE 23120/1
3539 CORNELIUS: Der Barbier von Bagdad: Arias. DONIZETTI: L'Elisir d'
amore: Arias. FLOTOW: Alessandro Stradella: Arias. Martha:
Arias. LEONCAVALLO: I Pagliacci: Arias. MAILLART: Das Glock-
chen des Eremiten: O schweige still o lasse dich erbitten. MAS-
CAGNI: Cavalleria rusticana: Arias. MASSENET: Manon: Arias.
MOZART: Cosi fan tutte, K 588: Arias. Die Entfuhrung aus dem
Serail, K 384: Arias. Don Giovanni, K 527: Arias. Die Zauber-
flote, K 620: Arias. PUCCINI: Manon Lescaut: Arias. Tosca:
Arias. Turandot: Arias. La fanciulla del West: Arias. SMETANA:
Die verkaufte Braut: Arias. STRAUSS, R.: Der Rosenkavalier, op.
59: Arias. TCHAIKOVSKY: Eugen Onegin, op. 24: Arias. VERDI: Il
trovatore: Arias. Luisa Miller: Arias. WEBER: Euryanthe: Arias.
Anton Dermota, t; BRSO; Robert Hager, Artur Rother.
      +-HFN 2-80 p101   +RR 2-80 p38

EA 23186
3540 DOWLAND: Lachrimae: Antiquae pavan. Galliard. LOSY VON LOSINTHAL:
Pieces, guitar (6). MILAN: Fantasias, nos. 1-3. REUSNER: Sonatina. SCHENK: Suite, A minor. VISEE: Suite, D minor. Siegfried
Behrend, gtr.
      +-RR 6-80 p80

23317
3541 BRAHMS: Geheimnis, op. 71, no. 3; Das Madchen spricht, op. 107, no.
3. DEBUSSY: Apparition; Clair de lune; Pantomime; Pierrot. HAN-
DEL: O sleep why dost thou leave me. MOZART: Exsultate jubilate,
K 165. SCHUBERT: An die Nachtigall, D 947; Lachen und Weine, D
777. STRAUSS, R.: Hamlet: Ophelia Lieder (3). WOLF: Auch kleine

Dinge; Ihr jungen Leute; Heb auf dein blondes Haupt; Mein Liebster singt; Mein Liebster hat zu Tische; Wir haben lange Zeit.
Erna Berger, s; Michael Raucheisen, pno.
        +HFN 5-80 p127   +RR 4-80 p109

ACCENT

ACC 7804
3542 BABELL: Sonata, oboe, no. 1, B major. BACH, C.P.E.: Sonata, oboe,
     G minor. FORSTER: Sonata, oboe, C minor. GEMINIANI: Sonata,
     oboe, no. 1, E minor. HANDEL: Sonata, oboe, F major. VINCENT:
     Sonata, oboe, op. 1, no. 2, A minor. Paul Dombrecht, ob; Robert
     Kohnen, hpd; Wieland Kuijken, vla da gamba.
             +FF 3/4-80 p198   +RR 6-80 p27
             +HFN 6-80 p101

ACC 7806
3543 BACH, J.C.: Quintet, D major. GALUPPI: Trio sonata, G major. HAN-
     DEL: Concerto a 4, D minor. JANITSCH: Quartet, F major. TELE-
     MANN: Trio sonata, G minor. Parnassus Ensemble.
             +FF 3/4-80 p198   +MT 11-79 p921
             +-HFN 6-80 p101   +RR 6-80 p27

ACC 7909
3544 BLAVET: Sonata, flute, op. 2, no. 2, F major. BOISMORTIER: Sonata,
     flute, op. 91, no. 2, G minor. GUIGNON: Sonata, flute, op. 1,
     no. 8, A major. LECLAIR: Sonata, flute, op. 9, no. 7, G major.
     MONTECLAIR: Concerto, flute, no. 12. Barthold Kuijken, flt;
     Wieland Kuijken, vla da gamba; Robert Kohnen, hpd.
             +-FF 5/6-80 p195   +RR 6-80 p27
             +HFN 6-80 p101

AFKA RECORDS

Unnumbered
3545 CLARKE: Trumpet voluntary (Prince of Denmark march). HANDEL: Verdi
     prati. HOVHANESS: Prayer of St. Gregory. KREBS: Wachet auf. MOU-
     RET: Sinfonies de fanfares. PURCELL: Trumpet tune. STANLEY:
     Voluntary, D major. STOLZEL: Bist du bei mir. TELEMANN: Air de
     trompette. VIVIANI: Sonata, trumpet and organ. Walter Chestnut,
     tpt; Ernest May, org.
             +MU 3-80 p8

ALPHA

DB 231
3546 BERNARDI: O quam tu pulchra es. BREVI: O spiritus angelici. DON-
     ATI: Psalmus, nos. 6. GABRIELI, A.: Canzon francese. GAGLIANO:
     Pastor levate su. GIAMBERTI: O belle lagrimette. GRANDI: Can-
     tabo domino. FRESCOBALDI: Sonnetti spirituali: Ohime che fur
     che sono; Dove sparir si ratto i di serani; Maddalena alla croce.
     KAPSBERGER: Nigra sum. ANON.: Ricercare (17th c.). Rene Jacobs,
     alto; Johan Huys, org, hpd.
             ++Gr 10-80 p528   +HFN 9-80 p113

DB 248
3547 BOISMORTIER: Concerto, op. 37, no. 6, E minor. DORNEL: Sonate en
      quatuor, D minor. FUX: Sinfonia, F major. GEMINIANI: Concerti
      grossi, op. 2, no. 4, D major. TELEMANN: Trio sonata, E minor.
      Parnassus Ensemble.
            +Gr 10-80 p504
DB 264
3548 ANON.: Credo. Gloria. Nunc diem festis. Je suis trestout. Pour
      leaulte maintenir. Qui n'a le cuer rainpli. Tijs soezas. Toe
      mpaloe. Huelgas Ensemble; Paul Van Nevel.
            +FF 11/12-80 p204

ANGEL

SZ 3896 (2) (From HMV originals, 1927-39)
3549 ALBENIZ: Suite, espanol, op. 47: Granada, Sevilla. BACH: Partita,
      violin, no. 3, S 1006, E major: Gavotte (arr. Segovia). Prelude,
      S 999, C minor (arr. Segovia, D minor). Sonata, violin, no. 1,
      S 1001, G minor: Fugue (arr. Segovia, A minor). Suite, lute, S
      996, E minor: Allemande (arr. Segovia). Suite, solo violoncello,
      no. 1, S 1007, G major: Prelude (arr. Ponce). Suite, solo vio-
      loncello, no. 3, S 1009, C major: Courante (arr. Segovia).
      CASTELNUOVO-TEDESCO: Sonata, guitar: Vivo ed energico. FROBERG-
      ER: Gigue. GRANADOS: Danzas espanolas, op. 37: Andaluza, Danza
      triste. MALATS: Serenata. MENDELSSOHN: Quartet, strings, no.
      1, op. 12, E flat major: Canzonetta (arr. Segovia). PONCE: Maz-
      urka. Petite valse. Sonata, guitar, no. 3. Suite, A major.
      Variations and fugue on "Folia de Espana". SOR: Variations on
      a theme by Mozart, op. 9. TARREGA: Recuerdos de la Alhambra.
      Estudio brillante, A major. TORROBA: Nocturno. Preludio. Sona-
      tina, A major: Allegretto. Suite castellana: Fandanguillo. TUR-
      INA: Fandanguillo. VISEE: Bourree. Menuet. Sarabande. Andres
      Segovia, gtr.
            +HF 7-80 p54   +-St 8-80 p93
            ++NR 6-80 p14
S 37324
3550 BRAHMS: Pieces, piano, op. 117: Intermezzi. CHOPIN: Fantasie, op.
      49, F minor. LISZT: Annees de pelerinage, 2nd year, G 161: Dan-
      te sonata. SCHUBERT: Soiree de Vienne, no. 6 (arr. Liszt).
      SCHUMANN: Arabesque, op. 18, C major. Leonard Pennario, pno.
            +-FF 3/4-80 p182   +NR 7-79 p14
SZ 37546 Tape (c) 4ZS 37546
3551 BARRERA Y CALLEJA: Adios Granada (arr. de los Angeles). BRAHMS:
      Liebestreu, op. 3, no. 1; Vergebliches Standchen, op. 84, no. 4.
      FALLA: Spanish popular songs: Jota; Polo. HANDEL: Radamisto:
      Vanne sorella ingrata. MONTEVERDI: Maledetto sia l'aspetto;
      Ohime Ch'io cado ohime. MONTSALVATGE: Canciones negras: Punto
      de habanera. NIN-CULMELL: Pano murciano; Asturiana. RODRIGO:
      Cancion del Grumete; De los alamos vengo madre; Trovadoresca.
      SCHUBERT: Lachen und Weinen, D 777; Mein. VALVERDE: Clavelitos.
      VAUGHAN WILLIAMS: The roadside fire. TRAD.: I will walk with my
      love; Blow the wind southerly (arr. Moore). ANON.: Una matica
      de ruda. Victoria de los Angeles, s; Gerald Moore, pno.
            ++Audio 3-80 p50   ++St 11-79 p90
            ++NYT 10-28-79 pD24

SZ 37560 (also HMV ASD 3810 Tape (c) TC ASD 3810, EMI 065 03645)
3552 BAZZINI: La ronde des lutins (Dance of the goblins), op. 25. CASTEL-
     NUOVO-TEDESCO: Tango (arr. Heifetz). DEBUSSY: Petite suite: En
     bateau (arr. Choisnel. FOSTER: Jeanie with the light brown hair
     (arr. Heifetz). GODOWSKY: Alt Wien (arr. Heifetz). PARADIS:
     Sicilienne (arr. Dushkin). RAFF: Cavatina, A flat major. STRAV-
     INSKY: Mavra: Chanson russe (arr. Dushkin). TCHAIKOVSKY: Souve-
     nir d'un lieu cher, op. 42: Melodie (arr. Flesch). VIEUXTEMPS:
     Souvenir d'Amerique, op. 7, no. 3. WIENIAWSKI: Mazurka, op. 19,
     no. 1. Polonaise brillante, no. 2, op. 21, A major. ANON.: Deep
     river (arr. Heifetz). Itzhak Perlman, vln; Samuel Sanders, pno.
              ++NR 4-80 p15   ++NYT 7-6-80 pD15
SZ 37676
3553 BIZET: Carmen: Et la garde descendante, La cloche a sonne...Dans l'
     air nous suivons. GOUNOD: Faust: Gloire immortelle de nos adieux.
     PUCCINI: Madama Butterfly: Humming chorus. Turandot: Perche tar-
     da la luna. VERDI: Aida: Gloria all egitto. Macbeth: Tre volte
     miagola. Nabucco: Va pensiero. Otello: Fuoco di gioia. Il tro-
     vatore: Vedi le fosche. WAGNER: Tannhauser: Freudig bergrussen.
     WEBBER: Der Freischutz: Was gleicht wohl auf Erden. Various
     choruses and orchestras.
              +NR 1-80 p10
SZ 37727 Tape (c) 4ZS 37727
3554 CHARPENTIER: Louise: Depuis le jour. DONIZETTI: Don Pasquale: Quel
     guardo il cavaliere...So anch'io la virtu magica. MASSENET:
     Thais: Ah je suis seule enfin...Dis-moi que je suis belle...Ah
     tais-toi voix impitovable. ROSSINI: Il barbiere di Siviglia:
     Ah se e ver...L'innocenza di Lindoro. Le siege de Corinth: Gius-
     to ciel, In tal pergiglio...Parmi vederlo ahi misero. VERDI:
     Rigoletto: Gualtier Malde...Caro nome. La traviata: Teneste la
     promessa...Addio del passato. Beverly Sills, s; Orchestral ac-
     companiment.
              +-ARG 10-80 p36   +-NR 4-80 p11
DS 37751
3555 ALBENIZ: Espana, op. 165: Tango (trans. Pourcel, Coignard). BACH:
     Siciliano (trans. Pourcel). BIZET: Carmen: Prelude. FALLA: El
     amor brujo: Ritual fire dance. GRIEG: Norwegian dance, no. 2
     (trans. Pourcel). MASCAGNI: Cavalleria rusticana: Intermezzo.
     MUSSORGSKY: Pictures at an exhibition: The great gate at Kiev.
     SATIE: Gymnopedie, nos. 1 and 3 (orch. Debussy). VERDI: I vespri
     siciliani: Overture. Franck Pourcel and His Orchestra.
              +-NR 8-80 p5
EAC 40070/9 (Japan) (10)
3556 BERLIOZ: Beatrice et Benedict: Overture. Benevenuto Cellini, op.
     23: Overture. Le carnaval romain, op. 9. Le Corsaire, op. 21.
     La damnation de Faust: Marche hongroise, Ballet de sylphes, Men-
     uet de follets. L'Enfance du Christ: Trio des jeunes. Romeo et
     Juliette, op. 17: Queen Mab scherzo. Les Troyens: Chasse royale
     et orage. DEBUSSY: Images pour orchestra: Gigues; Iberia; Rondes
     des printemps. Jeux. FRANCK: Les Djinns. Le chasseur maudit.
     Les Eolides. Redemption. RAVEL: Bolero. Daphnis et Chloe: Bal-
     let. Menuet antique. Miroirs: Alborada del gracioso; Une barque
     sur l'ocean. Ma mere l'oye: Ballet. Rapsodie espagnole. Le tom-
     beau de Couperin. Pavane pour une infante defunte. La valse.
     Valses nobles et sentimentales. ROUSSEL: Bacchus et Ariane, op.

43: Suite, no. 2. Le festin de l'araignee, op. 17. Sinfonietta, op. 52. Symphony, no. 3, op. 42, G minor. Symphony, no. 4, op. 53, A minor. WEBER: Invitation to the dance, op. 65. Orchestre National de la Radiodiffusion Francaise, OSCCP, Orchestre National de l'Opera, Orchestra National de l'Opera Comique, Orchestra National de Belgique; Orchestra; Andre Cluytens.
    +ARSC Vol 12, nos. 1-2, 1980 p78

EAC 47195/210 (Japan) (16)
3557 BIZET: L'Arlesienne: Suites, nos. 1 and 2. La jolie fille de Perth: Suite. Patrie overture. Symphony, C major. BERLIOZ: Symphonie fantastique, op. 14. DEBUSSY: La boite a joujoux. Children's corner. Le martyre de Saint Sebastian. DELIBES: Coppelia: Prelude, Act 1, Mazurka, Valse, Ballade de Epi, Theme slave varie, Valse de la poupee, Csardas. Sylvia: Prelude, Les chasseresses, Intermezzo, Valse lente, Pizzicati, Marche et cortege de Bacchus. FAURE: Requiem, op. 48. FRANCK: Psyche: Le sommeil de Psyche, Psyche enlevee par les zephyrs, Le jardin d'Eros, Psyche et Eros. Le chasseur maudit. Redemption. Symphony, D minor. Symphonic variations. d'INDY: Symphonie sur un chant montagnard Francais, op. 25. MASSENET: Les Erinnyes: Incidental music. Suites, orchestra: Scenes Alsaciennes, Scenes pittoresques. Phedre: Overture. RAVEL: Bolero. Daphnis et Chloe: Suites, nos. 1 and 2. L'Heure espagnole. Ma mere l'oye: Suite. Menuet antique. Miroirs: Alborada del gracioso. Pavane pour une infante defunte. Rapsodie espagnole. Le tombeau de Couperin. La valse. La valses nobles et sentimentales. SAINT-SAENS: Symphony, no. 3, op. 78, C minor. Martha Angelici, Mattiwilda Dobbs, Jacqueline Jourfier, Jacqueline Brumaire, Denise Duval, s; Rita Gorr, Solange Michel, con; Jean Giraudeau, Rene Herent, t; Jean Vieuille, Louis Noguera, bar; Charles Clavensy, bs; Aldo Ciccolini, Andre Collard, Monique Mercier, pno; Henriette Puig-Roget, Maurice Durufle, org; Henri Dionet, clt; Gaston Marchesini, vlc; Chanteurs de Saint Eustache; Orchestras; Andre Cluytens.
    +ARSC Vol 12, nos. 1-2, 1980 p78

ARABESQUE

8003 Tape (c) 9003 (From HMV originals)
3558 ADAM: Le postillon de Longjumeau: Mes amis ecoutez l'histoire. AUBER: Fra Diavolo: Pour toujours disait-elle. BEETHOVEN: Fidelio, op. 27: Gott welch Dunkel hier...In des Lebens Fruhlingstagen. LEHAR: Giuditta: Du bist miene Sonne; Freunde das Leben ist lebenswert. MOZART: Die Entfuhrung aus dem Serail, K 384: Hier soll ich dich denn sehen. STRAUSS, R.: Der Rosenkavalier, op. 59: Di rigori armato. TCHAIKOVSKY: Eugen Onegin, op. 24: Faint echo of my youth. WAGNER: Lohengrin: In fernem Land; Mein lieber Schwan. WEBER: Der Freischutz: Nein langer trag ich nicht ...Durch die Walder. Oberon: Seit fruhster Jugend; Du der diese Prufung schickt. Helge Roswange, t; Various accompaniments.
        +ARG 7/8-80 p48   +MUM 11/12-80 p35
        +-FF 11/12-80 p196   +NYT 1-6-80 pD18
        +-HF 10-80 p94

8013
3559 ADAM: Le toreador: Ah vous dirai-je Maman, variations. ALABIEV: The

nightingale. BENEDICT: Il carnevale di Venezi. DELIBES: Lakme:
Air des clochettes; Blanche Dourga; D'ou viens tu...C'est la
Dieu; Les filles de Cadiz. DONIZETTI: Lucia di Lammermoor: O
giusto cielo...Il dolce suono. La Zingara: Fra l'erbe cosparse.
OFFENBACH: Les contes d'Hoffman: Doll's song. PROCH: Air and
variations. ROSSINI: Il barbiere di Siviglia: Una voce poco fa.
Miliza Korjus, s.
> +ARG 6-80 p47   +NYT 1-6-80 pD18
> +-HF 7-80 p79

8027
3560 BROADWOOD: Birth of the flowers; The keys of heaven. DONIZETTI:
Lucrezia Borgia: Il segreto. DVORAK: Biblical songs, op. 99.
ELGAR: Dream of Gerontius, op. 35: Softly and gently. Sea pictures, op. 37: Where corals lie. Land of hope and glory. GLUCK:
Orfeo ed Euridice: Sposa Euridice...Che faro senza Euridice.
GOODHART: A fairy went a-marketing. HANDEL: Alessandro: Ne tri-
onfa d'Alessandro...Lusinghe...piu care. Sosarme: Rend'il sereno al ciglio. HATTON: The enchantress. HULLAH: Three fishers
went sailing. SULLIVAN: God shall wipe away all tears. Clara
Butt, con; Instrumental accompaniments.
> +NR 9-80 p8

8028 Tape (c) 9028 (From HMV originals)
3561 MOZART: Le nozze di Figaro, K 492: Porgi amor; Dove sono. STRAUSS,
R.: Arabella, op. 79: Ich mochte meinen fremden Mann; So wie Sie
sind. TCHAIKOVSKY: The sorceress: Mein los ist seltsam. VERDI:
Il trovatore: Tacea la notte; D'amor sull'ali rosee (in German).
WAGNER: Lohengrin: Das susse Lied verhalt. WEBER: Der Freischutz:
Wie nahte mir der Schlummer...Leise leise fromme Weise; Und ob
die Wolke. Tiana Lemnitz, s; Torsten Ralf, Helge Roswange, t;
Gerhard Husch, bar; Walter Lutz, vlc.
> +ARG 4-80 p47   +-HF 7-80 p78
> +FF 5/6-80 p179

8071
3562 BERKELEY: Poems of St. Teresa of Avila. BRITTEN: The rape of Lucretia, op. 37: Duet, Act 2. BRAHMS: Auf dem See, op. 59, no. 1.
Es Schauen die Blumen, op. 96, no. 3. Der Jager, op. 95, no. 4.
Ruhe Sussliebchen in Schatten. GLUCK: Orfeo ed Euridice: Che
faro senza Euridice. MOSS: The floral dance. PARRY: Love is a
bable. SCHUBERT: Rastlose Liebe, D 138; Wasserfluth. TRAD.:
The Spanish lady. "The early horn", excerpt from lecture-recital
July 28, 1955. Dennis Brain, Fr hn; Instrumental accompaniment.
> +NR 11-80 p8

ARGO

ZK 72/3 (2) Tape (c) KZKC 2 7063 (From ZRG 585, 699)
3563 ALBINONI: Concerto, trumpet, C major. ALBRECHTSBERGER: Concerto a
cinque, E flat major. FASCH: Concerto, trumpet, D major. HER-
TEL: Concerto a cinque, D major. HUMMEL: Concerto, trumpet, E
flat major. MOZART, L.: concerto, trumpet D major. TELEMANN:
Concerto, trumpet, D major. John Wilbraham, tpt; AMF; Neville
Marriner.
> +Gr 1-80 p1162   ++RR 1-80 p90
> +HFN 12-79 p179

ZK 92
3564 BACH, C.P.E.: Sonata, harp, G major (arr. Zingel). CAPLET: Diver-
tisssements. FLOTHUIS: Pour le tombeau d'Orphee. GURIDI: Viejo
zortzico. HOLLIGER: Sequenzen uber Johannes. SHERIFF: Mai ko
mashma lan. Emily Mitchell, hp; Kubbutz Chamber Orchestra; Noam
Sheriff.
           +HFN 8-80 p105   +RR 8-80 p37

ZRG 845 Tape (c) KZRC 845 (r) E 845
3565 BARBER: Quartet, strings, op. 11, B minor: Adagio. COPLAND: Quiet
city. COWELL: Hymn and fuguing tune, no. 10. CRESTON: A rumor.
IVES: Symphony, no. 3. Celia Nicklin, ob, cor anglais; Michael
Laird, tpt; AMF; Neville Marriner.
           ++Gr 7-76 p182   +—MT 2-77 p133
           ++Gr 11-76 p887 tape   ++NR 6-76 p5
           +—HF 10-76 p132   +NYT 7-4-76 pD1
           +HF 5-80 p90   +RR 7-76 p42
           +HFN 7-76 p84   ++St 10-76 p123
           +—MJ 7-76 p57

ZRG 870
3566 BRIAN: The Cenci: Fanfare (arr. MacDonald). BYRD: The Earl of
Salisbury pavan (arr. Wiggins). COPLAND: Ceremonial fanfare.
GERVAISE: Renaissance dances, nos. 1-6 (arr. Reeve). HOWARTH:
Processional fanfares (2). JOLIVET: Fanfares pour Britannicus:
Prelude. PURCELL: Trumpet tune (arr. Howarth). TIPPETT: Fan-
fare, brass. WALTON: The spitfire (arr. Howarth). ANON. (arr.
Howarth): Agincourt song. Greensleeves. Philip Jones Brass En-
semble.
           +ARG 9-79 p46   ++HFN 1-78 p121
           +Audio 6-78 p127   ++NR 3-80 p7
           ++FF 5/6-79 p127   +RR 1-78 p44
           ++Gr 1-78 p1258   +SFC 10-26-80 p20

ZRG 892
3567 ATTWOOD: Psalm, no. 98. DAVIES: Psalm, no. 121. SELBY: Psalm, no.
67. SKEATS: Psalm, no. 139. STANFORD: Psalms, nos. 95 and 150.
STEWART: Psalms, nos. 23, 39, 69, 90, 130. WALMISLEY: Psalm,
no. 49. WESLEY, S.: Psalm, no. 42. St. John's College Choir;
John Scott, org; George Guest.
           +FF 7/8-80 p163   +HFN 6-79 p111
           ++Gr 7-79 p243   ++RR 7-79 p111

ZRG 895 Tape (c) KZRC 895
3568 ABREU: Tico Tico (arr. Iveson). DEBUSSY: Le petit negre (arr. Emerson). HAZELL: Black Sam. Borage. Kraken. Mr. Jums. JOPLIN:
The easy winners. Ragtime dance (arr. Iveson). MONTI: Czardas
(arr. Jeames). MOZART: Serenade, no. 13, K 525, G major: Tuba
serenade (arr. Fletcher). PREMRU: Of nights and castles. Le
bateau sur Leman. Blues march. TRAD. (arr. Iveson): Frere Jacques. Philip Jones Brass Ensemble.
           ++Audio 6-79 p132   ++HFN 1-79 p125
           +FF 5/6-80 p197   ++HFN 2-79 p118 tape
           +Gr 1-79 p1334   ++RR 12-78 p58

ZRG 898 Tape (c) KZRC 898
3569 BACH, C.P.E.: March (arr. Jones). BACH, J.S.: Capriccio, S 992, B
flat major: Postillion's aria and fugue in imitation of the postillion's horn (arr. Breuer). Cantata, no. 79, Gott der Herr ist
Sonn und Schild (arr. Reeve). Suite, solo violoncello, no. 1, S

1007, G major: Menuetto and courante (arr. Fletcher). BIBER:
Sonata a 7 (arr. Hazell). FRANCK: Intrada (arr. Jones). HASS:
LER: Intrada a 5 (arr. Epps). SCARLATTI, D.: Sonatas, harpsichord, Kk 380, 430, 443 (arr. Dodgson). SCHEIDT: Canzona a 10
(arr. Jones). SPEER: Sonatas, nos. 1-4. ANON.: Die Bankelsangerlieder: Sonata (edit. King). Philips Jones Brass Ensemble.

    +Audio 12-79 p100   ++Gr 10-79 p727 tape
    ++FU 1/2-80 p173   +HFN 6-79 p113
    +-FU 5-80 p46   ++RR 6-79 p71
    +Gr 8-79 p348

ZRG 900 Tape (c) KZRC 900
3570 The play of Daniel. Pro Cantione Antiqua, Landini Consort.

    +FF 5/6-80 p182   +MT 1-80 p36
    +Gr 7-79 p234   ++NYT 8-17-80 pD20
    +Gr 9-79 p534 tape   +RR 9-79 p124
    +HF 1-80 p65   +St 1-80 p110
    ++HFN 7-79 p113

ZRG 912 Tape (c) KZRC 912
3571 BLISS: Fanfare for the Lord Mayor of London. BOURGEOIS: Wine symphony: Hock theme. BRITTEN: The eagle has two heads. Russian
funeral. CASALS: O vos omnes (trans. Stokowski). COPLAND: Fanfare for the common man. FRANCK: Piece heroique (trans. Fuller).
JANACEK: Sinfonietta: Allegretto. STRAUSS, R.: Festmusik der
Stadt Wien. TOMASI: Fanfares liturgiques: Procession du Vendredi-
Saint. UHL: Festfanfare. Philip Jonees Brass Ensemble.

    +Gr 3-80 p1398   +RR 3-80 p64
    +HFN 3-80 p103

ZRG 914
3572 Christmas songs: Child in a manger; Cradle song; The crown of roses;
Ding dong merrily on high; Donkey carol; Gabriel's message; I saw
a maiden; I saw three ships; In dulci jubilo; In the bleak midwinter; Jesus Christ the apple tree; The holly and the ivy; King
Jesus had a garden; Mary's lullaby; The noble stem of Jesse; Om-
nis mundus jocundetur; Quelle est cette odeur agreable; Up good
Christian folk and lis'en; Wassail song. Clare College, Cambridge, Orchestra and Chorus; John Rutter.

    +-FF 11/12-80 p200   +RR 12-79 p108
    +HFN 12-79 p173

ZRG 925
3573 BEETHOVEN: Aus Goethes Faust, op. 75, no. 3; Ich liebe dich, WoO
123. BRAHMS: Auf den Kirchhofe, op. 105, no. 4; Die Mainacht,
op. 43, no. 2. LISZT: Die drei Zigeuner, G 320. LOEWE: Edward,
op. 1, no. 1. MAHLER: Des Knaben Wunderhorn: Lob des honen Ver-
standes. MENDELSSOHN: Auf Flugeln des Gesanges, op. 34, no. 2.
SCHUBERT: Erlkonig, D 328; Wanderers Nachtlied, D 768. SCHUMANN:
Die beiden Grenadiere, op. 49, no. 1; Die Lotosblume, op. 25, no.
7. STRAUSS, R.: Allerseelen, op. 10, no. 8. WOLF: Morike Lieder: Gebet; Fussreise. Benjamin Luxon, bar; David Willison, pno.

    ++Gr 7-80 p161   +RR 7-80 p86
    +HFN 7-80 p113   +STL 9-14-80 p40

ARION

ARION 34348
3574 Gregorian chant: Noel Provencal. Provence of the Abbey Saint-Victor

Musicians.
            +ARG 12-77 p55   +RR 3-80 p32
38213
3575 Gregorian chants: Hymns, Graduals, Alleluias, Sequences, Offertor-
     ies, and Responsories for the Immaculate Conception and the Nat-
     ivity, the Annunciation, the Motherhood, the Compassion and the
     Assumption. Kergonan Abbey Choir; Dom Le Feuvre.
            +Gr 7-74 p270   +RR 3-80 p32
            +RR 3-74 p63

ARN 38470
3576 Gregorian chants: La nativite: Chants Gregoriens et Chants polyphon-
     iques. Louvain Chorale Concinite; Karel Aerts.
            +RR 3-80 p32

ARN 336 018 (3)
3577 BACH: Fugue, S 1000, G minor. Prelude, fugue and allegro, S 998,
     E flat major. Suite, lute, S 995, G minor. BATCHELAR: Mounsier's
     almayn. DOWLAND: Dowland's first galliard. Fantasias (2). The
     frog galliard. King of Denmark his galliard. Queen Elizabeth
     her galliard. Mr. John Langton's pavan. Sir John Smith's al-
     maine. Tarleton's riserrectione. MELII DA REGGIO: Capriccio
     cromatico. Capriccio detto "Il gran Matias". MILAN: Fantasia
     de redobles. Tento, no. 4. MILANO: Ricercare, nos. 1 and 2.
     Ricercare "La campagna". MUDARRA: Diferencias sobre el Conde
     claros (12). Fantasia que contrahace la harpa en la manera de
     Ludovico. Pavana. Pavana de Aleixandre y gallarda. NARVAEZ:
     Baxa de contrapunto. Cancion del Emperador. Diferencias sobre
     "El Conde claros (22). Diferencias sobre "El guardame las vacas"
     (7). ROBINSON: A gigue. A toye. SANZ: La cavalleria de Napoles
     con dos clarines. Folias. Fuga al ayre de giga. Fuga del pri-
     mer tono. Gallardas. La esfachata de Napoles. Giga al ayre
     de giga. Maricapalos. La minona de Cataluna. Paradetas. Pas-
     sacalles por la L, por el 2 bemolado y por primer tono punto bajo.
     Passacalles por la C, por cruzado y por quinto tono punto alto.
     Pavana. Preludio o capricho arpeado por la cruz. Rujero. Ses-
     quialtera. VISEE: Variations sur les Folies d'Espagne (6).
     WEISS: Fantasie. Rodrigo de Zayas, lt, theorbo, vihuela, gtr.
            +-Gr 3-80 p1423   +RR 3-80 p211

ARN 30A051
3578 Chants a la Cour de Charles Quint. Ana Maria Miranda, Le Groupe d'
     Instruments Anciens de Paris; Roger Cotte.
            +RR 3-80 p32

ARN 30A066
3579 Gregorian chants. Kergonan Abbey Monks Choir.
            +RR 3-80 p32

ARN 30A134
3580 Gregorian chants: Dans la joie de Paques. Kergonan Abbey Monks
     Choir.
            +RR 3-80 p32

                              AUDICOM

KM 1824
3581 BERLIOZ: Le carnival romain, op. 9. DELIUS: A village Romeo and
     Juliet: Walk into paradise garden. DVORAK: Symphony, no. 9, op.

95, E minor. RACHMANINOFF: Symphony, no. 2, op. 27, E minor.
ROSSINI: La cenerentola: Overture. TCHAIKOVSKY: Symphony, no. 4,
op. 36, F minor; Finale. WEBER: Concerto, clarinet, no. 2, op.
74, E flat major. John Mohler, clt; Morehead State University
Summer Music Camp Faculty; Gunnison, Colorado Summer Music Camp
Faculty; Robert Hawkins.
        ++IN 4-80 p14

AURORA

AUR 5055
3582 BOELLMANN: Suite gothique, op. 25: Toccata (arr. Curley). CAMIDGE:
    Gavotte (arr. Curley). DAVIES: Interlude, C major. GOUNOD: Sor-
    tie (arr. Curley). PURCELL: Trumpet tune and air (arr. Curley).
    SAINT-SAENS: Suite Algerienne, op. 60: Marche militaire fran-
    caise (arr. Curley). STANLEY: Introduction and trumpet tune
    (arr. Curley). VIERNE: Pieces en style libre, op. 31: Berceuse;
    Carillon de Longport. Symphony, no. 2, op. 20, E minor: Allegro.
    Carlo Curley, org.
        +-Gr 10-79 p724   +-RR 1-80 p103
        +-HFN 2-80 p103

BARBIROLLI SOCIETY

BS 03
3583 GIBBONS: Fantasias, nos. 3, 9. LOEILLET: Trio, oboe, violin and
    violoncello, B minor. POPPER: Duet, violoncello. PURCELL: Fan-
    tasia, C minor. Fantasia upon one note. VAUGHAN WILLIAMS: Fan-
    tasy quintet. Evelyn Rothwell Barbirolli, ob; Dorothy Kennedy,
    vln; John Barbirolli, Lauri Kennedy, vlc; Jean Pougnet, vla.
        +-ARG 2-80 p46

BASF

KBF 21490 (2) (also Acanta DE 21490)
3584 FLOTOW: Martha: Letze Rose...Mein Los mit Dir zu Teilen; Die Herrin
    rastet dort...Mag der Himmel Euch vergeben; Der Lenz ist gekom-
    men...Diese Hand die sich gewendet. GLUCK: Orfeo ed Euridice:
    Quest'asilo ameno e grato; Che fiero momento. HUMPERDINCK: Han-
    sel und Gretel: Suse liebe Suse...Bruderchen komm tanz mit mir.
    MOZART: Die Entfuhrung aus dem Serail, K 384: Welcher Kummer
    herrscht in meiner Selle...Traurigkeit ward mir zum Lose; Mar-
    tern aller Arten. Die Zauberflote, K 620: Der Holle rache kocht
    in meinem Herzen. OFFENBACH: Les contes d'Hoffmann: Sie entfloh
    die Taube so minnig, Hoffmann; Antonia...Ich wusst es ja Du lieb-
    est mich noch. STRAUSS, R.: Ariadne auf Naxos, op. 60: Gross-
    machtige Prinzessin. Der Rosenkavalier, op. 59: Ist ein Traum.
    VERDI: Rigoletto: Tochter...Mein Vater; Gualtier Malde...Tuerer
    Name dessen Klang; Wer ist statt hier im Sacke. Erna Berger,
    Tiana Lemnitz, s; Margarete Klose, con; Peter Anders, Helge Ros-
    wange, t; Josef Greindl, bs; Heinrich Schlussnus, bar; Various
    accompaniments.

+HF 9-74 p104   ++HR 2-74 p10
+HFN 5-80 p127   +ON 12-8-73 p60

BBC

<u>4001</u> (4) Tape (c) ZCBBC 4001 (From HMV DB 1934/5, 3257/9, 2795/6, 2191/3,
        333/7, 2253/7)
3585 BEETHOVEN: Symphony, no. 6, op. 68, F major. BERLIOZ: King Lear,
        op. 4. BLISS: Music for strings. BRAHMS: Symphony, no. 4, op.
        98, E minor. ELGAR: Cockaigne overture, op. 40. MOZART: Sym-
        phony, no. 36, K 425, C major. SIBELIUS: Night ride and sunrise,
        op. 55. VAUGHAN WILLIAMS: Fantasia on a theme by Thomas Tallis.
        BBC Symphony Orchestra; Bruno Walter, Adrian Boult, Arturo Tos-
        canini, Fritz Busch.
                +Gr 8-80 p233   +RR 8-80 p58

BIS

<u>LP 89</u>
3586 KOKKONEN: Evenings. KUUSISTO: Finnish husbandry. MADEJOTA: Come
        with me, op. 9, no. 3; Dark herbs, op. 9, no. 1; Since you left
        me, op. 2, no. 1; Swing swing, op. 60, no. 1; You thought I was
        watching you, op. 68, no. 3. PYLKKANEN: The swan of death, op.
        21. SALLINEN: Dream songs (4). Taru Valjakka, s; Ralf Gothoni,
        pno.
                +-HF 10-79 p122   +HFN 4-80 p112
<u>LP 102</u>
3587 HOLMBOE: Benedic domino, op. 59. JEPPESEN: Fjorden. JERSILD: Kaer-
        lighedsrosen. LEWKOVITCH: Madrigali di Torquato Tasso, op. 13.
        Tidligt forar. NIELSEN: Motets, op. 55 (3). RIISAGER: Snevind.
        SCHULTZ: Dansevise. Midsommervise. Kammerkoret Camerata; Per
        Enevold.
                +MUM 7/8-79 p36   +RR 3-80 p92
<u>LP 122</u>
3588 ARNOLD: Fantasy, op. 86. BOUTRY: Interference, bassoon and piano.
        BLOMDAHL: Little suite, bassoon and piano. HINDEMITH: Sonata,
        bassoon and piano. TANSMAN: Sonatina, bassoon and piano. VON
        KOCH: Monolog, no. 5. Knut Sonstevold, bsn; Eva Knardahl, pno.
                -FF 5/6-80 p194   ++NR 2-80 p7
                +-HFN 4-80 p116   +RR 4-80 p103
<u>LP 125</u>
3589 BACH: Suite, orchestra, S 1068, D major: Air. GRIEG: Varen (Spring).
        MOZART: Andante, K 315, C major. RACHMANINOFF: Vocalise, op. 34,
        no. 14. SOMMERFELDT: Varlater (Spring tunes), op. 44. VIVALDI:
        Concerto, piccolo, RV 444/P78, C major. VON KOCH: Cantilena, op.
        78. Gunilla von Bahr, flt; Roland Ostblom, org; Hans Fagius,
        org; Stockholm Chamber Ensemble; Jan-Olav Wedin.
                +-FF 3/4-80 p183   +-RR 7-79 p79
                +HFN 8-79 p119
<u>LP 126</u>
3590 AMMERBACH: Ich sag ade. ATTAIGNANT: Gaillard. CABEZON: Ave maris-
        stela. CARLETON: Praeludium. FACOLI: Padoana terza dita la fin-
        etta. Aria della comedia nuovo. Hor ch'io son gionto quivi. S'io

m'accorgo ben mio. GERLE: Ach Elslein, liebes Elselein. KLEBER:
Die Brunnlein die da fliessen. Zucht Ehr und Lob. LOFFELHOLTZ:
Es het ein Baur sein freylein vorlohren. Die kleine Schacht.
NORMIGER: Tantz Adelich und from. Viel Freuden mit sich bringet.
Von Gott will ich nicht lassen. PAIX: Der Keyserin Tantz. PEER-
SON: The fall of the leaf. The primrose. SCHMID: Alemando nov-
elle: Ein guter neuer Dantz. Der Imperial: Ein Furtlicher Hof-
dantz; Ein schoner Englisher Dantz; Wie schon Bluet uns der Maye.
ANON.: Entlaubet ist der Walde. Ich armes Kauzlein kleine. My
delyght. The nightingale. The Scots marche. Wanton season a
galyarde. Lena Jackson, org.

      -ARG 11-80 p39   +-NR 4-80 p14
    +-FF 9/10-80 p271   +-RR 8-80 p68
    +HFN 7-80 p113

LP 130
3591 BACH: Chorale preludes, S 599, Nun komm der Heiden Heiland; S 600,
    Gottes Sohn ist kommen; S 601, Herr Jesu Christ der ein'ge Gottes
    Sohn; S 603, Puer natus in Bethlehem; S 604, Gelobet seist du
    Jesu Christ; S 606, Vom Himmel hoch da komm ich her; S 607, Vom
    Himmel kam der Engel Schar; S 608, In dulci jubilo. DAQUIN: Liv-
    re de Noels: Noel etranger, Noel en trio et en dialogue, Noel
    grand jeu et duo. DUPRE: Variations sur un Noel, op. 20. PEPPING:
    Bearbeitungen uber Vom Himmel hoch da komm ich her. REGER: Pie-
    ces, organ, op. 145: Weihnachten. Hans Fagius, org.

       +-HFN 4-80 p117   +-NR 12-79 p2

LP 132
3592 BACH: Nain Jeesusta vain; Puer natus in Bethlehem. HANDEL: Rie-
    muitse tytar Siionin. PRAETORIUS: Veisatkaa. SIBELIUS: On han-
    gel korkeat nietokset, op. 1, no. 5. ANON.: Heinilla harkien
    kaukalon; Joudu satakiel; Maria Herran piikanen; The snow is
    falling. Tapiola Choir; Erkki Pohjola.

       +-HFN 4-80 p112   ++NR 12-79 p2

LP 135
3593 DOWLAND: Lacrimae pavan. FERRABOSCO: Pavane. HANDEL: Sonata, re-
    corder, A minor. MILANO: Ricercare. ORTIZ: Recercada, nos. 2
    and 4. Recercada felici occhi mei. TELEMANN: Sonata, recorder,
    C major. VAN EYCK: Amarilli mia bella. Engels Nachtgaeltje.
    Variations on "De-Lof-Zangh Marie". ANON.: Greensleeves to a
    ground. Clas Pehrsson, rec; Cecilia Peijel, gtr.

       +ARG 11-80 p39   ++NR 7-80 p7
       +-HFN 7-80 p115   +RR 8-80 p64

LP 140
3594 FAURE: Fantasy, op. 79. MESSIAEN: Le merle noir. POULENC: Sonata,
    flute and piano. RHENE-BATON: Passacaille, op. 35. ROUSSEL:
    Joueurs de flute, op. 27. Gunilla von Bahr, flt; Dag Achatz, pno.

       +FF 9/10-80 p281   +NR 4-80 p8
       +HFN 11-80 p127   +RR 3-80 p80

LP 141
3595 BYRD: Fantasia, C major. Prelude. Miserere. GIBBONS: Ground.
    A voluntary. KEEBLE: Double fugue, C major. PURCELL: Voluntary
    on the old 100th. TALLIS: Fantasia. Hymns: Es more docti mis-
    tico; Iam lucis orto sidere. WALOND: Voluntary, no. 5, G major.
    WESLEY, S.: Pieces, organ, nos. 6, 8-9, 11-12. WESLEY, S.S.:
    Choral song and fugue, C major. Hans Fagius, org.

       +-FF 5/6-80 p189   ++NR 2-80 p13

+Gr 8-80 p247   +RR 3-80 p77
+-HFN 4-80 p117

BONGIOVANNI

GB 9
3596 BELLINI: Almen se non poss'io; Malinconia ninfa gentile; Vaga luna
     che inargenti. DONIZETTI: Anna Bolena: Al dolce guidame. Luc-
     rezia Borgia: Com'e bello. FAURE: Apres un reve, op. 7, no. 1.
     PUCCINI: La rondine: Chi il bel sogno. Tosca: Vissi d'arte.
     Turandot: Tu che di gel sei cinta. RAVEL: Vocalise en forme de
     habanera. TURINA: Cantares, op. 19, no. 3. VERDI: La forza del
     destino: Pace pace mio Dio. Katia Ricciarelli, s; Luciano Sil-
     vestri, pno.
          +-Gr 11-80 p736

CALLIOPE

CAL 101
3597 BANCHIERI: Fantasia terza decima. GESUALDO: Gagliarda. GHIZEGHEM:
     De tous biens playne (2). GUAMI: Ricercar. ISAAC: Wolauff.
     HANART: Le serviteur. LAPPI: La serafina. Fanfare. RUFFO: La
     gamba. La disparata. SUSATO: Bergerette. Galliarde. Hoboec-
     kentanz. Pavane. Mon ami, ronde. ANON.: La cornetta. De tous
     biens playne (2). La gamba. Mon ami. Paduana del re. Salta-
     rello. Le serviteur. Sur le Pont d'Avignon. Weit guy. Calli-
     ope Renaissance Band.
          +ARG 6-79 p42   +NYT 8-10-80 pD17
          +-Audio 9-79 p100   +St 10-79 p150

CAPRICE

CAP 1176
3598 HAMBRAEUS: Mikrogram. HERMANSON: Stadier, op. 5. MAROS: Oolit.
     SANDSTROM: Out of. SVEINSSON: Aria. Maros Ensemble; Miklos
     Maros.
          ++FF 11/12-80 p219   +NR 10-80 p6

CAVATA

CV 5011
3599 BROUWER: Canticum. Danza caracteristica. Elogio de la danza.
     RODRIGO: Pequenas piezas (3). SMITH-BRINDLE: El polifemo de
     oro. VAN: Elegy (Homage to Falla). VILLA-LOBOS: Etudes, nos.
     11-12. Jeffrey Van, gtr.
          +FF 5/6-80 p186   ++St 9-80 p87
CV 5012
3600 BEVILACQUA: Canzonette veneziane (3). BOTTEGARI: Morte da me Tant
     aspettata; Zefiro torna. CACCINI: Amarilli mia bella. CAMPIAN:
     Sweet exclude me not. CORKINE: Beauty sat bathing. DOWLAND:
     Can she excuse. FALLA: Homage a Debussy. MILAN: Pavan, no. 1.

RODRIGO: Canciones espanoles (3). ROSSETER: When Laura smiles.
SOR: Minuet, op. 5, no. 3, C major. Minuet, op. 24, no. 1, C
minor. VILLA-LOBOS: Bachianas brasileiras, no. 5: Aria. Modin-
ha. VISEE: Passacaille. Vern Sutton, t; Jeffrey Van, gtr.
    +FF 11/12-80 p199

                                CBS

M 35838 Tape (c) MT 35838
3601 BEETHOVEN: Deutsche Tanze, WoO 42 (6). BRAHMS: Hungarian dance, no.
    5, G minor (arr. Joachim). FIBICH: Poeme (arr. Kubelik). FISCH-
    ER: Amoroso. DINICU: Hora staccato (arr. Heifetz). KHANDOSHKIN:
    Sentimental aria (arr. Yampolsky). KREISLER: March miniature
    Viennoise. LISZT: La lugubre gondola, G 200. MUSSORGSKY: Songs
    and dances of death: Trepak (arr. Rachmaninoff). PAGANINI: Cap-
    rice, op. 1, no. 14, E flat major (arr. Schumann). SCHUBERT: Der
    Erlkonig, D 328 (trans. Ernst). SHOSTAKOVICH: Prelude, op. 34,
    no. 17, A flat major (arr. Tsyganov). TCHAIKOVSKY: Melodie, op.
    42, no. 3. VIEUXTEMPS: Romance, op. 7, no. 2. Gidon Kremer,
    vln; Oleg Maisenberg, pno.
                +-St 11-80 p104
M 35853
3602 ALBINONI: Adagio, G minor. BACH: Cantata, no. 147, Jesu joy of man's
    desiring. Cantata, no. 140: Sleepers awake. Suite, orchestra, S
    1068, D major: Air on the G string. CIMAROSA: Concerto, guitar,
    D major. MARCELLO, A.: Concerto, guitar, D minor. VIVALDI: Con-
    certo, RV 93, D major. Liona Boyd, gtr; ECO; Andrew Davis.
                -FF 9/10-80 p278
M 35857
3603 ALBENIZ (Lagoya): Suite espanola, op. 47: Cadiz. PUJOL VILARRUBI:
    Guajira. RODRIGO: Nocturne. Prelude. Scherzino. TARREGA: Et-
    ude (Dream). Grand waltz. Introduction and variations on the
    theme "Carnival in Venice". Two little sisters. Waltz. TOR-
    ROBA: Torija. Alexandre Lagoya, gtr.
                +FF 9/10-80 p275
M 35861
3604 DEBUSSY: Jeux, excerpts. Prelude to the afternoon of a faun.
    RIMSKY-KORSAKOV: Scheherazade, op. 35, excerpts. SCHUMANN:
    Carnaval, op. 9, excerpts. STRAVINSKY: Petrouchka, excerpts.
    Le sacre du printemps, excerpts. WEBER: Invitation to the dance,
    op. 65. Charles Rosen, pno; NYP, NPhO, Columbia Symphony Orches-
    tra; Leonard Bernstein, Pierre Boulez, Zubin Mehta, Igor Stravin-
    sky.
                +-ARG 12-80 p52
61885 Tape (c) 40-61885
3605 ADDINSELL: Warsaw concerto. BOCCHERINI: Minuet. BRAHMS: Symphony,
    no. 3, op. 90, F major: 3rd movement. CHOPIN: Waltz, op. 34, no.
    1, A flat major. DEBUSSY: Suite bergamasque: Clair de lune (arr.
    Caillet). DELIBES: Sylvia: Pizzicato divertissement, Act 3.
    GRIEG: Peer Gynt, op. 46: Morning. PROKOFIEV: Lieutenant Kije,
    op. 60: Troika. RACHAMANINOFF: Vocalise, op. 34, no. 14. SHOS-
    TAKOVICH: Concerto, piano, no. 2, op. 10, F major: 2nd movement.
    TCHAIKOVSKY: Sleeping beauty, op. 66: Rose adagio, Act 1. Leo-
    nard Bernstein, Ivan Davis, Philippe Entremont, pno; NYP, PO,

Orchestra; Leonard Bernstein, Eugene Ormandy, Andre Kostelanetz.
        +Gr 3-80 p1449   +HFN 6-80 p119 tape
        +HFN 3-80 p105   +-RR 3-80 p59

<u>61889</u> Tape (c) 40-61889
3606 COOLEY: Aria and dance. FAURE: Elegie, op. 24, C minor. GUILMANT:
        Morceau symphonique, op. 88. RUSAGER: Concertino, op. 29.
        SAINT-SAENS: Morceau de concert, op. 94 (orch. version). SARA-
        SATE: Introduction and tarantelle, op. 43. VANHAL: Concerto,
        double bass, E major: Allegro moderato. Anshel Brusilow, vln;
        Carlton Cooley, vla; Lorne Monroe, vlc; Roger Scott, bs; Gilbert
        Johnson, tpt; Mason Jones, hn; Henry Smith, trom; PO; Eugene Or-
        mandy
                +Gr 5-80 p1718   +RR 5-80 p69
                +-HFN 5-80 p131

<u>73879</u>
3607 ALBENIZ: Suite espanola, op. 47: Granada; Asturias. BARNES: Fant-
        asy. BARRIOS: Cancion de la hilandera. Waltz, op. 8, no. 4.
        DEBUSSY: The little shepherd. PAYET: Cabellos de oro. Lejania.
        SATIE: Gymnopedie, no. 1. SOR: Waltzes, nos. 1-3. TARREGA: Re-
        cuerdos de la Alhambra. Liona Boyd, gtr.
                ++HFN 1-80 p117   /+RR 2-80 p68

<u>73885</u>
3608 DEBUSSY: Jeux, excerpts. Prelude a l'apres-midi d-un faune. RIMSKY-
        KORSAKOV: Scheherazade, excerpts. SCHUMANN: Carnaval, op. 9, ex-
        cerpts. STRAVINSKY: Petrouchka, excerpts. Le sacre du printemps,
        excerpts. WEBER (orch. Berlioz): Invitation to the dance, op.
        65. NYP, NPhO, Columbia Symphony Orchestra; Charles Rosen, pno;
        Leonard Bernstein, Pierre Boulez, Zubin Mehta.
                +-HFN 7-80 p114

<u>73902</u>
3609 ALBENIZ, I.: Suite espanola, op. 47: Granada, Sevilla, Castilla.
        BARRIOS: Danza de la gitana. FALLA: El sombrero de tres picos:
        Miller's dance. GRANADOS: Danzas espanolas, op. 37: Oriental.
        HALFFTER: Danza de la pastora. SOR: Divertissement, no. 1.
        Albeniz Trio
                +Gr 10-80 p517   +HFN 10-80 p111

<u>76859</u> Tape (c) 40-76859
3610 BOISMORTIER: L'Hyver: Cantata, no. 4. CAMPRA: Tancrede: Suite. HAN-
        DEL: Concerto, oboe, G minor. MOURET: Symphonies de chasse.
        MOZART, L.: Sinfonia pastorella, A major. Sophie Boulin, s;
        Michel Henby, ob; Andre Both, Michel Garcin-Marrou, hn; Le Grande
        Ecurie et la Chambre du Roy; Jean-Claude Malgoire.
                +-Gr 3-80 p1398   ++HFN 11-80 p131 tape
                +HFN 3-80 p103   +MT 11-80 p709

<u>76868</u> Tape (c) 40-76868
3611 DUPARC: Au pays ou se fait la guerre; L'invitation au voyage; Le
        manoir. FAURE: Apres un reve, op. 7, no. 1; Nell, op. 18, no. 1.
        SCHUBERT: Gretchen am Spinnrade, D 118; Nacht und Traume, D 827;
        Rastlose Liebe, D 138. SCHUMANN: Myrthen, op. 25: Du bist wie
        eine Blume. Zwolf Gedichte, op. 35: Stille Tranen; Soldaten-
        braut. WALTON: Daphne; Old Sir Faulk; Through gilded trellises.
        WOLF: Blumengruss. Kiri Te Kanawa, s; Richard Amner, pno.
                +-Gr 11-79 p899   +HFN 2-80 p107 tape
                +Gr 2-80 p1302 tape   +-RR 1-80 p108
                +Gr 9-80 p413 tape   +STL 12-2-79 p37
                +HFN 12-79 p173

<u>79334</u> (3) Tape (c) 40-79334 (From 72798, 76369, 72661, 76634)
3612 CASTELNUOVO-TEDESCO: Concerto, guitar, no. 1, op. 99, D major.
     GIULIANI: Concerto, guitar, op. 30, A major. RODRIGO: Concierto
     de Aranjeuz. Fantasia para un gentilhombre. VILLA-LOBOS: Con-
     certo, guitar. VIVALDI: Concerti, guitar, D major, A major.
     John Williams, gtr; ECO; Charles Groves, Daniel Barenboim.
           +Gr 11-80 p683   +HFN 11-80 p129

                            CEZAME

<u>CEZ 1036</u>
3613 ADRIENSSEN: Fantasie. ATTAIGNANT: La guerre. La Magdalena. BAL-
     LARD: Ballet de Monsieur le Dauphin. Branles de village. COR-
     OSO: Bassa savella. FERRABOSCO: Pavane. HUWET: Fantasie. LE
     ROY: Ricercare la campagna. NEUSIDLER: Danse washa mesa. Mon
     coeur s'est d'amour rempli. Preambule et danse du plectre.
     ANON.: Italiana. Io m'accorgo d'un altro amante. Passemezzo.
     Arnaud Dumond, gtr.
           -RR 8-80 p36
<u>CEZ 1048</u>
3614 ACHAVAL: Milonga del andariego. BARRIOS: La catedral. Danza para-
     gaya. BROUWER: Danza caracteristica. LAURO: Prelude. Valse
     angostura. Valses, nos. 2 and 3. PERNAMBUCO: Sons de carril-
     hoes. SAVIO: Nesta rua. VILLA-LOBOS: Choro, no. 1, E minor:
     Prelude, no. 1. Arnaud Dumond, gtr.
           +-RR 7-80 p74

                            CHALFONT

<u>SDG 203</u>
3615 BACH: Fugue, S 577, G major. Toccata and fugue, S 565, D minor.
     CLARKE: Trumpet voluntary, D minor. MOZART: Fantasia, K 608, F
     minor. PIERNE: Scherzando. WIDOR: Symphony, organ, no. 5, op.
     42, no. 1, F minor: Toccata. Symphony, organ, no. 6, op. 42, no.
     2, G major: Finale. Carlo Curley, org.
           +-ARG 4-80 p51   +-RR 5-80 p85
<u>SDG 303</u>
3616 BACH: Fugue, S 577, G major. Toccata and fugue, S 565, D minor.
     CLARKE: Trumpet voluntary (arr. Curley). MOZART: Fantasia, K
     608, F minor. PIERNE: Scherzando (arr. Curley). WIDOR: Symphony,
     organ, no. 5, op. 42, no. 1, F major: Toccata. Symphony, organ,
     no. 6, op. 42, no. 2: Finale. Carlo Curley, digital computer
     organ.
           -FF 11/12-79 p14   +HFN 4-80 p117
           +-Gr 4-80 p1597   +St 10-79 p92
<u>C 77004</u>
3617 ALFORD: Old Panama. BIGELOW: Our director. DONAJOWSKY (Dunn):
     The Preobrajensky march. DUNN: The Mountbatten march. HALL:
     The new colonial. LANGFORD: Famous British marches. Marching
     with Sousa. Prince of Wales march. MANSFIELD: The red cloak.
     MATT (Godfrey): Fame and glory. STANLEY: The contemptibles.
     WILLIAMS: Blue devil. Royal Marines Band; J. R. Mason
           +FF 1/2-80 p180

C 77007
3618 BACH, C.P.E.: Fantasia and fugue, C minor. CAMIDGE (ed. Trevor):
Gavotte. DANDRIEU (arr. Thalben-Ball): La musette. DUBOIS:
Fiat lux. FESTING (arr. Thalben-Ball): Largo, allegro, aria and
2 variations. GIGOUT: Grand choeur dialogue. JOUBERT: Prelude
on "Picardy". REGER: Praise the Lord, chorale. STANLEY (arr.
Thalben-Ball): Minuet, D major. Trumpet tune. WESLEY: Holsworthy
church bells. George Thalben-Ball, org.
+−Audio 2-80 p93   +MU 9-78 p15
+−FF 11/12-79 p162   +−NR 10-78 p14

C 77008
3619 COATES (Duthoit): The seven seas. The dambusters (Mair). DUNN:
The captain general. HESPE: King o' the clouds. ISAAC: Warship
theme. LOFFLER: Ad astra. HOOD: The Nelson touch. ORD HUME:
The royal marine. SOUSA (Langford): Liberty bell. STOVIN (Bradford): Flying stations. ZEHLE (Hewitt): Army and Marine. Traf-
algar. Royal Marines Band; J. R. Mason.
+FF 1/2-80 p181

CHANDOS

BBR 1004 Tape (c) BBT 1004
3620 CALVERT: Introduction, elegy and caprice. GREGSON: Connotations.
HUBER: Symphonic music. SIMPSON: Volcano. VINTER: John O'Gaunt.
Black Dyke Mills Band; Peter Parkes.
+Gr 6-80 p69   +RR 6-80 p59

BBR 1005
3621 ALBENIZ: Iberia: Carnival in Seville (arr. Newsome). BERLIOZ: Le
carnaval romain, op. 9 (arr. Wright). DVORAK: Carnival over-
ture, op. 92 (arr. Newsome). SAINT-SAENS: Carnival of the animals:
Suite (arr. Langford). PERKIN: Carnival suite: Burlesque. VIN-
TER: Lisbon carnival. Sun Life Stanshaw Band; Brian Howard, Roy
Newsome.
−RR 8-80 p38

DBR 3001 (3)
3622 BALAKIREV: Islamey. BARBER: Sonata, piano, op. 26, E minor. CHOPIN:
Nocturne, op. 32, no. 1, B major. GINASTERA: Sonata, piano.
HAYDN: sonata, no. 33, C minor. LIADOV: Musical snuff-box, op.
32. LISZT: Annees de pelerinage, 2nd year, G 161: Sposalizio;
Supplement, G 162. Annees de pelerinage, 3rd year, G 163: Les
jeux d'eaux a la Villa d'Este. Hungarian rhapsody, no. 11, G
244, A minor. PROKOFIEV: Pieces, piano, op. 4, no. 4: Suggestion diabolique. RAVEL: Miroirs: Noctuelles; Oiseaux tristes;
La vallee des cloches. SCARLATTI: Sonata, harpsichord, Kk 39, A
major. TCHAIKOVSKY: Pieces, piano, op. 19, no. 6, F major: Theme
and variations. The months, op. 37: January. Terence Judd, pno.
+Gr 12-80 p859   +−HFN 12-80 p151

CLASSICS FOR PLEASURE

CFP 40320 Tape (c) TC CFP 40320
3623 BARBER: Adagio, strings. COPLAND: Fanfare for the common man.
GOUNOD: Mors et vita: Judex. KHACHATURIAN: Spartacus: Adagio of

Spartacus and Phrygia. MACCUNN: Land of the mountain and the
flood. MASSENET: Thais: Meditation. SATIE: Gymnopedies, nos.
1 and 3 (orch. Debussy). TRAD.: Suo gan (arr. Weldon). Richard
Simpson, ob; Martin Milner, vln; Halle Orchestra; Maurice Handford.

+Gr 11-79 p918   +-RR 11-79 p75
+Gr 12-79 p1065 tape   +RR 7-80 p97 tape
+HFN 11-79 p151   *STL 12-9-79 p41
+HFN 1-80 p123 tape

CFP 40324 (From Music for Pleasure MFP 57006)
3624 BACH: Cantata, no. 147, Jesu joy of man's desiring. Toccata and
fugue, S 565, D minor. Ave Maria (arr. Gounod). BOELLMANN:
Suite gothique, op. 25: Priere a Notre Dame. MENDELSSOHN: Wed-
ding march. REGER: Pieces, organ, op. 59, no. 9: Benedictus.
WIDOR: Symphony, organ, no. 5, op. 42, no. 1, F major: Toccata.
Symphony, organ, no. 8, op. 42, no. 4, B minor: Finale. Jane
Parker-Smith, org.

+Gr 1-80 p1172   -RR 12-79 p97
+HFN 1-80 p121

CFP 40332
3625 BACH: Toccata and fugue, S 565, D minor. BEETHOVEN: The ruins of
Athens, op. 113: Turkish march. BRUCH: Concerto, violin, no. 1,
op, 26, G minor: Adagio. CHOPIN: Nocturne, op. 15, no. 2, F
sharp major. DELIBES: Lakme: Bell song. ELGAR: Sea pictures,
op. 37: Where corals lie. PROKOFIEV: Lieutenant Kije, op. 60:
Troika. PUCCINI: La boheme: Che gelida manina. PURCELL: Come
ye sons of art: Sound the trumpet. SATIE: Gymnopedies, nos. 1
and 3 (orch. Debussy). Maria Callas, s; Janet Baker, ms; James
Bowman, Charles Brett, c-t; Nicolai Gedda, t; Yehudi Menuhin,
vln; Maurizio Pollini, pno; Fernando Germani, org; LSO, RPO,
Rome Opera Orchestra, Birmingham City Orchestra, PhO; Early Music
Consort; John Barbirolli, Andre Previn, Thomas Beecham, Thomas
Schippers, Louis Fremaux, Tullio Serafin, Walter Susskind, David
Munrow.

+-HFN 6-80 p119   +RR 5-80 p74
+HFN 8-80 p109 tape

CLAVES

P 702 Tape (c) MC 702
3626 BAUMGARTNER: O du mein Heimatland. GOLSON: I remember Clifford.
JOPLIN: Palm leaf rag. HAYDN: Divertimento, no. 8, C major.
MENDELSSOHN: Songs without words, op. 30, no. 6, F minor. MEYER:
Schanfigger Bauernhochzeit. Zu Ehren d'Alphorns. SCHUBIGER:
Cacilien march. SENFL: Mit Lust tat ich ausreiten. TELEMANN:
Partita, no. 6: Air, Allemande, Air. ANON.: Codes Robertsbridge:
Estampie. TRAD.: Al cjant il cjal. Altes Guggisbergerlied.
Monte Crappa. Greensleeves. Le ranz des vaches. Hannes Meyer,
org.

+HFN 3-78 p149   +RR 8-80 p23

D 811
3627 DAETWYLER: Marignan march. LANGFORD: Rhapsody. PRYOR: Love's enchantment. STAIGERS: Carnival of Venice. STONE: Mexican shuffle. TRENET: I wish you love (arr. Waterworth). WINDSOR: Al-

pine echoes. TRAD.: Early one morning. My love is like a red
red rose. Le ranz des vaches fribourgeois. Philip McCann, cor;
Branimir Slokar, trom, Alphorn; Bernese Oberland Brass Band; Markus Bach.
            +Gr 5-80 p1718

D 904
3628 BACH: Das wohltempierte Klavier, S 846: Prelude. BEETHOVEN: Prelude, op. 39, no. 1. CZERNY: Les heures du matin, op. 204.
Kunst der Fingerfertigkeit, no. 4, B major; no. 6. Der Pianist
im klassischen style, op. 856, nos. 1 and 2. Schule der Gelauf-
igkeit, op. 299: Auswahl. Die Schule des Virtuosen, op. 365:
Auswah. DEBUSSY: Etudes, no. 1. LISZT: Etudes d'execution
transcendente, G 139: Prelude. Franzpeter Goebels, pno.
            +HFN 5-80 p131

D 8005
3629 BURKHARD: Suite, op. 98. FUKUSHIMA: Mei. KARG-ELERT: Sonata appassionata, op. 140, F sharp minor. KUHLAU: Fantasia, D major.
STAMITZ: Capriccio sonata, A major. TELEMANN: Fantasias, no. 7,
D major; no. 12, G minor. Peter Lukas Graf, flt.
            +Gr 9-80 p379

                          CLUB

99-112
3630 BERLIOZ: Damnation de Faust: Autrefois un Roi de Thule; D'amour
l'ardente flamme. Romeo et Juliette: Premiers transports. GRI-
SAR: Les Porcherons: Romance de la lettre. HALEVY: La Juive: Il
va venir. MASSENET: Herodiade: Pour moi tout autre est le destin. Marie-Magdeleine: C'est ici meme; O bien-aime. MEYERBEER:
L'Africaine: Adieu mon doux rivage; Sur mes genoux; O grand St.
Dominique. Robert le diable: Va dit-elle va mon enfant; Robert
toi que j'aime. ROSSINI: Guillaume Tell; Sombres forets. Stabat
mater: Inflammatus. Berthe Auguez de Montelant, s.
            +-ARG 4-78 p40   +FF 1/2-80 p163

99-115
3631 ADAM: Le chalet: Vive le vin l'amour et le tabac. Le toreador: Qui
le vie. BERLIOZ: L'Enfance du Christ, op. 25: O misere des rois.
DEBUSSY: Pelleas et Melisande: Je n'en dis rien. FLEGIER: Le
cor. GOUNOD: Philemon et Baucis: Ecoutez ecoutez; D'est l'orage;
Au bruit des lourds marteaux. Songs: Le vallon. Reine de Saba:
Sous les pieds d'une femme. MASSENET: Le Cid: Il a fait noble-
ment. Herodiade: Astres etincelants. MEYERBEER: Les Huguenots:
Seigneur rampart et seul soutien; Piff paff. L'Etoile du nord:
O jours heureux. Robert le diable: Nonnes qui reposez. SAINT-
SAENS: Le pas d'armes du Roi Jean. THOMAS: Le Caid: L'amour de
dieu profane. Armand Narcon, bs.
            +-ARG 3-79 p52   +FF 9/10-80 p244

99-118
3632 BERLIOZ: La damnation de Faust, op. 24: D'amour l'ardente flamme.
GEORGES: Miarka: L'eau qui nourt; Nuages. MASSENET: Le Cid: Alleluia. Herodiade: Il est doux. Manon: Gavotte. Thais: Mirror
aria; L'Amour est une vertu rare; Scene de l'Oasis. PUCCINI:
Tosca: Non la sospiri; Vissi d'arte. ROSSINI: William Tell: Sombre foret. VERDI: Aida: Ritorna vincitor. Rigoletto: Figlia mio

padre; Tutte le feste. Yvonne Gall, s.
    +—FF 11/12-80 p197

CO

367
3633 DONIZETTI: L'Elisir d'amore: Una furtiva lagrima. DVORAK: Rusalka,
     op. 114: Vidino divna presladka. LEONCAVALLO: I Pagliacci: Ves-
     ti la giubba. SMETANA: The bartered bride: Marenka-Jenik duets;
     Jenik's aria, Act 2. The devil's wall: Where can I flee. The
     kiss: If I knew how to redeem my guilt. The secret: You cast
     down your sweet eyes. The two widows: Ladislav's aria. TCHAI-
     KOVSKY: Eugen Onegin, op. 42: Lensky's arias. Ottokar Marak, t.
         -Op 7-80 p688

COLUMBIA

M 35123
3634 BARRIOS: Danza paraguaya. CRESPO: Nortena (Segovia). DODGSON:
     Fantasy divisions. LAURO: Vals criollo. PONCE: Sonatina meri-
     dional. SOJO: Pieces from Venezuela (5). VILLA-LOBOS: Choros,
     no. 1, E minor. YOKO: Theme and variations on "Sakura". John
     Williams, gtr.
         ++FF 1/2-80 p166
M 35137 (also CBS 73879 Tape (c) 40-73879)
3635 ALBENIZ: Suite espanola: Granada (arr. Boyd); Asturias. BARRIOS:
     Cancion de la hilandera (arr. Boyd). Waltz, op. 8, no. 4 (arr.
     Boyd). BARNES: Fantasy. DEBUSSY: Childrens corner: The little
     shepherd (arr. Boyd). PAYET: Cabellos de oro. Lejania. SATIE:
     Gymnopedie, no. 1 (arr. Boyd). SOR: Waltzes, nos. 1-3 (arr.
     Boyd). TARREGA: Recuerdos de la Alhambra. Liona Boyd, gtr.
         +—FF 9/10-79 p170   ++HFN 8-80 p109 tape
         +Gr 1-80 p1172   +NR 10-79 p14
M 35138 (also CBS 76800 Tape (c) 40-76800)
3636 BROSCHI: Idapse: Ombra fedele anch'io. LEONCAVALLO: La boheme: E
     destin. MONTEVERDI: Il ritorno d'Ulisse in patria: Torna torna.
     PAISIELLO: Nina: Il mio ben quando vera. ROSSINI: Semiramide:
     Wie glanzte so freundlich mir. Tancredi: Di tanto palpiti.
     Frederica von Stade, s; National Arts Centre Orchestra.
         +ARG 5-80 p49   +MUM 3/4-80 p36
         +—FF 5/6-80 p174   +—NR 1-80 p10
         +Gr 1-80 p1195   +NYT 10-28-79 pD24
         +Gr 3-80 p1446 tape   +ON 2-23-80 p45
         +HFN 1-80 p115   ++Op 3-80 p271
         +HFN 2-80 p107 tape   ++RR 1-80 p60
M 35159
3637 BACH: Presto (Brahms, Ricci). ERNST: Concerto variations on "The
     last rose of summer". PAGANINI: Variations on "Nel cor piu non
     mi santo". KREISLER: Recitative and scherzo. SAINT-LUBIN:
     Fantasy on the sextet from Donizetti's "Lucia di Lammermoor".
     TARREGA (arr. Ricci): Recuerdos de la Alhambra. WIENIAWSKI:
     La cadenza. ZITO: La cumparsita. TRAD. (arr. Ricci): Spanish
     ballad. Ruggiero Ricci, vln.

+NR 10-79 p13   +NYT 7-6-80 pD15

MG 35188 (2)

3638 BERNSTEIN: Candide: Overture. BIZET: Carmen: Prelude. GLINKA:
Russlan and Ludmilla: Overture. HEROLD: Zampa: Overture. MOZ-
ART: Le nozze di Figaro, K 492: Overture. OFFENBACH: Orphee aux
enfers: Overture. ROSSINI: Il barbiere di Siviglia: Overture.
Guglielmo Tell: Overture. SMETANA: The bartered bride: Overture.
STRAUSS, J. II: Die Fledermaus, op. 363: Overture. SUPPE: Light
cavalry: Overture. Poet and peasant: Overture. NYP, CO, PO;
Leonard Bernstein, Georg Szell, Eugene Ormandy.

+FF 7/8-80 p190   +NR 3-79 p4

MG 35190

3639 BOYCE: Symphony, no. 4, F major. DELIUS: Hassan: Intermezzo, Sere-
nade (arr. Beecham). ELGAR: Chanson de matin, op. 15, no. 2.
Chanson de nuit, op. 15, no. 1. HANDEL: Solomon: Arrival of the
Queen of Sheba. PURCELL: Chacony, G minor (ed. Britten). Dido
and Aeneas: Suite. VAUGHAN WILLIAMS: Fantasia on "Greensleeves"
(arr. Greaves). VIVALDI: Concerti, P 74, C major; P 86, D minor;
P 42, A minor; P 208, D major; P 119, E minor; P 118, G major.
WARLOCK: Capriol suite. ECO; Jose Luis Garcia.

+-ARG 5-79 p49   +MUM 1/2-80 p33
++FF 7/8-80 p190   +NR 5-79 p5
+MJ 11/12-79 p48

M 35821

3640 BACH: Cantata, no. 147, Jesu joy of man's desiring. Cantata, no.
208, Sheep may safely graze. Suite, orchestra, S 1067, B minor:
Badinerie. CLARKE: Trumpet voluntary. CORELLI: Concerto (Christmas): Pastorale. HANDEL: Water music suite: Allegro. MARCELLO:
Concerto, oboe, C minor: Adagio. MARTINI IL TEDESCO: Plaisir
d'amour. VIVALDI: Concerto, op. 4: Largo. Concerto, 2 trumpets:
Allegro. Philharmonia Virtuosi; Richard Kapp.

+FF 5/6-80 p199   +NR 3-80 p5

M 35830 Tape (c) MT 35830 (also CBS 76829)

3641 FLOTOW: Alessandro Stradella: Jungfrau Maria. MEYERBEER: L'Afrai-
caine: Land so wunderbar. MOZART: Die Zauberflote, K 620: Dies
Bildnis ist bezaubernd schon. SMETANA: The bartered bride: Hans
aria, Act 2. TCHAIKOVSKY: Eugen Onegin, op. 24: Lenski's aria.
WAGNER: Lohengrin: In fernem Land; Mein lieber Schwan. Die Meistersinger von Nurnberg: Prize song. WEBER: Oberon: Huon's recitative and aria, Act 1; Huons prayer, Act 2. Siegfried Jerusalem, t; Munich Radio Orchestra; Gabriel Chmura.

+-ARG 11-80 p49   +Op 5-80 p508
+Gr 4-80 p1594   +RR 5-80 p50
+HFN 4-80 p113   ++SFC 3-30-80 p39
+NR 4-80 p11   +St 7-80 p86
+ON 4-5-80 p29

MS 80030

3642 CASTELNUOVO-TEDESCO: Fantasia. FEUERSTEIN: Io. Philip and Eva.
To thee. Transmutations, nos. 1 and 2. GALLES: Sonata, guitar,
C major. MONDONVILLE: Tambourikne. PONCE: Andantino. SATIE:
Can-can grand mondain. Gnossienne. STRAUBE: Minuet. VIVALDI:
Sonata, guitar, G major. Robert Feuerstein, gtr; Sarah Feuer-
stein, hpd and pno.

+FF 7/8-80 p155   +MUM 7/8-80 p30
+FU 5-80 p52

CORNELL

CUWE 23
3643 BERNSTEIN: West side story: Prologue (arr. Gilmore). FLAGELLO: Sym-
phony of winds. LEEMANS (arr. Wiley): Marche des parachutistes
Belges. MAIS: Fantasy on Jewish tunes. SOUSA: Cubaland suite:
Under the Spanish flag. VON BLON (ed. Wiley): Die Wacht am Rhein.
Cornell University Wind Ensemble; Marice Stith.
+FF 11/12-79 p68   +NR 2-80 p14

CORNUCOPIA

IJ 100
3644 BAKER: Cantilena. COOKE: Rondo, B flat major. DUNHILL: Cornucopia.
ECCLES: Sonata, horn, G minor (arr. Eger). GWILT: Sonatina.
STIRLING: Horncore. Variations on a Tyrolean theme. VINTER:
Hunter's moon. TRAD.: Carnival in Venice (arr. Stirling). Ifor
James, hn; John McCabe, Wilfrid Parry, pno.
+Gr 10-80 p517

CORONET

LPS 3062
3645 CAMPOS: Danzas. DEBUSSY: Petite suite. DELANO: La bruja de Loiza:
Fiesta en el pueblo; La novia desconsolada; Las viejas chismosas.
LISZT: Concerto pathetique, G 258, E minor. RACHMANINOFF: Pieces,
op. 11: Barcarolle, Waltz. Gloria Whitney, Marilu Alvarado, pno.
-NR 5-80 p13

COURT OPERA CLASSICS

CO 380
3646 BIZET: Carmen: Sonntag war's. CORNELIUS: Barbier von Bagdad: O
holdes Bild in Engelschone. MOZART: Die Entfuhrung aus dem
Serail, K 384: Martern aller arten...Welch ein Geschick. Die
Zauberflote, K 620: O zittre nicht. PUCCINI: La boheme: Leb wohl
denn und ohne Hass. ROSSINI: Il barbiere di Siviglia: Frag ich
mein beklomnen Herz. VERDI: Rigoletto: Teurer Namen dessen Klang.
La traviata: 'S ist seltsam...Er ist es...'S ist Torheit...Von der
Freude Blumenkranzen. O lass uns fliehen. Maria Ivogun, s.
+-ARSC Vol VI, no. 2-3   +RR 8-80 p12
1979

CRD

CRD 1019 Tape (c) CRDC 4019
3647 ALFONSO X, El Sabio: Rosa das rosas. DOWLAND: Captain Digorie Piper's galliard. The King of Denmark's galliard. PRAETORIUS:
Peasant dances. Terpsichore: Fire dance; Stepping dance; Wind-
mills; Village dance; Sailor's dance; Fishermens dance; Festive
march. SOTHCOTT: Fanfare. TRAD.: (English) Good King Wencelas
pavane. The dressed ship. Staines Morris. Here we come a-

wassailing. Green garters. Fandango. God rest you merry gentle-
men. I saw three ships. All hail to the days. TRAD. (French)
Branle de l'official. ANON. (English) Edi beo thu. Ductia. As
I lay. ANON. (French) Alle psallite cum luya. ANON. (Italian)
La Manfredina. Saltarello. St. George's Canzona; John Sothcott.
                ++HFN 12-75 p167   ++RR 12-75 p93
                +HFN 2-80 p107 tape   +St 1-77 p132
CRD 1050 Tape (c) CRDC 4050
3648 English music for harpsichord and virginals. BULL: My grief. My
     self. The king's hunt. BYRD: The Carmans whistle. Lord Wil-
     loughby's welcome home. Watkin's ale (attrib. Byrd). DOWLAND:
     Can she excuse. FARNABY: Loath to depart. Muscadin. GIBBONS:
     The fairest nymph. Lord of Salisbury his pavan and galliardo.
     The woods so wild. MORLEY: La volta. TALLIS: O ye tenderest
     babes. TOMKINS: Barafostus dream. ANON.: My Lady Careys dompe.
     Trevor Pinnock, hpd and virginals.
                ++Gr 11-78 p934   +MT 5-79 p410
                +HFN 10-78 p135   +RR 11-78 p89
                +HFN 12-80 p159 tape

                            CRI

SD 423
3649 JULIAN: Wave canon. ROCHBERG: La bocca della verita. SCHULLER:
     Trio. SEEGER: Diaphonic suite, no. 1. SINGER: Work. SHAPEY:
     Rhapsodie. James Ostryniec, ob; Charles Wuorinen, pno; Noah
     Chaves, vla; David Bakkegard, Fr hn; Prerecorded tape.
                +FF 11/12-80 p222   +NR 10-80 p6

                        CRITICS CHOICE

CC 1709
3650 BUCHT: Klarinettstudie, op. 59. CAMERON: Variations. CORELLI:
     Trio sonata, op. 3, no. 8 (Limoli). DEBUSSY: Petite piece.
     GOEDICKE: Etude, op. 28, no. 2. MOZART: Quintet, clarinet, K
     581, A major. Michael Limoli, clt; Andrea Swan, pno; New Cham-
     ber Players, Cantilena Quartet.
                +ARG 11-79 p59   +NR 6-79 p9
                +-FF 1/2-80 p169   +NYT 12-2-79 pD22

                            CRYSTAL

S 106
3651 DIAMOND: Night music. EFFINGER: Nocturne. GART: Vivo. LANG: Pre-
     lude and fugue, C major. LOCKWOOD: Sonata fantasy. PINO: Con-
     certino. SEIBER: Introduction and allegro. VOLPI: Preludio,
     op. 31. Robert Davine, accord; James Carroll, bs; Lamont String
     Quartet.
                +Audio 11-80 p85   +St 2-80 p136
                +FF 1/2-80 p180
S 366
3652 DE LA VEGA: Para-tangents. DODGE: Extensions. HENZE: sonatina.

KUPFERMAN: Three ideas. LAZAROF: Concertazioni. Thomas Stevens, tpt; Anne Diener Giles, flt; Merritt Buxbaum, clt; Ralph Pyle, hn; Daniel Rothmuller, vlc; Dorothy Remsen, hp; Mitchell Peters, perc; Chet Swiatkowski, pno; Henri Lazarof.
+ARG 2-80 p56   +FF 1/2-80 p168

S 385
3653 BOUTRY: Pieces a quatre (5). CASTEREDE: Sonatine. CHAYNES: Impulsions. DEFAYE: Danses (2). SALZEDO: Piece concertante. Miles Anderson, trom; Los Angeles Slide Trombone Ensemble; Virko Baley, pno.
+-FF 5/6-80 p187   +NYT 5-18-80 pD42
+NR 5-80 p16

S 395
3654 CLARKE: From the shores of the mighty Pacific. HINDEMITH: Easy pieces (3). RECK: Studies for tuba alone (4). STEVENS: Dances. TELEMANN: Fantasy, C minor. TOMASI: To be or not to be. Toby Hanks, tuba; New York Tuba Quartet, New York City Ballet Orchestra Trombone Section; Gary Kirkpatrick, pno.
+FF 5/6-80 p187   +NYT 5-18-80 pD24
+NR 5-80 p16

S 532
3655 BAKER: Before assemblages III. MURRAY: Songs. O'BRIEN: Lingual. WATSON: Recital suite. WEIDENAAR: The tinsel chicken coop. Michiko Hirayama, s; Seth McCoy, t; Richard Shirey, Chet Swiatkowski, pno; Kenneth Watson, marimba; Anne-Beate Zimmer, flt; Frances Marie Uitti, vlc; Studio tape David Peelle; Indiana Chamber Orchestra Members; Thomas Briccetti.
+FF 9/10-80 p295   +NR 4-79 p10

S 700
3656 ALCOCK: Voluntary, D major. BRUHNS: Prelude and fugue. FANTINI: Dances (5). WALOND: Voluntary, D major. VIVIANI: Sonatas, trumpet, nos. 1 and 2. Fred Sautter, tpt; Roger Sherman, org.
+ARG 7-79 p49   ++NR 5-79 p15
+-Audio 11-79 p128   +St 9-79 p106
+-FF 1/2-80 p165

CRYSTAL CLEAR

CCS 6004/5
3657 Flamenco: Tango antiguo; Levante; Caribe aflamencao; Fandango; Taranto; Variaciones; Aires de Genil; Malaga; Jerez; Macarena en tango; Saeta; Solea-Cana; Zambra; Zapateao. Carlos Montoya, gtr.
++St 10-80 p129

7001/2 (2)
3658 ALAIN: Litanies, op. 79. BACH: Toccata, adagio and fugue, S 564, C major. Toccata and fugue, S 565, D minor. DUPRE: Prelude and fugue, G minor. FRANCK: Piece heroique. GIGOUT: Toccata. JONGEN: Symphonie concertante: Toccata. VIERNE: Symphony, no. 6, op. 59, B major: Finale. WIDOR: Symphony, organ, no. 5, op. 42, no. 1, F major: Toccata. Virgil Fox, org.
+-ARG 4-80 p51   +MU 2-79 p12
++Audio 1-79 p108   +NR 10-78 p15
++Audio 8-79 p86   -SFC 6-3-79 p49
+-FF 3/4-79 p14   +St 11-79 p98
+Gr 6-78 p90

CCS 7007
3659 BACH: Preludes, S 933-938: Little preludes (2). Clavierubung, Pt 1.
     Partita, harpsichord, no. 1, S 825, B flat major: Minuets (2).
     HANDEL: Suite, harpsichord, D minor: Sarabande. PURCELL: Suite,
     harpsichord, G major. RAMEAU: Les fetes d'Hebe. Suite, E major:
     Musette; Tambourin. SCARLATTI: Sonatas, harpsichord, nos. 9,
     132, 133, 146, 419. SOLER: Sonata, harpsichord, G major. Fer-
     nando Valenti, hpd.
                    +ARG 4-80 p50   +SFC 12-23-79 p40
                    +FF 11/12-79 p16

CCS 7010
3660 BACH: Toccata and fugue, S 565, D minor. BLISS: Salute (arr. Tulan).
     BRAHMS: Let nothing ever grieve thee, op. 30 (arr. Morris). COP-
     LAND: Fanfare for the common man. GIGOUT: Grand choeur dialogue
     (arr. Morris). Richard Morris, org; Atlanta Brass Ensemble;
     Jere Flint.
                    +ARG 11-79 p30   +SFC 12-23-79 p40
                    +Audio 12-79 p120   +St 2-80 p141
                    +NR 6-80 p14

CCS 7011
3661 COUPERIN, L.: Chaconne (arr. Morris). DUPRE: Poeme heroique. MOU-
     RET: Rondeau (arr. Morris). STANLEY: Trumpet tune and aires:
     Voluntaries (3). STRAUSS, R.: Also sprach Zarathustra, op. 30:
     Opening fanfare. WIDOR: Symphony, organ, no. 5, op. 42, no. 1,
     F major: Toccata. Richard Morris, org; Atlanta Brass Ensemble;
     Jere Flint.
                    +ARG 11-79 p31   +NR 6-80 p14
                    +Audio 12-79 p120   +SFC 12-23-79 p40

                          DA CAMERA IMPROMPTU

SM 194 055
3662 BARBE: Ein Jager langs dem Weiher ging. BRAHMS: Der eifersuchtige
     Knabe; All meine Herzgedanken. BRESGEN: Die Jagd. CHEMIN-PETIT:
     Und in dem Schneegebirge. GASTOLDI: Amor in Nachen. HERRMANN:
     Es steht ein Lind. LANG: Das Lieben bringt. MORLEY: Nun strahlt
     der Mai den Herzen. SCHMIDT-MANNHEIM: Die Hexen; Waldfreuden;
     Der verirrte Jager. SCHRAMM: Ein edler Jager wohlgemut. WEY-
     RAUCH: All mein gedanken; Weiss mir ein Blumlein blaue. Bayreuth
     Madrigalchor; Hans Schmidt.
                    +FF 7/8-80 p162

                               DECCA

SPA 554
3663 BACH: Cantatas, no. 147, Jesu joy of man's desiring. Chorale pre-
     lude, S 615, In dir ist Freude. Suite, orchestra, S 1068, D
     major: Air on the G string. CLARKE: Trumpet voluntary. BRAHMS:
     A rose has bloomed. GUILMANT: Grand choeur, D major. HANDEL:
     Largo. Water music: Hornpipe. MENDELSSOHN: Wedding march.
     WAGNER: Bridal chorus. WESLEY: Air and govotte. WIDOR: Symph-
     ony, organ, no. 5, op. 42, no. 1, F major: Toccata. Stephen
     Cleobury, org.
                    +-HFN 1-80 p119   /RR 12-79 p104

SPA 583 Tape (c) 583
3664 BACH: Toccata, adagio and fugue, S 564, C major. Toccata and fugue,
S 565, D minor. BOELLMANN: Suite gothique, op. 25: Toccata.
BUXTEHUDE: Toccata and fugue, F major. DUBOIS: Toccata, G major.
MULET: Toccata "Tu es Petrus". REGER: Toccata and fugue, op. 59,
nos. 5 and 6. WIDOR: Symphony, no. 5, op. 42, no. 1, F minor:
Toccata. Alan Wicks, Gillian Weir, Peter Hurford, Simon Preston,
Michael Nicholas, org.
            +Gr 10-80 p523   +HFN 11-80 p131
DPA 629/30
3665 ALBENIZ: Iberia: El corpus en Sevilla (orch. Arbos). Navarra. Pie-
zas caracteristicas: Torre bermeja. Recuerdos de viaje, op. 71:
Rumores de la caleta. BIZET: Carmen: Fantaisie. FALLA: El amor
brujo: Pantomime; Ritual fire dance. The three cornered hat:
Neighbours dance; Millers dance; Final dance. La vida breve:
Interlude and Spanish dance. GRANADOS: Goyescas: Maiden and the
nightingale. Spanish dances, op. 37: Andaluza. Tonadillas al
estilo antiguo: El tra la la; El maja timido. GURIDI: Como
quieres que adivine. MUDARRA: Fantasia. SARASATE: Danzas espanolas, op. 23: Zapateado. TARREGA: La alborada. Lagrima.
Recuerdos de la Alhambra. TURINA: Danzas fantasticas. Consuelo
Rubio, s; Teresa Berganza, ms; Felix Lavilla, pno; Ruggiero Ricci, vln; Timothy Walker, gtr; Marisa Robles, hp; Alfredo Campoli,
vln; Daphne Ibbott, pno; LSO, Spanish National Orchestra, OSR;
Ataulfo Argenta, Ernest Ansermet, Pierino Gamba.
            +HFN 1-80 p121   +RR 12-79 p71
DPA 631/2
3666 Music of France. ADAM: Giselle: Peasant pas de deux. BERLIOZ: Le
carnival romain, op. 9. BIZET: Carmen: Prelude; L'amour est un
oiseau rebelle. CHABRIER: Marche joyeuse. DEBUSSY: Prelude a
l'apres-midi d'un faune. Suite bergamasque: Clair de lune.
DELIBES: Coppelia: Mazurka. DUKAS: The sorcerer's apprentice.
FAURE: Pavane, op. 50. GOUNOD: Faust: Ballet music. Sapho: O
mon lyre. RAVEL: Pavane pour une infante defunte. La valse.
SAINT-SAENS: Danse macabre, op. 40. SATIE: Gymnopedie, no. 1.
Regine Crespin, s; Ilana Vered, pno; Geneva Grand Theatre Chorus;
OSCCP, OSR, NPhO, ROHO, NSL; Jean Martinon, Ernest Ansermet,
Alain Lombard, Charles Munch, Georg Solti, Raymond Agoult.
            +HFN 1-80 p121   +RR 12-79 p66
SXL 6870 Tape (c) KSXC 6870 (also London OS 26560 Tape (c) OS 5-26560)
3667 d'ANNIBALE: O paese d'o sole. CANNIO: O surdato 'nnammurato.
CAPUA: Maria Mari; O sole mio. CURTIS: Torna a Surriento; Tu
ca nun chiagne. DENZA: Funiculi funicula. GAMBARDELLA: O Mare-
nariello. PENNINO: Pecche. TAGLIAFERRI: Piscatore e pussileco.
TOSTI: A vucchella; Marechiare. ANON.: Fenesta vascia. Luciano
Pavarotti, Bologna Teatro Communale Orchestra, National Philharmonic Orchestra; Anton Guadagno, Giancarlo Chiaramello.
            +-Gr 10-79 p724   +NYT 10-28-79 pD24
            +Gr 2-80 p1302 tape   +-ON 12-15-79 p36
            -HF 1-80 p90   ++RR 10-79 p140
            +HFN 10-79 p165   ++SFC 9-16-79 p61
            +-NR 12-79 p11   ++St 12-79 p155
SXL 6923
3668 FALLA: La vida breve: Vivan los que rien; Alliesta riyenda junto
a esa mujer. GRANADOS: Goyescas: La maja y el ruisenor. MOZART:

Don Giovanni, K 527: Don Ottavio son morta...Or sai chi l'onore.
PUCCINI: Madama Butterfly: Tu tu piccolo iddio. Manon Lescaut:
Sola perduta abbandonata. Suor Angelica: Senza mamma. Tosca:
Vissi d'arte. VERDI: Don Carlo: Tu che le vanita. WAGNER: Loh-
engrin: Einsam in truben Tagen. Pilar Lorengar, s; LPO; Jesus
Lopez Cobos.

   +-Gr 8-80 p270   -Op 11-80 p1148
   +-HFN 8-80 p103   +RR 8-80 p29
   +NYT 9-14-80 pD42

SXL R 6936 (also London OS 26618)
3669 COSTANZI: Eupatra: Lusinga la speme. GIORDANI: Caro mio ben. LOT-
TI: Pur dicesti. MARCELLO: Quella fiamma che m'accende. PAIS-
IELLO: Nel cor piu non mi sento. PERGOLESI: Se tu m'ami. VIV-
ALDI: Bajazet: Sposa son disprezzata. L'Ateneide: Un certo non
so che. Ercole sul Termodonte: Onde chiare. La Griselda: Agitata da due venti; Da due venti. Ottone in Villa: Vieni vieni
o mio diletto. Montserrat Caballe, s; Miguel Zanetti, pno.

   +FF 9/10-80 p240   +-NYT 6-15-80 pD29
   +-Gr 3-80 p1445   ++RR 4-80 p51
   +HF 8-80 p84   +St 9-80 p84
   ++HFN 3-80 p101

SXL 6942 (also London OS 26591)
3670 MASCAGNI: L'Amico Fritz: Son pochi fiori. MOZART: Le nozze di Fig-
aro, K 492: Dove sono. PUCCINI: La boheme: Si mi chiamano Mimi.
Gianni Schicchi: O mio babbino caro. Madama Butterfly: Un bel
di vedremo. La rondine: Chi il bel sogno di Doretta. Turandot:
Tu che di gel sei cinta. ROSSINI: Guglielmo Tell: Selva opaca.
VERDI: Ernani: Ernani involami. Leona Mitchell, s; National
Philharmonic Orchestra; Kurt Herbert Adler.

   +FF 11/12-80 p196   +NYT 9-14-80 pD42
   +-Gr 4-80 p1594   +-RR 4-80 p49
   +-HFN 4-80 p113   +SFC 8-10-80 p29

SXDL 7504 Tape (c) KSXDC 7504 (also London LDR 10020)
3671 BOITO: Mefistofele: Dai campi dai prati; Ogni mortal mister gustai
...Giunto sul passo estremo. CILEA: Adriana Lecouvreur: La dolcissima effigie; L'anima ho stanca. GIORDANO: Andrea Chenier:
Colpito que m'avete...Un di all'azzurro spazio; Come un bel di di
maggio; Si fui soldato. Fedora: Amor ti vieta. MASCAGNI: Iris:
Apri la tua finestra. MASSENET: Werther: Pourquoi me reveiller.
MEYERBEER: L'Africaine: Mi batte il cor...O paradiso. PUCCINI:
La fanciulla del West: Ch'ella mi creda. Manon Lescaut: Ma se
vi talenta...Tra voi belle; Donna non vidi mai; Ah non v'avvici-
nate...No no pazzo son. Luciano Pavarotti, t; Neil Howlett, bar;
National Philharmonic Orchestra; Olivero de Fabritis, Riccardo
Chailly.

   +Gr 12-80 p878   +SFC 12-7-80 p33
   +HFN 12-80 p149

D129D2 (2) Tape (c) K129K22 (From SET 528/30, D 9603, SET 372/3, 503/5,
     565/6, 562/3, SXL 6649, SET 418/21, 484/6, D82D3, SET
     606/8, SXL 6828, SET 542/4, 374/5, 587/9)
3672 BELLINI: I puritani: A te o cara. DONIZETTI: La favorita: Favorita
del re...Spirto gentil. La fille du regiment: Ah mes amis; Pour
me rapprocher de Marie. L'Elisir d'amore: Chiedi all'aura lus-
inghiera. Lucia di Lammermoor: Chi mi frena; Tu che a Dio.
PUCCINI: La boheme: In un coupe...O Mimi tu piu non torni. Tos-

ca: E lucevan le stelle. Turandot: Non piangere liu. STRAUSS,
R.: Der Rosenkavalier, op. 59: Di rigori armato. VERDI: Un
ballo in maschera: La rivedra nell'estasi; E scherzo od e follia.
Luisa Miller: O fede negar potessi...Quando le sere al placido.
Requiem: Ingemisco. Rigoletto: Ella mi fu rapita...Parmi veder
le lagrime; La donna e mobile...Bella figlia dell'amore. La
traviata: Brindisi; Un di felice. Il trovatore: Se m'ami ancor
...Ai nostri monti. Joan Sutherland, Huguette Tourangeau, Helen
Donath, Montserrat Caballe, Marilyn Horne, s; Regina Resnik, con;
Ryland Davies, Luciano Pavarotti, t; Sherrill Milnes, Roland Pane-
rai, bar; Nicolai Ghiaurov, Giancarlo Luccardi, bs; ROHO and Chor-
us, VPO, National Philharmonic Orchestra, LSO, LPO, RPO, Teatro
Comunale Orchestra, Bologna, ECO, Santa Cecilia Orchestra and
Chorus, BPhO; Richard Bonynge, Herbert von Karajan, Bruno Barto-
letti, Peter Maag, Georg Solti, Zubin Mehta.
          +--Gr 8-80 p27   +RR 8-80 p28
          +HFN 8-80 p107

                              DELOS

FY 001
3673 Grandes Heures Liturgiques. La Maitrise de Notre Dame Cathedral
        Choir; Various organists.
               +FF 9/10-80 p270   +NR 7-77 p14
               ++MU 6-79 p9

DMS 3002
3674 ALTENBURG: Concerto, trumpet, D major. BIBER: Sonata, trumpet, C
        major. TELEMANN: concerto, trumpet, D major. TORELLI: Sonata,
        no. 1, C major. VIVALDI: Concerto, trumpet, C major. Gerard
        Schwarz, Mark Gould, Ed Carroll, Robert Sirinek, Norman Smith,
        James Miller, Neil Balm, Raymond Mase, tpt; Sayoko Aki, vln;
        Frederick Zlotkin, vlc; Loren Glickman, bsn; Linda Skernick, hpd;
        Gordon Gottlieb, timpani; New York Y Chamber Symphony Orchestra.
               +--FF 11/12-79 p15   +NR 12-79 p5
               +HF 2-80 p100   +--RR 4-80 p60
               ++HFN 4-80 p113   ++St 2-80 p136

D/DMS 3003
3675 BACH: The art of the fugue, S 1080: Contrapunctus, nos. 3 and 9.
        COPERARIO: Al primo giorno. Fancie a 5. DOWLAND: Volta. FER-
        RABOSCO: Almayne. Dovehouse pavan. GABRIELI, A.: Ricercar del
        sesto tuono. GABRIELI, G.: Canzon per sonare, nos. 4 and 5.
        Canzon per sonare "La spiritata". HOLBORNE: The widows myte.
        MORLEY: Joyne hands. SCHEIDT: Battle suite. SIMPSON: Allemande.
        SPEER: Sonatas, brass quintet (2). STORL: Sonata, brass quintet.
        WEELKES: Why are you ladies staying. Hark I hear some dancing.
        American Brass Quintet.
               +HFN 4-80 p115   +--RR 4-80 p60
               ++NR 3-80 p7   ++St 7-80 p84

DMS 3005
3676 ALBENIZ, I.: Recuerdos de viaje, op. 71: Rumores de la caleta. AL-
        BENIZ, M.: Sonata, D major. ALVARS (arr. McDonald): La mandoline.
        DEBUSSY (arr. McDonald): Preludes, Bk 1: La fille aux cheveux de
        lin. FRANCISQUE: Courante. Pavane et bransles. GRANDJANY: Sic-
        iliana. ORTIZ: La guabina. Llanos. SALZEDO: Song in the night.

TOURNIER: Etude de concert. WATKINS: Fire dance. ZABEL (arr.
McDonald): La source. TRAD. (arr. McDonald): Believe me if all
those endearing young charms. Irish gigue. Greensleeves. Sus-
ann McDonald, hp, Irish hp, Paraguayan hp.
  +HFN 4-80 p116   ++RR 4-80 p101
  +NR 2-80 p6   ++St 5-80 p95

DENON

<u>OX 7177</u>
3677 BEETHOVEN: Bagatelle, no. 25, A minor. CHOPIN: Nocturnes, op. 9,
  no. 2, E flat major; op. 72, E minor. DEBUSSY: Suite bergamasque: Clair de lune. HANDEL: Air and variations (The harmonious
  blacksmith). MOZART: Sonata, piano, no. 11, K 331, A major:
  Turkish march. Fantasia, K 397, D minor. SCHUBERT: Moment musicaux, op. 94, no. 3, D 780, F minor. SCHUMANN: Kinderscenen,
  op. 15: Traumerei. Romance, op. 28, no. 2, F sharp major. SIB-
  ELIUS: Romance, op. 24, no. 9, D flat major. John O'Connor, pno.
   +-FF 9/10-80 p263

DESMAR

<u>GHP 4001/2</u> (2)
3678 BALAKIREV: Islamey. BUSONI: Elegie, no. 5. CHOPIN: Etude, op. 10,
  no. 4, C sharp minor. Etudes, op. 25, nos. 1 and 2. Prelude,
  op. 28, no. 23, F major. Chants polonaise, op. 74: My joys
  (Liszt). Tarantelle, op. 43, A flat major. Waltz, op. 34, no.
  3, F major. DEBUSSY: Preludes, Bk 2: La puerta del vino. LISZT:
  Annees de pelerinage, 1st year, G 160: Au bord d'une source. Annees de pelerinage, 3rd year, G 163: Les jeux d'eau a la Villa
  d'Este. Etudes de concert, no. 2, G 144, F minor: La leggier-
  ezza. Etudes d'execution transcendente d'apres Paganini, nos.
  1-2, 5-6, G 140. Rhapsodie espagnole, G 254. SCHUBERT: Fantasia, op. 15, D 760, C major. Hark hark the lark (Liszt). STRA-
  VINSKY: Petrouchka: Danse russe. Claudio Arrau, pno.
   +-ARG 3-80 p47   ++Gr 5-80 p1694
   +-ARSC Vol 11, no. 2-3 +HF 1-80 p63
    1979 p196   +-St 1-80 p112

DESTO

<u>7181</u>
3679 BAUER: X-N-trick rag. BLAKE: The chevy chase. BRAHMS: Hungarian
  dance, no. 5, G minor. COLLICHIO: Go-go. JOPLIN: Eugenia.
  Gladiolus rag. Heliotrope bouquet (Chauvin). LANSING: The
  darkie'd dream. MATTHEWS: Pastime rag, no. 5. MORATH: Polyrag-
  mic. James Tyler, banjo and mand; New Excelsior Talking Machine.
   +FF 7/8-80 p183

<u>DC 7183</u>
3680 Mediaeval and Renaissance sounds, vol. 1. David Munrow, Chinese
  shawm, bagpipes, flutes, recorders, pipe and tabor, gemshorn,
  crumhorns, cornamuses, rauschpfeifen, dulcinas, kortholts, racketts, nicolo shawm, garkleinflotlein; Gillian Reid, psaltery,

Mediaeval bells, perc; Christopher Hogwood, regal, hpd.
+ARG 11-80 p43   ++NYT 8-17-80 pD18
+-FF 9/10-80 p256

DC 7184
3681 Mediaeval and Renaissance sounds, vol. 2. Musica Antiqua; Michael
Uridge.
+ARG 11-80 p43   -FF 9/10-80 p256

DC 7191
3682 BACH: Chorale prelude, S 751, In dulci jubilo. COUPERIN, L.: Carillon. DANDRIEU: Chanton de voix hautaine. HAYDN, M.: Pieces,
glockenspiel (3). KERLL: Capriccio "Cucu". LEBEGUE: Les cloches. MARTINI: Pastorale, G major. MUFFAT: Nova cyclopeias harmonica. MURSCHAUSER: Lasst uns das Kindlein wiegen. SCHEIDT:
Echo ad manuale duplex, fote et lene. SCRONX: Echo, C major.
STORACE: Ballo della battaglia. Franz Haselbock, org.
+-FF 11/12-80 p209

DC 7194
3683 ARCADELT: Ancidetimi pur. Da si felice sorte. Donna quando pietosa. ATTAIGNANT: Branles (5). DALLA CASA: Ancor che col partire. CRECQUILLON: Toutes les nuictz. FONTANA: Madonna mia
pieta. MILANO: Fantasia. Ricercar. NOLA: Chi la gagliarda.
LASSUS: Bonjour mon coeur. La nuit groide et sombre. ROQUELAY:
Ta bonne grace. RORE: Anchor che col partire. SERMISY: A douce
amour. London Pro Musica.
+St 10-80 p128

DC 7199 Tape (c) 47199
3684 CORELLI: Sonata, op. 5, no. 10, F major. GLIERE: Intermezzo, op.
35, no. 11. MASSENET: Elegie, op. 10. MENDELSSOHN: Auf flugeln des Gesanges, op. 34, no. 2. ROSSINI: Prelude, theme and
variations. SAINT-SAENS: Romance, op. 36. SCHMIDT: Im Tiefsten
Walde, op. 34. SCHUMANN: Fantasiestucke, op. 73. Casswell Neal,
hn; Armen Guzelimian, pno.
+-FF 11/12-80 p214

DEUTSCHE GRAMMOPHON

2531 051 Tape (c) 3301 051
3685 DAMASE: Sicilienne variee. DEBUSSY: Arabesque, no. 1. RAVEL: Pav-
ane pour une infante defunte. ROUSSEAU: Pastoral variations on
an old Christmas carol. ROUSSEL: Impromptu, op. 21. SALZEDO:
Chanson dans la nuit. TAILLEFERRE: Sonata, harp. TOURNIER:
Christmas songs, op. 32 (6). Nicanor Zabaleta, hp.
++Gr 11-78 p934   ++NR 10-79 p15
++HF 4-80 p104 tape   +RR 11-78 p88
++HFN 10-78 p135   ++SFC 8-12-79 p49

2531 113
3686 BROUWER: Tarantos. CARULLI: Divertimento per il Decacordo. CONGE:
La mort de Berenguer (arr. Yepes). KUHNEL: Suite, A major. ROB-
INSON: Religious songs (4). SOR: Fantaisie villageoise. ANON.:
Irish march (arr. Yepes). Narciso Yepes, gtr.
+-FF 9/10-80 p275   +-NR 8-80 p14
++Gr 8-79 p356   /-RR 8-79 p109
+HFN 8-79 p117   +St 9-80 p87

2531 192
3687 CALDARA: La costanza in amor vince l'inganno: Selve amiche; Come
     raggio sol. CARISSIMI: No non mi speri; Vittoria mio cuore (arr.
     Darumsgaard, Dallapiccola). CAVALLI: Lamento di Cassandra: L'
     alma fiacca svani; Son ancor pargoletta (arr. Leppard, Dorums-
     gaard). PERGOLESI: Se tu m'ami; Aria di Martia (arr. Parisotti,
     Spicker). SCARLATTI, A.: La donna ancora e fedele: Se Florindo
     e fedele (arr. Parissoti). Pirro e Demetrio: Le violette. Songs:
     Se delitto e l'adorarti (arr. Lavilla). Flavio: Canzonetta.
     VIVALDI: Un certo non so che: Piango gemo. Teresa Berganza, ms;
     Ricardo Requejo, pno.
                   +Gr 3-80 p1433
2531 215 Tape (c) 3301 215 (*From 2530 940)
3688 MENDELSSOHN: A midsummer night's dream, opp. 21/61: Overture. MOZ-
     ART: The marriage of Figaro, K 492: Overture. NICOLAI: The
     merry wives of Windsor: Overture. SCHUMANN: Manfred overture,
     op. 115.* WEBER: Invitation to the dance, op. 65. Rondo bril-
     lant, D flat major. Oberon: Overture. CSO; Daniel Barenboim;
     Frank Miller, vlc.
                   +FF 11/12-80 p225   +NR 6-80 p6
                   +Gr 12-79 p1023   +RR 1-80 p83
                   +-HFN 1-80 p115
2533 413
3689 Greek orthodox music: Easter on Mount Athos. Abbot Alexios; Com-
     munity of the Xenophontos Monastery, Mount Athos.
                   +-Audio 4-80 p46   ++HFN 4-79 p129
                   ++FF 9/10-79 p163   ++RR 8-79 p115
                   +Gr 5-79 p1939
2533 420
3690 BUONAMENTE: Sonata, 3 violini. FARINA: Sonata detta la Polacca.
     FONTANA: Sonata, 3 violini. GABRIELI: Sonata, 3 violini. MAR-
     INI: Capriccio. Eco, 3 violini. Passacaglia a 4. Sonata sopra
     la Monica. ROSSI: Sonata sopra l'aria di Ruggiero. Cologne
     Musica Antiqua.
                   +-FF 7/8-80 p172   +NR 8-80 p9
                   +Gr 1-80 p1168   +RR 1-80 p101
                   +HFN 1-80 p117   +ST 7-80 p195
2533 423
3691 ARNE: Concerto, harpsichord, G minor. BOYCE: Symphony, no. 1, B
     flat major. GEMINIANI: Concerto grosso, D minor. HELLENDAAL:
     Concerto, harpsichord, op. 3, no. 4, E flat major. STANLEY:
     Concerto, op. 2, no. 3, G major. English Concert; Trevor Pin-
     nock, hpd.
                   +ARG 11-80 p39   +MT 8-80 p505
                   +FF 7/8-80 p189   ++NR 6-80 p6
                   +Gr 1-80 p1162   ++RR 1-80 p86
                   +HFN 1-80 p117   +STL 2-10-80 p40
2533 446
3692 Easter on Mount Athos: Office of Easter. Xenophontos Monastery Com-
     munity; Abbot Alexios.
                   +HFN 6-80 p113   +-RR 5-80 p95
2533 451
3693 Russian orthodox music: Liturgy for All Saints Day. Trinity St.
     Sergius Monastery Priests Choir.
                   +-Gr 11-80 p731   +HFN 11-80 p125

2535 326
3694 DVORAK: Melodia, op. 55, no. 4. Serenade, op. 22, E major. FIBICH:
     Poeme, op. 41, no. 4. PROKOFIEV: War and peace, op. 91: Waltz.
     RACHMANINOFF: Vocalise, op. 34, no. 14. RIMSKY-KORSAKOV: The
     tale of the Tsar Sultan, op. 57: flight of the bumblebee. RUBIN-
     STEIN: Melody, op. 3, no. 1, F major. SVETLANOV: Aria. SHOSTA-
     KOVICH: The gadfly, op. 97a: Romance. Bolshoi Theatre Violin En-
     semble; Juli Reyentovich.
          +NR 5-80 p3
2535 367 Tape (c) 3335 367 (From 136011)
3695 ARDITI: Parla waltz. DVORAK: Rusalka, op. 114: O silver moon. GOD-
     ARD: Jocelyn: Berceuse. MEYERBEER: Dinorah: Ombra leggiera.
     SAINT-SAENS: Le rossignol et la rose. STRAUSS, J. II: Fruhlings-
     stimmen, op. 410. Geschichten aus dem Wiener Wald, op. 325. Die
     Fledermaus, op. 363: Mein Herr Marquis; Spiel ich die unschuld
     vom Lande. SUPPE: Boccaccio: Hab ich nur deine Liebe. VERDI:
     Lo spazzocamino. Rita Streich, s; RIAS Chamber Chorus; BRSO;
     Kurt Gaebel.
          +Gr 2-80 p1305   +RR 2-80 p42
          +HFN 2-80 p105
2535 801
3696 BIZET: The pearl fishers, excerpts. LORTZING: Der Waffenschmied.
     PUCCINI: La boheme, excerpts. Tosca, excerpts. ROSSINI: Il
     barbiere di Siviglia, excerpts. VERDI: Don carlo, excerpts.
     Rigoletto, excerpts. Fritz Wunderlich, t; Hermann Prey, bar;
     Erika Koth, s; Munich Radio Orchestra, Sudwestfunk Orchestra;
     Kurt Eichhorn, Horst Stein, Emmerich Smola, Hans Moltkau.
          +RR 8-80 p14
2536 410 Tape (c) 3336 410
3697 ECCARD: Over the mountains Mary goes; Von der Geburt Christi.
     FREUNDT: Wie schon singt uns der Engel Schar. GABRIELI, G.:
     Benedixisti domine. GUMPELZHAIMER: Vom Himmel hoch. GRUBER: Stil-
     le Nacht heilige Nacht. HASSLER: Verbum caro factum est. LOEWE:
     Quem pastores laudavere. PALESTRINA: Hodie Christus natus est.
     PRAETORIUS: Est is ein Ros entsprungen. REICHARDT: Heilige
     Nacht. RUDIGER: Still O Himmel; Es bluhen die Maien. SCHEIDT:
     O Jesulein zart. THIEL: Adeste fideles; Freu dich Erd und Stern-
     enzelt. TRAD.: Auf dem Berge da geht der Wind; O sanctissima;
     O schlafe gottlicher Knabe. Regensburger Domspatzen; Georg Rat-
     zinger.
          +Gr 12-80 p889 tape   +HFN 12-80 p159 tape
          +HFN 11-80 p124   +SFC 12-14-80 p20
          +NR 11-80 p1
2542 135 Tape (c) 3342 135 (From 2530 598)
3698 ANCHIETA: Con amores la mi madre. ESTEVE: Alma sintamos. GRANADOS:
     Tonadillas: La maja dolorosa; El majo discreto; El tra la la y
     el punteado; El majo timido. GURIDI: Canciones castellanas:
     Llamale con el panuelo; No quiero tus avellanas; Como quieres
     que adivine. MONTSALVATGE: Canciones negras. TORRE: Pampano
     verde. TURINA: Canto a Sevilla: El fatasma; Poema en forma de
     canciones; Cantares; Saeta en forma de Salve a la virgen de la
     esperanza. Teresa Berganza, ms; Felix Lavilla, pno.
          +Gr 6-80 p65   +HFN 8-80 p109 tape
          ++HFN 6-80 p119   +RR 6-80 p89

2547 001 Tape (c) 3347 001 (From 198036)
3699 Gregorian chant: The third Christmas mass. St. Martin Abbey Benedictine Monks Choir; Maurus Pfaff.
       +Gr 8-80 p258   +HFN 11-80 p131 tape
       +HFN 8-80 p107   +RR 8-80 p83
2547 016 Tape (c) 3347 016 (From APM 14017)
3700 Gregorian chant: Easter Sunday mass. St. Martin Abbey Choir; Maurus
Pfaff.
       +Gr 4-80 p1595   +HFN 7-80 p119
2547 028 Tape (c) 3347 028 (From APM 14002)
3701 Gregorian chant: Prima missa in commeratione omnium fidelium de-
functorum. Benedictine Abbey of St. Martin Monks Choir; Maurus
Pfaff.
          +-Gr 11-80 p728
2547 029 Tape (c) 3347 029 (From SAPM 198323)
3702 BRUMEL: Noe noe; Tandernac. FESTA: Quis dabit oculis nostris. HOF-
HAIMER: Tandernaken. ISAAC: a la bataglia; An buos; Carmen in
fa; Fortuna in mi; Imperii proceres; Innsbruck ich muss dich lassen; J'ay pris amours; La morra; San Sancti spiritus assit nobis
gratia. JOSQUIN DES PRES: Comment peult. OBRECHT: Vavilment.
RUE: Fors seulement. SENFL: Carmen in la; Carmen in re; Nasci
pati mori. ANON.: Carmen Hercules; En l'ombre d'un buissonet;
Naves pont; Si je perdu. Vienna Boys Choir, Vienna Chorus; VCM;
Nikolaus Harnoncourt.
          +Gr 11-80 p731
2723 068 (3)
3703 CANNABICH: Sinfonia concertante, C major. Sinfonia, B flat major.
FILTZ: Concerto, violoncello, G major. HOLZBAUER: Sinfonia, op.
4, no. 3, E flat major. Sinfonia concertante, A major. LEBRUN:
Concerto, oboe, D minor. RICHTER: Concerto, flute, E minor.
Sinfonia, B flat major. STAMITZ, J.: Concerto, violin, C major.
Trio, op. 1, no. 5, B flat major. Thomas Furi, vln; Jorg Dahler,
hpd; Heinz Holliger, ob; Berne Camerata; Thomas Furi.
          ++Gr 11-80 p684   +HFN 11-80 p127
2723 071 (6)
3704 Gregorian chants: Chants of the Proper of the Mass; The responsoria
of matins at Christmas; Palm Sunday chants; Proper and office for
the dedication of a church; Ancient Spanish chants; Ambrosian
chants. Various choirs and conductors.
          +Gr 9-80 p407
2740 229 (5) (From 2530 225, 2530 901, 2530 531, 2530 803, 2530 436,
              2531 004)
3705 BARTOK: Concerti, piano, nos. 1 and 2. BOULEZ: Sonata, piano, no.
2. NONO: Como una ola de fuerza y luz. Sofferte onde serene.
PROKOFIEV: Sonata, piano, no. 7, op. 83, B flat major. SCHOEN-
BERG: Pieces, piano, op. 11 (3); op. 19 (6); op. 23 (5); op. 33
(2). Suite, op. 25. STRAVINSKY: Petrouchka: Movements (3).
WEBERN: Variations, op. 27. Slava Taskova, s; Maurizio Pollini,
pno; CSO, Bavarian Radio Orchestra; Claudio Abbado.
          +Gr 8-80 p242   +STL 8-10-80 p30
          +HFN 10-80 p115

DISQUES PIERRE VERANY

PV 4801
3706 AYALA: Serie americaine. BROUWER: Airs populaires cubaine (3).
    LAURO: Valse. MALDONADO: Air de huella. PONCE: Valse. POWELL:
    Valsa sem nome. PUJOL-VILLARRUBI: Evocation cubaine. SEMENZATO:
    Divagando. Lucien Battaglia, gtr.
         +FF 11/12-80 p216

ELDORADO

No. 1
3707 BELSAYAGA: Magnificat. BLASCO: Piece, 2 flutes and harpsichord.
    DURAN DE LA MOTA: Laudate pueri. FERNANDES: Eso rigor e repente.
    FERNANDEZ HIDALGO: Salve regina a 5. LOPEZ CAPILLAS: Gloria
    laud et honor. NUNES GARCIA: Lauda Sion salvatorem. VICTORIA:
    Marian antiphon, excerpts. ZIPOLI: Mass: Gloria. Roger Wagner
    Chorale; UCLA Faculty; Thomas Harmon, org; Bess Karp, hpd; Joh-
    annes Wilbert, Roger Wagner.
         +LAMR Spring/Summer 1980 p119

No. 2
3708 ARAUJO: Villancico. BERMUDEZ: Domine ad adjuvandum me festina. DE
    LA SERNA: Tiento, 6th tone. FERNANDES: Song. Motet. MELLO
    JESUS: Se o canto enfraquecido. Roger Wagner Chorale; Thomas
    Harmon, org; Richard Wagner.
         +LAMR Spring/Summer 1980 p120

EMI

1C 137 53505/7 (3)
3709 BERLIOZ: La damnation of Faust, op. 25: Rakoczy march. BRAHMS: Con-
    certo, piano, no. 2, op. 83, B flat major. Concerto, violin, op.
    77, D major. Hungarian dances, nos. 5-6. LORTZING: Zar und
    Zimmermann: Dance. Undine: Ballet music. SCHUBERT: Marche mili-
    taire, no. 1, op. 51, D 733, D major. SCHUMANN: Concerto, piano,
    op. 54, A minor. TCHAIKOVSKY: Capriccio italien, op. 45, abridg-
    ed. Wilhelm Backhaus, Walter Gieseking, pno; Wolfgang Schneid-
    erhan, vln; Dresden Staatskapelle; Karl Bohm.
         +FF 9/10-80 p291

1C 137 53508/13 (6)
3710 BEETHOVEN: Symphony, no. 9, op. 125, D minor. BERGER: Rondino gio-
    coso, op. 4. BRAHMS: Symphony, no. 4, op. 98, E minor. BRUCK-
    NER: Symphony, no. 4, E flat major. Symphony, no. 5, B flat
    major. PFITZNER: Symphony, op. 46, C major. REGER: Variations
    and fugue on a theme by Mozart, op. 132, A major. STRAUSS, R.:
    Till Eulenspiegels lustige Streiche, op. 28. Don Juan, op. 20.
    Margarete Teschemacher, s; Elisabeth Hongen, con; Torsten Ralf,
    t; Josef Herrmann, bar; Dresden State Opera Chorus; Dresden
    Staatskapelle; Karl Bohm.
         +FF 9/10-80 p291

1C 147 03580/1 (2)
3711 ARNOLD: Wenn der Herrgott net will. DOMANIC-ROLL-ALLMEDER: Seht's
    Leut'in do war's anno dreissig in Wien. EYSLER: Die Schutzan-

liesel: Mutterl lieb's Mutterl. FIEBRICH: Das silberne Kanderln.
FELLNER-SCHNEIDER: 's Mussdorfer Sterndl. FODERL-HOCHMT-WERNER:
In Grinzing gibt's a Himmelstrass'n. GRUBER: Mei Mautterl war
a Weanerin. KRAKAUER: Du gauter Himmelvater. KRATZL-BICZO:
Das Gluck is' a Vogerl. LEHAR: Das Land des Lachelns: Als Gott
die Welt erschuf...Miene Liebe deine Liebe. Die lustige Witwe:
O Vaterland...Da geh ich zu Maxim. LORTZING: Waffenschmied: Auch
ich war ein Jungling. Wildschutz: Funftausend Taler. Zur und
Zimmermann: O sancta justitia. MOZART: Cosi fan tutte, K 588:
Questa piccola offerta...Il core vi dono bell'idole mio. Le
nozze di Figoro, K 492: Se vuol ballare; Non piu andrai. Don
Giovannai, K 527: Madamina il catalogo. Die Zauberflote, K 620:
Der Vogelfanger bin ich ja...Ein Madchen oder Weibchen...Papa-
gena Papagena. PICK: Fiakerlied. STRAUSS, J. II: Die Fledermaus, op. 363: Kommt mit mir zum Souper. Der lustige Krieg: Nur
fur Natur. Eine Nacht in Venedig: Komm in die Gondel...Ach wie so
herrlich zu schau'm. Der Zigeunerbaron, op. 420: Ja das Schreiben
und das Lesen. Wiener Blut: Wunsch gut'n Morgen Herr von Pepi.
WAGNER: Die Meistersinger von Nurnberg: Ein Werbelied; Von Sachs;
Ist's wahr. ZELLER: Der Vogelhandler: Wie mein Ahnl zwanzig
Jahr. Emmy Loose, Hermine Steinmassi, s; Eleanore Dorpinghaus,
ms; Annelies Scuckl, con; Blanche Thebom, ms; Nicolai Gedda, t;
Otto Edelmann, Erich Kunz, bs-bar; Orchestra and conductors.
          +ARSC Vol 12, nos. 1-2, 1980 p98
1C 147 30135/6 (2)
3712 BEETHOVEN: Fidelio, op. 72: Hat man nich auch Gold beneben. CORNEL-
IUS: Barbier von Bagdad: Ergreift den Alten...Heil diesem Haus
denn du tratst ein Salam aleikum. HALEVY: La juive: Wenn ew'ger
Hass. LORTZING: Zar und Zimmermann: O sancta justitia,..Den hoh-
en Herrscher wurdig zu empfangen...Heil sei dem Tag. Wildschutz:
Funftausend Taler. Waffenschmied: Auch ich war ein Jungling.
MOZART: Die Entfuhrung aus dem Serail, K 384: Wer ein Liebchen
hat gefunden...O wie will ich triumphieren. Le nozze di Figaro,
K 492: Susse Rache ja susse Rache. Die Zauberflote, K 620: O
Isis und Osiris...In diesen heil'gen Hallen. NICOLAI: Die lustigen Weiber von Windsor: Als Bublein klein. ROSSINI: Il barbiere
di Siviglia: Die Verleumdung sie ist ein Luftchen...Einen Doktor
meinesgleichen. TCHAIKOVSKY: Eugen Onegin, op. 24: Ein jeder
kennt die Lieb auf Erden. VERDI: Nabucco: Warum klagt ihr und
seid so verzweifelt. Don Carlo: Sie hat mich nie geliebt. Simon
Boccanegra: Leb wohl auf ewig...Palast der Vater. I vespres sic-
iliennes: O Heimat...O main Palermo. WAGNER: Gotterdammerung:
Hoiho Hoiho; Ihr Gibischmannen machet euch auf. Lohengrin: Mein
Herr und Gott. Die Meistersinger von Nurnberg: Das schone Fest
Johannistag. Rheingold: Halt du Gieriger...Gonne mir auch was.
Die Walkure: Mud am Herd fand ich den Mann. Maud Cunitz, s;
Margarete Klose, con; Rudolf Schock, Manfred Schmidt, Leopold
Clam, Harold Kraus, Wolfgang Windgassen, t; Josef Metternich,
Horst Gunter, Ferdinand Frantz, Horst Wilhelm, Benno Kusche, bar;
Walter Stoll, Robert Koffmane, Anton Metternich, Josef Greindl,
Gottlob Frick, bs; Various orchestras and conductors.
          +ARSC Vol 12, nos. 1-2, 1980 p94
1C 165 30796/9 (4)
3713 DALLAPICCOLA: Cori di Michelangelo Buonarroti. EDLUND: Elegie.
JOLIVET: Empithaleme. MARTIN: Ballade, piano. Mass. MESSIAEN:

Rechants (5). MONTEVERDI: Lagrime d'amante al sepolcro dell'
amata. POULENC: Chansons (9). STRAUSS, R.: Der Abend; Die Gott
in im Putzzimer. PIZZETTI: Composizioni corali (3). TALLIS:
Spem in alium. Stockholm Radio Choir, Stockholm Chamber Choir;
Eric Ericson.
+—ARSC Vol 12, nos. 1-2, 1980 p126

ENIGMA

K 23538
3714 BOZZA: Agrestide. DEBUSSY: Syrinx. FAURE: Fantasie, op. 79. IBERT:
     Piece, flute. MESSIAEN: Le merle noir. POULENC: Sonata, flute
     and piano. ROUSSEL: Joueurs de flute, op. 27. Susan Milan, flt;
     Clifford Benson, pno.
+Gr 9-80 p368   +HFN 9-80 p114

K 53589
3715 BACH: Suite, orchestra, S 1068, D major: Air on a G string. FAURE:
     Pavane. GLUCK: Orfeo ed Euridice: Dance of the blessed spirits.
     GRIEG: Holberg suite, op. 40: 1st movement. HANDEL: Solomon:
     Arrival of the Queen of Sheba. LOCKE: The tempest: Lilk and
     curtain tune. MOZART: Serenade, no. 13, K 525, G major: 1st
     movement. PACHELBEL: Canon, D major. PURCELL: Abdelazer: Rond-
     eau. St. John's Smith Square Orchestra; John Lubbock.
+Gr 4-80 p1597   +RR 3-80 p54
+—HFN 3-80 p103

ERATO

ERA 9512
3716 CAZZATI: Sonata, trumpet and strings. COLONNA: O lucidissima dies,
     motet. GABRIELI, D.: Sonata, trumpet and strings. PERTI: Quan-
     do si belle, aria. Aestuat mundi mare, motet. TORELLI: concerto
     a 4, 2 violins and strings. VITALI: Sinfonia, 2 trumpets, 2
     oboes and strings (attrib.). Mirella Freni, Reri Grist, s; Gab-
     riella Armuzzi-Romei, Christiane Rosse, vln; Maurice Andre, Mar-
     cel Lagorce, tpt; Marina Mauriella, Nicole Schnoebelen, hpd;
     Luigi Fernando Tagliavini, Achille Berruti, org; Bologna Commun-
     ity Theater Orchestra; Tito Gotti.
+FF 5/6-80 p185

STU 71127
3717 GINASTERA: Cancion al arbol del Olvido. IBERT: Entr'acte. HANDEL:
     Sonata, flute and harpsichord, op. 1, no. 4, A minor. PEPUSCH:
     Sonate, guitar. SCHEIDLER: Sonata, guitar, D major (arr. Scheit).
     VILLA-LOBOS: Distribuicao de flores. ANON.: Greensleeves (rev.
     Fleury). Christian Larde, flt; Turibio Santos, gtr.
+Gr 4-80 p1568   +RR 4-80 p94
+HFN 4-80 p115

ESQ

AS 31
3718 ABSIL: Pieces en quatuor. BYRD (arr. Houghton): Dances (2). BOZZA:

Nuages. ELLIS: Satyric suite. FRANCAIX: Quartet, saxophones.
GERSHWIN (arr. Houghton): Porgy and Bess: Summertime. JOPLIN
(arr. Houghton): Magnetic rag. NESTICO: A study in contrasts.
SATIE (arr. Lewis): Gymnopedie, no. 1. English Saxophone Quartet.
                +RR 6-80 p66

                        EVEREST

3444
3719 BULL: Fancy. BYRD: In fields abroad. Galiarda. CAMPIAN: Fair if
     you expect admiring. DOWLAND: Flow not so fast ye fountains.
     FARMER: Fair Phyllis I saw sitting all alone; Sweet friend thy
     absence. FARNABY: Carters now cast down your whips; Construe my
     meaning; Daphne on the rainbow. INGLOTT: The leaves be greene.
     JOHNSON: Defiled is my name. MORLEY: Thyrsis and Milla. PHIL-
     LIPS: Amarilli di Julio Romano. RAVENSCROFT: A bellman's song.
     ROSSETER: When Laura smiles. ANON.: Dance. Sacred ende. Jan-
     tina Noorman, ms; Nigel Rogers, t; Andrew Brunt, treble; Desmond
     Dupre, lt; John Beckett, virginals and organ; Jaye Consort of
     Viols.
                +ARG 7-79 p49   +NR 1-80 p6
                +-FF 7/8-80 p178
SDBR 3452
3720 Gregorian chants: Elegies for kings and princes. Deller Consort.
                /FF 5/6-80 p181   +NR 10-79 p7
SDBR 3457
3721 Gregorian chants: The wedding of Cana. Deller Consort.
                +-ARG 6-80 p49   +NR 3-80 p10
                /FF 5/6-80 p181
SDBR 3459 Tape (c) 3459
3722 ALBENIZ: Piezas caracteristicas: Torre bermeja. BACH: Suite, solo
     violoncello, no. 3, S 1009, C major: Suite. CRESPO: Nortena,
     homenaje a Julian Aguirre. DUARTE: Variations on a Catalan folk
     song, op. 25. PONCE: Mexican popular songs (3). SCARLATTI, A.:
     Gavotte. VILLA-LOBOS: Etude, guitar, no. 1, E minor. John Wil-
     liams, gtr.
                ++HF 11-80 p88 tape   +NR 8-80 p14
SDBR 3460
3723 CHERUBINI: Medea: O amore viene a me. DONIZETTI: Lucia di Lammer-
     moor: Regnava nel silenzio; Mad scene. PERGOLESI: La serva pad-
     rona: Stizzoso mio stizzoso; A serpina penserete. ROSSINI:
     Petite messe solennelle: Crucifixus. VERDI: Rigoletto: Caro
     nome; Tutte le feste. Renata Scotto, s; Orchestral Accompaniment.
                +ARG 6-80 p48   +-NR 4-80 p11
                +-FF 5/6-80 p173   +St 4-80 p145
SDBR 3469
3724 Christmas songs: Silent night; Hark the herald angels sing; See
     amid the winter snow; We three kings; Away in a manger; The first
     noel; Good King Wencelas; The holly and the ivy; While shepherds
     watched; God rest ye merry gentlemen. St. Paul's and St. Mary's
     Cathedral Choirs.
                +NR 12-80 p1

FESTIVO

<u>074</u>
3725 DUPRE: Prelude and fugue, op. 7, no. 1, B major. MULET: Carillon
        sortie. RALPH-DRIFFILL: Toccata. SAINT-SAENS: Fantaisie, E
        flat major. VAN OPSTAL: Scherzo. WIDOR: Symphony, no. 4, op.
        13, no. 4, F major: Andante cantabile; Finale. Herman Van Vliet,
        org.
                +Gr 11-80 p710

FINLANDIA

FA 308 (From Finnlevy SFX 32)
3726 ENGLUND: Passacaglia. KOKKONEN: Lux aeterna. MERIKANTO: Passacag-
        lia, op. 80. KUUSISTO: Ramus virens olivarum, op. 55, no. 1.
        PARVIAINEN: Toccata and fugue. SALONEN: Sen suuven suloisuutta.
        Tauno Aikaa, org.
                +FF 11/12-80 p210   +-HFN 12-80 p151

FINNADAR

SR 2720 (2)
3727 COWELL: Piece, piano, Paris 1924. FELDMAN: Verticle thoughts IV.
        Piece, piano (To Philip Guston). HAYS: Sunday nights. MIMARO-
        GLU: Rosa. ORNSTEIN: Impressions de Notre Dame. PECK: Suspend-
        ed sentence. Doris Hays, pno.
                +FF 9/10-80 p263   ++St 9-80 p85
                +NR 12-80 p10

GREAT AMERICAN GRAMOPHONE COMPANY

<u>GADD 1040</u>
3728 BACH: Prelude and fugue, E minor. CUNDICK: Fanfare. FRANCK: Piece
        heroique. KARG-ELERT: Clair de lune, op. 72, no. 2. HANDEL:
        Forest music. SCHUMANN: Sketch, op. 58, no. 4, D flat major.
        VIERNE: Berceuse. WALOND: Voluntary, no. 1. Robert Cundick,
        org.
                +ARG 4-80 p51   ++MU 9-78 p14
                +-HFN 1-79 p75

GASPARO

<u>GS 206</u>
3729 ARIOSTI: La profezia d'Eliseo nel'assedio di Amaria: Ma per destin
        peggiore...Prole tenera. BIBER: Sonata, solo violin, no. 6.
        FUX: Gli ossequi della notte: Caro mio ben. LIDL: Trio, violin,
        violoncello and viola da gamba, E major. SCHENCK: L'Echo du
        Danube: Sonata, no. 2. Oberlin Baroque Performance Institute
        Members; August Wenzinger.
                +FF 9/10-80 p284   ++St 9-80 p84
                ++NR 10-80 p7

GOLDEN AGE

1014
3730 BEETHOVEN: Sonatina, C major. DIABELLI: Sonatina, op. 168, no. 7,
     A major. DUSSEK: Sonatina, G major. HOPKINS: Sonatina. KUHLAU:
     Sonatina, op. 20, no. 2, G major. KHACHATURIAN: Sonatina, C maj-
     or. WEISS: Sonata, piano, op. 8, no. 1, D major. Eugenia Evans,
     pno.
                    +NR 10-80 p13

GOLDEN CREST

CRS 4191
3731 GIBSON: Quintet, winds. IANNACONNE: Parodies. PERLE: Quintet,
     woodwinds, no. 3. ROSS: Divertimento. SCHICKELE: Diversions.
     TANG: A little suite. Clarion Wind Quintet.
                    +ARG 11-80 p49

GOTHIC

D 87904 (2)
3732 BACH: Choral prelude, S 768, Sei gegrusset Jesu gutig: Partita.
     Fantasia and fugue, S 542, G minor. DISTLER: Partita on "Wachet
     auf ruft uns die Stimme". HINDEMITH: Sonata, organ, no. 1.
     ROREM: A Quaker reader: First-day thoughts; Mary Dyer did hang
     as a flag; Evidence of things not seen; There is a spirit that
     delights to do no evil...; A secret power; The world of silence.
     SOKOLA: Passacaglia quasi toccata on B-A-C-H. Catherine Crozier,
     org.
          +FF 7/8-80 p168   +-NR 3-80 p15
          +-MU 9-80 p12   +-St 6-80 p125

GRACE CATHEDRAL

Grace Cathedral, San Francisco
3733 ALAIN: Litanies, op. 79. BALBASTRE: Votre bonte. DANDRIEU: Offer-
     toire. GUILIAN: Suite in the 1st tone. VIERNE: Symphonie, no.
     2, op. 20, E minor: Choral. WIDOR: Symphony, no. 6, op. 42, no.
     2, B major: Adagio. John Fenstermaker, org.
                    +MU 7-80 p9

GRAND ORGUE

RLM 760910
3734 BARBLAN: Canon, D minor. Chaconne on BACH. BLOCH: Prelude. CHAIX:
     Chorales (2). GAGNEBIN: Carillon. Psalm, no. 89. REICHEL: Pas-
     torale, G major. SEGOND: Psalm, no. 24. Francois Rabot, org.
                    +ARG 10-79 p53   +-HFN 5-80 p135
LCM 770511
3735 GIGOUT: Grand choeur dialogue. LISZT: Adagio, G 263, D flat major.
     Prelude and fugue on the name B-A-C-H, G 260. MENDELSSOHN: Son-

ata, organ, op. 65, no. 2, C minor. ROUSSEL: Prelude and fugue, op. 41. VIERNE: Improvisations (3) (recons. by M. Durufle). Pierre Labric, org.
   -FF 1/2-80 p172

791205

3736 BACH: Chorale preludes, S 630, Heut triumphiere Gottes Sohn; S 712, In dich hab ich gehoffet. BLANCHARD: Prelude avec trompette du "Te deum". MOURET: Suite en re. SENNY: Vitrail pour Jeanne d' Arc. TELEMANN: Sonata en re. Michel Morisset, tpt; Marie-Andree Morisset-Balier, org.
  +-FF 9/10-80 p271   +-MU 11-80 p17

GRAND PRIX

GP 9002

3737 BACH: Cantata, no. 147, Jesu joy of man's desiring. The well-tempered clavier, S 846: Prelude and fugue, no. 6, D minor. BARNHART: When stars looked down. CROSSAN: Concertino, multiple keyboards. Prismatic rag. KOHS: Variations, piano. SCHUBERT: Valses nobles, D 969. WEBER: Sonata, piano, no. 1, op. 24, C major: Prepetuum mobile. Jack Crossan, pno, electric piano, clavichord, hpd.
   -FF 9/10-80 p265

GP 9003

3738 BENATZKY: Ich muss wider einma. BLECH: Telefonische Bestellung. DEBUSSY: Ballade des femmes de Paris; C'est l'extase langoureuse. DUPARC: Phidyle. DVORAK: Songs, op. 55: Songs my mother taught me. GRIEG: Thanks for advice. KLAMAN: Komm Zigany. RONTANI: Or ch'io non seguo piu. ROSA: To be near thee. STOLZ: Im Prater bluh'n wieder die Baume. STRAUSS, R.: Morgen, op. 27, no. 4; Standchen, op. 17, no. 2. VELLONES: Le posson volant. TRAD.: Echo song; Eriskay love lilt; Let us break bread together; Malurous qu'o uno fenno. Dorothy Warenskjold, s; Rolin Jensen, pno.
  +FF 9/10-80 p241

GRENADILLA

GS 1029/30

3739 AMRAM: Portraits. FELDMAN: Instruments (4). HADJU: Sketches in a sentimental mood (5). KOPYTMAN: About an old tune. KUPFERMAN: Abracadabra. ORGAD: Shaar Shaar. PARTOS: Quartet, piano. SIEGMEISTER: Songs of experience. Cantilena Chamber Players.
  +FF 3/4-80 p195   +NR 12-79 p6

GS 1040

3740 AMRAM: Fanfare. CALVERT: The Monteregian hills: Suite. CHASE: Fugue for brass sextet. HERMANN: Quintet, brass, no. 1. HOVHANESS: Sharagan and fugue, op. 58. KAUFMAN: A solemn music. KRAFT: Suite for brass. LIEB: Feature suite. The Brass Guild.
  /FF 7/8-80 p187   +NR 7-78 p7

GS 1041

3741 BRAHMS: Canons (4). HEINRICH: The minstrel's catch. HINDEMITH: Sine musica nulla disciplina. HOLST: Evening on the Moselle; If t'were the time of lilies. MOZART: Canons (2). SCHOENBERG:

Canons (2). ANON.: Welcome to our music feast. Wille wille
will. Gregg Smith Singers; Gregg Smith.
        +-FF 1/2-80 p163   +NR 10-79 p8
        +MJ 9/10-79 p50

GUILD

GSP 7014
3742 BACH: Chorale preludes, S 622, O Mensch bewein dein Sunde gross; S
     632, Herr Jesu Christ dich zu uns wend. BRUHNS: Prelude and
     fugue, E minor. BUXTEHUDE: Prelude and fugue, D major. KEE:
     choral prelude "Aus tiefer Not schrei ich zu Dir". Fantasia
     on "Wachet auf ruft uns die Stimme". KODALY: Praeludium. MEN-
     DELSSOHN: Sonata, organ, op. 65, no. 2, C minor. Piet Kee, org.
        ++Gr 9-79 p488   +MT 1-80 p37
        ++HFN 9-79 p119   ++RR 9-79 p105
GRSP 7016
3743 BACH: Toccata and fugue, S 565, D minor. KITSON: Communion on an
     Irish air "Alone with none but thee my God". LANG, C.S.: Tuba
     tune, op. 15, D major. STANFORD: Sonata, organ, no. 4, op. 153.
     WIDOR: Symphony, no. 5, op. 42, no. 1, F minor: Toccata. TRAD.
     (Irish): Londonderry air (arr. Dexter). John Dexter, org.
        +Gr 10-80 p523   +HFN 9-80 p114

HARMONIA MUNDI

HMD 204
3744 CORNYSHE: Ah Robin; Hoyda jolly Rutterkin. GENTIAN: Je suis Robert.
     GIBBONS: The cries of London. JOHNSON: Care-charming sleep.
     MONTEVERDI: Baci soavi e cari; Lamento dell Ninfa. SERMISY:
     Tant que vivray. VAUTOR: Mother I will have a husband. WEELKES:
     Cease sorrows now. WILBYE: Lady when I behold the roses. Del-
     ler Consort, Bulgarian Quartet; Rene Saorgin, hpd, org; Raphael
     Perulli, vla da gamba.
        +-Gr 11-75 p888   +RR 2-76 p59
        +-HFN 7-80 p113
HM 227
3745 ARNE: Sonatas, harpsichord, F major, E minor. HANDEL: Grand lesson
     on an air from "Rinaldo" (arr. Babell). BLOW: Suite, D minor.
     BULL: Piper's galliard. BYRD: Calino custurame. Malt's come
     down. FARNABY: Rosasolis. LOCKE: Suite, C major. Harold Les-
     ter, pno, hpd.
        +-Gr 4-80 p1572   +RR 4-80 p98
        +HFN 4-80 p116
HM 235
3746 Gregorian chants: Prague Easter play. Deller Consort.
        +ARG 11-80 p39   +-NR 6-80 p9
        +-FF 7/8-80 p161   +RR 4-79 p32
        +HFN 6-80 p113
HM 339
3747 Carmina Burana: Plaintes mariales du jeu de la passion. Clemencic
     Consort; Choralschola der Winer Hofburgkapelle; Rene Clemencic.
        +FF 1/2-80 p176   +NYT 8-10-80 pD17
        +HFN 2-79 p109

HM 396
3748 BERNARD DE VENTADORN: Quand vei la lauzeta mover. PEIROL: Quant
     amors trobet partit. VAQUEIRAS: Kalenda meia; Vida. VIDAL:
     Vida et razos; Barons de mon dan convit. ANON.: A l'entrada del
     temps clar. Clemencic Consort; Rene Clemencic.
             +FF 7/8-80 p176   +RR 10-78 p99
             +Gr 2-78 p1455   ++RR 4-78 p983
HM 397 Tape (c) 40-397
3749 AZALAIS DE PORCAIRAGUES: Ar em al freg temps vengut; Vida. BERNARD
     DE VENTADORN: Can l'erba; Vida. DIA: A chantar; Vida. FOLQUET
     DE MARSELHA: Sitot me sol; Vida. GUILHEM DE CABESTANH: Vida.
     Clemencic Consort; Rene Clemencic.
             ++FF 11/12-80 p203   +HFN 6-79 p117 tape
             +Gr 8-78 p368   ++RR 4-78 p93
             +HFN 7-78 p105   +RR 7-78 p89
HM 441 (From HM 440)
3750 Monks and troubadors: Plainsong hymns, Psalm verses and mass move-
     ments from the Gregorian, Ambrosian and Frankish rites; Trouba-
     dour and trouvere songs. Schola Cantorum; Denis Stevens.
             +HFN 6-80 p113   +-RR 7-80 p90
HM 490
3751 BACH: Chromatic fantasia and fugue, S 903, D minor. CROFT: Suite,
     C minor. FROBERGER: Suite, D major. LE ROUX: Suite, F major.
     ROSSI: Toccata settima. Emer Buckley, hpd.
             ++FF 5/6-80 p183   ++HFN 7-79 p116
             +Gr 9-79 p487   +RR 8-79 p106
HM 509
3752 CERNOHORSKY: Fuga moderato. LINEK: Concerto, organ, D major. Fan-
     fares, nos. 1-3, 5-6, 13-14. MYSLIVECEK: Suite, strings. TUMA:
     Parthia, D major. WOTJA: Introduzione et aria. ZACH: Sonata a
     tre, A major. Pro Arte Antiqua Prague.
             +-FF 9/10-80 p285   ++RR 7-78 p52
             +HFN 7-78 p95
HM 589
3753 BACH, C.P.E.: Sonata, oboe, G minor. HOTTETERRE: Sonata, oboe, op.
     5, no. 3, D major. LAVIGNE: Sonata, oboe. LOEILLET: Sonata,
     oboe, op. 5, no. 1, E minor. TELEMANN: Sonata, oboe, A minor.
     Michel Piguet, ob; Hansjurg Lange, bsn; Lionel Rogg, hpd.
             +HFN 2-80 p103   +-RR 2-80 p69
HMU 610
3754 ATTAINGNANT: Tordion. Pavane et galliarde. DEMANTIUS: Polnischer
     Tanz und Galliarda. FRANCK, M.: Pavane et galliarde. GERVAISE:
     Branle. HASSLER: Intradas (3). MODERNE: Branle gay nouveau.
     Branles de Bourgogne. PHALESE: L'Arboscello ballo furlano. SUS-
     ATO: Hoboecken dans. Il estoit une fillette, ronde. Mille re-
     gretz, pavane. Ronde et salterelle. Si pas souffrir, pavane.
     Ronde. Clemencic Consort; Rene Clemencic.
             -HFN 1-76 p105   +RR 5-80 p40
             +-RR 8-76 p42
HM 754
3755 BULL: Galliarda. Lord Lumleys paven and galliard. Pavana. BYRD:
     Almand. Calino casturame. Galiardas passamezzo. John come
     kiss me now. Miserere. La volta. FARNABY: Fantasia. Pawles
     wharf. Quodlings delight. Tower Hill. Up tails all. MUNDY:
     Robin. TOMKINS: A short verse. ANON.: Why aske you. Muscain.

Lionel Rogg, hpd, positiv organ.
+FF 9/10-80 p266   +RR 5-79 p90
+HFN 6-79 p115

HM 793
3756 AGUILERA DE HEREDIA: Pange lingua a tres voces. Salve de lleno.
Tiento de falsas de quarto tono. Tiento lleno de primer tono.
BRUNA: Tiento sobre la letania de la virgen. Tiento de falsas
de segundo tono. CORREA DE ARAUXO: Tiento de medio registro de
tiple de septimo tono. CABANILLES: Corrente italiana. SOLA:
Medio registro de mano derecho. DURON: Gaitilla de mano izquer-
da. MENALT: Tiento de falsas de sexio tono. Francis Chapelet,
org.
+RR 6-80 p77

HM 948
3757 BOHM: Christ lag in Todesbanden, chorale. FISCHER: Ricercari for
Advent, Quadragesima, Easter and Pentecost. PACHELBEL: Ricercare, C minor. SCHEIDEMANN: Chorales: Ach Gott von Himmel sieh
darein; Durch Adams fall ist ganz verderbt; Es ist das Heil uns
kommen her. SCHEIDT: Variations on "Von der fortuna". SWEEL-
INCK: Von der fortuna variations. Fantasia cromatica. Ballet
of the Grand Duke. Francis Chapelet, org.
+-Gr 4-80 p1572   ++RR 4-80 p103
+-HFN 4-80 p117

1003 Tape (c) 40-1003
3758 Danses anciennes de Hongrie et de Transylvanie. Clemencic Consort;
Rene Clemencic.
+FF 5/6-80 p193   +HFN 4-79 p134 tape
+HFN 1-79 p124   +RR 12-78 p92

HM 1013
3759 DIABELLI: Wiener Tanz. LANNER: Neue Wiener Landler, op. 1. Die Wer-
ber, op. 103. MAYER: Schnofler Tanz. STELZMULLER: Stelzmuller
Tanz. STRAUSS, J. I: Sperl polka, op. 133. STRAUSS, J. II: Neue
pizzicato polka, op. 449. STROHMAHER: Schone Ida. Die Tanzlustigen. ANON.: Linzer Tanz. Tanze (2). Vienna Bella Musica Ensemble; Michael Dittrich.
++FF 9/10-80 p285   +HFN 4-80 p115
+Gr 3-80 p1449   ++RR 3-80 p65

HM 1019
3760 ALFONSO X, El sabio: Cantigas, nos. 159, 200, 277, 281. BEAUCARNE:
Christopher Colomb. BUDEL: Lancan li jorn. ELUARD: Nous deux.
KUNZE: Refuge. OSNOWYCZ: Impro mi. RIFFARD: A la cambrousse.
ZOSSO: Une maison. ANON.: Chi vuol lo mondo. Dans Paris. En
leve. Ex adae vito. La-bas. Le garcon jardinier. Petite maz-
urka. Stella splendens. Rene Zosso, Anne Osnowycz, voice, hurdy
gurdy, Hungarian citera.
+-Gr 11-79 p18   +-RR 2-80 p78
+-HFN 1-80 p119   +-RR 5-80 p40

HM 1039
3761 Popular tunes of 17th century England: Londone tunes: Hyde Park;
Mayden Lane; St. Paul's wharf; Tower Hill; Gray's Inn. Country
dances: Cuckolds all in a row; Merry milkmaids we; Woodick; Newcastle. Ballads mentioned by Shakespeare: Callino Casturame;
Come live with me and be my love; Light o love; Jog on. 17th
century top three-greensleeves: Fortune my foe; Packington's
pound. Across the Channel: Che passa; All in a garden green; La

folia; Quarte branles. Across the border: The clean contrary
way; Gilderoy; Gillecrankie; The miller of the Dee. Braodside
Band; Jeremy Barlow.

    +FF 9/10-80 p257   +RR 7-80 p60
    +HFN 6-80 p113   ++SFC 12-21-80 p22
    *NYT 8-10-80 pD17

HM 1212
3762 BELLINI: Sonata, organ. FRESCOBALDI: Ricercare decimo on La, fa,
sol, la, re. Toccatas, nos. 4, 6. MALVEZZI: Canzone on the 2nd
tone. PETRALLI: Versets (2). SCARLATTI: Sonata, organ, K 288,
D major. ZIPOLI: Elevazione. Rene Saorgin, org.

    +-FF 9/10-80 p268   +RR 7-80 p75
    +HFN 7-80 p115

1C 065 99601
3763 ANERIO: Christus factus est. BERCHEM: O vos omnes. CLEMENS NON
PAPA: O crux benedicta. FUX: Ad te domine levavi. JOSQUIN DES
PREZ: Tu solus qui facis mirabilia. LASSUS: Tui sunt coeli.
MANGON: Salve regina. PALESTRINA: Terra tremuit. VICTORIA:
Ave Maria, vidi speciosam. WILLAERT: O magnum mysterium. ANON.:
Ave Maria Keiserin. Gregorian chants: Alma redemptoris mater.
Syte willekomen heire Kirst. Aachen Cathedral Choir; Rudolf
Pohl.

    +-Gr 2-80 p1282   +RR 2-80 p83
    +HFN 1-80 p121

1C 065 99648 (From HM 30616)
3764 BOUSSET: Air a boire. FESCH: Tu fai la superbetta. GORNER: Der
ordentliche Haussant; Der Kuss. GRAUN: Das Tochterchen. HAM-
MERSCHMIDT: Die Kunst des Kussens. KRIEGER: Coridon in Noten;
Ein Kussgen in Ehren; Im Dunkeln ist gut munkeln; Die schlimmen
Manner. RATHGEBER: Von den Weibsbildern. ROUSSEAU: Echo.
SPERONTES: Blaustrumpflied; Liebe mich redlich. TELEMANN: Ein
reiches Weib; Geld; Das Frauenzimmer; Die Lieb und auch die Floh;
Ein reiches Weib; Die ungekammte Phillis. Edith Mathis, s; Benno
Kursche, bar; Fritz Neumeyer, hpd; Reinhold Buhl, vlc.

    +-Gr 3-80 p1434   +-HFN 1-80 p121

1C 065 99745 (also HMS 30836, 30313-1, BASF DC 219569)
3765 BRUCK: O du armer Judas. BURGK: Der Herr mit seinen Jungern. DE-
MANTIUS: St. John Passion. LECHNER: Allein zu dir Herr Jesu
Christ. PRAETORIUS: O vos omnes. SCHUTZ: Die Wort der Einset-
zung des heiligen Abandmahls. Stuttgart Kantatenchor; August
Langenbeck.

    +FF 3/4-80 p80

1C 065 99807
3766 CIMAROSA: Quoniam tu solus Sanctus; Gloria patri. DONIZETTI: Don
Pasquale: Quel guardo il cavaliere. HANDEL: Alcina: Overture.
MOZART: Le nozze di Figaro, K 492: Deh vieni non tardar. Il re
pastore, K 208: L'amero saro costante. ROSSINI: Il barbiere di
Siviglia: Una voce poco fa. Arleen Auger, s; Stuttgart Radio
Orchestra; Argeo Quadri.

    +FF 1/2-80 p162   +-RR 7-80 p56
    +HFN 7-80 p111

1C 065 99824
3767 BIBER: Harmonia artificiosa ariosa, no. 1, D minor. BUXTEHUDE:
Sonata, 2 violins, op. 1, no. 5, C major. KUHNEL: Sonata, 2
viola da gamba, E minor. ROSENMULLER: Sonata, 2 violins, no. 2,

E minor. SCHENK: La nymphe di Rehno, op. 8: Chaconne, G major.
Janine Rubinlicht, vln; Sigiswald Kuijken, vln, vla da gamba;
Wieland Kuijken, vla, vla da gamba; Robert Kohnen, hpd.
+FF 5/6-80 p195   ++RR 6-80 p72
+HFN 5-80 p133

1C 065 99833
3768 Songs for the Tudor Kings: CORNYSH: My love she moun'th. DAVY: Joan
is sick and ill at ease. HENRY, VIII, King: Adieu madame et ma
maistresse; Alas what shall I do for love; Helas madame; O my
heart is sore. ANON.: Come o'er the burn Bessy; England be glad;
In wilderness; Hey trolly lolly lo; If I had wit for to endite;
Let not us that young men be; Time to pass with goodly sport; Up
I arose in verno tempore; Who shall have my fair lady. Pro Cantione Antiqua.
+HFN 4-80 p112   .   +-RR 3-80 p90

HELDEN RECORDS

HR 109/10
3769 FRANZ: Delight of melancholy. GRIEG: Peer Gynt, op. 46: Solveig's
song. A swan. JENSEN: Press thy cheek against my own. Row
gently here my gondolier. MASSENET: Elegy. MENDELSSOHN: Consolation. MUZIO: Mazurka. PIERNE: Serenade. RIMSKY-KORSAKOV:
The tale of the Tsar Sultan, op. 57: Flight of the bumblebee.
ROSSINI: The barber of Seville: Una voce poco fa. SCHUBERT: My
peace thou art. Serenade. SCHUMANN: Dedication. THOMAS: Mignon: Rondo gavotte. Milan Yancich, French hn; Edwin McArthur,
pno.
/FF 9/10-80 p283

HMV

RLS 724 (12) plus 243 page book
3770 The record of singing. ALABIEV: Songs: Die Nachtigall (Gertrude
Forstel s,); Solovei (Alma Fohrstrom, con). d'ALBERT: Tiefland:
Pedro's dream (Erik Schmedes, t). ARDITI: songs: Il bacio (Ade-
lina Patti, s; Landon Ronald, pno); L'incantrice (Maria Galvany,
s); Leggiero invisible (Ernestine Schumann-Heink, con). AUBER:
Fra Diavolo: Romanze (Wilhelm Herold, t); Welches Gluck ich arme
(Hermine Bosetti, s). Manon Lescaut: L'eclat de rire (Ellen
Beach Yaw, s). La muette de Portici: Air du sommeil (Georges
Imbart de la Tour, t). BACH (Gounod): Ave Maria (Alessandro
Moreschi, castrato). BELLINI: I Capuleti ed i Montecchi: Se
Romeo t'uccise (Guerrina Fabbri, con; Salvatore Cottone, pno).
Norma: Casta diva; Ah bello a me ritorna (Giannina Russ, s). I
Puritani: A te o cara (Aristodemo Giorgini, t); Ah viene al
tempio (Reginia Pacini, s); Qui la voce (Marcella Sembrich, s).
La sonnambula: Ah non credea (Adelina Patti, s; Alfred Barili,
pno); Ah perche non posso odiarti (Fernando de Lucia, t,) Vi rav-
viso (Andres de Segurola, bs). BEMBERG: Songs: Les anges pleur-
ent; Chant venitien (Nelli Belba, s; Gabriel Lapierre, pno);
Chanson des baisers (Emma Eames, s). BERLIOZ: La damnation de
Faust: Maintenant chantons a cette belle...Devant la maison

(Maurice Renaud, bar). Les Troyens: Chers Tyriens (Marie Delna, con.). BILLI: E canta il grillo (Titta Ruffo, bar). BIZET: Carmen: Dut-il m'en couter la vie (Lucien Muratore, t); En vain pour eviter (Gemma Bellincioni, s); Habanera (Emma Calve, s). La jolie fille de Perth: Quand la flamme de l'amour (Jean-Francois Delmas, bs). BLANGINI: Per valli per boschi (Nelli Melba, s; Charles Gilibert, bar). BOIELDIEU: La dame blanche: Ce domaine (Marie Gutheil-Schoder, s). BOITO: Mefistofele: Spunta l'aurora pallida (Teresa Arkel, s; Salvatore Cottone, pno). BOTTESINI: Ero e Leandro: Romanza d'Ero (Amelia Pinto, s). BRETON: La Dolores: Estratto del duetto (Florencio Constantino, t). CATALANI: La Wally: Ebben, ne andro lontano (Solomea Krusceniski, s). CHAMINADE: Songs: L'ete (Emma Albani, s); Chanson slave (Jeanne Gervillereache, con). CHARPENTIER: Louise: Depuis le jour (Julia Guiraudon, s). COSTA: Eli: I will extol thee (Agnes Nicholls, s). COWAN: At the mid-hour of night (Agnes Nicholls, s; Hamilton Harty, pno). BERIOT: Prendi per me sei libero (Fanny Torresella, s). DE LARA: Messaline: O nuit d'mour (Lawrence Whitehill, bar). DELIBES: Lakme: Fantasie aux divins mensonges (Edmond Clement, t). DESSAUER: La retour des promis (Lillian Blauvelt, s). DONIZETTI: Don Pasquale: Va ben ma riflette...Cheti, cheti, immantinente (Giuseppe de Luca, bar; Ferruccio Corradetti, bs). L' Elisir d'amore: Come paride vizzoso (Antonio Scotti, bar); Udite udite (Antonio Pini Corsi, bar); Una furtiva lagrima (Enrico Caruso, t; Salvatore Cottone, pno). La favorita: A tanto amor (Mario Ancona, bar). Lucrezia Borgia: Come e bello (Celestina Broninsegna, s); M'odi ah m'odi (Ines de Frate, s); M'odi ah m'odi (Elena Teodorini, s); Separati a l'alba...Vieni la mia vendetta (Francesco Navarini, bs). Poliuto: Di quai soavi lacrime (Maria de Macchi, s). LUcia di Lammermoor: Regnava nel silenzio... Quando rapita in estasi (Frieda Hempel, s). ERKEL: Hunyadi Laszlo: Ah rebeges a mi vadul (Lilian Nordica, s; Romayne Simmons, pno). FLOTOW: Alessandro Stradella: Seid mener Wonne (Hedwig Francillo-Kaufmann, s). Martha: Chi me dira (Edouard de Reszke, bs); Ja seit fruhester Kindheit Tagen (Karl Jorn, t; Paul Knupfer, bs). GIANELLI: Olga: E io sapevi (Olimpia Boronat, s). GIORDANO: Andrea Chenier: Un di all'azzurro spazio (Giovanni Zenatello, t); Un di m'era di gioia (Eugenio Giraldoni, bar). Fedora: Amor ti vieta (Amadeo Bassi, t). Siberia: Nel suo amor (Emma Carelli, s). GLINKA: A life of the Tsar: I do not grieve about that dear friends (Eugenia Zbrujeva, con); I look into empty fields (Marie Michailova, s); They guess the truth (Vladimir Kastorsky, bs). GLUCK: Alceste: J'enieve un tendre epoux (Maria Gay, con). Paride ed Elena: Spiagge amate (Alessandro Bonci, t). Orfeo ed Euridice: Away with mourning and crying (Louise Homer, con). GODARD: Chanson d'Estelle (Angelica Pandolfini, s); Embarquez-vous (Pol Plancon, bs). Jocelyn: Berceuse (Victor Capoul, t). GOLDMARK: Die Konigin von Saba: Magische Tone (Leo Slezak, t). GOLDSCHMIDT: Im mai (Blanche Marchesi, s). GOUNOD: Cinq-Mars: Sur les flots vous entraine (Henri Albers, bar). Faust: Salve dimora (Ben Davies, t); Le parlate d'amor (Eugenia Mantelli, con); Vous que faites l'endormie (Pedro Gailhard, bs). Mireille: Oh d'amour messagerra (Luisa Tetrazzini, s). The Queen of Sheba: How frail and weak...Lend me your aid (Edward Lloyd, t). Romeo et Juliette: Que fais-tu blanche tourterelle (Nina Friede,

con). Sappho: O ma lyre immortelle (Ernestine Schumann-Heink,
con). GRETCHANINOV: Dobrynia Nikitich: Flowers were blooming
(Leonid Sobinov, t). GRETRY: Richard Coeur de Leon: Une fievre
brillante (Charles Rousseliere, t). HAHN: Si mes vers (Marcella
Sembrich, s; Frank La Forge, pno). HALEVY: La Juive: Dieu que
ma voix tremblante (Agustarello Affre, t); Eudoxie's aria (Janina Korolewicz-Wayda, s); Rachel quand du Seigneur (Alexander
Davidov, t); Voi che del Dio (Adamo Didur, bs). HANDEL: Acis
and Galatea: Lo hear...Love in her eyes sits playing (Evan Williams, t). Alessandro: Ne trionfi d'Alessandro...Lusinghe piu
care (Clara Butt, con). Judas Maccabaeus: The Lord worketh wonders (Robert Watkin-Mills, bs). Serse: Va godendo (Giuseppe Anselmi, t). HATTON: Simon the cellarer (Charles Antley, bar).
ISOUARD: La Joconde: Dans un delire extreme (Lucien Fugere, bar).
KIENZL: Der Evangelimann: O schone Jugendtage (Edyth Walker, con).
LALO: Le Roy d'Ys: Chanson de l'epousee (Marguerite Carre, s;
Xavier Leroux, pno). LEONCAVALLO: La boheme: Mimi Pinson (Ronsina Storchio, s). I Pagliacci: Warum denn hielst du mich (Bap-
tist Hoffmann, bar; Emilie Herzog, s). Songs: Notte ha steso il
gran vel (Tadeusz Leliva, bar). Zaza: Buono Zaza (Mario Sammar-
co, bar); E un riso gentil (Edoardo Garbin, t). LISZT: Songs:
Oh quand je dors (Emmy Destinn, s). LORTZING: Der Waffenschmied:
Auch ich war ein Jungling (Theodor Bertram, bs). MAILLART: Les
dragons de Villars: Chanson a boire (Leon Melchissendec, bar).
MASCAGNI: Cavalleria rusticana: Siciliana (Fernando Valero, t).
MASINI: I mulatieri (Antonio Cotogni, bar). MASSENET: Le Cid:
Air de l'infante (Alice Verlet, s); C'est vous que l'on benit
(Jean Note, bar); Pleurez mes yeux (Felia Litvinne, s; Alfred
Cortot, pno). Herodiade: Celui dont la parole...Il est doux,
il est bon (Ada Adini, s); Vision fugitive (Maurice Renaud, bar).
Le jongleur de Notre Dame: Liberte (Mary Garden, s; Adolphe
Marechal, t). Manon: Helas, helas...N'est-ce plus ma main (Sig-
rid Arnoldson, s); Je suis encore tout etourdie (Lucette Korsoff,
s). Songs: Marquise (Victor Maurel, bar); Chant provencal (Jean
Lasalle, bar). Werther: C'est moi...J'aurais sur ma poitrine
(Emile Scaremberg, t); Pourquoi me reveiller (Ernest van Dyck,
t). MENDELSSOHN: Elijah, op. 70: Then shall the righteous shine
forth (Dan Beddoe, t). MESSAGER: Songs: Si j'avais vos ailes
(Aino Ackate, s). Veronique: Adieu je pars (Jean Perier, bar).
MEYERBEER: L'Africaine: Figlia di regi; Quando amor acende (Mat-
tia Battistini, bar); Schlummer arie (Margarete Matzenauer, con).
Dinorah: Schattentanz(Margarethe Siems, s). L'Etoile du nord:
Cadenza (Ellen Beach Yaw, s; W.A. Fransella, pno). Les Hugue-
nots: No no giammai (Armida Parsipettinella, con); Plus blanche
que la blanche ermine (Ivan Erschov, t). Le prophete: Ach mein
Sohn (Marianne Brandt, con); Sopra Berta (Francesco Vignas, t).
Robert le diable: Evocazione (Giovanni Gravina, bs); Sicilienne
(Leon Escalais, t); Valse infernale (Juste Nivette, bs). MONI-
USZKO: The haunted castle: Polonaise (Waclav Brzezinski, bar).
MOZART: Cosi fan tutte, K 588: Un'aura amorosa (Felix Senius, t).
Don Giovanni, K 527: Bravo bravo archibravo...Finch han dal vano
(Francesco d'Andrade, bar); Deh vieni alla finestra (Emilio de
Gogorza, bar; Henri Gilles, pno); Don Ottavio, son morta...Or
sai chi l'onore; Non mi dir (Lilli Lehmann, s); In quali accessi
...Mi tradi (Johanna Gadski, s). Die Entfuhrung aus dem serail,

K 384: O wie will ich triumphieren (Wilhelm Hesch, bs). Le nozze di Figaro, K 492: Eh Capitano...Non piu andrai (Charles Santley, bar); Sull'aria...Che soave zeffirettto (Marcella Sembrich,
Emma Eames, s). NICOLAI: Die lustigen Weiber von Windsor: Ver-
fuhrer warum (Erika Wedekind, s); Wie freu ich mich (Leopold
Demuth, bs; Wilhelm Hesch, bs). OFFENBACH: La chanson de fortunio: La chanson de fortunio (Emilio de Gogorza, bar). La perichole: O mon cher amant (Emma Calve, s). PAER: Le maitre de
Chapelle: Pour limiter (Gabriel Soulacroix, bar). O dolce con-
cento: Variations (Ellen Beach Yaw, s). PALADILHE: Psyche (Susan
Strongs, s). PONCHIELLI: La Gioconda: Enzo Grimaldo...Principe
di Santafior...O grido di quest'anima (Pasquale Amato, bar; Gio-
vanni Zenatelli, t). PUCCINI: La boheme: Si mi chiamano Mimi
(Cesira Ferrani, s). Manon Lescaut: In quelle trine morbide
(Lina Cavalieri, s). Tosca: Vissi d'arte (Felice Kaschowska, s).
RICCIARDI: Luna'lu (Fernando de Luca, t). RICO: Stella (Jose-
fina Huguet, s). RIMSKY-KORSAKOV: The golden cockerel: Hymn to
the sun (Antonina Nezhdanova, s). RONALD: Rosy morn (Zelie de
Lussan, s). ROSSINI: Il barbiere di Siviglia: Dunque io son
(Antonio Magini-Coletti, bar; Regina Pinkert, ms). Semiramide:
Bel raggio lusinghier (Irene Abendroth, con). RUBINSTEIN: The
demon: Accursed world (Joachim Tartakov, bar); On desire's soft
fleeing wing (Andrei Labinsky, t). Nero: Epitalamio (Nicholai
Shevelev, bar). SAINT-SAENS: Samson et Dalila: Arretez o mes
freres (Charles Dalmores, t); Mon coeur s'ouvre a ta voix (Blan-
che Deschamps-Jehin, con). Songs: Sabre en main au cimitiere
(Albert Vaguet, t). SCHUBERT: Gretchen am Spinnrade, D 118
(Emma Eames, s; Henri Gilles, pno). Schwanengesang: Abschied
(Harry Plunkett Greene, bar); Am Meer (Gustav Walter, bar).
Songs: Hark hark the lark (David Bispham, bar); Wohin, D 795
(Marcella Sembrich, s; Frank La Forge, pno). SCHUMANN: Dichter-
liebe, op. 48: Ich grolle nicht. Lied eines Schiedes (George
Henschel, bar). SEROV: Judith: I put on my garments (Natalia
Yuzhina, s). SMETANA: Dalibor: Blickst du mein Freund (Hermann
Winkelmann, t); Jakje mi (Emmy Destinn, s). STERN: Coquette
(Suzanne Adams, s). SULLIVAN: The sorcerer: Time was when love
and I (Andre Black, bs). TCHAIKOVSKY: Iolanthe, op. 69: My Lord
if I offend (Lev Sibiriakov, bar). The Opritchnik: As before
God and thee (Nicolai Figner, t). Queen of spades: It is mid-
night (Medea Mei-Figner, s). THOMAS: Le Caid: Air du Tambour-
Major (Pol Plancon, bs); Vive le mariage (Lise Landouzy, s).
Mignon: Ihr Schwalben in der Luften (Leon Rains, bs). Songs:
Le songe d'une nuit d'ete (Hippolyte Belhomme, bs). Hamlet:
Brindisi (Titta Ruffo, bar). TOSTI: Songs: Amour; Aprile (Luisa
Tetrazzini, s; Percy Pitt, pno; Mattia Battatistani, bar); In-
vano (Antonio Scotti, bar); Mattinata (Geraldine Farrar, s).
VALVERDE: Clavelitos (de Gogorza, bar). VARNEY: L'Amour mouille:
Valse d'oiseau (Blanche Arral, s). VERDI: Aida: Gia i sacerdoti
(Rosa Olitzka, con). Un ballo in maschera: Saper vorreste (Luisa
Tetrazzini, s). I due foscari: Questa dunque (Pasquale Amato,
bar). Ernani: O dei verdi'anni miei (Giuseppe Kaschmann, bar;
Salvatore Cottone, pno). La forza del destino: Pace pace mio
Dio (Eugenia Burzio, s). Luisa Miller: Quando le sere (Fiorello
Giraud, t; Salvatore Cottone, pno). Otello: Era la notte (Vic-
tor Maurel, bar; Esultate; Niun mi tema (Francesco Tamagno, t);

Niun mi tema (Giovanni de Negri, t); Ora e per sempre addio (Albert Alvarez, t). Requiem: Ingemisco (Francesco Marconi, t; Salvatore Cottone, pno. Rigoletto: Caro nome (Selma Kurz, s). Il trovatore: Dass nur fur dich; Il balen del suo sorriso (Giuseppe Pacini, bar). VRANGEL: O what a glorious night (Anastasia Vialtzeva, con). WAGNER: Der fliegende Hollander: Senta's ballad (Sophie Sedlmair, s). Lohengrin: Cessare i canti alfin (Fernando de Lucia, t); Deh non t'incanten (Giuseppe Borgatti, t); Euch Luften die mein Klagen (Katharina Senger-Bettaque, s); In fernam land (Ivan Altchevsky, t); Mein lieber Schwan (Andreas Dippel, t). Rienzi: Erstehe, hohe Roma (Jacques Urlus, t); Gerechter Gott...In seiner Bluthe bleicht (Louise Kirkby-Lunn, con). Tannhauser: Als du in kuhnem Sange (Karl Scheidemantel, bar); Dich teure Halle (Olive Fremstad, s). Siegfried: Heil dir Sonne (Thila Plaichinger, s). Tristan und Isolde: Dein Werk; O thorich'ge Magd (Pelagie Greef-Andreiessen, s); Wohin nun Tristan scheidet (Karel Burrian, t). Die Walkure: Du bist der Lenz (Katherin Fleischer-Edel, s); Ho-jo-to-ho (Ellen Gulbranson, s); Leb wohl du kuhnes, herrliches Kind (Anton van Rooy, bar); Siegmund heiss ich (Alfred von Bary, t; Bruno Seidler-Winkler, pno). WEBER: Oberon: Ozean du Ungeheuer (Anna Bahr-Mildenburg, s); Ozean du Ungeheuer (Lucie Weidt, s). WHITE: A youth once loved a maiden; The tears that night (Clara Butt, con). TRAD.: Ma Lisette (Emma Calve, s); They won't let Masha walk by the brook (Feodor Chaliapin, bs). Various accompaniments.

+ARSC Vol 12, nos. 1-2   +HFN 2-78 p99
    1980 p112   +NYT 1-15-78 pD15
+Gr 1-78 p1289   +RR 2-78 p18
+Gr 3-78 p1539
+-HF 4-78 p115

RLS 738 (3) Tape (c) TC RLS 738
3771 The art of Tito Gobbi. BELLINI: Fenesta che lucive (arr. de Meglio). BERLIOZ: La damnation de Faust, op. 24: Song of the flea; La Valanga che volge. CAPUA: O sole mio. CILEA: L'Arlesiana: Come due tizzi accesi. COTTRAU: Santa Lucia (arr. Gibilaro). DENZA: Occhi di fata. DONIZETTI: L'Elisir d'amore: La donna e un animale...Venti scudi. FALVO: Dicintencello vuje. GASTALDON: Musica proibita. GIORDANO: Andrea Chenier: Nemico della patria. Fedora: La Donna Russa. LEONCAVALLO: Zaza: Buona Zaza; Zaza piccola zingara. MOZART: Le nozze di Figaro, K 492: Aprite un po quegli'occhi. OLIVIERI: Canzona a due voci: Menia d'amore. ORTELLI: The glass mountain: Song of the mountains. PUCCINI: La fanciulla del West: Minnie dalla mia casa. RESPIGHI: Nebbie. ROSSINI: Guglielmo Tell: Resta immobile. ROTA: The glass mountain: Take the sun. SADERO: Gondoliera Veneziana; Amuri amuri. TOSTI: Songs: A vucchella; Marechiare; Malia; Donna vorrei morir; Ideale. VALENTE: Torna. VERDI: Un ballo in maschera: Alzati la tuo figlio...Eri tu. Don Carlo: O Carlo ascolta...Io morro. La forza del destino: Urna fatale del mio destino. Macbeth: Perfidi...Pieta rispetto amore. Otello: Credo in un Dio crudel; Era la notte. Nabucco: Ah prigioniero io sono...Dio di Giuda. WOLF-FERRARI: I gioielli della madonna: Aprile o bella. Songs: Se gli ableri; Serenata; Commiato. Tito Gobbi, bar; Various accompaniments.

+ARSC Vol 12, nos. 1-2, 1980 p96

```
+-Gr 6-79 p107              +Op 7-79 p682
+Gr 11-79 p924 tape       ++RR 6-79 p60
+HFN 6-79 p111             +RR 11-79 p127 tape
```

RLS 739 (4)

3772 BACH, W.F.: AIR (arr. Kreisler). BRAHMS: Concerto, violin, op. 77,
D major. CHAUSSON: Poeme, op. 25, E major. CHOPIN: Nocturne,
op. posth., C sharp minor (arr. Rodionov) (2). DEBUSSY: Sonata,
violin and piano, G minor. DINICU: Hora staccato (arr. Heifetz).
FALLA: La vida breve: Danse espagnole (arr. Kreisler). GLUCK:
Orfeo ed Euridice: Melodie. PARADIS: Sicilienne (arr. Dushkin).
RAVEL: Piece en forme de habanera. TZIGANE. SCARLATESCU: Baga-
telle. SIBELIUS: Concerto, violin, op. 47, D minor. STRAUSS,
R.: Sonata, violin and piano, op. 18, E flat major. SUK: Pieces,
op. 17. TARTINI: Variations on a theme by Corelli (arr. Kreis-
ler). Ginette Neveu, vln; Jean Neveu, Gustaf Beck, pno; PhO;
Walter Susskind.
                    +Gr 9-80 p354

RLS 742 (3)

3773 BOITO: Mefistofele: Ave Signore degli angeli e del santi...Ave Signor; Son lo spirito che nega. GOUNOD: Faust: Rien, En vain
j'interroge; Allons amis point de vaines alarmes...Le veau d'or;
Nous nous retrouverons mes amis...Ainsi que la brise; Salut demeure chaste et pure; Il etait temps; Qu' attendezvous encore...
Vous qui faites l'endormie. MUSSORGSKY: Boris Godunov: Coronation scene; And you my son; Ouf I suffocate; Well shall we vote;
Leave us alone. PUCCINI: La boheme: Gioventu mia; Dormo; Ripose;
Entrate...C'e Rodolfo; Donde lieta usci; Addio dolce svegliare
all mattina. VERDI: Otello: Piangea cantando...Ave Maria; Inaffia l'ugola; Mio Signore...che brani; Atroce...Ora e per sempre addio; Ah mille vite...Si pel ciel mormoreo; Dio mio potevi
scagliar; Niun mi tema. WAGNER: Gotterdammerung: Hier sitz ich
zur Wacht. Die Meistersinger von Nurnberg: Da zu dir der Heiland
kam; Wach' auf es nahet gender Tag; Morgenlich leuchtend. Nellie
Melba's farewell speech. Margaret Sheridan, Aurora Rettore, Nellie Melba, Jane Langier, Margherita Carosio, Tiana Lemnitz, s;
Angelo Minghetti, Browning Mummery, Joseph Hislop, Luigi Cilla,
Octave Dua, Giovanni Zenatello, Angelo Bada, Torsten Ralf, t;
Jane Bourguignon, ms; Giuseppe Nota, Ernesto Badini, John Brownlee, Franklyn Kelsey, Rudolf Bockelmann, bar; Pompilio Malatesta,
Feodor Chaliapin, Ludwig Weber, bs; ROHO; Eugene Goossens, Thom-
as Beecham.
          ++ARSC Vol. 12, nos. 1-2   +MT 1-80 p37
              1980 p92   +Op 12-79 p1170
          +Gr 9-79 p522   +RR 9-79 p56
          +HFN 10-79 p171   +STL 12-2-79 p37

RLS 743 (13) (From various originals, 1914-25)

3774 d'ALBERT: Tiefland: Sein bin ich (Hafgren-Dinkela). ANDERSON, S.:
Der flyvver saa mange Flugle (Melchior). BACH: Cantata, no. 201,
O yes just so (Paikin). BALFE: Come into the garden Maud (Coat-
es). BARTHELEMY: Pesca d'amore (Schipa). BEETHOVEN: Fidelio,
op. 72: Abscheulicher wo eilst du hin (Wildbrunn); Hat man nicht
auch Gold beineben (Mayr). Songs: In quest tomba oscura (Metz-
ger). BELLINI: Norma: Keusche Gottin (Kiurina). I puritani:
Viene fra queste braccia (Lazaro). La sonnambula: A te diletta
...Come per me sereno...Suvra il sen la man mi posa (Galli-Curci).
BEMBERG: Nymphes et Sylvains (Vincent). BISHOP: The pilgrim of

love (Hyde). BIZET: Carmen: La fleur que tu m'avais jetee (Fleta). BOITO: Mefistofele: L'Altra notte (Raisa); Dai campi dai
prati (Gigli). BORODIN: Prince Igor: Lentement baissee le jour
(Friant). BRAHMS: Die schone Magelone, op. 33, no. 12: Muss es
ein Trennung (Culp). BRUCH: Odysseus: Ich wob dies Gewand (Leisner). BUZZI-PECCIA: Mal d'amore (Muzio). CABALLERO: El cabo
primero: Yo quiero un hombre (Barientos). CATALANI: Loreley: Ah
dunque ei m'amera (Alda). CHARPENTIER: Louise: Depuis le jour
(Edvina); Depuis longtemps j'habitais cettre chambre (Gauther,
Harrold). CILEA: Adriana Lecouvreur: Del sultano Amuratte...Io
son l'umile ancella (Muzio). CORNELIUS: Der Barbier von Bagdad:
Heil sei der Schonen (Bohnen). CUI: Prisoner of the Caucasus:
The sun was brightly shining (Grizunov). DEL RIEGO: O dry those
tears (Mason). DIAZ: Le coupe du Roi de Thule: Il est venu ce
jour de lutte (Gilly). DONIZETTI: La favorita: Fernando dove mai
lo trovero (Anitua); A tanto amor (Zanelli). Don Pasquale: Quel
guardo...So anch'io la virtu magica (Pareto). Lucrezia Borgia:
Hor mein Flehen (Von Seeboek). Robert il diavolo: O Roberto tu
che adoro (White). DUPARC: Chanson triste (Gauthier). DUPONT:
Antar: Air de l'oasis (Heldy). DVORAK: Songs, op. 55: Songs my
mother taught me (Reimers). ELGAR: Pleading, op. 48, no. 1
(Buckman). FEVRIER: Monna Vanna: Ce n'est pas un vieillard
(Vanni-Marcoux). FRANCHETTI: Germania: Ascolta io moriro (Stracciari). GIORDANO: Andrea Chenier: Come un bel di di maggio (Lap-
pas); Un di all'azzurro spazio (Muro). GLINKA: Russlan and Ludmilla: O my Ratmir (Tcherkasskaya). GLUCK: Paride ed Elena:
Spiagge amate (Lashanska). GOLDMARK: Ein Wintermarchen: O Mensch-
engluck du gleischet der schwanken Blute (Schwarz). GORING-
THOMAS: Nadeshka: My heart is weary (Thornton). GOUNOD: Faust:
Faites lui mes aveux (Tugarinova); Ah je ris (Mason). Le Reine
de Saba: Sous les pieds (Journet); Plus grand dans son obscurite
(Gall). Romeo et Juliette: Que fais-tu blanche tourtourelle (Pe-
trenko); Salut tombeau (Franz). GRANADOS: Goyescas: La maja y
el ruisenor (Fitziu). GRIEG: Peer Gynt: Solveig's song (Bryhn-
Langaard). HALEVY: L'Eclair: Call me thine own (Garrison). La
Juive: Recha als Gott dich einst (Mann); Er kommt zuruck (Morena).
HALSEY: Swedish love song (Braslau). HANDEL: Messiah: Rejoice
greatly (Case). Israel in Egypt: The Lord is a man of war (Daw-
son, Radford). d'HARDELOT: Roses of forgiveness (Hill). HEISE:
Twelfth night: Den gang jeg var kun saa stor saa (Melchior).
HENSCHEL: Morning hymn (Elwes). HORNE: I know a bank (Allen,
Thornton). HORN: I've been roaming (Culp). JANACEK: Jenufa:
Mutter un habe den Kopf schwer (Jurjevskaya). KORNGOLD: Die
tote Stadt, op. 12: Mein sehen mein Wahnen (Duhan). KROTKOV:
The poet: I have long despised all women (Bragin). LALO: Le Roi
d'Ys: Vainement ma bien aimee (Devries). LEHAR: Alone at last:
Waltz entrancing (Kline). Paganini: Liebe du Himmel auf Erden
(Schwarz). LEONCAVALLO: I Pagliacci: Vesti la giubba (Ferrari-
Fontana); Si puo (Schwarz). Zaza: O mio piccolo tavolo (Crimi).
LOEWE: Fredericus Rex, op. 61, no. 1 (Von Raatz-Brockmann); Can-
zonetta (Gluck); Der Mummelsee (Bender). LULLY: Amadis: Bois
epais (Leblanc-Maeterlinck). MSACAGNI: Isabeau: Questo mio biano
manto (Dalla-Rizza). Lodoletta: Ah il suo nome Flammen perdon-
ami (Caracciolo). MALASHKIN: O could I in song tell my sorrow
(Chaliapin). MASSE: Variations on "Carnival of Venice" (Ritter-
Ciampi). MASSENET: Ariane: La fine grace (Merentie). Cendril-

lon: Ma pauvre enfant cherie...Nous quitterons cette ville (Brohly, Payan). Manon: Je ne suis que faiblesse...Adieu notre petite
table (Kuznetsova); Ah rands-moi ton amour...N'est-ce plus ma
main (Melis). Griselidis: Je suis l'oiseau (Cazette); La mer et
sur les flots toujours bleus...Il partit au printemps (Vallandri).
Herodiade: Salome...Demande au prisonnier (Lestelly). Marie-
Magdeleine: O mes soeurs...C'est ici meme a cette (Brohly).
Therese: Jour de juin (Megane). Thais: L'amour est une vertu
rare (Brozia); Voila donc la terrible cite (Dufranne). Werther:
Air des larmes (Vix). Songs: O si les fleurs avaient des yeux
(Namara); Pensee d'automne (Aquistapace); Crepuscule (Galli-
Curci). MAZZA: Campanone: Senorita amigos mios (Sagi-Barba).
MESSAGER: Fortunio: J'aimais le vieille maison grise; Si vous
croyez (Francell). Meyerbeer: Dinorah: Sei vendicata assai
(De Luca); Scena e canzonetta del capraio (Lazzari). L'Africaine:
Adieu mon beau rivage (Auguez de Montalant); Pays merveilleux...
O paradis (Ansseau); Wie hat mein Herz amato (Groenen); Von hier
seh ich das Meer (Kemp). Les Huguenots: Nobles seigneurs (Cis-
neros); Ihr Wangenpaar (Pattiera). Le prophete: Donnez donnez
pour un pauvre ame (Charbonnel); Non non...O toi que m'abandon-
nes (Royer); Air de Baal (Kalter); Church scene (Arndt-Ober).
Robert le diable: Invocation (Chaliapin). MONIUSZKO: The haunted
castle: The clock scene (Dygas). MOZART: Don Giovanni, K 527:
Schmale tobe aus; Wenn du fein fromm bist (Artot de Padilla).
Zaide, K 344: Ruhe sanft (Stueckgold). Die Zauberflote, K 620:
Ach ich fuhls (Perard-Petzl); Dies Bildnis ist bezaubernd schon
(Sembach). Idomeneo, Re di Creta, K 366: Noch tont mir ein Meer
in Busen (Jadlowker). NAPRAVNIK: Dubrovsky: O give me oblivion
(Smirnov). NOUGES: Quo Vadis: Viens pres de moi (Maguenat).
OFFENBACH: La belle Helene: Dis-moi Venus (Chenal). PINSUTI:
Queen of the earth (Hislop). PONCHIELLI: La Gioconda: Voce di
donna (Besanzoni). PUCCINI: La boheme: Che gelida manina (Hack-
ett). La fanciulla del West: Ch'ella mi creda (Calleja). Gian-
ni Schicchi: O mio babbino caro (Easton). Madama Butterfly: Un
bel di (Miura). Tosca: Se la giurata fede (Ivantzov); Vissi d'
arte (Agostinelli); Nur der Schonheit (Lehmann). Suor Angelica:
Senza mama (Poli-Randaccio). La Villi: Anima santa (Viglione-
Borghese). RABAUD: Marouf, Savatier du Caire: A travers le
desert (Crabbe). RACHMANINOFF: Before my window, op. 26, no. 10
(McCormack). REEVE: I am a friar of order grey (Dawson). REYER:
Sigurd: La bruit des chants...Esprits gardiens (Fontaine). RICCI:
La prigione d'Edimburgo: Sulla poppa (Stevens). RIMSKY-KORSAKOV:
The Tsar's bride: I bade farewell to my only true love (Gluck).
ROSSINI: Il barbiere di Siviglia: Se il mio nome (Carpi); All'
idea di quel metallo (Carpi, Stracciari); Una voce poco fa (Scotney). ROBERTS: Pierrot (Macbeth). ROUSSEAU: Tarass Bulba: Non
je n'ai pas (Kuznetsova). RUBINSTEIN: The demon: In the quiet
of the night (Koshetz). Nero: Epithalamium (Baklanov). SCAR-
LATTI, A.: Il Pompeo: O cessate di piargame (Werrenrath). SCHUB-
ERT: Sei mir gegrusset (Broderson). SCHUMANN: Sechs Gedichte,
op. 90, no. 2: Meine Rose (Rehkemper). SERRANO: El principe
carneval: Cancion espanola (Hidalgo). SMETANA: Dalibor: Slysel's
to priteli (Marak). SPONTINI: La vestale: Tu che invoco (Mazzoleni). STEVENSON: Tell me where if fancy bred (Marsh, Werrenrath). STRAUSS, R.: Ariadne auf Naxos: Es gibt ein Reich (Jerit-

za). Der Rosenkavalier, op. 59: Di rigori armato il seno (Tauber). Songs: Traum durch die Dammerung, op. 29, no. 1 (Tauber); Wiegenlied (Gerhardt); Freundliche Vision, op. 48, no. 1 (Rethberg). TCHAIKOVSKY: Eugen Onegin, op. 24: Gremin's aria (Kipnis). Iolanthe, op. 69: Why did I not know this before (Lipkowska). Jean d'Arc: Farewell in the forests (Petrova-Zvanceva). Pique Dame: Je crains de lui parler la nuit (Tugarinova). Songs: Lullaby (Koshetz). THOMAS: Hamlet: Doute de la lumiere (Lipkowska, Baklanov). Le songe d'une nuit d'ete: Ou suis-je (Lepelletrie). Mignon: Adieu Mignon (Chamlee); Elle ne croyait pas (McCormack); Dort bein ihm is sie jetz (Dux). TOSTI: Mattinata (Labia). VERDI: Aida: Bald kommt Radames...Azurne Blaue (Bindernagel); Fuggiam gli adori inospiti...La tra foreste vergini (Ruszkowska, Barrera); O patria mia (Rethberg). Un ballo in maschera: Ja du warst's (Weil); Wenn das Kraut wie hier ward (Kurt). Don Carlo: Dio che nell'alma infondere (Martinelli, De Luca). Ernani: Come rugiada al cespite (Martinelli); Ernani involami (Ponselle). Falstaff: Dal labbro il canto (Schipa). La forza del destino: Madre pietosa vergine (Heinrich); La vergine degl angeli (Ruszkowska). Nabucco: O chi piange...Del futuro nel buio (Mardones). Otello: Esultate; Ora e per sempre addio (O'Sullivan); Stilled by the gathering darkness (Licette, Mullings); Du neigst dich zum Gebet (Bland). Rigoletto: Teurer Name (Ivoguen). La traviata: E strano...Ah fors' e lui (Bronskaya); Parigi o cara (Bori, McCormack). Il trovatore: Loderne Flammen (Horvat). WAGNER: Lohengrin: Hochstes Vertrau'n hast du mir schon zu danken (Schubert); Nun sei bedankt (Kirchhoff); Einsam in truben Tagen (Von Der Osten). Parsifal: Nur eine Waffe taugt (Melchior). Tannhauser: Als du in kuhnem Sange (Bronsgeest); Blick ich umher (Soomer). Die Walkure: Mit acht Schwestern zog ich dich auf (Braun); Wintersturme (Martin); Ho jo to ho (Kappel). WALLACE: Lurline: Oh thou to whom this heart...Sweet spirit hear my pray-34 (Jones-Hudson). Maritana: Scenes that are brightest (Ponselle); Hear me gentle Maritana...The mariner and his barque (McEachern). WEBER: Der Freischutz: Trube Augen (Schumann). Oberon: Ozean du Ungeheuer (Leider); Vater Hor mein Fieh'n zu dir (Kirchner). Silvana: So soll denn dieses Herz (Piccaver). WEINGARTNER: Thou art a child (Marcel). WOLF: Italianisches Liederbuch: Und willst du deinen Liebsten sterben sehen (Gerhardt). WOLF-FERRARI: Il segreto di Susanna: O gioia nube (Bori). WRIGHTON: Her bright smile haunts me still (Johnson). YRADIER: La perla di trianna (Hildago). TRAD.: Mi ranchito (Bertana). When love is kind (Bori). Maria Kuznetsova, Nina Koshetz, Lydia Lipkowska, Eugenia Bronskaya, Marie Louise Edvina, Marthe Chenal, Yvonne Gall, Fanny Heldy, Marguerite Merentie, Aline Vallandri, Zina Brozia, Gabrielle Ritter-Ciampi, Berthe Auguez de Montalant, Georgette Leblanc-Maeterlinck, Claudia Muzio, Rosa Raisa, Elena Ruszkowska, Maria Labia, Adelina Agostinelli, Ester Mazzoleni, Tina Poli-Randaccio, Carmen Melis, Juanita Caracciolo, Golda Dalla-Rizza, Amelita Galli-Curci, Maria Barrientos, Marianne Tcherkasskaya, Florence Easton, Graziella Pareto, Elvira de Hidalgo, Lucrezia Bori, Frances Alda, Edith Mason, Alma Gluck, Hulda Lashanska, Anna Case, Eva Gauthier, Anna Fitziu, Carolina White, Lucille Marcel, Julia Heinrich, Marguerite Namara, Eleanor Jones-Hudson, Ruth Vincent, Lucy Isabelle Marsh, Olive Kline, Evelyn

Scotney, Mabel Garrison, Florence Macbeth, Luella Paikin, Maud
Perceval Allen, Rosina Buckman, Tamaki Miura, Borghild Bryhn-
Langaard, Rosa Ponselle, Carolina Lazzari, Eva von der Osten,
Luise Perard-Petzl, Zinaida Jurjevskaya, Elisabeth Rethberg,
Grete Stueckgold, Elsa Bland, Luly Hafgren-Dinkela, Barbara Kemp,
Charlotte von Seeboek, Melanie Kurt, Berta Moreno, Helene Wild-
brunn, Gertrude Bindernagel, Gertrude Kappel, Frida Leider,
Elisabeth Schumann, Berta Kiurina, Lola Artot de Padilla, Clair
Dux, Vera Schwarz, Maria Ivoguen, Maria Jeritza, Lotte Lehmann,
Elena Gerhardt, Miriam Licette, s; Elisaveta Petrenko, Vera
Petrova-Zvanceva, Klavdia Tugarinova, Suzanne Brohly, Jacqueline
Royer, Genevieve Vix, Gabriella Besanzoni, Fanny Anitua, Carmen
Hill, Leila Megane, Eleonora de Cisneros, Margarethe Arndt-Ober,
Ottilie Metzger, Ankar Horvat, Sabine Kalter, Emmi Leisner, Julia
Culp, ms; Marie Charbonnel, Luisa Bertana, Edna Thornton, Sophie
Braslau, con; Dimitri Smirnov, Paul Franz, Fernand Ansseau,
Charles Fontaine, David Devries, Fernand Francell, Charles Friant,
Louis Cazette, Rene Lapelletrie, Carlo Barrera, John McCormack,
Tito Schipa, Fernando Carpi, Hipolito Lazaro, Beniamino Gigli,
Miguel Fleta, Giulio Crimi, Ulysses Lappas, Bernardo de Muro,
Edoardo Ferrari-Fontana, Icilio Calleja, Giovanni Martinelli,
Riccardo Martin, Orville Harrold, Charles Hackett, Mario Chamlee,
Edward Johnson, Alfred Piccaver, Joseph Hislop, John O'Sullivan,
Frank Mullings, John Coates, Gervase Elwes, Walter Hyde, Paul
Reimers, Richard Tauber, Alexander Kirchner, Johannes Sembach, Her-
mann Jadlowker, Ottokar Marak, Ignazy Dygas, Joseph Mann, Tino
Pattiera, Richard Schubert, Walter Kirchoff, Lauritz Melchior,
t; George Baklanov, Alexander Bragin, Ivan Grizunov, Dinh Gilly,
Louis Lestelly, Alfred Maguenat, Armand Crabbe, Giuseppe de Luca,
Riccardo Stracciari, Domenico Viglione-Borghese, Renato Zanelli,
Emilio Sagi-Barba, Reinald Werrenrath, Horace Stevens, Julius
von Raatz-Brockmann, Friedrich Broderson, Heinrich Rehkemper,
Hans Duhan, Hermann Weil, Cornelis Bronsgeest, Joseph Groenen,
Joseph Schwarz, Walter Soomer, bar; Ivan Ivantzov, Hector Du-
franne, Peter Dawson, bs-bar; Robert Radford, Malcolm McEachern,
Michael Bohnen, Paul Bender, Richard Mayr, Carl Braun, Feodor
Chaliapin, Marcel Journet, Paul Payan, Jean-Emile Vanni-Marcoux,
Jean Aquistapace, Jose Mardones, Alexander Kipnis, bs; Various
accompaniments.

+ARSC Vol 12, nos. 1-2	++HFN 1-80 p113
1980 p112	++NYT 2-17-80 pD19
+Gr 1-80 p1196	++RR 2-80 p32
+HF 5-80 p63	+STL 1-27-80 p39

RLS 745 (2) (also Angel ZB 3896)
3775 ALBENIZ: Suite espanola: Granada; Sevilla. BACH: Clavierbuchlein
fur. W. F. Bach. Prelude, S 926, D minor. Sonata, violin, no.
1, S 1001, G minor: Fugue. Partita, violin, no. 3, S 1006, E
major: Gavotte. Suite, lute, S 996, E minor: Allemande. Suite,
solo violoncello, no. 1, S 1007, G major: Prelude. Suite, solo
violoncello, no. 3, S 1009, C major: Courante. CASTELNUOVO-
TEDESCO: Sonata, guitar: Vivo ed energico. FROBERGER: Gigue.
GRANADOS: Danzas espanolas, op. 37: Andaluza; Danza triste. MAL-
ATS: Serenata. MENDELSSOHN: Quartet, strings, no. 1, op. 12, E
flat major: Canzonetta (arr. Segovia). PONCE (Weiss): Suite,
A major. Mazurka. Folies d'Espagne: Theme, variations and fugue.

Petite valse. Sonata, guitar, no. 3: 1st movement; 2nd movement:
Cancion, Postlude. SOR: Theme varie, op. 9. TARREGA: Recuer-
dos de la Alhambra. Etude, A major. TORROBA: Sonatina, A major:
Allegretto. Nocturno. Preludio. Suite castellana: Fandanguil-
lo. TURINA: Fandanguillo. VISEE: Bourree. Menuet. Sarabande.
Andres Segovia, gtr.

+FF 11/12-80 p215   +HFN 8-80 p109 tape
++Gr 3-80 p1423   ++RR 4-80 p89
+HFN 3-80 p104

RLS 748
3776 BRITTEN: Songs: Come you not from Newcastle; The foggy foggy dew;
The holy sonnets of John Donne, op. 35; The king is gone a-hunt-
ing; O waly waly; The ploughboy; Sonnets of Michelangelo, op. 22
(7). COPLAND: Old American songs. GRAINGER: The jolly-sailor
song; Six dukes went a-fishing. PURCELL (arr. Britten): The
queen's epicedium. Fantasia, no. 13, F major. SCHUBERT: Auf der
Bruck, D 853; Im Fruhling, D 882. Peter Pears, t; Benjamin Britten, pno, vla; Zorian Quartet.

++Gr 6-80 p60   ++RR 6-80 p83
++HFN 6-80 p113   +STL 7-13-80 p38
+NYT 9-21-80 pD22

RLS 749 (4) Tape (c) TC RLS 749.
3777 BACH: Cantata, no. 147, Jesu joy of man's desiring. Chorale preludes, S 599, Nun komm der Heiden Heiland; S 639, Ich ruf zu dir.
Partita, harpsichrod, no. 1, S 825, B flat major. Sonata, flute
and harpsichord, S 1031, E flat major: Siciliano. CHOPIN: Barcarolle, op. 60, F sharp minor. Concerto, piano, no. 1, op. 11,
E minor. Nocturne, op. 27, no. 2, D flat major. Mazurka, op.
50, no. 3, C sharp minor. Sonata, piano, no. 3, op. 58, B minor.
Waltz, op. 34, no. 1, A flat major. ENESCO: Sonata, piano, no.
3, op. 24, D major. LISZT: Annees de pelerinage, 2nd year, G
161: Sonetto del Petrarca. MOZART: Concerto, piano, no. 21, K
467, C major. Sonata, piano, no. 8, K 310, A minor. RAVEL: Miroirs: Alborado del gracioso. SCARLATTI, D.: Sonatas, harpsichord,
E major, D minor. Dinu Lipatti, pno.

+Gr 5-80 p1694   +MT 12-80 p788
+HFN 6-80 p117   ++RR 6-80 p69
+HFN 8-80 p109   +-STL 6-8-80 p38

HQS 1091 (also Angel S 36457)
3778 ARNE: Where the bee sucks. BOYCE (Poston): Tell me lovely shepherd.
BUSCH: Rest. BRITTEN: Corpus Christi carol. CAMPIAN: If you
longst so much to learn; Fain would I wed; Never love unless you
can; Oft have I sighed. DOWLAND: Come again. GURNEY: The fields
are full. IRELAND: Down the Salley gardens. MONRO: My lovely
Celia. PARRY: O mistress mine; Proud Maisie. PURCELL: Lord what
is man; Sleep Adam sleep. QUILTER: Love's philosophy, op. 3, no.
1. STANFORD: La belle dame sans merci. VAUGHAN WILLIAMS: Linden
Lea. WARLOCK: Pretty ring time. Janet Baker, ms; Gerald Moore,
pno; Martin Isepp, hpd; Robert Spencer, lt; Ambrose Gauntless,
vla da gamba; Douglas Whittaker, flt.

+-FF 7/8-80 p158

ASD 2938 Tape (c) TC ASD 2938
3779 FRANCESCHINI: Sonata, 2 trumpets and strings, D major. HAYDN: Concerto, trumpet, E flat major. TELEMANN: Concerto, trumpet, D
major. TORELLI: Suite, no. 7, a cinque, D major. VIVIANI: Son-

ata, trumpet, no. 1, C major. Sonata, trumpet, no. 2, D major.
John Wilbraham, Michael Laird, tpt; Christopher Hodwood, hpd;
Kenneth Heath, vlc; AMF; Neville Marriner.

+Gr 4-74 p1862   +RR 3-74 p39
+Gr 10-75 p721 tape   +RR 11-75 p92 tape
+HFN 3-74 p122   +RR 4-80 p128 tape
+-HFN 10-75 p155 tape

SXDW 3049 (2) Tape (c) TC SXDW 3049 (From Columbia SAX 2300, 5286)
3780 PUCCINI: La boheme: Si mi chiamano Mimi. Gianni Schicchi: O mio
babbino caro. SMETANA: Die Verkaufte Braut: Endlich allein...
Wie fremd und tot. TCHAIKOVSKY: Eugen Onegin, op. 24: Tatiana's
letter scene. VERDI: Otello: Emilia te ne prego...Piangea cantando. WAGNER: Lohengrin: Einsam in truben Tagen; Euch Luften
die mein Klagen. Tannhauser: Dich teure Halle; Allmacht'ge Jungfrau. WEBER: Der Freischutz: Wie nahte mir der Schlummer...Leise
leise; Und ob die Wolke. Elisabeth Schwarzkopf, s; Christa Ludwig, Margreta Elkins, ms; PhO, LSO; Walter Susskind, Heinrich
Schmidt, Alceo Galliera.

++Gr 10-79 p716   +Op 3-80 p271
+HFN 11-79 p155   +RR 10-79 p70
+-HFN 1-80 p123 tape   ++STL 12-9-79 p41

ASD 3633
3781 BACH: Prelude and fugue, S 552, E flat major (Schoenberg). JANACEK:
The cunning little vixen: Suite. PANUFNIK: Hommage to Chopin.
IVES: The unanswered question. SHOSTAKOVICH: Christopher Colum-
bus, op. 19, no. 1: Overture. WEBERN: Pieces, orchestra, op. 10
(5). Leningrad Philharmonic Orchestra, Leningrad Philharmonic
Chamber Orchestra, MRSO, USSR, Moscow Conservatoire Students
Orchestra; Radik Suleimanov, flt; Gennady Rozhdestvensky.

+Gr 3-79 p1579   +Te 9-80 p86
++HFN 4-79 p129

ASD 3744 Tape (c) TC ASD 3744
3782 DOPPLER: L'Oiseau des bois, op. 21. FURSTENAU: Rondo brillant, op.
38. KUMMER: Divertissement, op. 13. POPP: Scherzo fantastique,
op. 423. TULOU: L'Angelus, op. 46. SAINT-SAENS: Romance, op.
37, D flat major. John Solum, flt; PhO; Neville Dilkes.

++Gr 9-79 p477   +HFN 1-80 p123 tape
+HFN 12-79 p173   +RR 10-79 p101

ASD 3764 Tape (c) TC ASD 3764
3783 BACH: Chorale prelude, S 734, Nun freut euch. BYRD: Alleluia ascendit Deus. GIGOUT: Toccata, B minor. GIBBONS: O clap your
hands. PHILLIPS: Ascendit Deus. RUBBRA: Magnificat and nunc
dimittis, op. 65, A flat major. TRAD. (Barnby): Psalm, no. 24.
English hymnal: Hymns nos. 147, 148. King's College Choir; Thomas Trotter, org; Philip Ledger.

+Gr 2-80 p1288   +HFN 4-80 p121 tape
+Gr 5-80 p1717 tape   +MT 10-80 p638
+HFN 2-80 p101   +RR 2-80 p84

ASD 3778 Tape (c) TC ASD 3778
3784 Festival of lessons and carols: Adam lay ybounden; Angels from the
realms of glory; Adeste fidelis; A baby is born; Chester carol;
Hark the herald angels sing; Joseph and Mary; A maiden most gentle; Once in Royal David's city; Resonet in laudibus; Sussex carol. BACH: Chorale prelude, S 729, In dulce jubilo. Thomas
Trotter, org; King's College Chapel Choir; Philip Ledger.

                        +HFN 1-80 p113   +RR 12-79 p109
                        +HFN 2-80 p107 tape

ASD 3785
3785 BARTOK: Rumanian folk dances (trans. Szekely). COPLAND: Rodeo: Hoe-
      down. DVORAK: Songs, op. 55: Songs my mother taught me (trans.
      Kreisler). HALFFTER: Danza de la gitana (trans. Heifetz). MEN-
      DELSSOHN: On wings of song, op. 34, no. 2 (trans. Larsen). PAGA-
      NINI: Concerto, violin, no. 2, op. 7, B minor: La clochette (ed.
      Kreisler). RAVEL: Piece en forme de habanera, op. 21, no. 2.
      SARASATE: Danza espanola, op. 23, no. 2: Zapateado (ed. Frances-
      catti). SCHUBERT: Ave Maria, D 839 (trans. Wilhelmj). WEBER:
      Air russe and rondo (trans. Szigeti). Ida Haendel, vln; Geoffrey
      Parsons, pno.
                        +Gr 5-80 p1689   ++RR 5-80 p88
                        ++HFN 5-80 p134

ASD 3797 Tape (c) TC ASD 3797
3786 ADDISON: A bridge too far. BAX: Malta GC: Introduction and march.
      BENNETT: Lady Caroline lamb, theme. Yanks, theme. BENJAMIN:
      An ideal husband. BLISS: Christopher Columbus suite. FARNON:
      Colditz march. GOODWIN: Frenzy. IRELAND: The overlanders.
      Romance. Intermezzo. MORLEY: Watership down: Kehaars theme.
      WALTON: Battle of Britain: Battle in the air. Birmingham Sym-
      phony Orchestra; Marcus Dods.
                        ++Gr 12-79 p1024   +HFN 2-80 p107 tape
                        +Gr 3-80 p1446 tape

ASD 3798
3787 Christmas songs: Easter alleluia; The first Nowell; I saw three
      ships; In dulci jubilo; In einem kuhlem Grunde; Maria auf dem
      Berge; O come all ye faithful; O du frohliche; Panis Angelicus;
      Stille Nacht; Sandmannchen; Vom Himmel hoch; Weihnachten. Elisa-
      beth Schwarzkopf, s; Orchestra and Chorus; Charles Mackerras.
                        +HFN 1-80 p121   +RR 12-79 p109
                        +-HFN 2-80 p107 tape

ASD 3810 Tape (c) TC ASD 3810
3788 BAZZINI: La ronde des lutins, op. 25. CASTELNUOVO-TEDESCO: Tango
      (arr. Heifetz). DEBUSSY: Petite suite: En bateau (arr. Choisnel).
      FOSTER: Jeanie with the light brown hair (arr. Heifetz). GOD-
      OWSKY: Alt Wien (arr. Heifetz). PARADIS: Sicilienne (arr. Dush-
      kin). RAFF: Cavatina. STRAVINSKY: Chanson russe. TCHAIKOVSKY:
      Melodie (arr. Flesch). VIEUXTEMPS: Souvenir d'Amerique, op. 7,
      no. 3. WIENIAWSKI: Mazurka, op. 19, no. 1. Polonaise brillante,
      op. 21, no. 2, A major. TRAD.: Deep river (arr. Heifetz). Itz-
      hak Perlman, vln; Samuel Sanders, pno.
                        +Gr 3-80 p1450   +RR 3-80 p89
                        +HFN 4-80 p115   +RR 7-80 p97 tape
                        ++HFN 6-80 p119 tape

ALP 3824 Tape (c) TC ALP 3824 (From Columbia 33CS 1231)
3789 BOITO: Mefistofele: L'altra notte in fondo al mare. CATALANI: La
      Wally: Ebben, ne andro lontana. CILEA: Adriana Lecouvreur: Ecco
      respiro appena...io son l'umile ancella; Poveri fiori. DELIBES:
      Lakme: Dov'e l'Indiana bruna. GIORDANO: Andrea Chenier: La mamma
      morta. MEYERBEER: Dinorah: Ombra leggiera. ROSSINI: Il barbiere
      di Siviglia: Una voce poco fa. VERDI: I vespri siciliani: Merce
      dilette amiche. Maria Callas; s; PhO; Tullio Serafin.
                        +Gr 3-80 p1445   +-Op 7-80 p686
                        +-HFN 6-80 p119 tape   +-RR 3-80 p40

ASD 3862 Tape (c) TC ASD 3862 (also Angel SZ 37757)
3790 ADDINSELL: Dangerous moonlight: Warsaw concerto. BATH: Love story:
     Cornish rhapsody. GERSHWIN: Rhapsody in blue. ROZSA: Spell-
     bound: Spellbound concerto. WILLIAMS: While I live: The dream
     of Olwen. Daniel Adni, pno; Bournemouth Symphony Orchestra; Ken-
     neth Alwyn.
               +FF 11/12-80 p239   +NR 10-80 p3
               +Gr 5-80 p1718   ++RR 5-80 p52
               +HFN 8-80 p109 tape   +SFC 8-24-80 p36
ASD 3865 Tape (c) TC ASD 3865
3791 ABT: Laughing. BARNBY: Home they brought her warrior dead. BRIDGE:
     The goslings. CALKIN: Breathe soft ye winds. CLARKE: Street
     music. HATTON: He that hath a pleasant face; The letter; The way
     to build a boat or Jack's opinion. HOBBS: Phyllis is my only joy
     (arr. Smith). LESLIE: Charm me asleep. MARTIN: Let maids be
     false so wine be true. MACY: Jenk's vegetable compound. PEAR-
     SALL: Light of my soul; Waters of Elle (arr.). PINSUTI: Good-
     night beloved. ROGERS: Hears not my Phyllis. STEVENS: All my
     sense thy sweetness gained. SULIVAN: The long day closes. SUT-
     TON: Come sweet Marguerite. The King's Singers.
               ++Gr 3-80 p1449   ++HFN 6-80 p119 tape
               +Gr 5-80 p1717 tape   ++RR 4-80 p119
               ++HFN 3-80 p103
ASD 3908 Tape (c) TC ASD 3908 (From HMV SLS 5113, Columbia SAX 2412/4,
               SLS 943, 956, 977, 5170, 5187, SAN 242/3)
3792 BELLINI: Norma: Mira Norma. BIZET: Les pecheurs de perles: C'Etait
     le soir...Au fond du temple saint. GOUNOD: Faust: Il se fait
     tard. LEONCAVALLO: I Pagliacci: E fra quest'ansie...Decido il
     mio destino. MASCAGNI: L'Amico Fritz: Suzel buon di. VERDI:
     Aida: La fatal pietra...O terra addio. Don Carlo: Dio che nell'
     anima infondere. La forza del destino: Solenne in quest'ora.
     Maria Callas, Montserrat Caballe, Mirella Freni, Renata Scotto,
     s; Christa Ludwig, Fiorenza Cossotto, ms; Alain Vanzo, Carlo
     Bergonzi, Placido Domingo, Luciano Pavarotti, t; Guillermo Sara-
     bia, Piero Cappuccilli, Sherrill Milnes, Thomas Allen, bar;
     Paris Opera Orchestra; La Scala Orchestra, RPO, ROHO, PhO; Geor-
     ges Pretre, Tullio Serafin, Lamberto Gardelli, Carlo Maria Giu-
     lini, Riccardo Muti, Gianandrea Gavazzeni.
               +Gr 9-80 p407
ASD 3915 Tape (c) TC ASD 3915 (From SAN 184/6, 103/6, Columbia SAX 2369/
               72, 2284, SAN 114/6, 131/2, SAX 2316/7, SLS 5113, 977)
3793 BIZET: Les pecheurs de perles: Me voila seule dans la nuit...Comme
     autrefois. DONIZETTI: Lucia di Lammermoor: Sparsa e di rose...
     Il dolce suono...Spargi d'amaro pianto. MOZART: Cosi fan tutte,
     K 588: Come scoglio. Don Giovanni, K 527: Troppo mi spiace...
     Non mi dir. PUCCINI: La boheme: Si mi chiamano Mimi. Madama
     Butterfly: Un bel di vedremo. ROSSINI: Il barbiere di Siviglia:
     Una voce poco fa. VERDI: Aida: Qui Radames verra...O patria mia.
     WEBER: Oberon: Ozean du Ungeheuer. Renata Scotto, Elisabeth
     Schwarzkopf, Joan Sutherland, Birgit Nilsson, Victoria de los
     Angeles, Mirella Freni, Maria Callas, Ileana Cotrubas, Montserrat
     Caballe; Rome Opera Orchestra, PhO, RPO, Paris Opera Orchestra,
     NPhO; John Barbirolli, Karl Bohm, Carlo Maria Giulini, Heinz
     Wallberg, Vittorio Gui, Thomas Schippers, Tullio Serafin, Georges
     Pretre, Riccardo Muti.
               +Gr 11-80 p736   +-HFN 11-80 p129

ASD 3943 Tape (c) TC ASD 3943 (also Angel DS 37758)
3794 BOCCHERINI: Quintet, strings, op. 13, no. 5, E major: Minuet (arr.
    Woodhouse). DVORAK: Nocturne, op. 40, B minor. FAURE: Pavane,
    op. 50. GRIEG: Elegiac melodies, op. 34 (2). TCHAIKOVSKY: Quar-
    tet, strings, no. 1, op. 11, D major: Andante cantabile. WAGNER:
    Siegfried Idyll. AMF; Neville Marriner.
                    +Gr 6-80 p43   ++HFN 10-80 p117 tape
                    +Gr 12-80 p889 tape   +NR 8-80 p5
                    ++HFN 6-80 p114   +-RR 6-80 p64

SLS 5022 (2) Tape (c) TC SLS 5022 (also Angel SB 3861)
3795 ARNE: As you like it: Under the greenwood tree. BACH: Cantata, no.
    208, Schafe konnen sicher weiden. Cantata, no. 106: Sonatina.
    Magnificat, S 243, D major: Esurientes. BARBIREAU: Eeen vrolic
    Wesen. BASTON: Concerto, D major. BRITTEN: Scherzo. BUTTERLY:
    The white throated warbler. BYRD: The leaves be green. COUPER-
    IN, F.: Livre de clavecin, Bk III, Ordre no. 15: Musete de choisi;
    Musete de taverni. DICKINSON: Recorder music. HANDEL: Acis and
    Galatea: O ruddier than the cherry. LE HEURTEUR: Troys jeunes
    bourgeoises. HINDEMITH: Trio, soprano and 2 alto recorders.
    HOLBORNE: The choice. Muylinda. Pavan and galliard. Sic semper
    soleo. JACOTIN: Voyant souffrir. PURCELL: Three parts upon a
    ground: Fantasia. SCHMELZER: Sonata a 7 flauti. SERMISY: Allez
    souspirs. Amour me voyant. VIVALDI: Concerto, P 77, A minor.
    ANON.: English dance. Saltarello. Early Music Consort; David
    Munrow.
                    +-ARG 11-78 p51   +HFN 8-76 p95 tape
                    +FF 9/10-80 p280   +MM 3-76 p43
                    +Gr 9-75 p479   ++NR 1-79 p16
                    +Gr 12-76 p1066 tape   +RR 9-75 p51
                    +HFN 9-75 p91   ++SFC 1-28-79 p43

SLS 5196 (2)
3796 DARGOMIZHSKY: Russalka: Miller's aria. The stone guest (Cui, orch.
    Rimsky-Korsakov). NAPRAVNIK: Dubrovsky: Vladimir's recitative
    and romance. RIMSKY-KORSAKOV: Servilia: Servilia's aria. RUB-
    INSTEIN: The demon: Tamara's song. SEROV: The power of evil:
    Yeromka's song. VERSTOVSKY: The tomb of Askold: Stranger's aria
    and chorus. Tamara Milashkina, Maria Beishu, Zoe Khristich, s;
    Tamara Sinyavskaya, ms; Vladimir Atlantov, Vitaly Vlasov, t;
    Alexander Vedernikov, Lev Vernigora, Vitaly Nartov, Mark Reshet-
    in, bs; Vladimir Valaitis, Nicolay Kondratyuk, bar; Bolshoi
    Theatre Orchestra and Chorus; Mark Ermler, Boris Khaikin.
                    +Gr 12-80 p872

ESD 7078 Tape (c) TC ESD 7078 (From ASD 3131, 2784, 3097, 3338)
3797 BERNSTEIN: Candide: Overture. DUKAS: The sorcerer's apprentice.
    ENESCO: Roumanian rhapsody, op. 11, no. 1, A major. FALLA: The
    three cornered hat: The neighbours dance; The miller's dance;
    Final dance. HOLST: The perfect fool, op. 39. VAUGHAN WILLIAMS:
    Fantasia on "Greensleeves". LSO; Andre Previn.
                    +Gr 10-79 p662   +RR 11-79 p71
                    ++HFN 11-79 p155   +RR 3-80 p104 tape
                    ++HFN 1-80 p123 tape

HLM 7134 (From Columbia LX 1404/6, 1229, 1275, 1248, 1229, LB 130)
3798 CASTELNUOVO-TEDESCO: Concerto, guitar, no. 1, op. 99, D major.
    Tarantella, A minor. CRESPO: Nortena, homenaje a Julian Aguirre.
    PONCE: Sonatina meridional. TORROBA: Suite castellana: Arada
    and fandanguillo (arr. Segovia). TURINA: Fandanguillo, op. 36.

VILLA-LOBOS: Etudes (2). Andres Segovia, gtr; New London Orchestra; Alec Sherman.
          +ARSC Vol 12, nos. 1-2   +-HFN 7-78 p109
             1980 p121   +RR 7-78 p49
          +Gr 7-78 p213

SXLP 30299 Tape (c) TC SXLP 30299 (From ALP 1533, 1843, ASD 259, 432,
             518, HQS 1136)
3799 CHABRIER: March joyeuse. DEBUSSY: L'Enfant prodigue: Cortege et
     air de danse. Prelude a l'apres-midi d'un faune. FAURE: Dolly
     suite, op. 56 (arr. Rabaud). Pavane, op. 50. GOUNOD: Romeo et
     Juliette: Le sommeil de Juliette. SAINT-SAENS: Samson et Dalila:
     Danse des pretresses de Dagon; Bacchanale. Le rouet d'Omphale,
     op. 31. RPO, French Radio Orchestra; Thomas Beecham.
          +ARSC Vol 12, no. 3,   +HFN 2-80 p105
             1980 p253   +HFN 4-80 p121 tape
          +Gr 2-80 p1275   +RR 3-80 p53
          +Gr 5-80 p1717 tape   +RR 7-80 p97 tape

                              HNH

4019
3800 Roman de Fauvel: Motets, rondeaus, ballades, lais and hymns. Rene
     Zosso, hurdy gurdy; Clemencic Consort.
          +NYT 8-10-80 pD17

4076
3801 COATES: The dambusters. DELIUS: Marche caprice. GRAINGER: Over the
     hills and far away. HOLST (Jacob): Suite, no. 1, op. 28, no. 1,
     E flat major: 1st movement march. HOWELLS: Procession, op. 38.
     PARRY: The birds: Bridal march. ROSSINI (Britten): Soirees musi-
     cales: March. VAUGHAN WILLIAMS: The wasps: March past of the
     kitchen utensils. STANFORD: Becket: The martyrdom. WALTON: Ham-
     let: Funeral march. LPO, NPhO; Adrian Boult.
          +FF 3/4-80 p200

                           HUNGAROTON

11477
3802 Gregorian chant from Hungary: Ave spes nostra, Antiphon; Veni, Re-
     demptor gentium, Hymn; Christus natus est nobis, Invitatorium;
     Jubilamen, Lesson; Descendit de caelis, Responsorium; Genealogia
     Christi, Evangelium; Lux fulgebit, Introitus; Alleluja, Dominus
     regnavit; Eia, recolamus, Sequentia; Procedentium sponsum, Bene-
     dicamus tropus; Verbum caro factum est, Responsorium; Hodie
     Christus natus est Antiphon; Dies est laetitiae, Cantio; Te
     Deum. Schola Hungarica Ensemble; Janka Szendrei, Laszlo Dobszay.
          +FF 7/8-80 p160   +Gr 1-75 p1392

SLPX 11723
3803 BALAZS: Song; Spring landscape; Carillon. BARDOS: Fire-rainbow.
     FARKAS: Butterflies reposed; Hark the sun whispers; Madrigal of
     the rose. FEHER: Homo sapiens, no. 1. LENDVAY: The feller.
     MAROS: Distances. PERTIS: Unfaithful girl. PETROVICS: Slow
     dancing tune. SARY: Lied in Lyd. SZOKOLAY: Revelation. HRT
     Chorus; Ferenc Sapszon.
          +FF 9/10-80 p246   +NR 3-80 p10

SLPX 11972
3804 BOISMORTIER: Sonata, bassoon, E minor. FASCH: Concerto, bassoon, C
major. STAMITZ: Quartet, op. 19, no. 6, F major. VIVALDI: Trio,
flute and bassoon, A minor. ZACHAU: Trio, flute and bassoon, F
major. Laszlo Hara, bsn; Csaba Vegvari, hpd; Tatrai Quartet,
Hungarian Baroque Trio.
+FF 5/6-80 p185   +NR 2-80 p7

SLPX 11983/4 (2)
3805 GREFINGER: Ach Gott; Ich stel leicht ab; Wol kumbt der mey. FINCK:
Greiner zanner; Ich stund an einem morgen; Ich wird erlost; Der
Ludel und der Hensel. Instrumental pieces (3). HOFHAIMER: Carmen
in re; Carmen magistri Pauli; Cupido; Der Hundt; Man hat bisher;
Greiner zanner; Nach willen dein. LUBLIN: Dances. Mon mary.
SERMISY: Tant que vivray. STOLTZER: Es mut vil leut; Ich klag
den Tag; Man sicht nun wol. WILLAERT: A quand; Allons, allons
gay; Ricercari (2); Villanelle. Ars Renata, Camerata Hungarica;
Laszlo Czidra.
++FF 7/8-80 p179   +NR 12-80 p9

SLPX 11987
3806 ARCADELT: Che piu foc'al. CLEMENS NON PAPA: Jesu nomen, Sit nomen.
GOMBERT: Cantibus organicis; Fundite cantores; Servite domino;
Venite filii. JOSQUIN DES PRES: Faulte d'argent. LASSUS: Veni
in hortum meum. ANON.: Fantasia, no. 2. Daniel Benko, lt.
+NR 8-80 p15

SLPX 12032
3807 BORODIN: Prince Igor: Polovtsian dances. GOUNOD: Faust: Walpurgis-
nacht. MUSSORGSKY: Khovanschina: Dance of the Persian slaves.
PONCHIELLI: La Gioconda: Dance of the hours. TCHAIKOVSKY: Eugen
Onegin, op. 24: Polonaise. Ferenc Beganyi, bs; Hungarian State
Opera Orchestra and Chorus; Janos Sandor.
-FF 7/8-80 p191   +NR 5-80 p2

SLPX 12048
3808 Gregorian chants from Hungary: Chants for Advent; Christmas; Pentecost. Schola Hungarica.
+FF 7/8-80 p160   +NR 3-80 p10

SLPX 12049
3809 Gregorian chants from Hungary. Schola Hungarica.
+FF 7/8-80 p160   ++NR 6-80 p9

SLPX 12065
3810 DUBROVAY: Duets, violin and percussion. KALMAR: Anera. KOSA: Divertimento. Two. PATACHICH: Metamorphoses. SARY: Sonata, percussion, no. 2. Gabor Kosa, perc.
-NR 12-80 p11

LPX 12085/6 (2)
3811 BEETHOVEN: Sonata, piano, no. 8, op. 13, C minor. Sonata, piano,
no. 14, op. 27, no. 2, C sharp minor. Sonata, piano, no. 28, op.
101, A major: Allegretto ma non troppo. BRAHMS: Pieces, op. 117:
Intermezzo. CHOPIN: Impromptu, no. 2, op. 36, F sharp major.
Mazurka, op. 56, no. 2, C major. Nocturne, op. 62, no. 1, B
major. DOHNANYI: Cascades, op. 41, no. 4. Humoresque, op. 17,
no. 1. Pastorale. Rhapsody, op. 11, no. 2, F sharp minor.
LISZT: Consolation, no. 3, G 172, D flat major. MOZART: Sonata,
piano, no. 11, K 331, A major. SCHUBERT (Dohnanyi): Valses nobles, op. 77, D 969. Erno Dohnanyi, pno.
+-FF 9/10-80 p261

LPX 12094
3812 DONIZETTI: La favorita: Vien Leonora. MOZART: Le nozze di Figaro,
     K 492: Se vuol ballare; Non piu andrai. ROSSINI: Il barbiere di
     Siviglia: Largo al factotum. Guglielmo Tell: Resta immobile.
     VERDI: La forza del destino: Urna fatale. Macbeth: Perfidi; All'
     Anglo contro me v'unite...Pieta rispetto amore. Rigoletto: Cor-
     tigiani vil razza dannata. WAGNER: Tannhauser: Wie Todesahnung
     ...O du mein holder Abendstern. Die Walkure: Leb wohl du kuhnes
     herrliches Kind. Alexander Sved, bar; Hungarian State Opera Or-
     chestra.
               -NR 4-80 p10
SLPX 12108
3813 BANCHIERI: Ricercare del 5 and 6 tuono. BELL'HAVER: Toccata del 1
     tuono. DIRUTA: Ricercare del 7, 8, 11, 12 tuono. Toccata del
     11 and 12 tuono. FATTORINI: Ricercare del 10 and 11 tuono.
     GABRIELI, A.: Toccata del 10 tuono. GABRIELI, G.: Canzone. Toc-
     cata del 2 tuono. GUAMI: Toccata del 2 tuono. LUZZASCHI: Ricer-
     care del 1 and 2 tuono. Toccata del 4 tuono. MORTARO: Canzone.
     QUAGLIATI: Toccata del 8 tuono. Tamas Zaszkalicsky, org.
               +FF 9/10-80 p99   +NR 9-80 p9
SLPX 12163
3814 AICHINGER: Laudate dominum. BOYCE: Alleluia. FRIDERICI: Ladilom.
     GALLUS: Pueri concinite. KODALY: Esti dal; Egyetem-Begyetem;
     Zold erdoben. LASSUS: Unnepelni jojjeted. LASZLO: Ma come bali
     bella bimba. LESUR: A kecske. LOTTI: Ecce panis angelorum.
     MORLEY: Ti edes majus-Fenyek. NAKADA: A behavazott Varosban.
     PALESTRINA: Anyai sziv; Jesu rex admirabilis. PITONI: Boldog
     Aki-Enekel. REGNART: Megbabonaz Sok Szivet. SALLINEN: Simpati.
     SAJNSZKIJ: Kiszamolo. SANDIG: A kis ponilo. SCHEIN: Ebreszto.
     VALERIA: Jalo jalo. VECCHI: Neked zeng ez a dal. WHITE/JAI:
     Utazo muzsikusok. YOULL: Majusi viragok. Hungarian Children's
     Choir; Valeria Botka, Laszlo Csanyi.
               +NR 10-80 p9

                         HYPERION

A 66012
3815 ATTWOOD: Come holy ghost. PARRY: I was glad. STAINER: Evening
     canticles, B flat major. STANFORD: Evening canticles, G major.
     WESLEY, S.: Exultate deo. WESLEY, S.S.: Blessed be the God and
     father. WOOD: O thou the central orb. Ely Cathedral Choir;
     Stephen le Prevost, org; Arthur Wills.
               +Gr 12-80 p871   +HFN 11-80 p125

                         ICARUS

1002
3816 ALBENIZ: Cantos de Espana, op. 232: Baja la palmera; Cordoba (trans.
     Llobet and Pujol). BROUWER: Micro piezas. GALLES: Sonata, gui-
     tar, E minor (trans. Castellani-Andriaccio). GRANADOS: Goyescas:
     Intermezzo (trans. Pujol). SCARLATTI, D.: Sonata, guitar, K 9,
     E minor (trans. Pujol). Sonata, guitar, K 380, E major (trans.
     Castellani-Andriaccio). Joanne Castellani, Michael Andriaccio,

gtr.
+NR 8-80 p15

IKON

IKO 9
3817 Russian Orthodox church music: Vespers of Good Friday. The Most
     Reverend Metropolitan Anthony of Sourozh, celebrant; London Rus-
     sian Orthodox Cathedral Choir; Michael Fortounatto.
          +—Gr 11-79 p900   +RR 7-79 p112
          +—HFN 10-80 p131

IMPORT MUSIC SERVICE

Import Music Service 901/906 (also Philips 6812 901/6)
3818 400 years of Dutch music. ANDRIESSEN: Variations and fugue on a
     theme by Kuhnau. BRANDTS BUYS: Serenade, op. 25, D minor. BUNS:
     Sonata finalis, op. 5, no. 15. CONRADUS: Canzon a 8. DIEPEN-
     BROCK: Im grossen Schweigen. ESCHER: Univers de Rimbaud. FODOR:
     Symphony, no. 4, op. 19, C minor. HELLENDAAL: Concerto grosso,
     op. 3, no. 1, G minor. JANSSEN: Dans van de Melic Matrijzen.
     LENTZ: Concerto, harpsichord, no. 2, C major. LOEVENDIE: Turkish
     folk poems (6). MEDER: Sympony, op. 3, no. 1, C major. ROSIER:
     Sonata, C major. RUYNEMAN: Hieroglyphen. VAN BAAREN: Septet.
     VAN BREE: Allegro moderato. VAN DER HORST: La nuit, op. 67.
     VAN VLIJMEN: Sonata, piano and 3 groups of instruments. VERHEY:
     Concerto, flute, no. 1, op. 43, D minor. VERMEULEN: Symphony,
     no. 3. WAGENAAR: Cyrano de Bergerac, op. 23. ZWEERS: Symphony,
     no. 3. Dorothy Dorow, s; Jean Giraudeau, t; Ruud von der Meer,
     bar; Willem Noske, Piet Nijland, Jaring Walta, vln; Herbert van
     der Velde, vla; Godfried Hoogeveen, vlc; Koos Verheul, Jolie de
     Wit, flt; Frank Minderaa, ob; Aart Rozeboom, clt; Kathleen White,
     bsn; Vicente Zarzo, hn; Peter Stotijn, bs; Ton Koopman, hpd; Guus
     Janssen, Theo Bruins, pno; Hague Philharmonic Orchestra; Nikolaus
     Harnoncourt, Ton Koopman, Antal Dorati, Ernest Bour, Ferdinand
     Leitner, Hans Vonk, Alain Lombard, Lucas Vis, Adam Medveczky.
          +HFN 7-80 p115   +RR 7-80 p24

ITALIA

ITL 70067
3819 BACH, C.P.E. Sonata, harp, F major (arr. Grandjany). BEETHOVEN:
     Variations on a Swiss air, F major (6). CLEMENTI: Andante con
     variazioni. ROSSINI: Sonata, harp, E flat major. VIOTTI: Son-
     ata, harp, B flat major. Claudio Antonelli, hp.
          -Gr 9-80 p380

LAUREL

LR 01150
3820 BEETHOVEN: Rondo, op. 51, no. 1, C major. CHOPIN: Ballade, no. 4,

op. 52, F minor. DEBUSSY: L'Isle joyeuse. RACHMANINOFF: Preludes, op. 23, nos. 3, 7; op. 32, nos. 5, 12. SCRIABIN: Sonata,
piano, no. 5, op. 53, F sharp major. Sedmara Zakarian (Rutsh-
tein), pno.
>   ++NR 8-80 p12

LEONARDA

LP1 102
3821 BREHM: Colloquy and chorale. HOOVER: Sinfonia. NELHYBEL: Concert
     etudes. PALMER: Contrasts. SCHICKELE: Last tango in Bayreuth.
     New York Bassoon Quartet.
>   +ARG 3-80 p52   +NR 4-80 p7
>   +FF 3/4-80 p195
LP1 104
3822 BOULANGER: D'un matin de printemps. Nocturne. FARRENC: Trio, op.
     45, E minor. HOOVER: On the betrothal of Princess Isabelle of
     France, aged six. TAILLEFERRE: Pastorale. ULEHLA: Elegy for a
     whale. Katherine Hoover, flt; Carter Brey, vlc; Barbara Wein-
     traub, Virginia Eskin, pno.
>   +-FF 9/10-80 p287   +St 10-80 p126
>   +-NR 8-80 p10

LONDON

SPA 4097 (From Argo ZRG 5450)
3823 FRICKER: A babe is born. GAUNTLETT: Once in royal David's city.
     HOLST: Lullay my liking. MATHIAS: Wassail. MENDELSSOHN: Hark
     the herald angels sing. PETTMAN: O babe divine. WISHART: Al-
     leluya. ANON.: Corde natus ex parentis. Infant holy. O little
     town of Bethlehem. There is no rose. King's College Choir;
     David Willcocks; Andrew Davis, org.
>   +FF 11/12-80 p256
CS 7133 (also Decca SXL 6909)
3824 GOLDMARK: Merlin: Overture. GOETZ: Francesca da Rimini. NICOLAI:
     The temple knight. SHREKER: Die Gezeichneten. WEBER: Die drei
     pintos: Intermezzo. WOLF: Der Corregidor: Overture. National
     Philharmonic Orchestra; Kurt Herbert Adler.
>   +FF 11/12-80 p225   +-ON 1-5-80 p37
>   +Gr 2-80 p1275   ++RR 3-80 p57
>   +HFN 3-80 p104   +SFC 11-12-78 p49
>   ++NR 10-79 p1   ++St 4-79 p159
CS 7147
3825 ALBENIZ: Iberia: Triana. BACH: Fantasia, S 921, C minor. CHOPIN:
     Berceuse, op. 57, D flat major. FALLA: El amor brujo: Ritual
     fire dance. GRANADOS: Goyescas: Maiden and the nightingale.
     GRIEG: Lyric pieces, op. 54: Nocturne, C major. MOZART: Fantas-
     ia, D 397, D minor. Sonata, piano, no. 11, K 331, A major: Rondo
     alla turca. Rondo, piano, K 485, D major. SCHUMANN: Noveletten,
     op. 21, no. 8. Alicia de Larrocha, pno.
>   +FF 1/2-80 p167   +-NR 3-80 p13
STS 15501
3826 LANNER: Huntsman's pleasure galop, op. 82. Pest waltz, op. 93.

SCHUBERT: Ecossaises (6). Waltzes (8). STRAUSS, J. I: Exeter
polka, op. 249. Indians galop, op. 111. Tivoli slide waltz,
op. 39. Youthful fire galop, op. 90. STRAUSS, J. II: Lovesong
waltz, op. 114. STRAUSS, Josef: The good old days waltz, op. 26.
Boskovsky Ensemble; Willi Boskovsky.
+FF 7/8-80 p183

STS 15511 (From London OS 25075)
3827 CILEA: Adriana Lecouvreur: La dolcissima effigie; L'anima ho stanca.
GIORDANO: Andrea Chenier: Come un bel di di maggio. MEYERBEER:
L'Africaine: O paradiso. PUCCINI: Manon Lescaut: Donna non vidi
mai. Tosca: Recondita armonia; E lucevan le stelle. VERDI: Aida:
Celeste Aida. La forza del destino: O tu che in seno agli ange-
li. Un ballo in maschero: Ma se m'e forza perderti. Luisa Mil-
ler: Quando le sere al placido. Il trovatore: Ah si ben io.
Carlo Bergonzi, t; Santa Cecilia Orchestra; Gianandrea Gavazzeni.
+FF 11/12-80 p195

OS 26603
3828 DELIBES: Lakme: Bell song. DONIZETTI: La fille du regiment: Par le
rang...Salut a la France. Maria Stuarda: O nube, che lieve per
l'aria. MASSENET: Esclarmonde: Esprits de l'air. OFFENBACH:
Les contes de Hoffman: Doll song. PUCCINI: Tosca: Vissi d'arte.
Turandot: In questa reggia. VERDI: Il trovatore: D'amor sull'
ali rosee...Tu vedrai. Joan Sutherland, s; Huguette Tourangeau,
ms; Luciano Pavarotti, t; Various orchestras; Richard Bonynge,
Zubin Mehta.
+-FF 3/4-80 p180   +NR 7-80 p9

LYRITA

SRCS 95
3829 ALWYN: Derby day. ARNOLD: Beckus the dandipratt. BUSH: Yorick.
CHAGRIN: Helter skelter. LEIGH: Agincourt. RAWSTHORNE: Street
corner. LPO, LSO, NPhO; William Alwyn, Nicholas Braithwaite,
Norman Handley, John Pritchard.
+Gr 1-80 p1162   +RR 12-79 p72
+HFN 12-79 p175

MDP

019
3830 DONIZETTI: L'Elisir d'amore: Una furtiva lagrima. GOUNOD: Faust:
O nuit d'amour. PUCCINI: La boheme: Che gelida manina; Mi chi-
amano Mimi; O soave fanciulla. Madama Butterfly: Act 1, finale.
Tosca: Recondita armonia; E lucevan le stella. STRAUSS, J. II:
Der Zigeunerbaron: Waltz song. VERDI: Rigoletto: La donna e mob-
ile. Grace Moore, s; Joseph Schmidt.
+-ARG 2-80 p54

029
3831 BLAND: Carry me back to old Virginny. BOND: I love you truly. DEL
RIEGO: Homing. EDEN: What's in the air today. GRANT-SCHAEFER:
The cuckoo clock. GRIEG: I love thee. GRISELLE/YOUNG: The cuckoo clock. HERBERT: Kiss me again. MASCAGNI: Cavalleria rusticana: Ave Maria. NANA-ZUCCA: The big brown bear. REGER: Maria's

Wiegenlied. SANDOVAL: Ave Maria. SERRADELL: La golondrina.
STRAUSS, O.: Chocolate soldier: My hero. STRAUSS, J. II: The blue
Danube,   op. 314. TOSTI: La ultima canzone; Marechiare. VAL-
VERDE: Clavelitos. TRAD.: Coming thro the rye. Rosa Ponselle,
s.
            +ARG 10-80 p37   -FF 9/10-80 p244

                            MELODIYA

S10 05519/20
3832 BEETHOVEN: Sonata, piano, no. 7, op. 10, no. 3, D major: Largo e
     mesto. CHOPIN: Sonata, piano, no. 3, op. 58, B minor: Scherzo
     molto vivace; Largo. LIADOV: Prelude, op. 11, no. 1, B minor.
     RUBINSTEIN: Impromptu, op. 16, no. 1, F major. SCHUBERT: Moment
     musicaux, op. 94, no. 4, D 780, C sharp minor. TCHAIKOVSKY:
     Berceuse, op. 16, no. 1, A flat minor (Pabst). Aveu passione, E
     minor. Morceau, op. 19: Reverie du soir. Sonata, piano, op. 37,
     G major: Andante non troppo quasi moderato. Konstantin Igumnov,
     pno.
            +ARSC Vol 12, nos. 1-2, 1980 p110
S10 05521/2
3833 CHOPIN: Mazurka, op. 56, no. 1, B major. RUBINSTEIN: Melancholy,
     op. 51, no. 1, G minor. Prelude, op. 75, no. 9, D minor. RACH-
     MANINOFF: Barcarolle, op. 10, no. 3, G minor. SCHUMANN: Kreis-
     leriana, op. 16. SCRIABIN: Mazurka, op. 25, no. 7, F sharp minor.
     Poem, op. 32, no. 2, F sharp major. Konstantin Igumnov, pno.
            +ARSC Vol 12, nos. 1-2, 1980 p110
S10 09715-6
3834 BACH, J.C.F.: Sonata, harpsichord, A major. KEFALIDI: Trio a quat-
     tro. LACHNER: Fugue, D minor. SCHOENBERG: Pieces, piano, 4
     hands (6). SCHUBERT: Fugue, D 952, E minor. Victoria Postni-
     kova, Gennady Rozdestvensky, hpd, org, pno, celesta; Leonid Miro-
     novich, flt; Nicolai Mironov, trom.
            +-FF 3/4-80 p191

                            MERIDIAN

E 77025
3835 BACH: Cantata, no. 147, Jesu joy of man's desiring. BRAHMS: Ein
     deutsches Requiem, op. 45: How lovely is thy dwelling place.
     BYRD: Ave verum corpus. MENDELSSOHN: Hear my prayer, op. 39,
     no. 1. MOZART: Ave verum corpus, K 618. PARRY: I was glad.
     PURCELL: Rejoice in the Lord alway. WESLEY, S.S.: Blessed be
     the God and Father. Robert Johnston, treble; Salisbury Cathed-
     ral Choir; Colin Walsh, org; Richard Seal.
            +Gr 3-80 p1433   +RR 3-80 p90
            +HFN 2-80 p101

E 77028
3836 BACH: Chorale preludes, S 608/729/751, In dulci jubilo. DAQUIN:
     Noel, no. 10, G major. EDMUNDSON: Preludes on old chorales (2).
     GIGOUT: Rhapsodie sur des noels. KARG-ELERT: In dulci jubilo,
     op. 75, no. 2. MESSIAEN: La nativite du Seigneur: Les anges;
     Dieu parmi nous. PEETERS: Chorale prelude on "How brightly

shines the morning star", op. 68, no. 7. David Sanger, org.
          ++Gr 4-80 p1575   +-RR 4-80 p79

E 77031/2 (4)
3837 BAX: Far in a western brookland. BUTTERWORTH: A Shropshire lad:
     Loveliest of trees; When I was one and twenty; Look not in my
     eyes; Think no more lad; The lads in their hundreds; Is my team
     ploughing. GIBBS: When I was one and twenty. GURNEY: The wes-
     tern playland: Reveille; Lovelist of trees; Golden friends; Twice
     a week; The aspens; Is my team ploughing; The far country; March.
     IRELAND: The boys are up in the woods all day. MOERAN: Ludlow
     town: When smoke stood up from Ludlow; Farewell to barn and stack
     and tree; Say lad have you things to do; The lads in their hund-
     reds. Songs: Tis time I think by Wenlock town. ORR, C.W.:
     Songs: Along the field; The lent lily; Oh when I was in love with
     you. PEEL: In summertime on Bredon; Reveille; When the lad for
     longing sighs. SOMERVELL: A Shropshire lad: Loveliest of trees;
     When I was one and twenty; There pass the careless people; In
     summertime on Bredon; The street sounds to the soldiers tread;
     On the idle hill of summer; White in the moon the long road lies;
     Think no more lad laugh be jolly; Into my heart an air that kills;
     The lads in their hundreds. Graham Trew, bar; Roger Vignoles,
     pno; Coull Quartet.
          ++Gr 4-80 p1583   ++STL 5-11-80 p39
          +HFN 4-80 p113

E 77034
3838 BACH: Toccata and fugue, S 565, D minor. BOELLMANN: Suite gothique,
     op. 25: Toccata. HOLLINS: Trumpet minuet. LANGLAIS: Paraphrases
     gregoriennes, op. 5: Te deum. MULET: Carillon sortie. PEETERS:
     Suite modale, op. 43: Adagio. SAINT-SAENS: Rhapsodies sur des
     cantiques bretons, op. 7, no. 3 (3). WIDOR: Symphony, no. 5, op.
     42, no. 1, F minor: Toccata. Christopher Herrick, org.
          +-Gr 11-80 p710   +HFN 11-80 p127

                         METRONOME

168016
3839 CHERUBINI: Sonatas, horn. KALLIWODA: Introduction and rondo, op.
     51, F major. REGER: Scherzino. SCHUMANN (orch. Ansermet): Ad-
     agio and allegro, op. 70, A flat major. WEISMANN: Concertino,
     horn, op. 118, E flat major. Hermann Baumann, hn; Munich Phil-
     harmonic Orchestra; Marinus Voorberg.
          +HFN 7-80 p114   +RR 7-80 p50

                      MOSS MUSIC GROUP

MMG 1118
3840 ARNE: Where the bee sucks. DIBDIN: Come away death. HOLBORNE:
     When daffodils begin to peere. ROBINSON: Bonny sweet Robin or
     Robin is to the greenwode gone. VERNON: When that I was a tiny
     boy. WEIGAND: Farewell dear love. ANON.: Almaine. Carman's
     whistle. The fryar and the nun. Jog on. Kemp's kegge or jig.
     New nothing. Night peece. O mistress mine. Robin Hood and the
     tanner. Sounds and sweet ayres. Willow song. Martin Best,

voice, lute, guitar; Barlow Baroque Players.
                    +ARG 12-80 p50
MMG 1119 Tape (c) CMG 1119
3841 BACH: Magnificat, S 243, D major: The cathedral. GILLIS: The joust.
     En sueno. HANDEL Royal fireworks music: A royal firework (arr.
     Gillis). SATIE: Gymnopedie, no. 1. TRAD.: Amazing grace; Bour-
     bon Street medley (arr. Gillis). Liona Boyd, gtr; Erica Goodman,
     hp; Don Gillis, pno; Canadian Brass.
               -FF 7/8-80 p185   ++St 9-80 p74
               +MUM 10-80 p34

                    MUSIC GALLERY EDITIONS

MGE 21
3842 FLOYD: Blues, horn and piano. FREEDMAN: Mono, solo horn. MONTGOM-
     ERY: Chaser, 2 horns and electronics. RIMMER: Extro-Intro, horn
     and electronics. SERMILA: Monody, horn and percussion. TRUAX:
     Sonic landscape, no. 1. James MacDonald, James Montgomery, hn;
     Monica Gaylord, pno; Russell Hartenberger, perc.
               +-ARG 6-80 p50   +MUM 10-80 p33

                    MUSICAL HERITAGE SOCIETY

MHS 3908
3843 BEETHOVEN (Godzinsky): Coriolan overture, op. 62. GRIEG (Godzinsky):
     Elegaic melodies, op. 34, no. 2. KETELBY (Chiapparin): In a Per-
     sian market. MASCAGNI (Chiapparin): Cavalleria rusticana: In-
     termezzo. SUPPE (Godzinsky): Light cavalry: Overture. Altti,
     Veikko, Pentti Laiho, accord.
               -FF 3/4-80 p199
MHS 4030
3844 BEETHOVEN: Masonic march. Opferlied, op. 121b. GIROUST: Le deluge.
     HIMMEL: Maurerlied. MOZART: Dir Seele des Weltalls, K 429. Mas-
     onic songs, K 148, K 468, K Anh 623. TASKIN: Masonic funeral
     march. S. Hamilton, P. Gianotti, t; R. Terrasson, bs; J. ver
     Hasselt, fortepiano; Les Chantres de la Tradition; Les Musiciens
     de Paris.
               -HF 12-79 p109   +St 5-80 p95
MHS 4044
3845 BACH: Partita, flute, C minor. GOLDBERG: Trio, 2 violins and con-
     tinuo, G minor. KREBS: Trio sonata, flute and violin, D major.
     KIRNBERGER: Cembalostucke. MUTHEL: Sonata, flute. NICHELMANN:
     Cembalostucke. Alfred Trippner, Richard Amboden, vln; Herbert
     Schafer, vlc; Martin Gotthart Schneider, cembalo; Leonore Weh-
     rung, flt.
               +-FF 1/2-80 p177
MHS 4064
3846 CIMA: Canzona francese. MERULA: Canzona IV. Capriccio. Sonata
     cromatica. MAYONE: Toccata, no 5. ROSSI: Toccatas, nos. 6, 14.
     SALVATORE: Canzona frances, no. 3. Toccata, no. 1. STORACE:
     Toccata a canzona. TRABACI: Canzona francese. Canto fermo, no.
     2. Durezze e legature. Stefano Innocenti, org.
               /FF 3/4-80 p192

MHS 4067
3847 BOIELDIEU: The Caliph of Baghdad: Overture. LEONCAVALLO: I Pagli-
acci: Intermezzo. MASCAGNI: Cavalleria rusticana: Intermezzo.
L'Amico Fritz: Intermezzo, Act 3. MASSENET: Thais: Meditation.
NICOLAI: The merry wives of Windsor: Overture. PUCCINI: Manon
Lescaut: Intermezzo, Act 3. REZNICEK: Donna Diana: Overture.
THOMAS: Mignon: Entr'acte. VERDI: La traviata: Prelude, Act 1.
Viktor Simcisko, vln; Slovak Madrigalists; Bratislava Radio Or-
chestra; Ondrej Lenard.
+FF 1/2-80 p181

MHS 4070
3848 BATES: Come life Shaker life; Mount Zion; Ode to contentment; Rights
of conscience. BILLINGS: The bird; Thanksgiving anthem, O praise
the Lord of heaven (Psalm, no. 148). BOURGEOIS: Psalm, no. 8.
BRACKETT: Simple gifts. CROFT: Psalm tune, no. 149. EADES: A
dream. HAMPTON: Doxology. HOLDEN: The Lord is good to all.
RUPE: Gentle words. RUSSELL: Millennial praise. TANS'UR: Westerham tune (Psalm, no. 81). TUFTS: Psalm tune, no. 100. BAY
PSALM BOOK: Psalms, nos. 23, 100. STERNHOLD AND HOPKINS PSALTER:
Psalms, nos. 7, 85, 115. ANON.: Love is little. March. A prayer for the captive. Supplication. Christina Price, s; Carolyn
Dickson, ms; Edward Anderson, t; Leonhard Hart, bs; Barbara Deni-
son, org; Plymouth Church Chancel Choir; John Herr.
+St 5-80 p95

MHS 4077 Tape (c) 6077
3849 ARAUJO: Los cofla desde la estleya. BELCHER: Carol. BILLINGS:
Bethlehem; Boston; Judea. DENNIS: Of a rose. FRANCO: Salve
regina. IVES: A Christmas carol. NOBRE: Ago lona. PRADO: Magnificat. READ: Expression; He is king of kings; I believe this
is Jesus; Star in the East; Rise up shepherd and follow; Sherburne. XIMENO: Ay ay galeguinos. Western Wind.
+AR 8-80 p85   +ARG 12-79 p14

MHS 4080
3850 BERBERIAN: Prelude. CHUKHAJIAN: Impromptus. ELMAS: Nocturne.
GHORGHANIAN: Bayati. KOMITAS: Dances. MANAS: Petite suite.
MIKULI: Etude. Lied. NOVA: Songs (2). PAPELYAN: La fin d'un
reve. SPENTIARIAN: Enzeli. Lullaby. TIGRANIAN: Et-Arhaj.
Sahan Arzunri, pno.
+FF 5/6-80 p184

MHS 4110
3851 ARZRUNI: Invocation. Mentations, no. 1. Heterophonic suite, ex-
cerpts. BARTEVIAN: For children. GAZAROSSIAN: Prelude. GELA-
LIAN: Andantino. HOVHANESS: Achtamar. Farewell to the mountains.
Mystic flute. Vanadour. KARAMANUK: Admiration. KALAJIAN: Song.
TERZIAN: Danza criolla. Juegos para Diana. Toccata. TJEKNA-
VORIAN: Armenian dance, no. 2. YARDUMIAN: Preludes (2). Sahan
Arzruni, pno.
+FF 9/10-80 p262

MHS 4121
3852 DE COURGES: Fantasie. DE LA BARRE: Sarabande. DU MONT: Pavanne, D
minor. Prelude, D minor. RACQUET: Fantasie. RICHARD: Prelude,
D minor. ROBERDAY: Fugues, nos. 10, 12. Fugue and caprice,
nos. 1 and 3. THOMELIN: Duo. ANON.: Ave maris stella. Fantasie. Andre Isoir, org.
+-FF 7/8-80 p168

MHS 4123
3853 DERING: Pavan. GIBBONS: The queen's command. HOLBORNE: Coranto,
     heigh ho holiday. Pavana ploravit. HUME: Touch me lightly.
     Death. Life. JOHNSON: Where the bee sucks. LUPO: Fantasia.
     RAVENSCROFT: Fantasia, no. 4. SIMPSON: Bonny sweet robin. TOM-
     KINS: Alman. Barafostus dream. ANON.: Fortune my foe. Green-
     sleeves. O death rock me asleep. Ophelia's songs. Robin is
     to the green wood gone. When Daphne from fair Phoebus did fly.
     Whoope do me no harm. SHAKESPEARE: Sonnets and plays, excerpts.
     Sheila Schonbrun, s; Edward Smith, hpd; New York Consort of Viols;
     Tom Klunis, actor.
             +-FF 11/12-80 p206   ++St 7-80 p87
MHS 4180 Tape (c) MHS 6180
3854 DEBUSSY: Syrinx. ENESCO: Cantabile et presto. FAURE: Fantaisie,
     op. 79. Morceau de concours. GAUBERT: Sonata, flute and piano,
     no. 1, A major. HONEGGER: Danse de la chevre. POULENC: Sonata,
     flute and piano. Carol Wincenc, flt; Andras Schiff, pno.
             +-FF 11/12-80 p212   +St 10-80 p127
             +HF 10-80 p96

                         MUSICAPHON

BM 30 SL 1209 (From Cantate 047704, Oryx 3C 301)
3855 BULL: Fantasia. In nomine. BYRD: Coranto. Galliard. Pavan.
     FARNABY: A toye. Loth to depart. GIBBONS: Pavan. PURCELL:
     Musick's hand-maid: March; Song tune; Air; Minuet; New minuet;
     New Scotch tune; Minuet; Sefauchi's farewell; Minuet rigadoon;
     A new ground; Minuet; A new Irish tune; Suite, G minor; Toccata;
     Hornpipe; Air. Fitzwilliam virginal book: Pieces. ANON.: Now-
     ells galliard. Why aske you. George Malcolm, hpd.
             +HFN 8-80 p101   +-RR 8-80 p73

                           MUZA

SX 0684
3856 BEETHOVEN: Sonata, piano, no. 14, op. 27, no. 2, C sharp minor.
     CHOPIN: Nocturne, op. 15, no. 2, F sharp major. Waltz, op. 18,
     E flat major. LISZT: Etudes d'execution transecendente d'apres
     Paganini, G 140: La campanella. PADEREWSKI: Minuet, op. 14, no.
     1, G major. SCHUBERT: Moment musicaux, op. 94, no. 2, A flat
     major. Ignace Jan Paderewski, pno.
             +-FF 9/10-80 p259
SXL 1135/7 (4)
3857 BACEWICZ: Divertimento. BLOCH: Meditations. BAIRD: Songs (5).
     DOBROWOLSKI: Music, strings, 2 groups of wind instruments, 2
     loudspeakers. GORECKI: Ad matrem. KILAR: Dipthongos. KOTONSKI:
     Mikrostriktury. LUTOSLAWSKI: Livre. MALAWSKI: Overture. MEYER:
     Quartettino. PENDERECKI: Threnody to the victims of Hiroshima.
     Stabat mater. PERKOWSKI: Nocturne. RUDZINSKI, W.: The dismisal
     of the Grecian envoys: Recitative and duet. RUDZINSKI, Z.: Con-
     tra fidem. SEROCKI: Fantasia elegiaca. SIKORSKI, T.: Prologues.
     SZABELSKI: Aphorisms "9". SAZLONEK: Improvisations sonoristiques.
     WISZNIEWSKI: Pezzi della tradizione (3). Stefania Woytowicz, s;

Halina Lukomska, Augustyn Block, org; Jerzy Wozniak, perc; Polish
Radio Orchestra, Warasw Chamber Orchestra, Silesian Philharmonic
Orchestra, Warsaw State Opera Orchestra, Warsaw Philharmonic Or-
chestra, National Philharmonic Orchestra and Chorus, Cracow MW2
Ensemble, Wroclaw Philharmonic Orchestra, Cracow Philharmonic
Orchestra and Chorus, ORTF, Music Workshops, Hessian Radio Orch-
estra; Jan Krenz, Karol Teutsch, Karol Stryja, Antoni Wicherek,
Witold Rowicki, Andrzej Markowski, Adam Kaczynski, Roman Kukle-
wicz, Sygmunt Drauze.
        +FF 9/10-80 p297

MW RECORDS

MW 920
3858 BRAHMS: Fugue, A flat minor. ELGAR: Enigma variations, op. 36:
        Nimrod. HANDEL: Judas Maccabaeus: See the conquering hero comes
        (arr. Best). Concerto, organ, op. 4, no. 1, G major: Finale
        (arr. Dearnley). FLETCHER: Festival toccata. LISZT: Prelude
        and fugue on the name B-A-C-H, G 260. REGER: Pieces, organ, op.
        59: Toccata. WESLEY, S.S.: Andante cantabile. Christopher
        Dearnley, org.
        +Gr 11-80 p710

NEW WORLD

NW 304
3859 ADLER: Sonata breve. Canto VIII. COWELL: Exultation. EVETT:
        Chaconne. GOOSSEN: Fantasy, aria and fugue. KEENEY: Sonatina.
        PERLE: Etudes (6). Bradford Gowen, pno.
        +ARG 5-80 p48   ++St 4-80 p141

NEW YORK PHILHARMONIC

Unnumbered
3860 BACH: Cantata, no. 208, Sheep may safely graze (Barbirolli). BEET-
        HOVEN: Egmont, op. 84: Overture. GOULD: Philharmonic waltzes.
        MENDELSSOHN: Midsummer night's dream, opp. 21/61: Scherzo. MOZ-
        ART: Cosi fan tutti, K 588: Overture. MUSSORGSKY: Fair at Soro-
        chinsk: Gopak. STRAVINSKY: Norwegian moods (4). THOMAS: Ray-
        mond: Overture. WAGNER: The flying Dutchman: Overture. NYP;
        Joseph Stransky, Arturo Toscanini, Willem Mengelberg, John Barb-
        irolli, Bruno Walter, Igor Stravinsky, Artur Rodzinski, Leopold
        Stokowski, Dimitri Mitropoulos.
        +FF 9/10-80 p293

NIMBUS

2112
3861 CAPLET: Ballades francaises (5). CHABRIER: Songs: Ballade de gros
        dindons; Les cigales; L'Isle heureuse; Pastorale des cochons
        roses; Villanelle des petits canards. HONEGGER: Salute du Bar-
        tas. MENASCE: Lettres d'enfants (2). SATIE: Songs: Ludions;

Melodies (3). Hughes Cuenod, t; Geoffrey Parsons, pno.
            +RR 11-78 p36   +STL 8-10-80 p30
           ++RR 4-79 p112

2118
3862 AURIC: Interludes (3). MANZIARLY: Fables de la Fontaine: La cigale
     et la fourmi; L'oiseau blesse d'une fleche; La grenoulliere.
     MILHAUD: Catalogue de fleurs. Poemes de Leo Latil (4). POULENC:
     Bleuet; C; A sa guitare; Priez pour paix; La grenouilliere.
     ROUSSEL: Le bachelier de Salamanque; Coeur en peril; Jazz dans
     la nuit. Hughes Cuenod, t; Geoffrey Parsons, pno.
            +Gr 4-79 p1762   +STL 8-10-80 p30
           ++RR 4-79 p112

45001/4
3863 BRAHMS: Songs: Vier ernste Gesange, op. 121; Sapphische Ode, op. 94,
     no. 4; Komm bald, op. 97, no. 5. FAURE: Apres un reve; Mirages.
     GOUNOD: Aubade; Au rossignol; Boire a l'ombre; O ma belle re-
     belle; Au bruit des lourdes marteaux; Madje; O ma belle rebelle;
     Le premier jour de Mai; Venise. SCHUBERT: An den Mond; An die
     Musik, D 547; Du bist die Ruh, D 776; Die Forelle, D 550; Der
     Jungling am Bache, D 30; Gruppe aus dem Tartarus, D 583; Im
     Fruhling, K 882; An Silvia, D 891; Fischerweise, D 881; Litanei,
     D 343; Meeres Stille, D 216; Der Tod und das Madchen, D 531; Der
     Wanderer an dem Mond, D 870. Schwanengesang, D 957. SCHUMANN:
     Dichterliebe, op. 48. Shura Gehrman, bs; Nina Walker, pno.
            +-HFN 10-80 p111   ++RR 11-79 p26

                        NONESUCH

H 71326 Tape (c) N5-1326
3864 Courtly art of the trouveres: ADAM DE LA HALLE: Fines amouretes ai;
     Tant con je vivrai. MUSET: Quant je voy yver. ANON.: Ductia;
     La sexte estampie real; Souvent souspire mon cuer. Burgundian
     Court of Philip the Good: DUFAY: Vergine bella. GULIELMUS: Falla
     con misuras. LEGRANT: Entre vous noviaux maries. German Court
     of Emperor Maximilian I: ISAAC: Innsbruck ich muss dich lassen.
     SENFL: Nun wollt ihr horen neue Mar. WECK: Spanyoler Tanz. An
     Hopper dancz. Italian music of the Medici Court: CARA: Non e
     tempo. FO: Tua voisi esser sempre mai. SCOTTO: O fallace sper-
     anza. ZESSO: E quando andarete al monte. ANON.: Polyphonic
     dances (6). Spanish Courts in the early sixteenth century:
     ALONSO: La tricotea Samartin. CABEZON: Diferencias sobre "La
     dama le demanda". ENCINA: Ay triste que vengo. ORTIZ: Recer-
     cadas primera y segunda. ANON.: Pase el agoa ma Julieta; Rodrigo
     Martines. Early Music Consort; David Munrow.
            +Gr 12-76 p1042   +NR 4-77 p12
            +HF 1-80 p91 tape   +NYT 8-15-76 pD15
            +HF 2-77 p108   +-RR 10-76 p91
            +HFN 11-76 p165   ++SFC 8-22-76 p38
            +-MT 1-77 p47   +St 3-77 p148

H 71354
3865 Christmas songs: Nowel owt of your slepe; Ad cantus leticie; Angel-
     us ad virginem; Singe we to this mery compane; Nova nova; Aue
     fitt es Eva; Mervele nought Josep; Exultemus et letemus; The mid-
     night cry; Sunny bank; All sons of Adams; Greensleeves; Lullay
     thou tiny little child; The Coventry carol; While Sheperds wat-

ched; Sherburne; Fulfillment; My little sweet darling; Gloucestershire wassail. Readings: And the Aungel Gabriel was sent from
God, Gabriel from evene king, Jesu swete sone dere; Make we mere
as we may. Boston Camerata; Joel Cohen.
                    +NR 11-80 p2
H 71356 Tape (c) N5-1356
3866 BARRETT: Voluntary, C major. CLARKE: English suite, D major. FAN-
     TINI: Sonatas, trumpet and organ, nos. 1-2, 7. KREBS: Chorale
     preludes, no. 2, Wachet auf; no. 5, Komm heiliger Geist, Herre
     Gott. PEZEL: Sonatinas, 2 trumpets and violoncello, nos. 4 and
     5, C major. TARR (ed.): Suite of trumpet voluntaries, C major
     (Stanley, Stubley, Handel, Boyce). ANON.: Sinfonia, D major.
     Edward Tarr, Marc Ullrich, baroque trumpets; George Kent, org;
     Anne Apostle, vlc.
                    +FF 1/2-80 p165   ++MT 11-79 p925
                    +Gr 8-79 p351   +NR 5-79 p15
                    ++HF 7-79 p158   ++RR 7-79 p83
                    +HF 10-79 p126 tape   +St 9-79 p106
                    +HFN 7-79 p115
H 71387
3867 DOWLAND: Fine knacks for ladies. GIBBONS: The silver swan. MORLEY:
     April is in my mistress face; Daemon and Phyllis; Fire fire; I
     love alas; Leave this tormenting; My bonny lass; Now is the month
     of maying; O grief; Those dainty daffadillies; Though Philomela
     lost her love. MUNDY: Were I a king. VAUTOR: Sweet Suffolk owl.
     WEELKES: Cease sorrows now; Come sirrah, Jack ho; Since Robin
     Hood. WILBYE: Thus saith my Cloris bright; Adieu sweet Amaryllis.
     The Scholars.
                    +FF 11/12-80 p206   +St 12-80 p138
N 78003
3868 The play of Daniel. Clerkes of Oxenford; David Wulstan.
          ++Audio 12-80 p86   ++SFC 9-28-80 p23

                              OASI

639
3869 BOITO: Mefistofele: L'altra notte. CILEA: Adriana Lecouvreur: Io
     sono l'umile ancella. FUENTES: Tu habanera. PONCHIELLI: La
     gioconda: Suicidio. PUCCINI: La boheme: Mi chiamano Mimi; Mus-
     etta's waltz. Manon Lescaut: In quelle trine morbide. Tosca:
     Vissa d'arte. TOSTI: Non ti ricordi piu; L'ultimo baccio. VERDI:
     Aida: O patria mia. La forza del destino: Pace pace mio Dio.
     YRADIER: La paloma. Elda Cavalieri, s.
                    +-ARG 3-80 p48
642
3870 CZIBULKA: Stephanie gavotte. GANNE: Extase. LEHAR: Die lustige
     Witwe: Vilia. RUBINSTEIN: Kamennoi ostrow, op. 10. SCHUBERT:
     Serenade. SCHUMANN: Kinderscenen, op. 15: Traumerei. TCHAIKOV-
     SKY: Autumn song; At evening; Romance; Waltz of the flowers.
     WALDTEUFEL: Barcarolle. Emmy Bettendorf, s.
                    +-FF 9/10-80 p242

ODEON

HG 183

3871 ALVARADO: Tiento. ECHEVERRIA: Sonata de 6 tono. LARRANAGA: Sonata
de 5 tono. OXINAGA: Sonata de 5 tono. OLAGUE: Sonata de 8 tono.
SOLA: Tiento, no. 1, de 1 tono. Esteban Elisondo Iriarte, org.
+-MU 7-80 p9

1C 147 30819/20 (2)

3872 ADAM: Toreador: Ach Mama. ALABIEV: Nightingale. DELIBES: Fille de
Cadiz. Lakme: Weisse Durga; Duet; Bell song. DELL'ACQUA: Villanelle. DONIZETTI: Lucia di Lammermoor: Mad scene. The gypsy:
Das Laub nur zum Lager. GOUNOD: Mireille: Waltz. MACKEBEN:
Warum. MEYERBEER: Dinorah: Mad scene. MOSZKOWSKI: Serenade, no.
15. MOZART: Abduction from the Seraglio, K 384: Martern aller
arten. Die Zauberflote, K 620: Der Holle Rache. MULLER: The
girl from Biberach: Jetz gang i ans Brunnele. OFFENBACH: Les
contes d'Hoffman: Doll song. PROCH: Variations on "Torno mio
bene". RIMSKY-KORSAKOV: Le coq d'or: Hymn to the sun. The legend of Sadko, op. 5: Song of India. The Tsar's bride: Martha's
aria. ROSSINI: The barber of Seville: Una voce poco fa. STRAUSS,
J. II: A thousand and one nights, op. 346. Voices of spring, op.
410. VERDI: Ernani: Ernani involami. Rigoletto: Duet and caro
nome. I vespri siciliani: Siciliana. WEBER: Invitation to the
dance, op. 65. Meliza Korjus, s; Various orchestras and conductors.
+-FF 3/4-80 p180

L'OISEAU-LYRE

DSLO 33 Tape (c) KDSLC 33

3873 ATTWOOD: To all that breathe the air of heaven. BATTISHILL: Amidst
the myrtles. BEALE: The humble tenant. CALLCOTT: O snatch me
swift. COOKE: Deh dove; In paper case. DANBY: The nightingale
who tunes her warbling notes. LINLEY: Let me care less. WALM-
ISLEY: Music all powerful. WEBBE: When winds breathe soft; You
gave me your heart. The Scholars.
　　　　　+ARG 3-80 p51　　　　　　　++Gr 7-79 p259 tape
　　　　　+FF 7/8-80 p162　　　　　　+HFN 4-79 p129
　　　　　++Gr 4-79 p1761　　　　　　+-RR 9-79 p121

DSLO 42 Tape (c) KDSLC 42

3874 ADAMS: The star of Bethlehem; Thora. BALFE: Come into my garden
Maud. DANKS: Silver threads among the gold. FOSTER: I dream of
Jeanie with the light brown hair. HANDEL: Silent worship.
JOHNSON: When you and I were young Maggie. LINTON: I give
thanks to you. MARSHALL: I hear you calling me. RAY: The sun-
shine of your smile. SANDERSON: As I sit here. TOURS: Mother
o' mine. WOOD: Roses of Picardy. TRAD.: Danny boy. Stuart
Burrows, t; John Constable, pno.
　　　　　+-Gr 4-80 p1596　　　　　　+RR 4-80 p117

DSLO 43 Tape (c) KDSLC 43

3875 AITKIN: Maire my girl. COATES: I heard you singing. DEL RIEGO: O
dry those tears. GREEN: Gortnamona. HARRISON: In the gloaming.
KOVEN: O promise me. MOLLOY: The Kerry dance. MURRAY: I'11
walk beside you. MURRELLS: Sitting by the window. PENN: Smilin
through. PURCELL, E.: Passing by. RASBACH: Trees. SHARP: Dear-

est of all. TOSTI: Parted. YOUNG: Mother Machree. Stuart Burrows, t; John Constable, pno.
    +Gr 6-80 p60   ++RR 6-80 p89

DSLO 545
3876 CAMPIAN: Jack and Joan. HUME: Tobacco, tobacco. JOHNSON: O let us
howle. MAYNARD: The twelve wonders of the world: The courtier;
Divine; The souldiour; The lawyer; The marchant; The countrey
gentleman; The batchelar; The marryed man; The wife; The widow;
The maid. PARSONS: Joan quoth John. RAVENSCROFT: Yonder comes
a courteous knight. ANON.: A poor soul sat sighing. The dark
is my delight. Come live with me and be my love. What is't ye
lack. Consort of Musicke; Anthony Rooley.
    +Gr 3-80 p1434   +MT 9-80 p567
    +HFN 2-80 p95   +RR 3-80 094

DSLO 559
3877 BARTLETT: Sweet birdes deprive us never. CAMPIAN: Come let us
sound; When to her lute. DANYEL: Like as the lute delights.
DOWLAND: I saw my lady weepe; In this trembling shadow. EDWARDS:
Where griping griefs. JONES, R.: If in this flesh. MORLEY: I
saw my ladye weeping. PILKINGTON: Come all ye; Musick deare solace; Rest sweet nimphs. Emma Kirkby, s; Anthony Rooley, lt.
    ++Audio 3-80 p46   +HFN 9-79 p116
    +Gr 10-79 p695   ++RR 9-79 p122

DSLO 575
3878 CORKINE: Fly swift my thoughts; We yet agree. DOWLAND: Die not before thy day; Mourne day is with darkness fled; Sorrow stay.
FALCONIERI: Perche piangi pastore. GRANDI: surge propera. d'
INDIA: Che farai Meliseo; Odi quel rossignuolo; Qual fiera si
crudel. JOHNSON, R.: As I walked forth; Charon O Charon; Tis
late and cold. JONES, R.: Whither runneth my sweetheart. LAWES,
W.: Daphne and Strephon; Venus and Vulcan. MERULA: No ch'io non
mi fido. PERI: Al fonte al prato. RADESCA: Non miri io mio bel
sole. ROVETTA: Uccidetemi pur bella. Emma Kirkby, s; David
Thomas, bs; Trevor Jones, bs viol; Anthony Rooley, lt.
    +Gr 9-80 p386   +HFN 8-80 p103

DSLO 587
3879 BARTLETT: Whither runneth my sweetheart. FERRARI: Amar io ti con-
siglio; Amanti io vi so dire. FONTEI: Dio ti salvi pastor.
FORD: Shut not sweet breast. FERRABOSCO: Fayre cruell nimph;
Tell me o love. GAGLIANO: Bel pastor. d'INDIA: Da l'onde del
mio pianto. LAWES, H.: Among thy fancies; Aged man that moves
these fields. MORLEY: Who is it that this dark night. MONTE-
VERDI: Bel pastor. Emma Kirkby, s; Martyn Hill, t; Consort of
Musicke; Anthony Rooley.
    +Gr 11-80 p727   +STL 11-9-80 p40
    ++HFN 11-80 p124

D186D4 (4)
BARBINGANT: L'Omme bany de sa plaisance. BEDYNGHAM: Mon seul plaisir
3880 ma doulce joye; Zentil madona. BINCHOIS (?): Je ne veis onques
la pareille. BUSNOIS: Est il mercy de quoy l'on puest finer;
J'ay moins de bien. CARON: Cent mille escus. DUFAY: Dona gentile; Le serviteur hault guerdonne; Vostre bruit et vostre grant
fame. DUNSTABLE (? Bedyngham): O rosa bella. FRYE: Tout a par
moy. MORTON: N'aray je jamais mieulx; Le souvenir de vous me
tue. OCKEGHEM: L'autre d'antan l'autrier passa; Ma bouche rit.
REGIS: S'il vous plaist que vostre je soye. VAN GHIZEGHEM: De

tous biens plaine. VINCENET: Fortune par tu cruaulte. ANON.:
Adieu vous dy; Ben lo sa Dio; Chiara fontana; Comme femme desconfortee; De mon povoir vous veul complaire; Faites moy scavoir
de la belle; Finir voglio la mia vita; La gracia de voi; Helas
je n'ay pas ose dire; Helas n'aray je jamais mieulx; Hora grider
oime; J'ay pris amours; L'aultre jour par ung matin; Ma bouche
plaint; Mort merce; O meschin inamorati; O pelegrina luce; Or ay
je perdu; Perla mia cara; Terriblement suis fortunee; Vray dieu
d'amours. Consort of Musicke; Anthony Rooley.
        +Gr 11-80 p727

OLYMPIC

6152
3881 Christmas songs: Silent night; Twelve days of Christmas; We wish you
a merry Christmas; O little town of Bethlehem; O Tannenbaum;
Away in the manger; Jingle bells; Greenseeves; God rest ye merry
gentlemen; Hark the herald angels sing; It came upon a midnight
clear; Deck the halls; Adeste fideles; Auld lang syne.
        +-NR 11-80 p2

OMNISOUND

N 1017
3882 ARENSKY: Valse. BRAHMS: Waltzes, op. 39 (8). CARMICHAEL: Stardust.
FALLA: El amor brujo: Dance of terror. GERSHWIN: Concerto, piano,
F major: finale, excerpt. I got rhythm. GLIERE: The red poppy:
Sailor's dance. KERN: All the things you are. PROKOFIEV: The
love for three oranges, op. 33: March. RAVEL: Piece en forme de
habanera. STRAUSS, R.: Der Rosenkavalier, op. 59: Waltzes.
TRAD.: Three blind mice. (all arr. Gearhart). Virginia Morley,
Livingston Gearhart, pno.
        -FF 7/8-79 p120   +NR 10-80 p13

OPUS

37810
3883 ALBENIZ: Suite espanola, op. 47: Sevillanas. BACH: Brandenburg
concerto, no. 3, S 1048, G major: 1st movement. Inventions, 2
part, S 772-786. DEBUSSY: Preludes, Bk 1: La fille aux cheveux
de lin. DOWLAND: The Earl of Essex galliard. Lachrimae pavane.
GRANADOS: Tonadillas al estilo antiguo: La maja de Goya. GRIEG:
Norwegian dance, no. 4. PACHELBEL: Fughetta. RAVEL: Ma mere
l'oye: Pavane de la belle a bois dormant. Pavane pour une infante defunte. Peder Siis, Peter Augustesen, Henry Forsblom, Anders
Kagg, gtr.
        +-FF 11/12-80 p217

ORION

ORS 78323 Tape (c) OC 828
3884 BACON: Parting. HARRIS: Suite. KNEUBUHL: Variations on a pretty

bird. KRENEK: Suite, solo guitar. NORMAN: Samba. Moods in 12
tone. Toccata. STRAVINSKY, S.: Sonatina. John Kneubuhl, gtr.
+HF 8-80 p87 tape   ++NR 9-80 p11 tape
+NR 10-79 p14

ORS 79350
3885 DONIZETTI: Sonata, flute and piano, C major. GAUBERT: Madrigal.
MOZART, F.X.: Rondo, E minor. PETROVICS: Hungarian children's
songs (15). RAVEL: Piece en forme de habanera. SCHUMANN: Romances, op. 94 (3). Paul Douglas, flt; Robert Rogers, pno.
+FF 1/2-80 p179

ORS 79351
3886 BIZET: Les pecheurs de perles: Me voila seule dans la nuit. CHAR-
PENTIER: Louise: Depuis le jour. DONIZETTI: La fille du regi-
ment: Deciso e dunque. Linda de Chamounix: Ah tardai troppo.
ISOUARD: Le billet de lotterie: Non je ne veux pas chanter. MAS-
SENET: Manon: Restons ici; Je suis encore tout etourdie. MEYER-
BEER: Dinorah: Ombra leggiera. Les Huguenots: Noble seigneurs
salut. ROSSINI: Guglielmo Tell: Selva opaca. THOMAS: Mignon:
Je suis Titania. Yolanda Marcoulescou, s; Orchestral accompani-
ment.
+NR 12-79 p10   +St 2-80 p80

ORS 79352
3887 CUI: Causerie, op. 40, no. 6. HAYDN: Sonata, piano, E flat major.
IBERT: Little white donkey. GRIFFES: Roman sketches, op. 7.
RACHAMANINOFF: Floods of spring, op. 14, no. 11 (arr. Stearns).
Duncan Stearns, pno.
+FF 7/8-80 p167   +St 11-80 p104
+NR 7-80 p11

ORS 79357
3888 BIZET: Agnus dei. FREIRE: Ay ay ay; El nino perdido; Yo quisiera.
GOUNOD: Ave Maria. GIORDANO: Andrea Chenier: Nemico della patria. GUERRERO: Cancion del sembrador. SERRANO: Alma de Dios.
STRADELLA: Pieta signore. VERDI: Otello: Credo. Rigoletto: Cor-
tigioni. VERT: La leyenda del beso: Brindisi. Herman Pelayo,
bar; Orchestra, organ and chorus.
-FF 9/10-80 p245   *NR 1-80 p11

ORS 79361
3889 BARTSCH: Bagatelles. BOECK: Menuet. d'HOOGHE: The little Geisha.
HUYBRECHTS: Sicilienne. MEESTER: Toccata. MORTELMANS: Like a
singing bird. LONQUE: Sonatina, op. 36, G major. VERMEIREN:
Polytonal study. Pierre Huybrechts, pno.
+CL 3-80 p14   +NR 5-80 p13
+FF 3/4-80 p19

ORS 79364
3890 BIZET: L'Arlesienne: Suite, no. 2: Menuet. Carmen: Entr'acte, Act
3. DEBUSSY: Valse romantique (trans. Laskine). FALLA: El amor
brujo: Ritual fire dance. MOZART: Divertimento, K 439b. PES-
CETTI: Sonata, harp, C minor (trans. Salzedo). SCHUBERT: Waltzes (3). Nancy Kay, hp; Paul Haemig, flt.
++NR 5-80 p7

ORS 80367
3891 CASCARINO: Songs (8). IBERT: Lyric aria. REGER: Sonata, clarinet
and piano, op. 49, no. 1, A major. RIMSKY-KORSAKOV: The tale of
the Tsar Sultan, op. 57: The flight of the bumblebee. RUSSO:
Songs (3). John Russo, clt; Lydia Ignacio, pno; Joan Monasevitch,

Dolores Ferraro, s; Romeo Cascarino, pno.
                    +FF 7/8-80 p174   +NR 8-80 p2
ORS 80371
3892 BERLINSKY: Psalm, no. 23. CAPLET: Ecoute. DRAGANSKI: The bestiary:
     Weathervane cock; Fish and the river; Fish eggs; Ic ane geseah
     idese sittan; Book worm. IBERT: Steles orientees: Mon amant a
     la vertus dans l'eau; On me dit. Aria (Vocalise). MORTARI:
     Canzone. ROLAND-MANUEL: Elegies: Charmant rossignol; Chanson.
     RODRIGO: Verde, verderol; Pajaro del agua. ROUSSEL: Poemes de
     Ronsard: Rossignol mon mignon; Ciel aer et vens. Yolanda Marc-
     oulescou, s; Robert Goodberg, flt.
                    +-FF 9/10-80 p199   +NR 8-80 p12

                    OXFORD UNIVERSITY PRESS

OUP 151/2 (2) (also Peters PLE 133/4)
3893 BATESON: Those sweet delightful lilies. BENNET: Weep O mine eyes.
     BYRD: Lullaby my sweet little baby; Though Amaryllis dance.
     CAVENDISH: come gentle swains. EAST: No haste but good, pt 2;
     Quick quick away, pt 1. FARMER: Fair Phyllis. FARNABY: Con-
     strue my meaning. GIBBONS: Ah dear heart; O that the learned
     poets; The silver swan; What is our life. GREAVES: Come away
     sweet love. KIRKBYE: See what a maze of error. MORLEY: Fyer
     fyer April is my mistress face; My bonny lass she smileth; Now
     is the month of maying; Sing we and chant it. RAMSEY: Sleep
     fleshly birth. TOMKINS: Music divine; Oyez has any found a lad;
     Too much I once lamented. VAUTOR: Sweet Suffolk owl. WARD: Come
     sable night; Out from the vale. WEELKES: Hark all ye lovely
     saints; Hence care thou art too cruel, pt 2; Sing we at pleasure;
     O care thou wilt despatch me, pt 1; Thus sings my dearest jewel.
     WILBYE: Adieu sweet Amaryllis; Draw on sweet night; Flora gave
     me fairest flowers; Sweet honey-sucking bees, pt 1; Weep weep
     mine eyes; Yet sweet take heed, pt. 2. Pro Cantione Antiqua;
     Philip Ledger.
                    ++ARG 6-80 p126   +MT 11-79 p925
                    +FF 9/10-80 p251   +NYT 8-17-80 pD20
                    +Gr 8-79 p367   ++RR 10-79 p51
                    +HFN 7-79 p113   ++SFC 1-13-80 p40
                    +-MM 7-79 p39   +ST 6-80 p126
OUP 153 (also Peters PLE 132)
3894 BYRD: The day Christ was born; Haec dies. DERING: Factum est sil-
     entium. FARRANT: Lord for thy tender mercy's sake (attrib.).
     GIBBONS: Hosanna to the son of David; O Lord in thy wrath rebuke
     me not. MUNDY: O Lord the maker of all things. PARSONS: Ave
     Maria. PHILLIPS: Ascendit Deus. TALLIS: Salvator mundi. TOM-
     KINS: When David heard. WEELKES: Hosanna to the son of David;
     When David heard. Christ Church Cathedral Choir; Simon Preston.
                    +FF 9/10-80 p251   +MT 8-79 p661
                    +Gr 7-79 p243   +MU 6-80 p8
                    +HFN 7-79 p115   ++RR 10-79 p51
                    +-MM 7-79 p39   ++SFC 1-13-80 p40
OUP 154
3895 HANDEL: Rigadoon. CLARKE: Trumpet voluntary. HAYDN: Pieces, musi-
     clock: March. HURFORD: Fanfare on "Old 100th". JACKSON: The

Archbishop's fanfare. MOZART: Le nozze de Figaro, K 492: Wedding
march. PURCELL: King Arthur: Trumpet tune (arr. Jackson). Trumpet tune and almand. RAVENSCROFT: Hornpipe. REUBKE: Sonata on
the 94th psalm. STANLEY: Trumpet voluntary (arr. Willcocks).
WILLCOCKS: Fanfare on "Gopsal". ANON.: The Lord Mayor's swan
hopping trumpet tune. Prince Eugen's march. Southwark Grenadiers march. Trumpet tune. Christopher Dearnley, org.
               ++Gr 10-80 p523   ++HFN 11-80 p127
OUP 164 (also Peters PLE 115)
3896 Medieval music, Ars Antiqua Polyphony. Pro Cantione Antiqua; Edgar
     Fleet.
          +Gr 2-79 p1459   +NYT 8-17-80 pD20
          +HFN 11-78 p181   +RR 7-79 p26
          +MT 6-79 p493

                          PAST MASTERS

PM 30
3897 BEETHOVEN: Symphony, no. 8, op. 93, F major: Allegretto. Deutsche
     Tanze, no. 12. BERLIOZ: La damnation de Faust, op. 24: Rakoczy
     march. HEUBERGER: Der Opernball: Overture. JANACEK: Lachian
     dance, no. 1. LISZT: Tarantelle. Annees de pelerinage, 2nd
     year, G 162: Venezia e Napoli. REZNICEK: Donna Diana: Overture.
     STRAUSS, J. II: Die Fledermaus, op. 363: Overture. STRAVINSKY:
     Fireworks. BPhO; Erich Kleiber.
               +NR 10-80 p3
PM 32
3898 BEETHOVEN: Coriolan overture, op. 62. BERGER: Legend of Prince Eu-
     gen. DOHNANYI: Symphonic minutes, op. 36. VERDI: La forza del
     destino: Overture. WAGNER: Albumblatt, C major. Traume. Munich
     Philharmonic Orchestra; Oswald Kabasta.
               +FF 3/4-80 p200

                            PEARL

GEMM 162/3 (2)
3899 BELLINI: Norma: Al del tebro. I Puritani: Cinta de fiori. BIZET:
     Carmen: Toreador song. BOITO: Mefistofele: Ave Signor, Son lo
     spirito. DONIZETTI: La favorita: Non sai tu; Splendon piu belle.
     Lucia di Lammermoor: Dalle stanze. GOUNOD: Faust: Le veau d'or;
     Ebben che ti pare...Io voglio il piacer. HALVEY: La Juive: So
     oppressi ognor; Voi che del Dio vivante. MOZART: Don Giovanni,
     K 527: Finch han dal vino; Deh vieni alla finestra. Die Zauber-
     flote, K 620: Possenti numi. ROSSINI: Il barbiere di Siviglia:
     La calunnia. SAINT-SAENS: Samson et Dalila: J'ai gravi la mon-
     tagne. THOMAS: Le Caid: Drum major's aria. Mignon: Del suo cor
     calmai. MEYERBEER: Roberto il diavolo: Le rovine son queste...
     Suore che riposte. VERDI: Aida: Mortal diletto ai numi; Nume
     custode e vindice. Don Carlo: Dormiro sol nel manto mio regal.
     Ernani: Che mai vegg'io...Infelice. Requiem: Confutatis male-
     dictis. Simon Boccanegra: A te l'estremo addio...Il lacerato
     spirito. Il trovatore: Di due figli...Abietta zingara. I ves-
     pri siciliani: O patria...O tu Palermo. Ezio Pinza, bs.

```
     +Gr 5-80 p1712              +NR 5-80 p9
     +HFN 2-80 p101             +RR 3-80 p26
```

GEMM 165 (Reissues)
3900 BIZET: Les pecheurs de perles: Del tempio al timitar. CAPUA: Maria
     Mari. COTTRAU: Addio a Napoli. CRESCENZO: Quanno a femmena vo.
     CURTIS: Canta pe'me; Voce e notte. DONAUDY: O bel nidi d'amore.
     DONIZETTI: Lucia di Lammermoor: Che mi frena. MARIO: Santa Lucia
     luntana. MEYERBEER: L'Africaine: O paradiso. THOMAS: Mignon:
     Adieu Mignon; Ah non credevi tu. VERDI: Rigoletto: Bella figlia
     dell'amore. Beniamino Gigli, t; Orchestral accompaniment.
                ++Gr 12-79 p1055   +RR 3-80 p26

GEMM 166
3901 ALVAREZ: La mantilla. CARISSIMI: Vittoria: Vittoria mio core.
     GLUCK: Paride ed Elena: O del mio dolce ardor. GOUNOD: Faust:
     O santa medaglia...Dio possente. HEROLD: Zampa: Perche tremar.
     MASSENET: Herodiade: Visione fuggitiva. Werther: Ah non mi ride-
     star. MOZART: Don Giovanni, K 527: Finch han del vino; Deh vieni
     alla finestra. PONCHIELLI: La gioconda: Ebbrezza delirio. VERDI:
     Ernani: O de verd'anni miei; O sommo Carlo. La forza del des-
     tino: Egli e salvo. Il trovatore: Qual voce...Come tu donna;
     Conte...Ne cessi. WAGNER: Tannhauser: Allor che tu coll'estro.
     Mattia Battistini, bar; Carlo Sabajno, pno.
                +-Gr 4-80 p1594   +RR 3-80 p26

GEMM 167 (Reissues)
3902 CHOPIN: Berceuse, op. 57, D flat major. Chant polonaise, op. 74:
     My joys (arr. Liszt). Etudes, op. 10, no. 5, G flat major; op.
     25, nos. 2 and 9. Fantasie-Impromptu, op. 66, C sharp minor.
     Impromptu, no. 1, op. 29, A flat major. Nocturne, op. 9, no. 2
     E flat major. Polonaise, op. 40, no. 1, A major. Waltzes, op.
     18, E flat major; op. 42, A flat major; op. 64, no. 2, C sharp
     minor. HENSELT: Berceuse, F sharp major. MENDELSSOHN: Introduc-
     tion and rondo capriccioso, op. 14, E flat major. RUBINSTEIN:
     Reve angelique. Serenade, D minor. SCHUBERT: Gute Nacht (arr.
     Godowsky). Hark hark the lark (arr. Liszt). Marche militaire
     (arr. Tausig). Morgengruss (arr. Godowsky). Leopold Godowsky,
     pno.
                ++Gr 1-80 p1181   +-RR 1-80 p102

GEMM 168
3903 BEETHOVEN: Songs: In questa tomba oscura. BREWER: The fairy pipers.
     DONIZETTI: La favorita: O mio Fernando. Lucrezia Borgia: Il
     segreto por esser felice. GORING-THOMAS: Nadeshka: Dear love of
     mine. A summer night. GOUNOD: Faust: When all was young. HAN-
     DEL: Serse: Ombra mai fu. OLIVER: Yonder. SAINT-SAENS: Samson
     et Dalila: Mon coeur s'ouvre a ta voix. SANDERSON: My dear soul.
     SULLIVAN: The willow song. VERDI: Don Carlo: O don fatale.
     Clara Butt, con; Various accompaniments.
                +Gr 2-80 p1301   +RR 3-80 p26
                +HFN 2-80 p101

GEMM 170
3904 DELISLE: La marseillaise. DARGOMIZKSHY: The old corporal. DONI-
     ZETTI: Lucrezia Borgia: Vieni la mia vendetta. FLEGIER: Le cor.
     GLINKA: A life for the Tsar: Now I am alone; They guess the truth.
     GOUNOD: Faust: Seigneur daignez permettre; Quand du Seigneur.
     KOENEMANN: When the king went forth to war. MUSSORGSKY: Boris
     Godunov: Yet one more tale (arr. Rimsky-Korsakov). Songs and

dances of death: Trepak. RIMSKY-KORSAKOV: O fearful crags; Ari-
osos, op. 49: The prophet. SCHUMANN: Songs: The two grenadiers,
op. 49, no. 1. VERDI: Ernani: Che mai vegg'io...infelice. TRAD.:
Dubinushka; Down the Petersky. Feodor Chaliapin, bs; Orchestral
accompaniment.
+Gr 12-79 p1055   +RR 3-80 p26

GEMM 173
3905 BEETHOVEN: Fidelio, op. 72: Life is nothing without money. GLINKA:
The midnight review. GOUNOD: Philemon and Baucis: Vulcan's song.
HAHN: Invictus. HALEVY: La Juive: Tho faithless men. HATTON:
Simon the cellarer. KNIGHT: Rocked in the cradle of the deep.
LOEWE: Edward. MOZART: Die Zauberflote, K 620: Within this hal-
lowed dwelling. PETRIE: Roll on thou deep and dark blue ocean.
SCHUBERT: Death and the maiden, D 531; The organ grinder, D 911.
STANFORD: Father O'Flynn. WAGNER: Gotterdammerung: Hagen's watch;
Hagen's call. Norman Allin, bs; Various orchestras and choruses.
+Gr 2-80 p1301

GEMM 175
3906 BEETHOVEN: Variations on a theme from Mozart's "Die Zauberflote".
BRAHMS: Concerto, violin and violoncello, op. 102, A minor.
CHOPIN: Nocturne, op. 9, no. 2, E flat major. Prelude, op. 28,
no. 15, D flat major. FAURE: Apres au reve, op. 7, no. 1. HIL-
LEMACHER: Gavotte tendre. SAINT-SAENS: Carnival of the animals:
Le cygne. SCHUBERT: Moment musicaux, F minor. Jacques Thibaud,
vln; Pablo Casals, vlc; Alfred Cortot, Nicholas Mednikoff, pno;
Casals Orchestra, Barcelona; Alfred Cortot.
+FF 9/10-80 p87   ++RR 5-80 p57
+Gr 9-80 p408

GEMM 179
3907 BEETHOVEN: Sonata, piano, no. 14, op. 27, no. 2, C sharp minor: 1st
movement. CHOPIN: Etudes, op. 10, nos. 3, 5, 12. Prelude, op.
28, no. 15, D flat major. Prelude, op. 28, no. 17, A flat major.
Waltz, op. 18, E flat major. DEBUSSY: Images: Reflets dans l'
eau. PADEREWSKI: Minuet, op. 14, no. 1, G major. SCHELLING:
Nocture a Raguze. SCHUBERT: Impromptu, op. 142, no. 2, D 935,
A flat major. SCHUMANN: Waldscenen, op. 82: Prophet bird. STOJ-
OWSKI: Chant d'amour, op. 26, no. 3: By the brookside. Ignaz
Paderewski, pno.
+FF 9/10-80 p259   +-HFN 6-80 p114
+Gr 9-80 p408   +RR 5-80 p88

SHE 554/5
3908 AURIC: Les facheux. MILHAUD: Le train bleu. POULENC: Les biches.
SATIE: Jack in the box (rch. Milhaud). SAUGUET: Le chatte. Monte Carlo Orchestra and Chorus; Igor Markevitch.
+-Gr 9-80 p352   +-STL 8-10-80 p30

PEPITA

SLPX 17576
3909 BOCCHERINI: Minuet. GRIEG: Peer Gynt, op. 46, excerpts. LISZT:
Hungarian rhapsody, no. 2, G 244, C sharp minor. MILCHBERG/ROB-
LES/SIMON: El condor pasa. MONTI: Czardas. SAINT-SAENS: Samson
and Delila, excerpt. TCHAIKOVSKY: Swan Lake, op. 20, excerpts.
VERDI: Aida: Triumphal march. TRAD.: Ex a. Greensleeves. Shep-

herd's dance. Volga song. Tamas Hacki, whistle; Instrumental
and vocal accompaniment.
      +St 7-80 p86

PETERS

PLE 068 (also Arion ARN 38396)
3910 ADAM DE LA HALLE: Rondeaux (4). DUFAY: Missa l'homme arme: Kyrie.
      HAYNE VAN GHIZEGHEM: Chanson (2). OCKEGHEM: Deploration sur la
      mort de Binchois. Missa "Cuiusivis toni". PEROTINUS LE GRAND:
      Organum "Virgo". ANON.: Motets "O virgo pia"; Belle Ysabellot.
      Da Camera Vocal Ensemble Francais; Daniel Meier.
            ++FF 5/6-79 p113   ++SFC 3-9-80 p40
PLE 108
3911 Gregorian chant: Good Friday tenebrae responsories. Abbey of St.
      Pierre de Solesmes Monks Choir; Joseph Gajard.
            ++FF 9/10-80 p253
PLE 111
3912 ALBINONI: Adagio, G minor (arr. Giazotto). BACH: Cantata, no. 147,
      Jesu joy of man's desiring. Chorale preludes, Jesu meine Freude;
      O haupt voll blut und Wunden; Herzlieber Jesu was hast du Verbro-
      chen. Suite, orchestra, S 1068, D major: Air on the G string.
      CORELLI: Grave. PURCELL: Sonata, trumpet, D major. VIVALDI: Con-
      certo, trumpet and organ, G minor (after Thilde's arrangement of
      op. 13, no. 6, Movements 1, 3-4). VIVIANI: Sonata, trumpet, op.
      4, no. 1, G major. Andre Bernard, tpt; Jean-Louis Gil, Edgar
      Krapp, org; Andre Bernard Brass Ensemble, Instrumental Ensemble
      of France; Jean-Pierre Wallez.
            +FF 5/6-80 p185

PLE 120
3913 Gregorian chant: Mass of the Annunciation; Mass of St. Joseph. Ab-
      bey of St. Pierre de Solesmes Monks Choir; Joseph Gajard.
            ++FF 9/10-80 p253

PHILIPS

6570 154 Tape (c) 7310 154
3914 Gregorian chant: Magnificat; Tu es pastor ovium; Stabat mater; Lauda
      Sion; Te deum; Adoro te devote; O sacrum convivium; Ave verum
      corpus; Tantum ergo; O salutaris hostia; Salve regina; Ave Maria;
      Sub tuum praesidium; Alma redemptoris mater; Inviolata; Regina
      caeli; Victimae paschali laudes; Veni creator spiritus. St.
      Maurice and St. Maur Abbey Benedictine Monks, Clervaux, Luxem-
      bourg.
            +-Gr 12-79 p1039   +HFN 3-80 p107 tape
            ++HFN 12-79 p179   /RR 1-80 p105
6757 394 (2)
3915 ALFVEN: Swedish rhapsody, no. 1, op. 19. BARTOK: Rhapsody, no. 1.
      ENESCO: Roumanian rhapsody, op. 11, no. 1, A major. GERSHWIN:
      Rhapsody in blue. LALO: Rapsodie norvegienne. LISZT (arr.
      Muller-Berghaus): Hungarian rhapsody, no. 4, G 244, E flat major.
      RACHMANINOFF: Rhapsody on a theme by Paganini, op. 43. Eugene
      List, Werner Haas, pno; Henryk Szeryng, vln; VSO, LSO, Lamoureux

Orchestra, Eastman-Rochester Orchestra, Frankfurt Radio Orchestra,
Monte Carlo Opera Orchestra, COA; Oivin Fjeldstad, Antal Dorati,
Roberto Benzi, Howard Hanson, Eliahu Inbal, Antonio de Almeida,
Bernard Haitink.
<table>
<tr><td>+-HFN 1-80 p121</td><td>+-RR 12-79 p44</td></tr>
</table>

6833 260
3916 BACH: Musical offering, S 1079, C minor: Ricercare a 6. CLARKE:
Trumpet voluntary. HANDEL: Solomon: Arrival of the Queen of
Sheba. PURCELL: Abdelazer: Rondeau. The Indian Queen: Trumpet
overture. RAMEAU: La poule, G minor. RICCIOTTI: Concertino, no.
4, F minor. TORELLI: Sonata a 5, D major. VIVALDI: Concerto
grosso, RV 562a, D major. John Wilbraham, Don Smithers, tpt;
Carmel Kaine, vln; AMF; Neville Marriner.

| +Gr 3-80 p1449 | +-RR 3-80 p49 |
| +HFN 2-80 p105 | |

9500 351 Tape (c) 7300 602
3917 MILAN: Fantasia. Pavanas. MUDARRA: Gallarda. NARVAEZ: Diferencias
sobre "Guardame las vacas". PISADOR: Pavana. SANZ: Suite espanola. VALDERRABANO: Soneto, no. 1. Pepe Romero, gtr.

+-Gr 9-80 p380	+-MJ 3/4-79 p46
+HFN 7-80 p115	+NR 11-78 p15
+HFN 11-80 p131 tape	+RR 7-80 p81

9500 358 Tape (c) 7300 740 (From various Philips originals)
3918 DONIZETTI: Lucia di Lammermoor: Eccola...Il dolce suono. MOZART:
Cosi fan tutte, K 588: Come scoglio. PUCCINI: Tosca: Vissi d'
arte. ROSSINI: Elisabetta, Regina d'Inghilterra: Indegno; Fellon la pena avrai. VERDI: Il Corsaro: Ne sulla terra. I Masnadieri: Venerabile o padre...Lo sguardo; Oh ma la pace...Tu del
mio Carlo. Montserrat Caballe, Valerie Masterson, s; Rosanne
Creffield, ms; John Sandor, Alexander Oliver, Vincenzo Bello,
Jose Carreras, Neil Jenkins, t; Ingvar Wixell, bar; Samuel Ramey,
bs; ROHO, NPhO, LSO: Colin Davis, Lamberto Gardelli, Jesus Lopez-
Cobos, Gianfranco Masini.

++Gr 4-80 p1593	+HFN 4-80 p119
+HF 8-80 p85	+RR 4-80 p48
+HFN 1-80 p123 tape	

9500 649 Tape (c) 7300 751
3919 CHAPI Y LORENTE: La bruja: Jota. Moreno. GURIDI: El caserio: Romanza. GUERRERO: El huesped del sevillano: Raquel. LUNA: La pic-
ara molinera: Paxarin tu que vuelas. SERRANO: La alegria del
batallon: Cancion guijira. Alma de Dios: Cancion hungara. Los
de Aragon: Cuantas veces solo. SOUTULLO/VERT: El ultimo roman-
tico: Noche de amor noche misteriosa. TORROBA: Luisa Fernanda:
De este apacible rincon de Madrid. VIVES: Dona Francisquita:
Por el humo. Jose Carreras, t; ECO; Antonio Ros-Marba.

+-FF 1/2-80 p161	+NR 12-79 p10
+Gr 10-79 p724	+RR 10-79 p145
++Gr 12-79 p1065 tape	++SFC 10-7-79 p50
+HFN 10-79 p165	++SFC 12-30-79 p33
+HFN 11-79 p157 tape	+SR 3-1-80 p29

9500 651 Tape (c) 7300 752
3920 Spirituals: Do Lawd, oh do Lawd; Ev'ry time I feel de spirit; Give
me Jesus; Gospel train; Great day; Hush somebody's callin' my
name; I couldn't hear nobody pray; Live a humble; Mary had a
baby; My Lord what a morning; Soon ah will be done; There is a

balm in Gilead; There's a man going round; Walk together children; Were you there. Jessye Norman, s; Dalton Baldwin, pno; Ambrosian Singers; Willis Patterson.
> +NR 7-80 p10   ++St 3-80 p102

9500 764
3921 ALVAREZ: Suspiros de Espana. CHOVI: Petite greus. JAVALOYES: El
abanico. LOPE: Gallito. Gerona. MARQUINA: Espana cani. ROIG:
La gracia de Dios. SOUTULLO: Puenteareas. TEIXIDOR: Amparito
roca. ZAVALA: Viva el rumbo. ECO; Enrique Garcia Asensio.
> +NR 11-80 p4

PLEASURE RECORDS

104
3922 ALTER: Akavyah. BERLINSKY: Sing joyfully, psalm, no. 81. CLONICK:
Be strong swift and brave. CHICOREL: Let your house. HELFMAN:
Odon Olam. JANOWSKI: Sim shalom, Kol nidre, Sh'ma Koleynu, Avinu
Malkeynu. ISAACSON: Sh'nayhem, B'amkom. PIKET: Shomeir Yisraeil.
STEINBERG: Shalom Rav. WEILL: Kiddush. Cantor Donald Roberts;
Sullivan Chamber Ensemble; Charles Sullivan, org and cond.
> +ARG 7/8-80 p48

PREISER

LV 142
3923 MOZART: Le nozze di Figaro, K 492: Non so piu; Voi che sapete.
PUCCINI: La boheme: Si mi chiamano Mimi; Addio senza rancor.
VERDI: Otello: Salce. WAGNER: Die Meistersinger von Nurnberg:
O Sachs mein Freund. Lohengrin: Einsam in truben Tagen; Euch
Luften die mein Klagen. Tannhauser: Dich teure Halle. Die Wal-
kure: Der Manner Sippe. WEBER: Der Freischutz: Und ob die Wolke.
Delia Reinhardt, s.
> +Op 7-80 p688

LV 176
3924 MASCAGNI: Cavalleria rusticana: Voi lo sapete. PUCCINI: Madama
Butterfly: Un bel di vedremo. Tosca: Ora stammi a sentir.
STRAUSS, R.: Salome, op. 54: Ah du wolltest mich nicht deinen
Mund kussen lassen. VERDI: La forza del destino: Madre madre
pietosa vergine; Pace pace mio Dio. WAGNER: Parsifal: Ich sah
das Kind an seiner Mutter Brust; Seit Ewigkeiten harre ich deiner. Tristan und Isolde: Die Wunde; Wo; Lass sich mich heilen;
Milde und leise. Gota Ljungberg, s.
> +ON 2-21-76 p32   +Op 7-80 p688

LV 229
3925 GIORDANO: Andrea Chenier: Nemico della patria. MASCAGNI: Isabeau:
Gia per terra e castella. MASSENET: Le jongleur de Notre Dame:
Fleurissait une rose au bord du chemin. Thais: Helas enfant en-
core; Voila donc la terrible cite. PUCCINI: La fanciulla des
West: Minnie della mia casa. Tosca: Ella vera...Ha piu forte
sapore; Gia mi dicon venal. SAINT-SAENS: Samson et Dalila: Maud-
ite a jamais soit la race des enfants d'Israel. VERDI: Otello:
Credo in un Dio crudel. Rigoletto: Pari siamo; Figlia mio padre
...Deh non parlare al misero; Cortigiani vil razza dannata. La

traviata: Di provenza il mar. WAGNER: Die Walkure: Wotan's farewell. Cesare Formichi, bar.
+Op 7-80 p688

LV 239
3926 BIZET: Les pecheurs de perles: Je crois entendre encore; De mon amie
fluer endormie. BORODIN: Prince Igor: Vladimir's aria. GLUCK:
Orfeo ed Euridice: Malheureux qu'ai-je fait...J'ai perdu mon
Euridice. GOUNOD: Faust: Rien...En vain j'interroge en mon ardente veille. LALO: Le Roi d'Ys: Vainement ma bien-aimee. MAS-
SENET: Manon: En fermant les yeux; Ah fuyez douce image. Werther: O nature pleine de grace; Lorsque l'enfant revient d'un voyage avant l'heure; Pourquoi me reviller. RIMSKY-KORSAKOV: May
night: Levko's aria. TCHAIKOVSKY: Pique dame: Herman's arias.
Joseph Rogatchevsky.
+Op 7-80 p688

LV 261
3927 BOITO: Mefistofele: Ave Signor; Son lo spirito che nega; Ecco il
mondo. DONIZETTI: La favorita: Spendon piu belle. GOUNOD:
Faust: Le veau d'or; Serenade. MOZART: Don Giovanni, K 527:
Catalogue aria. PONCHIELLI: La gioconda: Bella cosi, madonna.
PORRINI: Gli Orazi: Io per l'amico diritto. VERDI: Luisa Miller:
Il mio sangue. Nabucco: Tu sul labbro. Rigoletto: Quel vecchio
maledicami. Simon Boccanegra: Il lacerato spirito. WAGNER: Loh-
engrin: King Henry's prayer. Tancredi Pasero, bs-bar; Various
Orchestras and Conductors.
+-FF 5/6-80 p173

LV 266
3928 ALFANO: Risurrezione: Katyusha's scene. BIZET: Carmen: Habanera;
Seguidilla; Card scene. BRAHMS: Wiegenlied, op. 49, no. 4. CIL-
EA: L'Arlesiana: Esser madre. DONIZETTI: La favorita: In questo
suolo a lusinghar tua cara. FALLA: Canciones populares espanol-
as: Jota. GIORDANO: Crepuscolo triste. LUALDI: La canzone di
Fraciscio. MASSENET: Werther: Letter scene. MOZART: Le nozze
di Figaro, K 492: Non so piu; Voi che sapete. PIERACCINI: Bep-
pino rubacori. STRAUSS, R.: Standchen, op. 17, no. 2. VERDI:
La forza del destino: Al suon del tamburo; Rataplan. Gianna
Pederzini, ms; Orchestras and Conductors
+-FF 9/10-80 p243

LV 267
3929 MASCAGNI: Cavalleria rusticana: Voi lo sapete; Tu qui Santuzza.
PONCHIELLI: La gioconda: Suicidio; L'amo come il fulgor. PUC-
CINI: La boheme: Si mi chiamano Mimi. Tosca: Vissi d'arte.
ROSSINI: Guillaume Tell: Selva opaca. VERDI: Aida: O cieli az-
zurri. Un ballo in maschera: Ma dall'arido stelo; Morro ma
prima in grazia. Ernani: Da quel di. Il trovatore: Tacea la
notte placida; D'amor sull'ali rosee. Giannini Arangi Lombardi,
s.
+FF 7/8-80 p158

LV 268
3930 ANGLADA: Brindo a tu salud. BELLINI: Norma: Ite sul colle o Druidi.
DONIZETTI: Lucrezia Borgia: Vieni; La mia vendetta. FERRARI:
Pipele: Questa notte mentra a letto. GOMEZ: Salvator Rosa: Die
sposo. MEYERBEER: Etoile du nord: Peter's romance. MOZART: Die
Zauberflote, K 620: O Iris und Osiris. MUGUERZA: Tristes amores.
ROSSINI: Stabat mater: Pro peccatis. SERRANO: La alegria del

batallon. VERDI: Nabucco: Tu sul labbro; Del futuro nel buio
discerno. Requiem: Confutatis. I vespri siciliani: O tu Palermo. Jose Mardones, bs.
          ++FF 7/8-80 p159

PR 135005
3931 BEETHOVEN: Fidelio, op. 72: Abscheulicher. GLUCK: Alceste: Divini-
     tes du Styx. GOETZ: Taming of the shrew: Die Kraft versagt.
     STRAUSS, R.: Elektra, op. 58: Allein Weh ganz allein. SUTER-
     MEISTER: Romeo and Juliet: Balcony scene. VERDI: Aida: Ritorna
     vincitor; O patria mia. WEBER: Oberon: Ozean du Ungeheuer.
     Christel Goltz, s; Various orchestras and conductors.
          +-FF 11/12-80 p198

                          PROPRIUS

7761
3932 DUBEN: Suite, no. 5, G minor. PURCELL: Songs (3). ROMAN: Swedish
     mass, excerpt. SCHEIDT: Suite, strings. VERDIER: Lamento. An-
     drew Dalton, c-t; Drottningholms Barockensemble.
          +FF 1/2-80 p165   +RR 12-78 p32

PROP 7762
3933 ADAM: The blessed day; O holy night. BERLIN: White Christmas. BOS-
     SI: Cantate domino. GRUBER: silent night. HANDEL: Rejoice
     daughter of Zion. OLSSON: Advent; Christmas. REGER: Mary's
     cradle song. RUTTER: Il est ne le divin enfant. SARGENT: Lul-
     laby; Zither carol. VOLGER: Hosanna son of David; Rejoice you
     bride of Christ; Korean folksong (arr.). WALTHER: Concerto, or-
     gan, A major. Marianne Mellnas, s; Alf Linder, org; Oscars
     Church Motet Choir, Stockholm; Torsten Nilsson.
          +ARG 5-80 p52

PROP 7816
3934 ARCADELT: Ave Maria. BADINGS: Stabat mater. DURUFLE: Tota pulcra
     es Maria. FOLK: Fungfru Maria till Betlehem gick (arr. Forsberg).
     GUARNIERI: Ave Maria. LANGLAIS: Ave mundi gloria. LECHNER:
     Magnificat primi toni. MILVEDEN: Barn av Guds karlek. OLSSON:
     Ave maris stella, op. 42. SALONEN: Frukta icke Maria. SORENSON:
     Barn av Guds karlet. SORIANO: Regina caeli. TRAD.: Var halsad
     Herrens Moder (arr. Edlund). Mariakoren; Bror Samuelson.
          ++FF 5/6-80 p180

                          PROTONE

PR 148
3935 ALBENIZ: Espana, op. 165: Tango (arr. Godowsky). CHOPIN: Waltz, op.
     42, A flat major. GLUCK: Melodie Orpheus (arr. Chasins). LISZT:
     Etudes de concert, nos. 1-2, G 145: Waldesrauschen; Gnomenreigen.
     Paraphrases: Chopin: My joys; The maiden's wish. RACHMANINOFF:
     Polichinelle. SAINT-SAENS: The carnival of the animals: The
     swan (arr. Godowsky). SCHUBERT: Moment musicaux, op. 94, no. 3,
     D 780 (arr. Godowsky). WEINBERGER: Schwanda the bagpiper: Fan-
     tasia (arr. Chasins). Constance Keene, pno.
          +NR 10-80 p13

PVA RECORDINGS

4917 545
3936 BACH: Cantata, no. 208, Flocks in pastures green abiding (arr. Rop-
      er). BULLIVANT: Te deum laudamus, E flat major. DAVIES: Tarry
      no longer. ELGAR: The light of life, op. 29: Doubt not thy fat-
      her's care. MORLEY: Nolo mortem peccatoris. SCHUBERT: Where
      thou reignest. SHAW, M.: The greater light. THALBEN-BALL: Elegy,
      B flat major. Gloria patria, E flat major. Jubilate Deo, B flat
      major. The Lord God omnipotent reigneth. Psalm, no. 48: Chant,
      E flat major. Psalm, no. 130: Chant, D minor. VULPIUS: The
      strife is o'er (arr. Ley). George Thalben-Ball, org; Temple
      Church Choir; George Thalben-Ball.
                    +Gr 4-80 p1584   +MT 10-80 p638

PYE

QS PCNHX 10
3937 Coronation music. GIBBONS: O clap your hands together. HANDEL:
      The king shall rejoice. Zadok the priest. PARRY: I was glad.
      STANFORD: Gloria in excelsis. VAUGHAN WILLIAMS: O taste and see;
      The old hundredth. WALTON: A queen's fanfare. WESLEY, S.S.:
      Thou wilt keep him. Winchester Cathedral Choir, Waynflete Sing-
      ers, Winchester College Commoners, Bournemouth Sinfonietta; Mar-
      tin Neary; James Lancelot, org.
                    +Gr 11-77 p880   +-MU 4-80 p10
                    -HFN 8-77 p85
GH 589 Tape (c) CZGH 589 (ct) Y8GH 589
3938 BACH: St. Matthew Passion, S 244: O sacred head surrounded. Can-
      tata, no. 147, Jesu joy of man's desiring. Toccata and fugue,
      S 565, D minor. DAVIES: Psalm, no. 121. GOUNOD: Ave Maria.
      HANDEL: Messiah: I know that my redeemer liveth. HUMFREY: A
      hymne to God the father. MENDELSSOHN: Hear my prayer, op. 39,
      no. 1. Oh for the wings of a dove. MOZART: Ave verum corpus,
      K 618. WESLEY, S.S.: Blessed be the God and father. WIDOR: Sym-
      phony, organ, no. 5, op. 42, no. 1, F minor: Toccata. Timothy
      Wilson, treble; Winchester Cathedral Choir; Martin Neary, Clement
      McWilliam, org; Martin Neary.
                    +Gr 2-75 p1541   +-MU 4-80 p10
GH 629
3939 ALLEGRI: Miserere. BACH: Chorale prelude, S 727, Herzlich tut mich
      verlangen. Prelude and fugue, S 552, E flat major. St. Matthew
      Passion, S 244: Be near me Lord. DAVIES: God be in my head.
      GRANT/ROSS: The Lord's my shepherd. PARRY: Jerusalem, op. 208.
      PURCELL: Hear my prayer. STANFORD: Beati quorum via, op. 51, no.
      3. Magnificat and nunc dimittis, G major. Wesley, S.: Ascribe
      unto the Lord. Winchester Cathedral Choir, Waynflete Singers;
      BBC Academy; James Lancelot, Martin Neary, org; Martin Neary.
                    +-MU 4-80 p10
TPLS 13066
3940 BACH: Fantasia and fugue, S 542, G minor. DUPRE: Prelude and fugue,
      op. 7, no. 3, G minor. FRANCK: Chorale, no. 3, A minor. MES-
      SIAEN: Les corps glorieux: Joie et clarte des corps glorieux.
      WALOND: Voluntary, no. 5, G major. Martin Neary, org.
                    +Gr 10-75 p661   +-MU 4-80 p11

+—HFN 11-75 p171   +—RR 11-75 p67

QUINTESSENCE

PMC 7143
3941 BYRD: Ave verum corpus; Lullaby my sweet little baby. DERING: The
cryes of London. DOWLAND: Mrs. White's nothing; Tarleton's ris-
urrectione. MORLEY: I go before my darling; My bonny lass she
smileth; Sweet nymph come to thy lover. PARSONS: Pandolpho.
PEERSON: Upon my lap. TALLIS: Salvator mundi. WARD: Out from
the vale. WEELKES: The nightingale, the organ of delight. WIL-
BYE: Draw on sweet night; Sweet honeysucking bees. Deller Consort.
        ++ARG 3-80 p50   +HF 4-80 p102
        ++FF 5/6-80 p181

PMC 7145
3942 ALBINONI: Adagio, G minor (trans. Witold). ANGLES: Adagio, D minor.
FANCOUER: Concertino, G minor. GRETRY: Concerto, flute, C major.
Danse suite. RAMEAU: Suite en concert. SWEELINCK: Chorale and
variations. Jean-Pierre Rampal, flt; Instrumental Ensemble;
Jean-Pierre Rampal, Armand Birbaum.
        +FF 9/10-80 p278

PMC 7154
3943 ALBINONI: Adagio, G minor. BACH: Cantata, no. 4: Sinfonia. Con-
certo, 2 violins: Largo. Suite, orchestra, S 1068, D major: Air
on the G string. CORELLI: Christmas concerto: Pastorale. HAN-
DEL: Water music: Air. Serse: Largo. MARCELLO: Concerto, oboe,
C minor: Adagio. PACHELBEL: Canon, D major. TELEMANN: Overture,
C minor: Sommeille. VIVALDI: Concerto, op. 8: Winter largo.
German Bach Soloists; Helmut Winschermann.
        +FF 5/6-80 p200

2 PMC 2708 (2) Tape (c) 4P4C 2708
3944 BACH: Prelude, D minor (Siloti). Prelude and fugue, D major (Busoni). BEETHOVEN: Sonata, piano, no. 14, op. 27, no. 2, C sharp
minor. Variations, C minor (32). CHOPIN: Etude, op. 25, no. 2,
F minor. Etude, op. posth., A flat major. MEDTNER: Sonata rem-
iniscenza, op. 38, A minor. PROKOFIEV: The love for three oranges, op. 33: Scherzo; March. RAVEL: Jeux d'eau. Pavane pour
une infante defunte. Emil Gilels, pno.
        +—FF 7/8-80 p166   +—St 7-80 p88
        +HF 7-80 p82 tape

RCA

ARM 1-2766/7 Tape (c) RK 12766 (From Victor originals)
3945 BARTHELEMY: Adorables tourments; Triste ritorno. BIZET: Les pecheurs de perles: Del tempio al limitar. BUZZI-PECCIA: Lolita.
DONIZETTI: La favorita: Spirto gentil. Lucia di Lammermoor: Chi
mi frena. Don Sebastien: Deserto in terra (2 versions). FLOTOW:
Martha: M'appari. GIORDANO: Andrea Chenier: Un di all'azzurro
spazio. GOUNOD: Faust: Salut demeure. LEONCAVALLO: I Pagliacci:
Recitar...Vesti la giubba. MEYERBEER: L'Africaine: Mi batte il
cor...O paradiso. PUCCINI: La boheme: Che gelida manina; O Mimi
tu piu non torni; O soave fanciulla; Addio dolce svegliare. Mad-

ama Butterfly: Un po di vero c'e. Tosca: Recondita armonia: E
lucevan le stelle. TOSTI: Ideale; Pour un baiser. VERDI: Aida:
Celeste Aida (2). La forza del destino: Solenne in quest'ora.
Rigoletto: Bella figlia dell'amore; La donna e mobile; Questa o
quella. Il trovatore: Ah si ben mio; Se m'ami ancor...Ai nostri
monti; Di quella pira. Enrico Caruso, t; Orchestral accompaniment.

+ARG 11-78 p53	+–HFN 11-80 p124
++FF 11/12-78 p134	+MJ 9/10-79 p50
++Gr 9-80 p407	+MUM 7/8-80 p30
+Gr 11-80 p736	+–NR 10-78 p9
+HF 10-78 p96	+ON 10-78 p68
+HFN 8-80 p109 tape	+RR 8-80 p12
+HFN 7-80 p111	

ARM 1-3373/4 (From Victor originals, 1909/1910)
3946 BIZET: Carmen: La fleur que tu m'avais jetee; Il fior che avevi a
     me dato. FLOTOW: Martha: Solo profugo reietto. FRANCHETTI: Ger-
     mania: Studenti udite; Ah vieni qui...No non chiuder gli occhi
     vaghi. GEEHL: For you alone. GOLDMARK: Die Konigin von Saba:
     Magische note. GOUNOD: Faust: Seigneur Dieu que vois-je; Eh
     quoi toujours seule; Il se fait tard...Eternelle o nuit d'amour;
     O merveille; Que voulez-vous messieurs; Mon coeur est penetre d'
     epouvante; Attends; Voici la rue; Alerte ou vous etes perdus.
     LEONCAVALLO: I Pagliacci: No Pagliaccio non son. MASCAGNI: Cav-
     alleria rusticana: Siciliana. MEYERBEER: Les Huguenots: Ah qual
     soave vision...Bianca al par di neve alpina. NUTILE: Mamma mia
     che vo sape. PONCHIELLI: La gioconda: Cielo e mar. PUCCINI:
     Madama Butterfly: Amore o grillo; Non ve l'avevo detto. VERDI:
     Aida: La fatal pietra; O terra addio. La forza del destino: Dal-
     la natal sua terra...O tu che in seno agli angeli. Otello: Nell'
     ore arcane...Ora e per sempre addio. Il trovatore: Miserere.
     Enrico Caruso, t; Various accompaniments.

++FF 11/12-79 p149	++NR 10-79 p9
+–HF 12-79 p106	+ON 8-80 p36
+MUM 7/8-80 p30	

RL 1-3442 Tape (c) RK 1-3442
3947 BALFE: Killarney. BARNARD: Come back to Erin. DUFFERIN: Irish
     emigrant. LOUGHBOROUGH: Ireland mother Ireland. O'CONNOR: The
     old house. O'BRIEN: The fair tree. TRAD.: Bard of Armagh; Be-
     lieve me if all those endearing charms; Danny boy; The harp that
     once through Tara's halls; My lagan love; Next market day; She
     moved through the fair; Trottin to the fair. Robert White, t;
     National Philharmonic Orchestra; Charles Gerhardt.

+–FF 7/8-80 p157	+NYT 6-15-80 pD31
+Gr 5-80 p1718	

ARL 1-3522 Tape (c) ARK 1-3522
3948 BELLINI: Norma: Sediziose voci...Casta diva...Ah bello a me ritorna.
     BRITTEN: Gloriana: Soliloquy and prayer. HANDEL: Semele: Where'
     er you walk. LEONCAVALLO: I Pagliacci: Qual fiamma...Stridono
     lassu. VERDI: Rigoletto: Gualtier Malde...Caro nome. WAGNER:
     Tristan und Isolde: Liebestod. WEBER: Oberon: Ozean du Ungeheuer.
     Leontyne Price, s; Boris Martinovich, bs; Ambrosian Opera Chorus;
     PhO; Henry Lewis.

+–ARG 12-80 p51	+–NYT 6-15-80 pD29
+–FF 11/12-80 p194	+–ON 9-80 p68

+−HF 9−80 p102   +−SFC 5−25−80 p41
+NR 7−80 p10

ARM 1-3570/1 (2)
3949 CARDILLO: Cor 'ngrato. CRESCENZO: Tarantella sincera. CURTIS:
     Canta pe me. DONIZETTI: L'Elisir d'amore: Una furtiva lagrima.
     FAURE: Crucifix. FLOTOW: Martha: Sima giunti o giovinette; Ques-
     to cameo e per voi; Che vuol dir cio; Presto presto andiam; T'ho
     raggiunta sciagurata. GOMES: Lo schiavo: L'importuna insistenza;
     Quanto nascesti tu. LEONCAVALLO: La boheme: Musette; O gioia del-
     la mia dimora; Io non ho che una povera stanzetta; Testa adorata.
     MASCHERONI: Eternamente. MASSENET: Manon: Je suis seul; Ah fuy-
     ez douce image. TESCHEMACHER-GARTNER: Love is mine. TOSTI: Ad-
     dio. VERDI: Aida: Gia i sacerdoti adunansi; Misero appien mi
     festi; Se quel guerrier io fossi; Celeste Aida. Un ballo in mas-
     chera: Di tu se fedele; Forse la soglia attinse; Ma se m'e forza
     perderti. La forza del destino: Invano Alvaro; Le minaccie i
     fieri accenti. I Lombardi: Qual vo'uta transcorrere. Il trova-
     tore: Mal reggendo; Se m'ami ancor; Ai nostri monti. Enrico
     Caruso, t; Orchestral accompaniment.
               +NR 9−80 p6   +NYT 8-3-80 pD20
XRC 1-3624
3950 BRAHMS: Hungarian dances, nos. 11-16. MENDELSSOHN: Hebrides over-
     ture, op. 26. MOZART: Concerto, piano, no. 20, K 466, D minor:
     1st movement, excerpt. SCHUMANN: Symphony, no. 1, op. 38, B
     flat major: 1st movement. STRAVINSKY: Suites, nos. 1 and 2.
     Emanuel Ax, pno; PO, Dallas Symphony Orchestra; James Levine,
     Eugene Ormandy, Eduardo Mata.
               +FF 11/12−80 p226   +St 12−80 p138
               +NR 8−80 p5
LRL 1-5094 Tape (c) RK 11719 (also LRK 1-5094 (ct) LRS 1-5094)
3951 BACH: Suite, orchestra, S 1067, B minor: Minuet; Badinerie. CHOPIN:
     Waltz, op. 64, no. 1, D flat major (arr. and orch. Gerhardt).
     DINICU: Hora staccato (arr. and orch. Gerhardt). DOPPLER: Fan-
     taisie pastorale hongroise, op. 26. DRIGO: Les millions d'Arle-
     quin: Serenade (arr. and orch. Gamley). GLUCK: Orfeo ed Euridi-
     ce: Dance of the blessed spirits. GODARD: Pieces, op. 116: Waltz.
     MIYAGI: Haru no umi (arr. and orch. Gerhardt). PAGANINI: Moto
     perpetuo, op. 11, no. 2 (arr. and orch. Gerhardt). RIMSKY-
     KORSAKOV: The tale of the Tsar Sultan, op. 57: Flight of the
     bumblebee (arr. and orch. Gerhardt). SAINT-SAENS: Ascanio: Bal-
     let music, Adagio and variation. Games Galway, flt; National
     Philharmonic Orchestra; Charles Gerhardt.
               ++AR 2−80 p176   +−HFN 12−75 p164
               ++Gr 11−75 p915   +MJ 11−76 p60
               +Gr 1−76 p1244   ++NR 11−76 p16
               +Gr 7−76 p230 tape   +−RR 10−75 p38
               +−HF 3−77 p123 tape   +RR 1−77 p91 tape
PRL 1-9034 Tape (c) PRK 1-9034 (ct) 1-9034
3952 BRAHMS: Am Wildbach die Weiden; Die Berge sind spitz; Nun stehn die
     Rosen in Blute; Und gehst du uber den Kirchhof. DRECHSLER: Der
     Bauer als Millionar: Bruderlein fein. MOZART: Due pupille ama-
     bile, K 439; Luci care luci belle, K 346; Mi lagnero tacendo, K
     437; Piu non si trovano, K 459. SCHUBERT: Gott meine Zuversicht,
     D 706; Die Nachtigall, D 724; La Pastorella, D 513; Standchen, D
     921; Widerspruch, D 865. SCHUMANN: Zigeunerleben, op. 29. Vien-

na Boys Choir; Hans Gillesberger.

+Gr 10-79 p694   +HFN 1-80 p123 tape
+HF 8-76 p98   +NR 4-76 p8
+HFN 10-79 p165   ++RR 10-79 p143

RL 2-2359 (2) Tape (c) RK 2-2359 (From SB 6578, 6703, 6885, 6600, 6640, 6874, 6855, 6504, 6840, 6845, RB 16238, GL 42708)

3953 BRAHMS: Ballade, op. 10, no. 1, D minor. Pieces, piano, op. 76: Capriccio. Pieces, piano, op. 118: Romance. CHABRIER: Pieces pittoresques: Scherzo valse. CHOPIN: Berceuse, op. 57, D flat major. Fantaisie-Impromptu, op. 66, C sharp minor. Mazurka, op. 33, no. 2, D major. Waltz, op. 64, no. 1, D flat major. Polonaise, op. 40, no. 1, A major. DEBUSSY: Images: Poissons d'or. Preludes, Bk 1: La catedrale engloutie. FAURE: Nocturne, op. 33, no. 3, A flat major. FALLA: Love the magician: Ritual fire dance (arr. Rubinstein). LISZT: Valse oubliee, no. 1, G 215, F sharp minor. POULENC: Mouvements perpetuels. Intermezzo, A flat major. PROKOFIEV: The love of three oranges, op. 33: March (arr. Rubinstein). RAVEL: Miroirs: La vallee des cloches. SCHUBERT: Impromptu, op. 90, no. 3, D 899, G flat major. SCHUMANN: Forest scenes, op. 82: The prophet bird. Arabesque, op. 18, C major. VILLA-LOBOS: A prole do bebe: Polichinelle. Artur Rubinstein, pno.

+ARG 6-79 p43   +-HFN 7-79 p119 tape
+FF 7/8-80 p164   +NR 12-79 p12
+Gr 5-79 p1917   +RR 7-79 p81

CRL 2-3384 (2) (Reissues)
3954 BRITTEN: Young person's guide to the orchestra. DEBUSSY: Prelude a l'apres-midi d'un faun. FALLA: El sombrero de tres picos: Neighbour's dance; Miller's dance; Final dance. GINASTERA: Estancia: Dance final. KAHACHATURIAN: Gayaneh: Lesginka; Dance of the rose maidens; Dance of the Kurds; Sabre dance. MILHAUD: La creation du monde. RAVEL: La valse. STRAVINSKY: L'Oiseau de feu: Suite. WEBER: Invitation to the dance, op. 65. CSO, BPO, BSO, PO; Seiji Ozawa, Arthur Fiedler, Charles Munch, Eugene Ormandy, Fritz Reiner.

+/FF 1/2-80 p184

RL 2-5199 Tape (c) RK 2-5199
3955 BANCHIERI: Sonata sopra l'aria musical del Gran Duca. CALVI: La bertazzina. FARINA: Pavana. GARSI DA PARMA: La Lisfeltina. NEGRI: La nizzarda. RORE (arr. Rogniono): Anchor che col partire. STEFANI: Pargoletta che non sai. VECCHI: So ben mi chi ha bon tempo. ZANNETTI: Fuggi fuggi; La Mantovana. ANON.: Pavaniglia; Spagnoletta; Va pur superba va. Paul Elliot, t; London Early Music Group; James Tyler.

+Gr 9-79 p502   +MT 3-80 p181
+HFN 7-79 p116   ++RR 8-79 p98
+HFN 10-79 p171 tape

GL 2-5240 Tape (c) GK 2-5240
3956 GLUCK: Orfeo ed Euridice: Dance; Minuet. HAYDN, M.: Nocturne, F major. ISAAC (arr. Redel): Innsbruck ich muss dich lassen. MOZART: Rondo, violin, K 373, C major. PACHELBEL: Canon, D major. Chaconne, F minor. TELEMANN: Minuet, G minor. VIVALDI: Largo, D minor. Kurt Redel, flt; Georg Retyi, vln; Leonard Hokanson, hpd; Munich Pro Arte Chamber Orchestra; Kurt Redel.

+Gr 10-79 p662   +-RR 10-79 p127

+HFN 10-79 p167   +-RR 4-80 p127 tape
+HFN 2-80 p107 tape

RL 2-5247 Tape (c) RK 2-5247 (also ARL 1-3556 Tape (c) ARK 1-3556)
3957 BOELLMANN: Suite gothique, op. 25. BONNET: Pieces, op. 7: Elves.
GIGOUT: Grand choeur dialogue. GUILMANT: March on a theme by
Handel, op. 15. SAINT-SAENS: Fantaisie, E flat major. VIERNE:
Fantasiestucke, op. 54: Carillon de Westminster. Fantasiestucke,
op. 53: Clair de lune. Carlo Curley, org.
            -FF 9/10-80 p267   ++NR 6-80 p13
            +Gr 1-80 p1172   +-St 11-80 p267
            +Gr 12-79 p1065 tape

GL 2-5308 Tape (c) GK 2-5308 (From 2-5081)
3958 BLISS: Fanfare for a coming of age. Fanfare for a dignified occasion. Fanfare for the bride. Fanfare for heroes. Fanfare for
the Lord Mayor of London. Fanfare, homage to Shakespeare. Interlude. Royal fanfare. Royal fanfare, no. 1: Sovereign's fanfare. Royal fanfares, nos. 5, 6. BENJAMIN: Fanfare for a festive occasion. Fanfares: For a state occasion; For a brilliant
occasion; For a gala occasion. BRIAN: Festival fanfare. ELGAR:
Civic fanfare. JACOB: Music for a festival: Interludes for trumpets and trombones, no. 1, Intrada; no. 2, Round of seven parts;
no. 3, Interlude; no. 4, Saraband; no. 5, Madrigal. RUBBRA:
Fanfare for Europe, op. 142. SIMPSON: Canzona for brass. TIP-
PETT: Fanfare, brass no. 1. WALTON: Fanfare "Hamlet" (arr. Sargent). A queen's fanfare. TRAD.: National anthem (arr. Coe).
Locke Brass Consort; James Stobart.
            +Gr 10-80 p533   +HFN 10-80 p115

RL 3-0336
3959 ABAELARD: O quanta qualia. GAUTIER DE CHATILLON: Ver pacis apperit.
GUIDO OF AREZZO: Ut queant laxis resonare. PHILIPPE DE CHANCE-
LIER: Mundus a munditia. ANON.: Ave Maris stella Cum animadverterem; De ramis cadunt folia; Flos in monte cerintur; In saeculum viellatoris; Magne deus potencie; Mater summi domini; Novus
miles sequitur; O Roma nobilis; Olim in armonia; Quinte estampie
real; Stantipes; Veris ad imperia. Munich Capella Antiqua; Konrad Ruhland.
            +Gr 4-80 p1583   +RR 6-80 p87
            +-HFN 4-80 p113

RL 3-0469
3960 BACH (Gounod): Ave Maria. BIZET: Agnus Dei: Intermezzo. EYBLER:
Omnes. FAURE: Crucifix. FRANCK: Panis angelicus. HANDEL: Serse:
Largo. KIENZL: Der Evangelimann: Selig sind die Verfolgung leid-
en. LUTHER: Ein feste Vurg ist unser Gott. SCHUBERT: Ave Maria,
D 839. RITTER VON HERBECK: Adeste fideles; Pueri concinite.
Placido Domingo, t; Vienna Boys Choir, Vienna Chorus; VSO; Joh-
annes Sonnleitner, org; Helmuth Froschauer.
            +Gr 3-80 p145   +HFN 8-80 p109 tape
            +HFN 4-80 p112   ++RR 4-80 p112

CRL 3-3599 (3) Tape (c) CRK 3-3599 (From RCA originals)
3961 ANDERSON: Fiddle faddle. The syncopated clock. BERLIOZ: La damnation de Faust, op. 24: Rakoczy march. BOSC: Rose mousse: Entr'
acte. BORODIN: In the Steppes of Central Asia. CAILLIET: Variations on "Pop goes the weasel". DANOFF/NIVERT/DENVER: Take me
home country roads. ELLINGTON: Solitude. FAURE: Apres un reve,
op. 7, no. 1. FRIDAY/TOUSSAINT/TYLER: Java. GADE: Jalousie.

GERSHWIN: Rhapsody in blue, abridged. Variations on "I got rhythm". GOULD: Latin American sinfoniette: Conga. IVANOVICI:
Waves of the Danube. KHACHATURIAN: Masquerade: Mazurka; Galop.
KINGSLEY: Popcorn. LENNON/MCCARTNEY: And I love her. I want to
hold your hand. LEONCAVALLO: I Pagliacci: Prologue. LITOLFF:
Scherzo. MANCINI: Moon river. MOSZKOWSKI: Spanish dance, op.
12, no. 2, G minor. OFFENBACH: La belle Helene: Oveture. Gene-
vieve de Brabant: Galop. RODGERS: South Pacific: Medley. ROSSI-
NI: La boutique fantasque: Tarantella (Respighi). SCHUMAN: New
England triptych: Chester. SCHONHERR: Die seiben Sprunge.
SOUSA: High school cadets march. Stars and stripes forever.
STRAUSS, J. II: Artists life, op. 316. Ritter Pasman, op. 441:
Polka. STRAUSS, Josef: Fireproof polka. VERDI: La forza del
destino: Pace pace mio Dio. WOLF-FERRARI: Il segreto de Susanna:
Overture. I gioiella della Madonna: Dance of the Camorristi.
Patrice Munsel, s; Jesus Maria Sanroma, Earl Wild, Edward Elling-
ton, pno; Robert Merrill, bar; Helen Traubel, s; Al Hirt, tpt;
Nathan Milstein, vln; BPO, RCA Orchestra; Arthur Fiedler.
              +HF 9-80 p88   +-St 10-80 p125
RL 3-7354
3962 ALAIN: Danses (2). BOELLMAN: Menuet gothique. CAMPIAN: Suites,
     nos. 1-3. COUPERIN: Chaconne en re mineur. LUBLIN: Danse, no.
     8. MUFFAT: Passacaglia en sol mineur. Odile Pierre, org.
              +MU 5-80 p12
ARM 4-2942/7
3963 The Heifetz collection, vol. 1, Acoustic recordings complete: ACH-
     RON: Hebrew dance, op. 35, no. 1. Hebrew lullaby, op. 35, no.
     2. Hebrew melody, op. 33. Stimmung, op. 32, no. 1. d'AMBROSIO:
     Serenade, no. 4. BAZZINI: La ronde des lutins, op. 25. BEET-
     HOVEN: The ruins of Athens, op. 113: Chorus of the dervishes Tur-
     kish march. BOULANGER: Cortege. Nocturne, F major. BRAHMS:
     Hungarian dance, no. 1, G minor. CHOPIN: Nocturne, op. 27, D flat
     major. Nocturne, op. 9, no. 2, E flat major. DRIGO: Airs de
     ballet, no. 2: Valse bluette. DVORAK: Slavonic dance, op. 46,
     no. 2, E minor. Slavonic dance, op. 72, no. 2, E minor. Slavon-
     ic dance, op. 72, no. 8, A major. ELGAR: La capricieuse, op. 17.
     GLAZUNOV: Meditation, op. 32. Raymonda, op. 57: Valse grande
     adagio. GODOWSKY: Waltz, D major. GOLDMARK: Concerto, violin,
     op. 28, A minor: Andante. GRANADOS: Danza espanola, op. 37: An-
     daluza. HAYDN: Quartet, strings, op. 64, no. 5, D major: Vivace.
     JUON: Berceuse. KREISLER: Minuet, in the style of Niccolo Por-
     pora. Sicilienne et rigaudon. LALO: Symphonie espagnole, op.
     21, D minor: Andante. MENDELSSOHN: Concerto, violin, op. 64, E
     minor: Finale. On wings of song, op. 34, no. 2. MOSZKOWSKI:
     Stucke, op. 45, no. 2: Guitarre. MOZART: Divertimento, no. 17,
     K 334, D major: Minuet. Serenade, no. 7, K 250, D major: Rondo.
     PAGANINI: Caprices, op. 1, nos. 13, 20. Moto perpetuo, op. 11.
     SARASATE: Carmen fantasy, op. 25. Danzas espanolas, op. 21:
     Malaguena, Habanera; op. 23, Zapateado. Introduction and taran-
     telle, op. 43. Zigeunerweisen, op. 20, no. 1. SCHUBERT: Ave
     Maria, D 839. SCHUMANN: Myrthen, op. 25: Widmung. SCOTT: The
     gentle maiden. TCHAIKOVSKY: Concerto, violin, op. 35, D major:
     Canzonetta. Serenade melancolique, op. 26. Souvenir d'un lieu
     cher, op. 42: Scherzo. Serenade, strings, op. 48, C major: Valse.
     WIENIAWSKI: Concerto, violin, no. 2, op. 22, D minor: Romance.

Scherzo tarantelle, op. 16. Vol. 2, The first electrical recordings: ACHRON: Hebrew melody, op. 33. ALBENIZ: Suite espanola:
Sevillanas. BACH: Partita, violin, no. 3, S 1006, E major: Minuets, nos. 1 and 2. English suite, no. 3, S 808, G minor: Sarabande, Govotte, Musette. CASTELNUOVO-TEDESCO: Etudes d'ondes:
Sea murmurs. Valse. CLERAMBAULT: Largo on the G string. COUP-
ERIN: Livres de clavecin, Bk IV, Ordre no. 17: Les petits Moulins
a vent. DEBUSSY: L'Enfant prodigue: Prelude. Preludes, Bk I:
La fille aux cheveux de lin. La plus que lente. DOHNANYI: Ruralia Hungarica, op. 32: Gypsy andante. DRIGO: Airs de ballet,
no. 2: Valse bluette. ELGAR: La capricieuse, op. 17. FALLA:
Spanish popular songs: Jota. GLAZUNOV: Concerto, violin, op.
82, A minor. Meditation, op. 32. GODOWSKY: Alt Wien. GRIEG:
Lyric piece, op. 54: Scherzo. Lyric pieces, op. 71: Puck. Sonata, violin and piano, no. 3, op. 45, C minor. HUMMEL: Rondo,
op. 11, E flat major. KORNGOLD: Much ado about nothing, op. 11:
Holzapfel und Schlehwein. MENDELSSOHN: On wings of song, op.
34, no. 2. MILHAUD: Saudades do Brasil: Sumare. MOSZKOWSKI:
Stucke, op. 45, no. 2: Guitarre. MOZART: Concerto, violin, no.
5, K 219, A major. PAGANINI: Caprices, op. 1, nos. 13, 24, 20.
PONCE: Estrellita. RAVEL: Tzigane. RIMSKY-KORSAKOV: Tale of
the Tsar Sultan, op. 57: Flight of the bumblebee. SARASATE:
Danza espanola, op. 23: Zapateado. SCHUBERT: Ave Maria, D 839.
Impromptu, op. 90, no. 3, D 899, G flat major. Sonatina, violin
and piano, op. 137, D 384, D major: Rondo. STRAUSS: Sonata,
violin and piano, op. 18, E flat major. Stimmungsbilder, op. 90:
An einsamer Quelle. VIVALDI: Sonata, violin, op. 2, no. 2, C
major. WIENIAWSKI: Scherzo tarantelle, op. 16, G minor. Vol. 3,
1935-1937: BACH: Sonata, violin, no. 1, S 1001, G minor. Sonata,
violin, no. 3, S 1005, C major. BAZZINI: La ronde des lutins, op.
25. BRAHMS: Sonata, violin and piano, no. 2, op. 104, A major.
DINICU: Hora staccato. FAURE: Sonata, violin and piano, no. 1,
op. 13, A major. FALLA: La vida breve: Danza no. 1. GRIEG:
Sonata, violin, no. 2, op. 13, G minor. POULENC: Mouvements perpetuels, no. 1. SAINT-SAENS: Introduction and rondo capriccioso,
op. 28. SCOTT: Tallahassee suite. SZYMANOWSKI: Le Roi Roger,
op. 46: Chant do Roxane. VIEUXTEMPS: Concerto, violin, no. 4,
op. 31, D minor. WIENIAWSKI: Concerto, violin, no. 2, op. 22, D
minor. Polonaise, op. 4, D major. Vol. 4, 1937-1941: BEETHOVEN:
Concerto, violin, op. 61, D major. BRAHMS: Concerto, violin, op.
77, D major. Concerto, violin and violoncello, op. 102, A minor.
CHAUSSON: Concerto, violin, piano and string quartet, op. 21, D
major. PROKOFIEV: Concerto, violin, no. 2, op. 63, G minor.
SAINT-SAENS: Havanaise, op. 83. SARASATE: Zigeunerweisen, op.
20, no. 1. WALTON: Concerto, violin, B minor. Vol. 5, 1946-
1949: ARENSKY: Concerto, violin, A minor: Tempo di valse. BACH:
Concerto, 2 violins and strings, S 1043, D minor. English suite,
no. 6, S 811, D minor: Gavottes, nos. 1 and 2. BAX: Mediterranean. BEETHOVEN: Duetsche Tanze, no. 6. BRUCH: Scottish fantasia, op. 46. CASTELNUOVO-TEDESCO: Etudes d'ondes: Sea murmurs.
Tango. CHOPIN: Nocturne, op. 9, no. 2, E minor. DEBUSSY: Chanson de Bilitis: La chevelure. Songs: Ariettes oubliees; Il ple-
ure dans mon coeur. Prelude, Bk 1: La fille aux cheveux de lin.
ELGAR: Concerto, violin, op. 61, B minor. FALLA: El amor brujo:
Pantomime. Spanish popular songs: Jota. HALFFTER: Danza de la

gitana. KORNGOLD: Much ado about nothing, op. 11: Holzapfel und
Schlehwein, Garden scene. MEDTNER: Fairy tale, B flat minor.
MENDELSSOHN: Trio, piano, no. 1, op. 49, D minor: Scherzo. Sweet
remembrance. MILHAUD: Saudades do Brasil: Corcovada. MOZART:
Divertimento, no. 17, K 334, D major: Minuet. NIN-CULMELL: Cantilena asturiana. POLDOWSKY: Tango. PROKOFIEV: Gavotte. March,
F minor. RACHMANINOFF: Daisies, op. 38, no. 3. Etudes tableux,
op. 39, no. 2. Oriental sketch. RAVEL: Valses nobles et sentimentales, nos. 6 and 7. RIMSKY-KORSAKOV: The tale of the Tsar
Sultan: Flight of the bumblebee. TANSMAN: Mouvement perpetuel.
VIEUXTEMPS: Concerto, violin, no. 5, op. 37, A minor. Vol. 6,
1950-1955: BEETHOVEN: Romance, no. 1, op. 40, G major. Romance,
no. 2, op. 50, F major. Sonata, violin and piano, no. 9, op. 47,
A major. BLOCH: Sonatas, violin, nos. 1 and 2. BRAHMS: Sonata,
violin and piano, no. 3, op. 108, D minor. BRUCH: Concerto, violin, no. 1, op. 26, G minor. HANDEL: Sonata, violin, op. 1, no.
13, D major. RAVEL: Tzigane. SAINT-SAENS: Sonata, violin, no.
1, op. 75, D minor. SCHUBERT: Sonatina, violin and piano, no. 3,
op. 137, K 408, G minor. TCHAIKOVSKY: Concerto, violin, op. 35,
D major. WIENIAWSKI: Polonaise, op. 4, D major. Jascha Heifetz,
vln; With assisting artists.

++FF 9/10-80 p335	+NYT 6-29-75 pD17
+HF 8-75 p71	+SR 10-4-75 p51
++NR 7-75 p12	+St 1-76 p112

GL 4-2922
3964 BRAGA: Engenho novo (arr.). BUCHARDO: Jujena. DEBUSSY: Noel des
enfants qui n'ont plus de jouets. FAURE: Serenade Toscane.
GUARNIERI: Declaracao. HAHN: Infidelite; Le rossingol des lilas.
LISZT: Ihr Glocken von Marling; Himm einem Strahl der Sonne; Oh
quand je dors. RACHMANINOFF: My love; Oh stay; When yesterday
we met. TCHAIKOVSKY: At the ball; Don Juan's serenade. VILLA-
LOBOS: Serenata. Gerard Souzay, bar; Dalton Baldwin, pno.

+-HFN 4-80 p121	+RR 4-80 p118

GL 4-2952 (From SB 6698)
3965 BAKFARK: Fantasia. BESARD: Air de cour. Branle. Guillemette.
Volte. DLUGORAJ: Fantasia. Finales (2). Villanellas, nos. 1
and 2. DOWLAND: Fantasia. Queen Elizabeth's galliard. FERRA-
BOSCO: Pavan. HOWETT: Fantasia. LANDGRAVE OF HESSE: Pavan.
MOLINARO: Ballo detto "Il Conte Orlando". Fantasia. Saltarel-
los (2). MUDARRA: Fantasia. NEUSEIDLER: Hie folget ein welscher
Tanz. Ich klag den Tag. Der Judentanz. Mein Herz hat sich mit
Lieb verpflicht. PHILIPS: Galliard and chromatic pavan. Julian
Bream, lt.

+Gr 4-80 p1575	+HFN 8-80 p109 tape
+-HFN 4-80 p119	+-RR 4-80 p97

RL 4-3373 Tape (c) 4-3373 (From SB 6723)
3966 BRINDLE: El polifemo de oro. BRITTEN: Nocturnal, op. 70. HENZE:
Kammermusik 1958: Tentos (3). MARTIN: Pieces breves (4). VILLA-
LOBOS: Etudes, no. 5, C major; no. 7, E major. Julian Bream, gtr.

++Gr 11-80 p710	+HFN 12-80 p153

CRL 6-0720 (6)
3967 BACH: Concerto, 2 violins and strings, S 1043, D minor. BEETHOVEN:
Concerto, violin, op. 61, D major. BRAHMS: Concerto, violin,
op. 77, D major. BRUCH: Concerto, violin, no. 1, op. 26, G min-
or. GLAZUNOV: Concerto, violin, op. 82, A minor. MENDELSSOHN:

Concerto, violin, op. 64, E minor. MOZART: Concerto, violin, no.
5, K 219, A major. PROKOFIEV: Concerto, violin, no. 2, op. 63,
G minor. SIBELIUS: Concerto, violin, op. 47, D minor. TCHAI-
KOVSKY: Concerto, violin, op. 35, D major. Jascha Heifetz, Erik
Friedman, vln; NSO, BSO, CSO, RCA Symphony Orchestra; Malcolm
Sargent, Charles Munch, Fritz Reiner, Walter Hendl.
            +Gr 9-80 p352   ++SFC 1-12-75 p26
         ++HFN 11-80 p129

REALTIME

RT 203
3968 BERLIOZ: The damnation of Faust, op. 24: Rakoczy march. BIZET:
     Carmen: Prelude. BRAHMS: Hungarian dance, no. 5, G minor. GIN-
     ASTERA: Panambi: Suite. RIMSKY-KORSAKOV: Mlada: Procession of
     the nobles. PH; Zoltan Rozsnyai.
            +-ARG 5-80 p45   +HF 5-80 p70
            +-FF 9/10-80 p42

RICHARDSON

RRS 1
3969 AICHINGER: Sing to the Lord. BACH: Chorale prelude, O sacred head
     surrounded. BRAHMS: Let nothing ever grieve thee, op. 30.
     DYKES: The navy hymn. FRANCK: Psalm, no. 150. IPPOLITOV-IVANOV:
     Bless the Lord, o my soul. LANGLAIS: Chant de paix. PITONI:
     Cantate domino. RAMEAU: Tambourin. SCHUTZ: Christ to thee be
     glory. STANLEY: Trumpet voluntary. TALLIS: If ye love me.
     VIERNE: Symphony, no. 6, op. 59, B major: Final. James Dale,
     org; U.S. Naval Academy Protestant Choirs.
            +NR 8-80 p11

RRS 3
3970 BAND: General Burgoyne's march. BILLINGS: Thus saith the Lord, the
     lofty one. BUXTEHUDE: Prelude and fugue, A minor. CARR: Trump-
     ets of victory. HASSLER: Songs: Cantate domino; Alleluia, the
     lord is king; A-roving; Shenandoah; Old man Noah; America the
     beautiful. HAYDN: Divertimento, no. 1, B flat major. HOPKIN-
     SON: The toast. MORLEY: Now is the month of maying. PASSEREAU:
     Il est bel et bon. PURCELL: Nymphs and shepherds. PHILE: The
     president's march. REINAGLE: Gavotte. WEELKES: Though my car-
     riage be but careless. ANON.: Summer is icumen in. Yankee dood-
     le. United States Naval Academy Glee Club; John Cooper, org;
     Singers Madrigale; Annapolis Brass Quintet, Aeolian Woodwind
     Quintet; John Talley.
            +FF 11/12-80 p227

RRS 5
3971 BACH: Chorale prelude, Vom Himmel hoch. Songs: English medley: Deck
     the hall; Gloucestshire Wassail, Wassail song; Swiss chansons
     (3); Adeste fideles; Joy to the world; El cant dels ocells; The
     twelve days of Christmas; O come Emanuel; Spanish medley: Las
     posades, Ya viene Lavieta, A la nanita nana; The first noel;
     Good King Wenceslas; O holy night; We wish you a merry Christmas.
     Annapolis Brass Quintet.

+-FF 11/12-80 p22   +-NR 11-80 p1

RRS 6
3972 BACH: Chorale prelude, Nun komm der Heiden Heiland. DYKES: Eternal
     father. FRANCK: Piece herioque. GRETCHANINOFF: Glory to God,
     Credo, Nunc dimittis. HANDL: Confirma hoc deus. HASSLER: Laet-
     entur coeli. LANGLAIS: Poemes evangeliques, op. 2: La nativite.
     RIEGGER: Evel shall not prevail. ANON.: Amazing grace. Mother-
     less child. James Dale, org; Protestant Choirs U. S. Naval Aca-
     demy.

+-FF 11/12-80 p227   +NR 8-80 p11

RRS 7/8 (2)
3973 Anchors aweigh; A-roving; Blow the man down; Lowlands; What shall we
     do with a drunken sailor; Farewell to grog; Old man Noah; Shenan-
     doah; High Barbary; Navy blue and gold; We saw the sea; We are
     from Crabtown, We are the old nyvee, Don't give up the ship (med-
     ley); Down down underneath the ocean; Bless em all; Eyes of the
     fleet, Navy victory march, Up and at 'em Navee (medley); America
     the beautiful; Eternal father (Navy hymn); National anthem (Glee
     Club). Battle; Auld lang syne; Anchors aweigh; Marine hymn (Drum
     and Bugle Corps). Hey look me over; Goodbye my Coney Island baby;
     If you knew Susie; Sweet Sue (Barbershop Quartet). Song of the
     fishes; Rhyme of the chivalarous shark; Cat's in the cradle (Full
     Sail Trio). Marine Corps hymn; Noble men; The footlifter; Ameri-
     can Legion; Christopher Columbus; Army of the Nile; Anchors awe-
     igh (Band). U. S. Naval Academy Band, Glee Club and Drum and
     Bugle Corps.

+-FF 11/12-80 p227   +NR 9/80 p8

RICHMOND RECORDS

WRC 1-808
3974 BACH: Suite, solo violoncello, no. 1, S 1007, A major: 3 movements.
     ALBENIZ: Espana, op. 165: Capricho Catalan. Suite espanola, op.
     47: Asturias. HAUG: Alba. MILAN: Pavanas. VILLA-LOBOS: Prel-
     ude, no. 3. Louis Lawlor, gtr.

-FU 6-80 p45

ROCOCO

2122
3975 BACH (Busoni): Chaconne. BRAHMS: Variations on a theme by Paganini,
     op. 35, A minor. BEETHOVEN: Sonata, piano, no. 3, op. 2, no. 3,
     C major. CHOPIN: Waltz, op. posth., E flat major. DEBUSSY: Im-
     ages: Hommage a Rameau. MOMPOU: Cancion y danza, no. 1. SCHU-
     MANN: Concerto, piano, op. 54, A minor. Faschingsschwank aus
     Wien, op. 26. SCARLATTI: Sonatas, harpsichord (2). Arturo Ben-
     edetti Michelangeli, pno; Warsaw Philharmonic Orchestra; Witold
     Rowicki.

++NR 1-80 p15

5391
3976 BELLINI: La sonnambula: Prendi l'anel. CIMAROSA: Il matrimonio seg-
     reto: Pria che spunti. DONIZETTI: Don Pasquale: Povero Ernesto
     ...Cerchero lontana terra. L'Elisir d'amore: Una furtiva lag-
     rima. Lucia di Lammermoor: Tombe degl'avi...Fra poco a me.

GLUCK: Begrogene Kadi: Arietta amorosa. MOZART: Cosi fan tutte,
K 588: In aura amorosa. Die Entfuhrung aus dem Serail, K 384: O
wie angstlich. Don Giovanni, K 527: Dalla sua pace. ROSSINI:
L'Italiana in Algeri: Languir per una bella. Il barbiere di Siviglia: Se il mio nome. VERDI: Luisa Miller: O fedelta...Quando
le sere. Rigoletto: La donna e mobile. La traviata: Lunga da
lei...De miei bollenti spiriti. Petre Munteanu, t.
    +NR 1-80 p8

RUBINI

GV 34
3977 COCCIA: Per la patria: Bella Italia. DENZA: Culto; Occhi di fata.
    HEROLD: Zampa: Perche tremar. NOUGES: Quo vadis: Amica l'ora.
    QUARANTA: O ma charmante. ROTOLI: La gondola nera; Mia sposa
    sara la mia bandiera. VERDI: Don Carlo: Per me giunto; Morro
    ma lieta in corre. Il trovatore: Mira d'acerbe; Vivra contende.
    Mattia Battistini, bar.
        +NYT 8-3-80 pD20   +RR 8-77 p20

RV 39
3978 ADAM: Le chalet: Vallons de l'Helvetie. BERLIOZ: La damnation de
    Faust, op. 24: Serenade. FLOTOW: Martha: Canzone del porter.
    GODARD: Embarquez-vous. GOUNOD: Faust: Serenade; Le veau d'or.
    Romeo et Juliette: Allons jeunes gens. MEYERBEER: L'Etoile du
    nord: O jours heureux. Robert le diable: Invocation. ROSSINI:
    Stabat mater: Pro peccatis. SCHUMANN: Les deux grenadiers.
    THOMAS: Le Caid: Air du Tambour-major (2 versions). VERDI: Don
    Carlo: Monologue of Philip. Pol Plancon, bs.
        +RR 8-77 p20   +NYT 8-3-80 pD20

GV 79
3979 BERLIOZ: Damnation of Faust, op. 24: Su queste rose. DONIZETTI:
    Maria di Rohan: Bella e di sol vestita. Maria di Rudenz: Ah non
    avea piu. MARCHETTI: Ruy Blas: Ai miei rivale cedere. MASSENET:
    Re di Lahore: O casto fior. Werther: Ah non mi ridestar. MOZ-
    ART: Don Giovanni, K 527: Finch'han dal vino. NOUGES: Quo vadis:
    Errar sull'ampio mar. ROSSINI: Il barbiere di Siviglia: Largo
    al factotum. TOSTI: Malia; Non m'ama piu. VERDI: La forza del
    destino: Urna fatale. Macbeth: Pieta rispetta. Mattia Battis-
    tini, bar.
        +RR 4-80 p30

RS 305 (5)
3980 BALDELLI: A suon di baci. BARTHELEMY: Sulla bocca amorosa; Triste
    ritorno; Serenamente. BELLINI: La sonnambula: Ah perche non
    posso odiarti; Prendi l'anel ti dono; Son geloso. BIZET: Carmen:
    Il fior che avevi a me (2); La tua madre...Mia madre vedo ancor.
    Les pecheurs de perles: Della mia vita; Mi par d'udir ancora; Non
    hai compreso. CAPUA: O sole mio. CILEA: Adriana Lecouvreur: L'
    anima ho stanca. Songs: Lontananza. COSTA: Napulitanata; Tu sei
    morta nella vita mia; Oili oila; Era de maggio. COTTRAU: Fen-
    esta che lucive. CURTIS: Carmela; A surrentina. DENZA: Occhi
    de fata. DONIZETTI: L'Elisir d'amore: Ecco il magico liquore...
    Obbligato obbligato. La favorita: Una vergine un angel di Dio.
    GAMBARDELLA: Nun me guardate chiu. GIORDANO: Fedora: Amor ti
    vieta; Mia madre la mia vecchia madre; Vedi io piangi. GOUNOD:

Faust: Tardi si fa; Salve dimora casta e pura; Tardi si fa. Romeo et Juliette: Deh sorgi il luce in ciel. MASCAGNI: Cavalleria
rusticana: O Lola ch' hai di latti. MASSENET: Manon: Chiudo gli
occhi (2). Werther: Ah non mi ridestar. MOZART: Don Giovanni,
K 527: Dalla sua pace; Il mio tesoro. PUCCINI: Tosca: Recondita
armonia. RICCIARDI: Luna lu. ROSSINI: Il barbiere di Siviglia:
Se il mio nome; Ecco ridente in cielo; Numero quindici; All'idea
di quel metallo; Ah qual colpo; Se il mio nome; Ah qual colpo;
Ecco ridente in cielo. Songs: Pieta signore. THOMAS: Mignon:
Ah non credivi tu (2). TOSTI: Ideale; Marechiare; La serenata.
VERDI: Luisa Miller: Quando le sere al placido. Rigoletto: La
donna e mobile; E il sol dell anima. La travaita: Ah si da un
anno...Un di felice eterea; Parigi o cara; De miei bollenti spir-
iti. WAGNER: Lohengrin: Merce merce cigno gentil; Di non t'incanta; S'el torna alfin; Cessaro i canti alfin; Mio salvatore...
Mai devi domandarmi; Merce merce cigno gentil. Fernando de
Lucia, t; Various accompaniments.

++Gr 3-80 p1442	++NYT 8-3-80 pD20
++HF 12-80 p62	++RR 2-80 p20

RV 501

3981 BERLIOZ: Damnation de Faust, op. 24: Serenade. CATALANI: La Wally:
T'amo ben mio. DONIZETTI: La favorita: A tanto amor; Vien Leonora. Lucia di Lammermoor: Cruda funesta smania. MEYERBEER:
L'Africana: Figlia di regi. ROSSINI: Il barbiere di Siviglia:
Largo al factotum. THOMAS: Hamlet: Come romito fior. VERDI:
Aida: Quest assisa. I due Foscari: O vecchio cor. Ernani: O de
verd'anni miei; Lo vedremo o veglio audace. Rigoletto: Pari
siamo; Cortigiani vil razza dannata. La traviata: Di provenza
il mar. Riccardo Stracciari, bar; With accompaniments.

+Gr 2-79 p1466	+NYT 8-3-80 pD20
+ON 10-80 p42	

GV 504

3892 COHEN: Over there. CHAPI Y LORENTE: El milagro de la virgen: Flores
purisimas. COTTRAU: Addio a Napoli. CURTIS: Tu ca non chaigne;
Senza nisciuno; Canta pe'me. FUCITO: Scordame. LEONCAVALLO:
Lasciata amar; Mattinata. NIEDERMEYER: Pieta signore. OLIVIERI:
Garibaldi hymn. PASADAS: Noche felix. RICCIARDI: Amor mio.
ROSSINI: Petite messe solennelle: Crucifixus. TOSTI: L'alba
separa dalla luce l'ombra. Enrico Caruso, t; Orchestral accom-
paniment.

+Gr 3-80 p1445	+NYT 8-3-80 pD20
+-HFN 9-80 p113	+ON 8-80 p36

GV 505

3983 BOITO: Nerone: Queste ad un lido; Ecco la Dea. DONIZETTI: Lucia di
Lammermoor: Fra poco a me; Tu che a dio. MASCAGNI: Cavalleria
rusticana: Siciliana. Iris: Apri la tua finestra. PONCHIELLI: La
gioconda: Cielo e mar. PUCCINI: La boheme: Che gelida manina.
VERDI: Un ballo in maschera: E scherzo; La rivedra. Il trovatore: Ah si ben mio; Di quella pira. Aureliano Pertile, t;
Orchestral accompaniment.

++Gr 8-79 p374	+-RR 4-80 p30
+NYT 8-3-80 pD20	

GV 509

3984 BACHELET: Chere nuit. CHARPENTIER: Louise: Depuis le jour. DUPARC:
Chanson triste, op. 2, no. 2. FALLA: El amor brujo: Cancion de

amor dolido; Cancion de fuego fatuo; Danza del jungo de amor.
GOUNOD: Faust: Il etait un Roi de Thule; Air des Bijoux. MASSEN-
ET: Heroidade: Il est doux il est bon. RIMSKY-KORSAKOV: Snegur-
ochka: Chanson de Lehl. SAINT-SAENS: Le timbre d'Argent: Le bo-
heur est une chose legere. THOMAS: Mignon: Connais tu le pays;
Elle est aimee. Ninon Vallin, s.
> +Gr 9-80 p408   +-RR 4-80 p30

GV 529
3985 GORING-THOMAS: Esmeralda: O vision entrancing. HAGEMAN: Do not go
my love. HANDEL: Judas Maccabaeus: Sound an alarm. HAHN: The
hour. MOZART: Don Giovanni, K 527: On her contentment; To her I
love. The magic flute, K 620: O loveliness beyond compare; O
voice of magic melody. OFFENBACH: Les contes de Hoffman: Legend
of Kleinsack. WALLACE: Maritana: Yes let me like a soldier fall.
WEBER: Oberon: Oh to the glorious sight. The freeshooter: Through the forest. Tudor Davies, t.
> +RR 4-80 p30

GV 530
3986 BIZET: Micael's aria. MASSENET: Thais: Te souvient-il. PUCCINI:
Madama Butterfly: Ancora un passo; Iera son salita; Un po di vero;
Un bel di vedremo; Ora a noi; Sai cos'ebbe cuore...Che tua madre;
Tutti i fior; Con onor muore...Tu tu piccolo addio. Tosca: Vissi
d'arte. THOMAS: Mignon: Legeres hirondelles; Styrienne. WAGNER:
Tannhauser: Allmachte Jungfrau. Geraldine Farrar, s; Enrico Car-
uso, t.
> +RR 4-80 p30

GV 531 (From Pearl GEMM 146, 165, HMV HQM 1194, COLH 146)
3987 BIZET: I pescatore di perle: Mi par d'udir ancora. BOITO: Mefistof-
ele: Dai campi dai prati; Giunto sui passo. CAPUA: Maria Mari.
CATALANI: Loreley: Nel verde maggio. DENZA: Funiculi funicula.
DONIZETTI: Lucia di Lammermoor: Tombe degli...Fra poco; Tu che a
Dio. PONCHIELLI: La Gioconda: Enzo Grimaldo. PUCCINI: La boh-
eme: In un coupe O Mimi tu piu non torni. Tosca: Tu di tua mano
...O dolci mano. SAINT-SAENS: Il canto del cigno. VERDI: La
forza del destino: Solenne in quest'ora. Beniamino Gigli, t;
Various accompaniments.
> +Gr 3-80 p1441   +RR 3-80 p30
> +NYT 8-3-80 pD20

                              SAGA

5411
3988 BEETHOVEN: Modlinger dances, nos. 1-4, 6, 8. HAYDN: German dances,
nos. 4, 10-11. LANNER: The parting of the ways. Summer night's
dream, op. 90. MOZART: Landler, K 606 (6). SCHUBERT: German
dances with coda and 7 trios. STRAUSS, J. I: Vienna carnival.
Vienna Volksoper Orchestra; Paul Angerer.
> +Gr 1-76 p1248   +HFN 10-80 p115
> +HFN 2-76 p115   +RR 12-75 p50

SAGA 5465
3989 BARSANTI: Sonatas, recorder, G minor. BONONCINI: Divertimento, F
major. CORELLI: Sonata, op. 5, no. 4, F major. MARCELLO, B.:
Sonata, recorder, op. 2, no. 2, D minor. MATTEIS: Ayres with
divisions. VIVALDI: Sonata, recorder, op. 13, no. 6, G minor

(attrib.). Philip Pickett, rec; Anthony Pleeth, vlc; David Rob-
lou, hpd.
+Gr 9-79 p484   ++MT 3-80 p180
+-HFN 9-79 p119   +-RR 9-79 p110
5473 (From XIP 7011, STXID 5211, 5260, 5207)
3990 BUTTERWORTH: A Shropshire lad: Songs (6). IRELAND: I have twelve
oxen; Love and friendship; My fair; The Sally gardens; Sea fever.
KEEL: Sea water ballads: Trade winds. STANFORD: Drake's drum.
VAUGHAN WILLIAMS: Linden Lea; Silent noon; Songs of travel. WAR-
LOCK: Captain Stratton's fancy. John Shirley-Quirk, bar; Viola
Tunnard, Martin Isepp, Eric Parkin, pno.
+Gr 11-80 p728   +-HFN 6-80 p119

ST. JOHN'S CATHEDRAL RECORD FUND

Unnumbered
3991 BACH: Chorale prelude, Prepare thyself Zion. BRITTEN: Corpus Christi carol. HARRIS: Behold the tabernacle. Simple gifts. Come
thou fount. Vox ultima crucis. HOWELLS: Like as the hart. IRE-
LAND: Greater love. NEAR: O magnum mysterium. VAUGHAN WILLIAMS:
The call. WILLAN: O sacred feast. PLAINSONG: Domine quis habitabit. Herbert Tinney, org and director; Wilmington Cathedral
Choirs.
+MU 10-80 p10

ST. MARY'S CATHEDRAL GIFT SHOP

Unnumbered
3992 BIELAWA: Sweet was the songs. DANDRIEU: Noels (3). DIRKSEN: Nativity. GUERRERO: Carols (3). HOOPER: Psalm, no. 96, Responsorial psalm for midnight mass. NIXON: By-by-baby. PACHELBEL: Vom
Himmel hoch. PALESTRINA: Dies sanctificatus. POULENC: O magnum
mysterium. SARGENT: Silent night. WILLCOCKS: Adeste fideles.
St. Mary's Cathedral Choir, San Francisco; Organ, harp, flute
and brass.
++MU 6-80 p8

SCHUDI ORGAN COMPANY

Unnumbered
3993 COULTER: Concentric preludes (2). FRANCK: Prelude, fugue and variations. GRIGNY: Veni creator. LANGLAIS: Hymn d'actions de
graces: Te deum. TOURNEMIRE/DURUFLE: Improvisation on "Te deum".
VIERNE: Fantasiestucke, op. 54: Impromptu. George Baker, org.
+MU 3-80 p8

SCHWANN

VMS 2038
3994 BENNET: All creatures now are merry-minded. Eliza, her name gives
honor. BYRD: The queen's alman. The sweet and merry month of

May. DERING: Cries of London. JOHNSON, E.: Eliza is the fairest
queen. JOHNSON, R.: Benedicam domino. HILTON: Fair Oriana, beauty's queen. MORLEY: Blow shepherds blow your pipes. Will ye
buy a fine dog. RAVENSCROFT: Where are you fair maids. Maids
to be and cover coal. TYE: In nomine "Crye". WHYTHORNE: Buy a
new broom. Accademia Monteverdiana; Instrumental Ensemble; Denis
Stevens.

+ARG 3-79 p50   +NR 9-80 p8

VMS 2075
3995 BRIDGE: Sally in our alley. BRITTEN: Lachrymae, op. 43. HOLST:
St. Paul's suite, op. 29, no. 2. PARRY: English suite. WARLOCK:
Capriol suite. Rainer Moog, vla; RIAS Sinfonietta; David Atherton.

+FF 11/12-80 p224

SERAPHIM

S 60323
3996 BUSATTI: Morte son io. BYRD: The noble famous queen. DOWLAND: A-
way with those self-loving lads. In darkness let me dwell. Lasso vita mia. Melancholy galliard. Mr. George Whitehead his almand. Now O now I needs must part. FRESCOBALDI: Se l'aura
spira. GALILEI: Fantasia, lute. JOHNSON, E.: Eliza is the fairest queen. JOHNSON, R.: Full fathom five; Where the bee sucks.
MORLEY: O mistress mine. PIETRAGRUA: Tortorella. PIERCE: The
queen's galliard. VECCHI: So ben mio c'ha bon tempo. WILSON:
Take o take those lips away. ANON.: Gairda la royne d'Escosse.
Gray's Inn masque. Miserere my maker. Wilson's wild. James
Bowman, c-t; Robert Spencer, lt and chitarrone; Dennis Nesbitt,
treble viol; Oliver Brookes, bs viol.

+ARG 9-79 p49   ++SFC 5-18-80 p38

1750 ARCH

1783
3997 DINICU (Heifetz): Hora staccato. DVORAK: Humoresques, op. 101.
GABRIEL-MARIE: La cinquantaine. HAYDN: Quartet, strings, op. 3,
no. 5, F major: Andante cantabile. KREISLER: Schon Rosmarin.
MONTI: Czardas. PACHELBEL: Canon, D major. PURCELL: Chacony,
G minor. SATIE: Gymnopedie, no. 1. SCHUBERT: Moment musicaux,
op. 94, no. 3, D 780, F minor. TCHAIKOVSKY: Quartet, strings,
no. 1, op. 11, D major: Andante cantabile. San Francisco String
Quartet.

+NR 12-80 p7

SINE QUA NON

DIGI 101
3998 ALBINONI: Adagio, G minor. Concerto, trumpet, F major. BACH: Brandenburg concerto, S 1047, F major: 3rd movement. Cantata, no.
147, Jesu joy of man's desiring. Suite, orchestra, S 1067, B
minor: Rondeau and Badinerie. CORELLI: Gigue, op. 5. HANDEL:
Serse: Aria. PACHELBEL: Canon, D major. Rolf Smedvig, tpt;

Emanual Borok, vln; Paul Fried, flt; Alfred Genovese, ob; Cambridge Chamber Orchestra, Empire Brass Quintet; Rolf Smedvig.
+−FF 7/8-80 p188

DIGI 102
3999 ADSON: Courtly masquing ayres (3). BRADE: Festive dances (2).
GABRIELI, A.: Ricercar del duodecimo tuono. GABRIELI, G.: Canzona, no. 3. GHISELIN: La Alfonsina. GUAMI: Canzona, no. 19.
HOLBORNE: The fairy round. The honeysuckle. The image of melancholy. Wanton. The widows myte. ISAAC: Instrumental piece
without title. Maudit seyt. Der Welte fundt. LOCKE: Musick for
His Majesty's sackbutts and cornetts. PEZEL: Sonata hora decima,
no. 22. SCHEIDT: Canzona on a French theme. ANON.: Fanfares, 2
trumpets (2). Daniel Katzen, Fr hn; Thomas Gauger, perc; Empire
Brass Quintet.
++St 7-80 p86

SA 2014 (also DBX SS 3001)
4000 ALBINONI: Suite en sol. BACH: Die Kunst der Fuge, S 1080: Contrapunctus, no. 9. Fantasia, C major. BYRD: Alleluia. GABRIELI,
G.: Canzona per sonare, no. 2. HANDEL: Aria. JOSQUIN DES PREZ:
Heth sold ein meiskin. HOLBORNE: Maire-Golde. Patienca. The
choise. Last will and testament. The new yeres gift. PALESTRINA: Ricercare del primo tuono. PEUERL: Intrade, sarabande and
bal. PRIOLI: Canzone seconda a b. PURCELL: King Arthur: Allegro and air. SCHEIDT: Canzona bergamasca. SCHEIN: Paduana and
galliard. Empire Brass Quintet.
+Audio 6-80 p113   +−HF 4-78 p112
+−FF 5/6-78 p106   +HF 11-79 p94

SAS 2040 Tape (c) C 2040
4001 ALONSO: La tricotea. BAENA: Arcangel San Miguel. ENCINA: Ay triste
que vengo. Isi abra en este baldres. Mi libertad en sosiego.
Oy comamos y bebamos. Qu'es de ti desconsolado. Pedro i bien
te quiero. Tan buen ganadico. Vuestros amores e senora. GARCIMUNOS: Pues bien para esta. ANON.: Works (10). Greenwood
Consort.
+−ARG 8-79 p50   +−FF 1/2-80 p177

SONIC ARTS

13
4002 CHOPIN: Nocturne. HAYDN: Divertimento. PIATIGORSKY: Variations
on a theme by Paganini (14). TCHAIKOVSKY: Morceau, op. 51: Sentimentale. WEBER: Adagio and rondo. Stephen Kates, vlc; Brooks
Smith, pno.
+ARG 1-80 p51

SPECTRUM

SR 107 Tape (c) SC 207
4003 FINCK: Greiner zanner. HOFHAIMER: Ach lieb mit leyd. Ain frewlich
Wesenn. Greyner zanner. ISAAC: Innsbruck. La martinella. Es
het ein Bauer, ein Tochterlein. L'ombre. La la ho ho. MAHU:
Es gieng. SENFL: Fortuna ad voces musicales. Ich armes. Im
Maien. O Elslein liebe Elselein. STOLTZER: Ich klag den Tag.

Ricercar. Musica Antiqua, Vienna; Bernhard Klebel.
        +FF 3/4-80 p199   +HF 6-80 p96 tape
SR 110 (From Omega 153011)
4004 Gregorian chant: Laudes Mariae. Cathedral of St. Salvator Scola
        Gregoriana; Roger Deruwe.
        +FF 9/10-80 p253

SR 112
4005 BACH, C.P.E.: Sonata, flute, A minor. DAHL: Variations on a Swed-
        ish folktune. HINDEMITH: Pieces, flute (8). KUHLAU: Fantasia.
        MARAIS: Le folies d'Espagne. Bonita Boyd, flt.
          +-FF 5/6-80 p189

SUNDAY OPERA

SYO 1
4006 BREVELLE-SMITH: The witch of Bowden. ELLIOTT: Hybrius the Cretan.
        GOUNOD: Faust: The calf of gold. GOULD: The curfew. HANDEL:
        Alexander's feast: Behold a ghastly band...Revenge Timotheus
        cries. Scipio: Hear me ye winds and waves. JUDE: The mighty
        deep. LEHMANN: Myself when young. MENDELSSOHN: Elijah, op. 70:
        It is enough. SARJEANT: Blow blow thou winter wind. SLATER:
        From Oberon in fairyland. VERDI: Nabucco: Sperate o figli. I
        vespri siciliani: O tu Palermo. WALLACE: Maritana: Hear me
        gentle Maritana...The mariner in his barque. Malcolm McEachern,
        bs; Various orchestras and accompanists.
          +RR 1-80 p62

SYO 2
4007 DONIZETTI: Don Sebastiano: Deserto sulla terra. L'Elisir d'amore:
        Una furtiva lagrima. La favorita: Spirto gentil. GOLDMARK: Re-
        gina de Saba: Magiche note. MASSENET: Werther: Ah non mi ride-
        star. MEYERBEER: L'Africaine: O paradiso. Les Huguenots: Bianca
        al par. PENNINO: Pecche. PONCHIELLI: La Gioconda: Cielo e mar.
        PUCCINI: Madama Butterfly: Addio fiorito asil. Tosca: Recondita
        armonia; E lucevan le stelle; O dolci mani. TOSTI: Ideale.
        VERDI: Un ballo in maschera: Di tu se fedele. La forza del des-
        tino: Solenne in quest'ora. Costa Milona, t; Various orchestras.
          +-RR 4-80 p47

SUPRAPHON

110 2199
4008 BEETHOVEN: Romance, no. 2, op. 50, F major. BERLIOZ: Reverie et
        caprice, op. 8. FIBICH: Romance, op. 10, B flat major. SVEND-
        SEN: Romance, op. 26, G major. TCHAIKOVSKY: Serenade melanchol-
        ique, op. 26, B flat minor. WIENIAWSKI: Concerto, violin, no. 2,
        op. 22, D minor: Romance. Josef Suk, vln; PSO; Vaclav Smetacek.
          +FF 3/4-80 p189   +NR 10-79 p13
          +Gr 10-79 p723   +RR 10-79 p106
          +-HFN 11-79 p151   +SFC 5-25-80 p41
111 2327
4009 KUBIK: Inventions (2). KURZ: Sonata, violin and piano. RIEDLBAUCH:
        Allegri e pastorali. RYBAR: Elementi continuali (7). SLAVICKY:
        Brightening I. Jan Riedlbauch, flt; Milan Zelenka, gtr; Jana

Nacovska, pno; Jiri Tomacek, vln; Josef Ruzicka, pno; New Prague
Trio, Quintet '74.
+FF 9/10-80 p208   /+NR 8-80 p8

SWINSTY RECORDS

FEW 01
4010 DUSSEK: Rondo on "O dear what can the matter be". FIELD: Fantasie,
op. 3. HERZ: Contradanses: Le pantalon, La poule, La trenise,
Valse. KALKBRENNER: Nocturne, op. 129. PINTO: Sonata, op. 3,
no. 2: Romance. REISSIGER: A favourite waltz by Weber. Alan
Cuckston, pno.
-FF 7/8-80 p166   +RR 3-80 p77

TELARC

DC 10043
4011 BARBER: Commando march. GANNE: Marche Lorraine. GRAFULLA: Washing-
ton greys. FUCIK: Florentiner, op. 214. KING: Barnum and Bail-
ey's favorite. LEEMANS: Belgian paratroopers. SEITZ: University
of Pennsylvania march. SOUSA: The stars and stripes forever.
STRAUSS, J. I: Radtezky march, op. 228. VAUGHAN WILLIAMS: Sea
songs. ZIMMERMANN: Anchors away (Miles). Cleveland Symphony
Winds; Frederick Fennell.
+-ARG 9-79 p53   +NR 10-80 p15
+FF 7/8-79 p129   +HFN 8-80 p105
+Gr 4-80 p1597   ++RR 4-80 p56
+HF 11-79 p114

TELEFUNKEN

EK 6-35417 (2)
4012 GALLOT: Dauphine, gavotte. Le bout de l'an de M. Gaultier. Le
Doge de Venice, chaconne sans chanterelle. La divine, sarabande.
Prelude. Tombeau de Madame, courante. Le tombeau de muses, allemande. GAULTIER, D.: La chevre canaries. Cleopatre amante,
courante. Tombeau de Mademoiselle Gaultier. GAULTIER, E.: Prelude. Testament de Mezangeau, gigue. Canaries. Courante. Tombeau de Mezangeau. MOUTON: Canarie. Les cabrioles, courante.
Gavotte. Prelude. La princesse, sarabande. Tombeau de Gogo,
allemande. Tombeau de Madam, pavanne. VISEE: Courante. Gigue
grave. Prelude. Rondeau. Tombeau de vieux Gallot, allemande.
Tombeau de M. Mouton, allemande. Tombeau de du But, allemande.
Tombeau de Tonty, allemande. La Montsermeil, rondeau. La Veni-
tienne de M. Fourqueray. La muzette de M. Forquerary. Toyohiko
Satoh, lt.
-FF 9/10-80 p273   ++RR 7-79 p90
++Gr 8-79 p357   +St 2-80 p141
+HFN 8-79 p117
6-42074 Tape (c) 4-42074
4013 BULL: Lord Lumley's paven and galliard. Prelude and fantasia. The
prince's galliard. GIBBONS: Fantasia, A minor. Ground, A minor.
LASSUS: Susanne un jour. MORLEY: Lachrymae pavane and galliard.

SCHEIDT: Bergamasca. SWEELINCK: Praeludium toccata. TISDALE:
Coranto. ANON.: Almains (2). Coranto. Irish dance. The king's
morisco. The Lord's masque. Miserere. Bradford Tracey, virginal.
          +FF 5/6-80 p192   +St 5-80 p94

AW 6-42129
4014 DRAGHI: Trio sonata, G minor. HILTON: Fantasies, nos. 1-3. LOCKE:
Suites, nos. 1 and 2.   PURCEL: Chaconne "Two in one upon a
ground". Symphonies, nos. 1 and 2. WILLIAMS: Sonata, recorder,
no. 4, A minor. Quadro Hotteterre.
          +FF 3/4-80 p193   +-MM 9-78 p29
          +Gr 9-77 p452   +RR 9-77 p78
          +HFN 9-77 p141

AW 6-42229
4015 CORELLI: Sonata, op. 2, no. 12, G major: Ciacona. DORNEL: Sonata,
op. 3, no. 2, D major. HACQUART: Sonata, op. 3, no. 2, F major.
HANDEL: Trio sonata, op. 2, no. 6, G major. UCCELLINI: Sonata,
op. 5, B flat major. Musica da Camera, Amsterdam; Ton Koopman.
          +FF 3/4-80 p193   +HFN 9-78 p151
          +Gr 11-78 p921   ++RR 9-78 p77

AP 6-42364
4016 BERIO: Sequenza I. EDER: Sonatine. JOLIVET: Suite en concert.
MARTIN: Ballade. MESSIAEN: Le merle noir. Wolfgang Schulz, flt;
Helmut Deutsch, pno; Kurt Prihode, Roland Altmann, Gerald Fromme,
Rudolf Schmidinger, perc.
          ++FF 7/8-80 p182   +RR 9-79 p102
          +Gr 11-79 p873   ++SFC 4-6-80 p31
          +HFN 8-79 p119

6-42365 Tape (c) 4-43265
4017 DORNEL: Sonata, 3 recorders, B flat major. MATTHESON: Sonata, op.
1, no. 3, G minor. PURCELL: Chaconne, F major. RICCIO: La ros-
ignola. Sonata a 4, A minor. SCHEIDT: Paduan a 4, D minor.
SCARLATTI, A.: Sonata, 3 recorders, F major. ANON.: Sonata, 3
recorders, G major. Frans Bruggen, rec; Hotteterre Quartet.
          ++FF 5/6-80 p193   ++St 6-80 p126

                    THEATRE RECORDS

QCR 8818 (2)
4018 BAIRSTOW: Jesu the very though of thee. ELGAR: The apostles: Prologue. Give unto the Lord. GARDINER: Evening hymn. HARRIS,
W.H.: Faire is the heaven. HOWELLS: Like as the hart. SCHOLE-
FIELD: The day thou gavest. STANFORD: Magnificat and nunc dimittis, G major. VAUGHAN WILLIAMS: Lord thou hast been our refuge. Hymns: Dear lord and father of mankind. Phillip Coad,
org; Queens College Choir; Stephen Armstrong.
          +-HFN 5-80 p129   +-RR 6-80 p88

                    TITANIC

TI 35
4019 BACH: Sonata, flute and harpsichord, S 1035, F major. CORELLI:
Sonata, op. 5, no. 12, G minor. DE LA BARRE: Suite, no. 9, G

G major. LOEILLET: Sonata, recorder, op. 3, no. 4, A minor.
TELEMANN: Sonata, recorder, D minor. Marion Verbruggen, rec;
John Gibbons, hpd; Christina Mahler, vlc.
+AR 8-80 p85   +FF 9/10-80 p280

TI 37
4020 CABEZON: Diferencias sobre el canto Llano del caballero. CORREA DE
ARAUXO: Tiento de medio registro. GABRIELI, A.: Cancone francese.
MERULO: Toccata quarta del 6 tono. PASQUINI: Partita sopra al
Aria della Folia da Espagna. SCHEIDT: Hymnus de Sancto spiritu:
Veni creator spiritus. SWEELINCK: Mein junges Leben hat ein End.
Psalm, no. 36. VALENTE: Romanesca. Mireille Lagace, org.
-FF 9/10-80 p269

TOCCATA

53623
4021 BACH, J.C.: Aria and 15 variations, A minor. BUXTEHUDE: Prelude and
fugue, G minor. FISCHER: Musikalisches Blumenbuschlein: Suite,
no. 6, D major. HANDEL: Suite, harpsichord, no. 3, D minor.
ZACHAU: Suite, B minor. Bradford Tracy, hpd.
+HFN 5-80 p131   +MQ 10-77 p570

TOWERHILL

T 1002
4022 ALAIN: Choral Dorien, op. 47. LANGLAIS: Chant de paix. LIDON:
Sonata de primo tono. MENDELSSOHN: Preludes and fugues, op. 37,
C minor, G major, D minor. PASQUINI: Partita sopra la Aria della
Folia de Espagna. VALENTE: La Romenesca con cinque mutanze.
VIERNE: Berceuse. John Rose, org.
+-ARG 1-80 p50   +-MU 2-80 p10
+-FF 9/10-80 p266

TURNABOUT

TV 34685
4023 BACEWICZ: Kleine Triptychon. BACKER-GRONDAHL: Undomssang, op. 36,
no. 6. Visnet, op. 39, no. 9. BEACH: Improvisation, op. 118.
CARRENO: Reverie-Barcarolle "Venise", op. 33. Intermezzo scherz-
so, op. 34. CIBBINI-KOZELUH: Valses, op. 6 (6). CHAMINADE:
Air de ballet, no. 3, op. 47. L'Enjoleuse, op. 50. JACQUET DE
LA GUERRE: Rondeau, G minor. MENDELSSOHN, F.: Prelude, E minor.
SCHUMANN, C.: Variations on a theme by Robert Schumann, op. 20.
SZYMANOWSKA: Nocturnes, B flat major, A flat major. TAILLEFERRE:
Sicilienne. VON BRONSART: Valse caprice. VON PARADIS: Sicili-
enne, E flat major. Rosario Marciano, pno.
+-FF 11/12-79 p164   +-NYT 4-13-79 pD26
+-MUM 1/2-80 p34

TV 34709
4024 BYRD: Ah silly soul; All is as a sea; O dear life; When I was other-
wise. COPERARIO: Fantasy, 6 viols, F major. DOWLAND: Earl of
Essex, his galliard. John Langton's pavan. FERRABOSCO: Fantasy.

GIBBONS: In nomine. GILES: Cease now vain thoughts. JENKINS:
Fantasia. LEETHERLAND: Pavan. PURCELL: Fantasias, D minor, G
major. In nomine. ANON.: O death rock me to sleep. James Bowman, c-t; English Consort of Viols.
<table>
<tr><td>+FF 9/10-79 p182</td><td>+-HFN 4-80 p115</td></tr>
<tr><td>+Gr 4-80 p1584</td><td>+RR 6-80 p68</td></tr>
</table>

TV 34727
4025 BLUMENFELD: Rilke. CAGE: Wonderful widow of 18 springs. CARTER:
Tell me where is fancy bred. HARRISON: Serenade. IMBRIE: Tell
me where is fancy bred. KOLB: The sentences. SCHUMAN: Orpheus
and his lute. SMITH: Steps. STAROBIN: Song for David. STRA-
VINSKY: Songs (4). Rosalind Rees, s; David Starobin, gtr.
<table>
<tr><td>+MQ 1-80 p153</td><td>+NR 3-79 p13</td></tr>
</table>

TV 34755
4026 BACH, J.C. Sonata, 2 organs, C major. CHERUBINI: Sonata, 2 organs,
G major. LUCHINETTI: Sonata, 2 organs, D major. PIAZZA: Son-
ata, 2 organs, F major. ANON.: Intradas, no. 1, D major; no. 5,
D major; no. 14, D major. Rudolf Ewerhart, Hans Haselbock, org;
Wolfgard Bash, Albert Oesterle, clarin tpts; Walter Lexutt, Ralf
Wanre, hn; Karl Peinkofer, timpani.
                    +-FF 9/10-80 p271

TV 34762
4027 BACH: Brandenburg concerto, no. 6, S 1051, B major: Allegro II.
Concerto, harpsichord, S 971, F major: Allegro. CORELLI: Concerto grosso, op. 6, no. 8, G major/minor: Pastorale. CORRETTE:
Concerto, flute and harpsichord, op. 26, no. 6, D minor: Allegro.
DAQUIN: Le coucou. HANDEL: Concerto, harp, op. 4, no. 6, B flat
major: Allegro. Concerto grosso, op. 6, no. 12, B minor: Allegro. Water music: Allegro. LOCATELLI: Concerto, violin, op. 3,
no. 2: Andante capriccio. MANFREDINI: Concerti grossi, op. 3,
no. 12, C major: Pastorale; Allegro. MARCELLO, A.: Concerto,
oboe, op. 1, D minor: Adagio. TELEMANN: Concerto, viola: Allegro. VIVALDI: concerto, mandolin: Allegro. Concerto, 2 trumpets:
Allegro. Concerto, op. 8: Spring allegro. Various soloists,
orchestras and conductors.
                    +-FF 7/8-80 p188

                              UNICORN

RHS 354 Tape (c) UKC 354
4028 BASHFORD: Cavalry walk. BEETHOVEN: Zapfenstreich, no. 2, C major.
BLISS: Music for an investiture. CLARKE: Trumpet voluntary.
JOHNSON: Vivat regina, site. PLANQUETTE: Le regiment de Sambre
et meuse (arr. Rauski). REED: The music makers. SHARPE: Nulli
secundus. Royal jubilee. (arr. Sharpe): Ceremonial occasion.
Soldiers: Fantasia. SOUSA: Stars and stripes forever. STARKE:
The sword and lance. YOUNG: Kneller Hall slow march. TRAD.:
The buff coat hath no fellow. The girl I left behind me. Lilli-
burlero. The royal Scots polka. Royal Military School of Music
Band and Trumpeters; Caledonian Highlanders Fifes and Drums;
Trevor Sharpe.
<table>
<tr><td>+-FF 5/6-80 p197</td><td>++RR 8-78 p54</td></tr>
<tr><td>+Gr 7-78 p262</td><td>++SFC 12-30-79 p33</td></tr>
<tr><td>+HFN 12-80 p159 tape</td><td>+St 4-80 p140</td></tr>
</table>

MS 1000
4029 ALBINONI: Adagio, G minor (arr. Giazotto). BACH: Suite, orchestra,
     S 1068, D major: Air on the G string. BARRIOS: Aconquija Maxixa.
     BOYCE: Symphony, no. 4, F major. CLARKE: Trumpet voluntary.
     DEBUSSY: Suite bergamasque: Clair de lune. GLUCK: Orfeo ed Euri-
     dice: Dance of the blessed spirits. JACOB: Concertino, clarinet:
     3rd and 4th movements. LAURO: Vals criollo. SAINT-SAENS: Carni-
     val of the animaux: The swan. VAUGHAN WILLIAMS: Fantasia on
     Greensleeves. VIVALDI: Concerti, op. 8: Winter. PARADIS: Sici-
     lienne (arr. Dushkin). Leon Goossens, ob; Sidonie Goossens, hp;
     John Williams, gtr; John Wilbraham, tpt; Jack Brymer, clt; Lon-
     don Junior Chamber Orchestra; Malcolm Henderson.
                    +Gr 2-80 p1305   +RR 12-79 p54
                    +HFN 12-79 p175

                    UNITED ARTISTS

UACL 10010 (also Peters PLE 112)
4030 CILEA: L'Arlesiana: E la solita storia. DONIZETTI: Lucia di Lam-
     mermoor: Tombe degl'ave miei...Fra poco a me ricovere. FLOTOW:
     Martha: Ach so fromm. GOUNOD: Faust: C'est ici...Salut demeure
     chaste et pure. MASSENET: Werther: Pourquoi me reveiller. PUC-
     CINI: La boheme: Che gelida manina. Tosca: E lucevan le stelle.
     VERDI: Rigoletto: Questa o quella; Ella mi fu rapita...Parmi
     veder le lagrime. La traviata: Lunga da lei...De miei bollenti
     spiriti. Petr Dvorsky, t; Bratislava Radio Orchestra; Ondrej
     Lenard.
                    +-Gr 12-79 p1055   +-ON 2-23-80 p45
                    +-HFN 6-79 p117   +-RR 6-79 p64

                    UNIVERSITY OF EAST ANGLIA

UEA 78001
4031 BARTOLINO DA PADOVA: Per un verde boschetto. GIOVANNI DA CASCIA:
     De come dolcemente. DONATO DA FIRENZE: Come in sul fonte. JAC-
     OPO DA BOLOGNA: Vola el bel sparve. I'Sent'za. LANDINI: Caro
     signor pales. Donna i prego. In somm' alteca. Ochi dolenti
     mie. ANON.: Estampitta Isabella. La Manfredina. Su la Rivera.
     Landini Consort; Peter Syrus.
                    +RR 2-80 p91

                    UNIVERSITY OF MICHIGAN RECORDS

SM 0011
4032 BYRD: Agnus Dei (Anon.). HOLMES: Quintet, tubas. MOZART: The mari-
     age of Figaro, K 492: Overture (Gottschalk). PAYNE: Quartet,
     tuba. STEVENS: Manhattan suite. University of Michigan Tuba
     and Euphonium Ensemble; Abe Torchinsky.
                    +FF 7/8-80 p185

URSINA MOTETTE

M 1006
4033 BAUMANN: Sonatina, organ, no. 2: Toccata II, allegro vivace. Suite,
op. 67, no. 1: Toccata I, agitato brillante. BOELLMANN: Suite
gothique, op. 25: Toccata. GIGOUT: Pieces, organ, no. 4, B min-
or: Toccata. LANGLAIS: Incantataion pour un jour saint. Paraphrases Gregoriennes, op. 5: Te deum. VIERNE: Fantasiestucke,
op. 51, A minor: Andantino. Fantasiestucke, op. 53: Toccata.
WIDOR: Symphony, organ, no. 5, op. 42, no. 1, F major: Toccata.
Ludger Mai, org.
      +ARG 2-80 p48   +MU 1-78 p15
      +FF 11/12-79 p160

M 1007
4034 BACH: Canons, S 1087 (14). BLANCO: Concerto, organ, G major. BOS-
SLER: Kaleidoskop. HASSLER: Canzona, C major. HEILMANN: Passacaglia. MOZART: Fugue, K 426, C minor. Helmut Scheller, Hermann
Harrassowitz, org.
      +-ARG 2-80 p48   +-FF 1/2-80 p169

M 1008
4035 AHRENS: Es kommt ein Schiff geladen. BRAHMS: Chorale preludes, op.
122: Herzliebster Jesu was hast du verbrochen; O Welt ich muss
dich lassen; Schmucke dich o liebe Seele; Herzlich tut mich ver-
lange. Aus vier fruhe Kompositionen: O Traurigkeit o Herzelied.
BUXTEHUDE: Nun bitten wir den heiligen Geist. FLEURY: Variations
sur un Noel Bourguignon. PEPPING: Sollt ich meinem Gott ich singen. REGER: Valet will ich dir geben; Wunderbarer Konig. SCHE-
IDEMANN: Es ist gewisslich an der Zeit. SCHROEDER: Gott heilger
Schopfer aller Stern. ZEHM: Choralbearbeitung: Erschienen ist der
herrliche Tag. ANON.: Christ ist erstanden. Herbert Heine, Hans
Kunz, Peter Kempin, Hanns Brendel, org.
      +ARG 9-80 p48   /FF 7/8-80 p169

M 1018
4036 Improvisations: Es ist ein Reis entsprungen; Lasst uns das Kindlein
wiegen; Zu Betlehem geboren; In dulci jubilo; Preis sei Gott;
Lobt Gott ihr Christen allzugleich; Partita uber "O Jesulein
suss"; Gelobet seist du Jesu Christ; Kleine Tripelfuge; Auf gla-
bige Seelen; Von Himmel hoch; Fier Intermezzi; Fantasia meditat-
iva super Puer natus est und Stille Nacht. Heinz Bernhard Orlinski, org.
      +FF 9/10-80 p269

M 1020
4037 BACH: Chorale preludes, S 645, Wachet auf ruft uns die Stimme; S
667, Komm Gott Schopfer; S 668, Vor deinen Thron tret ich hiermit.
BRANDMULLER: Hommage a Perotin. COUPERIN, R.: Messe pour les
paroisses: Gloria; Kyrie. FRANCK: Chorale, no. 2, B minor.
IMPROVISATION: Noel musicale. Theo Brandmuller, org.
      +FF 9/10-80 p269   +MJ 11-80 p18

M 1021
4038 BACH: Concerto, organ, A minor (Vivaldi). KELLNER: Jesu meine
Zuversicht. Prelude, C major. KREBS: Mein Gott das Herze bring
ich dir. Fantasia, F major. Trio, C minor. MUTHEL: O Traurigkeit. VIERLING: Trio, C major. Ewald Kooiman, org.
      +-FF 9/10-80 p268   ++MU 8-79 p13

M 1030
4039 BACH: Chorale prelude, S 605, Der Tag der ist so freudenreich.
CLERAMBAULT: Suite du 2nd ton. DAQUIN: Livre de Noels, no. 6.
DUPRE: Ballade. Canzona. Sortie. STRATEGIER: Inventions: En-
tree. TELEMANN: Vater unser im Himmelreich. WALTHER, J.G.: Lobe
den Herren den machitgen Konig der Ehren. Johannes Ricken, org;
Makiko Takeda, pno.
+ARG 10-80 p53   +FF 7/8-80 p169

M 2001
4040 ALCOCK: Voluntary, D major. BUXTEHUDE: Erschienen ist der herrlich
Tag. MARTINI: Largo, E major. TELEMANN: Allein Gott in der Hoh
sei Ehr. Air de trompette, C major. Marches (4). Vater unser
im Himmelreich. WALOND: Voluntary, no. 3, D minor. ZIPOLI: Pastorale, C major. Wolfgang Brasch, tpt; Johannes Ricken, org.
+MU 11-80 p17

VANGUARD

VSD 71223
4041 AZZAIOLO: Chi passa per sta strada. DALZA: Recercar. Tastar de
corde. DUNSTABLE: O Rosa bella. CERTON: J'ay le rebours. FRYE:
Tout a par moy. MORTON: Il sera pour vous conbatu, L'ome arme.
OTHMAYR: Mir ist ein feins Brauns Maidelein. SENFL: Es taget vor
dem Walde. SERMISY: Dont vient cela. VAQUEIRAS: Kalenda miea.
ANON.: Aime sospiri. Amor potest, ad amorem. Blame not my lute.
Belle qui tiens ma vie. Amors amors. Danse royale. Es taget
vor dem Walde. Galliard after Lavecha. L'Homme arme. Hoftanz
und Haupfauff. Me lykyth ever. Pavana "La bataille". Patrie
pacis. Saltarello. Tant apart. Musica Reservata; Michael Mor-
row.
+ARG 11-80 p43   +NYT 8-17-80 pD18
+FF 11/12-80 p207   ++St 11-80 p90
+NR 10-80 p8

VSD 71254
4042 BACH: Fantasia, C major. Fugue, G minor. CALVERT: Chanson melancolique. GABRIELI, G.: Canzona prima a cinque. HOLBORNE: Muy
linda. Galliard. JOPLIN: the favorite. Pleasant moments.
JOSQUIN DES PREZ: Royal fanfare. LEJEUNE: Revecy venir du printemps. MCCAULEY: Miniature overture. MENDEZ: La virgin de la
macarena. PEZEL: Intradas, nos. 1, 3, 8, 10. Sarabande.
SCHEIDT: Canzaona Aechiopicam. Galliard battaglia. Canadian
Brass.
+-FF 7/8-80 p186   +-NR 7-80 p6

VSD 71262
4043 BULL: The king's hunt. My grief. My self. BYRD: Carmans whistle.
Lavolta, Lady Morley. Rowland, or Lord Willoughby's welcome
home. Watkin's ale (attrib.). DOWLAND (arr. Randall): Can she
excuse lachrimae and galliard. FARNABY: Loath to depart. Mus-
cadin, or Kempe's morris. GIBBONS: The fairest nymph. Lord
Salisburgy's pavan and galliard. The woods so wild. TALLIS: O
ye tender babes. TOMKINS: Barafostus dream. ANON.: My Lady
Careys dompe. Trevor Pinnock, hpd, virginal.
+ARG 5-80 p47   +NR 3-80 p15
+-FF 3/4-80 p181   +St 5-80 p94
+-HF 4-80 p102

VSD 79429
4044 ARNDT: Marionette. AUFDERHEIDE: Pelham waltzes. EUROPE: Castles
     half and half. FARWELL: Wa-Wan choral. JOPLIN: Bethena. Sol-
     ace. MACDOWELL: Woodland sketches, op. 51: To a wild rose.
     NEVIN: Ein Liechen. O'HARA: The perfect melody. RUIFROK: Song
     without words, op. 5, no. 2. Minuet, op. 4, no. 1. Max Morath,
     pno.
              +-FF 7/8-80 p165   +ARG 10-80 p51

                              VARESE

DBX VCDM 1000.20/PS 1008
4045 BLISS: Things to come: Epilogue. COPLAND: The red pony: Morning
     on the ranch. GOULD: Windjammer: Main theme. MOROSS: The big
     country: Main theme. NEWMAN: Airport: Main theme. ROZSA: That
     Hamilton woman: Love theme. Tribute to a badman: suite. VAUGHAN
     WILLIAMS: The 49th parallel: Prelude and fugue. WALTON: Spit-
     fire: Prelude and fugue. WILLIAMS: Star wars: Main theme. LSO;
     Morton Gould.
              +-FF 7/8-80 p193   +-St 11-80 p94

                              VISTA

VPS 1033
4046 COUPERIN: Dialogue sur les grands jeux. KARG-ELERT: Jerusalem, du
     hochgebaute Stadt, op. 65. MESSIAEN: La nativite du Seigneur:
     Dieu parmi nous. PEETERS: Koncertstuck, op. 52a. SALOME: Grand
     choeur. WILLAN: Introduction, passacaglia and fugue, E flat min-
     or. WILLS: Piece, organ: Processional. Richard Galloway, David
     Harrison, Ronald Perrin, John Turner, Allan Wicks, Arthur Wills,
     org.
              *Gr 3-77 p1444   ++NR 2-80 p13
              +-HF 7-77 p95   +-RR 4-77 p77
              +MU 8-77 p10

VPS 1034
4047 BENNETT: Alba. GUILMANT: Sonata, organ, no. 3, op. 56, C minor.
     LANG: Tuba tune, op. 15, D major. LEIGHTON: Festival fanfare.
     PARRY: Toccata and fugue (The wanderer). VIERNE: Pieces en style
     libre, op. 31: Prelude. YON: Toccatina, flute. Jonathon Bielby,
     org.
              +Gr 3-77 p1446   ++NR 2-80 p13
              +-HF 7-77 p95   +RR 4-77 p76
              +MU 8-77 p10

VPS 1042
4048 GUILMANT: Sonata, organ, no. 5, op. 80, C minor. HOLLINS: Trumpet
     minuet. HARWOOD: Paean, op. 15, no. 2. KELLNER: Was Gott tut.
     SWEELINCK: Balletto del Granduca. Peter Goodman, org.
              +Gr 3-77 p1444   +MU 7-77 p14
              +-HF 7-77 p95   +NR 1-80 p12
              +HFN 4-77 p141   +RR 3-77 p82

VPS 1045
4049 BACH: Fugue sopra il Magnificat, S 733. DUPRE: Lamento. HOWELLS:
     Rhapsody, op. 17, no. 3. PACHELBEL: Ciacona, D minor. PARRY:

Chorale prelude, no. 4: The old 104th. When I survey the wondrous cross, chorale fantasia. STANFORD: Sonata britannica, op.
152, D minor: Benedictus. VIERNE: Fantasiestucke, op. 54: Carillon de Westminster. Garth Benson, org.
          +NR 2-80 p12

VPS 1046
4050 COOK: Fanfare, organ. CRESTON: Toccata. DE MONFRED: In paradisum.
REUBKE: Sonata on the 94th psalm. THALBEN-BALL: Tune, E major.
TREDINNICK: Brief encounters. George Thalben-Ball, org.
          +Gr 12-77 p1118   +MU 4-78 p14
          ++HF 8-78 p93   +NR 2-80 p12
          +HFN 12-77 p175   +RR 11-77 p91

VPS 1047
4051 GIBBONS: Fantasia of 4 parts. HEWITT-JONES: Fanfare. HOWELLS:
Psalm prelude, op. 32, no. 1. MIDDLETON: Fantasie. PURCELL:
Voluntary, G major. STANFORD: Postlude, D minor. STANLEY: Voluntary, op. 5, no. 1, C major. VAUGHAN-WILLIAMS: Prelude on
Welsh hymn tunes: Rhosymedre. WEITZ: Grand choeur. ANON.: Upon
la mi re. Christopher Herrick, org.
          +Gr 11-77 p867   +NR 2-80 p12
          +-HFN 12-77 p175   +-RR 11-77 p93
          +MU 4-78 p14

VPS 1051
4052 BRIDGE: First book of organ pieces. PARRY: Chorale prelude on "St.
Thomas". STANFORD: Postlude, D minor. VIERNE: Symphony, no. 3,
op. 28, F minor. WHITLOCK: Plymouth suite: Salix. Geoffrey
Tristram, org.
          +Gr 11-77 p868   ++NR 4-80 p14
          +-HFN 12-77 p175   +-RR 11-77 p92

VPS 1059
4053 BACH: Cantata, no. 80, Ein feste Burg ist unser Gott. DAVIES: Interlude, C major. EDMUNDSON: Vom Himmel hoch. KARG-ELERT: Chorale improvisation, op. 65, no. 5. LANG: Tuba tune, op. 15, D
major. SCHUMANN: Sketch, op. 58, no. 2, C major. THALBEN BALL:
Elegy. Variations on a theme by Paganini. Birmingham pieces:
Poema; Toccata Beorma. WEITZ: Symphony, no. 1: Ave maris stella,
final movement. George Thalben Ball, org.
          ++ARG 3-80 p50   +-HFN 8-79 p119
          +Gr 4-79 p1749   ++NR 5-80 p14

VPS 1060
4054 BACH: Chorale prelude, S 680, Wir glauben all an einen Gott. COUP-
ERIN, F.: Plein jeu. Recit de tierce en taille. DAQUIN: Noel
suisse. HINE: A flute piece. HOWELLS: Master Tallis testament.
MUSHEL: Toccata. PIERNE: Pieces, op. 29 (3). VERSCHRAEGEN: Partita octavi toni super Veni Creator. WIDOR: Symphony, organ, no.
6, op. 42, no. 2, G major: Allegro. Donald Hunt, John Sanders,
Roy Massey, org.
          +-Gr 12-77 p1118   +NR 8-80 p13
          +-HFN 2-78 p113   /-RR 11-77 p93

VPS 1064
4055 DURUFLE: Prelude and fugue on the name Alain, op. 7. JANACEK:
Chorale preludes: Auf Fels gebaut; O Jesu Christ. JONGEN: Im-
promptu-Caprice, op. 37, no. 2. MULET: Tu es petra. PEETERS:
Chorale prelude on "How brightly shines the morning star", op.
68, no. 7. WIDOR: Symphony, organ, no. 5, op. 42, no. 1, F

major: Toccata. Harrison Oxley, org.
               +FF 11/12-79 p162   +NR 8-80 p13
               +HFN 8-79 p117

VPS 1065
4056 BACH: Komm heiliger Geist fantasia, S 651. EDMUNDSON: Gargoyles.
     KARGES: O mensch bewein. PEETERS: Ave maris stella, op. 28.
     SUNDERLAND: Fanfare, march and fugue. VIERNE: Fantasiestucke,
     op. 54: Carillon de Westminster. WIDOR: Symphony, no. 6, op.
     42, B major: Finale. WILLAN: Elegy and chaconne. Mangus Black,
     Melville Cook, Garth Benson, Ray Maulkin, Raymond Sunderland,
     Conrad Eden, org.
               -FF 11/12-79 p162   +NR 5-80 p14
               +-HFN 8-79 p117

VPS 1070 Tape (c) CPS 1070
4057 FRANCK: Fantaisie, A major. KING: Fanfare to the tongue of fires.
     REGER: Toccata and fugue, op. 59, no. 5. SIFLER: The despair
     and agony of Dachau as envisioned by Psalm XXII. SOWERBY: Pas-
     sacaglia. ANON.: The Agincourt hymn (arr. Swann). Frederick
     Swann, org.
               +ARG 10-79 p50   ++MU 2-79 p11
               +Gr 1-79 p1310   +NR 7-80 p12
               +HF 5-79 p75   ++RR 12-78 p96
               +HFN 1-79 p126

VPS 1072
4058 CASALS: O vos omnes. DIRKSEN: Christ our passover. FRIEDELL: The
     way to Jerusalem. LEISRING: O sons and daughters. PETRICH: Ah
     holy Jesus. OSSEWAARDE: Fanfare for Easter Day. PARKER: Love
     is come again. SCHEIN: Intrada. WYTON: Palm Sunday. This joy-
     ful Eastertide. HYMNS: All glory laud and honor; Christ the Lord
     is risen today. Riverside Church Choir; Frederick Swann, org
     and cond.
               ++MU 5-80 p12

VPS 1073
4059 DAVIE: Come holy ghost; There is a balm. ELGAR: Apostles: Prologue.
     RIDOUT: Let us with a gladsome mind. VAUGHAN WILLIAMS: Festival
     Te deum. PILGRIM HYMNAL: Hymns nos. 1, 12-13, 15, 23, 58, 84,
     227. Riverside Church Choir; Frederick Swann, org and cond.
               ++MU 5-80 p12

VPS 1075
4060 BOELY: Reveillez-vous, pastoreaux. COUPERIN, L.: Fantaisie. DAND-
     RIEU: Fugue sur "Ave maris stella". DUPRE: Antiennes: Lumen ad
     revelationem. FRANCK: Andantino poco mosso. Andante cantabile
     (arr. Vierne). GUILMANT: Sonata, organ, no. 1, op. 42, D minor:
     Pastorale. MESSIAEN: La nativite du Seigneur: Desseins eternels.
     RAISON: Trio en passacaille. SAINT-SAENS: Improvisation. TOUR-
     NEMIRE: L'Orgue mystique: Fantaisie sur le Te Deum; Guirlandes
     alleluiatiques. WIDOR: Symphony, organ, op. 73: Final. ANON.:
     Verses on the Te Deum. Robert Grogan, org.
               +-ARG 10-79 p50   ++MU 2-79 p13
               +Gr 1-79 p1309   +NR 7-80 p12
               +-HF 5-79 p76   +RR 12-78 p95
               +HFN 1-79 p126

VPS 1076
4061 ALAIN: Litanies, op. 79. BACH: Cantata, no. 29: Sinfonia (arr.
     Dupre). CORRETTE, M.: A la venue de Noel. DAQUIN: Noel etran-

ger. DURUFLE: Prelude et fugue sur le nom d'Alain, op. 7.
FRANCK: Chorale, no. 2, B minor. PAINE: Concert variations on
"Austria", op. 3. Eileen Morris Gunther, org.

+—ARG 10-79 p50	+HFN 1-79 p126
+—FF 7/8-79 p117	+—MU 2-79 p13
+—Gr 1-79 p1310	+NR 7-80 p12
+HF 5-79 p75	+RR 12-78 p95

VPS 1091
4062 BACH: Fantasia, S 562, C minor. Trio sonata, no. 4, S 528, E minor.
GERMANI: Toccata. KARG-ELERT: Valse mignonne, op. 142, no. 2.
MESSIAEN: Diptyque. REGER: Pieces, organ, op. 59: Pastorale.
Pieces, organ, op. 80: Perpetuum mobile. Works, organ, op. 65:
Scherzo. Graham Barber, org.

+HFN 1-80 p117	+RR 4-80 p99
+MT 11-80 p712	

VPS 1097
4063 BREWER: Marche heroique. CORRETTE: Magnificat du 3 and 4 ton. DU-
BOIS: Toccata, G major. GUILMANT: Marche funebre et chant sera-
phique. LLOYD, C.H.: Allegretto. PARRY: Fantasia on the old
104th. SANDERS: Toccata. STANLEY: Trumpet voluntary, D major.
WESLEY, S.S.: An air composed for Holsworthy church bells with
variations. John Sanders, org.

+Gr 11-80 p704

VOX

SVBX 5112 (3)
4064 BEACH: Trio, op. 150. CARRENO: Quartet, strings, B minor. BOULAN-
GER, L.: Cortege. Nocturne. CHAMINADE: Trio, no. 1, op. 11, G
minor. MENDELSSOHN-HENSEL: Trio, op. 11, D minor. SCHUMANN, C.:
Trio, op. 17, G minor. TAILLEFERRE: Sonata, violin and piano, C
sharp minor. Joseph Roche, Robert Zelnick, vln; Tamas Strasser,
vla; Camilla Heller, vlc; Paul Freed, pno; Macalester Trio.

-FF 9/10-80 p287	+—NYT 4-13-79 pD26
+—HF 5-80 p86	

WEALDEN

WS 156
4065 BACH: Chorale prelude: In dulci jubilo: Fantasia. DARKE: In the
bleak midwinter. DAVIES: A sacred cradle song; O little town
of Bethlehem. HAAS: Kirchensonate on "In dulci jubilo". HOLST:
Chrissemas day in the morning; Jesu sweet; I sing of a maiden.
HOWELLS: Here is the little door. LEIGHTON: Lully lulla thou
little tiny child. MARTIN: Chants de Noel (3). POSTON: Jesus
Christ the apple tree. TERRY: Myn liking. TRAD: The holly and
the ivy; Infant holy infant lowly; Ding dong merrily on high;
Away in the manger. Charles Meinardi, Petronella Dittmer, vln;
Lyn McLarin, flt; Andrew Ball, pno; Richard Coulson, org; Kens-
ington Gore Singers; Petronella Dittmer.

+RR 1-80 p107

WS 190
4066 ALAIN: March in the style of Handel. CLARKE: Trumpet voluntary.

HAYDN: Allegretto, flute clock. KARG-ELERT: Marche triomphale.
KLICKA: Fantasia de concert, op. 65: Final. LOVELOCK: Concerto, organ: Toccata. NOVAK: Prelude on a Wallachian love song.
PEETERS: Chorale prelude, O God thou faithful God. PIERNE: Pastorale. SCHICKHARDT: La tricoteuse. VIERLING: Melodia. Christopher Daly Atkinson, org.
+-RR 4-80 p100

WESTMINSTER

MCA 1418 (From Decca DL 79427
4067 BUXTEHUDE: In dulci jubilo. CHARPENTIER: In nativitatem Domini
canticum. HAMMERSCHMIDT: O ihr lieben Hirten. HAYDN, M.: Lauft
ihr Hirten. PACHELBEL, C.: Magnificat. PRAETORIUS: In dulci
jubilo. SCHEIN: Vom Himmel hoch. Elizabeth Humes, s; Melinda
Kessler, alto; Anthony Tamburello, bs; Amor Artis Chorale; Johannes Somary.
+ARG 12-80 p53   +NR 11-80 p1
+FF 11/12-80 p200

WORLD RECORDS

SHB 55 (5) Tape (c) TGSHB 55 (From Columbia LX 880, 823/4, 541/2, 614,
317/8, 885, 530, 805, 702/3)
4068 BERLIOZ: The damnation of Faust: Hungarian march; Dance of the syl-
phs; Minuet of the will o' the wisps. BIZET: L'Arlesienne:
Suites, nos. 1 and 2. Carmen: Suite no. 1. The fair maid of
Perth: Suite. CHABRIER: Espana: Rhapsody. DEBUSSY: Prelude a
l'apres-midi d'un faune. GRETRY: Zemire et Azor: Air de ballet.
OFFENBACH: Les contes de Hoffman: Epilogue; Barcarolle; Entr'
acte; Duet, Giulietta and Hoffman; Intermezzo, Act 1. LPO;
Thomas Beecham.
+ARSC Vol 12, no. 3,   +HFN 12-79 p173
1980 p246   ++RR 1-80 p74
++Gr 9-79 p474

SH 306
4069 BALFE: Killarney. BINGHAM: Green isle of Erin. BARNARD: Come back
to Erin. CROUCH: Kathleen Mavourneen. DAVIS: A nation once
again. DE VERE: The snow breasted pearl. DUFFERIN: Terence's
farewell to Kathleen. GRAVES: The foggy dew; Trottin' to the
fair. JACKSON: The dear little shamrock. MACMURROUGH: Eileen
Aroon. NEEDHAM: My dark Rosaleen. TRAD.: The boys of Wexford;
The croppy boy; God save Ireland; Savourneen Deelish. John
McCormack, t; Orchestral accompaniment.
+-Gr 4-80 p1596   +RR 5-80 p101

SH 1001
4070 ATTERBERG: Symphony, no. 6, op. 31, C major. d'ALBERT: Tiefland,
excerpts. GERMAN: Have you news of my boy Jack. MISSA: Muguet-
te: Entr'acte. OFFENBACH: Les contes de Hoffman: Doll's song.
STRAUSS, J. II: Die Fledermaus, op. 363: Overture. STRAVINSKY:
L'Oiseau de eau: Dance of the firebird; Scherzo; Infernal dance.
RPO; Thomas Beecham.
+ARSC Vol. 12, no. 3, 1980 p240

SH 1002
4071 BERLIOZ: Le carnival romain, op. 9.   BORODIN: Prince Igor: Polov-
          stian dances (arr. Rimsky-Korsakov, Glazunov).   HANDEL: The ori-
          gin of design: Ballet suite (arr. Beecham).   Soloman: Arrival of
          the Queen of Sheba.   HAYDN: Symphony, no. 40, F major.   WEBER:
          Oberon: Overture.   RPO; Thomas Beecham.
                    +ARSC Vol 12, no. 3, 1980 p240

SECTION III

ANONYMOUS WORKS

A l'entrada del temps clar. See no. 3748

Adieu vous dy. See no. 3880

Agincourt hymn. See no. 4058. See no. 3566

Aime sospiri. See no. 4042

Al cjant il cjal. See no. 3626

All hail the days. See no. 3647

Alle psallite cum luya. See no. 3647

Alleluja Christus resurgens with the clausula "Mors". See no. 2500

Almaine. See no. 3840. See no. 4014

Altes Guggisbergerlied. See no. 3626

Amazing grace. See no. 3841. See no. 3973

Amor potest, ad amorem. See no. 4042

Amors amors. See no. 4042

Archers (The). See no. 776

As I lay. See no. 3647

Auf dem Berge da geht der Wind. See 3697

L'aultre jour par ung matin. See no. 3880

Ave Maria Keiserin. See no. 3763

Ave maris stella. See no. 3852. See no. 3960

Away in the manger. See no. 4066

Bankelsangerlieder: Sonata. See no. 3569.

Bankelsangerlieder: Sonata, excerpt. See no. 1027

Bard of Armagh. See no. 3947

Believe me if all those endearing young charms. See no. 3676. See no. 3947

Belle qui tiens ma vie. See no. 4042

Ben lo sa Dio. See no. 3880

Blame not my lute. See no. 4042

Blow the wind southerly. See no. 3551

Bourbon Street medley. See no. 3841

Boys of Wexford. See no. 4070

Branle de l'official. See no. 3647

Buff coat hath no fellow. See no. 4029

Carmen Hercules. See no. 3702

Carman's whistle. See no. 3840

Carnival in Venice. See no. 3644

Cherubic hymn: Old chant. See no. 776

Chi vuol lo mondo. See no. 3760

Chiara fontana. See no. 3880

Christ ist erstanden. See no. 4036

Codes Robertsbridge: Estampie. See no. 3626

Come and let us bless Joseph. See no. 776

Come live with me and be my love. See no. 3876

Come o'er the burn Bessy. See no. 3768

Coming thro the rye. See no. 3831

Comme femme desconfortee. See no. 3880.

Comme ung homme desconfortee. See no. 3880

Coranto. See no. 4014

Corde natus ex parentis. See no. 3823

Cornetta. See no. 3597

Credo. See no. 3548

Croppy boy. See no. 4070

Cum animadverterem. See no. 3960

Dance. See no. 3719

Danny boy. See no. 3874. See no. 3947

Dans Paris. See no. 3760

Danse royale. See no. 4042

Dark is my delight. See no. 3876

De battle ob Jerico. See no. 3527

De mon povoir vous veul complaire. See no. 3880

De ramis cadunt folia. See no. 3960

De tous biens playne. See no. 3597

De virgin Mary. See no. 3527

Deep river. See no. 3552. See no. 3788

Dic Christi veritas. See no. 2500

Ding dong merrily on high. See no. 4066

Dio s'e fatto fanciullo. See no. 391

Down the Petersky. See no. 3904

Doxology. See no. 3532

Dressed ship. See no. 3647

Dubinushka. See no. 3904

Ductia. See no. 3647. See no. 3864

Early one morning. See no. 3627

Echo song. See no. 3738

Edi beo thu. See no. 3647

En leve. See no. 3760

En l'ombre d'un buissonet. See no. 3702

England be glad. See no. 3768

English carols: Deck the halls; Ding dong merrily on high; Away in the manger; I saw three ships; Coventry carol; Once in Royal David's city; We've been awhile a-wandering. See no. 904

English dance. See no. 3795

English hymnal: Hymns, nos. 147, 148. See no. 3783

Entlaubet ist der Walde. See no. 3590

Eriskay love lilt. See no. 3738

Es taget vor dem Walde. See no. 4042

Estampie royal, no. 6. See no. 3864

Ex a. See no. 3909

Ex adae vito. See no. 3760

Faites moy scavoir de la belle. See no. 3880

Fandango. See no. 3647

Fanfare, 2 trumpets. See no. 4000

Fantasia. See no. 3852

Fantasia, no. 2. See no. 3806

Fenesta vascia. See no. 3667

Finir voglio la mia vita. See no. 3880

Flos in monte cernitur. See no. 3960

Fortuna desperata. See no. 2439

Fortune my foe. See no. 3853

Frere Jacques. See no. 3568

Fryar and the nun. See no. 3840

Gaillard after Lavecha. See no. 4042

Gairda la royne d'Escosse. See no. 3997

La gamba. See no. 3597

Le garcon jardinier. See no. 3760

The girl I left behind me. See no. 4029

Give rest with the righteous. See no. 776

Gloria. See no. 3548

God rest you merry gentlemen. See no. 3647

God save Ireland. See no. 4070

God save the queen. See no. 2388

Good King Wencelas, pavan. See no. 3647

Gracia de voi. See no. 3880

Gray's Inn masque. See no. 3997

Greek chant: Let my prayer be set forth. See no. 776

Green garters. See no. 3647

Greensleeves. See no. 3566. See no. 3626. See no. 3676. See no. 3717. See no. 3853. See no. 3909

Greensleeves to a ground. See no. 3593

The harp that once through Tara's halls. See no. 3947

Heinilla harkien kaukalon. See no. 3592

Helas je n'ay pas ose dire. See no. 3880

Helas n'aray je jamais mieulx. See no. 3880

Here we come a'wassailing. See no. 3647

Hey trolly lolly lo. See no. 3768

Hoftanz und Hupfauff. See no. 4042

Holly and the ivy. See no. 4066

L'Homme arme. See no. 4042

Hora gridar oime. See no. 3880

Hymns: All glory laud and honor; Christ the Lord is risen today. See no. 4059

I saw three ships. See no. 3647

I will give my love an apple. See no. 3527

I will walk with my love. See no. 3551

Ich armes Kauzlein kleine. See no. 3590

If I had wit for to endite. See no. 3768

In saeculum viellatoris. See no. 3960

In wilderness. See no. 3768

Infant holy. See no. 3823. See no. 4066

Intradas, D major.   See no. 2010

Intradas, no. 1, D major; no. 5, D major; no. 14, D major. See no. 4027

Io m'accorgo d'un altro amante. See no. 3612

Irish dance. See no. 4014

Irish gigue. See no. 3676

Irish march. See no. 3686

Istampitta Isabella. See no. 4032

Italiana. See no. 3612

J'ay pris amours. See no. 3880

Je suis trestout. See no. 3548

Jog on. See no. 3840

Joudu satakiel. See no. 3592

Kate of Bardie. See no. 1139

Kemp's kegge or jog. See no. 3840

King's morisco. See no. 4014

King's procession. See no. 2978

La-bas. See no. 3760

Lancashire pipes. See no. 1139

Let God arise and Christ is risen. See no. 776

Let not us that young men be. See no. 3768

Let us break bread together. See no. 3738

Lilliburlero. See no. 4029

Linzer Tanz. See no. 3759

Londonderry air. See no. 3743

Lord Mayor's swan hopping trumpet tune. See no. 3895

Lord's maske. See no. 4014

Love is little. See no. 3848

Ma bouche plaint. See no. 3880

Ma Lisette. See no. 3770

Ma tredol rosignol. See no. 766

Magne deus potencie. See no. 3960

Malurous qu'o uno fenno. See no. 3738

Manfredina (La). See no. 3647. See no. 4032

March. See no. 3848

Maria Herran piikanen. See no. 3592

Mass of Barcelona. See no. 766

Mater summi domini. See no. 3960

Me lykyth ever. See no. 4042

Messe de Toulouse. See no. 1006

Messe de Tournai. See no. 1006

Mi ranchito. See no. 3774

Miserere. See no. 4014

Miserere my maker. See no. 3997

Mon ami. See no. 3597

Monte Crappa. See no. 3626

Mort merce. See no. 3880

Motets: O virgo pia; Belle ysabellot

See no. 3910

Motherless child. See no. 3973

Muscain. See no. 3755

My delyght. See no. 3590

My Lady Careys dompe. See no. 3648. See no. 4044

My lagan love. See no. 3947

My love is like a red red rose. See no. 3627

National anthem. See no. 3959

Naves pont. See no. 3702

New nothing. See no. 3840

Next market day. See no. 3947

Night peece. See no. 3840

Nightingale (The). See no. 3590

Novel amor. See no. 1842

Novus miles sequitur. See no. 3960

Nowells galliard. See no. 3855

Nunc diem festis. See no. 3548

O death rock me asleep. See no. 3853. See no. 4025

O little town of Bethlehem. See no. 3823

O meschin inamorati. See no. 3880

O mistress mine. See no. 3840

O pelegrina luce. See no. 3880

O Roma nobilis. See no. 3960

O sanctissima. See no. 3697

O schlafe Gottlicher Knabe. See no. 3697

Olim in armonia. See no. 3960

Once as I remember. See no. 3530

Ophelia's songs. See no. 3853

Or ay je perdu. See no. 3880

Paduana del Re. See no. 3597

Pase el agoa, ma Julieta. See no. 3864

Passemezzo. See no. 3612

Pater Noster commiserans. See no. 2500

Patrie pacis. See no. 4042

Pavan "La bataille". See no. 4042

Pavaniglia. See no. 3956

Perla mia cara. See no. 3880

Petite mazurka. See no. 3760

Pilgrim Hymnal: Hymns nos. 1, 12-13, 15, 23, 58, 84, 227. See no. 4060

Pipes of Rumsey. See no. 1139

Plainsong: Domine quis habitabit. See no. 3992

Pointe or preludium to be played before the Lancashire pipes. See no. 1139

Polyphonic dances. See no. 3864

A poor soul sat sighing. See no.

3876
Pour leaulte maintenir. See no. 3548

Prayer for the captive. See no. 3848

Prince Eugen's march. See no. 3895

Psalm, no. 24. See no. 3783

Qui n'a le cuer rainpli. See no. 3548

Quinte estampie real. See no. 3960

Ranz des vaches (Le). See no. 3626

Ranz des vaches fribourgeois (Le). See no. 3627

Resurrection O Christ our saviour. See no. 776

Ricercare (17th century). See no. 3546

Robin Hood and the tanner. See no. 3840

Robin is to the green wood gone. See no. 3853

Rodrigo Martines. See no. 3864

Royal Scots polka. See no. 4029

Sacred ende. See no. 3719

Saltarello. See no. 3597. See no. 3647. See no. 3795. See no. 4042

Savourneen Deelish. See no. 4070

Scots marche. See no. 3590

Serviteur (Le). See no. 3597

She moved through the fair. See no. 3947

Shepherd's dance. See no. 3909

Si je perdu. See no. 3702

Simonov Monastery melody. See no. 776

Sinfonia, D major. See no. 3866

Snow is falling. See no. 3592

Sonata, piano, E flat major. See no. 1696

Sonata, 3 recorders, G major. See no. 4018

Songs (English medley): Deck the hall; Gloucestershire Wassail song; Swiss chansons (3); Adeste fideles; Joy to the world; El cant dels ocells; The twelve days of Christmas; O come Emanuel; Spanish medley: Las posades, Ya viene Lavieta, A la nanita nana; The first noel; Good King Wence-las; O holy night; We wish you a merry Christmas. See no. 3972

Sounds and sweet ayres. See no. 3840

Southwark Grenadiers march. See no.

3895
Souvent souspire mon cuer. See no. 3864

Spagnoletta. See no. 3956

Spanish ballad. See no. 3637

Spanish lady. See no. 3562

Staines Morris. See no. 3647

Stantipes. See no. 3960

Stella splendens. See no. 3760

Su la Rivera. See no. 4032

Sumer is icumen in. See no. 3971

Suo gan. See no. 3623

Supplication. See no. 3848

Supra il fieno colcato. See no. 391

Sur le Pont d'Avignon. See no. 3597

Syt willekomen heire Kirst. See no. 3763

Tant apart. See no. 4042

Tanze (2). See no. 3759

Terriblement suis fortunee. See no. 3880

There is no rose. See no. 3823

They won't let Masha walk by the brook. See no. 3770

Three blind mice. See no. 3882

Tijs soezas. See no. 3548

Time to pass with goodly sport. See no. 3768

Toe mpaloe. See no. 3548

Trottin to the fair. See no. 3947

Trumpet tune. See no. 3895

Una magica de ruda. See no. 3551

Up I arose in verno tempore. See no. 3768

Upon la mi re. See no. 4052

Va pur superba va. See no. 3956

Var halsad Herrens Moder. See no. 3934

Veris ad imperia. See no. 3960

Verses on the Te Deum. See no. 4061

Volga song. See no. 3909

Vray dieu d'amours. See no. 3880

Wanton season a galyarde. See no. 3590

Weit guy. See no. 3597

Welcome to our music feast. See no. 3741

What is't ye lack. See no. 3876

When Daphne from fair Phoebus did fly. See no. 3853

When love is kind. See no. 3774

Who shall have my fair lady. See no. 3768

Whoope de me no harm. See no. 3853

Why aske you. See no. 3755. See no. 3855

Wille wille will. See no. 3741
Willow song. See no. 3840
Wilson's wilde. See no. 3997
Yankee doodle. See no. 3971

Section IV

PERFORMER INDEX

Aachen Cathedral Choir 139, 3763
Abbado, Claudio, conductor 367, 597,
  868, 886, 2050, 2390, 2529, 2924,
  3139, 3361, 3705
Abbey of Bec Hellouin Schola 165,
  1394
Abbey Saint-Pierre de Solesmes Monk'
  s Choir 3911, 3913
Abdullayev, Kemal, conductor 2534
Abel, Bruce, bass-baritone 109
Abel, Jenny, violin 385, 848
Abendroth, Irene, contralto 3770
Aberg, Kerstin, piano 1962
Abravanel, Maurice conductor 1506,
  1545, 1571, 3118, 3313
Academy of Ancient Music 88, 230,
  1241, 1587, 1628, 1648, 1692,
  2368, 2369, 2577, 2578, 2579,
  2584, 2602, 3435
Academy of St. Martin-in-the-Fields
  65, 104, 232, 240, 298, 373, 446,
  734, 754, 786, 1233, 1264, 1538,
  1546, 1588, 1590, 1603, 1607,
  1623, 1625, 1651, 1665, 1693,
  1710, 1722, 1727, 1736, 1789,
  2003, 2106, 2121, 2245, 2252,
  2271, 2272, 2277, 2300, 2313,
  2352, 2370, 2376, 2523, 2715,
  2737, 2972, 3320, 3329, 3406,
  3443, 3563, 3565, 3779, 3794,
  3916
Academy of St. Martin-in-the-Fields
  Chorus 232, 1623, 2313
Academy of St. Martin-in-the-Fields
  Chamber Ensemble 746, 2130
Accademia Monteverdiana Chorus 1468
Accademia Monteverdiana Orchestra
  549, 1468, 3994
Accardo, Salvatore, violin 807, 815,
  916, 920, 921, 923, 2474, 2995
Achatz, Dag, piano 1997, 2966, 3594
Ackate, Aino, soprano 3770
Ackerman, Otto, conductor 961, 3067,
  3080
Adam, Theo, bass-baritone 128, 323,

452, 456, 2222, 2306, 3467, 3475
Adamec, Petri, piano 2873
Adami, Madame, piano 1383
Adams, Donald, bass 3161
Adams, Suzanne, soprano 3770
Addison, Adele, soprano 609, 1128,
  1628
Adelaide Chamber Orchestra 375
Adelaide Symphony Orchestra 1516
Adeney, Richard, flute 51, 105, 2209,
  2325
Adini, Ada, soprano 3770
Adler, Kurt, conductor 113, 2088,
  3670, 3824
Adni, Daniel, piano 1829, 3790
Adorjan, Andras, flute 1268, 1941,
  2211, 2234
Aeolian Quartet 477, 1698, 1700,
  1703, 2338
Aeolian Woodwind Quintet 3970
Aerts, Karel, conductor 3576
Affre, Agustarello, tenor 3770
Agostinelli, Adelina, soprano 3774
Agoult, Raymond, conductor 3666
Ahlersmeyer, Matthieu, baritone 454,
  2319, 3354
Ahnsjo, Claes, tenor 1666, 1686,
  2355
Ahronovitch, Yuri, conductor 3193
Aikaa, Tauno, organ 3726
Aitchison, Marian, soprano 3503
Aitken, Robert, conductor 2799
Aitkin, Robert, flute 1269, 1270,
  1271, 1457, 3169
Aix-en-Provence Festival Chorus 1524
Ajemian, Maro, piano 974
Aki, Sayoko, violin 3674
Akiyama, Kazuyoshi, conductor 2685
Aks, Catherine, soprano 2787
Akulov, E., conductor 1502
Akulov, Yevgeni, conductor 2697
Alain, Marie-Claire, organ 221,
  1486, 1572, 1670, 1672, 3505
Alard Quartet 399, 1791
Alarie, Pierette, soprano 723

Albanese, Licia, soprano 724, 2322
Albani, Emma, soprano 3770
Albeniz Trio 3609
Alberni Quartet 1267
Albers, Henri, tenor 3770
Albrecht, Gerd, conductor 2680
Albrecht, Kenneth, French horn 2117
Albrecht, Otto, tenor 3167
Albright, William, organ 1033
Alda, Frances, soprano 3774
Aldea, Dolores, soprano 1763
Aldenhoff, Bernd, tenor 3469, 3488
Aldwinkle, Robert, harpsichord 1601
Alexander, Carlos, bass-baritone
    2452, 2462
Alexander, John, tenor 605
Alexander, Sylvia, flute 1960
Alexeev, Dmitri, piano 2532
Allard, Maurice, bassoon 2760
Alldis, John, Choir 412, 2311, 2397,
    3440, 3441, 3442, 3494
Allegri, Maria Gracia, soprano 2570
Allegri Quartet 475, 837, 1230, 2847
    2849, 2852
Allen, Maud Perceval, soprano 3774
Allen, Mildred, soprano 3128
Allen, Nancy, harp 1658
Allen, Thomas, baritone 1522, 1589,
    1955, 2591, 3792
Allers, Franz, conductor 2184
Allessandro, Victor, conductor 374
Allin, Norman, bass 3905
Alliot-Lugaz, Colette, mezzo-soprano
    992, 1008, 1197
Allister, Jean, contralto 3153
Almeida, Antonio de, conductor 1253,
    3915
Almeida, Laurindo, guitar 324
Alsen, Herbert, bass 3354
Altchevsky, Ivan, tenor 3770
Altenberger, Christian, violin 200
Altmann, Roland, percussion 4016
Altmeyer, Theo, tenor 131, 142, 143,
    151, 172, 228, 963, 2312, 2879,
    2962, 3302
d'Alton, Hugo, mandolin 403
Alva, Luigi, tenor 3351
Alvarado, Marilu, piano 3645
Alvarez, Albert, tenor 3770
Alwyn, Kenneth, conductor 3790
Alwyn, William, conductor 3829
Amadeus Quartet 835, 902, 1704,
    1706, 2318, 2854, 3234
Amadi, Sergio, conductor 3025
Amara, Lucine, soprano 605

Amati Quartet 1266
Amato, Pasquale, baritone 3770
Amboden, Richard, violin 3845
Ambrosian Opera Chorus 626, 1263,
    1955, 2089, 2091, 2563, 2734,
    2974, 3334, 3363, 3365, 3948
Ambrosian Singers 628, 1404, 1654,
    1809, 1948, 2042, 2617, 3920
Ambroziak, Delfina, soprano 2494
Ameling, Elly, soprano 139, 142,
    143, 146, 173, 855, 1100, 1223,
    1824, 2045, 2366, 2397, 2877,
    2878, 2916
American Art Quartet 1419
American Brass Quintet 3478, 3675
American Composers Orchestra 789,
    976
American Concert Choir 3128
American Symphony Orchestra 1177,
    1878
Amici Quartet 395
Amner, Richard, piano 1098, 3611
Amor Artis Chorale 141, 4067
Amoyal, Pierre, violin 918, 1407,
    2164, 2761, 2993, 3044
Amphion Wind Ensemble 3502
Amsterdam Electric Circus 2800
Amsterdam Ensemble 1166
Amsterdam Steelband Circle Ensemble
    2800
Amsterdam Studio Silver Strings 2800
Amsterdam University Chorus 2062
Ancerl, Karel, conductor 364, 490,
    1304, 1316, 1839, 2036
Ancona, Mario, baritone 3770
Anda, Geza, conductor 2259
Anda, Geza, piano 443, 799, 2259
Anderko, Laszlo, baritone 2103
Anders, Peter, tenor 454, 545, 2804,
    3538, 3584
Anders, Sylvia 1354
Andersen, Ellen Westberg, soprano
    1549
Andersen, Harald, conductor 1915
Andersen, Karsten, conductor 1585,
    3169, 3171, 3172
Anderson, Alfred, bass-baritone 402
Anderson, Angus, violin 3392
Anderson, Christine, soprano 393
Anderson, Edward, tenor 3848
Anderson, Eric, euphonium 295
Anderson, James, tenor 1351
Anderson, Miles, trombone 3653
Anderson, Roberta, soprano 2583
Anderson, Sylvia, alto 3059

d'Andrade, Francesco, baritone 3770
Andre, Maurice, trumpet 27, 30, 31,
    120, 1398, 1451, 1670, 1675, 3716
Andreae, Marc, conductor 425, 1676,
    2406, 2908, 2959
Andreolli, Florindo, tenor 2475
Andreyeva, Eleanora, soprano 41
Andriaccio, Michael, guitar 3816
Angas, Richard, bass 1229
Angeleri, Franco, piano 1897
Angeleri, Michaela Mignardo, piano
    1897
Angelici, Martha, soprano 717, 3557
Angelicum String Orchestra 199
Angelis, Brigitte, violin 197
Angelis, Giovanni de, bass 2564
d'Angelo, Louis, bass-baritone 716
Angerer, Paul, conductor 33, 38, 624
    1265, 2174, 3988
Anievas, Agustin, piano 1040
Anitua, Fanny, mezzo-soprano 3774
Annapolis Brass Quintet 1906, 3970,
    3971
Annheisser, Wolfgang, baritone 2514,
    3073
Anselmi, Giuseppe, tenor 3770
Ansermet, Ernest, conductor 556,
    1196, 1510, 2414, 2998, 3147,
    3224, 3239, 3458, 3665, 3666
Ansseau, Fernand, tenor 3774
Antiqua Musica 1242
Anton, Walton, tenor 2911
Antonelli, Claudia, harp 3819
Antonini, Alfredo, conductor 1159
Antonioli, Doro, tenor 1259
Apostle, Anne, violoncello 3866
Apostoli, Arnoldo, violin 3298
Appel, Toby, viola 2199
Appleton, Jon, synclavier 44
Apter, David, piano 1520
Apter, Deborah, piano 1520
Aquistapace, Jean, bass 3774
Arad, Atar, viola 1800, 1883
Aragall, Giacomo, tenor 1257
Araiza, Francisco, tenor 673, 2401
d'Archambeau, Pierre, violin 1020
d'Arco, Annie, piano 751, 2760, 2765
Ardal, Alf, conductor 134
Arditti, Irvine, violin 2701
Argenta, Ataulfo, conductor 3665
Argeo Quadri 3766
Argerich, Martha, piano 208, 366,
    1050, 1060, 1084, 2927, 3204
Argo Chamber Orchestra 1708, 2498,
    2689

Arita, Masahiro, flute 253
Arizcuren, Elias, violoncello 1013
Arizona Chamber Orchestra 735
Arkel, Teresa, soprano 3770
Arkhipova, Irina, mezzo-soprano
    2116, 2697
Armenian, Raffi, conductor 910
Armstrong, Nancy, soprano 2583
Armstrong, Richard, conductor 3374
Armstrong, Sheila, soprano 129, 2191,
    2581, 2830, 3334
Armstrong, Stephen, conductor 4018
Armuzzi-Romei, Gabriella, violin
    3716
Arndt-Ober, Margarethe, mezzo-sopr-
    ano 3774
Arnold, Malcolm, conductor 54, 57,
    58
Arnold, Robert, organ 1406
Arnoldson, Sigrid, soprano 3770
Aronowitz, Cecil, viola 2325
Arral, Blanche, soprano 3770
Arrau, Claudio, piano 11, 418, 444,
    540, 541, 542, 796, 1061, 1078,
    1095, 1208, 3206, 3678
Arrignon, M., clarinet 2712
Arroyo, Martina, soprano 1406, 2032,
    2296
Ars Europea Choeur National 2963
Ars Nova Brass Quintet 1027
Ars Nova Ensemble 1845
Ars Nova Woodwind Quintet 2678
Ars Rediviva Orchestra 98
Ars Renata 3805
Artaud, P. flute 1873
Artot de Padilla, Lola, soprano 3774
Arts Florissants Vocal and Instru-
    mental Ensembles 1015
Artymiw, Lydia, piano 618
Artzt, Alice, guitar 3197
Arzunri, Sahan, piano 2199, 3850,
    3851
Ashforth, Alden, synthesizers 61
Ashkenasi, Shmuel, violin 2471
Ashkenazy, Vladimir, conductor 2256,
    2923, 2992, 3004, 3218, 3263
Ashkenazy, Vladimir, piano 505, 515,
    1043, 1064, 1065, 1435, 1536,
    2256, 2618, 2621, 2622, 2923,
    2967
Ashrafi, Mukhtar, conductor 62
Assayas, Irit, violoncello 2640
Atamian, Dickran, piano 3145
Athena Ensemble 1527, 2183, 2424
Atherton, David, conductor 52, 636,

709, 1963, 2346, 2481, 2822, 3517
3995
Atkins, David, clarinet 2501
Atkinson, Christopher Daly, organ
4066
Atlanta Brass Ensemble 3660, 3661
Atlanta Symphony Chorus 757
Atlanta Symphony Orchestra 757, 771
Atlantov, Vladimir, tenor 1173, 3214
3796
Atrium Musicae, Madrid 766, 3311
Atzmon, Moshe, conductor 1871
Aubin, Tony, conductor 1291
Auger, Arleen, soprano 130, 1098,
1708, 2103, 2308, 2454, 2458,
3491, 3766
Auguez de Montalant, Berthe, soprano
3630, 3774
August, Veronica, mezzo-soprano 2719
Augustesen, Peter, guitar 3883
Aulos Wind Quintet 1658
Austbo, Haakon, piano 1202
Austin, Frederic, baritone 1469
Austin, Michael, organ 1868
Austrian Radio Orchestra 648, 2970
Avdeyeva, Larissa, mezzo-soprano
2530, 2697, 3214
Avery, James, piano 1514
Ax, Emanuel, piano 1315, 3950
Ayldon, John, bass-baritone 3152,
3165
Ayo, Felix, violin 19, 284, 3298,
3394, 3403
Ayres, Thomas, clarinet 1514
Babikian, Virginia, soprano 2455
Babino, Italo, violoncello 1913
Baccaloni, Salvatore, bass 2322,
2724
Bach Choir 263, 636, 2150
Bach Collegium, Stuttgart 130, 148,
150, 151, 963
Bach Ensemble 130
Bach, Markus, conductor 3627
Bachauer, Gina, piano 1983
Bachtiar, Alexandra, violoncello
2072
Bacon, Joseph, guitar 3384
Bacquier, Gabriel, bass-baritone
1525, 2094, 2293
Bada, Angelo, tenor 3773
Baden Baden Ensemble 13 39, 2163,
2371, 3120
Bader, Roland, conductor 1797, 2881
Badev, Georgi, violin 204
Badini, Ernesto, baritone 3773

Badura Skoda, Paul, conductor 2261
Badura Skoda, Paul, fortepiano 2323
Badura Skoda, Paul, hammerflugel
2817
Badura Skoda, Paul, piano 519, 530,
2261, 2262, 2363, 2659, 2840
Bagdasarian, Rafael, clarinet 1877
Bahr-Mildenburg, Anna, soprano 3770
Bailes, Anthony, lute 1273
Bailey, Norman, baritone 548, 603
Bainbridge, Elizabeth, mezzo-soprano
632
Baines, Francis, bass 237
Baker, George, baritone 1383, 3154,
3156, 3157, 3160
Baker, George, organ 3993
Baker, Janet, mezzo-soprano (contral-
to) 142, 143, 232, 265, 671, 858,
902, 1596, 1618, 1637, 2000,
2223, 2275, 3483, 3625, 3778
Baker, Julius, flute 3418
Baker, Margaret, soprano (mezzo-
soprano) 2171
Baker, Mark, bass 2583
Baker, Polly Jo, soprano 1922, 1925
Baker Quartet 1951
Baker-Genovesi, Margaret, soprano
2581
Bakkegard, David, horn 3649
Baklanov, George, baritone 3774
Balaban, Emanuel, conductor 2170
Baldin, Aldo, tenor 1797, 2276
Baldner, Thomas, conductor 1351
Baldwin, Dalton, piano 855, 902,
1223, 3920, 3964
Baley, Virko, piano 1532, 3653
Balint, Maria, violin 205, 2692
Ball, Andrew, piano 4065
Ball, Christopher, conductor 1802
Ball, David, organ 3338
Ballet Theatre Orchestra 695
Ballista, Antonio, piano 652, 3142
Balm, Neil, trumpet 3674
Balsam, Artur, piano 1576
Baltimore Symphony Orchestra 2507,
2508, 3226
Baltsa, Agnes, contralto 226, 3340,
3348, 3363
Bamberg Symphony Chamber Music En-
semble 2131
Bamberg Symphony Orchestra 625, 1501,
1508, 2377. 2379, 3272
Banchetto Musicale 3290
Banda, Ede, violoncello 1471, 1895
Banfield, Volker, piano 1425

Barabas, Sari, soprano 2730
Baraldi Trio 1383
Baran, Ayhan, bass 6
Barbato, Elisabetta, soprano 2568
Barbaux, Christine, bass 1198, 1525, 2102
Barber, Graham, organ 1175, 1238, 3501, 4062
Barber, Samuel, piano 3128
Barbieri, Fedora, mezzo-soprano 724, 3351
Barbirolli, Evelyn, oboe 3330, 3583
Barbirolli, John, conductor 396, 622 1230, 1332, 2646, 3097, 3330, 3337, 3625, 3793, 3860
Barbirolli, John, violoncello 2583
Barbizet, Pierre, piano 817
Barbosa, Antonio, piano 1072
Barda, Henri, piano 1980
Bardon, Pierre, organ 1154, 1168
Barenboim, Daniel, conductor 370, 424, 663, 670, 673, 679, 803, 823, 933, 904, 1098, 1194, 1221, 1356, 1368, 1370, 1377, 1380, 1726, 2020, 2203, 2239, 2763, 3084, 3612, 3688
Barenboim, Daniel, piano 412, 532, 2144, 2176, 2239, 2912, 2917, 2920, 3513
Bares, Peter, organ 354
Barili, Alfredo, piano 3770
Barkey, Karl, tenor 3056
Barlow Baroque Players 3840
Barlow, Jeremy, conductor 3761
Barmen-Gemarke Kantorei 235, 853
Barnes, Darrel, viola 487
Baron, Samuel, flute 1604, 2326, 3306
Baroque Consort 29
Baroque Ensemble 140, 3307
Barraud, Dany, soprano 1853
Barrera, Carlo, tenor 3774
Barrientos, Maria, soprano 3774
Barry, George, bassoon 487
Barshai, Rudolf, conductor 2978
Barsony, Laszlo, viola 1395
Barta, Mihaly, violin 2692
Bartel, Reinhold, tenor 3168
Bartholdy Quartet 2118, 2133, 2134
Bartok, Bela, piano 377
Bartoletti, Bruno, conductor 2570, 3373, 3672
Bartoli, Rene, guitar 1495
Bartolucci, Domenico, conductor 391
Bartz, Huub, conductor 2062

Barwahser, Hubert, flute 2214
Bash, Wolfgard, clarin trumpet 4026
Bashmet, Yuri, viola 2031, 2273
Basile, Arturo, conductor 63
Basiola, Mario, baritone 3372
Basle Symphony Orchestra 1871
Bassi, Amadeo, tenor 3770
Bastian, Gert, baritone 2427
Bastin, Jules, bass 644, 660, 663, 673, 2091, 2097, 2102, 2320, 3129, 3328
Bate, Jennifer, organ 209
Bate, John, conductor 3502
Bath Festival Orchestra 907
Bathy, Anna 229
Batigne, Jean, percussion 780
Batigne, Jean, timpani 3059
Battaglia, Lucien, guitar 3706
Battersby, Edmund, piano 2814
Battistini, Mattia, baritone 3770, 3901, 3977, 3979
Baucomont, Janette, soprano 655
Baudean, Christian, tenor 2100
Baudo, Serge, conductor 1811
Baum, Carol, harp 1925
Baumann, Christiane, soprano 126, 2141
Baumann, Hermann, horn 42, 127, 1762, 2205, 2238, 2328, 2807, 3839
Baumgartner, Bernard, conductor 192
Baumgartner, Rudolf, conductor 73, 320, 706, 3391, 3400
Baumgartner, Rudolf, violin 320
Baur, Elizabeth, flute 393
Bavarian Radio Chorus 173, 634, 1785, 1894, 1945, 1947, 2032, 2038, 2126, 2452, 2457, 2461, 2462, 3373, 3459, 3491
Bavarian Radio Orchestra 546, 561, 633, 1785, 2009, 2032, 2038, 2054, 2126, 2184, 2452, 2457, 2462, 2510, 2549, 2947, 3076, 3102, 3373, 3459, 3491, 3705
Bavarian State Opera Chorus 451, 453, 1866, 2301, 2680, 3073, 3105, 3166, 3215, 3448
Bavarian State Opera Orchestra 451, 453, 2301, 2680, 3103, 3105, 3166, 3215, 3448
Bavarian Symphony Orchestra 173, 359, 2219, 2468
Bay Bones Trombone Choir 896
Bayer Staatsoper Orchestra 2874
Bayreuth Festival Chorus 554, 3449, 3450, 3452, 3457, 3469, 3472

Bayreuth Festival Orchestra 554, 3449, 3450, 3452, 3457, 3465, 3467, 3469, 3470, 3471, 3472, 3475
Bayreuth Madrigalchor 3662
Bayreuth Radio Orchestra 565
B.B.C. Academy 3939
B.B.C. Concert Orchestra 1229
B.B.C. Northern Singers 3336
B.B.C. Radio Orchestra 1383
B.B.C. Singers 1229
B.B.C. Symphony Chorus 362, 1691
B.B.C. Symlhony Orchestra 362, 366, 374, 417, 423, 652, 660, 670, 1383, 1691, 2391, 2397, 2505, 2812, 2961, 3001, 3237, 3585
B.B.C. Welsh Symphony Orchestra 1855 3510
Bean, Hugh, violin 1359, 2702, 3332
Beardslee, Bethany, soprano 2499
Beattie, Mavis, soprano 970, 3326
Beaucoudray, Marc, flute 270
Beaumadier, Jean-Louis, piccolo 1167, 3420
Beaux Arts Trio 616, 833, 895, 1091, 1347, 1758, 1759, 2167, 2394, 2660, 2914
Beavon, Constance, mezzo-soprano 1410
Bechterev, Boris, piano 824
Beck, Gustaf, piano 3772
Beckedor, Horst, violoncello 2291
Beckensteiner, Anne-Marie, harpsichord 120
Becker, Peter, countertenor 2787
Becker, Werner, baritone 2464
Beckett, John, fortepiano 403
Beckett, John, organ 3719
Beckett, John, virginals 3719
Beddoe, Dan, tenor 3770
Bedford, Steuart, conductor 32, 3481
Beecham, Betty Humby, piano 1236
Beecham Choral Society 340, 346, 458, 1232, 1560, 1639, 1690, 2299
Beecham, Thomas, conductor 340, 344, 346, 428, 458, 562, 596, 685, 720, 877, 1213, 1227, 1230, 1232, 1236, 1355, 1560, 1622, 1639, 1690, 1723, 1741, 1742, 2225, 2236, 2299, 2388, 2393, 2705, 2889, 2991, 2994, 3001, 3013, 3083, 3086, 3093, 3099, 3101, 3252, 3625, 3773, 3799, 4068, 4070, 4071
Beganyi, Ferenc, bass 3807

Begg, Heather, mezzo-soprano 691, 906
Behrend, Siegfried, guitar 743, 745, 3540
Behrens, Hildegard, soprano 452
Beilke, Irma, soprano 3488
Beinl, Ludwig, violoncello 546
Beishu, Maria, soprano 3796
Beissel, Heribert, conductor 1069
Beker, Israel, violin 1952
Bel'Arte String Trio 2131
Belgian Radio and Television Orchestra and Chorus 3328
Belgrade Philharmonic Orchestra 427
Belhomme, Hippolyte, bass 3770
Belkin, Boris, violin 2992
Bell, Donald, bass-baritone 609
Bell, Kenneth, bass-baritone 2405
Bella, Dagmar, piano 2262
Bell'Arte String Trio See Bel'Arte String Trio
Bellary, Marie Luce 1199
Bellincioni, Gemma, soprano 3770
Bello, Vicenzo, tenor 1956, 3918
Bellugi, Piero, conductor 2728
Belohlavek, Jiri, conductor 769, 994, 1847, 2081, 2175, 2488
Belorussian State Opera and Ballet Theatre Orchestra and Chorus 3189
Beltrando, S., harp 1873
Bende, Zsolt, baritone 1260
Bender, Paul, bass 3774
Benedetti, Fernand, violoncello 3382
Benelli, Ugo, tenor 1955, 2728
Benko, Daniel, lute 335, 3806
Bennett, Brenda, soprano 3158
Bennett, Sabrina, flute 1821
Bennett, William, flute 3443
Bennett, William, piccolo 3443
Bennici, Aldo, viola 668
Benningsen, Lilian, soprano 2321
Benoit, Jean-Christoph, baritone 1775, 1940, 2774
Ben-Sedira, Leila, soprano 1200
Benson, Catherine, soprano 906
Benson, Clifford, piano 3714
Benson, Garth, organ 4049, 4056
Benyamini, Daniel, viola 370
Benzi, Roberto, conductor 774, 2443, 3915
Berberian, Cathy, mezzo-soprano 653
Berbie, Jane, mezzo-soprano 660, 2320, 2448
Berdini, Cannarile 2684
Berg, Alban, Quartet 468, 2333, 2336

Berg, Jacob, flute 487
Berganza, Teresa, contralto 1512, 2222, 2292, 2295, 3139, 3665, 3687, 3698
Bergen Symphony Orchestra 1585, 3171, 3172
Berger, Agnes 1865
Berger, Erna, Soprano 1784, 3538, 3541, 3584
Bergh, Oivind, conductor 1584
Berglund, Paavo, conductor 1890, 2981, 2985
Bergmann, Maria, piano 3054
Bergonzi, Carlo tenor 3350, 3792, 3827
Bergio, Luciano, conductor 653, 654, 655
Berkeley Contemporary Chamber Players 1287
Berkes, Kalman, clarinet 2290
Berkey, Jackson, piano 1176
Berkman, Louis, baritone 736
Berlin Chamber Orchestra 128, 1678, 1818
Berlin German Opera Chorus 226, 1198 1946, 2401, 2458, 3348
Berlin Motet Choir 2400
Berlin Opera Chorus 2571
Berlin Philharmonic Octet 895, 2279
Berlin Philharmonic Orchestra 117, 226, 379, 416, 420, 433, 435, 436, 442, 450, 462, 551, 554, 561, 565, 567, 568, 569, 584, 588, 601, 602, 665, 680, 793, 799, 805, 818, 825, 862, 867, 870, 886, 894, 927, 929, 937, 949, 1037, 1047, 1198, 1307, 1047, 1198, 1307, 1323, 1330, 1333, 1338, 1543, 1622, 1786, 1946, 2019, 2044, 2157, 2253, 2374, 2375, 2380, 2381, 2389, 2401, 2571, 2725, 2883, 2888, 2895, 2900, 2904, 2956, 2958, 2996, 3007, 3012, 3088, 3200, 3209, 3240, 3246, 3248, 3249, 3253, 3253, 3258, 3265, 3279, 3348, 3390, 3462, 3672, 3897
Berlin Radio Symphony Chorus 233, 3486
Berlin Radio Symphony Orchestra 291, 443, 450, 938, 1447, 1740, 2294, 2321, 2373, 2728, 2881, 2898, 2906, 3122, 3446, 3468, 3486, 3539, 3695
Berlin Reichsender Orchestra 432
Berlin Solistenvereinigung 128
Berlin State Opera Chorus 2728, 3466
Berlin State Opera Orchestra 1818, 1819, 3446, 3466
Berlin Symphony Orchestra 1035, 1280, 3019, 3071, 3072, 3277, 3477, 3487
Berlin Theatre des Westens 1891
Berman, Boris, piano 1443
Berman, Karel, bass-baritone 1312, 2048
Berman, Lazar, piano 1071, 1988, 2411, 2540, 2615, 2938
Bern Chamber Choir 1463
Bern City Choir 961
Bernard, Andre, Brass Ensemble 3912
Bernard, Andre, trumpet 3912
Bernardi, Mario, conductor 1353, 1750
Bernardin, Anna, soprano 3433
Bernat-Klein, Gundula, soprano 2962
Berne Camerata 3703
Berneking, Vicki, piano 295
Bernese Oberland Brass Band 3627
Bernet, Dietfried, conductor 2807, 3043
Bernius Stuttgart Chamber Choir 2127
Bernstein, Leonard, conductor 460, 483, 553, 676, 695, 696, 1288, 1629, 1748, 1805, 2023, 2152, 2156, 2263, 2376, 2554, 2645, 2971, 2980, 3216, 3604, 3605, 3608, 3638
Bernstein, Leonard, piano 2263, 3605
Beroff, Michel, piano 1441
Berruti, Achille, organ 3716
Berry, George, bassoon 2339
Berry, Walter, bass-baritone 267, 268, 602, 643, 649, 1817, 1820, 1894, 2911, 3082, 3166
Bertana, Luisa, contralto 3774
Berton, Liliane, soprano 1775
Bertona, Sylvia, soprano 3368
Bertovsky, Ernst, conductor 1831
Bertovsky, Ernst, violoncello 1831
Bertram, Theodor, bass 3770
Berv, Arthur, horn 356
Besanzoni, Gabriella, mezzo-soprano 3774
Bessac, Francine, soprano 2013
Best, Martin, guitar, lute, voice 3840
Best, Michael, tenor 3485
Bettendorf, Emmy, soprano 3870
Bettoni, Vicenzo, bass 2724

Beuerle, Hans Michael, conductor 925
Beusker, Gerd, baritone 3302
Bevan, Maurice, baritone 1592, 1694, 2587
Bex, Robert, violoncello 75
Bialkin, Maurice, violoncello 3316
Bianchi, Bonifacio, mandolin 1897
Bianco, Rene, baritone 723
Biedermeyer Concert Orchestra 1777
Bielby, Jonathan, organ 4047
Bihan, Jean, conductor 3375
Bilek, Ales, piano 2080
Bilgram, Hedwig, organ 320, 322, 323 1595
Bilik, Jerry, conductor 708
Bilson, Malcolm, fortepiano 514
Bilson, Malcolm, piano 1713
Bima, Jeanne Marie, soprano 3436
Bindernagel, Gertrude, soprano 3774
Bingham, John, piano 39, 1987
Binns, Malcolm, fortepiano 497
Binns, Malcolm, piano 2608
Birbaum, Armand, conductor 3942
Birch, John, harmonium 2738
Biret, Idil, piano 683
Birmingham Symphony Orchestra 58, 731, 962, 2092, 2758, 3625, 3786
Bishop-Kovacevich, Stephen, piano 366, 417, 423, 531, 801
Bispham, David, baritone 3770
Bister, Veli-Pekka, violoncello 4
Bjorkegren, Ulf, tenor 140
Bjorlin, Ulf, conductor 703
Bjorling, Jussi, tenor 724
Bjorling, Sigurd, tenor 3469
Blachly, Alexander, conductor 1286
Blachut, Beno, tenor 1312, 1834, 1836
Black, Andrew, bass 1383, 3770
Black Diamonds Band 1383
Black Dyke Mills Band 3620
Black, Mangus, organ 4056
Black, Neil, oboe 3084, 3443
Black, Stanley, conductor 1876
Blackwell, Derek, tenor 660
Blair Quartet 1490
Blanco, Diego, guitar 355, 3040
Bland, Elsa, soprano 3774
Blandford, Jeremy, organ 3527
Blankenheim, Toni, baritone 644
Blarr, Oskar Gottlieb, organ 3148
Blaser, Pierre-Andre, tenor 2141
Blauvelt, Lilian, soprano 3770
Blazer, Pierre-Andre, baritone 3129
Blegen, Judith, soprano 645, 2171,

2302, 2755
Bles, Theo, piano 2062
Bloch, Augustyn, organ 3857
Blomstedt, Herbert, conductor 456, 702, 1557
Blum, David, conductor 1732
Blumenthal, Felicja (Felicia), piano 2143, 2169, 2700
Boardman, Roger, piano 1412
Boas, Irmgard, soprano 3490
Bochum Symphony Orchestra 2438
Bock, Josef, organ 2309
Bockelmann, Rudolf, baritone 3538, 3773
Bocquillon, P., flute 1873
Bode, Hannelore, soprano 2464
Bodet, Catherine, conductor 2071
Bodin, Esther, piano 1455
Bodin, Lars-Gunnar, synthesizer 1851
Boegner, Michele, piano 190
Boehm, Mary Louise, piano 1815
Boeke, Kees, recorder 3299
Boepple, Hans, piano 406
Boese, Ursula, contralto 2126
Boettcher, Wolfgang, violoncello 1912
Boeykens, Walter, clarinet 2960
Bogacheva, Irina, mezzo-soprano 2978
Bogard, Carole, soprano 1292
Bogatin, Barbara, violoncello 998
Bohan, Edmund, tenor 3153
Bohm, Karl, conductor 421, 422, 430, 718, 792, 1340, 1689, 2222, 2319, 2344, 2374, 2375, 2381, 2386, 2396, 2883, 2894, 2895, 2900, 3075, 3079, 3081, 3088, 3096, 3264, 3278, 3354, 3355, 3449, 3457, 3464, 3467, 3470, 3475, 3709, 3710, 3793
Bohme, Kurt, bass 545, 1866, 2301, 2319, 3166, 3446, 3467, 3470, 3488, 3489, 3512
Bohn, Ole, violin 1941
Bohnen, Michael, bass 3486, 3774
Boivin-Beluse, Edith, piano 1252
Bokov, Anatoly, baritone 3189
Boldrey, Richard, piano 339
Bolet, Jorge, piano 1977
Bolle, James, conductor 1769
Bollen, Ria, mezzo-soprano 1463, 2788
Bolling, Claude, piano 760
Bologna Teatro Comunale Orchestra 1683, 2353, 3426, 3667, 3672,

3716
Bolshoi Theatre Orchestra 1173, 1505
    2623, 2697, 3024, 3214, 3796
Bolshoi Theatre Orchestra Chorus
    1173, 2623, 3024, 3214, 3796
Bolshoi Theatre Violin Ensemble 3694
Bonaventura, Anthony di, piano 1087
Bonavolonta, Nino, conductor 1492
Bonazzi, Elaine, mezzo-soprano 2720,
    3497
Bonci, Alessandro, tenor 3770
Bond, Dorothy, soprano 1236
Bonifaccio, Maddalena, soprano 2496
Bonisolli, Franco, tenor 3364, 3535
Bony, Guillaume, Choir 1572
Bonynge, Richard, conductor 105,
    1256, 1257, 1512, 1948, 2093,
    2099, 2218, 2569, 3225, 3238,
    3447, 3672, 3828
Bor, Christiaan, violin 1567
Bordas, Gyorgy, baritone 3126
Bordeau Acquitaine Orchestra 2443
Borg, Kim, bass 2400 2452, 3360
Borgatti, Giuseppe, tenor 3770
Borgioli, Dino, tenor 2574, 2724
Bori, Lucrezia, soprano 3774
Borielli, Mario, baritone 2575
Borkh, Inge, soprano 2452
Bormida, Ida, contralto 1956
Borodin Quartet 840, 3182
Borok, Emanual, violin 3998
Boronat, Olimpia, soprano 3770
Borsamsky, Ernst, conductor 657
Bosetti, Hermine, soprano 3770
Boskovsky, Willi 894
Boskovsky, Willi, conductor 1996,
    2221, 2278, 2280, 2281, 2282,
    2284, 2287, 2856, 3166, 3826
Boskovsky Ensemble 3826
Bossert, James, organ 61
Boston Boys Choir 1386
Boston Camerata 959, 996, 1012, 1573
    2583, 3865
Boston Museum Trio 214, 2638
Boston Musica Viva 3018
Boston Pops Orchestra 1478, 2444,
    2694, 3954, 3961
Boston Symphony Chamber Players 639,
    2810, 3064
Boston Symphony Orchestra 585, 640,
    1159, 1188, 1582, 2224, 2258,
    2682, 2687, 2811, 3000, 3027,
    3144, 3184, 3206, 3243, 3954
Both, Andre, horn 3610
Botka, Valeria, conductor 3814

Bottcher, Else 3354
Bottone, Robert, piano 903
Boulay, Laurence, harpsichord 2598
Boulez, Pierre, conductor 75, 644,
    645, 647, 649, 652, 670, 780,
    987, 1598, 2812, 3493, 3494,
    3604, 3608
Boulfroy, Alain 3411
Boulin, Sophie, soprano 3610
Boult, Adrian, conductor 842, 1363,
    1367, 1379, 1381, 1383, 1808,
    2486, 2748, 3461, 3482, 3585,
    3801
Bour, Ernest, conductor 3818
Bourdin, Roger, flute 291
Bourgue, Maurice, oboe 19, 1642,
    2760, 3423, 3521
Bourgue, Maurice, Wind Ensemble
    1526
Bourguignon, Jane, mezzo-soprano
    3773
Bournemouth Sinfonietta 51, 57, 66,
    347, 489, 788, 1228, 1235, 1684,
    1738, 3396, 3937
Bournemouth Sinfonietta Chorus 1228
Bournemouth Symphony Orchestra 1226,
    1672, 2059, 2836, 2981, 2985,
    3790
Boutry, Roger, conductor 2097, 2100
Bouvier, Helene, mezzo-soprano 2764
Bowen, Kenneth, tenor 2105
Bowman, James, countertenor 980,
    1275, 1586, 1596, 1625, 2584,
    3625, 3996, 4024
Bowman, Peter, oboe 2339
Boyd, Bonita, flute 4005
Boyd, Liona, guitar 17, 3602, 3607,
    3635, 3841
Boysen, Bjorn, organ 2001
Braaten, Geir Henning, piano 1269,
    1270, 1271
Brabec, Emanuel 894
Bradford Cathedral Choirs 3528
Bragin, Alexander, baritone 3774
Brain, Dennis, horn 3562
Brainin, Norbert, violin 1810
Braithwaite, Nicholas, conductor
    901, 1822, 3829
Brancart, Evelyne, piano 1883
Brandis, Thomas, violin 3390
Brandmuller, Theo, organ 4037
Brandt, Marianne, contralto 3770
Brandt, Volker 1891
Branson, David, piano 1418
Brasch, Wolfgang, trumpet 4040

Braslau, Sophie, contralto 3774
Brass Guild 3740
Brasseur, Elisabeth, Chorale 723
Brassus Chorale 1031
Bratislava Chamber Harmony 1282
Bratislava Radio Orchestra 3847, 4030
Bratlie, Jens Harald, piano 1549
Brauchli, Bernard, clavichord 3036
Braun, Carl, bass 3774
Bream, Julian, guitar 902, 3966
Bream, Julian, lute 2181, 3965
Brecknock, John, tenor 1948
Breitner, Tamas, conductor 1954
Brendel, Alfred, piano 419, 501, 503, 504, 2245, 2252, 2924
Brendel, Hanns, organ 4035
Brendel, Wolfgang, baritone 2468, 3066
Brennand, Charles, violoncello 694, 1470
Bressler, Charles, tenor 350, 3519
Brett, Charles, countertenor 1617, 1626, 1627, 1648, 1653, 2591, 3625
Brewer, Bruce, tenor 2448
Brewer, Edward, harpsichord 1641, 2601, 3306
Brewer, Edward, orgn 2787
Brewer, Virginia, oboe 1631
Brey, Carter, violoncello 3822
Briccetti, Thomas, conductor 3655
Bridier, Jean, Vocal Ensemble 1638
Briercliffe, Nellie, soprano 3154, 3156, 3157, 3160
Briggs, John, piano 1783
Brighton Festival Chorus 603, 1687
Brings, Allen, piano 1768
Britten, Benjamin, conductor 2376
Britten, Benjamin, piano 911, 1810, 3776
Britton, David, organ 1575
Brno Philharmonic Orchestra 769, 1303, 1312, 1417, 2080, 2488
Brno State Theatre Opera Chorus 1833
Brno State Theatre Opera Orchestra 1833
Broadside Band 3761
Brocheler, John, bass 1257
Brodard, Michel, bass 1013, 3434
Brodersen, Edith, soprano 2427
Broderson, Friedrich, baritone 3774
Brodie, Paul, saxophone 46
Brohly, Suzanne, mezzo-soprano 3774

Brokmeier, Willi, tenor 1272, 1866, 3073, 3166
Broninsegna, Celestina, soprano 3770
Bronsgeest, Cornelis, baritone 3466, 3774
Bronskaya, Eugenia, soprano 3774
Brooke, Gwydion, bassoon 2225
Brookes, Oliver, bass viol 3996
Brooks, Nigel, Chorale 3196
Broome, Oliver, bass 3334
Brough, George, piano 46
Brouwenstijn, Gre, soprano 16, 551
Brown, Ian, piano 1527
Brown, Iona, conductor 754, 1607, 2272, 2523, 3406, 3443
Brown, Iona, violin 65, 2271, 2272, 3406, 3443
Brown, James, oboe 105
Brown, Loren, violoncello 376
Brown, Ray, bass 759
Brown, Timothy, horn 3443
Brown, Wilfred, tenor 1647
Brownlee, John, baritone 3773
Brownridge, Angela, piano 979, 2965
Brozia, Zina, soprano 3774
Bruce, Neely, conductor 3484
Bruck, Charles, conductor 1873
Brudrin, I., 41
Bruggen, Frans, flute 96, 3310
Bruggen, Frans, recorder 986, 3310
Bruins, Theo, piano 955, 3818
Brumaire, Jacqueline, soprano 3557
Brunell, David, piano 983
Brunetti, Vito Maria, bass 1259
Brunner, Evelyn, soprano 1007, 2142
Bruscantini, Sesto, baritone 2728
Brusilow, Anshel, violin 3606
Bruson, Renato, baritone 1258, 2565, 2763, 3353
Bryant, Dinah, soprano 3074
Bryhn-Langaard, Borghild, soprano 3774
Brymer, Jack, clarinet 837, 2225, 4029
Bryn-Julson, Phyllis, soprano 709, 2822
Brzezinski, Waclav, baritone 3770
Buccarella, Lucio, double-bass 3521
Buccheri, Elizabeth, piano 339
Buchanan, Isabel, soprano 2569
Buchbinder, Rudolf, piano 619, 2824
Buchla, Donald, synthesizer 2722
Buchner, Eberhard, tenor 456
Buchner, Otto, violin 320, 322
Buchner, Paula, mezzo-soprano 3446

Buchta, Hubert, tenor 2319
Buckel, Ursula, soprano 131, 149, 1709, 2880
Buckley, Emer, harpsichord 3751
Buckman, Rosina, soprano 1383, 3774
Buckner, Tom, tenor 1165
Budapest Chamber Ensemble 1297, 3039 3126
Budapest Children's Chorus 262
Budapest Chorus 220, 262, 1711
Budapest Philharmonic Orchestra 6, 205, 361, 368, 1211, 2227, 2692
Budapest Quartet 466, 2340, 2518
Budapest Symphony Chorus 220
Budapest Symphony Orchestra 220, 343, 1028, 1249, 1296, 1954, 2736, 2809
Buen, Knud, fiddle 1556
Buffalo Philharmonic Orchestra 2755
Buhl, Reinhold, violoncello 3764
Buketoff, Igor, conductor 2617
Bulgarian A Capella Choir 3217
Bulgarian Quartet 2341, 2855, 3744
Bulgarian Radio & TV Orchestra 1029
Bulgarian Radio and TV Vocal Ensem- le 2606
Bumbry, Grace, mezzo-soprano 3471, 3472
Bunemann, Emmerich, violoncello 2234
Bunin, Victor, piano 2750
Buoso, Ennio 2684
Burge, David, piano 782, 1350
Burge, Lois, piano 1350
Burgess, Grayston, conductor 2188
Burgess, Sally, soprano 1589, 2148, 3334, 3440, 3442
Burke, Hilda, soprano 716
Burkh, Dennis, conductor 1473, 1523
Burles, Charles, tenor 2448, 3328
Burmeister, Annelies, mezzo-soprano (contralto) 323, 557, 3457, 3467, 3475
Burnett, Richard, fortepiano 1714
Burrian, Karel, tenor 3770
Burrowes, Norma, soprano 1422, 1596, 1637, 1653, 1666, 1817, 1820, 2300, 3082
Burrows, Brian, tenor 2317
Burrows, Stuart, tenor 603, 2223, 2293, 2296, 2300, 3874, 3875
Burton, John, violoncello 393
Burzio, Eugenia, soprano 3770
Busch Chamber Players 293
Busch, Fritz, conductor 293, 2307, 3585

Busch Qartet 471, 474
Buschmann, Eberhard, bassoon 1300
Busoni, Ferruccio, piano 1983
Busse, Barry, tenor 2405
Buswell, James, violin 3331
Butler, Richard, Northumbrian pipes 3503
Butt, Clara, contralto 3560, 3903
Buxbaum, Merritt, clarinet 3652
Byelikh, Valerii, bass 2973
Bylsma, Anner, violoncello 42, 986, 1059, 1217, 1911, 1917, 2690, 3046, 3310, 3432
Byng, George, conductor 1383
Caballe, Montserrat, soprano 630, 1392, 1955, 2122, 2194, 2275, 3089, 3344, 3345, 3473, 3669, 3672, 3792, 3793, 3918
Cabanel, Paul, bass 1200, 2764
Cable, Margaret, mezzo-soprano 1468, 1587, 2786
Caddy, Ian, bass 3433
Caecilian Trio 1921
Caillard, Philippe Chorale 1405
Caillet, Stephane, Chorale 3375
Caillat, Stephane, conductor 3375
Cakar, Mahir, horn 42, 2205, 2807
Calabrese, Franco, bass 724, 2567
Caledonian Highlanders Fifes and Drums 4028
Callas, Maria, soprano 627, 629, 2521, 2561, 2567, 2575, 3349, 3371, 3625, 3789, 3792, 3793
Calleja, Icilio, tenor 3774
Calliope Renaissance Band 3597
Calusdian, George, piano 1909
Calve, Emma, soprano 3770
Camarata, Salvador, conductor 2566
Cambreling, Sylvain, conductor 2098
Cambridge Chamber Orchestra 3998
Cambridge University Chamber Choir 1237
Camerata Bern 23
Camerata Hungarica 3805
Cameron, John, baritone 346, 1232, 1639
Campaneez, Irene, contralto 2521
Campbell, James, clarinet 46
Campbell, Susan, soprano 2437
Campi, Enrico, bass 724, 2732
Campoli, Alfredo, violin 3507, 3665
Campora, Giuseppe, tenor 63, 3368
Canadian Brass 145, 3841, 4042
Canfiedl, David 983
Caniglia, Maria, soprano 3372

Canino, Bruno, piano 652, 741, 3142, 3356

Canne-Meijer, Cora, mezzo-soprano 2730

Cantelli, Guido, conductor 873, 882, 883, 1450, 2160, 3235, 3275

Canterbury Cathedral Choir 2532

Canticum Novum Kammerorkester 134

Cantilena 783, 3392

Cantilena Chamber Players 2720, 3739

Cantilena Quartet 3650

Capderou, Janine 1940

Capecchi, Renato, baritone 2321, 2475, 2563

Capella Amsterdam 2062

Capella Nova 2014, 2440, 2441

Capitol University Symphonic Wind Ensemble 2060

Caplan, Joan, mezzo-soprano 2078

Capoul, Victor, tenor 3770

Cappella Coloniensis 1610, 1611

Cappuccilli, Piero, baritone 1956, 2521, 3340, 3348, 3366, 3792

Capsir, Mercedes, soprano 2724

Caracciolo, Juanita, soprano 3774

Carbou, Francois, organ 1115

Cardenes, Andres, violin 983

Cardon, Stephane, conductor 1026

Carelli, Emma, soprano 3770

Carey, Michel, baritone 778, 2097

Caridis, Miltiades, conductor 3171

Carleton Contemporary Ensemble 393

Carlos, Wendy, synthesizer 115

Carlsen, Toril, soprano 1555, 1556

Carlson, Claudine, mezzo-soprano 2528

Carmeli, Boris, bass 2494, 3058

Carmignola, Giuliano, violin 28, 3414

Carmirelli, Pina, violin 744, 1667, 3430

Carno, Zita, piano 761, 765

Carol, Henri, organ 1405

Carol, Norman, violin 2709

Caroli, Paolo, tenor 3368

Carosio, Margherita, soprano 3773

Carp, David, recorder 2601

Carpi, Fernando, tenor 3774

Carral, Dora, soprano 1259

Carre, Marguerite, soprano 3770

Carrelli, Gabor, tenor 3362

Carreras, Jose, tenor 1263, 1955, 2564, 2571, 2734, 3321, 3340, 3345, 3347, 3348, 3370, 3918, 3919

Carroll, James, bass 3651

Carter, John, baritone 3155, 3161

Carteri, Rossana, soprano 2497

Caruso, Enrico, tenor 3770, 3945, 3946, 3949, 3982, 3986

Casademunt, Sergei, viol 1483

Casadesus, Gaby, piano 2658, 2759

Casadesus, Jean-Claude, conductor 1302, 2654

Casadesus, Robert, piano 2658

Casals Orchestra Barcelona 620, 3906

Casals, Pablo, violoncello 620, 3906

Casapietra, Celestina, soprano 2145

Cascarino, Romeo, piano 3891

Case, Anna, soprano 3774

Caskel, Christoph, timpani 2010

Casoni, Bianca Maria, mezzo-soprano 2728

Cassado, Gaspar, violoncello 1307

Cassilly, Richard, tenor 456, 2022, 3483

Castellani, Joanne, guitar 3816

Catalani, Nestore 3025

Catelinet, Philip, tuba 3330

Cathedral Church of St. Paul, Detroit 266

Cathedral of St. Salvator Scola Gregoriana 4004

Cathedral Singers of Ottawa 966

Causse, Gerard, viola 2960

Cavalieri, Elda, soprano 3869

Cavalieri, Lina, soprano 3770

Cazalet, A., horn 1873

Cazette, Louis, tenor 3774

C.B.S. Festival Orchestra 919

Cebotari, Maria, soprano 454, 2319, 3083, 3538

Ceccato, Aldo, conductor 1501, 1508

Cecchele, Gianfranco, tenor 3344

Cehanovsky, George, baritone 716

Celea, Jean-Paul, double bass 3296

Celibidache, Sergiu, conductor 383, 1752, 2549

Celine, Annette, soprano 2143, 2169

Celli, Joseph, oboe 993

Cellier, Alexandre, organ 2768

Cellini, Renato, conductor 724

Central City Opera Festival Orchestra and Chorus 344

Centurione, Maria, violoncello 3430

Cernay, Germaine, mezzo-soprano 1200

Cervena, Sona, mezzo-soprano 3475

Cervera, Marcel, viola da gamba 274

Cervera, Marcel, violoncello, 269

Chailly, Riccardo, conductor 2103,

2148, 2731, 3124, 3671
Chaliapin, Feodor, bass 3770, 3773, 3774, 3904
Challis, Philip, piano 348
Chamberlain, Anne, piano 1960
Chambon, Charles, baritone 2764
Chambon, Jacques, oboe 31, 197, 1814
Chamlee, Mario, tenor 3774
Chant de Mond 45
Chanteurs de Saint Eustache 3557
Chantres de la Tradition 3844
Chapelet, Francis, organ 1141, 3756, 3757
Chapuis, Gerard, bass 2447
Charbonnel, Maria, contralto 3774
Charlston, Elsa, soprano 3018
Chateau, Christiane, soprano 3328
Chatman, Maura, Piano 393, 1016
Chaves, Noah, viola 3649
Chavez, Carlos, conductor 695
Chedel, Arlette, alto 3129
Cheek, John, bass 757, 2572
Chellet, Germain, soprano 717
Chenal, Marthe, soprano 3774
Cherkassky, Shura, piano 825, 1042
Chester, Richard, flute 3392
Chestnut, Walter, trumpet 3545
Chiaramello, Giancarlo, conductor 3667
Chicago Symphony Chorus 452, 819, 940, 3357
Chicago Symphony Orchestra 261, 367, 452, 819, 823, 861, 905, 933, 936, 940, 1128, 1329, 1838, 1878, 2050, 2413, 2892, 3357, 3688, 3705, 3954
Chichester Cathedral Choir 3479
Chilingirian Quartet 700, 2332
Chinn, Genevieve, piano 1768
Chkoniya, Lamara, soprano 2478
Chmura, Gabriel, conductor 3641
Chookasian, Lili, contralto 605, 2022
Chorale du Brassus 556
Choralschola der Winer Hofburgkapel-le 3747
Chorzempa, Daniel, organ, 1606, 2397
Christ Church Cathedral Choir 230, 1628, 1648, 1692, 3435, 3894
Christ, Peter, oboe 2501
Christ, Rudolf, tenor 2460
Christensen, Roy, violoncello 48
Christian, Thomas, violin 3043
Christie, William, conductor 1015
Christie, William, harpsichord 270,

997, 1009, 1010, 1295, 1424, 1599, 1957, 2186, 2593, 2723
Christie, William, organ 1009, 1010, 2723
Christin, Judith, mezzo-soprano 402
Christoff, Boris, bass 724, 3368
Chuchro, Josef, violoncello 2079
Chung, Kyung-Wha, violin 434, 1019, 1219, 2165
Ciani, Dino, piano 1206
Ciccolini, Aldo, piano 1967, 2098, 2774, 3557
Cilla, Luigi, tenor 3773
Cimara, Pietro, conductor 3372
Cincinnati May Festival Chorus 2743
Cincinnati Pops Orchestra 1475
Cincinnati Symphony Orchestra 945, 1731, 2022, 2473, 2743, 2899, 3202
Cisneros, Eleonora de, mezzo-soprano 3774
Civil, Alan, horn 902
Clabassi, Plinio, bass 2733, 3341
Clam, Leopold, tenor 3712
Clamp, Joan, oboe 1527
Clare College, Cambridge, Orchestra and Chorus 3572
Clarion Wind Quintet 3509, 3731
Clark, Barry, tenor 3165
Clark, Graham, tenor 1257
Clark, Patricia, soprano 1468
Clarke, Christina, soprano 2587
Clarkson, Julian, countertenor 1621
Clavensy, Charles, bass 3557
Clayton, Jay, singer 977
Clemencic Consort 36, 1104, 1285, 1842, 2439, 2442, 3747, 3748, 3749, 3754, 3758, 3800
Clemencic, Rene, conductor 36, 1285, 1842, 2439, 2442, 3747, 3748, 3749, 3754, 3758
Clemencic, Rene, recorder 2072
Clement, Edmond, tenor 3770
Cleobury, Stephen, organ 3663
Clerkes of Oxenford 1484, 3187, 3868
Cleva, Fausto, conductor 3343
Cleve, George, conductor 2385
Cleveland Orchestra 558, 573, 581, 585, 606, 609, 672, 712, 1018, 1190, 1193, 1320, 1325, 2408, 2556, 2557, 2695, 2907, 3087, 3146, 3269, 3638
Cleveland Orchestra Chorus 606, 609, 672, 1190
Cleveland Quartet 465, 469, 1315

Cleveland Symphony Winds 49, 4011
Clevenger, Dale, horn 905
Clinton, Gordon, bass-baritone 1236
Cloemeke, Karl-Heinz, conductor 2666
Cluytens, Andre, cnductor 437, 551,
    567, 717, 1524, 2651, 3556, 3557
Coad, Phillip, organ 4018
Coates, Albert, conductor 2537, 3259
Coates, John, tenor 1383, 3774
Cochereau, Pierre, organ 1116
Cochran, William, tenor 1785
Coertse, Mimi, soprano 2055
A Coeur Joi Vocal Ensemble of Val-
    ence 2013
Cohen, Joel, conductor 959, 996,
    1012, 1573, 2583, 3865
Cohen, Robert, violoncello 1361
Coin, Christophe, viol 1483
Coin, Christophe, viola da gamba
    1398, 1428, 2063
Colandrea, Italo, violin 3298
Cold, Ulrik, bass 992, 1586, 1626,
    1627, 1638
Cole, Martin, lute 1170
Collard, Andre, piano 3557
Collard, Jean-Philippe, piano 1402,
    2650
Collectif de Musique Ancienne de
    Paris 1276
College of the Desert Vocal Ensem-
    ble 1909
Collegiate Church of St. Mary Choir
    1011
Collegium Aureum 76, 77, 106, 107,
    118, 121, 139, 146, 172, 228,
    235, 292, 1120. 1134, 1602, 1668,
    1709, 1735, 1746, 2226, 2250,
    2274, 2285, 2305, 2312, 2349,
    2354, 2382, 2496, 2636, 3049,
    3308, 3339, 3395, 3409, 3431,
    3432
Collegium Aureum Quartet 2843
Collegium Musicum Italicum 2475
Collegium Musicum, Paris 18, 1671
Collegium Musicum, Prague 491, 2090
Collegium St. Emmeram 171
Collegium Terpsichore 2527
Collegium Vocale 135, 138, 1932
Collins, Anne, contralto 2569, 3440,
    3441, 3442
Collins, Philip, trumpet 1353
Collot, Serge, viola 780
Cologne Chamber Orchestra 2247
Cologne Civic Theatre Chorus 1272
Cologne Gurzenich Orchestra 1816

Cologne Kantorei 2076
Cologne Opera Children's Chorus 1816,
    2103
Cologne Philharmonic Orchestra 189
Cologne Radio Chorus 654, 1140,
    1797, 1846, 1862, 1864, 2464,
    2493, 3168, 3495
Cologne Radio Orchestra 641, 654,
    947, 950, 1140, 1772, 1797,
    1846, 1862, 1864, 2103, 2464,
    2493, 3168, 3495
Coloton, Diane, mezzo-soprano 1351
Columbia Chamber Ensemble 3128
Columbia Chamber Orchestra 1123
Columbia Percussion Ensemble 3128
Columbia String Quartet 1960
Columbia Symphony Orchestra 572,
    598, 720, 951, 1739, 1769, 1794,
    1863, 2971, 3343, 3604, 3608
Comissiona, Sergiu, conductor 1850,
    2507, 2508, 2509, 3226
Command, Michele, soprano 1223,
    1522, 1525, 2094, 2448, 3328
Complesso Barocco 1586
Concentus Felices 983
Concert Arts Orchestra 2711
Concert Royal 1112
Concertgebouw Orchestra, Amsterdam
    267, 268, 418, 439, 440, 460,
    563, 574, 593, 642, 664, 687,
    727, 772, 796, 806, 813, 942,
    1191, 1255, 1317, 1334, 1335,
    1345, 1449, 1650, 1737, 1747,
    1751, 1809, 1874, 2024, 2026,
    2215, 2372, 2708, 2800, 2801,
    3131, 3229, 3266, 3283, 3915
Concerto Amsterdam 1171, 1606, 1679,
    1798, 2205, 3444, 3445
Concerto Vocale 1599, 1826, 2193,
    2723
Concord Quartet 1705, 1937
Condo, Nucci, soprano 2734
Connell, Elizabeth, mezzo-soprano
    2569, 2731
Conrad, Ferdinand, recorder 2006
Consorte of Musicke 1274, 1277,
    1801, 1844, 1935, 1936, 2074,
    3876, 3879, 3880
Consortium Classicum 1244, 3046
Consortium Musicum 142, 143
Constable, John, harpsichord 1669
Constable, John, organ 2311, 3440,
    3442
Constable, John, piano 548, 2738,
    3874, 3875

Constant, Marius, conductor 1192
Constantino, Florencio, tenor 3770
Cook, Brian Rayner, baritone 1228,
  1376, 2429
Cook, Deborah, soprano 2177, 3082
Cook, Jean Carrington, piano 1180
Cooke de Varon, Lorna, conductor
  1033
Cooley, Carlton, viola 3606
Cooper, Carol, harpsichord 1856
Cooper, Imogen, piano 2245, 2841
Cooper, John, organ 3970
Cooper, Kenneth, harpsichord 1640
Cope, David, conductor 1122
Cope, David, piano, 1122
Copenhagen Philharmonic Orchestra
  1770
Copenhagen Quartet 1564
Copland, Aaron, conductor 1123, 1128
  1129
Copland, Aaron, piano 1128, 3128
Coppola, Piero, conductor 2768
Corato, Luigi de, tenor 3353
Corboz, Michel, conductor 126, 193,
  227, 857, 992, 1007, 1013, 1674,
  1695, 2141, 2142, 2830, 3387,
  3388, 3434
Corboz, Philippe, organ 3434
Cordes, Marcel, baritone 2460
Corelli, Franco, tenor 627
Corena, Fernando, bass-baritone 2571
Corey, Gerald, bassoon 1353
Corfield, Tom, organ 1375
Cornell University Wind Ensemble
  1387, 1533, 3643
Cornut, Guy, conductor 1143
Corradetti, Ferruccio, bass 3770
Cors d'Esprits 1174
Corsi, Antonio Pini, baritone 3770
Cortez, Viorica, mezzo-soprano 3364
Cortis, Marcello, bass-baritone
  1524, 2732
Cortot, Alfred, conductor 620, 3906
Cortot, Alfred, piano 602, 1056,
  1070, 1081, 1983, 3770, 3906
Cossotto, Fiorenza, mezzo-soprano
  2521, 2567, 2570, 3792
Costa, Othmar, conductor 3325
Costel, Morris Moshe, piano 1144
Cotlow, Marilyn 2170
Cotogni, Anna Maria, violin 3430
Cotogni, Antonio, baritone 3770
Cotrubas, Ileana, soprano 1687, 1816
  2320, 2856, 3366, 3793
Cotte, Roger, conductor 3578

Cottone, Salvatore, piano 3770
Coull Quartet 3837
Coulson, Richard, organ 4065
Coursier, Gilbert, trombone 2760
Covey-Crump, Rogers, tenor 1648,
  2495
Cowan, Robert, piano 2182
Coward, Henry, conductor 1383
Crabbe, Armand, baritone 3774
Cracow MW 2 Ensemble 3857
Cracow Philharmonic Orchestra and
  Chorus 2491, 3857
Crafoord Quartet 332
Craft, Robert, conductor 261
Craig, Charles, tenor 3346
Crantz, Gunnar, violin 189
Crass, Franz, bass 267, 2032, 3450,
  3452, 3471
Craxton, Janet, oboe 900
Credico, Iscar di 1258
Creffield, Rosanne, mezzo-soprano
  3918
Crespin, Regine, soprano 2094, 3104,
  3666
Crimi, Giulio, tenor 3774
Croft, James, conductor 1825
Crook, Howard, tenor 2601
Crook, Paul, tenor 626, 2563
Crossan, Jack, clavichord, harpsi-
  chord, piano 3737
Crossley, Paul, piano 1408
Croxford, Eileen, violoncello 3332
Crozier, Catherine, organ 3732
Cruts, Hubert, horn 2226
Csanyi, Janos, tenor 1954
Csanyi, Laszlo, conductor 3814
Csapo, Eva, soprano 2276
Csengery, Adrienne, soprano 3126
Csik, Erzsebet, flute 3038
Cubaynes, Jean-Jacques, bass 1525
Cuckston, Alan, piano 4010
Cuenod, Hugues, tenor 1222, 3861,
  3862
Culbertson, Mel, tuba 3287
Culp, Julia, mezzo-soprano 3774
Cundick, Robert, piano 3728
Cunitz, Maud, soprano 3712
Curley, Carlo, organ 3582, 3615,
  3616, 3957
Curry, Diane, mezzo-soprano 958
Curtis, Alan, conductor 1586
Curtis, Alan, harpsichord 77, 207,
  1111
Curtis, Josephine, soprano 3158
Curzon, Clifford, piano 902, 2818,

2825, 3205
Cutner, Solomon, piano 512, 524,
  615, 1541, 1983
Cybriwsky, Oresta, piano 914
Cyr, Mary, viola da gamba 273
Czajkowski, Renard, conductor 1162
Czakova, Anna, mezzo-soprano 1836
Czech Chamber Orchestra 2254, 2419
Czech Philharmonic Chorus 557, 1032,
  1316, 1811, 2081, 2456, 2476,
  2745, 3359
Czech Philharmonic Orchestra 364,
  490, 557, 576, 887, 994, 1017,
  1032, 1304, 1305, 1306, 1309,
  1311, 1316, 1326, 1336, 1348,
  1429, 1445, 1811, 1839, 1840,
  2036, 2048, 2053, 2079, 2082,
  2085, 2086, 2159, 2265, 2456,
  2551, 2745, 3213, 3284, 3359
Czech Philharmonic Orchestra Ensem-
  ble 2348
Czech Radio Orchestra, Bratislava
  1212
Czerwenka, Oskar, bass-baritone
  16, 3489
Czidra, Laszlo, conductor 3805
Czidra, Laszlo, recorder 3294
Czyz, Henryk, conductor 2493, 3178
Da Camera Vocal Ensemble Francais
  3910
Da Capo Chamber Players 789
Dachary, Lina, mezzo-soprano 1775,
  1940, 2447
Dahinden, Clemens, conductor 1576
Dahler, Jorg Ewald, conductor 1463
Dahler, Jorg Ewald, harpsichord 22,
  1464, 3417, 3439, 3703
Dalberg, Frederick 3469
Dalberto, Michel, piano 2866
Dale, James, organ 1630, 3969, 3972
Dalis, Irene, mezzo-soprano 3465
Dallapozza, Adolf, tenor 2219, 2306,
  3102, 3166
Dalla-Rizza, Gilda, soprano 3774
Dallas Symphony Chorus 2653
Dallas Symphony Orchestra 2649,
  2653, 3132, 3950
Dalmores, Charles, tenor 3770
Dalton, Andrew, countertenor 3932
Dame, Beverly 2170
Damiano, Guilherme 2568
Dams, Rita, alto 1586
Daniel, Susan, mezzo-soprano 3440,
  3442
Danieli, Lucia, contralto 2733

Danish Radio Chorus 2427
Danish Radio Orchestra 360, 943,
  2427
Danish Wind Quintet 1782
Danzi Quintet 1172, 1917, 2690, 3046
Darden, Charles, conductor 2437
Dari, Paolo, baritone 3368
Davia, Federico, bass 2728
Davidov, Alexander, tenor 3770
Davidovich, Bella, piano 407, 1080,
  2921
Davies, Andrew, conductor 3112
Davies, Andrew, piano 1418
Davies, Ben, tenor 3770
Davies, Dennis Russell, conductor
  915, 977
Davies, Maldwyn, tenor 1593
Davies, Ryland, tenor 632, 1098,
  1691, 2311, 3672
Davies, Tudor, tenor 1383, 3985
Davine, Robert, accordion 3651
Davis, Adrian, piano 1858
Davis, Andrew, conductor 17, 1328,
  1404, 2021, 3223, 3602
Davis, Andrew, harpsichord 1618,
  2188
Davis, Andrew, organ 3823
Davis, Colin, conductor 366, 417,
  423, 459, 595, 632, 660, 669,
  671, 687, 688, 691, 719, 801,
  1335, 1345, 1358, 1685, 1691,
  1737, 1751, 2214, 2223, 2255,
  2296, 2300, 2311, 2376, 2387,
  2391, 2397, 2564, 2801, 2995,
  3000, 3131, 3206, 3345, 3918
Davis, Ivan, piano 3605
Davis, Lynne, organ 659
Davis, Michael, violin 733, 1374
Davis, Robin, horn 3443
Davis, Sharon, piano 2501
Davison, Arthur, conductor 2409,
  3397
Dawson, Peter, bass-baritone 3160,
  3774
de los Angeles, Victoria, soprano
  14, 3368, 3382, 3551, 3793
Deakey, Zsolt, violoncello 646
Dean, Stafford, bass 2191, 2311
Dearnley, Caroline, violoncello 3534
Dearnley, Christopher, organ 3858,
  3895
Debray, Lucien, oboe 2071
Debrecen Philharmonic Orchestra 1559
Decoust, Michel, conductor 2712
Deffayet, Daniel, saxophone 1192

DeGaetani, Jan, mezzo-soprano 709, 1023, 2200, 2822

Deinzer, Hans, clarinet 611, 2226, 2878

Delfosse, Michele, harpsichord 108

Deller, Alfred, conductor 1481, 1592 2197, 2587, 2589, 2592, 2594, 2595, 3339, 3496

Deller, Alfred, countertenor 2500, 2587, 2593

Deller Choir 2592

Deller Consort 1481, 1633, 2197, 2500, 2589, 2592, 2594, 2595, 3339, 3496, 3720, 3721, 3744, 3746, 3941

Deller, Mark, conductor 1633

Del Mar, Norman, conductor 347, 1226, 1229, 1361, 1922, 3095, 3236, 3271

Delmas, Jean-Francois, bass 3770

Delna, Marie, contralto 3770

Delogu, Gaetano, conductor 2034, 2159, 3359

Del Vescova, Pierre, horn 46

DeMain, John, conductor 789

Demin, Antatoly, horn 7

Dempster, Stuart, trombone 1239

Demus, Jorg, hammerflugel 1044

Demus, Jorg, piano 404, 409, 529, 611, 2250, 2366, 2367, 2817, 2840 2851, 2878, 2913, 2915, 2916

Demuth, Leopold, bass 3770

Denison, Barbara, organ 3848

Denize, Nadine, soprano 1198, 2654

Dens, Michel, baritone 717, 1524

Denysenko, Wiodzimierz, baritone 2494

Deplus, Guy, clarinet 1192, 2877

Depraz, Xavier, bass-baritone 723

Derbina, Nina, mezzo-soprano 3241

Derksen, Jan, baritone 3346

Dermota, Anton, tenor 556, 3114, 3538, 3539

Dernesch, Helga, soprano 2680, 3457, 3467, 3475

Deroubaix, Jean, mezzo-soprano 780

DeRusha, Stanley, conductor 1823

Deruwe, Roger, conductor 4004

Dervaux, Pierre, conductor 1827, 2517, 2604, 2770

Deschamps-Jehin, Blanche, contralto 3770

Desmormiere, Roger, conductor 1200

Desser, Hermann, conductor 1280

Destinn, Emmy, soprano 3770

Desurmont, Claude, clarinet 2176

Detmond Wind Ensemble 1663

Detroit Symphony Orchestra 389, 1322, 3074

Dettwyler, Urs, tenor 109

Deutekom, Cristina, soprano 3346

Deutsch, Helmut, piano 4016

Devendra, Anand, clarinet 67

DeVoll, Ray, tenor 2078

Devos, Louis, tenor 2013

Devoyon, Pascal, piano 2655

De Vries, Han, oboe 3422

Devries, David, tenor 3774

Dexter, John, organ 3743

Deyanova, Marta, piano 2620

Dichter, Misha, piano 511, 797, 798, 800, 1993, 2928

Dickerson, Bernard, tenor 2191

Dickie, Murray, tenor 2029

Dickinson, Meriel, mezzo-soprano 2689

Dickson, Carolyn, mezzo-soprano 3848

Dickson, Harry, conductor 1102

Dickson, Stephen, baritone 958

Didur, Adamo, bass 3770

Didusch, Reingard, soprano 1140

Diederich, Cyril, conductor 1513

Diederich Instrumental Ensemble 1513

Diedrichsen, Annegret, violin 2268, 2361, 2362, 2364

Diestchy, Veronique, mezzo-soprano 973

Dieterman, Harry, trombone 2062

Dilkes, Neville, conductor 1534, 3782

Dimov Quartet 2334

Dingfelder, Ingrid, flute 74, 1799

Dionet, Henri, clarinet 3557

Dippel, Andreas, tenor 3770

Di Rocco, Giovanna 2728

Dittmer, Petronella, conductor 4065

Dittmer, Petronella, violin 4065

Dittrich, Michael, conductor 3759

DiVinci Quartet 1466

Dixon, James, conductor 789

Dobbs, Mattiwilda, soprano 3557

Dobler, Charles, piano 1871

Dobos, Kalman, violoncello 3021

Dobszay, Laszlo, conductor 3802

Dods, Marcus, conductor 3153, 3786

Doerin, Boris, bass-baritone 3241

Dohnanyi, Erno, piano 3811

Dokschitser, Timofey, trumpet 707

Doley, Malcolm, conductor 3526

Dolukhanova, Zara, mezzo-soprano

2729
Dom Orchestra 2310, 2397
Dombrecht, Paul, oboe 3304, 3310, 3542
Domgraf-Fassbaender, Willi, baritone 3835
Domingo, Placido, tenor 663, 1522, 2089, 2103, 2576, 2763, 3353, 3361, 3366, 3491, 3792, 3960
Dominguez, Albert, piano 352
Dominguez, Oralia, alto 3362
Dominiak, Debra, mezzo-soprano 1351
Donath, Helen, soprano 148, 456, 820, 963, 1589, 1947, 2146, 2308, 2311, 2314, 3672
Donch, Karl, baritone 649, 3066, 3067, 3489
Dondeyne, Desire, conductor 689, 690, 3106
Doneux, Edgar, conductor 3328
Doniat, Aime, baritone 1775, 1940, 2447
Donskaya, Irina, harp 3317
Dooley, Jeffrey, countertenor 2601
Doormann, Ludwig, conductor 137
Dorati, Antal, conductor 362, 374, 389, 559, 571, 603, 642, 737, 1322, 1446, 1666, 1685, 1686, 1687, 1724, 1729, 1733, 1984, 2727, 3074, 3229, 3818, 3915
Doria, Renee, soprano 2100
Dorow, Dorothy, soprano 1166, 3818
Dorpinghaus, Eleonore, mezzo-soprano 3711
Dosch, Peter, zither 634
Dosse, Marylene, piano 1004
Dostal, Roman, conductor 1272
Douatte, Roland, conductor 18, 1671
Dougherty, Lee, soprano 1960
Douglas, Paul, flute 3885
Doumene, Jacques, bass 2100
Dourain, Lyne, mezzo-soprano 778
Doussard, Jean, conductor 1775, 2447
Dowling, Denis, bass-baritone 1236
Downes, Edward, conductor 582, 3454
Downes, Ralph, organ 156, 3479
D'Oyly Carte Opera Chorus 3152, 3156, 3157, 3158, 3162, 3165
D'Oyle Carte Opera Orchestra 3156, 3158, 3162, 3165
Draper, Charles, clarinet 2329
Drauze, Zygmunt, conductor 3857
Dreier, Per, conductor 1555, 1556, 2436
Dresden Boys Choir 2217

Dresden Kreuzchor 323
Dresden Philharmonic Orchestra 323
Dresden Staatskapelle Chorus 3364, 3488
Dresden Staatskapelle Orchestra 421, 456, 2306, 2856, 3364, 3488, 3709, 3710
Dresden State Opera Chorus 718, 3512
Dresden State Orchestra 718, 872, 879, 926, 939, 1557, 2217, 2222, 3094, 3446, 3512
Dreyfus, Huguette, harpsichord 75, 78, 219
Driehuys, Leo, oboe 19
Driscoll, Loren, tenor 3128
Drottingholm, Baroque Ensemble 3932
Drouet, Jean-Pierre, percussion 2676, 2712
Drummond-Grant, Ann, contralto 3162
Druzhinin, Fyodor, viola 2977
Dua, Octave, tenor 3773
Dubrovay, Laszlo, organ 1283
Dubrovay, Laszlo, piano 1283
Dubrovin, Ivan, tenor 3189
Duchable, Francois, piano 681
Duclos, Rene, Choir 2651, 2774
Dudarova, Veronika, conductor 2178, 2902
Dudley, Anna Carol, soprano 698, 1165, 2596, 3177
Dudley, John, tenor 970
Dufallo, Richard, conductor 43
Duffy, Philip, conductor 3531
Duffy, Terence, organ 3531
Dufranne, Hector, bass-baritone 3774
Dufrene, Fernand, flute 3382
Duhan, Hans, baritone 3774
Duke, John, piano 1292
Duke, Vernon, piano 1951
Dumond, Arnaud, guitar 3613, 3614
Dunan, Gerard, tenor 649
Dunkel, Paul, flute 1433
Dunn, Mignon, soprano 3365
Dunn, Richard, conductor 356
Dunn, Thomas, conductor 3480
Dunn, Vivian, conductor 2092
Duo Antiqua 1856
Duo Crommelynck 826
Dupre, Desmond, lute 3719
Duran, Elena, flute 1235
Durling, Ken, piano 1122
Durrler, Brigitte, soprano 2464
Durufle, Maurice, organ 3557
Dussert, J. J., clarinet 1873
Dutertre, Annick, soprano 2094

Dutoit, Charles, conductor 1019, 1252, 2474, 2993, 3129, 3135, 3204
Dutoit, Laurence, soprano 2911
Duval, Denise, soprano 3557
Dux, Clair, soprano 3774
Dvorak Chamber Orchestra 3123
Dvorakova, Ludmila, soprano 3457
Dvorsky, Petr, tenor 1836, 4030
Dye, Theresa, piano 1109
Dyer, Lorely, soprano 1236
Dygas, Ignazy, tenor 3774
Dyson, Ruth, harpsichord 1856
Eames, Emma, soprano 3770
Earle, Roderick, bass 1414, 2600
Early Music Consort 3625, 3795, 3864
Eastman Jazz Ensemble 1924
Eastman Musica Nova 1016, 1796
Eastman Percussion Ensemble 1961
Eastman Rochester Symphony Orchestra 737, 3915
Eastman Wind Ensemble 1126, 2434
Easton, Florence, soprano 3774
Eathorne, Wendy, soprano 2191, 2786
Eberly, Helen-Kay, soprano 3113
Eda-Pierre, Christiane, soprano 459, 660, 1538, 2300
Eddy, Timothy, violoncello 1640, 3306
Edelmann, Otto, bass-baritone 554, 2055, 3489, 3711
Eden, Conrad, organ 4056
Eder, Gyorgy, violoncello 2331
Eder, Pal, violin 2331
Edinburgh Quartet 2976
Edvina, Marie Louise, soprano 3774
Egerton, Francis, tenor 1948, 2564
Egger, Georg, violin 2664
Egorov, Youri, piano 2918, 2934
Ehmann, Wilhelm, conductor 234, 1245, 2962
Ehrling, Sixten, conductor 1159
Eichhorn, Kurt, conductor 2457, 2461, 3696
Eidus, Arnold, violin 1886
Eisenberg, Irwin, violin 1470
Eisler, Rudolf, conductor 3065
Ek, Harald, tenor 3449
Ekier, Jan, piano 3182
Elburn, Beatrice, soprano 3157
Elgar, Edward, conductor 1365, 1369
Elhorst, Hans, oboe 23
Elizondo Iriarte, Esteban, organ 3871
Elkins, Margreta, mezzo-soprano 1261, 3780
Ellane Lavall Aquitaine Vocal Ensemble 2443
Ellenbeck, Hans-Dieter, tenor 2881, 2962
Ellington, Edward, piano 3961
Elliott, Jack, conductor 1574
Elliott, Malia, vocals 3196
Elliott, Paul, tenor 230, 1587, 1621, 1628, 1648, 3955
Elliott, Robert, organ 2587
Elliott, Victoria, soprano 3063
Ellis, Osian, harp 734, 904
Elmendorff, Karl, conductor 3446
Elsing, Evelyn, violin 1906
Elvins, Peter, bass 2078
Elvira, Pablo, baritone 2089
Elwes, Gervase, tenor 126, 1695, 3774
Elwes, John, tenor 1013, 2588, 2600
Ely Cathedral Choir 785, 3815
Elzinga, Harry, conductor 1859
Emanuele di Pareira's Neapolitan Singers and Orchestra 3427
Emelianoff, Andre, violoncello 1016
Emerson Quartet 1159
Empire Brass Quintet 3998, 3999, 4000
Enevold, Per, conductor 3587
Engel, Karl, piano 2007
Engen, Keith, bass 170, 264, 323, 451, 2452, 2462
English Bach Festival Chorus 1008, 3433
English Bach Festival Orchestra 992, 1014, 3433
English Baroque Orchestra 1008
English Baroque Soloists 738, 982, 1593, 2588
English Chamber Orchestra 17, 24, 55, 72, 74, 80, 86, 105, 187, 188, 191, 195, 586, 1098, 1248, 1256, 1493, 1550, 1589, 1596, 1609, 1618, 1635, 1637, 1649, 1669, 1726, 1799, 1810, 1922, 2203, 2209, 2225, 2228, 2239, 2240, 2246, 2248, 2269, 2273, 2376, 2397, 2580, 3084, 3321, 3404, 3440, 3441, 3442, 3602, 3612, 3639, 3672, 3919, 3921
English Chorale 3153
English Concert 87, 124, 178, 289, 3398, 3408, 3410, 3691
English Consort of Viols 4024
English, Gerald, tenor 3, 146, 1828,

3483
English Guitar Duo 3061
English Saxophone Quartet 3718
English Sinfonia 1534
Enns, Harold, bass-baritone 3322
Ensemble A Sei Voci 2194
Ensemble Guillaume de Machaut 1467
Ensemble Per Cantar et Sonar 3375
Entremont, Philippe, conductor 2759, 2776
Entremont, Philippe, piano 1250, 1968, 2757, 2759, 3605
Enzsol, Tunde, cimbalom 1870
Eotvos, Peter, conductor 3518
Ephrikian, Angelo, conductor 1683, 2353, 3426
Epstein, Daniel, piano 1074
Epstein, David, conductor 1386
Equale Brass Ensemble 2591
Equiluz, Kurt, tenor 129, 135, 136, 138, 139, 2309, 2320, 3082
Erb, Karl, tenor 3512
Erbach, Ernst, bass 3083
Ercolani, Renato, tenor 2575
Erdelyi, Miklos, conductor 205, 262, 1743, 1895
Ericson, Eric, conductor 3713
Erikson, Greta, piano 699, 3508
Erkkila, Eero, tenor 2771
Ermler, Mark, conductor 1173, 2697, 3214, 3796
Eros, Peter, conductor 3485
Erschov, Ivan, tenor 3770
Escalais, Leon, tenor 3770
Eschenbach, Christoph, conductor 2243
Eschenbach, Christoph, piano 416, 2243, 2816, 2925, 2932, 2943, 2944, 2945, 2946
Eschweiler, Wilhelm, conductor 956, 2477
Eskin, Virginia, piano 1103, 3822
Esposito, Alessandro, organ 199
Esser, Herbert, conductor 2471
Esser, Hermin, tenor 3449, 3467
Esswood, Paul, countertenor 135, 136, 138, 762, 1623, 1624, 1638, 2581
Estellet-Brun, Michael, organ 1298
Esterhazy Baryton Trio 1754, 1756
Esterhazy Quartet 127, 2328
Estes, Simon, bass-baritone 2124
Estonian State Symphony Orchestra 2750
Etcheverry, H., baritone 1200

Etheridge, Brian, bass-baritone 1414
Eurich, Hans, viola 2663
Eusebio, Wilma de 2684
Evans, Eugenia, piano 3730
Evans, Nancy, contralto 1236
Evans, Wynford, tenor 982, 2786
Ewer, Graeme, tenor 1257, 1948
Ewerhart, Rudolf, organ 1602, 2010, 4026
Exon Singers 1297
Extempore String Ensemble 1803
Exultate Singers 1423
Eymar, Jacqueline, piano 2503
Eyre, Marjorie, soprano 3158
Fabbri, Guerrina, contralto 3770
Fabian, Marta, cimbalom 3039
Fabritiis, Olivero de, conductor 3671
Fadle, Jorg, clarinet 777, 1254
Faerber, Jorg, conductor 27, 1004, 1663, 1673, 2399, 2829, 3019
Fagius, Hans, organ 2451, 3589, 3591, 3595
Fahberg, Antonia, soprano 264
Fallis, Mary Lou, soprano 2799
Faltl, Fritz, bassoon 2396
Falvai, Sandor, piano 196, 3369
Fancourt, Darrell, bass-baritone 3154, 3156, 3158, 3162
Farberman, Harold, conductor 5, 1507
Fardink, Michael, piano 2749
Farkac, Hynek, conductor 3048
Farkas, Ferenc, piano 1395
Farley, Carole, soprano 603, 1863
Farncombe, Charles, conductor 1594
Farrar, Geraldine, soprano 3770, 3986
Farrell, Eileen, soprano 3343
Farrell, Timothy, organ 394, 1423, 3196
Fasano, Renato, conductor 2475, 3401
Fassbaender, Brigitte, mezzo-soprano 173, 643, 1817, 1820, 2740, 2784, 3073, 3215
Faulstich, Gerhard, baritone 3302
Favero, Mafalda 2568
Favres Solisten Vereinigung 1622
Fayer, Yuri, conductor 1505
Fearon, Alan, conductor 3503
Feder, Donn-Alexandre, piano 3179
Fedoseyev, Vladimir, conductor 3192
Fedotov, Victor, conductor 1390
Fehenberger, Lorenz, tenor 545
Fehr, Gottfried, bass 961

Fehring, Johannes, conductor 633
Fehringer, Franz, tenor 1846, 1864
Feicht, Johann 1865
Feigin, Grigori, violin 2421, 2751
Feldbrill, Victor, conductor 919
Feldman, Jonathan, piano 1440
Fell, Sidney, clarinet 3312
Fellegi, Adam, piano 2809
Felmlee, Jerry, flute 3291
Fenby, Eric, conductor 1235
Fenby, Eric, piano 1231
Fenice Teatro Orchestra and Chorus
    1258
Fennell, Frederick, conductor 49,
    4611
Fennell, Frederick, Orchestra 1479
Fennelly, Brian, piano 1412
Fenstermaker, John, organ 3733
Ferber, Albert, piano 1403
Ferencsik, Janos, conductor 361, 368
    1711, 1884, 1969, 1973, 2315,
    2896
Ferguson, Allyn, conductor 1574
Ferguson, Barry, conductor 3524
Ferrari, Cesira, soprano 2724
Ferrari-Fontana, Edoardo, tenor 3774
Ferraro, Dolores, soprano 3891
Ferraro, Pier, tenor 2521
Ferras, Christian, violin 285, 817
Ferrier, Kathleen, contralto 485,
    2027
Ferrin, Augostino, bass 1259
Ferro, Luigi, violin 3401
Ferschtmann, Dmitri, violoncello
    2031
Festival Orchestra and Chorus 3155,
    3161
Feuerstein, Robert, guitar 3642
Feuerstein, Sarah, harpsichord 3642
Feyerbend, Johannes, tenor 137
Fichtmuller, Wilma, contralto 2075
Fidler, Tamara, piano 3194
Fiedler, Arthur, conductor 1478,
    2444, 2694, 3954, 3961
Fiedler, Hans Herbert, bass 2319,
    3167
Field-Hyde, Margaret, soprano 3083
Fietz, Erhard, mandolin 2367
Figuralchor der Gedachtniskirche,
    Stuttgart 148, 150, 151
Filippeschi, Mario, tenor 2733
Finchley Children's Music Group 906
    2569
Findley, Chuck, flugelhorn 1466
Fine Arts Quartet 1279, 2326, 2538

Fink, Johannes, viola da gamba 322
Finke, Martin, tenor 3102
Finnie, Linda, contralto 1263, 3440,
    3442
Finnila, Birgit, contralto 227, 1100,
    2974, 3440, 3441
Finnish Radio Orchestra 1890, 2175
Fioravanti, Giulio, baritone 2567
Fioroni, Giovanna, mezzo-soprano 1259
Fires of London 2107
Firkusny, Rudolf, piano 1349
Fischer, Adam, conductor 2736
Fischer, Annie, piano 229, 2922
Fischer, Edward, conductor 1848
Fischer, Edwin, piano 894, 2876
Fischer, Georg, piano 851
Fischer, Ivan, conductor 2809
Fischer-Dieskau, Dietrich, bass-
    baritone 125, 128, 170, 264, 265,
    323, 353, 359, 451, 663, 818,
    1098, 1221, 1595, 1785, 2020,
    2029, 2032, 2294, 2321, 2400,
    2510, 2680, 2740, 2912, 2925,
    2943, 2944, 2945, 2946, 3102,
    3215, 3373, 3513, 3516
Fischer-Dieskau, Dietrich, conduc-
    tor 887
Fisher, Roger, organ 258
Fisk, Eliot, guitar 256
Fiske, Richard Allen, conductor 983
Fistoulari, Anatole, conductor 811
Fitelberg, Grzegorz, conductor 3182
Fithian, Bruce, tenor 2583
Fitziu, Anna, soprano 3774
Fitzwilliam Quartet 1439, 2975
Fjeldstad, Oivin, conductor 3020,
    3022, 3023, 3170, 3174, 3915
Flagello, Ezio, bass 3350
Flagstad, Kirsten, soprano 2582,
    3451, 3460, 3538
Flamig, Martin, conductor 323
Flax, Laura, clarinet 1433
Fleet, Edgar, conductor 3896
Fleet, Edgar, tenor 1468, 1647, 3326
Fleischer, Evan, mezzo-soprano 128
Fleischer-Edel, Katherine, soprano
    3770
Fleisher, Leon, piano 892
Flesch, Ella, soprano 3476
Fleta, Miguel, tenor 3774
Fletcher, John, tuba 3331
Flint, Jere, conductor 3660, 3661
Flood, David, organ 3532
Flowers, Herbie, guitar 1531
Flynn, Radley, baritone 3158, 3162

Fodor, Eugene, violin 1500
Fohrstrom, Alma, contralto 3770
Foldes, Andor, piano 2260
Follia Instrumental Ensemble 750,
    2012
Fontaine, Charles, tenor 3774
Forest, Rene, violoncello 1254
Forger, James, saxophone 1823
Formichi, Cesare, baritone 3925
Fornaciari, Marco, violin 3428
Forrell, Gene, conductor 3312
Forrester, Maureen, contralto 346,
    1232
Forsblom, Henry, guitar 3883
Forstel, Gertrude, soprano 3770
Forster, Karl, conductor 818
Forti, Carlo, bass 2521
Fortounatto, Michael, conductor 776,
    3817
Fortunato, D'Anna, mezzo-soprano
    2583
Foss, Lukas, piano 3128
Foster, Lawrence, conductor 3483
Fourestier, Louis, conductor 2764
Fournet, Jean, conductor 723
Fournier, Pierre, violoncello 302,
    322, 443, 614
Fowke, Philip, piano 722
Fox, Virgil, organ 3658
Frager, Malcolm, piano 1068
Francaix, Jean, conductor 1431
Francell, Fernand, tenor 3774
Francesch, Homero, piano 1772
Francillo-Kaufmann, Hedwig, soprano
    3770
Francis, Alun, conductor 1421, 2228
Francis, Sarah, oboe 1468
Franco, Carlos, flute 1013
Francois, R., flute 2712
Frandsen, John, conductor 1461, 2426
Frank, Ernest, baritone 1622
Frank, Hannerle, soprano 2319
Frankfurt Cantata Orchestra 137
Frankfurt Chamber Orchestra 3302
Frankfurt Madrigal Ensemble 3302
Frankfurt Radio Orchestra 441, 1781,
    2969, 3915
Frankl, Peter, piano 890, 2839, 2937
    3084
Fransella, W. A., piano 3770
Frantz, Ferdinand, baritone 3462,
    3712
Frantz, Justus, piano 3816
Franz, Paul, tenor 3774
Franzen, Georg, bassoon 3292, 3293

Frate, Ines de, soprano 3770
Fredonia Singers 1925
Free University Chamber Chorus 2062
Freed, Paul, piano 4064
Freeman, Paul, conductor 1005, 1092,
    1682, 1913, 2120, 2182, 3316,
    3478
Freiburg Baroque Soloists 328, 331
Fremaux, Louis, conductor 63, 1405,
    2092, 2758, 3625
Fremeau, Jean-Marie, baritone 2094,
    2097
Fremstad, Olive, soprano 3770
Fremy, Gerard, piano 2781
French National Orchestra 1289, 2645,
    2650, 3420
French Radio and Television Orches-
    tra 1875, 2773, 3799
French Radio Orchestra 437, 685,
    2767, 3382
Freni, Mirella, soprano 1522, 1525,
    1956, 2296, 2565, 2573, 2731,
    2739, 3340, 3348, 3716, 3792,
    3793
Friant, Charles, tenor 3774
Frick, Gottlob, bass 451, 818, 2299,
    2460, 3462, 3512, 3712
Fricsay, Gerenc, conductor 363, 443,
    450, 767, 1688, 1887, 2258, 2294,
    2321, 2400, 3141, 3360, 3362
Fridheim, Henrik, violin 2706
Fried, Paul, flute 3998
Friedauer, Harry, tenor 1945
Friede, Nina, contralto 3770
Friedli, Thomas, clarinet 2174
Friedman, Erik, violin 2211
Friedman, Ignaz, piano 1983
Friedman, Leonard, conductor 740,
    908, 2208
Friedman, Viktor, piano 528, 1719
Friedrich, Karl, tenor 3083
Friedrich, Roswitha, viola da gamba
    1459
Friend, Rodney, violin 2399
Frieser, Erika, piano 3108
Friesl, Karel, piano 1788
Friisholm, Lavard, conductor 360
Froelich, Ralph, horn 350
Froelich, Thomas, organ 1767
Froget, N., soprano 1873
Froment, Louis de, conductor 1388,
    1503, 1918, 2438, 2531, 2766
Fromenteau, Michele, hurdy gurdy
    1026
Fromme, Gerald, percussion 4016

Froschauer, Helmuth, conductor 3960
Frosunde Wind Quintet 60
Fry, Tristan, drum 1531
Fry, Tristan, percussion 906
Fryatt, John, tenor 1948
Frykberg, Sten, conductor 1929
Fuchs, Gabriele, soprano 3102
Fuchs, Joseph, violin 2298
Fuchs, Lillian, viola 2298
Fuchs, Marta, soprano 545, 3512
Fuente, Miguel de la, conductor 750, 2012
Fuente, Miguel de la, violin 2012
Fugere, Lucien, bass-baritone 3770
Fujihara, Hinako, soprano 1812
Fulop, Attila, tenor 1721, 1895
Furi, Thomas, conductor 3703
Furi, Thomas, violin, 3703
Furlanetto, Ferruccio, bass 1258
Furtwangler, Wilhelm, conductor 433,
    554, 578, 580, 810, 867, 870,
    894, 927, 1543, 2262, 2958, 3279,
    3489
Fusco, Cecilia, soprano 63
Futterer, Iwona, harpsichord 320
Fyson, Leslie, tenor 3334
Gabai, Maurice, clarinet 2760
Gabard, Catherine, violin, 197
Gabon, Georges, conductor 711
Gabrieli, Anna, soprano 631, 2078
Gabrieli Quartet 476, 900, 1837,
    2135, 2845, 3233
Gachinger Kantorei 129, 130, 151
Gadski, Johanna, soprano 3770
Gaebel, Kurt, conductor 3695
Gage, Irwin, piano 2877
Gaifa, Carlo, tenor 1259
Gailhard, Pedro, bass 3770
Gajard, Joseph, conductor 3911, 3913
Gale, Elizabeth, soprano 1624, 2125
Gall, Yvonne, soprano 3632, 3774
Galland, Danielle, soprano 1293,
    1400
Gallet, Anne, harpsichord 2064
Galli-Curci, Amelita, soprano 3774
Galliera, Alceo, conductor 430,
    1544, 3780
Galloway, Richard, organ 4046
Galushkina, Lidiya, contralto 3189
Galvany, Maria, soprano 3770
Galvez, Genoveva, harpsichord 3032
Galway, James, flute 89, 706, 1937,
    2229, 2232, 2233, 2717, 3289,
    3951
Gamard, Jean-Marie, violoncello 2960

Gamba, Piero, conductor 449, 3665
Gamboa, Rene, baritone 2100
Gandolfi, Alfred, baritone 2574
Gandolfo, Romano, conductor 2739
Ganestova, Lyudmila, soprano 3189
Ganoci, Anton, mandolin 3418
Ganzarolli, Wladimiro, baritone
    2275, 2296, 3353
Garatti, Maria Teresa, harpsichord
    19, 1667
Garaventa, Ottavio, tenor 1258
Garazzi, Peyo, tenor 2094
Garbin, Edoardo, tenor 3770
Garbousova, Raya, violoncello 350
Garcia, Jose Luis, conductor 3639
Garcia Asensio, Enrique, conductor
    3921
Garcin-Marrou, Michel, horn 3610
Gardelli, Lamberto, conductor 628,
    1028, 1030, 1263, 2726, 3347,
    3370, 3792, 3918
Garden, Claude, harmonica 1252
Garden, Mary, soprano 3770
Gardiner, John Eliot, conductor 738,
    982, 1593, 1617, 1621, 1653,
    2095, 2104, 2588, 2591, 2600,
    2633
Gardner, Guy, baritone 2455
Gardner, Jake, baritone 2405
Garrison, Jon, tenor 2405
Garrison, Mabel, soprano 3774
Garrott, Alice, alto 344
Garside, Gwladys, contralto 3083
Gartner, Andras, timpani 1895
Gartner, Wendelin, clarinet 2663
Garvey, David, piano 2875
Gasser, Denis, harpsichord 2519
Gati, Istvan, bass-baritone 1954,
    3437
Gatt, Martin, bassoon 3443
Gatto, Armando, conductor 1259,
    2565
Gauger, Thomas, percussion 3999
Gauntless, Ambrose, viola da gamba
    3778
Gauthier, Eva, soprano 3774
Gavazzeni, Gianandrea, conductor
    1956, 3792, 3827
Gavoty, Bernard, organ 2767
Gavrilov, Andrei, piano 2542, 2543,
    2977, 3203
Gawriloff, Saschko, violin 3059,
    3521
Gay, Maria, contralto 3770
Gayer, Catherine, soprano 2784

Gaylord, Monica, piano 3842
Gayraud, Christiane, mezzo-soprano 1524
Gazzelloni, Severino, flute 739, 780, 1752, 3298, 3356, 3412, 3413
Gearhart, Livingston, piano 3882
Gedda, Nicolai, tenor 231, 461, 551, 660, 776, 1524, 1866, 1945, 2091, 2184, 2275, 2306, 2974, 3067, 3073, 3625, 3711
Gehly, Philipp, tenor 1864
Gehrman, Shura, bass 3863
Geissler, Melanie, mezzo-soprano 961
Gelashvili, Aedischer, tenor 2478
Gelmetti, Gianluigi, conductor 1258
Gencer, Leyla, soprano 1258
Gendron, Maurice, violoncello 301, 1308, 3286
Geneva, Grand Theatre Chorus 3666
Genovese, Alfred, oboe 3998
Genualdi, Joseph, violin 744
Genuit, Werner, piano 1911, 1971, 3046
Georgiadis, John, conductor 3062, 3070
Georgiadis, John, violin 1876, 2704
Georgina, Karine, violoncello 2031
Gerbrandt, Carl, bass 1603
Gerdes, Otto, conductor 3215
Gerecz, Arpad, conductor 202, 3405
Gerhardt, Charles, conductor 1049, 3947, 3951
Gerhardt, Elena, soprano 3774
Geri, Iska 1891
German Bach Soloists 131, 149, 200, 325, 1397, 2397, 3943
German Opera Orchestra and Chorus See Berlin German Opera Orchestra and Chorus
German Philharmonic Youth Orchestra 834
Germani, Fernando, organ 3625
Gerville-Reache, Jean, mezzo-soprano 3770
Gerwig, Walter, lute, 286, 319
Ghazarian, Sona, soprano 452, 2123
Ghedin, Cino, viola 3298
Gheorghiu, Valentin, piano 2119
Ghiaurov, Nicolai, bass 1522, 2094, 2099, 2731, 3348, 3361, 3366, 3672
Ghione, Franco, conductor 3371
Ghiuselev, Nikolai, bass 3347
Giacomini, Giuseppe, tenor 626
Gianattosio, Ron, piano 2199

Gianotti, P., tenor 3844
Gibbons, John, harpsichord 317, 4019
Gibson. Alexander, condutor 411, 722, 1360, 1362, 1512, 1806, 2150, 2206, 2404, 2431, 2608, 3346
Giebel, Agnes, soprano 267, 268, 818
Gieseking, Walter, piano 425, 432, 527, 827, 1185, 1543, 1781, 2356, 2365, 2656
Giesen, Hubert, piano 543, 544
Gifford, Gerald, conductor 3051
Gifford, Gerald, organ 85, 198, 3051
Gigli, Beniamino, tenor 2568, 3372, 3774, 3900, 3987
Gil, Jean-Louis, organ 3912
Gilbert, Kenneth, fortepiano 3033
Gilbert, Kenneth, harpsichord 213, 1113, 1146, 1148, 1151, 1152, 1646, 2635, 3033
Gilels, Elena, piano 2815
Gilels, Emil, piano 793, 835, 1045, 1075, 1553, 1760, 1815, 3944
Giles, Anne Diener, flute 3652
Gilibert, Charles, baritone 3770
Gill, Dorothy, contralto 3160
Gilles, Henri, piano 3770
Gillesberger, Hans, conductor 2309, 3952
Gillespie, Rhondda, piano 2002, 2175
Gillig, Charles, bass 961
Gillis, Don, piano 3841
Gilly, Dinh, baritone 3774
Ginzburg, Leo, conductor 1502
Giorgetti, Giorgio, bass-baritone 2562
Giorgini, Aristodemo, tenor 3770
Giovanni String Quartet 2339
Giraldoni, Eugenio, baritone 3770
Giraud, Fiorello, tenor 3770
Giraudeau, Jean, tenor 3557, 3818
Girod, Vincent, tenor 126
Giulini, Carlo Maria, conductor 415, 587, 591, 869, 876, 880, 905, 1036, 1046, 1195, 1329, 1331, 1343, 1448, 1745, 2242, 2314, 2376, 2497, 2732, 2892, 2903, 2954, 3254, 3280, 3366, 3792, 3793
Glass, Philip, Ensemble 1497
Glatt, Adelheid, viol 1010
Glawitsch, Rupert, tenor 3167
Glickman, Loren, bassoon 3674
Glinka Quartet 1958
Globokar, Vinko, trombone 1413
Glossop, Peter, baritone 632, 691

Gluck, Alma, soprano 3774
Glusel'nikov, Igor, piano 2116
Glushkova, Rimma, soprano 3241
Glyndebourne Festival Chorus 2307,
2730, 3163, 3164
Glyndebourne Festival Orchestra
2307, 2730
Glyndebourne Opera Chorus 2191
Glynne, Howell, bass 344
Gmunder, Martha, harpsichord 1459
Gobbi, Tito, baritone 2562, 3351,
3368, 3771
Gobel, Horst, piano 3134
Goberman, Max, conductor 2580
Godburn, Dennis, bassoon 2601
Godburn, Dennis, recorder 2601
Godfrey, Isidore, conductor 3158,
3162
Godowsky, Leopold, piano 3902
Goebel, Reinhard, conductor 239
Goebel, Reinhard, violin 1111
Goebels, Franzpeter, harpsichord
1619
Goebels, Franzpeter, piano 384, 1795
3628
Goehr, Walter, conductor 349, 1968
Gogorza, Emilio de, tenor 3770
Gold, Diane, flute 399
Goldberg, Laurette, harpsichord 2596
Goldberg, Laurette, piano 1992
Goldberg, Rainer, tenor 456, 3490
Goldberg, Szymon, conductor 201
Goldberg, Szymon, violin 201
Goldsmith, Harris, piano 526
Goldstein, Mark, percussion 1910
Goldstein, Martha, lute 287
Goldthorpe, Michael, tenor 1008
Golschmann, Vladimir, conductor 1861
Goltz, Christel, soprano 3096, 3931
Gomez, Jill, soprano 2429, 2633,
2689
Gonnenwein, Wolfgang, conductor 142,
143, 820, 2880
Gonzales, Carmen, mezzo-soprano 1956
Gonzalez Mantichi, Enrique, conduc-
tor 2718
Goodberg, Robert, flute 3892
Goodman Andrea, recorder 2187
Goodman, Andrea, singer 2187
Goodman, Benny, clarinet 377
Goodman, Erica, harp 3841
Goodman, Peter, organ 4048
Goossens, Eugene, conductor 1383,
3773
Goossens, Leon, oboe 2329, 4029

Goossens, Sidonie, harp 4029
Gordon, Brian, countertenor 1621
Gordon, Steven, piano 1086
Goritzki, Ingo, oboe 22, 200, 1776,
3439
Goritzki, Johannes, viola 3439
Gorner, Christine, soprano 1262
Gorog, Andre, piano 822, 3137
Gorr, Rita, soprano 3341, 3557
Gorvin, Carl, conductor 91
Goss, Julia, soprano 3152
Goteborg Symphony Orchestra 1850
Gothenburg Symphony Orchestra 2509
Gothoni, Ralf, piano 2083, 2084,
2544, 3586
Gotti, Tito, conductor 3716
Gottingen State Kantorei 137
Gottlieb, Gordon, percussion 914
Cottlieb, Gordon, timpani 3674
Gottlieb, Gordon, vibraphone 789
Goudswaard, Willy, percussion 366
Gould, Glenn, piano 305, 306, 494,
2357
Gould, Morton, conductor 12, 1488,
1521, 4045
Goulding, Charles, tenor 3154
Gouverne, Yvonne, Choeurs 1200
Gowen, Bradford, piano 3859
Gowers, Patrick, organ 1531
Gracis, Ettore, conductor 2612,
2782
Graeme, Peter, oboe 105
Graf, Heinz-Otto, viola 2291
Graf, Peter-Lukas, flute 189, 2603,
3629
Graffman, Gary, piano 390, 1477,
3207
Graham, Daniel, piano 821, 2114
Graham, John, viola 1016
Gramm, Donald, bass-baritone 3128
Grancher, Micheline 1199
Grand Prix Festival Orchestra 194
Grande Ecurie et la Chambre du Roy
1011, 1614, 1626, 1627, 1638,
2599, 3402, 3610
Grandi, Margherita, soprano 1622
Grant, Clifford, bass-baritone 2311
Granville, Sydney, baritone 3154,
3156, 3157, 3158
Gratovich, Eugene, violin 1532
Graunke Symphony Orchestra 1866,
1945, 3073
Gravina, Giovanni, bass 3770
Gray, Gary, clarinet 693, 761
Grayson, Richard, piano 761

Graz Concert Choir 2699
Graz Mozart Ensemble 2699
Greef-Andriessen, Pelagia, soprano 3770
Green, Alan, tenor 1694
Green, Christopher, violoncello 2691
Green, Martyn, baritone 3158, 3162
Greene, Daryl, soprano 1621
Greene, Harry Plunkett, baritone 3770
Greene, Leon, bass 719
Greenhouse, Bernard, violoncello 895
Greenwood Consort 4001
Gregor, Bohumil, conductor 1835
Gregor, Jozsef, bass 1711, 2315
Grehling, Ulrich, violin 3049
Greindl, Josef, bass 1688, 2400, 3450, 3452, 3457, 3471, 3584, 3712
Greindl-Rosner, Gudrun, soprano 3102
Grenacher, Karl, conductor 2808
Grenacher, Karl, piano 2808
Grenoble Ensemble Instrumental 1026
Grew, John, harpsichord 273
Grey, Joel 3497
Gridenko, Tatiana, violin 2031, 2543 2806
Grier, Francis, piano 734, 906
Grierson, Ralph, piano 1899
Griffin, Elsie, soprano 3154, 3160
Griffith, David, tenor 1925
Grigolo, Romano, tenor 63
Grigorov, Vladimir, horn 847
Grimbert, Jacques, conductor 2963
Grimes, Frederick, conductor 133
Grimes, Frederick, organ 133
Grin, Freddy, trumpet 1926
Grist, Reri, soprano 3716
Grizunov, Ivan, baritone 3774
Grobe, Donald, tenor 1946, 2032, 2464, 3491
Groenen, Joseph, baritone 3774
Grogan, Robert, organ 4060
Groppenberger, Walter, piano 2699
Grosgurin, Daniel, violoncello 3434
Grosses Wiener Rundfunkorchestra 1944
Grosskurth, Kurt 3168
Grossman, Arthur, bassoon 693, 1470
Grossman, Ferdinand, conductor 2310 2397, 2911
Grossman, Jerry, violoncello 744
Group for Contemporary Music 67
Groupe Choral Gregorien 3375

Groupe d'Instruments Anciens de Paris 3578
Groves, Charles, conductor 55, 1248, 1359, 1382, 3334, 3612
Gruber, Arthur, conductor 2804
Gruber, Ferry, baritone 3168
Gruber, Edita, soprano 1817, 1820, 2123, 2355, 2468, 3082, 3348
Gruenberg, Erich, violin 438, 1296
Grumbach, Raimund, baritone 3102
Grumiaux, Arthur, violin 202, 278, 439, 540, 541, 542, 642, 895, 1408, 1442, 1643, 1919, 2660, 3301, 3405
Grummer, Elisabeth, soprano 818, 3462, 3489
Grundheber, Franz, bass 2103
Grunfarb, Josef, violin 699, 2503
Guadagno, Anton, conductor 3667
Guarneri, Mario, trumpet 3149
Guarneri Quartet 488, 1701
Guarneri Trio 1024
Gudgeon, Susan, soprano 2799
Gueden, Hilde, soprano 3104, 3373
Guerrini, Adrianna, soprano 2568
Guest, George, conductor 762, 1693, 2498, 2786, 3376, 3567
Guggia, Mario 1258
Gui, Vittorio, conductor 2730, 3368, 3793
Guicher, Yvonne, recorder, tin whistle, 3-holed flute, bodhran 2519
Guildhall Waits 1801
Guillou, Jean, organ 1965
Guindon, Jean-Pierre, conductor 1581
Guiraudon, Julia, soprano 3770
Guise, P., percussion 1873
Gulbenkian Foundation Chamber Orchestra 193
Gulbenkian Foundation Chorus 1007, 1013, 2141, 2142
Gulbenkian Foundation Symphony Orchestra 857, 1007, 1013, 2141, 2142
Gulbranson, Ellen, soprano 3770
Gulda, Friedrich, piano 182
Gullet, Daniel, violin 895
Gulyas, Denes, tenor 1954, 3126
Gunnison, Colorado Summer Music Faculty 3581
Gunter, Horst, baritone 3167, 3712
Gunter, Kurt, violin 322
Gunther, Eileen Morris, organ 4061
Guschlbauer, Theodor, conductor

1672, 1684, 2212
Gustetto, Martha, piano 2641
Gutheil-Schoder, Marie, soprano 3770
Guthrie, Frederick, bass 551
Gutierrez, Horacio, piano 1966
Guzelimian, Armen, piano 3684
Gyuzelev, Nikola, bass 2606
Haas, Arthur, harpsichord 1957
Haas, Werner, piano 3915
Hacker, Alan, conductor 2351
Hackett, Charles, tenor 3774
Hacki, Tamas, whistle 3909
Haebler, Ingrid, piano 539, 2255,
    2257, 2324
Haemig, Paul, flute 3890
Haendel, Ida, violin 3785
Haffner, Barbara, violoncello 1016
Hafgren-Dinkela, Lily, soprano 3774
Hafliger, Ernst, tenor 128, 233, 264
    267, 268, 323, 451, 1688, 2024,
    2025, 2026, 2294, 2400, 2452,
    2802
Hagegard, Hakan, baritone 104, 1929,
    2564
Hager, Clyde, tenor 2455
Hager, Leopold, conductor 2238, 2267
    2268, 2308, 2355, 2392
Hager, Robert, conductor 3446, 3539
Hagerman, Karen, soprano 983
Hague Philharmonic Orchestra 3818
Haitink, Bernard, conductor 418, 419
    439, 440, 564, 583, 727, 796, 806
    813, 942, 1191, 1308, 1317, 1334,
    1747, 1874, 2147, 2154, 2156,
    2162, 2979, 2986, 2988, 3266,
    3283, 3915
Hajdu, Istvan, piano 2660
Hajossyova, Magdalena, soprano 1833
Hala, Josef, harpsichord 2090
Hala, Josef, piano 1017, 1473
Hall, Carol, mezzo-soprano 2600
Hall, Peter, tenor 1414, 1468
Halle Orchestra 662, 692, 794, 860,
    1332, 2110, 2646, 3068, 3330,
    3337, 3623
Hallin, Margareta, soprano 140, 2317
Halling, Patrick, violin 1531
Hallstein, Ingeborg, soprano 633,
    3111
Halman, Ella, contralto 3162
Hamari, Julia, mezzo-soprano 555,
    630, 1098, 1511, 1817, 1820,
    1955, 2032, 3350, 3491
Hambourg, Mark, piano 1983
Hamburg Monteverdi Choir 2581

Hamburg Philharmonic Orchestra 1786,
    3535
Hamburg Radio Orchestra 3167
Hamburg Symphony Orchestra 1069
Hames, Richard, conductor 1119
Hamilton, S., tenor 3844
Hamm-Albrecht, Helga, mezzo-soprano
    3056
Hammersmith Lyric Theatre Orchestra
    and Chorus 1469
Hampe, Veronica, viola da gamba 253
Hampton, Bonnie, violoncello 492
Hancock, David, piano 2525
Hancock, Judith, organ 1294
Hand, Frederick, guitar 2580
Handel Opera Society Chorus 1594
Handel Opera Society Orchestra 1594
Handford, Maurice, conductor 3623
Handley, Norman, conductor 3829
Handley, Vernon, conductor 731, 962,
    1228, 1234, 1341, 1357, 1378,
    2748, 2761, 3338, 3510
Hanks, Toby, tuba 3654
Hanly, Brian, violin 1130
Hann, Georg, bass-baritone 2075,
    3105, 3448, 3512
Hannikainen, Tauno, conductor 3002
Hanover Boys Choir 135, 138 1932
Hansen, Ib, bass-baritone 2427
Hansen, Ornulf Boye, violin 3170,
    3393
Hansen, Ove Verner, baritone 2427
Hansen, Paul, bass 1894, 2457
Hansen, Randy, tenor 1351
Hansen, Terje Boye, bassoon 3393
Hansli, Asbjorn, baritone 1555, 1556
Hansmann, Rotraud, soprano 2146
Hanson, Howard, conductor 737, 3915
Hanssen, Vessa, mezzo-soprano 1555,
    1556
Hara, Laszlo, bassoon 3804
Harassowitz, Hermann, organ 160
Hardy, Francis, trumpet 158
Hardy, Rosemary, soprano 1414, 2600
Harmann, Karl-Otto, bassoon 3445
Harmon, Thomas, organ 761, 1661,
    3707, 3708
Harnett, James, bass 1470
Harnoncourt, Alice, pardessus de
    viole 3299
Harnoncourt, Alice, piccolo 3299
Harnoncourt, Alice, violin 3299
Harnoncourt, Alice, violono 3299
Harnoncourt, Nikolaus, conductor
    127, 135, 136, 138, 705, 1591,

1624, 1631, 3702, 3818,
Harnoncourt, Nikolaus, viola da gam-
    ba 986
Harnoncourt, Nikolaus, violoncello
    138
Harper, Edward, conductor 1659
Harper, Heather, soprano 1691, 1710,
    3494
Harper, James, tenor 2462
Harper, Nelson, piano 733
Harras, Manfred, recorder 1459
Harrassowitz, Hermann, organ 4034
Harrell, Lynn, violoncello 80, 617
Harrell, Mack, baritone 3315
Harrer, Uwe, conductor 904
Harris, Dinah, soprano 982
Harris, Johana, piano 1660, 1661
Harris, Roy, conductor 1660, 1661
Harrison, David, organ 4046
Harrison, Elisabeth, mezzo-soprano
    1414
Harrold, Jack 3497
Harrold, Orville, tenor 3774
Hart, Freda, soprano 1236
Hart, Leonhard, bass 3848
Hartemann, Jean-Claude, conductor
    190
Hartenberger, Russell, percussion
    3842
Hartle, Enid, mezzo-soprano 2569,
    3082
Hartman, Gerda, soprano 2220
Hartmann, Karl Otto, bassoon 1171,
    1911
Hartmann, Rudolf, violin 895
Hartung, Gretel, soprano 1862
Harty, Hamilton, conductor 692
Harty, Hamilton, piano 3770
Harvard de la Montagne, Joachim,
    conductor 1528
Harvey, Brian, bass 2762
Harvey, Keith, violoncello 105
Harwood, Elizabeth, soprano 1946,
    2786
Haselbock, Franz, organ 3682, 4026
Haselbock, Martin, organ 2132, 2669
Haskil, Clara, piano 2251, 2258
Hasseman, Frauke, alto 1245, 2962
Haudebourg, Brigitte, harpsichord
    392, 1720
Haughn, Jeanne, contralto 1630
Haugland, Aage, bass 2427, 2974
Hauptmann, Norbert, horn 2956
Hauschild, Wolf-Dieter, conductor
    1678
Haussler, Gunter, bass 2457

Havlikova, Klara, piano 3150
Hawkins, Robert, conductor 3581
Hay, Patricia, soprano 3346
Hayakawa, Masaaki, conductor 3407
Hayami, Kazuko, piano 1656, 3478
Haydn Trio 2168
Hays, Doris, piano 3727
Hazelzet, Wilbert, flute 1111
Heald-Smith, Geoffrey, conductor
    348, 897
Healey, Peter, oboe 1013
Heath, Dennis, tenor 61
Heath, Kenneth, violoncello 2271,
    3779
Heather, Alfred, tenor 1469
Heger, Robert, conductor 425, 2513,
    2804, 3103, 3468
Hehrmann, Gudrunn, violin 1460
Heidelberg Baroque Ensemble 103
Heidelberg Chamber Orchestra 25,
    1182, 2210, 3291, 3292, 3293,
    3297
Heifetz, Jascha, violin 428, 3963,
    3967
Heiller, Anton, organ 167, 1779
Heine, Herbert, organ 4035
Heinemann, Rudolf, organ 260
Heinrich, Julia, soprano 3774
Heldy, Fanny, soprano 3774
Helffer, Claude, piano 1202
Heller, Camilla, violoncello 4064
Heller, Joan, soprano 1117
Hellmann, Claudio, soprano 2452
Hellwig, Judith, soprano 16
Hellwig, Klaus, piano 1985
Helm, Karl, tenor 2680
Helmerson, Frans, violoncello 304
Helmrich, Dennis, piano 1908
Helsingborg Concert House Chorus
    1929
Helsingborg Symphony Orchestra 1929
Helsinki Chamber Orchestra 1682
Helsinki Philharmonic Orchestra 651,
    1682, 1882, 2018, 2175, 3009
Heltay, Laszlo, conductor 1708,
    2689, 2738
Hempel, Frieda, soprano 3770
Hempfling, Volker, conductor 2076
Hemsley, Thomas, bass-baritone 1647,
    2582
Henby, Michel, oboe 3610
Hendel, Georg-Friedrich, violin 31
Henderson, Malcolm, conductor 4029
Hendl, Walter, conductor 1582
Hendricks, Barbara 1221, 2043, 3074
Henking, Arwed, organ 152

Henschel, George, baritone 3770
Henzi, Hans Werner, conductor 1772
Herbert, Giselle, harp 1182, 2482, 3047
Herbillon, Jacques, baritone 1409
Herbrecht, Denise, piano 2768
Herent, Rene, tenor 3557
Herincx, Raimund, baritone 632, 719
Hermann, Roland, bass-baritone 1090, 2049
Herold, Wilhelm, tenor 3770
Herr, John, conductor 3848
Herreweghe, Philippe, conductor 1932
Herrick, Christopher, organ 394, 3838, 4051
Herrmann, Josef, bass-baritone 3512
Hersh, Paul, piano 698, 3177
Hert, Tamara, soprano 750
Herzog, Colette, soprano 2631
Herzog, Emilie, soprano 3770
Hesch, Wilhelm, bass 3770
Hesse, Ruth, mezzo-soprano 1894, 3182, 3467
Hessian Radio Orchestra 3857
Hetu, Pierre, conductor 1764
Heusser, Hedda, soprano 1864
Hickman, David, trumpet 29, 1580
Hickox, Richard, conductor 1421, 1422
Hickox, Richard, Singers 1422
Hicks, Malcolm, organ 1621, 1653
Hidalgo, Elvira de, soprano 3774
Higginbotham, Diane, soprano 133
Higginbottom, Edward, conductor 3188
Highgate String Quartet 3312
Hilbish, Thomas, conductor 2173
Hill, Carmen, mezzo-soprano 3774
Hill, David, organ 2498
Hill, Eric, guitar 3383
Hill, Martyn, tenor 984, 1228, 1595, 1627, 1632, 1653, 1692, 2577, 2579, 2584, 2588, 2974, 3492, 3879
Hill, Valerie, soprano 3326
Hill-Smith, Marilyn, mezzo-soprano 992
Hillebrand, Nikolaus, bass 171, 1797
Hillen, Jaap, conductor 2062
Hilliard, Kathleen, mezzo-soprano 1469
Himmel, Harald, violin 2699
Himmler, Esther, soprano 109, 1245
Hindar Quartet 1563, 3173
Hindart, Kerstin, piano 1455
Hindemith, Paul, conductor 1786, 1792
Hinds, Esther, soprano 2919, 3015
Hinreiner, Ernst, conductor 1763
Hinson, Nina, mezzo-soprano 2832
Hiolski, Andrzej, baritone 333, 2493, 3182
Hirayama, Michiko, soprano 3655
Hirsch, Hans Ludwig, conductor 22, 2788, 3417
Hirsch, Hans Ludwig, piano 2740
Hirst, Grayson, tenor 402
Hirt, Al, trumpet 3961
Hirte, Klaus, bass-baritone 3102
Hislop, Joseph, tenor 3773, 3774
Hlavacek, Libor, conductor 2828
Hoban, John, conductor 970, 3326
Hoberman, Arthur, flute 2640, 2641
Hobson, Jane, mezzo-soprano 609
Hochstein, Wolfgang, harpsichord 325
Hochstrasser, Alois, conductor 2699
Hodgson, Alfreda, contralto 263, 603, 1362, 1623, 1654, 1708, 2191, 2498, 2738
Hodkinson, Sydney, conductor 1016
Hoefflin, Johannes, tenor 2962
Hoekmeyer, Peter, horn 2062
Hoelscher, Ulf, violin 641, 1441, 2770
Hoff, Brynjar, oboe 134
Hoffgen, Marga, contralto 231, 267, 268, 818, 3457, 3462
Hoffman, Baptist, baritone 3770
Hoffmann, Bruno, glass harp 2090
Hoffmann, Karl, bassoon, 3418
Hoffmann, Ludwig, piano 2324
Hoffmann, Paul, piano 1910
Hoffmeister, Frank, tenor 2803
Hofmann, Ludwig, bass 3446, 3466
Hofmann, Peter, tenor 452
Hofmann, Willy, tenor 1846, 1862, 1864
Hofner, Gunther, horn 2396
Hogwood, Christopher, conductor 88, 1241, 1587, 1628, 2368, 2577, 2578, 2579, 2584, 2602, 3443
Hogwood, Christopher, fortepiano 2872, 3492
Hogwood, Christopher, harpsichord 97, 968, 969, 984, 1241, 2004, 2073, 2369, 2584, 3779
Hogwood, Christopher, organ 969, 984, 1147, 3443
Hogwood, Christopher, virginal 969
Hokanson, Leonard, harpsichord 3956

Hokanson, Leonard, piano 848, 849, 902
Holdridge, Lee, conductor 3196
Holecek, Alfred, piano 1306
Holecek, Heinz, bass-baritone 3104
Holford, Sylvia, piano 2738
Holl, Robert, bass 555, 2699, 3440, 3441
Holliger, Heinz, cor anglais 493, 625, 1255
Holliger, Heinz, oboe 19, 23, 24, 26, 269, 320, 493, 625, 653, 1255, 1642, 1963, 2230, 3305, 3423, 3425, 3521, 3703
Holloway, John, violin 3402
Hollreiser, Heinrich, conductor 2075
Hollweg, Ilse, soprano 1560, 2299
Hollweg, Werner, tenor 1624, 1946
Holm, Renate, soprano 1945, 2184, 3168
Holm, Richard, tenor 2680
Holman, Peter, conductor 1845
Holmes, Donald, baritone 1375
Holmes, Ralph, violin 1664
Holst, Henry, violin 615
Holst, Imogen, conductor 1810
Holt, Hazel, soprano 3511
Holy Trinity Cathedral Mixed Choir 775
Holy Trinity Lutheran Church Bach Orchestra and Choir 133
Holy Trinity-St. Sergius Monastery Choir 775
Holy, Walter, trumpet 2010
Holzgraf, Lloyd, organ 162, 309
Holzman, Carrie, viola 1910
Homer, Louise, contralto 3770
Hongen, Elizabeth, contralto 554, 718, 859, 3354
Hongne, Paul, bassoon 621
Hood College Choir 1630
Hoogeveen, Godfried, violoncello 3818
Hoover, Katherine, flute 3822
Hopf, Gertrud, mezzo-soprano 3475
Hopf, Hans, tenor 16, 554, 3096, 3489, 3538
Hopferwieser, Josef, tenor 643
Hopfner, Heiner, tenor 171, 2788
Hopkins, Sue, percussion 1910
Horacek, Jaroslav, bass-baritone 3029
Horak, Marina, piano 2933
Horenstein, Jascha, conductor 438, 961, 1787, 2035, 2042, 2052,

2479, 2609, 3017
Horne, Marilyn, soprano 552, 1257, 2030, 3672
Hornik, Gottfried, bass-baritone 2401, 2571
Hornung, Dieter, piano 2857
Horowitz, Vladimir, piano 509, 1718, 1970
Horsley, Colin, piano 1039
Hortobagyi, Gyorgy, bassoon 2290
Horvat, Ankar, mezzo-soprano 3774
Horvat, Milan, conductor 1779, 2688
Horvath, Jozsef, tenor 3437
Horvath, Laszlo, clarinet 2185
Hosking, Arthur, tenor 3154, 3157
Hostettler, Nicole, spinet 3305
Hotter, Hans, bass-baritone 607, 643, 852, 859, 2075, 3448, 3465, 3538
Hotteterre Quartet 2067, 2069, 4014, 4017
Houbart, Francois-Henri, organ 158, 1986
Houston Chorale 2455
Houston Symphony Orchestra 2455
Houston Youth Symphony Boys Choir 2455
Houte de Lange, Michiel ten, tenor 2189
Houtmann, Jacques, conductor 1517
Hovhaness, Alan, conductor 1812
Hovora, Daria, piano 2140, 2960
Howard, Brian, conductor 3621
Howarth, Elgar, conductor 1414, 3125
Howat, Roy, piano 1203
Howell, Gwynne, bass-baritone 452, 1708, 2313, 3353
Howells, Anne, soprano 632
Howlett, Neil, baritone 3671
Hrdina, Emanuel, horn 2679
Hucke, Helmut, oboe 76, 189, 3395, 3409
Huddersfield Choral Society 1615
Hudemann, Hans-Olaf, bass 137
Hudson, Benjamin, violin 2199
Hudson, Paul, bass-baritone 2573
Huehn, Julius, baritone 716
Huelgas Ensemble 3548
Huffman, Kat, bassoon 1821
Hughes, Robert, conductor 1165
Huguet, Josefina, soprano 3770
Hull, Robert, conductor 735
Hull Youth Orchestra 348, 897
Hultberg, Cortland, conductor 393
Humair, Daniel, drums 760

Humes, Elizabeth, soprano 4067
Humphreys, Sydney, violin 2188
Hundemer, Thomas, horn 1514
Hungarian Baroque Trio 3804
Hungarian Children's Choir 3814
Hungarian Harp Trio 1895
Hungarian People's Army Male Chorus 1973
Hungarian Quartet 380
Hungarian Radio and Television Chorus 343, 1028, 2315, 3066, 3803
Hungarian Radio and Television Female (Women's) Chorus 1296
Hungarian Radio and Television Orchestra 3038, 3066
Hungarian State Opera Chorus 1296, 1511, 3807
Hungarian State Opera Orchestra 1296, 1511, 3807, 3812
Hungarian State Symphony Orchestra 262, 368, 1711, 1743, 1884, 1964, 1973, 2231, 2315, 2896
Hunsberger, Donald, conductor 1126, 2434
Hunt, Donald, conductor 784, 2762, 3511, 3529
Hunt, Donald, organ 4054
Hunteler, Konrad, flute 1459
Hunter, Rita, soprano 719
Hurford, Peter, organ 241, 243, 244, 245, 246, 3664
Hurst, Linda, mezzo-soprano 1414
Hurwitz, Emanuel, violin 105
Husa, Karel, conductor 1823
Husch, Gerhard, baritone 1819, 3561
Husson, Robert, organ 1869
Huttenlocher, Philippe, bass-baritone 126, 136, 138, 227, 1007, 1013, 1097, 1197, 2013, 2142, 2830, 3129
Huybregts, Pierre, piano 3889
Huys, Johan, harpsichord 3546
Huys, Johan, organ 3546
Hyde, Walter, tenor 3774
Hyldgaard, Tove, soprano 2427
Hylton, Brent, organ 2674
Hyman, Dick, piano 1477
Hynes, Elizabeth 3497
Iacopucci, Fernando, tenor 3350
Ibbott, Daphne, piano 3507, 3665
Iceland Symphony Orchestra 1949, 3169
Iglitzin, alan, viola 1470
Ignazio, Lydia Walton, piano 697, 2137, 3891

Ignal, Madeleine, soprano 1524
Igumnov, Konstantin, piano 2926, 3222, 3832, 3833
Ihara, Naoko, contralto 126, 1007, 2142
Iliev, Constantin, conductor 457
Illinois Contemporary Chamber Players 1580
Imanov, L. 41
Imbart de la Tour, Georges, tenor 3770
Immer, Friedemann, trumpet 3297
Inbal, Eliahu, conductor 444, 2950, 2952, 2957, 2969
Indiana Chamber Orchestra 3655
Indiana University Opera Theater Orchestra and Chorus 1351
Ingebretsen, Kjell, conductor 9, 1540, 3170
Ingebretsen, Kjell, piano 1540
Ingham, Michael, baritone 1906
Inghelbrecht, D. E., conductor 1199
Ingram, Nelly and Jaime, piano 1131
Innocenti, Stefano, organ 3846
Innsbruck Chamber Orchestra 3325
Instrumental Ensemble et Choeurs de la Madeleine 1528
Instrumental Ensemble of France 3912
International Festival Youth Orchestra 3270
International String Congress Orchestra, 1960 1660
Irving, Robert, conductor 907, 1498
Isaak, Donald, piano 3109, 3113
Isaeva, L. 41
Isakadze, Liana, violin 3186
Isepp, Martin, harpsichord 858, 1222, 3778
Isepp, Martin, piano 3990
Ishikawa, Shizuka, violin 3213
Isoir, Andre, organ 242, 252, 307, 312, 3852
Israel Music Centre Chamber Orchestra 2213
Israel Philharmonic Orchestra 414, 426, 429, 696, 2023, 2043, 2129, 2152, 2263, 2376, 2554, 2884, 2897, 3216, 3227
Italian Radio-Television Chamber Choir 3436
Ivanovsky, Vladimir, tenor 2698
Ivantzov, Ivan, bass-baritone 3774
Ives, Eugene, baritone 2713
Ivogun, Maria, soprano 3646, 3774
Jaccottet, Christiane, harpsichord

279, 322, 1642, 1674, 2072, 3305, 3434, 3521

Jacksch, Werner, violoncello 1182

Jackson, Francis, organ 1375

Jackson, Lena, organ 3590

Jackson, Nicholas, harpsichord 1145

Jackson, Nicholas, organ 251

Jackson, Richard, bass 1008

Jacob, Werner, organ 820, 2671

Jacobs, Paul, piano 155, 1186

Jacobs, Rene, countertenor 101, 763, 997, 1009, 1010, 1295, 1586, 1599, 1632, 2189, 2590, 3546

Jacquin, Christiane, soprano 1524

Jadlowker, Hermann, tenor 3774

Jahn, Jorg-Wolfgang, violin 1182, 1460

Jalas, Jussi, conductor 1949

James, David, alto 2495

James, Ifor, horn 3644

James, Judith, soprano 2719

Jamet, Marie-Clair, Quintet 2746

Jando, Jeno, piano 1395, 1969

Janigro, Antonio, conductor 1725, 1728, 1730, 3418

Janota, Gabor, bassoon 102

Janowitz, Gundula, soprano 170, 602, 1689, 3459

Janowski, Marek, conductor 1894

Jansen, Jacques, tenor 1200

Janska, Jaroslava, soprano 1834

Janssen, Guus, piano 3818

Janssen, Herbert, baritone 1622, 3451

Japan Chorus Union 2109

Japridze, Anton, bass 3214

Jarred, Mary, mezzo-soprano 3451

Jarry, Gerard, violin 120, 197, 1681, 1938

Jarsky, I., soprano 2712

Jarvi, Neimi, conductor 2750

Jarvis, Gerald, violin 1226

Jaye Consort of Viols 3, 3496, 3719

Jedlicka, Dalibor, bass 1834, 1836

Jenkins, Angela, singer 1468

Jenkins, Neil, tenor 263, 2587, 3334, 3918

Jenkins, Philips, piano 2541

Jensen, Rolin, piano 3738

Jerger, Alfred, baritone 3476

Jeritza, Maria, soprano 3774

Jerusalem Music Center Chamber Orchestra 2216

Jerusalem, Siegfried, tenor 730, 1894, 1947, 2148, 2468, 3641

Jeugden Muziek Middleburg 3518

Jeunesses Musicales de France Chorale 1486

Jeunesses Musicales Nordrhein-Westfalen Orchestra 2666

Jewel, Ian, viola 3332

Jewell, Kenneth, Chorale 3074

Jilek, Frantisek, conductor 1303, 1833, 3029

Joachim, Irene, soprano 1200

Jobin, Raoul, tenor 717

Jochims, Wilfrid, tenor 148

Jochum, Eugen, conductor 173, 267, 268, 555, 561, 563, 565, 574, 584, 593, 594, 793, 802, 926, 929, 938, 939, 946, 947, 2024, 2301, 2458

Johannes, William, bass 3534

Johannesen, Grant, piano 1077, 1399, 1545

Johansen, Mogens Schmidt, bass 2427

Johansson, Marianne, soprano 1850

Johns, Michele, piano 1020

Johnsen, Kjell, organ 9

Johnson, Edward, tenor 3774

Johnson, Gilbert, trumpet 2968, 3606

Johnson, Graham, piano 902

Johnson, James, piano 1005, 2120

Johnson, Laurie, conductor 1774

Johnson, Lucile, harp 1181

Johnson, Patricia, mezzo-soprano 719, 2581

Johnson, Robert, tenor 452

Johnston, David, tenor 3334

Joineau, Jacques, conductor 3318

Jonas, Diethelm, oboe 2234

Jonasson, Ingvar, viola 1415

Jones, Della, mezzo-soprano 1686, 2177, 2569

Jones, Gareth, baritone 3152, 3165

Jones, Geraint, conductor 1647, 2582

Jones, Geraint, Singers 1647

Jones, Gwyneth, soprano 553, 3074, 3449

Jones, Isola, mezzo-soprano 2089

Jones, Joela, piano 1092

Jones, Karon, violin 2640

Jones, Leslie, conductor 3050

Jones, Leslie, organ 3050

Jones, Leslie, tenor 1236

Jones, Mason, horn 1765, 3606

Jones, Philip, Brass Ensemble 59, 3566, 3568, 3569, 3571

Jones, Rowland, tenor 3063

Jones, Trevor, bass viol 3878

Jones, Trevor, conductor 1801, 2074
Jones, Trevor, viola da gamba 984
Jones-Hudson, Eleanor, soprano 3774
Jordan, Armin, conductor 1097, 1197, 2249, 3044
Jordan, Gary, bass 344
Jorn, Karl, tenor 3770
Jourfier, Jacqueline, soprano 3557
Journet, Marcel, bass 3774
Jubeau, Jean, piano 2960
Judd, James, conductor 1261, 2177
Judd, Roger, conductor 3525
Judd, Terence, piano 3622
Juilliard Ensemble 653
Juilliard Orchestra 1159
Juillard Percussion Orchestra 3327
Juilliard Quartet 353, 1419, 1699, 2340, 2850, 3494
Junghanel, Konrad, lute 215, 3500
Junghanel, Konrad, theorbo 997, 1000, 1010, 1599, 2590
Junghanns, Rolf, clavichord 92
Junghanns, Rolf, hammerklavier 2879
Junghanns, Rolf, harpsichord 81
Junghanns, Rolf, piano 537
Jungkind, Lisa, soprano 3167
Jungwirth, Manfred, bass 3082
Jurinac, Sena, soprano 453, 851, 2294, 2307
Jurjevskaya, Zinaida, soprano 3774
Jurrens, James, conductor 3030
Kabaiwanska, Raina, soprano 2565
Kabasta, Oswald, conductor 3898
Kacso, Diana, piano 1057
Kaczynski, Adam, conductor 3857
Kadinskaya, Klara, soprano 2697
Kagg, Anders, guitar 3883
Kahlhofer, Helmut, conductor 853
Kaine, Carmel, violin 2271, 3916
Kalichstein, Joseph, piano 2821
Kalish, Gilbert, piano 1023, 1715, 1717, 2810, 2867
Kaliszewska, Jadwiga, violin 1162
Kalmar, Magda, soprano 1721, 2315
Kalter, Sabine, mezzo-soprano 3774
Kamasa, Stefan, viola 333
Kamenev, Christo, tenor 457
Kammerkoret Camerata 3587
Kammermusiker Zurich 375
Kampe, Susan 2187
Kamu, Okko, violin 134, 1250
Kanawa, Kiri Te, contralto 555, 819, 1816, 2292, 2295, 2296, 3112, 3611
Kaniak, Jiri, oboe 2488

Kann, Hans, fortepiano 329
Kansas City Philharmonic Orchestra 2535
Kantilena Childrens Chorus 1312
Kantorow, Jean-Jacques, violin 1980, 2234
Kapanadze, Nikolay, bass 2478
Kaplan, Arnold, piano 1877
Kaplan, Gyorgy, tenor 3437
Kaplan, Leigh, piano 1281
Kapp, Richard, conductor 1990, 2343, 3640
Kapp Sinfonietta 356
Kappel, Gertrude, soprano 3774
Kaproff, Armand, violoncello 1952
Karabtchevksy, Isaac, conductor 2435
Karnobatlova-Dobreva, Blagovesta, soprano 2606
Karolyi, Sandor, violin 2663
Karp, Bess, harpsichord 3707
Karper, Laszlo, guitar 1471
Karr, Gary, double bass 1159
Karuza, Marjan, violin 3293
Kasandjiev, Vassil, conductor 3211
Kaschmann, Giuseppe, baritone 3770
Kaschowska, Felice, soprano 3770
Kasprzyk, Jacek, conductor 333
Kassebaum, Wilfried, piano 1301
Kassel State Theatre Orchestra 1780
Kassel Vocal Ensemble 131
Kastorksy, Vladimir, bass 3770
Kastu, Matti, tenor 3074
Katchen, Julius, piano 369
Kates, Stephen, violoncello 53, 1961, 4002
Katims, Milton, conductor 1504
Katims, Milton, viola 2342
Katin, Peter, piano 722, 2616
Katlewicz, Jerzy, conductor 2491
Katzen, Daniel, horn 3999
Kaufman, Louis, conductor 1576
Kaufman, Louis, violin 349, 1576
Kavafian, Ida, violin 547
Kavrakos, Dimitri, bass 3347
Kay, Nancy, harp 3890
Kazandjiev, Vassil, conductor 204
Kecskes, Andras, lute 2072
Kee, Piet, organ 3742
Keene, Christopher, conductor 958, 1518
Keene, Constance, piano 185, 3935
Keenlyside, Raymond, violin 2188
Kegel, Herbert, conductor 657, 2119, 2397, 3358, 3490
Kehr, Gunter, conductor 2503

Kehr Trio 2503
Keilberth, Joseph, conductor 425, 1786, 2804
Kejmar, Miroslav, trumpet 3417
Kelemen, Zoltan, bass-baritone 1946
Keller, Evelyn 2170
Keller, Irma, alto 131
Keller Quartet 3514
Keller, Roland, piano 3019, 3487
Kelsey, Franklyn, baritone 3773
Kelterborn, Rudolf, conductor 1871
Keltsch, Werner, Instrumental Ensemble 925
Kemp, Barbara, soprano 3774
Kempe, Rudolf, conductor 818, 928, 934, 1338, 1893, 3094, 3462, 3488
Kempff, Wilhelm, piano. 420, 499, 507, 510, 516, 523, 613, 614, 2823, 2861
Kempin, Peter, organ 4035
Kendall, William, tenor 1621
Kennard, Julie, soprano 1694
Kennedy, Dorothy, violin 3583
Kennedy, Lauri, violoncello 3583
Kensington Gore Singers 4065
Kent, George, organ 3866
Keonch, Boldizsar, tenor 3126
Kergonan Abbey Choir 3575, 3579, 3580
Kern, Adele, soprano 3105
Kerstens, Huub, conductor 1773, 2062 2801
Kertesz, Istvan, conductor 369, 1512 2376, 2885, 2886, 2891, 2901, 2905, 2983
Kertesz, Tamas, tenor 1954
Kessler, Melinda, alto 4067
Kessler, Thomas, conductor 1873
Ketchum, Anne Marie, soprano 1909
Ketelaars, Leo, bass 267, 268
Keyte, Christopher, bass-baritone 762, 1623, 1654, 2191, 2437, 2577 2579, 2786, 3511
Khaikin, Boris, conductor 2718, 3796
Khristich, Zoe, soprano 3796
Khristova, Tony, contralto 2606
Khuner, Jonathan, conductor 1287
Kibbutz Chamber Orchestra 3564
Kienzler, Iris, oboe 3292, 3293
Kiknadze, Shota, baritone 2478
Killebrew, Gwendolyn, mezzo-soprano 1797
Kim, Chang-Kook, flute 2210
Kincses, Veronica, soprano 1028, 1511, 1711, 1721

King, Andrew, tenor 1627
King Edward VI School Choir 3527
King, James, tenor 552, 1785, 3459, 3475
King, Malcolm, bass-baritone 2292, 2295, 2738, 2822
King, Peter, organ 34
King, Thea, clarinet 1420, 2228, 2338
King's College Chapel Choir, Cambridge 237, 1589, 1618, 1625, 1710, 3783, 3784, 3823
King's College Choral Scholars 906
King's House School Choir 2480
King's Music 1633, 2589
King's Singers 967, 3791
Kipnis, Alexander, bass 3774
Kipnis, Igor, clavichord 2798
Kipnis, Igor, harpsichord 2798, 3399
Kirby-Lunn, Louise, contralto 3770
Kirchner, Alexander, tenor 3774
Kirchoff, Walter, tenor 3774
Kirkby, Emma, soprano 230, 1147, 1587, 1623, 1628, 1648, 2074, 2584, 3435, 3877, 3878, 3879
Kirkpatrick, Gary, piano 3654
Kirkpatrick, John, piano 2755
Kirkpatrick, Ralph, harpsichord 192, 217, 218, 219, 320
Kirschbaum, Ralph, violoncello 890, 1360, 2770
Kiskalt, Fritz, violoncello 322
Kiurina, Berta, soprano 3774
Kjorkoy, Kare, tenor 1556
Klaas, Rainer, piano 2559
Klamanda, Olfa, horn 3417
Klarwein, Franz, tenor 3448
Klas, Eri, conductor 3024
Klebanow, Susan, soprano 2583
Klebel, Bernhard, conductor 4003
Klebl, Heidi, soprano 2787
Klecka, Paul, horn 3292, 3293
Klee, Bernhard, conductor 2217, 2303
Kleiber, Carlos, conductor 2887
Kleiber, Erich, conductor 570, 3897
Klein, Kenneth, conductor 1025
Klein, Peter, tenor 3067, 3538
Klemens, Mario, conductor 994
Klementti Institute Chamber Chorus 1915
Klemperer, Otto, conductor 229, 412, 607, 608, 930, 2345, 2347, 2922, 3091, 3455
Klenov, Oleg, baritone 3241
Klepac, Rudolf, bassoon 3418

Kleshcheva, Antonina, mezzo-soprano 2697
Kletzki, Paul, conductor 557, 817, 1048, 2029, 2628, 2630, 2702, 3276
Klein, Walter, piano 2339, 2358, 2851
Klier, Manfred, horn 2318, 2956
Klinda, Ferdinand, organ 257, 1860
Kline, Olive, soprano 3774
Kling, Paul, violin 53
Klint, Jergen, bass 2427
Klocker, Dieter, clarinet 1171, 1798 1911, 3445
Klomp, Dick, organ 1926
Klose, Margarete, contralto 2075, 2400, 3446, 3468, 3584, 3712
Klotz, Hans, organ 2667
Kmentt, Waldemar, tenor 16, 602, 607, 2146
Knappertsbusch, Hans, conductor 453, 3456, 3460, 3465, 3474
Knardahl, Eva, piano 1539, 1540, 1551, 1552, 1554, 1558, 1561, 1562, 1565, 3020, 3588
Kneubuhl, John, guitar 1910, 3884
Knibbs, Jean, soprano 1621
Knight, Gillian, mezzo-soprano 2311
Knupfer, Paul, bass 3770
Knushevitzky, Sviatoslav, violon-cello 2926
Koban, Gisela, soprano 2276
Kobayashi, Takanori, piano 1456
Koch, Helmut, conductor 128
Koch, Johannes, viola da gamba 90, 1645, 2006, 3308
Koch, Ulrich, viola 1431, 2664, 3049
Kocsis, Zoltan, piano 196, 3038
Kodousek, Josef, viola 1788, 2270, 3048
Koeckert, Rudolf, violin 3108
Koerner, Jean, piano 1167
Koetsier, Jan, conductor 546
Koffmane, Robert, bass 3712
Kogan, Leonid, violin 1760
Kohler, Christoph, horn 42, 2205, 2956
Kohler, Siegfried, conductor 3487
Kohn, Karl, bass 2294, 2462
Kohnen, Robert, harpsichord 271, 763, 1251, 1427, 3304, 3542, 3544, 3767
Kollo, Rene, tenor 460, 553, 1846,

1946, 2023, 3082
Kolniak, Angela, soprano 2319
Kolomyzeva, Tatyana, conductor 3189
Kondrashin, Kiril (Kyril), conductor 434, 1339, 2037, 2047, 2179, 2297, 2623, 2708, 2984
Kondratyuk, Nicolay, baritone 3796
Konetzni, Hilde, soprano 3355
Kontarsky, Alfons, piano 846, 1964, 2871
Kontarsky, Aloys, piano 846, 1964, 2871, 3059
Konwitschny, Franz, conductor 804
Kooiman, Ewald, organ 4038
Koopman, Ton, conductor 1597, 3818, 4015
Koopman, Ton, harpsichord 330, 978, 1158, 1428, 2063, 2069, 2515, 3818
Koopman, Ton, organ 177, 1155
Kord, Kazimierz, conductor 1920, 2094, 2998
Korjus, Meliza, soprano 3559, 3872
Kormendi, Klara, piano 3039
Korody (Korodi), Andras, conductor 368, 1296, 2227
Korolewicz-Wayda, Janina, soprano 3770
Korolyov, Aleksei, bass 2697
Korondy, Gyorgy, tenor 1711, 1973, 2315
Korsoff, Lucette, soprano 3770
Kosa, Gabor, percussion 1283, 3810
Kosa, Gyorgy, piano 1895
Koshetz, Nina, soprano 3774
Kosler, Zdenek, conductor 1017, 1311, 1326, 1344, 1840, 2079, 2551, 2745, 3213
Kosmala, Jerzy, viola 1089
Kostelanetz, Andre, conductor 1863, 3605
Koszut, Ursula, soprano 1785, 2468
Koth, Erika, soprano 633, 1864, 2301, 3470, 3696
Koussevitzky, Serge, conductor 1159
Kovacs, Bela, clarinet 1395, 2227, 2692
Kovacs, Denes, violin 205
Kovacs, Lorant, flute 196, 2231
Kovacs, Peter, bass 1895
Kovalyov, Alexei, conductor 2697
Kovats, Kolos, bass 358, 1028, 3437
Koves-Steiner, Toni, cimbalom 3128
Kozikova, Marcela, harp 1181
Kozina, Zdenek, piano 3123

Kozlovsky, Alexei, conductor 1898
Kozlovsky, Ivan, tenor 2926
Krahmer, Renate, soprano 323
Krainev, Vladimir, piano 2418
Krainis, Bernard, recorder 1608
Kramar, Magda, soprano 1028
Kramer, Nicholas, harpsichord 65, 2633
Krapp, Edgar, organ 3912
Krasavin, Sergei, bassoon 7
Kraus, Adalbert, tenor 130, 2009, 3302
Kraus, Alfredo, tenor 630, 2102, 2563, 3365, 3371
Kraus, Eberhard, organ 2032
Kraus, Harold, tenor 3712
Kraus, Lili, piano 2359, 2360, 2864, 2870
Kraus, Peter, tenor 634
Kraus, Philip, baritone 452
Krause, Tom, baritone 2123, 2320
Krauss, Clemens, conductor 2075, 2874, 3085, 3105, 3448
Krebbers, Hermann, violin 202, 440, 806
Krebs, Helmut, tenor 3360
Kreger, James, violoncello 1103
Kreil, Karl, tenor 2457
Kreiselman, Jack, clarinet 1412
Krejcik, Vladimir, tenor 1834, 1836
Kremer, Gidon, violin 387, 410, 696, 2031, 2543, 2806, 2977, 3209, 3601
Krenek, Ernst, conductor 1907, 1910
Krenn, Werner, tenor 150, 1687, 1946, 1948, 2009, 2123, 2308, 2974
Krenz, Jan, conductor 333, 3857
Krepelova, Libuse, piano 2752
Kreppel, Walter, bass 2294
Krips, Josef, conductor 447, 2372, 3121
Krist, Michael, piano 3287
Kroll, Mark, harpsichord 281
Kronos String Quartet 2753
Krumbach, Wilhelm, organ 100
Krusceniski, Solomeo, soprano 3770
Kruysen, Bernard, baritone 1293, 1405
Ktitorov, Leonid, bass-baritone 2697
Kubalek, Antonin, piano 2467
Kubelik, Rafael, conductor 569, 585, 589, 1323, 1330, 1785, 1838, 2032, 2038, 2054, 2126, 2462, 2947, 3027, 3459, 3491

Kubler, David, tenor 452
Kucera, Joseph, percussion 1910
Kuchl, Rainer, violin 3098
Kuehn, Robert, baritone 2803
Kuen, Paul, tenor 2321, 2460, 3469
Kuerti, Anton, piano 498, 500
Kuhn Chorus 1312
Kuhn Female Choir 1832
Kuhne, Rolf, bass-baritone 557
Kuijken, Barthold, flute 1757, 3300, 3310, 3544
Kuijken Consort 101
Kuijken, Sigiswald, conductor 1133, 1135, 1632, 2634
Kuijken, Sigiswald, viol 1427
Kuijken, Sigiswald, viola da gamba 1251, 3767
Kuijken, Sigiswald, violin 277, 763, 1137, 1427, 1757, 3432, 3767
Kuijken, Wieland, pardessus de viole 3310
Kuijken, Wieland, viol 1009, 1010, 1427, 2593, 2723
Kuijken, Wieland, viola da gamba 1251, 2590, 3310, 3542, 3544, 3767
Kuijken, Wieland, violin 1427, 3767
Kuijken, Wieland, violoncello 763, 1137, 1295, 1599, 1757, 3304
Kuklewicz, Roman, conductor 3857
Kulenkampff, Georg, violin 805
Kulka, Janos, conductor 1037
Kulka, Konstanty, violin 1902, 3180, 3399
Kullmann, Charles, tenor 2028
Kuney, Scott, mandolin 2580
Kunth, Bodo, horn 3292, 3293
Kuntzsch, Matthias, conductor 2438
Kunz, Erich, bass-baritone 3067, 3081, 3711
Kunz, Hans, organ 4035
Kunzel, Erich, conductor 1475, 3202
Kuoppala, Mats, keyed fiddle 1850
Kupferman, Meyer, clarinet 1656, 1913, 3478
Kurpe, Nikolai, tenor 2973
Kurshumov, Pavel, tenor 2606
Kurt, Melanie, soprano 3774
Kurtz, Efrem, conductor 2550, 3244
Kurz, Dieter, conductor 2276
Kurz, Selma, soprano 3770
Kusche, Benno, baritone 1846, 1862, 1864, 1947, 2460, 3462, 3712, 3764
Kussmaul, Jurgen, viola 1911

Kussmaul, Jurgen, violin 200
Kussmaul, Rainer, violin 189, 325
Kussmaul, Wolfgang, violin 200
Kuster-Jordon, Karin, soprano 1763
Kuszenova, Olga, mezzo-soprano 2478
Kuznetsov, Lev, tenor 3214, 3241
Kuznetsova, Maria, soprano 3774
Kvalbein, Aage, violoncello 3393
Kvapil, Radoslav, piano 1303
Kweksilber, Marianne, soprano 1597, 2189
Kwella, Payrizia, soprano 1593
Kynaston, Nicholas, organ 1371, 2207, 3381
Labadie, P., percussion 1873
Labia, Maria, soprano 3774
Labinsky, Andrei, tenor 3770
Labounsky, Ann, organ 1928
Labric, Pierre, organ 212, 3377, 3379, 3380, 3735
Lachance, Janine, piano 1003, 1022, 1444, 1529, 1581, 2101
Lachert, Hanna, violin 386, 3183
Ladysz, Bernard, bass-baritone 2490, 2493, 2494
Lafont, Jean-Philippe, baritone 2102
Lagace, Bernard, organ 791, 964
Lagace, Mireille, harpsichord 179, 756
Lagace, Mireille, organ 4020
Lagger, Peter, bass 2494
Lagorce, Marcel, trumpet 3716
Lagoya, Alexandre, guitar 760, 3603
Lahota, Gabor, organ 163
Laiho, Altti, Pentti, Veikko, accordian 3834
Laird, Michael, trumpet 3565, 3779
Lajos, Attila, flute 1296
Laky, Krisztina, soprano 1632, 1797
Lamont String Quartet 3651
La Montaine, John, piano 1923, 1924, 1925
Lamoureux Concerts Orchestra 713, 723, 1919
Lamoureux Orchestra 3915
Lampe, Oscar, violin 3101
Lancashire Schools Symphony Orchestra 3526
Lancelot, James, organ 3937, 3939
Lanchbery, John, conductor 1114, 2777
Landau, Siegfried, conductor 1499, 1892
Landesjungendorchester Nordhein-Westfalen 1793

Landini Consort 3570, 4031
Landis, Helen, contralto 3155
Landouzy, Lise, soprano 3770
Landy, Tonny, tenor 2427
Lane, Elizabeth 1468
Lane, Martin, alto 1618
Lang, Wilhelm, bass 2075
Lang, William, trumpet 1680
Langan, Kevin, bass 1351
Langbein, Brenton, conductor 375
Langdon, John, organ 1618
Langdon, Michael, bass 1690
Lange, Hansjurg, bassoon 3753
Langenbeck, August, conductor 3765
Langier, Jane, soprano 3773
Langlais, Jean, organ 1927
Langridge, Philip, tenor 5, 709, 762, 1421, 1637, 1813, 2102
Lanigan, John, tenor 629
Lannerholm, Torlief, oboe 1455
Lantos, Istvan, organ, 1711
Lantos, Istvan, piano 1249
Lapelletrie, Rene, tenor 3774
Lapierre, Gabriel, piano 3770
Laplante, Bruno, baritone 1003, 1022, 1444, 1529, 1581, 2101
Lappas, Ulysses, tenor 3774
Larde, Christian, flute 621, 1938, 3717
Laredo, Carlos, violin 1013
Laredo, Jaime, violin 2939
Laredo, Ruth, piano 2613, 2939
Larrocha, Alicia de, piano 408, 431, 1535, 2264, 2826, 3037, 3825
Larsens, Gunars, violin 3400
Lasalle, Jean, baritone 3770
LaSalle Quartet 482, 836, 2853, 3522
Lashanska, Hulda, soprano 3774
Laskine, Lily, harp 1183, 2236
Lasser, Ingeborg, contralto 649
Latchem, Malcolm, violin 65, 3443
Latvian Radio and Television Orchestra 1867
Latvian Radio Orchestra 1831
Latvian S.S.R. Philharmonic Cello Ensemble 1831
Laubacher Kantorei 925
Laubenthal, Horst, tenor 173, 643, 1894, 2123, 2464
Laugs, Richard, piano 2663
Lauke, Michael, guitar 637
Lauri-Volpi, Giacomo, tenor 1491
Laurich, Hildegard, contralto 925, 1797
Lausanne Chamber Orchestra 126, 227,

1097, 1100, 1666, 1685, 1686, 1695, 2249, 3044, 3387, 3388, 3434
Lausanne Instrumental Ensemble 1674
Lausanne Orchestra 2830
Lausanne Pro Arte Chorus 1031
Lausanne University Chorus 3129
Lausanne Vocal Ensemble 126, 227, 1695, 2830, 3387, 3388, 3434
Lautenbacher, Susanne, violin 1413, 1645, 1663, 2664, 2829
Lavilla, Felix, piano 3665, 3698
Lavotha, Elemer, violoncello 1962
Lawlor, Louis, guitar 3974
Lawson, Peter, piano 238, 2778
Lawson, Winifred, soprano 3154, 3156, 3157
Lazarev, Alexander, conductor 2611
Lazaro, Hipolito, tenor 3774
Lazarof, Henri, conductor 3652
Lazzari, Agostino, tenor 2733
Lazzari, Carolina, soprano 3774
Lea, Yvonne, mezzo-soprano 908
Leandre, J., bass 1873
Lear, Evelyn, soprano 264, 2942, 3215
Lebherz, Louis, bass 3344
Lebranc-Maeterlinck, Georgette, soprano 3774
Ledger, Philip, conductor 906, 1589, 3783, 3784, 3893
Ledger, Philip, piano 734, 2487
Lee, Fred, vibraphone 1910
Lee, Noel, harpsichord 1941
Lee, Noel, piano 1293, 1941
Lee, Sung-Sook, soprano 2743
Leeds Parish Church Choir 1375
Leeuw, Reinbert de, conductor 1166
Leeuw, Reinbert, piano 2775
Le Floc, Herve, violin 3296
Leggatt, Robin, tenor 1666
Legrand, Christiane, soprano 655
Legrand, Michel, conductor 1942
Legrand Michel, piano 1942
Le Grice, Ian, organ 3534
Lehane, Maureen, mezzo-soprano 139, 1709, 2962
Lehel, Gyorgy, conductor 343, 1249, 1296, 1721
Lehmann, Fritz, conductor 2260
Lehmann, Lilli, soprano 3770
Lehmann, Lotte, soprano 3476, 3774
Lehmayer, Walter, oboe 2396
Lehotka, Gabor, organ 159, 250, 1870
Lehrndorfer, Franz, organ 1673

Leib, Gunter, bass 128
Leicestershire Schools Symphony Orchestra 898
Leider, Frida, soprano 3774
Leinsdorf, Erich, conductor 2395, 2711
Leipzig Gewandhaus Orchestra 128, 132, 236, 238, 560, 575, 592, 600, 797, 798, 800, 807, 815, 863, 916, 920, 921, 923, 931, 935, 944, 952, 2145, 2951, 2953
Leipzig Radio Chorus 456, 657, 1557, 2145, 2222, 2306, 2397, 2856, 3358
Leipzig Radio Orchestra 657, 2397, 3358, 3490
Leisner, Emmi, mezzo-soprano 545, 3774
Leitner, Ferdinand, conductor 420, 2452, 2464, 3818
Lejsek, Vlastimil, piano 2080
Lejskova, Vera, piano 2080
Leliva, Tadeusz, baritone 3770
Lemaigre, Philippe, guitar 3042
Lemmen, Gunther, viola d'amore 47
Lemnitz, Tiana, soprano 1622, 3538, 3561, 3584, 3773
Lenard, Ondrej, conductor 1212, 3847, 4030
Lener String Quartet 2329
Leningrad Chamber Orchestra 1389, 3781
Leningrad Orchestra of Old and New Music 1390, 3317
Leningrad Philharmonic Academic Symphony 1389, 1390
Leningrad Philharmonic Orchestra 2973, 3008, 3136, 3781
Lennox, David, tenor 632
Lensky, Margaret, contralto 2581
Lenz, Friedrich, tenor 451, 1947, 2301, 2321, 3166
Leonard, Lawrence, conductor 1799
Leonard, Patricia, mezzo-soprano 3165
Leonard, Peter, conductor 2719
Leonard, Ronald, violoncello 761
Leonhardt Consort   96, 122, 127, 135, 136, 138
Leonhardt, Gustav, conductor 96, 122, 127, 135, 136, 138, 2189
Leonhardt, Gustav, harpsichord 76, 77, 96, 183, 223, 254, 277, 316, 986, 1157, 1452, 1453, 1679, 2189, 2792, 3310

Leonhardt, Gustav, organ 95, 96, 1452, 3175
Leonhardt, Marie, violin 96
Leoz, Alfonso, tenor 2734
Lepetit, Jean-Pierre, horn 2807
Leppard, Raymond, conductor 86, 188, 195, 1550, 1596, 1609, 1637, 1649 2125, 2190, 2191, 2192, 2209, 2397, 2580
Leppard, Raymond, harpsichord 195
Leprin, Frederic, tenor 717
Lerdahl, Fred, conductor 1287
Le Roux, Jean-Louis, conductor 1287, 1937
Leroux, Xavier, piano 3770
Leroy, Jean-Paul, trumpet 1897
Le Roy, Rene, flute 2236, 3327
Lessing, Alfred, viola da gamba 47
Lestelly, Louis, baritone 3774
Lester, Harold, harpsichord 3050, 3745
Lettvin, Theodore, piano 445
Leuba, Christopher, conductor 1174
Leussink, Jos, conductor 1773
Levin, Robert, piano 1568
Levinas, Michael, conductor 1873
Levinas, Michael, piano 1873
Levine, James, conductor 626, 2051, 2057, 2089, 2563, 3127, 3950
Levine, James, piano 2330
Levinzon, Iosif, violoncello 3194
Levitzki, Mischa, piano 1983
Levy, Robert, synthesizer 3484
Levy, Robert, trumpet 3484, 3509
Lewin, Michael, theorbo 1653
Lewis, Bertha, contralto 3154, 3156, 3157
Lewis, Henry, conductor 3948
Lewis, Keith, tenor 2734
Lewis, Richard, tenor 458, 609, 1118 2192, 2307
Lewis, Robert Hall, conductor 5
Lexutt, Walter, horn 4026
Leyetchkiss, Vladimir, piano 2545
Liberman, Victor, violin 1390
Libove, Charles, violin 2643
Licette, Miriam, soprano 3774
Lichfield Cathedral Choir 34
Lichtenberger, Hannes, bass 3347
Lieberman, Carol, violin 281
Lieder Quartett 1720
Liege Symphony Orchestra 1517
Lill, John, piano 411, 794
Lille Philharmonic Orchestra 1302, 2654

Lilleslatten, Asbjorn, viola 3173
Lilley, Barbara, soprano 3165
Lilowa, Margarita, mezzo-soprano 2123
Lima, Luis, tenor 2099
Limoli, Michael, clarinet 3650
Lind, Gitta, soprano 1846
Lind, Loren, flute 697
Lindberg, Jakob, lute 1273
Lindblom, Rolf, piano 1454
Lindbloom, Christopher, baritone 3485
Linde, Hans-Martin, flute 73, 90, 292, 1668, 2230
Linde, Hans-Martin, recorder 3308
Linden, Magnus, bass 2317
Linder, Alf, organ 2721, 3933
Linder, Brigitte, soprano 2219
Lindholm, Berit, soprano 632, 691
Lindley, Simon, conductor 1375
Lindley, Simon, organ 2691
Lindquist, Karen, harp 1907
Lindsay Quartet 467
Linos, Lenys, mezzo-soprano 1624
Linz City Theater Operetta Ensemble 1865
Lipatti, Dinu, piano 1544, 3774
Lipkowska, Lydia, soprano 3774
Lipp, Wilma, soprano 3469
Lippe, Rosanna, soprano 2570
Lippincott, Joan, organ 308
Lipson-Gruzen, Berenice, piano 1184
Liptak, David, piano 988
List, Emmanuel, bass 3476
List, Eugene, piano 3915
Liszt, Ferenc, Chamber Orchestra 79, 102, 1675, 1721, 2185, 2241, 2244 2286, 2289, 3294
Liszt, Ferenc, Choir 1870, 1931
Liszt Music Academy Orchestra 196
Litaize, Gaston, organ 2774
Littasy, Gyorgy 229
Litvinne, Felia, soprano 3770
Litz, Gisela, soprano 3166
Liverpool Cathedral Choir 3531
Liverpool Radio Orchestra 2119
Livingston, William, tenor 1630
Ljungberg, Gota, soprano 3924
Llewellyn, Redvers, baritone 1236
Lloyd, David, tenor 1629, 2582
Lloyd, Edward, tenor 3770
Lloyd, Robert, bass 660, 906, 2223, 2300, 2314, 2564, 2763, 3334
Lloyd Webber, Julian, violoncello 901, 1220

Loban, John, violin 1016
Locke Brass Consort 3116, 3950
Lockhart, James, conductor 1780
Lodeon, Frederic, violoncello 1684,
   2140, 2164, 2960
Lodz Philharmonic Orchestra 3178
Lohman, Judy, harp 912
Lohmeyer, Gerd, piano 2880
Loibner, Wilhelm, conductor 812
Loman, Judy, harp 912
Lombard, Alain, conductor 3089,
   3473, 3666, 3818
Lombardi, Giannini Arangi, soprano
   3929
London Bach Choir 610
London Bach Orchestra 1694
London Camerata 981
London Chamber Choir 1708, 2738
London Chamber Orchestra 2689
London Chorale 736, 3323
London Concert Orchestra 3062, 3153
London Concord Singers 736
London Early Music Group 3955
London, George, bass-baritone 1792
London Junior Chamber Orchestra 4029
London, Little Orchestra 3050
London Master Virtuosi 3312
London Music Group 2835, 3335
London Music Players 1170
London Opera Chorus 2293, 2569, 2573
London Oratory Choir 970, 3326
London Philharmonic Chorus 1807,
   2148, 3479
London Philharmonic Orchestra 30, 54
   358, 413, 419, 424, 562, 564, 583
   670, 692, 795, 842, 877, 901,
   1234, 1308, 1318, 1324, 1342,
   1356, 1357, 1361, 1363, 1366,
   1367, 1368, 1370, 1377, 1378,
   1379, 1380, 1381, 1622, 1807,
   1808, 1822, 1996, 2021, 2033,
   2034, 2039, 2046, 2056, 2102,
   2125, 2147, 2148, 2154, 2162,
   2192, 2243, 2264, 2293, 2384,
   2409, 2474, 2486, 2552, 2558,
   2608, 2624, 2629, 2682, 2748,
   2974, 2979, 2986, 2988, 3801,
   3829, 3082, 3093, 3095, 3159,
   3219, 3236, 3271, 3274, 3338,
   3454, 3461, 3479, 3482, 3668,
   3672
London Philomusica 762, 3419
London Pro Musica 3683
London Russian Orthodox Cathedral
   Choir 3817

London Sinfonia (Symphonica) 1230,
   1422, 2049, 2058, 3002
London Sinfonietta 52, 709, 1414,
   1963, 2346, 2350, 2822, 3124
London Sinfonietta Chorus 2822
London Soloists Vocal Ensemble 3502
London Strings 1608
London Studio Symphony Orchestra
   1774
London Symphony Chorus 459, 1421,
   2397, 2529
London Symphony Orchestra 5, 12, 296
   326, 362, 366, 369, 396, 410, 413
   447, 459, 555, 559, 579, 582, 594
   604, 610, 642, 652, 671, 684, 688
   714, 736, 801, 808, 878, 886,
   1092, 1189, 1230, 1263, 1319,
   1357, 1364, 1365, 1369, 1421,
   1488, 1500, 1512, 1521, 1542,
   1555, 1787, 1876, 1942, 1984,
   2035, 2042, 2051, 2148, 2158,
   2214, 2229, 2237, 2255, 2257,
   2311, 2387, 2390, 2391, 2395,
   2397, 2407, 2429, 2430, 2479,
   2481, 2524, 2529, 2533, 2537,
   2555, 2644, 2647, 2652, 2696,
   2701, 2703, 2704, 2707, 2710,
   2726, 2748, 2806, 2923, 2924,
   2955, 3017, 3070, 3092, 3097,
   3112, 3135, 3139, 3193, 3196,
   3221, 3245, 3257, 3259, 3264,
   3278, 3285, 3330, 3331, 3493,
   3494, 3625, 3665, 3672, 3780,
   3797, 3829, 3915, 3918, 4045,
   4068
London Symphony Winds 3110
London Voices 1257, 1596, 1637, 1956
   2099
London Wind Orchestra 1804, 2345
Long, Nancy, soprano 970, 3326
Longfield, Susan, soprano 1654
Loose, Emmy, soprano 3067, 3711
Lopez-Cobos, Jesus, conductor 30,
   1685, 2682, 2734, 3668, 3918
Lorand, Colette, soprano 2680
Lorengar, Pilar, soprano 3668
Lorenz, Max, tenor 456, 3081, 3446,
   3451, 3468, 3538
Lorenz, Siegfried, bass 128
Lorincz, Edith, violin 646
Los Angeles Baroque Players 310
Los Angeles Camerata 2832
Los Angeles Chamber Orchestra 114,
   294, 1841, 1907
Los Angeles Festival Orchestra and

Chorus 3117
Los Angeles Philharmonic Orchestra 371, 431, 587, 917, 1036, 1046, 1195, 1939, 2030, 2040, 2686, 3231, 3242, 3247, 3250, 3260, 3282
Los Angeles Slide Trombone Ensemble 3653
Los Angeles String Quartet 1790
Losch, Liselotte, soprano 2400
Lott, Felicity, soprano 263, 1637, 2591, 3440, 3442
Loughran, James, conductor 794, 860, 898, 2110, 3068
Louisville Orchestra 43, 53, 336, 1662, 1764, 2011, 2117, 2172
Loup, Francois, bass 1197
Louvain Chorale Concinite 3576
Lovaas, Kari, soprano 730, 1090, 2740, 2788, 3166
Lovberg, Aase Nordmo, soprano 607
Loveday, Alan, violin 2271, 2352, 3443
Lowenthal, Jerome, piano 1567
Lubbock, John, conductor 2153, 2204 3119, 3715
Lubik, Hedi, harp 1895, 2692
Luca, Giuseppe de, baritone 3770, 3774
Luca, Sergiu, violin 998, 2821
Lucas, Brenda, piano 2121
Luccardi, Giancarlo, bass 3672
Luccioni, Jose, tenor 2764
Lucerne Festival Orchestra 349
Lucerne Festival Strings 73, 144, 192, 320, 706, 810, 3391, 3400
Luchetti, Veriano, tenor 1028, 3363
Lucia, Fernando de, tenor 3770, 3980
Ludewig-Verdehr, Elsa, lute 988
Ludwig, Christa, mezzo-soprano 170, 461, 607, 627, 1816, 2019, 2023, 2314, 2569, 3513, 3780, 3792
Ludwig, Hanna, soprano 3067
Ludwig, Leopold, conductor 3486
Ludwig, Walther, tenor 545, 3446, 3538
Ludwigsburger Festspiele Orchester 820
Lugovoy, Nina, piano 2643
Lukacs, Ervin, conductor 1511, 2231, 2692
Lukacs, Peter, viola 1895
Lukomska, Halina, soprano 3494, 3857
Lukowski, Guy, guitar 3042
Lunds Studentsangare 2504

Lupu, Radu, piano 414, 426, 429, 829, 1219, 1542, 2862
Lush, Ernest, piano 859
Lussan, Zelie de, soprano 3770
Lutz, Volker, organ 84
Lutz, Walter, violoncello 3561
Luvisi, Lee, piano 463, 2833
Luxembourg Radio Orchestra 1388, 1431, 1503, 1918, 2438, 2531, 2766
Luxon, Benjamin, baritone 226, 1362, 1625, 1637, 1686, 3479, 3483, 3573
Lyman-Silbiger, Gian, viola da gamba 1152
Lynn, Nalga, soprano 896
Lyon Vocal and Instrumental Ensemble 1143
Lysell, Bernt, violin 1455
Lytton, Henry, baritone 3154
Lyubimov, Aleksei, piano 2031
Lyubimov, Anatoly, oboe 7
Ma, Yo Yo, violoncello 442, 547
Maag, Peter, conductor 625, 2237, 2468, 3672
Maazel, Lorin, conductor 233, 291, 558, 581, 588, 606, 672, 712, 1018, 1190, 1193, 1289, 1447, 1740, 2292, 2295, 2373, 2408, 2556, 2576, 2650, 2695, 2895, 3087, 3122, 3146, 3209, 3269, 3353, 3453
Macalester Trio 4064
Macbeth, Florence, soprano 3774
Macchi, Maria de, soprano 3770
MacCourt, Donald, bassoon 1641
MacDonald, James, horn 3842
MacDonnel, Frances, conductor 966
Macerollo, Joseph, accordian 1905
Machata, Siegfried, horn 3292, 3293
Machotkova, Marcela, soprano 1312, 2081, 3029
Mackerras, Charles, conductor 74, 1612, 1834, 1836, 2384, 2446, 2581, 3159, 3787
MacNeil, Cornell, baritone 2572
MacPhail, Jean, mezzo-soprano 2799
Macurdy, John, bass 605, 2292, 2295
Madden, Ronald, baritone 2719
Madge, Geoffrey Douglas, piano 2062, 3518
Madison String Quartet 1908
Maerzendorfer, Ernst, conductor 2511, 3066
Maestri, Gigino, violin 1013

Magaloff, Nikita, piano 1051, 1073, 1079, 1096

Magdalen College Choir, Oxford 2495, 3319

Maggio Musical Fiorentino Chorus 2562

Maggio Musicale Fiorentino Orchestra 1512, 2560

Magiera, Leone, conductor 3535

Magiera, Leone, piano 2739

Magini-Coletti, Antonio, baritone 3770

Magnin, Alexandre, flute 25, 2083

Magnusson, Bob, double bass 1466

Maguenat, Alfred, baritone 3774

Maguire, Hugh, violin 2325, 3245

Magyar, Thomas, violin 201

Mahkhov, Vladimir, tenor 3241

Mahler, Christina, violoncello 4019

Mahon, Arnold, organ 659

Mai, Ludger, organ 4033

Maia, Carolyn mezzo-soprano 3061

Maier, Franzjosef, conductor 76, 106 121, 292, 1602, 1735, 2226, 2250, 2382, 3409

Maier, Franzjosef, violin 107, 611, 2291, 3395, 3432

Maile, Hans, violin 1254

Mainz Chamber Orchestra 2503

Maisenberg, Oleg, piano 3601

Maiste, Armas, piano 46

Maitrise de Notre Dame Cathedral Choir 3673

Maitrise Gabriel Faure 1400

Maison, Rene, tenor 716

Maklari, Jozsef, conductor 1260

Maksymiuk, Jerzy, conductor 119, 1548

Malacek, Alfred, violin 895

Malafronte, Judith, mezzo-soprano 2787

Malaniuk, Ira, mezzo-soprano 2055

Malatesta, Pompilio, bass 3773

Malcolm, George, conductor 24, 191, 297, 1613

Malcolm, George, harpsichord 175, 2523, 3855

Malcolm, George, organ 1603, 2523

Malgoire, Jean-Claude, conductor 1011, 1614, 1626, 1627, 1638, 2599, 3402, 3433, 3610

Mali, Istvan, clarinet 2290

Malko, Nicolai, conductor 2547

Mallebrera, Andre, countertenor 778, 2448

Malmo Kammarkor 2504

Malone, Carol, soprano 2464

Malt, Alexander, bass 2974

Maly, Lubomir, viola 32, 2752

Mancini, Caterina, soprano 2733

Mandalka, Rudolf, violoncello 611

Mandel, Alan, piano 3015

Mandikian, Arda, mezzo-soprano 2582

Mann, Joseph, tenor 3774

Mannberg, Karl-Ove, violin 2506

Manne, Shelly, drums 759

Manneke, Daan, conductor 2062

Manning, Jane, soprano 636, 1659

Manolov, Dimiter, conductor 3211

Mantel, Gerhard, violoncello 3108

Mantelli, Eugenia, contralto 3770

Manuguerra, Matteo, baritone 630, 2102, 2563, 3347

Manz, Lorraine, mezzo-soprano 393

Marak, Ottokar, tenor 3633, 3774

Marburg Vocal Ensemble 854

Marcel, Lucille, soprano 3774

Marchand, Charles, trombone 1873

Marchesi, Blanche, soprano 3770

Marchesini, Gaston, violoncello 3557

Marchwinski, J., piano 3180

Marciano, Rosario, piano 1243, 2837, 3021, 4023

Marconi, Francesco, tenor 3770

Marcoulescou, Yolanda, soprano 3886, 3892

Mardones, Jose, bass 3774, 3930

Marechal, Adolphe, tenor 3770

Margalit, Israela, piano 1018

Margittay, Sandor, organ 2315

Margolis, Sanford, piano 2008

Marheineke, Regina, soprano 2788

Mariakoren 3934

Marion, Alain, flute 621

Mariotti, Alfredo, bass 63, 2728

Mark, Alan, piano 781

Mark, Peter, conductor 2403, 2405

Markevitch, Igor, conductor 64, 642, 713, 772, 778, 1032, 2522, 2696, 2707, 3908

Markova, Emilija, soprano 457

Markowski, Andrzej, conductor 2490, 2494, 3857

Marlboro Music Festival 748

Marlow, Anthony, tenor 344

Marlow, Richard, conductor 1237

Maros, Miklos, conductor 3598

Maros, Miklos, Ensemble 3598

Marova, Libuse, mezzo-soprano 1832

Marquesita, Violet, soprano 1469

Marriner, Neville, conductor 65, 104
  232, 240, 298, 373, 446, 714, 734
  786, 1233, 1264, 1538, 1546, 1588
  1590, 1603, 1608, 1623, 1651,
  1665, 1722, 1727, 1736, 1789,
  1809, 1841, 2003, 2106, 2121,
  2245, 2252, 2271, 2277, 2313,
  2352, 2370, 2376, 2715, 2737,
  2972, 3320, 3329, 3443, 3563,
  3565, 3779, 3794, 3916
Mars, Jacques 1199
Marschner, Kurt, baritone 3167
Marsh, Lucy Isabelle, soprano 3774
Marshall, Lois, soprano 1639, 2299
Marshall, Margaret, soprano 232,
  1617, 1623, 1686, 2313, 2738,
  3440, 3441, 3442
Marszalek, Franz, conductor 1846,
  1862, 1864, 3168
Martin, Andrew, violin 3392
Martin, Riccardo, tenor 3774
Martin, Thomas, conductor 402
Martin, William, tenor 344
Martin, Wolfgang, conductor 1818
Martinelli, Giovanni, tenor 3352,
  3367, 3774
Martini, Louis, conductor 1486
Martinon, Jean, conductor 725, 1875,
  2744, 2767, 3666
Martinotti, Bruno, conductor 2565
Martinovich, Boris, bass 3948
Martinu Piano Quartet 464
Marton, Eva, soprano 1894
Marty, Jean-Pierre, conductor 1941
Marvin, Frederick, piano 1299
Marx, Joseph, piano 859
Mase, Raymond, trumpet 3674
Maserati, Ellen, harpsichord 2066
Masini, Gianfranco, conductor 3918
Masini, Mafalda, mezzo-soprano 2732
Mason, Barry, lute, 981
Mason, Edith, soprano 3774
Mason, Frances, violin 3332
Mason, J. R., conductor 3617, 3619
Mason, Marilyn, organ 1020
Massard, Robert, baritone 660
Masseta Maiaenco Tambourine Players
  3318
Massey, Roy, organ 2485, 2762, 4054
Masson, Diego, conductor 779
Masterson, Valerie, soprano 1948,
  3155, 3161, 3918
Mastilovic, Daniza, soprano 3475
Masur, Kurt, conductor 560, 575,
  592, 600, 797, 798, 800, 807,

815, 863, 916, 920, 921, 923,
  931, 935, 944, 952, 2145, 2951,
  2953
Mata, Eduardo, conductor 1500, 2229,
  2649, 2653, 2717, 3132, 3950
Mater, Ad, oboe 127
Mathis, Edith, soprano 125, 128,
  151, 265, 1596, 2032, 2038, 2044,
  2126, 2217, 2222, 2268, 2303,
  2308, 2355, 2401, 3764
Matiffa, Elisabeth, viola da gamba
  2066, 3296
Matousek, Bohuslav, violin 2873
Mattes, Willi, conductor 634, 1866,
  1945
Mattioli, Renata 3025
Matuz, Istvan, flute 196, 3039
Matyas, Miroslav, conductor 2419
Matzenauer, Margarete, soprano 3770
Mauersberger, Edhard, conductor 132
Maulkin, Ray, organ 4056
Maurane, Camille 1199
Maurel, Victor, baritone 3770
Maurer, Jean-Pierre, tenor 3388,
  3434
Maurette, Ariane, viola da gamba
  978, 1158
Mauri, Giulio, bass 2575
Mauriella, Marina, harpsichord 3716
Mawby, Colin, conductor 658
Maxen, Toni, tenor 2464
Maximilien, Wanda, piano 1164
Maxwell Davies, Peter, conductor
  2107
May, Angelica, violoncello 107, 849,
  1780
May, Ernest, organ 3545
Mayer-Schierning, Ernst, violin 200
Mayes, Samuel, violoncello 445, 2444
Mayr, Ingrid, alto 1763
Mayr, Richard, bass 3774
Mazura, Franz, baritone 644
Mazurok, Yuri, baritone 2697, 3214
Mazzini, Guido 3025
Mazzoleni, Ester, soprano 3774
Mazzotta, Palo, baritone 63
McArthur, Edwin, piano 3769
McCabe, John, piano 1696, 2779,
  2780, 3644
McCabe, Robin, piano 2416
McCann, Philip, cornet 3627
McCormack, John, tenor 3774, 4069
McCoy, Seth, tenor 3655
McCracken, James, tenor 2811
McCracken, Kay, soprano 1951

McCue, William, bass 3346
McDaniel, Barry, bass-baritone 139, 172, 2581, 3494
McDonald, Lawrence, clarinet 2008
McDonald, Susann, harp 1509, 3676
McEachern, Malcolm, bass 3774, 4006
McFrederick, Michael, piano 991
McGegan, Nicholas, flute 97, 2004
McHugh, Peter, violin 53
McInnes, Donald, viola 3324
McLarin, Lyn, flute 4065
McLaughlin, Marie, soprano 1593, 2569
McNab, Eilidh, soprano 2582
McNeil, Dorothy, soprano 2307
McRae, Donna, soprano 2713
McWilliam, Clement, organ 903, 3938
Mdivani, Marina, piano 3186
Measham, David, conductor 1516, 1828
Medici Quartet 906
Medieval Ensemble of London 2502
Medjimorec, Heinz, piano 2337
Medlam, Charles, viola da gamba 1111
Mednikoff, Nicholas, piano 620, 3906
Medus, Henri, bass 2764
Medveczky, Adam, conductor 3818
Megane, Leila, mezzo-soprano 3774
Mehta, Dady, piano 698
Mehta, Zubin, conductor 371, 414, 426, 429, 431, 566, 678, 686, 866, 875, 884, 885, 917, 1477, 2030, 2040, 2043, 2129, 2376, 2410, 2884, 2897, 3133, 3227, 3231, 3247, 3250, 3260, 3282, 3604, 3608, 3672, 3828
Meidhof, Adolf, oboe 1460
Mei-Figner, Medea, soprano 3770
Meier, Daniel, conductor 3910
Meier, Gustav, conductor 445
Meinardi, Charles, violin 4065
Meinecke, Siegfried, viola 322
Meints, Catharina, violoncello 272
Melba, Nellie, soprano 3770, 3773
Melchior, Lauritz, tenor 3476, 3774
Melchissedec, Leon, baritone 3770
Melenteva, Tatiana, soprano 3317
Melik-Pashayev, Aleksandr, conductor 2697
Melis, Carmen, soprano 3774
Melkus, Eduard, conductor 320
Melkus, Eduard, violin 320, 2422
Mellnas, Marianne, soprano 2433, 3933
Melos Ensemble 2128, 2681
Melos Quartet 924, 1215

Melsted, Linda, violin 1812
Melzer, Friedreich, tenor 925, 2962
Mendelssohn Club of Philadelphia 2124, 2968
Meneguzzer, Jolanda, soprano 2562
Mengelberg, Willem, conductor 664, 3860
Menges, Herbert, conductor 1541
Menuhin Festival Orchestra 787, 1654, 2122
Menuhin, Hephzibah, piano 895, 1373, 2122, 3286
Menuhin, Yehudi, conductor 787, 907, 1654, 2122
Menuhin, Yehudi, viola 669
Menuhin, Yehudi, violin 810, 894, 1231, 1373, 2122, 3244, 3286, 3625
Mercier, Monique, piano 3557
Merentie, Marguerite, soprano 3774
Merfeld, Robert, piano 2989
Meriweather, Annette, soprano 3058
Mermaid Singers and Orchestra 2582
Mermoud, Philippe, violoncello 3305
Merola, Gaetano, conductor 2574
Merrill, Robert, baritone 724, 3341, 3961
Merriman, Eric, conductor 3527
Merriman, Nan, mezzo-soprano 2024, 2026, 3351
Mersiovsky, Gertrud, organ 972, 1142
Mertens, Theo, trumpet 1679
Mesple, Mady, soprano 1223, 2448, 2774, 3328
Messana, John, countertenor 1617
Messiereur, Petr, violin 1847
Mester, Jorge, conductor 53, 336, 1662, 2117, 2171, 2172
Metcalfe, Jane, mezzo-soprano 3152, 3165
Metropolitan Opera Orchestra 716, 2322
Metropolitan Symphony Orchestra 1049
Metsala, Kerttu, soprano 16
Metternich, Anton, bass 3712
Metternich, Joseph, baritone 3712
Metzger, Ottilie, mezzo-soprano 3774
Meunier, Claudine, contralto 655
Meyendorf, Werner, horn 127, 1911
Meyer, Hannes, organ 3626
Meyer, Kerstin, mezzo-soprano 551
Meyer-Welfing, Hugo, tenor 859
Meyerdorf, Werner, horn 2807
Mezo, Laszlo, violoncello 3038
Mezzena, Bruno, piano 677, 2741

Michael, Audrey, mezzo-soprano 3353
Michael, Hermann, conductor 441
Michaels, Jost, conductor 1663
Michailova, Marie, soprano 3770
Michel, Catherine, harp 1503
Michel, Solange, mezzo-soprano 717, 3557
Michelangeli, Arturo Benedetti, piano 415, 427, 2612, 3975
Michelucci, Roberto, violin 19
Michigan State Symphony Band 1823
Michigan State Wind Symphony Orchestra 1823
Michigan University Chamber Choir 2173
Michigan University Instrumental Ensemble 2173
Michigan University Symphony Orchestra 445
Michigan University Wind Ensemble 1163
Midgley, Vernon, tenor 1468
Migdal, Marian, piano 637, 703
Mihaly, Andras, conductor 1296, 3039, 3126
Mihule, Jiri, oboe 1900
Mikkonen, Pentii, viola 4
Milan, Susan, flute 3714
Milanov, Zinka, soprano 724
Milanova, Dora, piano 847
Milanova, Stoika, violin 204, 847
Milashkina, Tamara, soprano 1173, 2697, 3214, 3796
Mildonian, Susanna, harp 2234
Miljakovic, Olivera, soprano 1866
Millard, Janet, flute 376
Miller, Frank, violoncello 3688
Miller, James, trumpet 3674
Miller, Lajos, baritone 3437
Miller, Mildred, mezzo-soprano 2025
Miller, Robert, piano 1433
Miller, Rodney, trumpet 3287
Miller, Tess, oboe 2271
Millington, Andrew, organ 3525
Milner, Martin, violin 3623
Milnes, Sherrill, baritone 2099, 2563, 2573, 2731, 3365, 3672, 3792
Milona, Costa, tenor 4007
Milstein, Nathan, violin 802, 811, 816, 3961
Minarchi, Dora 3025
Minderaa, Frank, oboe 3818
Minghetti, Angelo, tenor 3773
Minich, Peter, tenor 634

Minneapolis Symphony Orchestra 737
Minnesota Orchestra 2492, 2536, 2662, 3140
Minton, Yvonne, contralto 644, 663, 670, 673, 992, 1368, 2223
Minty, Shirley, contralto 3334
Miranda, Ana Maria, soprano 1463, 3578
Mironov, Nicolai, trombone 3834
Mironovich, Leonid, flute 3834
Mirzchulava, Didim, conductor 2478
M.I.T. Symphony Orchestra 1386
Mitchell, Emily, harp 3564
Mitchell, Geoffrey, Choir 1261
Mitchell, Leona (Leonie), mezzo-soprano 2088, 3670
Mitchell, Margaret, soprano 3162
Mitchinson, John, tenor 1229
Mitropoulos, Dmitri, conductor 2041, 2055, 2549, 3860
Mitzelfelt, H. Vincent, conductor 2832
Miura, Tamaki, soprano 3774
Mixa, Ruth, soprano 16
Mixova, Ivana, mezzo-soprano 1312
Modesti, Giuseppe, bass 2562
Modl, Martha, mezzo-soprano 3457
Moeller, Jobst, bass 1945
Moffo, Anna, soprano 1878, 3351
Moglia, Alain, violin 3296
Mohler, John, clarinet 3581
Moisewitsch, Benno, piano 2417, 2610
Mok, Judith, mezzo-soprano 973
Molajoli, Lorenzo, conductor 2724
Molard Quartet 741
Molinari, Helga Muller 1632
Molinari-Pradelli, Francesco, conductor 3364
Moll, Kurt, bass 128, 459, 460, 553, 643, 2103, 2219, 2293, 3102, 3366
Molodtsova, Galina, soprano 3241
Moltkau, Hans, conductor 3696
Monachesi, Walter, baritone 3368
Monasevitch, Joan, soprano 3891
Monden, Godelieve, guitar 2716
Monk, Meredith, piano 2187
Monoyios, Ann, soprano 1112
Monreale, Leonardo, bass 2475, 2521
Monroe, Lorne, violoncello 3606
Monte Carlo National Orchestra 64
Monte Carlo Opera Chorus 778, 2097, 2522, 3908
Monte Carlo Opera Orchestra 63, 758, 774, 778, 1197, 1262, 1268, 1400,

1405, 2095, 2097, 2098, 2104, 2522, 3908, 3915
Monteux, Claude, flute 296
Monteux, Pierre, conductor 296, 582, 610, 808, 878, 2647, 2652, 2703, 3245
Monteverdi Choir 738, 982, 1593, 1617, 1621, 1653, 2588, 2591, 2600, 2633
Monteverdi Instrumental Academy 22, 3417
Monteverdi Orchestra 1617, 1621, 1653, 2591, 2600, 2633
Montgomery, James, horn 3842
Monti, Nicola, tenor 2475
Montoya, Carlos, guitar 3657
Montreal Symphony Orchestra 1252
Montreux Festival Chorus 1100
Montserrat, Capella and Escolania de Musica 995, 1480, 2196
Moog, Rainer, viola 3995
Moore, David, violoncello 1412, 1913
Moore, Gerald, piano 3515, 3516, 3551, 3778
Moore, Grace, soprano 3830
Moore, John, trombone 3287
Moore, Kenneth, conductor 2008
Moralt, Rudolf, conductor 16
Morath, Max, piano 4044
Moravec, Ivan, piano 1062, 1445, 2254, 2265
Mordkovich, Lydia, violin 809
Morehead State University Summer Music Camp Faculty 3581
Morehouse Spelman Chorus 757
Moreno, Berta, soprano 3774
Moreschi, Alessandro, castrato 3770
Morgan, Beverly, mezzo-soprano 1287, 2755
Morgan, Carole, flute 1016
Morgan, Geoffrey, organ 3319
Morison, Elsie, soprano 1639, 1690, 2032
Morisset, Michel, trumpet 165, 1394, 3736
Morisset-Balier, Marie-Andree, organ 165, 1394, 3736
Morley Consort 2197
Morley, Virginia, piano 3882
Mormon Tabernacle Choir of Salt Lake City 605, 2997
Morris, Richard, organ 3660, 3661
Morris, Wyn, conductor 2049, 2058
Morrison, Mary, soprano 1905
Morrow, Michael, conductor 4041

Morski Zvutsi Chorus 1029
Morton, James, clarinet 1353
Morton, Richard tenor 1617
Moscovicz, Jacob, piano 1566
Moscow Academic Philharmonic Orchestra 2902
Moscow Chamber Orchestra 707, 2978
Moscow Conservatoire Students Orchestra 3781
Moscow Philharmonic Orchestra 2037, 2179, 2297, 2472, 2611, 2623, 2984, 3212
Moscow Radio and TV Symphony Orchestra 2534, 3192
Moscow Radio Symphony Chorus 41, 2697, 3241
Moscow Radio Symphony Orchestra 41, 342, 661, 1021, 1502, 1537, 2047, 2113, 2548, 2553, 2697, 2718, 2750, 2978, 3006, 3008, 3010, 3241, 3781
Moscow State Musical Theatre Chorus 2534
Moscow Symphony Orchestra 2178
Moser, Edda, soprano 456, 460, 1866, 1947, 2292, 2295, 2306, 3073, 3166
Moser, Thomas, tenor 2355, 2699
Moskvitina, Emilia, harp 7
Moss, Eileen, soprano 3485
Moss, Phyllis, piano 893
Mostly Mozart Orchestra 1749, 2302, 2383
Mouillere, Jean, violin 2960
Mowakowski, Marian, bass 458
Moxon, Alice, soprano 3157
Moyle, Julian, baritone 719
Moyse, Marcel, flute 293
Mozart Boys Choir 1624
Mozart Festival Orchestra 2385
Mozzato, Guido, violin 3401
Mroz, Leonard, bass 2974
Muck, Karl, conductor 3466
Mugdan, Albrect, trumpet 3297
Muhle, Anne-Marie, alto 2317
Muller, Edoardo, conductor 3321
Muller, Eduard, harpsichord 322
Muller, Eduard, organ 1605
Muller, Franz, conductor 1773
Muller, Hannelore, viola da gamba 2005
Muller, Hans Udo, piano 1819
Muller, Hartje, bass 3350
Muller, Maria, soprano 545, 3538
Muller, Philippe violoncello 2084

Muller, Wouter, violoncello 3444
Muller-Brincken, Jochen, oboe 22
Muller-Bruhl, Helmut, conductor 189, 2247
Muller-Lampertz, Richard, conductor 1818
Mullings, Frank, tenor 3774
Mummery, Browning, tenor 3773
Munch, Charles, conductor 864, 2258, 3666, 3954
Munchinger, Karl, conductor 116, 2378, 2890, 3399
Munchner Nonett 2834
Munchner Vokalisten 2740
Munclinger, Milan, conductor 635
Munich Bach Choir 125, 128, 170, 264 265, 323
Munich Bach Orchestra 125, 128, 170, 264, 265, 288, 320, 323
Munich Baryton Trio 1753, 1755
Munich Boys Choir 264
Munich Capella Antiqua 3536, 3959
Munich Chamber Orchestra 1595, 1779, 2211, 2230, 2234, 2784, 2788
Munich Children's Choir 634
Munich Motet Choir Womens Voices 2032
Munich Philharmonic Orchestra 928, 934, 1676, 1893, 2406, 2908, 2959 3456, 3839, 3898
Munich Pro Arte Chamber Orchestra 3956
Munich Radio Orchestra 633, 634, 1894, 1947, 2461, 3641, 3696
Munich Vocal Soloists 2788
Munro, Leigh, soprano 344
Munrow, David, Chinese shawm, bag-pipes, flutes, recorders, pipe and tabor, gemshorn, crumhorns, cornamuses, tauschpfeifen, dul-cinas, kortholts, racketts, nic-olo shawm, garkleinflotlein 3680
Mundrow, David, conductor 2197, 3625, 3795, 3864
Munsel, Patrice, soprano 3961
Munteanu, Petre, tenor 3976
Muntyan, Michael, piano 2977
Muraco, Thomas, piano 650
Murail, Tristan, percussion 1872
Murail, Tristan, piano 1873
Muratore, Lucien, tenor 3770
Muro, Bernardo de, tenor 3774
Murphy, William, baritone 3128
Murray, Ann, mezzo-soprano 626, 2125, 2192, 3347, 3440, 3441

Murray, Matthew, bass 2787
Murray, Michael, organ 157, 2769
Murray, Peter, conductor 3155, 3161
Murray, Thomas, organ 1372, 2138
Musgrave, Thea, conductor 2404
Music for a While 2015
Music Party (The) 2351
Music Workshop 3857
Musica Aeterna Chorus 1406
Musica Aeterna Orchestra 350, 1310, 1406, 1604
Musica Antiqua 3681
Musica Antiqua, Amsterdam 1597
Musica Antiqua, Cologne 239, 3295, 3690
Musica Antiqua, Vienna 4003
Musica da Camera, Amsterdam 4015
Musica da Camera, Prague 1416
Musica Holmiae 1156
Musica Reservata 4041
Musica Sveciae 1850
Musici (I) 19, 26, 351, 739, 764, 1132, 1136, 1667, 2783, 3298, 3389, 3394, 3403, 3412, 3413, 3416, 3423, 3425, 3430
Musici of Prague 1848
Musiciens de l'Opera (Les) 711
Musiciens de Paris 2071, 3844
Musikverein Quartet 1888, 2335
Musique des Gardiens de la Paix 689, 690, 3106
Musique Vivante Ensemble 655, 779
Muszely, Melitta, soprano 961
Muthel, Angela 1891
Muti, Riccardo, conductor 590, 630, 1001, 1955, 2161, 2454, 2948, 2955, 3143, 3203, 3262, 3273, 3281, 3363, 3792, 3793
Mutter, Anne-Sophie, violin 435, 442
Muzio, Claudia, soprano 2574, 3774
Nacovska, Jana, piano 4009
Nadien, David, violin 1288
Naegele, Philipp, viola 744, 2083, 3047
Naegele, Philipp, violin 3297
Naidenov, Asen, conductor 2697
Namara, Marguerite, soprano 3774
Nanzetta, Virginia, flute 3509
Naples Orchestra 1734, 2882, 2893
Naples Orchestra Chorus 2882
Narcon, Armand, bass 1200, 3631
Nartov, Vitaly, bass 3796
Nasedkin, Alexei, piano 7
Nash Ensemble 486, 701, 3045, 3125
Hash, John Heddle, tenor 3063

Nash, Royston, conductor 3152, 3165
National Arts Centre Orchestra 1353, 1750, 3636
National Philharmonic Chorus 3857
National Philharmonic Orchestra 113, 626, 628, 874, 1250, 1257, 1956, 2088, 2089, 2093, 2099, 2218, 2563, 2566, 2569, 2573, 2576, 3208, 3225, 3238, 3268, 3447, 3667, 3670, 3671, 3672, 3821, 3857, 3947, 3951
National Symphony Orchestra 1050
National Symphony Orchestra of Mexico 695, 1025
Navarini, Francesco, bass 3770
Navarra, Andre, violoncello 300, 751 2765
Navarra, Garcia, conductor 187, 1493 2716
Naveau, Claude, viola 2960
Navratil, Constance, soprano 1910
N.B.C. Symphony Orchestra 577, 1450
NDR Rundfunkorchester 1616
Neal, Casswell, horn 3684
Neary, Martin, conductor 903, 3937, 3938, 3939
Neary, Martin, organ 3938, 3939, 3940
Neblett, Carol, soprano 2563
Nebolsin, Vasili, conductor 2698
Neel, Boyd, conductor 50
Negri, Giovanni de, tenor 3770
Negri, Vittorio, conductor 1100, 3440, 3441, 3442
Negro, Lucia, piano 1902
Negyesy, Janos, violin 1873
Neidlinger, Gustav, bass 453, 2460, 3167, 3457, 3462, 3465, 3467, 3470
Neikrug, George, violoncello 1218, 2399
Neil, William, organ 29
Neill, William 3497
Nelis, Sylvia, soprano 1469
Nelson, Judith, soprano 230, 982, 997, 1009, 1010, 1147, 1295, 1587, 1599, 1628, 1648, 1692, 2186, 2577, 2584, 2723, 2913, 3435
Nelson, Nelda, soprano 1351
Nelsova, Zara, violoncello 1349
Nemeckova, Kvetoslava, soprano 3358
Nemeth, Gabor, baritone 1895
Nemeth, Geza, viola 368
Neriki, Shigeo, piano 990

Nesbitt, Dennis, viol 3996
Nesbitt, Dennis, viola da gamba 2188
Nessi, Giuseppe, tenor 2575
Nestorenko, Yevgeny, bass 2418, 2978, 3214, 3363
Netherlands Broadcasting Foundation Chorus 460
Netherlands Chamber Choir 1773
Netherlands Chamber Orchestra 71, 201
Netherlands Choir 2800
Netherlands Horn Quartet 3287
Netherlands National Ballet 2800
Netherlands Radio Chorus 267, 268
Netherlands Saxophone Quartet 1874
Netherlands Vocal Ensemble 1773
Netherlands Wind Ensemble 1901
Neuhaus, Werner, violin 3409
Neumann, Gunter, tenor 3490
Neumann, Vaclav, conductor 1017, 1305, 1306, 1309, 1336, 1348, 1445, 2036, 2048, 2053, 2079, 2082, 2085, 2086
Neumeyer, Fritz, clavichord 82
Neumeyer, Fritz, conductor 2527
Neumeyer, Fritz, hammerklavier 2879
Neumeyer, Fritz, harpsichord 47, 3764
Neveu, Ginette, violin 3772
Neveu, Jean, piano 3772
New Budapest Quartet 1395, 2844
New Cavendish Quintet 2432
New Chamber Players 3650
New Chamber Soloists 297
New City Ensemble 2111
New College Choir, Oxford 3188
New England Conservatory Chorus 1033
New England Conservatory Contemporary Ensemble 1117
New England Contemporary Ensemble 2200
New Excelsior Talking Machine 3679
New Hampshire Symphony Orchestra 1769
New Hungarian Quartet 470, 1216
New Irish Chamber Orchestra 89, 2232, 2233
New Koto Ensemble 1634
New London Orchestra 3798
New Music Group of Scotland 1659
New Philharmonia Chorus 2146
New Philharmonia Orchestra 412, 438, 439, 444, 591, 662, 1092, 1341, 1948, 2105, 2146, 2149, 2206, 2617, 2731, 2761, 2770, 2950,

2952, 2957, 2998, 3218, 3349, 3461, 3478, 3604, 3608, 3666, 3793, 3801, 3829, 3918
New Philharmonia Wind Ensemble 2345, 2347, 2700
New Prague Trio 4009
New String Trio 2675
New Symphony, London 3666
New Vienna Octet 2337
New York Bassoon Quartet 3821
New York Brass Quintet 99
New York City Ballet Orchestra 3654
New York City Opera Orchestra 3497
New York Consort of Viols 3853
New York Opera Orchestra 3344
New York Philharmonic Orchestra 353, 386, 566, 645, 647, 676, 678, 686 814, 875, 884, 885, 941, 987, 1288, 1477. 1598, 1629, 1748, 1792, 1805, 2025, 2263, 2316, 2410, 2980, 3093, 3133, 3604, 3605, 3608, 3638, 3860
New York Sinfonietta 2580
New York Stadium Orchestra 3220
New York String Orchestra 1796
New York Tuba Quartet 3654
New York Wind Ensemble 3327
New York Y Chamber Orchestra 1677, 3674
Newell, Jonathan, organ 3528
Newman, Anthony, organ 259, 1636
Newman, Michael, guitar 13
Newsome, Roy, conductor 3621
Ney, Tibor, violin 229
Nezhdanova, Antonina, soprano 3770
NHK Symphony Orchestra 2109
Nicholas, Michael, organ 3664
Nicholls, Agnes, soprano 3770
Nichols, William, clarinet 1908
Nickell-Lean, Elizabeth, soprano 3158
Nicklin, Celia, cor anglais 3565
Nicklin, Celia, oboe 3329, 3443, 3565
Nicolai, Elena, mezzo-soprano 3355
Nicolet, Aurele, flute 320, 322, 625, 1443, 1963, 2215, 2664
Nicolet, Christiane, flute 322
Nielsen, Carl, String Quartet 2428
Nieminen, Tuula, mezzo-soprano 2771
Nienstedt, Gerd, bass-baritone 644, 3459, 3467, 3471
Niggemann, Hans-Ulrich, flute 91
Nigoghossian, Sonia, soprano 1411
Nijland, Piet, violin 3818

Nikolayeva, Tatiana, piano 2113, 3232
Nilson, Goran, conductor 1930
Nilsson, Birgit, soprano 360, 582, 3457, 3470, 3474, 3475, 3793
Nilsson, Torsten, conductor 2433, 3933
Nilsson, Ulf, clarinet 1455
Nimsgern, Siegmund, bass-baritone 146, 228, 1140, 1404, 1816, 2496
Nitsche, Horst, tenor 3348
Nivette, Juste, bass 3770
Noble, John 1468
Noble, Robert, piano 1942
Noble, Tim, baritone 1351
Nocker, Hans, bass-baritone 2462, 2464, 2680
Nocodemus, Verne, trumpet 1812
Noeth, Ortwin, violin 1013
Noguera, Louis, baritone 3557
Nolan, Bruce, clarinet 844
Noll, Dietrich, clarinet 1354
Noll, Dietrich, piano 1354
Noni, Alda, soprano 3081
Noorman, Jantina, mezzo-soprano 3719
Noras, Arto, violoncello 1682, 1882, 2859
Norberg, Edith, Carillon Choristers 915
Nordica, Lilian, soprano 3770
Nordin, Birgit, soprano 1929
Nordmann, Marielle, harp 392, 2235, 3044
Norell, Judith, harpsichord 2399, 2785
Norman, Jerold, tenor 2124
Norman, Jessye, soprano 645, 856, 1666, 2811, 3920
Norman, John, conductor 1909
Norrington, Roger, conductor 1400
Norris, Harry, conductor 3154, 3157
North German Radio Chamber Orchestra 2581
North German Radio Chorus 2032, 3167
North German Radio Orchestra 2017
North, Nigel, lute 1273
Northern Sinfonia Orchestra 1613, 1615, 1680, 2758, 3051
Northwest Chamber Orchestra 1812
Norton, John, clarinet 1462
Norwegian Broadcasting Orchestra 1584
Norwegian Chamber Orchestra 1547, 2450
Noske, Willem, violin 3818

Nota, Giuseppe, tenor 3773
Note, Jean, baritone 3770
Notti, Raymonde, mezzo-soprano 717
Nouvel Philharmonic Orchestra 1941, 2712
Nova Saxophone Quartet 2
Novaes, Guiomar, piano 517, 518
Novak, Richard, bass 1834
Novotna, Jarmila, soprano 2322
Novotny, Jan, piano 1788, 1848, 1849
Nurmela, Kari, baritone 1955
Nurnberg Symphony Orchestra 2671
Nurnberg Teachers Choral Society 2671
Nyffenegger, Esther, violoncello 3288
Nyquist, Roger, organ 1436
Oberg, David, conductor 1160
Oberlin Baroque Ensemble 2065, 3729
Oberlin, Russell, countertenor 1629
Oborin, Lev, piano 538
Obraztsova, Elena (Yelena), mezzo-soprano 606, 2103, 2529, 2763, 3353, 3366
O'Brien, Garrett, conductor 1423
Ochman, Wieslaw, tenor 2458
O'Connor, John, piano 3677
Odeon Trio 3195
O'Dette, Paul, lute 971
Oesterle, Albert, clarin trumpet 4026
Ogdon, John, piano 2121, 2619, 2972
Ogeas, Francoise 1199
Ogston, Bruce, baritone 1813, 3334
Ohlsson, Garrick, piano 795, 1063
Ohrwall, Anders, conductor 140
Oien, Per, flute 1269, 1270, 1271, 2450
Oistrakh, David, conductor 3212
Oistrakh, David, viola 2297
Oistrakh, David, violin 276, 437, 490, 538, 804, 850, 2363, 2926
Oistrakh, Igor, violin 1021, 1974, 2297, 3212
O'Keefe, Suzanne, mezzo-soprano 3165
Olbertz, Walter, piano 2858
Oldham, Derek, tenor 3154, 3156, 3157, 3158, 3160
Oldheim, Helen, mezzo-soprano 716
Oleg, Raphael, violin 2940
Olitzka, Rosa, contralto 3770
Oliveira, Elmar, viola 1440
Oliver, Alexander, tenor 1261, 1596, 1637, 2177, 2192, 3918
Oliver, Robert, bass 3128

Olivero, Magda, soprano 2572
Olofsson, Ake, violoncello 1455
Olshansky, Ludwig, piano 533, 832
Oncina, Juan, tenor 2730
Onofrey, Robert, clarinet 1016
Oosterhout Chamber Choir 2062
Orchestra of Our Time 656
Orchestre de la Societe des Concerts du Conservatoire de Paris 550, 1524, 2651, 3556, 3666
Orchestre de la Suisse Romande 1031, 1196, 1510, 2094, 2414, 2624, 2628, 2630, 2983, 2998, 3147, 3224, 3239, 3458, 3665, 3666
Orchestre de la Suisse Romande Chorus 1031, 2094
Orchestre de Paris 370, 589, 663, 673, 679, 803, 864, 1194, 1221, 2657, 2763, 2774
Orchestre de Paris Chorus 663, 673, 1194, 1221, 2763
Orchestre National de Belgique 3556
Orchestre National de l'Opera 2764, 3556
Orchestre National de l'Opera Comique 3556
Orchestre National de la Radiodiffusion Francaise 3556
Orchestre Philharmonique de Pays de Loire 1827, 2517, 2604
Orchestre Symphonique de Gramophone 2768
Orebro Symphony Orchestra 1930
Orff, Carl, conductor 2459, 2463
Orford, John, bassoon 1572
Orford Quartet 401, 480
Oriana Concert Orchestra and Choir 1592
Orkis, Lambert, harpsichord 1016
Orliac, Jean-Claude, tenor 750, 982, 2633
Orlinski, Heinz Bernhard, organ 4036
Orloff, Penny, percussion 761
Orloff, Penny, soprano 761
Ormandy, Eugene, conductor 365, 378, 605, 715, 728, 932, 1045, 1327, 1778, 1885, 2124, 2626, 2709, 2769, 2968, 2997, 2999, 3005, 3077, 3100, 3207, 3210, 3228, 3256, 3315, 3605, 3606, 3638, 3950, 3954
Ornstein, Doris, harpsichord 272
Ornstein, Suzanne, violin 1103
Orquesta Sinfonica del Brasil 2435
Orr, Linda, flute 1812

O.R.T.F. Orchestra 725, 1030, 1192, 1199, 1779, 2511, 2744, 3347, 3370, 3857

O.R.T.F. Orchestra Chorus 1030, 1199 2511, 3347

Orth, Norbert, tenor 634, 1947, 2468

Orth, Robert, baritone 2172

Ortiz, Cristina, piano 1435

Ory, Gisele, mezzo-soprano 2100

Osa, Sigbjorn Bernhoft, hardingfele 1584

Osborn, Leonard, tenor 3162

Oscar's Motet Choir 2433, 3933

Oshita, Kumiko, soprano 750

Oslo Chamber Orchestra 3393

Oslo Philharmonic Orchestra 1159, 1555, 1556, 3020, 3022, 3023, 3170, 3171, 3174

Osnowycz, Anne, hurdy gurdy, Hungarian citera 3760

Ostblom, Roland, organ 3589

Osterloh, Klaus, trumpet 3297

Ostertag, Karl, tenor 2075, 3448

Ostman, Arnold, conductor 1570

Ostman, Arnold, piano 1570

Ostryniec, James, oboe 1907, 1010, 3649

O'Sullivan, John, tenor 3774

Otava, Zdenek, bass-baritone 1311

Ott, Karen, soprano 2401

Otto, Hans, harpsichord 2217

Otto, Hans, organ 2217

Otto, Lisa, soprano 2400

Otvos, Csabo, baritone 1296

Ousset, Cecile, piano 999

Ovcharek, Vladimir, violin 3194

Owen, Trevor, tenor 2762

Oxley, Harrison, organ 4055

Ozawa, Seiji, conductor 640, 674, 675, 1838, 2224, 2683, 2687, 2811, 3144, 3184, 3243

Ozolins, Arthur, piano 1041

Pacific Arts Woodwind Quintet 400

Pacini, Reginia, soprano 3770

Paderewski, Ignace, piano 520, 3856, 3907

Paikin, Luella, soprano 3774

Paillard Jean-Francois, Chamber Orchestra 20, 120, 197, 222, 1183, 1398, 1451, 1652, 1670, 1681, 1814, 1938, 2013, 2288

Paillard, Jean-Francois, conductor 20, 120, 197, 222, 1183, 1398, 1451, 1652, 1681, 1814, 1938, 2013, 2288

Paillard-Francais, Claude, piano 1431

Pal, Tamas, conductor 1981

Palacio, Ernesto, tenor 1259

Palankay, Klara, mezzo-soprano 361

Palenicek, Josef, piano 1832

Palivcova, Jarmila, mezzo-soprano 1833

Palli, Olavi, violin 4

Palma, Pierro de, tenor 627, 1257, 2575, 2733

Palmer, Felicity, soprano 1591, 1617, 1631, 2313, 2498

Palmer, Larry, organ 1246

Palsson, Pall, conductor 3169

Paltrinieri, Giordano, tenor 716

Pampuch, Helmut, tenor 579, 644

Pandolfi, Roland, horn 487, 2339

Pandolfini, Angelica, soprano 3770

Panenka, Jan, piano 1430, 2079

Panerai, Rolando, baritone 2475, 3351, 3364, 3672

Paniagua, Gregorio, conductor 766, 3311

Panizza, Ettore, conductor 2322, 3367

Panocha Quartet 1314

Panula, Jorma, conductor 651, 1882, 2018, 3009

Paolis, Alessio de, tenor 2322

Papi, Gennaro, conductor 716

Parachivkova, Lilijana, contralto 457

Paraskivesco, Theodore, piano 1179, 1205, 1409, 1410, 1411

Paratore, Anthony, piano 1518

Paratore, Joseph, piano 1518

Parcher, William, bass-baritone 1351

Pareto, Graziella, soprano 3774

Parikian, Manoug, violin 3517

Paris, Dominique, Northumbrian pipes 2519

Paris Opera Chorus 649, 717, 1522, 2292, 2295

Paris Opera Orchestra 644, 649, 717, 1522, 2096, 2100, 2292, 2295, 2764, 3792, 3793

Parkai, Istvan, conductor 1931

Parker, Louise, contralto 1792

Parker-Smith, Jane, organ 32, 3504, 3624

Parkes, Peter, conductor 3620

Parkhouse, David, piano 2204, 3332

Parkin, Eric, piano 899, 1813, 1822, 3990

Parnassus Ensemble 3543, 3547
Parrella, Nancianne, organ 133
Parry, Wilfred, piano 3644
Parsi-Pettinella, Armida, mezzo-soprano 3770
Parsons, Geoffrey, piano 14, 856, 1090, 2000, 3785, 3861, 3862
Partridge, Ian, tenor 632, 1654, 3335, 3433
Pasdeloup Orchestra 1486
Pasero, Tancredi, bass-baritone 3927
Paskuda, George, tenor 2680, 3450, 3471
Pasquier, Regis, violin 2909
Passaquet, Raphael, conductor 1934
Passaquet, Raphael, Vocal Ensemble 1934
Passaro, Joseph, percussion 914
Passin, Gunther, oboe 1254
Passin, Gunther, oboe d'amore 1254
Pastine, Gianfranco, tenor 2734
Paszthy, Julia, soprano 1260, 1954
Patane, Giuseppe, conductor 1956, 3342
Patterson, Willis, conductor 3920
Patti, Adelina, soprano 3770
Pattiera, Tino, tenor 3774
Patzak, Julius, tenor 2027, 2874, 3537
Pau, Maria de la, piano 2661
Pauk, Gyorgy, violin 890
Paul, Richard, baritone 3524
Pavarotti, Luciano, tenor 113, 1256, 1956, 2572, 2573, 2731, 2739, 3342, 3667, 3671, 3672, 3792, 3828
Pavlik, Justus, conductor 1282
Pavlinek, Ferdo, mandolin 3418
Pay, Anthony, conductor 2350
Payan, Paul, bass 3774
Payne, Joseph, harpsichord 1396, 1485
Payne, Patricia, mezzo-soprano 459, 3345
Pearlman, Martin, harpsichord 3290
Pears, Peter, tenor 902, 911, 1810, 2436, 2935, 3776
Pearson, Beth, violoncello 2989
Pearson, Keith, clarinet 2405
Pearson, Leslie, harpsichord 1468, 1609
Pearson, Leslie, organ 1404
Peclard, Etienne, violoncello 2445, 3296
Pedersen, Guy, double bass 760
Pederzini, Gianna, mezzo-soprano 3928
Peerce, Jan, tenor 453
Peeters, Hans, conductor 194
Peeters, Wiel, viola 42, 1917, 2690
Pegram, Wayne, conductor 708
Pehrsson, Clas, recorder 3593
Peijel, Cecilia, guitar 3593
Peinkofer, Karl, timpani 4026
Pekkanen, Pertti, conductor 1384
Pelayo, Herman, baritone 3888
Peltzer, Dwight, piano 704, 1161, 2754, 2756, 3316
Pena, Michele, soprano 2448
Penn Contemporary Players 1961
Pennario, Leonard, piano 1093, 3550
Pennetier, Jean Claude, piano 2909
Penzel, Erich, horn 1668, 2010
Perahia, Murray, conductor 2240, 2246, 2248
Perahia, Murray, piano 2440, 2446, 2248, 2935
Perantoni, Daniel, tuba 1580
Perard - Petzl, Luise, soprano 3774
Percussions de Strasbourg 3057
Perenyi, Eszter, violin 3039
Perenyi, Miklos, violoncello 622, 3039
Perier, Jean, baritone 3770
Perinelli, Rene, trumpet 1853
Perle, George, piano 2499
Perlea, Jonel, conductor 724, 3220
Perlman, Itzhak, violin 617, 640, 813, 1393, 2202, 2990, 3210, 3552, 3788
Perret, Anne, mezzo-soprano 973
Perrin, Ronald, organ 2489, 4046
Perry, Elisabeth, violin 1468
Perry, Janet, soprano 2401
Perry, John, piano 2526
Persichetti, Vincent, conductor 1796
Persson, Mats, keyboard 1851
Pertile, Aureliano, tenor 1240, 3983
Perulli, Raphael, viola da gamba 3744
Pesko, Zoltan, conductor 2505
Peters, Manfred, recorder 1460
Peters, Mitchell, percussion 3652
Peters, Reinhard, conductor 107, 1499, 1602, 1800
Peters, Roberta, soprano 344, 724
Peters, Wolfgang, conductor 1891
Peterson, Wayne, piano 376
Petijean, Lucien, piano 2768
Petit, Annie, piano 1004
Petite Bande (La) 1133, 1135, 1137,

1632, 2634
Petkov, Dimiter, bass 2606, 2974
Petrenko, Elisaveta, mezzo-soprano
    3774
Petri, Mario, bass 2475, 2732, 2742
Petri, Michala, recorder 1607
Petro, Janos, conductor 726, 1870
Petrov, Ivan, bass-baritone 457,
    2698
Petrov, Nicolai, piano 1082, 2546
Petrova-Zvanceva, Vera, mezzo-
    soprano 3774
Pettinger, Peter, piano 388
Peyer, Gervase de, conductor 3110
Peyron, Joseph, tenor 1940
Peysang, Andre, tenor 2464
Pezzani, Romana, violin 199
Pezzino, Leonardo, tenor 1220
Pfaff, Maurus, conductor 3699, 3700,
    3701
Pfeiffer, Thomas, baritone 2857
Pfluger, Hans, organ 168
Philadelphia Orchestra 365, 378,
    590, 605, 715, 728, 865, 932,
    1001, 1045, 1327, 2057, 2091,
    2124, 2626, 2709, 2769, 2968,
    2997, 2999, 3005, 3077, 3100,
    3143, 3207, 3210, 3228, 3244,
    3256, 3315, 3605, 3606, 3638,
    3950, 3954
Philadelphia Trio 1881
Philarte Quartet 1489, 1765
Philharmonia Chamber Orchestra 1598
Philharmonia Hungarica 299, 666, 667
    1002, 1272, 1321, 1499, 1724,
    1729, 1733, 1762, 1800, 1990,
    1996, 3230, 3968
Philharmonia Orchestra 231, 341,
    362, 461, 607, 608, 629, 630,
    636, 669, 682, 770, 809, 810,
    811, 817, 869, 873, 876, 880,
    882, 883, 905, 907, 913, 930,
    1048, 1110, 1118, 1129, 1230,
    1253, 1328, 1331, 1343, 1404,
    1435, 1448, 1541, 1544, 1685,
    1745, 1778, 1885, 1955, 1995,
    2029, 2108, 2160, 2161, 2177,
    2256, 2314, 2446, 2454, 2460,
    2547, 2550, 2561, 2610, 2612,
    2702, 1716, 2717, 2734, 2735,
    2820, 2903, 2948, 2954, 2955,
    2992, 2993, 3003, 3004, 3011,
    3067, 3080, 3091, 3121, 3203,
    3235, 3254, 3262, 3263, 3273,
    3275, 3276, 3280, 3281, 3363,
3363, 3365, 3453, 3455, 3625,
    3772, 3780, 3782, 3789, 3792,
    3793, 3948
Philharmonia Orchestra Chorus 607,
    2314, 2454, 3067, 3351
Philharmonia Virtuosi 2343, 3640
Philharmonic Vocal Ensemble 730
Philipp, Gunther, piano 633
Philippot, Michel, conductor 2712
Philips, Peter, conductor 40
Phillips, Daniel, violin 744
Phillips, Paul, conductor 1796
Phillips, Robert, piano 1474
Piatigorsky, Gregor, violoncello
    816, 3494
Piccaver, Alfred, tenor 3774
Picchi, Mirto, tenor 2742
Picht-Axenfeld, Edith, harpsichord
    269
Pickens, Jo Ann, soprano 3357
Pickett, Philip, recorder 3989
Pidoux, Roland, violoncello 1683,
    2445, 2855, 2909
Pierce, Jacqueline, mezzo-soprano
    133
Pierce, Joshua, conductor 977
Pierce, Joshua, piano 974, 977
Pierlot, Pierre, oboe 1671, 2235,
    2960, 3414, 3424
Pierre, Odile, organ 1578, 3962
Piguet, Michel, oboe 2328, 3444, 3753
Pikaizen, Viktor, violin 1877
Pilgram, Neva, soprano 1908
Pilponnen, Matti, tenor 1880
Pini, Anthony, violoncello 615
Pini, Carl, conductor 3419
Pinkas, Jiri, conductor 1312
Pinkert, Regina, mezzo-soprano 3770
Pinkett, Eric, conductor 898
Pinnock, Trevor, conductor 87, 178,
    289, 3398
Pinnock, Trevor, fortepiano 3033
Pinnock, Trevor, harpsichord 124,
    178, 181, 314, 2632, 2637, 2639,
    3033, 3398, 3408, 3410, 3648,
    3691, 4043
Pinnock, Trevor, virginal 3648, 4043
Pinto, Amelia, soprano 3770
Pinza, Ezio, bass 2322, 3899
Pioneer Choir 2494
Pirazzini, Miriam, mezzo-soprano 2742
Pires, Maria-Joao, piano 193, 2249
Pirzchalava, Abrek, tenor 2478
Pischner, Hans, harpsichord 276
Pishchayev, Gennady, tenor 2697

Pistor, Gotthelf, tenor 3466
Pitt, Percy, conductor 1383
Pitt, Percy, piano 3770
Pittman, Richard, conductor 3018
Pitts, Susan, piano 1281
Pittsburgh Symphony Orchestra 1124,
  1515, 1744, 2045, 2714, 2990
Piveteau, Roseline, violin 753
Plaichinger, Thila, soprano 3770
Plancon, Pol, bass 3770, 3978
Plantey, Bernard, baritone 2447
Plasson, Michel, conductor 1525,
  1530, 2102, 2448, 2757
Platt, Rosemary, piano 1374
Pleeth, Anthony, violoncello 97, 902
  2004, 2073, 2854, 3410, 3989
Pleshakov, Vladimir, piano 1125,
  1978
Plesner, Gurli, contralto 2427
Plessier, Rene, bassoon 3382
Plessis, Christian du, baritone
  1261, 2177
Plishka, Paul, bass 626, 2563, 2743
Plovdiv Symphony Orchestra 2606
Plumacher, Hetty, contralto 151,
  2452
Plymouth Church Chancel Choir 3848
Plzen Radio Orchestra 994
Poduschka, Walter, bass 649
Poell, Alfred, baritone 3114, 3489
Poggi, Gianni, tenor 2562
Pohjola, Erkki, conductor 3592
Pohl, Gunther, flute 1301
Pohl, Rudolf, conductor 139, 3763
Polgar, Laszlo, bass 1954, 3126
Poli-Randaccio, Tina, soprano 3774
Polish Chamber Orchestra 119, 1548
Polish Philharmonic Orchestra 1162
Polish Radio Orchestra 333, 1920,
  3182, 3857
Polisi, Joseph, bassoon 710
Polivnick, Paul, conductor 344
Pollack, Anna, contralto 2582, 3063
Pollain, Rene, viola 3093
Pollard, Brian, bassoon 127, 3310
Pollini, Maurizio, piano 367, 422,
  430, 792, 839, 1048, 1054, 3625,
  3705
Polster Hermann-Christian, bass 456
Poltoratsky, Viktor, piano 2421,
  2751
Polyakov, Aleksander, bass 2697
Polyphonic Chorus 2570
Polyskova, Nina, soprano 2697
Pomerium Musices 1286

Pommerien, Wilhelm, bass 2962
Pongracz, Peter, oboe 79
Pons, Juan, bass 3344
Ponselle, Rosa, soprano 716, 3774,
  3831
Ponti, Michael, piano 38, 1035, 1499
Pool for Modern Music 1773
Popov, Valery, bassoon 1854
Popp, Lucia, soprano 606, 1404, 1817,
  1820, 2009, 2223, 2293, 2355,
  2457, 2461, 2893
Popper, Jan, conductor 3322
Portal, Michel, clarinet 779
Post, Carl, conductor 194
Post, Carl, piano 194
Postnikova, Victoria, piano 338,
  3834
Pougnet, Jean, viola 1236
Poulter, David, organ 3524
Pourcel, Franck, and His Orchestra
  3555
Poutanen, Risto, violoncello 4
Powers, Marie 2170
Poznan Percussion Ensemble 1162
Pozzi, Pina, piano 349
Praetorius Consort 1802
Prague Chamber Orchestra 32, 635,
  1612, 1656, 2261, 2266, 2270,
  3411
Prague National Orchestra 1835
Prague National Theatre Orchestra
  and Chorus 3029
Prague Quartet 2846
Prague Radio Orchestra 490
Prague Symphony Orchestra 729, 1311,
  1391, 2080, 2081, 2488, 2828,
  4008
Prague Symphony Orchestra Wind En-
  semble 1847
Prappacher, Ernst, bassoon 1460
Pratt, Daniel, baritone 133
Pratz, Albert, violin 919
Pressler, Menahem, piano 895
Preston, Simon, conductor 230, 1648,
  1692, 3435, 3894
Preston, Simon, harpsichord 104, 734
Preston, Simon, organ 237, 2524,
  3664
Preston, Stephen, flute 97, 124, 178,
  1916, 2004, 3410
Pretre, Georges, conductor 1522,
  3792, 3793
Preucil, William, viola 1514
Previn, Andre, conductor 684, 1189,
  1364, 1515, 1542, 1744, 2045,

2158, 2430, 2524, 2555, 2644,
2710, 2714, 2990, 3092, 3221,
3257, 3331, 3625, 3797
Previn, Andre, piano 2165, 2618
Previtali, Fernando, conductor 1259
Prevost, Stephen le, organ 3815
Prey, Hermann, bass-baritone 173,
264, 902, 1406, 1947, 1999, 2007,
2009, 2055, 2184, 2457, 2460,
2461, 3166, 3462, 3491, 3696
Pribyl, Vilem, tenor 1312, 1832,
1833
Price, Christina, soprano 3848
Price, Janet, soprano 2105, 2569
Price, Leontyne, soprano 2875, 3082,
3341, 3350, 3948
Price, Margaret, soprano 2148, 2293
Price, Paul, Percussion Ensemble 977
Priday, Elisabeth, soprano 1621
Prieur, Andre, conductor 89, 2232,
2233
Prihode, Kurt, percussion 4016
Primavera String Quartet 3015
Primrose, William, viola 1794
Pring, Katherine, contralto 1229
Prinz, Alfred, clarinet 2396, 2913
Pritchard, John, conductor 1512,
1615, 1794, 1816, 2409, 3829
Pro Arte Antiqua Prague 3752
Pro Arte Orchestra 3163, 3164
Pro Arte Quartet 789, 1121, 2518
Pro Arte Trio 889
Pro Cantione Antiqua 1011, 1120,
1933, 2599, 3570, 3768, 3893,
3896
Pro Musica Orchestra 1000
Procter, Norma, contralto 129, 556,
2032, 2038, 2042
Proebstl, Max, bass 264
Proglhof, Harald, bass 643
Prohaska, Jaro, baritone 3446, 3468
Prohle, Henrik, flute 1895
Protero, Dodi, soprano 16
Provatorov, Gennady, conductor 3241
Provence of the Abbey Saint-Victor
Musicians 3574
Prunnbauer, Sonja, guitar 2470
Prusa, Karel, bass 1312, 2081
Puchelt, Gerhard, piano 1784
Puglisi, Lino 2684
Puig-Roget, Henriette, organ 3557
Purcell Consort of Voices 2188
Purcell Singers 1810
Purcell String Quartet 1905
Pustelak, Kazimierz, tenor 2490,

2494
Putnam, Ashley, soprano 2405, 2564
Puyana, Rafael, harpsichord 274,
1248, 3032
Pyle, Ralph, horn 3652
Quan, Linda, violin 1016, 1433
Quartetto Italiano 742, 839, 895,
1707
Queens College Choir 4018
Queffelec, Anne, piano 1407, 1814,
2164, 2841
Queler, Eve, conductor 3344
Quintet '74 4009
Quintetto Boccherini 747
Quivar, Florence, mezzo-soprano 2743
Rabbath, Francois, double bass 2605
Rabinovitsi, Max, violin 487
Rabot, Francois, organ 3734
Rabus, Kathrin, violin 189
Radev, Mariana, mezzo-soprano 3360
Radford, Robert, bass 3774
Radio Wind Ensemble 2801
Radivonik, Yaroslav, baritone 2973
Rados, Ferenc, piano 2241
Raffalli, Tibere, tenor 2097
Raffalt, Reinhard, harmonium 2740
Raffell, Anthony, bass 632
RAI Symphony Orchestra 1259, 1492,
2742
RAI Symphony Orchestra Chorus 1259,
2742
Raimondi, Gianni, tenor 2565
Raimondi, Ruggero, bass 1198, 2292,
2295, 2571, 2739, 3340, 3348
Rains, Leon, bass 3770
Raisa, Rosa, soprano 3774
Rajna, Thomas, piano 1975
Rajter, Ludovic, conductor 871, 881,
1860
Ralf, Torsten, tenor 718, 3355,
3561, 3773
Ramalho, Ricardo, flute 1013
Ramey, Samuel, bass 232, 1596, 1666,
2734, 3365, 3918
Ramirez, Alejandro, tenor 1007,
2142, 2830
Ramor Quartet 646
Rampal, Jean-Pierre, conductor 2235,
2383, 3420, 3942
Rampal, Jean-Pierre, flute 18, 75,
120, 203, 311, 621, 635, 760,
1242, 1268, 1482, 1495, 1671,
1875, 2212, 2213, 2216, 2235,
2426, 3198, 3421, 3942
Rampal, Jean-Pierre, piccolo 3421

Rampal, Joseph, flute 3421
Randall, Darrel, oboe 2713
Rands, Leslie, baritone 3156, 3157, 3158
Raninger, Walter, bass-baritone 1763
Ranki, Dezso, piano 368, 622, 2244, 2331, 3138
Rantos, Spiros, violin 320
Rapf, Kurt, organ 2805
Raphael Trio 1346
Raphaele Concert Orchestra 2449
Raphaelis, Enrico, oboe 3291, 3292, 3293
Raskin, Judith, soprano 789, 3499
Rattle, Simon, conductor 2059, 2108
Ratzinger, Georg, conductor 3697
Rauch, Fantisek, piano 1058, 3026
Raucheisen, Michael, piano 852, 2874 3537, 3541
Rault, Yves, piano 2940
Rautio, Erkki, violoncello 2544
Ravaglia, Emilia 2684
Ravel Trio 2166
Raver, Leonard, organ 2755
Ravinia Festival Orchestra 2330, 3127
Rawsthorne, Noel, organ 249
Rayam, Curtis, tenor 3074
Raychev, Russlan, conductor 2606
Rayner, Michael, baritone 3152, 3165
R.C.A. Italiana Opera Chorus 3350
R.C.A. Italiana Opera Orchestra 3350
R.C.A. Symphony Orchestra 724, 816, 3961
Reardon, John, baritone 2171
Redaelli, Robert, piano 111
Redd, Paula, alto 1351
Redel, Julius, conductor 3365
Redel, Kurt, conductor 3956
Redel, Kurt, flute 3956
Reed, Daniel, violin 2601
Reed, John, baritone 3165
Rees, Rosalind, soprano 4025
Rees-Williams, Jonathan, conductor 34
Reese, Rebecca, trumpet 1387
Regensburg Cathedral Choir 171, 265, 323
Regensburg Domspatzen 3697
Rehfuss, Heinz, bass-baritone 231
Rehkemper, Heinrich, baritone 3774
Reich, Gunter, bass 925
Reichelt, Ingeborg, soprano 137
Reichert, Manfred, conductor 39, 2163, 2371, 3120

Reid, Gillian, psaltery, Mediaeval bells, percussion 3680
Reid, Meston, tenor 3152, 3165
Reilly, Tommy, harmonica 52
Reimers, Paul, tenor 3774
Reiner, Fritz, conductor 816, 3451, 3954
Reinhardt, Carole, trumpet 1397, 1676
Reinhardt, Delia, soprano 3923
Reinhardt, Rolf, conductor 1709, 3049, 3308
Reining, Maria, soprano 3081, 3446
Remsen, Dorothy, harp 3652
Renar, Karl, bass 1946
Renaud, Maurice, baritone 3770
Rendall, David, tenor 1596
Renon-McLaughlin, G., viola 1873
Renzulli, Franco, piano 1474
Requejo, Ricardo, piano 10, 1088, 1776, 3687
Rescigno, Nocola, conductor 629, 2573, 3349
Reshetin, Mark, bass-baritone 3796
Resnik, Georgine, soprano 1630
Resnik, Regina, contralto 610, 1948, 3672
Reszke, Edouard de, bass 3770
Retchitzka, Basia, soprano 3129
Rethberg, Elisabeth, soprano 3367, 3774
Rettore, Aurora, soprano 3773
Retyi, Georg, violin 3956
Rev, Livia, piano 1178, 1204, 1209, 1210
Rex, Sheila, soprano 2582
Reyentovich, Yuli, conductor 3694
Reyes, Angel, violin 445
Reynolds, Anna, mezzo-soprano 125, 128, 233, 2171
Reynolds, H. Robert, conductor 1163
Reynolds, Veda, violin 1470
Rhodes, Jane, soprano 1525, 2443, 2448
Rhodes, Keith, conductor 3528
Rhodes, Keith, organ 1615, 3528
RIAS Chamber Chorus 233, 2294, 2321, 2400, 2881, 3360, 3695
RIAS Sinfonietta 777, 1254, 3995
RIAS Symphony Orchestra 2258, 2400, 3360
Ribari, Antal, piano 2692
Ribassenko, Vladimir, bass 2973
Ribera, Jose, piano 1472
Ricci, Ruggiero, violin 1349, 1388,

1499, 2438, 2469, 2473, 2772, 3637, 3665
Ricciardi, Franco, tenor 3341
Ricciarelli, Katia, soprano 1263, 2564, 2565, 2570, 2571, 3340, 3342, 3347, 3353, 3361, 3596
Richards, Bernard, violoncello 237
Richardson, Lynda, soprano 3334
Richman, James, conductor 1112
Richman, James, harpsichord 998
Richter, Georg, conductor 2407
Richter, Karl, conductor 125, 170, 264, 265, 288, 320, 322, 323
Richter, Karl, harpsichord 218, 320, 321, 322
Richter, Karl, organ 151, 169
Richter, Konrad, piano 1912
Richter, Sviatoslav, piano 513, 535, 536, 840, 850, 902, 1083, 2614, 2819, 2868
Richter, Werner, flute 2663
Richter-Hasser, Hans, piano 2865
Ricken, Johannes, organ 4039, 4040
Ricou, Claude, vibraphone 780
Ridder, Anton de, tenor 1272
Ridderbusch, Karl, bass 456, 706, 2009, 2461, 3449, 3459
Riedel-Pax, Rotraud, soprano 1245
Riedlbauch, Jan, flute 4009
Riegel, Kenneth, tenor 644, 672, 2292, 2295, 2743
Rieu, Andre, conductor 1679
Rifkin, Joshua, piano 1857
Rigai, Amiram, piano 1519
Rignold, Hugo, conductor 2610
Riley, Terry, organ 2693
Rilling, Helmuth, conductor 129, 130, 148, 150, 151, 963, 2802
Rinaldi, Alberto, baritone 1098
Rinaldi, Margherita, soprano 1259, 3364
Ringeissen, Bernard, piano 1, 3137
Rippon, Michael, bass-baritone 2105, 3334
Ristenpart, Karl, conductor 31, 78, 203, 843
Ritchie, Margaret, soprano 1236
Ritchie, Stanley, violin 2186
Ritt, Morey, piano 2499, 3499
Ritter-Ciampi, Gabrielle, soprano 3774
Ritzkowsky, Johannes, horn 2807
Ritzman, Martin, tenor 557
Rivaz, Antony de, countertenor 2762
Rivera, Daniel, piano 668

Riverside Church Choir 4058, 4059
Rizzi, Lucia, contralto 3436
Rizzoli, Bruna, soprano 2732
Robert, George, piano 2713
Roberts, Bernard, piano 496, 506, 521
Roberts, Elisabeth, lute 279, 345
Roberts, Guy, lute 345, 2066
Roberts, Guy, theorbo 2066
Roberts, Joy, soprano 2602
Roberts, Stephen, bass-baritone 263, 709, 982, 1591
Robertson, Duncan, tenor 629
Robertson, John, tenor 3346
Robertson, Linnhe, harpsichord 3396
Robertson, Stuart, baritone 3154, 3160
Robev (Robey), Georgi, conductor 3217
Robin Hood Dell Orchestra 816
Robinson, McNeil, conductor 1006, 2787
Robinson, McNeil, organ 1006
Robison, Paula, flute 1640, 2327
Robles, Marisa, harp 754, 903, 2229, 3665
Roblou, David, harpsichord 3989
Robson, Ann, mezzo-soprano 719
Robson, Christopher, alto 3326
Robson, Elizabeth, soprano 719
Roccino, Teresa 2728
Roche, Joseph, violin 4064
Rochester Cathedral Choir 3524
Rodde, Anne-Marie, soprano 1410, 1411, 1638, 2633
Roden, Anthony, tenor 1008
Rodin, Gustaf, tenor 3468
Rodin, Margot, contralto 140
Rodina Choir 457
Roehr, Gideon, viola 1455
Rogatchevsky, Joseph 3926
Rogeri Trio 1103
Rogers, Nigel, tenor 1468, 2074, 2581, 3719
Rogers, Robert, piano 3885
Rogg, Lionel, harpsichord 3753, 3755
Rogg, Lionel, organ 166, 210, 3755
Rogier, Frank 2170
Rogner, Heinz, conductor 2898, 2906
Rogoff, Ilan, piano 2820
Rohan, Jindrich, conductor 729, 2080, 2488
Rohmann, Imre, piano 196, 2930
Rohn, Erich, violin 433
Rohrig, Wolfram, conductor 2671

Roi, Daniele, harpsichord 28
Rolfe Johnson, Anthony, tenor 227,
    1591, 1623, 1631, 1666, 1708,
    2313, 2822, 3333, 3440, 3441,
    3442
Rolla, Janos, conductor 102, 2185,
    2286, 2289
Rolla, Janos, violin 1870
Rolle, Antony, piano 2115
Romani, Augusto, bass 2742
Rome Opera Chorus 3341, 3368
Rome Opera Orchestra 724, 3341, 3368
    3625, 3793
Romero, Angel, guitar 15, 759, 1487,
    1494
Romero, Celedonio, guitar 1487
Romero, Celin, guitar 1487
Romero Guitar Quartet 2715
Romero, Pepe, guitar 746, 1487, 1496
    2715, 3041, 3917
The Romeros 3320
Rommerts, Floris, bass 2189
Ronald, Landon, piano 3770
Roni, Luigi, bass 2296
Ronneback, Tore, bassoon 1455
Roo, Michael de, percussion 368
Rooley, Anthony, conductor 1274,
    1277, 1801, 1844, 1935, 2074,
    3876, 3879, 3880
Rooley, Anthony, lute 1273, 3877,
    3878
Roon, Elisabeth, soprano 2911
Ropek, Jiri, organ 1352
Roque-Alsina, Carlos, piano 2712
Roquin, L., trumpet 1873
Ros, Ad, trumpet 2062
Rosat, Karine, soprano 1013
Rosbaud, Hans, conductor 1874
Rose, Barry, conductor 1694
Rose, Bernard, conductor 2495, 3319
Rose, Jerome, piano 1990
Rose, John, organ 1438, 3031, 4022
Rose, Leonard, violoncello 814
Rose, Margot, alto 2803
Rose, Werner, piano 1130
Roseman, Ronald, oboe 710, 789,
    1641, 3306
Rosen, Charles, piano 1716, 3494,
    3604, 3608
Rosen, Marcy, violoncello 744
Rosen, Michael, percussion 2008
Rosenberger, Carol, piano 1187
Rosenblith, Eric, violin 1117
Rosenboom, David, piano 2722
Rosenthal, Manuel, conductor 1919

Rosenthal, Maurice, conductor 2773
Rosenthal, Willi, mandolin 2366
Rosetta, Vittorio, harmonium 2739
Ros-Marba, Antonio, conductor 3919
Rosner, Anton, baritone 2457
Ross, Alastair, harpsichord 1621
Ross, Alastair, organ 3440
Ross, Scott, harpsichord 2790
Rossi, Christiane, violin 3716
Rossi-Lemeni, Nicola, bass 2497,
    2733
Rossini Orchestra 1512
Rossl-Majdan, Hilde, contralto 602
Rossler, Almut, organ 8
Rostal, Max, violin 3094
Rostropovich, Mstislav, conductor
    1050, 1324, 1342, 2974, 3200,
    3208, 3219, 3240
Rostropovich, Mstislav, violoncello
    813, 1309, 1760, 3200
Roswange, Helge, tenor 1622, 2075,
    3538, 3558, 3561, 3584
Rota, Anna Maria, contralto 724
Roth, Daniel, organ 1853
Roth, Gottfried, horn 3293
Rothenberger, Anneliese, soprano
    634, 1866, 1945, 2306, 3073, 3166
Rother, Artur, conductor 432, 2075,
    2804, 3446, 3539
Rothmuller, Daniel, violoncello 3652
Rothweiler, Margot 1891
Rott, Helena, contralto 545
Rotterdam Philharmonic Orchestra
    1225, 1290, 2625, 2627
Rottgen Chamber Choir 1247
Rotzsch, Hans Joachim, tenor 128
Rouleau, Joseph, bass 629
Round, Thomas, tenor 3155, 3161
Roussel, Jacques, conductor 1242
Rousseleire, Charles, tenor 3770
Roux, Michel, baritone 2730
Rowicki, Witold, conductor 69, 70,
    334, 1870, 2255, 2257, 3181,
    3182, 3857, 3975
Rowland, Gilbert, harpsichord 2795,
    2797, 3034, 3035
Roy, Will, bass 344
Royal Albert Hall Orchestra 1365
Royal Choral Society 1118, 1383
Royal College of Music Orchestra
    3534
Royal Liverpool Philharmonic Orch-
    estra 1359, 1382, 2087, 2436,
    3517
Royal Marines Band 3617, 3619

Royal Military School of Music Band and Trumpeters 4028

Royal Opera House Chorus, Covent Garden 632, 660, 691, 2223, 2564, 2652, 3345, 3353, 3483, 3672

Royal Opera House Orchestra, Covent Garden 344, 582, 632, 691, 1512, 1685, 2223, 2296, 2564, 2777, 3345, 3353, 3451, 3483, 3666, 3672, 3773, 3792, 3918

Royal Philharmonic Chorus 3083, 3322

Royal Philharmonic Orchestra 5, 340, 346, 428, 458, 559, 571, 595, 596, 603, 703, 720, 918, 961, 1005, 1019, 1049, 1227, 1230, 1232, 1236, 1338, 1355, 1446, 1498, 1507, 1540, 1560, 1622, 1639, 1687, 1690, 1723, 1741, 1742, 1794, 1838, 1913, 2120, 2182, 2225, 2236, 2299, 2388, 2393, 2532, 2609, 2705, 2727, 2747, 2776, 2889, 2991, 2994, 3013, 3083, 3086, 3099, 3101, 3152, 3204, 3252, 3316, 3322, 3334, 3625, 3672, 3792, 3793, 3799, 4070, 4071

Royall, Christopher, countertenor 1621

Royer, Jacqueline, mezzo-soprano 3774

Rozeboom, Aart, clarinet 3818

Rozhdestvenskaya, Nadia, soprano 2698

Rozhdestvensky, Gennady, celesta 3834

Rozhdestvensky, Gennady, conductor 342, 661, 1021, 1389, 1854, 2047, 2533, 2539, 2548, 2553, 2806, 2973, 3006, 3008, 3010, 3237, 3781

Rozhdestvensky, Gennady, harpsichord 3834

Rozhdestvensky, Gennady, organ 3834

Rozhdestvensky, Gennady, piano 338, 3834

Rozsa, Miklos, conductor 2747

Rozsnyai, Zoltan, conductor 299, 666, 667, 1002, 1321, 1769, 3230, 3968

Rozsos, Istvan, tenor 1721

RSFSR Russian Chorus 2530

RTF Boys Choir 3318

Rubinlicht, Janine, violin 2519, 3767

Rubinow, Ruth, violoncello 2078

Rubinstein, Artur, piano 255, 424, 428, 2929, 3953, 3954

Rubio, Consuelo, soprano 3665

Rubsam, Wolfgang, organ 224, 1577, 2665

Rudel, Julius, conductor 2091, 3497

Rudolf, Max, conductor 945, 1731, 2473

Ruf, Hugo, harpsichord 90, 1645, 2006

Ruffo, Titta, baritone 3770

Ruhland, Konrad, conductor 3536, 3959

Rumbo, Luigi 3025

Rumpler, Harry, viola 2640

Rundel, Peter, violin 3291

Rundgren, Bengt, bass 3364

Russ, Ingeborg, contralto 109

Russel, Lynda, soprano 1008

Russian Cathedral Choir, London 776

Russill, Patrick, organ 970

Russo, John, clarinet 697, 2137, 3891

Ruszkowska, Elena, soprano 3774

Rutter, John, conductor 3572

Ruzicka, Josef, piano 4009

Ruzickova, Zuzana, harpsichord 206, 275, 280, 1620, 1644, 2791

Ryan, Jane, viola da gamba 97, 1147

Rybin, Juan Carlos, violin 3414, 3429

Rydberg, Goran, percussion 1851

Rysanek, Leonie, soprano 451, 3475

Ryshna, Natalie, piano 1951, 1952

Rzewski, Frederic, piano 1852

Saar Chamber Orchestra 203

Saar Radio Chamber Orchestra 31, 78

Saarinen, Gloria, piano 46

Saarne, Hilja, violoncello 1579

Sabajno, Carlo, conductor 1383

Sabouret, Jean-Pierre, violin 2960

Saccomano, Lorenzo, baritone 1956

Sackson, David, violin 3316

Sadler's Wells Orchestra and Chorus 719, 3063

Sadlo, Milos, violoncello 303, 490, 1306

Sagi-Barba, Emilio, baritone 3774

St. Bavo Cathedral Boys Choir 3229

Saint-Clivier, Andre, mandolin 1814

St. George's Canzona 3647

St. George's Chapel Choir 2105

St. Hedwig's Cathedral Choir 551, 818, 1688, 3360, 3362 3462

St. Jacob Choir, Stockholm 2317

St. Jacobi Kantorei Chorus 1616
St. John's College Chapel Choir,
    Cambridge 762, 1693, 2498, 2786,
    3376, 3567
St. John's Episcopal Church Choir,
    Los Angeles 3016
St. John's Orchestra 2153, 2204,
    3119
St. John'S Smith Square Orchestra
    3715
St. Louis Symphony Orchestra 721,
    838, 1349, 1476, 2578, 2607, 2949
St. Martin Benedictine Abbey Monks
    Choir 3699, 3700, 3701
St. Mary of Warwick Choir 2599
St. Mary's Cathedral Choir 3724,
    3992
St. Maurice and St. Maur Abbey Ben-
    edictine Monks Choir 3914
St. Michael's College Choir 3525
St. Paul Chamber Orchestra 915
St. Paul's Cathedral Choir 263, 1694
    3334, 3724
St. Peter ad Vincula Choir 3530
St. Thomas Choir 132, 236
St. Willibrord Church Boys Chorus
    267, 268
Saks, Toby, violoncello 693
Sala, Oskar, mixtur-trautonium 1779
Salber, Gunther, violin 634
Salisbury Cathedral Choir 3479, 3835
Salminen, Matti, baritone 265, 2771
Salmon, Godfrey, conductor 1531
Salvi, Bruno, violin 199
Salzburg Camerata Academica 1763,
    2259
Salzburg Chamber Choir 2355
Salzburg City Theatre Operetta Ens-
    emble 3065
Salzburg Mozarteum Chorus 2308
Salzburg Mozarteum Orchestra 2238,
    2267, 2268, 2308, 2355, 2392
Salzburg Radio Chorus 2308
Salzer, Daniele, harpsichord 3296
Sammarco, G. Mario, baritone 3770
Samuel, Gerhard, conductor 896
Samuel, Harold, piano 220
Samuelson, Bror, conductor 3934
San Antonio Symphony Orchestra 374
San Carlo Opera Orchestra and Chorus
    2733, 3371
San Diego Master Chorale 3485
San Diego Symphony Orchestra 3485
San Francisco Contemporary Music
    Players 1287, 1937

San Francisco Opera Orchestra 2574
San Francisco String Quartet 3997
San Francisco Symphony Orchestra
    674, 675
San Francisco Trio 891
Sanderling, Kurt, conductor 809,
    872, 879, 943, 2820, 3277
Sanders, John, organ 4054, 4063
Sanders, Samuel, piano 547, 1393,
    2202, 3552, 3788
Sandford, Kenneth, bass-baritone
    3152, 3165
Sandor, Frigyes, conductor 1675,
    2241, 2244, 3294
Sandor, Janos, conductor 79, 1211,
    3807
Sandor, John, tenor 3918
Sandor, Judit 229
Sanger, David, organ 752, 3378,
    3506, 3836
Sanroma, Jesus Maria, piano 3961
Sansom, Marilyn, violoncello 1621,
    2633
Santa Cecilia Chorus 3672
Santa Cecilia Orchestra 2570, 3672,
    3827
Santa Cruz Chamber Symphony 1122
Santiago, Enrique, viola 924
Santini, Gabriele, conductor 2742,
    3368
Santley, Charles, baritone 3770
Santos, Turibio, guitar 3717
Santunione, Orianna, soprano 1259
Sanvoisin, Michel, recorder 1026,
    3296
Saorgin, Rene, harpsichord 3744
Saorgin, Rene, organ 1434, 2402,
    3744, 3762
Saperstein (Saperton), David, piano
    1055
Sapin, D., horn 1873
Sapszon, Ferenc, conductor 3803
Sarabia, Guillermo, baritone 3792
Saram, Rohan de, violoncello 2432,
    2748
Sardi, Ivan, bass 2294, 2321, 3362
Saretzki, Hans Dieter, tenor 1245,
    2962
Sarfaty, Regina, mezzo-soprano 3128
Sargent, Malcolm, conductor 413,
    1049, 1118, 1230, 1383, 1794,
    3154, 3156, 3160, 3163, 3164
Sarkissov, Ashot, bass 2973
Sass, Sylvia, soprano 358, 628,
    1028, 1296, 2293, 3370

Satava, Oldrich, percussion 1656
Satoh, Toyohiko, lute 1824, 4012
Saulesco, Mircea, violin 1455
Saulesco Quartet 985
Sautter, Fred, trumpet 3656
Savaga, Susan, piano 761
Savall, Jordi, lyra 1139
Savall, Jordi, viol 1139, 1483
Savall, Jordi, viola da gamba 978,
    1158, 1428, 1916, 2016, 2063,
    2064, 2069
Savaria Symphony Orchestra 726
Savchenko, Arkady, baritone 3189
Savonlinna Opera Festival Orchestra
    and Chorus 2771
Savouret, Alain, harpsichord 2781
Savouret, Alain, organ 2781
Sawallisch, Wolfgang, conductor 359,
    2460, 2510, 2740, 3102, 3450,
    3452, 3471, 3472
Sawallish, Wolfgang, piano 2146,
    2149, 2740
Sax, Manfred, bassoon 1642, 3305,
    3439
Saxon State Orchestra 3075
La Scala Chorus 627, 1383, 2521,
    2567, 2575, 2724, 2732, 3361
La Scala Coro Polifonico 2739
La Scala Orchestra 627, 1383, 2497,
    2521, 2567, 2575, 2724, 2732,
    3275, 3361, 3792
Scaletti, Carla, harp 1160
Scaremberg, Emile, tenor 3770
Scarlatti Orchestra 2782
Schadle, Lotte, soprano 2301
Schaeffer, Steve, drums 1466
Schaer, Hanna, contralto 1013, 1695,
    2830, 3388, 3434
Schafer, Herbert, violoncello 3845
Schartel, Elisabeth, contralto 3475
Schary, Elke, mezzo-soprano 634,
    3066
Schaude, Rolf, timpani 3297
Schech, Marianne, soprano 2400
Scheidemantel, Karl, baritone 3770
Schellenberg, Arno, bass-baritone
    545
Scheller, Helmut, organ 4034
Schenck, Manfred, bass 643
Scheppan, Hilde, soprano 2075, 3446,
    3468
Scherchen, Hermann, conductor 123
Scherler, Barbara, contralto 1140
Schernus, Herbert, conductor 1140
Scheurich, Marga, harpsichord 700,

1460
Schickele, Peter, conductor 2803
Schickele, Peter, piano 2803
Schiff, Andras, piano 180, 191, 196,
    2793, 3854
Schiff, Heinrich, violoncello 815
Schiml, Marga, contralto 2222, 3491
Schipa, Tito, tenor 1099, 3774
Schippers, Thomas, conductor 353,
    2743, 2899, 3350, 3625, 3793
Schirp, Wilhelm, bass 2075
Schlemm, Anny, mezzo-soprano 1817
Schlusnus, Heinrich, baritone 3538,
    3584
Schluter, Erna, soprano 3083
Schluter, Karl-Heinz, piano 2831
Schluter, Michael, piano 2831
Schmalfuss, Gernot, oboe 1911
Schmedes, Erik, tenor 3770
Schmidinger, Rudolf, percussion 4016
Schmidl, Peter, clarinet 2337, 2396
Schmidt, Hans, conductor 3662
Schmidt, Hans, harpsichord 1460
Schmidt, Heinrich, conductor 3780
Schmidt, Heinrich, piano 546
Schmidt, Ingus, trumpet 2010
Schmidt, Joseph, tenor 3830
Schmidt, Manfred, tenor 1140, 1894,
    3462, 3712
Schmidt, Ole, conductor 1770, 2429
Schmidt, Thomas, piano 710
Schmidt, Trudeliese, mezzo-soprano
    643
Schmidt-Gaden, Gerhard, conductor
    172, 228, 2312
Schmidt-Gertenbach, Volker, conduc-
    tor 1035
Schmidt-Isserstedt, Hans, conductor
    454, 552, 805, 1307, 2306, 2377,
    2379
Schmitt-Walter, Karl, baritone 545,
    3446, 3538
Schmitz, Otto, horn 3417
Schmitz, Paul, conductor 2260
Schnabel, Artur, piano 413, 495, 502
Schneeberger, Hansheinz, violin 957
Schneider, Martin Gotthart, cembalo
    3845
Schneiderhan, Wolfgang, violin 321,
    436, 443, 2851
Schneidt, Hanns-Martin, conductor
    171, 323
Schnoebelen, Nicole, harpsichord
    3716
Schock, Rudolf, tenor 633, 3462,

3712

Schoenberg, Arnold, Choir 1624

Schoener, Eberhard, conductor 2219

Schoettler, Frederick, piano 1109

Schoffler, Paul, bass-baritone 16, 2319, 3081, 3083, 3096, 3355

Schola Cantorum Basiliensis 1605, 1610, 3303, 3309

Schola Cantorum, New York 1006, 1792

Schola Cantorum of Church of St. Mary the Virgin 2787

Schola Cantorum Sankt Foillan, Aachen 956, 2477

Schola Hungarica Ensemble 3802, 3808 3809

Scholars 345, 3867, 3873

Scholz, Kristine, keyboard 1851

Schonbrun, Sheila, soprano 3853

Schonstedt, Arno, organ 153

Schoof, Armin, organ 965

Schopper, Michael, bass 2312

Schorg, Gretl, soprano 1846

Schott, Ulricke, harpsichord 320

Schramm, Ernst, bass 2881

Schramm, Margit, soprano 1272

Schreier, Peter, conductor 144

Schreier, Peter, tenor 125, 128, 144, 265, 323, 1689, 2145, 2222, 2306, 2308, 2355, 2367, 2740, 2858, 2936

Schrello, Mark, trumpet 1455

Schroder, Andreas, organ 2670

Schroder, Jaap, conductor 1171, 1606 1798, 2205, 3444, 3445

Schroder, Jaap, viola 1217

Schroder, Jaap, violin 42, 1217, 1917, 2369, 2690, 2872, 3046, 3444

Schroeder, Kurt, conductor 1781

Schuback, Peter, violoncello 1851

Schubart, Marianne, soprano 1846

Schubert Quartet 2851

Schubert, Richard, tenor 3774

Schuchter, Gilbert, piano 2838

Schuchter, Wilhelm, conductor 3167

Schuler, Johannes, conductor 3446, 3468

Schuller, Gunther, conductor 1117

Schulte, Rolf, violin 1433

Schulz, Gerhard, violin 1697

Schulz, Otto, conductor 1777

Schulz, Ulla, viola 1697

Schulz, Walther, violoncello 1697

Schulz, Wolfgang, flute 1697, 2396, 4016

Schumann, Elisabeth, soprano 3774

Schumann-Heink, Ernestine, contralto 3770

Schuricht, Carl, conductor 350

Schurmann, Gerard, conductor 2961

Schwartz, Nathan, piano 492

Schwarz, Gerard, Brass Ensemble 2755

Schwarz, Gerard, conductor 114, 1679, 2200

Schwarz, Gerard, trumpet 650, 1677, 3674

Schwarz, Hanna, mezzo-soprano 460, 553, 644, 2461

Schwarz, Joseph, baritone 3774

Schwarz, Rudolf, conductor 2836

Schwarz, Vera, soprano 3774

Schwarzkopf, Elisabeth, soprano 147, 231, 461, 554, 2365, 2460, 2575, 2582, 2876, 3080, 3351, 3486, 3515, 3516, 3538, 3780, 3787, 3793

Schweiger, Hans, conductor 2535

Schweizer, Verena, soprano 3388

Schwenk, Georg, mandolin 634

Scimone, Claudio, conductor 21, 28, 758, 918, 1110, 1262, 1268, 1482, 1897, 2631, 3198, 3199, 3414, 3415, 3421, 3424, 3428, 3429, 3436, 3438

Sciutti, Graziella, soprano 2475, 2732

Scot-Shepherd, Stephen, bass 3485

Scotney, Evelyn, soprano 3774

Scott, John, flute 1531

Scott, John, organ 1693, 3567

Scott, John, saxophone 1531

Scott, Roger, bass 3606

Scotti, Antonio, baritone 3770

Scottish Baroque Ensemble 740, 908, 2208

Scottish Chamber Orchestra 1659

Scottish National Chorus 1362, 1806

Scottish National Orchestra 411, 722, 1360, 1362, 1806, 2150, 2404, 2431, 3346

Scottish Opera Chorus 1659, 3346

Scotto, Renata, soprano 626, 1955, 2088, 2562, 2563, 2576, 3363, 3723, 3792, 3793

Scovotti, Jeannette, soprano 3066

Scuckl, Annelies, contralto 3711

Seal, Richard, conductor 3835

Seaman, Christopher, conductor 1680

Seattle Symphony Orchestra 1504

Sebastian, Georges, conductor 2096

Sebestyen, Janos, harpsichord 1471
Sebok, Gyorgy, piano 895, 1442
Sebon, Karl-Bernhard, flute 1254
Sedlmair, Sophie, soprano 3770
Seefried, Irmgard, soprano 264, 451, 859, 2294, 2316, 2321, 3081, 3538
Seemann, Carl, piano 2260
Segarra, Ireneu, conductor 995, 1480, 2196
Segerstam, Hannele, violin 4, 2970
Segerstam, Leif, conductor 648, 2642, 2970
Segovia, Andres, guitar 3549, 3775, 3798
Seguin, J. P. bassoon 1873
Segurola, Andres de, bass 3770
Seibel, Paul, soprano 2172
Seidler-Winkler, Bruno, piano 3770
Seifert, Gerd, horn 2010, 2318, 2956
Seiler, Emil, Chamber Orchestra 91
Sellers, Michael, piano 2465
Sellick, Phyllis, piano 1401
Sembach, Johannes, tenor 3774
Sembrich, Marcella, soprano 3770
Semkov, Jerzy, conductor 1047, 2949
Senechal, Michel, tenor 2448, 2573
Senger-Bettaque, Katharina, soprano 3770
Senior, Marion, piano 3503
Senius, Felix, tenor 3770
Senofsky, Ellen Mack, piano 1961
Sentance, Joseph, organ 3530
Seow, Yitkin, piano 1220, 2432
Sequoia String Quartet 381
Serafim, Fernando, tenor 1013
Serafin, Josef, organ 2668
Serafin, Tullio, conductor 627, 2561, 2567, 2575, 2733, 3625, 3789, 3792, 3793
Serebrier, Jose, conductor 1337
Sereni, Mario, baritone 3350, 3371
Serkin, Peter, piano 1067
Serkin, Rudolf, piano 508, 830, 2827
Serov, Eduard, conductor 1390, 2750, 3317
Sessions, Roger, piano 3128
Severin, Julius, piano 2514
Seward, Steven, tuba 295
Seymour, Peter, organ 164
Sgrizzi, Luciano, harpsichord 108, 197, 2796
Sgrizzi, Luciano, piano 1107
Shakhovskaya, Natalia, violoncello 1877
Shanley, Gretel, flute 2501

Shann, Edgar, oboe 320
Shannon, Gordon, tenor 2787
Shapey, Ralph, conductor 2200
Sharon, Boaz, piano 1889
Sharp, Frederick, baritone 1236, 3063
Sharpe, Trevor, conductor 4028
Shatskes, A., piano 2112
Shaw, John, baritone 2617
Shaw, Robert, conductor 757, 771
Shaw, Verena, violin 3021
Shearer, Mary, soprano 1351
Shearing, George, piano 759
Sheffield Choir 1383
Sheffield, Leo, bass-baritone 3154, 3157, 3160
Shelley, Anthony, baritone 970, 3326
Shelton, Lucy, soprano 2803
Shenderovich, Yevgeny, piano 2418
Shepherd, Adrian, conductor 3392
Shepherd, Adrian, violoncello 783, 3392
Shepherd Quartet 1121
Shepherd, Scott, percussion 761
Sheppard, Honor, soprano 1592, 2587
Sheridan, Margaret, soprano 3773
Sheriff, Noam, conductor 3564
Sherman, Alec, conductor 3798
Sherman, Roger, organ 3656
Sherman, S., organ 1502
Shetler, Norman, piano 2936
Shevelev, Nicholai, baritone 3770
Shiesley, Robert, baritone 402
Shifrin, David, clarinet 1163
Shimko, Tamara, soprano 3189
Shingles, Stephen, viola 1531, 2352
Shirey, Richard, piano 3655
Shirley, George, tenor 3128
Shirley-Quirk, John, baritone 233, 263, 1422, 1618, 1637, 1691, 1710, 2621, 3990
Shirvan, Harriet, piano 1569
Shostakovich, Dmitri, piano 490
Shostakovich, Maxim, conductor 2978
Shovelton, Geoffrey, tenor 3152, 3165
Shreiner, Alexander, organ 3313
Shulman, Louis, violin 2601
Shumsky, Oscar, violin 283
Shurtleff, Lynn, conductor 1436
Shushaniya, Irakli, bass 2478
Sibertin-Blanc, Antoine, organ 1013
Sibiriakov, Lev, baritone 3770
Sibirtsev, Alexander, baritone 2984

Siebert, Dorothea, soprano 3457, 3467
Siebert, Renee, flute, 2399
Siede, Mathias, organ 2010
Siegel, Jeffry, piano 1476
Siegl, Henry, violin 1504
Siems, Margarethe, soprano 3770
Sifler, Paul, organ 3016
Sighele, Mietta, soprano 3341
Signor, Franco 1258
Siis, Peder, guitar 3883
Siki, Bela, piano 3324
Silesian Philharmonic Orchestra 3857
Silfies, George, clarinet 487, 838,
    2339
Silja, Anja, soprano 643, 3450, 3452
    3457, 3467, 3471, 3472
Sillem, Maurits, fortepiano 1691
Sillem, Maurits, harpsichord 2384
Sillito, Kenneth, violin 3397
Sills, Beverly, soprano 3554
Silva, Joana, soprano 2141
Silverman, Robert, piano 2077
Silverstein, Joseph, violin 1569,
    2810
Silvestri, Constantin, conductor
    1995, 3121
Silvestri, Luciano, piano 3596
Simcisko, Viktor, violin 3847
Simionato, Giulietta, mezzo-soprano
    2732
Simmons, Romayne, piano 3770
Simon, Abbey, piano 487, 1069, 2607
Simon, Albert, conductor 196
Simon, Geoffrey, conductor 736
Simon, Laszlo, piano 1108
Simoncini, Margaret, soprano 63
Simoneau, Leopold, tenor 723, 2299,
    2316
Simonova, Lyudmila, mezzo-soprano
    41, 3241
Simonsen, Irene, flute 1412
Simpson, Glenda, soprano 981
Simpson, Richard, oboe 3623
Simsek, Hikmet, conductor 6
Sinclair, Jeannette, soprano 2730
Sinclair, Monica, contralto 458,
    629, 2730
Sinfonia of London See London Sin-
    fonia
Singers Madrigale 3970
Sinnhoffer Quartet 2512
Sinopoli, Giuseppe, conductor 2017
Sinta, Donald, saxophone 1163
Sinyavskaya, Tamara, contralto 3214
    3796

Sirera, Gines, tenor 2100
Sistine Chapel Choir 391
Siu, Leon, guitar 3196
Siu, Leon, vocals 3196
Sjaellands Symphony Orchestra 2426
Sjogren, Thorsten, double bass 1455
Skeaping, Adam, violone 2188
Skeaping, Roderick, violin 2593
Skernick, Linda, harpsichord 3674
Skinner, John, countertenor 1632
Skold, Stefa, conductor 2317
Skowronek, Felix, flute 693
Skowronski, Vincent, violin 3109
Skram, Knut, bass-baritone 134
Skrowaczewski, Stanislaw, conductor
    2492, 2536, 2662, 3140
Slater, Vivien, piano 1768
Slatford, Rodney, double bass 902
Slatkin, Leonard, conductor 721,
    1476, 2528, 2607
Sleeper, Tom, trombone 1821
Slezak, Leo, tenor 3770
Slokar, Branimir, alphorn 3627
Slokar, Branimir, trombone 33, 624,
    3627
Slovak Chamber Orchestra 1138
Slovak Madrigalists 3847
Slovak Philharmonic Chorus 1260
Slovak Philharmonic Orchestra 871,
    881, 1260, 1344, 1473, 1523, 1860
Slovak Quartet 382
Sluys, Jozef, organ 68, 1872, 1953
Smati, Xavier, bass 717
Smedvig, Rolf, conductor 3998
Smedvig, Rolf, trumpet 3998
Smendzianka, Regina, piano 70
Smetacek, Vaclav, conductor 1429,
    2456, 4008
Smetana Quartet 472, 2848, 3028
Smirnov, Dimitri, tenor 3774
Smirnov, Yuri, piano 387, 2031
Smit, Leo, piano 1127, 1582
Smith, Brooks, piano 2772, 4002
Smith, Cyril, piano 1401
Smith, Donald, tenor 719
Smith, Edward, harpsichord 3853
Smith, Gregg, conductor 638, 914,
    3741
Smith, Gregg, Singers 638, 914,
    2755, 3741
Smith, Henry, trombone 3606
Smith, Hopkinson, guitar 978, 2069,
    3386
Smith, Hopkinson, lute 1284, 3386
Smith, Hopkinson, theorbo 978, 1916,

2063, 2064, 2069, 3385, 3386
Smith, Jennifer, soprano 227, 1013,
  1593, 1626, 1627, 1693, 2013,
  2588, 2600
Smith, Marilyn Hill, soprano 3433
Smith, Peter, horn 1527
Smith, Robert, harpsichord 176
Smithers, Don, trumpet 1678, 3916
Smola, Emmerich, conductor 3696
Smylie, Dennis, clarinet 67
Sneberger, Karel, violin 1930
Snell, Howard, conductor 59
Snitil, Vaclav, violin 1656, 2828
Snow, John, English horn 710
Snowden, Philip, baritone 3323
Snyder, Amy, voice 896
Snyder, Barry, piano 1089, 2139
Soames, Rene, tenor 1236
Sobinov, Leonid, tenor 3770
Sobolev, A., mandolin 2116
Soderblom, Ulf, conductor 2175, 2771
Sodergren, Inger, piano 534, 848,
  2919
Soderstrom, Elisabeth, soprano 37,
  610, 1536, 1816, 1836, 2622, 3104
Sofia Chamber Orchestra 204
Sofia Philharmonic Orchestra 457,
  3211
Sofia Soloists 3211
Sokoloff, Vladimir, piano 2968
Sokolov, Vladimir, clarinet 7
Soldh, Anita, soprano 1570
Solem, Paul, tenor 2787
Solistes de France (Les) 190
Solistes Romands 202, 3405
Solisti di Zagreb (I) 3289, 3418,
  3422
Solisti Veneti (I) 21, 28, 1482,
  1897, 2631, 3198, 3199, 3414,
  3415, 3421, 3424, 3428, 3429,
  3436, 3438
Sollberger, Harvey, conductor 67
Sollner, Franz, horn 2913
Sollscher, Goran, guitar 216
Solomón, piano See Cutner, Solomon,
  piano
Solomon, Jeff, horn 1821
Solow, Jeffrey, violoncello 352
Solti, Georg, conductor 358, 452,
  819, 861, 936, 1366, 1807, 1817,
  1820, 2264, 2293, 2413, 3076,
  3082, 3098, 3205, 3341, 3357,
  3463, 3666, 3672
Solyom, Janos, piano 612
Som, Laszlo, double bass 1895

Somary, Johannes, conductor 141,
  1635, 1749, 4067
Somer, Hilde, piano 374
Somogyvari, Labos 229
Soni Ventorum 693
Sonnersted, Bernard, baritone 360
Sonnleitner, Johannes, organ 1483,
  3960
Sonstevold, Knut, bassoon 3588
Soomer, Walter, baritone 3774
Sorensen, Christian, tenor 2427
Sormova, Nada, soprano 3029
Sortomme, Richard, violin 2199
Sothcott, John, conductor 3647
Sotin, Hans, bass 142, 143, 452,
  1687
Sotkilava, Surab, tenor 2478
Soto Chavvaria, Carlos Manuel, tenor
  973
Soukupova, Vera, contralto 3467,
  3470
Soulacroix, Gabriel, baritone 3770
Sounova, Daniela, soprano 1312, 3029
Sousa Band 1101
South German Madrigal Choir 142,
  143, 2880
South German Philharmonic Orchestra
  843
South German Radio Chorus 2437
South German Radio Orchestra 2437
Southend Boys Choir 1623, 2039
Southwest German Chamber Orchestra
  33, 38, 624, 1265, 1463
Southwest German Radio Orchestra
  3054, 3059
Southwest German Radio Orchestra
  Wind Octet 455
Southwest German Symphony Orchestra
  2174
Southwestern State University Wind
  Symphony 3030
Souzay, Gerard, baritone 1223, 3964
Soyer, Roger, bass-baritone 632,
  660, 691
Spalding, Albert, violin 812
Spandauer Kantorei 2802
Spanish National Orchestra 3665
Speculum Musicae 987, 1657, 2516,
  2755
Speiser, Elisabeth, soprano 128,
  148, 323
Spelina, Karel, viola 1788
Spencer, Robert, chitarrone 3443,
  3996
Spencer, Robert, lute 980, 984,

1275, 3778, 3996
Spencer, Roderick, organ 3502
Sperry, Paul, tenor 650
Spierer, Leon, conductor 3390
Spierer, Leon, violin 441, 3390
Spiering, Gert, tenor 2962
Spillman, Robert, piano 844
Spivakov, Vladimir, conductor 2273
Spivakov, Vladimir, violin 824, 2269
   2273
Spoorenberg, Erna, soprano 150, 2032
Spreckelsen, Uta, soprano 126, 1695,
   3302, 3388, 3434
Springer, Ingeborg, mezzo-soprano
   128
Springfels, Mary, viola da gamba
   2601
Sprunk, Petr, timpani 1656
Sramek, Alfred, bass 643, 2123, 2293
Srubar, Teodor, baritone 2456
Stacy, Thomas, English horn 1796
Stader, Maria, soprano 323, 453,
   1688, 2294, 2321, 2400, 3360,
   3362
Stadler, Vilmos, recorder 2072
Stadlmair, Hans, conductor 1595,
   1779, 2211, 2230, 2234, 2784
Stafford, Ashley, countertenor 1621,
   1694, 3326
Stafford, LeAnn, marimba 1821
Stagliano, James, horn 356
Stahl, Kerstin, singer 1851
Stalder Quintet 1871
Stampfli, Jakob, bass 131, 148, 151,
   963
Standage, Simón, violin 124, 178,
   1422, 3398, 3408, 3410
Stanic, Jelka, violin 3418
Starck, Claude, violoncello 1088
Starek, Jiri, conductor 777, 1254
Starke, Joachim, harp 1182
Starke, Ute, piano 1880
Starker, Janos, violoncello 275,
   444, 895, 990, 1886
Starobin, David, guitar 744, 914,
   1913, 4025
Starr, Susan, piano 2931
Staryk, Steven, violin 3099
Stasio, Anna di, mezzo-soprano 2570
Stearns, Duncan, piano 3887
Steed, Graham, organ 1437
Stefano, Giuseppe di, tenor 2567
Steffner, Raymond, baritone 649
Stegenga, Jan, violoncello 753
Steigerwalt, Gary, piano 3519

Stein, Andreas, alto 172, 228
Stein, Horst, conductor 1031, 3272,
   3696
Steinberg, Marja, flute 3412
Steinberg, William, conductor 1124
Steiner, Elisabeth, contralto 3066
Steiner, Oliver, violin 2139
Steiner, Peter, violoncello 895
Steingruber, Ilona, soprano 2911
Steinmassi, Hermine, soprano 3711
Stempnik, Gerard, cor anglais 3007
Stenlund, Dan-Olof, conductor 2504
Stenstadvold, Erik, guitar 3393
Stepan, Pavel, piano 3151
Stepelman, Rena, piano 3014
Stephani, Martin, conductor 1793
Stephens, Suzanne, clarinet 3055
Stephens, Suzanne, Japanese rin
   3054, 3058
Stern, Isaac, conductor 2213, 2216
Stern, Isaac, violin 814, 2492,
   2714, 2991, 2994, 3208, 3494
Stevens, Delores, piano 761
Stevens, Denis, conductor 549, 1468,
   3750, 3994
Stevens, Horace, baritone 3774
Stevens, Thomas, trumpet 3652
Stevenson, Delcina, soprano 2832
Stevensson, Kjell-Inge, clarinet
   1851
Stewart, Charles, bass 1621
Stewart, Thomas, bass-baritone
   3449, 3457, 3459
Stich-Randall, Teresa, soprano 233
Stiehler, Kurt, violin 657
Stiftner, Walter, bassoon 2072
Still, Ray, oboe 2526
Stilwell, Richard, baritone 1198,
   2192
Stingl, Anton, guitar 780
Stiot, Monique 1940
Stith, Marice, conductor 1387, 1533,
   3643
Stobart, James, conductor 3116, 3950
Stockhausen, Karlheinz, conductor
   3054, 3056, 3058, 3060
Stockhausen, Markus, trumpet 3058
Stockholm Bach Choir 140, 1591,
   1631
Stockholm Chamber Choir 3713
Stockholm Chamber Ensemble 3589
Stockholm Conservatory Musicians
   2317
Stockholm Philharmonic Orchestra
   37, 554, 2052, 3053

Stockholm Radio Choir 3713
Stocklassa, Gertraud, soprano 1894
Stoddart, John, tenor 719
Stoker, Richard, piano 3061
Stokman, Abraham, piano 3523
Stokman, Arlene, piano 3523
Stokowski, Leopold, conductor 326,
    599, 841, 865, 874, 1177, 1318,
    1878, 2455, 3220, 3270, 3285,
    3860
Stoll, Walter, bass 3462, 3712
Stolte, Adele, soprano 128, 2145
Stoltzman, Richard, clarinet 1201,
    2803
Stolz, Robert, conductor 1944, 3071,
    3072, 3477
Stolze, Gerhard, tenor 2452, 2462,
    3471
Stone, Frederick, piano 859
Storchio, Ronsina, soprano 3770
Stotijn, Peter, bass 3818
Stour Music Festival Chorus 2587
Stour Music Festival Orchestra 2587
Stout, Gordon, marimba 3509
Stoutz, Edmond de 2603
Stracciari, Riccardo, baritone 3774,
    3981
Stradivari Quartet 1514
Strano, Francesco, violoncello 3430
Stransky, Joseph, conductor 3860
Strasbourg Philharmonic Orchestra
    3089, 3473
Strasser, Tamas, viola 4064
Stratas, Teresa, soprano 644
Stratford Ensemble 910
Strauss, Isabel, soprano 649
Strauss, Richard, conductor 2874,
    3078, 3090, 3107, 3115
Strauss, Richard, piano 3114
Stravinsky, Igor, conductor 3117,
    3128, 3604, 3860
Streich, Rita, soprano 2184, 2400,
    3167, 3489, 3695
Streicher, Ludwig, double bass 3325
Stricker, Frieder, tenor 3066
Striegler, Kurt, conductor 3512
Strienz, Wilhelm, bass 1622
Stringer, Alan, trumpet 1665
Strongs, Susan, soprano 3770
Strummer, Peter, bass 344
Stryja, Karol, conductor 3857
Stuckey, Michael, conductor 2480
Studebaker, Julia, horn 2877
Studer, Michael, piano 2247
Studer, Ulrich, bass 1638

Studholme, Marion, soprano 3063,
    3153
Stueckgold, Grete, soprano 3774
Stuller, Gyula, violin 1283
Stumacher, Eric, piano 2989
Stuttgart Cantata Choir 3765
Stuttgart Chamber Music Ensemble 91
Stuttgart Chamber Orchestra 116,
    3399
Stuttgart Philharmonic Orchestra
    730, 2378
Stuttgart Radio Chorus 2319
Stuttgart Radio Orchestra 1871,
    2319, 3766
Stuyvesant Quartet 1903
Subotnik, Morton, conductor 3149
Subrtova, Milada, soprano 2456
Suddaby, Elsie, soprano 1236
Suddendorf, Richard, conductor 2060
Sudwestfunk Wind Players 1871
Suk Chamber Orchestra 3048
Suk, Josef, conductor 2266
Suk, Josef, violin 280, 1304, 1305,
    1430, 1644, 2079, 2266, 2270,
    3048, 4008
Suk Quartet 1847
Suk Trio 883
Suleimanov, Radik, flute 3781
Sullivan Chamber Ensemble 3922
Sullivan, Charles, conductor 3922
Sullivan, Charles, organ 3922
Sultan, Grete, piano 975
Summers, Jonathan, baritone 2454,
    3347
Sun Life Stanshaw Band 3621
Sunderland, Raymond, organ 4056
Susca, Vito, baritone 63
Susskind, Walter, conductor 1349,
    2022, 2899, 3625, 3772, 3780
Sussman, Ellen, soprano 344
Sutherland, Joan, soprano 552, 556,
    1256, 1257, 1948, 2099, 2218,
    2569, 3447, 3672, 3793, 3828
Sutton, Vern, tenor 3600
Sved, Alexancer, baritone 3812
Svehla, Zdenek, tenor 1836, 3029
Sveinbjornsson, Einar, violin 1415,
    3169
Svetlanov, Yevgeny, conductor 337,
    768, 2112, 2113, 2180, 2530,
    2546, 2623, 2697, 2704, 2706,
    2982, 2987, 3201, 3251, 3255,
    3261, 3267
Svihlikova, Viktorie, harpsichord
    635

Svolkovskis, Juris, violin 1831
Swan, Andrea, piano 3650
Swann, Frederick, conductor 4058,
    4059
Swann, Frederick, organ 4057, 4058,
    4059
Swedish Radio Orchestra 702, 2642,
    3052, 3508
Swedish Royal Orchestra 9
Sweelinck Conservatory Students
    Orchestra 2062
Swiatkowski, Chet, piano 3652, 3655
Sydney Symphony Orchestra 1114, 1337
Syme, David, piano 1092
Symphony of the Air 599, 841
Syracuse Symphony Orchestra 958,
    1518
Syre, Wolfram, organ 953
Syrus, Peter, conductor 4031
Szabo, Laszlo, conductor 1559
Szasz, Arpad, violoncello 1895
Szczepanska, Krystyna, mezzo-soprano
    2494, 3182
Szebenyi, Janos, flute 229
Szeged Symphony Orchestra 1981
Szekely, Mihaly, bass 361, 362
Szekeres, Ferenc, conductor 3437
Szelecsenyi, Norbert, piano 2692
Szell, Georg, conductor 573, 609,
    1320, 1325, 2557, 2907, 3638
Szendrei, Janka, conductor 3802
Szenthelyi, Judith, piano 1904
Szenthelyi, Miklos, violin 1904
Szeryng, Henryk, conductor 3404
Szeryng, Henryk, violin 278, 321,
    444, 539, 613, 614, 808, 2206,
    2533, 3404, 3915
Szeverenyi, Ilona, cimbalom 1283,
    1870
Szidon, Roberto, piano 385, 1982
Szigeti, Joseph, violin 377
Sziklay, Erika, soprano 2692
Szokefalvy-Nagy, Katalin, soprano
    1028, 1895
Szombathely Symphony Orchestra 1870
Szonyi, Ferenc, tenor 1296
Szonyi, Olga, soprano 362
Szostek-Radkowa, Krystyna, mezzo-
    soprano 334
Taber, John, trumpet 3287
Tacchino, Gabriel, piano 2531
Tachezi, Herbert, harpsichord 3418
Tadeo, Giorgio, bass 2468, 2733
Tagliavini, Luigi, organ 3716
Taggart, Mark, saxophone 1387

Taillon, Jocelyne, mezzo-soprano
    1197, 1221, 1522
Tajo, Italo, bass 2563, 2572, 2573
Takacs, Klara, soprano 1028, 1395,
    1711, 1895, 2315, 3369, 3437
Takahashi, Yuji, piano 1457
Takeda, Makiko, piano 4039
Taktakishvili, Otar, conductor 3186
Talich Quartet 473, 478, 479, 481,
    484, 1313
Talich, Vaclav, conductor 1309
Tall, John, organ 3433
Talley, John, conductor 1630, 3970
Tallis Scholars 40
Talmi, Yoav, conductor 1762
Talvela, Martti, bass 552, 606, 3215
Tamagno, Francesco, tenor 3770
Tamburello, Anthony, bass 4067
Taneyev Quartet 1389, 3190, 3191
Tanglewood Festival Chorus 2811
Tanguy, Jean-Michel, flute 3291
Tapiola Choir 3592
Tappy, Eric, tenor 1197, 3129
Tarack, Gerald, violin 2525
Tarjani, Ferenc, horn 1870, 3039
Tarkhov, Boris, tenor 2698, 2973
Tarr, Edward, trumpet 35, 3866
Tarres, Enriqueta, soprano 2464
Tartak, Marvin, piano 698, 3177
Tartakov, Joachim, baritone 3770
Tarushkin, Richard, conductor 2014
Taschke, Carl, violin 657
Tashi Ensemble 3184, 3185
Taskin Harpsichord Trio 282
Tassinari, Arrigo, flute 2070
Tate, Jeffrey, organ 3440
Tatishvili, Liano, mezzo-soprano
    2478
Tatishvili, Zisana, soprano 2478
Tatrai Quartet 1702, 2692, 3804
Tatton, Thomas, viola 1923
Taube, Werner, violoncello 1413
Taube, Richard, tenor 1943, 3538,
    3774
Tausky, Vilem, conductor 3063
Taverner Choir 2578
Taylor, Christopher, flute 3419
Taylor, Rose, mezzo-soprano 2124
Tchakarov, Emil, conductor 410
Tcherkasskaya, Marianne, soprano
    3774
Tear, Robert, tenor 232, 263, 459,
    644, 905, 906, 962, 1362, 1589,
    1618, 1625, 1637, 1693, 1710,
    2191, 2300, 2314, 2487, 2689,

2738, 2974, 3334
Teatro delle Novita Orchestra 1259
Teatro Giuseppe Verdi Orchestra and
  Chorus 63, 3025
Teatro Regio di Parma Orchestra 3342
Tebaldi, Renata, soprano 2742
Teikari, Jauko, oboe 4
Teixeira, Jean, conductor 1572
Teixeira, Paulo, oboe 1013
Tel Aviv Quartet 2673
Tellefsen, Arve, violin 703, 1568,
  3171
Temirkanov, Yuri, conductor 2532,
  3136
Temple Church Choir, London 3534,
  3936
Tennessee Tech University Band 708
Tennstedt, Klaus, conductor 795,
  2033, 2039, 2046, 2056, 2956
Teodorini, Elena, soprano 3770
Ter Linden, Jaap, violoncello 997,
  1824
Terebesi, Gyorgy, violin 2470
Terrasson, R., bass 3844
Terrell, Kathy, mezzo-soprano 2799
Terry, Vera, soprano 1622
Terzieff, Laurent 2676
Teschemacher, Margarete, soprano
  2319, 3446, 3512
Tessmer, Heinrich, tenor 1622
Tetrazzini, Luisa, soprano 3770
Teutsch, Karol, conductor 3857
Thalben-Ball, George, conductor
  3534, 3936
Thalben-Ball, George, organ 3533,
  3618, 3936, 4050, 4053
Thallaug, Edith, mezzo-soprano 1557
Thames Chamber Orchestra 263, 3326
Thames Youth Ensemble 2480
Thau, Pierre, bass 632, 2763
Theatre Royal de Monnaie Chorus 3328
Thebom, Blanche, mezzo-soprano 3711
Thibaud, Jacques, violin 620, 3906
Thimmig, Leslie, clarinet 67
Thirache, Julien, baritone 717
Thiry, Louis, organ 3176
Thoday, Gillian, violoncello 348
Thomas, David, bass 230, 1587, 1628
  1648, 1692, 2584, 2588, 2600,
  3878
Thomas, Francis, bass 1229
Thomas, Jess, tenor 3465
Thomas, Kurt, conductor 236, 238
Thomas, Marjorie, contralto 1236,
  2032

Thomas, Michael Tilson, conductor
  586, 1188, 2686, 2755, 3242
Thomas, Michael Tilson, piano 2755
Thomas, Milton, viola 693
Thomas, Pascal, bass 1198
Thomas, Ronald, conductor 51, 66,
  788, 1738, 3396
Thomas, Ronald, violin 489, 1228
Thomaschke, Thomas, bass 3440, 3442
Thomatos Guitar Trio 1224
Thome, Joel, conductor 656
Thompson, Alastair, tenor 1617, 3511
Thomson, Bryden, conductor 1664,
  1855
Thomson, Virgil, conductor 3315
Thorborg, Kerstin, mezzo-soprano
  2028
Thornton, Edna, contralto 1383, 3774
Thune, Daniel, harpsichord 3418
Thunemann, Klaus. bassoon 3521
Thurlow, Deidree, soprano 3162
Tibbett, Lawrence, baritone 3367
Tihanyi, Gellert, clarinet 3039
Tilney, Colin, clavichord 83
Tilney, Colin, harpsichord 1278,
  1588, 2597, 3443
Tilney, Colin, organ 3443
Tinney, Herbert, conductor 3991
Tinney, Herbert, organ 3991
Tipo, Maria, piano 2794
Tirimo, Martino, piano 2863
Tiszay, Magda 229
Tivoli Symphony Orchestra 1461
Tjeknavorian, Loris, conductor 1319,
  2701, 3268, 3274
Tkachenko, Nelly, soprano 3189
Toivanen, Heikki, bass 2771
Tokyo Quartet 1214, 2327
Tollefson, Arthur, piano 3314
Tolley, Christopher, conductor 1297
Tolzer Boys Choir (Tolzer Knaben-
  chor) 135, 136, 138, 172, 173,
  228, 1709, 2032, 2312, 2459,
  2463, 2493
Tomacek, Jiri, violin 4009
Tomanek, Jaroslav, tenor 2456
Tomatz, David, violoncello 1130
Tomita Isao, electronic synthesi-
  zer 2648
Tomlinson, John, bass 992, 1008,
  2573
Tomowa (Tomova-Sintow), Anna sop-
  rano 226, 2320
Tonhalle Orchestra Brass Players
  2808

Tonnesen, Terje, conductor 1547
Tons, E., conductor 1831
Topler-Marizy, Anne Marie, soprano 2962
Topper, Hertha, mezzo-soprano 128, 170, 264, 323, 2321
Tora, Riccardo, harpsichord 2070
Torchinsky, Abe, conductor 4032
Toronto Chamber Orchestra 50
Toronto Children's Chorus 3223
Toronto Symphony Orchestra 3223
Torresella, Fanny, soprano 3770
Tortelier, Paul, violoncello 817, 2165, 2661, 2758, 3094
Tortelier, Yan Pascal, conductor 2758
Tortelier, Yan Pascal, violin 2661
Toscanini, Arturo, conductor 577, 3585, 3860
Toso, Piero, violin 28, 3198, 3199, 3428, 3429
Toth, Zoltan, viola 2331
Toulon, Jacques, trombone 2760
Toulouse Capitole Theatre Chorus 1525, 2448
Toulouse Capitole Theatre Orchestra 1525, 1530, 2448, 2757
Tourangeau, Huguette soprano 2099, 3672, 3828
Tourel, Jennie, mezzo-soprano 2316
Toyama, Shigeru, violin 3407
Tozzi, Giorgio, bass 3341
Tracey, Bradford, harpsichord 81, 1458, 4021
Tracey, Bradford, organ 1458
Tracey, Bradford, piano 537
Tracey, Bradford, virginal 4013
Traey, Sylvia, piano 831
Trampler, Walter, viola 833, 2342, 2399
Traubel, Helen, soprano 3961
Traxel, Josef, tenor 818
Trempont, Michel, baritone 2448, 3328
Trenkner, Evelinde, piano 357, 960, 989, 1125
Trepte, Paul, organ 2762, 3511, 3529
Tretyakov, Victor, violin 2472
Trew, Graham, baritone 3837
Trieste Teatro Verdi Orchestra 2171
Trimarchi, Domenico, baritone 1686
Trinity Boys Choir 2563
Trinity St. Sergius Monastery Priests Choir 3693

Trio di Milano 2860, 2910
Tripp, Werner, flute 2396
Trippner, Alfred, violin 3845
Tristram, Geoffrey, organ 4052
Tropin, Robert, bass 1524
Trossingen Martin-Luther-Kirche Chor 109
Troth, Marilyn, soprano 1621
Trotschel, Elfriede, soprano 3488
Trotter, Thomas, organ 3783, 3784
Troy, Dermot, tenor 2730
Troyanos, Tatiana, soprano 626, 2102, 2581, 2811, 3082
Trubashnik, Lara, piano 56
Trubashnik, Sonia, oboe 56
Tryon, Valerie, piano 1976
Ts'ong, Fou, piano 1052, 1076
Tsuchiya, Kunio, viola 895
Tucapsky, Antonin, conductor 3323
Tucapsky, Beryl, soprano 3323
Tucek, Rene, baritone 1312
Tucker, Gene, tenor 133
Tucker, Richard, tenor 3343
Tuckwell, Barry, conductor 1669
Tuckwell, Barry, horn 1665, 1669, 1776, 2237, 2404
Tugarinova, Klavdia, mezzo-soprano 3774
Tugarinova, Tatiana, mezzo-soprano 3214
Tuller, Niklaus, bass 130
Tung, Ling, conductor 682
Tunnard, Viola, piano 3990
Tureck, Rosalyn, harpsichord 112, 313
Tureck, Rosalyn, piano 174, 184
Turetschek, Gerhard, oboe 2396
Turetzky, Bertram, double bass 1532
Turicchi, Franco, bass 3436
Turkovic, Milan, bassoon 2526
Turku Philharmonic Orchestra 1384
Turner, Bruno, conductor 1120, 1933
Turner, John, organ 4046
Tweed, Pauline, soprano 3485
Twentieth Century Players 3149
Tyler, James, banjo 3679
Tyler, James, cittern 2188
Tyler, James. conductor 3955
Tyler, James, flute 2188
Tyler, James, mandolin 3679
Tylsar, Bedrich, horn 2679
Tylsar, Zdenek, horn 888, 2679
Tyte, Susan, oboe 3392
Uhl, Fritz, tenor 649, 961, 3450
Uhlhorn, Herman, piano 2062

Uittenbosch, Anneke, harpsichord 253, 330, 1679, 1824
Uittenbosch, Anneke, organ 1824
Uitti, Frances Marie, violoncello 3655
Ullrich, Marc, trumpet 3866
Ulmer, Ernest, piano 1207
Ulsamer Collegium 2585
Ulster Orchestra 1664
Unger, Gerhard, tenor 2194, 2299, 3462
U. S. Air Force Academy Band 1661
U. S. Naval Academy Band 3973
U. S. Naval Academy Choir 1630, 3969, 3972
U. S. Naval Academy Drum and Bugle Corps 3973
U. S. Naval Academy Glee Club 3970, 3973
University of British Columbia Chamber Singers 393
University of California, Los Angeles Brass Ensemble 1661
University of California, Los Angeles Men's Glee Club 1033
University of California, Los Angeles Wind Ensemble 1660
University of Chicago Contemporary Chamber Players 2200
University of South Florida Winds 1825
Urbain, Luc, flute 3411
Urbanner, Erich, conductor 3325
Urfer, Christine 1865
Uridge, Michael, conductor 3681
Urlus, Jacques, tenor 3770
Ursuleac, Viorica, soprano 2075, 3105, 3448
Usedruuf, Bernhard, conductor 2210, 3297
USKO Orchestra 2062
U.S.S.R. Radio and Television Orchestra 3186
U.S.S.R. Radio Chorus 2478, 2698
U.S.S.R. Radio Orchestra 1898, 2478 2698
U.S.S.R. State Academic Orchestra 2987
U.S.S.R. Symphony Orchestra 337, 768, 2112, 2180, 2530, 2546, 2706, 2982, 3201, 3251, 3255, 3261, 3267, 3781
Utah Chorale 3313
Utah Symphony Orchestra 1545, 1571, 3118, 3313

Uto, Endre, bass-baritone 1296
Uzbek Navoi Bolshoi Theatre Orchestra 62
Uzbek Philharmonic Orchestra 1898
Vadstena Instrumental Ensemble 1570
Vaguet, Albert, tenor 3770
Vainio, Mati, organ 1896
Vajda, Jozsef, bassoon 3294
Vajnar, Frantisek, conductor 1900, 2090
Valaitis, Vladimir, baritone 3796
Valek, Vladimir, conductor 3123
Valenti, Fernando, harpsichord 3659
Valentini-Terrani, Lucia, contralto 2739
Valero, Fernando, tenor 3770
Valjakka, Taru, soprano 648, 1557, 2771, 2974, 3586
Valkki, Anita, alto 2771
Vallandri, Aline, soprano 3774
Vallecillo, Irma, piano 1201, 1764
Valletti, Cesare, tenor 2732
Vallin, Ninon, soprano 3984
Valls Santos, Francisco, baritone 973
Valsta, Tapani, piano 2859
Van, Jeffry, guitar 3599, 3600
Van Allan, Richard, bass 1257, 2275, 2296, 2573, 2731
Van Altena, Marius, tenor 2189
Van Asperen, Bob, harpsichord 93, 3299, 3310
Van Beinum, Eduard, conductor 1650, 2026
Van Blerk, Gerard, piano 1059, 1217
Van Dael, Lucy, violin 763, 1137
Van Dam, Jose, bass 227, 1198, 1525, 2292, 2295, 2320, 2401, 3340, 3348
Van de Kamp, Harry, baritone 1452
Van den Berg, Pieter, bass 3346
Van den Berg, William, violoncello 1951
Van den Hombergh, Hans, conductor 1773
Van der Meer, Ruud, bass 135, 136, 3818
Van der Velde, Herbert, viola 3818
Van Dyck, Ernest, tenor 3770
Van Egmond, Max, bass 135, 136, 138, 1586, 1824, 2309
Van Gucht, Georges, timpani 3059
Van Gucht, Georges, xylorimba 780
Van Hauwe, Walter, recorder 3310
Van Immerseel, Jos, piano 1106

Van Juten, Grit, soprano 634
Van Kempen, Paul, conductor 436
Van Kesteren, John. tenor 267, 2454, 2457, 2468
Van Mill, Arnold, bass 556
Van Nevel, Paul, conductor 3548
Van Rooy, Anton, baritone 3770
Van Vliet, Herman, organ 3725
Van Vrooman, Richard, tenor 649, 1100, 1709
Van Woudenberg, Adriaan, horn 127
Vancouver Symphony Orchestra 2685
Vandenburg, Howard, tenor 2400
Vandersteene, Zeger, tenor 2013
Vandeville, Jacques, oboe d'amore 1026
Vanerette, Edith, soprano 1351
Vanne-Marcoux, Jean-Emile, bass 3774
Vantin, Martin, tenor 2400
Vanzo, Alain, tenor 1525, 2097, 3793
Varady, Julia, soprano 359, 1098, 1956, 2222, 2308, 2680
Varcoe, Stephen, bass-baritone 1593, 1621, 1632, 1653, 2588, 2600
Vardi, Emanuel, viol 732, 922
Varga, Laszlo, violoncello 2531
Varga, Tibor, violin 372
Varnay, Astrid, soprano 1955, 2462, 3469, 3538
Varviso, Silvio, conductor 1512, 3104
Vas, Katalin, violoncello 1283
Vasary, Tamas, conductor 2253
Vasary, Tamas, piano 1037, 1038, 1047, 1053, 1085, 1994, 2253
Vasquez, Alejandro, tenor 2103
Vasseur, Jean-Philippe, viola 'amore 1026
Vater, Wolfgang, tenor 2103
Vatican Boys Choir 391
Vaughan, Denis, clavichord 94
Vaughan, Denis, conductor 1734, 2882, 2893
Veasey, Josephine, soprano 632, 691
Vecchi, Guido, violoncello 1415, 1579
Vedernikov, Alexander, bass 1173, 3796
Vegh, Sandor, violin 388
Vegvari, Csaba, harpsichord 3804
Veilhan, Jean-Claude, flute 2066
Veilhan, Jean-Claude, recorder 2066
Vel, Peter, violoncello 1468
Velin, Andrea, tenor 2572
Vento, Marc, bass 1525, 2097

Ver Hasselt, J., fortepiano 3844
Verbruggen, Marion, recorder 4019
Verde, Sven, conductor 1850
Vered, Ilana, piano 525, 2201, 3666
Verheul, Koos, flute 3818
Veritch, Alan de, viola 2501
Verkinderen, Anne, soprano 1009, 1010
Verlet, Alice, soprano 3770
Verlet, Blandine, harpsichord 186, 315, 1149, 1153, 1916, 2789
Vernigora, Lev, bass 3796
Verona Arena Orchestra 2565
Verrett, Shirley, mezzo-soprano 3361
Vescovo, Pierre del, horn 2960
Veselka, Josef, conductor 2476
Vessieres, Andre, bass 1524
Vester, Frans, flute 1217, 1911
Veyron-Lacroix, Robert, harpsichord 78
Veyron-Lacroix, Robert, piano 78, 311, 621, 1643
Vezzani, Cesar, tenor 1583
Via Nova Quartet 2960
Vialtzeva, Anastasia, contralto 3770
Vickers, Jon, tenor 606, 610, 632, 691, 2762, 3341
Victor Orchestra 1101
Victorian Time Machine 1119
Vida, Gabor, flute 2692
Vieira, Helena, soprano 1007
Vienna Bella Musica Ensemble 448, 3759
Vienna Boys Choir (Vienna Sanger-knaben) 127, 904, 1817, 1820, 2309, 2310, 2397, 2511, 3702, 3952, 3960
Vienna Capella Academica 320, 323, 2422, 2911
Vienna Chorus (Chorus Viennensis) 127, 2309, 3370, 3702, 3960
Vienna Concentus Musicus 127, 135, 138, 705, 1591, 1624, 1631, 2309, 3702
Vienna Festival Orchestra and Chorus 2055
Vienna Gesellschaft Orchestra and Chorus 231
Vienna Mozart Ensemble 2221, 2278, 2280, 2281, 2282, 2284, 2287
Vienna Octet 773
Vienna Philharmonic Orchestra 422, 430, 434, 485, 552, 553, 554, 570, 578, 579, 580, 597, 643,

792, 802, 866, 868, 875, 894,
927, 1339, 1340, 1817, 1820, 1834
1836, 2027, 2028, 2123, 2151,
2155, 2262, 2320, 2344, 2376,
2386, 2396, 2560, 2885, 2886,
2887, 2890, 2891, 2894, 2901
2905, 3069, 3078, 3085, 3090,
3096, 3098, 3104, 3107, 3115,
3130, 3134, 3205, 3340, 3366,
3460, 3463, 3464, 3474, 3476,
3489, 3672
Vienna Philharmonic Quartet 2842
Vienna Philharmonic Quintet 2136
Vienna Philharmonic Wind Soloists
  2283
Vienna Singverein 461, 602, 1689,
  2123
Veinna State Opera Chorus 16, 552,
  553, 1834, 1836, 2123, 2320,
  3104, 3340, 3354, 3355, 3463,
  3489
Vienna State Opera Orchestra 123,
  1512, 1861, 2874, 3079, 3081,
  3354, 3355
Vienna Symphony Orchestra 16, 415,
  1582, 1689, 2212, 2242, 2471,
  2807, 2911, 3043, 3071, 3072,
  3220, 3915, 3960
Vienna Tonkunstler Orchestra 812
Vienna Volksoper Orchestra 3988
Vienna Wind Soloists 1432
Viera, Silvio 2568
Vieuille, Jean, baritone 717, 3557
Vigay, Dennis, violoncello 65, 3531
Viglione-Borghese, Domenico, bari-
  tone 3774
Vignas, Francesco, tenor 3770
Vigneron, Jacques 1199
Vigners, Leonids, conductor 1867
Vignoles, Roger, piano 1376, 2942,
  3837
Viitanan, Usko, baritone 2771
Vilker, Valeria, violin 2989
Villa, Joseph, piano 1989
Villa-Lobos, Heitor, conductor 3382
Vincent, Ruth, soprano 3774
Vincenzi, Edda, soprano 627
Vinco, Ivo, bass 2521
Violette, Andrew, piano 1160
Virginia Opera Orchestra 2403, 2405
Virtuosi di Roma (I) 2475, 3401
Virtuosi of England 3397
Vis, Lucas, conductor 3818
Vishnevskaya, Galina, soprano 2974
Visser, Lieuwe, bass 1257

Vivalda, Janetta, soprano 1524
Vivaldi Ensemble 3407
Vix, Genevieve, mezzo-soprano 3774
Vlach, Josef, conductor 2254, 2265
Vladimirov, Yevgeny, bass 3241
Vlasov, Vitali, tenor 3796
Voge, Richard, organ 2667
Voisin, Roger, trumpet 1102
Vokalensemble Marburg 2941
Volker, Franz, tenor 3538
Von Alpenheim, Ilse, piano 1446,
  1712
Von Bahr, Gunilla, flute 355, 3589,
  3594
Von Bary, Alfred, tenor 3770
Von Benda, Hans, violin 1818
Von Borries, Melchior, conductor
  1247
Von der Linde, Robert, bass 3468
Von der Osten, Eva, soprano 3774
Von Dohnanyi, Christoph, conductor
  643, 2123, 2151, 2155, 2608,
  3130, 3134
Von Garaguly, Carl, conductor 1850
Von Halem, Victor, bass 2571
Von Karajan, Herbert, conductor 117,
  226, 231, 341, 379, 416, 435,
  442, 461, 462, 568, 602, 665,
  680, 770, 799, 825, 862, 913,
  937, 949, 1198, 1333, 1544, 1946,
  2019, 2044, 2157, 2320, 2376,
  2380, 2389, 2401, 2560, 2571,
  2657, 2725, 2735, 2888, 2904,
  2996, 3003, 3007, 3011, 3012,
  3069, 3246, 3248, 3249, 3253,
  3258, 3265, 3340, 3348, 3351,
  3469, 3672
Von Matacic, Lovro, conductor 576,
  3080, 3283
Von Milinkovic, Georgine, contralto
  3105
Von Nordberg, Hermann, piano 859
Von Ottenthal, Gertrud, mezzo-sop-
  ano 2103
Von Raatz-Brockmann, Julius, baritone 3774
Von Saalfeld, Monica, piano 1300
Von Seeboek, Charlotte, soprano
  3774
Von Stade, Frederica, mezzo-soprano
  1198, 1223, 1685, 1816, 2021,
  2091, 2192, 2223, 2320, 2734,
  3636
Von Wrochem, Ulrich, viola 856
Vonk, Hans, conductor 2800, 3818

Voorberg, Marinus, conductor 3839
Voorhorst, Lucius, flute 253
Votapek, Ralph, piano 988, 1478
Votipka, Thelma, soprano 716
Votto, Antonino, conductor 2521, 2568
Vronsky, Petr, conductor 1391
Vyvyan, Jennifer, soprano 458
Waart, Edo de, conductor 1449, 2625, 2627
Wachter, Eberhard, baritone 3471, 3472
Wagemann, Rose, mezzo-soprano 1785, 2461
Wagner, Richard, baritone 2832
Wagner, Roger, Chorale 3707, 3708
Wagner, Roger, conductor 3707, 3708
Wagner, Sieglinde, contralto 3449, 3457, 3475
Waisman, Elya, soprano 2100
Waitzmann, Kurt 1891
Wakasugi, Hiroshi, conductor 641, 3495
Wakehan, Michael, baritone 3155
Walcha, Helmut 211, 218, 247, 248, 278, 318
Waldeland, Hege, violoncello 3171
Walden, Peter, conductor 2449
Walden Trio 2803
Waldenau, Elisabeth, mezzo-soprano 2319
Waldhans, Jiri, conductor 1417, 2080
Waldman, Frederic, conductor 350, 1310, 1406, 1604, 3327
Wales, Roy, conductor 3323
Walker, Edyth, contralto 3770
Walker, Frances, piano 2008
Walker, George, piano 1913, 3478
Walker, Nellie, contralto 1469, 3156, 3157, 3160
Walker, Nina, piano 3863
Walker, Timothy, guitar 3665
Wallace, Ian, bass-baritone 2730, 3153
Wallberg, Heinz, conductor 1947, 2009, 3793
Wallen, Martti, bass 2771
Wallenstein, Alfred, violoncello 3093
Wallez, Jean-Pierre, conductor 3912
Walsh, Colin, organ 3835
Walt, Sherman, bassoon 2224
Walter, Bruno, conductor 572, 598, 604, 814, 941, 951, 1739, 2025, 2027, 2028, 2316, 3476, 3585, 3860
Walter, Gustav, baritone 3770
Walters, Valerie, mezzo-soprano 2078
Walther, Hans-Jurgen, conductor 1000
Wand, Gunter, conductor 947, 950
Wandsworth School Boys Choir 2042, 2573
Wangler, Rudolf, guitar 957
Wanre, Ralf, horn 4026
Warchal, Bohdan, conductor 1138
Ward, David, bass 610
Ward, David, piano 2304
Warenskjold, Dorothy, soprano 3738
Warfield, William, baritone 1128, 1629, 2316
Warland, Dale, Singers 915
Warren, Leonard, baritone 724, 3367
Warsaw Chamber Orchestra 3857
Warsaw Opera Orchestra 3857
Warsaw Philharmonic Chorus 2490, 2494, 3181
Warsaw Philharmonic Orchestra 69, 70, 334, 1879, 2490, 2494, 3181, 3182, 3857, 3975
Watkin-Mills, Robert, bass 3770
Watkinson, Carolyn, contralto 230, 1628, 1638, 1692, 3435
Watson, Donald, clarinet 1527
Watson, Kenneth, marimba 3655
Watson, Lilian, soprano 2191
Watson, Richard, bass 3162
Watters, Mark, saxophone 755
Watts, Anthony, conductor 1858
Watts, Helen, contralto 130, 1637, 1647, 1693, 2191, 3334, 3433
Watts, John, synthesizer 3484
Waugh, Nigel, baritone 1659
Wayneberg, Daniel, piano 2608
Waynflete Singers 3937, 3939
Wearing, Catherin, soprano 906
Weatherley, Denis, bass-baritone 3503
Weatherley, Eleanor, piano 3503
Weaver, James, conductor 2065
Webb, Richard, violoncello 2073
Weber, Heinrich, tenor 1894, 2457
Weber, Josef, bass 2457
Weber, Ludwig, bass 3105, 3451, 3773
Wedekind, Erika, soprano 3770
Wedin, Jan-Olav, conductor 3589
Wegner, Walburga, soprano 454
Wehrung, Herrad, soprano 925, 2962
Wehrung, Leonore, flute 3845
Weichert, Gregor, piano 1991
Weidt, Lucie, soprano 3770

Weigand, George, conductor 1803
Weigand, John, clarinet 922
Weikenmeier, Albert, tenor 649
Weikl, Bernd, baritone 819, 2293
Weil, Hermann, baritone 3774
Weil, Terence, violoncello 2325
Weingartner, Felix, conductor 579
Weinrich, Carl, organ 110
Weinstock, Frank, piano 732, 922
Weintraub, Barbara, piano 3822
Weir, Gillian, organ 954, 1169, 3336
    3664
Weirich, Robert, piano 393
Weisbach, Hans, conductor 2075
Weisberg, Arthur, bassoon 3306
Weisbrod, Annette, piano 3288
Weiss, Abraham, bassoon 765
Weiss, Alan, piano 2869
Weiss, David, oboe 706, 765
Weiss, Dawn, flute 765
Weiss, Don, conductor 1033
Weissenberg, Alexis, piano 1999,
    2194, 2242
Weiter, Georg, baritone 2460
Welin, Karl Erik, organ 2433
Welitsch, Ljuba, soprano 859, 3083
Weller, Walter, conductor 2087,
    2552, 2558, 2624, 2629
Wellington, Christopher, viola 3332
Wells, David, violoncello 1960
Wells, Mary, soprano 906
Wells, William, conductor 393
Welsby, Norman, baritone 1229
Welsh, Moray, violoncello 740, 2852,
    3517
Welsh National Opera Orchestra and
    Chorus 3374
Welting, Ruth, soprano 940, 1816,
    2091
Wenglor, Ingeborg, soprano 557
Wenk, Erich, bass 129, 150
Wenkel, Ortrun, contralto 1638, 2039
Wentworth, Jean, piano 1914
Wentworth, Kenneth, piano 1914
Wenzinger, August, conductor 1605,
    1610, 1611, 2065, 2422, 3303,
    3309, 3729
Wenzinger, August, viola da gamba
    322, 2005
Werba, Erik, piano 3111
Werfel, Franz, conductor 1865
Werrenrath, Reinald, baritone 3774
Wesleyan Singers 3484
Wesseley, Karl, tenor 2319, 3512
West Australian Symphony Orchestra
    1828
West German Radio Chorus 2032
West Jutland Chamber Ensemble 909,
    2423
West, Lucretia, soprano 2055
West Virginia University Collegium
    Musicum 1859
Westbrook, James, conductor 1660,
    1661
Westenholz, Elisabeth, organ 35,
    2425
Westerberg, Stig, conductor 37,
    3052, 3053, 3508
Western Brass Quintet 3523
Western Wind 3894
Westminster Cathedral String Orch-
    estra 658
Westminster Choir 234, 1629, 2316
Westphalian Kantorei 1245, 2962
Westphalian Symphony Orchestra 1499,
    1892
Wettinger College Choir 2808
Wheeler, Gerald, organ 1426
Wheeler, John, bass 1375
White, Carolina, soprano 3774
White, Kathleen, soprano 3818
White, Robert, tenor 547, 3947
White, Willard, bass 3074
Whitehill, Lawrence, baritone 3770
Whitelaw, John, fortepiano 2220
Whitney, Gloria, piano 3645
Whitney, Robert, conductor 2011
Whittaker, Douglas, flute 3778
Wicherek, Antoni, conductor 3857
Wicks, Allan, conductor 3532
Wicks, Allan, organ 3664, 4046
Wicks, Denis, bass 632
Wicks, Denis, conductor 1804
Widdop, Walter, tenor 3083
Widensky, Peter, positiv organ 2072
Widmer, Kurt, bass-baritone 820,
    1100
Wilanow Quartet 3180
Wilber, Bob, clarinet 612
Wilbert, Johannes, conductor 3707
Wilbraham, John, trumpet 2972,
    3563, 3779, 3916, 4029
Wilbrink, Hans, bass-baritone 2680
Wilcox, Carol, soprano 402
Wild, Earl, piano 790, 1049, 1066,
    2609, 3961
Wildbrunn, Helene, soprano 3774
Wilde, David, piano 1998
Wilhelm, Horst, baritone 3462, 3712
Wilkinson, Stephen, conductor 3336

Willcocks, David, conductor 237, 263
  636, 1618, 1625, 1710, 2105,
  3534, 3823
Willens, Michael, bass 914
Willer, Luise, alto 3105, 3448
Williams, Evan, tenor 3770
Williams, John, countertenor 2591
Williams, John, guitar 55, 225, 1248
  1531, 2520, 3612, 3634, 3722,
  4029
Williams, John, organ 3530
Williams, Trevor, violin 2691
Willis, Katherine, soprano 906
Willison, David, piano 3333, 3573
Wills, Arthur, conductor 785
Wills, Arthur, organ 785, 2412,
  3815, 4046
Wilmington Cathedral Choirs 3991
Wilson, Carol, soprano 393
Wilson, Christopher lute 1273
Wilson, Gran, tenor 1351
Wilson, Ransom, flute 294
Winbergh, Gosta, tenor 37
Wincenc, Carol, flute 1658, 3854
Winchester Cathedral Choir 903, 3479
  3937, 3938, 3939
Winchester College Commoners 3937
Windgassen, Wolfgang, tenor 3467,
  3470, 3471, 3472, 3712
Winkelmann, Hermann, tenor 3770
Winland, Leo, violoncello 612, 1455
Winnipeg Symphony Orchestra 449
Winschermann, Helmut, conductor 149,
  200, 290, 325, 1397, 2397, 3943
Winschermann, Helmut, oboe 325
Winter, Helmut, organ 2466
Winterbourne, Carol, flute 1910
Winterthur String Orchestra 1576
Wislocki, Stanislaw, conductor 70
Wit, Jolie de, flute 3818
Witoszynskyi, Leo, guitar 1243
Witsenburg, Edward, harp 1217
Witt, Josef, tenor 3354
Witte, Erich, tenor 3486
Witte, Gerd, conductor 109
Wittrisch, Marcel, tenor 3538
Wixell, Ingvar, baritone 1257, 1956,
  2296, 2564, 3052, 3345, 3918
Wohlfahrt, Irwin, tenor 3467, 3470
Wolf, Gary, piano 1462
Wolf, Harold, violin 2640, 2641
Wolf, Ilse, soprano 1647, 2495
Wolf, Jurgen, violoncello 1460
Wolf-Matthaus, Lotte, contralto 137
Wolfenden, Guy, conductor 1972

Wollitz, Eduard, bass 1709
Wolny, Piotr, piano 631
Wood, Henry, conductor 1230
Woodhams, Richard, oboe 487
Woodrow, Anthony, bass 2690, 3310
Woodward, Roger, piano 2976
Woolley, Robert, harpsichord 1150,
  1600, 2586
Worcester Cathedral Academy Choir
  784, 1626, 1627, 2762, 3511,
  3529
Worcester Cathedral Academy Orch-
  estra 784
Worcester Festival Choral Society
  3511
Worthley, Max, tenor 1592
Woytowicz, Stefania, soprano 2490,
  2491, 2493, 2494, 3182, 3857
Wozniak, Jerzy, percussion 3857
Wren Orchestra 2495, 2786
Wright, Desmond, fortepiano 2362,
  2364
Wright, Desmond, hammerflugel 2361
Wright, Edmund, organ 161
Wright, Harold, clarinet 2224
Wright, John, Jew's harp 2519
Wright, John, violin 2519
Wright, John, vocals 2519
Wright, Rayburn, conductor 1924
Wroclaw Philharmonic Orchestra 3857
Wuhrer, Friedrich, conductor 859
Wulstan, David, conductor 1484,
  3187, 3868
Wunderlich, Fritz, tenor 543, 544,
  1862, 2301, 3215, 3373, 3696
Wuorinen, Charles, piano 3649
Wurttemberg Chamber Orchestra 27,
  1004, 1663, 1673, 2276, 2399,
  2829
Wustenhagen, Harry 1891
Wyatt, Keith, tenor 2832
Wyner, Susan Davenny, soprano 1959
Wyner, Yehudi, conductor 1959
Wyttenbach, Jurg, conductor 1413
Wyttenbach, Jurg, piano 493, 1413
Xenophontos Monastery Community
  3689, 3692
Yablonskaya, Oxana, piano 405, 1979,
  2415
Yakar, Rachel, soprano 227, 1111,
  1197, 1586
Yamada, Kazuo, conductor 2109
Yamaoka, Shigenobu, conductor 1456,
  2198
Yancich, Milan, horn 3769

Yarbrough, Joan, piano 2182
Yaron, Yuval, violin 3014
Yaroslavtsev, Valery, bass-baritone 3214
Yarvy, Neimye, conductor 2472
Yaw, Ellen Beach, soprano 3770
Yelnikov, Yuri, tenor 2697
Yepes, Narciso, guitar 1493, 2716, 3686
Yepes, Narciso, lute 321
Yomiuri Nippon Symphony Orchestra 1456, 2198
Yordanoff, Ruben, violin 2176
York-Skinner, John, alto 1008
Young, Alexander, tenor 1639, 1690, 2307, 3063
Young Singers of Callanwolde 757
Yuzhina, Natalia, soprano 3770
Zabaleta, Nicanor, harp 187, 372, 2396, 3685
Zaccaria, Nicolas, bass 461, 627, 1257, 2575
Zadek, Hilde, soprano 2055
Zaepffel, Alain, countertenor 1007
Zagreb Philharmonic Orchestra 2688
Zagreb Quartet 743, 745, 2672
Zagreb Radio Orchestra 1725, 1728, 1730
Zagreb RTV Choir 1830, 1843
Zagreb Symphony Orchestra 1830, 1843
Zahradnicek, Jiri, tenor 1834, 2081, 3029
Zahradnik, Bohuslav, clarinet 1900
Zaimont, Judith, piano 3519
Zakarian, Sedmara, piano 3820
Zampiere, Giuseppe, tenor 2055
Zanelli, Renato, baritone 3774
Zanetti, Miguel, piano 1392, 3669
Zannerini, Severino, violoncello 3198, 3199
Zanotelli, Hans, conductor 730
Zapf, Gerd, trumpet 3417
Zarzo, Vicente, horn 3818
Zaszkaliczky, Tamas, organ 262, 3813
Zayas, Rodrigo de, conductor 973
Zayas, Rodrigo de, lute, theorbo, vihuela, guitar 3577
Zbrujeva, Eugenia, contralto 3770
Zedda, Alberto, conductor 199
Zednik, Heinz, tenor 2320, 2571
Zehetmair, Thomas, violin 2267
Zeitlin, Denny, piano 3520
Zelenka, Milan, guitar 327, 4009

Zelnick, Robert, violin 4064
Zeltser, Mark, piano 442
Zeman, Dietmar, bassoon 2396
Zemel Choir 736
Zempleni, Maria, soprano 1395, 1511, 3437
Zenatello, Giovanni, tenor 3770, 3773
Zender, Hans, conductor 834
Zepperitz, Rainer, double bass 2318
Zertsalova, Natalia, piano 1974
Zeumer, Gerti, soprano 2881
Zhukov, Igor, piano 2750
Zhuraitis, Algis, conductor 5, 1532, 1537
Zidek, Ivo, tenor 1834
Ziegler, Klaus Martin, conductor 131
Zikmundova, Eva, mezzo-soprano 1834
Zimerman, Krystian, piano 845, 1036, 1046, 1094
Zimmer, Anne-Beate, flute 3655
Zinman, David, conductor 71, 1225, 1255, 1290, 2215
Zitek, Vaclav, baritone 1312, 1836, 2081
Zlotkin, Frances, flute 2199
Zlotkin, Frederick, violoncello 2199, 3674
Zoghby, Linda, soprano 1686
Zoller, Karl, flute 1912
Zorian Quartet 3776
Zosso, Rene, hurdy gurdy 3760, 3800
Zsigmond, Gabriella, contralto 1895
Zukerman, Eugenia, flute 72
Zukerman, Pinchas, conductor 72, 1939, 2302
Zukerman, Pinchas, viola 80, 488, 617
Zukerman, Pinchas, violin 371, 803, 917, 1218, 1939, 2202
Zurich Chamber Orchestra 2603
Zurich Radio Orchestra 1968
Zuyderduin, Albert, trombone 3287
Zverov, Valentin, clarinet 7
Zylis-Gara, Teresa, soprano 1618